MMPI-2 Correlates for Outpatient Community Mental Health Settings

MMPI-2 Correlates for Outpatient Community Mental Health Settings

John R. Graham, Yossef S. Ben-Porath,
and John L. McNulty

Foreword by James N. Butcher

University of Minnesota Press
Minneapolis • London

Published by the University of Minnesota Press
111 Third Avenue South, Suite 290
Minneapolis, MN 55401-2520
http://www.upress.umn.edu

Printed in the United States of America on acid-free paper

Library of Congress Cataloging-in-Publication Data

Graham, John R. (John Robert), 1940–
MMPI-2 correlates for outpatient community mental health settings / John R. Graham, Yossef S. Ben-Porath, and John L. McNulty ; foreword by James N. Butcher.
p. cm.
Includes bibliographical references and index.
ISBN 0-8166-2564-6 (hardcover)
1. Minnesota Multiphasic Personality Inventory. 2. Minnesota Multiphasic Personality Inventory—Validity. I. Ben-Porath, Yossef S. II. McNulty, John L. III. Title.
[DNLM: 1. Community Mental Health Services 2. MMPI. WM 145.5.M6 G739m 1999]
RC473.M5G733 1999
616.89'075—dc21
DNLM/DLC
for Library of Congress 99-20293

11 10 09 08 07 06 05 04 03 02 01 00 99 10 9 8 7 6 5 4 3 2 1

Contents

Tables

Figures

Foreword

James N. Butcher

Psychologists who use the Minnesota Multiphasic Personality Inventory-2 (MMPI-2) in their practice do so with the confidence that they have more than a half-century of research to support their decisions and recommendations. This empirical foundation for the traditional MMPI scales was built through thousands of investigations over the earlier years of the MMPI's life. When the revision of the test was undertaken in the 1980s, a major goal, both implicit and explicit, was to preserve and maintain the clinical scales, with this established interpretive lore, with as little item change as possible to preserve continuity with the past.

The MMPI-2 and MMPI-A, published respectively in 1989 and 1992, were completed after almost a decade of research and redevelopment. With the initial publication of these revised versions, interpretation relied largely on the continuity that was maintained with the original research base on the MMPI clinical scales and code types. The MMPI-2 clinical scales could be reliably interpreted with the original database. A few studies of the revised instrument addressed the external validity of the MMPI-2 clinical scales, providing some reassurance of continuity. However, no extensive studies of the empirical validity of the original scales and newly minted measures were possible at that time because such research requires very large samples and a very cost-intensive data collection program for sufficient data to be collected. With the revision of the instrument came a whisper of concern that the new version of the test might not produce the same "true" results as the original. Some questioned whether the traditional scales measured the original constructs sufficiently given the new norms.

The definitive MMPI-2 empirical study has now been published. This book will likely quell any remaining doubts about the robustness of the MMPI-2 scales. The study represents the most important research program for the empirical description of personality since the early work on MMPI "cookbooks" in the 1950s and 1960s. The Portage Path study by Graham, Ben-Porath, and McNulty, addressing an important clinical population, community mental health center patients, will serve as the primary outpatient research base for external correlates of the MMPI-2 indices for years to come.

Monumental empirical research contributions like the Portage Path study do not happen by chance or accrue out of samples of convenience. Rather, they are built by careful design and dogged persistence in accumulating the information essential to the development of an abundant database. The development of such an empirical database demands a number of things of investigators: a sound conceptualization and tenable rationale for the overall plan of the research, methodological sophistication in selecting the most potentially fruitful indices, meticulous detail in cataloging the observations on which the results hinge, and a persistent tracking and management of an enormous quantity of information to ensure that the results are interpretable. An empirical research program such as this is difficult to initiate, maintain, and bring to fruition. The authors are to be commended for their major scientific accomplishment.

The research base for this study is unsurpassed in the MMPI empirical literature. The community-based patient sample employed in this study was carefully selected to provide a broad basis for generalizing to future samples. A large midwestern community mental health center that provided comprehensive mental health services was selected as the primary population for the study. Of a total population of 2,482 clients, 1,219 were administered the MMPI-2—every testable client over a 21-month period. Each of these participants was initially evaluated at intake and followed over several months to obtain extensive therapists' ratings, appropriate demographic data, and other information about them. Over 1,000 of these individuals produced valid MMPI-2s and had sufficient external information about their psychological problems and progress in treatment. The population studied was quite heterogeneous, unlike the earlier MMPI codebook studies, and the results can confidently be applied to a broad sample of mental health patients.

This research program will firmly establish the empirical basis for the MMPI-2 clinical scales, as the Gilberstadt and Duker (1963) and Marks, Seeman, and Haller (1975) codebooks did for the original MMPI. The conclusions drawn from these data will be cited for decades as the definitive empirical study for the MMPI-2. As one would expect, based on the "doctrine of continuity" between the MMPI-2 and the original instrument, the clinical scales were found to be robust measures of the traditional characteristics. The results of this study clearly showed that the MMPI-2 can be relied on to assess the clinical dimensions that were addressed by the original MMPI. The external correlates of the MMPI-2 scales bear very strong resemblance to those characteristically obtained for the original MMPI clinical scales.

Moreover, this study provided clear external support for the validity of many of the newer scales developed for the MMPI-2. With the publication of the MMPI-2 came a number of new measures, particularly the MMPI-2 Content Scales, the Addiction Potential Scale, and the Addiction Acknowledgment Scale. The scale construction strategies employed were very different from those used in the development of the traditional clinical scales. Empirical validation was not the primary criterion for their development. However, ultimately for a scale to survive, it is necessary to establish external correlates. This study is the first major proving ground for these scales—the first substantial correlate research establishing the external validity of these newer measures alongside the clinical scales. This research substantially expands our knowledge base on the empirical correlates for the MMPI-2 Content Scales.

This research represents a clear methodological improvement over the earlier MMPI codebook studies in terms of research design and quality of sample obtained. This is the first MMPI codebook research that implemented practical scale definition criteria for ensuring the reliability of the prototypes being evaluated. This is also the first MMPI-based codebook research that incorporated ethnicity as a variable and showed that the MMPI-2 correlates apply equally well to African Americans and Caucasians.

Of the myriad books published each year, only a few stand out as unique or monumental works that will survive the test that time so strenuously puts to all new works. The volume by Graham, Ben-Porath, and McNulty is one of those likely survivors destined to be consulted as a reference work for decades to come. This book is one of the most important works published on the most widely used personality test, the MMPI-2, and it firmly establishes the instrument's empirical interpretive base for contemporary personality description.

Preface

This book reports the major results of a research project concerning the use of the Minnesota Multiphasic Personality Inventory-2 (MMPI-2) in an outpatient community mental health center setting. Although the MMPI and MMPI-2 have been widely used in such settings, the bulk of the empirical research concerning the meanings of scores and configurations of scores on the instruments has been conducted in other settings, especially inpatient psychiatric hospitals. The major purpose of the research was to identify correlates of MMPI-2 scales and code types in a community mental health setting and to determine whether the interpretive information available from other settings in which MMPI and MMPI-2 research has been conducted can be applied to the MMPI-2 results of community mental health outpatients.

All clients seeking services at a large outpatient community mental health center for a period of 21 months were potential participants in our study. We obtained valid MMPI-2s and extra-test information from more than 1,000 clients, their intake workers, and their therapists. Characteristics of persons having high scores on individual MMPI-2 scales and having specific MMPI-2 code types were determined and are reported in this book.

The results of our research project indicate clearly that the scales and code types of the MMPI-2 have essentially the same meanings in an outpatient community mental health setting as in other settings where MMPI and MMPI-2 research has been conducted in the past. Thus, clinicians using the MMPI-2 in outpatient mental health settings should feel confident in applying the large database that has accumulated concerning the interpretation of the MMPI and MMPI-2.

Our research project also addressed other important issues concerning the use of the MMPI-2. We determined that the scales and code types have essentially the same meanings for African American as for Caucasian clients. We concluded that most scales and code types have very similar meanings for both male and female clients, but we also identified gender-specific correlates for some scales. We investigated the implications of utilizing defined code types (i.e., those in which the lowest scale in the code type is at least five T-score points higher than the next highest scale in the profile) rather than unrestricted ones and concluded that defined code types have stronger and more homogeneous correlates than unrestricted ones. Finally, we examined the meaning of relatively low scores on MMPI-2 scales and concluded that low scores on some scales contribute important information about clients.

In this book we present narrative summaries of correlates for the MMPI-2 scales and code types that we studied as well as detailed results of statistical analyses on which the summaries are based. In doing so, we hope that the book will be a useful reference guide for persons who use the MMPI-2 clinically as well as those who are involved in conducting MMPI-2 research. We also present data concerning the frequency and severity with which extra-test characteristics occurred for high scores on individual scales and for code types. These additional data should be helpful in determining how likely it is that a listed correlate will apply to persons with a specific high score or code type. Although our study took place in an outpatient community mental health center setting, the similarity of our results to those previously reported for other settings indicates that much of the interpretive material presented in this book would apply to MMPI-2s completed in other settings as well. Thus, the book should be a valuable reference to anyone studying, researching, or using the MMPI-2 clinically.

Many organizations and individuals contributed significantly to the research project on which this book is based. Beverly Kaemmer and the University of Minnesota Press have provided support for the project. National Computer Systems contributed testing materials, scoring services, and hardware and software that made this large-scale project feasible. Of course, the project could never have been completed without the cooperation and participation of the clients, staff, and administrators at the Portage Path Community Mental Health Center in Akron, Ohio, which was the site for the research project.

There also are individuals who deserve credit and thanks for their contributions to the research project on which this book is based. Dr. Elizabeth K. Ott was instrumental in our gaining access to the mental health center where the project took place. Nancy Sherwood, Kristen Shepherd, and Heather Chapman served as research assistants for the project and coordinated data collection, processing, and analysis at the mental health center and on the Kent State University campus. Numerous undergraduate and graduate students at Kent State contributed to the research project in various ways. To all of these organizations and individuals we express our sincere thanks and appreciation.

J. R. G., Y. S. B.-P., J. L. M.
Kent, Ohio

Chapter 1

Introduction

Historical Background

At the time of its revision in 1989, the MMPI was the most widely used self-report measure of personality (Brown & McGuire, 1976; Harrison, Kaufman, Hickman, & Kaufman, 1988; Lubin, Larsen, & Matarazzo, 1984; Piotrowski & Keller, 1989; Piotrowski, Sherry, & Keller, 1985; Watkins, Campbell, & McGregor, 1988). Not coincidentally, it was also one of the most widely researched psychological tests (Reynolds & Sundberg, 1976). Recent surveys indicate that the revised and updated version of the inventory, the MMPI-2 (Butcher, Dahlstrom, Graham, Tellegen, & Kaemmer, 1989), is also used widely and, for the most part, has supplanted the original MMPI (Gallagher, Somwaru, Briggs, & Ben-Porath, 1996; Piotrowski & Keller, 1992; Piotrowski & Zalewski, 1993; Watkins, Campbell, Nieberding, & Hallmark, 1995; Webb, Levitt, & Rodjdev, 1993). It also continues to be one of the most widely researched psychological measures (Butcher & Rouse, 1996).

Although intended originally for use as screening devices for differential diagnosis, soon after their development it became evident that the MMPI clinical scales (Hathaway & McKinley, 1940) were only marginally successful at predicting diagnostic group membership (Hathaway, 1960). Rather than fading away, as had many of its predecessors, the MMPI underwent a transformation from a test designed to predict membership in known diagnostic classes to an instrument that both defined class membership on the basis of code types and permitted the description of persons within classes through the determination of empirical correlates of code-type group membership. In a series of studies, the test's authors and their students identified relatively homogeneous groups of individuals who produced similar patterns of scores on the clinical scales. These authors also identified empirical correlates of membership in these classes of profile patterns or code types (e.g., Black, 1953; Gough, 1946; Hathaway & Meehl, 1951; Meehl, 1946; Schmidt, 1945).

The psychometric theory underlying the empirical correlate approach to psychological testing was explicated first by Meehl (1945), who stated that "a self-rating constitutes an intrinsically interesting and significant bit of verbal behavior, the non-test correlates of which must be discovered by empirical means" (p. 297). Thus, according to Meehl (1945), the meaning and interpretation of MMPI scale scores and patterns were to be derived through empirical research designed to identify their correlates. This approach to test construction and interpretation assumed that MMPI scales measured certain psychological constructs whose nature was to be explored and determined through empirical research designed to establish the scales' construct validity (Cronbach & Meehl, 1955).

Just over a decade after the MMPI's initial publication, Meehl (1954) argued and demonstrated that assessment based on empirical correlates (the statistical or actuarial approach to test interpretation) was at least equal and mostly superior to clinical, non-psychometrically based forms of assessment. Subsequently, he issued his well-known call for the development of "MMPI Cookbooks" (Meehl, 1956). These would be research-based documents designed to inform MMPI users of the empirical correlates of various patterns of scores on the instrument. The task of the test interpreter would be primarily clerical: determine to which class of MMPI profiles a given set of scores belongs (i.e., identify the code type) and describe the person who produced those scores based on the empirical correlates of their MMPI code type.

Meehl's (1956) call for a cookbook sparked a flurry of research activity culminating in the publication of three monographs designed to serve as MMPI cookbooks (Drake & Oetting, 1959; Gilberstadt & Duker, 1965; Marks & Seeman, 1963). The authors of these monographs used somewhat different approaches in responding to Meehl's challenge. A review of these efforts, and the differences among them, will help set the stage for several decisions that needed to be made in developing the methodology for the present investigation. The two primary methodological issues faced by developers of MMPI codebooks were (1) how to classify profiles into code types, and (2) how to identify symptomatic and personality characteristics associated with code-type membership.

Early approaches to code-type classification were based on the two highest scales in the MMPI profile. Hathaway and Meehl (1951) identified clinical characteristics associated with nine two-point code types, defined simply on the basis of the two highest scales on the profile. They noted that the incidence of psychopathology was considerably greater when T scores on both the scales in the code type exceeded 70. They did not, however, propose any specific rules or impose any restrictive criteria for including a profile in a code type. Subsequent investigators introduced varying degrees of restriction in developing their methods for code-type classification. As reviewed below, authors of the three MMPI codebooks developed in response to Meehl's challenge differed in their approach to code-type definition.

Two general approaches were used to identify empirically grounded characteristics of MMPI code types. One method relied on generating descriptive frequency or mean data for members of various code types. We refer to characteristics identified in this manner as *descriptors.* A second approach to identifying code-type characteristics involved data comparisons. Using this method, researchers compared frequency or mean data identified for a given code type with similar data obtained for samples of individuals who did not belong to the code type. Statistical tests typically were conducted to identify characteristics that differed significantly across groups defined by code-type membership. This approach relied, essentially, on correlational analyses that identified an association between code-type membership and extra-test data. We refer to characteristics identified in this manner as *correlates.* Hathaway and Meehl (1951) relied on absolute frequency data to produce descriptors for their two-point code types. They cautioned, however, that "the actual absolute values of these fractions [i.e., frequencies] are practically meaningless. It is only the relative probabilities of symptoms that make any real difference" (Hathaway & Meehl, 1951, p. 139).

The first of the comprehensive MMPI codebooks was published by Drake and Oetting (1959). These authors identified empirical correlates for a sample of 2,634 men and 1,546 women who had completed the MMPI and received services at a college counseling center. They reviewed the treatment records of their participants and identified characteristics that were associated statistically with membership in various MMPI code types. Code-type classification was based on individuals' highest and lowest scores on the profile. Code-type characteristics were identified using essentially correlational analyses, yielding lists of empirical correlates for the code types included in their investigation. Drake and Oetting's codebook served as an important reference source for counselors at college and university clinics.

Marks and Seeman (1963) published the next extensive empirically grounded MMPI codebook. Their project, which was based on a sample of approximately 350 psychiatric inpatients (59%) and outpatients (41%), remains one of the most comprehensive efforts at establishing an empirical basis for MMPI interpretation. Unlike Drake and Oetting (1959), Marks and Seeman used very strict rules for classifying MMPI code types. For example, to be classified as a *27* code type, the following criteria had to be met: (1) scales 2 and 7 above T score 70, (2) scale 2 greater than scale 7, (3) scale 2 at least 15 T-score points greater than scale 8, (4) scale 7 greater than scales 1 and 3, (5) scale 7 at least 10 T-score points greater than scales 4, 6, and 8, (6) scale 9 less than T score 60, and (7) scales L, F, and K less than T score 70.

Marks and Seeman (1963) relied primarily on descriptive analyses in identifying code-type characteristics. Using Q-sorts generated by participants' therapists, they identified the five (or so) most prototypical participants in each code-type group and generated descriptions for the code type based on these patients' Q-sorts. In addition, they provided a comprehensive list of descriptive clinical and psychometric data based on somewhat larger code-type groups. Thus, most of the code-type characteristics identified by Marks and Seeman were descriptors rather than correlates. However, these investigators did provide some correlational data by identifying those code-type descriptors that deviated beyond certain levels from the overall base rates for their sample.

Gilberstadt and Duker (1965) published a similarly comprehensive set of empirically derived characteristics for profiles of approximately 360 male inpatients at a VA hospital. Like Marks and Seeman (1963), these authors developed restrictive rules for code-type classification. For example, to be classified as a *27* code type under the Gilberstadt and Duker rules, a profile had to satisfy the following criteria: (1) scales 2 and 7 greater than T score 70, (2) scale 2 greater than scale 7, (3) scale 7 at least 15 T-score points greater than scale 8, (4) scale 0 less than T score 70, and (5) scales 4 and 6 less than T score 80 unless scales 2 and/or 7 are not greater than T score 85, in which instance scales 4 and 6 had to be less than T score 70.

Gilberstadt and Duker (1965) relied primarily on correlational analyses in developing their codebook. Unlike Marks and Seeman (1963), who used their entire sample as the contrast group for their correlational analyses, these authors relied on a "general abnormal sample" for this purpose. Code-type correlates were identified through statistical significance testing. Because of the relatively high base rate of some characteristics in the general abnormal sample, certain commonly occurring characteristics were not identified as correlates (because they appeared with similar frequency in the target code type and comparison groups). Gilberstadt and Duker added these features to their list of code-type characteristics if they occurred in more than 50% of the cases for a given code type. Like Marks and Seeman, these authors excluded from their analyses participants who deviated markedly from expectations for their code types.

The codebooks written by Marks and Seeman (1963) and Gilberstadt and Duker (1965) served for many years as primary resources for MMPI interpretation in a variety of clinical settings. Current interpretive guides (e.g., Butcher & Williams, 1992; Graham, 1993; Greene, 1991) continue to rely, in part, on these sources. However, shortly after Marks and Seeman published their codebook, questions were raised concerning the scope of coverage of the code types defined in their monograph. Whereas Marks and Seeman stated initially that nearly 80% of the patients at their facility could be classified into 1 of their 16 code types, Briggs, Taylor, and Tellegen (1966) reported that as many as 80% of patients at other facilities could not be classified according to Marks and Seeman's stringent rules for code-type classification. Fowler and Coyle (1968), Huff (1965), and Meikle and Gerritse (1970) raised similar concerns.

In response to these concerns, researchers began to use less stringent rules for code-type classification in an effort to increase the proportion of profiles that could be classified. Approaches reemerged that were based on the identification of MMPI high-point, two-point, and three-point code types (e.g., Gynther, Altman, & Sletten, 1973; Lewandowski & Graham, 1972). Boerger, Graham, and Lilly (1974) demonstrated that reliable empirical correlates could be identified for single scales. Marks, Seeman, and Haller (1974) developed an alternative classification system that relied on loosely defined two-point codes for profile classification. Profiles were assigned to two-point codes based on the two highest scores among the clinical scales.

In addition to relaxing their criteria for code-type classification, Marks, Seeman, and Haller (1974) developed narrative summaries of code-type characteristics. In doing so, they shifted from their original emphasis on frequency-based descriptors and relied primarily on characteristics identified through correlational analyses. They included in their narrative summaries those code-type characteristics that deviated significantly from the overall base rates in their sample. Nonetheless, they continued to provide a rich set of descriptive extra-test data in addition to the correlationally based summaries. Gynther, Altman, and Sletten (1973) and Lewandowski and Graham (1972) reported code-type correlates generated by contrasting information about code-type members with similar data on remaining participants in their samples.

At the time of its revision in 1989, the one-, two-, and three-point code-type classification scheme was the most common approach to MMPI interpretation, and code-type characteristics were identified mainly through correlational analyses. Summarized in various interpretive guides (e.g., Graham, 1977, 1987; Greene, 1980), an unparalleled source of empirical information was available to guide test users' interpretation of original MMPI profiles. Therefore, it was a matter of great interest to determine the extent to which protocols scored with the new MMPI-2 norms yielded the same code-type classification as would have been derived if profiles had been generated based on the original MMPI norms.

This question stirred considerable debate in the literature. Initial reports in the MMPI-2 manual indicated that code types varied across the two sets of norms in approximately one third of clinical and nonclinical cases. However, Graham, Timbrook, Ben-Porath, and Butcher (1991) reanalyzed these data and determined that congruence in code-type classification across the two sets of norms is considerably greater when some restrictions are placed on code-type class membership. Specifically Graham, Timbrook, et al. recommended that to be classified to a code type, a set of scores has to be *well defined,* meaning that the lowest scale used to define the code type has to be at least 5 T-score points greater than the next highest scale in the profile.

Dahlstrom (1992) rejected Graham, Timbrook, et al.'s (1991) recommendation on the grounds that it was unprecedented and arbitrary. Tellegen and Ben-Porath (1993) provided further psychometric justification for implementing the recommendation that only well-defined code types be interpreted, and cited literature showing that some restriction of code-type membership was necessary and consistent with past practice. As detailed in chapter 2, in the current investigation we used well-defined code types as recommended by Graham, Timbrook, et al. Although some disagreement over the optimal way to classify MMPI-2 code types continues, all of the participants in these exchanges have agreed that what is most needed at this time are studies of the empirical correlates of code types based on MMPI-2 norms.

A second question that has emerged from the code-type congruence debate is the extent to which it is necessary to rely on code types for MMPI-2 interpretation. Over the years of the test's existence, hundreds of studies have been published reporting the empirical correlates of individual MMPI clinical scales and various supplementary scales. These also were summarized in MMPI interpretive guides and are incorporated in current resources designed to guide clinicians in MMPI-2 interpretation.

Tellegen and Ben-Porath (1993) argued that in those cases where an individual profile cannot be classified into a well-defined code type, profile interpretation was still possible by relying on the empirical correlates of the individual clinical and supplementary scales of the MMPI-2. Further, even in cases that are readily classified into well-defined code types, additional important information may be gleaned from individual clinical and supplementary scales.

Goals of the Study

The overall aim of the study reported in this book was to identify an up-to-date, comprehensive set of empirical correlates in an outpatient community mental health setting to guide clinicians in the interpretation of MMPI-2 profiles. We provide a list of empirical correlates for both scales carried over from the original MMPI as well as for new scales developed specifically for the MMPI-2. We augment this information by providing frequency and other descriptive extra-test data. To develop an up-to-date empirical list of MMPI-2 correlates, we established four primary goals for the study. Our first goal was to conduct the research at an outpatient community mental health facility because most of the past comprehensive empirical correlate studies were conducted with inpatients, and a need exists to establish the empirical correlates of MMPI-2 scale scores and code types generated by outpatients. At the time when the original MMPI codebook studies were conducted, mental health services were considerably more likely to be delivered on an inpatient basis than they are today. The facility where data were collected for this project is described in detail in chapter 2.

The second goal of this investigation was to collect a large enough sample of MMPI-2 profiles to allow the data to be analyzed separately by gender. This is important because prior studies have suggested that some empirical correlates may be moderated by gender (Graham, 1993). Similarly, we wanted to collect a large enough sample to allow us to identify empirical correlates for a large number of well-defined code types. Unfortunately, although we tested and obtained collateral information on over 1,200 individuals, we were unable to identify reasonably sized groups of participants for all possible two- and three-point code types. Further, to provide adequate power for the analyses involving code types, we had to combine genders. Nevertheless, we were able to identify empirical correlates for the most common MMPI-2 code types in this setting.

The third goal of this project was to obtain a rich, multisource set of extra-test data to be used to identify empirical correlates for MMPI-2 scales and code types. As described in detail in chapter 2, we obtained data from the participants themselves, from mental health workers who conducted intake interviews with the participants, and from clinicians who provided therapy for these outpatients. We constructed several measures designed to obtain reliable and comprehensive information to be used in the correlate analyses.

The final goal of this study was to compare the correlates identified in this research with those that had been cataloged in previous studies with the original MMPI. Such a comparison is provided in the final chapter of this monograph, leading to the conclusion that the empirical correlates identified in the present investigation correspond well to those that had been found in prior comprehensive studies of the original version of this instrument.

Scales Included in the Study

We chose to be comprehensive in the number of MMPI-2 variables investigated in this study. However, we decided not to include the MMPI-2 validity scales in our analyses. This decision reflects our view that these scales are used most appropriately to assess test-taking attitudes rather than to generate information about individuals' personality or psychopathology. Although prior studies have identified empirical correlates for some MMPI-2 validity scales, none of these characteristics is associated uniquely with elevations on these scales. Therefore, no important interpretive information is lost by limiting the role of the validity scales to provide information regarding individual profile validity. A list of the MMPI-2 measures studied, and our rationale for including them in the investigation, follows.

Clinical Scales

Early in their work on the revision of the inventory, members of the MMPI restandardization committee decided to maintain the clinical scales as closely as possible to their original form. Thus, no new items were added to these scales, a few items were deleted from some of the clinical scales, and minor cosmetic changes were made to a small proportion of the remaining items. Ben-Porath and Butcher (1989b) demonstrated that rewriting of several MMPI-2 items did not alter their psychometric functioning. These authors also found that the two versions of the inventory yielded very comparable scores on the clinical scales (Ben-Porath & Butcher, 1989a).

The present investigation identified empirical correlates for the clinical scales individually, for several MMPI-2 well-defined code types, and for subscales of the clinical scales, including the Harris and Lingoes (1955) subscales and the scale 0 subscales developed by Ben-Porath, Hostetler, Butcher, and Graham (1989). None of the comprehensive MMPI studies conducted to date has identified empirical correlates for these subscales. Although subscales are interpreted primarily on the basis of their content, identifying their empirical correlates can generate additional interpretive information.

Content Scales and Content Component Subscales

The MMPI-2 Content Scales (Butcher, Graham, Williams, & Ben-Porath, 1990) follow in a tradition of scale construction that varies dramatically from the original clinical scales of the instrument. Welsh (1956) was one of the first MMPI authors to rely on the item content of MMPI scales (scales A and R) in suggesting how they should be interpreted. Development of the Harris and Lingoes (1955) subscales also was predicated on the premise that it is possible to rely on item content to explicate the meaning of elevated scores on MMPI clinical scales.

Wiggins (1966) was the first to develop a comprehensive set of content scales for the MMPI. He offered cogent arguments in favor of constructing content-based scales, citing research in the area of personality assessment that had demonstrated equivalence, if not superiority, of content-based measures compared to empirically derived ones. The MMPI-2 Content Scales (Butcher et al., 1990) follow in the tradition of, and were constructed similarly to, the Wiggins content scales.

The fundamental rationale of content-based scale construction and interpretation deviates markedly from the empirical correlate approach that characterizes construction and interpretation of the MMPI-2 clinical scales. In constructing the MMPI-2 Content Scales, their developers sought to identify, by means of rational/conceptual analysis, items that are related to specific domains of personality and psychopathology. Although they used statistical techniques to refine and improve the resultant scales, primary consideration was given to their content in selecting items to assign to a given scale.

Content-based scale interpretation relies on the content of items that make up a scale to derive the meaning of elevated scores on that scale. For example, individuals who produce elevated scores on the MMPI-2 Depression (DEP) content scale can be described as reporting a large number of symptoms of depression, and, by inference, as likely experiencing a depressive disorder. Note that in content-based interpretation the clinician uses the scales to characterize what the test-taker *reports* about himself or herself. One need not take these reports at face value and assume blindly that they are accurate. Careful examination of scores on the validity scales of the MMPI-2 is necessary to determine the extent to which content-based interpretations may be accurate.

As was the case with the original clinical scales, publication of the MMPI-2 Content Scales represented a starting, not an end, point in our understanding of the scales and knowledge of how best to interpret them. In the initial publication introducing these scales, Butcher et al. (1990) reported empirical correlates along with content-based descriptors for these scales. By identifying empirical correlates for the Content Scales, it is possible to augment their content-based interpretation by reference to empirically derived correlates. Since their publication, a growing body of literature on the empirical correlates of the MMPI-2 Content Scales has begun to accumulate (e.g., Archer, Aiduk, Griffin, & Elkins, 1996; Ben-Porath, Butcher, & Graham, 1991; Ben-Porath, McCully, & Almagor, 1993; Clark, 1994, 1996; Endler, Parker, & Butcher, 1993; Strassberg, Clutton, & Korboot, 1991; Zonderman, Siegler, Barefoot, & Williams, 1993). The current study seeks to add to this literature by identifying empirical correlates for the MMPI-2 Content Scales in an outpatient community mental health setting.

Although the MMPI-2 Content Scales were developed by methods designed to enhance their internal consistency, Ben-Porath and Sherwood (1993) found that most of them could be divided meaningfully into subscales. They developed the MMPI-2 Content Component scales to assist in the interpretation of elevated scores on the full Content Scales. The MMPI-2 Content Component scales function similarly to the Harris and Lingoes (1955) subscales for the clinical scales. Like the parent MMPI-2 Content Scales, the component scales are interpreted primarily on the basis of their item content. They can be particularly helpful in identifying the primary content source of moderate elevations on the parent content scale. Ben-Porath and Sherwood reported some initial empirical correlates of these scales based on data provided by couples in the MMPI-2 normative sample. In this book, we provide the first report of correlates for the component scales in a clinical sample.

Supplementary Scales

One problematic aspect of the history of MMPI research was the proliferation of invalid and/or redundant scales that were developed with the test's item pool. One of the tasks of the committee that revised and restandardized the MMPI was to identify which scales, among the multitude that had been developed with the MMPI item pool, would be retained and normed with the new version of the test. The criteria used in making these decisions centered on the need to reduce substantially the number of supplementary scales and retain only those scales that were supported by a research base indicating that they were valid and nonredundant.

In the current study, we report empirical correlates for several of the MMPI-2 supplementary scales, those that would be most relevant for the assessment of community mental health outpatients. The following scales were included: Welsh's (1956) Anxiety (A) and Repression (R) scales; Baron's (1953) Ego Strength (Es) scale; a slightly modified version of the MacAndrew (1965) Alcoholism scale (MAC-R); two new substance abuse scales developed by Weed, Butcher, McKenna, and Ben-Porath (1992)—the Addiction Potential Scale (APS) and the Addiction Acknowledgment Scale (AAS); the Dominance (Do) and Social Responsibility (Re) scales (Gough, McCloskey, & Meehl, 1951, 1952); the Overcontrolled Hostility (O-H) scale (Megargee, Cook, & Mendelsohn, 1967); the MMPI-2 version of the PTSD scale developed by Keane, Malloy, and Fairbank (1984); and the recently developed Marital Distress Scale (MDS) (Hjemboe, Almagor, & Butcher, 1992).

Conclusion

This book represents the first systematic effort to identify a comprehensive list of empirical correlates for MMPI-2 scales and code types in an outpatient community mental health setting. It follows in the tradition of the codebook studies mentioned earlier and reflects our view that to maintain the MMPI-2 as a vital clinical assessment instrument, it is essential that its empirical correlates be continually investigated and updated. We turn next to a detailed description of the method of this investigation.

Chapter 2

Description of the Research Project

Study Setting

The research project was conducted at a large urban community mental health center (CMHC) in northeast Ohio. The center served clients with a wide range of diagnoses and from diverse backgrounds. Its staff of 55 mental health professionals included psychologists, psychiatrists, registered nurses, licensed professional clinical counselors, social workers, and certified chemical dependency counselors.

A variety of treatment programs was available to clients of the CMHC. The most frequently used treatment approach involved individual and/or group outpatient counseling or therapy. The particular therapeutic orientation varied considerably among the professional staff. Psychiatric consultations, often to assess the appropriateness of medication, were frequently utilized. An intensive treatment service provided partial (day) hospitalization for clients who needed more comprehensive treatment than the typical outpatient program offered. Clients usually were referred to this program to try to prevent hospitalization or for aftercare following hospitalization. A specialized program was available for dual diagnosis clients (i.e., those with both psychiatric and substance abuse disorders). This program involved individual counseling, group education/therapy, family education/counseling, support groups, and referral to Alcoholics Anonymous, Narcotics Anonymous, and Al-Anon. However, clients for whom the primary referral problem involved substance abuse exclusively were referred for treatment to other agencies for services. Another specialized program was available for persons referred by the courts because of family/child abuse. There also was a program that offered counseling to first-time shoplifters in lieu of jail sentences.

Participants

All persons seeking services at the CMHC between April 1, 1991, and December 31, 1992, were potential participants in the study. Figure 2.1 summarizes the numbers of participants for whom the various study measures were available.

During the 21-month study period, standardized intake forms were completed for 2,482 clients (1,035 men, 1,447 women). This represented virtually everyone who requested services during the study period. Information concerning demographic characteristics and mental health history and status of the 2,482 clients is reported in Tables 2.1 and 2.2.

The average age of the clients was approximately 33 years, and they had completed,

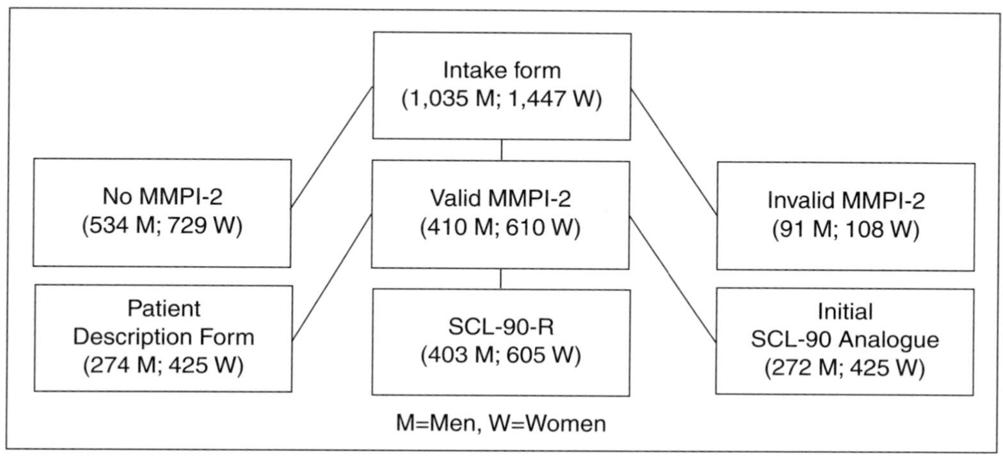

2.1. Number of clients for whom study measures were available

Table 2.1. Demographic characteristics (all intakes)

Demographic characteristic	Men (n = 1,035)	Women (n = 1,447)
Age		
Mean	33.16	33.05
SD	10.46	10.73
Years of education		
Mean	11.57	11.85
SD	2.25	2.08
Race		
Caucasian	75%	74%
African American/Other	25%	26%
Marital status		
Married	20%	21%
Widowed	1%	2%
Divorced	22%	26%
Separated	9%	11%
Never married	48%	40%
Employment status[1]		
Full-time	24%	16%
Part-time	9%	12%
Not employed	52%	54%
Disabled	10%	5%
Other	10%	19%

[1]Categories do not sum to 100% as they are not mutually exclusive.

Table 2.2. Mental health history and status (all intakes)

Variable	Men (n = 1,035)	Women (n = 1,447)
Current level of functioning (Axis V)		
Mean	60.59	61.07
SD	11.79	10.54
Previous psychiatric hospitalizations	36%	32%
Number of previous psychiatric hospitalizations		
Range	0–39	0–16
Mean	0.82	0.73
Mode	0	0
Median	0	0
Previous outpatient treatment	48%	61%
Current medications		
Antipsychotic	6%	5%
Antidepressant	13%	17%
Lithium	4%	3%
Antianxiety	9%	14%
Other	13%	15%
Any Axis I diagnosis	88%	89%
Multiple Axis I diagnoses	26%	20%
Specific Axis I diagnoses[1]		
Adjustment disorders	27%	32%
Depression	23%	28%
Anxiety disorders	14%	17%
Substance abuse/dependence	25%	15%
V codes	6%	5%
Psychotic disorders	5%	4%
Bipolar disorders	5%	4%
Any Axis II diagnosis	27%	30%

[1]The sum of the specific Axis I diagnoses is greater than 100% because some participants had more than one Axis I diagnosis.

on average, just under 12 years of formal education. Three fourths of the sample was Caucasian, and almost all of the remaining participants were African American. Relatively few of the clients were currently married (20% of men and 21% of women), and many had never been married (48% of men and 40% of women). Only 24% of the men and 16% of the women were currently employed on a full-time basis, and more than half of both the men and women were not currently employed at all.

Approximately one third of the clients reported having had psychiatric hospitalizations, with the modal number of hospitalizations being one for both men and women. Many clients (48% of men and 61% of women) reported prior involvement in outpatient mental health treatment, and many were taking psychotropic medications at the time that they requested services at the CMHC. Most of the clients (88% of the men and 89% of the women) were given an Axis I diagnosis at admission, with adjustment disorders, depression, anxiety disorders, and substance abuse/dependence disorders

Table 2.3. Reasons MMPI-2 not completed

Reason	Men	Women
Did not keep testing appointments	26%	32%
MMPI-2 not scheduled by intake workers	22%	23%
Terminated treatment before MMPI-2 completed	15%	16%
Refused to complete MMPI-2	13%	10%
MMPI-2 deferred	6%	5%
MMPI-2 recently completed	5%	4%
Referred elsewhere for treatment	3%	3%
MMPI-2 started but not completed	3%	3%
Other/unknown	7%	4%

Note: Percentages are of those who did not complete the MMPI-2.

being most common. Approximately 26% of the men and 20% of the women had multiple Axis I diagnoses.[1] Axis II diagnoses were assigned to approximately 27% of the men and 30% of the women.

Of the 2,484 clients for whom standardized intake information was available, 1,219 were scheduled for and completed the MMPI-2. Table 2.3 reports reasons that MMPI-2s were not completed. The most common reasons for the MMPI-2 not being completed were that clients failed to keep testing appointments, testing was not scheduled by intake workers, or treatment at the mental health center was terminated before testing was completed. Relatively few clients, 13% of the man and 10% of the women, refused to complete the MMPI-2. Only 3% of the men and 3% of the women who did not complete the MMPI-2 started the test but did not finish it.

MMPI-2s that met the following criteria were considered valid: (a) 30 or fewer items omitted; (b) Variable Response Inconsistency (VRIN) scale T score equal to or less than 80; (c) True Response Inconsistency (TRIN) raw score between 6 and 12; F scale raw score less than 27 for men or less than 29 for women; and Fb scale raw score less than 23 for men or less than 24 for women. Criteria for identifying invalid profiles were based on recommendations in the MMPI-2 manual (Butcher et al., 1989) for the Cannot Say, VRIN, and TRIN scales and recommendations by Graham, Watts, and Timbrook (1991) for the F and Fb scales. Based on these criteria, 199 clients were eliminated from the study, resulting in a sample of 410 men and 610 women for whom standardized intake information and valid MMPI-2s were available. All subsequent analyses were conducted on this sample of 1,020 clients or some portion of it.

Table 2.4 summarizes information comparing demographic characteristics of clients who completed valid MMPI-2s, clients who completed invalid MMPI-2s, and clients

[1]All references to diagnoses in this book use categories from the *Diagnostic and Statistical Manual of Mental Disorders, Third Edition-Revised (DSM-III-R)* (American Psychiatric Association, 1987), because this was the nosology in use at the time that the data were collected. Although some changes were introduced in *DSM-IV* (American Psychiatric Association, 1994), for the most part the criteria for the major diagnostic categories remained essentially the same.

Table 2.4. Demographic characteristics:
Valid MMPI-2, invalid MMPI-2, and no MMPI-2

	Men				Women			
	Valid MMPI-2 (410)	Invalid MMPI-2 (91)	No MMPI-2 (534)	p[1]	Valid MMPI-2 (610)	Invalid MMPI-2 (108)	No MMPI-2 (729)	p[1]
Age								
Mean	33.55	32.16	33.04	.481	32.54	33.89	33.36	.264
SD	10.80	9.50	10.36		9.88	11.00	11.35	
Education								
Mean	11.98_a	10.67_b	11.41_c	.0001	12.10_a	11.12_b	11.74_c	.000
SD	2.10	2.08	2.32		2.04	1.99	2.10	
Race								
Caucasian	$81\%_a$	$58\%_b$	$72\%_c$	.000	$79\%_b$	$66\%_a$	$70\%_a$	.001
African American	$17\%_a$	$39\%_b$	$26\%_c$		$20\%_b$	$32\%_a$	$29\%_a$	
Other	$2\%_a$	$2\%_a$	$1\%_a$		$1\%_a$	$2\%_a$	$2\%_a$	
Marital status								
Married	18%	25%	20%	.046	21%	27%	20%	.276
Widowed	2%	0%	1%		3%	1%	2%	
Divorced	22%	12%	23%		26%	26%	26%	
Separated	10%	10%	9%		13%	7%	10%	
Never married	47%	53%	47%		37%	39%	42%	
Employment status[2]								
Full-time	$28\%_a$	$10\%_b$	$24\%_a$	.003	18%	9%	15%	.037
Part-time	12%	6%	7%	.011	14%	9%	11%	.205
Not employed	$45\%_b$	$67\%_a$	$55\%_a$	.000	$50\%_a$	$65\%_b$	$56\%_{ab}$	.007
Disabled	9%	14%	11%	.294	5%	6%	6%	.566
Other	13%	8%	9%	.109	21%	18%	18%	.327

[1] *t* tests for continuous variables; x^2 for categorical variables.

[2] Categories do not sum to 100% as they are not mutually exclusive.

Note: Values in rows with same subscript do not differ significantly from each other.

who did not complete MMPI-2s. The three groups of clients did not differ significantly in terms of age, marital status, or employment status. The valid MMPI-2 group was significantly more educated than the other groups, but the differences in education were not great. All three groups had mean education levels between 10.5 and 12 years. The valid MMPI-2 group included a larger proportion of Caucasians than did the other groups.

Table 2.5 summarizes information concerning mental health history and status for the valid MMPI-2, invalid MMPI-2, and no MMPI-2 groups. It appears that the group with valid MMPI-2s was somewhat less emotionally disturbed than the other groups. Clients with valid MMPI-2s were functioning at a higher level and were less likely to have had previous psychiatric hospitalizations. However, the three groups of clients did not differ in terms of having had previous outpatient treatment or the percentages who were assigned Axis I or Axis II diagnoses at admission.

In summary, clients who completed valid MMPI-2s were not substantially different

Table 2.5. Mental health history and status: Valid MMPI-2, invalid MMPI-2, and no MMPI-2

	Men				Women			
	Valid MMPI-2 (410)	Invalid MMPI-2 (91)	No MMPI-2 (534)	p[1]	Valid MMPI-2 (610)	Invalid MMPI-2 (108)	No MMPI-2 (729)	p[1]
Current level of functioning								
Mean	62.96_b	57.28_a	59.31_a	.000	62.33_b	58.42_a	60.42_a	.000
SD	10.09	14.89	12.11		9.88	1.77	10.76	
Number of sessions								
Mean	10.66_a	11.69_a	3.85_b	.000	10.47_a	9.11_a	4.68_b	.000
SD	10.37	11.39	6.04		9.94	10.17	7.55	
Previous hospitalization	$29\%_a$	$39\%_{ab}$	$41\%_b$	.001	$27\%_b$	$39\%_a$	$36\%_a$	.001
Previous outpatient treatment	47%	52%	49%	.681	60%	58%	62%	.741
Current medications								
Antipsychotic	$4\%_a$	$3\%_{ab}$	$9\%_b$	.007	$3\%_a$	$6\%_{ab}$	$7\%_b$	.007
Antidepressant	11%	15%	14%	.262	16%	26%	17%	.067
Lithium	3%	2%	5%	.196	2%	6%	4%	.131
Antianxiety	6%	10%	12%	.017	12%	21%	14%	.050
Any Axis I diagnosis	87%	87%	89%	.660	89%	91%	89%	.892
Specific Axis I diagnoses								
Adjustment disorder	27%	24%	28%	.738	34%	34%	29%	.216
Depression	21%	31%	24%	.081	30%	22%	27%	.221
Anxiety disorder	17%	7%	13%	.040	15%	19%	18%	.402
Substance abuse/ dependence	21%	31%	27%	.022	12%	16%	17%	.023
Psychotic disorder	3%	4%	7%	.023	$1\%_a$	$11\%_b$	$6\%_a$	.000
V codes	$10\%_a$	$3\%_{ab}$	$4\%_b$	.002	7%	6%	4%	.189
Bipolar disorder	5%	3%	5%	.824	3%	7%	4%	.280
Any Axis II diagnosis	29%	32%	24%	.166	32%	27%	29%	.297

[1] *t* tests for continuous variables; x^2 for categorical variables.
Note: Values in rows with same subscript do not differ significantly from each other.

from those who did not in terms of demographic characteristics such as age, education, marital status, and employment status. However, according to some measures, those who completed valid MMPI-2s were somewhat less psychologically disturbed than those who did not. It is possible that this greater disturbance was involved in the unwillingness and/or inability of some clients to complete the MMPI-2 and other study measures. However, the clients in the study setting who completed valid MMPI-2s are likely to be representative of all clients in the setting who might reasonably be expected to complete valid MMPI-2 in the course of their treatment at the CMHC. Thus, although perhaps not representative of the entire population of clients at the CMHC, the current sample does represent those individuals whose MMPI-2s will be interpreted.

To gauge the representativeness of our final sample, we compared its demographic makeup with the population of community mental health center clients in the state of

Ohio. Data provided by the Ohio Department of Mental Health on their World Wide Web page indicate that our sample represents well the population of service receivers at community mental health centers statewide. The proportions of ethnic minority clients and those who are not employed were nearly identical for our sample and all community mental health centers in Ohio in 1996. Data regarding marital status and education were not available for the entire state. A comparison of the educational level and marital status of our sample with data available for an ongoing study of the MMPI-2 in psychiatric inpatients in Minnesota (Arbisi & Ben-Porath, 1998) indicated that the two samples are very similar in terms of levels of education and marital status. Overall, the demographic composition of our sample seems to represent appropriately the population of individuals to whom the MMPI-2 is likely to be administered at community agencies. As would be expected, this population is somewhat less educated and has larger proportions of unmarried, not employed, and ethnic minority individuals than the general population.

Study Measures

Minnesota Multiphasic Personality Inventory-2 (MMPI-2)

The MMPI-2 is a 567-item personality inventory (Butcher et al., 1989). It is a revised and updated version of the original MMPI (Hathaway & McKinley, 1940). The MMPI-2 includes the validity and clinical scales of the original MMPI, some new validity scales developed specifically for the MMPI-2, content scales, content component subscales, and other supplementary scales. Norms were developed for the MMPI-2 that were representative of the population of the United States. The internal consistencies and test-retest reliability coefficients of the MMPI-2 scales have been reported in the test manual (Butcher et al., 1989).

Intake Form

The intake form was developed specifically for this study (Appendix A). It was designed to be completed on the basis of a personal interview with the client. The intake form includes demographic information such as age, education, marital status, employment status, and ethnicity. It also includes information concerning mental health history (e.g., prior psychiatric hospitalizations, prior outpatient treatment), and substance abuse history. Diagnostic impressions are provided for all five axes of DSM-III-R. Ratings are made on a variety of mental status variables including orientation, memory, thought processes, insight, and mood. All persons completing the intake forms were licensed professionals (e.g., social workers, psychologists, nurses) who had considerable experience in conducting intake interviews and who were trained specifically to complete the intake form used in this study. Although it would have been very desirable to demonstrate interrater reliability for the intake ratings, reliability checks were not feasible in this applied clinical setting.

SCL-90-R

The SCL-90-R is a 90-item self-report inventory designed to reflect the psychological symptom patterns of psychiatric and medical patients (Derogatis, 1983). Clients rate on a five-point scale (not at all, a little bit, moderately, quite a bit, extremely) how much they were distressed by various symptoms during the past seven days. The following nine primary symptom dimensions were identified through a combination of clinical/rational and empirical/analytic procedures: Somatization, Obsessive-Compulsive, Interpersonal Sensitivity, Depression, Anxiety, Hostility, Phobic Anxiety, Paranoid Ideation, and Psychoticism.

Derogatis (1983) reported internal consistency (Alpha) coefficients for the dimension scales ranging from .77 for Psychoticism to .90 for Depression. One week test-retest coefficients for psychiatric patients were between .80 and .90 (Derogatism, 1983). Validation studies have indicated that the SCL-90-R scales are related to conceptually relevant MMPI scales (Derogatis, Rickels, & Rock, 1976) and are sensitive to differences in levels of depression (e.g., Weissman, Slobetz, Prusoff, Mezritz, & Howard, 1976) and to stress-related conditions (e.g., Carrington, et al., 1980).

SCL-90 Analogue

The SCL-90 Analogue is a visual analogue scale by which each of the nine primary dimensions of the SCL-90-R is rated by health professionals (Derogatis, 1983). Each dimension is represented on a 100-mm line, with "not at all" at one end and "extremely" at the other. Brief descriptions of each dimension are provided for raters. Derogatis reported interrater reliability coefficients ranging from .83 to .96 for a sample of 72 outpatients. Although validity data for this analogue version of the SCL-90 have not been reported, previous research provides general support for the use of visual analogue scales to measure clinical phenomena (see Wewers & Lowe, 1990, for a review).

Patient Description Form

The Patient Description Form (PDF) was developed specifically for this study (Appendix B). Its 188 items are rated (not at all, slight, moderate, high, very high) by therapists to describe personality and symptomatic characteristics of patients. The items were selected on the basis of a review of previous research and current interpretive reference sources. They represent commonly identified symptoms and characteristics associated with MMPI-2 scales and code types.

Using a combined rational/statistical approach, we developed 25 scales to assess the major content dimensions of the instrument. Internal consistency (Alpha) coefficients for these scales, based on the clients in this study with valid MMPI-2s and for whom the PDF had been completed, are reported in Table 2.6. The data indicate that the scales are internally consistent. A listing of the items included in each of its scales is presented in Appendix C.

Procedures

During clients' first visits to the CMHC, comprehensive intake interviews were conducted by experienced professional mental health workers, primarily social workers and nurses. Although a standardized interview was not required, all intake workers were familiar with the standard intake form that was to be completed on the basis of the interview. The intake workers had been trained to complete the intake form by research project staff. Intake workers did not have access to MMPI-2 results.

Following the intake interviews, clients were scheduled for another appointment to

Table 2.6. Patient Description Form scales

Scale	No. items	Alpha Men (n = 274)	Alpha Women (n = 425)
Angry resentment	7	.92	.90
Critical/Argumentative	6	.91	.90
Narcissistic	8	.92	.93
Defensive	8	.89	.89
Histrionic	8	.89	.90
Aggressive	4	.82	.77
Insecure	7	.87	.91
Anxious	6	.87	.87
Pessimistic	2	.73	.72
Depressed	6	.86	.87
Achievement-oriented	8	.84	.87
Passive-submissive	4	.85	.86
Introverted	3	.84	.86
Emotionally controlled	5	.88	.85
Antisocial	6	.90	.87
Negative treatment attitudes	6	.89	.86
Somatic symptoms	5	.92	.91
Psychotic symptoms	5	.80	.87
Family problems	4	.89	.90
Obsessive-compulsive	6	.83	.85
Stereotypic masculine interests	2	.92	.84
Procrastinates	3	.75	.72
Suspicious	3	.83	.79
Agitated	3	.69	.75
Work problems	3	.78	.78

complete the MMPI-2 and the SCL-90-R. The median length of time between the intake interview and the administration of the MMPI-2 was seven days. The MMPI-2 and the SCL-90-R were administered to clients individually or in small groups. Research project staff or psychology interns typically monitored test administration. If needed, an audiotape version of the MMPI-2 was utilized.

Treatment program and staff assignments were made upon completion of the intake interview or shortly thereafter. Client status at the CMHC was monitored by project staff, and after three treatment appointments had been kept, therapists were asked to complete the SCL-90 Analogue and the Patient Description Form (PDF). The median length of time between MMPI-2 administration and completion of these forms by therapists was 38 days. Therapists did not have access to MMPI-2 data until after these forms were completed. In a few instances (less than 3%), psychologists reviewing computerized interpretations of the MMPI-2 results identified specific serious concerns (e.g., suicide potential) and brought them to the attention of the therapists. In these cases, therapists were not given specific MMPI-2 scores and did not have access to computerized interpretations until after their ratings of clients were completed.

Data Analyses

Extra-test correlates of MMPI-2 scales and code types were determined using subsets of the sample of clients for whom valid MMPI-2s were available. The size of these various subsets was determined by the number of persons for whom each set of extra-test measures (e.g., intake information, therapist ratings) was available (see Figure 2.1). K-corrected T scores for MMPI-2 scales were used for all analyses. Although evidence concerning the relative superiority of K-corrected and non-K-corrected scores has been inconsistent (e.g., Dahlstrom, Welsh, & Dahlstrom, 1972; Weed & Han, 1992), we decided to use corrected scores because the existing research base concerning correlates of MMPI and MMPI-2 scales has been generated using K-corrected scores. By using K-corrected scores in our study, our results are directly comparable to those of earlier studies.

Correlations with Individual Scales

For individual MMPI-2 clinical, Harris and Lingoes, Content, Content Component, and supplementary scales or subscales, correlations were calculated between scores on the scales or subscales and measures from the various extra-test instruments that were available for clients. The MMPI-2 scale scores were treated as dichotomous variables ($T \geq 65$ versus $T < 65$). Treating MMPI-2 scales as dichotomous variables provides a direct comparison of individuals who have clinically significant elevations on the scales and those who do not. The correlation coefficients provide effect size information for the identified correlates.

Correlations are not reported for several scales because there were inadequate numbers of clients in the higher ($T \geq 65$) groups. For the Ego Strength (Es), Dominance (Do), and Responsibility (Re) supplementary scales, lower scores typically are associated with more symptoms, problems, and negative characteristics. For these scales, the categories for the dichotomous variable were low ($T \leq 40$) versus other ($T > 40$), and correlates are presented for lower scorers.

Correlations with Code Type

In trying to identify correlates of code types, several important issues had to be considered. We limited our analyses to two- and three-point code types. We also conducted some preliminary analyses of correlates of one-point code types. Because the correlates were almost completely redundant with those for individual clinical scales, we decided not to report data for one-point code types. We also decided to limit our analyses to code types that were well defined (i.e., at least 5 T-score points between the lowest score in the code type and the next highest clinical score in the profile) and elevated (all scales in the code type greater than $T = 64$). Graham, Timbrook, Ben-Porath, and Butcher (1991), Ben-Porath and Tellegen (1995), and Tellegen and Ben-Porath (1993) have stressed the importance of limiting code-type interpretation to those that are well defined. The basic issue is that the clinical scales of the MMPI-2 are not perfectly reliable. Given the standard error of measurement of the scales, differences of less than 5 T-score points between scales should not be considered meaningful. By limiting analyses to well-defined code types, the homogeneity of persons within a code-type category was increased. This greater homogeneity increases the likelihood that the correlates identified for a code-type category will apply to specific individuals with that code type. Using a subset of data from the current study setting, McNulty, Ben-Porath, and Graham (1999) found that well-defined code types had stronger and conceptually more relevant correlates than undefined code types.

Graham, Smith, and Schwartz (1986) demonstrated that MMPI code types are more stable temporally when the original code type included at least one scale that was significantly elevated. In addition, Graham (1993) has pointed out that both the symptomatic descriptors and the personality characteristics associated with code types are more likely to apply to persons with particular code types when their scores on the scales in the code type are significantly elevated. Based on both of these considerations, we decided to limit our analyses to code types that were also elevated (i.e., all of the scales in the code type greater than T = 64).

Another important issue had to do with the frequencies with which code types occurred in the setting where the study was conducted. As is usually the case, not all code types occurred equally frequently in our study. In order to have sufficient statistical power to identify correlates of code types, we limited our analyses to those with at least 10 clients having the code type in our study. Table 2.7 reports the frequencies of the two- and three-point code types included in the analyses of correlates of code types. It should be noted that the order of the scales in the code type was not considered (e.g., 12/21 includes both 12 and 21 codes; 123 includes 123, 132, 231, 213, 312, and 321 codes).

Another issue involved selecting a group of clients with whom clients with a particular code type could be compared and contrasted. Several options were available to us. Most previous code-type research has used a comparison group consisting of all participants in a study except for those in the target code type for which correlates were being identified (Archer, Griffin, & Aiduk, 1995; Gilberstadt & Duker, 1965; Lewandowski & Graham, 1972; Marks & Seeman, 1963). Using such a comparison group has the advantage of permitting the identification of correlates that are unique to the target code type. However, it has the disadvantage of not identifying characteristics of persons with the target code type if those characteristics are shared by other persons in the setting where the research is done. For example, clinical depression was characteristic of persons in our study setting with the 12/21 code type, but it would not have been identified for this code because it also was characteristic of most other clients in our study setting.

Another approach would be to compare each target code type with a nonpathological contrast group. This would permit the identification of symptoms, problems, and personality characteristics that are likely to be shared by persons with a particular code type, even if they occurred frequently among persons with other code types. It is unlikely that we will ever be able to have individuals from the general population complete the MMPI-2, go through a clinical intake interview, and have enough subsequent contact with mental health professionals to permit meaningful ratings of their psychological functioning.

One way to approximate such a nonpathological contrast group is to identify clients seeking clinical services who are not experiencing serious psychopathology. Toward this end, we decided to use in our code-type analyses a contrast group consisting of clients in the study setting who produced nondefensive, within-normal-limits (WNL) profiles (i.e., no clinical scale score greater than T = 64). This approach has the advantage of identifying all characteristics of persons with a particular code type, regardless of whether they are shared with persons with different code types. Because the primary goal of our research was to identify a comprehensive list of descriptors for CMHC clients with particular code types, we decided that using the WNL comparison group was more

Table 2.7. Frequencies of two-point and three-point code types

Code type	Men	Women	Total
12/21	5	10	15
13/31	7	13	20
23/32	3	17	20
24/42	10	20	30
26/62	5	10	15
27/72	10	25	35
34/43	8	7	15
46/64	14	21	35
48/84	5	11	16
49/94	2	10	12
68/86	15	13	28
78/87	11	9	20
123	9	18	27
247	8	9	17
278	8	21	29
468	11	9	20
478	4	8	12
Within normal limits	48	42	90

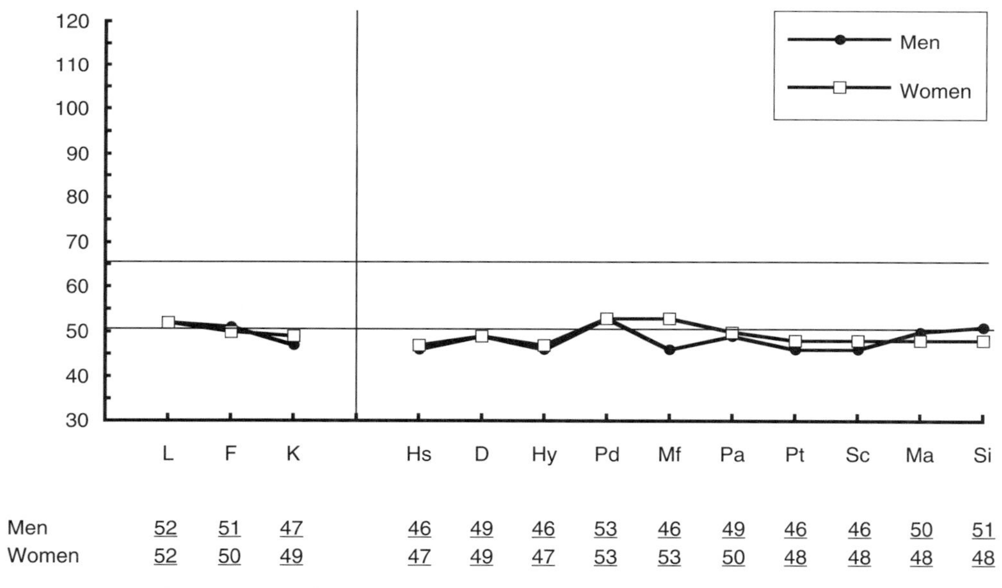

2.2. Mean standard scales profiles for within-normal-limits groups

appropriate than using a general comparison group that would yield only unique correlates for the code types.

The WNL group that we used consisted of 48 male and 42 female clients in the study setting who had no clinical scale T scores greater than 64. Recognizing that some clients produce WNL profiles because of underreporting of symptoms and problems, we excluded from our WNL contrast group clients with L or K scale T scores greater than 64. The mean profiles for men and women in the WNL group are presented in Figures 2.2 and 2.3. It should be noted that the mean scores for men or women in this WNL

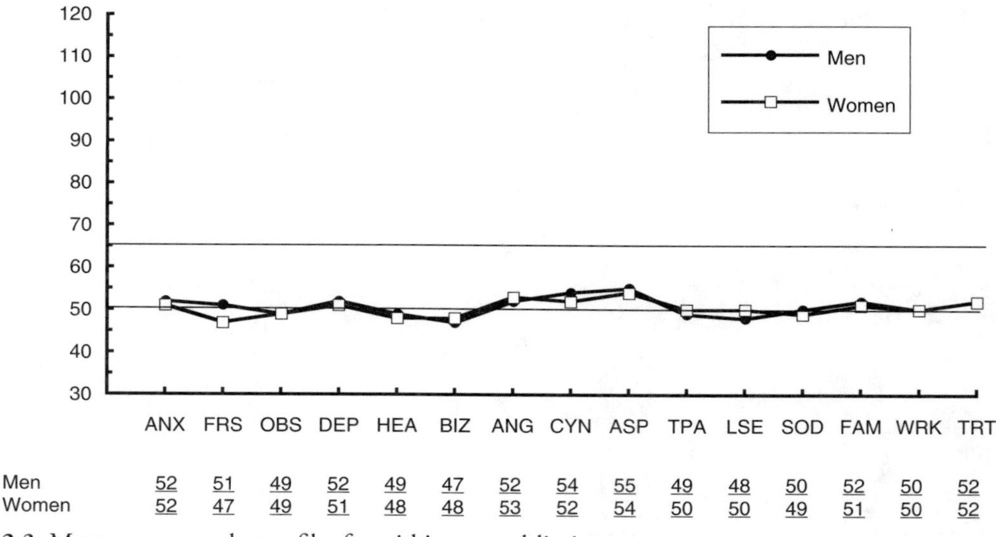

2.3. Mean content scales profiles for within-normal-limits groups

group did not differ more than 5 T-score points above or below the mean for the MMPI-2 normative sample.

The most common Axis I diagnoses for the WNL clients were adjustment disorder (40%) and V codes, that is, conditions such as marital or occupational problems not attributable to a mental disorder that are a focus of attention or treatment (25%). Clients in the WNL group were more likely than others to have been referred by the courts or a probation officer and to hold full-time jobs. They were less likely than others to have had previous psychiatric hospitalizations or treatment or to be taking psychotropic medications.

Because of the large sample sizes, even modest (and probably not clinically meaningful) correlations between group membership and external criteria are statistically significant. Therefore, only correlations equal to or greater than .15 (and p values less than .001) were considered to be potentially meaningful and are reported. For the PDF items, for which large numbers of correlations exceeded this criterion, only the 10 strongest correlations for each gender are reported for each MMPI-2 scale. For the code-type analyses, the 10 strongest PDF item correlations for the combined genders are reported.

Significant correlations between an MMPI-2 scale or code type and extra-test variables indicate that persons with high (or for a few scales low) scores on the scale or who have the code type are more likely to have these characteristics than persons with other scores on the scale or with a WNL profile. However, the correlational data do not address the issue of just how common or how strong the associated characteristics are for persons in the target group. We also calculated the frequencies (categorical variables) and average values (continuous variables) for each extra-test measure separately for the entire sample of persons with valid MMPI-2s, for the WNL contrast group, and for each high/other score and code-type group. These descriptive data can be very helpful in understanding how likely it is that each correlate will apply to persons in the target groups. These summary data are reported in appendixes along with the correlate data. Examples illustrating the use of these descriptive data are provided in chapter 6.

Chapter 3

Correlates of Clinical Scales and Harris-Lingoes and Scale 0 Subscales

In this chapter we provide summary descriptions of correlates for each of the MMPI-2 clinical scales and the Harris-Lingoes and scale 0 subscales. The descriptions are based on the correlations between MMPI-2 scale and subscale scores and extra-test measures that are reported in Appendixes D, E, and F. Because the MMPI-2 scales and subscale scores were dichotomized (T ≥ 65 versus T < 65), the descriptions that follow compare clients with clinically elevated scores on each scale or subscale with clients who did not have such elevated scores on that scale or subscale. Unless otherwise specified, the correlates applied to both male and female clients. The correlates are organized primarily according to source of information (e.g., history, self-report, intake worker ratings, therapist ratings), and the order of their presentation in the summaries does not necessarily correspond to the relative magnitude of the correlations between the MMPI-2 scales and subscales and the extra-test measures.

Although high scorers are more likely than other scorers to have the characteristics included in the summaries and/or to have them to a greater extent, not every high scorer on a scale or subscale will have every extra-test characteristic that is presented. Reference to Appendixes K-1, K-2, L-1, or L-2, in which we report frequencies (categorical variables) and average values (continuous variables) for each extra-test variable for the high score and other score groups, can be of additional help in determining the likelihood that a specific characteristic will apply to high scorers on a particular clinical scale or subscale.

Clinical Scales

Scale 1: Hypochondriasis (Hs)

Compared with clients with T scores below 65 on this scale, those with T scores equal to or greater than 65 were more likely to have diagnoses of depression or dysthymia. Female clients with high scores on this scale were more likely to have histories of having been physically abused and of suicide attempts, and they were more likely to be taking anxiolytic medications. Both male and female clients with high scale 1 scores reported multiple somatic symptoms. Male clients with high scores on this scale also reported feeling anxious.

High scale 1 scorers were rated as depressed and as having sad mood during intake interviews, and later their therapists also characterized them as depressed. They were also seen as preoccupied with health problems and as developing physical symptoms in response to stress. High scorers were also characterized as feeling hopeless and pessimistic. They reported sleep disturbances, fatigue, lack of energy, and low sex drive. Female clients with high scale 1 scores were also seen by their therapists as not coping well with stress, not having many interests, and not having high aspirations.

Scale 2: Depression (D)

Compared with clients with T scores below 65 on this scale, those with T scores equal to or greater than 65 were more likely to have diagnoses of depression or dysthymia. Male clients were also more likely to have anxiety disorder diagnoses and histories of previous outpatient and inpatient mental health treatment. Female clients scoring high on this scale were more likely to have histories of suicide attempts and to have few or no friends. Both male and female clients who scored high on this scale reported anxiety, depression, and obsessive-compulsive symptoms.

High scorers on this scale were rated as depressed and sad during intake interviews, and their therapists characterized them similarly. They were seen by therapists as having suicidal ideation and as feeling hopeless and pessimistic. These clients did not have much energy, their sleep was disturbed, and they reported feeling fatigued much of the time. High scorers were also seen as anxious and preoccupied with health problems. Therapists saw high scorers as feeling that life is a strain and as not coping well with stress. High scorers appeared to be insecure and introverted, and they were not very achievement oriented. High-scoring male clients were described by therapists as feeling nervous and agitated and as having obsessive-compulsive symptoms. These men were characterized as interpersonally sensitive and as not having strong stereotypically masculine interests.

Scale 3: Hysteria (Hy)

Compared with clients with T scores below 65 on this scale, those with T scores equal to or greater than 65 were more likely to have diagnoses of depression or dysthymia. High-scoring female clients were more likely to be taking antidepressant and/or anxiolytic medications. Both male and female clients who scored high on this scale reported multiple somatic complaints.

Male and female clients who scored high on this scale were rated as depressed and sad during intake interviews, and the female clients were also rated as anxious. High-scoring male and female clients were characterized by therapists as feeling sad, depressed, and hopeless. They tended to have sleep disturbances and to feel fatigued much of the time. Therapists also reported that high scorers on this scale seemed to be preoccupied with health problems, presented multiple somatic symptoms, and tended to develop physical symptoms in response to stress. High scorers were also described by therapists as feeling overwhelmed and anxious and as having trouble concentrating. Male clients who scored high on this scale were characterized by therapists as pessimistic, angry, resentful, and having low sex drive. Female clients who scored high on this scale were characterized by therapists as interpersonally sensitive.

Scale 4: Psychopathic Deviate (Pd)

Compared with clients with T scores below 65 on this scale, those with T scores equal to or greater than 65 were more likely to have histories of outpatient mental health treatment and of having been physically abused. High-scoring male clients were more likely to have histories of previous psychiatric hospitalizations. High-scoring female clients were more likely to have diagnoses of depression or dysthymia. These women were also more likely to have histories of alcohol abuse, suicide attempts, having few or no friends, and having been sexually abused.

Male and female clients scoring high on this scale were rated as depressed during intake interviews, and their therapists later described depression and suicidal ideation. These clients were seen as feeling sad, hopeless, and pessimistic. High-scoring male clients were characterized by therapists as agitated, self-degrading, and interpersonally sensitive. These men were more likely to have work-related problems. High-scoring female clients were characterized by therapists as histrionic, over-reactive, and lonely. They were also seen as angry, resentful, critical, argumentative, cynical, and sarcastic. These women felt that they were getting a raw deal from life, were suspicious of others, and had difficulty trusting other people.

Scale 5: Masculinity-Femininity (Mf)

Compared with the other clinical scales, there were very few extra-test correlates for scale 5. Compared with clients with T scores below 65 on this scale, men with high scores on this scale were less likely to have been arrested, and women with high scores were more likely to have antisocial personality disorder diagnoses. High-scoring men were described by therapists as not having stereotypically masculine interests and behaviors and as rejecting a traditional gender role. These men were also characterized as having exaggerated needs for attention, and they were more likely to express concerns about homosexuality. High-scoring female clients were characterized by therapists as more likely than other female clients to have stereotypically masculine interests.

Scale 6: Paranoia (Pa)

Compared with clients with T scores below 65 on this scale, those with T scores equal to or greater than 65 were more likely to have diagnoses of depression or dysthymia and histories of previous hospitalizations and of having few or no friends. Female clients scoring high on this scale were more likely to have histories of suicide attempts and of having been sexually abused. High-scoring male and female clients described themselves as depressed and interpersonally sensitive, and they were more likely to report psychotic symptoms, including paranoid ideation.

High scorers on this scale were rated as sad and depressed during intake interviews and later by their therapists. High-scoring men were also rated as angry and unhappy during intake interviews. High-scoring men and women were characterized by therapists as tearful, and they were more likely to have suicidal ideation. Therapists indicated that high-scoring male clients were anxious and had sleep disturbances. These men were described as hostile, angry, and resentful, and they tended to have family problems. They were seen as pessimistic and insecure. They often felt inferior and did not have strong achievement orientations. High-scoring women were characterized by therapists as lacking in energy.

Scale 7: Psychasthenia (Pt)

Compared with clients with T scores below 65 on this scale, those with T scores equal to or greater than 65 were more likely to have diagnoses of depression or dysthymia. High-scoring male clients were more likely to have histories of outpatient and inpatient mental health treatment. High-scoring female clients were more likely to have histories of suicide attempts, and they were more likely to be taking anxiolytic and/or antidepressant medications. Both male and female clients with high scores on this scale described themselves as interpersonally sensitive, and they reported symptoms of anxiety, depression, and obsessive-compulsive disorders. Some high scorers also reported having psychotic symptoms.

Intake workers and therapists agreed that high scorers on this scale were depressed, sad, and anxious. These clients were also seen by therapists as feeling pessimistic and hopeless and as having suicidal ideation. They reported somatic symptoms and sleep disturbances. They were characterized as nervous, anxious, and worried, and they had difficulty concentrating. High scorers seemed to feel that life is a strain, they felt overwhelmed much of the time, and they did not cope well with stress. They were described by therapists as having strong feelings of inferiority and insecurity, and they engaged in self-degrading behaviors. These clients were also seen as interpersonally sensitive. Male clients scoring high on this scale were seen by therapists as not having strong achievement needs or strong stereotypically masculine interests. Female clients scoring high on this scale were described by therapists as introverted and overly sensitive to criticism.

Scale 8: Schizophrenia (Sc)

Compared with clients with T scores below 65 on this scale, those with T scores equal to or greater than 65 were more likely to have diagnoses of depression or dysthymia. They were also more likely to have had psychiatric hospitalizations and to report having few or no friends. Male clients scoring high on this scale were more likely to have histories of outpatient mental health treatment. Female clients scoring high on this scale were more likely to have histories of suicide attempts, and they were more likely to be taking antidepressant and/or anxiolytic medications. Both male and female clients with high scores on this scale described themselves as interpersonally sensitive, and they reported symptoms of anxiety, depression, obsessive-compulsive disorder, and psychosis.

Both male and female clients with high scores on this scale were rated as sad and depressed during the intake interview, and the female clients were also rated as anxious. Therapists described high scorers on this scale as depressed and sad, as feeling pessimistic and hopeless, and as having suicidal ideation. High scorers were also anxious, seemed to be preoccupied with health problems, and had sleep disturbances. Therapists characterized high scorers as insecure persons who did not have strong achievement needs and who tended to feel like failures and make self-degrading comments. High scorers also tended to feel overwhelmed and that life is a strain, and they did not cope well with stress. Therapists described male clients who scored high on this scale as having obsessive-compulsive symptoms and family problems. Female clients with high scores on this scale were characterized as histrionic, overly sensitive persons who were suspicious of others and felt that they were getting a raw deal from life.

Scale 9: Hypomania (Ma)

Compared with clients with T scores below 65 on this scale, those with T scores equal to or greater than 65 were more likely to have histories of marijuana abuse. Female clients with high scores on this scale were more likely to have substance abuse or dependence diagnoses and histories of abusing heroin, cocaine, and alcohol. These women were also more likely to have had psychiatric hospitalizations.

Clients with high scores on this scale were rated by therapists as antisocial and aggressive. They tended to overevaluate their own worth, and they did not get along with coworkers. Male clients with high scores on this scale were rated as aloof and as displaying circumstantial speech during intake interviews. Male clients with high scores on this scale were described by therapists as having psychotic symptoms, including poor reality testing. These men tended to be restless, to have stormy interpersonal relationships, and to display temper tantrums. Female clients who scored high on this scale were described by therapists as narcissistic, egocentric, grandiose, and not likable. They were seen as psychopathic and having work problems. These women tended to be evasive and defensive. They had negative attitudes about treatment and were difficult to motivate.

Scale 0: Social Introversion (Si)

Compared with clients with T scores below 65 on this scale, those with T scores equal to or greater than 65 were more likely to have diagnoses of depression or dysthymia. Female clients were more likely to have histories of having few or no friends and of suicide attempts, and they were more likely to be taking antidepressant and/or anxiolytic medications. High-scoring men and women described themselves as interpersonally sensitive.

Clients with high scores on this scale were rated as sad and depressed during intake interviews, and their therapists characterized them as feeling depressed and hopeless. These clients were also described by therapists as insecure, introverted, shy, and socially awkward. Male clients with high scores on this scale were described by therapists as anxious, worried, and pessimistic. They were preoccupied with health problems and had sleep disturbances and obsessive-compulsive symptoms. These men tended to feel that life was a strain, and they felt overwhelmed much of the time. Female clients with high scores on this scale displayed slowed speech during intake interviews. Their therapists indicated that they were passive-submissive in relationships and did not make good first impressions. These women lacked energy, had narrow interests, did not have high aspirations, and were not very competitive.

Harris-Lingoes Subscales

Correlations between MMPI-2 Harris-Lingoes subscales and the extra-test measures available for clients (Appendix E) provided the basis for summaries of correlates included in this section. Correlations between several Harris-Lingoes subscales and extra-test measures were not computed. As Krishnamurthy, Archer, and Huddleston (1995) pointed out, the distribution of scores for the Hy_1 (Denial of Social Anxiety) subscale is such that it is not possible to obtain T scores greater than 65 on this subscale. Therefore, no correlations were calculated between scores on this subscale and the extra-test variables. For two additional Harris-Lingoes subscales, Hy_5 (Inhibition of Aggression) and Pd_3 (Social Imperturbability), there were too few clients in the high score group to permit meaningful analyses of data.

We concur with Graham's (1993) recommendation that Harris-Lingoes subscales should be interpreted only when scores on their parent scales are significantly elevated

(T > 65). Interpretation of the Harris-Lingoes subscales should be limited to trying to understand why elevated scores were obtained on the parent scales.

Subjective Depression (D_1)

Compared with clients with T scores below 65 on this subscale, those with T scores equal to or greater than 65 were more likely to have diagnoses of depression or dysthymia. Male clients with high scores on this subscale were also more likely to have histories of previous inpatient and outpatient mental health treatment. Female clients with high scores on this subscale were more likely to have histories of having few or no friends and of suicide attempts, and less likely to have histories of arrests. Both male and female clients with high scores on this subscale reported anxiety, depression, and obsessive-compulsive symptoms, and they described themselves as interpersonally sensitive.

High scorers on this subscale were rated during intake interviews as sad and depressed, and therapists later rated them similarly. Therapists also described high scorers as feeling overwhelmed and that life is a strain, and as not coping well with stress. They were seen as feeling sad, hopeless, and anxious, and they tended to have suicidal ideation. High scorers also reported fatigue, somatic symptoms, and sleep disturbances. They were characterized as interpersonally sensitive and insecure persons who often felt like failures and did not have strong achievement orientations. Male clients with high scores on this subscale were rated as unhappy during intake interviews, and therapists later rated them as histrionic, agitated, angry, and resentful. These men were seen as having obsessive-compulsive symptoms and family problems. Female clients with high scores on this subscale were rated as anxious during intake interviews, and therapists described them as introverted.

Psychomotor Retardation (D_2)

Compared with male clients with T scores below 65 on this subscale, clients with T scores equal to or greater than 65 were seen by therapists as not being very energetic. Male clients were more likely to have had previous psychiatric hospitalizations. These male clients reported symptoms of depression and were described by their therapists as depressed. They felt pessimistic and hopeless, and they experienced fatigue and sleep disturbances. These men were also seen as anxious and nervous. They were preoccupied with health problems, had multiple somatic complaints, and were prone to develop physical symptoms in response to stress. They were characterized by therapists as insecure. Female clients with high scores on this subscale were described by therapists as having suicidal ideation and as not being very competitive.

Physical Malfunctioning (D_3)

Compared with clients with T scores below 65 on this subscale, those with T scores equal to or greater than 65 were more likely to have diagnoses of depression or dysthymia. Male clients with high scores on this subscale were more likely to have histories of having few or no friends. Female clients with high scores on this subscale were more likely to have histories of suicide attempts, and they were more likely to be taking antidepressant and/or anxiolytic medications currently. Both male and female high scorers on this subscale reported anxiety and somatic complaints.

In intake interviews high scorers on this subscale were rated as sad and depressed, and therapists later rated them similarly. These clients were also described by therapists as feeling hopeless and as experiencing fatigue, sleep disturbances, and problems with concentration. They were seen as being preoccupied with health problems, having multiple somatic symptoms, and prone to develop physical symptoms in response to stress. Male clients with high scores on this subscale were characterized as feeling that life is a strain. They tended to feel anxious and pessimistic. They were seen by therapists as insecure, histrionic, angry, and resentful. Female clients with high scores on this subscale were described by therapists as lacking energy and having low sex drive. These women did not have many interests and did not have strong achievement orientation or high aspirations.

Mental Dullness (D_4)

Compared with clients with T scores below 65 on this subscale, those with T scores equal to or greater than 65 were more likely to have diagnoses of depression or dysthymia. They were also more likely to have histories of previous psychiatric hospitalizations and of having been physically abused. Male clients with high scores on this subscale were more likely to have histories of outpatient mental health treatment. Female clients with high scores on this subscale were more likely to have histories of suicide attempts, having few or no friends, and having been sexually abused. These women were also more likely to be taking antidepressant and/or anxiolytic medications currently. Both male and female high scorers on this subscale reported depression and obsessive-compulsive symptoms.

High scorers on this subscale were rated as depressed and sad during intake interviews. Male clients with high scores on this subscale were also rated as unhappy, and female clients with high scores were also rated as anxious. Therapists described high scorers on this subscale as feeling overwhelmed by life and that life is a strain. They felt that they were getting a raw deal from life, and they did not cope well with stress. These clients were seen as sad and depressed and as feeling pessimistic and hopeless. They tended to experience fatigue, sleep disturbances, and suicidal ideation. They were seen as preoccupied with health problems, and they reported multiple somatic symptoms. They were characterized by therapists as insecure persons who often felt like failures. They tended to be self-punishing and to make self-degrading comments. Female clients with high scores on this subscale were characterized by therapists as interpersonally sensitive, overly sensitive to criticism, and suspicious. They were also seen as histrionic, introverted, and agitated.

Brooding (D_5)

Compared with clients with T scores below 65 on this subscale, those with T scores equal to or greater than 65 were more likely to have diagnoses of depression or dysthymia. They were also more likely to have histories of having few or no friends and of suicide attempts. Female clients with high scores on this subscale were more likely to be taking antidepressant and/or anxiolytic medications currently. Both male and female clients with high scores on this subscale described themselves as interpersonally sensitive, and they reported feeling anxious and depressed. They reported obsessive-compulsive symptoms, and some of them reported psychotic symptoms.

High scorers on this subscale were rated as sad and depressed during intake interviews. Male clients with high scores on this subscale were also rated as unhappy, and female clients with high scores were also rated as anxious. Therapists described high scorers as feeling that life is a strain and as not coping well with stress. They tended to feel sad, depressed, and hopeless. They were not very energetic and experienced sleep disturbances and suicidal ideation. Therapists characterized high scorers as interpersonally sensitive and insecure persons. They made self-degrading statements, often felt like failures, and were not very achievement oriented. Male clients with high scores on this subscale were described by therapists as anxious and worried. They reported somatic complaints and obsessive-compulsive symptoms. These men were characterized as histrionic, pessimistic, angry, and resentful. Female clients with high scores on this subscale were described by therapists as not making good first impressions.

Denial of Social Anxiety (Hy_1)

Because it is not possible to obtain T scores greater than 65 on this subscale, no correlations were calculated between subscale scores and extra-test variables.

Need for Affection (Hy_2)

There were very few correlates for this subscale. Both male and female clients with high scores on this subscale were rated by therapists as more empathic than other clients. Male clients with high scores on this subscale were rated by intake interviewers as having tics and by therapists as creating good first impressions. Female clients with high scores on this subscale were described by therapists as moralistic.

Lassitude-Malaise (Hy_3)

Compared with clients with T scores below 65 on this subscale, those with T scores equal to or greater than 65 were more likely to have diagnoses of depression or dysthymia and histories of suicide attempts. Male clients with high scores on this subscale were more likely to have had previous inpatient and outpatient mental health treatment. Female clients with high scores on this subscale were more likely to have histories of having few or no friends and of having been physically abused, and they were more likely to be taking antidepressant medications currently. Both male and female high scorers on this subscale described themselves as anxious and depressed, and they reported having obsessive-compulsive symptoms.

High scorers on this subscale were rated as sad and depressed during intake interviews, and therapists later rated them similarly. Therapists also saw high scorers as feeling overwhelmed by life, that life is a strain, and that they were getting a raw deal from life. High scorers were described as feeling hopeless and pessimistic and as experiencing anxiety, suicidal ideation, fatigue, and sleep disturbances. High scorers seemed to be preoccupied with health problems and reported somatic complaints. They were characterized as insecure, lonely people who were interpersonally sensitive. Male clients with high scores on this subscale were described as agitated and as having obsessive-compulsive symptoms. They were seen by therapists as angry, resentful, critical, and argumentative. They tended to be histrionic and did not have strong achievement orientations. They were also seen as reporting family problems.

Somatic Complaints (Hy_4)

Compared with clients with T scores below 65 on this subscale, those with T scores equal to or greater than 65 were more likely to have diagnoses of depression or dysthymia. Female clients with high scores on this subscale were more likely to have histories of few or no friends, suicide attempts, and having been physically abused. These women were also more likely to be taking anxiolytic medications currently. Both male and female high scorers on this subscale reported feeling anxious, and they had somatic complaints and obsessive-compulsive symptoms.

High scorers on this subscale were rated as depressed and sad during intake interviews. Male clients with high scores were also rated as unhappy. Therapists indicated that both male and female high scorers tended to feel that life was a strain. They seemed to be preoccupied with health problems, presented multiple somatic complaints, and were prone to develop physical symptoms in response to stress. High scorers were also described by therapists as anxious and depressed. They tended to feel pessimistic and hopeless, and they experienced fatigue and sleep disturbances. Male clients with high scores on this subscale seemed to be agitated and to feel overwhelmed. Female clients with high scores on this subscale were characterized as not having many interests, not having strong achievement orientations, and not coping well with stress.

Inhibition of Aggression (Hy_5)

Because there were so few clients with T scores equal to or greater than 65 on this subscale, correlations between subscale scores and extra-test variables were not calculated.

Familial Discord (Pd_1)

Compared with clients with T scores below 65 on this subscale, those with T scores equal to or greater than 65 were more likely to have histories of having few or no friends, having been physically abused, and suicide attempts. High-scoring male clients were rated as displaying sad mood and circumstantial speech during intake interviews.

Therapists described high scorers on this subscale as histrionic persons who had family problems, indicated that their families lacked love, and resented family members. Male clients with high scores on this subscale were described by therapists as depressed, anxious, and ruminative, and they displayed obsessive-compulsive symptoms. These men were seen as lonely, insecure persons who often felt rejected. They were also seen as angry persons who had stormy interpersonal relationships and did not get along with coworkers. Female clients with high scores on this subscale were characterized by therapists as argumentative and demanding of attention. They tended to blame their families for their difficulties, and they had histories of having been fired from jobs.

Authority Problems (Pd_2)

Compared with clients with T scores below 65 on this subscale, those with T scores equal to or greater than 65 were more likely to have Axis I diagnoses of substance abuse or dependence and Axis II diagnoses of antisocial personality disorder. High scorers were more likely to have histories of alcohol, marijuana, and heroin abuse. They were also more likely to have histories of arrests and misdemeanor convictions. Female clients with high scores on this subscale were also more likely to have histories of cocaine abuse.

Male clients with high scores on this subscale were rated as anxious during intake interviews, and female clients with high scores were rated as aggressive. Therapists described both male and female high scorers on this subscale as sociopathic persons who engaged in antisocial, acting-out behavior. These clients were seen as self-indulgent and impulsive, and they showed poor judgment. Therapists saw male clients with high scores on this subscale as aggressive, emotionally labile persons who had stormy interpersonal relationships, displayed temper tantrums, and were physically abusive. Female clients with high scores on this subscale were seen by therapists as hostile, suspicious persons who experienced hallucinations and paranoid ideation. These women also tended to have low tolerance for frustration and often did not complete projects. They were also described as self-defeating.

Social Imperturbability (Pd_3)

Because there were so few clients with T scores equal to or greater than 65 on this subscale, correlations were not calculated between subscale scores and extra-test variables.

Social Alienation (Pd_4)

Compared with clients with T scores below 65 on this subscale, those with T scores equal to or greater than 65 were more likely to have diagnoses of depression or dysthymia and histories of having few or no friends. Female clients with high scores on this subscale were more likely to have had previous outpatient mental health treatment and histories of having been sexually abused. High scorers on this subscale described themselves as interpersonally sensitive. They reported experiencing paranoid ideation and symptoms of depression.

High scorers on this subscale were rated as sad and depressed during intake interviews. Therapists described these clients as feeling that life is a strain and that they were getting a raw deal from life. They were seen as feeling depressed, hopeless, and rejected. Male clients with high scores on this subscale were described by therapists as having suicidal ideation. They were characterized as insecure persons who often feel like failures. They were seen as having family problems, feeling that their families were lacking in love, and resenting family members. They tended not to get along with coworkers. Female clients with high scores on this subscale were described by therapists as not having many interests and not making good first impressions.

Self-Alienation (Pd_5)

Compared with clients with T scores below 65 on this subscale, those with T scores equal to or greater than 65 were more likely to have diagnoses of depression or dysthymia. They were also more likely to have histories of previous psychiatric hospitalizations and suicide attempts. Female clients with high scores on this subscale were more likely to have histories of alcohol abuse and of having few or no friends. Both male and female high scorers on this subscale described themselves as depressed.

High scorers on this subscale were rated as depressed and sad during intake interviews. Male clients with high scores were also rated as unhappy, and female clients with high scores were rated as anxious. Therapists described both male and female high scorers as being in acute psychological turmoil. They were seen as feeling depressed, hopeless, and pessimistic, and they tended to have suicidal ideation. High scorers were characterized as insecure persons who felt like failures much of the time. They were self-degrading, self-doubting, and self-punishing. Male clients with high scores on this subscale were described by therapists as feeling overwhelmed and that life is a strain. They were seen as anxious and agitated, and they reported sleep disturbances, somatic complaints, and obsessive-compulsive symptoms. Female clients with high scores on this subscale were described by therapists as interpersonally sensitive.

Persecutory Ideas (Pa_1)

Compared with clients with T scores below 65 on this subscale, those with T scores equal to or greater than 65 were more likely to have histories of having few or no friends. Male clients with high scores on this subscale were more likely to have histories of having been physically abused and of committing domestic violence. Female clients with high scores on this subscale were more likely to have histories of suicide attempts. Both male and female high scorers on this subscale reported having paranoid ideation.

High scorers on this subscale were rated as sad and depressed during intake interviews. Therapists described male clients with high scores on this subscale as feeling that life is a strain. They were seen as anxious and depressed, and they tended to ruminate and feel sad and hopeless. High-scoring male clients were described as having family problems and resenting family members. They were characterized as insecure persons who felt inferior and felt like failures much of the time. They tended not to get along with coworkers. Female clients with high scores on this subscale were described by therapists as lacking energy and as sexually maladjusted. They did not make good first impressions and were not likable. These women did not have many interests, did not have high aspirations, and did not have strong achievement orientations. They did not communicate effectively and did not seem to have insight into their own problems.

Poignancy (Pa_2)

Compared with clients with T scores below 65 on this subscale, those with T scores equal to or greater than 65 were more likely to have diagnoses of depression or dysthymia. Male clients with high scores on this subscale were more likely to have anxiety disorder diagnoses. Female clients with high scores were more likely to have histories of suicide attempts and of having few or no friends.

Therapists characterized high scorers on this subscale as feeling that life is a strain and that they were getting a raw deal from life. These clients were seen as feeling sad, depressed, hopeless, and pessimistic. They tended to be tearful and to have suicidal ideation. They often felt rejected and like failures. Male clients with high scores on this subscale were described as anxious, insecure, and pessimistic. They had obsessive-compulsive symptoms and nightmares. They were characterized by therapists as insecure and self-punishing and as harboring angry resentment.

Naïveté (Pa_3)

Compared with clients with T scores below 65 on this subscale, those with T scores equal to or greater than 65 were more likely to be described by therapists as having paranoid ideation. During intake interviews male clients with high scores on this subscale were rated as having tics, and female clients with high scores were rated as having obsessions. Therapists described male clients with high scores on this subscale as having psychotic, obsessive-compulsive, and somatic symptoms. They were characterized as hostile and interpersonally sensitive.

Social Alienation (Sc_1)

Compared with clients with T scores below 65 on this subscale, those with T scores equal to or greater than 65 were more likely to have diagnoses of depression or dysthymia and histories of having few or no friends. Male clients with high scores on this subscale were more likely to have histories of previous inpatient and outpatient mental health treatment and having been physically abused. Female clients with high scores on this subscale were more likely to have histories of suicide attempts and having been sexually abused. Both male and female high scorers on this subscale described themselves as interpersonally sensitive and having paranoid ideation.

During intake interviews high scorers on this subscale were rated as depressed and sad. Therapists characterized these clients as feeling that life is a strain and as not coping well with stress. They were also seen as feeling pessimistic and hopeless and having family problems. They did not have strong achievement orientations and did not make good first impressions. Male clients with high scores on this subscale were described by therapists as sad, depressed, and ruminative and having suicidal ideation. They were also seen as anxious, nervous, and worried and having obsessive-compulsive symptoms. They were characterized as insecure, introverted persons who often felt like failures. They did not have strong stereotypically masculine interests. They seemed to feel that their families were lacking in love. Female clients with high scores on this subscale were seen by therapists as not having many interests and as giving up easily. They were also described as angry, resentful, critical, and argumentative. These women seemed to have negative feelings toward men and did not have much insight into their own problems.

Emotional Alienation (Sc_2)

Compared with clients with T scores below 65 on this subscale, those with T scores equal to or greater than 65 were more likely to have diagnoses of depression or dysthymia and histories of inpatient mental health treatment. Male clients with high scores on this subscale were more likely to have histories of previous outpatient mental health treatment. Female clients with high scores on this subscale were more likely to have histories of having few or no friends and were more likely to be taking antidepressant medications currently. High scorers on this subscale described themselves as depressed.

High scorers on this subscale were rated as sad and depressed during intake interviews. In addition, male clients with high scores were rated as unhappy, and female clients with high scores were rated as anxious. Therapists described both male and female high scorers as feeling that life is a strain. They were seen as feeling sad, depressed, pessimistic, and hopeless and as experiencing sleep disturbances and suicidal ideation. High scorers were described as anxious, insecure persons who were interpersonally sensitive and often felt like failures. Male clients with high scores on this subscale were described by therapists as anxious and agitated. They were preoccupied with health problems and reported somatic complaints. They also reported phobic anxiety and obsessive-compulsive symptoms. These men were seen as histrionic persons who tended to make self-degrading comments. Female clients with high scores on this subscale were described as feeling inferior.

Lack of Ego Mastery, Cognitive (Sc_3)

Compared with clients with T scores below 65, those with T scores equal to or greater than 65 on this subscale were more likely to have histories of previous psychiatric hospitalizations and having few or no friends. Male clients with high scores on this subscale were more likely to have histories of marijuana abuse. Female clients with high scores on this subscale were more likely to have histories of suicide attempts and of having been sexually abused, and they were more likely to be taking anxiolytic medications currently. Both male and female high scorers on this subscale reported anxiety, depression, and obsessive-compulsive thoughts and behaviors. Some of the high scorers also reported psychotic symptoms.

Clients with high scores on this subscale were rated as sad and depressed during intake interviews. Male clients with high scores were also rated as angry, and female clients with high scores were also rated as anxious. Therapists described both male and female high scorers on this subscale as being in acute psychological turmoil and not coping well with stress. High scorers were seen as feeling depressed, sad, pessimistic, and hopeless, and as reporting suicidal ideation and sleep disturbances. These clients were characterized as insecure, self-punishing people. Male clients with high scores on this subscale were seen as feeling overwhelmed. They felt lonely and lacked energy. They reported family problems and said that their families were lacking in love. Female clients with high scores on this subscale were seen as agitated and as feeling that they were getting a raw deal from life.

Lack of Ego Mastery, Conative (Sc_4)

Compared with clients with T scores below 65 on this subscale, those with T scores equal to or greater than 65 were more likely to have diagnoses of depression or dysthymia. They were also more likely to have histories of prior psychiatric hospitalizations and suicide attempts. Female clients with high scores on this subscale were more likely to have histories of having few or no friends. Both male and female high scorers on this subscale described themselves as interpersonally sensitive, and they felt depressed and anxious. They reported obsessive-compulsive thoughts and behaviors, and some of them reported psychotic symptoms.

High scorers on this subscale were rated as sad and depressed during intake interviews. Male clients with high scores were also rated as unhappy, and female clients with high scores were rated as anxious. Therapists described both male and female high scorers on this subscale as feeling overwhelmed and that life is a strain. These clients were seen by therapists as feeling sad, depressed, pessimistic, and hopeless and as experiencing suicidal ideation and sleep disturbances. They also felt anxious and reported somatic complaints. High scorers were characterized by therapists as interpersonally sensitive people who often felt insecure and inferior. They made self-degrading comments and often felt like failures. Male clients with high scores on this subscale were seen as having obsessive-compulsive symptoms. Female clients with high scores on this subscale were characterized as histrionic and needing attention.

Lack of Ego Mastery, Defective Inhibition (Sc_5)

Compared with clients with T scores below 65 on this subscale, those with T scores equal to or greater than 65 were more likely to have diagnoses of depression or dysthymia. Male clients with high scores on this subscale were more likely to have had previous outpatient mental health treatment. Female clients with high scores on this subscale were more likely to have borderline personality disorder diagnoses. These women were also more likely to have histories of previous psychiatric hospitalizations, suicide attempts, and having been sexually abused.

Female clients with high scores on this subscale were rated as depressed during intake interviews. Therapists described both male and female high scorers as tearful and depressed. They were seen as experiencing suicidal ideation and sleep disturbances, and they had difficulty concentrating. Male clients with high scores on this subscale were described as feeling overwhelmed, anxious, sad, and hopeless. They reported multiple somatic complaints and were prone to develop physical symptoms in response to stress. These men often reported feeling like failures. Female clients with high scores on this subscale were described by therapists as having low tolerance for frustration and not coping well with stress. In addition, they seemed to be disoriented.

Bizarre Sensory Experiences (Sc_6)

Compared with clients with T scores below 65 on this subscale, those with T scores equal to or greater than 65 were more likely to have diagnoses of depression or dysthymia. Male clients with high scores on this subscale were more likely to have histories of previous psychiatric hospitalizations and of having few or no friends. Female clients with high scores on this subscale were more likely to have histories of suicide attempts and having been sexually abused. Both male and female high scorers on this subscale reported somatic symptoms.

High scorers on this subscale were rated as depressed during intake interviews. Female clients with high scores were also rated as having sad mood. Therapists characterized both male and female high scorers on this subscale as preoccupied with health problems, reporting multiple somatic complaints, and prone to develop physical symptoms in response to stress. High scorers were also seen as feeling depressed, anxious, and pessimistic. They reported feeling fatigued and had difficulty concentrating. Male clients with high scores on this subscale were described as feeling overwhelmed. They were seen as feeling angry, resentful, and hopeless, and they experienced sleep disturbances. Female clients with high scores on this subscale were characterized by therapists as not coping well with stress. These women were seen as not having many interests, not being very achievement oriented, and not having high aspirations.

Amorality (Ma_1)

Compared with clients with T scores below 65 on this subscale, those with T scores equal to or greater than 65 were more likely to have histories of alcohol abuse. Male clients with high scores on this subscale were more likely to have histories of being physically abusive and being convicted of domestic violence. Female clients with high scores on this subscale were more likely to have Axis I diagnoses of substance abuse or dependence and Axis II diagnoses of antisocial personality disorder. These women were also more likely to have histories of marijuana and/or cocaine abuse and misdemeanor convictions. Male clients with high scores on this subscale were rated as angry during intake interviews, and their therapists indicated that they tended to act out and to experience sleep disturbances.

Psychomotor Acceleration (Ma_2)

Compared with clients with T scores below 65 on this subscale, those with T scores equal to or greater than 65 were more likely to have histories of cocaine abuse. Male clients with high scores on this subscale were more likely to have histories of being physically abusive and of being convicted of domestic violence. Female clients with high scores on this subscale were rated as evasive during intake interviews, and they were more likely to have borderline personality disorder diagnoses and histories of alcohol abuse.

Imperturbability (Ma_3)

Compared with clients with T scores below 65 on this subscale, those with T scores equal to or greater than 65 were rated as less depressed during intake interviews, and therapists later described them similarly. Female clients with high scores on this subscale were rated as less sad and as having unusual gait during intake interviews. These women were described by their therapists as feeling less anxious, nervous, worried, sad, and hopeless than other female clients. They were also described as less shy, insecure, introverted, passive-submissive, and lonely than other female clients and as having stronger stereotypically masculine interests than other female clients.

Ego Inflation (Ma_4)

Compared with male clients with T scores below 65 on this subscale, men with T scores equal to or greater than 65 were described by therapists as excitable persons who had difficulty making decisions and did not get along with coworkers. Female clients with high scores on this subscale were characterized by therapists as sociopathic persons who did not cope well with stress. These women were described as easily bored, and they tended to give up easily. They were characterized as narcissistic, histrionic, whiny women who did not make good first impressions. They were difficult to motivate, and they were unable to see their own limitations.

Scale 0 Subscales

Correlations between scale 0 subscale scores and the extra-test measures available for clients provided the basis for summaries of correlates included in this chapter (Appendix F). As with the Harris-Lingoes subscales, we recommend that scale 0 subscale scores be interpreted only when scores on the parent scale are significantly elevated (T > 65) and that interpretation be limited to trying to understand why elevated scores were obtained on scale 0.

Shyness/Self-Consciousness (Si_1)

Compared with male clients with T scores below 65 on this subscale, men with T scores equal to or greater than 65 were more likely to have diagnoses of bipolar disorder or cyclothymia. Female clients with high scores on this subscale were more likely than other female clients to have diagnoses of depression or dysthymia and histories of suicide attempts and having few or no friends. These women were also more likely to be taking antidepressant medications currently.

Female clients with high scores on this subscale were rated as sad and having slowed speech during intake interviews. Both male and female clients with high scores on this subscale were described by therapists as introverted and shy. Male clients with high scores on this subscale were described by therapists as depressed, anxious, worried, and nervous. These men also tended to have sleep disturbances. They were seen by therapists as insecure, self-degrading, and self-punishing, and they seemed to be uncomfortable around women. Female clients with high scores on this subscale were described by therapists as unassertive and passive in relationships. They did not have many interests, and they did not have strong achievement needs or high aspirations. These women did not make good first impressions.

Social Avoidance (Si_2)

Compared with female clients with T scores below 65 on this subscale, women with T scores equal to or greater than 65 were more likely to have histories of having few or no friends. These women were also more likely to be taking antidepressant and/or anxiolytic medications currently. Female clients with high scores on this subscale were rated as depressed during intake interviews.

Therapists described both male and female high scorers on this subscale as depressed and as having suicidal ideation. High scorers were characterized as introverted persons who lacked energy and did not have many interests. Male clients with high scores on this subscale were seen as feeling that life is a strain. These men seemed to be preoccupied with health problems and displayed restricted affect. Female clients with high scores on this subscale were described as not coping well with stress. These women were seen as sexually maladjusted, and they experienced sleep disturbances. They were not very concerned about status, did not have strong achievement orientations, and did not have high aspirations.

Self/Other Alienation (Si_3)

Compared with female clients with T scores below 65, women with T scores equal to or greater than 65 were more likely to have histories of suicide attempts and having few or no friends. Both male and female clients with high scores on this subscale were rated as depressed during intake interviews. High scorers were described by therapists as insecure persons who experienced suicidal ideation. Male clients with high scores on this subscale were described as guilt-prone persons who felt depressed, hopeless, anxious, and nervous. These men had difficulty making decisions, and they experienced sleep disturbances. They were characterized by therapists as passive and insecure. Female clients with high scores on this subscale were described by therapists as having many specific fears and as not coping well with stress. These women were pessimistic, lacked energy, and were introverted. They were not very self-reliant, did not have many interests, did not have strong achievement orientations, and did not have high aspirations.

Chapter 4

Correlates of MMPI-2 Code Types

In order to determine extra-test correlates of two- and three-point code types, clients with each code type were compared with a group of clients having within-normal-limits (WNL) profiles. Because of relatively small sample sizes, data for male and female clients were combined for these analyses. Only code types that were well defined (i.e., at least 5 T-score points between the lowest scale in the code type and the next highest clinical scale) and elevated (i.e., all scales in the code type with T > 64) and for which there were at least 10 cases were included in these analyses. The order of scales within the code type was not considered (e.g., 12 and 21 codes were combined). Mean standard scale and content scale profiles were calculated for each code type and are presented in this chapter along with the summaries of the correlates.

Point-biserial correlations were computed with MMPI-2 group (specific two- or three-point code type versus WNL profiles) as one variable and extra-test measures for clients as the other variable. Extra-test measures that were significantly related to specific code-type membership provided the basis for the descriptions that follow (Appendix G). It should be understood that the descriptions are comparing clients with each specific code type with clients with WNL profiles. As we discussed in chapter 2, the advantage of using this comparison group, rather than one composed of clients with other code types, is that it permitted us to identify symptoms, problems, and personality characteristics that are common among persons with a particular code type, even if the characteristics are frequently found among other patients as well. For example, because depression was such a common symptom among the clients in the setting where our study was conducted, we would not have identified depression as a characteristic of persons with the 12/21 code type if we had used a comparison group composed of patients with code types other than the 12/21.

For some of the code types included in our analyses there was gender imbalance. For example, the 49/94 code type included 2 men and 12 women. In cases such as this, where gender imbalance is marked, special caution must be exercised in applying the correlates to the underrepresented gender. However, the marked similarity of correlates of the individual clinical scales for men and women offers some evidence that the correlates identified for code types may very well apply to both genders. In later sections of this chapter we will examine this issue in relation to several code types for which gender imbalance was more marked.

Although persons with a particular code type are more likely to have the characteristics included in the summaries and/or have them to a greater extent, not every person with the code type will have every extra-test characteristic presented. In Appendixes K-3 and L-3 we report frequencies (categorical variables) and average values (continuous variables) for all of our extra-test measures for each code-type group, including the WNL group. Reference to these data can be of additional help in determining how likely it is that specific characteristics will apply to persons with a particular code type. An example of how these additional data might be used is provided in chapter 6.

It is important to know how the characteristics of the code types in our study are similar to or different from those previously reported in codebooks such as those authored by Marks and Seeman (1963) and Gilberstadt and Duker (1965). Such information is helpful in determining to what extent the findings of our study can be generalized to other settings. Although we will discuss this matter generally in chapter 6, in this chapter we will compare the characteristics of clients with each of our code types with those previously reported in these other codebooks. Of course, not all of our code types were included in the earlier studies. In particular, Marks and Seeman's codebook did not include any three-point code types.

Two-Point Code Types

12/21 Code Type

Manifestations of depression and somatization were the primary features associated with having the 12/21 code type. In contrast to clients having WNL profiles, the 12/21 code-type clients were more likely to have diagnoses of depression or dysthymia. These clients reported anxiety, phobias, somatic symptoms, depression, and obsessive-compulsive thoughts and behaviors. They were rated as depressed and angry and as having tremors during intake interviews. Their therapists described them as preoccupied with health

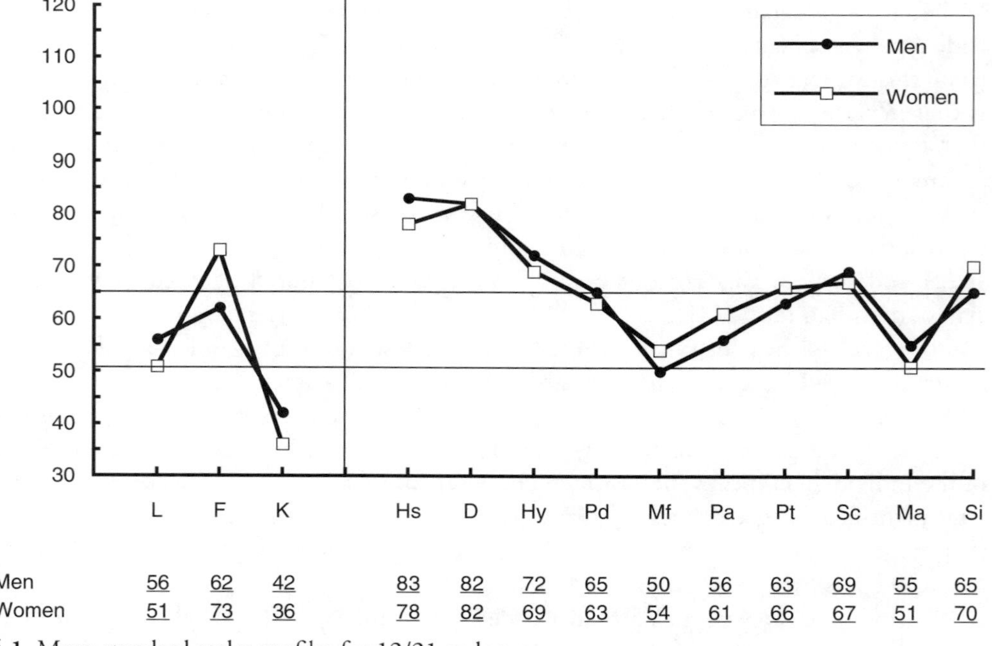

4.1. Mean standard scales profiles for 12/21 code type

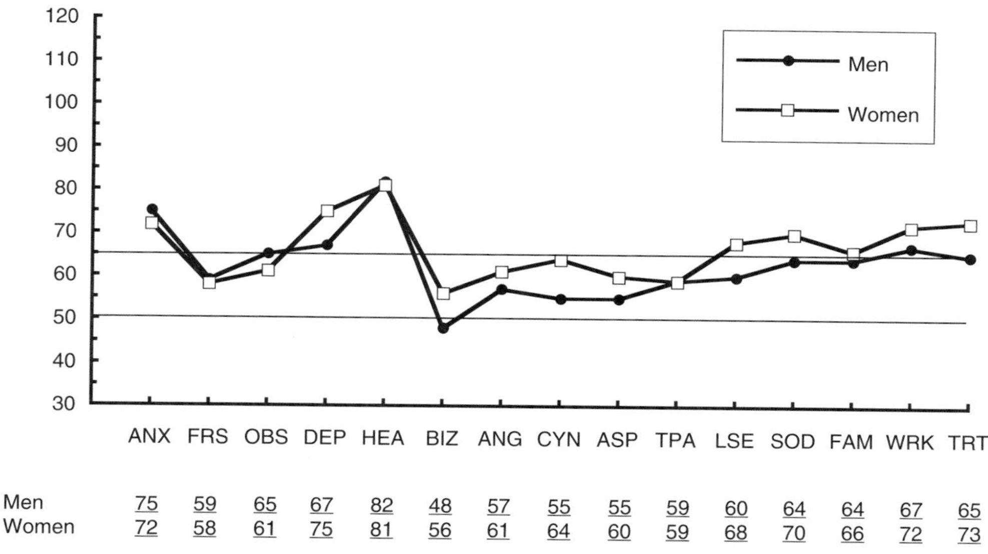

4.2. Mean content scales profiles for 12/21 code type

problems, having multiple somatic complaints, and prone to develop physical symptoms in response to stress. They were also seen by therapists as depressed and fatigued.

Depression-related correlates were found for most of the code types included in this study, particularly the ones in which scale 2 was one of the code-type's defining scales. Angry mood and tremors during intake were associated uniquely with membership in this code type.

Neither Marks and Seeman (1963) nor Gilberstadt and Duker (1965) included the 12/21 code type in their studies. Gilberstadt and Duker included a 123 code type in their study, and the characteristics of patients with that code type will be compared later in this chapter with those clients in our study who had the 123 code type.

13/31 Code Type

Somatization was the primary feature associated with membership in this code type. Compared with clients having WNL profiles, those with the 13/31 code type reported anxiety and somatic symptoms. Their therapists described them as preoccupied with health problems, having multiple somatic complaints, and prone to develop physical symptoms in response to stress. Therapists reported also that these patients were anxious, worried, and depressed. They tended to have sleep disturbances and low sex drive. They were also characterized as histrionic.

Although somatization-related features were found as correlates for a number of other code types, in most of these cases either scale 1 or scale 3 was involved. Moreover, the highest correlations with somatization were associated with membership in the 13/31 code type. A therapist rating of phobic anxiety was associated uniquely with membership in this code type. Correlations with other manifestations of anxiety and depression were shared with most other code types.

The correlates for our 13/31 code type are quite congruent with those reported in earlier codebooks. Somatic symptoms, depression, and anxiety, which characterized

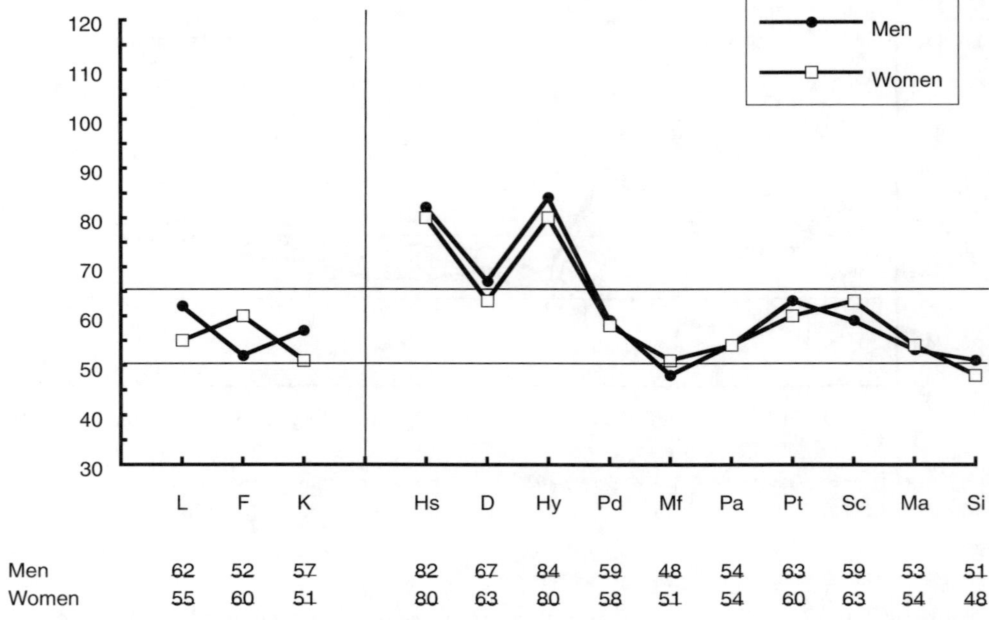

4.3. Mean standard scales profiles for 13/31 code type

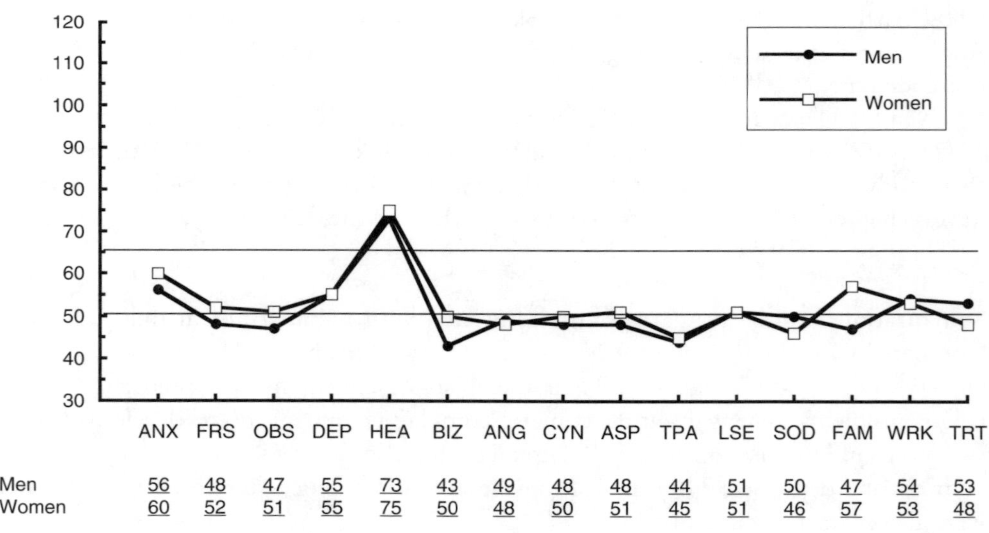

4.4. Mean content scales profiles for 13/31 code type

clients in our study with this code type, were also reported for this code type in other studies. Somatic complaints of various kinds were reported in large percentages of cases by Marks and Seeman (1963) and Gilberstadt and Duker (1965). Although many clinicians might not associate depression with the 13/31 code type, depression was reported for many clients with this code type (32% by Gilberstadt and Duker; 70% by Marks and Seeman). Fatigue characterized our 13/31 clients and also was reported as a frequent symptom by Gilberstadt and Duker and Marks and Seeman. The sleep disturbance reported by our 13/31 clients also was present for 50% of the 13/31 individuals in the Marks and Seeman study. Several of the correlates of this code type in our study, for example, low sex drive, were not included as possible correlates in the other codebook studies. Thus, it would appear that the characteristics of our 13/31 clients are consistent with those identified for persons with this code type in other studies that included both inpatients and outpatients.

23/32 Code Type

Dysphoric mood was the primary feature associated with this code type. Clients with the 23/32 code type were rated as depressed and sad during intake interviews, and their therapists described them similarly. Therapists also reported that these clients were preoccupied with health problems, had multiple somatic complaints, and tended to develop physical symptoms in response to stress. They often felt fatigued, reported sleep disturbances, and had low sex drive. They were characterized by therapists as insecure and feeling like failures.

Sadness, self-depreciation, and low sex drive were among the more unique correlates of membership in this code type. Somatic preoccupation was found in members of this code type to a degree similar to members of the 12/21 code type and to a lesser extent than was found in members of the 13/31 code type. This is a code type with marked gender imbalance in our study (3 men and 17 women). Thus, some caution is advised in applying the correlates of this code type to men. However, the correlates for both scales 2 and 3 individually were markedly similar for men and women, offering some support for their application to men with the 23/32 code type.

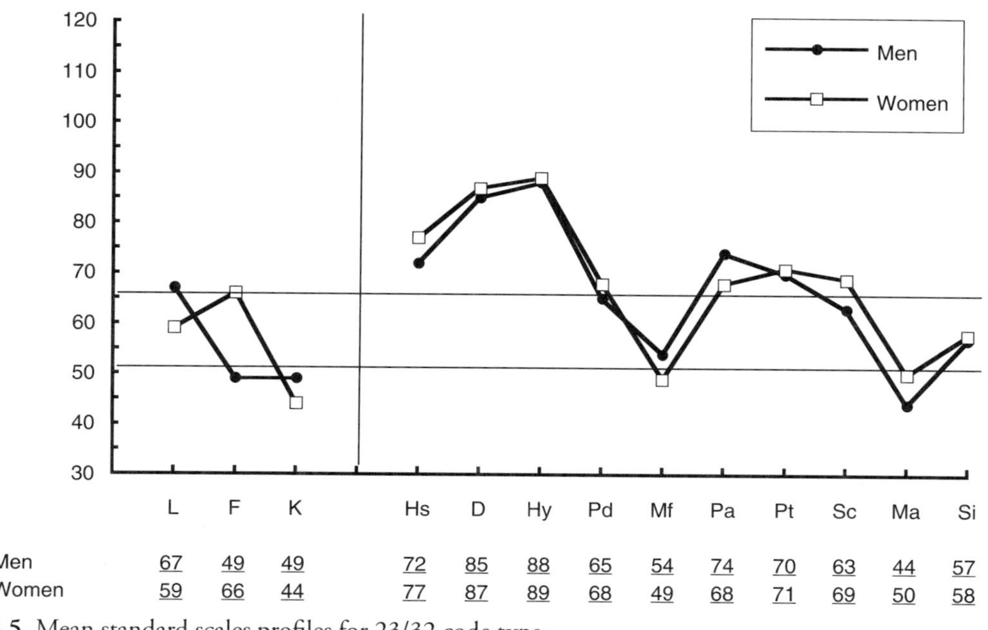

	L	F	K	Hs	D	Hy	Pd	Mf	Pa	Pt	Sc	Ma	Si
Men	67	49	49	72	85	88	65	54	74	70	63	44	57
Women	59	66	44	77	87	89	68	49	68	71	69	50	58

4.5. Mean standard scales profiles for 23/32 code type

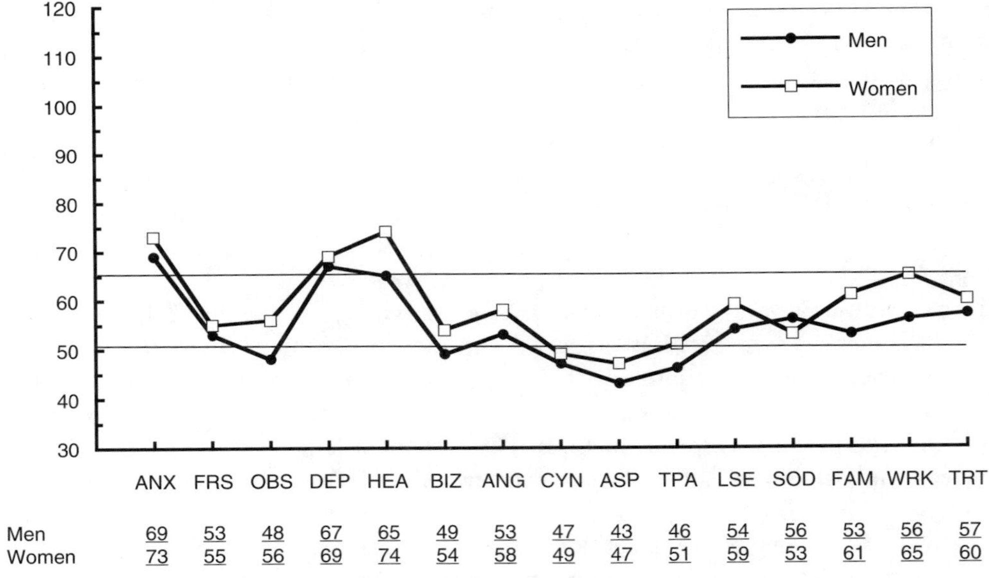

4.6. Mean content scales profiles for 23/32 code type

The most salient characteristics of clients with the 23/32 code type in our study were reported previously by Marks and Seeman (1963) for both their 231/213 and 321 code types. It should be noted that Gilberstadt and Duker (1965) did not include the 23/32 code type in their study. Depression and somatic complaints were strong correlates for both Marks and Seeman code types. Sleep disturbance, fatigue, and insecurity were reported for the Marks and Seeman 231/213 code type. Although suicidal ideation and low sex drive were not correlates for either of the Marks and Seeman code types, these characteristics are consistent with the correlates that were reported for these code types. Likewise, we did not find several of the correlates reported by Marks and Seeman for the two code types, but many of these correlates are consistent with those reported in our study for the 23/32 code type. It is noteworthy that Marks and Seeman reported schizoid and paranoid features for the 321 code type, and these were not correlates of our 23/32 code type. However, only 5% of Marks and Seeman's 321 cases were described as being paranoid or schizoid. It would appear that the most salient correlates that we identified for clients with the 23/32 code type in our study (e.g., depression, somatization, and insecurity) are quite congruent with those previously reported by Marks and Seeman.

24/42 Code Type

Anger, depression, and anxious rumination were the primary features associated with membership in this code type. Clients having the 24/42 code type were more likely than clients having WNL profiles to have diagnoses of depression or dysthymia. They described themselves as depressed and anxious. Their therapists characterized them as depressed and pessimistic. They tended to ruminate excessively, to feel hopeless, and to have suicidal ideation. They were also described as anxious and worried. They tended to

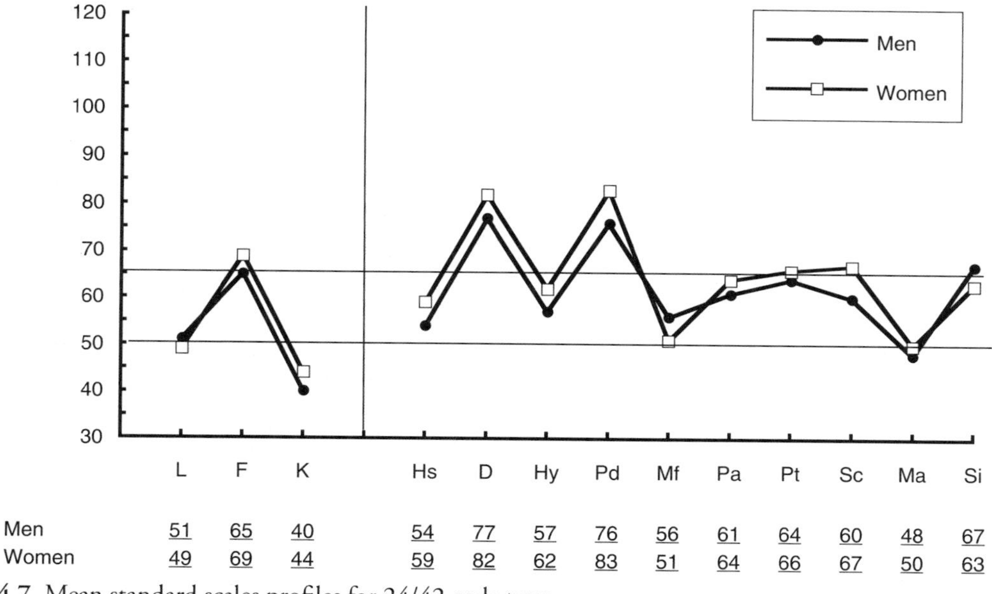

4.7. Mean standard scales profiles for 24/42 code type

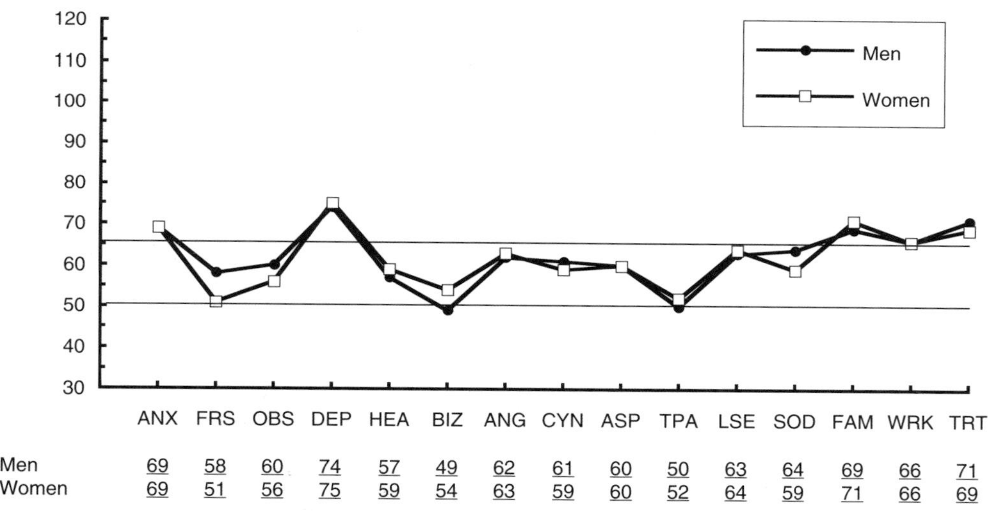

4.8. Mean content scales profiles for 24/42 code type

be critical, angry, argumentative, and resentful. They were characterized by therapists as insecure persons who often felt inferior and made self-degrading comments. They were also seen as histrionic and emotionally labile.

Therapists' rating of suicidal ideation was correlated more highly with the 24/42 code type than with most other code types included in this study. Although it shared its depression- and anxiety-related correlates with several other code types, the 24/42 code type was more uniquely associated with manifestations of anger and argumentativeness. Feelings of inferiority and rumination were associated uniquely with membership in this code type. Neither Marks and Seeman (1963) nor Gilberstadt and Duker (1965) included the 24/42 code type in their studies.

26/62 Code Type

Depression and somatic preoccupation were primary among the relatively small number of correlates identified for this code type. Clients having the 26/62 code type were more likely than clients having WNL profiles to have histories of suicide attempts. They tended to describe themselves as anxious. They were rated as more depressed during intake interviews. Their therapists also saw them as depressed and feeling hopeless. They were preoccupied with health problems and reported multiple somatic complaints and sleep disturbances. Therapists indicated that these clients did not cope well with stress, did not create good first impressions, and did not have much energy.

Low energy, a history of suicide attempts, poor coping skills, and a reduced likelihood of generating a favorable first impression were features relatively unique to this code type. Neither Marks and Seeman (1963) nor Gilberstadt and Duker (1965) included the 26/62 code type in their studies.

27/72 Code Type

Depression, anxiety, and self-degradation were the primary features associated with this code type. Clients having the 27/72 code type were more likely than clients having WNL profiles to have diagnoses of depression or dysthymia, to have histories of previous psychiatric hospitalizations, and to be taking antidepressant medications. They tended to report symptoms of anxiety and depression and obsessive-compulsive thoughts and behaviors. In intake interviews they were rated as sad and depressed, and

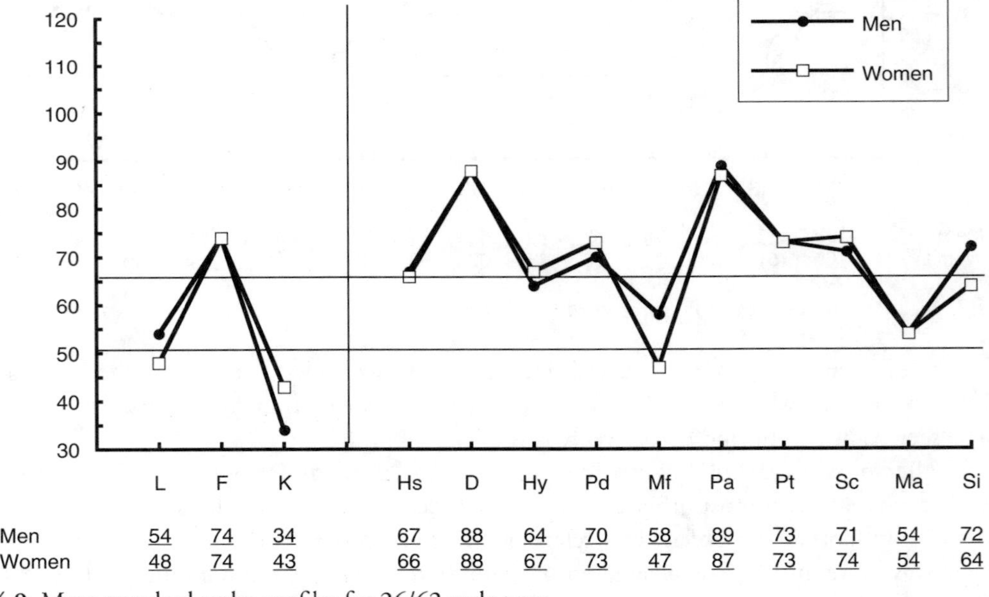

4.9. Mean standard scales profiles for 26/62 code type

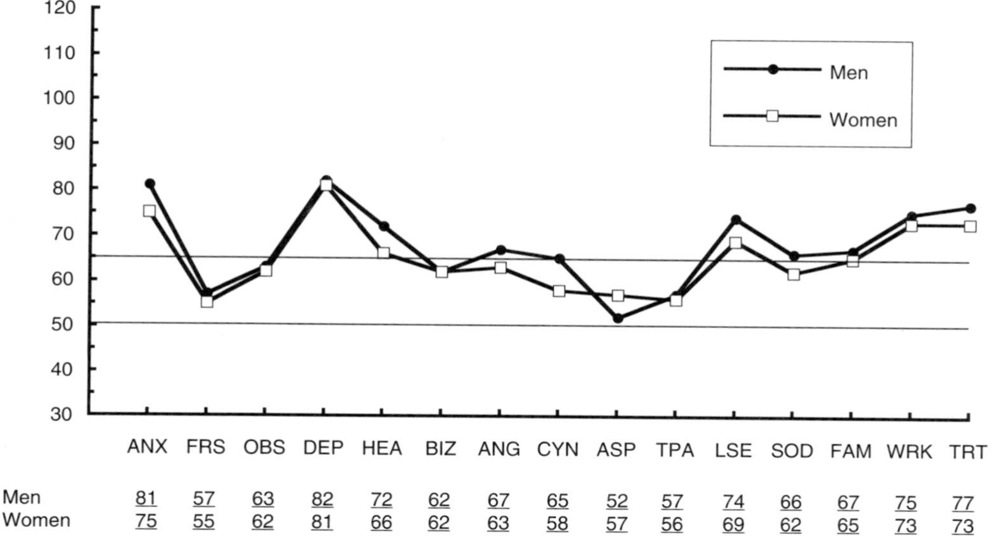

4.10. Mean content scales profiles for 26/62 code type

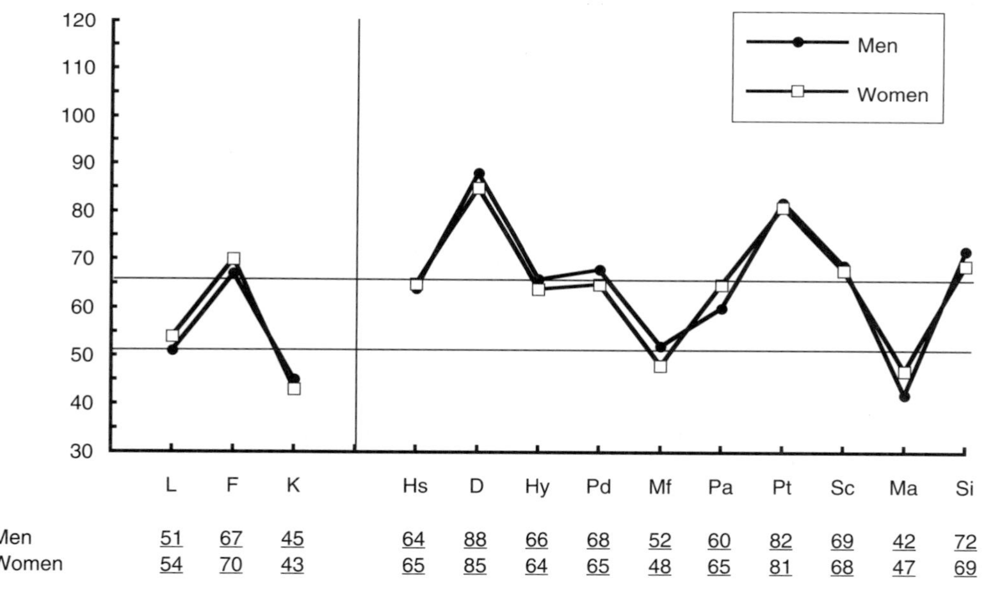

4.11. Mean standard scales profiles for 27/72 code type

they were described similarly by therapists. They were also seen by therapists as feeling hopeless, lacking energy, experiencing sleep disturbances and fatigue, and having suicidal ideation. They were also described as anxious and tending to develop physical symptoms in response to stress. They were not very achievement or work oriented and tended to make self-degrading comments. There was marked gender imbalance for this code type in our study (5 men, 10 women). Caution is advised in applying the correlates of the 27/72 code type to men. However, it should be noted that the correlates for scales 2

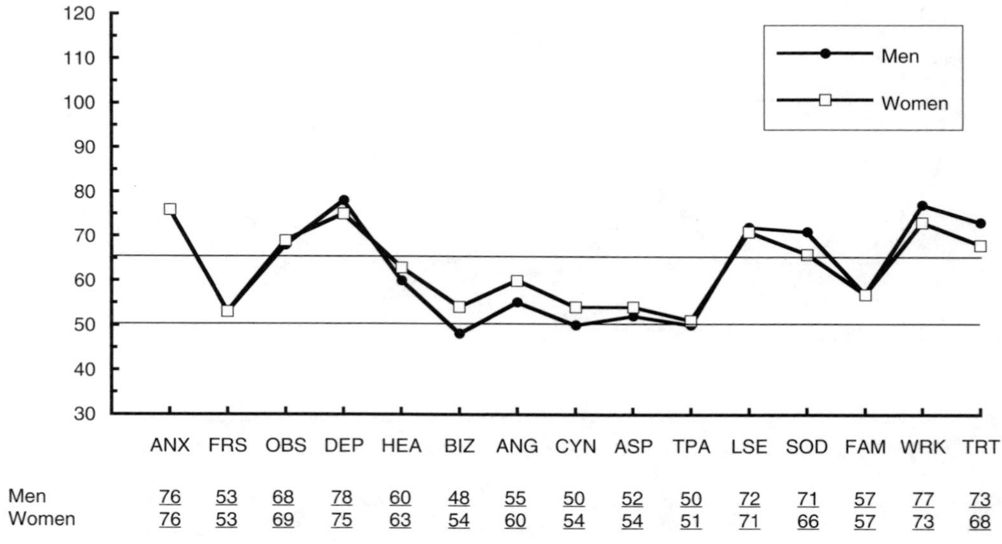

4.12. Mean content scales profiles for 27/72 code type

and 7 individually were remarkably similar for men and women, suggesting that the 27/72 correlates may also apply to both men and women.

Compared with other code types that included scale 2, the 27/72 had stronger correlations with having a sad mood during intake and previous psychiatric hospitalization. Individuals who generated this code type were less likely to be achievement oriented. This was the only two-point code type correlated with a current prescription of antidepressant medication. A tendency toward somatic preoccupation was shared with several other two-point code types.

Both Marks and Seeman's (1963) and Gilberstadt and Duker's (1965) codebooks included the 27/72 code type. The characteristics of the 27/72 clients in our study overlap almost completely with those of the 27/72 individuals in the other studies. In all of the studies 27/72 individuals are characterized by depression, anxiety, somatic complaints, and obsessive thinking. Fatigue and self-degradation also are common to all three studies. Although suicidal ideation, taking antidepressant medications, and not being achievement oriented were not mentioned specifically in Marks and Seeman's and Gilberstadt and Duker's codebooks for the 27/72 code type, these characteristics are consistent with the descriptors that were reported.

34/43 Code Type

Clients having the 34/43 code type were more likely than clients having WNL profiles to have substance abuse/dependence diagnoses and histories of recent alcohol abuse. These clients reported anxiety, depression, and somatic symptoms. Their therapists indicated that these clients were worried, preoccupied with health problems, and had multiple somatic complaints. Therapists reported that some of these clients also had psychotic symptoms. Therapists characterized these clients as cynical, histrionic, excitable, and emotionally labile.

Histrionic tendencies, excitability, alcohol and substance abuse, cynicism, and

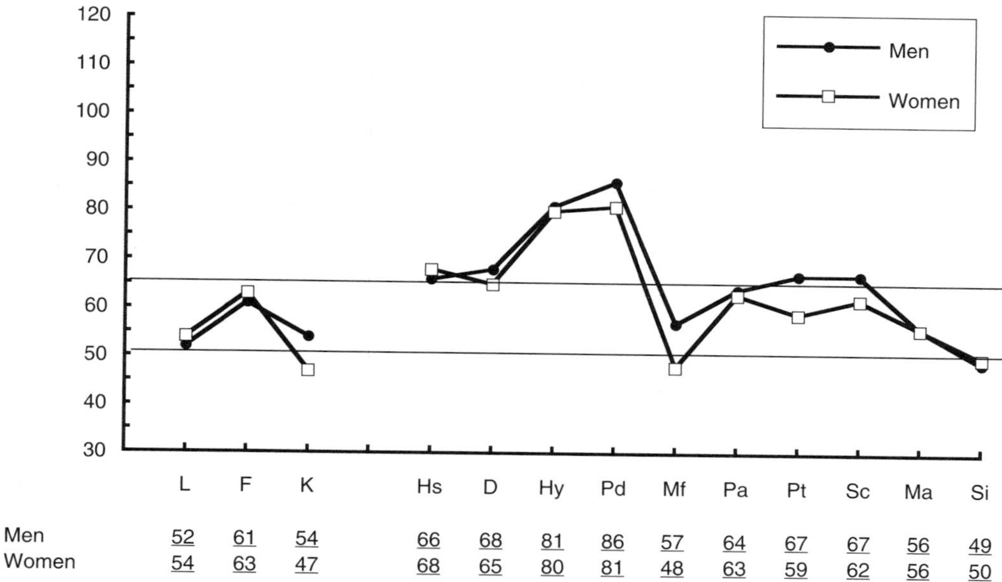

4.13. Mean standard scales profiles for 34/43 code type

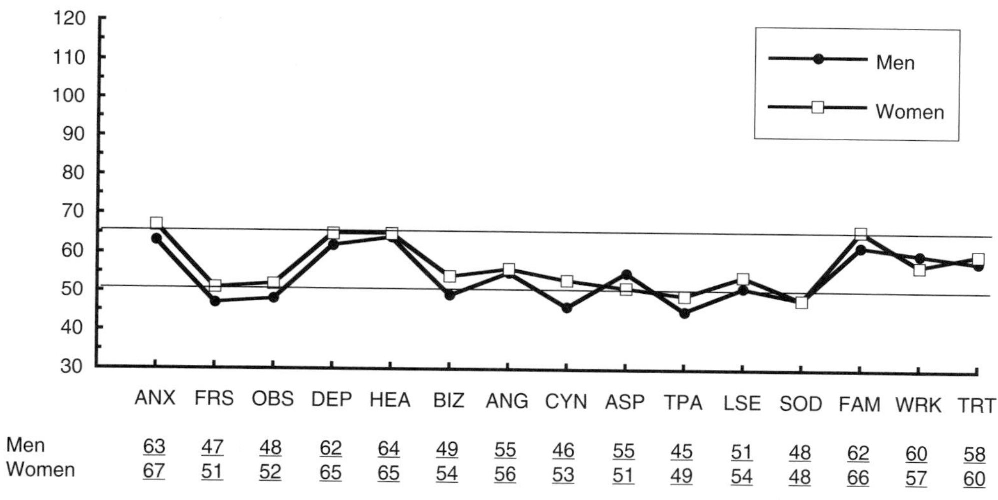

4.14. Mean content scales profiles for 34/43 code type

psychotic symptomatology were among the more unique features associated with membership in this code type. This was one of the few code types not associated with therapist ratings of depression or anxiety. Several of its correlates suggested some somatic preoccupation.

The Marks and Seeman codebook (1963) did not include the 34/43 code type, but the Gilberstadt and Duker codebook (1965) included a 43 code type. There are some similarities and some differences between our 34/43 clients and the 43 patients of Gilberstadt and Duker. Both studies found that persons with this code type were likely to use alcohol excessively. Although the Gilberstadt and Duker patients with the 43 code type were described as hostile and assaultive, our 34/43 clients did not tend to have these characteristics. These differences may reflect the fact that we included persons with scale 3 higher than scale 4 as well as those with scale 4 higher than scale 3. It is not clear from the Gilberstadt and Duker data how many of their 43 patients actually had scale 4 higher than scale 3. However, their classification rules for the 43 code type did not require that scale 4 be higher than scale 3. Although we had too few clients in the separate 34 and 43 code-type groups to compare correlates between them formally, we noted that angry resentment and irritability were correlates of the 43 code type but not of the 34 code type.

Several other differences between our 34/43 correlates and those of the Gilberstadt and Duker 43 characteristics were noted. Our 34/43 clients tended to report anxiety and depression, and their therapists reported that these patients sometimes had psychotic symptoms, and this was not noted for the Gilberstadt and Duker 43 code type. Suicide attempts were listed as characteristic of the Gilberstadt and Duker 43 code type, but we did not find this for our 34/43 clients. However, previous suicide attempts were characteristic of a subgroup of our 43 code-type clients.

46/64 Code Type

Clients having the 46/64 code type were more likely than clients having WNL profiles to have had previous psychiatric hospitalizations. These clients reported anxiety, depression, and obsessive-compulsive symptoms. They also described themselves as interpersonally sensitive, and some of them reported psychotic symptoms, including paranoid ideation. These clients were rated as depressed during intake interviews and later by their therapists. They were also seen by therapists as nonconforming and feeling that they

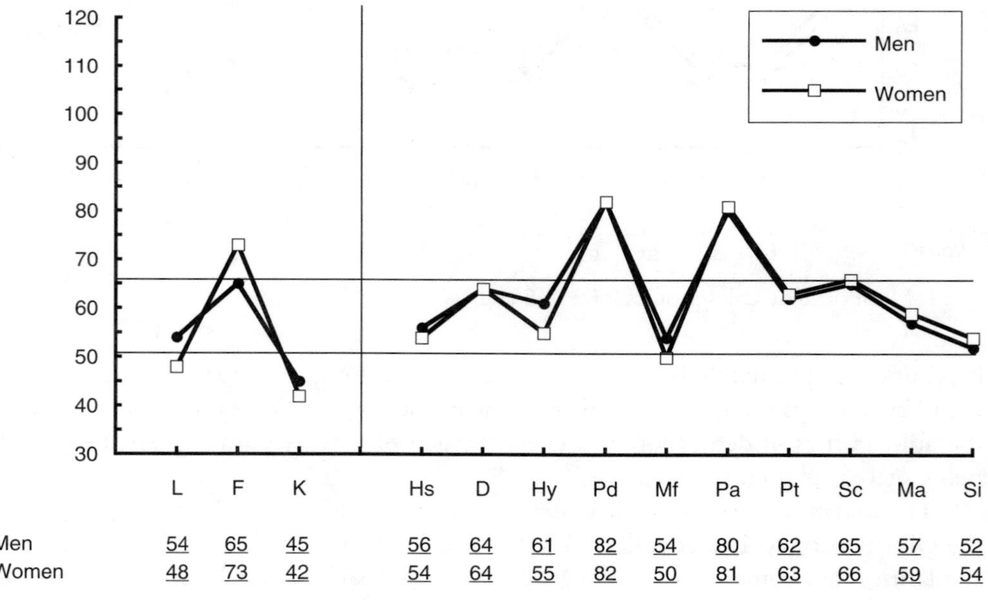

4.15. Mean standard scales profiles for 46/64 code type

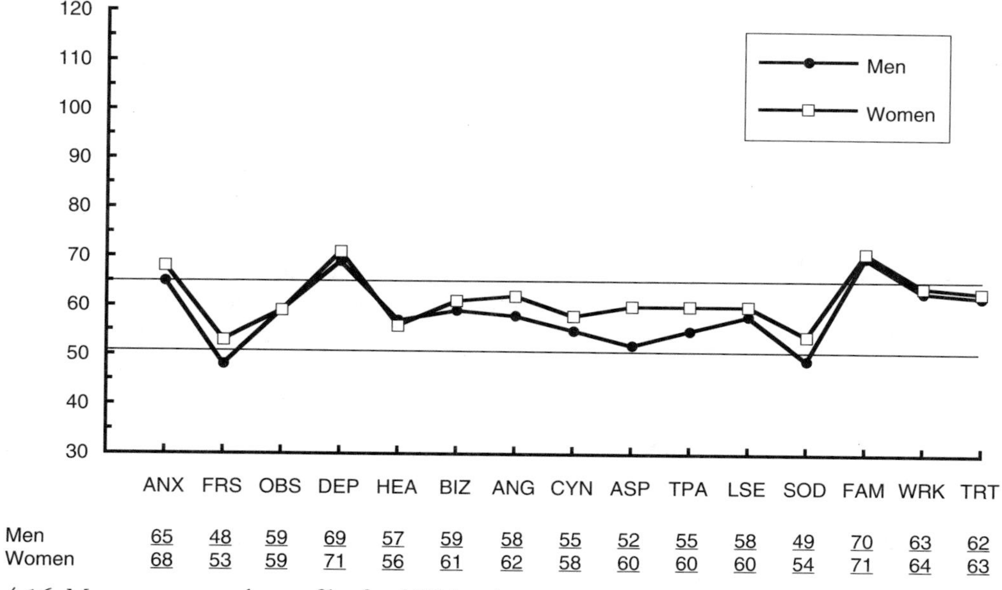

4.16. Mean content scales profiles for 46/64 code type

were getting a raw deal from life. They described their families as lacking in love, they resented family members, and they blamed families for their difficulties.

Family conflict, projection of blame onto family members, nonconformity, and psychotic symptomatology were among the more unique correlates associated with membership in this code type. Manifestations of depression and anxiety were correlated with membership in this code type as they were with most other groups included in this study. A history of prior psychiatric hospitalization was shared with code types associated with more severe symptomatology.

Gilberstadt and Duker (1965) did not include the 46/64 code type in their study, but Marks and Seeman (1963) did include this code type in their study. Our 46/64 clients' acknowledgment of paranoid ideation is consistent with the diagnosis of paranoid schizophrenia that was most common for the 46/64 individuals in the Marks and Seeman study. Likewise, that our 46/64 clients tended to blame family for problems is consistent with the defensiveness and rationalization described for the 46/64 code in the Marks and Seeman study. Although Marks and Seeman did not report depression and anxiety as primary characteristics of their 46/64s, approximately 78% of the Marks and Seeman 46/64 individuals were anxious and approximately 67% were depressed or despondent. Marks and Seeman also described their 46/64 individuals as self-centered, self-indulgent, conflicted about sexuality, insecure, resentful of authority, having strong needs for attention and affection, and using projection as a defense. Although these specific characteristics were not identified for 46/64 clients in our study, they are consistent with the general picture of the 46/64 clients that emerged in our study. Additionally, a subgroup of our clients with the 64 code were characterized as angry, immodest, sociopathic, and nonconforming.

48/84 Code Type

Clients having the 48/84 code type were more likely than clients having WNL profiles to have had previous psychiatric hospitalizations and histories of having been sexually abused. These clients reported somatic complaints, anxiety, and depression. They also reported psychotic symptoms and obsessive-compulsive thoughts and behaviors. Therapists described these clients as experiencing acute psychological turmoil, including anxiety, depression, agitation, and sleep disturbances. They often felt hopeless and had suicidal ideation. Therapists characterized these clients as having psychotic symptoms, including suspiciousness, paranoid ideation, hallucinations, and delusional thinking. They tended to feel insecure and like failures, and they daydreamed excessively.

Psychotic symptomatology including hallucinations and delusional thinking, paranoid tendencies, a significant likelihood of prior psychiatric hospitalization, a history of having been abused sexually, daydreaming, and a negative self-view were among the relatively unique correlates of this scale. Among the two-point codes, the strongest correlations with severe psychotic symptomatology were found for this code type. Depression appeared as a correlate of the 48/84 code type, as it did for most other code types.

Gilberstadt and Duker (1965) did not include the 48/84 code type in their codebook. Marks and Seeman (1963) included a 482/842/824 code type that seems to be similar to our 48/84 code type. Salient characteristics of our 48/84 clients included paranoid ideations, delusions, and hallucinations. Although Marks and Seeman did not include these characteristics as primary characteristics of their 482/842/824 individuals, they described these persons as having schizoid and paranoid features. Approximately 30% of persons with this code type in the Marks and Seeman study had delusions, and approximately 25% had hallucinations. Our 48/84 clients were also characterized as depressed and anxious. Interestingly, although Marks and Seeman did not list these symp-

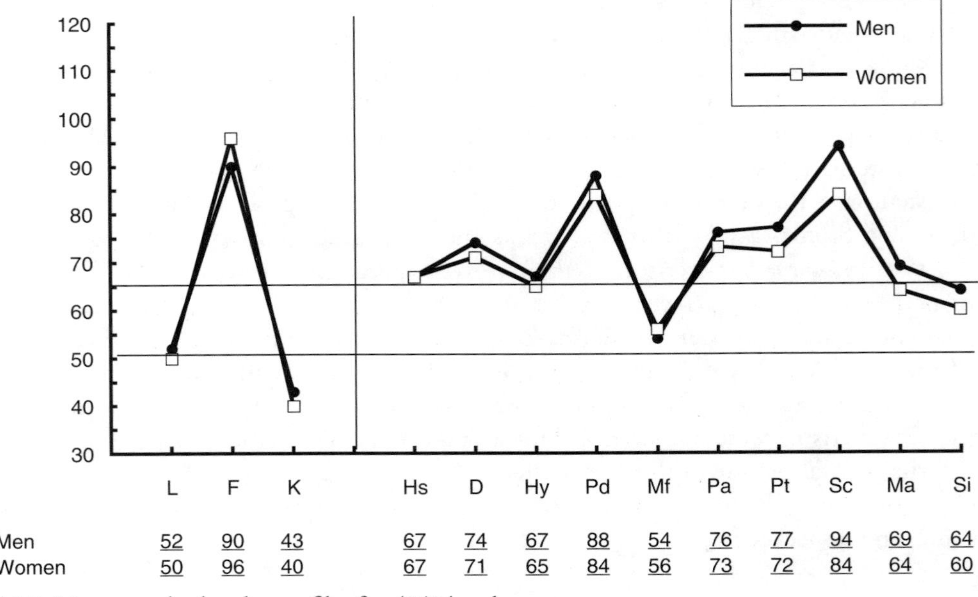

4.17. Mean standard scales profiles for 48/84 code type

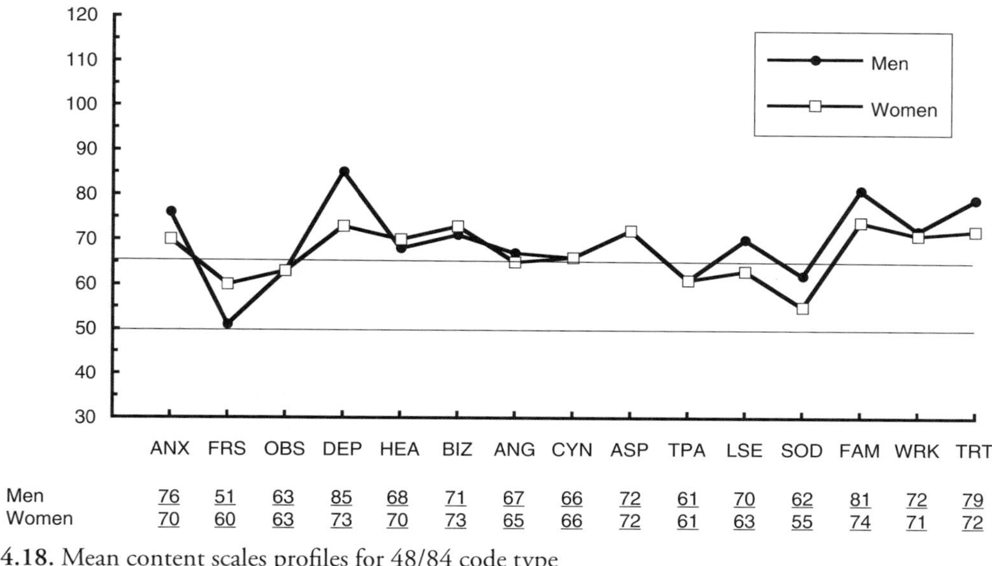

4.18. Mean content scales profiles for 48/84 code type

toms as primary characteristics of persons with their 482/842/824 code type, approximately 80% of persons in their study with this code type had symptoms of depression, and 75% had symptoms of anxiety.

49/94 Code Type

Problems with authority figures, impulsivity, and having superficial relationships were associated uniquely with membership in this code type. These clients were characterized by therapists as eccentric, cynical, and narcissistic. They tended to have superficial relationships and to feel uncomfortable with members of the opposite sex. Other relatively

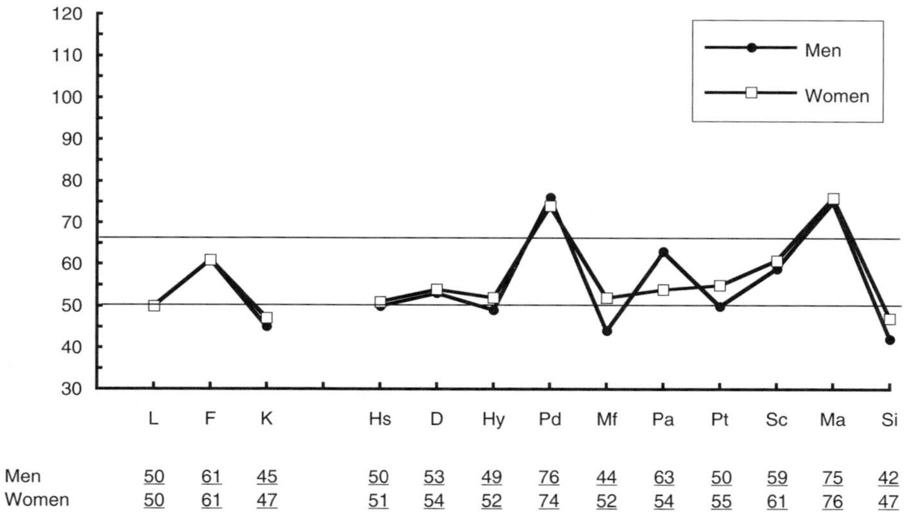

4.19. Mean standard scales profiles for 49/94 code type

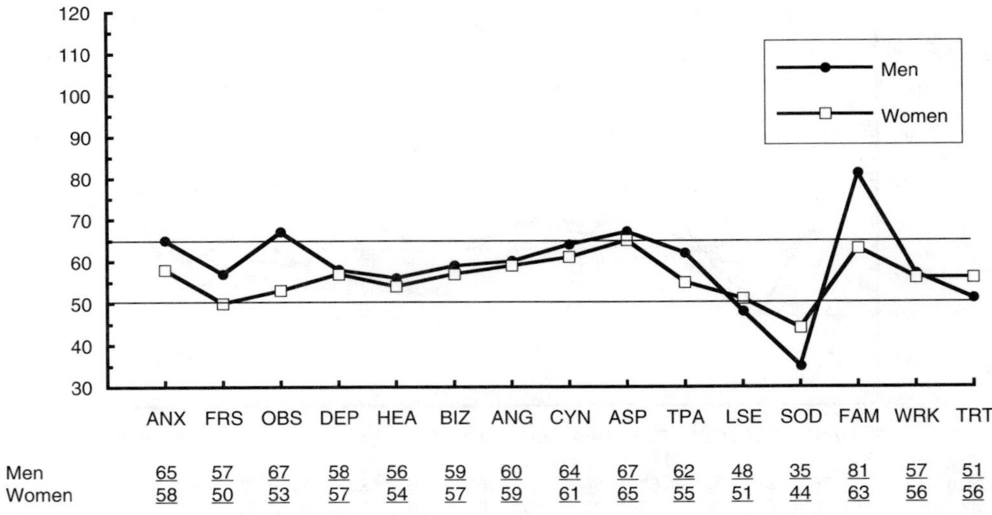

4.20. Mean content scales profiles for 49/94 code type

unique features of the 49/94 group included cynicism, narcissism, being eccentric, and being uncomfortable with members of the opposite sex. Members of this code type were also more likely to be described as being emotionally labile; however, unlike most other code types, manifestations of depression and anxiety were not associated with producing a 49/94 profile. Clients having the 49/94 code type were more likely than clients having WNL profiles to be described by their therapists as having psychotic symptoms, including paranoid ideation and poor reality testing. Because there was marked gender imbalance for this code type in our study (2 men, 10 women), caution is advised in applying the 49/94 correlates to men. The concern is greater here than for other code types with gender imbalance because the correlates for scales 4 and 9 individually were not very similar for men and women. In addition, many of the correlates for the 49/94 code type were not identified for scales 4 and 9 individually.

Both Marks and Seeman (1963) and Gilberstadt and Duker (1965) included the 49/94 code type in their studies. Consistent with the results of our study, their 49/94 individuals were characterized as narcissistic, impulsive, and hostile. Further, they were seen as resenting authority and having superficial relationships. At first glance, it might seem surprising that our 49/94 clients were characterized as having psychotic symptoms including paranoid ideation and problems with reality testing. However, the Marks and Seeman and Gilberstadt and Duker studies also reported similar symptoms for many of their 49/94 individuals. For example, 30% of the Marks and Seeman 49/94s had hallucinations, and 25% had ideas of reference. Gilberstadt and Duker reported that their 49/94s tended to have paranoid psychotic episodes related to excessive drinking, and 30% of their 49/94s had paranoid delusions or paranoid trends.

68/86 Code Type

General dysfunction, manifested in depression, low tolerance for frustration, poor work and achievement orientation, and a lesser likelihood of creating a favorable first impres-

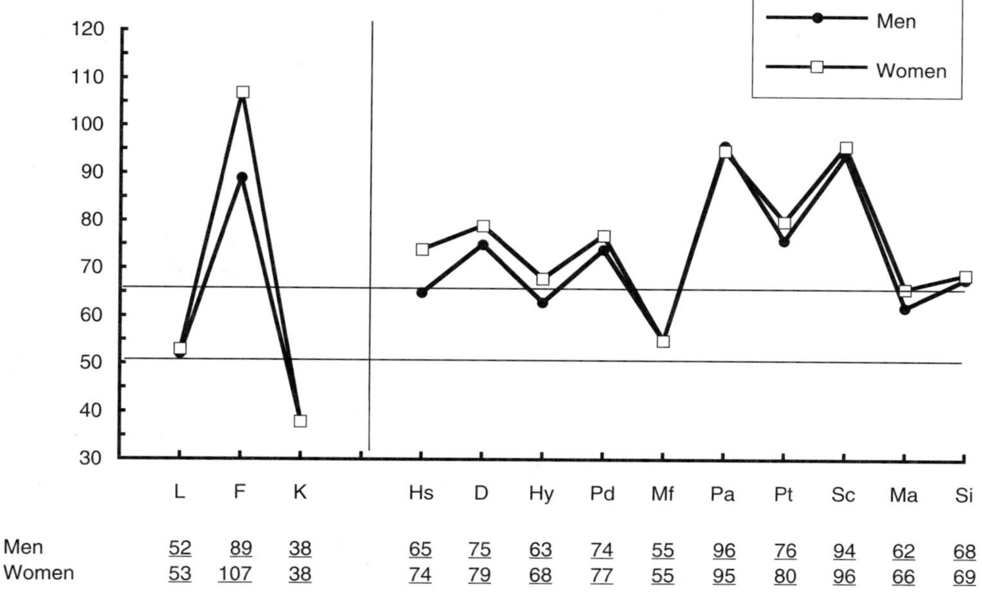

	L	F	K	Hs	D	Hy	Pd	Mf	Pa	Pt	Sc	Ma	Si
Men	52	89	38	65	75	63	74	55	96	76	94	62	68
Women	53	107	38	74	79	68	77	55	95	80	96	66	69

4.21. Mean standard scales profiles for 68/86 code type

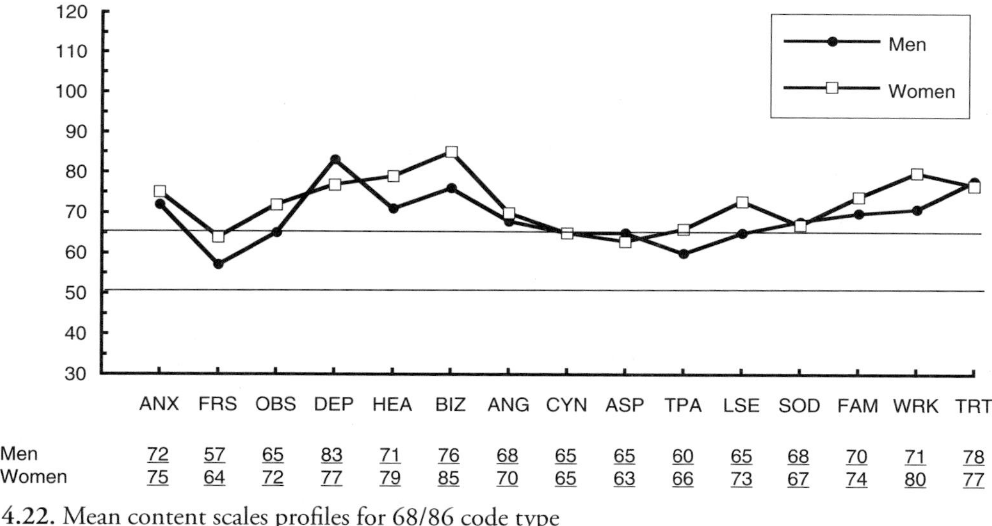

	ANX	FRS	OBS	DEP	HEA	BIZ	ANG	CYN	ASP	TPA	LSE	SOD	FAM	WRK	TRT
Men	72	57	65	83	71	76	68	65	65	60	65	68	70	71	78
Women	75	64	72	77	79	85	70	65	63	66	73	67	74	80	77

4.22. Mean content scales profiles for 68/86 code type

sion were the primary features associated with membership in this code type. Clients having the 68/86 code type were more likely than clients having WNL profiles to have diagnoses of depression or dysthymia. They were also more likely to have had previous psychiatric hospitalizations and histories of having few or no friends. These clients reported multiple symptoms including anxiety, somatic complaints, and obsessive-compulsive thoughts and behaviors. They described themselves as hostile. During intake interviews these clients were described as depressed. Their therapists later characterized them as depressed and as feeling hopeless and pessimistic. They tended to have sleep disturbances and to feel fatigued much of the time. Therapists indicated that these clients tended to feel that life was a strain and that they had low frustration tolerance and gave up easily. These clients were not very work or achievement oriented and did not make good first impressions.

There were very few correlates associated uniquely, or even relatively uniquely, with membership in this code type. Compared with members of other code types, this group produced the highest average elevation on scale F, the clinical scales, and the content scales. This is consistent with the overall level of dysfunction reflected in the 68/86 code-type correlates.

The profiles of the Marks and Seeman (1963) 86/68 code type and the Gilberstadt and Duker (1965) 86 code type were very similar to the profile for our 68/86 code type. Our 68/86s were similar to those of the other two studies in that they were characterized as inadequate persons who did not function well generally and who did not have close relationships with other people. Although the depression that was a salient characteristic of 68/86s in our study was not reported as a primary characteristic for the corresponding code types in the other two studies, it is interesting to note that depression was characteristic of 85% of the 86/68s in the Marks and Seeman study and 40% of the 86s in the Gilberstadt and Duker study. It is quite striking that whereas persons with the Marks and Seeman 86/68 code type or the Gilberstadt and Duker 86 code type had blatant psychotic symptoms including delusions and hallucinations, our clients with the 68/86 code type were not described as having these kinds of symptoms. However, as we reported earlier, persons with such blatant psychotic symptoms who sought services at our study agency were referred to other community agencies for treatment. When this kind of systematic selection does not occur, the blatant psychotic symptoms are likely to be encountered in persons with the 68/86 code type.

78/87 Code Type

Compared with clients having WNL profiles, clients having the 78/87 code type tended to report anxiety, depression, somatic complaints, and obsessive-compulsive symptoms. They also described themselves as interpersonally sensitive. Therapists described these clients as experiencing acute psychological turmoil. They were anxious, nervous, and worried, and they engaged in obsessive thinking. They were preoccupied with health problems and reported multiple somatic complaints. Therapists also described these clients as depressed and pessimistic. They were more likely to have sleep disturbances and suicidal ideation. Therapists reported that some of these clients experienced hallucinations.

Anxiety, tension, rumination, and significant manifestation of depression were the primary features associated with membership in this code type. Somatic preoccupation and concern and psychotic symptomatology were also correlated with the 78/87 code type. All of the features associated with membership in this group were correlated with several other code types. There were virtually no features associated uniquely with producing a 78/87 code type.

Marks and Seeman (1963) did not include the 78/87 code type in their study. The characteristics of the 78/87 clients in our study are quite consistent with those previously reported by Gilberstadt and Duker (1965) for their 78 code type. In both studies these

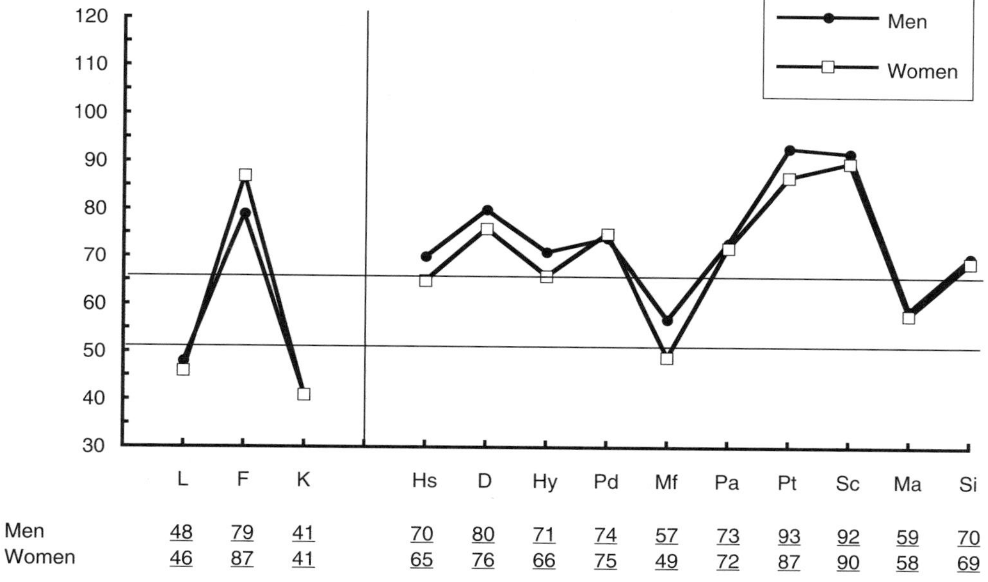

	L	F	K	Hs	D	Hy	Pd	Mf	Pa	Pt	Sc	Ma	Si
Men	48	79	41	70	80	71	74	57	73	93	92	59	70
Women	46	87	41	65	76	66	75	49	72	87	90	58	69

4.23. Mean standard scales profiles for 78/87 code type

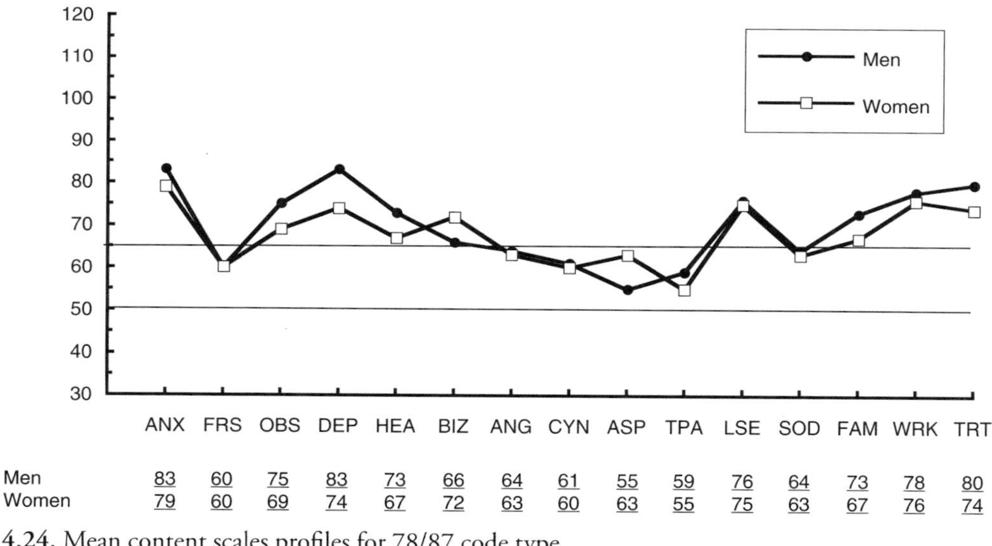

	ANX	FRS	OBS	DEP	HEA	BIZ	ANG	CYN	ASP	TPA	LSE	SOD	FAM	WRK	TRT
Men	83	60	75	83	73	66	64	61	55	59	76	64	73	78	80
Women	79	60	69	74	67	72	63	60	63	55	75	63	67	76	74

4.24. Mean content scales profiles for 78/87 code type

clients were characterized as experiencing a great deal of psychological turmoil, including anxiety and depression. The somatic and obsessive-compulsive symptoms characteristic of our 78/87 clients also were reported for the Gilberstadt and Duker 78 code type. Although patients with the 78 code type in the Gilberstadt and Duker study did not frequently report hallucinations, secondary diagnoses for this code type included schizoid personality and chronic, borderline schizophrenia.

Three-Point Code Types

123 Code Type

Clients having the 123 code type were more likely than clients having WNL profiles to report anxiety, depression, and somatic symptoms. In intake interviews these clients were rated as sad and depressed. Their therapists described them as feeling that life is a

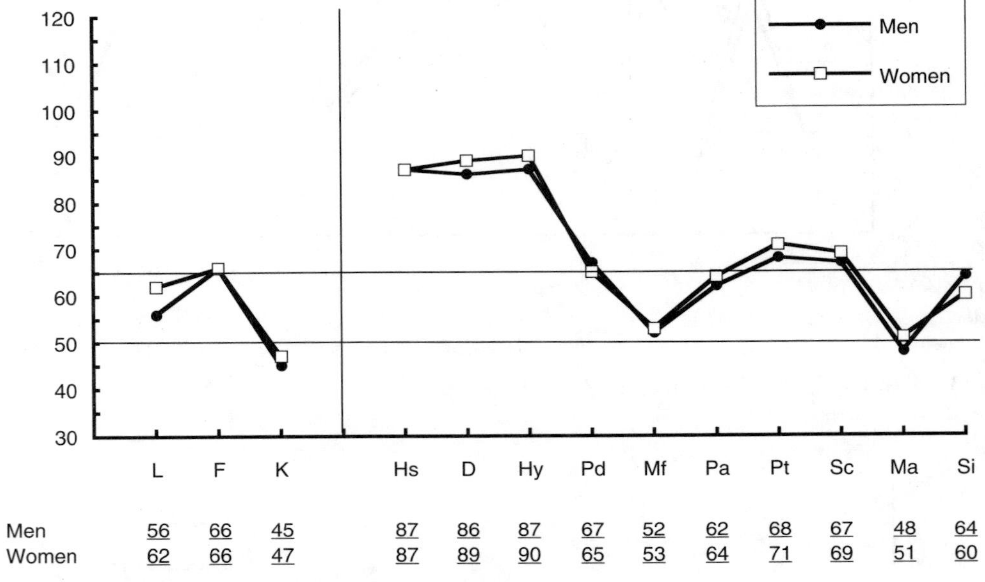

4.25. Mean standard scales profiles for 123 code type

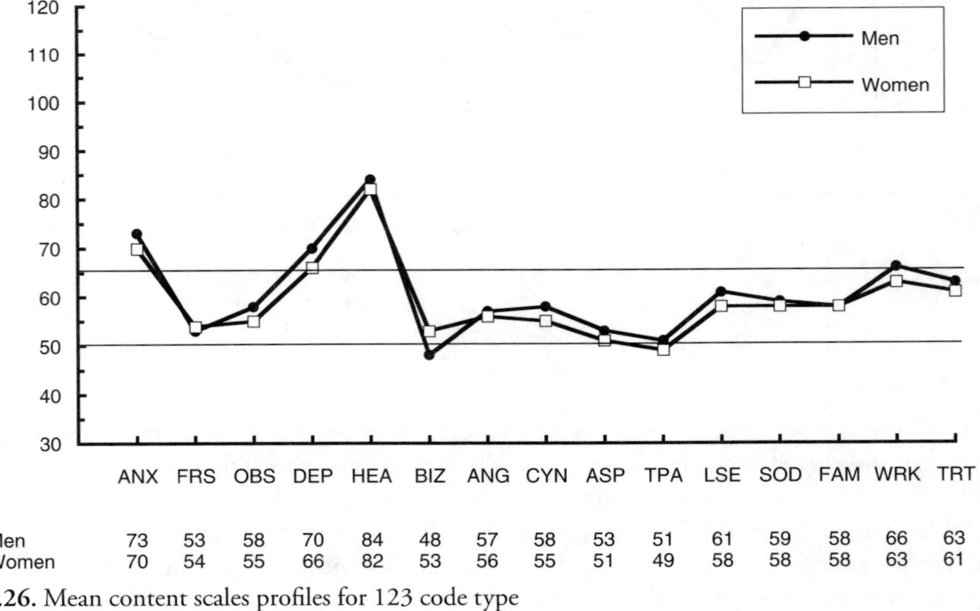

4.26. Mean content scales profiles for 123 code type

strain. Therapists indicated also that these clients tended to feel depressed, pessimistic, and hopeless. They also experienced anxiety, fatigue, sleep disturbances, and lack of energy. Therapists characterized these clients as preoccupied with health problems, reporting multiple somatic complaints, and prone to develop physical symptoms in response to stress. These clients were not very achievement oriented.

Very substantial manifestations of somatization, poor achievement orientation, low energy, depression, and anxiety were the primary features associated with membership in this code type. Correlations with various manifestations of somatization were stronger for the 123 code type than they were for any of the two-point codes made up of these scales.

The characteristics of the 123 clients in our study are remarkably similar to those reported by Gilberstadt and Duker (1965) for their patients with the 123 code type. In both studies persons with this code type were described as anxious and preoccupied with somatic concerns. Both studies described the 123 persons as lacking in energy and experiencing sleep disturbances. Although Gilberstadt and Duker did not include depression as a primary characteristic of the patients with the 123 code type, approximately 45% of their patients with this code type were described as depressed.

247 Code Type

Clients having the 247 code type were more likely than clients having WNL profiles to have diagnoses of depression or dysthymia. These clients reported multiple symptoms including anxiety, phobias, somatic complaints, and obsessive-compulsive thoughts and behaviors. They described themselves as interpersonally sensitive. Therapists described these clients as feeling that life is a strain and that they are getting a raw deal from life.

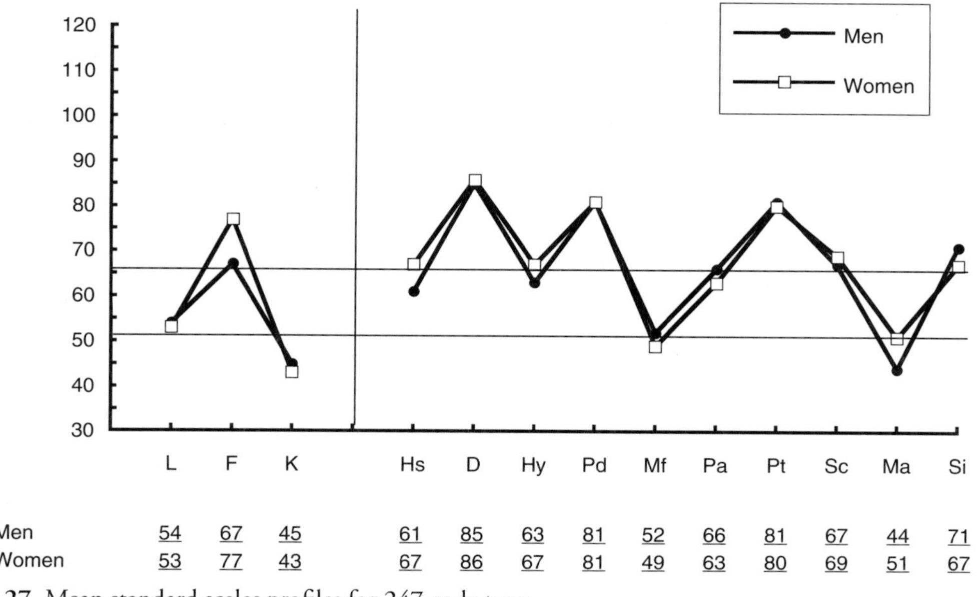

4.27. Mean standard scales profiles for 247 code type

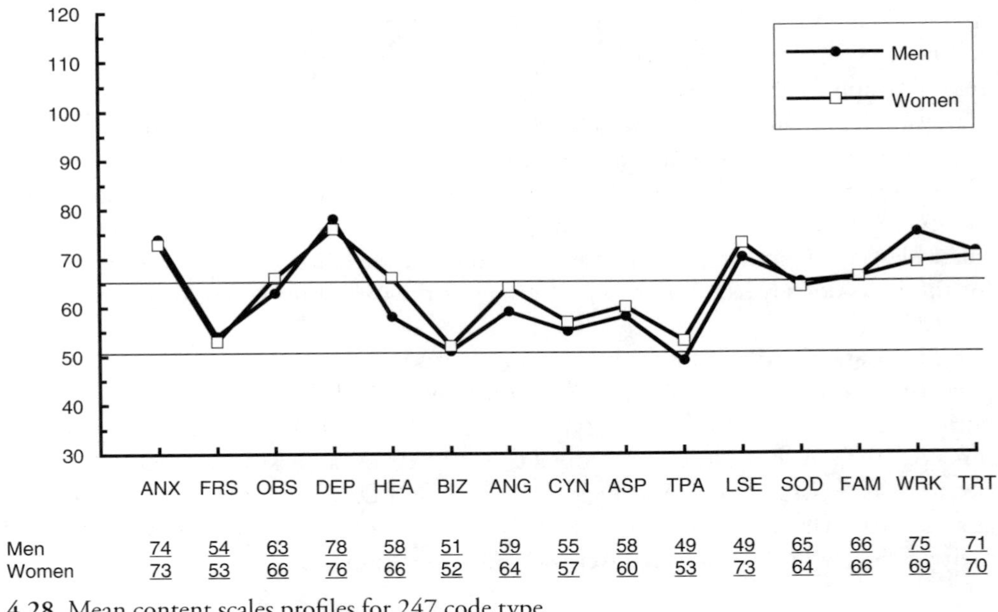

4.28. Mean content scales profiles for 247 code type

They tended to feel depressed and pessimistic and to have suicidal ideation. They were rather uncomfortable around members of the opposite sex.

Depression, feeling that life is a strain, being pessimistic and feeling like a failure, suicidal ideation, and being uncomfortable with members of the opposite sex were the primary features associated with membership in this code type. There were relatively few correlates associated with membership in this code type. Correlates identified for this code type were related similarly with the various two-point codes made up of scales 2, 4, and 7.

The mean profile for our 247 code type is quite similar to that of the 274 code type in the Gilberstadt and Duker (1965) study. Individuals with these code types were quite similar in that they were described as depressed. However, a major difference between the two studies is that the excessive use of alcohol that was characteristic of the 274 patients in the Gilberstadt and Duker study was not a frequent problem for our clients with the 247 code type. Although in our setting persons whose primary problem was substance abuse were referred to other agencies for treatment, substance abuse problems were frequent enough in our sample that it emerged as characteristic of persons with other code types. Perhaps having scale 4 as a more prominent feature in the Gilberstadt and Duker code type increased the likelihood that substance abuse problems would be present.

278 Code Type

Clients having the 278 code type were more likely than clients having WNL profiles to have diagnoses of depression or dysthymia and histories of previous psychiatric hospitalizations and having been sexually abused. These clients reported depression, anxiety, phobias, and obsessive-compulsive symptoms, and they described themselves as interpersonally sensitive. During intake interviews these clients were described as sad and depressed,

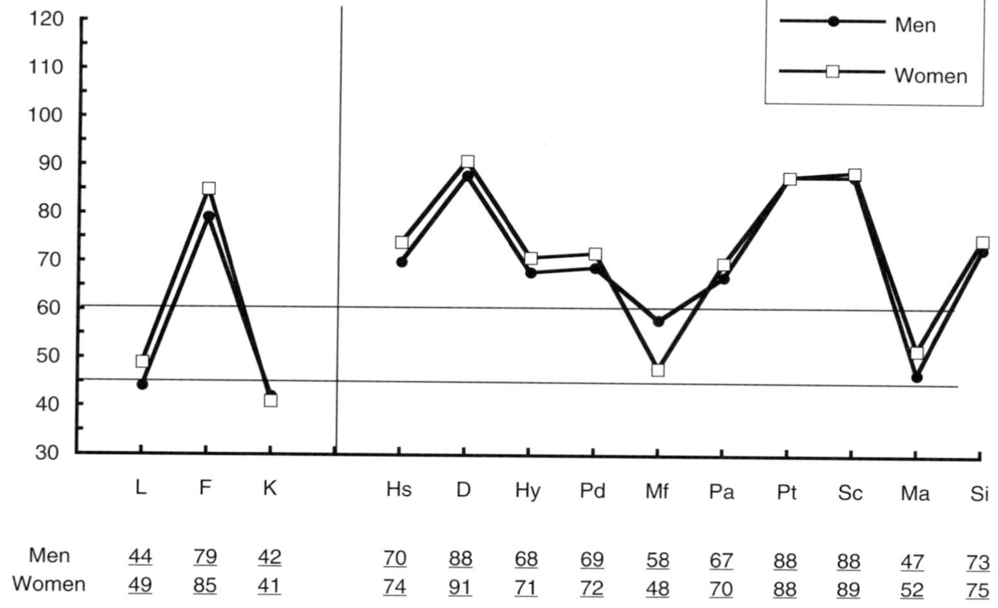

4.29. Mean standard scales profiles for 278 code type

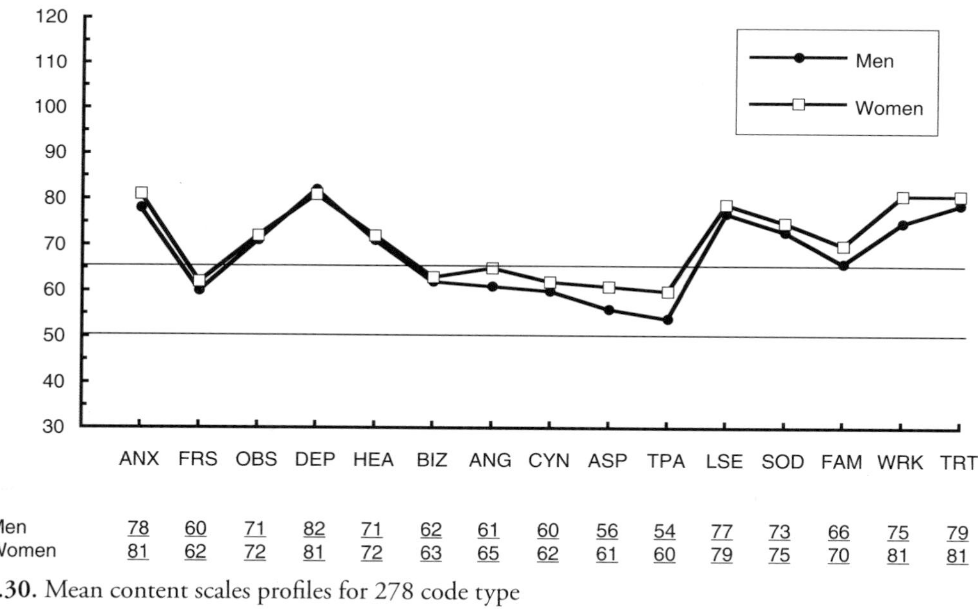

4.30. Mean content scales profiles for 278 code type

and later their therapists described them similarly. Therapists also indicated that these clients felt fatigued, pessimistic, and hopeless, and they tended to have sleep disturbances and suicidal ideation. These clients were also seen as preoccupied with health problems and reporting multiple somatic complaints. They were rather insecure persons who made self-degrading comments and were not very achievement oriented.

Depression, hopelessness, and suicidal ideation were the primary features associated with membership in this code type. Somatic preoccupation and a history of requiring psychiatric hospitalization and having been abused sexually were also associated with producing a 278 code type. Correlations with various manifestations of depression were higher for the 278 code type than for any other code type in this study.

In some ways the clients in our study with the 278 code type were similar to the patients in the Gilberstadt and Duker (1965) study who had this code type, and in some ways they were noticeably different. The anxiety and depression reported for our 278s were reported by Gilberstadt and Duker for this code type. Also, both studies characterized the 278s as rather insecure persons who felt inadequate and inferior. However, our study did not identify the psychotic symptoms, including ideas of reference, that Gilberstadt and Duker reported for their 278 code type. This difference probably reflects the fact that persons with blatant psychotic symptoms were referred to other community agencies and were not treated in our study setting. Another difference in correlates between our study and Gilberstadt and Duker's is that somatic complaints were quite common for our 278 clients, and such complaints were not very common for the Gilberstadt and Duker 278 code type.

468 Code Type

Clients having the 468 code type were more likely than clients having WNL profiles to have Axis I diagnoses of depression or dysthymia and an Axis II diagnosis of antisocial personality disorder. They were also more likely to be taking antidepressant medications and to have histories of previous psychiatric hospitalizations, suicide attempts, and having been physically abused. These clients reported psychotic symptoms, including paranoid ideation, as well as anxiety, depression, and hostility. In intake interviews these

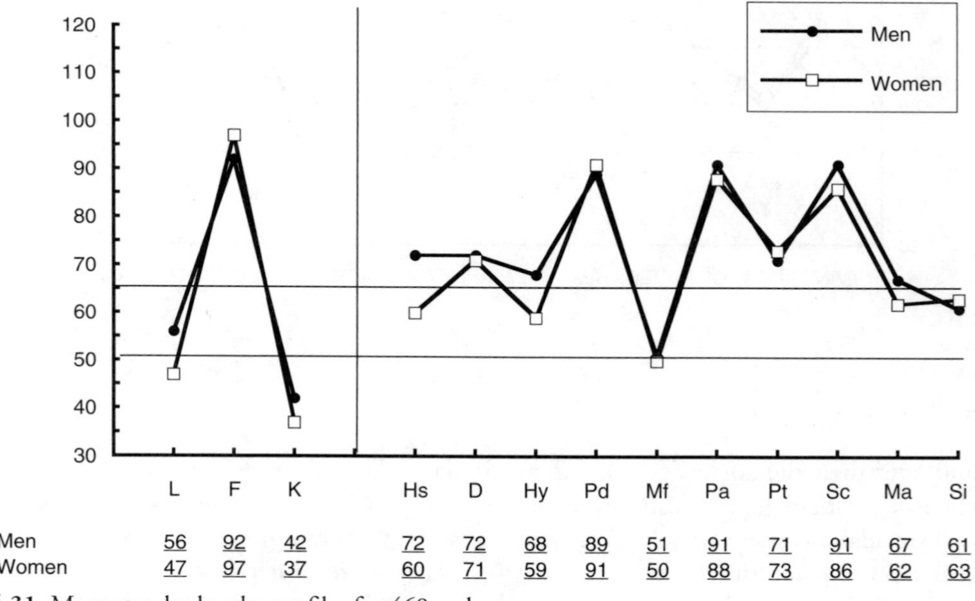

4.31. Mean standard scales profiles for 468 code type

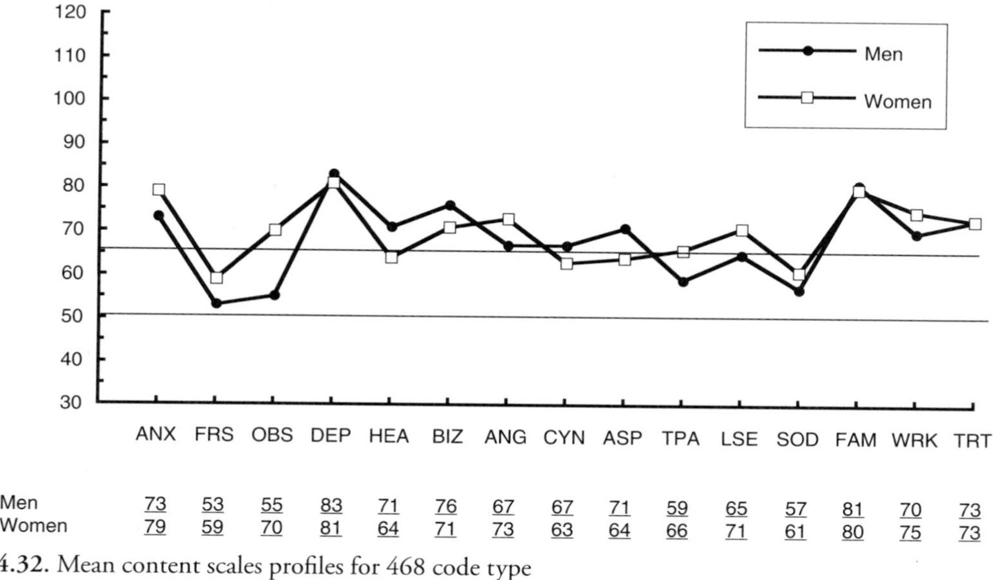

4.32. Mean content scales profiles for 468 code type

clients were rated as having circumstantial and tangential speech. Therapists characterized these clients as having acute psychological turmoil. They reported that these clients tended to feel anxious and agitated and to have obsessive-compulsive symptoms. They were also seen by therapists as sad, depressed, and pessimistic, and they tended to have suicidal ideation. These clients were characterized by therapists as defensive and histrionic and as demanding attention. They tended to be antisocial and to have low tolerance for frustration. They were described as critical, angry, aggressive, argumentative, and resentful. Therapists indicated that these clients reported psychotic symptoms, including suspiciousness and feeling that they were getting a raw deal from life. These clients had work and family problems. They were insecure and often felt like failures.

Many of the correlates identified for this code type were unique. A diagnosis of antisocial personality disorder, social isolation, a history of having been abused physically, circumstantial and tangential speech, being described by therapists as aggressive, having significant antisocial features, being angry and resentful, being agitated, being defensive, and having significant family problems were features associated exclusively or relatively uniquely with membership in this code type. The 468 code type generated many correlates beyond those found for the two-point codes that consist of these three scales. The Gilberstadt and Duker (1965) codebook did not include the 468 code type.

478 Code Type

Clients having the 478 code type were more likely than clients having WNL profiles to have had previous psychiatric hospitalizations. They reported anxiety, phobias, depression, and obsessive-compulsive symptoms. They described themselves as interpersonally sensitive, and they reported psychotic symptoms. During intake interviews these clients were rated as having delusions, hallucinations, and loose cognitive associations. Therapists described these clients as eccentric and suspicious and as having psychotic symptoms,

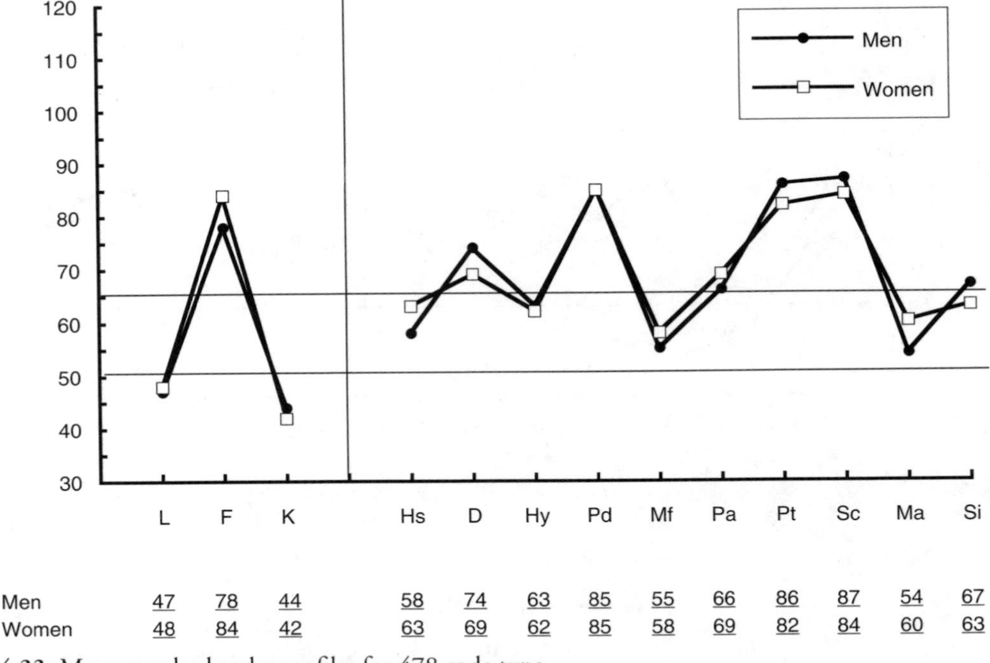

4.33. Mean standard scales profiles for 478 code type

	ANX	FRS	OBS	DEP	HEA	BIZ	ANG	CYN	ASP	TPA	LSE	SOD	FAM	WRK	TRT
Men	75	56	67	82	57	59	66	62	62	53	73	65	71	75	77
Women	72	55	72	74	64	69	65	64	69	61	69	60	72	73	75

4.34. Mean content scales profiles for 478 code type

including disorientation and poor reality testing. Therapists also characterized these clients as anxious and agitated and as having obsessive-compulsive symptoms, many specific fears, and problems with concentration. They were also seen by therapists as depressed, having suicidal ideation, and not showing deep emotions. They were characterized by therapists as histrionic, insecure, and introverted, and also as self-degrading and self-punishing.

Delusions, hallucinations, loose associations, disorientation, introversion, the absence of deep emotions, having many specific fears, and being self-punitive were features associated uniquely with membership in this code type. Manifestations of depression and anxiety were not associated with producing a 478 code type in this study. The Gilberstadt and Duker (1965) codebook did not include the 478 code type.

Chapter 5

Correlates of the MMPI-2 Content Scales, Content Component Scales, and Supplementary Scales

In this chapter we provide summary descriptions of correlates for each of the MMPI-2 Content Scales, Content Component scales, and supplementary scales. The descriptions are based on the correlations between the relevant MMPI-2 scales and component scales and extra-test measures. These are reported in Appendixes H, I, and J. Because the MMPI-2 scales were dichotomized, the descriptions that follow compare clients with high scores on each of the scales with clients who did not produce high scores on the same scale. For all but three of the supplementary scales, dichotomization was performed such that T scores at or above 65 were treated as high.

The three exceptions were supplementary scales Ego Strength (Es), Dominance (Do), and Social Responsibility (Re). Unlike most other MMPI-2 scales, these measures are keyed such that *lower* scores are related to psychopathology. For these scales, dichotomization was performed at a T score of 40. Those with T scores lower than 40 on these scales were compared on the extra-test measures with clients who had T scores at or above 40 on the same scale. A positive correlation between these scales and the extra-test measures (see Appendix J) indicates that low scorers on these scales were more likely to have the characteristic indicated by a given measure.

Unless otherwise specified, the descriptions applied to both male and female clients. The narratives are organized primarily according to source of information (e.g., history, self-report, intake worker ratings, therapist ratings), and the order of the characteristics' presentation in the summaries does not necessarily correspond to the relative correlations between the MMPI-2 scales and the extra-test measures.

Although high scorers are more likely than those who do not have high scores on a scale to have the characteristic included in the summaries for that scale and/or to have these features to a greater extent, not every high scorer on a scale will have every extra-test characteristic that is described. Reference to Appendixes K-1, K-2, L-1, and L-2, in which we report frequencies (for categorical variables) and average values (for continuous variables) for each extra-test variable for the high score and nonelevated score groups, can be of additional help in determining the likelihood that a specific characteristic will apply to high scorers on a particular Content, Content Component, or supplementary scale.

Content Scales

Anxiety (ANX)

Compared with clients with T scores below 65 on this scale, those with high scores on ANX were more likely to receive a depressive or dysthymic disorder diagnosis at intake.

Men with elevations on this scale were more likely to have had previous psychiatric hospitalizations, whereas women were more likely to have had histories characterized by suicide attempts and having few or no friends. These women were also more likely to be receiving anxiolytic medication. Members of both genders reported higher levels of anxiety, depression, and obsessive-compulsive tendencies.

High scorers on ANX were more likely to be described during intake as being sad and depressed. Their therapists were more likely to describe these individuals as being anxious, depressed, and pessimistic. Therapists reported that these individuals were more likely to be complaining of sleep disturbance and somatic concerns and to be feeling sad, hopeless, and overwhelmed. High ANX scorers were also described as experiencing suicidal ideation, being prone to worry, and feeling that life is a strain. They believed that they were failures, and they had lower levels of energy. These individuals were less likely to be described as coping well with stress. Women who scored high on ANX were less likely to be described by their therapists as being achievement oriented.

Fears (FRS)

Very few empirical correlates were found for clients with high scores on FRS. Compared with clients who score below 65 on this scale, these individuals were more likely to report phobic fears. Men with elevations on this scale were more likely to receive a diagnosis of schizophrenia, be placed on antipsychotic medication, and be described during intake as experiencing hallucinations and obsessions. Women who scored high on this scale were described by their therapists as lacking in achievement and work orientation, less likely to be competitive, and less likely to cope well with stress.

Obsessiveness (OBS)

Compared with clients who scored below 65 on this scale, individuals who had high scores on OBS were more likely to be viewed as being depressed during their intake interview, and they were more likely to present with obsessive-compulsive tendencies, anxiety, and some psychotic symptoms. Women with high scores on this scale were more likely to have histories of having been sexually abused and having few or no friends.

Therapists described male clients with high scores on OBS as depressed, anxious, nervous, feeling hopeless, and complaining of sleep disturbance. Women with high scores on this scale were described by their therapists as being less likely to have high aspirations and many interests.

Depression (DEP)

Compared with individuals who score below 65 on this scale, clients with high scores on DEP were more likely to receive a depression or dysthymia diagnosis and to have histories of suicide attempts and having few or no friends. They were also more likely to have had prior psychiatric hospitalizations. These clients presented with a considerable amount of depressive symptomatology. Men who scored high on this scale were also more likely to have had prior outpatient mental health treatment and to receive multiple Axis I diagnoses. Women were more likely to be prescribed antidepressant and anxiolytic medications.

Clients who scored high on DEP were more likely to be viewed during intake as being depressed and sad. Men were less likely to be described as being happy. Their therapists described high scorers on DEP as depressed, feeling hopeless and sad, complaining of sleep disturbance, having suicidal ideation, feeling like a failure, being more pessimistic and less optimistic, and having lower levels of energy. They also described these clients as being insecure, lacking in achievement orientation, feeling that life is a strain, and being less likely to cope well with stress. Male clients who scored high on DEP were also described as being anxious, overwhelmed, and overly sensitive in interpersonal situations, and as being inclined toward somatization. Women with high scores on this scale were more likely to be described as being introverted.

Health Concerns (HEA)

Compared with individuals who score below 65 on this scale, clients who had high scores on HEA were more likely to receive a depression or dysthymia diagnosis and to present with multiple somatic complaints. Men were more likely to receive multiple Axis I diagnoses, and women were more likely to have histories of suicide attempts and to be placed on antidepressant and anxiolytic medication.

Clients with high scores on HEA were likely to be viewed during intake as being sad and depressed. Men were less likely to be viewed as happy. The primary characteristics attributed to high HEA scorers by their therapists were somatic symptoms and complaints. They were described as being preoccupied with health problems, presenting with multiple somatic complaints, developing physical symptoms in response to stress, being hypochondriacal, and inclined toward somatization. These clients were also described as being depressed, anxious, and pessimistic; complaining of fatigue, low energy, and difficulties concentrating; feeling overwhelmed; and being less likely to cope well with stress. Men who scored high on HEA were also described by their therapists as being agitated, angry, resentful, anxious, and histrionic. Female clients with high scores on this scale were less likely to be described as having many interests.

Bizarre Mentation (BIZ)

Compared with individuals who score below 65 on this scale, clients who scored high on BIZ were more likely to present with psychotic symptoms, paranoid ideation, and anxiety. Men with high scores on this scale were more likely to receive a depression or dysthymia diagnosis, to have histories of having been physically abused, and to have lifetime and recent histories of cocaine abuse. Women with high scores on BIZ were more likely to have histories of having been sexually abused, making suicide attempts, and being hospitalized for psychiatric treatment.

Men who scored high on BIZ were more likely to be described at intake as presenting with loose cognitive associations and angry mood. Their therapists saw these men as feeling that life is a strain. Women with high scores on this scale had a greater likelihood of being viewed as presenting initially with hallucinations. Their therapists described these women as having psychotic symptoms and low tolerance for frustration. They also described them as being less likely to create a good first impression; less likely to be work and achievement oriented, competitive, and self-reliant; and less likely to communicate effectively.

Anger (ANG)

Compared with individuals who scored below 65 on this scale, clients with high scores on ANG had a greater likelihood of having been physically abusive. They also had higher rates of substance abuse and dependence. These individuals presented with a great deal of hostility at intake. Men who scored high on this scale were more likely to have histories of committing acts of domestic violence. Women who scored high on ANG were more likely to have histories of having been sexually abused and making suicide attempts.

Clients who scored high on ANG were more likely to be described by their therapists as having temper tantrums. Men were also described as being physically abusive, agitated, resenting family members, coming from families lacking in love, having low tolerance for frustration, reporting many nightmares, feeling hopeless, and complaining of sleep disturbance. Women with high scores on ANG were more likely to be described as grouchy.

Cynicism (CYN)

Compared with individuals who scored below 65 on this scale, high scorers on CYN were more likely to present with paranoid ideation and interpersonal hostility. Men with high scores on this scale were more likely to receive diagnoses of depression or dysthymia, and to have histories of having been physically abused and having few or no friends. Women were more likely to have made suicide attempts.

At intake, men with high CYN scores were more likely to be described as being sad and depressed. Their therapists were more likely to report that these men have many nightmares and complained of sleep disturbance. Women with high scores on this scale were less likely to be viewed as being likable and dependable, less likely to have insight into their own problems, less likely to create a good first impression, and less likely to be idealistic and achievement oriented. They were less likely to be described as having many interests or high aspirations. Their therapists were more likely to describe these women as being difficult to motivate, psychologically immature, and antisocial.

Antisocial Practices (ASP)

Compared with individuals who scored below 65 on this scale, individuals with high scores on ASP were more likely to have histories of having been arrested and to present initially with interpersonal hostility. Men who scored high on this scale were more likely to have histories of committing acts of domestic violence and being physically abusive, and they had a greater likelihood of receiving an antisocial personality disorder and a substance abuse disorder diagnosis at intake. Women with high scores on ASP were more likely to have histories of misdemeanor convictions and cocaine abuse, and they had a greater likelihood of having made a suicide attempt.

At intake, men who scored high on ASP were more likely to be viewed as being angry, demonstrating poor judgment, and being defensive. Women were more likely to be viewed as experiencing hallucinations. Therapists viewed individuals who produced high scores on ASP as displaying antisocial behavior, acting out, and having low tolerance for frustration. They were also viewed as being physically abusive and having family problems. Men who scored high on this scale were more likely to be described as having stormy interpersonal relationships and feeling lonely. Women who scored high on ASP were described as being sociopathic, having problems with authority figures, being deceptive and psychologically immature, having superficial relationships, getting bored easily, and being defensive.

Type A Behaviors (TPA)

Compared with individuals who scored below 65 on this scale, high scorers on TPA were more likely to present with interpersonal hostility. Men were likely to be viewed by their therapists as being excitable and developing physical symptoms in response to stress. Women were less likely to be viewed as creating a good first impression or being likable.

Low Self-Esteem (LSE)

Compared with individuals who scored below 65 on this scale, clients with high scores on LSE were more likely to receive a depression or dysthymia diagnosis. They presented with greater levels of interpersonal sensitivity and symptoms of depression. Men who scored high on this scale were more likely to have histories of outpatient treatment and of having been physically abused. They were also more likely to receive a bipolar or cyclothymia diagnosis as well as multiple Axis I diagnoses. Women who scored high on LSE were more likely to have a history of suicide attempts and of having few or no friends and to be receiving antidepressant medication at the time of intake.

Individuals with high scores on LSE were more likely during intake to be viewed as depressed. Men were more likely to be described as anxious, and women as sad. Their therapists described these clients as being insecure, passive-submissive, self-degrading, and self-doubting, and as feeling inferior and like a failure. They also viewed them as being depressed, anxious, and pessimistic, as feeling hopeless and overwhelmed, and as being introverted. Men who scored high on this scale were also described by their therapists as being inclined to somatize, preoccupied with health problems, and complaining of sleep disturbance. Women with high scores on LSE were viewed as more likely to be passive in interpersonal relationships, giving up easily, and being tearful. They were less likely to be viewed as being achievement oriented or self-reliant, or as coping well with stress.

Social Discomfort (SOD)

Compared with individuals who scored below 65 on this scale, those with high scores on SOD were more likely to present with interpersonal sensitivity. Women were more likely to be taking antidepressant or anxiolytic medications at intake and to have histories of having few or no friends.

Therapists working with individuals who scored high on SOD were more likely to describe them as being introverted, shy, and socially awkward. They were less likely to rate them as being extroverted. These individuals were also described as being depressed and more likely to have suicidal ideation. Men who scored high on this scale were also described as being insecure, uncomfortable with members of the opposite sex, pessimistic, anxious, suspicious, angry, resentful, and emotionally controlled. In addition, they were viewed by their therapists as more likely to feel hopeless, to be self-degrading, and to be self-punishing. Women with high scores on SOD were less likely to be described as achievement oriented, to create a good first impression, or to be energetic or concerned about status.

Family Problems (FAM)

Compared with individuals who scored below 65 on this scale, clients with high scores on FAM were more likely to have a history of having been physically abused and of having few or no friends. They were more likely to present with paranoid ideation, hostility, interpersonal sensitivity, and depression. Men also had a greater likelihood of having abused marijuana and women of having been sexually abused.

During intake, men with high scores on FAM were more likely to be viewed as presenting with circumstantial speech, depression, and sad mood. Therapists described clients who scored high on FAM as having family problems, coming from families lacking in love and characterized by discord, resenting family members, and blaming family for their difficulties. Men were also described by their therapists as depressed, insecure, anxious, and agitated. They were viewed as being sad and self-degrading, prone to rumination, and feeling hopeless. They were also described as not getting along with coworkers. Women who scored high on FAM were more likely to be described by their therapists as being critical and argumentative, grouchy, overbearing in relationships, having difficulty trusting others, and feeling that they get a raw deal from life.

Work Interference (WRK)

Compared with those who scored below 65 on this scale, individuals with high scores on WRK were more likely to receive a depression or dysthymia diagnosis at intake and to present with depression, interpersonal sensitivity, and obsessive-compulsive tendencies. Men who scored high on this scale also were more likely to receive multiple Axis I diagnoses and to have histories of outpatient psychiatric treatment. Women with high scores on WRK were more likely to have made past suicide attempts, to have histories of having few or no friends, and to be taking anxiolytic medication at the time of intake.

Individuals who produce elevated scores on WRK were more likely to be described as sad and depressed during intake. Men with high scores on this scale were also described as being angry. Therapists described clients who scored high on WRK as being less achievement oriented, energetic, or extroverted, and less likely to cope well with stress. They also described these individuals as being depressed, sad, and insecure, and feeling hopeless and like a failure. Men with high scores on this scale were also viewed by their therapists as being anxious, complaining of sleep disturbance, and feeling overwhelmed. Additionally, these men were described as prone to somatization, preoccupied with health problems, and having multiple somatic complaints. Women with high scores on WRK were less likely to be described as self-reliant, to have high aspirations, or to create good first impressions. They were more likely to be viewed as overly sensitive to criticism and being passive in relationships.

Negative Treatment Indicators (TRT)

Compared with clients who scored below 65 on this scale, high scorers on TRT were more likely to receive an intake diagnosis of depression or dysthymia, to have had previous psychiatric hospitalizations, and to present with depression and interpersonal sensitivity. Male clients were also more likely to receive multiple Axis I diagnoses.

At intake, individuals with high scores on TRT were more likely to be viewed as sad and depressed. Men were also more likely to be described as angry. Therapists rated high scorers on TRT as depressed, anxious, insecure, and pessimistic. They described them as feeling hopeless and overwhelmed, feeling like a failure and that life is a strain, having suicidal ideation, and being sad. They also described these clients as giving up easily. Therapists were less likely to describe high TRT individuals as energetic and coping well with stress. Men with high scores on this scale were also more likely to complain of sleep disturbance and to present with somatic symptoms, and were described as being anxious, angry, resentful, and obsessive-compulsive. Female clients who scored high on TRT were viewed as being introverted and were less likely to be described as being achievement oriented, having high aspirations or many interests, or creating a good first impression.

Content Component Scales

The Content Component scales can be helpful in understanding which correlates of the parent Content Scales should be emphasized for particular clients. The component scales should be interpreted only when T scores on the parent Content Scale are greater than 60. In addition, greater emphasis should be placed on the correlates of a component scale when it is at least 10 T-score points higher than other component scales of the parent scale.

Generalized Fearfulness (FRS_1)

Compared with clients who scored below 65 on this component scale, individuals with high scores on FRS_1 were more likely to have histories of having few or no friends and to present with symptoms of phobic anxiety. Women who scored high on this scale were more likely to have histories of having been physically and sexually abused and of having made suicide attempts.

High scorers on FRS_1 were more likely to be viewed by their therapists as being anxious. Men with high scores on this scale were described by therapists as presenting with multiple somatic complaints, developing physical symptoms in response to stress, and having difficulties concentrating. Women scoring high on FRS_1 were more likely to be characterized as having many specific fears; having many nightmares; being depressed, nervous, socially awkward, and introverted; and experiencing suicidal ideation. They were less likely to be described as achievement oriented, communicating effectively, or coping well with stress.

Multiple Fears (FRS_2)

No correlates common to both women and men were found for this component scale. Compared with men who scored below 65 on FRS_2, men with high scores on this scale were more likely to receive a diagnosis of schizophrenia and to be receiving antipsychotic medication at intake. They were also more likely to be characterized as experiencing hallucinations. Their therapists were less likely to view these men as exhibiting stereotypic masculine behavior. Women with high scores on FRS_2 were more likely to present with symptoms of phobic anxiety.

Lack of Drive (DEP_1)

Compared with individuals who scored below 65 on this component scale, clients who scored high on DEP_1 were more likely to receive a depression or dysthymia diagnosis at intake. They were also more likely to present with symptoms of depression. Men were more likely to receive multiple Axis I diagnoses, whereas women had a greater likelihood of having histories of suicide attempts, of having few or no friends, and of having previous psychiatric hospitalizations. At intake, these women were more likely to be receiving antidepressant or anxiolytic medications.

Clients who scored high on DEP_1 had a greater likelihood of being described as depressed and sad at intake. Their therapists viewed these clients as depressed, sad, pessimistic, feeling hopeless, and experiencing suicidal ideation. They also viewed high DEP_1 scorers as complaining of somatic symptoms and being preoccupied with health problems. Therapists also described these clients as complaining of fatigue, feeling overwhelmed, and feeling that they get a raw deal from life. These individuals were less likely to be characterized as energetic, optimistic, having many interests, or being achievement oriented. Men with high scores on this component scale were also more likely to be described as anxious, insecure, histrionic, obsessive-compulsive, and procrastinating. Women were less likely to be described as creating a good first impression.

Dysphoria (DEP_2)

Compared with individuals who scored below 65 on this component scale, those with high scores on DEP_2 were more likely to receive a depression or dysthymia diagnosis and to present with symptoms of depression. Male clients who scored high on this scale also had a greater likelihood of having had prior outpatient treatment. Women with high scores on DEP_2 were more likely to have histories of suicide attempts and of having few or no friends, and they were less likely to have ever been arrested or to have abused marijuana. These women were likely to be taking antidepressant medication at intake.

Clients with high scores on DEP_2 had a greater likelihood of being viewed as sad and depressed during their intake interviews. Male clients were less likely to be viewed as happy. Therapists characterized high scorers on this component scale as depressed and sad, feeling hopeless and inferior, feeling that life is a strain, and feeling rejected and like a failure. These clients complained of sleep disturbance, were viewed as insecure, self-degrading, and pessimistic, and experienced suicidal ideation. Men who produced high scores on DEP_2 were also characterized as anxious, presenting with somatic complaints and interpersonal sensitivity, and being obsessive-compulsive. Female clients who scored high on this scale were viewed as being overly sensitive to criticism.

Self-Depreciation (DEP_3)

Compared with clients who scored below 65 on this component scale, those with high scores on DEP_3 were more likely to receive a depression or dysthymia diagnosis and to have histories of suicide attempts. They also presented with many symptoms of depression. Women with high scores on this scale were also more likely to have histories of having few or no friends and to have abused alcohol over the course of their lives.

Clients with high scores on DEP_3 were more likely to be viewed at intake as being sad and depressed. Their therapists described these individuals as self-doubting, insecure, self-degrading, self-punishing, giving up easily, and feeling inferior and like a failure. These clients were viewed as being depressed, as feeling hopeless, pessimistic, and that life is a strain, and as having suicidal ideation. They were less likely to be viewed as being achievement oriented. Men with high scores on DEP_3 were more likely to be characterized as being anxious, presenting somatic problems, complaining of sleep disturbance, being obsessive-compulsive, being histrionic, and experiencing anger and resentment. In addition, these male clients were viewed as being sad and ruminating. Women with high scores on this scale were less likely to be viewed as having many interests.

Suicidal Ideation (DEP_4)

Compared with clients who scored below 65 on this component scale, high DEP_4 scorers were more likely to have histories of suicide attempts and previous psychiatric hospitalizations. They also had a greater likelihood of receiving a depression or dysthymia diagnosis and being placed on antidepressant medication. These clients presented with multiple symptoms of depression. Men with high scores on this scale were also more likely to have abused cocaine during the six-month period prior to their intake interviews.

High scorers on DEP_4 were described at intake as being sad and depressed. Their therapists were more likely to view these individuals as being depressed and tearful and experiencing hopelessness and suicidal ideation. They were less likely to be viewed as optimistic or energetic. Men who scored high on this component scale were also more likely to be described as pessimistic, anxious, insecure, angry, resentful, and agitated. They were more likely to complain of sleep disturbance, feel anxious and overwhelmed, and feel like a failure. Female clients with high scores on DEP_4 were more likely to give up easily and less likely to be achievement oriented, create a good first impression, or be self-reliant. They also were less likely to be sexually well adjusted.

Gastrointestinal Symptoms (HEA_1)

Compared with those who scored below 65 on this component scale, high scorers on HEA_1 were more likely to present with somatization. Women who scored high on this scale had a greater likelihood of receiving antidepressant medication at intake.

Intake workers viewed women who scored high on HEA_1 as being anxious and depressed during their interviews. Therapists characterized high HEA_1 scorers as somatizing, presenting multiple somatic complaints, and being preoccupied with health problems. They also viewed these clients as being depressed and described them as complaining of sleep disturbance. Male clients who scored high on the scale were additionally described as being sad, feeling that life is a strain, complaining of fatigue, being anxious, and experiencing suicidal ideation. Women with high scores on HEA_1 were more likely to be described as having difficulties concentrating, and they were less likely to be viewed as being energetic and having multiple interests.

Neurological Symptoms (HEA_2)

Compared with clients who scored below 65 on this scale, those with high scores on HEA_2 were more likely to present with indications of somatization and to receive a depression or dysthymia diagnosis. Men with high scores on this scale had a greater likelihood of receiving multiple Axis I diagnoses. Women more often had histories of being sexually and physically abused and being the victims of domestic violence. They were also more likely to have histories of suicide attempts and of having few or no friends and to be taking antidepressant medication at intake.

At intake, high HEA_2 scorers were more likely to be viewed as depressed. Women were also described as sad. Therapists more likely viewed high scorers on this component scale as somatizing, being preoccupied with health problems, presenting multiple somatic complaints, developing physical symptoms in response to stress, having difficulties concentrating, and being hypochondriacal. High scorers were also characterized as depressed, anxious, and pessimistic, and they were more likely to complain of sleep disturbance and fatigue. They also had a greater likelihood of feeling hopeless and overwhelmed, and of having suicidal ideation. Men with high scores on HEA_2 were viewed as agitated and more likely to have a low sex drive. Women were less likely to be described as achievement oriented.

General Health Concerns (HEA_3)

Compared with individuals who scored below 65 on this component scale, those with high scores on HEA_3 were more likely to present with somatization and to receive a depression or dysthymia diagnosis. Male clients who scored high on this scale had a greater likelihood of having received previous outpatient treatment, and female clients were more likely to have been sexually abused, to have had a history of suicide attempts, and to be taking antidepressant medication.

At intake, individuals who scored high on HEA_3 were more likely to be viewed as being sad and depressed. Their therapists characterized these clients as somatizing, presenting multiple physical complaints, being preoccupied with health problems, developing physical symptoms in response to stress, and being hypochondriacal. They also viewed these individuals as being depressed, anxious, and pessimistic, and feeling hopeless and overwhelmed. Men scoring high on this scale were described as being angry and resentful. Women were less likely to have been characterized as being energetic, having many interests, or as having high aspirations.

Psychotic Symptomatology (BIZ_1)

Compared with those who scored below 65 on the scale, clients with high scores on BIZ_1 were more likely to present with symptoms of psychosis and paranoid ideation. Men were more likely to receive a psychotic disorder diagnosis, and women had a greater likelihood of having had prior psychiatric hospitalizations.

At intake, men who scored high on BIZ_1 were more likely to be described as being angry, and women had a greater likelihood of being characterized as experiencing hallucinations. Therapists characterized men with high scores on BIZ_1 as experiencing delusional thinking and being undercontrolled. They were less likely to describe women with high scores on this scale as communicating effectively and more likely to view them as having low tolerance for frustration.

Schizotypal Characteristics (BIZ_2)

Compared with individuals who scored below 65 on this scale, clients who scored high on BIZ_2 were more likely to have been previously hospitalized for psychiatric treatment and to present with symptoms of psychosis, paranoid ideation, and anxiety. Men with high scores on this scale were more likely to have a history of having been physically abused and to receive a depression or dysthymia diagnosis at intake. Women who scored high on BIZ_2 were more likely to have histories of having been sexually abused and having made suicide attempts, and they had a greater likelihood of receiving an Axis II, Cluster B diagnosis.

At intake, high scorers on BIZ_2 were more likely to be described as presenting with loose cognitive associations. Therapists were more likely to describe men who scored high on this scale as feeling overwhelmed and that life is a strain, coming from families lacking in love, being anxious, and having difficulties making decisions. Female clients with high scores on BIZ_2 were more likely to be viewed as suspicious, sociopathic, and having suicidal ideation. They were less likely to be characterized as being achievement oriented, creating a good first impression, coping well with stress, being work oriented, or being self-reliant.

Explosive Behavior (ANG_1)

Compared with those who scored below 65 on this component scale, clients who produced high scores on ANG_1 were more likely to have histories of being physically abusive and abusing alcohol over the course of their lives, and they were also more likely to receive substance abuse or dependence diagnoses. These clients presented with significant levels of hostility. Men who scored high on this scale were more likely to have committed acts of domestic violence and to have been convicted of such crimes. They also had a greater likelihood of having been abused physically. These men received multiple Axis I diagnoses and had histories of abusing marijuana over the course of their lives and alcohol within the past six months. Female clients who scored high on ANG_1 were more likely to have had histories of having been sexually abused and of making suicide attempts, and they had a greater likelihood of having misdemeanor convictions.

Clients who scored high on ANG_1 were more likely to be described by therapists as having temper tantrums. Men with high scores on this component scale were described as being hostile, physically abusive, aggressive, angry, and resentful, as harboring grudges, as having stormy interpersonal relationships, and as having a low level of tolerance for frustration. These men were also characterized as having family problems, coming from families lacking in love, and resenting members of their family. They were viewed as depressed and described as having many nightmares.

Irritability (ANG_2)

Compared with individuals who scored below 65 on this component sale, clients who scored high on ANG_2 were more likely to present with indications of hostility and to receive a depression or dysthymia diagnosis. Men had a greater likelihood of receiving multiple Axis I diagnoses, whereas women were more likely to have histories of suicide attempts and previous outpatient treatment.

Clients who scored high on ANG_2 were more likely to be described as sad during their intake interview. Male clients scoring high on this scale were also more likely to be described as being depressed. Therapists viewed high ANG_2 clients as depressed and self-degrading. Men with high scores on this scale were also characterized as being angry, resentful, and anxious, as having family problems and coming from families lacking in love, and as having many somatic complaints and developing physical problems in response to stress. These men were also more likely to be described as complaining of sleep disturbance and having many nightmares, as having suicidal ideation, and as being sad. Women with high scores on ANG_2 were viewed as feeling inferior and being less likely to cope well with stress.

Misanthropic Beliefs (CYN_1)

Compared with those who scored below 65 on this component scale, clients who scored high on CYN_1 were more likely to present with paranoid ideation. Women who scored high on this scale were also more likely to have histories of suicide attempts.

Men with high scores on this component scale were more likely to be described by their therapists as ruminating, being socially awkward, having many nightmares, and being depressed. Women with high scores on CYN_1 were more likely to be viewed as having a negative attitude toward treatment and as being difficult to motivate, psychologically immature, and antisocial. These women were less likely to be characterized as being achievement oriented, having insight into their problems, creating a favorable first impression, being likable, communicating effectively, having many interests, being a reliable informant, or being work oriented.

Interpersonal Suspiciousness (CYN_2)

Compared with clients who scored below 65 on this component scale, those with high scores on CYN_2 were more likely to present with paranoid ideation. Men were likely to have histories of having few or no friends and to receive a depression or dysthymia diagnosis. Women who scored high on CYN_2 were less likely to be viewed by therapists as having insight into their problems or being dependable.

Antisocial Attitudes (ASP_1)

Compared with clients who scored below 65 on this component scale, high scorers on ASP_1 were more likely to present with hostility. Men were more likely to have histories of having few or no friends, and women were more likely to have made suicide attempts.

At intake, men who scored high on this scale were more likely to be described as having poor judgment, and women with high scores on ASP_1 had a greater likelihood of being characterized as having hallucinations. Therapists viewed these men as having a low level of tolerance for frustration and described them as having many nightmares. Female clients with high scores on this component scale were characterized as antisocial, defensive, unable to see their own limitations, psychologically immature, having superficial relationships, being sociopathic, and difficult to motivate. Women with high scores on ASP_1 were less likely to be described as having insight into their problems or as being a reliable informant, dependable, or likable.

Antisocial Behavior (ASP_2)

Compared with individuals who scored below 65 on this component scale, clients with high ASP_2 scores were more likely to have histories of being arrested; they had a greater number of arrests, and they were more likely to have a history of misdemeanor convictions. These clients also had a greater likelihood of abusing alcohol, marijuana, or cocaine during their lives, and they were more likely to receive a substance abuse or dependence diagnosis. They also were more likely to receive an antisocial personality disorder diagnosis. These individuals presented with interpersonal hostility. Men with high scores on this scale were more likely to have a history of felony convictions, of committing and being convicted of domestic violence, and of being physically abusive. They were also more likely to receive an Axis II, Cluster B diagnosis. Women with high scores on ASP_2 were more likely to have histories of having been sexually and/or physically abused, and they had a greater likelihood of heroin abuse in their past.

Therapists were more likely to describe high ASP_2 scorers as antisocial, hostile, aggressive, angry, resentful, and suspicious. They also characterized clients with high scores on this component scale as acting out, being impulsive, having temper tantrums, harboring grudges, being sociopathic, having a low level of tolerance for frustration, and experiencing stormy interpersonal relationships. Men with high scores on this scale were more likely to be viewed as physically abusive and self-indulgent. Women who scored high on ASP_2 had a greater likelihood of being characterized as having family problems, and as being narcissistic, critical, and argumentative. They were also likely to be described as being agitated, defensive, manipulative, deceptive, and paranoid, and as having many nightmares.

Impatience (TPA_1)

Compared with those who scored below 65 on this component scale, clients with high scores on TPA_1 presented with higher levels of hostility. They were more likely to be described by their therapists as developing physical symptoms in response to stress. Men with high scores on this scale had a greater likelihood of being characterized as displaying unusual gestures at intake. Female clients who scored high on TPA_1 were more likely to be described by their therapists as depressed, complaining of somatic symptoms, being overly sensitive to criticism, histrionic, insecure, agitated, being a worrier, nervous, grouchy, self-degrading, socially awkward, restless, and giving up easily. These women were less likely to be viewed as coping well with stress.

Competitive Drive (TPA_2)

Very few empirical correlates were identified for this component scale in this study. Compared with clients who scored lower than 65 on this scale, those with high scores were more likely to present with paranoid ideation. Female clients with high scores were more likely to be described by their therapists as having problems with authority figures and being psychologically immature.

Self-Doubt (LSE_1)

Compared with individuals who scored below 65 on this component scale, high scorers on LSE_1 were more likely to receive a diagnosis of depression or dysthymia and to have a history of suicide attempts. They presented with symptoms of depression and an increased level of interpersonal sensitivity.

High LSE_1 scorers were more likely to be characterized as sad and depressed during intake. Their therapists were more likely to view these individuals as depressed and insecure. They described them as self-degrading and self-doubting, and as feeling inferior, hopeless, and like a failure. High LSE_1 scorers were less likely to be viewed as coping well with stress. Male clients with high scores on this scale were also characterized as anxious, obsessive-compulsive, pessimistic, agitated, histrionic, angry, resentful, complaining of sleep disturbance, and having somatic complaints. Therapists were also more likely to view these men as worriers who feel overwhelmed and that life is a strain. Women who scored high on LSE_1 were more likely to be described as passive-submissive and interpersonally sensitive, and they were less likely to be viewed as being achievement oriented, having many interests, having high aspirations, or being extroverted.

Submissiveness (LSE_2)

Compared with clients who scored below 65 on this component scale, individuals with high scores on LSE_2 were more likely to present with significant interpersonal sensitivity. Men with high scores on this scale had a greater likelihood of having been physically abused. Female clients with high scores on LSE_2 were more likely to be identified as having few or no friends and as having histories of suicide attempts.

Therapists described men who scored high on this scale as anxious, nervous, passive, and complaining of sleep disturbance. Women with high scores on LSE_2 were characterized as submissive, passive in relationships, and overly compliant. These women were less likely to be viewed as assertive, self-reliant, or achievement oriented.

Introversion (SOD_1)

Compared with those who scored below 65 on this component scale, individuals with high scores on SOD_1 presented with increased levels of interpersonal sensitivity. Women with high scores on this scale were more likely at intake to be receiving antidepressant or anxiolytic medications and to be assigned a depression or dysthymia diagnosis. These women also had a greater likelihood of having histories characterized by having few or no friends.

At intake, women with high scores on SOD_1 had a greater likelihood of being viewed as sad and depressed. Therapists characterized high SOD_1 scorers as introverted, depressed, feeling hopeless and pessimistic, and presenting with sleep disturbance and suicidal ideation. Men with high scores on this scale were viewed as insecure, pessimistic, obsessive-compulsive, anxious, suspicious, and more likely to report somatic problems. These men tended to feel like failures. They were self-doubting, self-degrading, and self-punishing, and they were preoccupied with physical health concerns. Women with high scores on SOD_1 were less likely to be achievement oriented, energetic, or extroverted. They also had a smaller likelihood of having high aspirations, and they tended not to be concerned with social status issues. These women had a greater likelihood of being viewed as socially awkward.

Shyness (SOD_2)

Compared with clients who scored below 65 on this component scale, clients with high scores on SOD_2 presented with indications of interpersonal sensitivity. Male clients with high scores on this scale had a greater likelihood of being viewed by their therapists as being passive. Female clients were more likely to be described as shy and introverted. They were less likely to be characterized as achievement oriented, having high aspirations, being extroverted and energetic, having many interests, being competitive, or creating a favorable first impression.

Family Discord (FAM_1)

Compared with clients who scored below 65 on this component scale, individuals with high scores on FAM_1 were more likely to present with hostility, paranoid ideation, and interpersonal sensitivity. Men were more likely to have been sexually abused, and women with high scores on FAM_1 had a greater likelihood of having made suicide attempts.

Men with high scores on FAM_1 were more likely to be described by their therapists as having family problems, coming from families lacking in love, resenting family members, blaming family members for their problems, and complaining of family discord. These men also had a greater likelihood of being viewed as depressed, insecure, feeling hopeless, sad, and rejected, and having low tolerance for frustration. High FAM_1 men were also more likely not to get along well with coworkers. Women with high scores on this scale were described as critical, argumentative, and grouchy.

Familial Alienation (FAM_2)

Compared with those who scored below 65 on this component scale, clients with high scores on FAM_2 were more likely to have histories of having few or no friends. Male clients also had a greater likelihood of having been physically abused and of abusing alcohol and marijuana over the course of their lives. Women with elevated scores on FAM_2 were more likely to have been sexually abused and to have made past suicide attempts.

Therapists were more likely to describe high FAM_2 scorers as having family problems, coming from families lacking in love, and being lonely. Men were additionally viewed as experiencing familial discord and being self-degrading. Female clients with high scores on FAM_2 were also characterized as being critical, argumentative, histrionic, suspicious, angry, and resentful. Therapists were also more likely to describe these women as feeling that they get a raw deal from life, having difficulty trusting others, demanding of attention, psychologically immature, having an exaggerated need for affection, needing attention, being narcissistic, and being overly sensitive to criticism.

Low Motivation (TRT_1)

Compared with individuals who scored below 65 on this component scale, clients with high scores on TRT_1 were more likely to receive a diagnosis of depression or dysthymia and to present with symptoms of depression. Male clients who scored high on this scale had a greater likelihood of having had prior outpatient treatment. Women with high scores on TRT_1 were more likely to have histories of suicide attempts and of having few or no friends.

Clients with high scores on TRT_1 were more likely to be viewed during intake as being sad and depressed. They were also likely to be described as anxious. Therapists characterized high TRT_1 individuals as depressed, insecure, anxious, and pessimistic. They viewed them as feeling hopeless, pessimistic, giving up easily, and having suicidal ideation. These clients were less likely to be described by their therapists as coping well with stress or being optimistic. Men with high TRT_1 scores were more likely to be viewed as being obsessive-compulsive, presenting somatic complaints, feeling overwhelmed and that life is a strain, self-degrading, anxious, and sad. Women with high scores on TRT_1 were less likely to be described as being achievement oriented, having many interests, having high aspirations, or being self-reliant.

Inability to Disclose (TRT_2)

Compared with female clients who scored below 65 on this component scale, women with high scores on TRT_2 were more likely to have histories characterized by suicide attempts and misdemeanor convictions, having been abused physically and sexually, having few or no friends, requiring prior psychiatric hospitalization, and having abused alcohol during their lives.

Clients who scored high on TRT_2 were more likely to be described by their therapists as having suicidal ideation and feeling that life is a strain. Men with high scores on this scale were described as depressed, complaining of sleep disturbance and fatigue, and developing physical problems in response to stress. Women with high scores on TRT_2 were more likely to be characterized as introverted and shy and less likely to be viewed as having high aspirations.

Supplementary Scales

Anxiety (A)

Compared with individuals who scored below 65 on this scale, those with high scores on A were more likely to receive a diagnosis of depression or dysthymia, to have histories of previous psychiatric hospitalizations, and to have few or no friends. Men with high scores on this scale were more likely to receive multiple Axis I diagnoses and to have had prior outpatient treatment. Women with high scores on A were more likely to have histories of suicide attempts. High A clients reported multiple symptoms of depression and anxiety at intake.

Intake workers viewed high A clients as sad and depressed. They were less likely to view high A men as happy. Therapists viewed individuals with high scores on A as depressed and insecure. They were more likely to describe these clients as feeling hopeless and like failures, as self-degrading, and as experiencing suicidal ideation. They were less likely to characterize them as extroverted, energetic, or coping well with stress. Men who produced high scores on this scale were viewed as anxious, worriers, sad, feeling overwhelmed and that life is a strain, and complaining of sleep disturbance. Women with high scores on A were more likely to be described as passive in relationships and giving up, and they were less likely to be viewed as being self-reliant.

Repression (R)

Compared with clients who scored below 65 on this scale, individuals with high scores on R were more likely to be described by their therapists as presenting with somatic symptoms and being preoccupied with physical health concerns. Male clients were also more likely to be characterized as having a low sex drive, nervous, complaining of fatigue, pessimistic, depressed, and demonstrating restricted affect. Female clients with high scores on R were more likely to be taking antidepressant medication at intake. They were described by their therapists as anxious, introverted, shy, feeling overwhelmed and that life is a strain, having many specific fears, and demonstrating concrete thinking. These women were less likely to be described as energetic.

Ego Strength (Es): Description of Low Scorers

Compared with individuals who scored above 39 on this scale, clients with low scores on Es were more likely to receive a depression or dysthymia diagnosis and to have histories characterized by having few or no friends and prior psychiatric hospitalizations. Women with low scores on Es also had a greater likelihood of having been physically and sexually abused in the past, having made suicide attempts, and receiving antidepressant medication at intake. Low Es clients presented with multiple symptoms of psychopathology including psychoticism, depression, and somatization.

Low Es scorers were described at intake as depressed and sad. Low Es women were also characterized as anxious. Therapists were more likely to view low Es clients as depressed, anxious, insecure, somatizing, preoccupied with health problems, presenting multiple physical complaints, complaining of sleep disturbance, feeling hopeless and that life is a strain, and pessimistic. They were less likely to characterize these clients as coping well with stress, being work oriented, or being energetic. Male clients who scored below 40 were more likely to be described as having family problems and being passive and submissive. Women with low scores were viewed as having an increased level of interpersonal sensitivity and being less likely to be achievement oriented, to have many interests, to have high aspirations, or to be competitive.

MacAndrew Alcoholism Scale-Revised (MAC-R)

Compared with clients who produced scores below 65 on this scale, high MAC-R scorers were more likely to receive a substance abuse or dependence diagnosis as well as multiple Axis I diagnoses. These individuals had a greater likelihood of having abused alcohol, marijuana, and cocaine over the course of their lives and alcohol within the six months prior to their intake. Women with high scores on MAC-R were also more likely to have abused cocaine within the past six months and to have a history of arrests, a larger number of arrests, histories of felony and misdemeanor convictions, and a history of having been physically abused.

Clients with high scores on MAC-R were more likely to be viewed by their therapists as engaging in antisocial behavior, acting out, and having problems with authority figures. Men with high scores on this scale were also described as having stormy interpersonal relationships, and as being physically abusive, hostile, and agitated. Female clients who scored high on MAC-R were more likely to be viewed by their therapists as aggressive, having family problems, coming from families lacking in love, suspicious, having a low tolerance for frustration, impulsive, showing poor judgment, excitable, and sociopathic. At intake, these women were more likely to be viewed as experiencing hallucinations.

Addiction Acknowledgment Scale (AAS)

Compared with clients who scored below 65 on this scale, those with high scores on AAS were more likely to receive a substance abuse or dependence diagnosis as well as multiple Axis I diagnoses. These clients were more likely to have abused alcohol, marijuana, and cocaine during their lives, as well as within the past six months. They also had a greater likelihood of past suicide attempts. Women with high scores on AAS were more likely to have had previous psychiatric hospitalizations and a history of misdemeanor convictions.

Therapists were more likely to describe high AAS scorers as coming from families lacking in love, acting out, having difficulties trusting others, and being histrionic. Male clients were also more likely to be viewed as agitated, insecure, self-punishing, restless, self-defeating, feeling like a failure, and prone to having temper tantrums. At intake, these men were more likely to be viewed as depressed. Women with high AAS scores were more likely to be characterized as antisocial, impulsive, manipulative, narcissistic, critical, argumentative, having family problems, being preoccupied sexually, giving up easily, sarcastic, cynical, moody, and procrastinating.

Addiction Potential Scale (APS)

Compared with individuals who scored below 65 on this scale, high scorers on APS were more likely to receive a substance abuse or dependence diagnosis and to have abused alcohol during their lives and within the past six months. Women with high scores on this scale had a greater likelihood of receiving multiple Axis I diagnoses. Therapists were more likely to describe high APS women as power oriented, concerned about status, preoccupied sexually, histrionic, nervous, obsessive, using intellectualization, self-defeating, giving up easily, extroverted, and feeling like a failure.

Overcontrolled Hostility (O-H)

Very few empirical correlates were found for the O-H scale in this study. Compared with those who scored below 65 on this scale, men who scored high on O-H were more likely to have been arrested in the past and less likely to be viewed as depressed during their intake interview. Female clients who scored high on O-H were more likely to be viewed by their therapists as being optimistic.

Dominance (Do): Description of Low Scorers

Compared with those who scored above 39 on this scale, low scorers on Do were more likely to have been abused physically in the past. Women with low scores on this scale were more likely to receive depression or dysthymia diagnoses, to be taking antidepressant medication at intake, and to have histories of having few or no friends, making suicide attempts, being sexually abused, and having psychiatric hospitalizations.

Therapists were more likely to describe low Do clients as depressed, anxious, worriers, complaining of somatic symptoms and sleep disturbance, being preoccupied with health problems, having suicidal ideation, and being socially awkward. These individuals were more likely to be viewed as being depressed during their intake. Low-scoring male clients were also more likely to be characterized as insecure, feeling rejected, experiencing acute psychological turmoil, and having family problems. Female clients who were low scorers on Do were described as pessimistic, introverted, passive, and submissive. They were less likely to be viewed as being achievement oriented, having many interests, communicating effectively, being self-reliant and work oriented, or coping well with stress.

Social Responsibility (Re): Description of Low Scorers

Compared with individuals who scored above 39 on this scale, low scorers on Re were more likely to receive substance abuse or dependence diagnoses, to have abused alcohol, marijuana, and cocaine during their lives, to have been arrested and have a greater number of arrests, and to have been physically abused. Men who scored low on this scale were also more likely to have been physically abusive and to have abused alcohol within the six months prior to intake. Women with low scores on Re had a greater likelihood of having histories characterized by having few or no friends, being sexually abused, and having misdemeanor convictions.

Clients who scored low on Re were more likely to be described by their therapists as aggressive, antisocial, angry, resentful, suspicious, and having family problems and coming from families lacking in love. They were described as engaging in antisocial behavior and acting out, exercising poor judgment, having problems with authority figures as well as difficulties trusting others, and having stormy interpersonal relationships. Men with low scores on this scale were also characterized as having work problems, being physically abusive, harboring grudges, and being hostile and agitated. Female clients with low scores on Re were described as being narcissistic, defensive, critical, argumentative, having superficial relationships, feigning remorse when in trouble, being preoccupied sexually, and sociopathic. Intake workers were more likely to see these women as demonstrating poor judgment.

Marital Distress Scale (MDS)

Compared with individuals who scored below 65 on this scale, clients with high scores on MDS were more likely to receive a depression or dysthymia diagnosis and to have histories of having few or no friends. These clients presented with an increased level of interpersonal sensitivity and depression. Male clients with high scores on this scale were more likely to have histories of having been physically abused and of receiving outpatient treatment. Women with high scores on MDS were more likely to have made suicide attempts in the past.

At intake, high MDS scorers were more likely to be viewed as sad or depressed. Therapists were more likely to describe high MDS scorers as angry, resentful, feeling rejected and that life is a strain, depressed, and having suicidal ideation. Male clients with high scores on this scale were more likely to be viewed as interpersonally sensitive, insecure, having family problems, anxious, histrionic, pessimistic, and agitated. These men were described further as feeling mistreated and that they get a raw deal from life, being sad, experiencing emotional lability, pessimistic, hopeless, self-degrading, agitated, and coming from families lacking in love. Female clients with high scores on MDS were more likely to be characterized as argumentative and grouchy.

Post-Traumatic Stress Disorder (PK)

Compared with clients who scored below 65 on this scale, high scorers on PK were more likely to receive depression or dysthymia diagnoses at intake. These clients were also more likely to have histories of having few or no friends. They presented with significant symptoms of depression. Male clients with high scores on PK had a greater likelihood of having had prior psychiatric hospitalizations and of receiving multiple diagnoses on Axis I. Women with high scores on this scale were more likely to have histories of having been abused physically and sexually and having made suicide attempts in the past.

High scorers on PK were more likely to be viewed as sad and depressed during intake. Male clients with high scores on this scale were also more likely to be described by intake workers as angry and less likely to be characterized as happy. Therapists were more likely to describe high PK scorers as having increased levels of interpersonal sensitivity, and as depressed, insecure, feeling hopeless and that life is a strain, complaining of sleep disturbance, feeling that they get a raw deal from life, self-degrading, experiencing suicidal ideation, feeling like a failure, sad, and pessimistic. These clients were less likely to be viewed as coping well with stress, optimistic, or having many interests. Male clients with high scores on PK were also described as anxious, hostile, somatizing and complaining about somatic problems, having family problems, angry, resentful, histrionic, suspicious, worriers, and obsessive-compulsive.

Chapter 6

Discussion and Conclusions

In this chapter we will summarize the major findings of our research as they relate to the goals of the project. Several specific research questions are addressed:

1. Are there meaningful and useful empirical correlates of MMPI-2 scales and code types in an outpatient community mental health center setting?
2. Are correlates of the MMPI-2 scales and code types identified in this study comparable to those previously reported for the original MMPI?
3. Are correlates of the MMPI-2 scales and code types identified in an outpatient community mental health center setting comparable to those previously identified for the MMPI and MMPI-2 in other settings (e.g., psychiatric inpatient)?
4. Are stronger and more homogeneous correlates identified when code types are defined than when code types are unrestricted?
5. Do low scores on the MMPI-2 scales contribute important information concerning clients in this setting?
6. Should MMPI-2 results of ethnic minority clients be interpreted similarly to those of other clients in this setting?

In addition to addressing these research questions, this chapter will discuss some of the limitations of our research project and suggest directions for future research concerning the use of the MMPI-2 in outpatient mental health settings.

Correlates of MMPI-2 Scales and Code Types in an Outpatient Community Mental Health Setting

Data from the present study clearly indicate that there are meaningful and useful empirical correlates of MMPI-2 scales and code types in an outpatient community mental health center setting. For virtually every scale and code type considered, numerous significant correlates were identified. It is particularly encouraging that similar correlates were identified across various sources of criterion information (i.e., clients' self-report on the SCL-90-R, intake workers' ratings, therapists' ratings). As expected, relationships were stronger when MMPI-2 scale scores and code types, which are based on self-report, were correlated with other self-report measures (i.e., SCL-90-R scales) than when they were correlated with ratings of intake workers and therapists. However, the patterns of correlations were very similar for the self-report criterion measures and those based on ratings provided by mental health professionals.

As described in chapter 2, in addition to determining correlates of scales and code types, we also calculated frequencies and mean scores for extra-test variables separately for each high score and code-type group, as well as for the entire sample of clients, for those with valid MMPI-2s, and for a subgroup of clients with nondefensive within-normal-limits (WNL) profiles. These additional data can be very helpful in determining the likelihood that specific correlates will characterize persons with high scores on a particular scale or with a particular code type. For example, having a high score on scale 2 was significantly correlated (.31 for men; .20 for women) with having an Axis I diagnosis of depression or dysthymia (Appendix D). Reference to the frequency data reveals that 32% of the male clients and 37% of the female clients with high scale 2 scores had these diagnoses, compared with 23% of men and 28% of women in the total sample and 9% of men and 5% of women with WNL profiles (Appendixes K-1 and K-2). Although diagnoses of depression or dysthymia were more frequent among clients with elevated scale 2 scores than among clients in general and especially among clients producing WNL profiles, only about one third of clients with elevated scale 2 scores actually had these diagnoses.

Another example of the complementary nature of the frequency data involves the 48/84 code type. Membership in this code type versus the WNL group was correlated ($r = .63$) with having a history of previous psychiatric hospitalization (Appendix G). Reference to the frequency data (Appendix K-3) reveals that 69% of clients with the 48/84 code type had histories of previous psychiatric hospitalizations, compared with 34% of all clients and 6% of clients having WNL profiles. These examples again emphasize that the correlates listed are more likely to characterize these clients with elevated scores on the scales or with the code types than other clients, but they will not apply to everyone with the elevated scales or with the code types.

Because previous researchers (e.g., Graham, 1988) reported different correlates for men and women for some MMPI-2 scales, we conducted all of our single-scale analyses separately for male and female clients. Only for the code-type analyses, where sample sizes were relatively small, were combined-gender analyses conducted. Summing across all of the scales that we analyzed in our study, there clearly were more similarities than differences in the correlates for male and female clients. For example, both male and female clients with high scores on scale 1 were more likely to have somatic symptoms (Appendix D), both male and female clients with high scores on the MacAndrew Alcoholism Scale-Revised were more likely to have histories of abusing alcohol and other substances (Appendix J), and both male and female clients with high scores on the Depression content scale were more likely to have Axis I diagnoses of depression or dysthymia than were those male and female participants with T scores below 65 on this scale (Appendix H).

For most scales, the major differences in correlates between male and female clients had to do with the magnitude of the correlations with criterion measures. However, the patterns of correlations were usually very similar. Scale 5 appeared to be an exception, but it should be noted that higher raw scores on scale 5 are associated with higher T scores for men and lower T scores for women. Because we used T scores in all of our analyses, the scale 5 correlations were often in opposite directions for male and female clients. For example, female clients with elevated scores on scale 5 were rated as having stronger stereotypic masculine interests than those with T scores below 65, but male clients with high scores on scale 5 were rated as having weaker stereotypic masculine interests when compared with those who did not have elevated scores on this scale (Appendix D).

In spite of the general finding that the correlates for male and female clients were very similar, there were some scales for which there were some gender differences. For example, male clients with high scores on scale 6 were rated by intake workers and therapists as more angry than lower scorers, but there was virtually no relationship between scale 6 scores and ratings of anger for female clients (Appendix D). Female clients with high scores on scale 9 were more likely than lower scorers to have histories of alcohol, cocaine, and heroin abuse, but there was no meaningful relationship between scale 9 scores and abuse of these substances for male clients (Appendix D).

Because of the relatively small sample sizes for specific code types, we were not able to conduct code-type analyses separately for men and women. Therefore, it is not clear to what extent the correlates identified for the mixed-gender groups will apply equally well to male and female clients. The marked similarity of correlates for the individual clinical scales that are involved in the code types suggests that the correlates for code types may be similar for men and women. However, additional research will be needed utilizing samples large enough to permit separate analyses for men and women. For now, clinicians using our data to guide their interpretations of MMPI-2 results should examine carefully the correlates of each scale that is elevated in a profile to determine the extent to which there are gender differences. They should also apply the code-type correlates cautiously, particularly in cases where there is marked gender imbalance.

One of the salient findings of our study is that some particular symptoms and behaviors were associated with higher scores on many of the MMPI-2 scales. For example, various manifestations of depression were identified as correlates for a majority of the scales studied. This probably reflects the high rate of occurrence of this disorder among clients at the mental health center. Regardless of the unique symptoms, problems, and behaviors that clients had, most of them reported symptoms of depression.

The ubiquity of depression among our participants is consistent with epidemiological data on this phenomenon. In a recent literature review, Mineka, Watson, and Clark (1998) cite data indicating that depressive and anxiety disorders are more likely to be comorbid than to appear on their own and that both conditions show substantial comorbidity with other conditions, including substance abuse, somatization, and eating, conduct, personality, and attention deficit disorders. The considerable redundancy in depression and anxiety as correlates across different MMPI-2 scales and code types is consistent with levels of syndromal and, even more so, symptomatic comorbidity reported in the epidemiological literature.

One might argue that the MMPI-2 scales are not very useful if depression is a correlate for most of them. We maintain that it is very important for clinicians to know if clients are likely to be depressed, even if depression is very common at the treatment facility. Not to report depression as a characteristic indicated by the MMPI-2 simply because most clients at the center are depressed would not be responsible practice. It should also be noted that in addition to the common correlates for MMPI-2 scales, many scales had unique correlates, that is, symptoms and behaviors associated with higher scores on a particular scale that were not associated with higher scores on other scales.

For some of the MMPI-2 scales studied, the absence of conceptually relevant correlates is apparent. For example, for neither male nor female clients was there a significant relationship between scale 8 and the PDF Psychotic Symptoms scale (Appendix D). Similarly, psychotic symptomatology was unrelated to the 68/86 code type, although it did appear as a correlate for several other code types involving scale 8. This absence is likely due, in part, to the relatively low occurrence of psychotic disorders among the mental health center clients. Psychotic clients seeking services at the mental health center typically were referred to another community agency for treatment. The absence can also be explained in part by the heterogeneity of the content of scale 8 items. Although the scale includes some items dealing with clearly psychotic behaviors, many items in the scale have to do with other problem behaviors, including depression, somatic complaints, and feelings of alienation. In those instances where psychotic symptoms appeared as scale or code-type correlates, substance abuse may be implicated.

For some MMPI-2 scales and code types we identified extra-test correlates that were not expected based on previous research studies. For example, in our study men and women with high scores on scale 4 were more likely to feel like failures (Appendix D), and clients with the 34/43 code type were more likely than those with WNL profiles to have psychotic symptoms (Appendix G). These and other unexpected correlates need to be replicated in other samples before they are used routinely in MMPI-2 interpretation.

Comparability of Scale and Code-Type Correlates for the MMPI and MMPI-2

Early studies with the MMPI-2 focused on establishing the comparability of MMPI-2 and MMPI scales and code types in order to boost confidence that the large research base that is available for the MMPI could be utilized in interpreting the MMPI-2. However, Graham (1990) pointed out the importance of also establishing empirically extra-test correlates for the MMPI-2.

A review of previous MMPI studies indicates that the correlates of most of the MMPI-2 scales and code types in our study are clearly comparable to those previously identified for the original MMPI. This is not surprising because the scales carried over to the MMPI-2 are essentially the same as the versions that were in the MMPI. For example, early research indicated that correlations between MMPI scales and their corresponding MMPI-2 scales were very high (typically greater than .95) for persons in the normative sample (Graham, 1988), college students (Ben-Porath and Butcher, 1989a), and psychiatric inpatients (Graham, 1988).

Some examples may help to illustrate the comparability of correlates for the MMPI and MMPI-2. Our findings that high scorers on scale 1 were more likely to be preoccupied with health problems, to report multiple somatic complaints, and to develop physical symptoms in response to stress are entirely consistent with findings for scale 1 of the original MMPI (Appendix D). That high scale 4 scorers in our study were more likely to report family and work problems and to be critical and argumentative (Appendix D) is also consistent with findings for scale 4 of the original MMPI. Research with the original MMPI indicated that high scale 0 scorers tend to be introverted, insecure, and not very achievement oriented. Our findings for scale 0 are very consistent with these previous data (Appendix D).

Some examples of the comparability of code-type correlates can also be offered. In our study, membership in the 27/72 code type was associated with symptoms of depression and anxiety (Appendix G). Again, these correlates are very consistent with those previously reported for this code type in MMPI codebooks (e.g., Marks & Seeman, 1963; Gilberstadt & Duker, 1965). The PDF scale that was related most strongly to the 48/84 code type in our study was Psychotic Symptoms (Appendix G). Gilberstadt and Duker (1965) and other investigators have reported that psychotic symptoms and behaviors typically have been associated with this code type with the original MMPI.

There were some code types in our study for which the correlates do not seem to be so directly congruent with those identified in earlier studies. For example, correlates for the 49/94 code type in our study included paranoid ideation and poor reality testing. These correlates may appear to be inconsistent with the findings of Marks and Seeman (1963) and Gilberstadt and Duker (1965). However, these two codebooks also reported relatively high frequencies of psychotic symptoms for the 49/94 code type. In the Marks and Seeman study, 30% of the 49/94s had hallucinations and 25% had ideas of reference. Gilberstadt and Duker reported that their 49/94s tended to have paranoid psychotic episodes related to excessive drinking, and 30% of their 49/94s had paranoid delusions or paranoid trends.

It may also seem surprising that clients in our study with the 68/86 code type did not display the blatant psychotic symptoms that were reported for this code type by Marks and Seeman (1963) and Gilberstadt and Duker (1965). However, it should be remembered that persons with blatant psychotic symptoms who requested services at the agency where our study was conducted were routinely referred to other agencies for services. Because neither Marks and Seeman nor Gilberstadt and Duker reported depression as a primary characteristic of persons with the 68/86 code type in their studies, it may seem surprising that depression was such a strong correlate of this code type in our study. However, close examination of the data from these earlier studies reveals that depression was characteristic of 85% of the 86/68s in the Marks and Seeman study and 49% of the 86s in the Gilberstadt and Duker study. It is important to remember that in these earlier studies persons with this code type were compared with all other patients. Thus, symptoms such as depression, which occurred with a high base rate in the settings where these earlier studies were conducted, did not emerge as a unique characteristic of the 68/86.

The failure of Marks and Seeman (1963) and Gilberstadt and Duker (1965) to report depression as a correlate for the 68/86 code type, in spite of its widespread prevalence among persons with this code type, underscores the disadvantage of reporting a code type's unique characteristics while ignoring ones that are shared with members of other code types. Our methodology allowed for the identification of a full complement of correlates for all of the code types in our study.

Graham (1993) summarized the correlates of the MMPI-2 supplementary scales that were carried over from the original MMPI. Because virtually all of the information summarized by Graham was based on scales from the original MMPI, comparison of our supplementary scale correlates with his information about these scales can inform us concerning the comparability of correlates for MMPI and MMPI-2 versions of the supplementary scales.

In general, the correlates of the MMPI-2 supplementary scales were very similar to those of the corresponding MMPI measures. Because the items in these scales are not very different in the two versions of the test, this similarity is not at all surprising. A few examples are informative. Graham (1993) described Welsh's Anxiety (A) scale as a measure of general maladjustment of which anxiety is just one symptom. In our study, higher A scale scores were associated with a wide variety of symptoms and problems, including anxiety (Appendix J). The MacAndrew Alcoholism Scale-Revised (MAC-R) was described by Graham as being associated with various kinds of substance abuse and also with problems with the law. In our study higher MAC-R scores also were associated with substance abuse problems and with antisocial, acting-out behaviors (Appendix J). The Overcontrolled Hostility (O-H) scale was described by Graham as a measure of the tendency for persons to be not hostile most of the time, and then to respond in overly hostile ways on some occasions. We did not have very relevant extra-test measures for this scale in our study. Higher O-H scale scorers in our study tended to deny problems of almost all kinds, and there were not significant relationships between O-H scale scores and our extra-test measures of anger, aggression, and hostility (Appendix J). It is not clear if the differences in correlates between those in our study and those described by Graham indicate that the O-H scale should be interpreted differently in different settings or whether we simply did not have appropriate measures in our study to assess the construct.

Although not at all surprising, it is encouraging and important that the correlates of most of the MMPI-2 scales and code types are quite comparable to their counterparts in the original MMPI. Because T-score cutoffs were utilized in our analyses, these findings also support earlier research suggesting that the use of uniform T scores does not lead to differences in the correlates of MMPI-2 scales and code types. Although the MMPI-2 norms generally lead to lower T scores than for the original MMPI, Graham, Timbrook, Ben-Porath, and Butcher et al. (1991) found that the configuration of scores on the scales remained essentially unchanged. Our data also suggest that the correlates of those configurations are usually the same for the MMPI and MMPI-2.

Comparability of Correlates of MMPI-2 Scales and Code Types in a Mental Health Center Setting and Other Settings

Of special interest in our study is the extent to which correlates identified in an outpatient community mental health center are similar to, or different from, those previously identified in other settings. If the correlates are very similar, the data previously reported for other settings can also be used in interpreting MMPI-2s in outpatient mental health settings and our data can be applied to MMPI-2 results in other settings.

Because the MMPI-2 has not been in use very long, most studies reported in the literature have used the original MMPI. Thus, comparing our data, which were based on the MMPI-2 in an outpatient setting, with older studies that used the original MMPI in other kinds of settings involves both instrument differences (i.e., MMPI vs. MMPI-2) and setting differences (e.g., inpatient vs. outpatient). Although earlier in this chapter we concluded that the correlates based on MMPI scales and code types are very similar to those based on MMPI-2 scales and code types, the most direct assessment of setting similarities and differences can be made by comparing our results to those of studies that used the MMPI-2 in settings other than outpatient mental health centers.

Clinical Scales

The most comprehensive previous study of correlates of MMPI-2 scales was reported by Graham (1988) and involved the identification of descriptors of MMPI-2 scales in inpatient psychiatric hospital settings. Although the current study and the inpatient study involved somewhat different extra-test measures, there was enough similarity in the content of these measures to permit some comparisons.

In general, the correlates that we identified for MMPI-2 clinical scales in our outpatient mental health setting are very similar to those reported for the inpatient setting. For example, in both settings, higher scores on both scales 1 and 3 were associated with somatic symptoms and worries about health, and higher scores on scale 2 were related to symptoms of depression and anxiety (Appendix D). Higher scale 4 scores were indicative of anger and some antisocial characteristics in both outpatient and inpatient settings (Appendix D). As expected, higher scores on scale 0 were associated with characteristics of introversion for both inpatients and outpatients (Appendix D).

There were also some interesting differences in the patterns of descriptors for the outpatient and inpatient settings. For example, in the outpatient setting, scale 4 elevations were also associated with symptoms of depression, whereas this pattern did not emerge in the inpatient setting (Appendix D). This difference may reflect the higher base rate of depression in the outpatient setting.

Code Types

It also is important to determine if the correlates associated with code types in our outpatient setting are similar to those previously reported in other settings. Only one other study has been published concerning the correlates of MMPI-2 code types. Archer, Griffin, and Aiduk (1995) determined correlates for nine commonly occurring two-point code types in an inpatient psychiatric setting. Patients' self-reports of symptoms and ratings of symptoms and problems by psychologists and nurses were compared for patients having each code type versus all other patients. Protocols were included in code types only if both scales in the code type had T scores greater than 65, but these investigators did not require that code types be well defined. Eight of the code types analyzed by Archer et al. (1995) were also included in our study. The correlates of the code types in these two different kinds of settings were remarkably similar. For example, in both settings the 12/21 code type was associated with anxiety and depression, and the 49/94 code type was associated with impulse control problems and difficulties with authority figures. Thus, there is some initial evidence that correlates of MMPI-2 code types are similar in inpatient and outpatient settings.

Given the similarity of correlates for the individual scales of the MMPI and MMPI-2, we can also compare our code-type correlate data to data previously reported for MMPI code types in settings other than outpatient mental health centers. Two of the most comprehensive code-type correlate studies using the original MMPI were conducted by Lewandowski and Graham (1972) and Gynther, Altman, and Sletten (1973). Both studies were completed in state psychiatric hospital settings, and both used methodologies in which patients with a particular code type were compared with all other patients in the samples.

In addition to the fact that Lewandowski and Graham's (1972) and Gynther et al.'s (1973) studies used the MMPI and our study used the MMPI-2, several other differences between our study and the two earlier ones make comparisons of results difficult. One important consideration is that each of the three studies used different extra-test measures. Lewandowski and Graham utilized data provided by psychiatrists who used the Brief Psychiatric Rating Scale and by nurses who used the Nurses Observation Scale for Inpatient Evaluation. While there is some overlap of content between their measures and ours, clearly some content areas covered by the measures in one study are not covered in the others.

The group with which a particular code type was compared also differed. As mentioned earlier, the Lewandowski and Graham (1972) and Gynther et al. (1973) studies both compared patients with a particular code type with all other patients in the sample. This approach identified descriptors that were unique to a particular code type. We chose to compare clients having a particular code type with a group of clients having WNL profiles. Our approach identified all characteristics associated with a code type, whether or not those characteristics were shared by clients with different code types. Thus, the absence of particular characteristics for a code type in the Lewandowski and Graham and Gynther et al. studies could mean either that patients with that code type did not have the characteristics or that they had the characteristics but that patients with other code types also had them.

Another factor that makes it difficult to compare our results with the earlier studies is that the kinds of persons included as participants were different. As stated earlier, state hospital psychiatric patients were used in both the Lewandowski and Graham (1972) and Gynther et al. (1973) studies. Our study used community mental health center outpatients, and more seriously disturbed persons were served by a different agency. Thus, our sample did not include many psychotic persons. This difference could account for the absence of psychotic symptoms as characteristics of our clients with the 68/86 code type, when both of the earlier studies identified psychotic symptoms as characteristic of the 68/86 code type.

A code-type–by–code-type comparison of our results with those of Lewandowski and Graham (1972) and Gynther et al. (1973) identified only one instance where our results were directly inconsistent with theirs. We found that clients with the 12/21 code type were more likely to have symptoms of depression (Appendix G), whereas Lewandowski and Graham reported that patients with the 12/21 code type were less likely to be depressed. Interestingly, Gynther et al. did not report that their patients with the 12/21 code type were either more or less depressed than other patients.

For many code types there were common correlates for our clients and the patients in the Lewandowski and Graham (1972) and Gynther et al. (1973) studies. For example, somatic symptoms were characteristic of persons with the 13/31 code type in all three studies. Depression was characteristic of persons with the 27/72 code type in all three studies.

The most typical finding when comparing our data with those of Lewandowski and Graham (1972) and Gynther et al. (1973) was that there were some common correlates between our study and those of one or both of the other studies, but there were additional descriptors that were identified for one study but not for the others. For example, depression was characteristic of persons with the 27/72 code type in all three studies. However, anxiety also was characteristic of our clients who had the 27/72 code type (Appendix G). This difference is probably explained by our use of a WNL control group. Our methodology permitted us to identify characteristics of clients with the 27/72 code type even if those characteristics were shared by clients with other code types. It may well be that the 27/72 patients in the other two studies also were characterized by anxiety, but that it did not appear as a correlate because anxiety was prevalent among patients with other code types as well.

In general, there were more similarities than differences between our results and those of the two inpatient studies with which our results were compared. Cardinal characteristics of code types, such as somatic concerns for the 13/31 code type and depression for the 27/72 code type, were identified across settings. However, some of the characteristics that we identified for code types were not reported in the earlier studies and vice versa. These differences could mean that the code types should be interpreted differently in outpatient and inpatient settings, but they just as well could have resulted from the differences in the groups with which a code type was contrasted or in the extra-test measures utilized in the various studies. To reach more definitive conclusions about the generalizability of code-type correlates across settings, we will need multisite research in which the same extra-test measures are used across settings and the same methodologies, especially in terms of the group with which a particular code type is compared, are employed.

Harris-Lingoes Subscales

The results of our study indicate that there are reliable correlates of many of the Harris-Lingoes subscales and that the patterns of the correlations are sometimes different from those of the parent scales. Unfortunately, no comprehensive study of the correlates of the Harris-Lingoes subscales in other settings is available for comparison with our results. Graham (1993) has summarized the meaning of higher scores on the Harris-Lingoes subscales. His summaries are syntheses of information based primarily on the content of items in the subscales with some additional descriptors added on the basis of correlates of some subscales with external measures. Although this does not represent a direct comparison of our findings with those from other settings, it is informative to determine to what extent the correlates of the Harris-Lingoes subscales in our study are consistent with the descriptors previously presented by Graham.

A scale-by-scale comparison of the correlates of the Harris-Lingoes subscales in our study and the summaries presented by Graham (1993) indicates marked similarities. For no subscale were our correlates and Graham's summaries inconsistent. There were some subscales for which some descriptors suggested by Graham were not found in our study. These tended to involve characteristics that were not represented in our extra-test measures or symptoms that were not very prevalent among the clients in our study setting.

An example involving two scale 4 subscales serves to illustrate the similarities between our findings and the descriptors previously reported by Graham (1993). It has been suggested that examining the relationship between Pd_1 (Familial Discord) and Pd_2 (Authority Problems) can be helpful in determining if higher scale 4 scores are more likely to indicate antisocial characteristics or problematic family circumstances. Graham indicated that higher scorers on Pd_1 are likely to be experiencing a variety of family problems, including a lack of love. In our study correlates of the Pd_1 subscale included the PDF Family Problems scale and PDF items suggesting familial discord, lack of family love, and resentment of family members (Appendix E). By contrast, Graham indicated that higher scorers on Pd_2 are likely to resent societal standards and to have been in trouble in school and with the law. In our study the correlates of the Pd_2 scale included higher scores on the PDF Antisocial scale and histories of arrests and misdemeanor and felony convictions (Appendix E).

In summary, our findings offer support for previously reported descriptors for most of the Harris-Lingoes subscales. However, because there has been no comprehensive study of the subscales in settings different from our mental health center setting, we should be somewhat cautious in concluding that the correlates identified in our study apply directly in all other settings where the MMPI-2 is used.

Supplementary Scales

Because there has been no previous comprehensive study of the correlates of MMPI-2 supplementary scales in other kinds of settings, it is not possible to determine directly the extent to which the correlates of MMPI-2 supplementary scales in our outpatient study are similar to correlates in other kinds of settings. However, we concluded earlier in this chapter that the correlates of supplementary scales that were carried over from MMPI to MMPI-2 were similar in our study and in previous studies that were summarized by Graham (1993). Because these previous studies were conducted in a variety of settings, the similarity of our correlates to those identified in these other studies offers some support for the generalizability of our findings to other settings. For supplementary scales developed specifically for the MMPI-2, there is not yet an appropriate database from other settings that can be used for comparison.

Content Scales

Two previous comprehensive studies of the correlates of the MMPI-2 Content Scales are available for comparison with our data. Butcher, Graham, Williams, and Ben-Porath (1990) reported correlates of the Content Scales based on spousal ratings of a subset of men and women in the MMPI-2 normative sample. Dwyer, Graham, and Ott (1991) reported Content Scale correlates for male and female inpatients in a state psychiatric hospital. A direct comparison of our results with these two earlier studies is difficult because our study and the other two investigations used different extra-test measures. However, there is enough similarity of content in the measures utilized that some comparisons are possible.

For some Content Scales (Anxiety [ANX], Depression [DEP], Health Concerns [HEA]), the correlates were similar across all three settings (i.e., outpatient, inpatient, normative). High scorers on ANX were more likely to be rated as anxious, high scorers on DEP were more likely to report various symptoms of depression, and high scorers on HEA were more likely to have somatic symptoms and concerns about health. For other Content Scales, there were marked similarities in correlates for the outpatient and inpatient settings but not for the normative participants. This seems to be accounted for by the absence of significant psychopathology among normative persons. For example, the Bizarre Mentation (BIZ) content scale was related to some psychotic symptoms, including hallucinations, in both clinical samples (Appendix H). For still other scales, there were similarities between the outpatient and normative correlates but not the inpatient ones. This seemed to occur when the extra-test measures used in the inpatient study did not include conceptually relevant scales for the Content Scales.

For example, the Anger (ANG) content scale was related to ratings of anger and irritability in both the outpatient and normative settings but not in the inpatient setting. Likewise, the Low Self-Esteem (LSE) content scale was related to ratings of insecurity and poor self-concept in the outpatient and normative settings but not in the inpatient setting. In these examples, conceptually relevant measures were not included in the inpatient study. Several Content Scales had some correlates in our outpatient study that were not found in either the inpatient or normative settings. In our study high male scorers on the Fears (FRS) content scale were more likely to be taking antipsychotic medication, and high female scorers on this scale were less likely to be achievement oriented or competitive (Appendix H). These relationships were not found in either of the other two studies. The Family Problems (FAM) content scale was related to ratings of family problems and histories of having been physically abused in our study (Appendix H). In the normative study, higher FAM scorers were rated as more irritable, fearful, and moody and more likely to have temper tantrums. There were no correlates of the FAM scale in the inpatient study.

Finally, there were several scales (Work Problems [WRK], Negative Treatment Indicators [TRT]) that were not related to conceptually relevant measures in our outpatient study but which had relevant correlates in one of the other studies. Higher scorers on WRK in our study were seen as more depressed and anxious (Appendix H). Interestingly, the WRK scale was not related to the measures of work problems that were included in our study. It should be noted that possibly because of uncertainty about how to rate clients who were not employed, therapists often omitted large numbers of items from this scale. In the normative study, high WRK scorers were seen as indecisive, lacking in interests, and giving up easily. In the inpatient study, high WRK scorers were seen as more depressed. High TRT scorers in our study were seen as more anxious, depressed, and insecure (Appendix H). In the inpatient study, high TRT scorers also were rated as more depressed. High TRT scorers in the normative study were rated as more worried, more hostile, lacking in interests, and likely to give up easily.

In summary, the correlates of the Content Scales in our outpatient study are very similar to those previously reported for inpatients and for participants in the MMPI-2 normative study. Many of the differences that were found between settings could be accounted for by differences in the extra-test measures used in the studies. A more direct comparison of the correlates of the Content Scales across settings will require a multisite study in which the same extra-test measures are employed at all sites.

Content Component Scales

For the most part, the correlates of the Content Component scales in our outpatient study were very similar to those of their parent scales. This finding was not unexpected, because our correlational analyses included all clients whether or not they had differences between component scales within a parent Content Scale. We probably would have found more differences in extra-test measures if we had compared persons who had meaningful differences between component scale scores. A study to determine if the Content Component scales contribute to the prediction of extra-test characteristics for persons who have meaningful differences between component scale scores was conducted by McNulty, Ben-Porath, and Graham (1997). Using a subsample of clients from our larger project, we first identified clients with T scores of at least 60 on a parent Content Scale. We then identified subgroups of these clients who had component scale T scores of at least 65 and for whom there was at least a 10 T-score point difference between a particular component scale and other component scales for that parent scale. We then compared extra-test variable means for the higher component-scale group with corresponding means for clients who scored high on the parent Content Scale. We reasoned that extra-test variables on which the high component scale group scored two or more standard errors from the mean for the parent Content Scale group should be emphasized or de-emphasized in interpreting high scores on the parent scale. Using this procedure, we were able to identify correlates of the parent Content Scales that should be emphasized or de-emphasized for 9 of the 12 Content Scales for which component scales were developed. The results of our study suggest that the interpretation of high scores on some of the Content Scales can be enhanced when a differential pattern of scores exists among the relevant component scales. Of course, these findings should be replicated in other settings before they are routinely used in the interpretation of the MMPI-2 Content Scale scores.

Effects of Code-Type Definition on Correlates of MMPI-2 Scales and Code Types

As discussed in chapter 2, there has been extensive debate concerning the criteria for establishing membership in code types. Graham, Timbrook, et al. (1991) suggested that clinicians should interpret only well-defined code types, that is, those with at least 5 T-score points between the lowest scale in the code type and the next highest scale in the profile. Consideration of the standard errors of measurement of the clinical scales, as well as the increased homogeneity, temporal stability, and greater applicability of both symptom and personality characteristics of defined code types, suggests that greater interpretive confidence should be placed on inferences based on defined code types. Dahlstrom and his colleagues (Dahlstrom, 1992; Dahlstrom & Humphrey, 1996; Humphrey & Dahlstrom, 1995) disagreed with this recommendation and indicated that it is arbitrary and unwarranted. Tellegen and Ben-Porath (1993) and Ben-Porath and Tellegen (1995) offered some compelling arguments in favor of interpreting only defined code types. Based on their arguments, we decided to use well-defined code types in our major analyses.

Prior research concerning the advantages and disadvantages of code-type definition has primarily addressed the effects of definition on congruence of MMPI and MMPI-2 code types. No research to date has addressed the effects of code-type definition on the correlates of code types. Using a subset of data from the current study, McNulty, Ben-Porath, and Graham (1999) investigated the effects of code-type definition on correlates of four frequently occurring code types. Correlates of defined code types were compared with correlates of code types that were not defined. It was expected that conceptually relevant descriptors would have stronger relationships to defined code types than to code types that were not defined. By contrast, descriptors that were judged not to be conceptually relevant were expected to have weaker relationships with defined code types than with code types that were not defined. Code types were included in the McNulty et al. study if there were at least 15 profiles in the larger database that met the criteria for definition and an additional 15 profiles that did not meet those criteria. Only the 13/31, 24/42, 27/72, and 46/64 code types met the criteria frequently enough to be included.

Research concerning the correlates of code types is affected by the selection of the comparison group. As discussed in chapter 2, previous research typically has identified correlates of a particular code type in comparison with all other profiles in a sample. While this approach will identify correlates specific to the particular code type, descriptors that apply to several code types are much less likely to be identified as characteristic of any particular code type. If the purpose of a study is to identify all relevant extra-test correlates, a different comparison group is needed. The comparison group in all of our code-type analyses included nondefensive persons having WNL profiles, that is, none of the clinical scales exceeded a T score of 65. Choosing a WNL comparison group allowed for all symptoms and personality characteristics relevant to a code type to emerge as correlates. For most assessment purposes, it is more important to identify all characteristics of persons with a particular code type than to identify only those that are unique to that code type.

The results of the correlational analyses in the McNulty et al. (1999) study suggested that both the strength and number of conceptually relevant descriptors were greater for the well-defined code types. These results supported our decision to examine defined code types in the present study. In addition, they suggested that clinicians should place greater confidence in the accuracy of correlates that are based on defined code types than in those based on code types that are not defined. Descriptors for code types that are not defined should be more carefully verified against other sources of information.

It is interesting to note that in our larger study 42% of the male clients and 44% of the female clients had a defined and elevated two- or three-point code type. Because of redundancy of correlates for high-point code types and individual clinical scales, we chose not to emphasize the former in this book. However, if one-, two-, or three-point codes are considered, 69% of both male and female clients in our study had defined and elevated code types. Of course, for clients who do not have defined and elevated code types, interpretation of MMPI-2 scores is still possible by considering correlates of individual scales on which these clients have clinically elevated scores.

The Meaning of Low Scores on MMPI-2 Scales

Because low scores on MMPI-2 scales are statistically deviant from the norm, it has long been felt that low scores may provide important information about persons who are assessed with the MMPI and now the MMPI-2. Keiller and Graham (1993) summarized the various possible meanings of low scores that had been suggested previously. First, low scores on the clinical scales of MMPI-2 could indicate favorable characteristics that are conceptually related to the meaning of high scores on those scales. In this case, the relationship between scores on a scale and conceptually relevant extra-test measure are assumed to be linear, such that higher scores would indicate more than an average amount of the characteristic and lower scores would indicate less than an average amount of the characteristic. For example, higher scores on scale 2 would indicate more than an average amount of depression, whereas lower scores on that scale would indicate less than an average amount of depression.

A second possibility is that low scores represent unfavorable characteristics that are conceptually related to the meaning of higher scores on the scales. Low scores would suggest too much or not enough of some characteristic that persons with high scores possess to an extreme degree. For example, if high scale 2 scores indicate psychomotor retardation, low scores on this scale could indicate agitation or manic behavior.

A third possibility is that low scores indicate good general adjustment but not behaviors and characteristics that are specific to a particular scale. For example, low scores on all or many of the clinical scales could be associated with the same indicators of good overall adjustment.

A fourth possibility is that low scores indicate general maladjustment or unfavorable characteristics that are not conceptually related to the meaning of high scores on particular scales. For example, low scores on scale 2 could be associated with descriptors such as suspicious or antisocial.

A fifth possibility is that scores on the scales have curvilinear relationships with extra-test characteristics such that high and low scores on a particular scale have similar meaning. For example, both high and low scorers on scale 6 might be described as suspicious and untrusting.

Finally, low scores could provide no useful information. If this were the case, the extra-test characteristics of low scorers on a scale would not differ from those of persons with average scores on the scale. However, high scorers might differ from both average and low scorers. For example, high scale 2 scorers might be rated as more depressed than both average and low scorers, whose depression ratings would not differ from each other.

In order to investigate more directly the meaning of low scores on MMPI-2 scales, Graham, Ben-Porath, and McNulty (1997) completed a study using a subset of data from the current project. Participants in the study were 274 male and 425 female clients from the larger project who completed valid MMPI-2s and whose therapists provided information about them using the Patient Description Form (PDF). MMPI-2 validity criteria and the construction and psychometric properties of the PDF scales were described in chapter 2.

For each MMPI-2 clinical, content, and supplementary scale separately, clients were categorized into high (T > 64), medium (T = 41–64), and low (T < 41) groups based on their scores on that scale. These three groups were then compared for each of the PDF scales. Because in this clinical sample there were very few low scorers on some scales (and very few high scorers on scales for which high scores indicate favorable characteristics), we did not have enough statistical power to permit analyses for all scales. We had enough clients in all three groups for clinical scales 9 and 0; for Content Scales FRS, OBS, BIZ, ANG, CYN, TPA, LSE, and SOD; and for supplementary scales A, R, MAC-R, APS, and O-H.

The results of our study did not support a single explanation for the meaning of low scores on MMPI-2 scales. Rather, the meaning of low scores seemed to differ from one scale to another. For clinical scale 9, as expected, high scores were associated with characteristics suggestive of acting out, agitation, and self-centeredness. Interestingly, low scorers on scale 9 did not differ from medium scorers for any of the PDF scales, suggesting that low scores on this scale do not provide any useful information about the clients. A somewhat different picture emerged for clinical scale 0. There seemed to be a linear relationship between scale 0 scores and conceptually relevant PDF scales, with higher scale 0 scorers being seen as more introverted, insecure, anxious, depressed, and passive-submissive and less achievement oriented than medium scorers, and lower scale 0 scorers being seen as basically the opposite of higher scorers on these characteristics.

As with the clinical scales, a single explanation of the meaning of low scores on the Content Scales was not suggested by our data. For one Content Scale (BIZ), low scorers did not differ on any of the PDF scales from medium scorers, but high BIZ scorers were seen as having more symptoms, including psychotic symptoms, than medium scorers. For several other Content Scales (FRS, ANG, CYN, OBS) low scores seemed to suggest better overall adjustment but not necessarily in ways that are conceptually relevant to what these scales were designed to measure. For still other Content Scales (LSE, SOD) characteristics of lower scorers were very much the opposite of higher scorers in ways that are conceptually related to what the scales were designed to measure. For example, high scorers on LSE were seen as more insecure than medium scorers, and low scorers were seen as less insecure than medium scorers. High SOD scorers were seen as more introverted, insecure, and passive-submissive than medium scorers, whereas low scorers were seen as less introverted, insecure, and passive-submissive than medium scorers.

For two supplementary scales (APS, O-H), low scorers did not differ significantly from medium scorers on the PDF scales, suggesting that low scores on these scales did not communicate important information about clients. For the A scale, low scorers were seen as having less anxiety than medium scorers, but they also were rated as having better general adjustment than medium scorers. Similarly, low SOD scorers were rated as being less introverted than medium scorers. For both the A and SOD scales, high and low scorers were seen as very much the opposite of each other on both conceptually relevant characteristics and on overall adjustment. The final supplementary scale that we studied was the MAC-R. Information concerning the abuse of alcohol and other substances was not available from therapist ratings, so we could not assess the meaning of high, medium, and low scores on this highly relevant characteristic. However, low scorers differed from medium scorers on the conceptually relevant characteristic of antisocial behaviors and also on less conceptually relevant characteristics such as suspiciousness, defensiveness, and narcissism.

The basic conclusion that can be reached from our study of low scores on the MMPI-2 scales is that no single explanation of the meaning of low scores applies to all of the MMPI-2 scales. For some scales, low scores seem to provide no useful information about the clients. For other scales, low scorers appear to have fewer of the symptoms and negative characteristics that average scorers have. For still other scales, low scores seem to suggest better general adjustment but not necessarily in ways that are conceptually related to the particular scales studied. Our study offered no support for curvilinear relationships between MMPI-2 scores and relevant extra-test measures.

There are several aspects of the Graham et al. (1997) study of the meaning of low scores that limit the generalizability of its results. First, we did not have enough clients in the three groups to permit comparisons of low, medium, and high scorers for all scales. Clearly, there is need for additional research concerning the scales that we were not able to study. Second, the small numbers of clients in some groups necessitated combined-gender analyses. Thus, we do not know if our results would apply equally well to both male and female clients. Finally, our database did not include relevant extra-test measures for all of the MMPI-2 scales. Future studies should focus on collecting information that is conceptually relevant to these scales.

Based on our study, we recommend that low MMPI-2 scores in an outpatient mental health center setting be interpreted cautiously. One should not assume that low scores on a particular scale necessarily indicate the opposite of high scores on that scale. The inferences that can be made based on low scores will differ from one scale to another. One general finding of our study was that for none of the scales that we were able to analyze did low scores indicate more negative characteristics or poorer adjustment than medium or high scores. We would expect that if we had been able to include scales such as Ego Strength, Dominance, or Social Responsibility, where higher scores are indicative of more positive characteristics, low scores might have been associated with poorer adjustment and more negative characteristics than medium or high scores.

Relationship of Correlates of MMPI-2 Scales and Code Types to Ethnic Minority Status

Considerable research over the past 50 years has been devoted to determining if the MMPI was biased against members of ethnic minority groups, particularly African Americans. While the most consistently reported mean scale differences between Caucasians and African Americans have been for scales F, 4, 8, and 9, Greene's (1987) review concluded that there were more findings of no mean differences between these groups than there were of differences. In addition, as suggested by Dahlstrom, Lachar, and Dahlstrom (1986), when the effects of moderator variables (e.g., age, education, socioeconomic status) are controlled, differences between Caucasians and African Americans lessen or disappear. Dahlstrom et al. concluded that real attitudinal and/or clinical differences between groups are better explanations than test bias for observed MMPI differences between Caucasians and African Americans.

Timbrook and Graham (1994) argued that analyzing mean differences between groups on a personality test scale is not a sufficient test of bias. A more appropriate approach is to examine possible differences between Caucasians and African Americans in the relationships between test scores and conceptually relevant extra-test measures. Using matched samples of Caucasians and African Americans from the MMPI-2 normative sample, Timbrook and Graham found no differential accuracy in the prediction of conceptually relevant extra-test characteristics, even though the groups differed in mean scores. However, they concluded that additional research with clinical groups was needed to determine the generalizability of their findings.

In the current project, data for ethnic minority clients were not analyzed separately. This decision was made in part because of the relatively small number of minority clients in the sample. Another consideration was our desire to identify correlates that would apply broadly to the clientele of a mental health center setting. However, a separate study was conducted to determine if the correlates of MMPI-2 scales and code types were similar or different for Caucasian and African American mental health center clients.

McNulty, Graham, and Ben-Porath (1997) used a subset of 561 Caucasians and 123 African Americans who had valid MMPI-2s and rating information provided by their therapists using the Patient Description Form (PDF). There were not enough study participants to consider any other ethnic minority group. Following the recommendation of

Baron and Kenny (1986), the possibility of test bias was assessed by comparing the correlations of conceptually relevant PDF scales and MMPI-2 scales between the two groups. For example, the PDF Somatic Symptoms scale was correlated with scale 1, and the PDF Anxious scale was correlated with the Anxiety (ANX) content scale. Because of limitations of sample size, the correlational analyses were conducted with genders combined, but mean score differences were examined separately for male and female clients within each ethnic minority group.

African American women obtained significantly higher scores than Caucasian women on scale 9 and significantly lower scores on the Low Self-Esteem content scale. African American men scored significantly higher than their Caucasian counterparts on the L scale and the Fears content scale. However, there were no significant differences in the correlations between any MMPI-2 and PDF scales between the two groups. These results were interpreted as indicating that differences in MMPI-2 scores for Caucasians and African Americans are indicative of real differences in the characteristics of these two groups of clients and not suggestive of test bias. The results also indicated that the correlates of the MMPI-2 scales and code types in the current study are applicable to both Caucasian and African American clients. Differences in scores between these two groups were uncommon. However, those that did emerge are likely to reflect meaningful differences in symptom presentation and personality characteristics that have important implications for treatment planning.

Limitations of the Study and Future Research Directions

This research project has provided valuable empirical information concerning the correlates of MMPI-2 scales and code types in outpatient community mental health settings. It is, we believe, the most comprehensive study of MMPI-2 correlates published to date. Nevertheless, this study has several limitations that should be addressed in future investigations. In this final section we identify some limitations of this study and suggest directions for future research efforts.

Sample Size

In spite of tremendous efforts and expenditure of resources, our final sample was not large enough to address all of the research goals of this project. Specifically, when categorized by code type, our sample did not provide a sufficient number of clients to permit the identification of correlates for all two-point code types or to conduct code-type correlate analyses separately by gender. Although we began with approximately 2,500 clients who yielded 1,020 valid MMPI-2 profiles, when classified by well-defined code types, our sample permitted analyses of only some code types. Larger samples will be needed in future investigations. Based on our experience with this project, we suggest that samples well in excess of 10,000 participants are needed to allow for a detailed analysis of code-type correlates by gender. Because of the widespread use of the MMPI-2, it would not be very difficult to collect such large samples. It would be a far more challenging task, however, to collect the rich set of extra-test data that are, of course, necessary for the identification of empirical correlates.

Our experiences with this project suggest that it will not be possible for a single investigator or one group of investigators to compile the requisite data at a single research site. To compile a sufficiently large set of MMPI-2 and extra-test data, multisite collaborative studies will be necessary. Such projects, in which teams of investigators use the same set of extra-test measures to collect data at various geographical locations and in different types of clinical settings, would require funding of imposing magnitude. Nevertheless, this scope of research is called for if we want to study in detail the empirical correlates of all MMPI-2 code types.

Sample Demographics

The sample used in our project provides a very useful cross section of the population that is likely to be tested with the MMPI-2. The outpatient community mental health center where data for this project were collected serves a relatively large catchment area that encompasses both urban and rural communities and includes a relatively large African American population. A comparison with data available from the Ohio Department of Mental Health indicated that our sample was very similar to the population of individuals receiving community mental health services in Ohio (about 3% of the state's population on an annual basis). Moreover, data published by the U.S. Census Bureau indicate that the state of Ohio represents well the demographic characteristics of the United States. Thus, we feel confident concluding that our sample represents a large segment of the population of individuals who receive mental health services in the United States. However, some components of the U.S. population, including Hispanic Americans, Asian Americans, and American Indians, were not represented adequately in our sample. Further, to the extent that one might expect regional differences to affect some of the findings of this investigation, the current sample presents additional demographic limitations.

This, again, points to the need for multisite collaborative investigations that span the geographical regions of the United States. Such an approach was used in the MMPI Restandardization Project, yielding a sample that provided better representation of various demographic characteristics of the general population of the United States than does the sample available for the present investigation. Encouragingly, as reviewed in a previous section of this chapter, it does not appear that the MMPI-2 functions very differently across ethnic groups. Further, there do not appear, a priori, to be reasons to expect vast regional differences in MMPI-2 characteristics. Nevertheless, by including a more diverse subsample of ethnic minorities than was available in this study and by conducting multisite collaborative studies, future investigators will be able to avert misgivings about the limiting effects of underrepresentation of ethnic groups or geographical regions.

The Question of Gender Differences

The correlates identified for individual scales in this study suggest both a great deal of comparability across genders as well as some gender-specific findings. However, we still do not know to what extent the gender differences in MMPI-2 correlates that were identified in this project reflect differential base rates of clinical phenomena across genders versus a tendency for clinical observers to perceive differences across genders where such differences do not actually exist. To the extent, for example, that women in clinical settings are more likely than men to experience suicidal ideation, then the greater prevalence of this correlate among women than men in our findings reflects a genuine gender difference in the proclivity to experience suicidal ideation. However, to the extent that women and men do not differ substantially along these lines, then our findings may reflect either gender differences in the willingness to acknowledge suicidal ideation to one's therapist, and/or bias-driven differences in therapists' tendencies to attribute suicidal ideation to male and female clients. To the extent that either of the latter two scenarios (and they are not mutually exclusive) account for the observed gender differences for this correlate, then this difference is artifactual and should not be used to generate different MMPI-2 interpretations for women and men.

Because of relatively small sample sizes, it was not feasible for us to conduct our code-type analyses separately for men and women. Therefore, we were not able to compare the correlates for male and female clients. An additional concern is that there was marked gender imbalance for some of the code types included in our analysis. As discussed in chapter 4, caution is indicated in applying the correlates to the underrepresented gender. However, the marked similarity of correlates between male and female clients for the individual scales offers some evidence that many of the correlates are likely to apply to both men and women.

Additional research is needed to assess the various explanations just proposed for gender differences in MMPI-2 correlates. It will be especially important to conduct studies with large enough samples to permit separate analysis of code-type correlates for men and women. In these studies, investigators should attend to the gender of participants and raters, and efforts will be required to come up with creative ways to obtain accurate estimates of the actual base rates of the clinical phenomena in question.

Generalizability to Other Settings

Earlier in this chapter, we discussed the extent to which our findings correspond to those that were reported in prior studies that were conducted in other types of settings. Our conclusion was that there is considerable comparability between previous findings and our own. However, presently we are able to comment on the issue of comparability only by inference, through a qualitative comparison of the present correlates with those that were reported previously.

To address questions pertaining to cross-setting correlate comparability more directly, we point once more toward multisite collaborative research as the best possible approach. By using the same extra-test measures and procedures across a variety of settings serving psychiatric, medical, substance abuse, and forensic populations in both inpatient and outpatient environments, future investigators will be able to address more directly questions regarding the generalizability of MMPI-2 correlates across settings. We expect that such research will reflect a great deal of comparability with a lesser, albeit important, degree of specificity of MMPI-2 correlates across settings.

Scale Proliferation

We have reported in this book empirical correlates for a large number of MMPI-2 scales and code types. Users and students of the original MMPI will recall that by the 1970s the number of MMPI "special" scales had already exceeded the number of items in the test. To avoid a similar situation with the MMPI-2, it has been suggested that new scales that are proposed for the MMPI-2 must possess incremental validity in reference to scales that are already available on the test (Butcher, Graham, & Ben-Porath, 1995). Thus, for example, Ben-Porath, Butcher, and Graham (1991) and Ben-Porath, McCully, and Almagor (1993) reported on the incremental validity of some of the MMPI-2 Content Scales in reference to the clinical scales.

The data set collected for the present investigation yielded additional information on the incremental validity of the MMPI-2 Content Scales (Barthlow, Graham, Ben-Porath, & McNulty, 1999). Similarly, a study of the incremental validity of recently developed MMPI-2 substance abuse scales in reference to the MacAndrew Alcoholism Scale-Revised revealed that the new substance abuse scales add incrementally to the MAC-R scale (Stein, Graham, Ben-Porath, & McNulty, 1999). We hope that the data set from the current study will be a fruitful resource for these and further investigations of the incremental validity of new scales that are proposed for the MMPI-2. The availability of this and similar data sets for incremental validity studies should help prevent undue proliferation of MMPI-2 scales.

Treatment Outcome

The MMPI/MMPI-2 has long played an important role in treatment planning and other aspects of psychotherapy. Prior investigations (reviewed by Butcher, 1990) demonstrated that certain scales and code types can be used to generate predictions about therapy outcome and to suggest that certain therapy modalities may be more appropriate for particular clients. Most of this research was conducted with the original MMPI.

Using a subset of data from our larger project, a comprehensive investigation of the MMPI-2's potential contributions to treatment planning and the prediction of therapy outcome is being conducted. In addition to providing information about clients' clinical history, current mental status, personality and behavioral characteristics, and termination status, therapists who participated in this study conveyed detailed information regarding clients' presenting problems and their severity, along with periodic updates on whether and how their clients were progressing in treatment. Therapists also described the treatment modalities they used with their clients.

These data will be used to provide empirical information on the prognostic power of MMPI-2 data as well as to investigate whether clients who produce certain patterns of scores on the test may stand to benefit more from one mode of treatment than they might from others. We hope that this research will highlight the utility of data that are available to clinicians who rely on psychological assessment to guide them in the process of problem formulation and treatment planning.

Conclusions

This project was undertaken to generate information that would be useful to psychologists who rely on the MMPI-2 as a source of information in scientifically grounded psychological assessment. The data presented, summarized, and discussed in this book follow in the tradition of prior efforts that serve as the empirical foundation of MMPI-2 interpretation. We believe that these data will add to this foundation. The use of relatively large samples and the inclusion of multiple sources of extra-test information were especially important aspects of the project. The results of our study should be helpful to clinicians faced with the task of interpreting MMPI-2 scores of community mental health outpatients, and more generally the study adds incrementally to the very large empirical database that demonstrates the validity of the MMPI-2. Future researchers may find some of our measures and methods useful as they add even more information to this database.

References

American Psychiatric Association. (1987). *Diagnostic and statistical manual of mental disorders: DSM-III-R* (3rd ed.). Washington, DC: American Psychiatric Association.

American Psychiatric Association. (1994). *Diagnostic and statistical manual of mental disorders: DSM-IV* (4th ed.). Washington, DC: American Psychiatric Association.

Arbisi, P. A., & Ben-Porath, Y. S. (1998). [A study of the MMPI-2 in inpatients]. Unpublished data.

Archer, R. P., Aiduk, R., Griffin, R., & Elkins, D. E. (1996). Incremental validity of the MMPI-2 Content Scales in a psychiatric sample. *Assessment, 3,* 79–90.

Archer, R. P., Griffin, R., & Aiduk, R. (1995). MMPI-2 codes. *Journal of Personality Assessment, 65,* 391–407.

Baron, F. (1953). An ego strength scale which predicts response to psychotherapy. *Journal of Consulting Psychology, 17,* 327–333.

Baron, R. M., & Kenny, D. A. (1986). The moderator-mediator variable distinction in social psychological research: Conceptual, strategic, and statistical considerations. *Journal of Personality and Social Psychology, 51,* 1173–1182.

Barthlow, D., Graham, J. R., Ben-Porath, Y. S., & McNulty, J. L. (1999). Incremental validity of the MMPI-2 Content Scales in an outpatient mental health setting. *Psychological Assessment: A Journal of Consulting and Clinical Psychology, 11,* 39–47.

Ben-Porath, Y. S., & Butcher, J. N. (1989a). The comparability of MMPI and MMPI-2 scales and profiles. *Psychological Assessment: A Journal of Consulting and Clinical Psychology, 1,* 345–347.

Ben-Porath, Y. S., & Butcher, J. N. (1989b). Psychometric stability of rewritten MMPI items. *Journal of Personality Assessment, 53,* 645–653.

Ben-Porath, Y. S., Butcher, J. N., & Graham, J. R. (1991). Contribution of the MMPI-2 Content Scales to the differential diagnosis of psychopathology. *Psychological Assessment: A Journal of Consulting and Clinical Psychology, 3,* 634–640.

Ben-Porath, Y. S., Hostetler, K., Butcher, J. N., & Graham, J. R. (1989). New subscales for the MMPI-2 Social Introversion (Si) scale. *Psychological Assessment: A Journal of Consulting and Clinical Psychology, 1,* 169–174.

Ben-Porath, Y. S., McCully, E., & Almagor, M. (1993). Incremental validity of the MMPI-2 Content Scales in the assessment of personality and psychopathology by self-report. *Journal of Personality Assessment, 61,* 557–575.

Ben-Porath, Y. S., & Sherwood, N. E. (1993). *The MMPI-2 Content Component Scales:*

Development, psychometric characteristics, and clinical application. Minneapolis: University of Minnesota Press.

Ben-Porath, Y. S., & Tellegen, A. (1995). How (not) to evaluate the comparability of MMPI and MMPI-2 profile configurations: A reply to Humphrey and Dahlstrom. *Journal of Personality Assessment, 65,* 52–58.

Black, J. D. (1953). The interpretation of MMPI profiles of college women. *Dissertation Abstracts, 13,* 870–871.

Boerger, A. R., Graham, J. R., & Lilly, R. S. (1974). Behavioral correlates of single-scale MMPI code types. *Journal of Consulting and Clinical Psychology, 42,* 398–402.

Briggs, P. F., Taylor, M., & Tellegen, A. (1966). *A study of the Marks and Seeman MMPI profile types as applied to a sample of 2,875 psychiatric patients* (Report Number PR-66-5). Minneapolis: University of Minnesota, Research Laboratories of the Department of Psychiatry.

Brown, W. R., & McGuire, J. M. (1976). Current psychological assessment practices. *Professional Psychology, 7,* 475–484.

Butcher, J. N. (1990). *MMPI-2 in psychological treatment.* New York: Oxford University Press.

Butcher, J. N., Dahlstrom, W. G., Graham, J. R., Tellegen, A., & Kaemmer, B. (1989). *Minnesota Multiphasic Personality Inventory-2 (MMPI-2): Manual for administration and scoring.* Minneapolis: University of Minnesota Press.

Butcher, J. N., Graham, J. R., & Ben-Porath, Y. S. (1995). Methodological problems and issues in MMPI, MMPI-2, and MMPI-A research. *Psychological Assessment, 7,* 320–329.

Butcher, J. N., Graham, J. R., Williams, C. L., & Ben-Porath, Y. S. (1990). *Development and use of the MMPI-2 Content Scales.* Minneapolis: University of Minnesota Press.

Butcher, J. N., & Rouse, S. V. (1996). Personality: Individual differences and clinical assessment. *Annual Review of Psychology, 47,* 87–111.

Butcher, J. N., & Williams, C. L. (1992). *Essentials of MMPI-2 and MMPI-A interpretation.* Minneapolis: University of Minnesota Press.

Carrington, P., Collings, G. H., Benson, H., Robinson, H., Wood, L. W., Lehrer, P. M., Woolfolk, R. L., & Cole, J. (1980). The use of meditation-relaxation techniques for the management of stress in a working population. *Journal of Occupational Medicine, 22,* 221–231.

Clark, M. E. (1994). Interpretive limitations of the MMPI-2 Anger and Cynicism scales. *Journal of Personality Assessment, 63,* 89–96.

Clark, M. E. (1996). MMPI-2 Negative Treatment Indicators content and content component scales: Clinical correlates and outcome prediction for men with chronic pain. *Psychological Assessment, 8,* 32–38.

Cronbach, L. J., & Meehl, P. E. (1955). Construct validity in psychology tests. *Psychological Bulletin, 52,* 281–302.

Dahlstrom, W. G. (1992). Comparability of two-point high-point code patterns from original MMPI norms to MMPI-2 norms for the restandardization sample. *Journal of Personality Assessment, 59,* 153–164.

Dahlstrom, W. G., & Humphrey, D. (1996). Comparability of MMPI and MMPI-2 profile patterns: Ben-Porath and Tellegen's inappropriate invocation of Mahalanobis's D^2 function. *Journal of Personality Assessment, 66,* 350–354.

Dahlstrom, W. G., Lachar, D., & Dahlstrom, L. E. (1986). *MMPI patterns of American minorities.* Minneapolis: University of Minnesota Press.

Dahlstrom, W. G., Welsh, G. S., & Dahlstrom, L. E. (1972). *An MMPI handbook: Vol. I. Clinical interpretation.* Minneapolis: University of Minnesota Press.

Derogatis, L. R. (1983). *SCL-90-R: Administration, scoring, and procedures manual - II for the R(evised) version.* Towson, MD: Clinical Psychometric Research.

Derogatis, L. R., Rickels, K., & Rock, A. (1976). The SCL-90 and the MMPI: A step in the validation of a new self-report scale. *British Journal of Psychiatry, 128,* 280–289.

Drake, L. E., & Oetting, E. R. (1959). *An MMPI codebook for counselors.* Minneapolis: University of Minnesota Press.

Dwyer, S. A., Graham, J. R., & Ott, E. K. (1991). *Psychiatric symptoms associated with the MMPI-2 Content Scales.* Unpublished manuscript, Kent State University, Kent, OH.

Endler, N. S., Parker, J. D. A., & Butcher, J. N. (1993). A factor analytic study of coping styles and the MMPI-2 Content Scales. *Journal of Clinical Psychology, 49,* 523–527.

Fowler, R. D., & Coyle, F. A. (1968). Overlap as a problem in atlas classification of MMPI profiles. *Journal of Clinical Psychology, 24,* 435.

Gallagher, R., Somwaru, D., Briggs, S., & Ben-Porath, Y. S. (1996). *A survey of psychological test usage in state correctional institutions.* Paper presented at the Biennium Meeting of the American Law Society, Hilton Head, SC.

Gilberstadt, H., & Duker, J. (1965). *A handbook for clinical and actuarial MMPI interpretation.* Philadelphia: Saunders.

Gough, H. G. (1946). Diagnostic patterns on the MMPI. *Journal of Clinical Psychology, 2,* 23–37.

Gough, H. G., McClosky, H., & Meehl, P. E. (1951). A personality scale for dominance. *Journal of Abnormal and Social Psychology, 46,* 360–366.

Gough, H. G., McClosky, H., & Meehl, P. E. (1952). A personality scale for social responsibility. *Journal of Abnormal and Social Psychology, 47,* 73–80.

Graham, J. R. (1977). *The MMPI: A practical guide.* New York: Oxford University Press.

Graham, J. R. (1987). *The MMPI: A practical guide* (2nd ed.). New York: Oxford University Press.

Graham, J. R. (1988, August). *Establishing validity of the revised form of the MMPI.* Symposium presentation at the 96th Annual Convention of the American Psychological Association, Atlanta, GA.

Graham, J. R. (1990). *MMPI-2: Assessing personality and psychopathology.* New York: Oxford University Press.

Graham, J. R. (1993). *MMPI-2: Assessing personality and psychopathology* (2nd ed.). New York: Oxford University Press.

Graham, J. R., Ben-Porath, Y. S., & McNulty, J. L. (1997). Empirical correlates of low scores on MMPI-2 scales in an outpatient mental health setting. *Psychological Assessment, 9,* 386–391.

Graham, J. R., Smith, R. L., & Schwartz, G. F. (1986). Stability of MMPI configurations for psychiatric inpatients. *Journal of Consulting and Clinical Psychology, 54,* 375–380.

Graham, J. R., Timbrook, R. E., Ben-Porath, Y. S., & Butcher, J. N. (1991). Code-type congruence between MMPI and MMPI-2: Separating fact from artifact. *Journal of Personality Assessment, 57,* 205–215.

Graham, J. R., Watts, D., & Timbrook, R. (1991). Detecting fake-good and fake-bad MMPI-2 profiles. *Journal of Personality Assessment, 57,* 264–277.

Greene, R. L. (1980). *The MMPI: An interpretive manual.* New York: Grune and Straton.

Greene, R. L. (1987). Ethnicity and MMPI performance: A review. *Journal of Consulting and Clinical Psychology, 55,* 497–512.

Greene, R. L. (1991). *MMPI/MMPI-2: An interpretive manual.* New York: Grune and Straton.

Gynther, M. D., Altman, H., & Sletten, I. W. (1973). Replicated correlates of MMPI two-point types: The Missouri Actuarial System. *Journal of Clinical Psychology, 29,* 263–289.

Harris, R., & Lingoes, J. (1955). *Subscales for the Minnesota Multiphasic Personality Inventory.* Mimeographed materials, The Langley Porter Clinic.

Harrison, P. L., Kaufman, A. S., Hickman, J. A., & Kaufman, N. L. (1988). A survey of tests for adult assessment. *Journal of Psychoeducational Assessment, 6,* 188–198.

Hathaway, S. R. (1960). Foreword to first edition. In W. G. Dahlstrom & G. S. Welsh (Eds.), *An MMPI handbook: A guide to use in clinical practice and research* (pp. vii-xi). Minneapolis: University of Minnesota Press.

Hathaway, S. R., & McKinley, J. C. (1940). A multiphasic personality schedule (Minnesota): I. Construction of the schedule. *Journal of Psychology, 10,* 249–254.

Hathaway, S. R., & Meehl, P. E. (1951). The Minnesota Multiphasic Personality Inventory. In *Military Clinical Psychology* (Department of the Army Technical Manual TM 8:242; Department of the Air Force Manual AFM 160-145). Washington, DC: U.S. Government Printing Office.

Hjemboe, S., Almagor, M., & Butcher, J. N. (1992). Empirical assessment of marital distress: The Marital Distress Scale (MDS) for the MMPI-2. In J. N. Butcher & C. D. Speilberger (Eds.), *Advances in personality assessment* (Vol. 9, pp. 141–152). Hillsdale, NJ: Erlbaum.

Huff, F. W. (1965). Use of actuarial description of abnormal personality in a mental hospital. *Psychological Reports, 17,* 224.

Humphrey, D. H., & Dahlstrom, W. G. (1995). The impact of changing from the MMPI to the MMPI-2 on the profile configurations. *Journal of Personality Assessment, 64,* 428–439.

Keane, T. M., Malloy, P. F., & Fairbank, J. A. (1984). Empirical development of an MMPI subscale for the assessment of combat-related post-traumatic stress disorder. *Journal of Consulting and Clinical Psychology, 52,* 888–891.

Keiller, S. W., & Graham, J. R. (1993). Interpreting low scores on the MMPI-2 clinical scales. *Journal of Personality Assessment, 61,* 211–223.

Krishnamurthy, P., Archer, R. P., & Huddleston, E. N. (1995). Clinical research note on psychometric limitations of two Harris-Lingoes subscales. *Assessment, 2,* 301–304.

Lewandowski, D., & Graham, J. R. (1972). Empirical correlates of frequently occurring two-point code types: A replicated study. *Journal of Consulting and Clinical Psychology, 39,* 467–472.

Lubin, B., Larsen, R. M., & Matarazzo, J. D. (1984). Patterns of psychological test usage in the United States: 1935–1982. *American Psychologist, 39,* 451–454.

MacAndrew, C. (1965). The differentiation of male alcoholic out-patients from nonalcoholic psychiatric patients by means of the MMPI. *Quarterly Journal of the Studies of Alcohol, 26,* 238–246.

Marks, P. A., & Seeman, W. (1963). *The actuarial description of abnormal personality: An atlas for use with the MMPI.* Baltimore: Williams and Wilkins.

Marks, P. A., Seeman, W., & Haller, D. L. (1974). *The actuarial use of the MMPI with adolescents and adults.* Baltimore: Williams and Wilkins.

McNulty, J. L., Ben-Porath, Y. S., & Graham, J. R. (1997, June). *Using the content component scales to facilitate content scale interpretation.* Paper presented at the 32nd annual MMPI-2 & MMPI-A Symposium, Minneapolis, MN.

McNulty, J. L., Ben-Porath, Y. S., & Graham, J. R. (1999). An empirical examination of the correlates of well-defined and not defined MMPI-2 code types. *Journal of Personality Assessment, 71,* 393–410.

McNulty, J. L., Graham, J. R., & Ben-Porath, Y. S. (1997). Comparative validity of MMPI-2 scores of African American and Caucasian mental health center clients. *Psychological Assessment, 9,* 464–470.

Meehl, P. E. (1945). The dynamics of "structured" personality tests. *Journal of Clinical Psychology, 1,* 296–303.

Meehl, P. E. (1946). Profile analysis of the MMPI in differential diagnosis. *Journal of Applied Psychology, 30,* 517–524.

Meehl, P. E. (1954). *Clinical versus statistical prediction: A theoretical analysis and a review of the evidence.* Minneapolis: University of Minnesota Press.

Meehl, P. E. (1956). Wanted—A good cookbook. *American Psychologist, 11,* 263–272.

Megargee, E. I., Cook, P. E., & Mendelsohn, G. A. (1967). Development and validation of an MMPI scale of assaultiveness in overcontrolled individuals. *Journal of Abnormal Psychology, 72,* 519–528.

Meikle, S., & Gerritse, R. (1970). MMPI cookbook pattern frequencies in a psychiatric unit. *Journal of Clinical Psychology, 26,* 82–84.

Mineka, S., Watson, D., & Clark, L. A. (1998). Comorbidity of anxiety and unipolar mood disorders. *Annual Review of Psychology, 49,* 377–412.

Piotrowski, C., & Keller, J. W. (1989). Psychological testing in outpatient mental health facilities. *Professional Psychology: Research and Practice, 20,* 423–425.

Piotrowski, C., & Keller, J. W. (1992). Psychological testing in applied settings: A literature review from 1982–1993. *Journal of Training & Practice in Professional Psychology, 6,* 74–82.

Piotrowski, C., Sherry, D., & Keller, J. W. (1985). Psychodiagnostic test usage: A survey for the Society for Personality Assessment. *Journal of Personality Assessment, 49,* 115–119.

Piotrowski, C., & Zalewski, C. (1993). Training in psychodiagnostic testing in APA-approved PsyD and PhD clinical psychology programs. *Journal of Personality Assessment, 61,* 394–405.

Reynolds, W. M., & Sundberg, N. D. (1976). Recent research trends in testing. *Journal of Personality Assessment, 40,* 228–233.

Schmidt, H. O. (1945). Test profiles as a diagnostic aid: The Minnesota Multiphasic Inventory. *Journal of Applied Psychology, 29,* 115–131.

Stein, L. A. R., Graham, J. R., Ben-Porath, Y. S., & McNulty, J. L. (1999). Using the MMPI-2 to detect substance abuse in an outpatient mental health setting. *Psychological Assessment, 11,* 94–100.

Strassberg, D. S., Clutton, S., & Korboot, P. (1991). A descriptive validity study of the Minnesota Multiphasic Personality Inventory-2 (MMPI-2) in an elderly Australian sample. *Journal of Psychopathology and Behavioral Assessment, 13,* 301–311.

Tellegen, A., & Ben-Porath, Y. S. (1993). Code-type comparability of the MMPI and MMPI-2: Analysis of recent findings and criticisms. *Journal of Personality Assessment, 61,* 489–500.

Timbrook, R. E., & Graham, J. R. (1994). Ethnic differences on the MMPI-2? *Psychological Assessment, 6,* 212–217.

Watkins, C., Campbell, V. L., & McGregor, P. (1988). Counseling psychologists' use of and opinions about psychological tests: A contemporary perspective. *Counseling Psychologist, 16,* 476–486.

Watkins, C., Campbell, V. L., Nieberding, R., & Hallmark, R. (1995). Contemporary practice of psychological assessment by clinical psychologists. *Professional Psychology: Research and Practice, 26,* 54–60.

Webb, J. T., Levitt, E. E., & Rojdev, R. (1993, March). *After three years: A comparison of the clinical use of the MMPI and MMPI-2.* Paper presented at the 53rd Annual Meeting of the Society for Personality Assessment, San Francisco, CA.

Weed, N. C., Butcher, J. N., McKenna, T., & Ben-Porath, Y. S. (1992). New measures for assessing alcohol and drug abuse with the MMPI-2: The APS and AAS. *Journal of Personality Assessment, 58,* 389–404.

Weed, N. C., & Han, K. (1992, May). *Is K correct?* Paper presented at the 27th Annual Symposium on Recent Developments in the Use of the MMPI (MMPI-2 and MMPI-A), Minneapolis, MN.

Weissman, M. M., Slobetz, F., Prusoff, B., Mezritz, M., & Howard, P. (1976). Clinical depression among narcotic addicts maintained on methadone in the community. *American Journal of Psychiatry, 133,* 1434–1439.

Welsh, G. S. (1956). Factor dimensions A and R. In G. S. Welsh & W. G. Dahlstrom (Eds.), *Basic Readings on the MMPI in Psychology and Medicine* (pp. 264–281). Minneapolis: University of Minnesota Press.

Wewers, M. E., & Lowe, N. K. (1990). A critical review of visual analogue scales in the measurement of clinical phenomena. *Research in Nursing and Health, 13,* 227–236.

Wiggins, J. S. (1966). Substantive dimensions of self-report in the MMPI item pool. *Psychological Monographs, 80,* (22, Whole No. 630).

Zonderman, A. B., Siegler, I. C., Barefoot, J. C., & Williams, R. B. (1993). Age and gender differences in the Content Scales of the Minnesota Multiphasic Personality Inventory. *Experimental Aging Research, 19,* 241–257.

Appendix A

Intake Form

Background Information

1. Date of intake ____________________
2. Patient number ____________________
3. Was patient previously admitted to Portage Path between April 1, 1991, and the above date? ___ yes ___ no
4. Referral source:
   ___ University of Akron
   ___ Family Services
   ___ ORIANNA House
   ___ INFO Line
   ___ Physician
   ___ Attorney
   ___ Other ____________________
   ___ Children's Services Board
   ___ Probation/Parole Officer
   ___ Friends, relatives, etc.
   ___ Court (e.g., Barberton, Cuyahoga Falls)
   ___ P.E.E.R.S, Crisis Hotline, Crisis Stabilization Unit
   ___ Hospital (Akron General, etc.)
5. Age ___
6. Sex: (1) Male (2) Female
7. Race: (1)___ Caucasian (2)___ African American (3)___ Hispanic (4)___ Asian-American (5)___ American Indian (6) Other
8. Number of years of education completed ___; if less than 12, has the patient completed the GED? ___ yes ___ no
9. Marital status: (1)___ married (2)___ widowed (3)___ divorced (4)___ separated (5)___ never married
10. Employment status (More than one may be checked if appropriate):
    ___ full-time ___ part-time ___ unemployed
    ___ retired ___ student ___ self-employed
    ___ disabled ___ on leave ___ housewife
11. Occupation: ____________________
12. Spouse's occupation: ____________________
13. Total family income: ____________________

Adult Legal History

14. Number of arrests ___
15. Number of misdemeanor convictions ___
16. Number of felony convictions ___
17. Ever convicted of domestic violence? (1)___ yes (2)___ no
18. If yes, time in jail? (1)___ yes (2)___ no
19. If yes, court-ordered treatment? (1)___ yes (2)___ no

Psychiatric History

20. Has patient had previous psychiatric hospitalization?
(1) ___yes (2) ___no

21. If yes, how many? _____

22. If yes, number of months since last hospitalization _____

23. Does patient have a history of outpatient psychiatric treatment?
(1) ___yes (2) ___no

24. If yes, how many times has the patient been involved in such treatment? _____

25. If the patient has had past outpatient treatment, what kind was it?
(Check all that apply)
___ (1) individual counseling or psychotherapy
___ (2) medication
___ (3) group therapy
___ (4) family/couples therapy

26. Medications patient is taking at present (check all that apply):
(1) ___ antipsychotic (2) ___ antidepressant
(3) ___ Lithium (4) ___ antianxiety
(5) ___ other (specify) ________________________

27. Check if patient has a history of:
___ being sexually abusive
___ being sexually abused
___ being physically abusive
___ committing domestic violence
___ being a victim of domestic violence
___ being physically abused
___ having few or no friends
___ suicide attempts (if so, how many) ___
___ eating disorder (binge eating, self-induced vomiting, use of laxatives or diuretics)

Substance Abuse History

28. Indicate substance use/abuse by the patient *at any time during his/her life:*

	No info.	No use	Some use	Possible abuse	Definite abuse
Alcohol	___	___	___	___	___
Marijuana	___	___	___	___	___
Cocaine (includes crack)	___	___	___	___	___
Heroin	___	___	___	___	___
Other	___	___	___	___	___

(specify)________________________

29 Indicate substance use/abuse by the patient *at any time during the past six months:*

	No info.	No use	Some abuse	Possible abuse	Definite abuse
Alcohol	___	___	___	___	___
Marijuana	___	___	___	___	___
Cocaine (includes crack)	___	___	___	___	___
Heroin	___	___	___	___	___
Other	___	___	___	___	___

(specify): ______________________________

30. How much confidence do you have that the information provided by the patient during the intake interview was accurate and reliable?

1	2	3	4	5
none	very little	little	some	a great deal

31. To what treatment program was the patient referred?

____

Diagnostic Impressions

Axis I: (include code; list primary impression first)

1.

2.

3.

Axis II: (include code; list primary impression first)

1.

2.

3.

Axis III: (include code)

Axis IV: Severity of psychosocial stressors in past year[1]
(circle the number corresponding to the most serious stressor)

[1] *Source: The severity of psychosocial stressor scales: adult. Diagnostic and statistical manual of mental disorders (Third Edition-Revised): DSM-III-R.* Washington, D.C. Copyright 1987 by the American Psychiatric Association. Reproduced by permission.

Examples of stressors

Code	Term	Acute events	Enduring circumstances
1	None	No acute events that may be relevant to the disorder	No enduring circumstances that may be relevant to the disorder
2	Mild	Broke up with boyfriend or girlfriend; started or graduated from school; child left home	Family arguments; job dissatisfaction; residence in high-crime neighborhood
3	Moderate	Marriage; marital separation; loss of job; retirement; miscarriage	Marital discord; serious financial problems; trouble with boss; being a single parent
4	Severe	Divorce; birth of first child	Unemployment; poverty
5	Extreme	Death of spouse; serious physical illness diagnosed; victim of rape	Serious chronic illness in self or child; ongoing physical or sexual abuse
6	Catastrophic	Death of child; suicide of spouse; devastating natural disaster	Captivity as hostage; concentration camp experience
0	Inadequate information, or no change in condition		

Axis V: Current psychological, social, and occupational functioning[2] _____

Highest level of psychological, social, and occupational functioning for at least a few months in past year _____

Write code in each blank above. You may use intermediate numbers (those not actually appearing on the scale below).

Code

90 Absent or minimal symptoms (e.g., mild anxiety before an exam), good functioning in all areas, interested and involved in a wide range of activities, socially effective, generally satisfied with life, no more than everyday problems or
81 concerns (e.g., an occasional argument with family members).

80 If symptoms are present, they are transient and expectable reactions to psychosocial stressors (e.g., difficulty concentrating after family argument); no more than slight impairment in social, occupational, or school functioning
71 (e.g., temporarily falling behind in school work).

[2] *Source: The global assessment of functioning scale (GAF scale). Diagnostic and statistical manual of mental disorders (Third Edition-Revised): DSM-III-R.* Washington, D.C. Copyright © 1987 by the American Psychiatric Association. Reproduced by permission.

70 Some mild symptoms (e.g., depressed mood and mild insomnia) OR some difficulty in social, occupational, or school functioning (e.g., occasional truancy, or theft within the household); but generally functioning pretty well, has some
61 meaningful interpersonal relationships.

60 Moderate symptoms (e.g., flat affect and circumstantial speech, occasional panic attacks) OR moderate difficulty in social, occupational, or school functioning
51 (e.g., few friends, conflicts with coworkers).

50 Serious symptoms (e.g., suicidal ideation, severe obsessional rituals, frequent shoplifting) OR any serious impairment in social, occupational, or school
41 functioning (e.g., no friends, unable to keep a job).

40 Some impairment in reality testing or communication (e.g., speech is at times illogical, obscure, or irrelevant) OR major impairment in several areas, such as work or school, family relations, judgment, thinking, or mood (e.g., depressed man avoids friends, neglects family, and is unable to work; child frequently
31 beats up younger children, is defiant at home, and is failing at school).

30 Behavior is considerably influenced by delusions or hallucinations OR serious impairment in communication or judgment (e.g., sometimes incoherent, acts grossly inappropriately, suicidal preoccupation) OR inability to function in almost
21 all areas (e.g., stays in bed all day; no job, home, or friends).

20 Some danger of hurting self or others (e.g., suicide attempts without clear expectation of death, frequently violent, manic excitement) OR occasionally fails to maintain minimal personal hygiene (e.g., smears feces) OR gross impairment in
11 communication (e.g., largely incoherent or mute).

10 Persistent danger of severely hurting self or others (e.g., recurrent violence) OR persistent inability to maintain minimal personal hygiene OR serious suicidal act
1 with clear expectation of death.

0 Inadequate information.

Mental Status

Note: The following ratings should be based on the patient's behavior *during your interview with him/her.*

1. Patient's Dress

1	2	3	4	5
very sloppily dressed	sloppily dressed	average dress	neatly dressed	very neatly dressed

2. Patient's Grooming

1	2	3	4	5
very poorly groomed	poorly groomed	average grooming	well groomed	very well groomed

3. Relationship with Examiner (check all that apply)

___ uncomfortable
___ cooperative
___ seductive
___ defensive
___ aggressive/hostile
___ evasive
___ aloof

4. Intelligence (as judged from interview)

1	**2**	**3**
below average	average	above average

5. Orientation (check all that apply)

___ oriented for time
___ oriented for place
___ oriented for person

6. Memory for Recent Events

1	**2**	**3**	**4**	**5**
very poor	poor	average	good	very good

7. Memory for Distant Events

1	**2**	**3**	**4**	**5**
very poor	poor	average	good	very good

8. Thought Processes and Content (check all that apply)

___ loose associations
___ delusions
___ hallucinations
___ poor judgment
___ obsessions
___ preoccupations
___ ideas of reference
___ blocking
___ tangential thinking
___ circumstantiality
___ flight of ideas
___ depersonalization
___ distortions of body

9. Patient Insight Concerning Presence of Mental Problems

1	**2**	**3**	**4**	**5**
none	very little	average	some	a great deal

10. Emotional Appropriateness (check all that apply)

___ emotional response is too sad for content of the conversation
___ emotional response is in keeping with the content of the conversation
___ emotional response is too happy for the content of the conversation
___ patient is emotionally flat

11. Prevailing Mood (check all that apply)

___ happy
___ sad
___ worried
___ anxious
___ angry

12. Patient Anxiety during Interview

1	2	3	4	5
none	mild	moderate	considerable	extreme

13. Patient Depression during Interview

1	2	3	4	5
none	mild	moderate	considerable	extreme

14. Patient Activity Level during Interview

1	2	3	4	5
extremely underactive	somewhat underactive	average activity	somewhat overactive	extremely overactive

15. Patient Speech during Interview

1	2	3	4	5
extremely slow	somewhat slow	average	somewhat fast	extremely fast

16. Mannerisms and Posturing (check all that apply)

____ tics ____ tremors
____ unusual gait ____ unusual gestures

Appendix B

Patient Description Form

Patient number:________________________ Date:_______________

Below is a list of personality and symptomatic characteristics that may be used to describe the patient. Please use the following scale to rate the degree to which the patient possesses each of these characteristics. (**Please make sure to rate 0 only when you have insufficient information to make a rating.**)

1 = Not at all 2 = Slight 3 = Moderate 4 = High 5 = Very high
0 = *Insufficient* information

1. anxious	1	2	3	4	5	0
2. problems with authority figures	1	2	3	4	5	0
3. has insight into own problems	1	2	3	4	5	0
4. fears losing control	1	2	3	4	5	0
5. extroverted	1	2	3	4	5	0
6. uses repression	1	2	3	4	5	0
7. submissive	1	2	3	4	5	0
8. difficulty concentrating	1	2	3	4	5	0
9. rigid	1	2	3	4	5	0
10. overly compliant	1	2	3	4	5	0
11. whiny	1	2	3	4	5	0
12. feels overwhelmed	1	2	3	4	5	0
13. manipulative	1	2	3	4	5	0
14. difficulty trusting others	1	2	3	4	5	0
15. insensitive to others	1	2	3	4	5	0
16. stereotypic masculine behavior	1	2	3	4	5	0
17. harbors grudges	1	2	3	4	5	0
18. evasive	1	2	3	4	5	0
19. disoriented	1	2	3	4	5	0
20. energetic	1	2	3	4	5	0
21. lonely	1	2	3	4	5	0
22. family lacks love	1	2	3	4	5	0
23. worrier	1	2	3	4	5	0
24. narcissistic	1	2	3	4	5	0
25. tearful	1	2	3	4	5	0
26. provocative	1	2	3	4	5	0
27. moralistic	1	2	3	4	5	0
28. socially awkward	1	2	3	4	5	0
29. hostile	1	2	3	4	5	0
30. overcontrolled	1	2	3	4	5	0
31. resistant to interpretations	1	2	3	4	5	0
32. antisocial behavior	1	2	3	4	5	0

33. sarcastic	1	2	3	4	5	0
34. rejects traditional gender role	1	2	3	4	5	0
35. feels gets raw deal from life	1	2	3	4	5	0
36. acute psychological turmoil	1	2	3	4	5	0
37. does not complete projects	1	2	3	4	5	0
38. uncomfortable with opposite sex	1	2	3	4	5	0
39. preoccupied with health problems	1	2	3	4	5	0
40. work-oriented	1	2	3	4	5	0
41. resents family members	1	2	3	4	5	0
42. demanding of attention	1	2	3	4	5	0
43. passive	1	2	3	4	5	0
44. self-punishing	1	2	3	4	5	0
45. needs to achieve	1	2	3	4	5	0
46. needs to be with others	1	2	3	4	5	0
47. irritable	1	2	3	4	5	0
48. self-defeating	1	2	3	4	5	0
49. delusional thinking	1	2	3	4	5	0
50. self-reliant	1	2	3	4	5	0
51. aggressive	1	2	3	4	5	0
52. competitive	1	2	3	4	5	0
53. suspicious	1	2	3	4	5	0
54. compulsive	1	2	3	4	5	0
55. dependable	1	2	3	4	5	0
56. multiple somatic complaints	1	2	3	4	5	0
57. complains of lack of time	1	2	3	4	5	0
58. poor work performance	1	2	3	4	5	0
59. insecure	1	2	3	4	5	0
60. discusses problems openly	1	2	3	4	5	0
61. sexually adjusted	1	2	3	4	5	0
62. exaggerated need for affection	1	2	3	4	5	0
63. resentful	1	2	3	4	5	0
64. uses denial	1	2	3	4	5	0
65. hypochondriacal	1	2	3	4	5	0
66. communicates effectively	1	2	3	4	5	0
67. has many nightmares	1	2	3	4	5	0
68. stormy interpersonal relationships	1	2	3	4	5	0
69. feigns remorse when in trouble	1	2	3	4	5	0
70. stereotypic masculine interests	1	2	3	4	5	0
71. guarded	1	2	3	4	5	0
72. feels inferior	1	2	3	4	5	0
73. low frustration tolerance	1	2	3	4	5	0
74. psychotic symptoms	1	2	3	4	5	0
75. fired from past jobs	1	2	3	4	5	0
76. needs attention	1	2	3	4	5	0
77. acts out	1	2	3	4	5	0

78. histrionic	1	2	3	4	5	0
79. self-indulgent	1	2	3	4	5	0
80. depressed	1	2	3	4	5	0
81. grandiose	1	2	3	4	5	0
82. cynical	1	2	3	4	5	0
83. sociopathic	1	2	3	4	5	0
84. agitated	1	2	3	4	5	0
85. marital problems	1	2	3	4	5	0
86. absence of deep emotions	1	2	3	4	5	0
87. uncomfortable dealing with emotions	1	2	3	4	5	0
88. sad	1	2	3	4	5	0
89. self-degrading	1	2	3	4	5	0
90. unable to express negative feelings	1	2	3	4	5	0
91. concrete in thinking	1	2	3	4	5	0
92. unable to see own limitations	1	2	3	4	5	0
93. power-oriented	1	2	3	4	5	0
94. grouchy	1	2	3	4	5	0
95. overbearing in relationships	1	2	3	4	5	0
96. uncertain about career	1	2	3	4	5	0
97. likable	1	2	3	4	5	0
98. procrastinator	1	2	3	4	5	0
99. negative feelings toward opposite sex	1	2	3	4	5	0
100. defensive	1	2	3	4	5	0
101. empathetic	1	2	3	4	5	0
102. perfectionistic	1	2	3	4	5	0
103. judgmental	1	2	3	4	5	0
104. copes well with stress	1	2	3	4	5	0
105. moody	1	2	3	4	5	0
106. selfish	1	2	3	4	5	0
107. gives up easily	1	2	3	4	5	0
108. physical symptoms in response to stress	1	2	3	4	5	0
109. blames family for difficulties	1	2	3	4	5	0
110. bored	1	2	3	4	5	0
111. idealistic	1	2	3	4	5	0
112. difficulty establishing therapeutic rapport	1	2	3	4	5	0
113. daydreams	1	2	3	4	5	0
114. concerned about status	1	2	3	4	5	0
115. creates good first impression	1	2	3	4	5	0
116. complains of sleep disturbance	1	2	3	4	5	0
117. has temper tantrums	1	2	3	4	5	0
118. holds grudges	1	2	3	4	5	0
119. overreactive	1	2	3	4	5	0
120. high aspirations	1	2	3	4	5	0
121. feels hopeless	1	2	3	4	5	0
122. keeps others at a distance	1	2	3	4	5	0

123. argumentative	1	2	3	4	5	0
124. paranoid features	1	2	3	4	5	0
125. restless	1	2	3	4	5	0
126. pessimistic	1	2	3	4	5	0
127. feels like a failure	1	2	3	4	5	0
128. hallucinations	1	2	3	4	5	0
129. restricted affect	1	2	3	4	5	0
130. impatient	1	2	3	4	5	0
131. assertive	1	2	3	4	5	0
132. modest	1	2	3	4	5	0
133. self-doubting	1	2	3	4	5	0
134. deceptive	1	2	3	4	5	0
135. feels that life is a strain	1	2	3	4	5	0
136. physically abusive	1	2	3	4	5	0
137. feels rejected	1	2	3	4	5	0
138. does not get along with coworkers	1	2	3	4	5	0
139. uses projection	1	2	3	4	5	0
140. complains of fatigue	1	2	3	4	5	0
141. uses rationalization	1	2	3	4	5	0
142. critical of others	1	2	3	4	5	0
143. egocentric	1	2	3	4	5	0
144. overevaluates own worth	1	2	3	4	5	0
145. optimistic	1	2	3	4	5	0
146. psychologically immature	1	2	3	4	5	0
147. poor judgment	1	2	3	4	5	0
148. low sex drive	1	2	3	4	5	0
149. feels mistreated	1	2	3	4	5	0
150. overly sensitive to criticism	1	2	3	4	5	0
151. sentimental	1	2	3	4	5	0
152. sexual preoccupation	1	2	3	4	5	0
153. accelerated speech	1	2	3	4	5	0
154. concerns about homosexuality	1	2	3	4	5	0
155. many specific fears	1	2	3	4	5	0
156. passive in relationships	1	2	3	4	5	0
157. negative attitudes toward therapy	1	2	3	4	5	0
158. guilt-prone	1	2	3	4	5	0
159. nervous	1	2	3	4	5	0
160. obsessive	1	2	3	4	5	0
161. shy	1	2	3	4	5	0
162. uses intellectualization	1	2	3	4	5	0
163. has many interests	1	2	3	4	5	0
164. difficulty making decisions	1	2	3	4	5	0
165. indirect expression of hostility	1	2	3	4	5	0
166. poor reality testing	1	2	3	4	5	0
167. angry	1	2	3	4	5	0

168. eccentric	1	2	3	4	5	0
169. emotional lability	1	2	3	4	5	0
170. dislikes change	1	2	3	4	5	0
171. believes cannot be helped	1	2	3	4	5	0
172. reliable informant	1	2	3	4	5	0
173. ignores problems	1	2	3	4	5	0
174. ruminates	1	2	3	4	5	0
175. excitable	1	2	3	4	5	0
176. conforming	1	2	3	4	5	0
177. ineffective at dealing with problems	1	2	3	4	5	0
178. introverted	1	2	3	4	5	0
179. superficial relationships	1	2	3	4	5	0
180. impulsive	1	2	3	4	5	0
181. stereotypic feminine behavior	1	2	3	4	5	0
182. resentful	1	2	3	4	5	0
183. stubborn	1	2	3	4	5	0
184. hostile toward therapist	1	2	3	4	5	0
185. difficult to motivate	1	2	3	4	5	0
186. suicidal ideations	1	2	3	4	5	0
187. familial discord	1	2	3	4	5	0
188. dogmatic	1	2	3	4	5	0

Note: Due to to an oversight, Item 63 (resentful) was repeated as Item 182. Also, the contents of Item 17 (harbors grudges) and Item 118 (holds grudges) are virtually identical.

Appendix C

Items in Patient Description Form Scales

Angry Resentment

29	hostile
35	feels gets raw deal from life
63	resentful
94	grouchy
118	holds grudges
149	feels mistreated
167	angry

Critical/Argumentative

33	sarcastic
47	irritable
82	cynical
123	argumentative
142	critical of others
183	stubborn

Narcissistic

13	manipulative
15	insensitive to others
24	narcissistic
79	self-indulgent
81	grandiose
106	selfish
143	egocentric
144	overevaluates own worth

Defensive

9	rigid
18	evasive
64	uses denial
71	guarded
91	concrete in thinking
92	unable to see own limitations
100	defensive
146	psychologically immature

Histrionic

11	whiny
42	demanding of attention
62	exaggerated need for affection
76	needs attention
78	histrionic
119	overreactive
169	emotional lability
175	excitable

Aggressive

51	aggressive
95	overbearing in relationships
117	has temper tantrums
136	physically abusive

Insecure

59	insecure
72	feels inferior
89	self-degrading
127	feels like a failure
133	self-doubting
137	feels rejected
158	guilt-prone

Anxious

1	anxious
8	difficulty concentrating
12	feels overwhelmed
23	worrier
155	many specific fears
159	nervous

Pessimistic

126	pessimistic
171	believes cannot be helped

Depressed

25	tearful
80	depressed
88	sad
116	complains of sleep disturbance
121	feels hopeless
186	suicidal ideation

Achievement-Oriented

20	energetic
40	work-oriented
45	needs to achieve
50	self-reliant
52	competitive
114	concerned about status
120	high aspirations
163	has many interests

Passive-Submissive

7	submissive
10	overly compliant
43	passive
156	passive in relationships

Introverted

28	socially awkward
161	shy
178	introverted

Emotionally Controlled

30	overcontrolled
86	absence of deep emotions
87	uncomfortable dealing with emotions
90	unable to express negative feelings
129	restricted affect

Antisocial

32	antisocial behavior
69	feigns remorse when in trouble
77	acts out
83	sociopathic
147	poor judgment
180	impulsive

Negative Treatment Attitudes

31	resistant to interpretations
112	difficulty establishing therapeutic rapport
157	negative attitude toward therapy
173	ignores problems
184	hostile toward therapist
185	difficult to motivate

Somatic Symptoms

39	preoccupied with health problems
56	multiple somatic problems
65	hypochondriacal
108	physical symptoms in response to stress
140	complains of fatigue

Psychotic Symptoms

19	disoriented
49	delusional thinking
74	psychotic symptoms
128	hallucinations
166	poor reality testing

Family Problems

22	family lacks love
41	resents family members
109	blames family for difficulties
187	familial discord

Obsessive-Compulsive

54	compulsive
102	perfectionistic
160	obsessive
164	difficulty making decisions
170	dislikes change
174	ruminates

Stereotypic Masculine Interests

16	stereotypic masculine behavior
70	stereotypic masculine interests

Procrastinates

37	does not complete projects
57	complains of lack of time
98	procrastinator

Suspicious

14	difficulty trusting others
53	suspicious
124	paranoid features

Agitated

84	agitated
125	restless
153	accelerated speech

Work Problems

58	poor work performance
75	fired from past jobs
138	does not get along with coworkers

Appendix D

Correlates for MMPI-2 Clinical Scales

Extra-test Characteristics	Clinical Scales																			
	1 (Hs)		2 (D)		3 (Hy)		4 (Pd)		5 (mf)		6 (Pa)		7 (PE)		8 (Sc)		9 (Ma)		0 (Si)	
	Men	Women	Men	Women	Men	Women	Men	Women	Men	Women	Men	Women	Men	Women	Men	Women	Men	Women	Men	Women
Intake Information																				
Axis I Anxiety Disorder	—	—	.17	—	—	—	—	—	—	—	—	—	—	—	—	—	—	—	—	—
Axis I Depression or Dysthymia	.23	.18	.31	.20	.21	.17	—	.21	—	—	.18	.20	.23	.23	.25	.21	—	—	.19	.17
Axis I Substance Abuse or Dependence	—	—	—	—	—	—	—	—	—	—	—	—	—	—	—	—	—	.17	—	—
Axis II Antisocial Personality Disorder	—	—	—	—	—	—	—	—	—	.15	—	—	—	—	—	—	—	—	—	—
Currently on Antidepressant Medication	—	.21	—	—	—	.16	—	—	—	—	—	—	—	.15	—	.18	—	—	—	.21
Currently on Anxiolytic Medication	—	.16	—	—	—	.16	—	—	—	—	—	—	—	.16	—	.17	—	—	—	.16
Ever Arrested	—	—	—	—	—	—	—	—	-.19	.09	—	—	—	—	—	—	—	—	—	—
History of Being Physically Abused	—	.17	—	—	—	—	.16	.13	—	—	—	—	—	—	—	—	—	—	—	—
History of Being Sexually Abused	—	—	—	—	—	—	—	.16	—	—	—	.16	—	—	—	.20	—	—	—	—
History of Having Few or No Friends	—	—	—	.17	—	—	—	.17	—	—	.17	.14	—	—	.17	.15	—	—	—	.23
History of Outpatient Psychiatric Treatment	—	—	.22	—	—	—	.20	.15	—	—	—	—	.19	—	.18	—	—	—	—	—
History of Suicide Attempts	—	.15	—	.19	—	—	—	.21	—	—	—	.22	—	.19	—	.24	—	—	—	.18
Lifetime History of Alcohol Abuse	—	—	—	—	—	—	.09	.20	—	—	—	—	—	—	—	—	—	.16	—	—
Lifetime History of Cocaine Abuse	—	—	—	—	—	—	—	—	—	—	—	—	—	—	—	—	—	.20	—	—
Lifetime History of Heroin Abuse	—	—	—	—	—	—	—	—	—	—	—	—	—	—	—	—	—	.21	—	—
Lifetime History of Marijuana Abuse	—	—	—	—	—	—	—	—	—	—	—	—	—	—	—	—	.16	.18	—	—
Previous Psychiatric Hospitalizations	—	—	.19	—	—	—	.25	—	—	—	.20	.16	.20	—	.26	.21	—	.16	—	—
Mental Status																				
Aloof During Interview	—	—	—	—	—	—	—	—	—	—	—	—	—	—	—	—	.17	—	—	—
Anxiety During Interview	—	—	—	—	—	.15	—	—	—	—	—	—	—	.18	—	.20	—	—	—	—
Circumstantial Speech	—	—	—	—	—	—	—	—	—	—	—	—	—	—	—	—	.18	—	—	—
Depression During Interview	.24	.27	.29	.30	.27	.27	.19	.21	—	—	.26	.24	.30	.30	.27	.29	—	—	.25	.13
Prevailing Mood Angry	—	—	—	—	—	—	—	—	—	—	.16	—	—	—	—	—	—	—	—	—
Prevailing Mood Anxious	—	—	—	—	—	—	—	—	—	—	—	—	.20	—	—	—	—	—	—	—
Prevailing Mood Happy	—	—	—	—	—	—	—	—	—	—	-.23	—	-.21	—	-.16	—	—	—	-.16	—
Prevailing Mood Sad	.27	.20	.25	.27	.23	.19	—	—	—	—	.29	.21	.24	.22	.21	.15	—	—	.18	.14
Speech During Interview	—	—	—	—	—	—	—	—	—	—	—	—	—	—	—	—	—	—	—	.15
SCL-90-R Scales																				
Anxiety	.52	.48	.57	.53	.47	.48	.41	.36	.17	—	.45	.47	.55	.58	.54	.56	—	—	.49	.41

Depression	.49	.45	.64	.62	.49	.44	.49	.44	.22	—	.48	.51	.61	.61	.59	.57	—	—	.48	.42
Hostility	.25	.27	.30	.40	.18	.26	.37	.33	—	—	.38	.43	.30	.46	.37	.44	.25	.17	—	—
Interpersonal Sensitivity	.41	.33	.53	.48	.33	.29	.43	.36	.24	—	.50	.49	.52	.54	.52	.50	—	—	.55	.50
Obsessive-Compulsive	.47	.48	.60	.55	.45	.44	.43	.32	.18	—	.43	.44	.58	.58	.59	.55	—	—	.47	.43
Paranoid Ideation	.32	.27	.38	.40	.23	.23	.41	.35	—	—	.53	.49	.37	.41	.48	.46	.24	.19	.38	.36
Phobic Anxiety	.41	.43	.41	.41	.34	.35	.31	.25	—	—	.34	.38	.41	.47	.44	.43	—	—	.43	.45
Psychoticism	.48	.38	.54	.46	.41	.34	.46	.37	.24	—	.52	.49	.53	.53	.58	.52	.16	.14	.41	.42
Somatization	.65	.65	.49	.51	.57	.58	.33	.26	—	—	.37	.37	.43	.52	.48	.51	—	—	.37	.34
Initial SCL-90 Analogue																				
Anxiety	.23	—	.37	—	.24	.18	.22	—	—	—	.24	—	.30	.16	.26	.19	—	—	—	—
Depression	.30	.19	.44	.23	.33	.23	.26	.18	—	—	.26	.17	.39	.23	.32	.24	—	—	—	—
Hostility	—	—	—	—	—	—	—	—	—	—	.19	—	—	—	—	—	—	.16	—	—
Interpersonal Sensitivity	—	—	.22	—	—	.17	.27	—	—	—	.20	—	.25	.21	—	.25	—	—	—	—
Somatization	.48	.28	.34	.17	.41	.25	—	—	—	—	—	—	.24	—	—	.16	—	—	—	—
Patient Description Form Scales																				
Achievement-Oriented	-.23	-.26	-.24	-.19	—	—	—	—	—	—	-.21	—	-.25	—	-.21	-.19	—	—	—	—
Aggressive	—	—	—	—	—	—	—	—	—	—	—	—	—	—	—	—	.22	.19	—	—
Agitated	—	—	.20	—	—	—	—	—	—	—	—	—	—	—	—	—	—	—	—	—
Angry Resentment	—	—	—	—	.20	—	—	.20	—	—	.22	—	—	—	—	—	—	.18	—	—
Antisocial	—	—	—	—	—	—	—	—	—	—	—	—	—	—	—	—	—	.22	—	—
Anxious	.32	.18	.42	.20	.28	.22	.27	.17	—	—	.27	—	.43	.22	.41	.23	—	—	—	—
Critical/Argumentative	—	—	—	—	—	—	—	.20	—	—	—	—	—	—	—	—	—	.18	—	—
Defensive	—	—	—	—	—	—	—	—	—	—	—	—	—	—	—	—	—	.18	—	—
Depressed	.40	.25	.53	.32	.38	.31	.31	.20	—	—	.35	.23	.49	.31	.48	.35	—	—	—	—
Family Problems	—	—	—	—	—	—	.21	.17	—	—	.22	—	—	—	.22	—	—	—	—	—
Histrionic	—	—	—	—	—	—	—	.23	—	—	—	—	—	—	—	.21	—	—	—	—
Insecure	—	—	.36	.18	—	—	.29	.17	—	—	.30	—	.32	.22	.29	.22	—	—	—	—
Introverted	—	—	.22	.17	—	—	—	—	—	—	—	—	—	.17	—	—	—	—	—	—
Narcissistic	—	—	—	—	—	—	—	—	—	—	—	—	—	—	—	—	.13	.25	—	—
Negative Treatment Attitudes	—	—	—	—	—	—	—	—	—	—	—	—	—	—	—	—	—	.18	—	—
Obsessive-Compulsive	—	—	.25	—	—	—	—	—	—	—	—	—	.21	—	.23	—	—	—	—	—
Pessimistic	.31	.18	.37	.17	.24	—	.20	.16	—	—	.21	—	.20	.17	.26	.23	—	—	—	—
Psychotic Symptoms	—	—	—	—	—	—	—	—	—	—	—	—	—	—	—	—	.20	.11	—	—
Somatic Symptoms	.53	.30	.37	.23	.46	.25	—	—	—	—	—	—	.29	.17	.28	.21	—	—	—	—
Stereotypic Masculine Interests	—	—	-.20	—	—	—	—	—	-.33	.16	—	—	-.19	—	—	—	—	—	—	—
Suspicious	—	—	—	—	—	—	—	.20	—	—	—	—	—	—	—	.17	—	—	—	—
Work Problems	—	—	—	—	—	—	.30	—	—	—	—	—	—	—	—	.22	—	.22	—	—
Patient Description Form Items																				
Agitated	—	—	—	—	—	—	.30	—	—	—	—	—	—	—	—	—	—	—	—	—

Correlates for MMPI-2 Clinical Scales (*continued*)

Extra-test Characteristics	Clinical Scales																			
	1 (Hs)		2 (D)		3 (Hy)		4 (Pd)		5 (mf)		6 (Pa)		7 (PE)		8 (Sc)		9 (Ma)		0 (Si)	
	Men	Women	Men	Women	Men	Women	Men	Women	Men	Women	Men	Women	Men	Women	Men	Women	Men	Women	Men	Women
Antisocial Behavior	—	—	—	—	—	—	—	—	—	—	—	—	—	—	—	—	.19	.23	—	—
Anxious	—	—	.43	—	—	—	—	—	—	—	.28	—	.44	.18	.39	.18	—	—	—	—
Complains of Fatigue	.38	.28	.37	.25	.32	.22	—	—	—	—	—	—	—	—	—	—	—	—	—	—
Complains of Sleep Disturbance	.39	.25	.43	.28	.33	.29	—	—	—	—	.26	—	.36	.22	.37	.29	—	—	—	—
Concerns About Homosexuality	—	—	—	—	—	—	—	—	.25	—	—	—	—	—	—	—	—	—	—	—
Copes Well with Stress	—	-.22	-.27	-.21	—	—	—	—	—	—	—	—	-.24	-.26	-.27	-.27	—	—	—	—
Cynical	—	—	—	—	—	—	—	.20	—	—	—	—	—	—	—	—	—	—	—	—
Depressed	.36	.27	.50	.28	.37	.33	.27	.19	—	—	.27	.19	.47	.29	.45	.30	—	—	—	—
Difficult to Motivate	—	—	—	—	—	—	—	—	—	—	—	—	—	—	—	—	—	.21	—	—
Difficulty Concentrating	—	—	—	—	.20	.20	—	—	—	—	—	—	.31	.20	—	—	—	—	—	—
Difficulty Trusting Others	—	—	—	—	—	—	—	.20	—	—	—	—	—	—	—	—	—	—	—	—
Does Not Get Along with Coworkers	—	—	—	—	—	—	—	—	—	—	—	—	—	—	—	—	.24	.22	—	—
Egocentric	—	—	—	—	—	—	—	—	—	—	—	—	—	—	—	—	—	.21	—	—
Energetic	-.29	-.26	-.30	-.23	—	—	—	—	—	—	—	-.17	—	—	—	—	—	—	—	—
Evasive	—	—	—	—	—	—	—	—	—	—	—	—	—	—	—	—	—	.21	—	—
Exaggerated Need for Affection	—	—	—	—	—	—	—	—	.22	—	—	—	—	—	—	—	—	—	—	—
Family Lacks Love	—	—	—	—	—	—	.27	.21	—	—	—	—	—	—	—	—	—	—	—	—
Feels Gets Raw Deal From Life	—	—	—	—	—	—	—	.20	—	—	—	—	—	—	—	.24	—	—	—	—
Feels Hopeless	.32	.20	.46	.28	.28	.22	.29	.19	—	—	.32	.16	.37	.28	.40	.28	—	—	—	—
Feels Inferior	—	—	—	—	—	—	.26	.17	—	—	.27	—	.21	.23	—	—	—	—	—	—
Feels Like a Failure	—	—	—	—	—	—	.29	.17	—	—	.28	—	—	—	.32	.20	—	—	—	—
Feels Overwhelmed	—	—	—	—	.27	.21	—	—	—	—	—	—	.31	.19	.34	.18	—	—	—	—
Feels Rejected	—	—	—	—	—	—	.26	.20	—	—	.28	—	—	—	—	—	—	—	—	—
Feels That Life is a Strain	—	—	.42	.22	—	—	.22	.21	—	—	.30	—	.30	.22	.31	.27	—	—	—	—
Grandiose	—	—	—	—	—	—	—	—	—	—	—	—	—	—	—	—	—	.19	—	—
Has Many Interests	—	-.26	—	—	—	—	—	—	—	—	—	—	—	—	—	—	—	—	—	—
Has Temper Tantrums	—	—	—	—	—	—	—	—	—	—	—	—	—	—	—	—	.21	—	—	—
High Aspirations	—	-.24	—	—	—	—	—	—	—	—	—	—	—	—	—	—	—	—	—	—
Hypochondriacal	.38	.20	—	—	.35	.18	—	—	—	—	—	—	—	—	—	—	—	—	—	—
Likable	—	—	—	—	—	—	—	—	—	—	—	—	—	—	—	—	—	-.21	—	—
Lonely	—	—	—	—	—	—	—	.20	—	—	—	—	—	—	—	—	—	—	—	—
Low Sex Drive	.35	—	—	—	.29	—	—	—	—	—	—	—	—	—	—	—	—	—	—	—
Multiple Somatic Complaints	.49	.26	—	—	.43	.23	—	—	—	—	—	—	—	—	—	—	—	—	—	—

Descriptor																				
Narcissistic	—	—	—	—	—	—	—	—	—	—	—	—	—	—	—	—	—	.24	—	—
Nervous	—	—	.39	—	—	—	—	—	—	—	—	—	.35	.17	—	—	—	—	—	—
Optimistic	—	—	—	—	—	—	—	—	—	—	—	—	-.33	—	—	—	—	—	—	—
Overevaluates Own Worth	—	—	—	—	—	—	—	—	—	—	—	—	—	—	—	—	.19	.22	—	—
Overly Sensitive to Criticism	—	—	—	—	—	—	—	—	—	—	—	—	—	.23	—	.25	—	—	—	—
Overreactive	—	—	—	—	—	—	—	.23	—	—	—	—	—	—	—	—	—	—	—	—
Pessimistic	.34	.20	.41	.18	—	—	.25	.17	—	—	.28	—	—	—	.32	.22	—	—	—	—
Physical Symptoms in Response to Stress	.48	.25	—	—	.41	.20	—	—	—	—	—	—	—	—	—	—	—	—	—	—
Poor Reality Testing	—	—	—	—	—	—	—	—	—	—	—	—	—	—	—	—	.26	—	—	—
Preoccupied with Health Problems	.52	.30	.38	.23	.42	.25	—	—	—	—	—	—	—	—	.32	.19	—	—	—	—
Rejects Traditional Gender Role	—	—	—	—	—	—	—	—	.31	—	—	—	—	—	—	—	—	—	—	—
Restless	—	—	—	—	—	—	—	—	—	—	—	—	—	—	—	—	.19	—	—	—
Sad	—	—	.38	.23	.28	.26	.27	.21	—	—	.27	.19	.35	.26	.36	.25	—	—	—	—
Sarcastic	—	—	—	—	—	—	—	.20	—	—	—	—	—	—	—	—	—	—	—	—
Self-Degrading	—	—	—	—	—	—	.35	—	—	—	—	—	.29	.25	.25	.23	—	—	—	—
Sociopathic	—	—	—	—	—	—	—	—	—	—	—	—	—	—	—	—	—	.20	—	—
Stereotypic Masculine Behavior	—	—	—	—	—	—	—	—	-.32	—	—	—	—	—	—	—	—	—	—	—
Stereotypic Masculine Interest	—	—	—	—	—	—	—	—	-.31	.19	—	—	—	—	—	—	—	—	—	—
Stormy Interpersonal Relationships	—	—	—	—	—	—	—	—	—	—	—	—	—	—	—	—	.23	—	—	—
Suicidal Ideations	—	—	.32	.24	—	—	.21	.20	—	—	.24	.24	.30	.26	.34	.31	—	—	—	—
Tearful	—	—	—	—	—	—	—	—	—	—	.26	.19	—	—	—	—	—	—	—	—
Worrier	—	—	—	—	—	—	—	—	—	—	—	—	.32	.21	—	—	—	—	—	—

Appendix E

Correlates for MMPI-2 Harris-Lingoes Subscales

Table E-1. Correlates for MMPI-2 Harris-Lingoes D Subscales

Extra-test Characteristics	Subjective Depression (D_1)		Psychomotor Retardation (D_2)		Physical Malfunctioning (D_3)		Mental Dullness (D_4)		Brooding (D_5)	
	Men	Women	Men	Women	Men	Women	Men	Women	Men	Women
Intake Information										
Alcohol Abuse in the Past Six Months	—	—	—	—	—	—	—	—	—	—
Axis I Anxiety Disorder	—	—	—	—	—	—	—	—	—	—
Axis I Depression or Dysthymia	.28	.24	—	—	.21	.19	.28	.19	.30	.29
Axis I Substance Abuse or Dependence	—	—	—	—	—	—	—	—	—	—
Axis II Antisocial Personality Disorder	—	—	—	—	—	—	—	—	—	—
Axis II Borderline Personality Disorder	—	—	—	—	—	—	—	—	—	—
Currently on Antidepressant Medication	—	—	—	—	—	.22	—	.15	—	.15
Currently on Anxiolytic Medication	—	—	—	—	—	.15	—	.16	—	.15
Ever Arrested	—	-.16	—	—	—	—	—	—	—	—
History of Being Physically Abused	—	—	—	—	—	—	.17	.16	—	—
History of Being Physically Abusive	—	—	—	—	—	—	—	—	—	—
History of Being Sexually Abused	—	—	—	—	—	—	—	.17	—	—
History of Committing Domestic Violence	—	—	—	—	—	—	—	—	—	—
History of Domestic Violence Conviction	—	—	—	—	—	—	—	—	—	—
History of Having Few or No Friends	—	.20	—	—	.17	—	—	.17	.16	.20
History of Misdemeanor Conviction(s)	—	—	—	—	—	—	—	—	—	—
History of Outpatient Psychiatric Treatment	.18	—	—	—	—	—	.20	—	—	—
History of Suicide Attempts	—	.22	—	—	—	.19	—	.19	.16	.23
Lifetime History of Alcohol Abuse	—	—	—	—	—	—	—	—	—	—
Lifetime History of Cocaine Abuse	—	—	—	—	—	—	—	—	—	—
Lifetime History of Heroin Abuse	—	—	—	—	—	—	—	—	—	—
Lifetime History of Marijuana Abuse	—	—	—	—	—	—	—	—	—	—
Marijuana Abuse in the Past Six Months	—	—	—	—	—	—	—	—	—	—
Number of Arrests	—	—	—	—	—	—	—	—	—	—
Previous Psychiatric Hospitalizations	.18	—	.17	—	—	—	.19	.15	—	—
Mental Status										
Aggressive During Interview	—	—	—	—	—	—	—	—	—	—
Anxiety During Interview	—	.15	—	—	—	—	—	.15	—	.17
Circumstantial Speech	—	—	—	—	—	—	—	—	—	—
Depression During Interview	.29	.28	.20	—	.18	.25	.30	.26	.32	.30

Evasive During Interview	—	—	—	—	—	—	—	—	—	—
Obsessions	—	—	—	—	—	—	—	—	—	—
Prevailing Mood Angry	—	—	—	—	—	—	—	—	—	—
Prevailing Mood Anxious	—	—	—	—	—	—	—	—	—	—
Prevailing Mood Happy	-.17	—	—	—	—	—	-.17	—	-.16	—
Prevailing Mood Sad	.27	.28	—	—	.19	.22	.24	.22	.29	.27
Tics	—	—	—	—	—	—	—	—	—	—
Unusual Gait	—	—	—	—	—	—	—	—	—	—
SCL-90-R Scales										
Anxiety	.57	.56	.29	.21	.51	.49	.57	.54	.54	.51
Depression	.69	.66	.34	.30	.51	.48	.63	.62	.66	.65
Hostility	.46	.46	—	—	.34	.37	.44	.46	.45	.46
Interpersonal Sensitivity	.57	.55	.27	.23	.43	.39	.51	.54	.58	.56
Obsessive-Compulsive	.62	.56	.32	.27	.48	.47	.62	.59	.54	.53
Paranoid Ideation	.46	.44	—	—	.37	.34	.43	.45	.45	.46
Phobic Anxiety	.42	.43	.28	.20	.39	.44	.41	.44	.35	.42
Psychoticism	.56	.50	.26	.19	.46	.45	.54	.54	.56	.53
Somatization	.47	.49	.21	.19	.55	.57	.50	.50	.41	.45
Initial SCL-90 Analogue										
Anxiety	.35	—	.26	—	.21	—	.25	—	.28	—
Depression	.46	.24	.26	—	.26	—	.37	.21	.41	.18
Hostility	—	—	—	—	—	—	—	—	—	—
Interpersonal Sensitivity	.25	.18	—	—	—	—	—	.21	.26	.16
Obsessive-Compulsive	—	—	—	—	—	—	—	—	—	—
Paranoid Ideation	—	—	—	—	—	—	—	—	—	—
Phobic Anxiety	—	—	—	—	—	—	—	—	—	—
Psychoticism	—	—	—	-.16	—	—	—	—	—	—
Somatization	.30	—	.22	—	.33	.21	.29	—	.20	—
Patient Description Form Scales										
Achievement-Oriented	-.25	-.18	—	-.19	—	-.25	-.22	—	-.23	-.21
Aggressive	—	—	—	—	—	—	—	—	—	—
Agitated	.19	—	—	—	—	—	—	.17	—	—
Angry Resentment	.22	—	—	—	.26	—	—	—	.23	—
Antisocial	—	—	—	—	—	—	—	—	—	—
Anxious	.43	.22	.21	—	.30	—	.37	.23	.38	—
Critical/Argumentative	—	—	—	—	—	—	—	—	—	—
Depressed	.58	.33	.29	—	.42	.23	.51	.30	.53	.29
Family Problems	.21	—	—	—	—	—	—	—	—	—
Histrionic	.20	—	—	—	.21	—	—	.19	.22	—

Table E-1. Correlates for MMPI-2 Harris-Lingoes D Subscales *(continued)*

Extra-test Characteristics	Subjective Depression (D_1)		Psychomotor Retardation (D_2)		Physical Malfunctioning (D_3)		Mental Dullness (D_4)		Brooding (D_5)	
	Men	Women	Men	Women	Men	Women	Men	Women	Men	Women
Insecure	.37	.23	.20	—	.23	—	.31	.23	.36	.18
Introverted	.19	.18	—	—	—	—	.17	.17	—	—
Narcissistic	—	—	—	—	—	—	—	—	—	—
Obsessive-Compulsive	.26	—	—	—	—	—	.23	.16	.22	—
Passive-Submissive	—	—	—	—	—	—	—	—	—	—
Pessimistic	.36	.22	—	—	.28	—	.29	.23	.31	—
Somatic Symptoms	.36	.22	.29	—	.38	.22	.36	.21	.21	—
Stereotypic Masculine Interests	—	—	—	—	—	—	—	—	—	—
Suspicious	—	—	—	—	—	—	—	.17	—	—
Patient Description Form Items										
Acts Out	—	—	—	—	—	—	—	—	—	—
Acute Psychological Turmoil	—	—	—	—	—	—	—	—	—	—
Aggressive	—	—	—	—	—	—	—	—	—	—
Angry	—	—	—	—	—	—	—	—	—	—
Antisocial Behavior	—	—	—	—	—	—	—	—	—	—
Anxious	.43	.16	—	—	—	—	.36	.17	.38	—
Argumentative	—	—	—	—	—	—	—	—	—	—
Blames Family For Difficulties	—	—	—	—	—	—	—	—	—	—
Bored	—	—	—	—	—	—	—	—	—	—
Communicates Effectively	—	—	—	—	—	—	—	—	—	—
Competitive	—	—	—	-.17	—	—	—	—	—	—
Complains of Fatigue	.35	.26	.29	—	.30	.20	.33	.24	—	—
Complains of Sleep Disturbance	.50	.26	.25	—	.41	.24	.44	.24	.42	.19
Copes Well with Stress	-.28	-.27	—	—	—	—	-.23	-.28	-.30	-.24
Creates Good First Impression	—	—	—	—	—	—	—	—	—	-.20
Demanding of Attention	—	—	—	—	—	—	—	—	—	—
Depressed	.52	.31	.28	—	.35	.23	.47	.26	.48	.25
Difficult to Motivate	—	—	—	—	—	—	—	—	—	—
Difficulty Concentrating	—	—	—	—	.28	.19	—	—	—	—
Difficulty Making Decisions	—	—	—	—	—	—	—	—	—	—
Disoriented	—	—	—	—	—	—	—	—	—	—
Does Not Complete Projects	—	—	—	—	—	—	—	—	—	—
Does Not Get Along with Coworkers	—	—	—	—	—	—	—	—	—	—
Emotional Lability	—	—	—	—	—	—	—	—	—	—
Empathetic	—	—	—	—	—	—	—	—	—	—

Energetic	—	—	-.22	-.19	—	-.23	—	—	-.29	-.22
Excitable	—	—	—	—	—	—	—	—	—	—
Extroverted	—	—	—	—	—	—	—	—	—	—
Familial Discord	—	—	—	—	—	—	—	—	—	—
Family Lacks Love	—	—	—	—	—	—	—	—	—	—
Feels Gets Raw Deal From Life	—	—	—	—	—	—	.22	.28	—	—
Feels Hopeless	.49	.31	.29	—	.35	.17	.43	.27	.44	.28
Feels Inferior	—	—	—	—	—	—	—	—	—	—
Feels Like a Failure	.40	.25	—	—	—	—	.32	.25	.38	.20
Feels Overwhelmed	.39	.25	—	—	—	—	.35	.20	—	—
Feels Rejected	—	—	—	—	—	—	—	—	—	—
Feels That Life is a Strain	.42	.28	—	—	.31	—	.33	.24	.33	.22
Fired From Past Jobs	—	—	—	—	—	—	—	—	—	—
Gives Up Easily	—	—	—	—	—	—	—	—	—	—
Hallucinations	—	—	—	—	—	—	—	—	—	—
Has Insight Into Own Problems	—	—	—	—	—	—	—	—	—	—
Has Many Interests	—	—	—	—	—	-.23	—	—	—	—
Has Many Nightmares	—	—	—	—	—	—	—	—	—	—
Has Temper Tantrums	—	—	—	—	—	—	—	—	—	—
High Aspirations	—	—	—	—	—	-.22	—	—	—	—
Hypochondriacal	—	—	—	—	—	—	—	—	—	—
Impulsive	—	—	—	—	—	—	—	—	—	—
Insecure	—	—	—	—	—	—	—	—	—	—
Likable	—	—	—	—	—	—	—	—	—	—
Lonely	—	—	—	—	—	—	—	—	—	—
Low Frustration Tolerance	—	—	—	—	—	—	—	—	—	—
Low Sex Drive	—	—	—	—	—	.22	—	—	—	—
Moralistic	—	—	—	—	—	—	—	—	—	—
Multiple Somatic Complaints	—	—	.30	—	.40	.20	.34	.16	—	—
Narcissistic	—	—	—	—	—	—	—	—	—	—
Needs Attention	—	—	—	—	—	—	—	—	—	—
Needs to Achieve	—	—	—	—	—	—	—	—	—	—
Negative Feelings Toward Opposite Sex	—	—	—	—	—	—	—	—	—	—
Nervous	—	—	.23	—	—	—	—	—	—	—
Optimistic	—	—	—	—	—	—	—	—	—	—
Overly Sensitive to Criticism	—	—	—	—	—	—	—	.25	—	—
Passive	—	—	—	—	—	—	—	—	—	—
Passive in Relationships	—	—	—	—	—	—	—	—	—	—
Pessimistic	.39	.23	.24	—	.31	—	—	—	.36	—
Physical Symptoms in Response to Stress	—	—	.22	—	.34	.19	—	—	—	—
Physically Abusive	—	—	—	—	—	—	—	—	—	—
Poor Judgment	—	—	—	—	—	—	—	—	—	—

Table E-1. Correlates for MMPI-2 Harris-Lingoes D Subscales *(continued)*

Extra-test Characteristics	Subjective Depression (D_1)		Psychomotor Retardation (D_2)		Physical Malfunctioning (D_3)		Mental Dullness (D_4)		Brooding (D_5)	
	Men	Women	Men	Women	Men	Women	Men	Women	Men	Women
Preoccupied with Health Problems	—	—	.29	—	.42	.25	.37	.18	—	—
Reliable Informant	—	—	—	—	—	—	—	—	—	—
Resents Family Members	—	—	—	—	—	—	—	—	—	—
Ruminates	—	—	—	—	—	—	—	—	—	—
Sad	.43	.24	—	—	.36	—	.38	.18	.37	.21
Self-Defeating	—	—	—	—	—	—	—	—	—	—
Self-Degrading	—	—	—	—	—	—	.30	.27	.32	.23
Self-Doubting	—	—	—	—	—	—	—	—	—	—
Self-Indulgent	—	—	—	—	—	—	—	—	—	—
Self-Punishing	—	—	—	—	—	—	.26	.26	—	—
Sexually Adjusted	—	—	—	—	—	—	—	—	—	—
Shy	—	—	—	—	—	—	—	—	—	—
Sociopathic	—	—	—	—	—	—	—	—	—	—
Stormy Interpersonal Relationships	—	—	—	—	—	—	—	—	—	—
Suicidal Ideations	.40	.28	—	.18	—	—	.36	.30	.41	.27
Superficial Relationships	—	—	—	—	—	—	—	—	—	—
Tearful	—	—	—	—	—	—	—	—	—	—
Unable to See Own Limitations	—	—	—	—	—	—	—	—	—	—
Whiny	—	—	—	—	—	—	—	—	—	—
Work-Oriented	—	—	—	—	—	—	—	—	—	—
Worrier	—	—	—	—	—	—	—	—	.34	—

Table E-2. Correlates for MMPI-2 Harris-Lingoes Hy Subscales

Extra-test Characteristics	Need for Affection (Hy_2)		Lassitude-Malaise (Hy_3)		Somatic Complaints (Hy_4)	
	Men	Women	Men	Women	Men	Women
Intake Information						
Alcohol Abuse in the Past Six Months	—	—	—	—	—	—
Axis I Anxiety Disorder	—	—	—	—	—	—
Axis I Depression or Dysthymia	—	—	.29	.23	.24	.17
Axis I Substance Abuse or Dependence	—	—	—	—	—	—
Axis II Antisocial Personality Disorder	—	—	—	—	—	—
Axis II Borderline Personality Disorder	—	—	—	—	—	—
Currently on Antidepressant Medication	—	—	—	.17	—	—
Currently on Anxiolytic Medication	—	—	—	—	—	.15
Ever Arrested	—	—	—	—	—	—
History of Being Physically Abused	—	—	—	.15	—	.16
History of Being Physically Abusive	—	—	—	—	—	—
History of Being Sexually Abused	—	—	—	—	—	—
History of Committing Domestic Violence	—	—	—	—	—	—
History of Domestic Violence Conviction	—	—	—	—	—	—
History of Having Few or No Friends	—	—	—	.17	—	.18
History of Misdemeanor Conviction(s)	—	—	—	—	—	—
History of Outpatient Psychiatric Treatment	—	—	.21	—	—	—
History of Suicide Attempts	—	—	.20	.19	—	.19
Lifetime History of Alcohol Abuse	—	—	—	—	—	—
Lifetime History of Cocaine Abuse	—	—	—	—	—	—
Lifetime History of Heroin Abuse	—	—	—	—	—	—
Lifetime History of Marijuana Abuse	—	—	—	—	—	—
Marijuana Abuse in the Past Six Months	—	—	—	—	—	—
Number of Arrests	—	—	—	—	—	—
Previous Psychiatric Hospitalizations	—	—	.19	—	—	—
Mental Status						
Aggressive During Interview	—	—	—	—	—	—
Anxiety During Interview	—	—	—	—	—	—
Circumstantial Speech	—	—	—	—	—	—
Depression During Interview	—	—	.33	.32	.23	.24
Evasive During Interview	—	—	—	—	—	—
Obsessions	—	—	—	—	—	—
Prevailing Mood Angry	—	—	—	—	—	—
Prevailing Mood Anxious	—	—	—	—	—	—

Table E-2. Correlates for MMPI-2 Harris-Lingoes Hy Subscales *(continued)*

Extra-test Characteristics	Need for Affection (Hy_2)		Lassitude-Malaise (Hy_3)		Somatic Complaints (Hy_4)	
	Men	Women	Men	Women	Men	Women
Prevailing Mood Happy	—	—	-.20	—	-.16	—
Prevailing Mood Sad	—	—	.26	.25	.22	.21
Tics	.22	—	—	—	—	—
Unusual Gait	—	—	—	—	—	—
SCL-90-R Scales						
Anxiety	—	-.16	.59	.54	.58	.52
Depression	—	-.18	.67	.63	.51	.48
Hostility	-.19	-.18	.46	.44	.32	.32
Interpersonal Sensitivity	-.18	-.19	.55	.49	.47	.38
Obsessive-Compulsive	-.17	-.16	.59	.53	.55	.51
Paranoid Ideation	-.20	-.20	.46	.41	.37	.36
Phobic Anxiety	—	—	.43	.41	.44	.46
Psychoticism	-.18	-.17	.58	.47	.49	.45
Somatization	—	-.17	.52	.54	.68	.68
Initial SCL-90 Analogue						
Anxiety	—	—	.28	—	.28	—
Depression	—	—	.42	.22	.32	—
Hostility	—	—	—	—	—	—
Interpersonal Sensitivity	—	—	.21	.16	—	—
Obsessive-Compulsive	—	—	.21	—	—	—
Paranoid Ideation	—	—	—	—	—	—
Phobic Anxiety	—	—	—	—	—	—
Psychoticism	—	—	—	—	—	—
Somatization	—	—	.38	.16	.39	.23
Patient Description Form Scales						
Achievement-Oriented	—	—	-.24	—	—	-.21
Aggressive	—	—	—	—	—	—
Agitated	—	—	.24	—	.20	—
Angry Resentment	—	—	.25	—	—	—
Antisocial	—	—	—	—	—	—
Anxious	—	—	.42	.18	.36	.20
Critical/Argumentative	—	—	.21	—	—	—
Depressed	—	—	.55	.30	.38	.24

Family Problems	—	—	.20	—	—	—
Histrionic	—	—	.28	—	—	—
Insecure	—	—	.36	.17	—	—
Introverted	—	—	—	—	—	—
Narcissistic	—	—	—	—	—	—
Obsessive-Compulsive	—	—	.32	—	—	—
Passive-Submissive	—	—	—	—	—	—
Pessimistic	—	—	.34	.18	.21	.17
Somatic Symptoms	—	—	.42	.20	.44	.27
Stereotypic Masculine Interests	—	—	—	—	—	—
Suspicious	—	—	—	—	—	—
Patient Description Form Items						
Acts Out	—	—	—	—	—	—
Acute Psychological Turmoil	—	—	—	—	—	—
Aggressive	—	—	—	—	—	—
Angry	—	—	—	—	—	—
Antisocial Behavior	—	—	—	—	—	—
Anxious	—	—	.40	—	.33	.15
Argumentative	—	—	—	—	—	—
Blames Family For Difficulties	—	—	—	—	—	—
Bored	—	—	—	—	—	—
Communicates Effectively	—	—	—	—	—	—
Competitive	—	—	—	—	—	—
Complains of Fatigue	—	—	.36	.23	.32	.24
Complains of Sleep Disturbance	—	—	.49	.26	.37	.22
Copes Well with Stress	—	—	—	—	—	-.22
Creates Good First Impression	.23	—	—	—	—	—
Demanding of Attention	—	—	—	—	—	—
Depressed	—	—	.51	.29	.38	.22
Difficult to Motivate	—	—	—	—	—	—
Difficulty Concentrating	—	—	—	—	—	—
Difficulty Making Decisions	—	—	—	—	—	—
Disoriented	—	—	—	—	—	—
Does Not Complete Projects	—	—	—	—	—	—
Does Not Get Along with Coworkers	—	—	—	—	—	—
Emotional Lability	—	—	—	—	—	—
Empathetic	.17	.16	—	—	—	—
Energetic	—	—	—	—	-.30	-.21
Excitable	—	—	—	—	—	—
Extroverted	—	—	—	—	—	—
Familial Discord	—	—	—	—	—	—
Family Lacks Love	—	—	—	—	—	—

Table E-2. Correlates for MMPI-2 Harris-Lingoes Hy Subscales *(continued)*

Extra-test Characteristics	Need for Affection (Hy_2)		Lassitude-Malaise (Hy_3)		Somatic Complaints (Hy_4)	
	Men	Women	Men	Women	Men	Women
Feels Gets Raw Deal From Life	—	—	.30	.21	—	—
Feels Hopeless	—	—	.46	.28	.27	.21
Feels Inferior	—	—	—	—	—	—
Feels Like a Failure	—	—	—	—	—	—
Feels Overwhelmed	—	—	.39	.22	.34	—
Feels Rejected	—	—	—	—	—	—
Feels That Life is a Strain	—	—	.40	.24	.30	.19
Fired From Past Jobs	—	—	—	—	—	—
Gives Up Easily	—	—	—	—	—	—
Hallucinations	—	—	—	—	—	—
Has Insight Into Own Problems	—	—	—	—	—	—
Has Many Interests	—	—	—	—	—	-.26
Has Many Nightmares	—	—	—	—	—	—
Has Temper Tantrums	—	—	—	—	—	—
High Aspirations	—	—	—	—	—	—
Hypochondriacal	—	—	—	—	.35	.19
Impulsive	—	—	—	—	—	—
Insecure	—	—	—	—	—	—
Likable	—	—	—	—	—	—
Lonely	—	—	.30	.21	—	—
Low Frustration Tolerance	—	—	—	—	—	—
Low Sex Drive	—	—	—	—	—	—
Moralistic	—	.17	—	—	—	—
Multiple Somatic Complaints	—	—	.41	—	.40	.24
Narcissistic	—	—	—	—	—	—
Needs Attention	—	—	—	—	—	—
Needs to Achieve	—	—	—	—	—	—
Negative Feelings Toward Opposite Sex	—	—	—	—	—	—
Nervous	—	—	—	—	—	—
Optimistic	—	—	—	—	—	—
Overly Sensitive to Criticism	—	—	—	—	—	—
Passive	—	—	—	—	—	—
Passive in Relationships	—	—	—	—	—	—
Pessimistic	—	—	.38	.20	—	—
Physical Symptoms in Response to Stress	—	—	—	—	.38	.24
Physically Abusive	—	—	—	—	—	—
Poor Judgment	—	—	—	—	—	—

Preoccupied with Health Problems	—	—	.40	.21	.44	.28
Reliable Informant	—	—	—	—	—	—
Resents Family Members	—	—	—	—	—	—
Ruminates	—	—	—	—	—	—
Sad	—	—	.41	.24	—	—
Self-Defeating	—	—	—	—	—	—
Self-Degrading	—	—	—	—	—	—
Self-Doubting	—	—	—	—	—	—
Self-Indulgent	—	—	—	—	—	—
Self-Punishing	—	—	—	—	—	—
Sexually Adjusted	—	—	—	—	—	—
Shy	—	—	—	—	—	—
Sociopathic	—	—	—	—	—	—
Stormy Interpersonal Relationships	—	—	—	—	—	—
Suicidal Ideations	—	—	.36	.22	—	—
Superficial Relationships	—	—	—	—	—	—
Tearful	—	—	—	—	—	—
Unable to See Own Limitations	—	—	—	—	—	—
Whiny	—	—	—	—	—	—
Work-Oriented	—	—	—	—	—	—
Worrier	—	—	—	—	—	—

Table E-3. Correlates for MMPI-2 Harris-Lingoes Pd Subscales

Extra-test Characteristics	Familial Discord (Pd_1)		Authority Problems (Pd_2)		Social Alienation (Pd_4)		Self-Alienation (Pd_5)	
	Men	Women	Men	Women	Men	Women	Men	Women
Intake Information								
Alcohol Abuse in the Past Six Months	—	—	.21	.16	—	—	—	.18
Axis I Anxiety Disorder	—	—	—	—	—	—	—	—
Axis I Depression or Dysthymia	—	—	—	—	.17	.19	.22	.25
Axis I Substance Abuse or Dependence	—	—	.24	.16	—	—	—	—
Axis II Antisocial Personality Disorder	—	—	.18	.16	—	—	—	—
Axis II Borderline Personality Disorder	—	—	—	—	—	—	—	—
Currently on Antidepressant Medication	—	—	—	—	—	—	—	—
Currently on Anxiolytic Medication	—	—	—	—	—	—	—	—
Ever Arrested	—	—	.27	.20	—	—	—	—
History of Being Physically Abused	.22	.14	—	—	—	—	—	—
History of Being Physically Abusive	—	—	—	—	—	—	—	—
History of Being Sexually Abused	—	—	—	—	—	.18	—	—
History of Committing Domestic Violence	—	—	—	—	—	—	—	—
History of Domestic Violence Conviction	—	—	—	—	—	—	—	—
History of Having Few or No Friends	.22	.14	—	—	.17	.20	—	.19
History of Misdemeanor Conviction(s)	—	—	.19	.17	—	—	—	—
History of Outpatient Psychiatric Treatment	—	—	—	—	—	.15	—	.16
History of Suicide Attempts	.18	.24	—	—	—	.22	.17	.27
Lifetime History of Alcohol Abuse	—	—	.24	.21	—	—	—	.21
Lifetime History of Cocaine Abuse	—	—	—	.18	—	—	—	—
Lifetime History of Heroin Abuse	—	—	.25	.15	—	—	—	—
Lifetime History of Marijuana Abuse	—	—	.20	.21	—	—	—	—
Marijuana Abuse in the Past Six Months	—	—	.19	—	—	—	—	—
Number of Arrests	—	—	.19	.19	—	—	—	—
Previous Psychiatric Hospitalizations	—	—	—	—	—	—	.17	.18
Mental Status								
Aggressive During Interview	—	—	—	.17	—	—	—	—
Anxiety During Interview	—	—	—	—	—	—	—	.16
Circumstantial Speech	.17	—	—	—	—	—	—	—
Depression During Interview	—	—	—	—	.19	.17	.29	.27
Evasive During Interview	—	—	—	—	—	—	—	—
Obsessions	—	—	—	—	—	—	—	—
Prevailing Mood Angry	—	—	—	—	—	—	—	—
Prevailing Mood Anxious	—	—	-.18	—	—	—	—	—

Prevailing Mood Happy	—	—	—	—	—	—	-.17	—
Prevailing Mood Sad	.21	—	—	—	.24	.19	.23	.18
Tics	—	—	—	—	—	—	—	—
Unusual Gait	—	—	—	—	—	—	—	—
SCL-90-R Scales								
Anxiety	.32	.23	—	—	.41	.42	.50	.47
Depression	.34	.28	—	—	.53	.51	.61	.59
Hostility	.37	.29	—	—	.40	.43	.41	.46
Interpersonal Sensitivity	.35	.28	—	—	.54	.51	.49	.53
Obsessive-Compulsive	.29	.21	—	—	.46	.42	.51	.48
Paranoid Ideation	.35	.30	—	—	.55	.51	.41	.45
Phobic Anxiety	.19	.19	—	—	.26	.33	.35	.40
Psychoticism	.33	.27	—	—	.48	.47	.53	.49
Somatization	.22	.22	—	—	.33	.35	.38	.42
Initial SCL-90 Analogue								
Anxiety	—	—	—	—	—	—	.22	—
Depression	—	—	—	—	.26	—	.33	.19
Hostility	—	—	—	.16	—	—	—	—
Interpersonal Sensitivity	—	—	—	—	—	—	.18	.16
Obsessive-Compulsive	—	—	—	—	—	—	—	—
Paranoid Ideation	—	—	—	.16	—	—	—	—
Phobic Anxiety	—	—	—	—	—	—	—	—
Psychoticism	—	—	—	—	—	—	—	—
Somatization	—	—	—	—	—	—	.22	—
Patient Description Form Scales								
Achievement-Oriented	—	—	—	—	—	—	—	—
Aggressive	—	—	.29	—	—	—	—	—
Agitated	—	—	—	—	—	—	.20	—
Angry Resentment	—	—	—	—	—	—	—	—
Antisocial	—	—	.33	.21	—	—	—	—
Anxious	.24	—	—	—	—	—	.36	—
Critical/Argumentative	—	—	—	—	—	—	—	—
Depressed	.25	—	—	—	.33	—	.47	.26
Family Problems	.27	.22	—	—	.24	—	—	—
Histrionic	.22	.17	—	—	—	—	—	—
Insecure	.26	—	—	—	.29	—	.35	.22
Introverted	—	—	—	—	—	—	—	—
Narcissistic	—	—	—	—	—	—	—	—
Obsessive-Compulsive	.21	—	—	—	—	—	.23	—

Table E-3. Correlates for MMPI-2 Harris-Lingoes Pd Subscales *(continued)*

Extra-test Characteristics	Familial Discord (Pd_1)		Authority Problems (Pd_2)		Social Alienation (Pd_4)		Self-Alienation (Pd_5)	
	Men	Women	Men	Women	Men	Women	Men	Women
Passive-Submissive	—	—	—	—	—	—	—	—
Pessimistic	—	—	—	—	—	—	.30	.17
Somatic Symptoms	—	—	—	—	—	—	.27	—
Stereotypic Masculine Interests	—	—	—	—	—	—	—	—
Suspicious	—	—	—	.19	—	—	—	—
Patient Description Form Items								
Acts Out	—	—	.27	.22	—	—	—	—
Acute Psychological Turmoil	—	—	—	—	—	—	.29	.19
Aggressive	—	—	.28	—	—	—	—	—
Angry	.23	—	—	—	—	—	—	—
Antisocial Behavior	—	—	.29	.20	—	—	—	—
Anxious	—	—	—	—	—	—	—	—
Argumentative	—	.15	—	—	—	—	—	—
Blames Family For Difficulties	—	.18	—	—	—	—	—	—
Bored	—	—	—	—	—	—	—	—
Communicates Effectively	—	—	—	—	—	—	—	—
Competitive	—	—	—	—	—	—	—	—
Complains of Fatigue	—	—	—	—	—	—	—	—
Complains of Sleep Disturbance	—	—	—	—	—	—	.39	—
Copes Well with Stress	—	—	—	—	—	—	—	—
Creates Good First Impression	—	—	—	—	—	-.17	—	—
Demanding of Attention	—	.18	—	—	—	—	—	—
Depressed	.22	—	—	—	.34	.18	.44	.23
Difficult to Motivate	—	—	—	—	—	—	—	—
Difficulty Concentrating	—	—	—	—	—	—	—	—
Difficulty Making Decisions	—	—	—	—	—	—	—	—
Disoriented	—	—	—	—	—	—	—	—
Does Not Complete Projects	—	—	—	.19	—	—	—	—
Does Not Get Along with Coworkers	.30	—	—	—	.28	—	—	—
Emotional Lability	—	—	.21	—	—	—	—	—
Empathetic	—	—	—	—	—	—	—	—
Energetic	—	—	—	—	—	—	—	—
Excitable	—	—	—	—	—	—	—	—
Extroverted	—	—	—	—	-.26	—	—	—
Familial Discord	.20	.21	—	—	—	—	—	—
Family Lacks Love	.30	.22	—	—	.25	—	—	—

Feels Gets Raw Deal From Life	—	—	—	—	.23	.19	—	—
Feels Hopeless	—	—	—	—	.26	.16	.41	.22
Feels Inferior	—	—	—	—	—	—	—	—
Feels Like a Failure	—	—	—	—	.28	—	.37	.23
Feels Overwhelmed	—	—	—	—	—	—	.32	—
Feels Rejected	.25	—	—	—	.25	.16	—	—
Feels That Life is a Strain	—	—	—	—	.26	.15	.32	.19
Fired From Past Jobs	—	.21	—	—	—	—	—	—
Gives Up Easily	—	—	—	—	—	—	—	—
Hallucinations	—	—	—	.20	—	—	—	—
Has Insight Into Own Problems	—	—	—	—	—	—	—	—
Has Many Interests	—	—	—	—	—	-.20	—	—
Has Many Nightmares	—	—	—	.22	—	—	—	—
Has Temper Tantrums	—	—	.22	—	—	—	—	—
High Aspirations	—	—	—	—	—	—	—	—
Hypochondriacal	—	—	—	—	—	—	—	—
Impulsive	—	—	.22	.21	—	—	—	—
Insecure	—	—	—	—	—	—	—	—
Likable	—	—	—	—	—	—	—	—
Lonely	.24	—	—	—	—	—	—	—
Low Frustration Tolerance	—	—	—	.19	—	—	—	—
Low Sex Drive	—	—	—	—	—	—	—	—
Moralistic	—	—	—	—	—	—	—	—
Multiple Somatic Complaints	—	—	—	—	—	—	—	—
Narcissistic	—	—	—	—	—	—	—	—
Needs Attention	—	.17	—	—	—	—	—	—
Needs to Achieve	—	—	—	—	—	—	—	—
Negative Feelings Toward Opposite Sex	—	—	—	—	—	—	—	—
Nervous	—	—	—	—	—	—	—	—
Optimistic	—	—	—	—	—	—	—	—
Overly Sensitive to Criticism	—	—	—	—	—	—	—	—
Passive	—	—	—	—	—	—	—	—
Passive in Relationships	—	—	—	—	—	—	—	—
Pessimistic	—	—	—	—	—	—	—	—
Physical Symptoms in Response to Stress	—	—	—	—	—	—	.32	.20
Physically Abusive	—	—	.29	—	—	—	—	—
Poor Judgment	—	—	.22	.16	—	—	—	—
Preoccupied with Health Problems	—	—	—	—	—	—	—	—
Reliable Informant	—	—	—	—	—	—	—	—
Resents Family Members	.25	.19	—	—	.25	—	—	—
Ruminates	.24	—	—	—	—	—	—	—
Sad	—	—	—	—	.32	—	—	—

Table E-3. Correlates for MMPI-2 Harris-Lingoes Pd Subscales *(continued)*

Extra-test Characteristics	Familial Discord (Pd_1)		Authority Problems (Pd_2)		Social Alienation (Pd_4)		Self-Alienation (Pd_5)	
	Men	Women	Men	Women	Men	Women	Men	Women
Self-Defeating	—	—	—	.19	—	—	—	—
Self-Degrading	.31	—	—	—	—	—	.34	.24
Self-Doubting	—	—	—	—	—	—	.32	.21
Self-Indulgent	—	—	.22	.16	—	—	—	—
Self-Punishing	—	—	—	—	—	—	.29	.20
Sexually Adjusted	—	—	—	—	—	—	—	—
Shy	—	—	—	—	—	—	—	—
Sociopathic	—	—	.20	.19	—	—	—	—
Stormy Interpersonal Relationships	.26	—	.22	—	—	—	—	—
Suicidal Ideations	—	—	—	—	.20	.16	.43	.30
Superficial Relationships	—	—	—	.20	—	—	—	—
Tearful	—	—	—	—	—	—	—	—
Unable to See Own Limitations	—	—	—	—	—	—	—	—
Whiny	—	—	—	—	—	—	—	—
Work-Oriented	—	—	—	—	—	—	—	—
Worrier	—	—	—	—	—	—	—	—

Table E-4. Correlates for MMPI-2 Harris-Lingoes Pa Subscales

Extra-test Characteristics	Persecutory Ideas (Pa_1)		Poignancy (Pa_2)		Naïveté (Pa_3)	
	Men	Women	Men	Women	Men	Women
Intake Information						
Alcohol Abuse in the Past Six Months	—	—	—	—	—	—
Axis I Anxiety Disorder	—	—	.18	—	—	—
Axis I Depression or Dysthymia	—	—	.19	.22	—	—
Axis I Substance Abuse or Dependence	—	—	—	—	—	—
Axis II Antisocial Personality Disorder	—	—	—	—	—	—
Axis II Borderline Personality Disorder	—	—	—	—	—	—
Currently on Antidepressant Medication	—	—	—	—	—	—
Currently on Anxiolytic Medication	—	—	—	—	—	—
Ever Arrested	—	—	—	—	—	—
History of Being Physically Abused	.20	—	—	—	—	—
History of Being Physically Abusive	—	—	—	—	—	—
History of Being Sexually Abused	—	—	—	—	—	—
History of Committing Domestic Violence	.16	—	—	—	—	—
History of Domestic Violence Conviction	—	—	—	—	—	—
History of Having Few or No Friends	.20	.17	—	.18	—	—
History of Misdemeanor Conviction(s)	—	—	—	—	—	—
History of Outpatient Psychiatric Treatment	—	—	—	—	—	—
History of Suicide Attempts	—	.22	—	.17	—	—
Lifetime History of Alcohol Abuse	—	—	—	—	—	—
Lifetime History of Cocaine Abuse	—	—	—	—	—	—
Lifetime History of Heroin Abuse	—	—	—	—	—	—
Lifetime History of Marijuana Abuse	—	—	—	—	—	—
Marijuana Abuse in the Past Six Months	—	—	—	—	—	—
Number of Arrests	—	—	—	—	—	—
Previous Psychiatric Hospitalizations	—	—	—	—	—	—
Mental Status						
Aggressive During Interview	—	—	—	—	—	—
Anxiety During Interview	—	—	—	—	—	—
Circumstantial Speech	—	—	—	—	—	—
Depression During Interview	.20	.16	.24	.21	—	—
Evasive During Interview	—	—	—	—	—	—
Obsessions	—	—	—	—	—	.16
Prevailing Mood Angry	—	—	—	—	—	—
Prevailing Mood Anxious	—	—	—	—	—	—

Table E-4. Correlates for MMPI-2 Harris-Lingoes Pa Subscales *(continued)*

Extra-test Characteristics	Persecutory Ideas (Pa_1)		Poignancy (Pa_2)		Naïveté (Pa_3)	
	Men	Women	Men	Women	Men	Women
Prevailing Mood Happy	—	—	-.19	—	—	—
Prevailing Mood Sad	.22	.17	.22	.21	—	—
Tics	—	—	—	—	.20	—
Unusual Gait	—	—	—	—	—	—
SCL-90-R Scales						
Anxiety	.44	.39	.52	.41	—	—
Depression	.44	.40	.55	.49	—	—
Hostility	.45	.39	.42	.36	-.20	—
Interpersonal Sensitivity	.52	.44	.51	.44	-.19	—
Obsessive-Compulsive	.45	.36	.45	.37	-.16	—
Paranoid Ideation	.63	.56	.46	.41	-.22	-.15
Phobic Anxiety	.39	.37	.33	.32	—	—
Psychoticism	.50	.48	.49	.44	-.19	—
Somatization	.40	.33	.41	.36	-.17	—
Initial SCL-90 Analogue						
Anxiety	—	—	—	—	—	—
Depression	.20	—	.20	.17	—	—
Hostility	—	—	—	—	—	—
Interpersonal Sensitivity	—	—	—	—	—	—
Obsessive-Compulsive	—	—	—	—	—	—
Paranoid Ideation	—	—	—	—	—	—
Phobic Anxiety	—	—	—	—	—	—
Psychoticism	—	—	—	—	—	—
Somatization	—	—	—	—	—	—
Patient Description Form Scales						
Achievement-Oriented	—	-.24	—	—	—	—
Aggressive	—	—	—	—	—	—
Agitated	—	—	—	—	—	—
Angry Resentment	—	—	.21	—	—	—
Antisocial	—	—	—	—	—	—
Anxious	.20	—	.29	—	—	—
Critical/Argumentative	—	—	—	—	—	—
Depressed	.27	—	.43	.22	—	—

Family Problems	.20	—	—	—	—	—
Histrionic	—	—	—	—	—	—
Insecure	.25	—	.28	—	—	—
Introverted	—	—	—	—	—	—
Narcissistic	—	—	—	—	—	—
Obsessive-Compulsive	—	—	.22	—	—	—
Passive-Submissive	—	—	—	—	—	—
Pessimistic	—	—	.21	—	—	—
Somatic Symptoms	—	—	—	—	—	—
Stereotypic Masculine Interests	—	—	—	—	—	—
Suspicious	—	—	—	—	—	—
Patient Description Form Items						
Acts Out	—	—	—	—	—	—
Acute Psychological Turmoil	—	—	—	—	—	—
Aggressive	—	—	—	—	—	—
Angry	—	—	—	—	—	—
Antisocial Behavior	—	—	—	—	—	—
Anxious	—	—	—	—	—	—
Argumentative	—	—	—	—	—	—
Blames Family For Difficulties	—	—	—	—	—	—
Bored	—	—	—	—	—	—
Communicates Effectively	—	-.18	—	—	—	—
Competitive	—	—	—	—	—	—
Complains of Fatigue	—	—	—	—	—	—
Complains of Sleep Disturbance	—	—	.37	.16	—	—
Copes Well with Stress	—	—	—	—	—	—
Creates Good First Impression	—	-.24	—	—	—	—
Demanding of Attention	—	—	—	—	—	—
Depressed	.27	—	.35	.23	—	—
Difficult to Motivate	—	—	—	—	—	—
Difficulty Concentrating	—	—	—	—	—	—
Difficulty Making Decisions	—	—	—	—	—	—
Disoriented	—	—	—	—	—	—
Does Not Complete Projects	—	—	—	—	—	—
Does Not Get Along with Coworkers	.26	—	—	—	—	—
Emotional Lability	—	—	—	—	—	—
Empathetic	—	—	—	—	—	—
Energetic	—	-.19	—	—	—	—
Excitable	—	—	—	—	—	—
Extroverted	—	—	—	—	—	—
Familial Discord	—	—	—	—	—	—

Table E-4. Correlates for MMPI-2 Harris-Lingoes Pa Subscales *(continued)*

Extra-test Characteristics	Persecutory Ideas (Pa_1)		Poignancy (Pa_2)		Naïveté (Pa_3)	
	Men	Women	Men	Women	Men	Women
Family Lacks Love	—	—	—	—	—	—
Feels Gets Raw Deal From Life	—	—	.25	.17	—	—
Feels Hopeless	.24	—	.32	.18	—	—
Feels Inferior	.25	—	—	—	—	—
Feels Like a Failure	.27	—	.25	.16	—	—
Feels Overwhelmed	—	—	—	—	—	—
Feels Rejected	—	—	.27	.17	—	—
Feels That Life is a Strain	.29	—	.28	.18	—	—
Fired From Past Jobs	—	—	—	—	—	—
Gives Up Easily	—	—	—	—	—	—
Hallucinations	—	—	—	—	—	—
Has Insight Into Own Problems	—	-.22	—	—	—	—
Has Many Interests	—	-.27	—	—	—	—
Has Many Nightmares	—	—	.28	—	—	—
Has Temper Tantrums	—	—	—	—	—	—
High Aspirations	—	-.22	—	—	—	—
Hypochondriacal	—	—	—	—	—	—
Impulsive	—	—	—	—	—	—
Insecure	.21	—	—	—	—	—
Likable	—	-.20	—	—	—	—
Lonely	—	—	—	—	—	—
Low Frustration Tolerance	—	—	—	—	—	—
Low Sex Drive	—	—	—	—	—	—
Moralistic	—	—	—	—	—	—
Multiple Somatic Complaints	—	—	—	—	—	—
Narcissistic	—	—	—	—	—	—
Needs Attention	—	—	—	—	—	—
Needs to Achieve	—	-.19	—	—	—	—
Negative Feelings Toward Opposite Sex	—	—	—	—	—	—
Nervous	—	—	—	—	—	—
Optimistic	—	—	—	—	—	—
Overly Sensitive to Criticism	—	—	—	—	—	—
Passive	—	—	—	—	—	—
Passive in Relationships	—	—	—	—	—	—
Pessimistic	—	—	.24	.17	—	—
Physical Symptoms in Response to Stress	—	—	—	—	—	—
Physically Abusive	—	—	—	—	—	—

Poor Judgment	—	—	—	—	—	—
Preoccupied with Health Problems	—	—	—	—	—	—
Reliable Informant	—	—	—	—	—	—
Resents Family Members	.23	—	—	—	—	—
Ruminates	.26	—	—	—	—	—
Sad	.24	—	.21	.17	—	—
Self-Defeating	—	—	—	—	—	—
Self-Degrading	—	—	.30	—	—	—
Self-Doubting	—	—	—	—	—	—
Self-Indulgent	—	—	—	—	—	—
Self-Punishing	—	—	.27	—	—	—
Sexually Adjusted	—	-.20	—	—	—	—
Shy	—	—	—	—	—	—
Sociopathic	—	—	—	—	—	—
Stormy Interpersonal Relationships	—	—	—	—	—	—
Suicidal Ideations	—	—	.29	.22	—	—
Superficial Relationships	—	—	—	—	—	—
Tearful	—	—	.32	.17	—	—
Unable to See Own Limitations	—	—	—	—	—	—
Whiny	—	—	—	—	—	—
Work-Oriented	—	-.22	—	—	—	—
Worrier	—	—	—	—	—	—

Table E-5. Correlates for MMPI-2 Harris-Lingoes Sc Subscales

Extra-test Characteristics	Social Alienation (Sc_1)		Emotional Alienation (Sc_2)		Lack of Ego Mastery, Cognitive (Sc_3)		Lack of Ego Mastery, Conative (Sc_4)		Lack of Ego Mastery, Defective Inhibition (Sc_5)		Bizarre Sensory Experiences (Sc_6)	
	Men	Women	Men	Women	Men	Women	Men	Women	Men	Women	Men	Women
Intake Information												
Alcohol Abuse in the Past Six Months	—	—	—	—	—	—	—	—	—	—	—	—
Axis I Anxiety Disorder	—	—	—	—	—	—	—	—	—	—	—	—
Axis I Depression or Dysthymia	.24	.20	.29	.21	.20	.18	.32	.20	.19	.14	.22	.16
Axis I Substance Abuse or Dependence	—	—	—	—	—	—	—	—	—	—	—	—
Axis II Antisocial Personality Disorder	—	—	—	—	—	—	—	—	—	—	—	—
Axis II Borderline Personality Disorder	—	—	—	—	—	—	—	—	—	.17	—	—
Currently on Antidepressant Medication	—	—	—	.20	—	—	—	.17	—	—	—	—
Currently on Anxiolytic Medication	—	—	—	—	—	.15	—	—	—	—	—	—
Ever Arrested	—	—	—	—	—	—	—	—	—	—	—	—
History of Being Physically Abused	.21	—	—	—	—	—	—	—	—	—	—	—
History of Being Physically Abusive	—	—	—	—	—	—	—	—	—	—	—	—
History of Being Sexually Abused	—	.17	—	—	—	.16	—	—	—	.20	—	.19
History of Committing Domestic Violence	—	—	—	—	—	—	—	—	—	—	—	—
History of Domestic Violence Conviction	—	—	—	—	—	—	—	—	—	—	—	—
History of Having Few or No Friends	.23	.23	—	.21	.16	.17	—	.19	—	—	.16	—
History of Misdemeanor Conviction(s)	—	—	—	—	—	—	—	—	—	—	—	—
History of Outpatient Psychiatric Treatment	.19	—	.21	—	—	—	.18	—	.16	—	—	—
History of Suicide Attempts	—	.26	.19	.20	—	.15	.16	.22	—	.23	—	.21
Lifetime History of Alcohol Abuse	—	—	—	—	—	—	—	—	—	—	—	—
Lifetime History of Cocaine Abuse	—	—	—	—	—	—	—	—	—	—	—	—
Lifetime History of Heroin Abuse	—	—	—	—	—	—	—	—	—	—	—	—
Lifetime History of Marijuana Abuse	—	—	—	—	.17	—	—	—	—	—	—	—
Marijuana Abuse in the Past Six Months	—	—	—	—	.18	—	—	—	—	—	—	—
Number of Arrests	—	—	—	—	—	—	—	—	—	—	—	—
Previous Psychiatric Hospitalizations	.16	—	—	.15	.17	.14	.18	.16	—	.18	.18	—
Mental Status												
Aggressive During Interview	—	—	—	—	—	—	—	—	—	—	—	—
Anxiety During Interview	—	—	—	.24	—	.18	—	.21	—	—	—	—
Circumstantial Speech	—	—	—	—	—	—	—	—	—	—	—	—
Depression During Interview	.22	.14	.31	.30	.26	.26	.33	.29	—	.16	.19	.19
Evasive During Interview	—	—	—	—	—	—	—	—	—	—	—	—
Obsessions	—	—	—	—	—	—	—	—	—	—	—	—
Prevailing Mood Angry	—	—	—	—	.20	—	—	—	—	—	—	—

Prevailing Mood Anxious	—	—	—	—	—	—	—	—	—	—	—	—
Prevailing Mood Happy	—	—	-.23	-.08	—	—	-.17	—	—	—	—	—
Prevailing Mood Sad	.22	—	.26	.24	.19	.20	.27	.22	—	—	.15	.15
Tics	—	—	—	—	—	—	—	—	—	—	—	—
Unusual Gait	—	—	—	—	—	—	—	—	—	—	—	—
SCL-90-R Scales												
Anxiety	.51	.39	.54	.49	.51	.57	.57	.54	.46	.49	.52	.54
Depression	.51	.48	.61	.61	.53	.56	.67	.62	.37	.40	.46	.39
Hostility	.46	.47	.41	.42	.45	.45	.45	.45	.41	.43	.38	.39
Interpersonal Sensitivity	.57	.51	.48	.52	.45	.48	.58	.55	.39	.39	.43	.38
Obsessive-Compulsive	.48	.39	.49	.47	.61	.63	.64	.58	.43	.41	.52	.53
Paranoid Ideation	.56	.53	.41	.41	.47	.43	.46	.42	.40	.44	.46	.42
Phobic Anxiety	.43	.36	.41	.40	.40	.47	.39	.44	.38	.45	.38	.47
Psychoticism	.51	.48	.53	.47	.53	.54	.57	.51	.45	.48	.51	.50
Somatization	.41	.35	.42	.45	.47	.53	.48	.50	.42	.37	.62	.61
Initial SCL-90 Analogue												
Anxiety	.25	—	.23	.16	—	—	.27	—	—	—	—	—
Depression	.25	—	.36	.24	.28	—	.37	.22	—	.18	.26	—
Hostility	—	—	—	—	—	—	—	—	—	—	—	—
Interpersonal Sensitivity	—	—	.20	.18	—	—	.22	.22	—	—	—	—
Obsessive-Compulsive	—	—	.20	—	—	—	—	—	—	—	—	—
Paranoid Ideation	—	—	—	—	—	—	—	—	—	—	—	—
Phobic Anxiety	—	—	.20	—	—	—	—	—	—	—	—	—
Psychoticism	—	—	—	—	—	—	—	—	—	—	—	—
Somatization	—	—	.23	—	—	—	.23	—	—	—	.26	.24
Patient Description Form Scales												
Achievement-Oriented	-.24	-.18	—	—	—	—	—	—	—	—	—	-.23
Aggressive	—	—	—	—	—	—	—	—	—	—	—	—
Agitated	—	—	.23	—	—	.17	—	—	—	—	—	—
Angry Resentment	.15	.18	—	—	—	—	—	—	—	—	.21	—
Antisocial	—	—	—	—	—	—	—	—	—	—	—	—
Anxious	.34	—	.33	.17	.31	.21	.36	.18	.25	—	.28	.17
Critical/Argumentative	—	.17	—	—	—	—	—	—	—	—	—	—
Depressed	.37	—	.48	.28	.42	.25	.53	.29	.33	.23	.36	.19
Family Problems	.27	.18	—	—	.21	—	—	—	—	—	—	—
Histrionic	—	—	.20	—	—	—	—	.19	—	—	—	—
Insecure	.28	—	.31	.18	.26	.17	.33	.24	—	—	—	—
Introverted	.22	—	—	—	—	—	—	—	—	—	—	—
Narcissistic	—	—	—	—	—	—	—	—	—	—	—	—

Table E-5. Correlates for MMPI-2 Harris-Lingoes Sc Subscales *(continued)*

Extra-test Characteristics	Social Alienation (Sc_1)		Emotional Alienation (Sc_2)		Lack of Ego Mastery, Cognitive (Sc_3)		Lack of Ego Mastery, Conative (Sc_4)		Lack of Ego Mastery, Defective Inhibition (Sc_5)		Bizarre Sensory Experiences (Sc_6)	
	Men	Women	Men	Women	Men	Women	Men	Women	Men	Women	Men	Women
Obsessive-Compulsive	.22	—	.21	—	.22	—	.22	—	—	—	—	—
Passive-Submissive	—	—	—	—	—	—	—	—	—	—	—	—
Pessimistic	.23	.17	.23	.20	.20	.17	.25	.21	—	—	.23	—
Somatic Symptoms	—	—	.29	—	.23	.19	.30	.19	.20	—	.35	.25
Stereotypic Masculine Interests	-.20	—	—	—	—	—	—	—	—	—	—	—
Suspicious	—	—	—	—	—	—	—	—	—	—	—	—
Patient Description Form Items												
Acts Out	—	—	—	—	—	—	—	—	—	—	—	—
Acute Psychological Turmoil	—	—	—	—	.20	.21	—	—	—	—	—	—
Aggressive	—	—	—	—	—	—	—	—	—	—	—	—
Angry	—	—	—	—	—	—	—	—	—	—	—	—
Antisocial Behavior	—	—	—	—	—	—	—	—	—	—	—	—
Anxious	.34	—	.33	—	—	—	.34	.17	.26	—	—	—
Argumentative	—	.19	—	—	—	—	—	—	—	—	—	—
Blames Family For Difficulties	—	—	—	—	—	—	—	—	—	—	—	—
Bored	—	—	—	—	—	—	—	—	—	—	—	—
Communicates Effectively	—	—	—	—	—	—	—	—	—	—	—	—
Competitive	—	—	—	—	—	—	—	—	—	—	—	—
Complains of Fatigue	—	—	—	—	—	—	—	—	—	—	.31	.18
Complains of Sleep Disturbance	—	—	.40	.22	.37	.20	.42	.20	.29	.17	.38	.15
Copes Well with Stress	-.27	-.21	—	—	-.20	-.24	—	—	—	-.17	—	-.20
Creates Good First Impression	-.19	-.20	—	—	—	—	—	—	—	—	—	—
Demanding of Attention	—	—	—	—	—	—	—	—	—	—	—	—
Depressed	.34	—	.43	.25	.38	.21	.47	.27	.30	.17	.33	.17
Difficult to Motivate	—	—	—	—	—	—	—	—	—	—	—	—
Difficulty Concentrating	—	—	—	—	—	—	—	—	.23	.17	.28	.21
Difficulty Making Decisions	—	—	—	—	—	—	—	—	—	—	—	—
Disoriented	—	—	—	—	—	—	—	—	—	.18	—	—
Does Not Complete Projects	—	—	—	—	—	—	—	—	—	—	—	—
Does Not Get Along with Coworkers	—	—	—	—	—	—	—	—	—	—	—	—
Emotional Lability	—	—	—	—	—	—	—	—	—	—	—	—
Empathetic	—	—	—	—	—	—	—	—	—	—	—	—
Energetic	—	—	—	—	-.29	—	—	—	—	—	.27	-.18
Excitable	—	—	—	—	—	—	—	—	—	—	—	—
Extroverted	—	—	—	—	—	—	—	—	—	—	—	—

Familial Discord	—	—	—	—	—	—	—	—	—	—	—	—
Family Lacks Love	.31	—	—	—	.29	—	—	—	—	—	—	—
Feels Gets Raw Deal From Life	—	.21	—	—	—	.20	—	—	—	—	—	—
Feels Hopeless	.34	.18	.39	.27	.36	.22	.45	.26	.26	—	.33	—
Feels Inferior	—	—	—	.21	—	—	.20	.23	—	—	—	—
Feels Like a Failure	.29	—	.30	.21	—	—	.33	.27	.24	—	—	—
Feels Overwhelmed	—	—	—	—	.28	—	.32	.17	.23	—	.28	—
Feels Rejected	—	—	—	—	—	—	—	—	—	—	—	—
Feels That Life is a Strain	.29	.18	.34	.23	—	—	.31	.20	—	—	—	—
Fired From Past Jobs	—	—	—	—	—	—	—	—	—	—	—	—
Gives Up Easily	.18	.20	—	—	—	—	—	—	—	—	—	—
Hallucinations	—	—	—	—	—	—	—	—	—	—	—	—
Has Insight Into Own Problems	—	-.18	—	—	—	—	—	—	—	—	—	—
Has Many Interests	—	-.18	—	—	—	—	—	—	—	—	—	-.24
Has Many Nightmares	—	—	—	—	.28	.20	—	—	.28	—	—	—
Has Temper Tantrums	—	—	—	—	—	—	—	—	—	—	—	—
High Aspirations	—	—	—	—	—	—	—	—	—	—	—	-.17
Hypochondriacal	—	—	—	—	—	—	—	—	—	—	—	.18
Impulsive	—	—	—	—	—	—	—	—	—	—	—	—
Insecure	—	—	—	—	.21	.22	—	—	—	—	—	—
Likable	—	—	—	—	—	—	—	—	—	—	—	—
Lonely	—	—	—	—	.28	—	—	—	—	—	—	—
Low Frustration Tolerance	—	—	—	—	—	—	—	—	—	.16	—	—
Low Sex Drive	—	—	—	—	—	—	—	—	—	—	—	—
Moralistic	—	—	—	—	—	—	—	—	—	—	—	—
Multiple Somatic Complaints	—	—	—	—	—	—	—	—	—	—	.36	.24
Narcissistic	—	—	—	—	—	—	—	—	—	—	—	—
Needs Attention	—	—	—	—	—	—	—	.21	—	—	—	—
Needs to Achieve	—	—	—	—	—	—	—	—	—	—	—	—
Negative Feelings Toward Opposite Sex	—	.18	—	—	—	—	—	—	—	—	—	—
Nervous	.31	—	—	—	—	—	—	—	—	—	—	—
Optimistic	—	—	-.24	-.22	—	—	—	—	—	—	—	—
Overly Sensitive to Criticism	—	—	—	—	—	—	—	—	—	—	—	—
Passive	—	—	—	—	—	—	—	—	—	—	—	—
Passive in Relationships	—	—	—	—	—	—	—	—	—	—	—	—
Pessimistic	—	—	.26	.22	—	—	.30	.22	—	—	.28	.16
Physical Symptoms in Response to Stress	—	—	—	—	—	—	—	—	.25	—	.31	.17
Physically Abusive	—	—	—	—	—	—	—	—	—	—	—	—
Poor Judgment	—	—	—	—	—	—	—	—	—	—	—	—
Preoccupied with Health Problems	—	—	.29	—	—	—	—	—	—	—	.37	.25
Reliable Informant	—	—	—	—	—	—	—	—	—	—	—	—
Resents Family Members	—	—	—	—	—	—	—	—	—	—	—	—

Table E-5. Correlates for MMPI-2 Harris-Lingoes Sc Subscales *(continued)*

Extra-test Characteristics	Social Alienation (Sc_1)		Emotional Alienation (Sc_2)		Lack of Ego Mastery, Cognitive (Sc_3)		Lack of Ego Mastery, Conative (Sc_4)		Lack of Ego Mastery, Defective Inhibition (Sc_5)		Bizarre Sensory Experiences (Sc_6)	
	Men	Women	Men	Women	Men	Women	Men	Women	Men	Women	Men	Women
Ruminates	.28	—	—	—	—	—	—	—	—	—	—	—
Sad	.30	—	.31	.21	.27	.19	.36	.20	.27	—	—	—
Self-Defeating	—	—	—	—	—	—	—	—	—	—	—	—
Self-Degrading	—	—	.29	—	—	—	.31	.23	—	—	—	—
Self-Doubting	—	—	—	—	—	—	—	—	—	—	—	—
Self-Indulgent	—	—	—	—	—	—	—	—	—	—	—	—
Self-Punishing	—	—	—	—	.20	.23	—	—	—	—	—	—
Sexually Adjusted	—	—	—	—	—	—	—	—	—	—	—	—
Shy	—	—	—	—	—	—	—	—	—	—	—	—
Sociopathic	—	—	—	—	—	—	—	—	—	—	—	—
Stormy Interpersonal Relationships	—	—	—	—	—	—	—	—	—	—	—	—
Suicidal Ideations	.27	.22	.38	.27	.30	.25	.38	.29	.23	.27	—	—
Superficial Relationships	—	—	—	—	—	—	—	—	—	—	—	—
Tearful	—	—	—	—	—	—	—	—	.20	.17	—	—
Unable to See Own Limitations	—	—	—	—	—	—	—	—	—	—	—	—
Whiny	—	—	—	—	—	—	—	—	—	—	—	—
Work-Oriented	—	—	—	—	—	—	—	—	—	—	—	—
Worrier	.28	—	—	—	.26	.22	—	—	—	—	—	—

Table E-6. Correlates for MMPI-2 Harris-Lingoes Ma Subscales

Extra-test Characteristics	Amorality (Ma_1)		Psychomotor Acceleration (Ma_2)		Imperturbability (Ma_3)		Ego Inflation (Ma_4)	
	Men	Women	Men	Women	Men	Women	Men	Women
Intake Information								
Alcohol Abuse in the Past Six Months	.20	.21	—	—	—	—	—	—
Axis I Anxiety Disorder	—	—	—	—	—	—	—	—
Axis I Depression or Dysthymia	—	—	—	—	—	—	—	—
Axis I Substance Abuse or Dependence	—	.22	—	—	—	—	—	—
Axis II Antisocial Personality Disorder	—	.19	—	—	—	—	—	—
Axis II Borderline Personality Disorder	—	—	—	.20	—	—	—	—
Currently on Antidepressant Medication	—	—	—	—	—	—	—	—
Currently on Anxiolytic Medication	—	—	—	—	—	—	—	—
Ever Arrested	—	—	—	—	—	—	—	—
History of Being Physically Abused	—	—	—	—	—	—	—	—
History of Being Physically Abusive	.17	—	.20	—	—	—	—	—
History of Being Sexually Abused	—	—	—	—	—	—	—	—
History of Committing Domestic Violence	.31	—	.25	—	—	—	—	—
History of Domestic Violence Conviction	.21	—	—	—	—	—	—	—
History of Having Few or No Friends	—	—	—	—	—	—	—	—
History of Misdemeanor Conviction(s)	—	.16	—	—	—	—	—	—
History of Outpatient Psychiatric Treatment	—	—	—	—	—	—	—	—
History of Suicide Attempts	—	—	—	—	—	—	—	—
Lifetime History of Alcohol Abuse	.18	.17	—	.18	—	—	—	—
Lifetime History of Cocaine Abuse	—	.20	.19	.17	—	—	—	—
Lifetime History of Heroin Abuse	—	—	—	—	—	—	—	—
Lifetime History of Marijuana Abuse	—	.15	—	—	—	—	—	—
Marijuana Abuse in the Past Six Months	—	—	—	—	—	—	—	—
Number of Arrests	—	—	—	—	—	—	—	—
Previous Psychiatric Hospitalizations	—	—	—	—	—	—	—	—
Mental Status								
Aggressive During Interview	—	—	—	—	—	—	—	—
Anxiety During Interview	—	—	—	—	—	—	—	—
Circumstantial Speech	—	—	—	—	—	—	—	—
Depression During Interview	—	—	—	—	-.25	-.14	—	—
Evasive During Interview	—	—	—	.16	—	—	—	—
Obsessions	—	—	—	—	—	—	—	—
Prevailing Mood Angry	.17	—	—	—	—	—	—	—
Prevailing Mood Anxious	—	—	—	—	—	—	—	—

Table E-6. Correlates for MMPI-2 Harris-Lingoes Ma Subscales *(continued)*

Extra-test Characteristics	Amorality (Ma_1)		Psychomotor Acceleration (Ma_2)		Imperturbability (Ma_3)		Ego Inflation (Ma_4)	
	Men	Women	Men	Women	Men	Women	Men	Women
Prevailing Mood Happy	—	—	—	—	—	—	—	—
Prevailing Mood Sad	—	—	—	—	—	-.16	—	—
Tics	—	—	—	—	—	—	—	—
Unusual Gait	—	—	—	—	—	.18	—	—
SCL-90-R Scales								
Anxiety	—	—	—	.19	-.22	-.22	—	—
Depression	—	—	—	—	-.29	-.26	—	—
Hostility	.24	—	.24	.20	-.20	-.19	.23	.18
Interpersonal Sensitivity	—	—	—	—	-.27	-.23	.16	.21
Obsessive-Compulsive	—	—	—	.15	-.22	-.21	.17	—
Paranoid Ideation	—	—	.16	.23	-.18	-.19	.29	.28
Phobic Anxiety	—	—	—	.15	—	-.15	—	—
Psychoticism	—	—	—	.17	-.20	-.19	.17	.23
Somatization	—	—	—	—	-.16	-.19	—	—
Initial SCL-90 Analogue								
Anxiety	—	—	—	—	—	—	—	—
Depression	—	—	—	—	—	-.18	—	—
Hostility	—	—	—	—	—	—	—	—
Interpersonal Sensitivity	—	—	—	—	—	—	—	—
Obsessive-Compulsive	—	—	—	—	—	—	—	—
Paranoid Ideation	—	—	—	—	—	—	—	—
Phobic Anxiety	—	—	—	—	—	—	—	—
Psychoticism	—	—	—	—	—	—	—	—
Somatization	—	—	—	—	—	—	—	—
Patient Description Form Scales								
Achievement-Oriented	—	—	—	—	—	—	—	—
Aggressive	—	—	—	—	—	—	—	—
Agitated	—	—	—	—	—	—	—	—
Angry Resentment	—	—	—	—	—	—	—	—
Antisocial	—	—	—	—	—	—	—	—
Anxious	—	—	—	—	—	-.20	—	—
Critical/Argumentative	—	—	—	—	—	—	—	—
Depressed	—	—	—	—	-.20	-.22	—	—

Family Problems	—	—	—	—	—	—	—	—
Histrionic	—	—	—	—	—	—	—	.17
Insecure	—	—	—	—	—	-.20	—	—
Introverted	—	—	—	—	—	-.16	—	—
Narcissistic	—	—	—	—	—	—	—	.18
Obsessive-Compulsive	—	—	—	—	—	—	—	—
Passive-Submissive	—	—	—	—	—	-.20	—	—
Pessimistic	—	—	—	—	—	—	—	—
Somatic Symptoms	—	—	—	—	—	—	—	—
Stereotypic Masculine Interests	—	—	—	—	—	.19	—	—
Suspicious	—	—	—	—	—	—	—	—
Patient Description Form Items								
Acts Out	.20	—	—	—	—	—	—	—
Acute Psychological Turmoil	—	—	—	—	—	—	—	—
Aggressive	—	—	—	—	—	—	—	—
Angry	—	—	—	—	—	—	—	—
Antisocial Behavior	—	—	—	—	—	—	—	—
Anxious	—	—	—	—	—	-.19	—	—
Argumentative	—	—	—	—	—	—	—	—
Blames Family For Difficulties	—	—	—	—	—	—	—	—
Bored	—	—	—	—	—	—	—	.17
Communicates Effectively	—	—	—	—	—	—	—	—
Competitive	—	—	—	—	—	—	—	—
Complains of Fatigue	—	—	—	—	—	—	—	—
Complains of Sleep Disturbance	.20	—	—	—	—	—	—	—
Copes Well with Stress	—	—	—	—	—	—	—	-.18
Creates Good First Impression	—	—	—	—	—	—	—	-.16
Demanding of Attention	—	—	—	—	—	—	—	—
Depressed	—	—	—	—	-.20	-.23	—	—
Difficult to Motivate	—	—	—	—	—	—	—	.20
Difficulty Concentrating	—	—	—	—	—	—	—	—
Difficulty Making Decisions	—	—	—	—	—	—	.18	—
Disoriented	—	—	—	—	—	—	—	—
Does Not Complete Projects	—	—	—	—	—	—	—	—
Does Not Get Along with Coworkers	—	—	—	—	—	—	.25	—
Emotional Lability	—	—	—	—	—	—	—	—
Empathetic	—	—	—	—	—	—	—	—
Energetic	—	—	—	—	—	—	—	—
Excitable	—	—	—	—	—	—	.21	—
Extroverted	—	—	—	—	—	—	—	—
Familial Discord	—	—	—	—	—	—	—	—
Family Lacks Love	—	—	—	—	—	—	—	—

E-6. Correlates for MMPI-2 Harris-Lingoes Ma Subscales *(continued)*

Extra-test Characteristics	Amorality (Ma_1)		Psychomotor Acceleration (Ma_2)		Imperturbability (Ma_3)		Ego Inflation (Ma_4)	
	Men	Women	Men	Women	Men	Women	Men	Women
Feels Gets Raw Deal From Life	—	—	—	—	—	—	—	—
Feels Hopeless	—	—	—	—	—	-.19	—	—
Feels Inferior	—	—	—	—	—	—	—	—
Feels Like a Failure	—	—	—	—	—	—	—	—
Feels Overwhelmed	—	—	—	—	—	—	—	—
Feels Rejected	—	—	—	—	—	—	—	—
Feels That Life is a Strain	—	—	—	—	—	—	—	—
Fired From Past Jobs	—	—	—	—	—	—	—	—
Gives Up Easily	—	—	—	—	—	—	—	.18
Hallucinations	—	—	—	—	—	—	—	—
Has Insight Into Own Problems	—	—	—	—	—	—	—	—
Has Many Interests	—	—	—	—	—	—	—	—
Has Many Nightmares	—	—	—	—	—	—	—	—
Has Temper Tantrums	—	—	—	—	—	—	—	—
High Aspirations	—	—	—	—	—	—	—	—
Hypochondriacal	—	—	—	—	—	—	—	—
Impulsive	—	—	—	—	—	—	—	—
Insecure	—	—	—	—	—	-.20	—	—
Likable	—	—	—	—	—	—	—	—
Lonely	—	—	—	—	—	-.19	—	—
Low Frustration Tolerance	—	—	—	—	—	—	—	—
Low Sex Drive	—	—	—	—	—	—	—	—
Moralistic	—	—	—	—	—	—	—	—
Multiple Somatic Complaints	—	—	—	—	—	—	—	—
Narcissistic	—	—	—	—	—	—	—	.20
Needs Attention	—	—	—	—	—	—	—	—
Needs to Achieve	—	—	—	—	—	—	—	—
Negative Feelings Toward Opposite Sex	—	—	—	—	—	—	—	—
Nervous	—	—	—	—	—	-.19	—	—
Optimistic	—	—	—	—	—	—	—	—
Overly Sensitive to Criticism	—	—	—	—	—	—	—	—
Passive	—	—	—	—	—	-.18	—	—
Passive in Relationships	—	—	—	—	—	-.21	—	—
Pessimistic	—	—	—	—	—	—	—	—
Physical Symptoms in Response to Stress	—	—	—	—	—	—	—	—
Physically Abusive	—	—	—	—	—	—	—	—
Poor Judgment	—	—	—	—	—	—	—	—

Preoccupied with Health Problems	—	—	—	—	—	—	—	—
Reliable Informant	—	—	—	—	—	—	—	-.18
Resents Family Members	—	—	—	—	—	—	—	—
Ruminates	—	—	—	—	—	—	—	—
Sad	—	—	—	—	—	-.22	—	—
Self-Defeating	—	—	—	—	—	—	—	—
Self-Degrading	—	—	—	—	—	—	—	—
Self-Doubting	—	—	—	—	—	—	—	—
Self-Indulgent	—	—	—	—	—	—	—	—
Self-Punishing	—	—	—	—	—	—	—	—
Sexually Adjusted	—	—	—	—	—	—	—	—
Shy	—	—	—	—	—	-.18	—	—
Sociopathic	—	—	—	—	—	—	—	.16
Stormy Interpersonal Relationships	—	—	—	—	—	—	—	—
Suicidal Ideations	—	—	—	—	—	—	—	—
Superficial Relationships	—	—	—	—	—	—	—	—
Tearful	—	—	—	—	—	—	—	—
Unable to See Own Limitations	—	—	—	—	—	—	—	.17
Whiny	—	—	—	—	—	—	—	.18
Work-Oriented	—	—	—	—	—	—	—	—
Worrier	—	—	—	—	—	-.17	—	—

Appendix F

Correlates for MMPI-2 Scale 0 Subscales

Extra-test Characteristics	Shyness/Self-Consciousness (Si_1)		Social Avoidance (Si_2)		Self/Other Alienation (Si_3)	
	Men	Women	Men	Women	Men	Women
Intake Information						
Axis I Bipolar or Cyclothymia	.16	—	—	—	—	—
Axis I Depression or Dysthymia	—	.15	—	—	—	—
Currently on Antidepressant Medication	—	.18	—	.19	—	—
Currently on Anxiolytic Medication	—	—	—	.17	—	—
History of Having Few or No Friends	—	.18	—	.17	—	.15
History of Suicide Attempts	—	.16	—	—	—	.21
Mental Status						
Depression During Interview	—	—	.20	—	.18	.13
Prevailing Mood Sad	—	.17	—	—	—	—
Speech During Interview	—	-.15	—	—	—	—
SCL-90-R Scales						
Anxiety	.33	.31	.25	.31	.49	.38
Depression	.34	.32	.27	.30	.46	.44
Hostility	.23	.21	.18	.21	.38	.39
Interpersonal Sensitivity	.41	.43	.29	.34	.47	.48
Obsessive-Compulsive	.31	.32	.24	.32	.47	.42
Paranoid Ideation	.18	.26	.19	.23	.43	.45
Phobic Anxiety	.30	.36	.28	.40	.35	.35
Psychoticism	.25	.30	.19	.28	.46	.49
Somatization	.17	.23	.17	.29	.40	.31
Patient Description Form Scales						
Achievement-Oriented	—	-.27	—	-.26	—	-.21
Anxious	.25	—	—	—	.24	—
Depressed	.25	—	.22	.18	.30	—
Insecure	.23	—	—	—	.26	.16
Introverted	.26	.25	—	.19	—	—
Patient Description Form Items						
Anxious	.26	—	—	—	.27	—
Assertive	—	-.21	—	—	—	—

Competitive	—	—	—	—	—	-.17
Complains of Sleep Disturbance	.23	—	—	.21	.27	—
Concerned About Status	—	—	—	-.20	—	—
Copes Well with Stress	—	—	—	-.18	—	-.24
Creates Good First Impression	—	-.20	—	—	—	—
Depressed	—	—	.20	.16	.27	—
Difficulty Making Decisions	—	—	—	—	.22	—
Energetic	—	-.27	-.20	-.24	—	-.20
Extroverted	-.21	-.27	-.22	-.22	—	-.18
Feels Hopeless	—	—	—	—	.22	—
Feels That Life is a Strain	—	—	.22	—	—	—
Guilt-prone	—	—	—	—	.25	—
Has Many Interests	—	-.25	-.23	-.20	—	-.20
Has Many Nightmares	.29	—	—	—	.26	—
High Aspirations	—	-.26	—	-.21	—	-.18
Insecure	—	—	—	—	.22	—
Introverted	.25	.26	.23	.18	—	—
Many Specific Fears	—	—	—	—	.12	.17
Needs to Achieve	—	-.20	—	—	—	—
Nervous	.24	—	—	—	.24	—
Optimistic	—	—	—	—	—	-.19
Passive	—	—	—	—	.22	—
Passive in Relationships	—	.19	—	—	—	—
Preoccupied with Health Problems	—	—	.21	—	—	—
Restricted Affect	—	—	.22	—	—	—
Self-Degrading	.23	—	—	—	—	—
Self-Punishing	.22	—	—	—	—	—
Self-Reliant	—	—	—	—	—	-.22
Sexually Adjusted	—	—	—	-.19	—	—
Shy	.22	.22	—	—	—	—
Suicidal Ideations	—	—	.21	.17	.19	.18
Uncomfortable with Opposite Sex	.22	—	—	—	—	—
Worrier	.25	—	—	—	—	—

Appendix G

Correlates for MMPI-2 Code Types (Men and Women Combined)

Extra-test Characteristics	Code Types							
	12/21	13/31	23/32	24/42	26/62	27/72	34/43	46/64
Intake Information								
Alcohol Abuse in the Past Six Months	—	—	—	—	—	—	.39	—
Axis I Depression or Dysthymia	.42	—	—	.34	—	.33	—	—
Axis I Substance Abuse or Dependence	—	—	—	—	—	—	.37	—
Axis II Antisocial Personality Disorder	—	—	—	—	—	—	—	—
Currently on Antidepressant Medication	—	—	—	—	—	.38	—	—
History of Being Physically Abused	—	—	—	—	—	—	—	—
History of Being Sexually Abused	—	—	—	—	—	—	—	—
History of Having Few or No Friends	—	—	—	—	—	—	—	—
History of Suicide Attempts	—	—	—	—	.41	—	—	—
Previous Psychiatric Hospitalizations	—	—	—	—	—	.34	—	.45
Mental Status								
Circumstantial Speech	—	—	—	—	—	—	—	—
Delusions	—	—	—	—	—	—	—	—
Depression During Interview	.42	—	.49	—	.36	.43	—	.31
Hallucinations	—	—	—	—	—	—	—	—
Loose Associations	—	—	—	—	—	—	—	—
Prevailing Mood Angry	.33	—	—	—	—	—	—	—
Prevailing Mood Sad	—	—	.38	—	—	.50	—	—
Tangential Speech	—	—	—	—	—	—	—	—
Tremors	.35	—	—	—	—	—	—	—
SCL-90-R Scales								
Anxiety	.74	.51	.77	.65	.72	.74	.62	.58
Depression	.66	.34	.78	.74	.78	.76	.57	.66
Hostility	—	—	.62	.56	.65	.53	.43	.49
Interpersonal Sensitivity	.50	—	.48	.60	.70	.60	.40	.61
Obsessive-Compulsive	.67	.42	.75	.56	.66	.68	.44	.56
Paranoid Ideation	.40	—	.46	.55	.64	—	.31	.63
Phobic Anxiety	.67	.41	.53	.43	.64	.59	—	.38
Psychoticism	.52	—	.58	.55	.67	.54	.40	.57
Somatization	.84	.75	.80	.47	.63	.60	.59	.48

Initial SCL-90 Analogue								
Anxiety	—	—	—	.36	—	—	—	—
Depression	.40	.34	.37	.48	—	.45	—	—
Paranoid Ideation	—	—	—	—	—	—	—	—
Phobic Anxiety	—	.33	—	—	—	—	—	—
Psychoticism	—	—	—	—	—	—	—	—
Somatization	.47	.63	.51	—	—	—	—	—
Patient Description Form Scales								
Achievement-Oriented	—	—	—	—	—	-.45	—	—
Aggressive	—	—	—	—	—	—	—	—
Agitated	—	—	—	—	—	—	—	—
Angry Resentment	—	—	—	.37	—	—	—	—
Antisocial	—	—	—	—	—	—	—	—
Anxious	—	.43	—	.45	—	.36	—	—
Critical/Argumentative	—	—	—	.37	—	—	—	—
Defensive	—	—	—	—	—	—	—	—
Depressed	—	.44	.54	.50	.43	.59	—	.35
Family Problems	—	—	—	—	—	—	—	—
Histrionic	—	—	—	.41	—	—	.36	—
Insecure	—	—	.37	.43	—	—	—	—
Introverted	—	—	—	—	—	—	—	—
Obsessive-Compulsive	—	—	—	—	—	—	—	—
Pessimistic	—	—	—	.41	—	—	—	—
Psychotic Symptoms	—	—	—	—	—	—	—	—
Somatic Symptoms	.54	.62	.54	—	.41	.43	—	—
Suspicious	—	—	—	—	—	—	—	—
Work Problems	—	—	—	—	—	—	—	—
Patient Description Form Items								
Absence of Deep Emotions	—	—	—	—	—	—	—	—
Acute Psychological Turmoil	—	—	—	—	—	—	—	—
Anxious	—	—	—	.48	—	—	—	—
Blames Family For Difficulties	—	—	—	—	—	—	—	.32
Complains of Fatigue	.45	.48	.48	—	—	.51	—	—
Complains of Sleep Disturbance	—	.52	.50	—	.51	.57	—	—
Conforming	—	—	—	—	—	—	—	-.35
Copes Well with Stress	—	—	—	—	-.36	—	—	—
Creates Good First Impression	—	—	—	—	-.36	—	—	—
Cynical	—	—	—	—	—	—	—	.37
Daydreams	—	—	—	—	—	—	—	—
Delusional Thinking	—	—	—	—	—	—	—	—

Correlates for MMPI-2 Code Types (Men and Women Combined) *(continued)*

Extra-test Characteristics	Code Types							
	12/21	13/31	23/32	24/42	26/62	27/72	34/43	46/64
Demanding of Attention	—	—	—	—	—	—	—	—
Depressed	.35	.46	.43	.50	.44	.58	—	.37
Difficulty Concentrating	—	—	—	—	—	—	—	—
Disoriented	—	—	—	—	—	—	—	—
Eccentric	—	—	—	—	—	—	—	—
Emotional Lability	—	—	—	.47	—	—	.45	—
Energetic	—	—	—	—	-.36	-.46	—	—
Excitable	—	—	—	—	—	—	.35	—
Family Lacks Love	—	—	—	—	—	—	—	.37
Feels Gets Raw Deal From Life	—	—	—	—	—	—	—	.33
Feels Hopeless	—	—	—	.44	.41	.48	—	—
Feels Inferior	—	—	—	.50	—	—	—	—
Feels Like a Failure	—	—	.47	—	—	—	—	—
Feels That Life is a Strain	—	—	—	—	—	—	—	—
Gives Up Easily	—	—	—	—	—	—	—	—
Hallucinations	—	—	—	—	—	—	—	—
Histrionic	—	.42	—	.52	—	—	—	—
Hypochondriacal	—	.49	—	—	—	—	—	—
Impulsive	—	—	—	—	—	—	—	—
Low Frustration Tolerance	—	—	—	—	—	—	—	—
Low Sex Drive	—	.44	.44	—	—	—	—	—
Many Specific Fears	—	—	—	—	—	—	—	—
Multiple Somatic Complaints	.61	.69	.55	—	.45	—	.35	—
Narcissistic	—	—	—	—	—	—	—	—
Needs to Achieve	—	—	—	—	—	—	—	—
Nervous	—	—	—	—	—	—	—	—
Obsessive	—	—	—	—	—	—	—	—
Paranoid Features	—	—	—	—	—	—	—	—
Pessimistic	—	—	—	—	—	—	—	—
Physical Symptoms in Response to Stress	.38	.51	.48	—	—	.42	—	—
Poor Reality Testing	—	—	—	—	—	—	—	—
Preoccupied with Health Problems	.55	.57	.52	—	.50	—	.37	—
Problems with Authority Figures	—	—	—	—	—	—	—	—
Psychotic Symptoms	—	—	—	—	—	—	.37	—
Resents Family Members	—	—	—	—	—	—	—	.37
Ruminates	—	—	—	.43	—	—	—	—

Sad	—	—	.42	—	—	.43	—	—
Self-Degrading	—	—	—	.45	—	.43	—	—
Self-Punishing	—	—	—	—	—	—	—	—
Suicidal Ideations	—	—	.43	.50	—	.49	—	—
Superficial Relationships	—	—	—	—	—	—	—	—
Uncomfortable with Opposite Sex	—	—	—	—	—	—	—	—
Work-Oriented	—	—	—	—	—	-.42	—	—
Worrier	—	.42	.45	—	—	—	—	.35

Extra-test Characteristics	Code Types (continued)								
	48/84	49/94	68/86	78/87	123	247	278	468	478
Intake Information									
Alcohol Abuse in the Past Six Months	—	—	—	—	—	—	—	—	—
Axis I Depression or Dysthymia	—	—	.44	—	—	.40	.50	.49	—
Axis I Substance Abuse or Dependence	—	—	—	—	—	—	—	—	—
Axis II Antisocial Personality Disorder	—	—	—	—	—	—	—	.36	—
Currently on Antidepressant Medication	—	—	—	—	—	—	—	.36	—
History of Being Physically Abused	—	—	—	—	—	—	—	.34	—
History of Being Sexually Abused	.35	—	—	—	—	—	.29	—	—
History of Having Few or No Friends	—	—	.34	—	—	—	—	.39	—
History of Suicide Attempts	—	—	—	—	—	—	—	.36	—
Previous Psychiatric Hospitalizations	.63	—	.49	—	—	—	.40	.58	.39
Mental Status									
Circumstantial Speech	—	—	—	—	—	—	—	.41	—
Delusions	—	—	—	—	—	—	—	—	.48
Depression During Interview	—	—	.30	—	.35	—	.41	—	—
Hallucinations	—	—	—	—	—	—	—	—	.48
Loose Associations	—	—	—	—	—	—	—	—	.39
Prevailing Mood Angry	—	—	—	—	—	—	—	—	—
Prevailing Mood Sad	—	—	—	—	.35	—	.38	—	—
Tangential Speech	—	—	—	—	—	—	—	.40	—
Tremors	—	—	—	—	—	—	—	—	—
SCL-90-R Scales									
Anxiety	.68	.35	.74	.79	.74	.66	.83	.79	.72
Depression	.64	—	.67	.69	.73	.79	.84	.73	.67
Hostility	.48	.33	.70	.55	.40	.57	.64	.73	.51
Interpersonal Sensitivity	.46	—	.63	.70	.46	.68	.80	.64	.60
Obsessive-Compulsive	.65	—	.70	.77	.68	.72	.85	.62	.67
Paranoid Ideation	.52	.33	.66	.54	.29	.52	.59	.70	.49
Phobic Anxiety	.53	—	.69	.66	.62	.67	.82	.68	.65
Psychoticism	.66	—	.71	.66	.53	.58	.80	.76	.63
Somatization	.68	—	.70	.71	.82	.61	.76	.69	.55
Initial SCL-90 Analogue									
Anxiety	.41	—	—	—	—	—	—	—	—
Depression	.44	—	—	—	.41	—	.49	.36	—

Paranoid Ideation	.49	.52	—	—	—	—	—	—	—
Phobic Anxiety	—	—	—	—	—	—	—	—	—
Psychoticism	.45	—	—	—	—	—	—	—	—
Somatization	—	—	—	—	.71	—	.46	—	—
Patient Description Form Scales									
Achievement-Oriented	—	—	-.47	—	-.57	—	-.36	—	—
Aggressive	—	—	—	—	—	—	—	.40	—
Agitated	.40	—	—	—	—	—	—	.43	.41
Angry Resentment	—	—	—	—	—	—	—	.44	—
Antisocial	—	—	—	—	—	—	—	.45	—
Anxious	—	—	—	.43	.35	—	.42	.47	.52
Critical/Argumentative	—	—	—	—	—	—	—	.46	—
Defensive	—	—	—	—	—	—	—	.35	—
Depressed	.51	—	.44	.40	.55	.36	.63	.63	.44
Family Problems	—	—	—	—	—	—	—	.42	—
Histrionic	—	—	—	—	—	—	—	.52	.39
Insecure	.38	—	—	—	—	—	.42	.47	.45
Introverted	—	—	—	—	—	—	—	—	.40
Obsessive-Compulsive	—	—	—	—	—	—	—	.40	.42
Pessimistic	—	—	.42	—	.42	—	—	.48	—
Psychotic Symptoms	.51	.38	—	—	—	—	—	.41	.51
Somatic Symptoms	—	—	—	.39	.78	—	.52	—	—
Suspicious	.42	—	—	—	—	—	—	.48	.39
Work Problems	—	—	—	—	—	—	—	.51	—
Patient Description Form Items									
Absence of Deep Emotions	—	—	—	—	—	—	—	—	.47
Acute Psychological Turmoil	.52	—	—	.42	—	—	—	.49	—
Anxious	—	—	—	.39	—	—	—	—	.44
Blames Family For Difficulties	—	—	—	—	—	—	—	—	—
Complains of Fatigue	—	—	.44	—	.61	—	.57	—	—
Complains of Sleep Disturbance	.51	—	.42	.43	.60	—	.60	—	—
Conforming	—	—	—	—	—	—	—	—	—
Copes Well with Stress	—	—	—	—	—	—	—	—	—
Creates Good First Impression	—	—	-.42	—	—	—	—	—	—
Cynical	—	.38	—	—	—	—	—	—	—
Daydreams	.42	—	—	—	—	—	—	—	—
Delusional Thinking	.53	—	—	—	—	—	—	—	—
Demanding of Attention	—	—	—	—	—	—	—	.54	—
Depressed	—	—	—	—	.51	.40	.58	.52	—
Difficulty Concentrating	—	—	—	—	—	—	—	—	.54

Extra-test Characteristics	Code Types *(continued)*								
	48/84	49/94	68/86	78/87	123	247	278	468	478
Disoriented	—	—	—	—	—	—	—	—	.45
Eccentric	—	.48	—	—	—	—	—	—	.56
Emotional Lability	—	.38	—	—	—	—	—	—	—
Energetic	—	—	—	—	-.55	—	—	—	—
Excitable	—	—	—	—	—	—	—	—	—
Family Lacks Love	—	—	—	—	—	—	—	—	—
Feels Gets Raw Deal From Life	—	—	—	—	—	.38	—	.55	—
Feels Hopeless	.49	—	.44	—	.47	—	.50	.54	—
Feels Inferior	—	—	—	—	—	—	—	—	—
Feels Like a Failure	.44	—	—	—	—	—	—	.57	—
Feels That Life is a Strain	—	—	.43	—	.48	.37	—	—	—
Gives Up Easily	—	—	.51	—	—	—	—	—	—
Hallucinations	.52	—	—	.41	—	—	—	—	—
Histrionic	—	—	—	—	—	—	—	—	—
Hypochondriacal	—	—	—	—	.60	—	—	—	—
Impulsive	—	.37	—	—	—	—	—	—	—
Low Frustration Tolerance	—	—	.44	—	—	—	—	.49	—
Low Sex Drive	—	—	—	—	—	—	—	—	—
Many Specific Fears	—	—	—	—	—	—	—	—	.46
Multiple Somatic Complaints	—	—	—	.43	.80	—	.43	—	—
Narcissistic	—	.36	—	—	—	—	—	—	—
Needs to Achieve	—	—	-.41	—	—	—	—	—	—
Nervous	—	—	—	.41	—	—	—	—	—
Obsessive	—	—	—	.42	—	—	—	—	—
Paranoid Features	.51	.48	—	—	—	—	—	—	—
Pessimistic	—	—	.49	.44	—	.44	.46	.51	—
Physical Symptoms in Response to Stress	—	—	—	—	.71	—	—	—	—
Poor Reality Testing	—	.36	—	—	—	—	—	—	.48
Preoccupied with Health Problems	—	—	—	.42	.76	—	.47	—	—
Problems with Authority Figures	—	.37	—	—	—	—	—	—	—
Psychotic Symptoms	.65	—	—	—	—	—	—	—	—
Resents Family Members	—	—	—	—	—	—	—	—	—
Ruminates	—	—	—	—	—	—	—	—	—
Sad	—	—	—	—	—	—	.46	.49	—
Self-Degrading	—	—	—	—	—	—	.43	—	.54
Self-Punishing	—	—	—	—	—	—	—	—	.51
Suicidal Ideations	.59	—	—	.52	—	.37	.58	.54	.56

Superficial Relationships	—	.39	—	—	—	—	—	—	—
Uncomfortable with Opposite Sex	—	.37	—	—	—	.39	—	—	—
Work-Oriented	—	—	-.47	—	—	—	—	—	—
Worrier	—	—	—	.42	—	—	—	—	—

Appendix H

Correlates for MMPI-2 Content Scales

Extra-test Characteristics	Content Scales															
	Anxiety (ANX)		Fears (FRS)		Obsessiveness (OBS)		Depression (DEP)		Health Concerns (HEA)		Bizarre Mentation (BIZ)		Anger (ANG)		Cynicism (CYN)	
	Men	Women	Men	Women	Men	Women	Men	Women	Men	Women	Men	Women	Men	Women	Men	Women
Intake Information																
Axis I Bipolar or Cyclothymia	—	—	—	—	—	—	—	—	—	—	—	—	—	—	—	—
Axis I Depression or Dysthymia	.22	.20	—	—	—	—	.27	.26	.27	.15	.18	—	—	—	.23	—
Axis I Multiple Diagnoses	—	—	—	—	—	—	—	—	—	—	—	—	—	—	—	—
Axis I Schizophrenia	—	—	.24	—	—	—	—	—	—	—	—	—	—	—	—	—
Axis I Substance Abuse or Dependence	—	—	—	—	—	—	—	—	—	—	—	—	.18	.13	—	—
Axis II Antisocial Personality Disorder	—	—	—	—	—	—	—	—	—	—	—	—	—	—	—	—
Cocaine Abuse in the Past Six Months	—	—	—	—	—	—	—	—	—	—	.18	—	—	—	—	—
Currently on Antidepressant Medication	—	—	—	—	—	—	—	.17	—	.17	—	—	—	—	—	—
Currently on Antipsychotic Medication	—	—	.22	—	—	—	—	—	—	—	—	—	—	—	—	—
Currently on Anxiolytic Medication	—	.15	—	—	—	—	—	.15	—	.17	—	—	—	—	—	—
Ever Arrested	—	—	—	—	—	—	—	—	—	—	—	—	—	—	—	—
History of Being Physically Abused	—	—	—	—	—	—	.20	—	—	—	.18	—	—	—	.17	—
History of Being Physically Abusive	—	—	—	—	—	—	—	—	—	—	—	—	.20	.16	—	—
History of Being Sexually Abused	—	—	—	—	—	.15	—	—	—	—	—	.16	—	.16	—	—
History of Committing Domestic Violence	—	—	—	—	—	—	—	—	—	—	—	—	.22	—	—	—
History of Having Few or No Friends	—	.18	—	—	—	.15	.17	.22	—	—	—	—	—	—	.16	—
History of Misdemeanor Conviction(s)	—	—	—	—	—	—	—	—	—	—	—	—	—	—	—	—
History of Outpatient Psychiatric Treatment	—	—	—	—	—	—	.21	—	—	—	—	—	—	—	—	—
History of Suicide Attempts	—	.19	—	—	—	.21	.16	.26	—	.18	—	.18	—	.18	—	.16
History of Victim of Domestic Violence	—	—	—	—	—	—	—	—	—	—	—	—	—	—	—	—
Lifetime History of Alcohol Abuse	—	—	—	—	—	—	—	—	—	—	—	—	.16	.19	—	—
Lifetime History of Cocaine Abuse	—	—	—	—	—	—	—	—	—	—	.17	—	—	—	—	—
Lifetime History of Marijuana Abuse	—	—	—	—	—	—	—	—	—	—	—	—	.21	—	—	—
Previous Psychiatric Hospitalizations	.17	—	—	—	.16	—	.21	.13	—	—	—	.16	—	—	—	—
Mental Status																
Anxiety During Interview	—	.16	—	—	—	—	—	—	—	—	—	—	—	—	—	—
Circumstantial Speech	—	—	—	—	—	—	—	—	—	—	—	—	—	—	—	—

Defensive During Interview	—	—	—	—	—	—	—	—	—	—	—	—	—	—	—	—
Depression During Interview	.29	.27	—	—	.25	.16	.32	.29	.23	.24	—	—	—	—	.16	—
Hallucinations	—	—	.17	—	—	—	—	—	—	—	—	.19	—	—	—	—
Loose Associations	—	—	—	—	—	—	—	—	—	—	.16	—	—	—	—	—
Obsessions	—	—	.16	—	—	—	—	—	—	—	—	—	—	—	—	—
Poor Judgment	—	—	—	—	—	—	—	—	—	—	—	—	—	—	—	—
Prevailing Mood Angry	.19	—	—	—	.16	—	—	—	—	—	.20	—	—	—	—	—
Prevailing Mood Happy	—	—	—	—	—	—	-.17	—	-.20	—	—	—	—	—	—	—
Prevailing Mood Sad	.21	.25	—	—	—	—	.25	.25	.22	.16	—	—	—	—	.16	—
SCL-90-R Scales																
Anxiety	.61	.62	.16	.36	.51	.46	.56	.50	.59	.54	.47	.42	.36	.29	.34	.27
Depression	.65	.65	—	.28	.46	.45	.70	.69	.49	.47	.33	.29	.31	.29	.25	.21
Hostility	.51	.49	—	.25	.36	.38	.48	.47	.34	.32	.31	.37	.64	.53	.38	.28
Interpersonal Sensitivity	.56	.54	.16	.31	.50	.50	.59	.58	.45	.40	.38	.33	.30	.33	.33	.29
Obsessive-Compulsive	.59	.60	.18	.34	.54	.48	.59	.52	.54	.53	.42	.35	.33	.23	.31	.23
Paranoid Ideation	.54	.51	—	.31	.42	.43	.51	.49	.39	.38	.48	.46	.40	.34	.44	.40
Phobic Anxiety	.41	.46	.26	.48	.36	.42	.42	.40	.47	.48	.39	.38	—	.23	.30	.30
Psychoticism	.56	.52	.19	.34	.41	.51	.58	.54	.48	.46	.52	.49	.31	.32	.30	.37
Somatization	.50	.51	.18	.36	.37	.38	.46	.46	.71	.72	.45	.33	.31	.24	.30	.26
Initial SCL-90 Analogue																
Anxiety	.24	—	—	—	—	—	.26	—	.30	—	—	—	—	—	—	—
Depression	.33	.16	—	—	—	—	.42	.19	.34	—	—	—	—	—	—	—
Interpersonal Sensitivity	—	—	—	—	—	—	.24	—	—	—	—	—	—	—	—	—
Phobic Anxiety	—	—	—	—	—	—	—	—	.20	—	—	—	—	—	—	—
Somatization	.27	—	—	—	—	—	.28	—	.46	.29	—	—	—	—	—	—
Patient Description Form Scales																
Achievement-Oriented	—	-.18	—	-.18	—	—	-.24	-.19	-.20	-.22	—	-.20	—	—	—	-.18
Aggressive	—	—	—	—	—	—	—	—	—	—	—	—	.27	—	—	—
Agitated	—	—	—	—	—	—	—	—	.25	—	—	—	—	—	—	—
Angry Resentment	.21	—	—	—	—	—	.23	—	.23	—	—	—	.24	—	—	—
Antisocial	—	—	—	—	—	—	—	—	—	—	—	—	—	—	—	—
Anxious	.33	.18	—	—	.21	—	.37	—	.38	.18	—	—	—	—	—	—
Critical/Argumentative	—	—	—	—	—	—	—	—	—	—	—	—	—	—	—	—
Defensive	—	—	—	—	—	—	—	—	—	—	—	—	—	—	—	—
Depressed	.48	.26	—	—	.26	—	.55	.26	.41	.22	—	—	.25	—	—	—
Emotionally Controlled	—	—	—	—	—	—	—	—	—	—	—	—	—	—	—	—
Family Problems	—	—	—	—	—	—	—	—	—	—	—	—	.25	—	—	—
Histrionic	—	—	—	—	—	—	—	—	.21	—	—	—	—	—	—	—
Insecure	.26	—	—	—	—	—	.38	.23	—	—	—	—	—	—	—	—

Correlates for MMPI-2 Content Scales *(continued)*

Extra-test Characteristics	Content Scales															
	Anxiety (ANX)		Fears (FRS)		Obsessiveness (OBS)		Depression (DEP)		Health Concerns (HEA)		Bizarre Mentation (BIZ)		Anger (ANG)		Cynicism (CYN)	
	Men	Women	Men	Women	Men	Women	Men	Women	Men	Women	Men	Women	Men	Women	Men	Women
Introverted	—	—	—	—	—	—	—	.16	—	—	—	—	—	—	—	—
Narcissistic	—	—	—	—	—	—	—	—	—	—	—	—	—	—	—	—
Negative Treatment Attitudes	—	—	—	—	—	—	—	—	—	—	—	—	—	—	—	—
Obsessive-Compulsive	—	—	—	—	—	—	.23	—	.22	—	—	—	—	—	—	—
Passive-Submissive	—	—	—	—	—	—	—	—	—	—	—	—	—	—	—	—
Pessimistic	.21	.16	—	—	—	—	.33	.22	.31	.17	—	—	—	—	—	—
Somatic Symptoms	.31	.17	—	—	—	—	.31	—	.49	.33	—	—	—	—	—	—
Suspicious	—	—	—	—	—	—	—	—	—	—	—	—	—	—	—	—
Patient Description Form Items																
Acts Out	—	—	—	—	—	—	—	—	—	—	—	—	—	—	—	—
Agitated	—	—	—	—	—	—	—	—	—	—	—	—	.24	—	—	—
Angry	—	—	—	—	—	—	—	—	—	—	—	—	.29	—	—	—
Antisocial Behavior	—	—	—	—	—	—	—	—	—	—	—	—	—	—	.06	.17
Anxious	.34	—	—	—	.23	—	.35	—	.38	—	—	—	—	—	—	—
Argumentative	—	—	—	—	—	—	—	—	—	—	—	—	—	—	—	—
Blames Family For Difficulties	—	—	—	—	—	—	—	—	—	—	—	—	—	—	—	—
Bored	—	—	—	—	—	—	—	—	—	—	—	—	—	—	—	—
Communicates Effectively	—	—	—	—	—	—	—	—	—	—	—	-.18	—	—	—	—
Competitive	—	—	—	-.17	—	—	—	—	—	—	—	-.16	—	—	—	—
Complains of Fatigue	—	—	—	—	—	—	—	—	.35	.28	—	—	—	—	—	—
Complains of Sleep Disturbance	.44	.22	—	—	.25	—	.43	.17	.41	.21	—	—	.27	—	.24	—
Concerned About Status	—	—	—	—	—	—	—	—	—	—	—	—	—	—	—	—
Copes Well with Stress	-.26	-.23	—	-.17	—	—	-.26	-.23	-.20	-.22	-.21	—	—	—	—	—
Creates Good First Impression	—	—	—	—	—	—	—	—	—	—	—	-.23	—	—	—	-.19
Deceptive	—	—	—	—	—	—	—	—	—	—	—	—	—	—	—	—
Defensive	—	—	—	—	—	—	—	—	—	—	—	—	—	—	—	—
Dependable	—	—	—	—	—	—	—	—	—	—	—	—	—	—	—	-.20
Depressed	.41	.25	—	—	—	—	.51	.24	.38	.21	—	—	—	—	—	—
Difficult to Motivate	—	—	—	—	—	—	—	—	—	—	—	—	—	—	—	.18
Difficulty Concentrating	—	—	—	—	—	—	—	—	.34	.18	—	—	—	—	—	—
Difficulty Trusting Others	—	—	—	—	—	—	—	—	—	—	—	—	—	—	—	—

Does Not Get Along with Coworkers	—	—	—	—	—	—	—	—	—	—	—	—	—	—	—	—
Energetic	-.21	-.19	—	—	—	—	-.29	-.24	-.24	-.23	—	—	—	—	—	—
Excitable	—	—	—	—	—	—	—	—	—	—	—	—	—	—	—	—
Extroverted	—	—	—	—	—	—	—	—	—	—	—	—	—	—	—	—
Familial Discord	—	—	—	—	—	—	—	—	—	—	—	—	—	—	—	—
Family Lacks Love	—	—	—	—	—	—	—	—	—	—	—	—	.26	—	—	—
Feels Gets Raw Deal From Life	—	—	—	—	—	—	.31	.23	—	—	—	—	—	—	—	—
Feels Hopeless	.37	.24	—	—	.23	—	.46	.27	—	—	—	—	.24	—	—	—
Feels Inferior	—	—	—	—	—	—	—	—	—	—	—	—	—	—	—	—
Feels Like a Failure	.29	.18	—	—	—	—	.40	.25	—	—	—	—	—	—	—	—
Feels Overwhelmed	.34	.19	—	—	—	—	.36	—	.33	.17	—	—	—	—	—	—
Feels That Life is a Strain	.31	.23	—	—	—	—	.38	.26	—	—	.19	—	—	—	—	—
Fired From Past Jobs	—	—	—	—	—	—	—	—	—	—	—	—	—	—	—	—
Gives Up Easily	—	—	—	—	—	—	—	—	—	—	—	—	—	—	—	—
Grouchy	—	—	—	—	—	—	—	—	—	—	—	—	—	.16	—	—
Has Insight Into Own Problems	—	—	—	—	—	—	—	—	—	—	—	—	—	—	—	-.25
Has Many Interests	—	—	—	-.18	—	-.17	—	—	—	-.26	—	—	—	—	—	-.20
Has Many Nightmares	—	—	—	—	—	—	—	—	—	—	—	—	.26	—	.25	—
Has Temper Tantrums	—	—	—	—	—	—	—	—	—	—	—	—	.29	.23	—	—
High Aspirations	—	—	—	—	—	-.18	—	—	—	—	—	—	—	—	—	-.18
Hypochondriacal	—	—	—	—	—	—	—	—	.37	.22	—	—	—	—	—	—
Idealistic	—	—	—	—	—	—	—	—	—	—	—	—	—	—	—	-.18
Introverted	—	—	—	—	—	—	—	—	—	—	—	—	—	—	—	—
Likable	—	—	—	—	—	—	—	—	—	—	—	—	—	—	—	-.22
Lonely	—	—	—	—	—	—	—	—	—	—	—	—	—	—	—	—
Low Frustration Tolerance	—	—	—	—	—	—	—	—	—	—	—	.19	.25	—	—	—
Multiple Somatic Complaints	—	—	—	—	—	—	—	—	.47	.30	—	—	—	—	—	—
Needs to Achieve	—	—	—	—	—	—	—	—	—	—	—	—	—	—	—	—
Nervous	—	—	—	—	.25	—	—	—	—	—	—	—	—	—	—	—
Optimistic	—	—	—	—	—	—	-.32	-.24	—	—	—	—	—	—	—	—
Overbearing in Relationships	—	—	—	—	—	—	—	—	—	—	—	—	—	—	—	—
Overly Sensitive to Criticism	—	—	—	—	—	—	—	—	—	—	—	—	—	—	—	—
Passive in Relationships	—	—	—	—	—	—	—	—	—	—	—	—	—	—	—	—
Pessimistic	—	—	—	—	—	—	.37	.26	—	—	—	—	—	—	—	—
Physical Symptoms in Response to Stress	—	—	—	—	—	—	—	—	.43	.28	—	—	—	—	—	—
Physically Abusive	—	—	—	—	—	—	—	—	—	—	—	—	.25	—	—	—
Preoccupied with Health Problems	—	—	—	—	—	—	—	—	.49	.30	—	—	—	—	—	—
Problems with Authority Figures	—	—	—	—	—	—	—	—	—	—	—	—	—	—	—	—
Psychologically Immature	—	—	—	—	—	—	—	—	—	—	—	—	—	—	—	.16
Psychotic Symptoms	—	—	—	—	—	—	—	—	—	—	—	.19	—	—	—	—
Resents Family Members	—	—	—	—	—	—	—	—	—	—	—	—	.26	—	—	—
Ruminates	—	—	—	—	—	—	—	—	—	—	—	—	—	—	—	—

Correlates for MMPI-2 Content Scales *(continued)*

Extra-test Characteristics	Content Scales: Anxiety (ANX) Men	Anxiety (ANX) Women	Fears (FRS) Men	Fears (FRS) Women	Obsessiveness (OBS) Men	Obsessiveness (OBS) Women	Depression (DEP) Men	Depression (DEP) Women	Health Concerns (HEA) Men	Health Concerns (HEA) Women	Bizarre Mentation (BIZ) Men	Bizarre Mentation (BIZ) Women	Anger (ANG) Men	Anger (ANG) Women	Cynicism (CYN) Men	Cynicism (CYN) Women
Sad	.35	.20	—	—	.19	—	.43	.20	—	—	—	—	—	—	—	—
Self-Degrading	—	—	—	—	—	—	—	—	—	—	—	—	—	—	—	—
Self-Doubting	—	—	—	—	—	—	—	—	—	—	—	—	—	—	—	—
Self-Punishing	—	—	—	—	—	—	—	—	—	—	—	-.18	—	—	—	—
Self-Reliant	—	—	—	—	—	—	—	—	—	—	—	—	—	—	—	—
Shy	—	—	—	—	—	—	—	—	—	—	—	—	—	—	—	—
Socially Awkward	—	—	—	—	—	—	—	—	—	—	—	—	—	—	—	—
Sociopathic	—	—	—	—	—	—	—	—	—	—	—	—	—	—	—	—
Stormy Interpersonal Relationships	—	—	—	—	—	—	—	—	—	—	—	—	—	—	—	—
Suicidal Ideations	.33	.21	—	—	—	—	.40	.26	—	—	—	—	—	—	—	—
Superficial Relationships	—	—	—	—	—	—	—	—	—	—	—	—	—	—	—	—
Tearful	—	—	—	—	—	—	—	—	—	—	—	—	—	—	—	—
Uncomfortable with Opposite Sex	—	—	—	—	—	—	—	—	—	—	—	—	—	—	—	—
Work-Oriented	—	—	—	-.16	—	—	—	—	—	—	—	-.18	—	—	—	—
Worrier	.32	.19	—	—	—	—	—	—	—	—	—	—	—	—	—	—

Extra-test Characteristics	Content Scales (continued)													
	Antisocial Practices (ASP)		Type A Behavior (TPA)		Low Self-Esteem (LSE)		Social Discomfort (SOD)		Family Problems (FAM)		Work Interference (WRK)		Negative Treatment Indicators (TRT)	
	Men	Women	Men	Women	Men	Women	Men	Women	Men	Women	Men	Women	Men	Women
Intake Information														
Axis I Bipolar or Cyclothymia	—	—	—	—	.16	—	—	—	—	—	—	—	—	—
Axis I Depression or Dysthymia	—	—	—	—	.17	.18	—	—	—	—	.27	.15	.20	.23
Axis I Multiple Diagnoses	—	—	—	—	—	—	—	—	—	—	.16	—	—	—
Axis I Schizophrenia	—	—	—	—	—	—	—	—	—	—	—	—	—	—
Axis I Substance Abuse or Dependence	.20	—	—	—	—	—	—	—	—	—	—	—	—	—
Axis II Antisocial Personality Disorder	.17	—	—	—	—	—	—	—	—	—	—	—	—	—
Cocaine Abuse in the Past Six Months	—	—	—	—	—	—	—	—	—	—	—	—	—	—
Currently on Antidepressant Medication	—	—	—	—	—	.15	—	.21	—	—	—	—	—	—
Currently on Antipsychotic Medication	—	—	—	—	—	—	—	—	—	—	—	—	—	—
Currently on Anxiolytic Medication	—	—	—	—	—	—	—	.16	—	—	—	.13	—	—
Ever Arrested	.17	.19	—	—	—	—	—	—	—	—	—	—	—	—
History of Being Physically Abused	—	—	—	—	.17	—	—	—	.26	.20	—	—	—	—
History of Being Physically Abusive	.21	—	—	—	—	—	—	—	—	—	—	—	—	—
History of Being Sexually Abused	—	—	—	—	—	—	—	—	—	.20	—	—	—	—
History of Committing Domestic Violence	.24	—	—	—	—	—	—	—	—	—	—	—	—	—
History of Having Few or No Friends	—	—	—	—	—	.16	—	.20	.21	.16	—	.18	—	.23
History of Misdemeanor Conviction(s)	—	.20	—	—	—	—	—	—	—	—	—	—	—	—
History of Outpatient Psychiatric Treatment	—	—	—	—	.19	—	—	—	—	—	.16	—	—	—
History of Suicide Attempts	.14	.22	—	—	—	.20	—	—	—	.24	—	.21	—	.25
History of Victim of Domestic Violence	.18	—	—	—	—	—	—	—	—	—	—	—	—	—
Lifetime History of Alcohol Abuse	—	—	—	—	—	—	—	—	—	—	—	—	—	—
Lifetime History of Cocaine Abuse	—	.17	—	—	—	—	—	—	—	—	—	—	—	—
Lifetime History of Marijuana Abuse	.18	—	—	—	—	—	—	—	.18	—	—	—	—	—
Previous Psychiatric Hospitalizations	—	—	—	—	—	—	—	—	—	—	—	.16	.17	.15
Mental Status														
Anxiety During Interview	—	—	—	—	.16	—	—	—	—	—	—	—	—	—
Circumstantial Speech	—	—	—	—	—	—	—	—	.19	—	—	—	—	—
Defensive During Interview	.17	—	—	—	—	—	—	—	—	—	—	—	—	—
Depression During Interview	—	—	—	—	.22	.20	.16	—	.18	—	.30	.25	.26	.18

Extra-test Characteristics	Content Scales (continued)													
	Antisocial Practices (ASP)		Type A Behavior (TPA)		Low Self-Esteem (LSE)		Social Discomfort (SOD)		Family Problems (FAM)		Work Interference (WRK)		Negative Treatment Indicators (TRT)	
	Men	Women	Men	Women	Men	Women	Men	Women	Men	Women	Men	Women	Men	Women
Hallucinations	—	.15	—	—	—	—	—	—	—	—	—	—	—	—
Loose Associations	—	—	—	—	—	—	—	—	—	—	—	—	—	—
Obsessions	—	—	—	—	—	—	—	—	—	—	—	—	—	—
Poor Judgment	.19	—	—	—	—	—	—	—	—	—	—	—	—	—
Prevailing Mood Angry	.17	—	—	—	—	—	—	—	—	—	.18	—	.19	—
Prevailing Mood Happy	—	—	—	—	—	—	—	—	—	—	—	—	—	—
Prevailing Mood Sad	—	—	—	—	—	.19	—	—	.16	—	.22	.21	.19	.25
SCL-90-R Scales														
Anxiety	.17	—	.33	.21	.50	.43	.34	.35	.43	.32	.58	.52	.58	.45
Depression	—	—	.21	.15	.52	.51	.40	.37	.44	.41	.63	.62	.61	.58
Hostility	.33	.18	.45	.25	.29	.42	.26	.26	.45	.42	.43	.46	.49	.45
Interpersonal Sensitivity	—	—	.29	.24	.53	.58	.47	.46	.44	.42	.60	.58	.58	.55
Obsessive-Compulsive	—	—	.31	.19	.49	.47	.36	.36	.37	.34	.59	.57	.55	.48
Paranoid Ideation	.28	.17	.38	.29	.38	.43	.27	.28	.45	.46	.52	.48	.53	.46
Phobic Anxiety	—	—	.19	.18	.40	.39	.33	.43	.29	.28	.44	.45	.45	.41
Psychoticism	.16	.15	.26	.28	.47	.51	.32	.35	.41	.41	.56	.55	.56	.55
Somatization	.17	—	.30	.16	.39	.38	.19	.28	.31	.32	.49	.43	.46	.38
Initial SCL-90 Analogue														
Anxiety	—	—	—	—	—	—	—	—	—	—	—	—	.21	—
Depression	—	—	—	—	.20	.21	—	—	.20	.07	.29	.11	.28	.21
Interpersonal Sensitivity	—	—	—	—	.18	.20	—	—	—	—	—	—	—	—
Phobic Anxiety	—	—	—	—	—	—	—	—	—	—	—	—	—	—
Somatization	—	—	—	—	.21	.08	—	—	—	—	.21	.11	—	—
Patient Description Form Scales														
Achievement-Oriented	—	—	—	—	-.17	-.21	-.13	-.29	—	—	-.22	-.22	-.18	-.27
Aggressive	—	.23	—	—	—	—	—	—	—	—	—	—	—	—
Agitated	—	—	—	—	—	—	—	—	.19	—	—	—	—	—
Angry Resentment	—	.22	—	—	—	—	.20	—	—	—	—	—	.23	—
Antisocial	.19	.29	—	—	—	—	—	—	—	—	—	—	—	—

Anxious	—	—	—	—	.33	—	.23	—	.26	—	.29	—	.34	.18
Critical/Argumentative	—	.20	—	—	—	—	—	—	—	.18	—	—	—	—
Defensive	—	.24	—	—	—	—	—	—	—	—	—	—	—	—
Depressed	—	—	—	—	.35	.25	.35	.17	.33	—	.40	.21	.48	.24
Emotionally Controlled	—	—	—	—	—	—	.20	—	—	—	—	—	—	—
Family Problems	.26	.17	—	—	—	—	—	—	.31	.23	—	—	—	—
Histrionic	—	—	—	—	—	—	—	—	—	—	—	—	—	—
Insecure	—	—	—	—	.34	.24	.32	—	.27	—	.25	.17	.33	.17
Introverted	—	—	—	—	.20	.16	.27	.24	—	—	—	—	—	.18
Narcissistic	—	.23	—	—	—	—	—	—	—	—	—	—	—	—
Negative Treatment Attitudes	—	.18	—	—	—	—	—	—	—	—	—	—	—	—
Obsessive-Compulsive	—	—	—	—	—	—	—	—	—	—	—	—	.21	—
Passive-Submissive	—	—	—	—	.22	.23	—	—	—	—	—	—	—	—
Pessimistic	—	—	—	—	.25	.19	.26	—	—	—	—	—	.28	.19
Somatic Symptoms	—	—	—	—	.25	—	—	—	—	—	.26	—	.24	—
Suspicious	—	.21	—	—	—	—	.22	—	—	—	—	—	—	—
Patient Description Form Items														
Acts Out	.23	.20	—	—	—	—	—	—	—	—	—	—	—	—
Agitated	—	—	—	—	—	—	—	—	.27	—	—	—	—	—
Angry	—	—	—	—	—	—	—	—	—	—	—	—	—	—
Antisocial Behavior	.23	.29	—	—	—	—	—	—	—	—	—	—	—	—
Anxious	—	—	—	—	—	—	—	—	.27	—	.31	—	.32	—
Argumentative	—	—	—	—	—	—	—	—	—	.17	—	—	—	—
Blames Family For Difficulties	—	—	—	—	—	—	—	—	.23	.18	—	—	—	—
Bored	—	.22	—	—	—	—	—	—	—	—	—	—	—	—
Communicates Effectively	—	—	—	—	—	—	—	—	—	—	—	—	—	—
Competitive	—	—	—	—	—	—	—	—	—	—	—	—	—	—
Complains of Fatigue	—	—	—	—	—	—	—	—	—	—	—	—	—	—
Complains of Sleep Disturbance	—	—	—	—	.35	—	.27	.16	—	—	.35	—	.44	—
Concerned About Status	—	—	—	—	—	—	-.01	-.17	—	—	—	—	—	—
Copes Well with Stress	—	—	—	—	—	-.22	—	—	—	—	-.22	-.23	-.22	-.22
Creates Good First Impression	—	—	—	-.17	—	—	—	-.18	—	—	—	-.19	—	-.21
Deceptive	—	.25	—	—	—	—	—	—	—	—	—	—	—	—
Defensive	—	.24	—	—	—	—	—	—	—	—	—	—	—	—
Dependable	—	—	—	—	—	—	—	—	—	—	—	—	—	—
Depressed	—	—	—	—	.26	.24	.30	—	.26	—	.37	.18	.39	.22
Difficult to Motivate	—	—	—	—	—	—	—	—	—	—	—	—	—	—
Difficulty Concentrating	—	—	—	—	—	—	—	—	—	—	—	—	—	—
Difficulty Trusting Others	—	—	—	—	—	—	—	—	—	.18	—	—	—	—
Does Not Get Along with Coworkers	—	—	—	—	—	—	—	—	.30	—	—	—	—	—
Energetic	—	—	—	—	—	—	—	-.28	—	—	-.26	-.24	-.24	-.25

Extra-test Characteristics	Content Scales (continued)													
	Antisocial Practices (ASP)		Type A Behavior (TPA)		Low Self-Esteem (LSE)		Social Discomfort (SOD)		Family Problems (FAM)		Work Interference (WRK)		Negative Treatment Indicators (TRT)	
	Men	Women	Men	Women	Men	Women	Men	Women	Men	Women	Men	Women	Men	Women
Excitable	—	.23	—	—	—	—	—	—	—	—	—	—	—	—
Extroverted	—	—	—	—	—	—	-.20	-.22	—	—	-.20	-.21	—	—
Familial Discord	.26	—	—	—	—	—	—	—	.23	.21	—	—	—	—
Family Lacks Love	.24	.16	—	—	—	—	—	—	.31	.25	—	—	—	—
Feels Gets Raw Deal From Life	—	—	—	—	—	—	—	—	—	.20	—	—	—	—
Feels Hopeless	—	—	—	—	.33	.21	.35	—	.30	—	.34	.19	.43	.24
Feels Inferior	—	—	—	—	.23	.28	—	—	—	—	—	—	—	—
Feels Like a Failure	—	—	—	—	.31	.24	.31	—	—	—	.27	.17	.35	.19
Feels Overwhelmed	—	—	—	—	.29	.17	—	—	—	—	.27	—	.34	.16
Feels That Life is a Strain	—	—	—	—	.33	.18	—	—	—	—	—	—	.36	.21
Fired From Past Jobs	—	—	—	—	—	—	—	—	—	—	—	—	—	—
Grouchy	—	—	—	—	—	—	—	—	—	.17	—	—	—	—
Gives Up Easily	—	—	—	—	—	.22	—	—	—	—	—	—	.21	.23
Has Insight Into Own Problems	—	—	—	—	—	—	—	—	—	—	—	—	—	—
Has Many Interests	—	—	—	—	—	—	—	-.20	—	—	—	—	—	-.23
Has Many Nightmares	—	—	—	—	—	—	—	—	—	—	—	—	—	—
Has Temper Tantrums	.23	.24	—	—	—	—	—	—	—	—	—	—	—	—
High Aspirations	—	—	—	—	—	—	—	-.25	—	—	—	-.20	—	-.26
Hypochondriacal	—	—	—	—	—	—	—	—	—	—	—	—	—	—
Idealistic	—	—	—	—	—	—	—	—	—	—	—	—	—	—
Introverted	—	—	—	—	—	—	.29	.21	—	—	—	—	—	—
Likable	—	—	—	-.16	—	—	—	—	—	—	—	—	—	—
Lonely	.22	—	—	—	—	—	—	—	—	—	—	—	—	—
Low Frustration Tolerance	.21	.22	—	—	—	—	—	—	—	—	—	—	—	—
Multiple Somatic Complaints	—	—	—	—	—	—	—	—	—	—	.27	—	—	—
Needs to Achieve	—	—	—	—	—	—	—	-.21	—	—	—	—	—	—
Nervous	—	—	—	—	—	—	—	—	—	—	—	—	—	—
Optimistic	—	—	—	—	—	—	—	—	—	—	—	—	—	—
Overbearing in Relationships	—	—	—	—	—	—	—	—	—	.17	—	—	—	—
Overly Sensitive to Criticism	—	—	—	—	—	—	—	—	—	—	—	.19	—	—
Passive in Relationships	—	—	—	—	—	.24	—	—	—	—	—	.18	—	—
Pessimistic	—	—	—	—	.29	.21	.29	—	—	—	—	—	.35	.18

Physical Symptoms in Response to Stress	—	—	.21	—	—	—	—	—	—	—	—	—	—	—
Physically Abusive	.25	.19	—	—	—	—	—	—	—	—	—	—	—	—
Preoccupied with Health Problems	—	—	—	—	.28	—	—	—	—	—	.30	—	—	—
Problems with Authority Figures	—	.25	—	—	—	—	—	—	—	—	—	—	—	—
Psychologically Immature	—	.24	—	—	—	—	—	—	—	—	—	—	—	—
Psychotic Symptoms	—	—	—	—	—	—	—	—	—	—	—	—	—	—
Resents Family Members	—	—	—	—	—	—	—	—	.31	.20	—	—	—	—
Ruminates	—	—	—	—	—	—	—	—	.28	—	—	—	—	—
Sad	—	—	—	—	—	—	—	—	.26	—	.30	.16	.34	.17
Self-Degrading	—	—	—	—	.28	.23	.32	—	.25	—	—	—	—	—
Self-Doubting	—	—	—	—	.28	.18	—	—	—	—	—	—	—	—
Self-Punishing	—	—	—	—	—	—	.29	—	—	—	—	—	—	—
Self-Reliant	—	—	—	—	—	-.22	—	—	—	—	—	-.21	—	—
Shy	—	—	—	—	—	—	.21	.21	—	—	—	—	—	—
Socially Awkward	—	—	—	—	—	—	.21	.21	—	—	—	—	—	—
Sociopathic	—	.24	—	—	—	—	—	—	—	—	—	—	—	—
Stormy Interpersonal Relationships	.23	—	—	—	—	—	—	—	—	—	—	—	—	—
Suicidal Ideations	—	—	—	—	—	—	.30	.17	—	—	.26	.19	.35	.26
Superficial Relationships	—	.23	—	—	—	—	—	—	—	—	—	—	—	—
Tearful	—	—	—	—	—	.22	—	—	—	—	—	—	—	—
Uncomfortable with Opposite Sex	—	—	—	—	—	—	.27	—	—	—	—	—	—	—
Work-Oriented	—	—	—	—	—	—	—	—	—	—	—	—	—	—
Worrier	—	—	—	—	.28	.20	—	—	—	—	—	—	—	—

Appendix I

Correlates for MMPI-2 Content Component Scales

Table I-1. Correlates for MMPI-2 Content Component FRS Scales

Extra-test Characteristics	Generalized Fearfulness (FRS_1)		Multiple Fears (FRS_2)	
	Men	Women	Men	Women
Intake Information				
Alcohol Abuse in the Past Six Months	—	—	—	—
Axis I Depression or Dysthymia	—	—	—	—
Axis I Other Psychotic Diagnosis	—	—	—	—
Axis I Schizophrenia	—	—	.19	—
Axis I Substance Abuse or Dependence	—	—	—	—
Axis II Antisocial Personality Disorder	—	—	—	—
Axis II Cluster B Diagnosis	—	—	—	—
Cocaine Abuse in the Past Six Months	—	—	—	—
Currently on Antidepressant Medication	—	—	—	—
Currently on Antipsychotic Medication	—	—	.19	—
Currently on Anxiolytic Medication	—	—	—	—
Ever Arrested	—	—	—	—
History of Being Physically Abused	—	.16	—	—
History of Being Physically Abusive	—	—	—	—
History of Being Sexually Abused	—	.16	—	—
History of Committing Domestic Violence	—	—	—	—
History of Domestic Violence Conviction	—	—	—	—
History of Felony Conviction(s)	—	—	—	—
History of Having Few or No Friends	.22	.14	—	—
History of Misdemeanor Conviction(s)	—	—	—	—
History of Outpatient Psychiatric Treatment	—	—	—	—
History of Suicide Attempts	—	.15	—	—
History of Victim of Domestic Violence	—	—	—	—
Lifetime History of Alcohol Abuse	—	—	—	—
Lifetime History of Cocaine Abuse	—	—	—	—
Lifetime History of Heroin Abuse	—	—	—	—
Lifetime History of Marijuana Abuse	—	—	—	—
Number of Arrests	—	—	—	—
Previous Psychiatric Hospitalizations	—	—	—	—

Mental Status				
Anxiety During Interview	—	—	—	—
Depression During Interview	—	—	—	—
Hallucinations	—	—	.17	—
Loose Associations	—	—	—	—
Poor Judgment	—	—	—	—
Prevailing Mood Angry	—	—	—	—
Prevailing Mood Happy	—	—	—	—
Prevailing Mood Sad	—	—	—	—
Speech During Interview	—	—	—	—
Unusual Gestures	—	—	—	—
SCL-90-R Scales				
Anxiety	.37	.36	—	.16
Depression	.22	.24	—	—
Hostility	.20	.26	—	—
Interpersonal Sensitivity	.29	.30	—	—
Obsessive-Compulsive	.32	.33	—	.16
Paranoid Ideation	.27	.28	—	.15
Phobic Anxiety	.49	.46	—	.25
Psychoticism	.36	.31	—	.16
Somatization	.30	.32	—	.18
Initial SCL-90 Analogue				
Anxiety	—	—	—	—
Depression	—	—	—	—
Hostility	—	—	—	—
Interpersonal Sensitivity	—	—	—	—
Paranoid Ideation	—	—	—	—
Somatization	—	—	—	—
Patient Description Form Scales				
Achievement-Oriented	—	-.17	—	—
Aggressive	—	—	—	—
Agitated	—	—	—	—
Angry Resentment	—	—	—	—
Antisocial	—	—	—	—
Anxious	.21	.17	—	—
Critical/Argumentative	—	—	—	—
Defensive	—	—	—	—
Depressed	—	.16	—	—
Family Problems	—	—	—	—

Table I-1. Correlates for MMPI-2 Content Component FRS Scales *(continued)*

Extra-test Characteristics	Generalized Fearfulness (FRS_1)		Multiple Fears (FRS_2)	
	Men	Women	Men	Women
Histrionic	—	—	—	—
Insecure	—	—	—	—
Introverted	—	.17	—	—
Narcissistic	—	—	—	—
Negative Treatment Attitudes	—	—	—	—
Obsessive-Compulsive	—	—	—	—
Passive-Submissive	—	—	—	—
Pessimistic	—	—	—	—
Procrastinates	—	—	—	—
Somatic Symptoms	.23	—	—	—
Suspicious	—	—	—	—
Patient Description Form Items				
Acts Out	—	—	—	—
Agitated	—	—	—	—
Angry	—	—	—	—
Antisocial Behavior	—	—	—	—
Anxious	.21	—	—	—
Argumentative	—	—	—	—
Assertive	—	—	—	—
Blames Family For Difficulties	—	—	—	—
Communicates Effectively	—	-.16	—	—
Competitive	—	—	—	—
Complains of Fatigue	—	—	—	—
Complains of Sleep Disturbance	—	—	—	—
Concerned About Status	—	—	—	—
Copes Well with Stress	—	-.17	—	—
Creates Good First Impression	—	—	—	—
Critical of Others	—	—	—	—
Deceptive	—	—	—	—
Defensive	—	—	—	—
Delusional Thinking	—	—	—	—
Demanding of Attention	—	—	—	—
Dependable	—	—	—	—
Depressed	—	—	—	—
Difficult to Motivate	—	—	—	—
Difficulty Concentrating	.20	—	—	—

Difficulty Making Decisions	—	—	—	—
Difficulty Trusting Others	—	—	—	—
Does Not Get Along with Coworkers	—	—	—	—
Energetic	—	—	—	—
Exaggerated Need for Affection	—	—	—	—
Extroverted	—	—	—	—
Familial Discord	—	—	—	—
Family Lacks Love	—	—	—	—
Feels Gets Raw Deal From Life	—	—	—	—
Feels Hopeless	—	—	—	—
Feels Inferior	—	—	—	—
Feels Like a Failure	—	—	—	—
Feels Overwhelmed	—	—	—	—
Feels Rejected	—	—	—	—
Feels That Life is a Strain	—	—	—	—
Gives Up Easily	—	—	—	—
Grouchy	—	—	—	—
Harbors Grudges	—	—	—	—
Has Insight Into Own Problems	—	—	—	—
Has Many Interests	—	—	—	—
Has Many Nightmares	—	.22	—	—
Has Temper Tantrums	—	—	—	—
High Aspirations	—	—	—	—
Hypochondriacal	—	—	—	—
Impulsive	—	—	—	—
Insecure	—	—	—	—
Introverted	—	—	—	—
Likable	—	—	—	—
Lonely	—	—	—	—
Low Frustration Tolerance	—	—	—	—
Low Sex Drive	—	—	—	—
Manipulative	—	—	—	—
Many Specific Fears	—	.17	—	—
Multiple Somatic Complaints	.23	—	—	—
Narcissistic	—	—	—	—
Needs Attention	—	—	—	—
Needs to Achieve	—	—	—	—
Nervous	—	.18	—	—
Optimistic	—	—	—	—
Overcontrolled	—	—	—	—
Overly Compliant	—	—	—	—
Overly Sensitive to Criticism	—	—	—	—
Paranoid Features	—	—	—	—

Table I-1. Correlates for MMPI-2 Content Component FRS Scales *(continued)*

Extra-test Characteristics	Generalized Fearfulness (FRS_1)		Multiple Fears (FRS_2)	
	Men	Women	Men	Women
Passive	—	—	—	—
Passive in Relationships	—	—	—	—
Pessimistic	—	—	—	—
Physical Symptoms in Response to Stress	.20	—	—	—
Physically Abusive	—	—	—	—
Preoccupied with Health Problems	.25	—	—	—
Problems with Authority Figures	—	—	—	—
Psychologically Immature	—	—	—	—
Reliable Informant	—	—	—	—
Resents Family Members	—	—	—	—
Restless	—	—	—	—
Ruminates	—	—	—	—
Sad	—	—	—	—
Self-Degrading	—	—	—	—
Self-Doubting	—	—	—	—
Self-Indulgent	—	—	—	—
Self-Punishing	—	—	—	—
Self-Reliant	—	—	—	—
Sexually Adjusted	—	—	—	—
Shy	—	—	—	—
Socially Awkward	—	.18	—	—
Sociopathic	—	—	—	—
Stereotypic Masculine Behavior	—	—	-.20	—
Stormy Interpersonal Relationships	—	—	—	—
Submissive	—	—	—	—
Suicidal Ideations	—	.19	—	—
Superficial Relationships	—	—	—	—
Tearful	—	—	—	—
Unable to See Own Limitations	—	—	—	—
Work-Oriented	—	—	—	—
Worrier	—	—	—	—

Table I-2. Correlates for MMPI-2 Content Component DEP Scales

Extra-test Characteristics	Lack of Drive (DEP_1)		Dysphoria (DEP_2)		Self-Depreciation (DEP_3)		Suicidal Ideation (DEP_4)	
	Men	Women	Men	Women	Men	Women	Men	Women
Intake Information								
Alcohol Abuse in the Past Six Months	—	—	—	—	—	—	—	—
Axis I Depression or Dysthymia	.29	.23	.27	.30	.19	.21	.27	.26
Axis I Other Psychotic Diagnosis	—	—	—	—	—	—	—	—
Axis I Schizophrenia	—	—	—	—	—	—	—	—
Axis I Substance Abuse or Dependence	—	—	—	—	—	—	—	—
Axis II Antisocial Personality Disorder	—	—	—	—	—	—	—	—
Axis II Cluster B Diagnosis	—	—	—	—	—	—	—	—
Cocaine Abuse in the Past Six Months	—	—	—	—	—	—	.17	—
Currently on Antidepressant Medication	—	.17	—	.16	—	—	.17	.16
Currently on Antipsychotic Medication	—	—	—	—	—	—	—	—
Currently on Anxiolytic Medication	—	.15	—	—	—	—	—	—
Ever Arrested	—	—	—	-.17	—	—	—	—
History of Being Physically Abused	—	—	—	—	—	—	—	—
History of Being Physically Abusive	—	—	—	—	—	—	—	—
History of Being Sexually Abused	—	—	—	—	—	—	—	—
History of Committing Domestic Violence	—	—	—	—	—	—	—	—
History of Domestic Violence Conviction	—	—	—	—	—	—	—	—
History of Felony Conviction(s)	—	—	—	—	—	—	—	—
History of Having Few or No Friends	—	.18	—	.18	—	.19	—	—
History of Misdemeanor Conviction(s)	—	—	—	—	—	—	—	—
History of Outpatient Psychiatric Treatment	—	—	.17	—	—	—	—	—
History of Suicide Attempts	—	.26	—	.22	.16	.21	—	.32
History of Victim of Domestic Violence	—	—	—	—	—	—	—	—
Lifetime History of Alcohol Abuse	—	—	—	—	—	.15	—	—
Lifetime History of Cocaine Abuse	—	—	—	—	—	—	—	—
Lifetime History of Heroin Abuse	—	—	—	—	—	—	—	—
Lifetime History of Marijuana Abuse	—	—	—	-.15	—	—	—	—
Number of Arrests	—	—	—	—	—	—	—	—
Previous Psychiatric Hospitalizations	—	.20	—	—	—	—	.19	.18
Mental Status								
Anxiety During Interview	—	—	—	—	—	—	—	—
Depression During Interview	.31	.27	.31	.30	.31	.19	.28	.23
Hallucinations	—	—	—	—	—	—	—	—
Loose Associations	—	—	—	—	—	—	—	—

Table I-2. Correlates for MMPI-2 Content Component DEP Scales *(continued)*

Extra-test Characteristics	Lack of Drive (DEP_1)		Dysphoria (DEP_2)		Self-Depreciation (DEP_3)		Suicidal Ideation (DEP_4)	
	Men	Women	Men	Women	Men	Women	Men	Women
Poor Judgment	—	—	—	—	—	—	—	—
Prevailing Mood Angry	—	—	—	—	—	—	—	—
Prevailing Mood Happy	—	—	-.18	—	—	—	—	—
Prevailing Mood Sad	.23	.23	.27	.26	.25	.19	.22	.20
Speech During Interview	—	—	—	—	—	—	—	—
Unusual Gestures	—	—	—	—	—	—	—	—
SCL-90-R Scales								
Anxiety	.57	.47	.53	.49	.43	.37	.48	.39
Depression	.65	.63	.65	.63	.54	.51	.59	.53
Hostility	.50	.46	.40	.43	.34	.39	.33	.40
Interpersonal Sensitivity	.55	.50	.53	.52	.46	.49	.45	.42
Obsessive-Compulsive	.59	.48	.52	.46	.44	.39	.46	.38
Paranoid Ideation	.46	.44	.45	.42	.40	.40	.39	.36
Phobic Anxiety	.42	.37	.35	.33	.30	.29	.34	.29
Psychoticism	.56	.49	.53	.44	.48	.46	.53	.46
Somatization	.50	.45	.38	.39	.32	.29	.41	.36
Initial SCL-90 Analogue								
Anxiety	.25	—	.29	—	.23	—	—	—
Depression	.39	.16	.43	.20	.34	.16	.25	—
Hostility	—	—	—	—	—	—	—	—
Interpersonal Sensitivity	.20	.17	.27	.15	—	.20	—	—
Paranoid Ideation	—	—	—	—	—	—	—	—
Somatization	.33	—	.27	—	.22	—	—	—
Patient Description Form Scales								
Achievement-Oriented	-.24	-.19	—	—	-.23	-.18	—	-.24
Aggressive	—	—	—	—	—	—	—	—
Agitated	—	—	—	—	—	—	.23	—
Angry Resentment	—	—	—	—	.20	—	.25	—
Antisocial	—	—	—	—	—	—	—	—
Anxious	.36	—	.35	—	.35	—	.37	—
Critical/Argumentative	—	—	—	—	—	—	—	—
Defensive	—	—	—	—	—	—	—	—
Depressed	.53	.25	.55	.27	.46	.18	.48	.24

Family Problems	—	—	—	—	—	—	—	—
Histrionic	.21	—	—	—	.21	—	.24	—
Insecure	.32	—	.34	.23	.39	.21	.33	—
Introverted	—	—	—	—	—	—	—	—
Narcissistic	—	—	—	—	—	—	—	—
Negative Treatment Attitudes	—	—	—	—	—	—	—	—
Obsessive-Compulsive	.23	—	.27	—	.24	—	—	—
Passive-Submissive	—	—	—	—	—	—	—	—
Pessimistic	.30	.19	.28	.19	.30	.19	.38	—
Procrastinates	.23	—	—	—	—	—	—	—
Somatic Symptoms	.39	.16	.28	—	.24	—	—	—
Suspicious	—	—	—	—	—	—	—	—
Patient Description Form Items								
Acts Out	—	—	—	—	—	—	—	—
Agitated	—	—	—	—	—	—	—	—
Angry	—	—	—	—	—	—	—	—
Antisocial Behavior	—	—	—	—	—	—	—	—
Anxious	—	—	.38	—	—	—	.32	—
Argumentative	—	—	—	—	—	—	—	—
Assertive	—	—	—	—	—	—	—	—
Blames Family For Difficulties	—	—	—	—	—	—	—	—
Communicates Effectively	—	—	—	—	—	—	—	—
Competitive	—	—	—	—	—	—	—	—
Complains of Fatigue	.35	.20	—	—	—	—	—	—
Complains of Sleep Disturbance	.45	.21	.41	.19	.39	—	.38	—
Concerned About Status	—	—	—	—	—	—	—	—
Copes Well with Stress	—	—	—	—	—	—	—	—
Creates Good First Impression	—	-.23	—	—	—	—	—	-.22
Critical of Others	—	—	—	—	—	—	—	—
Deceptive	—	—	—	—	—	—	—	—
Defensive	—	—	—	—	—	—	—	—
Delusional Thinking	—	—	—	—	—	—	—	—
Demanding of Attention	—	—	—	—	—	—	—	—
Dependable	—	—	—	—	—	—	—	—
Depressed	.50	.23	.52	.27	.40	.16	.35	.21
Difficult to Motivate	—	—	—	—	—	—	—	—
Difficulty Concentrating	—	—	—	—	—	—	—	—
Difficulty Making Decisions	—	—	—	—	—	—	—	—
Difficulty Trusting Others	—	—	—	—	—	—	—	—
Does Not Get Along with Coworkers	—	—	—	—	—	—	—	—
Energetic	-.25	-.23	—	—	-.31	—	-.20	-.21

Table I-2. Correlates for MMPI-2 Content Component DEP Scales *(continued)*

Extra-test Characteristics	Lack of Drive (DEP_1)		Dysphoria (DEP_2)		Self-Depreciation (DEP_3)		Suicidal Ideation (DEP_4)	
	Men	Women	Men	Women	Men	Women	Men	Women
Exaggerated Need for Affection	—	—	—	—	—	—	—	—
Extroverted	—	—	—	—	—	—	—	—
Familial Discord	—	—	—	—	—	—	—	—
Family Lacks Love	—	—	—	—	—	—	—	—
Feels Gets Raw Deal From Life	.23	.21	—	—	—	—	—	—
Feels Hopeless	.44	.26	.48	.27	.38	.20	.42	.22
Feels Inferior	—	—	.24	.22	.27	.21	—	—
Feels Like a Failure	—	—	.33	.23	.37	.20	.37	—
Feels Overwhelmed	.35	.15	—	—	—	—	.31	—
Feels Rejected	—	—	.27	.23	—	—	—	—
Feels That Life is a Strain	.33	.24	.34	.21	.34	.17	.34	—
Gives Up Easily	—	—	—	—	.24	.19	—	.17
Grouchy	—	—	—	—	—	—	—	—
Harbors Grudges	—	—	—	—	—	—	—	—
Has Insight Into Own Problems	—	—	—	—	—	—	—	—
Has Many Interests	-.20	-.22	—	—	—	-.23	—	—
Has Many Nightmares	—	—	—	—	—	—	—	—
Has Temper Tantrums	—	—	—	—	—	—	—	—
High Aspirations	—	—	—	—	—	—	—	—
Hypochondriacal	—	—	—	—	—	—	—	—
Impulsive	—	—	—	—	—	—	—	—
Insecure	—	—	—	—	.23	.19	—	—
Introverted	—	—	—	—	—	—	—	—
Likable	—	—	—	—	—	—	—	—
Lonely	—	—	—	—	—	—	—	—
Low Frustration Tolerance	—	—	—	—	—	—	—	—
Low Sex Drive	—	—	—	—	—	—	—	—
Manipulative	—	—	—	—	—	—	—	—
Many Specific Fears	—	—	—	—	—	—	—	—
Multiple Somatic Complaints	.37	—	—	—	—	—	—	—
Narcissistic	—	—	—	—	—	—	—	—
Needs Attention	—	—	—	—	—	—	—	—
Needs to Achieve	—	—	—	—	—	—	—	—
Nervous	—	—	—	—	—	—	—	—
Optimistic	-.24	-.24	—	—	—	—	-.29	-.19
Overcontrolled	—	—	—	—	—	—	—	—
Overly Compliant	—	—	—	—	—	—	—	—

Overly Sensitive to Criticism	—	—	—	.23	—	—	—	—
Paranoid Features	—	—	—	—	—	—	—	—
Passive	—	—	—	—	—	—	—	—
Passive in Relationships	—	—	—	—	—	—	—	—
Pessimistic	—	—	.33	.23	.30	.22	.42	—
Physical Symptoms in Response to Stress	.35	—	—	—	—	—	—	—
Physically Abusive	—	—	—	—	—	—	—	—
Preoccupied with Health Problems	.38	.17	—	—	—	—	—	—
Problems with Authority Figures	—	—	—	—	—	—	—	—
Psychologically Immature	—	—	—	—	—	—	—	—
Reliable Informant	—	—	—	—	—	—	—	—
Resents Family Members	—	—	—	—	—	—	—	—
Restless	—	—	—	—	—	—	—	—
Ruminates	—	—	—	—	.32	—	—	—
Sad	.42	.17	.37	.24	.34	—	.39	—
Self-Degrading	—	—	.35	.21	.34	.21	—	—
Self-Doubting	—	—	—	—	.31	.21	—	—
Self-Indulgent	—	—	—	—	—	—	—	—
Self-Punishing	—	—	—	—	.26	.19	—	—
Self-Reliant	—	—	—	—	—	—	—	-.18
Sexually Adjusted	—	—	—	—	—	—	—	-.20
Shy	—	—	—	—	—	—	—	—
Socially Awkward	—	—	—	—	—	—	—	—
Sociopathic	—	—	—	—	—	—	—	—
Stereotypic Masculine Behavior	—	—	—	—	—	—	—	—
Stormy Interpersonal Relationships	—	—	—	—	—	—	—	—
Submissive	—	—	—	—	—	—	—	—
Suicidal Ideations	.39	.23	.40	.22	.35	.18	.44	.27
Superficial Relationships	—	—	—	—	—	—	—	—
Tearful	—	—	—	—	—	—	.21	.16
Unable to See Own Limitations	—	—	—	—	—	—	—	—
Work-Oriented	—	—	—	—	—	—	—	—
Worrier	—	—	—	—	—	—	—	—

Table I-3. Correlates for MMPI-2 Content Component HEA Scales

Extra-test Characteristics	Gastrointestinal Symptoms (HEA_1)		Neurological Symptoms (HEA_2)		General Health Concerns (HEA_3)	
	Men	Women	Men	Women	Men	Women
Intake Information						
Alcohol Abuse in the Past Six Months	—	—	—	—	—	—
Axis I Depression or Dysthymia	—	—	.21	.19	.18	.18
Axis I Other Psychotic Diagnosis	—	—	—	—	—	—
Axis I Schizophrenia	—	—	—	—	—	—
Axis I Substance Abuse or Dependence	—	—	—	—	—	—
Axis II Antisocial Personality Disorder	—	—	—	—	—	—
Axis II Cluster B Diagnosis	—	—	—	—	—	—
Cocaine Abuse in the Past Six Months	—	—	—	—	—	—
Currently on Antidepressant Medication	—	.18	—	.16	—	.15
Currently on Antipsychotic Medication	—	—	—	—	—	—
Currently on Anxiolytic Medication	—	—	—	—	—	—
Ever Arrested	—	—	—	—	—	—
History of Being Physically Abused	—	—	—	.18	—	—
History of Being Physically Abusive	—	—	—	—	—	—
History of Being Sexually Abused	—	—	—	.18	—	.15
History of Committing Domestic Violence	—	—	—	—	—	—
History of Domestic Violence Conviction	—	—	—	—	—	—
History of Felony Conviction(s)	—	—	—	—	—	—
History of Having Few or No Friends	—	—	—	.17	—	—
History of Misdemeanor Conviction(s)	—	—	—	—	—	—
History of Outpatient Psychiatric Treatment	—	—	—	—	.17	—
History of Suicide Attempts	—	—	—	.20	—	.15
History of Victim of Domestic Violence	—	—	—	.15	—	—
Lifetime History of Alcohol Abuse	—	—	—	—	—	—
Lifetime History of Cocaine Abuse	—	—	—	—	—	—
Lifetime History of Heroin Abuse	—	—	—	—	—	—
Lifetime History of Marijuana Abuse	—	—	—	—	—	—
Number of Arrests	—	—	—	—	—	—
Previous Psychiatric Hospitalizations	—	—	—	—	—	—
Mental Status						
Anxiety During Interview	—	.16	—	—	—	—
Depression During Interview	—	.17	.23	.18	.19	.22
Hallucinations	—	—	—	—	—	—
Loose Associations	—	—	—	—	—	—

Poor Judgment	—	—	—	—	—	—
Prevailing Mood Angry	—	—	—	—	—	—
Prevailing Mood Happy	—	—	—	—	—	—
Prevailing Mood Sad	—	—	—	.15	.21	.17
Speech During Interview	—	—	—	—	—	—
Unusual Gestures	—	—	—	—	—	—
SCL-90-R Scales						
Anxiety	.41	.42	.51	.48	.45	.43
Depression	.35	.35	.43	.37	.43	.42
Hostility	.24	.25	.30	.31	.26	.29
Interpersonal Sensitivity	.31	.31	.39	.30	.42	.37
Obsessive-Compulsive	.32	.38	.50	.45	.48	.46
Paranoid Ideation	.29	.30	.34	.34	.32	.35
Phobic Anxiety	.27	.35	.43	.45	.36	.44
Psychoticism	.34	.34	.43	.39	.41	.42
Somatization	.48	.55	.64	.65	.56	.61
Initial SCL-90 Analogue						
Anxiety	—	—	.21	.19	.22	.12
Depression	.22	—	.29	.19	.27	.19
Hostility	—	—	—	—	—	—
Interpersonal Sensitivity	—	—	—	.17	—	—
Paranoid Ideation	—	—	—	—	—	—
Somatization	.26	.21	.41	.30	.40	.25
Patient Description Form Scales						
Achievement-Oriented	—	—	—	-.19	—	-.28
Aggressive	—	—	—	—	—	—
Agitated	—	—	.21	—	—	—
Angry Resentment	—	—	—	—	.20	—
Antisocial	—	—	—	—	—	—
Anxious	—	—	.32	.23	.33	.17
Critical/Argumentative	—	—	—	—	—	—
Defensive	—	—	—	—	—	—
Depressed	.29	.16	.38	.26	.36	.26
Family Problems	—	—	—	—	—	—
Histrionic	—	—	—	—	—	—
Insecure	—	—	—	—	—	—
Introverted	—	—	—	—	—	—
Narcissistic	—	—	—	—	—	—
Negative Treatment Attitudes	—	—	—	—	—	—

Table I-3. Correlates for MMPI-2 Content Component HEA Scales *(continued)*

Extra-test Characteristics	Gastrointestinal Symptoms (HEA_1)		Neurological Symptoms (HEA_2)		General Health Concerns (HEA_3)	
	Men	Women	Men	Women	Men	Women
Obsessive-Compulsive	—	—	—	—	—	—
Passive-Submissive	—	—	—	—	—	—
Pessimistic	—	—	.25	.21	.23	.17
Procrastinates	—	—	—	—	—	—
Somatic Symptoms	.26	.21	.46	.31	.46	.29
Suspicious	—	—	—	—	—	—
Patient Description Form Items						
Acts Out	—	—	—	—	—	—
Agitated	—	—	—	—	—	—
Angry	—	—	—	—	—	—
Antisocial Behavior	—	—	—	—	—	—
Anxious	.23	—	—	—	.31	—
Argumentative	—	—	—	—	—	—
Assertive	—	—	—	—	—	—
Blames Family For Difficulties	—	—	—	—	—	—
Communicates Effectively	—	—	—	—	—	—
Competitive	—	—	—	—	—	—
Complains of Fatigue	.23	—	.34	.30	.36	.26
Complains of Sleep Disturbance	.28	.16	.40	.30	.32	.23
Concerned About Status	—	—	—	—	—	—
Copes Well with Stress	—	—	—	—	—	—
Creates Good First Impression	—	—	—	—	—	—
Critical of Others	—	—	—	—	—	—
Deceptive	—	—	—	—	—	—
Defensive	—	—	—	—	—	—
Delusional Thinking	—	—	—	—	—	—
Demanding of Attention	—	—	—	—	—	—
Dependable	—	—	—	—	—	—
Depressed	.24	—	.34	.22	.31	.27
Difficult to Motivate	—	—	—	—	—	—
Difficulty Concentrating	—	.17	.30	.23	—	—
Difficulty Making Decisions	—	—	—	—	—	—
Difficulty Trusting Others	—	—	—	—	—	—
Does Not Get Along with Coworkers	—	—	—	—	—	—
Energetic	—	-.17	—	—	—	-.27
Exaggerated Need for Affection	—	—	—	—	—	—

Extroverted	—	—	—	—	—	—
Familial Discord	—	—	—	—	—	—
Family Lacks Love	—	—	—	—	—	—
Feels Gets Raw Deal From Life	—	—	—	—	—	—
Feels Hopeless	—	—	.31	.20	.32	.21
Feels Inferior	—	—	—	—	—	—
Feels Like a Failure	—	—	—	—	—	—
Feels Overwhelmed	—	—	.32	.18	.32	.18
Feels Rejected	—	—	—	—	—	—
Feels That Life is a Strain	.24	—	—	—	—	—
Gives Up Easily	—	—	—	—	—	—
Grouchy	—	—	—	—	—	—
Harbors Grudges	—	—	—	—	—	—
Has Insight Into Own Problems	—	—	—	—	—	—
Has Many Interests	—	-.16	—	—	—	-.27
Has Many Nightmares	—	—	—	—	—	—
Has Temper Tantrums	—	—	—	—	—	—
High Aspirations	—	—	—	—	—	-.24
Hypochondriacal	—	—	.35	.24	.32	.16
Impulsive	—	—	—	—	—	—
Insecure	—	—	—	—	—	—
Introverted	—	—	—	—	—	—
Likable	—	—	—	—	—	—
Lonely	—	—	—	—	—	—
Low Frustration Tolerance	—	—	—	—	—	—
Low Sex Drive	—	—	.34	—	—	—
Manipulative	—	—	—	—	—	—
Many Specific Fears	—	—	—	—	—	—
Multiple Somatic Complaints	.23	.20	.43	.28	.45	.28
Narcissistic	—	—	—	—	—	—
Needs Attention	—	—	—	—	—	—
Needs to Achieve	—	—	—	—	—	—
Nervous	—	—	—	—	—	—
Optimistic	—	—	—	—	—	—
Overcontrolled	—	—	—	—	—	—
Overly Compliant	—	—	—	—	—	—
Overly Sensitive to Criticism	—	—	—	—	—	—
Paranoid Features	—	—	—	—	—	—
Passive	—	—	—	—	—	—
Passive in Relationships	—	—	—	—	—	—
Pessimistic	—	—	.30	.22	—	—
Physical Symptoms in Response to Stress	.24	.16	.41	.24	.42	.24

Table I-3. Correlates for MMPI-2 Content Component HEA Scales *(continued)*

Extra-test Characteristics	Gastrointestinal Symptoms (HEA_1)		Neurological Symptoms (HEA_2)		General Health Concerns (HEA_3)	
	Men	Women	Men	Women	Men	Women
Physically Abusive	—	—	—	—	—	—
Preoccupied with Health Problems	.23	.19	.45	.29	.44	.29
Problems with Authority Figures	—	—	—	—	—	—
Psychologically Immature	—	—	—	—	—	—
Reliable Informant	—	—	—	—	—	—
Resents Family Members	—	—	—	—	—	—
Restless	—	—	—	—	—	—
Ruminates	—	—	—	—	—	—
Sad	.27	—	—	—	—	—
Self-Degrading	—	—	—	—	—	—
Self-Doubting	—	—	—	—	—	—
Self-Indulgent	—	—	—	—	—	—
Self-Punishing	—	—	—	—	—	—
Self-Reliant	—	—	—	—	—	—
Sexually Adjusted	—	—	—	—	—	—
Shy	—	—	—	—	—	—
Socially Awkward	—	—	—	—	—	—
Sociopathic	—	—	—	—	—	—
Stereotypic Masculine Behavior	—	—	—	—	—	—
Stormy Interpersonal Relationships	—	—	—	—	—	—
Submissive	—	—	—	—	—	—
Suicidal Ideations	.22	—	.24	.23	—	—
Superficial Relationships	—	—	—	—	—	—
Tearful	—	—	—	—	—	—
Unable to See Own Limitations	—	—	—	—	—	—
Work-Oriented	—	—	—	—	—	—
Worrier	—	—	—	—	—	—

Table I-4. Correlates for MMPI-2 Content Component BIZ Scales

Extra-test Characteristics	Psychotic Symptomatology (BIZ_1)		Schizotypal Characteristics (BIZ_2)	
	Men	Women	Men	Women
Intake Information				
Alcohol Abuse in the Past Six Months	—	—	—	—
Axis I Depression or Dysthymia	—	—	.18	—
Axis I Other Psychotic Diagnosis	.16	—	—	—
Axis I Schizophrenia	—	—	—	—
Axis I Substance Abuse or Dependence	—	—	—	—
Axis II Antisocial Personality Disorder	—	—	—	—
Axis II Cluster B Diagnosis	—	—	—	.17
Cocaine Abuse in the Past Six Months	—	—	—	—
Currently on Antidepressant Medication	—	—	—	—
Currently on Antipsychotic Medication	—	—	—	—
Currently on Anxiolytic Medication	—	—	—	—
Ever Arrested	—	—	—	—
History of Being Physically Abused	—	—	.19	—
History of Being Physically Abusive	—	—	—	—
History of Being Sexually Abused	—	—	—	.22
History of Committing Domestic Violence	—	—	—	—
History of Domestic Violence Conviction	—	—	—	—
History of Felony Conviction(s)	—	—	—	—
History of Having Few or No Friends	—	—	—	—
History of Misdemeanor Conviction(s)	—	—	—	—
History of Outpatient Psychiatric Treatment	—	—	—	—
History of Suicide Attempts	—	—	—	.25
History of Victim of Domestic Violence	—	—	—	—
Lifetime History of Alcohol Abuse	—	—	—	—
Lifetime History of Cocaine Abuse	—	—	—	—
Lifetime History of Heroin Abuse	—	—	—	—
Lifetime History of Marijuana Abuse	—	—	—	—
Number of Arrests	—	—	—	—
Previous Psychiatric Hospitalizations	—	.17	.18	.20
Mental Status				
Anxiety During Interview	—	—	—	—
Depression During Interview	—	—	—	—
Hallucinations	—	.15	—	.15
Loose Associations	—	—	.19	.14

Table I-4. Correlates for MMPI-2 Content Component BIZ Scales *(continued)*

Extra-test Characteristics	Psychotic Symptomatology (BIZ_1)		Schizotypal Characteristics (BIZ_2)	
	Men	Women	Men	Women
Poor Judgment	—	—	—	—
Prevailing Mood Angry	.17	—	—	—
Prevailing Mood Happy	—	—	—	—
Prevailing Mood Sad	—	—	—	—
Speech During Interview	—	—	—	—
Unusual Gestures	—	—	—	—
SCL-90-R Scales				
Anxiety	.37	.33	.43	.42
Depression	.25	.24	.33	.32
Hostility	.22	.28	.31	.42
Interpersonal Sensitivity	.32	.28	.39	.39
Obsessive-Compulsive	.32	.29	.40	.35
Paranoid Ideation	.43	.41	.46	.48
Phobic Anxiety	.35	.31	.36	.39
Psychoticism	.44	.43	.45	.49
Somatization	.36	.27	.38	.33
Initial SCL-90 Analogue				
Anxiety	—	—	—	—
Depression	—	—	—	—
Hostility	—	—	—	—
Interpersonal Sensitivity	—	—	—	—
Paranoid Ideation	—	—	—	—
Somatization	—	—	—	—
Patient Description Form Scales				
Achievement-Oriented	—	—	—	-.18
Aggressive	—	—	—	—
Agitated	—	—	—	—
Angry Resentment	—	—	—	—
Antisocial	—	—	—	—
Anxious	—	—	—	—
Critical/Argumentative	—	—	—	—
Defensive	—	—	—	—
Depressed	—	—	—	—

Family Problems	—	—	—	—
Histrionic	—	—	—	—
Insecure	—	—	—	—
Introverted	—	—	—	—
Narcissistic	—	—	—	—
Negative Treatment Attitudes	—	—	—	—
Obsessive-Compulsive	—	—	—	—
Passive-Submissive	—	—	—	—
Pessimistic	—	—	—	—
Procrastinates	—	—	—	—
Somatic Symptoms	—	—	—	—
Suspicious	—	—	—	.16
Patient Description Form Items				
Acts Out	—	—	—	—
Agitated	—	—	—	—
Angry	—	—	—	—
Antisocial Behavior	—	—	—	—
Anxious	—	—	.20	—
Argumentative	—	—	—	—
Assertive	—	—	—	—
Blames Family For Difficulties	—	—	—	—
Communicates Effectively	—	—	—	-.16
Competitive	—	—	—	—
Complains of Fatigue	—	—	—	—
Complains of Sleep Disturbance	—	—	—	—
Concerned About Status	—	—	—	—
Copes Well with Stress	—	—	—	-.16
Creates Good First Impression	—	—	—	-.18
Critical of Others	—	—	—	—
Deceptive	—	—	—	—
Defensive	—	—	—	—
Delusional Thinking	.20	—	—	—
Demanding of Attention	—	—	—	—
Dependable	—	—	—	—
Depressed	—	—	—	—
Difficult to Motivate	—	—	—	—
Difficulty Concentrating	—	—	—	—
Difficulty Making Decisions	—	—	.21	—
Difficulty Trusting Others	—	—	—	—
Does Not Get Along with Coworkers	—	—	—	—
Energetic	—	—	—	—

Table I-4. Correlates for MMPI-2 Content Component BIZ Scales *(continued)*

Extra-test Characteristics	Psychotic Symptomatology (BIZ_1)		Schizotypal Characteristics (BIZ_2)	
	Men	Women	Men	Women
Exaggerated Need for Affection	—	—	—	—
Extroverted	—	—	—	—
Familial Discord	—	—	—	—
Family Lacks Love	—	—	.21	—
Feels Gets Raw Deal From Life	—	—	—	—
Feels Hopeless	—	—	—	—
Feels Inferior	—	—	—	—
Feels Like a Failure	—	—	—	—
Feels Overwhelmed	—	—	.21	—
Feels Rejected	—	—	—	—
Feels That Life is a Strain	—	—	.22	—
Gives Up Easily	—	—	—	—
Grouchy	—	—	—	—
Harbors Grudges	—	—	—	—
Has Insight Into Own Problems	—	—	—	—
Has Many Interests	—	—	—	—
Has Many Nightmares	—	—	—	—
Has Temper Tantrums	—	—	—	—
High Aspirations	—	—	—	—
Hypochondriacal	—	—	—	—
Impulsive	—	—	—	—
Insecure	—	—	—	—
Introverted	—	—	—	—
Likable	—	—	—	—
Lonely	—	—	—	—
Low Frustration Tolerance	—	.17	—	—
Low Sex Drive	—	—	—	—
Manipulative	—	—	—	—
Many Specific Fears	—	—	—	—
Multiple Somatic Complaints	—	—	—	—
Narcissistic	—	—	—	—
Needs Attention	—	—	—	—
Needs to Achieve	—	—	—	—
Nervous	—	—	—	—
Optimistic	—	—	—	—
Overcontrolled	-.20	—	—	—
Overly Compliant	—	—	—	—

Overly Sensitive to Criticism	—	—	—	—
Paranoid Features	—	—	—	—
Passive	—	—	—	—
Passive in Relationships	—	—	—	—
Pessimistic	—	—	—	—
Physical Symptoms in Response to Stress	—	—	—	—
Physically Abusive	—	—	—	—
Preoccupied with Health Problems	—	—	—	—
Problems with Authority Figures	—	—	—	—
Psychologically Immature	—	—	—	—
Reliable Informant	—	—	—	—
Resents Family Members	—	—	—	—
Restless	—	—	—	—
Ruminates	—	—	—	—
Sad	—	—	—	—
Self-Degrading	—	—	—	—
Self-Doubting	—	—	—	—
Self-Indulgent	—	—	—	—
Self-Punishing	—	—	—	—
Self-Reliant	—	—	—	-.16
Sexually Adjusted	—	—	—	—
Shy	—	—	—	—
Socially Awkward	—	—	—	—
Sociopathic	—	—	—	.17
Stereotypic Masculine Behavior	—	—	—	—
Stormy Interpersonal Relationships	—	—	—	—
Submissive	—	—	—	—
Suicidal Ideations	—	—	—	.18
Superficial Relationships	—	—	—	—
Tearful	—	—	—	—
Unable to Express Negative Feelings	—	—	—	—
Work-Oriented	—	—	—	-.17
Worrier	—	—	—	—

Table I-5. Correlates for MMPI-2 Content Component ANG Scales

Extra-test Characteristics	Explosive Behavior (ANG_1)		Irritability (ANG_2)	
	Men	Women	Men	Women
Intake Information				
Alcohol Abuse in the Past Six Months	.20	—	—	—
Axis I Depression or Dysthymia	—	—	.17	.15
Axis I Other Psychotic Diagnosis	—	—	—	—
Axis I Schizophrenia	—	—	—	—
Axis I Substance Abuse or Dependence	.24	.16	—	—
Axis II Antisocial Personality Disorder	—	—	—	—
Axis II Cluster B Diagnosis	—	—	—	—
Cocaine Abuse in the Past Six Months	—	—	—	—
Currently on Antidepressant Medication	—	—	—	—
Currently on Antipsychotic Medication	—	—	—	—
Currently on Anxiolytic Medication	—	—	—	—
Ever Arrested	—	—	—	—
History of Being Physically Abused	.22	—	—	—
History of Being Physically Abusive	.27	.25	—	—
History of Being Sexually Abused	—	.16	—	—
History of Committing Domestic Violence	.29	—	—	—
History of Domestic Violence Conviction	.19	—	—	—
History of Felony Conviction(s)	—	—	—	—
History of Having Few or No Friends	—	—	—	—
History of Misdemeanor Conviction(s)	—	.14	—	—
History of Outpatient Psychiatric Treatment	—	—	—	.15
History of Suicide Attempts	—	.26	—	.15
History of Victim of Domestic Violence	—	—	—	—
Lifetime History of Alcohol Abuse	.24	.17	—	—
Lifetime History of Cocaine Abuse	—	—	—	—
Lifetime History of Heroin Abuse	—	—	—	—
Lifetime History of Marijuana Abuse	.21	—	—	—
Number of Arrests	—	—	—	—
Previous Psychiatric Hospitalizations	—	—	—	—
Mental Status				
Anxiety During Interview	—	—	—	—
Depression During Interview	—	—	.18	—
Hallucinations	—	—	—	—
Loose Associations	—	—	—	—

Poor Judgment	—	—	—	—
Prevailing Mood Angry	—	—	—	—
Prevailing Mood Happy	—	—	—	—
Prevailing Mood Sad	—	—	.21	.13
Speech During Interview	—	—	—	—
Unusual Gestures	—	—	—	—
SCL-90-R Scales				
Anxiety	.30	.28	.46	.33
Depression	.26	.27	.42	.39
Hostility	.63	.54	.60	.53
Interpersonal Sensitivity	.28	.32	.41	.39
Obsessive-Compulsive	.30	.21	.42	.32
Paranoid Ideation	.34	.34	.45	.34
Phobic Anxiety	—	.25	.26	.24
Psychoticism	.28	.33	.39	.34
Somatization	.28	.23	.45	.27
Initial SCL-90 Analogue				
Anxiety	—	—	—	—
Depression	—	—	—	—
Hostility	.22	—	—	—
Interpersonal Sensitivity	—	—	—	—
Paranoid Ideation	—	—	—	—
Somatization	—	—	—	—
Patient Description Form Scales				
Achievement-Oriented	—	—	—	—
Aggressive	.34	—	—	—
Agitated	—	—	—	—
Angry Resentment	.29	—	.22	—
Antisocial	—	—	—	—
Anxious	—	—	.22	—
Critical/Argumentative	—	—	—	—
Defensive	—	—	—	—
Depressed	.28	—	.33	.16
Family Problems	.28	—	.25	—
Histrionic	—	—	—	—
Insecure	—	—	—	—
Introverted	—	—	—	—

Table I-5. Correlates for MMPI-2 Content Component ANG Scales *(continued)*

Extra-test Characteristics	Explosive Behavior (ANG_1)		Irritability (ANG_2)	
	Men	Women	Men	Women
Narcissistic	—	—	—	—
Negative Treatment Attitudes	—	—	—	—
Obsessive-Compulsive	—	—	—	—
Passive-Submissive	—	—	—	—
Pessimistic	—	—	—	—
Procrastinates	—	—	—	—
Somatic Symptoms	—	—	—	.21
Suspicious	—	—	—	—
Patient Description Form Items				
Acts Out	—	—	—	—
Agitated	.30	—	—	—
Angry	.30	—	.27	—
Antisocial Behavior	—	—	—	—
Anxious	—	—	—	—
Argumentative	—	—	—	—
Assertive	—	—	—	—
Believes Cannot Be Helped	—	—	—	—
Communicates Effectively	—	—	—	—
Competitive	—	—	—	—
Complains of Fatigue	—	—	—	—
Complains of Sleep Disturbance	—	—	.35	—
Concerned About Status	—	—	—	—
Copes Well with Stress	—	—	—	-.18
Creates Good First Impression	—	—	—	—
Critical of Others	—	—	—	—
Deceptive	—	—	—	—
Defensive	—	—	—	—
Delusional Thinking	—	—	—	—
Demanding of Attention	—	—	—	—
Dependable	—	—	—	—
Depressed	—	—	.23	.16
Difficult to Motivate	—	—	—	—
Difficulty Concentrating	—	—	—	—
Difficulty Making Decisions	—	—	—	—
Difficulty Trusting Others	—	—	—	—
Does Not Get Along with Coworkers	—	—	—	—

Energetic	—	—	—	—
Exaggerated Need for Affection	—	—	—	—
Extroverted	—	—	—	—
Familial Discord	—	—	—	—
Family Lacks Love	.27	—	.26	—
Feels Gets Raw Deal From Life	—	—	—	—
Feels Hopeless	—	—	.26	—
Feels Inferior	—	—	—	.18
Feels Like a Failure	—	—	—	—
Feels Overwhelmed	—	—	—	—
Feels Rejected	—	—	—	—
Feels That Life is a Strain	—	—	—	—
Gives Up Easily	—	—	—	—
Grouchy	—	—	—	—
Harbors Grudges	.27	—	—	—
Has Insight Into Own Problems	—	—	—	—
Has Many Interests	—	—	—	—
Has Many Nightmares	.31	—	.32	—
Has Temper Tantrums	.36	.21	.22	—
High Aspirations	—	—	—	—
Hypochondriacal	—	—	—	—
Impulsive	—	—	—	—
Insecure	—	—	—	—
Introverted	—	—	—	—
Likable	—	—	—	—
Lonely	—	—	—	—
Low Frustration Tolerance	.26	—	.24	—
Low Sex Drive	—	—	—	—
Manipulative	—	—	—	—
Many Specific Fears	—	—	—	—
Multiple Somatic Complaints	—	—	—	—
Narcissistic	—	—	—	—
Needs Attention	—	—	—	—
Needs to Achieve	—	—	—	—
Nervous	—	—	—	—
Optimistic	—	—	—	—
Overcontrolled	—	—	—	—
Overly Compliant	—	—	—	—
Overly Sensitive to Criticism	—	—	—	—
Paranoid Features	—	—	—	—
Passive	—	—	—	—
Passive in Relationships	—	—	—	—

Table I-5. Correlates for MMPI-2 Content Component ANG Scales *(continued)*

Extra-test Characteristics	Explosive Behavior (ANG_1)		Irritability (ANG_2)	
	Men	Women	Men	Women
Pessimistic	—	—	—	—
Physical Symptoms in Response to Stress	—	—	.24	—
Physically Abusive	.33	—	—	—
Preoccupied with Health Problems	—	—	—	—
Problems with Authority Figures	—	—	—	—
Psychologically Immature	—	—	—	—
Reliable Informant	—	—	—	—
Resents Family Members	.26	—	—	—
Restless	—	—	—	—
Ruminates	—	—	.25	—
Sad	—	—	.21	.16
Self-Degrading	—	—	—	—
Self-Doubting	—	—	—	—
Self-Indulgent	—	—	—	—
Self-Punishing	—	—	—	—
Self-Reliant	—	—	—	—
Sexually Adjusted	—	—	—	—
Shy	—	—	—	—
Socially Awkward	—	—	—	—
Sociopathic	—	—	—	—
Stereotypic Masculine Behavior	—	—	—	—
Stormy Interpersonal Relationships	.25	—	—	—
Submissive	—	—	.25	—
Suicidal Ideations	—	—	—	—
Superficial Relationships	—	—	—	—
Tearful	—	—	—	—
Unable to See Own Limitations	—	—	—	—
Work-Oriented	—	—	.23	—
Worrier	—	—	—	—

Table I-6. Correlates for MMPI-2 Content Component CYN Scales

Extra-test Characteristics	Misanthropic Beliefs (CYN_1)		Interpersonal Suspiciousness (CYN_2)	
	Men	Women	Men	Women
Intake Information				
Alcohol Abuse in the Past Six Months	—	—	—	—
Axis I Depression or Dysthymia	—	—	.17	—
Axis I Other Psychotic Diagnosis	—	—	—	—
Axis I Schizophrenia	—	—	—	—
Axis I Substance Abuse or Dependence	—	—	—	—
Axis II Antisocial Personality Disorder	—	—	—	—
Axis II Cluster B Diagnosis	—	—	—	—
Cocaine Abuse in the Past Six Months	—	—	—	—
Currently on Antidepressant Medication	—	—	—	—
Currently on Antipsychotic Medication	—	—	—	—
Currently on Anxiolytic Medication	—	—	—	—
Ever Arrested	—	—	—	—
History of Being Physically Abused	—	—	—	—
History of Being Physically Abusive	—	—	—	—
History of Being Sexually Abused	—	—	—	—
History of Committing Domestic Violence	—	—	—	—
History of Domestic Violence Conviction	—	—	—	—
History of Felony Conviction(s)	—	—	—	—
History of Having Few or No Friends	—	—	.21	—
History of Misdemeanor Conviction(s)	—	—	—	—
History of Outpatient Psychiatric Treatment	—	—	—	—
History of Suicide Attempts	—	.18	—	—
History of Victim of Domestic Violence	—	—	—	—
Lifetime History of Alcohol Abuse	—	—	—	—
Lifetime History of Cocaine Abuse	—	—	—	—
Lifetime History of Heroin Abuse	—	—	—	—
Lifetime History of Marijuana Abuse	—	—	—	—
Number of Arrests	—	—	—	—
Previous Psychiatric Hospitalizations	—	—	—	—
Mental Status				
Anxiety During Interview	—	—	—	—
Depression During Interview	—	—	—	—
Hallucinations	—	—	—	—
Loose Associations	—	—	—	—

Table I-6. Correlates for MMPI-2 Content Component CYN Scales *(continued)*

Extra-test Characteristics	Misanthropic Beliefs (CYN_1)		Interpersonal Suspiciousness (CYN_2)	
	Men	Women	Men	Women
Poor Judgment	—	—	—	—
Prevailing Mood Angry	—	—	—	—
Prevailing Mood Happy	—	—	—	—
Prevailing Mood Sad	—	—	—	—
Speech During Interview	—	—	—	—
Unusual Gestures	—	—	—	—
SCL-90-R Scales				
Anxiety	.20	.22	.33	.23
Depression	—	.18	.24	.19
Hostility	.29	.26	.26	.21
Interpersonal Sensitivity	.20	.23	.32	.27
Obsessive-Compulsive	.17	.20	.30	.19
Paranoid Ideation	.29	.33	.38	.33
Phobic Anxiety	.20	.23	.26	.24
Psychoticism	.19	.31	.30	.32
Somatization	.16	.22	.23	.20
Initial SCL-90 Analogue				
Anxiety	—	—	—	—
Depression	—	—	—	—
Hostility	—	—	—	—
Interpersonal Sensitivity	—	—	—	—
Paranoid Ideation	—	—	—	—
Somatization	—	—	—	—
Patient Description Form Scales				
Achievement-Oriented	—	-.18	—	—
Aggressive	—	—	—	—
Agitated	—	—	—	—
Angry Resentment	—	—	—	—
Antisocial	—	.17	—	—
Anxious	—	—	—	—
Critical/Argumentative	—	—	—	—
Defensive	—	—	—	—
Depressed	.20	—	—	—

Family Problems	—	—	—	—
Histrionic	—	—	—	—
Insecure	—	—	—	—
Introverted	—	—	—	—
Narcissistic	—	—	—	—
Negative Treatment Attitudes	—	.17	—	—
Obsessive-Compulsive	—	—	—	—
Passive-Submissive	—	—	—	—
Pessimistic	—	—	—	—
Procrastinates	—	—	—	—
Somatic Symptoms	—	—	—	—
Suspicious	—	—	—	—
Patient Description Form Items				
Acts Out	—	—	—	—
Agitated	—	—	—	—
Angry	—	—	—	—
Antisocial Behavior	—	.18	—	—
Anxious	—	—	—	—
Argumentative	—	—	—	—
Assertive	—	—	—	—
Blames Family For Difficulties	—	—	—	—
Communicates Effectively	—	-.19	—	—
Competitive	—	—	—	—
Complains of Fatigue	—	—	—	—
Complains of Sleep Disturbance	.21	—	—	—
Concerned About Status	—	—	—	—
Copes Well with Stress	—	—	—	—
Creates Good First Impression	—	-.23	—	—
Critical of Others	—	—	—	—
Deceptive	—	—	—	—
Defensive	—	—	—	—
Delusional Thinking	—	—	—	—
Demanding of Attention	—	—	—	—
Dependable	—	—	—	-.17
Depressed	—	—	—	—
Difficult to Motivate	—	.22	—	—
Difficulty Concentrating	—	—	—	—
Difficulty Making Decisions	—	—	—	—
Difficulty Trusting Others	—	—	—	—
Does Not Get Along with Coworkers	—	—	—	—
Energetic	—	—	—	—

Table I-6. Correlates for MMPI-2 Content Component CYN Scales *(continued)*

Extra-test Characteristics	Misanthropic Beliefs (CYN_1)		Interpersonal Suspiciousness (CYN_2)	
	Men	Women	Men	Women
Exaggerated Need for Affection	—	—	—	—
Extroverted	—	—	—	—
Familial Discord	—	—	—	—
Family Lacks Love	—	—	—	—
Feels Gets Raw Deal From Life	—	—	—	—
Feels Hopeless	—	—	—	—
Feels Inferior	—	—	—	—
Feels Like a Failure	—	—	—	—
Feels Overwhelmed	—	—	—	—
Feels Rejected	—	—	—	—
Feels That Life is a Strain	—	—	—	—
Gives Up Easily	—	—	—	—
Grouchy	—	—	—	—
Harbors Grudges	—	—	—	—
Has Insight Into Own Problems	—	-.28	—	-.17
Has Many Interests	—	-.18	—	—
Has Many Nightmares	.25	—	—	—
Has Temper Tantrums	—	—	—	—
High Aspirations	—	—	—	—
Hypochondriacal	—	—	—	—
Impulsive	—	—	—	—
Insecure	—	—	—	—
Introverted	—	—	—	—
Likable	—	-.23	—	—
Lonely	—	—	—	—
Low Frustration Tolerance	—	—	—	—
Low Sex Drive	—	—	—	—
Manipulative	—	—	—	—
Many Specific Fears	—	—	—	—
Multiple Somatic Complaints	—	—	—	—
Narcissistic	—	—	—	—
Needs Attention	—	—	—	—
Needs to Achieve	—	—	—	—
Nervous	—	—	—	—
Optimistic	—	—	—	—
Overcontrolled	—	—	—	—
Overly Compliant	—	—	—	—

Overly Sensitive to Criticism	—	—	—	—
Paranoid Features	—	—	—	—
Passive	—	—	—	—
Passive in Relationships	—	—	—	—
Pessimistic	—	—	—	—
Physical Symptoms in Response to Stress	—	—	—	—
Physically Abusive	—	—	—	—
Preoccupied with Health Problems	—	—	—	—
Problems with Authority Figures	—	—	—	—
Psychologically Immature	—	.19	—	—
Reliable Informant	—	-.22	—	—
Resents Family Members	—	—	—	—
Restless	—	—	—	—
Ruminates	.24	—	—	—
Sad	—	—	—	—
Self-Degrading	—	—	—	—
Self-Doubting	—	—	—	—
Self-Indulgent	—	—	—	—
Self-Punishing	—	—	—	—
Self-Reliant	—	—	—	—
Sexually Adjusted	—	—	—	—
Shy	—	—	—	—
Socially Awkward	.19	—	—	—
Sociopathic	—	—	—	—
Stereotypic Masculine Behavior	—	—	—	—
Stormy Interpersonal Relationships	—	—	—	—
Submissive	—	—	—	—
Suicidal Ideations	—	—	—	—
Superficial Relationships	—	—	—	—
Tearful	—	—	—	—
Unable to See Own Limitations	—	—	—	—
Work-Oriented	—	-.18	—	—
Worrier	—	—	—	—

Table I-7. Correlates for MMPI-2 Content Component ASP Scales

Extra-test Characteristics	Antisocial Attitudes (ASP_1)		Antisocial Behavior (ASP_2)	
	Men	Women	Men	Women
Intake Information				
Alcohol Abuse in the Past Six Months	—	—	—	—
Axis I Depression or Dysthymia	—	—	—	—
Axis I Other Psychotic Diagnosis	—	—	—	—
Axis I Schizophrenia	—	—	—	—
Axis I Substance Abuse or Dependence	—	—	.20	.15
Axis II Antisocial Personality Disorder	—	—	.17	.13
Axis II Cluster B Diagnosis	—	—	.17	—
Cocaine Abuse in the Past Six Months	—	—	—	—
Currently on Antidepressant Medication	—	—	—	—
Currently on Antipsychotic Medication	—	—	—	—
Currently on Anxiolytic Medication	—	—	—	—
Ever Arrested	—	—	.22	.24
History of Being Physically Abused	—	—	—	.16
History of Being Physically Abusive	—	—	.21	—
History of Being Sexually Abused	—	—	—	.18
History of Committing Domestic Violence	—	—	.22	—
History of Domestic Violence Conviction	—	—	.22	—
History of Felony Conviction(s)	—	—	.28	—
History of Having Few or No Friends	.17	—	—	—
History of Misdemeanor Conviction(s)	—	—	.20	.19
History of Outpatient Psychiatric Treatment	—	—	—	—
History of Suicide Attempts	—	.18	.19	.18
History of Victim of Domestic Violence	—	—	—	—
Lifetime History of Alcohol Abuse	—	—	.17	.23
Lifetime History of Cocaine Abuse	—	—	.22	.23
Lifetime History of Heroin Abuse	—	—	—	.15
Lifetime History of Marijuana Abuse	—	—	.26	.24
Number of Arrests	—	—	.24	.20
Previous Psychiatric Hospitalizations	—	—	—	—
Mental Status				
Anxiety During Interview	—	—	—	—
Depression During Interview	—	—	—	—
Hallucinations	—	.16	—	—
Loose Associations	—	—	—	—

Poor Judgment	.17	—	—	—
Prevailing Mood Angry	—	—	—	—
Prevailing Mood Happy	—	—	—	—
Prevailing Mood Sad	—	—	—	—
Speech During Interview	—	—	—	—
Unusual Gestures	—	—	—	—
SCL-90-R Scales				
Anxiety	.17	—	—	—
Depression	—	—	—	—
Hostility	.32	.16	.23	.15
Interpersonal Sensitivity	—	—	—	—
Obsessive-Compulsive	—	—	—	—
Paranoid Ideation	.24	.18	—	.15
Phobic Anxiety	.16	.13	—	—
Psychoticism	.17	.16	—	—
Somatization	.17	—	—	—
Initial SCL-90 Analogue				
Anxiety	—	—	—	—
Depression	—	—	—	—
Hostility	—	—	.26	.17
Interpersonal Sensitivity	—	—	—	—
Paranoid Ideation	—	—	—	.19
Somatization	—	—	—	—
Patient Description Form Scales				
Achievement-Oriented	—	—	—	—
Aggressive	—	—	.30	.21
Agitated	—	—	—	.17
Angry Resentment	—	—	.22	.21
Antisocial	—	.19	.35	.29
Anxious	—	—	—	—
Critical/Argumentative	—	—	—	.20
Defensive	—	.17	—	.18
Depressed	—	—	—	—
Family Problems	—	—	—	.22
Histrionic	—	—	—	—
Insecure	—	—	—	—
Introverted	—	—	—	—
Narcissistic	—	—	—	.20
Negative Treatment Attitudes	—	—	—	—

Table I-7. Correlates for MMPI-2 Content Component ASP Scales *(continued)*

Extra-test Characteristics	Antisocial Attitudes (ASP_1)		Antisocial Behavior (ASP_2)	
	Men	Women	Men	Women
Obsessive-Compulsive	—	—	—	—
Passive-Submissive	—	—	—	—
Pessimistic	—	—	—	—
Procrastinates	—	—	—	—
Somatic Symptoms	—	—	—	—
Suspicious	—	—	.20	.26
Patient Description Form Items				
Acts Out	—	—	.32	.27
Agitated	—	—	—	—
Angry	—	—	—	—
Antisocial Behavior	—	.18	.34	.30
Anxious	—	—	—	—
Argumentative	—	—	—	—
Assertive	—	—	—	—
Blames Family For Difficulties	—	—	—	—
Communicates Effectively	—	—	—	—
Competitive	—	—	—	—
Complains of Fatigue	—	—	—	—
Complains of Sleep Disturbance	—	—	—	—
Concerned About Status	—	—	—	—
Copes Well with Stress	—	—	—	—
Creates Good First Impression	—	—	—	—
Critical of Others	—	—	—	—
Deceptive	—	—	—	.23
Defensive	—	—	—	.22
Delusional Thinking	—	—	—	—
Demanding of Attention	—	—	—	—
Dependable	—	-.17	—	—
Depressed	—	—	—	—
Difficult to Motivate	—	.16	—	—
Difficulty Concentrating	—	—	—	—
Difficulty Making Decisions	—	—	—	—
Difficulty Trusting Others	—	—	.28	.24
Does Not Get Along with Coworkers	—	—	—	—
Energetic	—	—	—	—
Exaggerated Need for Affection	—	—	—	—

Extroverted	—	—	—	—
Familial Discord	—	—	—	—
Family Lacks Love	—	—	.23	.25
Feels Gets Raw Deal From Life	—	—	—	—
Feels Hopeless	—	—	—	—
Feels Inferior	—	—	—	—
Feels Like a Failure	—	—	—	—
Feels Overwhelmed	—	—	—	—
Feels Rejected	—	—	—	—
Feels That Life is a Strain	—	—	—	—
Gives Up Easily	—	—	—	—
Grouchy	—	—	—	—
Harbors Grudges	—	—	.30	.21
Has Insight Into Own Problems	—	-.19	—	—
Has Many Interests	—	—	—	—
Has Many Nightmares	.28	—	—	.28
Has Temper Tantrums	—	—	.29	.19
High Aspirations	—	—	—	—
Hypochondriacal	—	—	—	—
Impulsive	—	—	.27	.18
Insecure	—	—	—	—
Introverted	—	—	—	—
Likable	—	-.17	—	—
Lonely	—	—	—	—
Low Frustration Tolerance	.20	—	.27	.21
Low Sex Drive	—	—	—	—
Manipulative	—	—	—	.23
Many Specific Fears	—	—	—	—
Multiple Somatic Complaints	—	—	—	—
Narcissistic	—	—	—	—
Needs Attention	—	—	—	—
Needs to Achieve	—	—	—	—
Nervous	—	—	—	—
Optimistic	—	—	—	—
Overcontrolled	—	—	—	—
Overly Compliant	—	—	—	—
Overly Sensitive to Criticism	—	—	—	—
Paranoid Features	—	—	—	.22
Passive	—	—	—	—
Passive in Relationships	—	—	—	—
Pessimistic	—	—	—	—
Physical Symptoms in Response to Stress	—	—	—	—
Physically Abusive	—	—	.31	—

Table I-7. Correlates for MMPI-2 Content Component ASP Scales *(continued)*

Extra-test Characteristics	Antisocial Attitudes (ASP_1)		Antisocial Behavior (ASP_2)	
	Men	Women	Men	Women
Preoccupied with Health Problems	—	—	—	—
Problems with Authority Figures	—	—	—	—
Psychologically Immature	—	.17	—	—
Reliable Informant	—	-.19	—	—
Resents Family Members	—	—	—	—
Restless	—	—	—	—
Ruminates	—	—	—	—
Sad	—	—	—	—
Self-Degrading	—	—	—	—
Self-Doubting	—	—	.27	—
Self-Indulgent	—	—	—	—
Self-Punishing	—	—	—	—
Self-Reliant	—	—	—	—
Sexually Adjusted	—	—	—	—
Shy	—	—	—	—
Socially Awkward	—	—	—	—
Sociopathic	—	.17	.24	.27
Stereotypic Masculine Behavior	—	—	—	—
Stormy Interpersonal Relationships	—	—	.32	.20
Submissive	—	—	—	—
Suicidal Ideations	—	—	—	—
Superficial Relationships	—	.17	—	—
Tearful	—	—	—	—
Unable to See Own Limitations	—	.19	—	—
Work-Oriented	—	—	—	—
Worrier	—	—	—	—

Table I-8. Correlates for MMPI-2 Content Component TPA Scales

Extra-test Characteristics	Impatience (TPA_1)		Competitive Drive (TPA_2)	
	Men	Women	Men	Women
Intake Information				
Alcohol Abuse in the Past Six Months	—	—	—	—
Axis I Depression or Dysthymia	—	—	—	—
Axis I Other Psychotic Diagnosis	—	—	—	—
Axis I Schizophrenia	—	—	—	—
Axis I Substance Abuse or Dependence	—	—	—	—
Axis II Antisocial Personality Disorder	—	—	—	—
Axis II Cluster B Diagnosis	—	—	—	—
Cocaine Abuse in the Past Six Months	—	—	—	—
Currently on Antidepressant Medication	—	—	—	—
Currently on Antipsychotic Medication	—	—	—	—
Currently on Anxiolytic Medication	—	—	—	—
Ever Arrested	—	—	—	—
History of Being Physically Abused	—	—	—	—
History of Being Physically Abusive	—	—	—	—
History of Being Sexually Abused	—	—	—	—
History of Committing Domestic Violence	—	—	—	—
History of Domestic Violence Conviction	—	—	—	—
History of Felony Conviction(s)	—	—	—	—
History of Having Few or No Friends	—	—	—	—
History of Misdemeanor Conviction(s)	—	—	—	—
History of Outpatient Psychiatric Treatment	—	—	—	—
History of Suicide Attempts	—	—	—	—
History of Victim of Domestic Violence	—	—	—	—
Lifetime History of Alcohol Abuse	—	—	—	—
Lifetime History of Cocaine Abuse	—	—	—	—
Lifetime History of Heroin Abuse	—	—	—	—
Lifetime History of Marijuana Abuse	—	—	—	—
Number of Arrests	—	—	—	—
Previous Psychiatric Hospitalizations	—	—	—	—
Mental Status				
Anxiety During Interview	—	—	—	—
Depression During Interview	—	—	—	—
Hallucinations	—	—	—	—
Loose Associations	—	—	—	—

Table I-8. Correlates for MMPI-2 Content Component TPA Scales *(continued)*

Extra-test Characteristics	Impatience (TPA_1)		Competitive Drive (TPA_2)	
	Men	Women	Men	Women
Poor Judgment	—	—	—	—
Prevailing Mood Angry	—	—	—	—
Prevailing Mood Happy	—	—	—	—
Prevailing Mood Sad	—	—	—	—
Speech During Interview	—	—	—	—
Unusual Gesture	.17	—	—	—
SCL-90-R Scales				
Anxiety	.35	.28	.18	.15
Depression	.28	.27	—	—
Hostility	.44	.35	.26	.20
Interpersonal Sensitivity	.30	.34	.20	.21
Obsessive-Compulsive	.28	.30	.21	.17
Paranoid Ideation	.35	.27	.27	.29
Phobic Anxiety	.19	.30	—	—
Psychoticism	.24	.30	.18	.26
Somatization	.26	.25	—	—
Initial SCL-90 Analogue				
Anxiety	—	—	—	—
Depression	—	—	—	—
Hostility	—	—	—	—
Interpersonal Sensitivity	—	—	—	—
Paranoid Ideation	—	—	—	—
Somatization	—	—	—	—
Patient Description Form Scales				
Achievement-Oriented	—	—	—	—
Aggressive	—	—	—	—
Agitated	—	.16	—	—
Angry Resentment	—	—	—	—
Antisocial	—	—	—	—
Anxious	—	—	—	—
Critical/Argumentative	—	—	—	—
Defensive	—	—	—	—
Depressed	—	.18	—	—

Family Problems	—	—	—	—
Histrionic	—	.17	—	—
Insecure	—	.17	—	—
Introverted	—	—	—	—
Narcissistic	—	—	—	—
Negative Treatment Attitudes	—	—	—	—
Obsessive-Compulsive	—	—	—	—
Passive-Submissive	—	—	—	—
Pessimistic	—	—	—	—
Procrastinates	—	—	—	—
Somatic Symptoms	—	.17	—	—
Suspicious	—	—	—	—
Patient Description Form Items				
Acts Out	—	—	—	—
Agitated	—	—	—	—
Angry	—	—	—	—
Antisocial Behavior	—	—	—	—
Anxious	—	—	—	—
Argumentative	—	—	—	—
Assertive	—	—	—	—
Blames Family For Difficulties	—	—	—	—
Communicates Effectively	—	—	—	—
Competitive	—	—	—	—
Complains of Fatigue	—	—	—	—
Complains of Sleep Disturbance	—	—	—	—
Concerned About Status	—	—	—	—
Copes Well with Stress	—	-.19	—	—
Creates Good First Impression	—	—	—	—
Critical of Others	—	—	—	—
Deceptive	—	—	—	—
Defensive	—	—	—	—
Delusional Thinking	—	—	—	—
Demanding of Attention	—	—	—	—
Dependable	—	—	—	—
Depressed	—	—	—	—
Difficult to Motivate	—	—	—	—
Difficulty Concentrating	—	—	—	—
Difficulty Making Decisions	—	—	—	—
Difficulty Trusting Others	—	—	—	—
Does Not Get Along with Coworkers	—	—	—	—
Energetic	—	—	—	—

Table I-8. Correlates for MMPI-2 Content Component TPA Scales *(continued)*

Extra-test Characteristics	Impatience (TPA_1)		Competitive Drive (TPA_2)	
	Men	Women	Men	Women
Exaggerated Need for Affection	—	—	—	—
Extroverted	—	—	—	—
Familial Discord	—	—	—	—
Family Lacks Love	—	—	—	—
Feels Gets Raw Deal From Life	—	—	—	—
Feels Hopeless	—	—	—	—
Feels Inferior	—	—	—	—
Feels Like a Failure	—	—	—	—
Feels Overwhelmed	—	—	—	—
Feels Rejected	—	—	—	—
Feels That Life is a Strain	—	—	—	—
Gives Up Easily	—	.17	—	—
Grouchy	—	.19	—	—
Harbors Grudges	—	—	—	—
Has Insight Into Own Problems	—	—	—	—
Has Many Interests	—	—	—	—
Has Many Nightmares	—	—	—	—
Has Temper Tantrums	—	—	—	—
High Aspirations	—	—	—	—
Hypochondriacal	—	—	—	—
Impulsive	—	—	—	—
Insecure	—	.18	—	—
Introverted	—	—	—	—
Likable	—	—	—	—
Lonely	—	—	—	—
Low Frustration Tolerance	—	—	—	—
Low Sex Drive	—	—	—	—
Manipulative	—	—	—	—
Many Specific Fears	—	—	—	—
Multiple Somatic Complaints	—	—	—	—
Narcissistic	—	—	—	—
Needs Attention	—	—	—	—
Needs to Achieve	—	—	—	—
Nervous	—	.19	—	—
Optimistic	—	—	—	—
Overcontrolled	—	—	—	—
Overly Compliant	—	—	—	—

Overly Sensitive to Criticism	—	.19	—	—
Paranoid Features	—	—	—	—
Passive	—	—	—	—
Passive in Relationships	—	—	—	—
Pessimistic	—	—	—	—
Physical Symptoms in Response to Stress	.25	.16	—	—
Physically Abusive	—	—	—	—
Preoccupied with Health Problems	—	—	—	—
Problems with Authority Figures	—	—	—	—
Psychologically Immature	—	—	—	.16
Reliable Informant	—	—	—	.16
Resents Family Members	—	—	—	—
Restless	—	.16	—	—
Ruminates	—	—	—	—
Sad	—	—	—	—
Self-Degrading	—	.18	—	—
Self-Doubting	—	—	—	—
Self-Indulgent	—	—	—	—
Self-Punishing	—	—	—	—
Self-Reliant	—	—	—	—
Sexually Adjusted	—	—	—	—
Shy	—	—	—	—
Socially Awkward	—	.17	—	—
Sociopathic	—	—	—	—
Stereotypic Masculine Behavior	—	—	—	—
Stormy Interpersonal Relationships	—	—	—	—
Submissive	—	—	—	—
Suicidal Ideations	—	—	—	—
Superficial Relationships	—	—	—	—
Tearful	—	—	—	—
Unable to See Own Limitations	—	—	—	—
Work-Oriented	—	—	—	—
Worrier	—	.22	—	—

Table I-9. Correlates for MMPI-2 Content Component LSE Scales

Extra-test Characteristics	Self-Doubt (LSE_1)		Submissiveness (LSE_2)	
	Men	Women	Men	Women
Intake Information				
Alcohol Abuse in the Past Six Months	—	—	—	—
Axis I Depression or Dysthymia	.21	.22	—	—
Axis I Other Psychotic Diagnosis	—	—	—	—
Axis I Schizophrenia	—	—	—	—
Axis I Substance Abuse or Dependence	—	—	—	—
Axis II Antisocial Personality Disorder	—	—	—	—
Axis II Cluster B Diagnosis	—	—	—	—
Cocaine Abuse in the Past Six Months	—	—	—	—
Currently on Antidepressant Medication	—	—	—	—
Currently on Antipsychotic Medication	—	—	—	—
Currently on Anxiolytic Medication	—	—	—	—
Ever Arrested	—	—	—	—
History of Being Physically Abused	—	—	.18	—
History of Being Physically Abusive	—	—	—	—
History of Being Sexually Abused	—	—	—	—
History of Committing Domestic Violence	—	—	—	—
History of Domestic Violence Conviction	—	—	—	—
History of Felony Conviction(s)	—	—	—	—
History of Having Few or No Friends	—	.19	—	.15
History of Misdemeanor Conviction(s)	—	—	—	—
History of Outpatient Psychiatric Treatment	.26	—	—	—
History of Suicide Attempts	.16	.25	—	.15
History of Victim of Domestic Violence	—	—	—	—
Lifetime History of Alcohol Abuse	—	—	—	—
Lifetime History of Cocaine Abuse	—	—	—	—
Lifetime History of Heroin Abuse	—	—	—	—
Lifetime History of Marijuana Abuse	—	—	—	—
Number of Arrests	—	—	—	—
Previous Psychiatric Hospitalizations	—	—	—	—
Mental Status				
Anxiety During Interview	—	—	—	—
Depression During Interview	.26	.24	—	—
Hallucinations	—	—	—	—
Loose Associations	—	—	—	—

Poor Judgment	—	—	—	—
Prevailing Mood Angry	—	—	—	—
Prevailing Mood Happy	—	—	—	—
Prevailing Mood Sad	.18	.21	—	.16
Speech During Interview	—	—	—	—
Unusual Gestures	—	—	—	—
SCL-90-R Scales				
Anxiety	.49	.39	.29	.31
Depression	.57	.53	.27	.33
Hostility	.35	.42	—	.26
Interpersonal Sensitivity	.52	.55	.35	.43
Obsessive-Compulsive	.48	.43	.32	.34
Paranoid Ideation	.39	.38	.25	.33
Phobic Anxiety	.36	.36	.28	.31
Psychoticism	.50	.45	.27	.41
Somatization	.39	.35	.21	.24
Initial SCL-90 Analogue				
Anxiety	—	—	—	—
Depression	.27	.23	—	—
Hostility	—	—	—	—
Interpersonal Sensitivity	—	.21	—	—
Paranoid Ideation	—	—	—	—
Somatization	—	—	—	—
Patient Description Form Scales				
Achievement-Oriented	—	-.24	—	-.17
Aggressive	—	—	—	—
Agitated	.25	—	—	—
Angry Resentment	.22	—	—	—
Antisocial	—	—	—	—
Anxious	.38	—	.21	—
Critical/Argumentative	—	—	—	—
Defensive	—	—	—	—
Depressed	.43	.21	—	—
Family Problems	—	—	—	—
Histrionic	.24	—	—	—
Insecure	.37	.21	—	—
Introverted	—	—	—	—
Narcissistic	—	—	—	—
Negative Treatment Attitudes	—	—	—	—

Table I-9. Correlates for MMPI-2 Content Component LSE Scales *(continued)*

Extra-test Characteristics	Self-Doubt (LSE_1)		Submissiveness (LSE_2)	
	Men	Women	Men	Women
Obsessive-Compulsive	.29	—	—	—
Passive-Submissive	—	.18	—	.21
Pessimistic	.27	—	—	—
Procrastinates	—	—	—	—
Somatic Symptoms	.21	—	—	—
Suspicious	—	—	—	—
Patient Description Form Items				
Acts Out	—	—	—	—
Agitated	—	—	—	—
Angry	—	—	—	—
Antisocial Behavior	—	—	—	—
Anxious	.34	—	—	—
Argumentative	—	—	—	—
Assertive	—	—	—	-.23
Blames Family For Difficulties	—	—	—	—
Communicates Effectively	—	—	—	—
Competitive	—	—	—	—
Complains of Fatigue	—	—	—	—
Complains of Sleep Disturbance	.36	—	.22	—
Concerned About Status	—	—	—	—
Copes Well with Stress	-.24	-.20	—	—
Creates Good First Impression	—	—	—	—
Critical of Others	—	—	—	—
Deceptive	—	—	—	—
Defensive	—	—	—	—
Delusional Thinking	—	—	—	—
Demanding of Attention	—	—	—	—
Dependable	—	—	—	—
Depressed	.36	.20	—	—
Difficult to Motivate	—	—	—	—
Difficulty Concentrating	—	—	—	—
Difficulty Making Decisions	—	—	—	—
Difficulty Trusting Others	—	—	—	—
Does Not Get Along with Coworkers	—	—	—	—
Energetic	—	—	—	—
Exaggerated Need for Affection	—	—	—	—

Extroverted	—	-.20	—	—
Familial Discord	—	—	—	—
Family Lacks Love	—	—	—	—
Feels Gets Raw Deal From Life	—	—	—	—
Feels Hopeless	.39	.19	—	—
Feels Inferior	.23	.23	—	—
Feels Like a Failure	.38	.20	—	—
Feels Overwhelmed	.33	—	—	—
Feels Rejected	—	—	—	—
Feels That Life is a Strain	.34	—	—	—
Gives Up Easily	—	—	—	—
Grouchy	—	—	—	—
Harbors Grudges	—	—	—	—
Has Insight Into Own Problems	—	—	—	—
Has Many Interests	—	-.23	—	—
Has Many Nightmares	—	—	—	—
Has Temper Tantrums	—	—	—	—
High Aspirations	—	-.22	—	-.19
Hypochondriacal	—	—	—	—
Impulsive	—	—	—	—
Insecure	—	—	—	—
Introverted	—	—	—	—
Likable	—	—	—	—
Lonely	—	—	—	—
Low Frustration Tolerance	—	—	—	—
Low Sex Drive	—	—	—	—
Manipulative	—	—	—	—
Many Specific Fears	—	—	—	—
Multiple Somatic Complaints	—	—	—	—
Narcissistic	—	—	—	—
Needs Attention	—	—	—	—
Needs to Achieve	—	—	—	—
Nervous	—	—	.20	—
Optimistic	—	—	—	—
Overcontrolled	—	—	—	—
Overly Compliant	—	—	—	.16
Overly Sensitive to Criticism	—	—	—	—
Paranoid Features	—	—	—	—
Passive	—	—	.21	—
Passive in Relationships	—	.20	—	.19
Pessimistic	—	—	—	—
Physical Symptoms in Response to Stress	—	—	—	—

Table I-9. Correlates for MMPI-2 Content Component LSE Scales *(continued)*

Extra-test Characteristics	Self-Doubt (LSE_1)		Submissiveness (LSE_2)	
	Men	Women	Men	Women
Physically Abusive	—	—	—	—
Preoccupied with Health Problems	—	—	—	—
Problems with Authority Figures	—	—	—	—
Psychologically Immature	—	—	—	—
Reliable Informant	—	—	—	—
Resents Family Members	—	—	—	—
Restless	—	—	—	—
Ruminates	—	—	—	—
Sad	—	—	—	—
Self-Degrading	.36	.20	—	—
Self-Doubting	.31	.20	—	—
Self-Indulgent	—	—	—	—
Self-Punishing	—	—	—	—
Self-Reliant	—	—	—	-.20
Sexually Adjusted	—	—	—	—
Shy	—	—	—	—
Socially Awkward	—	—	—	—
Sociopathic	—	—	—	—
Stereotypic Masculine Behavior	—	—	—	—
Stormy Interpersonal Relationships	—	—	—	—
Submissive	—	—	—	.19
Suicidal Ideations	.35	.18	—	—
Superficial Relationships	—	—	—	—
Tearful	—	—	—	—
Unable to See Own Limitations	—	—	—	—
Work-Oriented	—	—	—	—
Worrier	.32	—	—	—

Table I-10. Correlates for MMPI-2 Content Component SOD Scales

Extra-test Characteristics	Introversion (SOD_1)		Shyness (SOD_2)	
	Men	Women	Men	Women
Intake Information				
Alcohol Abuse in the Past Six Months	—	—	—	—
Axis I Depression or Dysthymia	—	.18	—	—
Axis I Other Psychotic Diagnosis	—	—	—	—
Axis I Schizophrenia	—	—	—	—
Axis I Substance Abuse or Dependence	—	—	—	—
Axis II Antisocial Personality Disorder	—	—	—	—
Axis II Cluster B Diagnosis	—	—	—	—
Cocaine Abuse in the Past Six Months	—	—	—	—
Currently on Antidepressant Medication	—	.23	—	—
Currently on Antipsychotic Medication	—	—	—	—
Currently on Anxiolytic Medication	—	.17	—	—
Ever Arrested	—	—	—	—
History of Being Physically Abused	—	—	—	—
History of Being Physically Abusive	—	—	—	—
History of Being Sexually Abused	—	—	—	—
History of Committing Domestic Violence	—	—	—	—
History of Domestic Violence Conviction	—	—	—	—
History of Felony Conviction(s)	—	—	—	—
History of Having Few or No Friends	—	.21	—	—
History of Misdemeanor Conviction(s)	—	—	—	—
History of Outpatient Psychiatric Treatment	—	—	—	—
History of Suicide Attempts	—	—	—	—
History of Victim of Domestic Violence	—	—	—	—
Lifetime History of Alcohol Abuse	—	—	—	—
Lifetime History of Cocaine Abuse	—	—	—	—
Lifetime History of Heroin Abuse	—	—	—	—
Lifetime History of Marijuana Abuse	—	—	—	—
Number of Arrests	—	—	—	—
Previous Psychiatric Hospitalizations	—	—	—	—
Mental Status				
Anxiety During Interview	—	—	—	—
Depression During Interview	—	.16	—	—
Hallucinations	—	—	—	—
Loose Associations	—	—	—	—

Table I-10. Correlates for MMPI-2 Content Component SOD Scales *(continued)*

Extra-test Characteristics	Introversion (SOD_1)		Shyness (SOD_2)	
	Men	Women	Men	Women
Poor Judgment	—	—	—	—
Prevailing Mood Angry	—	—	—	—
Prevailing Mood Happy	—	—	—	—
Prevailing Mood Sad	—	.17	—	—
Speech During Interview	—	-.15	—	—
Unusual Gait	—	—	—	—
SCL-90-R Scales				
Anxiety	.27	.37	.29	.29
Depression	.35	.38	.29	.29
Hostility	.24	.29	.22	.20
Interpersonal Sensitivity	.38	.41	.35	.37
Obsessive-Compulsive	.29	.38	.29	.30
Paranoid Ideation	.21	.28	.17	.21
Phobic Anxiety	.26	.42	.30	.36
Psychoticism	.25	.36	.22	.25
Somatization	.17	.32	.18	.22
Initial SCL-90 Analogue				
Anxiety	—	—	—	—
Depression	.19	—	—	—
Hostility	—	—	—	—
Interpersonal Sensitivity	—	—	—	—
Paranoid Ideation	—	—	—	—
Somatization	—	—	—	—
Patient Description Form Scales				
Achievement-Oriented	—	-.28	—	-.26
Aggressive	—	—	—	—
Agitated	—	—	—	—
Angry Resentment	—	—	—	—
Antisocial	—	—	—	—
Anxious	.21	—	—	—
Critical/Argumentative	—	—	—	—
Defensive	—	—	—	—
Depressed	.33	.21	—	—

Family Problems	—	—	—	—
Histrionic	—	—	—	—
Insecure	.28	—	—	—
Introverted	.22	.20	—	.23
Narcissistic	—	—	—	—
Negative Treatment Attitudes	—	—	—	—
Obsessive-Compulsive	.23	—	—	—
Passive-Submissive	—	—	—	—
Pessimistic	.25	—	—	—
Procrastinates	—	—	—	—
Somatic Symptoms	.21	—	—	—
Suspicious	.20	—	—	—
Patient Description Form Items				
Acts Out	—	—	—	—
Agitated	—	—	—	—
Angry	—	—	—	—
Antisocial Behavior	—	—	—	—
Anxious	—	—	—	—
Argumentative	—	—	—	—
Assertive	—	—	—	—
Blames Family For Difficulties	—	—	—	—
Communicates Effectively	—	—	—	—
Competitive	—	—	—	-.17
Complains of Fatigue	—	—	—	—
Complains of Sleep Disturbance	.26	.20	—	—
Concerned About Status	—	-.19	—	—
Copes Well with Stress	—	—	—	—
Creates Good First Impression	—	—	—	-.19
Critical of Others	—	—	—	—
Deceptive	—	—	—	—
Defensive	—	—	—	—
Delusional Thinking	—	—	—	—
Demanding of Attention	—	—	—	—
Dependable	—	—	—	—
Depressed	.28	.20	—	—
Difficult to Motivate	—	—	—	—
Difficulty Concentrating	—	—	—	—
Difficulty Making Decisions	—	—	—	—
Difficulty Trusting Others	—	—	—	—
Does Not Get Along with Coworkers	—	—	—	—
Energetic	—	-.27	—	-.22

Table I-10. Correlates for MMPI-2 Content Component SOD Scales *(continued)*

Extra-test Characteristics	Introversion (SOD_1)		Shyness (SOD_2)	
	Men	Women	Men	Women
Exaggerated Need for Affection	—	—	—	—
Extroverted	—	-.22	—	-.24
Familial Discord	—	—	—	—
Family Lacks Love	—	—	—	—
Feels Gets Raw Deal From Life	—	—	—	—
Feels Hopeless	.32	.17	—	—
Feels Inferior	—	—	—	—
Feels Like a Failure	.33	—	—	—
Feels Overwhelmed	—	—	—	—
Feels Rejected	—	—	—	—
Feels That Life is a Strain	—	—	—	—
Gives Up Easily	—	—	—	—
Grouchy	—	—	—	—
Harbors Grudges	—	—	—	—
Has Insight Into Own Problems	—	—	—	—
Has Many Interests	—	-.22	—	-.19
Has Many Nightmares	—	—	—	—
Has Temper Tantrums	—	—	—	—
High Aspirations	—	-.22	—	-.26
Hypochondriacal	—	—	—	—
Impulsive	—	—	—	—
Insecure	—	—	—	—
Introverted	.24	.19	—	.23
Likable	—	—	—	—
Lonely	—	—	—	—
Low Frustration Tolerance	—	—	—	—
Low Sex Drive	—	—	—	—
Manipulative	—	—	—	—
Many Specific Fears	—	—	—	—
Multiple Somatic Complaints	—	—	—	—
Narcissistic	—	—	—	—
Needs Attention	—	—	—	—
Needs to Achieve	—	—	—	-.20
Nervous	—	—	—	—
Optimistic	—	—	—	—
Overcontrolled	—	—	—	—
Overly Compliant	—	—	—	—

Overly Sensitive to Criticism	—	—	—	—
Paranoid Features	—	—	—	—
Passive	—	—	.22	—
Passive in Relationships	—	—	—	.17
Pessimistic	.26	—	—	—
Physical Symptoms in Response to Stress	—	—	—	—
Physically Abusive	—	—	—	—
Preoccupied with Health Problems	.25	—	—	—
Problems with Authority Figures	—	—	—	—
Psychologically Immature	—	—	—	—
Reliable Informant	—	—	—	—
Resents Family Members	—	—	—	—
Restless	—	—	—	—
Ruminates	—	—	—	—
Sad	—	—	—	—
Self-Degrading	.25	—	—	—
Self-Doubting	.26	—	—	—
Self-Indulgent	—	—	—	—
Self-Punishing	.27	—	—	—
Self-Reliant	—	—	—	—
Sexually Adjusted	—	—	—	—
Shy	—	—	—	.19
Socially Awkward	—	.19	—	—
Sociopathic	—	—	—	—
Stereotypic Masculine Behavior	—	—	—	—
Stormy Interpersonal Relationships	—	—	—	—
Submissive	—	—	—	—
Suicidal Ideations	.29	.20	—	—
Superficial Relationships	—	—	—	—
Tearful	—	—	—	—
Unable to See Own Limitations	—	—	—	—
Work-Oriented	—	—	—	—
Worrier	—	—	—	—

Table I-11. Correlates for MMPI-2 Content Component FAM Scales

Extra-test Characteristics	Family Discord (FAM_1)		Familial Alienation (FAM_2)	
	Men	Women	Men	Women
Intake Information				
Alcohol Abuse in the Past Six Months	—	—	—	—
Axis I Depression or Dysthymia	—	—	—	—
Axis I Other Psychotic Diagnosis	—	—	—	—
Axis I Schizophrenia	—	—	—	—
Axis I Substance Abuse or Dependence	—	—	—	—
Axis II Antisocial Personality Disorder	—	—	—	—
Axis II Cluster B Diagnosis	—	—	—	—
Cocaine Abuse in the Past Six Months	—	—	—	—
Currently on Antidepressant Medication	—	—	—	—
Currently on Antipsychotic Medication	—	—	—	—
Currently on Anxiolytic Medication	—	—	—	—
Ever Arrested	—	—	—	—
History of Being Physically Abused	.19	—	.16	.15
History of Being Physically Abusive	—	—	—	—
History of Being Sexually Abused	—	—	—	.16
History of Committing Domestic Violence	—	—	—	—
History of Domestic Violence Conviction	—	—	—	—
History of Felony Conviction(s)	—	—	—	—
History of Having Few or No Friends	—	—	.20	.17
History of Misdemeanor Conviction(s)	—	—	—	—
History of Outpatient Psychiatric Treatment	—	—	—	—
History of Suicide Attempts	—	.19	—	.15
History of Victim of Domestic Violence	—	—	—	—
Lifetime History of Alcohol Abuse	—	—	.19	—
Lifetime History of Cocaine Abuse	—	—	—	—
Lifetime History of Heroin Abuse	—	—	—	—
Lifetime History of Marijuana Abuse	—	—	.18	—
Number of Arrests	—	—	—	—
Previous Psychiatric Hospitalizations	—	—	—	—
Mental Status				
Anxiety During Interview	—	—	—	—
Depression During Interview	—	—	—	—
Hallucinations	—	—	—	—
Loose Associations	—	—	—	—

Poor Judgment	—	—	—	—
Prevailing Mood Angry	—	—	—	—
Prevailing Mood Happy	—	—	—	—
Prevailing Mood Sad	—	—	—	—
Speech During Interview	—	—	—	—
Unusual Gestures	—	—	—	—
SCL-90-R Scales				
Anxiety	.36	.27	.21	.20
Depression	.36	.30	.28	.24
Hostility	.46	.39	.20	.19
Interpersonal Sensitivity	.38	.34	.28	.23
Obsessive-Compulsive	.30	.24	—	.18
Paranoid Ideation	.42	.37	.28	.25
Phobic Anxiety	.23	.26	—	.16
Psychoticism	.34	.35	.25	.25
Somatization	.28	.22	—	.20
Initial SCL-90 Analogue				
Anxiety	—	—	—	—
Depression	—	—	—	—
Hostility	—	—	—	—
Interpersonal Sensitivity	—	—	—	.15
Paranoid Ideation	—	—	—	—
Somatization	—	—	—	—
Patient Description Form Scales				
Achievement-Oriented	—	—	—	—
Aggressive	—	—	—	—
Agitated	—	—	—	—
Angry Resentment	—	—	—	.16
Antisocial	—	—	—	—
Anxious	—	—	—	—
Critical/Argumentative	—	.16	—	.19
Defensive	—	—	—	—
Depressed	.24	—	—	—
Family Problems	.32	—	.26	.21
Histrionic	—	—	—	.18
Insecure	.21	—	—	—
Introverted	—	—	—	—
Narcissistic	—	—	—	—
Negative Treatment Attitudes	—	—	—	—

Table I-11. Correlates for MMPI-2 Content Component FAM Scales *(continued)*

Extra-test Characteristics	Family Discord (FAM_1)		Familial Alienation (FAM_2)	
	Men	Women	Men	Women
Obsessive-Compulsive	—	—	—	—
Passive-Submissive	—	—	—	—
Pessimistic	—	—	—	—
Procrastinates	—	—	—	—
Somatic Symptoms	—	—	—	—
Suspicious	—	—	—	.17
Patient Description Form Items				
Acts Out	—	—	—	—
Agitated	—	—	—	—
Angry	—	—	—	—
Antisocial Behavior	—	—	—	—
Anxious	—	—	—	—
Argumentative	—	.16	—	—
Assertive	—	—	—	—
Blames Family For Difficulties	.23	—	—	.22
Communicates Effectively	—	—	—	—
Competitive	—	—	—	—
Complains of Fatigue	—	—	—	—
Complains of Sleep Disturbance	—	—	—	—
Concerned About Status	—	—	—	—
Copes Well with Stress	—	—	—	—
Creates Good First Impression	—	—	—	—
Critical of Others	—	.18	—	—
Deceptive	—	—	—	—
Defensive	—	—	—	—
Delusional Thinking	—	—	—	—
Demanding of Attention	—	—	—	.21
Dependable	—	—	—	—
Depressed	—	—	—	—
Difficult to Motivate	—	—	—	—
Difficulty Concentrating	—	—	—	—
Difficulty Making Decisions	—	—	—	.23
Difficulty Trusting Others	—	—	—	—
Does Not Get Along with Coworkers	.28	—	—	—
Energetic	—	—	—	—
Exaggerated Need for Affection	—	—	—	.20

Extroverted	—	—	—	—
Familial Discord	.23	—	.24	—
Family Lacks Love	.29	—	.32	.25
Feels Gets Raw Deal From Life	—	—	—	.24
Feels Hopeless	.23	—	—	—
Feels Inferior	—	—	—	—
Feels Like a Failure	—	—	—	—
Feels Overwhelmed	—	—	—	—
Feels Rejected	.21	—	—	—
Feels That Life is a Strain	—	—	—	—
Gives Up Easily	—	—	—	—
Grouchy	—	.17	—	—
Harbors Grudges	—	—	—	—
Has Insight Into Own Problems	—	—	—	—
Has Many Interests	—	—	—	—
Has Many Nightmares	—	—	—	—
Has Temper Tantrums	—	—	—	—
High Aspirations	—	—	—	—
Hypochondriacal	—	—	—	—
Impulsive	—	—	—	—
Insecure	—	—	—	—
Introverted	—	—	—	—
Likable	—	—	—	—
Lonely	—	—	.21	.16
Low Frustration Tolerance	.22	—	—	—
Low Sex Drive	—	—	—	—
Manipulative	—	—	—	—
Many Specific Fears	—	—	—	—
Multiple Somatic Complaints	—	—	—	—
Narcissistic	—	—	—	.18
Needs Attention	—	—	—	.19
Needs to Achieve	—	—	—	—
Nervous	—	—	—	—
Optimistic	—	—	—	—
Overcontrolled	—	—	—	—
Overly Compliant	—	—	—	—
Overly Sensitive to Criticism	—	—	—	.17
Paranoid Features	—	—	—	—
Passive	—	—	—	—
Passive in Relationships	—	—	—	—
Pessimistic	—	—	—	—
Physical Symptoms in Response to Stress	—	—	—	—

Table I-11. Correlates for MMPI-2 Content Component FAM Scales *(continued)*

Extra-test Characteristics	Family Discord (FAM_1)		Familial Alienation (FAM_2)	
	Men	Women	Men	Women
Physically Abusive	—	—	—	—
Preoccupied with Health Problems	—	—	—	—
Problems with Authority Figures	—	—	—	—
Psychologically Immature	—	—	—	.20
Reliable Informant	—	—	—	—
Resents Family Members	.36	—	.24	.17
Restless	—	—	—	—
Ruminates	—	—	—	—
Sad	.22	—	—	—
Self-Degrading	.25	—	.21	—
Self-Doubting	—	—	—	—
Self-Indulgent	—	—	—	—
Self-Punishing	—	—	—	—
Self-Reliant	—	—	—	—
Sexually Adjusted	—	—	—	—
Shy	—	—	—	—
Socially Awkward	—	—	—	—
Sociopathic	—	—	—	—
Stereotypic Masculine Behavior	—	—	—	—
Stormy Interpersonal Relationships	—	—	—	—
Submissive	—	—	—	—
Suicidal Ideations	—	—	—	—
Superficial Relationships	—	—	—	—
Tearful	—	—	—	—
Unable to See Own Limitations	—	—	—	—
Work-Oriented	—	—	—	—
Worrier	—	—	—	—

Table I-12. Correlates for MMPI-2 Content Component TRT Scales

Extra-test Characteristics	Low Motivation (TRT_1)		Inability to Disclose (TRT_2)	
	Men	Women	Men	Women
Intake Information				
Alcohol Abuse in the Past Six Months	—	—	—	—
Axis I Depression or Dysthymia	.24	.18	—	—
Axis I Other Psychotic Diagnosis	—	—	—	—
Axis I Schizophrenia	—	—	—	—
Axis I Substance Abuse or Dependence	—	—	—	—
Axis II Antisocial Personality Disorder	—	—	—	—
Axis II Cluster B Diagnosis	—	—	—	—
Cocaine Abuse in the Past Six Months	—	—	—	—
Currently on Antidepressant Medication	—	—	—	—
Currently on Antipsychotic Medication	—	—	—	—
Currently on Anxiolytic Medication	—	—	—	—
Ever Arrested	—	—	—	—
History of Being Physically Abused	—	—	—	.17
History of Being Physically Abusive	—	—	—	—
History of Being Sexually Abused	—	—	—	.19
History of Committing Domestic Violence	—	—	—	—
History of Domestic Violence Conviction	—	—	—	—
History of Felony Conviction(s)	—	—	—	—
History of Having Few or No Friends	—	.19	—	.18
History of Misdemeanor Conviction(s)	—	—	—	.19
History of Outpatient Psychiatric Treatment	.17	—	—	—
History of Suicide Attempts	—	.23	—	.21
History of Victim of Domestic Violence	—	—	—	—
Lifetime History of Alcohol Abuse	—	—	—	.15
Lifetime History of Cocaine Abuse	—	—	—	—
Lifetime History of Heroin Abuse	—	—	—	—
Lifetime History of Marijuana Abuse	—	—	—	—
Number of Arrests	—	—	—	—
Previous Psychiatric Hospitalizations	—	—	—	.16
Mental Status				
Anxiety During Interview	.16	—	—	—
Depression During Interview	.28	.22	—	—
Hallucinations	—	—	—	—
Loose Associations	—	—	—	—

Table I-12. Correlates for MMPI-2 Content Component TRT Scales *(continued)*

Extra-test Characteristics	Low Motivation (TRT_1)		Inability to Disclose (TRT_2)	
	Men	Women	Men	Women
Poor Judgment	—	—	—	—
Prevailing Mood Angry	—	—	—	—
Prevailing Mood Happy	—	—	—	—
Prevailing Mood Sad	.18	.22	—	—
Speech During Interview	—	—	—	—
Unusual Gestures	—	—	—	—
SCL-90-R Scales				
Anxiety	.55	.45	.25	.31
Depression	.61	.55	.25	.31
Hostility	.39	.39	.24	.28
Interpersonal Sensitivity	.52	.50	.25	.33
Obsessive-Compulsive	.54	.47	.23	.26
Paranoid Ideation	.44	.41	.21	.30
Phobic Anxiety	.39	.38	—	.31
Psychoticism	.54	.50	.21	.37
Somatization	.45	.39	.27	.22
Initial SCL-90 Analogue				
Anxiety	.19	—	—	—
Depression	.30	—	—	—
Hostility	—	—	—	—
Interpersonal Sensitivity	—	—	—	—
Paranoid Ideation	—	—	—	—
Somatization	.20	—	—	—
Patient Description Form Scales				
Achievement-Oriented	—	-.30	—	—
Aggressive	—	—	—	—
Agitated	—	—	—	—
Angry Resentment	—	—	—	—
Antisocial	—	—	—	—
Anxious	.32	.16	—	—
Critical/Argumentative	—	—	—	—
Defensive	—	—	—	—
Depressed	.44	.20	.25	—

Family Problems	—	—	—	—
Histrionic	—	—	—	—
Insecure	.34	.16	—	—
Introverted	—	—	—	—
Narcissistic	—	—	—	.16
Negative Treatment Attitudes	—	—	—	—
Obsessive-Compulsive	.21	—	—	—
Passive-Submissive	—	—	—	—
Pessimistic	.26	.19	—	—
Procrastinates	—	—	—	—
Somatic Symptoms	.27	—	—	—
Suspicious	—	—	—	—
Patient Description Form Items				
Acts Out	—	—	—	—
Agitated	—	—	—	—
Angry	—	—	—	—
Antisocial Behavior	—	—	—	—
Anxious	.32	—	—	—
Argumentative	—	—	—	—
Assertive	—	—	—	—
Blames Family For Difficulties	—	—	—	—
Communicates Effectively	—	—	—	—
Competitive	—	—	—	—
Complains of Fatigue	—	—	.20	—
Complains of Sleep Disturbance	.37	—	.21	—
Concerned About Status	—	—	—	—
Copes Well with Stress	-.20	-.20	—	—
Creates Good First Impression	—	—	—	—
Critical of Others	—	—	—	—
Deceptive	—	—	—	—
Defensive	—	—	—	—
Delusional Thinking	—	—	—	—
Demanding of Attention	—	—	—	—
Dependable	—	—	—	—
Depressed	.42	.16	.26	—
Difficult to Motivate	—	—	—	—
Difficulty Concentrating	—	—	—	—
Difficulty Making Decisions	—	—	—	—
Difficulty Trusting Others	—	—	—	—
Does Not Get Along with Coworkers	—	—	—	—
Energetic	-.28	-.25	—	—

Table I-12. Correlates for MMPI-2 Content Component TRT Scales *(continued)*

Extra-test Characteristics	Low Motivation (TRT_1)		Inability to Disclose (TRT_2)	
	Men	Women	Men	Women
Exaggerated Need for Affection	—	—	—	—
Extroverted	—	—	—	—
Familial Discord	—	—	—	—
Family Lacks Love	—	—	—	—
Feels Gets Raw Deal From Life	—	—	—	—
Feels Hopeless	.42	.22	—	—
Feels Inferior	—	—	—	—
Feels Like a Failure	.32	.21	—	—
Feels Overwhelmed	.32	—	—	—
Feels Rejected	—	—	—	—
Feels That Life is a Strain	.32	—	.19	.13
Gives Up Easily	.21	.21	—	—
Grouchy	—	—	—	—
Harbors Grudges	—	—	—	—
Has Insight Into Own Problems	—	—	—	—
Has Many Interests	—	-.26	—	—
Has Many Nightmares	—	—	—	—
Has Temper Tantrums	—	—	—	—
High Aspirations	—	-.26	—	-.21
Hypochondriacal	—	—	—	—
Impulsive	—	—	—	—
Insecure	—	—	—	—
Introverted	—	—	—	—
Likable	—	—	—	—
Lonely	—	—	—	—
Low Frustration Tolerance	—	—	—	—
Low Sex Drive	—	—	—	—
Manipulative	—	—	—	—
Many Specific Fears	—	—	—	—
Multiple Somatic Complaints	—	—	—	—
Narcissistic	—	—	—	—
Needs Attention	—	—	—	—
Needs to Achieve	—	—	—	—
Nervous	—	—	—	—
Optimistic	-.22	-.21	—	—
Overcontrolled	—	—	—	—
Overly Compliant	—	—	—	—

Overly Sensitive to Criticism	—	—	—	—
Paranoid Features	—	—	—	—
Passive	—	—	—	—
Passive in Relationships	—	—	—	—
Pessimistic	.29	.20	—	—
Physical Symptoms in Response to Stress	—	—	.21	—
Physically Abusive	—	—	—	—
Preoccupied with Health Problems	—	—	—	—
Problems with Authority Figures	—	—	—	—
Psychologically Immature	—	—	—	—
Reliable Informant	—	—	—	—
Resents Family Members	—	—	—	—
Restless	—	—	—	—
Ruminates	—	—	—	—
Sad	.31	—	—	—
Self-Degrading	.32	—	—	—
Self-Doubting	—	—	—	—
Self-Indulgent	—	—	—	—
Self-Punishing	—	—	—	—
Self-Reliant	-.15	-.23	—	—
Sexually Adjusted	—	—	—	—
Shy	—	—	—	.16
Socially Awkward	—	—	—	—
Sociopathic	—	—	—	—
Stereotypic Masculine Behavior	—	—	—	—
Stormy Interpersonal Relationships	—	—	—	—
Submissive	—	—	—	—
Suicidal Ideations	.30	.20	.19	.13
Superficial Relationships	—	—	—	—
Tearful	—	—	—	—
Unable to See Own Limitations	—	—	—	—
Work-Oriented	—	—	—	—
Worrier	—	—	—	—

Appendix J

Correlates for MMPI-2 Supplementary Scales

Extra-test Characteristics	Supplementary Scales											
	Anxiety (A)		Repression (R)		Ego Strength (Es)		MacAndrew Alcoholism Scale-Revised (MAC-R)		Addiction Acknowledgment Scale (AAS)		Addiction Potential Scale (APS)	
	Men	Women	Men	Women	Men	Women	Men	Women	Men	Women	Men	Women
Intake Information												
Alcohol Abuse in the Past Six Months	—	—	—	—	—	—	.20	.14	.44	.34	.18	.15
Axis I Depression or Dysthymia	.22	.18	—	—	.23	.22	—	—	—	—	—	—
Axis I Substance Abuse or Dependence	—	—	—	—	—	—	.32	.22	.42	.42	.25	.15
Cocaine Abuse in the Past Six Months	—	—	—	—	—	—	—	.20	.22	.14	—	—
Currently on Antidepressant Medication	—	—	—	.15	—	.16	—	—	—	—	—	—
Ever Arrested	—	—	—	—	—	—	—	.21	—	—	—	—
History of Being Physically Abused	—	—	—	—	—	.15	—	.17	—	—	—	—
History of Being Physically Abusive	—	—	—	—	—	—	—	—	—	—	—	—
History of Being Sexually Abused	—	—	—	—	—	.22	—	—	—	—	—	—
History of Committing Domestic Violence	—	—	—	—	—	—	—	—	—	—	—	—
History of Domestic Violence Conviction	—	—	—	—	—	—	—	—	—	—	—	—
History of Felony Conviction(s)	—	—	—	—	—	—	—	.16	—	—	—	—
History of Having Few or No Friends	.20	.15	—	—	.19	.16	—	—	—	—	—	—
History of Misdemeanor Conviction(s)	—	—	—	—	—	—	—	.29	—	.21	—	—
History of Outpatient Psychiatric Treatment	.16	—	—	—	—	—	—	—	—	—	—	—
History of Suicide Attempts	—	.24	—	—	—	.21	—	—	.20	.23	—	—
Lifetime History of Alcohol Abuse	—	—	—	—	—	—	.26	.22	.33	.40	.18	.17
Lifetime History of Cocaine Abuse	—	—	—	—	—	—	.21	.17	.23	.32	—	—
Lifetime History of Marijuana Abuse	—	—	—	—	—	—	.25	.21	.29	.33	—	—
Marijuana Abuse in the Past Six Months	—	—	—	—	—	—	—	—	.23	.24	—	—
Number of Arrests	—	—	—	—	—	—	—	.18	—	—	—	—
Previous Psychiatric Hospitalizations	.20	.15	—	—	.17	.15	—	—	.14	.18	—	—
Mental Status												
Anxiety During Interview	—	—	—	—	—	.15	—	—	—	—	—	—
Depression During Interview	.28	.24	—	—	.25	.26	—	—	.17	—	—	—
Hallucinations	—	—	—	—	—	—	—	.17	—	—	—	—
Poor Judgment	—	—	—	—	—	—	—	—	—	—	—	—
Prevailing Mood Angry	—	—	—	—	—	—	—	—	—	—	—	—
Prevailing Mood Happy	-.17	—	—	—	—	—	—	—	—	—	—	—

Prevailing Mood Sad	.24	.17	—	—	.19	.23	—	—	—	—	—	—
SCL-90-R Scales												
Anxiety	.60	.52	—	—	.59	.54	.17	.13	.22	.18	—	—
Depression	.62	.61	—	—	.59	.55	—	—	.20	.17	—	—
Hostility	.42	.46	—	—	.42	.41	.21	—	.34	.19	—	—
Interpersonal Sensitivity	.59	.61	—	—	.57	.46	—	—	.16	.13	—	—
Obsessive-Compulsive	.58	.55	—	—	.59	.56	—	—	.19	.16	—	—
Paranoid Ideation	.49	.50	—	—	.50	.41	—	—	.25	.16	—	—
Phobic Anxiety	.43	.45	—	.17	.49	.47	—	—	—	—	—	—
Psychoticism	.55	.55	—	—	.58	.50	.16	.16	.25	.20	—	—
Somatization	.45	.42	—	—	.55	.55	.20	—	.20	.15	—	—
Initial SCL-90 Analogue												
Anxiety	—	—	—	—	.29	—	—	—	—	—	—	—
Depression	.23	—	—	—	.32	—	—	—	—	—	—	—
Hostility	—	—	—	—	—	—	—	—	—	—	—	—
Interpersonal Sensitivity	—	—	—	—	—	.18	—	—	—	—	—	—
Somatization	—	—	—	—	.32	.16	—	—	—	—	—	—
Patient Description Form Scales												
Achievement-Oriented	—	—	—	—	-.21	-.32	—	—	—	—	—	—
Aggressive	—	—	—	—	—	—	—	.22	—	—	—	—
Agitated	—	—	—	—	—	—	—	—	.23	—	—	—
Angry Resentment	—	—	—	—	.22	—	—	—	—	—	—	—
Antisocial	—	—	—	—	—	—	.21	.22	—	.20	—	—
Anxious	.28	—	—	.16	.33	.19	—	—	—	—	—	—
Critical/Argumentative	—	—	—	—	—	—	—	—	—	.17	—	—
Defensive	—	—	—	—	—	—	—	—	—	—	—	—
Depressed	.40	.20	—	—	.44	.26	—	—	—	—	—	—
Family Problems	—	—	—	—	.25	—	—	.18	—	.17	—	—
Histrionic	—	—	—	—	—	—	—	—	—	.18	—	.18
Insecure	.24	.17	—	—	.22	.16	—	—	.21	—	—	—
Introverted	—	—	—	.21	—	—	—	—	—	—	—	—
Narcissistic	—	—	—	—	—	—	—	—	—	.20	—	—
Obsessive-Compulsive	—	—	—	—	—	—	—	—	—	—	—	—
Passive-Submissive	—	—	—	—	—	.17	—	—	—	—	—	—
Pessimistic	—	—	—	—	.27	—	—	—	—	—	—	—
Procrastinates	—	—	—	—	—	—	—	—	—	.19	—	—
Somatic Symptoms	—	—	.21	.16	.37	.20	—	—	—	—	—	—
Suspicious	—	—	—	—	—	—	—	.17	—	—	—	—
Work Problems	—	—	—	—	—	—	—	—	—	—	—	—

Correlates for MMPI-2 Supplementary Scales *(continued)*

Extra-test Characteristics	Supplementary Scales: Anxiety (A)		Repression (R)		Ego Strength (Es)		MacAndrew Alcoholism Scale-Revised (MAC-R)		Addiction Acknowledgment Scale (AAS)		Addiction Potential Scale (APS)	
	Men	Women	Men	Women	Men	Women	Men	Women	Men	Women	Men	Women
Patient Description Form Items												
Accelerated Speech	—	—	—	—	—	—	—	—	—	—	—	—
Acts Out	—	—	—	—	—	—	.21	.18	.23	.17	—	—
Acute Psychological Turmoil	—	—	—	—	—	—	—	—	—	—	—	—
Agitated	—	—	—	—	—	—	.19	—	.23	—	—	—
Angry	—	—	—	—	—	—	—	—	—	—	—	—
Antisocial Behavior	—	—	—	—	—	—	.26	.25	—	—	—	—
Anxious	.30	—	—	—	.37	—	—	—	—	—	—	—
Argumentative	—	—	—	—	—	—	—	—	—	—	—	—
Communicates Effectively	—	—	—	—	—	—	—	—	—	—	—	—
Competitive	—	—	—	—	—	-.23	—	—	—	—	—	—
Complains of Fatigue	—	—	.21	—	—	—	—	—	—	—	—	—
Complains of Sleep Disturbance	.39	—	—	—	.39	.22	—	—	—	—	—	—
Concerned About Status	—	—	—	—	—	—	—	—	—	—	—	.22
Copes Well with Stress	-.19	-.19	—	—	-.26	-.28	—	—	—	—	—	—
Cynical	—	—	—	—	—	—	—	—	.11	.20	—	—
Depressed	.34	.19	.20	—	.41	.24	—	—	—	—	—	—
Difficulty Trusting Others	—	—	—	—	—	—	—	—	.20	.18	—	—
Does Not Get Along with Coworkers	—	—	—	—	—	—	—	—	—	—	—	—
Emotional Lability	—	—	—	—	—	—	—	—	—	—	—	—
Energetic	-.22	-.18	—	-.17	-.25	-.23	—	—	—	—	—	—
Excitable	—	—	—	—	—	—	—	.19	—	—	—	—
Extroverted	-.12	-.18	—	—	—	—	—	—	—	—	—	.17
Family Lacks Love	—	—	—	—	—	—	—	.19	.22	.22	—	—
Feels Gets Raw Deal From Life	—	—	—	—	—	—	—	—	—	—	—	—
Feels Hopeless	.33	.21	—	—	.37	.22	—	—	—	—	—	—
Feels Like a Failure	.25	.17	—	—	—	—	—	—	.21	—	—	.17
Feels Mistreated	—	—	—	—	—	—	—	—	—	—	—	—
Feels Overwhelmed	.26	—	—	.16	—	—	—	—	—	—	—	—
Feels Rejected	—	—	—	—	—	—	—	—	—	—	—	—
Feels That Life is a Strain	.26	.13	.15	.16	.32	.20	—	—	—	—	—	—
Feigns Remorse When in Trouble	—	—	—	—	—	—	—	—	—	—	—	—
Gives Up Easily	—	.18	—	—	—	—	—	—	—	.22	—	.17

Grouchy	—	—	—	—	—	—	—	—	—	—	—	—
Harbors Grudges	—	—	—	—	—	—	—	—	—	—	—	—
Has Many Interests	—	—	—	—	—	-.28	—	—	—	—	—	—
Has Temper Tantrums	—	—	—	—	—	—	—	—	.23	—	—	—
High Aspirations	—	—	—	—	—	-.26	—	—	—	—	—	—
Histrionic	—	—	—	—	—	—	—	—	.19	.19	—	—
Hostile	—	—	—	—	—	—	.20	—	—	—	—	—
Impulsive	—	—	—	—	—	—	—	.22	—	.20	—	—
Introverted	—	—	—	.18	—	—	—	—	—	—	—	—
Low Frustration Tolerance	—	—	—	—	—	—	—	.23	—	—	—	—
Low Sex Drive	—	—	.27	—	—	—	—	—	—	—	—	—
Manipulative	—	—	—	—	—	—	—	—	—	.20	—	—
Many Specific Fears	—	—	.13	.16	—	—	—	—	—	—	—	—
Moody	—	—	—	—	—	—	—	—	.16	.20	—	—
Multiple Somatic Complaints	—	—	.21	—	.36	.19	—	—	—	—	—	—
Needs to Achieve	—	—	—	—	—	—	—	—	—	—	—	—
Nervous	—	—	.21	—	—	—	—	—	—	—	—	.19
Obsessive	—	—	—	—	—	—	—	—	—	—	—	.17
Optimistic	—	—	—	—	—	—	—	—	—	—	—	—
Passive in Relationships	—	.19	—	—	—	—	—	—	—	—	—	—
Pessimistic	—	—	.21	—	.31	.16	—	—	—	—	—	—
Physical Symptoms in Response to Stress	—	—	—	—	.36	—	—	—	—	—	—	—
Physically Abusive	—	—	—	—	—	—	.23	—	—	—	—	—
Poor Judgment	—	—	—	—	—	—	—	.20	—	—	—	—
Power-Oriented	—	—	—	—	—	—	—	—	—	—	—	.23
Preoccupied with Health Problems	—	—	.24	.18	.39	.21	—	—	—	—	—	—
Problems with Authority Figures	—	—	—	—	—	—	.20	.18	—	—	—	—
Psychologically Immature	—	—	—	—	—	—	—	—	—	—	—	—
Restless	—	—	—	—	—	—	—	—	.25	—	—	—
Restricted Affect	—	—	.19	—	—	—	—	—	—	—	—	—
Sad	.27	—	—	—	.37	.20	—	—	—	—	—	—
Sarcastic	—	—	—	—	—	—	—	—	—	.20	—	—
Self-Defeating	—	—	—	—	—	—	—	—	.21	—	—	.17
Self-Degrading	.19	.18	—	—	—	—	—	—	—	—	—	—
Self-Punishing	—	—	—	—	—	—	—	—	.25	—	—	—
Self-Reliant	—	-.19	—	—	—	—	—	—	—	—	—	—
Sexual Preoccupation	—	—	—	—	—	—	—	—	.05	.26	.06	.19
Shy	—	—	—	.16	—	—	—	—	—	—	—	—
Socially Awkward	—	—	—	.22	—	—	—	—	—	—	—	—
Sociopathic	—	—	—	—	—	—	—	.19	—	—	—	—
Stormy Interpersonal Relationships	—	—	—	—	—	—	.25	—	—	—	—	—
Suicidal Ideations	.25	.18	—	—	—	—	—	—	—	—	—	—

Correlates for MMPI-2 Supplementary Scales *(continued)*

Extra-test Characteristics	Supplementary Scales											
	Anxiety (A)		Repression (R)		Ego Strength (Es)		MacAndrew Alcoholism Scale-Revised (MAC-R)		Addiction Acknowledgment Scale (AAS)		Addiction Potential Scale (APS)	
	Men	Women	Men	Women	Men	Women	Men	Women	Men	Women	Men	Women
Superficial Relationships	—	—	—	—	—	—	—	.18	—	.22	—	—
Uses Intellectualization	—	—	—	—	—	—	—	—	—	—	—	.17
Work-Oriented	—	—	—	—	-.21	-.24	—	—	—	—	—	—
Worrier	.27	—	—	—	—	—	—	—	—	—	—	—

Extra-test Characteristics	Supplementary Scales *(continued)*									
	Marital Distress Scale (MDS)		Overcontrolled Hostility (O-H)		Dominance (Do)		Social Responsibility (Re)		Post-Traumatic Stress Disorder (PK)	
	Men	Women	Men	Women	Men	Women	Men	Women	Men	Women
Intake Information										
Alcohol Abuse in the Past Six Months	—	—	—	—	—	—	.17	—	—	—
Axis I Depression or Dysthymia	.27	.21	—	—	—	.17	—	—	.24	.25
Axis I Substance Abuse or Dependence	—	—	—	—	—	—	.22	.17	—	—
Cocaine Abuse in the Past Six Months	—	—	—	—	—	—	—	—	—	—
Currently on Antidepressant Medication	—	—	—	—	—	.15	—	—	—	—
Ever Arrested	—	—	.17	—	—	—	.17	.16	—	—
History of Being Physically Abused	.18	—	—	—	.17	.19	.18	.15	—	.15
History of Being Physically Abusive	—	—	—	—	—	—	.23	—	—	—
History of Being Sexually Abused	—	—	—	—	—	.16	—	.20	—	.20
History of Committing Domestic Violence	—	—	—	—	—	—	.18	—	—	—
History of Domestic Violence Conviction	—	—	—	—	—	—	—	—	—	—
History of Felony Conviction(s)	—	—	—	—	—	—	—	—	—	—
History of Having Few or No Friends	.16	.22	—	—	—	.19	—	.17	.18	.21
History of Misdemeanor Conviction(s)	—	—	—	—	—	—	—	.18	—	—
History of Outpatient Psychiatric Treatment	.17	—	—	—	—	—	—	—	—	—
History of Suicide Attempts	—	.23	—	—	—	.22	—	—	—	.25
Lifetime History of Alcohol Abuse	—	—	—	—	—	—	.23	.20	—	—
Lifetime History of Cocaine Abuse	—	—	—	—	—	—	.19	.13	—	—
Lifetime History of Marijuana Abuse	—	—	—	—	—	—	.24	.15	—	—
Marijuana Abuse in the Past Six Months	—	—	—	—	—	—	—	—	—	—
Number of Arrests	—	—	—	—	—	—	.17	.17	—	—
Previous Psychiatric Hospitalizations	—	—	—	—	—	.17	—	—	.21	—
Mental Status										
Anxiety During Interview	—	—	—	—	—	—	—	—	—	—
Depression During Interview	.24	.18	-.20	—	.21	.15	—	—	.28	.28
Hallucinations	—	—	—	—	—	—	—	—	—	—
Poor Judgment	—	—	—	—	—	—	—	.16	—	—
Prevailing Mood Angry	—	—	—	—	—	—	—	—	.17	—
Prevailing Mood Happy	—	—	—	—	—	—	—	—	-.21	—
Prevailing Mood Sad	.25	.20	—	—	—	.17	—	—	.25	.22

Extra-test Characteristics	Supplementary Scales *(continued)*									
	Marital Distress Scale (MDS)		Overcontrolled Hostility (O-H)		Dominance (Do)		Social Responsibility (Re)		Post-Traumatic Stress Disorder (PK)	
	Men	Women	Men	Women	Men	Women	Men	Women	Men	Women
SCL-90-R Scales										
Anxiety	.49	.40	—	-.18	.40	.39	.23	.19	.58	.53
Depression	.59	.55	-.20	-.27	.42	.38	.22	.16	.66	.64
Hostility	.48	.43	-.18	-.20	.31	.32	.38	.27	.51	.53
Interpersonal Sensitivity	.54	.49	—	-.25	.37	.37	.27	.20	.57	.53
Obsessive-Compulsive	.52	.40	-.17	-.23	.42	.41	.20	.15	.59	.51
Paranoid Ideation	.49	.47	—	-.19	.34	.33	.40	.30	.54	.50
Phobic Anxiety	.33	.28	—	—	.33	.38	—	.18	.43	.44
Psychoticism	.54	.45	—	-.22	.39	.38	.24	.26	.60	.53
Somatization	.43	.35	—	-.17	.34	.36	.18	—	.49	.50
Initial SCL-90 Analogue										
Anxiety	—	—	—	—	—	—	—	—	.27	—
Depression	.23	—	—	—	.22	—	—	—	.36	.16
Hostility	—	—	—	—	—	—	.29	—	.20	—
Interpersonal Sensitivity	.22	—	—	—	—	—	—	—	.26	.17
Somatization	—	—	—	—	—	—	—	—	.21	—
Patient Description Form Scales										
Achievement-Oriented	-.21	—	—	—	—	-.30	—	—	-.24	-.19
Aggressive	—	—	—	—	—	—	.27	.18	—	—
Agitated	.20	—	—	—	—	—	—	—	—	—
Angry Resentment	.22	—	—	—	—	—	.24	.19	.24	—
Antisocial	—	—	—	—	—	—	.26	.28	—	—
Anxious	.25	—	—	—	.27	.17	—	—	.38	—
Critical/Argumentative	—	—	—	—	—	—	—	.17	—	—
Defensive	—	—	—	—	—	—	—	.17	—	—
Depressed	.38	—	—	—	.32	.17	—	—	.54	.26
Family Problems	.25	—	—	—	.22	—	.26	.20	.27	—
Histrionic	.24	—	—	—	—	—	—	—	.21	—
Insecure	.29	—	—	—	.24	—	—	—	.35	.18
Introverted	—	—	—	—	—	.20	—	—	—	—
Narcissistic	—	—	—	—	—	.20	—	—	—	—
Obsessive-Compulsive	—	—	—	—	—	—	—	—	.26	—

Passive-Submissive	—	—	—	—	—	.18	—	—	—	—
Pessimistic	.23	—	—	—	—	.16	—	—	.30	—
Procrastinates	—	—	—	—	—	—	—	—	—	—
Somatic Symptoms	—	—	—	—	.24	.18	—	—	.26	—
Suspicious	—	—	—	—	—	—	.20	.22	.20	—
Work Problems	—	—	—	—	—	—	.28	—	—	—
Patient Description Form Items										
Accelerated Speech	—	—	—	—	—	—	—	—	—	—
Acts Out	—	—	—	—	—	—	.25	.21	—	—
Acute Psychological Turmoil	—	—	—	—	.25	—	—	—	—	—
Agitated	.31	—	—	—	—	—	.26	—	—	—
Angry	—	—	—	—	—	—	.30	—	—	—
Antisocial Behavior	—	—	—	—	—	—	.28	.25	—	—
Anxious	—	—	—	—	.30	—	—	—	.39	—
Argumentative	—	.17	—	—	—	—	—	—	—	—
Communicates Effectively	—	—	—	—	—	-.26	—	—	—	—
Competitive	—	—	—	—	—	—	—	—	—	—
Complains of Fatigue	—	—	—	—	—	—	—	—	—	—
Complains of Sleep Disturbance	—	—	—	—	.28	.16	—	—	.42	.21
Concerned About Status	—	—	—	—	—	—	—	—	—	—
Copes Well with Stress	—	—	—	—	—	-.24	—	—	-.29	-.26
Cynical	—	—	—	—	—	—	—	—	—	—
Depressed	.32	.16	—	—	.27	—	—	—	.47	.22
Difficulty Trusting Others	—	—	—	—	—	—	.26	.21	—	—
Does Not Get Along with Coworkers	—	—	—	—	—	—	.27	—	—	—
Emotional Lability	.20	—	—	—	—	—	—	—	—	—
Energetic	—	—	—	—	—	-.22	—	—	—	—
Excitable	—	—	—	—	—	—	—	—	—	—
Extroverted	—	—	—	—	—	—	—	—	—	—
Family Lacks Love	.31	—	—	—	—	—	.27	.17	—	—
Feels Gets Raw Deal From Life	.26	—	—	—	—	—	—	—	.28	.20
Feels Hopeless	.35	—	—	—	.23	—	—	—	.46	.24
Feels Like a Failure	—	—	—	—	—	—	—	—	.35	.17
Feels Mistreated	.21	—	—	—	—	—	—	—	—	—
Feels Overwhelmed	—	—	—	—	—	—	—	—	—	—
Feels Rejected	.28	.18	—	—	.24	—	—	—	—	—
Feels That Life is a Strain	.28	.16	—	—	—	—	—	—	.34	.21
Feigns Remorse When in Trouble	—	—	—	—	—	—	—	.24	—	—
Gives Up Easily	—	—	—	—	—	—	—	—	—	—
Grouchy	—	.17	—	—	—	—	—	—	—	—
Harbors Grudges	—	—	—	—	—	—	.26	—	—	—

Extra-test Characteristics	Supplementary Scales (continued)									
	Marital Distress Scale (MDS)		Overcontrolled Hostility (O-H)		Dominance (Do)		Social Responsibility (Re)		Post-Traumatic Stress Disorder (PK)	
	Men	Women	Men	Women	Men	Women	Men	Women	Men	Women
Has Many Interests	—	—	—	—	—	-.27	—	—	-.20	-.18
Has Temper Tantrums	—	—	—	—	—	—	—	—	—	—
High Aspirations	—	—	—	—	—	-.26	—	—	—	—
Histrionic	—	—	—	—	—	—	—	—	—	—
Hostile	—	—	—	—	—	—	.25	—	—	—
Impulsive	—	—	—	—	—	—	—	—	—	—
Introverted	—	—	—	—	—	—	—	—	—	—
Low Frustration Tolerance	—	—	—	—	—	—	—	—	—	—
Low Sex Drive	—	—	—	—	—	—	—	—	—	—
Manipulative	—	—	—	—	—	—	—	—	—	—
Many Specific Fears	—	—	—	—	—	—	—	—	—	—
Moody	—	—	—	—	—	—	—	—	—	—
Multiple Somatic Complaints	—	—	—	—	—	—	—	—	—	—
Needs to Achieve	—	—	—	—	—	-.21	—	—	—	—
Nervous	—	—	—	—	.23	—	—	—	—	—
Obsessive	—	—	—	—	—	—	—	—	—	—
Optimistic	—	—	—	.20	—	—	—	—	-.30	-.20
Passive in Relationships	—	—	—	—	—	—	—	—	—	—
Pessimistic	.28	—	—	—	—	—	—	—	.35	.16
Physical Symptoms in Response to Stress	—	—	—	—	—	—	—	—	—	—
Physically Abusive	—	—	—	—	—	—	.31	—	—	—
Poor Judgment	—	—	—	—	—	—	.20	.23	—	—
Power-Oriented	—	—	—	—	—	—	—	—	—	—
Preoccupied with Health Problems	—	—	—	—	.23	.18	—	—	—	—
Problems with Authority Figures	—	—	—	—	—	—	.20	.22	—	—
Psychologically Immature	—	—	—	—	—	—	—	.23	—	—
Restless	—	—	—	—	—	—	—	—	—	—
Restricted Affect	—	—	—	—	—	—	—	—	—	—
Sad	.31	—	—	—	—	—	—	—	.39	.18
Sarcastic	—	—	—	—	—	—	—	—	—	—
Self-Defeating	—	—	—	—	—	—	—	—	—	—
Self-Degrading	.33	—	—	—	—	—	—	—	.31	.19
Self-Punishing	—	—	—	—	—	—	—	—	—	—
Self-Reliant	—	—	—	—	—	-.24	—	—	—	—
Sexual Preoccupation	—	—	—	—	—	—	—	.23	—	—

Shy	—	—	—	—	—	—	—	—	—	—
Socially Awkward	—	—	—	—	.19	.21	—	—	—	—
Sociopathic	—	—	—	—	—	—	—	.21	—	—
Stormy Interpersonal Relationships	—	—	—	—	—	—	.33	.20	—	—
Suicidal Ideations	.29	.18	—	—	.26	.22	—	—	—	—
Superficial Relationships	—	—	—	—	—	—	—	—	.41	.25
Uses Intellectualization	—	—	—	—	—	—	—	—	—	—
Work-Oriented	—	—	—	—	—	-.23	—	—	—	—
Worrier	—	—	—	—	.24	.17	—	—	.34	—

Appendix K

Percentages of Female and Male Clients with Categorical Extra-Test Characteristics: High Scores on Individual Scales and Two- and Three-Point Code Types

Table K-1a. Percentages of female clients with categorical extra-test characteristics: High scores on clinical scales

Extra-test Characteristics	Total Sample (n = 1,447)	Valid MMPI-2 (n = 610)	WNL (n = 42)	Clinical Scales 1 (Hs) (n = 325)	2 (D) (n = 404)	3 (Hy) (n = 319)	4 (Pd) (n = 221)	5 (Mf) (n = 60)
Intake Information								
Ever Arrested	25	27	29	26	23	21	26	40
History of Misdemeanor Conviction(s)	11	11	03	12	10	10	13	17
History of Felony Conviction(s)	09	08	03	08	08	07	09	08
History of Domestic Violence Conviction	01	01	00	01	01	00	01	00
Previous Psychiatric Hospitalizations	32	27	05	30	30	28	31	27
History of Outpatient Psychiatric Treatment	61	60	57	63	61	63	65	58
Currently on Antipsychotic Medication	05	03	03	02	02	03	03	03
Currently on Antidepressant Medication	17	16	03	24	20	22	19	14
Currently on Lithium	03	02	00	01	03	03	03	03
Currently on Anxiolytic Medication	14	12	05	17	15	17	14	07
History of Being Sexually Abusive	01	01	00	01	01	01	01	02
History of Being Sexually Abused	32	36	18	41	40	39	41	31
History of Being Physically Abusive	11	10	07	09	10	10	11	10
History of Committing Domestic Violence	04	04	05	04	04	03	04	00
History of Victim of Domestic Violence	27	33	24	37	34	36	33	21
History of Being Physically Abused	41	43	27	51	47	50	48	36
History of Having Few or No Friends	35	37	10	42	43	42	43	36
History of Suicide Attempts	28	29	07	36	35	34	36	29
Lifetime History of Alcohol Abuse	32	30	17	33	32	34	37	30
Lifetime History of Marijuana Abuse	14	15	18	15	13	16	16	17
Lifetime History of Cocaine Abuse	12	09	10	09	08	09	11	17
Lifetime History of Heroin Abuse	02	01	00	02	02	01	02	03
Alcohol Abuse in the Past Six Months	15	14	02	15	15	15	16	18
Marijuana Abuse in the Past Six Months	04	03	00	03	03	03	03	02
Cocaine Abuse in the Past Six Months	03	01	00	01	01	01	02	02
Heroin Abuse in the Past Six Months	00	00	00	00	00	00	00	00
Axis I Substance Abuse or Dependence	15	12	02	13	12	12	13	19
Axis I Schizophrenia	04	01	02	00	01	00	00	02
Axis I Depression or Dysthymia	28	30	05	38	37	38	37	27

Axis I Bipolar or Cyclothymia	04	03	00	02	04	03	04	03
Axis I Other Psychotic Diagnosis	01	00	00	01	01	01	01	00
Axis I Anxiety Disorder	17	15	07	17	17	17	15	12
Axis I Sexual Disorder	01	01	02	01	01	01	00	02
Axis I Adjustment Disorders	32	34	49	28	29	27	28	34
Axis I V Code Diagnosis	05	07	24	03	03	03	05	03
Axis I Any Diagnosis	89	89	88	87	89	88	89	90
Axis I No Diagnosis	00	00	00	00	00	00	00	00
Axis I Diagnosis Deferred	03	03	07	04	02	04	03	02
Axis I Rule Out Diagnosis	07	07	05	09	09	09	08	08
Axis I Multiple Diagnoses	20	17	07	19	18	19	19	24
Axis II Cluster A Diagnosis	01	01	00	00	01	01	01	00
Axis II Cluster B Diagnosis	09	08	03	08	08	09	10	08
Axis II Cluster C Diagnosis	11	13	18	14	13	14	15	19
Axis II Antisocial Personality Disorder	01	01	00	00	01	01	01	05
Axis II Borderline Personality Disorder	07	06	03	06	06	07	08	02
Axis II Dependent Personality Disorder	10	12	10	13	12	14	14	17
Axis II Personality Disorder NOS Diagnosis	09	10	08	12	11	12	11	07
Axis II Any Diagnosis	30	32	28	34	33	36	36	34
Axis II No Diagnosis	32	31	38	28	29	26	30	29
Axis II Deferred Diagnosis	29	28	28	29	28	29	26	29
Axis II Rule Out Diagnosis	09	09	05	09	09	09	09	10
Axis I and II Dual Diagnosis	28	30	21	31	31	32	33	34
Mental Status								
Uncomfortable During Interview	18	17	10	15	17	17	18	19
Defensive During Interview	07	05	05	04	04	04	05	07
Aloof During Interview	03	03	03	03	03	04	03	07
Cooperative During Interview	90	92	90	93	94	92	92	81
Aggressive During Interview	03	02	03	01	02	02	02	05
Evasive During Interview	09	07	08	07	07	08	08	14
Loose Associations	03	02	00	02	02	02	02	02
Thought Blocking	10	13	10	15	14	15	15	10
Delusions	03	02	00	02	02	02	02	00
Tangential Speech	05	05	03	06	05	06	06	03
Hallucinations	05	03	00	03	03	04	04	03
Circumstantial Speech	08	08	05	10	08	10	09	05
Poor Judgment	27	29	28	30	29	28	31	43
Obsessions	04	04	03	04	04	05	05	05
Preoccupations	17	15	21	15	16	17	17	18
Ideas of Reference	02	02	00	02	02	03	03	00
Too Sad for the Content of the Interview	02	02	03	04	03	04	02	03

Table K-1a. Percentages of female clients with categorical extra-test characteristics: High scores on clinical scales *(continued)*

				Clinical Scales				
Extra-test Characteristics	Total Sample (n = 1,447)	Valid MMPI-2 (n = 610)	WNL (n = 42)	1 (Hs) (n = 325)	2 (D) (n = 404)	3 (Hy) (n = 319)	4 (Pd) (n = 221)	5 (Mf) (n = 60)
Appropriate Emotional Response During Interview	91	92	87	91	93	91	92	88
Too Happy for the Content of the Interview	03	04	05	05	03	04	04	05
Emotionally Flat During Interview	05	04	03	04	04	05	05	05
Prevailing Mood Happy	07	08	10	07	07	07	07	08
Prevailing Mood Anxious	74	72	64	73	74	74	75	63
Prevailing Mood Sad	57	60	36	69	69	69	64	53
Prevailing Mood Angry	16	15	10	17	14	18	16	17
Prevailing Mood Worried	43	47	36	49	50	48	50	39
Unusual Gait	01	01	00	01	01	01	00	02
Unusual Gestures	02	02	03	02	02	02	01	03
Tics	00	00	00	00	00	00	00	00
Tremors	01	01	00	02	02	02	01	02

Extra-test Characteristics	Clinical Scales *(continued)* 6 (Pa) (n = 325)	7 (Pt) (n = 363)	8 (Sc) (n = 368)	9 (Ma) (n = 121)	0 (Si) (n = 230)
Intake Information					
Ever Arrested	27	24	25	34	26
History of Misdemeanor Conviction(s)	12	12	12	19	13
History of Felony Conviction(s)	09	08	09	12	09
History of Domestic Violence Conviction	01	01	01	01	00
Previous Psychiatric Hospitalizations	34	32	35	42	33
History of Outpatient Psychiatric Treatment	63	63	65	67	63
Currently on Antipsychotic Medication	03	03	03	05	03
Currently on Antidepressant Medication	21	21	22	12	26
Currently on Lithium	03	02	03	03	02
Currently on Anxiolytic Medication	13	16	16	10	19
History of Being Sexually Abusive	01	01	01	03	01
History of Being Sexually Abused	43	40	43	47	42
History of Being Physically Abusive	11	11	12	17	10
History of Committing Domestic Violence	04	04	05	07	03
History of Victim of Domestic Violence	36	34	34	33	38
History of Being Physically Abused	47	46	48	50	48
History of Having Few or No Friends	43	42	43	40	52
History of Suicide Attempts	39	37	38	38	40
Lifetime History of Alcohol Abuse	34	35	35	45	31
Lifetime History of Marijuana Abuse	15	16	16	28	11
Lifetime History of Cocaine Abuse	09	10	11	21	07
Lifetime History of Heroin Abuse	02	02	02	07	00
Alcohol Abuse in the Past Six Months	17	16	15	20	15
Marijuana Abuse in the Past Six Months	04	03	04	03	03
Cocaine Abuse in the Past Six Months	02	01	02	04	01
Heroin Abuse in the Past Six Months	00	00	00	00	00
Axis I Substance Abuse or Dependence	13	14	14	23	14
Axis I Schizophrenia	01	01	00	03	00
Axis I Depression or Dysthymia	38	39	38	36	40
Axis I Bipolar or Cyclothymia	05	03	04	05	02
Axis I Other Psychotic Diagnosis	01	00	01	00	00
Axis I Anxiety Disorder	17	18	18	11	18
Axis I Sexual Disorder	00	01	01	02	00
Axis I Adjustment Disorders	27	26	25	27	27
Axis I V Code Diagnosis	04	03	03	03	03

Extra-test Characteristics	Clinical Scales *(continued)* 6 (Pa) (n = 325)	7 (Pt) (n = 363)	8 (Sc) (n = 368)	9 (Ma) (n = 121)	0 (Si) (n = 230)
Axis I Any Diagnosis	90	89	88	86	89
Axis I No Diagnosis	00	00	00	00	00
Axis I Diagnosis Deferred	02	03	03	04	02
Axis I Rule Out Diagnosis	08	08	09	08	08
Axis I Multiple Diagnoses	18	20	20	25	18
Axis II Cluster A Diagnosis	01	01	01	03	00
Axis II Cluster B Diagnosis	11	09	10	14	08
Axis II Cluster C Diagnosis	13	14	13	15	14
Axis II Antisocial Personality Disorder	01	01	01	03	01
Axis II Borderline Personality Disorder	09	07	08	09	06
Axis II Dependent Personality Disorder	12	13	12	13	13
Axis II Personality Disorder NOS Diagnosis	10	13	11	10	12
Axis II Any Diagnosis	35	36	34	41	34
Axis II No Diagnosis	29	28	29	25	31
Axis II Deferred Diagnosis	28	28	27	23	27
Axis II Rule Out Diagnosis	08	08	10	11	08
Axis I and II Dual Diagnosis	32	34	32	38	31
Mental Status					
Uncomfortable During Interview	19	18	18	17	17
Defensive During Interview	05	04	04	06	03
Aloof During Interview	03	03	02	03	03
Cooperative During Interview	92	92	93	90	94
Aggressive During Interview	03	02	02	06	02
Evasive During Interview	08	08	08	10	07
Loose Associations	03	02	02	03	01
Thought Blocking	14	15	15	12	17
Delusions	02	02	02	03	02
Tangential Speech	06	05	06	08	04
Hallucinations	04	03	04	08	04
Circumstantial Speech	09	09	09	09	06
Poor Judgment	32	30	30	33	28
Obsessions	05	05	05	05	03
Preoccupations	17	15	16	14	13
Ideas of Reference	03	03	03	03	03
Too Sad for the Content of the Interview	03	03	03	01	03
Appropriate Emotional Response During Interview	92	92	92	92	92

Too Happy for the Content of the Interview	04	03	04	04	03
Emotionally Flat During Interview	05	05	04	03	03
Prevailing Mood Happy	05	07	06	12	04
Prevailing Mood Anxious	75	75	75	73	79
Prevailing Mood Sad	70	69	66	56	69
Prevailing Mood Angry	16	14	13	17	14
Prevailing Mood Worried	51	48	47	44	48
Unusual Gait	01	01	01	02	01
Unusual Gestures	02	03	02	01	02
Tics	00	00	00	00	00
Tremors	02	01	02	03	01

Table K-1b. Percentages of female clients with categorical extra-test characteristics: High scores on Harris-Lingoes subscales

Extra-test Characteristics	Harris-Lingoes Subscales							
	D_1 (n = 417)	D_2 (n = 176)	D_3 (n = 273)	D_4 (n = 388)	D_5 (n = 351)	Hy_2 (n = 20)	Hy_3 (n = 424)	Hy_4 (n = 305)
Intake Information								
Ever Arrested	22	24	23	23	23	26	24	24
History of Misdemeanor Conviction(s)	11	11	11	11	11	05	11	12
History of Felony Conviction(s)	07	07	06	08	07	11	08	07
History of Domestic Violence Conviction	01	01	01	01	01	00	01	00
Previous Psychiatric Hospitalizations	29	30	31	32	32	20	30	30
History of Outpatient Psychiatric Treatment	62	64	64	64	64	50	63	64
Currently on Antipsychotic Medication	03	01	02	03	03	05	03	02
Currently on Antidepressant Medication	20	24	25	20	21	10	20	21
Currently on Lithium	02	03	02	03	02	00	02	02
Currently on Anxiolytic Medication	15	17	17	16	16	00	15	17
History of Being Sexually Abusive	01	00	01	01	01	00	01	01
History of Being Sexually Abused	39	34	39	42	41	25	40	41
History of Being Physically Abusive	10	10	09	11	11	00	10	11
History of Committing Domestic Violence	03	05	04	03	04	00	04	04
History of Victim of Domestic Violence	33	36	32	33	35	40	34	37
History of Being Physically Abused	47	47	45	49	49	30	48	51
History of Having Few or No Friends	44	42	42	43	45	30	42	46
History of Suicide Attempts	36	33	39	36	38	05	35	38
Lifetime History of Alcohol Abuse	32	32	32	34	33	25	31	34
Lifetime History of Marijuana Abuse	13	13	14	15	13	17	13	15
Lifetime History of Cocaine Abuse	09	06	08	10	10	06	08	10
Lifetime History of Heroin Abuse	01	01	02	02	01	00	01	02
Alcohol Abuse in the Past Six Months	15	18	14	15	16	10	14	16
Marijuana Abuse in the Past Six Months	03	04	03	03	03	00	02	03
Cocaine Abuse in the Past Six Months	01	01	01	02	02	00	01	01
Heroin Abuse in the Past Six Months	00	00	00	00	00	00	00	00
Axis I Substance Abuse or Dependence	12	13	13	13	13	05	12	15
Axis I Schizophrenia	00	00	00	01	00	00	01	00
Axis I Depression or Dysthymia	38	34	40	37	41	15	37	38
Axis I Bipolar or Cyclothymia	03	03	03	04	03	00	03	03
Axis I Other Psychotic Diagnosis	00	01	01	00	00	05	00	00
Axis I Anxiety Disorder	17	18	16	17	17	10	17	16
Axis I Sexual Disorder	00	00	01	01	00	00	00	01
Axis I Adjustment Disorders	29	28	27	27	27	50	29	26
Axis I V Code Diagnosis	03	02	03	02	02	10	04	02

Axis I Any Diagnosis	89	87	89	88	90	95	89	86
Axis I No Diagnosis	00	00	00	00	00	00	00	00
Axis I Diagnosis Deferred	02	03	03	03	03	05	03	04
Axis I Rule Out Diagnosis	09	10	08	09	08	00	08	10
Axis I Multiple Diagnoses	18	18	19	18	18	15	18	19
Axis II Cluster A Diagnosis	00	00	01	01	00	00	00	00
Axis II Cluster B Diagnosis	09	07	09	09	10	00	09	09
Axis II Cluster C Diagnosis	14	10	14	13	15	15	14	14
Axis II Antisocial Personality Disorder	01	01	01	01	01	00	01	01
Axis II Borderline Personality Disorder	07	06	07	07	08	00	07	06
Axis II Dependent Personality Disorder	13	10	13	12	14	15	13	13
Axis II Personality Disorder NOS Diagnosis	12	14	12	12	14	15	12	12
Axis II Any Diagnosis	36	31	35	35	38	30	35	35
Axis II No Diagnosis	27	34	26	28	27	55	27	28
Axis II Deferred Diagnosis	27	28	30	28	27	15	29	28
Axis II Rule Out Diagnosis	10	07	09	09	08	00	08	09
Axis I and II Dual Diagnosis	33	28	33	32	36	30	33	32
Mental Status								
Uncomfortable During Interview	18	17	15	18	20	25	17	16
Defensive During Interview	04	04	04	04	04	05	04	04
Aloof During Interview	03	02	03	03	02	00	03	04
Cooperative During Interview	93	94	93	93	93	90	94	93
Aggressive During Interview	02	02	01	03	02	00	02	02
Evasive During Interview	07	07	09	07	07	00	07	08
Loose Associations	02	01	02	02	02	00	02	02
Thought Blocking	15	17	14	15	14	16	15	16
Delusions	01	01	02	02	01	00	01	02
Tangential Speech	05	05	05	06	06	05	06	06
Hallucinations	03	02	03	04	04	00	03	03
Circumstantial Speech	08	07	08	08	08	11	08	10
Poor Judgment	29	28	29	28	30	16	30	31
Obsessions	05	05	04	05	05	05	05	04
Preoccupations	16	13	15	15	17	21	15	14
Ideas of Reference	02	02	03	03	03	00	02	02
Too Sad for the Content of the Interview	03	02	04	03	03	05	03	03
Appropriate Emotional Response During Interview	93	95	91	92	93	85	92	91
Too Happy for the Content of the Interview	03	02	04	04	03	10	03	04
Emotionally Flat During Interview	04	04	04	04	04	10	04	05
Prevailing Mood Happy	06	05	06	07	06	05	07	07
Prevailing Mood Anxious	75	77	73	76	75	60	73	74
Prevailing Mood Sad	70	69	72	68	71	50	68	70

Table K-1b. Percentages of female clients with categorical extra-test characteristics: High scores on Harris-Lingoes subscales *(continued)*

Extra-test Characteristics	Harris-Lingoes Subscales							
	D_1 (n = 417)	D_2 (n = 176)	D_3 (n = 273)	D_4 (n = 388)	D_5 (n = 351)	Hy_2 (n = 20)	Hy_3 (n = 424)	Hy_4 (n = 305)
Prevailing Mood Angry	15	13	16	16	15	15	17	17
Prevailing Mood Worried	50	47	49	49	50	40	50	49
Unusual Gait	00	01	01	01	01	00	00	01
Unusual Gestures	02	01	03	02	02	05	02	02
Tics	00	00	00	00	00	00	00	00
Tremors	01	01	01	02	02	00	01	02

Extra-test Characteristics	Harris-Lingoes Subscales *(continued)*												
	Pd_1 (n = 286)	Pd_2 (n = 154)	Pd_4 (n = 369)	Pd_5 (n = 372)	Pa_1 (n = 295)	Pa_2 (n = 332)	Pa_3 (n = 36)	Sc_1 (n = 339)	Sc_2 (n = 256)	Sc_3 (n = 344)	Sc_4 (n = 393)	Sc_5 (n = 249)	Sc_6 (n = 245)
Intake Information													
Ever Arrested	26	42	25	25	26	24	33	26	24	23	25	27	28
History of Misdemeanor Conviction(s)	12	21	12	12	11	12	04	13	12	13	12	16	14
History of Felony Conviction(s)	09	14	09	09	09	08	10	09	08	08	08	09	10
History of Domestic Violence Conviction	00	00	01	01	00	01	00	01	01	01	01	01	01
Previous Psychiatric Hospitalizations	33	33	32	33	33	31	28	32	33	32	32	37	34
History of Outpatient Psychiatric Treatment	64	69	66	66	64	62	47	65	62	64	63	64	64
Currently on Antipsychotic Medication	04	07	02	03	04	02	06	03	02	04	03	04	03
Currently on Antidepressant Medication	18	15	20	20	21	19	11	19	22	20	21	21	22
Currently on Lithium	03	04	02	03	02	03	03	02	03	03	03	04	02
Currently on Anxiolytic Medication	14	13	14	15	14	14	11	15	15	16	15	15	15
History of Being Sexually Abusive	01	02	01	01	01	01	00	01	01	01	01	02	02
History of Being Sexually Abused	42	45	42	41	43	41	25	43	40	42	40	47	46
History of Being Physically Abusive	11	14	12	12	12	10	06	11	11	11	10	13	13
History of Committing Domestic Violence	03	05	04	04	03	04	00	04	04	04	03	03	04
History of Victim of Domestic Violence	34	34	36	36	37	34	36	36	34	34	34	32	34
History of Being Physically Abused	50	53	47	48	47	46	31	48	48	48	47	48	48
History of Having Few or No Friends	44	45	45	44	45	45	33	47	45	44	44	44	43
History of Suicide Attempts	41	35	38	39	40	37	17	40	37	35	37	42	41
Lifetime History of Alcohol Abuse	37	47	34	38	31	33	17	34	33	35	34	37	36
Lifetime History of Marijuana Abuse	15	28	15	17	13	14	14	13	12	16	15	19	17
Lifetime History of Cocaine Abuse	11	18	09	12	07	10	03	09	09	12	10	13	12
Lifetime History of Heroin Abuse	02	05	02	02	02	02	00	02	02	02	02	03	02
Alcohol Abuse in the Past Six Months	16	23	16	19	14	16	09	15	15	15	15	18	18
Marijuana Abuse in the Past Six Months	02	04	03	04	03	03	00	03	03	04	03	04	05
Cocaine Abuse in the Past Six Months	03	03	02	02	02	02	00	02	01	02	02	03	02
Heroin Abuse in the Past Six Months	00	00	00	00	00	00	00	00	00	00	00	00	00
Axis I Substance Abuse or Dependence	15	21	13	15	12	14	06	13	13	15	13	16	16
Axis I Schizophrenia	01	01	01	01	01	01	00	01	00	01	01	01	00
Axis I Depression or Dysthymia	34	33	37	39	36	39	26	38	38	37	37	38	39
Axis I Bipolar or Cyclothymia	04	05	04	04	03	05	06	03	04	04	04	05	04
Axis I Other Psychotic Diagnosis	00	00	00	00	00	00	00	00	00	00	00	00	00
Axis I Anxiety Disorder	15	18	15	16	17	18	09	17	17	17	17	20	18
Axis I Sexual Disorder	00	00	01	01	00	00	00	00	00	01	01	01	01
Axis I Adjustment Disorders	29	25	30	27	29	26	34	26	27	26	28	23	23
Axis I V Code Diagnosis	06	05	04	04	04	04	09	04	04	02	03	04	02

Extra-test Characteristics	Harris-Lingoes Subscales *(continued)*												
	Pd_1 (n = 286)	Pd_2 (n = 154)	Pd_4 (n = 369)	Pd_5 (n = 372)	Pa_1 (n = 295)	Pa_2 (n = 332)	Pa_3 (n = 36)	Sc_1 (n = 339)	Sc_2 (n = 256)	Sc_3 (n = 344)	Sc_4 (n = 393)	Sc_5 (n = 249)	Sc_6 (n = 245)
Axis I Any Diagnosis	89	87	90	89	89	91	89	90	89	88	88	91	88
Axis I No Diagnosis	01	01	00	00	00	00	00	00	00	00	00	00	00
Axis I Diagnosis Deferred	02	04	03	02	03	02	03	03	03	03	03	03	03
Axis I Rule Out Diagnosis	08	08	07	09	07	07	09	07	08	10	09	07	08
Axis I Multiple Diagnoses	20	26	17	21	17	19	11	18	19	20	19	21	21
Axis II Cluster A Diagnosis	01	02	01	01	01	01	00	01	00	01	00	01	01
Axis II Cluster B Diagnosis	10	13	10	10	11	11	06	11	09	10	09	13	12
Axis II Cluster C Diagnosis	15	13	14	14	15	13	09	15	14	12	15	11	13
Axis II Antisocial Personality Disorder	01	03	01	01	01	01	00	02	01	01	01	01	02
Axis II Borderline Personality Disorder	07	08	08	07	08	08	06	08	07	07	07	11	08
Axis II Dependent Personality Disorder	14	11	13	12	13	12	09	14	13	11	13	10	12
Axis II Personality Disorder NOS Diagnosis	11	07	13	13	10	11	06	10	12	11	11	12	10
Axis II Any Diagnosis	36	34	38	37	36	36	20	37	35	33	35	36	36
Axis II No Diagnosis	28	32	27	27	28	27	43	28	27	27	27	28	27
Axis II Deferred Diagnosis	25	28	26	27	26	28	29	25	31	29	29	28	28
Axis II Rule Out Diagnosis	10	07	08	09	10	09	09	10	08	10	09	08	09
Axis I and II Dual Diagnosis	34	28	35	35	34	34	20	35	33	31	33	33	33
Mental Status													
Uncomfortable During Interview	16	24	17	18	17	18	11	18	18	19	19	16	18
Defensive During Interview	05	07	04	04	06	04	00	05	04	04	04	04	06
Aloof During Interview	04	02	03	02	03	03	00	03	03	03	03	03	04
Cooperative During Interview	91	89	93	93	92	94	97	92	93	93	93	93	90
Aggressive During Interview	01	07	02	02	02	03	03	03	02	03	02	02	03
Evasive During Interview	08	11	07	07	10	07	00	09	07	08	07	08	10
Loose Associations	02	04	02	02	03	02	00	02	02	02	02	02	02
Thought Blocking	14	17	15	14	15	15	14	16	15	16	15	14	13
Delusions	01	03	02	02	02	02	03	02	02	02	02	01	02
Tangential Speech	06	06	05	06	06	05	03	06	06	06	06	05	06
Hallucinations	03	06	03	04	04	03	00	04	04	04	04	04	05
Circumstantial Speech	10	07	08	08	10	08	06	08	08	09	09	09	10
Poor Judgment	35	36	32	33	32	31	20	32	30	30	30	30	33
Obsessions	03	07	04	05	04	06	17	04	05	06	05	06	04
Preoccupations	13	16	16	15	17	15	14	16	16	15	15	14	14
Ideas of Reference	02	04	03	03	04	02	03	03	02	03	03	01	03
Too Sad for the Content of the Interview	02	01	02	02	03	03	03	02	03	03	03	03	03

Appropriate Emotional Response During Interview	91	90	92	93	92	93	94	93	93	92	93	91	91
Too Happy for the Content of the Interview	05	06	04	03	03	03	03	03	03	04	03	04	05
Emotionally Flat During Interview	05	04	04	04	05	05	03	05	04	05	04	04	05
Prevailing Mood Happy	08	05	06	07	05	05	09	07	06	07	07	07	07
Prevailing Mood Anxious	74	75	76	76	75	77	69	76	77	76	76	76	73
Prevailing Mood Sad	65	58	68	67	68	70	49	66	70	69	68	67	69
Prevailing Mood Angry	13	19	14	16	15	15	09	16	15	16	15	15	16
Prevailing Mood Worried	47	50	52	51	50	47	43	47	51	49	49	46	47
Unusual Gait	01	00	01	01	01	01	00	01	01	01	01	00	01
Unusual Gestures	02	01	02	02	02	02	00	02	02	02	02	02	03
Tics	00	00	00	00	00	00	00	00	00	00	00	00	00
Tremors	01	01	01	02	02	01	00	01	01	02	02	02	03

Extra-test Characteristics	Harris-Lingoes Subscales *(continued)*			
	Ma_1 (n = 42)	Ma_2 (n = 97)	Ma_3 (n = 31)	Ma_4 (n = 118)
Intake Information				
Ever Arrested	42	24	41	33
History of Misdemeanor Conviction(s)	30	18	13	17
History of Felony Conviction(s)	21	09	13	12
History of Domestic Violence Conviction	00	01	00	00
Previous Psychiatric Hospitalizations	50	35	27	36
History of Outpatient Psychiatric Treatment	55	69	61	64
Currently on Antipsychotic Medication	05	03	07	04
Currently on Antidepressant Medication	21	13	07	14
Currently on Lithium	02	02	00	03
Currently on Anxiolytic Medication	12	08	00	11
History of Being Sexually Abusive	05	02	00	01
History of Being Sexually Abused	34	45	39	49
History of Being Physically Abusive	15	16	13	15
History of Committing Domestic Violence	00	04	03	05
History of Victim of Domestic Violence	27	26	35	33
History of Being Physically Abused	34	50	48	48
History of Having Few or No Friends	51	39	39	48
History of Suicide Attempts	37	38	23	40
Lifetime History of Alcohol Abuse	60	49	26	40
Lifetime History of Marijuana Abuse	35	27	27	18
Lifetime History of Cocaine Abuse	32	21	10	14
Lifetime History of Heroin Abuse	06	05	00	03
Alcohol Abuse in the Past Six Months	41	20	06	16
Marijuana Abuse in the Past Six Months	08	03	03	05
Cocaine Abuse in the Past Six Months	05	03	00	04
Heroin Abuse in the Past Six Months	00	00	00	00
Axis I Substance Abuse or Dependence	38	21	16	16
Axis I Schizophrenia	02	01	00	01
Axis I Depression or Dysthymia	31	36	13	35
Axis I Bipolar or Cyclothymia	05	04	00	04
Axis I Other Psychotic Diagnosis	00	00	03	01
Axis I Anxiety Disorder	14	10	03	10
Axis I Sexual Disorder	00	02	03	01
Axis I Adjustment Disorders	31	32	55	27
Axis I V Code Diagnosis	02	04	06	03
Axis I Any Diagnosis	86	88	90	83

Axis I No Diagnosis	00	00	00	01
Axis I Diagnosis Deferred	05	05	06	06
Axis I Rule Out Diagnosis	10	06	03	10
Axis I Multiple Diagnoses	38	24	16	16
Axis II Cluster A Diagnosis	00	02	00	04
Axis II Cluster B Diagnosis	21	24	10	10
Axis II Cluster C Diagnosis	07	10	10	14
Axis II Antisocial Personality Disorder	07	03	00	02
Axis II Borderline Personality Disorder	10	17	06	07
Axis II Dependent Personality Disorder	07	10	03	12
Axis II Personality Disorder NOS Diagnosis	12	12	13	11
Axis II Any Diagnosis	40	47	32	38
Axis II No Diagnosis	24	18	23	26
Axis II Deferred Diagnosis	19	27	35	23
Axis II Rule Out Diagnosis	14	09	10	13
Axis I and II Dual Diagnosis	38	44	29	32
Mental Status				
Uncomfortable During Interview	17	22	21	14
Defensive During Interview	00	10	14	05
Aloof During Interview	05	05	11	02
Cooperative During Interview	88	86	79	90
Aggressive During Interview	02	05	04	03
Evasive During Interview	07	17	11	09
Loose Associations	05	05	00	02
Thought Blocking	14	20	07	11
Delusions	02	03	00	04
Tangential Speech	02	09	04	09
Hallucinations	02	05	04	08
Circumstantial Speech	05	14	14	15
Poor Judgment	40	38	39	36
Obsessions	07	06	04	03
Preoccupations	17	17	07	15
Ideas of Reference	02	03	07	05
Too Sad for the Content of the Interview	00	02	00	03
Appropriate Emotional Response During Interview	93	88	97	91
Too Happy for the Content of the Interview	02	07	03	03
Emotionally Flat During Interview	05	05	00	03
Prevailing Mood Happy	05	05	21	08
Prevailing Mood Anxious	64	71	43	74
Prevailing Mood Sad	55	59	25	67

Extra-test Characteristics	Harris-Lingoes Subscales *(continued)*			
	Ma_1 (n = 42)	Ma_2 (n = 97)	Ma_3 (n = 31)	Ma_4 (n = 118)
Prevailing Mood Angry	14	16	21	15
Prevailing Mood Worried	67	54	43	39
Unusual Gait	00	00	07	01
Unusual Gestures	05	00	00	03
Tics	00	00	00	00
Tremors	02	02	00	03

Table K-1c. Percentages of female clients with categorical extra-test characteristics: High scores on Si subscales

Extra-test Characteristics	Si Subscales		
	Si_1 (n = 173)	Si_2 (n = 211)	Si_3 (n = 236)
Intake Information			
Ever Arrested	26	25	43
History of Misdemeanor Conviction(s)	15	12	20
History of Felony Conviction(s)	08	08	18
History of Domestic Violence Conviction	00	01	05
Previous Psychiatric Hospitalizations	33	34	34
History of Outpatient Psychiatric Treatment	62	64	54
Currently on Antipsychotic Medication	03	04	03
Currently on Antidepressant Medication	27	26	11
Currently on Lithium	02	01	03
Currently on Anxiolytic Medication	19	20	08
History of Being Sexually Abusive	01	01	05
History of Being Sexually Abused	42	41	11
History of Being Physically Abusive	08	09	17
History of Committing Domestic Violence	02	04	13
History of Victim of Domestic Violence	38	37	09
History of Being Physically Abused	52	45	27
History of Having Few or No Friends	51	49	35
History of Suicide Attempts	41	35	21
Lifetime History of Alcohol Abuse	33	30	49
Lifetime History of Marijuana Abuse	11	10	26
Lifetime History of Cocaine Abuse	10	08	11
Lifetime History of Heroin Abuse	01	01	02
Alcohol Abuse in the Past Six Months	17	14	26
Marijuana Abuse in the Past Six Months	02	03	09
Cocaine Abuse in the Past Six Months	02	01	04
Heroin Abuse in the Past Six Months	00	00	01
Axis I Substance Abuse or Dependence	15	11	23
Axis I Schizophrenia	01	00	02
Axis I Depression or Dysthymia	41	38	27
Axis I Bipolar or Cyclothymia	02	03	07
Axis I Other Psychotic Diagnosis	00	00	00
Axis I Anxiety Disorder	21	20	20
Axis I Sexual Disorder	00	00	04
Axis I Adjustment Disorders	25	24	23

Table K-1c. Percentages of female clients with categorical extra-test characteristics: High scores on Si subscales *(continued)*

Extra-test Characteristics	Si Subscales		
	Si_1 (n = 173)	Si_2 (n = 211)	Si_3 (n = 236)
Axis I V Code Diagnosis	02	02	09
Axis I Any Diagnosis	89	85	90
Axis I No Diagnosis	00	01	00
Axis I Diagnosis Deferred	04	04	03
Axis I Rule Out Diagnosis	08	11	07
Axis I Multiple Diagnoses	21	19	29
Axis II Cluster A Diagnosis	00	01	01
Axis II Cluster B Diagnosis	09	06	13
Axis II Cluster C Diagnosis	15	16	06
Axis II Antisocial Personality Disorder	01	00	06
Axis II Borderline Personality Disorder	07	04	06
Axis II Dependent Personality Disorder	13	14	04
Axis II Personality Disorder NOS Diagnosis	13	09	12
Axis II Any Diagnosis	37	32	31
Axis II No Diagnosis	29	30	33
Axis II Deferred Diagnosis	28	30	24
Axis II Rule Out Diagnosis	06	08	11
Axis I and II Dual Diagnosis	34	28	29
Mental Status			
Uncomfortable During Interview	18	18	21
Defensive During Interview	04	05	06
Aloof During Interview	02	03	03
Cooperative During Interview	94	92	92
Aggressive During Interview	02	03	02
Evasive During Interview	07	07	08
Loose Associations	02	01	05
Thought Blocking	20	15	08
Delusions	02	02	04
Tangential Speech	04	05	06
Hallucinations	03	06	02
Circumstantial Speech	04	07	10
Poor Judgment	29	29	33
Obsessions	02	02	05
Preoccupations	12	17	19
Ideas of Reference	03	03	01

Too Sad for the Content of the Interview	04	03	01
Appropriate Emotional Response During Interview	92	92	92
Too Happy for the Content of the Interview	02	02	02
Emotionally Flat During Interview	04	03	04
Prevailing Mood Happy	04	07	06
Prevailing Mood Anxious	79	75	77
Prevailing Mood Sad	73	70	47
Prevailing Mood Angry	14	17	20
Prevailing Mood Worried	49	45	45
Unusual Gait	01	01	02
Unusual Gestures	02	03	03
Tics	00	00	00
Tremors	01	01	03

Table K-1d. Percentages of female clients with categorical extra-test characteristics: High scores on content scales

Extra-test Characteristics	Content Scales ANX (n = 396)	FRS (n = 130)	OBS (n = 219)	DEP (n = 376)	HEA (n = 286)	BIZ (n = 161)	ANG (n = 192)	CYN (n = 171)
Intake Information								
Ever Arrested	24	26	26	24	24	29	33	32
History of Misdemeanor Conviction(s)	13	13	14	11	11	15	17	16
History of Felony Conviction(s)	07	09	08	07	08	08	11	11
History of Domestic Violence Conviction	01	00	01	01	00	01	01	01
Previous Psychiatric Hospitalizations	31	32	33	32	32	39	31	36
History of Outpatient Psychiatric Treatment	63	64	64	63	63	66	68	58
Currently on Antipsychotic Medication	02	02	03	02	02	06	03	03
Currently on Antidepressant Medication	19	25	21	21	23	21	17	18
Currently on Lithium	02	01	01	02	01	04	03	02
Currently on Anxiolytic Medication	16	13	15	16	18	14	13	12
History of Being Sexually Abusive	01	02	02	01	01	02	02	01
History of Being Sexually Abused	40	48	45	40	43	48	47	44
History of Being Physically Abusive	11	12	14	11	11	15	17	12
History of Committing Domestic Violence	04	04	05	04	04	06	04	05
History of Victim of Domestic Violence	35	38	37	34	37	37	32	35
History of Being Physically Abused	48	52	48	47	50	49	51	48
History of Having Few or No Friends	43	48	46	45	43	47	43	44
History of Suicide Attempts	36	40	42	39	38	43	41	41
Lifetime History of Alcohol Abuse	33	37	39	33	35	38	43	32
Lifetime History of Marijuana Abuse	14	13	17	14	16	19	20	14
Lifetime History of Cocaine Abuse	10	07	11	09	10	13	14	12
Lifetime History of Heroin Abuse	01	01	02	02	02	03	02	03
Alcohol Abuse in the Past Six Months	15	19	17	16	15	20	19	17
Marijuana Abuse in the Past Six Months	03	02	04	03	04	04	05	03
Cocaine Abuse in the Past Six Months	01	02	02	01	01	02	03	02
Heroin Abuse in the Past Six Months	00	00	00	00	00	00	00	00
Axis I Substance Abuse or Dependence	13	15	17	13	14	19	18	17
Axis I Schizophrenia	00	00	01	00	00	02	00	01
Axis I Depression or Dysthymia	37	35	35	39	37	36	36	38
Axis I Bipolar or Cyclothymia	03	04	03	04	03	04	04	02
Axis I Other Psychotic Diagnosis	00	00	00	00	01	00	00	00
Axis I Anxiety Disorder	17	21	17	16	17	16	15	15
Axis I Sexual Disorder	01	00	00	00	01	00	00	00
Axis I Adjustment Disorders	30	27	29	28	27	25	26	30

Axis I V Code Diagnosis	03	03	04	04	02	04	05	03
Axis I Any Diagnosis	89	87	89	89	87	88	88	90
Axis I No Diagnosis	00	00	00	00	00	01	00	01
Axis I Diagnosis Deferred	03	07	03	03	04	04	03	04
Axis I Rule Out Diagnosis	08	06	07	08	09	07	09	06
Axis I Multiple Diagnoses	19	20	21	18	20	25	21	18
Axis II Cluster A Diagnosis	01	01	00	00	00	02	01	01
Axis II Cluster B Diagnosis	09	10	11	09	08	14	14	12
Axis II Cluster C Diagnosis	14	17	14	15	13	15	13	11
Axis II Antisocial Personality Disorder	01	01	00	01	01	02	02	02
Axis II Borderline Personality Disorder	07	07	09	07	05	10	09	10
Axis II Dependent Personality Disorder	12	15	12	13	12	13	11	09
Axis II Personality Disorder NOS Diagnosis	11	09	15	12	13	10	14	10
Axis II Any Diagnosis	34	36	39	36	35	40	42	33
Axis II No Diagnosis	26	28	28	28	28	22	26	30
Axis II Deferred Diagnosis	30	29	27	27	28	30	25	27
Axis II Rule Out Diagnosis	10	06	07	09	10	09	08	10
Axis I and II Dual Diagnosis	32	32	36	34	32	37	38	31
Mental Status								
Uncomfortable During Interview	17	16	19	18	15	21	19	18
Defensive During Interview	04	03	04	04	04	08	06	06
Aloof During Interview	03	02	02	02	03	05	03	04
Cooperative During Interview	93	91	93	94	93	88	91	90
Aggressive During Interview	02	03	02	02	01	03	04	04
Evasive During Interview	07	09	06	07	08	13	09	09
Loose Associations	02	03	02	02	02	03	01	01
Thought Blocking	15	20	15	14	14	14	15	12
Delusions	02	02	02	02	02	03	03	03
Tangential Speech	06	06	05	06	06	06	05	08
Hallucinations	03	06	05	04	03	08	06	05
Circumstantial Speech	09	12	09	08	10	09	07	09
Poor Judgment	32	34	33	31	32	37	36	36
Obsessions	05	05	04	05	04	07	04	02
Preoccupations	16	15	14	16	14	19	17	17
Ideas of Reference	03	02	02	02	02	04	03	04
Too Sad for the Content of the Interview	03	02	03	03	04	03	03	02
Appropriate Emotional Response During Interview	92	91	92	93	91	92	92	89
Too Happy for the Content of the Interview	04	03	05	03	04	04	04	05
Emotionally Flat During Interview	04	06	04	04	05	06	03	04
Prevailing Mood Happy	06	02	06	07	07	07	08	08
Prevailing Mood Anxious	75	76	76	75	75	72	73	75

Table K-1d. Percentages of female clients with categorical extra-test characteristics: High scores on content scales *(continued)*

	Content Scales							
Extra-test Characteristics	ANX (n = 396)	FRS (n = 130)	OBS (n = 219)	DEP (n = 376)	HEA (n = 286)	BIZ (n = 161)	ANG (n = 192)	CYN (n = 171)
Prevailing Mood Sad	69	67	69	70	68	64	64	63
Prevailing Mood Angry	15	19	13	15	16	14	16	17
Prevailing Mood Worried	50	52	49	49	49	49	47	44
Unusual Gait	01	01	00	01	01	01	01	01
Unusual Gestures	02	02	03	02	02	02	02	03
Tics	00	00	00	00	00	00	00	00
Tremors	02	02	02	01	03	02	03	02

Extra-test Characteristics	Content Scales *(continued)*						
	ASP (n = 158)	TPA (n = 84)	LSE (n = 263)	SOD (n = 202)	FAM (n = 311)	WRK (n = 315)	TRT (n = 284)
Intake Information							
Ever Arrested	41	26	42	48	47	42	47
History of Misdemeanor Conviction(s)	22	13	23	21	21	23	22
History of Felony Conviction(s)	13	10	18	26	23	18	23
History of Domestic Violence Conviction	00	02	05	06	08	07	07
Previous Psychiatric Hospitalizations	34	39	38	37	33	35	37
History of Outpatient Psychiatric Treatment	62	67	59	58	53	55	54
Currently on Antipsychotic Medication	05	02	03	03	02	03	03
Currently on Antidepressant Medication	18	20	14	14	13	15	14
Currently on Lithium	01	02	03	03	01	03	02
Currently on Anxiolytic Medication	15	11	10	08	06	08	08
History of Being Sexually Abusive	03	02	06	05	04	05	04
History of Being Sexually Abused	45	36	17	13	14	13	13
History of Being Physically Abusive	13	14	18	12	21	17	18
History of Committing Domestic Violence	04	04	11	11	16	13	13
History of Victim of Domestic Violence	32	29	07	05	10	08	07
History of Being Physically Abused	52	44	30	24	33	27	27
History of Having Few or No Friends	43	37	37	35	39	35	33
History of Suicide Attempts	46	37	27	25	23	22	24
Lifetime History of Alcohol Abuse	39	42	49	46	49	49	51
Lifetime History of Marijuana Abuse	22	14	28	27	30	27	28
Lifetime History of Cocaine Abuse	17	08	13	12	14	13	13
Lifetime History of Heroin Abuse	04	04	03	03	04	03	03
Alcohol Abuse in the Past Six Months	17	20	24	27	25	26	29
Marijuana Abuse in the Past Six Months	03	03	06	09	08	08	10
Cocaine Abuse in the Past Six Months	03	01	05	06	04	05	05
Heroin Abuse in the Past Six Months	00	00	01	01	01	01	01
Axis I Substance Abuse or Dependence	18	15	24	24	21	23	26
Axis I Schizophrenia	01	01	02	02	02	01	02
Axis I Depression or Dysthymia	35	32	30	31	26	31	29
Axis I Bipolar or Cyclothymia	03	02	09	10	04	06	06
Axis I Other Psychotic Diagnosis	00	01	00	01	01	00	01
Axis I Anxiety Disorder	15	15	19	19	19	20	21
Axis I Sexual Disorder	00	00	06	04	04	04	04
Axis I Adjustment Disorders	26	32	24	23	23	21	23
Axis I V Code Diagnosis	04	05	07	04	07	07	07

Extra-test Characteristics	Content Scales (continued)						
	ASP (n = 158)	TPA (n = 84)	LSE (n = 263)	SOD (n = 202)	FAM (n = 311)	WRK (n = 315)	TRT (n = 284)
Axis I Any Diagnosis	85	89	90	87	85	87	91
Axis I No Diagnosis	00	00	00	00	01	00	01
Axis I Diagnosis Deferred	05	05	01	04	04	02	02
Axis I Rule Out Diagnosis	10	06	08	09	09	09	07
Axis I Multiple Diagnoses	19	17	31	32	25	29	30
Axis II Cluster A Diagnosis	01	01	01	01	02	01	02
Axis II Cluster B Diagnosis	12	13	10	11	14	12	14
Axis II Cluster C Diagnosis	10	15	06	09	05	05	05
Axis II Antisocial Personality Disorder	02	01	04	05	06	07	07
Axis II Borderline Personality Disorder	08	09	05	05	07	04	06
Axis II Dependent Personality Disorder	09	11	04	04	03	03	03
Axis II Personality Disorder NOS Diagnosis	10	13	11	12	10	11	11
Axis II Any Diagnosis	34	41	27	32	29	28	31
Axis II No Diagnosis	27	25	31	29	31	34	31
Axis II Deferred Diagnosis	31	28	30	28	25	25	25
Axis II Rule Out Diagnosis	08	08	12	10	14	12	12
Axis I and II Dual Diagnosis	31	40	24	27	25	24	28
Mental Status							
Uncomfortable During Interview	20	16	22	22	22	21	20
Defensive During Interview	06	06	08	10	08	08	08
Aloof During Interview	03	00	02	03	04	05	05
Cooperative During Interview	90	92	90	91	90	89	89
Aggressive During Interview	04	04	01	03	03	02	03
Evasive During Interview	07	08	08	09	10	08	08
Loose Associations	02	01	06	03	06	04	04
Thought Blocking	12	10	08	07	11	08	08
Delusions	02	02	02	03	03	02	03
Tangential Speech	04	06	08	04	08	06	06
Hallucinations	07	06	01	03	00	01	02
Circumstantial Speech	06	10	12	06	15	11	10
Poor Judgment	32	33	31	25	36	33	32
Obsessions	05	04	04	03	06	05	03
Preoccupations	15	18	20	20	20	20	17
Ideas of Reference	04	01	01	02	03	01	02
Too Sad for the Content of the Interview	01	01	01	01	01	01	02
Appropriate Emotional Response During Interview	93	94	90	93	94	92	91

Too Happy for the Content of the Interview	05	02	02	02	01	02	03
Emotionally Flat During Interview	03	02	06	04	04	04	05
Prevailing Mood Happy	07	08	04	04	05	05	05
Prevailing Mood Anxious	74	77	78	76	79	77	76
Prevailing Mood Sad	62	56	48	48	47	49	48
Prevailing Mood Angry	13	11	17	16	20	20	21
Prevailing Mood Worried	49	45	50	47	43	44	46
Unusual Gait	00	01	01	03	01	02	02
Unusual Gestures	01	02	02	02	02	01	02
Tics	00	00	00	00	00	00	00
Tremors	01	01	03	03	02	02	03

Table K-1e. Percentages of female clients with categorical extra-test characteristics: High scores on content component scales

Extra-test Characteristics	Content Component Scales							
	FRS_1 (n = 178)	FRS_2 (n = 86)	DEP_1 (n = 382)	DEP_2 (n = 422)	DEP_3 (n = 319)	DEP_4 (n = 186)	HEA_1 (n = 301)	HEA_2 (n = 240)
Intake Information								
Ever Arrested	29	24	24	22	27	24	26	26
History of Misdemeanor Conviction(s)	16	11	12	11	12	10	12	13
History of Felony Conviction(s)	09	11	07	07	08	09	09	10
History of Domestic Violence Conviction	00	01	01	01	01	00	00	01
Previous Psychiatric Hospitalizations	33	31	34	29	31	39	30	33
History of Outpatient Psychiatric Treatment	63	54	63	61	64	65	63	63
Currently on Antipsychotic Medication	03	01	02	02	03	03	02	01
Currently on Antidepressant Medication	21	24	21	20	19	25	23	24
Currently on Lithium	01	01	03	02	03	02	02	02
Currently on Anxiolytic Medication	15	14	16	14	15	16	16	17
History of Being Sexually Abusive	01	00	01	01	01	02	00	01
History of Being Sexually Abused	47	40	40	37	41	43	41	46
History of Being Physically Abusive	11	12	12	10	11	11	09	14
History of Committing Domestic Violence	02	06	04	03	03	04	03	05
History of Victim of Domestic Violence	36	36	34	33	33	29	36	41
History of Being Physically Abused	55	42	47	45	48	44	49	54
History of Having Few or No Friends	47	36	44	43	46	45	42	47
History of Suicide Attempts	40	32	39	36	38	51	36	41
Lifetime History of Alcohol Abuse	36	31	34	30	37	30	32	37
Lifetime History of Marijuana Abuse	16	07	14	11	16	13	14	18
Lifetime History of Cocaine Abuse	09	05	11	09	11	08	09	12
Lifetime History of Heroin Abuse	01	01	02	01	03	01	02	02
Alcohol Abuse in the Past Six Months	16	19	16	14	18	15	14	17
Marijuana Abuse in the Past Six Months	03	02	03	02	04	03	03	04
Cocaine Abuse in the Past Six Months	02	01	01	01	02	02	01	02
Heroin Abuse in the Past Six Months	00	00	00	00	00	00	00	00
Axis I Substance Abuse or Dependence	18	14	13	12	15	14	13	16
Axis I Schizophrenia	01	00	00	00	01	00	00	00
Axis I Depression or Dysthymia	35	36	38	39	39	48	36	41
Axis I Bipolar or Cyclothymia	04	02	04	03	04	04	03	03
Axis I Other Psychotic Diagnosis	00	00	00	00	00	00	00	00
Axis I Anxiety Disorder	20	19	17	16	15	15	17	17
Axis I Sexual Disorder	01	00	00	00	00	01	01	01
Axis I Adjustment Disorders	26	30	27	30	28	21	28	25
Axis I V Code Diagnosis	02	06	03	04	05	05	03	02

Axis I Any Diagnosis	90	89	89	90	90	93	88	89
Axis I No Diagnosis	00	00	00	00	00	00	00	00
Axis I Diagnosis Deferred	05	05	03	03	02	01	04	03
Axis I Rule Out Diagnosis	05	06	09	08	08	07	08	08
Axis I Multiple Diagnoses	21	19	18	18	20	20	19	21
Axis II Cluster A Diagnosis	02	00	00	00	00	00	01	00
Axis II Cluster B Diagnosis	13	06	10	09	11	10	09	09
Axis II Cluster C Diagnosis	13	11	14	14	15	12	15	14
Axis II Antisocial Personality Disorder	02	00	01	01	01	00	01	01
Axis II Borderline Personality Disorder	09	04	08	07	08	09	07	06
Axis II Dependent Personality Disorder	11	11	13	13	14	11	13	12
Axis II Personality Disorder NOS Diagnosis	09	07	11	11	12	15	11	11
Axis II Any Diagnosis	36	25	35	35	37	37	35	35
Axis II No Diagnosis	26	33	27	29	27	29	27	27
Axis II Deferred Diagnosis	31	31	28	28	26	27	27	27
Axis II Rule Out Diagnosis	07	09	09	09	10	08	11	10
Axis I and II Dual Diagnosis	32	24	33	32	35	35	33	32
Mental Status								
Uncomfortable During Interview	18	14	18	17	17	18	17	17
Defensive During Interview	04	05	04	04	03	03	04	05
Aloof During Interview	02	04	03	03	02	03	03	04
Cooperative During Interview	91	92	92	94	94	94	93	91
Aggressive During Interview	03	01	03	02	02	01	02	02
Evasive During Interview	10	08	07	07	06	05	08	09
Loose Associations	03	01	02	02	01	02	02	02
Thought Blocking	17	17	13	14	13	09	13	14
Delusions	02	05	02	01	02	02	02	02
Tangential Speech	06	06	06	05	05	04	08	07
Hallucinations	05	05	04	03	04	05	03	04
Circumstantial Speech	11	10	09	08	07	08	11	11
Poor Judgment	32	30	31	28	32	32	30	32
Obsessions	05	06	04	04	04	05	04	03
Preoccupations	13	17	15	16	14	14	14	14
Ideas of Reference	01	01	02	02	03	02	02	02
Too Sad for the Content of the Interview	02	04	03	03	02	03	03	03
Appropriate Emotional Response During Interview	90	91	93	93	93	94	92	91
Too Happy for the Content of the Interview	04	01	03	03	04	02	04	05
Emotionally Flat During Interview	05	06	04	04	03	03	04	05
Prevailing Mood Happy	04	05	07	07	08	05	07	07
Prevailing Mood Anxious	75	80	74	76	73	72	76	73
Prevailing Mood Sad	67	61	69	68	69	75	67	69

Table K-1e. Percentages of female clients with categorical extra-test characteristics: High scores on content component scales *(continued)*

Extra-test Characteristics	Content Component Scales							
	FRS_1 (n = 178)	FRS_2 (n = 86)	DEP_1 (n = 382)	DEP_2 (n = 422)	DEP_3 (n = 319)	DEP_4 (n = 186)	HEA_1 (n = 301)	HEA_2 (n = 240)
Prevailing Mood Angry	16	19	16	15	15	12	17	17
Prevailing Mood Worried	49	51	48	49	51	48	48	48
Unusual Gait	01	01	01	00	01	01	01	01
Unusual Gestures	01	02	01	02	02	02	02	03
Tics	00	00	00	00	00	00	00	00
Tremors	01	02	02	01	02	02	02	03

Extra-test Characteristics	Content Component Scales (continued)												
	HEA_3 (n = 258)	BIZ_1 (n = 134)	BIZ_2 (n = 209)	ANG_1 (n = 165)	ANG_2 (n = 270)	CYN_1 (n = 203)	CYN_2 (n = 111)	ASP_1 (n = 88)	ASP_2 (n = 199)	TPA_1 (n = 192)	TPA_2 (n = 111)	LSE_1 (n = 263)	LSE_2 (n = 167)
Intake Information													
Ever Arrested	24	33	28	36	26	31	34	41	42	26	27	24	22
History of Misdemeanor Conviction(s)	11	17	14	19	13	16	16	22	21	15	15	11	11
History of Felony Conviction(s)	09	08	10	13	08	10	11	15	12	06	10	06	06
History of Domestic Violence Conviction	00	00	01	01	00	01	01	00	01	01	01	01	00
Previous Psychiatric Hospitalizations	31	41	39	30	29	34	38	39	33	29	33	33	30
History of Outpatient Psychiatric Treatment	62	65	67	68	68	59	61	62	64	63	65	66	64
Currently on Antipsychotic Medication	02	05	05	01	03	03	03	05	05	03	02	03	02
Currently on Antidepressant Medication	23	23	19	17	18	18	21	20	17	17	20	22	23
Currently on Lithium	01	05	03	01	03	03	02	03	03	03	04	02	02
Currently on Anxiolytic Medication	15	14	14	12	15	14	11	15	12	14	13	15	16
History of Being Sexually Abusive	01	02	02	02	01	01	00	02	02	01	02	02	01
History of Being Sexually Abused	44	44	50	48	43	43	43	45	48	36	42	41	44
History of Being Physically Abusive	11	17	13	22	14	14	12	15	15	14	16	10	08
History of Committing Domestic Violence	05	05	05	06	03	05	05	02	05	03	05	03	03
History of Victim of Domestic Violence	38	38	35	34	34	34	35	30	39	30	33	36	36
History of Being Physically Abused	49	52	50	52	48	47	43	45	55	46	50	46	47
History of Having Few or No Friends	40	48	45	47	44	47	42	48	40	42	45	48	48
History of Suicide Attempts	37	39	45	48	37	41	40	49	41	36	40	42	41
Lifetime History of Alcohol Abuse	32	38	38	43	35	30	34	35	45	38	35	34	33
Lifetime History of Marijuana Abuse	15	19	20	21	17	14	12	18	27	16	15	14	14
Lifetime History of Cocaine Abuse	10	11	15	15	12	11	11	16	19	10	11	09	08
Lifetime History of Heroin Abuse	01	03	03	03	01	02	02	05	04	02	04	02	01
Alcohol Abuse in the Past Six Months	14	18	18	21	16	15	14	17	20	20	13	16	16
Marijuana Abuse in the Past Six Months	04	05	05	05	05	02	02	02	06	04	01	03	05
Cocaine Abuse in the Past Six Months	01	02	03	03	02	02	03	04	03	02	02	01	01
Heroin Abuse in the Past Six Months	00	00	00	00	00	00	00	00	00	00	00	00	00
Axis I Substance Abuse or Dependence	11	16	18	20	14	15	16	19	19	16	11	14	12
Axis I Schizophrenia	00	02	01	00	00	01	01	02	02	01	02	00	01
Axis I Depression or Dysthymia	39	33	37	40	38	36	34	32	33	35	33	41	38
Axis I Bipolar or Cyclothymia	02	04	04	02	04	03	03	05	05	03	04	04	02
Axis I Other Psychotic Diagnosis	01	01	00	00	00	00	00	00	00	01	01	00	00
Axis I Anxiety Disorder	17	17	18	12	15	16	12	12	18	17	09	15	16
Axis I Sexual Disorder	00	00	00	00	01	00	00	00	01	00	00	00	00
Axis I Adjustment Disorders	29	28	24	29	30	29	33	32	27	29	35	25	31
Axis I V Code Diagnosis	02	04	03	06	05	04	03	03	04	04	04	04	04
Axis I Any Diagnosis	89	86	87	90	90	91	90	89	89	88	89	90	91

Extra-test Characteristics	Content Component Scales *(continued)*												
	HEA_3 (n = 258)	BIZ_1 (n = 134)	BIZ_2 (n = 209)	ANG_1 (n = 165)	ANG_2 (n = 270)	CYN_1 (n = 203)	CYN_2 (n = 111)	ASP_1 (n = 88)	ASP_2 (n = 199)	TPA_1 (n = 192)	TPA_2 (n = 111)	LSE_1 (n = 263)	LSE_2 (n = 167)
Axis I No Diagnosis	00	01	00	00	00	00	00	00	01	00	00	00	00
Axis I Diagnosis Deferred	04	04	03	03	03	03	02	05	04	03	05	03	02
Axis I Rule Out Diagnosis	08	09	09	07	07	05	07	07	07	09	05	07	06
Axis I Multiple Diagnoses	19	21	21	23	19	17	13	20	22	19	14	17	16
Axis II Cluster A Diagnosis	00	02	01	01	00	01	00	00	01	01	01	00	00
Axis II Cluster B Diagnosis	08	13	15	14	12	12	12	15	12	12	12	10	09
Axis II Cluster C Diagnosis	14	12	12	14	13	14	14	13	13	10	17	15	19
Axis II Antisocial Personality Disorder	01	02	02	03	02	02	02	02	03	02	01	00	00
Axis II Borderline Personality Disorder	05	09	10	08	08	09	08	10	08	09	08	08	08
Axis II Dependent Personality Disorder	13	11	12	12	11	12	10	10	12	08	14	13	17
Axis II Personality Disorder NOS Diagnosis	12	09	10	14	13	10	12	10	10	13	12	12	12
Axis II Any Diagnosis	34	36	38	43	38	35	37	38	36	36	42	37	39
Axis II No Diagnosis	29	25	27	23	28	29	30	29	26	30	23	26	23
Axis II Deferred Diagnosis	29	30	26	28	26	27	28	25	30	26	26	29	29
Axis II Rule Out Diagnosis	08	09	10	06	09	09	06	09	08	08	10	08	07
Axis I and II Dual Diagnosis	31	32	35	40	36	33	35	35	33	33	39	35	38
Mental Status													
Uncomfortable During Interview	14	16	19	18	17	18	15	24	17	19	18	20	18
Defensive During Interview	04	08	06	07	05	06	04	03	05	04	07	04	02
Aloof During Interview	02	03	04	03	03	03	01	02	03	02	02	02	01
Cooperative During Interview	94	90	90	89	94	91	95	93	92	93	93	93	95
Aggressive During Interview	02	03	03	04	03	04	05	06	04	04	03	02	01
Evasive During Interview	07	11	11	09	06	11	05	07	08	06	08	06	05
Loose Associations	02	02	04	01	01	01	01	02	02	01	01	01	01
Thought Blocking	13	13	15	15	14	15	11	15	16	14	14	15	15
Delusions	01	04	03	02	02	03	02	02	03	03	02	02	01
Tangential Speech	05	08	06	05	04	06	07	03	06	05	05	05	04
Hallucinations	04	08	06	06	04	05	07	09	05	04	05	04	03
Circumstantial Speech	09	10	09	08	07	10	09	05	07	10	07	07	06
Poor Judgment	28	36	34	38	33	36	40	32	35	32	31	32	33
Obsessions	03	06	05	04	05	06	03	07	05	04	04	05	02
Preoccupations	14	15	18	17	15	16	18	16	18	17	16	15	12
Ideas of Reference	02	05	04	02	03	03	04	05	04	03	03	04	04
Too Sad for the Content of the Interview	04	02	03	03	03	01	01	01	03	04	01	03	02
Appropriate Emotional Response During Interview	91	92	90	91	92	91	94	92	91	92	94	95	94
Too Happy for the Content of the Interview	04	03	05	05	03	04	05	06	05	02	04	02	04

Emotionally Flat During Interview	04	06	05	02	03	04	02	03	03	04	03	04	04
Prevailing Mood Happy	07	06	05	06	06	08	09	07	04	06	12	07	07
Prevailing Mood Anxious	75	76	75	74	76	76	76	73	77	76	77	75	72
Prevailing Mood Sad	70	63	64	67	67	62	64	61	60	66	62	72	73
Prevailing Mood Angry	14	14	14	19	14	16	17	15	15	13	14	14	12
Prevailing Mood Worried	46	50	48	50	48	47	46	52	47	48	49	51	48
Unusual Gait	01	01	01	01	00	01	01	00	00	01	01	00	01
Unusual Gestures	02	01	02	03	02	03	03	03	00	02	03	02	04
Tics	00	00	00	00	00	00	00	00	00	00	00	00	00
Tremors	02	02	02	03	02	02	02	02	01	03	02	03	02

Extra-test Characteristics	Content Component Scales *(continued)*					
	SOD_1 (n = 224)	SOD_2 (n = 176)	FAM_1 (n = 239)	FAM_2 (n = 275)	TRT_1 (n = 299)	TRT_2 (n = 162)
Intake Information						
Ever Arrested	25	27	27	27	25	32
History of Misdemeanor Conviction(s)	12	15	13	14	12	21
History of Felony Conviction(s)	08	08	11	09	08	10
History of Domestic Violence Conviction	01	00	01	00	00	01
Previous Psychiatric Hospitalizations	34	31	33	33	32	39
History of Outpatient Psychiatric Treatment	65	62	64	64	65	63
Currently on Antipsychotic Medication	02	03	03	03	02	03
Currently on Antidepressant Medication	27	23	17	19	21	24
Currently on Lithium	02	02	03	03	02	02
Currently on Anxiolytic Medication	19	18	13	12	15	16
History of Being Sexually Abusive	01	01	01	01	01	02
History of Being Sexually Abused	40	43	44	44	40	51
History of Being Physically Abusive	10	08	12	11	11	12
History of Committing Domestic Violence	04	02	04	04	04	03
History of Victim of Domestic Violence	37	40	33	36	34	42
History of Being Physically Abused	47	50	48	51	46	57
History of Having Few or No Friends	50	48	45	46	46	51
History of Suicide Attempts	37	38	40	37	40	45
Lifetime History of Alcohol Abuse	32	36	34	36	31	42
Lifetime History of Marijuana Abuse	12	11	13	15	14	16
Lifetime History of Cocaine Abuse	08	10	10	12	08	14
Lifetime History of Heroin Abuse	00	01	02	02	02	03
Alcohol Abuse in the Past Six Months	16	19	15	15	16	21
Marijuana Abuse in the Past Six Months	04	03	03	03	03	04
Cocaine Abuse in the Past Six Months	01	02	03	02	01	03
Heroin Abuse in the Past Six Months	00	00	00	00	00	00
Axis I Substance Abuse or Dependence	15	16	14	16	13	19
Axis I Schizophrenia	00	01	00	00	01	00
Axis I Depression or Dysthymia	41	36	35	35	39	40
Axis I Bipolar or Cyclothymia	03	02	04	05	03	03
Axis I Other Psychotic Diagnosis	00	00	00	00	00	00
Axis I Anxiety Disorder	20	23	18	16	14	15
Axis I Sexual Disorder	00	00	00	00	00	00
Axis I Adjustment Disorders	23	26	27	26	29	29
Axis I V Code Diagnosis	02	03	05	04	04	01
Axis I Any Diagnosis	86	89	91	88	90	90

Axis I No Diagnosis	00	00	00	01	00	01
Axis I Diagnosis Deferred	04	03	03	04	03	03
Axis I Rule Out Diagnosis	10	09	06	07	07	06
Axis I Multiple Diagnoses	22	21	17	20	18	22
Axis II Cluster A Diagnosis	00	00	00	01	00	01
Axis II Cluster B Diagnosis	07	09	12	09	10	08
Axis II Cluster C Diagnosis	13	16	14	13	17	10
Axis II Antisocial Personality Disorder	01	01	02	01	00	01
Axis II Borderline Personality Disorder	05	06	08	06	08	06
Axis II Dependent Personality Disorder	11	15	12	11	15	08
Axis II Personality Disorder NOS Diagnosis	10	13	11	13	11	12
Axis II Any Diagnosis	31	38	37	35	38	31
Axis II No Diagnosis	32	29	30	28	28	28
Axis II Deferred Diagnosis	29	28	23	27	26	30
Axis II Rule Out Diagnosis	08	05	10	09	09	11
Axis I and II Dual Diagnosis	29	34	34	32	35	29
Mental Status						
Uncomfortable During Interview	19	18	17	17	17	19
Defensive During Interview	05	03	05	05	04	06
Aloof During Interview	04	03	03	04	03	02
Cooperative During Interview	91	93	92	90	93	91
Aggressive During Interview	03	02	02	02	03	02
Evasive During Interview	08	07	08	08	08	11
Loose Associations	00	02	02	01	02	01
Thought Blocking	16	19	16	15	14	17
Delusions	02	02	02	01	02	03
Tangential Speech	06	04	03	06	04	05
Hallucinations	05	02	03	04	04	06
Circumstantial Speech	06	05	07	09	07	06
Poor Judgment	26	30	31	34	32	34
Obsessions	04	02	03	04	05	04
Preoccupations	17	14	16	16	15	14
Ideas of Reference	03	02	02	02	03	04
Too Sad for the Content of the Interview	04	04	02	02	03	04
Appropriate Emotional Response During Interview	92	91	92	93	93	90
Too Happy for the Content of the Interview	02	03	04	05	03	06
Emotionally Flat During Interview	05	04	04	03	04	03
Prevailing Mood Happy	06	04	08	09	08	08
Prevailing Mood Anxious	74	78	75	75	74	68
Prevailing Mood Sad	71	68	60	64	71	64
Prevailing Mood Angry	16	13	14	14	16	15

Extra-test Characteristics	Content Component Scales *(continued)*					
	SOD_1 (n = 224)	SOD_2 (n = 176)	FAM_1 (n = 239)	FAM_2 (n = 275)	TRT_1 (n = 299)	TRT_2 (n = 162)
Prevailing Mood Worried	48	49	47	45	49	48
Unusual Gait	01	01	01	01	01	01
Unusual Gestures	03	02	02	02	02	02
Tics	00	00	00	00	00	00
Tremors	01	01	01	01	02	01

Table K-1f. Percentages of female clients with categorical extra-test characteristics: High scores on supplementary scales

Extra-test Characteristics	Supplementary Scales							
	A (n = 300)	R (n = 129)	Es (n = 382)	MAC-R (n = 121)	AAS (n = 192)	APS (n = 87)	O-H (n = 64)	Do (n = 396)
Intake Information								
Ever Arrested	24	26	30	46	35	33	37	27
History of Misdemeanor Conviction(s)	11	06	11	30	21	17	11	10
History of Felony Conviction(s)	08	08	06	17	11	10	13	06
History of Domestic Violence Conviction	00	00	01	01	01	01	04	02
Previous Psychiatric Hospitalizations	34	27	19	38	39	34	09	17
History of Outpatient Psychiatric Treatment	64	63	57	67	64	63	52	54
Currently on Antipsychotic Medication	03	03	02	05	03	00	02	03
Currently on Antidepressant Medication	21	27	09	13	16	10	11	09
Currently on Lithium	02	02	04	03	03	04	02	02
Currently on Anxiolytic Medication	15	17	07	11	13	10	05	07
History of Being Sexually Abusive	01	01	00	03	02	00	00	01
History of Being Sexually Abused	41	30	22	44	42	37	35	25
History of Being Physically Abusive	11	09	07	13	14	09	13	08
History of Committing Domestic Violence	04	02	03	05	06	02	06	04
History of Victim of Domestic Violence	34	34	27	44	32	33	37	26
History of Being Physically Abused	46	41	33	60	48	42	43	31
History of Having Few or No Friends	44	45	27	36	41	30	35	24
History of Suicide Attempts	40	36	17	42	45	33	16	16
Lifetime History of Alcohol Abuse	36	21	27	50	57	50	23	25
Lifetime History of Marijuana Abuse	14	06	14	30	32	27	16	12
Lifetime History of Cocaine Abuse	10	04	08	20	23	16	03	07
Lifetime History of Heroin Abuse	02	00	01	05	04	03	00	02
Alcohol Abuse in the Past Six Months	17	11	13	24	31	26	08	11
Marijuana Abuse in the Past Six Months	04	01	02	07	09	09	07	02
Cocaine Abuse in the Past Six Months	02	01	00	06	04	01	02	00
Heroin Abuse in the Past Six Months	00	00	00	00	00	00	00	00
Axis I Substance Abuse or Dependence	14	08	10	26	32	24	06	09
Axis I Schizophrenia	01	00	01	02	01	00	00	01
Axis I Depression or Dysthymia	38	38	17	33	32	25	14	19
Axis I Bipolar or Cyclothymia	03	01	03	04	04	06	02	04
Axis I Other Psychotic Diagnosis	00	01	00	01	01	00	02	01
Axis I Anxiety Disorder	18	20	11	18	16	17	17	14
Axis I Sexual Disorder	00	00	01	00	01	01	02	01
Axis I Adjustment Disorders	27	24	42	26	27	35	38	39

Table K-1f. Percentages of female clients with categorical extra-test characteristics: High scores on supplementary scales *(continued)*

Extra-test Characteristics	Supplementary Scales							
	A (n = 300)	R (n = 129)	Es (n = 382)	MAC-R (n = 121)	AAS (n = 192)	APS (n = 87)	O-H (n = 64)	Do (n = 396)
Axis I V Code Diagnosis	03	05	13	04	05	06	13	11
Axis I Any Diagnosis	89	87	89	88	89	88	83	89
Axis I No Diagnosis	00	01	01	00	00	00	00	00
Axis I Diagnosis Deferred	03	02	04	04	03	05	06	05
Axis I Rule Out Diagnosis	08	10	06	08	08	07	11	06
Axis I Multiple Diagnoses	20	16	14	28	32	31	10	15
Axis II Cluster A Diagnosis	00	01	00	01	01	01	00	00
Axis II Cluster B Diagnosis	11	05	06	13	13	17	02	07
Axis II Cluster C Diagnosis	14	18	13	07	11	15	11	10
Axis II Antisocial Personality Disorder	01	01	01	03	03	01	00	00
Axis II Borderline Personality Disorder	09	04	05	08	08	14	02	06
Axis II Dependent Personality Disorder	13	16	11	05	10	15	11	09
Axis II Personality Disorder NOS Diagnosis	13	13	09	11	08	10	05	09
Axis II Any Diagnosis	39	36	29	31	33	43	18	26
Axis II No Diagnosis	27	35	35	26	35	25	36	39
Axis II Deferred Diagnosis	27	22	27	35	26	21	30	26
Axis II Rule Out Diagnosis	08	06	10	08	07	11	16	08
Axis I and II Dual Diagnosis	36	32	25	31	29	40	16	24
Mental Status								
Uncomfortable During Interview	18	17	15	14	19	15	15	16
Defensive During Interview	04	04	06	07	05	05	06	06
Aloof During Interview	03	04	04	03	03	05	05	03
Cooperative During Interview	93	93	92	92	90	89	94	92
Aggressive During Interview	02	02	03	03	02	04	02	02
Evasive During Interview	08	05	07	08	08	08	10	07
Loose Associations	02	01	00	03	02	04	02	01
Thought Blocking	15	17	10	08	11	12	13	10
Delusions	02	02	02	03	02	02	02	01
Tangential Speech	05	04	04	06	04	04	03	04
Hallucinations	03	02	01	08	05	04	00	01
Circumstantial Speech	07	09	08	08	06	08	07	08
Poor Judgment	32	27	28	38	37	36	23	25
Obsessions	05	02	05	02	04	05	02	06
Preoccupations	15	17	18	14	14	19	13	14
Ideas of Reference	03	03	02	05	03	02	00	01

Too Sad for the Content of the Interview	03	06	01	02	03	04	02	01
Appropriate Emotional Response During Interview	93	92	93	91	90	87	92	95
Too Happy for the Content of the Interview	03	03	04	05	06	06	08	02
Emotionally Flat During Interview	04	03	02	04	04	06	02	02
Prevailing Mood Happy	07	07	12	08	08	08	13	11
Prevailing Mood Anxious	75	70	69	73	72	72	65	71
Prevailing Mood Sad	69	67	45	59	60	53	40	49
Prevailing Mood Angry	13	14	13	15	13	19	13	15
Prevailing Mood Worried	48	53	40	45	47	53	50	43
Unusual Gait	01	02	01	00	01	00	02	00
Unusual Gestures	03	01	00	01	01	01	00	00
Tics	00	00	00	00	00	00	00	00
Tremors	02	00	00	03	02	04	00	00

Extra-test Characteristics	Supplementary Scales *(continued)* Re (n = 274)	MDS (n = 426)	PK (n = 379)
Intake Information			
Ever Arrested	21	23	25
History of Misdemeanor Conviction(s)	06	12	13
History of Felony Conviction(s)	05	08	08
History of Domestic Violence Conviction	01	01	01
Previous Psychiatric Hospitalizations	25	30	30
History of Outpatient Psychiatric Treatment	58	63	64
Currently on Antipsychotic Medication	02	02	02
Currently on Antidepressant Medication	16	18	19
Currently on Lithium	03	02	02
Currently on Anxiolytic Medication	12	13	15
History of Being Sexually Abusive	00	01	01
History of Being Sexually Abused	27	40	43
History of Being Physically Abusive	07	11	11
History of Committing Domestic Violence	03	04	04
History of Victim of Domestic Violence	29	35	36
History of Being Physically Abused	36	47	49
History of Having Few or No Friends	30	44	45
History of Suicide Attempts	24	36	38
Lifetime History of Alcohol Abuse	22	32	35
Lifetime History of Marijuana Abuse	10	13	15
Lifetime History of Cocaine Abuse	06	10	11
Lifetime History of Heroin Abuse	01	02	02
Alcohol Abuse in the Past Six Months	11	15	16
Marijuana Abuse in the Past Six Months	02	03	04
Cocaine Abuse in the Past Six Months	00	02	02
Heroin Abuse in the Past Six Months	00	00	00
Axis I Substance Abuse or Dependence	07	13	14
Axis I Schizophrenia	00	01	00
Axis I Depression or Dysthymia	28	36	39
Axis I Bipolar or Cyclothymia	04	03	03
Axis I Other Psychotic Diagnosis	01	00	00
Axis I Anxiety Disorder	14	16	16
Axis I Sexual Disorder	01	00	01
Axis I Adjustment Disorders	37	28	28
Axis I V Code Diagnosis	08	05	03
Axis I Any Diagnosis	90	89	89

Axis I No Diagnosis	00	00	00
Axis I Diagnosis Deferred	03	03	03
Axis I Rule Out Diagnosis	07	07	09
Axis I Multiple Diagnoses	14	17	19
Axis II Cluster A Diagnosis	01	01	01
Axis II Cluster B Diagnosis	06	10	10
Axis II Cluster C Diagnosis	13	15	14
Axis II Antisocial Personality Disorder	00	01	01
Axis II Borderline Personality Disorder	06	07	07
Axis II Dependent Personality Disorder	12	13	13
Axis II Personality Disorder NOS Diagnosis	10	11	12
Axis II Any Diagnosis	30	36	37
Axis II No Diagnosis	34	29	27
Axis II Deferred Diagnosis	27	25	27
Axis II Rule Out Diagnosis	09	10	09
Axis I and II Dual Diagnosis	27	33	34
Mental Status			
Uncomfortable During Interview	13	16	18
Defensive During Interview	04	04	04
Aloof During Interview	03	03	03
Cooperative During Interview	94	93	93
Aggressive During Interview	01	02	02
Evasive During Interview	06	07	07
Loose Associations	01	02	02
Thought Blocking	10	15	15
Delusions	01	02	02
Tangential Speech	05	06	06
Hallucinations	02	03	03
Circumstantial Speech	09	08	08
Poor Judgment	23	31	32
Obsessions	03	04	04
Preoccupations	15	15	16
Ideas of Reference	02	03	02
Too Sad for the Content of the Interview	02	02	03
Appropriate Emotional Response During Interview	92	94	93
Too Happy for the Content of the Interview	04	03	04
Emotionally Flat During Interview	03	04	04
Prevailing Mood Happy	10	07	06
Prevailing Mood Anxious	66	75	75
Prevailing Mood Sad	59	66	68
Prevailing Mood Angry	13	15	16

Extra-test Characteristics	Supplementary Scales *(continued)*		
	Re (n = 274)	MDS (n = 426)	PK (n = 379)
Prevailing Mood Worried	46	49	50
Unusual Gait	01	00	01
Unusual Gestures	02	02	02
Tics	00	00	00
Tremors	02	02	02

Table K-2a. Percentages of male clients with categorical extra-test characteristics: High scores on clinical scales

Extra-test Characteristics	Total Sample (n = 1,035)	Valid MMPI-2 (n = 410)	WNL (n = 48)	Clinical Scales 1 (Hs) (n = 169)	2 (D) (n = 227)	3 (Hy) (n = 181)	4 (Pd) (n = 243)	5 (Mf) (n = 156)
Intake Information								
Ever Arrested	52	49	62	50	44	49	50	25
History of Misdemeanor Conviction(s)	26	21	26	26	19	22	25	07
History of Felony Conviction(s)	26	21	20	23	20	22	24	12
History of Domestic Violence Conviction	08	06	10	04	05	04	07	03
Previous Psychiatric Hospitalizations	36	29	06	35	37	33	38	27
History of Outpatient Psychiatric Treatment	48	47	30	56	57	53	55	64
Currently on Antipsychotic Medication	06	04	00	04	04	03	03	02
Currently on Antidepressant Medication	13	11	02	14	15	13	13	11
Currently on Lithium	04	03	04	01	03	01	02	04
Currently on Anxiolytic Medication	09	06	00	10	09	08	08	04
History of Being Sexually Abusive	04	06	04	05	05	05	05	04
History of Being Sexually Abused	11	11	15	12	11	12	13	16
History of Being Physically Abusive	18	15	15	14	13	15	18	07
History of Committing Domestic Violence	14	11	15	11	09	11	14	09
History of Victim of Domestic Violence	06	06	04	07	06	07	08	11
History of Being Physically Abused	22	21	15	28	24	26	27	22
History of Having Few or No Friends	31	28	23	33	33	34	34	27
History of Suicide Attempts	24	19	13	26	22	24	23	31
Lifetime History of Alcohol Abuse	49	46	43	53	45	48	50	53
Lifetime History of Marijuana Abuse	24	22	14	27	21	21	27	25
Lifetime History of Cocaine Abuse	15	12	05	16	11	14	16	20
Lifetime History of Heroin Abuse	05	03	00	04	03	03	05	02
Alcohol Abuse in the Past Six Months	28	25	20	31	26	27	29	27
Marijuana Abuse in the Past Six Months	07	06	05	09	07	06	08	07
Cocaine Abuse in the Past Six Months	06	04	05	06	05	05	04	09
Heroin Abuse in the Past Six Months	00	00	00	01	00	00	00	00
Axis I Substance Abuse or Dependence	25	21	15	22	19	21	24	20
Axis I Schizophrenia	04	02	00	01	03	01	03	00
Axis I Depression or Dysthymia	23	21	09	32	32	30	25	27
Axis I Bipolar or Cyclothymia	05	04	04	04	06	03	05	09
Axis I Other Psychotic Diagnosis	01	01	00	01	01	01	01	02
Axis I Anxiety Disorder	14	17	07	18	22	21	18	20
Axis I Sexual Disorder	03	04	07	03	02	02	03	04
Axis I Adjustment Disorders	27	27	33	29	22	28	23	25

Table K-2a. Percentages of male clients with categorical extra-test characteristics: High scores on clinical scales *(continued)*

Extra-test Characteristics	Total Sample (n = 1,035)	Valid MMPI-2 (n = 410)	WNL (n = 48)	Clinical Scales 1 (Hs) (n = 169)	2 (D) (n = 227)	3 (Hy) (n = 181)	4 (Pd) (n = 243)	5 (Mf) (n = 156)
Axis I V Code Diagnosis	06	10	26	05	06	07	07	04
Axis I Any Diagnosis	88	87	89	88	89	88	88	87
Axis I No Diagnosis	01	01	02	00	00	00	01	00
Axis I Diagnosis Deferred	04	05	07	04	03	04	03	04
Axis I Rule Out Diagnosis	08	07	02	08	08	07	07	09
Axis I Multiple Diagnoses	26	22	13	31	25	26	24	24
Axis II Cluster A Diagnosis	02	02	00	01	01	03	03	02
Axis II Cluster B Diagnosis	12	11	09	10	11	10	13	05
Axis II Cluster C Diagnosis	05	06	11	06	06	05	06	07
Axis II Antisocial Personality Disorder	05	05	02	06	05	05	06	02
Axis II Borderline Personality Disorder	06	05	02	04	06	05	07	04
Axis II Dependent Personality Disorder	03	03	02	05	04	05	04	07
Axis II Personality Disorder NOS Diagnosis	07	10	07	10	11	10	10	13
Axis II Any Diagnosis	27	29	26	25	29	28	32	27
Axis II No Diagnosis	36	36	50	33	36	35	35	36
Axis II Deferred Diagnosis	26	26	17	30	25	25	23	20
Axis II Rule Out Diagnosis	10	10	07	10	10	11	10	16
Axis I and II Dual Diagnosis	24	24	17	22	26	24	28	25
Mental Status								
Uncomfortable During Interview	19	18	16	19	18	19	17	12
Defensive During Interview	07	07	04	05	06	06	07	04
Aloof During Interview	04	04	02	02	04	03	04	05
Cooperative During Interview	88	90	91	91	91	91	90	91
Aggressive During Interview	03	02	02	02	02	02	02	00
Evasive During Interview	10	08	02	10	08	09	08	09
Loose Associations	04	03	00	04	04	03	05	04
Thought Blocking	08	07	09	09	08	07	08	09
Delusions	05	03	00	02	03	02	04	00
Tangential Speech	05	05	00	08	06	07	07	05
Hallucinations	06	01	00	02	02	02	01	00
Circumstantial Speech	07	09	00	11	09	09	12	13
Poor Judgment	31	30	35	33	28	28	33	20
Obsessions	04	05	00	07	06	07	06	05
Preoccupations	18	18	13	22	20	23	19	29

Ideas of Reference	04	02	04	02	01	02	02	00
Too Sad for the Content of the Interview	01	01	00	02	02	02	01	00
Appropriate Emotional Response During Interview	92	92	93	92	93	92	92	96
Too Happy for the Content of the Interview	02	03	04	02	02	03	02	04
Emotionally Flat During Interview	05	03	02	04	03	03	05	02
Prevailing Mood Happy	08	09	11	04	05	04	07	04
Prevailing Mood Anxious	75	75	65	80	80	80	79	82
Prevailing Mood Sad	41	39	20	54	50	51	45	48
Prevailing Mood Angry	15	14	09	14	16	14	18	07
Prevailing Mood Worried	39	45	39	53	47	51	45	48
Unusual Gait	01	01	00	02	02	02	02	04
Unusual Gestures	02	02	05	02	01	02	01	02
Tics	00	00	00	00	00	00	00	00
Tremors	02	01	00	03	03	03	02	00

Extra-test Characteristics	Clinical Scales *(continued)*				
	6 (Pa) (n = 194)	7 (Pt) (n = 213)	8 (Sc) (n = 218)	9 (Ma) (n = 101)	0 (Si) (n = 145)
Intake Information					
Ever Arrested	50	46	46	51	43
History of Misdemeanor Conviction(s)	23	22	22	18	18
History of Felony Conviction(s)	24	19	20	22	23
History of Domestic Violence Conviction	07	05	06	10	06
Previous Psychiatric Hospitalizations	39	38	40	34	38
History of Outpatient Psychiatric Treatment	53	56	55	44	57
Currently on Antipsychotic Medication	03	04	05	03	03
Currently on Antidepressant Medication	14	14	15	09	14
Currently on Lithium	02	02	02	05	01
Currently on Anxiolytic Medication	09	08	08	05	08
History of Being Sexually Abusive	05	06	06	06	06
History of Being Sexually Abused	12	13	13	10	13
History of Being Physically Abusive	18	12	15	23	16
History of Committing Domestic Violence	15	11	13	17	14
History of Victim of Domestic Violence	09	07	08	11	06
History of Being Physically Abused	27	25	27	27	25
History of Having Few or No Friends	36	34	36	31	36
History of Suicide Attempts	23	23	24	26	26
Lifetime History of Alcohol Abuse	52	46	50	57	46
Lifetime History of Marijuana Abuse	25	23	26	33	27
Lifetime History of Cocaine Abuse	14	12	15	18	12
Lifetime History of Heroin Abuse	04	03	04	05	04
Alcohol Abuse in the Past Six Months	31	27	28	31	24
Marijuana Abuse in the Past Six Months	08	08	08	10	09
Cocaine Abuse in the Past Six Months	06	05	06	04	06
Heroin Abuse in the Past Six Months	01	00	00	00	01
Axis I Substance Abuse or Dependence	21	22	21	27	21
Axis I Schizophrenia	03	02	03	04	01
Axis I Depression or Dysthymia	28	30	30	24	31
Axis I Bipolar or Cyclothymia	05	07	07	07	08
Axis I Other Psychotic Diagnosis	01	00	01	00	00
Axis I Anxiety Disorder	19	21	19	16	23
Axis I Sexual Disorder	04	03	03	05	04
Axis I Adjustment Disorders	24	24	23	25	23
Axis I V Code Diagnosis	07	07	07	03	06
Axis I Any Diagnosis	89	89	89	87	86

Axis I No Diagnosis	01	00	00	01	01
Axis I Diagnosis Deferred	03	02	04	06	03
Axis I Rule Out Diagnosis	07	08	07	06	11
Axis I Multiple Diagnoses	25	29	29	27	32
Axis II Cluster A Diagnosis	03	02	01	02	01
Axis II Cluster B Diagnosis	14	13	12	15	11
Axis II Cluster C Diagnosis	06	07	06	04	08
Axis II Antisocial Personality Disorder	06	06	06	08	06
Axis II Borderline Personality Disorder	07	06	06	07	04
Axis II Dependent Personality Disorder	05	04	05	03	04
Axis II Personality Disorder NOS Diagnosis	12	12	13	10	14
Axis II Any Diagnosis	33	32	31	30	32
Axis II No Diagnosis	28	34	33	33	30
Axis II Deferred Diagnosis	25	23	24	23	26
Axis II Rule Out Diagnosis	14	11	11	15	11
Axis I and II Dual Diagnosis	31	29	27	24	26
Mental Status					
Uncomfortable During Interview	18	20	21	22	23
Defensive During Interview	08	06	07	08	07
Aloof During Interview	05	05	04	10	02
Cooperative During Interview	89	90	90	90	90
Aggressive During Interview	02	02	02	04	02
Evasive During Interview	10	09	09	11	07
Loose Associations	05	05	06	08	03
Thought Blocking	08	09	10	09	10
Delusions	04	02	04	03	02
Tangential Speech	06	05	07	08	06
Hallucinations	01	03	03	02	02
Circumstantial Speech	11	08	10	18	08
Poor Judgment	31	30	31	29	28
Obsessions	06	07	06	06	04
Preoccupations	18	20	20	18	18
Ideas of Reference	03	01	02	01	02
Too Sad for the Content of the Interview	03	01	01	02	01
Appropriate Emotional Response During Interview	91	93	93	92	93
Too Happy for the Content of the Interview	02	02	02	03	01
Emotionally Flat During Interview	04	03	03	02	04
Prevailing Mood Happy	02	03	05	11	03
Prevailing Mood Anxious	80	83	81	79	78
Prevailing Mood Sad	53	50	48	40	50
Prevailing Mood Angry	20	18	19	20	17

Extra-test Characteristics	Clinical Scales *(continued)*				
	6 (Pa) (n = 194)	7 (Pt) (n = 213)	8 (Sc) (n = 218)	9 (Ma) (n = 101)	0 (Si) (n = 145)
Prevailing Mood Worried	45	45	45	45	49
Unusual Gait	01	02	02	01	01
Unusual Gestures	02	02	02	02	01
Tics	01	00	00	00	00
Tremors	02	02	02	01	03

Table K-2b. Percentages of male clients with categorical extra-test characteristics: High scores on Harris-Lingoes subscales

Extra-test Characteristics	Harris-Lingoes Subscales							
	D_1 (n = 246)	D_2 (n = 149)	D_3 (n = 187)	D_4 (n = 221)	D_5 (n = 208)	Hy_2 (n = 19)	Hy_3 (n = 261)	Hy_4 (n = 171)
Intake Information								
Ever Arrested	44	46	45	44	44	53	46	45
History of Misdemeanor Conviction(s)	20	22	24	22	21	35	23	23
History of Felony Conviction(s)	20	24	20	19	20	18	20	20
History of Domestic Violence Conviction	06	04	07	06	07	00	07	05
Previous Psychiatric Hospitalizations	36	39	34	37	35	11	36	34
History of Outpatient Psychiatric Treatment	54	52	52	56	55	63	55	52
Currently on Antipsychotic Medication	03	07	04	03	03	05	04	04
Currently on Antidepressant Medication	14	13	14	14	15	00	14	14
Currently on Lithium	02	03	02	02	02	05	02	01
Currently on Anxiolytic Medication	08	10	09	08	08	05	08	10
History of Being Sexually Abusive	05	07	05	05	04	00	04	05
History of Being Sexually Abused	12	11	10	12	13	11	11	11
History of Being Physically Abusive	16	10	17	17	16	00	17	15
History of Committing Domestic Violence	12	09	11	13	13	00	13	11
History of Victim of Domestic Violence	07	05	10	08	07	00	08	07
History of Being Physically Abused	26	17	25	28	26	11	26	27
History of Having Few or No Friends	33	30	37	35	35	37	33	36
History of Suicide Attempts	23	22	23	22	25	05	25	26
Lifetime History of Alcohol Abuse	47	49	46	50	47	32	48	50
Lifetime History of Marijuana Abuse	23	21	24	27	25	05	25	24
Lifetime History of Cocaine Abuse	13	12	13	14	13	05	14	13
Lifetime History of Heroin Abuse	04	05	04	05	04	06	04	04
Alcohol Abuse in the Past Six Months	28	27	25	28	28	21	27	28
Marijuana Abuse in the Past Six Months	08	07	07	09	09	00	07	08
Cocaine Abuse in the Past Six Months	05	05	05	06	06	00	05	06
Heroin Abuse in the Past Six Months	00	01	01	00	01	00	00	01
Axis I Substance Abuse or Dependence	23	22	17	23	22	11	23	22
Axis I Schizophrenia	02	03	02	02	01	06	02	01
Axis I Depression or Dysthymia	30	28	30	31	33	11	29	32
Axis I Bipolar or Cyclothymia	05	07	04	06	06	00	05	05
Axis I Other Psychotic Diagnosis	01	01	01	00	00	00	01	01
Axis I Anxiety Disorder	21	21	21	20	20	22	19	22
Axis I Sexual Disorder	02	02	02	03	03	00	02	04
Axis I Adjustment Disorders	23	24	24	25	21	28	26	24

Table K-2b. Percentages of male clients with categorical extra-test characteristics: High scores on Harris-Lingoes subscales *(continued)*

Extra-test Characteristics	Harris-Lingoes Subscales							
	D_1 (n = 246)	D_2 (n = 149)	D_3 (n = 187)	D_4 (n = 221)	D_5 (n = 208)	Hy_2 (n = 19)	Hy_3 (n = 261)	Hy_4 (n = 171)
Axis I V Code Diagnosis	06	06	07	06	07	11	06	07
Axis I Any Diagnosis	88	87	87	90	89	89	89	88
Axis I No Diagnosis	00	00	00	00	00	00	00	00
Axis I Diagnosis Deferred	03	04	04	02	03	00	03	04
Axis I Rule Out Diagnosis	08	08	09	07	08	11	07	08
Axis I Multiple Diagnoses	27	28	26	29	29	00	27	31
Axis II Cluster A Diagnosis	02	02	01	01	03	06	02	01
Axis II Cluster B Diagnosis	11	09	10	11	11	06	11	13
Axis II Cluster C Diagnosis	06	06	06	06	07	11	07	05
Axis II Antisocial Personality Disorder	05	02	04	06	05	00	05	05
Axis II Borderline Personality Disorder	05	06	06	05	05	06	05	06
Axis II Dependent Personality Disorder	04	03	04	04	05	00	04	05
Axis II Personality Disorder NOS Diagnosis	11	11	12	12	11	06	11	09
Axis II Any Diagnosis	29	27	28	30	31	28	30	27
Axis II No Diagnosis	35	35	33	35	33	33	34	32
Axis II Deferred Diagnosis	24	28	28	25	23	28	24	28
Axis II Rule Out Diagnosis	12	09	11	10	12	11	11	12
Axis I and II Dual Diagnosis	26	24	25	27	29	28	27	24
Mental Status								
Uncomfortable During Interview	19	14	21	18	18	21	18	20
Defensive During Interview	07	07	06	07	08	05	07	04
Aloof During Interview	04	03	03	05	05	00	03	03
Cooperative During Interview	91	92	91	90	91	100	90	91
Aggressive During Interview	02	02	02	02	02	00	02	02
Evasive During Interview	08	08	11	07	06	05	08	08
Loose Associations	04	05	06	03	03	00	04	02
Thought Blocking	08	07	09	08	07	00	08	10
Delusions	03	04	03	03	02	05	03	02
Tangential Speech	06	07	08	05	06	05	07	05
Hallucinations	02	03	03	02	02	00	02	02
Circumstantial Speech	10	06	12	09	10	11	10	09
Poor Judgment	30	26	32	30	31	32	31	32
Obsessions	06	07	07	06	06	00	07	06
Preoccupations	20	21	20	19	20	42	19	20
Ideas of Reference	02	02	02	02	01	05	02	02

Too Sad for the Content of the Interview	02	01	01	02	01	00	02	02
Appropriate Emotional Response During Interview	93	93	90	93	92	100	92	93
Too Happy for the Content of the Interview	02	01	04	02	03	05	03	01
Emotionally Flat During Interview	03	04	04	04	04	00	04	04
Prevailing Mood Happy	05	06	06	05	04	16	05	04
Prevailing Mood Anxious	79	77	78	78	80	63	78	80
Prevailing Mood Sad	49	45	49	49	52	21	48	51
Prevailing Mood Angry	19	10	18	18	19	05	17	15
Prevailing Mood Worried	47	46	49	48	48	47	47	52
Unusual Gait	02	03	02	02	02	00	02	02
Unusual Gestures	02	01	01	01	01	00	02	02
Tics	00	00	00	00	00	05	00	00
Tremors	02	03	03	02	02	00	02	03

Extra-test Characteristics	Harris-Lingoes Subscales *(continued)*																
	Pd_1 (n = 219)	Pd_2 (n = 100)	Pd_4 (n = 222)	Pd_5 (n = 227)	Pa_1 (n = 189)	Pa_2 (n = 179)	Pa_3 (n = 23)	Sc_1 (n = 196)	Sc_2 (n = 218)	Sc_3 (n = 205)	Sc_4 (n = 225)	Sc_5 (n = 129)	Sc_6 (n = 176)	Ma_1 (n = 80)	Ma_2 (n = 41)	Ma_3 (n = 39)	Ma_4 (n = 74)
Intake Information																	
Ever Arrested	48	74	47	47	51	43	50	47	49	46	43	49	46	63	53	57	42
History of Misdemeanor Conviction(s)	21	35	20	23	23	19	16	23	23	23	22	22	20	30	17	22	18
History of Felony Conviction(s)	24	33	22	23	23	21	11	19	23	21	18	21	23	29	18	24	19
History of Domestic Violence Conviction	08	09	07	06	09	07	00	08	07	06	06	05	06	16	16	06	08
Previous Psychiatric Hospitalizations	34	33	33	36	36	37	26	36	36	37	36	37	38	43	37	16	35
History of Outpatient Psychiatric Treatment	53	53	53	51	53	51	61	56	57	54	55	59	51	47	59	26	51
Currently on Antipsychotic Medication	05	03	03	02	03	03	04	04	03	03	03	05	04	03	00	00	01
Currently on Antidepressant Medication	14	13	13	12	13	16	04	13	14	14	14	15	13	12	13	05	06
Currently on Lithium	02	03	02	02	01	03	13	02	02	02	03	03	02	05	05	03	03
Currently on Anxiolytic Medication	07	07	07	08	08	07	04	08	08	07	07	09	09	04	03	03	08
History of Being Sexually Abusive	04	05	03	05	03	05	00	04	04	05	05	05	04	06	05	14	04
History of Being Sexually Abused	14	11	11	13	13	13	04	13	11	12	12	11	12	15	03	11	12
History of Being Physically Abusive	20	22	20	17	20	16	04	18	17	17	14	18	17	28	37	16	23
History of Committing Domestic Violence	14	18	15	14	17	15	04	14	14	12	13	13	13	31	35	14	15
History of Victim of Domestic Violence	09	07	09	08	10	10	00	10	08	08	07	08	09	14	15	05	11
History of Being Physically Abused	30	28	26	25	30	26	00	30	26	27	23	28	27	31	23	16	33
History of Having Few or No Friends	37	35	35	33	38	31	22	39	33	36	33	35	37	36	28	16	34
History of Suicide Attempts	25	24	23	25	23	24	13	24	26	22	25	27	22	29	33	08	21
Lifetime History of Alcohol Abuse	50	67	46	50	48	47	52	48	49	51	47	54	53	65	68	26	50
Lifetime History of Marijuana Abuse	27	36	24	27	26	24	22	25	26	28	25	27	28	34	37	11	27
Lifetime History of Cocaine Abuse	15	20	15	16	15	14	04	12	13	17	13	16	16	22	31	06	12
Lifetime History of Heroin Abuse	03	11	04	05	04	04	05	04	04	06	03	03	05	03	06	03	05
Alcohol Abuse in the Past Six Months	28	41	25	30	28	29	22	27	28	28	26	31	29	43	40	18	25
Marijuana Abuse in the Past Six Months	08	15	07	08	08	08	09	08	09	11	08	09	10	09	08	00	08
Cocaine Abuse in the Past Six Months	05	05	06	06	06	07	00	04	05	06	05	07	07	07	10	00	01
Heroin Abuse in the Past Six Months	00	01	00	00	01	01	00	01	00	01	00	00	01	00	00	00	00
Axis I Substance Abuse or Dependence	24	38	24	26	24	20	18	20	23	23	23	22	23	31	34	08	26
Axis I Schizophrenia	04	01	02	02	03	01	09	03	02	02	01	02	02	01	00	00	04
Axis I Depression or Dysthymia	26	15	27	29	27	29	09	31	31	29	32	32	31	19	27	05	20
Axis I Bipolar or Cyclothymia	04	06	05	05	04	07	09	05	05	06	06	09	06	05	12	03	07
Axis I Other Psychotic Diagnosis	01	02	01	00	01	01	00	02	01	01	01	00	01	03	00	03	00
Axis I Anxiety Disorder	16	10	18	19	17	24	14	20	20	20	19	22	21	14	12	08	16
Axis I Sexual Disorder	04	02	04	03	04	03	00	03	04	03	03	04	04	07	02	08	05
Axis I Adjustment Disorders	25	22	26	25	26	22	27	21	23	24	23	22	25	29	27	28	22
Axis I V Code Diagnosis	08	08	07	07	06	06	09	08	05	07	06	05	06	04	05	18	12
Axis I Any Diagnosis	88	85	88	89	87	88	91	87	88	89	88	91	90	86	93	79	89

Axis I No Diagnosis	00	03	00	00	01	01	00	01	00	00	00	01	01	01	00	03	00
Axis I Diagnosis Deferred	05	07	04	02	04	03	05	04	04	03	03	04	03	05	02	13	03
Axis I Rule Out Diagnosis	06	05	07	08	07	08	05	08	07	07	08	05	06	07	05	05	07
Axis I Multiple Diagnoses	26	28	26	27	27	27	05	28	28	28	29	30	30	29	29	08	28
Axis II Cluster A Diagnosis	02	03	02	02	03	01	05	02	02	01	02	01	01	01	00	00	01
Axis II Cluster B Diagnosis	13	20	13	10	12	11	05	13	11	13	11	12	13	18	12	13	12
Axis II Cluster C Diagnosis	06	04	07	06	04	06	14	07	08	06	07	07	06	04	05	03	07
Axis II Antisocial Personality Disorder	05	11	06	04	06	05	00	06	05	07	06	07	07	11	05	08	07
Axis II Borderline Personality Disorder	07	07	06	05	05	07	05	06	05	06	05	05	06	06	05	05	05
Axis II Dependent Personality Disorder	04	03	05	04	04	05	00	05	05	05	05	05	05	01	00	00	05
Axis II Personality Disorder NOS Diagnosis	11	13	10	12	11	09	14	10	11	13	10	13	11	13	12	08	10
Axis II Any Diagnosis	31	40	32	29	30	26	36	31	31	32	29	32	31	34	29	23	29
Axis II No Diagnosis	32	32	33	34	30	35	41	32	32	34	36	33	33	28	32	46	38
Axis II Deferred Diagnosis	25	21	23	25	27	25	18	25	23	23	21	17	23	28	17	31	15
Axis II Rule Out Diagnosis	13	07	12	11	14	14	05	12	14	12	13	18	13	10	22	00	18
Axis I and II Dual Diagnosis	27	30	28	27	26	23	32	27	28	28	26	30	27	28	27	13	25
Mental Status																	
Uncomfortable During Interview	18	12	20	20	21	20	09	22	21	21	21	23	20	29	30	18	19
Defensive During Interview	08	11	08	08	09	07	00	08	07	07	06	07	07	10	15	05	03
Aloof During Interview	05	08	05	04	06	04	04	05	04	05	04	05	05	08	05	05	07
Cooperative During Interview	90	90	89	90	87	88	91	89	90	90	90	89	91	86	90	92	93
Aggressive During Interview	03	04	02	02	03	02	00	02	02	03	02	03	03	05	03	03	03
Evasive During Interview	08	11	08	08	10	11	04	09	08	07	07	07	09	13	10	13	07
Loose Associations	04	03	04	04	05	03	04	05	04	05	04	05	04	08	10	08	07
Thought Blocking	07	08	09	08	10	07	04	10	10	09	08	09	10	10	10	08	12
Delusions	03	03	04	03	05	03	04	05	04	04	03	05	04	01	02	03	04
Tangential Speech	07	05	05	05	06	04	09	07	06	06	06	07	06	08	07	08	07
Hallucinations	00	00	01	02	01	02	00	02	03	02	02	03	02	01	02	03	01
Circumstantial Speech	13	11	11	10	13	11	04	12	10	10	09	09	10	11	12	13	15
Poor Judgment	34	37	32	33	33	28	26	32	33	32	30	28	31	42	37	37	38
Obsessions	06	03	05	05	06	06	04	06	05	05	05	07	06	06	07	05	05
Preoccupations	17	17	17	17	16	17	26	18	18	19	17	20	17	23	17	08	12
Ideas of Reference	02	01	02	03	03	01	04	02	02	02	01	01	02	01	02	03	03
Too Sad for the Content of the Interview	00	00	02	01	02	03	00	02	02	01	02	02	02	01	02	00	01
Appropriate Emotional Response During Interview	93	90	92	92	91	91	96	94	94	92	93	93	92	91	88	92	92
Too Happy for the Content of the Interview	03	07	02	02	02	02	00	01	01	03	03	03	02	03	07	05	03
Emotionally Flat During Interview	04	02	04	04	03	04	04	03	03	04	03	02	03	05	02	03	04
Prevailing Mood Happy	08	14	05	04	06	03	17	05	03	06	04	03	04	10	10	16	10
Prevailing Mood Anxious	75	62	79	79	78	82	65	78	79	80	79	80	78	80	71	68	73
Prevailing Mood Sad	48	39	49	49	50	51	30	50	50	48	51	47	47	44	34	16	45

Extra-test Characteristics	Harris-Lingoes Subscales *(continued)*																
	Pd_1 (n = 219)	Pd_2 (n = 100)	Pd_4 (n = 222)	Pd_5 (n = 227)	Pa_1 (n = 189)	Pa_2 (n = 179)	Pa_3 (n = 23)	Sc_1 (n = 196)	Sc_2 (n = 218)	Sc_3 (n = 205)	Sc_4 (n = 225)	Sc_5 (n = 129)	Sc_6 (n = 176)	Ma_1 (n = 80)	Ma_2 (n = 41)	Ma_3 (n = 39)	Ma_4 (n = 74)
Prevailing Mood Angry	17	19	17	18	19	20	04	19	19	21	18	19	19	27	20	16	26
Prevailing Mood Worried	44	45	45	46	46	44	39	44	47	45	45	49	47	49	49	41	45
Unusual Gait	01	00	01	02	01	02	00	02	01	02	02	02	02	01	03	00	01
Unusual Gestures	02	01	02	01	02	02	00	03	02	02	02	04	02	03	05	00	01
Tics	00	00	00	00	00	00	04	00	00	00	00	00	00	00	00	00	00
Tremors	01	00	02	03	02	02	00	02	02	02	02	01	02	03	00	03	00

Table K-2c. Percentages of male clients with categorical extra-test characteristics: High scores on Si subscales

Extra-test Characteristics	Si Subscales		
	Si_1 (n = 116)	Si_2 (n = 112)	Si_3 (n = 162)
Intake Information			
Ever Arrested	40	49	43
History of Misdemeanor Conviction(s)	20	20	20
History of Felony Conviction(s)	19	25	18
History of Domestic Violence Conviction	03	07	05
Previous Psychiatric Hospitalizations	34	38	34
History of Outpatient Psychiatric Treatment	58	55	54
Currently on Antipsychotic Medication	02	05	03
Currently on Antidepressant Medication	16	13	11
Currently on Lithium	03	03	03
Currently on Anxiolytic Medication	08	06	08
History of Being Sexually Abusive	06	05	05
History of Being Sexually Abused	12	11	11
History of Being Physically Abusive	14	16	17
History of Committing Domestic Violence	11	12	13
History of Victim of Domestic Violence	05	07	09
History of Being Physically Abused	23	20	27
History of Having Few or No Friends	35	29	35
History of Suicide Attempts	23	18	21
Lifetime History of Alcohol Abuse	44	44	49
Lifetime History of Marijuana Abuse	25	21	26
Lifetime History of Cocaine Abuse	12	08	11
Lifetime History of Heroin Abuse	05	02	02
Alcohol Abuse in the Past Six Months	27	27	26
Marijuana Abuse in the Past Six Months	10	07	09
Cocaine Abuse in the Past Six Months	05	04	04
Heroin Abuse in the Past Six Months	01	00	01
Axis I Substance Abuse or Dependence	25	19	23
Axis I Schizophrenia	01	02	02
Axis I Depression or Dysthymia	28	27	27
Axis I Bipolar or Cyclothymia	10	06	07
Axis I Other Psychotic Diagnosis	00	01	00
Axis I Anxiety Disorder	24	24	20
Axis I Sexual Disorder	04	05	04
Axis I Adjustment Disorders	21	18	23

Table K-2c. Percentages of male clients with categorical extra-test characteristics: High scores on Si subscales *(continued)*

Extra-test Characteristics	Si Subscales		
	Si_1 (n = 116)	Si_2 (n = 112)	Si_3 (n = 162)
Axis I V Code Diagnosis	05	04	09
Axis I Any Diagnosis	87	86	90
Axis I No Diagnosis	00	01	00
Axis I Diagnosis Deferred	02	05	03
Axis I Rule Out Diagnosis	12	08	07
Axis I Multiple Diagnoses	34	23	29
Axis II Cluster A Diagnosis	01	02	01
Axis II Cluster B Diagnosis	07	13	13
Axis II Cluster C Diagnosis	10	07	06
Axis II Antisocial Personality Disorder	03	06	06
Axis II Borderline Personality Disorder	04	06	06
Axis II Dependent Personality Disorder	04	02	04
Axis II Personality Disorder NOS Diagnosis	13	12	12
Axis II Any Diagnosis	30	33	31
Axis II No Diagnosis	33	27	33
Axis II Deferred Diagnosis	28	29	24
Axis II Rule Out Diagnosis	08	10	11
Axis I and II Dual Diagnosis	27	28	29
Mental Status			
Uncomfortable During Interview	21	20	21
Defensive During Interview	06	12	06
Aloof During Interview	02	04	03
Cooperative During Interview	94	89	92
Aggressive During Interview	01	05	02
Evasive During Interview	07	08	08
Loose Associations	03	03	05
Thought Blocking	07	08	08
Delusions	01	05	04
Tangential Speech	05	05	06
Hallucinations	03	03	02
Circumstantial Speech	07	07	10
Poor Judgment	29	25	33
Obsessions	04	03	05
Preoccupations	17	24	19
Ideas of Reference	03	02	01

Too Sad for the Content of the Interview	01	02	01
Appropriate Emotional Response During Interview	92	93	92
Too Happy for the Content of the Interview	02	01	02
Emotionally Flat During Interview	05	05	04
Prevailing Mood Happy	04	05	06
Prevailing Mood Anxious	80	76	77
Prevailing Mood Sad	47	46	47
Prevailing Mood Angry	13	16	20
Prevailing Mood Worried	47	50	45
Unusual Gait	02	03	02
Unusual Gestures	02	02	03
Tics	00	00	00
Tremors	03	05	03

Table K-2d. Percentages of male clients with categorical extra-test characteristics: High scores on content scales

Extra-test Characteristics	Content Scales							
	ANX (n = 236)	FRS (n = 64)	OBS (n = 143)	DEP (n = 252)	HEA (n = 171)	BIZ (n = 96)	ANG (n = 136)	CYN (n = 133)
Intake Information								
Ever Arrested	45	55	46	45	46	54	54	47
History of Misdemeanor Conviction(s)	22	27	24	22	25	24	30	22
History of Felony Conviction(s)	20	28	18	21	21	26	22	19
History of Domestic Violence Conviction	08	04	05	06	05	09	10	07
Previous Psychiatric Hospitalizations	35	32	39	36	35	39	33	34
History of Outpatient Psychiatric Treatment	53	62	57	55	53	55	53	54
Currently on Antipsychotic Medication	04	14	04	04	04	03	02	03
Currently on Antidepressant Medication	15	16	14	14	15	13	11	11
Currently on Lithium	01	00	03	03	01	02	02	02
Currently on Anxiolytic Medication	07	11	11	08	09	09	06	05
History of Being Sexually Abusive	04	06	05	05	05	05	01	05
History of Being Sexually Abused	11	11	11	13	10	13	07	13
History of Being Physically Abusive	19	20	19	18	17	20	25	20
History of Committing Domestic Violence	15	09	12	14	12	15	21	14
History of Victim of Domestic Violence	08	09	10	08	08	11	10	07
History of Being Physically Abused	25	31	27	28	27	35	29	31
History of Having Few or No Friends	34	41	36	34	34	40	35	39
History of Suicide Attempts	23	20	19	24	25	29	24	24
Lifetime History of Alcohol Abuse	47	56	54	49	51	53	57	51
Lifetime History of Marijuana Abuse	25	23	28	26	26	26	33	27
Lifetime History of Cocaine Abuse	14	12	13	13	16	22	18	13
Lifetime History of Heroin Abuse	04	06	04	05	04	05	05	04
Alcohol Abuse in the Past Six Months	29	33	29	28	29	32	32	28
Marijuana Abuse in the Past Six Months	09	05	09	08	09	09	11	06
Cocaine Abuse in the Past Six Months	05	03	04	05	07	10	06	04
Heroin Abuse in the Past Six Months	00	00	01	00	01	00	00	00
Axis I Substance Abuse or Dependence	24	16	24	24	21	26	31	25
Axis I Schizophrenia	02	11	01	02	01	02	00	02
Axis I Depression or Dysthymia	28	30	29	29	34	33	27	34
Axis I Bipolar or Cyclothymia	05	05	08	06	04	06	06	04
Axis I Other Psychotic Diagnosis	00	00	00	00	01	01	00	00
Axis I Anxiety Disorder	21	22	19	19	21	19	19	17
Axis I Sexual Disorder	03	08	05	04	04	03	01	05
Axis I Adjustment Disorders	24	16	18	22	25	21	24	19
Axis I V Code Diagnosis	07	05	08	06	05	09	08	08

Axis I Any Diagnosis	89	92	88	89	88	90	90	89
Axis I No Diagnosis	00	00	00	00	00	01	01	01
Axis I Diagnosis Deferred	03	03	01	03	04	04	02	04
Axis I Rule Out Diagnosis	08	05	10	08	08	05	06	06
Axis I Multiple Diagnoses	27	27	29	28	30	32	33	29
Axis II Cluster A Diagnosis	01	02	01	03	01	01	02	00
Axis II Cluster B Diagnosis	13	11	14	11	14	15	16	12
Axis II Cluster C Diagnosis	05	03	07	06	06	09	05	06
Axis II Antisocial Personality Disorder	06	06	07	06	07	10	09	08
Axis II Borderline Personality Disorder	06	05	07	05	06	04	07	05
Axis II Dependent Personality Disorder	03	03	05	04	05	06	03	05
Axis II Personality Disorder NOS Diagnosis	13	11	14	11	10	13	14	11
Axis II Any Diagnosis	30	27	34	30	30	36	36	29
Axis II No Diagnosis	35	35	28	33	30	27	27	30
Axis II Deferred Diagnosis	23	32	27	24	28	22	26	28
Axis II Rule Out Diagnosis	12	05	11	12	11	15	11	14
Axis I and II Dual Diagnosis	27	27	30	27	26	33	34	24
Mental Status								
Uncomfortable During Interview	20	21	20	19	18	25	19	23
Defensive During Interview	07	06	08	08	05	11	09	07
Aloof During Interview	05	02	04	05	03	07	07	04
Cooperative During Interview	90	89	91	89	92	85	89	90
Aggressive During Interview	02	00	03	02	02	04	03	02
Evasive During Interview	09	14	07	08	08	06	07	07
Loose Associations	05	03	06	04	02	08	05	04
Thought Blocking	08	10	09	07	09	13	06	04
Delusions	02	06	04	02	02	06	04	03
Tangential Speech	06	08	05	06	05	08	07	08
Hallucinations	02	06	02	02	02	02	01	02
Circumstantial Speech	12	06	09	11	08	15	13	12
Poor Judgment	35	27	31	31	29	42	35	37
Obsessions	06	13	06	06	06	07	04	02
Preoccupations	20	24	17	20	19	19	18	18
Ideas of Reference	01	03	01	02	02	02	01	01
Too Sad for the Content of the Interview	02	00	01	02	02	02	01	01
Appropriate Emotional Response During Interview	93	92	91	92	94	89	93	94
Too Happy for the Content of the Interview	02	02	02	02	01	03	04	02
Emotionally Flat During Interview	03	06	05	04	02	05	02	04
Prevailing Mood Happy	05	10	05	05	02	04	08	04
Prevailing Mood Anxious	80	81	77	79	78	79	75	73
Prevailing Mood Sad	47	30	46	48	51	49	49	50

Table K-2d. Percentages of male clients with categorical extra-test characteristics: High scores on content scales *(continued)*

Extra-test Characteristics	Content Scales							
	ANX (n = 236)	FRS (n = 64)	OBS (n = 143)	DEP (n = 252)	HEA (n = 171)	BIZ (n = 96)	ANG (n = 136)	CYN (n = 133)
Prevailing Mood Angry	20	21	22	18	16	27	20	17
Prevailing Mood Worried	48	41	48	46	53	51	48	50
Unusual Gait	02	02	01	02	02	01	01	02
Unusual Gestures	02	03	02	02	02	02	03	03
Tics	00	00	00	00	00	00	00	00
Tremors	02	02	03	02	02	02	01	01

Extra-test Characteristics	Content Scales *(continued)*						
	ASP (n = 113)	TPA (n = 57)	LSE (n = 147)	SOD (n = 118)	FAM (n = 181)	WRK (n = 208)	TRT (n = 196)
Intake Information							
Ever Arrested	64	46	42	48	47	42	47
History of Misdemeanor Conviction(s)	31	24	23	21	21	23	22
History of Felony Conviction(s)	29	18	18	26	23	18	23
History of Domestic Violence Conviction	11	07	05	06	08	07	07
Previous Psychiatric Hospitalizations	38	36	38	37	33	35	37
History of Outpatient Psychiatric Treatment	53	61	59	58	53	55	54
Currently on Antipsychotic Medication	03	04	03	03	02	03	03
Currently on Antidepressant Medication	13	09	14	14	13	15	14
Currently on Lithium	03	02	03	03	01	03	02
Currently on Anxiolytic Medication	05	07	10	08	06	08	08
History of Being Sexually Abusive	03	02	06	05	04	05	04
History of Being Sexually Abused	10	09	17	13	14	13	13
History of Being Physically Abusive	28	20	18	12	21	17	18
History of Committing Domestic Violence	23	14	11	11	16	13	13
History of Victim of Domestic Violence	13	05	07	05	10	08	07
History of Being Physically Abused	31	27	30	24	33	27	27
History of Having Few or No Friends	37	41	37	35	39	35	33
History of Suicide Attempts	28	29	27	25	23	22	24
Lifetime History of Alcohol Abuse	54	48	49	46	49	49	51
Lifetime History of Marijuana Abuse	33	30	28	27	30	27	28
Lifetime History of Cocaine Abuse	17	19	13	12	14	13	13
Lifetime History of Heroin Abuse	04	06	03	03	04	03	03
Alcohol Abuse in the Past Six Months	35	29	24	27	25	26	29
Marijuana Abuse in the Past Six Months	11	05	06	09	08	08	10
Cocaine Abuse in the Past Six Months	04	04	05	06	04	05	05
Heroin Abuse in the Past Six Months	00	00	01	01	01	01	01
Axis I Substance Abuse or Dependence	34	30	24	24	21	23	26
Axis I Schizophrenia	03	02	02	02	02	01	02
Axis I Depression or Dysthymia	25	32	30	31	26	31	29
Axis I Bipolar or Cyclothymia	05	07	09	10	04	06	06
Axis I Other Psychotic Diagnosis	02	00	00	01	01	00	01
Axis I Anxiety Disorder	13	16	19	19	19	20	21
Axis I Sexual Disorder	04	02	06	04	04	04	04
Axis I Adjustment Disorders	22	16	24	23	23	21	23
Axis I V Code Diagnosis	06	14	07	04	07	07	07

Extra-test Characteristics	Content Scales *(continued)*						
	ASP (n = 113)	TPA (n = 57)	LSE (n = 147)	SOD (n = 118)	FAM (n = 181)	WRK (n = 208)	TRT (n = 196)
Axis I Any Diagnosis	89	89	90	87	85	87	91
Axis I No Diagnosis	02	02	00	00	01	00	01
Axis I Diagnosis Deferred	04	00	01	04	04	02	02
Axis I Rule Out Diagnosis	05	07	08	09	09	09	07
Axis I Multiple Diagnoses	30	35	31	32	25	29	30
Axis II Cluster A Diagnosis	03	00	01	01	02	01	02
Axis II Cluster B Diagnosis	17	19	10	11	14	12	14
Axis II Cluster C Diagnosis	07	09	06	09	05	05	05
Axis II Antisocial Personality Disorder	11	09	04	05	06	07	07
Axis II Borderline Personality Disorder	05	09	05	05	07	04	06
Axis II Dependent Personality Disorder	04	09	04	04	03	03	03
Axis II Personality Disorder NOS Diagnosis	10	12	11	12	10	11	11
Axis II Any Diagnosis	35	39	27	32	29	28	31
Axis II No Diagnosis	29	30	31	29	31	34	31
Axis II Deferred Diagnosis	25	16	30	28	25	25	25
Axis II Rule Out Diagnosis	12	16	12	10	14	12	12
Axis I and II Dual Diagnosis	29	35	24	27	25	24	28
Mental Status							
Uncomfortable During Interview	21	19	22	22	22	21	20
Defensive During Interview	14	05	08	10	08	08	08
Aloof During Interview	06	02	02	03	04	05	05
Cooperative During Interview	86	95	90	91	90	89	89
Aggressive During Interview	05	04	01	03	03	02	03
Evasive During Interview	10	04	08	09	10	08	08
Loose Associations	04	04	06	03	06	04	04
Thought Blocking	07	04	08	07	11	08	08
Delusions	04	00	02	03	03	02	03
Tangential Speech	04	11	08	04	08	06	06
Hallucinations	01	02	01	03	00	01	02
Circumstantial Speech	09	12	12	06	15	11	10
Poor Judgment	45	35	31	25	36	33	32
Obsessions	04	04	04	03	06	05	03
Preoccupations	15	14	20	20	20	20	17
Ideas of Reference	02	00	01	02	03	01	02
Too Sad for the Content of the Interview	01	00	01	01	01	01	02
Appropriate Emotional Response During Interview	93	95	90	93	94	92	91

Too Happy for the Content of the Interview	03	04	02	02	01	02	03
Emotionally Flat During Interview	04	02	06	04	04	04	05
Prevailing Mood Happy	07	07	04	04	05	05	05
Prevailing Mood Anxious	71	72	78	76	79	77	76
Prevailing Mood Sad	47	46	48	48	47	49	48
Prevailing Mood Angry	24	25	17	16	20	20	21
Prevailing Mood Worried	47	53	50	47	43	44	46
Unusual Gait	01	02	01	03	01	02	02
Unusual Gestures	02	02	02	02	02	01	02
Tics	00	00	00	00	00	00	00
Tremors	01	02	03	03	02	02	03

Table K-2e. Percentages of male clients with categorical extra-test characteristics: High scores on content component scales

Extra-test Characteristics	Content Component Scales							
	FRS_1 (n = 79)	FRS_2 (n = 65)	DEP_1 (n = 228)	DEP_2 (n = 241)	DEP_3 (n = 214)	DEP_4 (n = 119)	HEA_1 (n = 145)	HEA_2 (n = 164)
Intake Information								
Ever Arrested	51	53	46	46	45	47	48	46
History of Misdemeanor Conviction(s)	26	24	21	22	22	24	20	23
History of Felony Conviction(s)	26	24	21	19	22	22	20	21
History of Domestic Violence Conviction	06	02	06	06	06	05	03	05
Previous Psychiatric Hospitalizations	42	33	35	35	34	42	31	36
History of Outpatient Psychiatric Treatment	61	63	53	54	51	54	52	51
Currently on Antipsychotic Medication	10	13	03	03	03	04	03	05
Currently on Antidepressant Medication	18	13	14	13	13	19	13	13
Currently on Lithium	00	00	03	02	02	03	03	01
Currently on Anxiolytic Medication	11	09	08	08	08	10	06	09
History of Being Sexually Abusive	03	08	04	05	05	03	06	04
History of Being Sexually Abused	11	09	12	11	15	11	10	09
History of Being Physically Abusive	19	19	19	15	17	14	17	17
History of Committing Domestic Violence	14	08	13	13	13	13	10	12
History of Victim of Domestic Violence	09	05	08	07	08	08	08	09
History of Being Physically Abused	29	30	27	24	26	30	27	27
History of Having Few or No Friends	48	34	33	32	33	34	31	34
History of Suicide Attempts	22	20	22	24	25	28	22	21
Lifetime History of Alcohol Abuse	54	52	50	45	48	52	49	53
Lifetime History of Marijuana Abuse	20	24	26	23	25	28	25	27
Lifetime History of Cocaine Abuse	11	11	13	12	14	15	14	15
Lifetime History of Heroin Abuse	04	05	04	04	04	02	02	05
Alcohol Abuse in the Past Six Months	33	31	28	26	27	34	29	31
Marijuana Abuse in the Past Six Months	04	07	09	07	09	12	07	09
Cocaine Abuse in the Past Six Months	05	05	06	05	06	09	04	07
Heroin Abuse in the Past Six Months	00	00	00	00	01	01	00	01
Axis I Substance Abuse or Dependence	23	22	24	20	25	25	17	22
Axis I Schizophrenia	06	09	02	02	01	02	02	03
Axis I Depression or Dysthymia	29	30	31	30	28	37	27	31
Axis I Bipolar or Cyclothymia	05	03	06	05	05	08	06	05
Axis I Other Psychotic Diagnosis	00	00	00	00	00	00	01	01
Axis I Anxiety Disorder	27	19	20	21	18	17	24	21
Axis I Sexual Disorder	03	08	03	02	04	03	04	04
Axis I Adjustment Disorders	19	14	21	23	23	22	25	21
Axis I V Code Diagnosis	06	06	07	06	07	08	06	08

Axis I Any Diagnosis	87	97	90	87	89	89	88	88
Axis I No Diagnosis	01	00	00	00	00	00	00	00
Axis I Diagnosis Deferred	06	00	03	03	02	04	03	04
Axis I Rule Out Diagnosis	05	03	08	08	08	07	10	09
Axis I Multiple Diagnoses	30	25	29	26	26	32	27	31
Axis II Cluster A Diagnosis	01	02	02	03	01	04	01	00
Axis II Cluster B Diagnosis	13	11	12	12	12	13	12	12
Axis II Cluster C Diagnosis	05	02	06	08	05	05	07	06
Axis II Antisocial Personality Disorder	08	06	06	05	06	04	06	06
Axis II Borderline Personality Disorder	05	03	06	06	06	08	06	06
Axis II Dependent Personality Disorder	05	02	04	05	03	04	05	04
Axis II Personality Disorder NOS Diagnosis	16	11	10	10	11	10	10	11
Axis II Any Diagnosis	35	25	30	32	30	31	28	29
Axis II No Diagnosis	30	39	32	34	35	34	35	32
Axis II Deferred Diagnosis	26	28	25	22	24	24	26	29
Axis II Rule Out Diagnosis	09	06	13	12	11	10	10	10
Axis I and II Dual Diagnosis	27	25	28	28	27	28	24	25
Mental Status								
Uncomfortable During Interview	22	17	20	20	19	18	19	18
Defensive During Interview	06	03	08	07	08	08	04	07
Aloof During Interview	01	02	04	04	05	03	01	04
Cooperative During Interview	90	90	91	90	91	90	94	93
Aggressive During Interview	03	00	02	02	01	03	03	03
Evasive During Interview	06	10	07	09	06	07	07	08
Loose Associations	06	05	04	05	04	03	03	02
Thought Blocking	13	10	07	08	08	08	09	09
Delusions	04	03	03	03	03	03	01	02
Tangential Speech	08	10	06	06	06	06	06	06
Hallucinations	05	06	02	02	02	03	02	03
Circumstantial Speech	10	05	11	10	11	12	09	08
Poor Judgment	32	31	31	29	34	28	28	31
Obsessions	09	11	05	07	06	03	06	07
Preoccupations	17	23	18	21	18	19	19	19
Ideas of Reference	03	02	02	02	02	03	01	02
Too Sad for the Content of the Interview	01	00	02	02	02	01	01	02
Appropriate Emotional Response During Interview	90	95	92	93	92	93	93	93
Too Happy for the Content of the Interview	03	02	02	03	02	03	01	02
Emotionally Flat During Interview	06	03	04	03	04	03	04	03
Prevailing Mood Happy	01	10	06	05	05	03	06	06
Prevailing Mood Anxious	81	78	78	79	78	82	81	79
Prevailing Mood Sad	38	35	49	50	50	55	47	47

Table K-2e. Percentages of male clients with categorical extra-test characteristics: High scores on content component scales *(continued)*

Extra-test Characteristics	Content Component Scales							
	FRS_1 (n = 79)	FRS_2 (n = 65)	DEP_1 (n = 228)	DEP_2 (n = 241)	DEP_3 (n = 214)	DEP_4 (n = 119)	HEA_1 (n = 145)	HEA_2 (n = 164)
Prevailing Mood Angry	22	17	19	17	18	19	18	17
Prevailing Mood Worried	47	46	45	45	45	50	49	52
Unusual Gait	01	03	02	02	02	02	01	02
Unusual Gestures	03	00	02	02	01	02	02	02
Tics	00	00	00	00	00	00	00	00
Tremors	03	02	02	02	03	02	02	02

Extra-test Characteristics	Content Component Scales *(continued)*														
	HEA_3 (n = 214)	BIZ_1 (n = 89)	BIZ_2 (n = 121)	ANG_1 (n = 156)	ANG_2 (n = 132)	CYN_1 (n = 101)	CYN_2 (n = 89)	ASP_1 (n = 76)	ASP_2 (n = 152)	TPA_1 (n = 54)	TPA_2 (n = 53)	LSE_1 (n = 202)	LSE_2 (n = 86)	SOD_1 (n = 126)	SOD_2 (n = 81)
Intake Information															
Ever Arrested	47	56	53	55	46	50	47	63	64	37	49	43	42	47	44
History of Misdemeanor Conviction(s)	22	22	24	30	25	25	22	33	32	24	14	21	21	20	17
History of Felony Conviction(s)	20	26	22	23	20	19	17	27	36	11	23	20	16	26	23
History of Domestic Violence Conviction	05	08	09	11	07	06	07	11	13	07	08	05	03	06	00
Previous Psychiatric Hospitalizations	33	34	41	34	33	33	31	37	37	26	35	34	37	39	36
History of Outpatient Psychiatric Treatment	55	54	57	57	49	54	52	53	53	55	54	60	57	57	53
Currently on Antipsychotic Medication	04	03	03	02	02	04	03	04	02	00	06	03	05	03	01
Currently on Antidepressant Medication	14	13	14	15	12	13	08	14	13	09	10	15	12	14	16
Currently on Lithium	02	02	03	02	02	03	01	03	03	02	00	03	05	04	01
Currently on Anxiolytic Medication	08	11	08	05	07	06	06	05	05	04	08	09	07	08	09
History of Being Sexually Abusive	05	03	07	03	02	05	03	03	04	02	02	04	05	05	08
History of Being Sexually Abused	09	10	13	08	10	14	15	11	10	11	08	13	20	14	14
History of Being Physically Abusive	15	16	19	28	22	19	19	21	25	15	17	16	16	14	13
History of Committing Domestic Violence	11	13	17	23	17	12	16	20	20	17	13	11	11	12	09
History of Victim of Domestic Violence	07	06	12	10	10	06	06	09	09	06	08	05	07	06	05
History of Being Physically Abused	25	28	33	32	28	31	27	31	29	22	17	27	35	22	22
History of Having Few or No Friends	31	35	38	36	34	38	47	44	34	35	40	34	39	34	35
History of Suicide Attempts	23	24	28	26	24	26	26	29	29	24	19	26	27	22	22
Lifetime History of Alcohol Abuse	50	55	54	61	52	47	54	54	57	48	43	48	53	44	47
Lifetime History of Marijuana Abuse	22	23	26	32	27	28	24	34	35	32	22	27	27	24	25
Lifetime History of Cocaine Abuse	14	16	18	17	17	12	15	20	21	17	16	13	10	10	16
Lifetime History of Heroin Abuse	03	03	04	05	04	03	05	03	07	04	05	04	04	05	06
Alcohol Abuse in the Past Six Months	28	31	32	36	30	27	26	36	32	31	25	26	29	26	30
Marijuana Abuse in the Past Six Months	06	07	08	11	09	07	07	09	10	04	02	10	07	08	10
Cocaine Abuse in the Past Six Months	06	08	07	07	06	03	07	07	06	02	04	06	06	05	06
Heroin Abuse in the Past Six Months	01	00	00	01	00	00	01	00	01	00	00	01	01	01	01
Axis I Substance Abuse or Dependence	20	19	22	33	26	23	24	30	31	24	30	25	24	23	27
Axis I Schizophrenia	02	02	02	01	00	03	03	03	02	00	02	02	05	02	00
Axis I Depression or Dysthymia	28	24	31	26	31	27	34	28	23	35	26	29	32	25	25
Axis I Bipolar or Cyclothymia	05	04	07	06	05	05	03	07	06	06	04	07	11	08	10
Axis I Other Psychotic Diagnosis	01	03	01	01	00	02	00	03	02	00	00	01	00	01	00
Axis I Anxiety Disorder	20	19	20	17	21	18	10	13	13	22	11	20	19	21	22
Axis I Sexual Disorder	03	03	06	02	02	04	03	05	03	02	02	05	10	05	04
Axis I Adjustment Disorders	27	21	19	25	23	16	24	18	22	19	17	21	17	20	23
Axis I V Code Diagnosis	08	10	07	07	09	08	09	07	08	15	13	07	10	04	06
Axis I Any Diagnosis	88	85	91	89	89	88	87	88	87	91	85	89	92	85	86

Extra-test Characteristics	Content Component Scales *(continued)*														
	HEA_3 (n = 214)	BIZ_1 (n = 89)	BIZ_2 (n = 121)	ANG_1 (n = 156)	ANG_2 (n = 132)	CYN_1 (n = 101)	CYN_2 (n = 89)	ASP_1 (n = 76)	ASP_2 (n = 152)	TPA_1 (n = 54)	TPA_2 (n = 53)	LSE_1 (n = 202)	LSE_2 (n = 86)	SOD_1 (n = 126)	SOD_2 (n = 81)
Axis I No Diagnosis	00	01	01	01	00	02	00	01	01	00	02	01	00	00	00
Axis I Diagnosis Deferred	04	07	03	03	02	04	03	04	05	00	04	03	00	05	03
Axis I Rule Out Diagnosis	08	06	05	07	08	05	09	07	07	07	09	07	07	11	12
Axis I Multiple Diagnoses	28	22	27	34	34	25	28	33	30	35	28	28	35	28	34
Axis II Cluster A Diagnosis	01	01	01	02	00	00	01	03	02	00	00	02	00	01	00
Axis II Cluster B Diagnosis	12	10	13	15	16	10	09	17	18	13	13	12	07	11	08
Axis II Cluster C Diagnosis	05	08	05	06	06	06	08	07	04	09	08	06	05	07	08
Axis II Antisocial Personality Disorder	05	06	08	08	07	06	04	11	09	02	08	06	04	05	04
Axis II Borderline Personality Disorder	05	03	05	07	09	04	03	05	08	09	06	05	04	06	04
Axis II Dependent Personality Disorder	03	07	03	05	04	03	07	05	03	06	08	04	02	03	04
Axis II Personality Disorder NOS Diagnosis	11	14	15	13	14	13	10	09	11	15	17	12	16	13	13
Axis II Any Diagnosis	29	32	33	36	35	29	26	33	35	35	36	31	28	32	29
Axis II No Diagnosis	33	26	30	27	29	29	27	24	32	33	30	32	32	27	31
Axis II Deferred Diagnosis	26	25	24	26	23	28	29	28	22	20	19	25	27	29	30
Axis II Rule Out Diagnosis	12	16	13	10	13	14	18	16	11	11	15	11	12	11	09
Axis I and II Dual Diagnosis	26	29	29	33	33	25	22	29	30	35	28	28	26	26	25
Mental Status															
Uncomfortable During Interview	19	18	24	21	19	26	20	25	15	13	21	19	23	19	26
Defensive During Interview	04	07	09	10	08	09	09	12	11	11	06	07	06	09	04
Aloof During Interview	04	07	07	07	05	04	03	08	05	04	02	05	04	04	03
Cooperative During Interview	90	89	87	86	92	88	93	88	87	94	94	90	90	92	92
Aggressive During Interview	01	04	03	03	02	02	03	04	03	02	04	01	01	02	01
Evasive During Interview	09	06	07	09	05	05	07	11	11	02	04	07	11	08	09
Loose Associations	04	03	08	05	02	05	04	04	05	04	06	04	05	02	04
Thought Blocking	08	08	11	06	05	04	07	08	07	02	06	09	07	07	05
Delusions	02	07	06	04	02	04	04	04	05	00	00	03	02	03	01
Tangential Speech	06	08	08	07	06	08	07	04	05	09	06	06	10	06	05
Hallucinations	02	02	02	01	02	02	02	03	01	00	02	02	02	02	03
Circumstantial Speech	10	16	12	12	09	13	13	12	09	13	09	11	12	07	06
Poor Judgment	30	35	36	34	29	39	38	47	35	30	36	31	35	24	31
Obsessions	05	07	07	05	05	04	02	05	04	06	02	05	02	02	03
Preoccupations	19	18	19	16	21	18	17	19	15	17	09	19	21	21	19
Ideas of Reference	02	04	02	01	02	01	03	00	03	02	00	02	02	02	04
Too Sad for the Content of the Interview	01	01	02	01	02	00	01	00	00	00	00	02	00	02	03
Appropriate Emotional Response During Interview	92	93	92	92	92	93	92	92	91	94	92	91	95	94	89

Too Happy for the Content of the Interview	02	02	02	04	04	02	03	04	03	06	06	03	00	02	03
Emotionally Flat During Interview	04	01	04	03	02	05	02	04	05	00	02	05	06	04	08
Prevailing Mood Happy	06	06	07	08	07	07	03	08	08	07	11	05	05	06	05
Prevailing Mood Anxious	80	82	78	73	75	70	71	75	68	74	68	76	80	74	80
Prevailing Mood Sad	49	47	45	45	53	47	49	49	40	41	38	48	45	46	43
Prevailing Mood Angry	14	26	23	19	21	16	20	24	20	22	23	17	20	14	13
Prevailing Mood Worried	47	51	48	46	51	47	48	49	40	50	43	44	45	49	47
Unusual Gait	02	01	02	01	02	01	02	03	01	04	02	02	01	02	03
Unusual Gestures	02	02	02	01	03	03	03	05	02	08	00	02	02	02	03
Tics	00	00	00	00	00	00	00	00	00	00	00	00	00	00	00
Tremors	02	01	02	01	01	00	01	00	01	00	02	03	04	04	04

Extra-test Characteristics	Content Component Scales *(continued)*			
	FAM_1 (n = 171)	FAM_2 (n = 180)	TRT_1 (n = 206)	TRT_2 (n = 99)
Intake Information				
Ever Arrested	47	50	47	57
History of Misdemeanor Conviction(s)	19	25	23	26
History of Felony Conviction(s)	22	25	21	27
History of Domestic Violence Conviction	07	09	06	11
Previous Psychiatric Hospitalizations	31	33	36	41
History of Outpatient Psychiatric Treatment	51	54	56	56
Currently on Antipsychotic Medication	02	03	02	04
Currently on Antidepressant Medication	11	12	14	14
Currently on Lithium	02	02	02	02
Currently on Anxiolytic Medication	05	05	08	08
History of Being Sexually Abusive	03	03	04	04
History of Being Sexually Abused	13	14	12	11
History of Being Physically Abusive	20	21	14	17
History of Committing Domestic Violence	15	15	11	17
History of Victim of Domestic Violence	10	07	08	07
History of Being Physically Abused	30	29	26	28
History of Having Few or No Friends	35	38	31	38
History of Suicide Attempts	23	25	22	26
Lifetime History of Alcohol Abuse	51	57	50	52
Lifetime History of Marijuana Abuse	29	30	26	32
Lifetime History of Cocaine Abuse	14	16	14	14
Lifetime History of Heroin Abuse	03	05	04	02
Alcohol Abuse in the Past Six Months	28	28	29	36
Marijuana Abuse in the Past Six Months	10	10	08	12
Cocaine Abuse in the Past Six Months	02	06	05	05
Heroin Abuse in the Past Six Months	00	01	01	00
Axis I Substance Abuse or Dependence	23	25	24	25
Axis I Schizophrenia	02	03	02	02
Axis I Depression or Dysthymia	26	23	30	29
Axis I Bipolar or Cyclothymia	05	03	06	06
Axis I Other Psychotic Diagnosis	01	01	00	02
Axis I Anxiety Disorder	18	16	20	18
Axis I Sexual Disorder	02	05	04	03
Axis I Adjustment Disorders	23	26	22	18
Axis I V Code Diagnosis	10	07	07	06
Axis I Any Diagnosis	86	87	90	86

Axis I No Diagnosis	01	01	00	02
Axis I Diagnosis Deferred	05	06	02	04
Axis I Rule Out Diagnosis	08	06	08	08
Axis I Multiple Diagnoses	26	27	28	28
Axis II Cluster A Diagnosis	01	02	02	02
Axis II Cluster B Diagnosis	14	16	12	14
Axis II Cluster C Diagnosis	06	06	06	03
Axis II Antisocial Personality Disorder	07	07	06	10
Axis II Borderline Personality Disorder	07	07	06	04
Axis II Dependent Personality Disorder	05	04	04	02
Axis II Personality Disorder NOS Diagnosis	09	11	10	13
Axis II Any Diagnosis	30	35	30	32
Axis II No Diagnosis	33	29	31	32
Axis II Deferred Diagnosis	23	26	28	23
Axis II Rule Out Diagnosis	14	11	11	12
Axis I and II Dual Diagnosis	26	30	27	27
Mental Status				
Uncomfortable During Interview	20	20	21	23
Defensive During Interview	08	07	07	09
Aloof During Interview	05	05	05	03
Cooperative During Interview	89	90	90	86
Aggressive During Interview	02	03	02	02
Evasive During Interview	08	09	07	10
Loose Associations	04	05	04	04
Thought Blocking	08	10	08	05
Delusions	03	02	03	06
Tangential Speech	07	09	06	04
Hallucinations	00	01	02	03
Circumstantial Speech	14	14	10	06
Poor Judgment	35	36	31	33
Obsessions	05	05	05	02
Preoccupations	16	20	19	19
Ideas of Reference	02	02	02	01
Too Sad for the Content of the Interview	00	01	01	01
Appropriate Emotional Response During Interview	95	94	91	92
Too Happy for the Content of the Interview	02	02	03	03
Emotionally Flat During Interview	03	03	04	04
Prevailing Mood Happy	06	07	07	07
Prevailing Mood Anxious	77	76	79	75
Prevailing Mood Sad	46	47	47	47

Extra-test Characteristics	Content Component Scales *(continued)*			
	FAM_1 (n = 171)	FAM_2 (n = 180)	TRT_1 (n = 206)	TRT_2 (n = 99)
Prevailing Mood Angry	18	20	19	18
Prevailing Mood Worried	42	46	42	46
Unusual Gait	01	01	02	04
Unusual Gestures	02	02	02	02
Tics	00	00	00	00
Tremors	00	02	02	04

Table K-2f. Percentages of male clients with categorical extra-test characteristics: High scores on supplementary scales

Extra-test Characteristics	Supplementary Scales							
	A (n = 190)	R (n = 48)	Es (n = 239)	MAC-R (n = 79)	AAS (n = 127)	APS (n = 80)	O-H (n = 51)	Do (n = 227)
Intake Information								
Ever Arrested	43	44	53	62	56	51	71	52
History of Misdemeanor Conviction(s)	22	15	20	36	28	32	36	21
History of Felony Conviction(s)	17	26	19	34	29	16	28	21
History of Domestic Violence Conviction	06	02	06	11	12	03	08	06
Previous Psychiatric Hospitalizations	39	47	20	37	38	36	35	26
History of Outpatient Psychiatric Treatment	56	55	39	53	53	58	52	46
Currently on Antipsychotic Medication	04	10	03	01	03	03	08	06
Currently on Antidepressant Medication	16	13	05	14	14	15	08	11
Currently on Lithium	02	04	05	05	02	05	02	04
Currently on Anxiolytic Medication	09	08	04	08	07	08	08	06
History of Being Sexually Abusive	05	10	07	00	02	05	10	07
History of Being Sexually Abused	12	10	10	09	08	08	12	11
History of Being Physically Abusive	17	10	14	24	21	19	08	13
History of Committing Domestic Violence	14	08	10	15	18	20	12	09
History of Victim of Domestic Violence	07	04	04	13	09	09	04	03
History of Being Physically Abused	28	10	14	28	26	23	14	13
History of Having Few or No Friends	38	29	18	34	31	31	34	22
History of Suicide Attempts	25	23	14	30	31	20	24	17
Lifetime History of Alcohol Abuse	49	35	41	72	70	64	48	45
Lifetime History of Marijuana Abuse	27	14	15	42	39	28	23	16
Lifetime History of Cocaine Abuse	12	05	10	26	23	15	20	11
Lifetime History of Heroin Abuse	03	02	02	08	07	00	07	03
Alcohol Abuse in the Past Six Months	27	17	21	43	54	41	25	24
Marijuana Abuse in the Past Six Months	09	00	04	13	15	08	00	03
Cocaine Abuse in the Past Six Months	05	04	03	07	10	05	08	03
Heroin Abuse in the Past Six Months	01	00	00	00	01	00	00	00
Axis I Substance Abuse or Dependence	22	15	19	47	46	41	18	20
Axis I Schizophrenia	02	09	01	04	01	00	06	02
Axis I Depression or Dysthymia	30	19	10	27	25	28	12	14
Axis I Bipolar or Cyclothymia	06	09	04	06	05	07	02	04
Axis I Other Psychotic Diagnosis	00	02	01	00	02	00	04	01
Axis I Anxiety Disorder	21	19	11	15	17	15	10	14
Axis I Sexual Disorder	03	06	04	01	02	00	00	04
Axis I Adjustment Disorders	21	32	31	19	23	31	29	30

Table K-2f. Percentages of male clients with categorical extra-test characteristics: High scores on supplementary scales *(continued)*

Extra-test Characteristics	Supplementary Scales							
	A (n = 190)	R (n = 48)	Es (n = 239)	MAC-R (n = 79)	AAS (n = 127)	APS (n = 80)	O-H (n = 51)	Do (n = 227)
Axis I V Code Diagnosis	07	06	15	06	04	05	10	11
Axis I Any Diagnosis	86	91	85	91	88	94	80	86
Axis I No Diagnosis	01	00	02	00	01	00	04	01
Axis I Diagnosis Deferred	03	04	07	05	02	00	12	07
Axis I Rule Out Diagnosis	10	04	05	04	09	06	04	06
Axis I Multiple Diagnoses	29	28	15	41	37	35	14	17
Axis II Cluster A Diagnosis	02	02	03	03	02	03	02	03
Axis II Cluster B Diagnosis	13	09	10	18	13	10	12	08
Axis II Cluster C Diagnosis	06	04	06	04	04	09	10	07
Axis II Antisocial Personality Disorder	06	00	03	09	07	04	08	03
Axis II Borderline Personality Disorder	06	09	04	09	05	06	04	03
Axis II Dependent Personality Disorder	04	00	02	04	02	06	04	03
Axis II Personality Disorder NOS Diagnosis	12	13	08	09	14	16	04	10
Axis II Any Diagnosis	32	28	26	32	33	38	29	28
Axis II No Diagnosis	32	36	41	29	33	33	37	39
Axis II Deferred Diagnosis	22	32	27	27	24	19	33	25
Axis II Rule Out Diagnosis	13	04	07	12	11	10	02	09
Axis I and II Dual Diagnosis	28	26	19	31	30	37	18	22
Mental Status								
Uncomfortable During Interview	23	25	16	17	21	16	25	15
Defensive During Interview	08	10	07	13	07	09	12	07
Aloof During Interview	05	04	05	05	06	03	06	04
Cooperative During Interview	90	87	90	88	88	92	86	91
Aggressive During Interview	02	02	03	04	03	01	06	02
Evasive During Interview	08	17	08	10	08	05	16	08
Loose Associations	05	04	02	06	05	05	02	01
Thought Blocking	10	06	07	08	06	03	08	06
Delusions	03	02	01	05	02	01	04	02
Tangential Speech	06	06	04	06	04	05	06	06
Hallucinations	03	02	00	03	03	00	02	01
Circumstantial Speech	11	02	07	14	08	13	06	07
Poor Judgment	30	23	30	39	36	25	29	26
Obsessions	04	11	03	05	05	05	06	04
Preoccupations	18	32	16	13	16	13	14	19
Ideas of Reference	01	02	02	01	02	00	04	02

Too Sad for the Content of the Interview	02	02	01	01	01	01	00	02
Appropriate Emotional Response During Interview	92	90	93	87	92	94	90	91
Too Happy for the Content of the Interview	03	00	04	05	03	04	02	05
Emotionally Flat During Interview	04	08	02	06	04	03	06	03
Prevailing Mood Happy	04	02	14	09	09	08	16	12
Prevailing Mood Anxious	79	75	70	67	74	77	67	72
Prevailing Mood Sad	51	44	27	48	45	46	31	31
Prevailing Mood Angry	20	10	10	18	14	10	12	10
Prevailing Mood Worried	45	38	40	47	44	49	35	44
Unusual Gait	02	02	01	00	01	03	00	01
Unusual Gestures	02	00	01	03	02	00	00	02
Tics	00	02	01	00	00	00	02	01
Tremors	03	06	00	03	02	01	00	00

Extra-test Characteristics	Supplementary Subscales *(continued)*		
	Re (n = 195)	MDS (n = 249)	PK (n = 235)
Intake Information			
Ever Arrested	41	46	47
History of Misdemeanor Conviction(s)	16	20	23
History of Felony Conviction(s)	16	22	22
History of Domestic Violence Conviction	03	07	07
Previous Psychiatric Hospitalizations	23	34	37
History of Outpatient Psychiatric Treatment	43	54	54
Currently on Antipsychotic Medication	05	04	03
Currently on Antidepressant Medication	10	14	14
Currently on Lithium	03	02	02
Currently on Anxiolytic Medication	06	06	07
History of Being Sexually Abusive	06	04	04
History of Being Sexually Abused	09	11	12
History of Being Physically Abusive	08	18	19
History of Committing Domestic Violence	06	12	14
History of Victim of Domestic Violence	04	08	09
History of Being Physically Abused	14	27	27
History of Having Few or No Friends	22	34	35
History of Suicide Attempts	13	24	24
Lifetime History of Alcohol Abuse	35	49	50
Lifetime History of Marijuana Abuse	12	26	26
Lifetime History of Cocaine Abuse	06	13	14
Lifetime History of Heroin Abuse	02	03	04
Alcohol Abuse in the Past Six Months	18	28	30
Marijuana Abuse in the Past Six Months	04	08	09
Cocaine Abuse in the Past Six Months	03	05	05
Heroin Abuse in the Past Six Months	00	00	00
Axis I Substance Abuse or Dependence	12	22	24
Axis I Schizophrenia	03	02	02
Axis I Depression or Dysthymia	18	29	29
Axis I Bipolar or Cyclothymia	04	04	06
Axis I Other Psychotic Diagnosis	01	01	00
Axis I Anxiety Disorder	19	18	21
Axis I Sexual Disorder	04	04	03
Axis I Adjustment Disorders	30	25	23
Axis I V Code Diagnosis	11	07	06
Axis I Any Diagnosis	86	89	88

Axis I No Diagnosis	00	00	00
Axis I Diagnosis Deferred	06	04	03
Axis I Rule Out Diagnosis	08	07	08
Axis I Multiple Diagnoses	18	27	28
Axis II Cluster A Diagnosis	02	02	02
Axis II Cluster B Diagnosis	07	13	12
Axis II Cluster C Diagnosis	06	07	07
Axis II Antisocial Personality Disorder	02	05	06
Axis II Borderline Personality Disorder	04	07	06
Axis II Dependent Personality Disorder	02	05	04
Axis II Personality Disorder NOS Diagnosis	08	10	11
Axis II Any Diagnosis	22	31	31
Axis II No Diagnosis	41	32	32
Axis II Deferred Diagnosis	29	25	24
Axis II Rule Out Diagnosis	08	12	13
Axis I and II Dual Diagnosis	18	28	27
Mental Status			
Uncomfortable During Interview	17	20	20
Defensive During Interview	04	08	07
Aloof During Interview	03	04	04
Cooperative During Interview	92	89	90
Aggressive During Interview	02	02	02
Evasive During Interview	07	09	08
Loose Associations	01	04	04
Thought Blocking	06	07	09
Delusions	02	03	03
Tangential Speech	03	06	06
Hallucinations	02	02	02
Circumstantial Speech	06	11	11
Poor Judgment	26	31	33
Obsessions	05	06	06
Preoccupations	17	18	19
Ideas of Reference	02	02	02
Too Sad for the Content of the Interview	02	01	01
Appropriate Emotional Response During Interview	93	92	93
Too Happy for the Content of the Interview	03	03	02
Emotionally Flat During Interview	03	04	04
Prevailing Mood Happy	11	06	04
Prevailing Mood Anxious	77	78	80
Prevailing Mood Sad	32	48	49
Prevailing Mood Angry	11	19	19

Extra-test Characteristics	Supplementary Subscales *(continued)*		
	Re (n = 195)	MDS (n = 249)	PK (n = 235)
Prevailing Mood Worried	46	45	46
Unusual Gait	01	01	02
Unusual Gestures	01	02	02
Tics	00	00	00
Tremors	01	02	02

Table K-3. Percentages of clients with categorical extra-test characteristics (men and women combined): Two- and three-point code types

Extra-test Characteristics	Total Sample (N = 2,482)	Valid MMPI-2 (n = 1,020)	WNL (n = 90)	Code Types 12/21 (n = 15)	13/31 (n = 20)	23/32 (n = 20)	24/42 (n = 30)	26/62 (n = 15)
Intake Information								
Ever Arrested	36	36	47	18	25	07	34	27
History of Misdemeanor Conviction(s)	17	15	16	09	00	13	15	07
History of Felony Conviction(s)	16	13	13	17	00	00	19	07
History of Domestic Violence Conviction	04	03	05	00	00	06	08	00
Previous Psychiatric Hospitalizations	34	28	06	21	10	26	23	27
History of Outpatient Psychiatric Treatment	56	55	43	42	40	42	57	67
Currently on Antipsychotic Medication	06	03	01	07	00	00	00	00
Currently on Antidepressant Medication	16	14	02	20	20	11	13	07
Currently on Lithium	04	03	02	00	00	05	03	00
Currently on Anxiolytic Medication	12	10	02	13	05	05	03	00
History of Being Sexually Abusive	02	03	02	00	00	00	07	00
History of Being Sexually Abused	23	26	16	33	20	26	20	27
History of Being Physically Abusive	14	12	11	07	05	11	03	00
History of Committing Domestic Violence	08	07	10	00	00	11	10	07
History of Victim of Domestic Violence	19	22	14	20	30	26	20	33
History of Being Physically Abused	33	34	20	40	50	42	37	33
History of Having Few or No Friends	33	34	17	33	15	32	37	53
History of Suicide Attempts	26	25	10	20	05	21	30	53
Lifetime History of Alcohol Abuse	39	37	31	33	25	26	27	07
Lifetime History of Marijuana Abuse	18	17	16	07	10	06	14	14
Lifetime History of Cocaine Abuse	13	10	07	00	05	06	07	00
Lifetime History of Heroin Abuse	03	02	00	00	00	00	03	00
Alcohol Abuse in the Past Six Months	21	18	12	20	00	06	10	07
Marijuana Abuse in the Past Six Months	05	04	02	00	00	00	00	00
Cocaine Abuse in the Past Six Months	05	02	02	00	00	00	00	00
Heroin Abuse in the Past Six Months	00	00	00	00	00	00	00	00
Axis I Substance Abuse or Dependence	19	15	09	13	00	05	13	07
Axis I Schizophrenia	04	01	01	00	00	00	00	00
Axis I Depression or Dysthymia	26	26	07	47	20	21	33	33
Axis I Bipolar or Cyclothymia	04	04	02	00	00	11	00	00
Axis I Other Psychotic Diagnosis	01	01	00	00	00	00	00	00
Axis I Anxiety Disorder	16	16	07	33	30	16	17	13

Table K-3. Percentages of clients with categorical extra-test characteristics (men and women combined): Two- and three-point code types *(continued)*

Extra-test Characteristics	Total Sample (N = 2,482)	Valid MMPI-2 (n = 1,020)	WNL (n = 90)	Code Types 12/21 (n = 15)	13/31 (n = 20)	23/32 (n = 20)	24/42 (n = 30)	26/62 (n = 15)
Axis I Sexual Disorder	02	02	05	00	00	00	00	00
Axis I Adjustment Disorders	30	31	40	20	45	42	33	40
Axis I V Code Diagnosis	06	08	25	07	00	05	07	00
Axis I Any Diagnosis	89	88	89	87	95	79	93	93
Axis I No Diagnosis	01	00	01	00	00	00	00	00
Axis I Diagnosis Deferred	03	04	07	00	05	00	00	00
Axis I Rule Out Diagnosis	07	07	03	13	00	21	07	07
Axis I Multiple Diagnoses	22	19	10	40	10	21	10	00
Axis II Cluster A Diagnosis	02	01	00	00	00	00	00	00
Axis II Cluster B Diagnosis	10	09	06	07	11	00	10	00
Axis II Cluster C Diagnosis	08	10	14	07	11	06	10	07
Axis II Antisocial Personality Disorder	03	02	01	07	00	00	00	00
Axis II Borderline Personality Disorder	07	06	02	00	05	00	10	00
Axis II Dependent Personality Disorder	07	08	06	07	11	06	10	07
Axis II Personality Disorder NOS Diagnosis	08	10	07	00	00	06	07	20
Axis II Any Diagnosis	29	31	27	14	21	11	27	27
Axis II No Diagnosis	33	33	45	50	42	33	47	20
Axis II Deferred Diagnosis	28	27	22	29	32	33	17	47
Axis II Rule Out Diagnosis	10	09	06	07	05	22	10	07
Axis I and II Dual Diagnosis	26	27	19	07	16	11	23	27
Mental Status								
Uncomfortable During Interview	18	17	13	21	10	11	10	07
Defensive During Interview	07	06	05	14	00	00	00	00
Aloof During Interview	03	03	02	07	00	05	00	00
Cooperative During Interview	90	91	90	79	100	100	100	100
Aggressive During Interview	03	02	02	07	00	05	00	00
Evasive During Interview	09	08	05	14	00	05	00	00
Loose Associations	03	02	00	00	00	11	00	07
Thought Blocking	10	11	09	07	10	16	07	00
Delusions	04	02	00	00	00	00	00	00
Tangential Speech	05	05	01	07	15	11	03	13
Hallucinations	05	02	00	00	00	05	00	00
Circumstantial Speech	08	09	02	07	10	11	03	07

Poor Judgment	29	30	32	21	15	42	23	20
Obsessions	04	05	01	07	00	05	03	00
Preoccupations	17	16	16	21	10	21	13	27
Ideas of Reference	03	02	02	00	00	00	00	00
Too Sad for the Content of the Interview	02	02	01	07	00	16	00	00
Appropriate Emotional Response During Interview	91	92	91	93	90	84	97	100
Too Happy for the Content of the Interview	03	03	05	00	05	11	03	00
Emotionally Flat During Interview	05	03	02	00	10	05	00	07
Prevailing Mood Happy	08	08	11	07	10	05	13	00
Prevailing Mood Anxious	74	73	65	64	75	89	83	73
Prevailing Mood Sad	51	51	27	64	55	74	50	60
Prevailing Mood Angry	16	15	09	43	15	21	07	20
Prevailing Mood Worried	42	46	38	50	45	63	57	60
Unusual Gait	01	01	00	00	00	00	00	00
Unusual Gestures	02	02	04	14	00	00	00	07
Tics	00	00	00	00	00	00	00	00
Tremors	01	01	00	14	00	00	00	00

Extra-test Characteristics	Code Types *(continued)*											
	27/72 (n = 35)	34/43 (n = 15)	46/64 (n = 35)	48/84 (n = 16)	49/94 (n = 12)	68/86 (n = 28)	78/87 (n = 20)	123 (n = 35)	247 (n = 17)	278 (n = 29)	468 (n = 20)	478 (n = 12)
Intake Information												
Ever Arrested	19	47	39	64	50	57	26	17	27	19	50	36
History of Misdemeanor Conviction(s)	10	23	17	43	22	26	06	08	00	13	43	42
History of Felony Conviction(s)	07	17	14	23	20	22	06	08	21	08	23	10
History of Domestic Violence Conviction	00	00	03	07	11	13	00	04	00	00	17	11
Previous Psychiatric Hospitalizations	31	27	43	69	27	48	20	15	25	38	60	42
History of Outpatient Psychiatric Treatment	61	47	56	75	36	52	70	38	63	76	75	67
Currently on Antipsychotic Medication	03	00	00	13	08	00	10	00	00	03	00	17
Currently on Antidepressant Medication	26	07	12	19	00	19	05	11	20	17	25	17
Currently on Lithium	00	07	03	13	00	07	05	00	00	00	00	00
Currently on Anxiolytic Medication	18	07	15	06	00	15	05	15	20	10	15	17
History of Being Sexually Abusive	00	00	00	13	00	11	05	00	13	00	00	00
History of Being Sexually Abused	26	13	32	56	33	19	35	19	20	45	35	33
History of Being Physically Abusive	06	07	15	19	08	22	05	08	00	07	15	17
History of Committing Domestic Violence	00	07	09	13	08	15	10	04	00	00	15	17
History of Victim of Domestic Violence	18	13	21	31	33	19	30	15	13	38	15	17
History of Being Physically Abused	29	20	32	44	50	30	40	31	33	48	60	33
History of Having Few or No Friends	38	33	32	50	17	52	45	23	27	38	60	42
History of Suicide Attempts	24	33	26	25	08	26	30	15	27	31	45	42
Lifetime History of Alcohol Abuse	26	60	39	63	58	54	30	27	31	38	60	58
Lifetime History of Marijuana Abuse	03	29	15	44	25	21	16	08	07	19	30	42
Lifetime History of Cocaine Abuse	06	29	07	20	36	26	20	08	07	08	25	25
Lifetime History of Heroin Abuse	00	08	03	07	00	12	00	00	07	04	06	00
Alcohol Abuse in the Past Six Months	12	53	12	31	33	36	11	08	13	28	26	17
Marijuana Abuse in the Past Six Months	00	07	03	19	09	00	00	04	00	14	05	08
Cocaine Abuse in the Past Six Months	00	07	00	07	09	14	05	00	00	04	05	00
Heroin Abuse in the Past Six Months	00	00	00	00	00	00	00	00	00	04	00	00
Axis I Substance Abuse or Dependence	18	47	11	20	33	30	10	00	13	14	26	17
Axis I Schizophrenia	03	00	03	00	00	00	00	00	00	03	05	17
Axis I Depression or Dysthymia	32	13	23	20	33	44	25	22	44	52	53	17
Axis I Bipolar or Cyclothymia	03	07	03	20	00	07	15	00	00	00	05	00
Axis I Other Psychotic Diagnosis	00	00	00	00	00	00	00	00	00	03	05	00
Axis I Anxiety Disorder	15	13	23	07	00	11	25	22	06	28	16	17
Axis I Sexual Disorder	00	00	03	07	00	00	00	00	00	00	00	00
Axis I Adjustment Disorders	41	40	26	20	67	22	20	37	44	10	11	25
Axis I V Code Diagnosis	00	07	09	00	00	07	05	04	06	03	05	00
Axis I Any Diagnosis	88	93	91	80	92	93	95	78	100	83	89	83

Axis I No Diagnosis	00	00	00	07	00	00	00	00	00	00	05	00
Axis I Diagnosis Deferred	03	00	03	00	08	07	00	00	00	07	05	00
Axis I Rule Out Diagnosis	09	07	03	13	00	00	05	22	00	10	00	17
Axis I Multiple Diagnoses	21	33	20	20	33	33	10	11	13	28	37	17
Axis II Cluster A Diagnosis	00	00	06	00	00	00	00	00	00	00	00	08
Axis II Cluster B Diagnosis	12	20	09	07	25	22	15	04	06	07	37	08
Axis II Cluster C Diagnosis	15	00	06	00	17	04	15	00	13	10	05	17
Axis II Antisocial Personality Disorder	00	07	00	07	08	07	00	00	00	00	21	08
Axis II Borderline Personality Disorder	12	13	09	00	17	15	15	00	06	07	11	00
Axis II Dependent Personality Disorder	09	00	06	00	17	00	15	00	06	03	05	17
Axis II Personality Disorder NOS Diagnosis	15	00	03	00	08	11	10	11	13	28	11	17
Axis II Any Diagnosis	42	20	24	07	50	37	35	15	31	45	53	50
Axis II No Diagnosis	27	40	28	40	25	22	35	33	50	14	26	33
Axis II Deferred Diagnosis	24	27	32	27	25	30	25	41	19	38	11	08
Axis II Rule Out Diagnosis	06	13	12	27	00	11	05	11	00	03	11	08
Axis I and II Dual Diagnosis	39	20	24	00	42	33	35	15	31	45	47	42
Mental Status												
Uncomfortable During Interview	18	07	09	19	33	15	10	15	13	17	25	08
Defensive During Interview	00	07	09	00	00	15	05	00	06	00	15	00
Aloof During Interview	03	00	00	13	00	07	00	04	00	07	10	00
Cooperative During Interview	97	93	91	94	100	81	95	96	87	93	80	92
Aggressive During Interview	00	00	03	00	00	11	00	00	00	00	05	00
Evasive During Interview	00	13	06	06	08	15	00	15	00	07	10	08
Loose Associations	00	00	03	06	08	04	00	04	00	00	10	17
Thought Blocking	06	00	06	06	08	14	11	11	13	18	10	33
Delusions	03	07	03	00	00	04	05	00	00	04	10	25
Tangential Speech	00	00	12	00	08	07	00	07	00	00	25	17
Hallucinations	00	00	03	06	00	07	00	00	00	07	05	25
Circumstantial Speech	00	13	15	06	17	11	05	11	00	00	30	08
Poor Judgment	24	27	26	25	42	32	21	19	06	14	55	42
Obsessions	03	00	06	06	00	00	16	04	00	07	10	08
Preoccupations	09	07	24	00	17	07	11	22	06	07	30	42
Ideas of Reference	03	00	06	00	08	00	05	04	00	04	00	17
Too Sad for the Content of the Interview	06	00	00	00	00	00	00	07	00	00	00	00
Appropriate Emotional Response During Interview	91	100	97	94	92	86	95	93	93	93	95	73
Too Happy for the Content of the Interview	00	00	00	06	00	04	00	04	00	03	00	09
Emotionally Flat During Interview	03	00	06	00	08	11	05	04	00	03	00	18
Prevailing Mood Happy	00	07	00	13	17	07	05	04	00	00	00	25
Prevailing Mood Anxious	76	87	88	63	67	67	85	74	87	72	75	75
Prevailing Mood Sad	82	60	47	50	67	59	55	67	50	69	60	50
Prevailing Mood Angry	00	20	21	13	25	22	05	07	13	14	25	17

Extra-test Characteristics	Code Types *(continued)*											
	27/72 (n = 35)	34/43 (n = 15)	46/64 (n = 35)	48/84 (n = 16)	49/94 (n = 12)	68/86 (n = 28)	78/87 (n = 20)	123 (n = 35)	247 (n = 17)	278 (n = 29)	468 (n = 20)	478 (n = 12)
Prevailing Mood Worried	47	33	53	25	33	56	55	48	31	55	65	33
Unusual Gait	03	00	00	00	00	04	00	00	00	00	00	00
Unusual Gestures	00	00	00	00	00	04	00	00	00	03	00	17
Tics	00	00	00	00	00	00	00	00	00	00	00	00
Tremors	03	00	00	06	00	04	00	07	00	00	00	08

Appendix L

Means and Standard Deviations for Women and Men for Continuous Extra-Test Characteristics: High Scores on Individual Scales and Two- and Three-Point Code Types

Table L-1a. Means and standard deviations for continuous extra-test characteristics (women): High scores on clinical scales

Extra-test Characteristics	Total Sample		Valid MMPI-2		WNL		Clinical Scales: 1 (Hy)		Clinical Scales: 2 (D)	
	Mean	SD	Mean	SD	Mean	SD	Mean	SD	Mean	SD
Intake Information	(n = 1,447)		(n = 610)		(n = 42)		(n = 325)		(n = 404)	
Axis IV diagnosis	2.97	.96	2.97	.97	2.76	.92	3.13	1.03	3.06	.99
Axis V - Current Level of Functioning	61.07	10.54	62.33	9.88	68.10	9.15	60.17	10.08	60.63	10.05
Number of Arrests	.52	1.80	.49	1.46	.32	.53	.49	1.62	.39	1.01
Mental Status	(n = 1,447)		(n = 610)		(n = 42)		(n = 325)		(n = 404)	
Anxiety During Interview	2.42	.68	2.37	.67	2.26	.59	2.44	.71	2.44	.70
Depression During Interview	2.41	.74	2.42	.74	2.03	.74	2.60	.72	2.57	.73
Activity Level During Interview	2.99	.42	2.96	.36	2.95	.22	2.97	.41	2.96	.38
Speech During Interview	2.99	.42	2.98	.39	2.97	.16	2.97	.43	2.96	.40
SCL-90-R Scales	(n = 746)		(n = 605)		(n = 42)		(n = 324)		(n = 402)	
Somatization	1.28	.92	1.20	.87	.38	.28	1.72	.79	1.52	.85
Obsessive-Compulsive	1.58	.99	1.49	.94	.51	.43	1.90	.87	1.85	.86
Interpersonal Sensitivity	1.56	.96	1.48	.92	.65	.55	1.76	.89	1.80	.85
Depression	1.92	1.01	1.87	.98	.76	.53	2.29	.84	2.31	.80
Anxiety	1.43	1.02	1.34	.96	.33	.31	1.77	.92	1.70	.92
Hostility	1.33	1.04	1.25	.98	.45	.37	1.50	1.01	1.52	.97
Phobic Anxiety	.89	.99	.78	.89	.13	.21	1.14	.97	1.04	.96
Paranoid Ideation	1.46	1.01	1.37	.95	.65	.55	.1.61	.97	1.64	.94
Psychoticism	1.01	.83	.91	.72	.33	.35	1.17	.75	1.14	.72
Initial SCL-90 Analogue	(n = 716)		(n = 425)		(n = 35)		(n = 223)		(n = 269)	
Somatization	2.24	2.58	2.22	2.57	1.00	1.26	2.91	2.83	2.56	2.71
Obsessive-Compulsive	2.57	2.59	2.66	2.60	1.86	2.07	2.67	2.53	2.58	2.52
Interpersonal Sensitivity	4.74	2.71	4.70	2.72	3.63	2.73	4.99	2.60	5.01	2.58
Depression	4.34	2.58	4.43	2.57	3.09	2.05	4.89	2.55	4.88	2.49
Anxiety	4.29	2.59	4.28	2.63	3.40	2.20	4.60	2.69	4.51	2.70
Hostility	2.86	2.57	2.85	2.58	2.17	2.31	2.89	2.58	2.84	2.58

Table L-1a. Means and standard deviations for continuous extra-test characteristics (women): High scores on clinical scales *(continued)*

Extra-test Characteristics	Total Sample Mean	Total Sample SD	Valid MMPI-2 Mean	Valid MMPI-2 SD	WNL Mean	WNL SD	Clinical Scales 1 (Hy) Mean	Clinical Scales 1 (Hy) SD	Clinical Scales 2 (D) Mean	Clinical Scales 2 (D) SD
Phobic Anxiety	1.16	2.07	1.10	2.02	.51	1.09	1.32	2.16	1.20	2.13
Paranoid Ideation	1.21	1.98	1.12	1.92	.51	1.09	1.20	2.00	1.14	2.01
Psychoticism	.72	1.60	.70	1.65	.31	.76	.65	1.55	.66	1.67
Patient Description Form Scales	(n = 714)		(n = 425)		(n = 35)		(n = 223)		(n = 269)	
Angry Resentment	2.68	.88	2.65	.87	2.25	.80	2.66	.88	2.69	.87
Critical/Argumentative	2.29	.83	2.29	.84	1.92	.71	2.28	.85	2.32	.83
Narcissistic	1.95	.81	1.99	.83	1.72	.67	1.91	.77	1.97	.85
Defensive	2.48	.83	2.48	.82	2.10	.81	2.45	.83	2.49	.81
Histrionic	2.46	.83	2.44	.84	1.97	.72	2.47	.79	2.51	.84
Aggressive	1.83	.75	1.81	.72	1.67	.55	1.77	.71	1.82	.72
Insecure	3.03	.89	3.02	.89	2.54	.87	3.11	.87	3.15	.85
Anxious	2.94	.80	2.87	.81	2.46	.69	3.01	.79	3.00	.80
Pessimistic	2.20	.88	2.18	.88	1.75	.84	2.33	.90	2.29	.88
Depressed	2.55	.84	2.54	.87	1.91	.68	2.74	.83	2.74	.84
Achievement-Oriented	2.41	.74	2.49	.75	2.94	.62	2.30	.66	2.38	.71
Passive-Submissive	2.57	.95	2.59	.92	2.24	.85	2.69	.90	2.67	.89
Introverted	2.34	.97	2.37	.95	2.05	.84	2.48	.98	2.49	.97
Emotionally Controlled	2.29	.90	2.34	.88	2.27	.91	2.31	.88	2.34	.85
Antisocial	2.05	.81	2.07	.80	1.90	.71	1.97	.75	2.04	.78
Negative Treatment Attitudes	1.91	.73	1.91	.71	1.70	.71	1.90	.72	1.89	.71
Somatic Symptoms	2.11	1.04	2.08	1.02	1.50	.67	2.38	1.09	2.26	1.06
Psychotic Symptoms	1.33	.62	1.28	.59	1.05	.16	1.24	.45	1.28	.56
Family Problems	3.01	1.10	3.00	1.09	2.76	1.10	2.95	1.12	3.01	1.09
Obsessive-Compulsive	2.58	.83	2.55	.85	2.32	.76	2.55	.79	2.57	.83
Stereotypic Masculine Interests	1.40	.70	1.42	.71	1.41	.70	1.37	.69	1.36	.65
Procrastinates	2.19	.92	2.18	.90	2.03	.98	2.14	.88	2.18	.89
Suspicious	2.43	.92	2.40	.90	1.99	.71	2.43	.90	2.44	.91
Agitated	2.13	.81	2.12	.85	1.77	.79	2.15	.82	2.19	.85
Work Problems	1.60	.80	1.56	.75	1.35	.56	1.52	.76	1.62	.82
Patient Description Form Items	(n = 714)		(n = 14)		(n = 35)		(n = 223)		(n = 269)	
Anxious	3.19	.97	3.13	.99	2.86	.85	3.22	1.00	3.21	1.03
Problems with Authority Figures	2.68	1.19	2.69	1.20	2.31	1.02	2.60	1.25	2.72	1.23
Has Insight Into Own Problems	2.56	.90	2.61	.90	3.03	.82	2.55	.92	2.59	.90
Fears Losing Control	3.08	1.10	3.11	1.12	3.06	1.09	3.12	1.11	3.15	1.12

Extroverted	2.47	1.01	2.57	1.04	2.69	.99	2.43	1.00	2.48	1.07
Uses Repression	2.78	1.11	2.81	1.07	2.88	.93	2.80	1.07	2.76	1.06
Submissive	2.74	1.06	2.73	1.04	2.37	1.03	2.83	1.04	2.82	1.00
Difficulty Concentrating	2.69	1.12	2.63	1.12	1.83	.89	2.84	1.11	2.79	1.10
Rigid	2.41	1.03	2.43	1.03	2.09	1.08	2.51	1.01	2.45	1.00
Overly Compliant	2.16	1.06	2.17	1.04	1.83	.82	2.21	1.06	2.24	1.05
Whiny	2.02	1.02	1.97	1.01	1.56	.96	2.03	1.01	2.03	1.00
Feels Overwhelmed	3.38	1.10	3.33	1.10	2.83	1.15	3.52	1.04	3.51	1.04
Manipulative	2.31	1.12	2.35	1.13	2.06	1.00	2.30	1.10	2.34	1.13
Difficulty Trusting Others	3.15	1.12	3.17	1.12	2.76	1.02	3.20	1.13	3.24	1.14
Insensitive to Others	1.81	.89	1.83	.90	1.65	.69	1.76	.85	1.78	.87
Stereotypic Masculine Behavior	1.34	.70	1.36	.71	1.41	.78	1.33	.69	1.30	.64
Harbors Grudges	2.51	1.04	2.48	1.02	2.27	.80	2.42	1.01	2.48	1.03
Evasive	2.27	1.07	2.26	1.08	1.86	1.06	2.18	1.05	2.23	1.05
Disoriented	1.32	.70	1.29	.70	1.09	.28	1.32	.71	1.31	.71
Energetic	2.42	1.00	2.46	.96	2.97	.87	2.22	.89	2.29	.95
Lonely	2.81	1.11	2.82	1.09	2.21	1.08	3.01	1.07	2.99	1.05
Family Lacks Love	2.84	1.27	2.84	1.25	2.48	1.23	2.87	1.27	2.91	1.25
Worrier	3.34	1.04	3.29	1.05	2.91	.93	3.46	1.00	3.46	.99
Narcissistic	2.03	1.07	2.07	1.11	1.74	.95	1.94	.99	2.02	1.08
Tearful	2.28	1.16	2.30	1.18	1.86	1.03	2.46	1.17	2.48	1.17
Provocative	1.71	.96	1.76	.99	1.62	.89	1.66	.91	1.71	.95
Moralistic	2.30	.96	2.31	.98	2.27	1.01	2.37	.96	2.33	.94
Socially Awkward	2.37	1.07	2.38	1.03	1.94	.92	2.52	1.06	2.52	1.04
Hostile	2.13	1.09	2.12	1.07	1.91	1.04	2.09	1.05	2.08	1.04
Overcontrolled	2.39	1.16	2.47	1.16	2.49	1.07	2.39	1.14	2.45	1.14
Resistant to Interpretations	2.15	1.03	2.17	1.00	1.94	.98	2.15	.97	2.16	.98
Antisocial Behavior	1.70	.94	1.71	.93	1.59	.82	1.63	.90	1.64	.88
Sarcastic	1.81	.96	1.82	.98	1.53	1.02	1.81	1.00	1.84	.98
Rejects Traditional Gender Role	1.60	.94	1.63	.95	1.56	.96	1.57	.93	1.61	.94
Feels Gets Raw Deal From Life	2.83	1.18	2.83	1.17	2.22	1.13	2.94	1.16	2.98	1.15
Acute Psychological Turmoil	2.94	1.06	2.92	1.08	2.24	.82	3.05	1.07	3.08	1.08
Does Not Complete Projects	2.21	1.12	2.19	1.12	1.72	1.02	2.13	1.08	2.21	1.11
Uncomfortable with Opposite Sex	2.14	1.15	2.17	1.15	1.94	1.13	2.27	1.18	2.29	1.16
Preoccupied with Health Problems	1.99	1.23	1.98	1.23	1.43	.81	2.34	1.36	2.20	1.32
Work-Oriented	2.64	1.11	2.74	1.12	3.27	1.07	2.57	1.05	2.63	1.08
Resents Family Members	3.01	1.24	3.00	1.22	2.74	1.19	2.96	1.26	3.02	1.22
Demanding of Attention	2.48	1.10	2.50	1.08	2.14	.94	2.46	1.05	2.55	1.08
Passive	2.57	1.13	2.58	1.09	2.17	1.07	2.74	1.05	2.68	1.04
Self-Punishing	2.59	1.12	2.61	1.14	2.03	.93	2.74	1.16	2.80	1.13
Needs to Achieve	2.58	1.02	2.65	1.05	2.87	.81	2.50	1.00	2.60	1.05
Needs to Be with Others	3.05	1.01	3.07	1.00	2.94	.79	3.06	1.03	3.09	1.01

Table L-1a. Means and standard deviations for continuous extra-test characteristics (women): High scores on clinical scales *(continued)*

Extra-test Characteristics	Total Sample		Valid MMPI-2		WNL		Clinical Scales 1 (Hy)		Clinical Scales 2 (D)	
	Mean	SD	Mean	SD	Mean	SD	Mean	SD	Mean	SD
Irritable	2.57	1.00	2.54	1.03	2.00	.94	2.60	1.05	2.63	1.06
Self-Defeating	3.03	1.10	3.04	1.09	2.56	1.02	3.06	1.07	3.10	1.05
Delusional Thinking	1.34	.79	1.30	.79	1.03	.17	1.27	.69	1.30	.76
Self-Reliant	2.59	.95	2.70	.92	3.40	.85	2.62	.88	2.60	.85
Aggressive	1.98	.96	2.03	.97	1.94	1.00	1.95	.92	1.92	.91
Competitive	2.08	.97	2.19	1.00	2.55	.83	2.03	.93	2.07	.96
Suspicious	2.41	1.13	2.36	1.10	2.12	1.09	2.40	1.08	2.39	1.09
Compulsive	2.27	1.15	2.30	1.18	2.42	1.29	2.17	1.09	2.18	1.12
Dependable	2.97	.93	3.05	.90	3.36	.74	2.98	.89	3.00	.90
Multiple Somatic Complaints	1.94	1.21	1.93	1.18	1.38	.70	2.23	1.31	2.09	1.25
Complains of Lack of Time	2.00	1.13	2.04	1.13	2.00	1.11	2.02	1.14	2.03	1.14
Poor Work Performance	1.80	.99	1.75	.94	1.38	.73	1.76	.95	1.85	.99
Insecure	3.45	.97	3.43	.98	2.82	.94	3.52	.94	3.56	.93
Discusses Problems Openly	3.15	.89	3.22	.85	3.43	.78	3.19	.88	3.20	.84
Sexually Adjusted	2.50	.85	2.54	.85	2.79	.74	2.44	.90	2.46	.89
Exaggerated Need for Affection	2.34	1.14	2.35	1.14	1.91	1.00	2.39	1.12	2.41	1.14
Resentful	2.93	1.06	2.94	1.09	2.62	.95	2.91	1.08	2.97	1.08
Uses Denial	2.74	1.13	2.77	1.11	2.50	1.02	2.71	1.12	2.74	1.09
Hypochondriacal	1.68	1.01	1.64	.98	1.29	.62	1.83	1.09	1.73	1.04
Communicates Effectively	3.05	.90	3.09	.89	3.43	.78	2.97	.86	3.03	.88
Has Many Nightmares	1.97	1.08	1.94	1.07	1.59	.85	2.05	1.10	2.03	1.11
Stormy Interpersonal Relationships	3.12	1.15	3.10	1.18	2.86	1.09	3.02	1.22	3.08	1.22
Feigns Remorse When in Trouble	1.77	.97	1.79	.98	1.55	.87	1.66	.92	1.79	.98
Stereotypic Masculine Interests	1.46	.81	1.48	.81	1.41	.70	1.41	.77	1.42	.76
Guarded	2.50	1.14	2.48	1.12	2.24	1.07	2.42	1.14	2.49	1.15
Feels Inferior	3.14	1.12	3.13	1.13	2.48	.94	3.26	1.09	3.29	1.07
Low Frustration Tolerance	2.79	1.06	2.77	1.06	2.11	.90	2.84	1.08	2.86	1.06
Psychotic Symptoms	1.28	.74	1.22	.68	1.00	.00	1.20	.59	1.25	.70
Fired From Past Jobs	1.56	.97	1.51	.94	1.36	.64	1.50	.96	1.56	1.00
Needs Attention	2.95	1.02	2.94	1.02	2.56	.89	3.01	.94	3.04	1.01
Acts Out	2.24	1.11	2.24	1.08	1.97	.95	2.18	1.03	2.25	1.10
Histrionic	2.15	1.16	2.14	1.15	1.63	.91	2.11	1.08	2.16	1.14
Self-Indulgent	2.18	1.05	2.22	1.06	2.09	.98	2.06	.97	2.15	1.07
Depressed	3.15	1.04	3.14	1.06	2.41	.82	3.41	.97	3.36	.97
Grandiose	1.60	.87	1.62	.89	1.50	.79	1.53	.84	1.58	.89
Cynical	2.12	1.05	2.12	1.04	1.67	.82	2.16	1.02	2.15	1.01

Sociopathic	1.37	.71	1.40	.73	1.21	.48	1.35	.66	1.35	.67
Agitated	2.32	1.02	2.26	1.06	1.85	.89	2.38	1.04	2.37	1.05
Marital Problems	2.62	1.58	2.66	1.57	3.06	1.44	2.68	1.55	2.69	1.55
Absence of Deep Emotions	1.95	1.09	2.00	1.08	1.79	1.02	1.93	1.09	1.97	1.04
Uncomfortable Dealing with Emotions	2.78	1.14	2.83	1.12	2.82	1.21	2.81	1.13	2.83	1.10
Sad	2.95	1.06	2.95	1.06	2.26	.93	3.15	1.00	3.13	.99
Self-Degrading	2.50	1.14	2.50	1.15	1.91	1.03	2.58	1.14	2.67	1.15
Unable to Express Negative Feelings	2.17	1.11	2.25	1.10	2.18	.92	2.25	1.12	2.29	1.09
Concrete in Thinking	2.31	1.10	2.26	1.08	1.74	.93	2.33	1.10	2.33	1.09
Unable to See Own Limitations	2.16	1.04	2.15	1.04	1.65	.88	2.08	1.00	2.14	1.03
Power-Oriented	1.78	.92	1.86	.96	1.84	.95	1.75	.91	1.79	.94
Grouchy	2.06	.96	2.02	.96	1.48	.63	2.08	1.00	2.10	.99
Overbearing in Relationships	2.00	1.04	2.02	1.06	1.87	1.10	1.96	1.02	2.06	1.07
Uncertain About Career	2.88	1.32	2.85	1.31	2.77	1.38	2.86	1.29	2.93	1.30
Likable	3.29	.85	3.34	.82	3.56	.61	3.27	.85	3.30	.86
Procrastinator	2.42	1.11	2.39	1.06	2.21	1.17	2.36	1.00	2.36	.99
Negative Feelings Toward Opposite Sex	2.46	1.20	2.49	1.21	2.06	1.12	2.53	1.23	2.56	1.20
Defensive	2.64	1.11	2.67	1.07	2.30	.95	2.66	1.11	2.72	1.08
Empathetic	2.64	.78	2.66	.76	2.76	.79	2.67	.79	2.67	.74
Perfectionistic	2.42	1.13	2.48	1.16	2.41	1.01	2.37	1.09	2.44	1.14
Judgmental	2.46	1.02	2.49	.99	2.25	.84	2.44	.99	2.47	.99
Copes Well with Stress	2.01	.76	2.11	.76	2.56	.62	1.95	.73	1.99	.74
Moody	2.70	1.01	2.69	.99	2.27	.87	2.75	.99	2.81	1.00
Selfish	1.92	.92	1.93	.93	1.66	.70	1.86	.87	1.92	.94
Gives Up Easily	2.19	1.05	2.14	1.01	1.68	.91	2.26	1.02	2.24	1.02
Physical Symptoms in Response to Stress	2.23	1.22	2.20	1.20	1.69	.90	2.48	1.28	2.37	1.25
Blames Family For Difficulties	2.76	1.26	2.72	1.27	2.35	1.20	2.61	1.28	2.75	1.28
Bored	2.18	1.08	2.20	1.10	1.71	1.07	2.23	1.09	2.25	1.10
Idealistic	2.37	1.03	2.44	1.03	2.36	1.03	2.39	1.01	2.40	1.02
Difficulty Establishing Therapeutic Rapport	1.87	.96	1.84	.93	1.74	1.02	1.85	.95	1.84	.96
Daydreams	1.92	.99	1.92	.98	1.59	.73	1.94	.99	1.96	.98
Concerned About Status	2.16	1.09	2.19	1.10	2.36	1.08	2.07	1.04	2.14	1.07
Creates Good First Impression	2.86	.95	2.91	.96	3.53	.86	2.79	.95	2.82	.94
Complains of Sleep Disturbance	2.62	1.24	2.57	1.26	1.70	.95	2.88	1.25	2.84	1.25
Has Temper Tantrums	2.06	1.08	2.03	1.06	1.83	.89	2.03	1.09	2.07	1.07
Overreactive	2.68	1.12	2.66	1.10	2.09	.93	2.73	1.10	2.78	1.11
High Aspirations	2.37	1.09	2.47	1.10	2.85	1.09	2.22	1.00	2.42	1.10
Feels Hopeless	2.62	1.14	2.58	1.18	1.85	1.08	2.81	1.14	2.83	1.15
Keeps Others at a Distance	2.83	1.15	2.82	1.13	2.48	1.09	2.82	1.14	2.84	1.10
Argumentative	2.10	1.03	2.10	1.01	1.74	.79	2.06	1.01	2.12	1.04
Paranoid Features	1.70	.99	1.68	.97	1.15	.57	1.70	.98	1.68	.98
Restless	2.38	1.05	2.41	1.08	1.82	.85	2.47	1.04	2.50	1.10

Table L-1a. Means and standard deviations for continuous extra-test characteristics (women): High scores on clinical scales *(continued)*

Extra-test Characteristics	Total Sample		Valid MMPI-2		WNL		Clinical Scales 1 (Hy)		Clinical Scales 2 (D)	
	Mean	SD	Mean	SD	Mean	SD	Mean	SD	Mean	SD
Pessimistic	2.61	1.08	2.56	1.08	2.00	.87	2.76	1.10	2.70	1.07
Feels Like a Failure	2.85	1.12	2.86	1.12	2.15	1.08	3.00	1.14	3.03	1.10
Hallucinations	1.16	.61	1.11	.51	1.00	.00	1.09	.41	1.12	.52
Restricted Affect	2.12	1.12	2.14	1.11	1.97	1.03	2.16	1.09	2.15	1.07
Impatient	2.55	1.03	2.56	1.04	2.47	1.05	2.50	1.01	2.54	1.03
Assertive	2.11	.85	2.18	.87	2.26	.71	2.08	.83	2.14	.86
Modest	2.59	.84	2.58	.83	2.66	.70	2.61	.83	2.62	.85
Self-Doubting	3.12	1.03	3.08	1.04	2.65	.95	3.19	1.02	3.22	1.00
Deceptive	1.83	.94	1.84	.91	1.64	.99	1.75	.85	1.79	.88
Feels That Life is a Strain	3.03	1.09	3.00	1.08	2.33	1.14	3.16	1.05	3.18	1.05
Physically Abusive	1.33	.74	1.29	.65	1.19	.40	1.28	.60	1.29	.63
Feels Rejected	3.10	1.15	3.10	1.13	2.71	1.14	3.19	1.10	3.22	1.08
Does Not Get Along with Coworkers	1.61	.87	1.62	.87	1.46	.78	1.64	.91	1.67	.91
Uses Projection	2.34	1.06	2.34	1.06	2.06	1.00	2.22	1.04	2.30	1.05
Complains of Fatigue	2.56	1.25	2.52	1.27	1.64	.99	2.86	1.28	2.76	1.28
Uses Rationalization	2.60	1.06	2.67	1.07	2.62	.99	2.59	1.05	2.59	1.02
Critical of Others	2.39	1.05	2.41	1.03	2.18	.83	2.35	1.04	2.41	1.07
Egocentric	2.15	1.06	2.17	1.06	1.76	.89	2.10	1.04	2.16	1.08
Overevaluates Own Worth	1.60	.88	1.66	.91	1.38	.65	1.57	.85	1.67	.96
Optimistic	2.05	.81	2.13	.81	2.38	.70	1.97	.78	2.03	.78
Psychologically Immature	2.78	1.19	2.77	1.20	2.35	1.15	2.71	1.22	2.81	1.16
Poor Judgment	2.80	1.18	2.77	1.15	2.35	1.01	2.66	1.12	2.75	1.14
Low Sex Drive	2.18	1.21	2.13	1.19	1.95	1.23	2.23	1.24	2.25	1.22
Feels Mistreated	3.12	1.16	3.11	1.15	2.67	1.19	3.18	1.13	3.21	1.12
Overly Sensitive to Criticism	3.10	1.13	3.09	1.15	2.44	1.02	3.15	1.10	3.24	1.09
Sentimental	2.62	1.00	2.61	1.04	2.19	1.03	2.59	.98	2.67	1.01
Sexual Preoccupation	1.50	.90	1.54	.92	1.30	.72	1.49	.90	1.49	.89
Accelerated Speech	1.69	.96	1.68	.95	1.59	.96	1.59	.90	1.69	.99
Concerns About Homosexuality	1.15	.57	1.14	.57	1.00	.00	1.15	.59	1.17	.64
Many Specific Fears	2.08	1.08	2.04	1.08	1.61	.90	2.12	1.08	2.16	1.11
Passive in Relationships	2.79	1.19	2.81	1.17	2.50	1.24	2.92	1.12	2.92	1.11
Negative Attitudes Toward Therapy	1.65	.87	1.66	.85	1.47	.79	1.64	.86	1.64	.86
Guilt-Prone	2.98	1.19	3.00	1.18	2.70	1.31	3.06	1.16	3.10	1.14
Nervous	2.94	.97	2.86	.99	2.50	.90	3.00	.98	2.96	.99
Obsessive	2.38	1.14	2.39	1.14	1.94	.90	2.38	1.13	2.42	1.16
Shy	2.32	1.13	2.35	1.10	1.94	.85	2.46	1.16	2.50	1.15

Uses Intellectualization	2.24	1.07	2.33	1.06	2.35	.98	2.22	1.02	2.26	1.04
Has Many Interests	2.29	.93	2.36	.94	2.97	.82	2.13	.88	2.25	.93
Difficulty Making Decisions	2.92	1.08	2.88	1.11	2.56	1.05	2.95	1.06	2.98	1.08
Indirect Expression of Hostility	2.71	1.13	2.78	1.13	2.56	1.16	2.80	1.17	2.79	1.12
Poor Reality Testing	1.58	.94	1.54	.95	1.26	.71	1.48	.83	1.52	.90
Angry	2.96	1.15	2.97	1.15	2.56	1.08	3.01	1.16	3.02	1.15
Eccentric	1.64	.97	1.66	.98	1.29	.68	1.63	.95	1.64	.95
Emotional Lability	2.42	1.08	2.40	1.08	1.85	.82	2.49	1.05	2.54	1.10
Dislikes Change	2.64	.99	2.60	.99	2.31	1.00	2.68	.96	2.69	.93
Believes Cannot Be Helped	1.79	.92	1.81	.91	1.52	.94	1.89	.93	1.87	.90
Reliable Informant	3.23	.96	3.29	.93	3.62	.82	3.25	.97	3.29	.92
Ignores Problems	2.36	1.04	2.43	1.04	2.21	.98	2.36	1.01	2.39	1.04
Ruminates	2.80	1.04	2.78	1.03	2.19	.93	2.89	1.00	2.90	1.02
Excitable	2.57	1.01	2.55	1.03	2.09	.90	2.56	1.00	2.59	1.03
Conforming	2.57	.95	2.60	.93	2.61	.83	2.61	.95	2.62	.95
Ineffective at Dealing with Problems	3.04	1.06	3.01	1.03	2.55	.90	3.05	.98	3.05	1.01
Introverted	2.33	1.12	2.35	1.08	2.24	1.00	2.41	1.08	2.43	1.09
Superficial Relationships	2.60	1.09	2.68	1.09	2.25	1.05	2.60	1.07	2.67	1.07
Impulsive	2.64	1.21	2.67	1.19	2.52	1.28	2.60	1.16	2.63	1.17
Stereotypic Feminine Behavior	2.77	1.16	2.79	1.15	2.56	1.11	2.77	1.15	2.79	1.16
Stubborn	2.66	1.01	2.67	1.02	2.26	1.03	2.63	1.02	2.67	.98
Hostile Toward Therapist	1.33	.65	1.33	.65	1.24	.65	1.33	.66	1.31	.65
Difficult to Motivate	2.16	1.09	2.09	1.04	1.53	.75	2.16	1.04	2.11	1.02
Suicidal Ideations	1.62	.91	1.62	.92	1.12	.41	1.77	.99	1.79	1.00
Familial Discord	3.35	1.27	3.38	1.26	3.29	1.45	3.33	1.29	3.36	1.23
Dogmatic	1.98	.92	2.02	.94	1.81	.90	2.02	.96	1.98	.93

	Clinical Scales *(continued)*															
	3 (Hy)		4 (Pd)		5 (Mf)		6 (Pa)		7 (Pt)		8 (Sc)		9 (Ma)		0 (Si)	
	Mean	SD	Mean	SD	Mean	SD	Mean	SD	Mean	SD	Mean	SD	Mean	SD	Mean	SD
Intake Information	(n = 319)		(n = 407)		(n = 60)		(n = 325)		(n = 363)		(n = 368)		(n = 121)		(n = 230)	
Axis IV diagnosis	3.09	1.02	3.01	.93	2.88	.94	3.01	.93	3.04	1.01	3.03	1.01	3.07	.98	2.98	.96
Axis V - Current Level of Functioning	59.88	10.02	61.38	9.57	61.37	13.61	60.24	9.62	60.21	9.95	60.24	10.01	61.01	9.71	60.76	9.67
Number of Arrests	.33	.81	.53	1.66	1.11	3.17	.46	1.22	.40	1.04	.47	1.24	.82	1.77	.41	.97
Mental Status	(n = 319)		(n = 407)		(n = 60)		(n = 325)		(n = 363)		(n = 368)		(n = 121)		(n = 230)	
Anxiety During Interview	2.47	.71	2.42	.69	2.36	.78	2.46	.72	2.47	.72	2.48	.73	2.39	.70	2.45	.67
Depression During Interview	2.61	.73	2.53	.73	2.38	.83	2.59	.74	2.60	.73	2.59	.72	2.46	.71	2.55	.72
Activity Level During Interview	2.96	.41	2.94	.37	2.88	.42	2.96	.39	2.96	.39	2.96	.41	2.95	.37	2.95	.39
Speech During Interview	2.97	.42	2.97	.40	2.97	.45	2.97	.41	2.96	.42	2.97	.44	2.98	.43	2.90	.36
SCL-90-R Scales	(n = 318)		(n = 404)		(n = 58)		(n = 323)		(n = 361)		(n = 366)		(n = 119)		(n = 228)	
Somatization	1.68	.82	1.36	.87	1.18	.90	1.50	.88	1.57	.85	1.56	.85	1.37	.87	1.59	.85
Obsessive-Compulsive	1.88	.88	1.70	.90	1.32	1.00	1.87	.87	1.93	.84	1.90	.85	1.66	.97	2.00	.84
Interpersonal Sensitivity	1.74	.90	1.71	.90	1.15	.83	1.90	.86	1.89	.84	1.85	.87	1.59	.93	2.08	.84
Depression	2.29	.83	2.18	.90	1.55	.99	2.34	.82	2.36	.78	2.33	.81	1.92	.91	2.40	.85
Anxiety	1.78	.94	1.58	.95	1.19	.98	1.76	.93	1.80	.89	1.77	.90	1.49	.98	1.85	.92
Hostility	1.49	.97	1.48	1.00	1.21	1.04	1.64	1.01	1.62	.99	1.60	.99	1.59	1.05	1.66	1.00
Phobic Anxiety	1.08	.98	.94	.93	.75	.88	1.10	.98	1.13	.96	1.09	.95	.92	.95	1.30	.98
Paranoid Ideation	1.58	.97	1.61	.94	1.26	.94	1.81	.94	1.70	.93	1.73	.94	1.73	.99	1.81	.93
Psychoticism	1.14	.75	1.10	.74	.86	.79	1.24	.73	1.22	.71	1.21	.72	1.12	.81	1.30	.75
Initial SCL-90 Analogue	(n = 222)		(n = 273)		(n = 43)		(n = 224)		(n = 248)		(n = 252)		(n = 84)		(n = 146)	
Somatization	2.84	2.79	2.44	2.70	2.19	2.58	2.36	2.69	2.55	2.71	2.57	2.75	2.51	2.85	2.45	2.59
Obsessive-Compulsive	2.70	2.46	2.85	2.65	2.44	2.88	2.52	2.49	2.79	2.62	2.78	2.55	2.82	2.57	2.67	2.65
Interpersonal Sensitivity	5.13	2.68	5.00	2.61	4.49	2.77	4.88	2.66	5.18	2.55	5.27	2.52	4.93	2.81	5.07	2.50
Depression	5.00	2.48	4.79	2.51	3.95	2.57	4.83	2.55	4.94	2.54	4.94	2.51	4.52	2.67	4.93	2.41
Anxiety	4.73	2.68	4.55	2.64	4.44	2.24	4.56	2.73	4.63	2.66	4.70	2.68	4.45	2.70	4.69	2.68
Hostility	3.02	2.61	3.09	2.64	2.77	2.66	2.94	2.61	2.97	2.54	3.03	2.60	3.67	2.64	2.74	2.51
Phobic Anxiety	1.22	2.06	1.23	2.13	1.33	2.20	1.09	2.01	1.21	2.11	1.22	2.12	1.39	2.20	1.13	1.98
Paranoid Ideation	1.18	1.90	1.22	1.99	1.21	2.17	1.08	1.83	1.15	1.91	1.27	2.07	1.65	2.23	1.03	1.84
Psychoticism	.67	1.67	.78	1.78	.67	1.60	.69	1.62	.68	1.72	.73	1.76	1.04	2.03	.62	1.51
Patient Description Form Scales	(n = 221)		(n = 274)		(n = 43)		(n = 223)		(n = 248)		(n = 252)		(n = 85)		(n = 146)	
Angry Resentment	2.70	.88	2.78	.87	2.67	1.01	2.67	.86	2.72	.87	2.76	.87	2.94	.83	2.66	.87
Critical/Argumentative	2.32	.87	2.41	.88	2.36	.84	2.30	.85	2.35	.85	2.40	.85	2.58	.89	2.30	.86

Narcissistic	1.95	.82	2.08	.87	1.94	.65	1.97	.84	2.00	.86	2.08	.87	2.38	.90	1.88	.76
Defensive	2.45	.86	2.53	.82	2.65	.72	2.43	.83	2.51	.82	2.55	.83	2.76	.80	2.47	.82
Histrionic	2.51	.82	2.58	.83	2.28	.67	2.48	.88	2.54	.80	2.59	.84	2.68	.93	2.39	.79
Aggressive	1.78	.71	1.88	.75	1.99	.81	1.83	.74	1.80	.72	1.86	.73	2.09	.82	1.75	.69
Insecure	3.13	.87	3.13	.87	2.89	.92	3.11	.90	3.19	.85	3.18	.85	3.06	.90	3.19	.84
Anxious	3.05	.78	2.98	.80	2.72	.86	2.92	.79	3.02	.77	3.03	.78	2.87	.78	3.02	.82
Pessimistic	2.31	.89	2.28	.86	2.26	.89	2.22	.86	2.31	.89	2.34	.86	2.33	.89	2.35	.83
Depressed	2.79	.82	2.67	.86	2.45	.90	2.72	.87	2.76	.84	2.78	.83	2.49	.82	2.73	.82
Achievement-Oriented	2.40	.73	2.48	.76	2.29	.71	2.40	.74	2.40	.74	2.37	.74	2.51	.75	2.20	.71
Passive-Submissive	2.65	.90	2.61	.91	2.56	.92	2.61	.90	2.70	.89	2.69	.90	2.48	.96	2.79	.93
Introverted	2.40	.98	2.38	.93	2.48	.96	2.35	.94	2.50	.97	2.48	.96	2.24	.86	2.71	.98
Emotionally Controlled	2.34	.89	2.36	.89	2.40	.88	2.27	.87	2.39	.89	2.39	.92	2.44	.94	2.39	.89
Antisocial	1.97	.75	2.16	.82	2.20	.77	2.08	.83	2.07	.79	2.16	.82	2.43	.92	1.99	.74
Negative Treatment Attitudes	1.88	.72	1.93	.68	2.06	.62	1.84	.66	1.92	.71	1.96	.72	2.17	.71	1.88	.68
Somatic Symptoms	2.32	1.11	2.12	1.04	2.06	.90	2.14	1.03	2.23	1.06	2.26	1.07	2.17	1.10	2.17	1.05
Psychotic Symptoms	1.26	.58	1.32	.61	1.26	.45	1.29	.58	1.30	.60	1.31	.57	1.42	.72	1.24	.48
Family Problems	3.01	1.11	3.14	1.09	3.03	1.16	3.07	1.10	3.04	1.09	3.10	1.09	3.28	1.15	2.99	1.10
Obsessive-Compulsive	2.59	.82	2.63	.88	2.37	.80	2.51	.85	2.63	.85	2.62	.84	2.56	.79	2.57	.93
Stereotypic Masculine Interests	1.36	.66	1.43	.72	1.76	1.06	1.39	.69	1.39	.68	1.39	.67	1.51	.77	1.38	.71
Procrastinates	2.16	.94	2.26	.91	2.22	.85	2.14	.91	2.26	.92	2.26	.91	2.31	.86	2.14	.85
Suspicious	2.46	.91	2.53	.91	2.54	.92	2.43	.87	2.48	.91	2.53	.92	2.65	.89	2.44	.86
Agitated	2.23	.86	2.20	.88	2.19	.77	2.17	.86	2.19	.83	2.22	.85	2.27	.92	2.16	.81
Work Problems	1.51	.80	1.65	.80	1.65	.58	1.61	.80	1.63	.77	1.71	.87	1.94	.91	1.54	.76
Patient Description Form Items	(n = 221)		(n = 274)		(n = 43)		(n = 223)		(n = 248)		(n = 252)		(n = 85)		(n = 146)	
Anxious	3.29	.98	3.24	.99	3.02	.96	3.22	1.00	3.28	.98	3.28	1.00	3.19	.98	3.30	1.01
Problems with Authority Figures	2.60	1.25	2.83	1.22	2.93	1.30	2.65	1.23	2.74	1.26	2.77	1.22	3.11	1.12	2.64	1.20
Has Insight Into Own Problems	2.62	.91	2.63	.89	2.35	.78	2.57	.85	2.59	.89	2.56	.89	2.28	.83	2.58	.86
Fears Losing Control	3.19	1.15	3.20	1.07	3.10	1.08	3.10	1.12	3.21	1.12	3.20	1.12	3.12	1.03	3.10	1.09
Extroverted	2.52	1.07	2.62	1.10	2.37	1.02	2.48	1.09	2.46	1.06	2.48	1.11	2.79	1.07	2.16	.99
Uses Repression	2.77	1.08	2.87	1.08	2.76	.94	2.72	1.10	2.81	1.08	2.83	1.07	2.98	1.07	2.78	1.06
Submissive	2.80	1.03	2.79	1.02	2.63	1.02	2.75	1.02	2.85	1.01	2.83	1.03	2.65	1.08	2.90	1.06
Difficulty Concentrating	2.85	1.11	2.76	1.09	2.59	1.14	2.73	1.07	2.82	1.07	2.81	1.09	2.82	1.13	2.75	1.06
Rigid	2.50	1.03	2.46	1.04	2.48	1.04	2.34	.98	2.48	1.02	2.46	1.02	2.54	1.07	2.52	1.04
Overly Compliant	2.18	1.04	2.21	1.05	2.07	.97	2.18	1.07	2.21	1.05	2.24	1.06	2.13	1.10	2.33	1.06
Whiny	2.01	1.00	2.03	1.00	1.67	.79	2.01	1.02	2.04	1.02	2.08	1.03	2.21	1.10	1.99	1.03
Feels Overwhelmed	3.55	1.02	3.46	1.07	3.05	1.21	3.40	1.05	3.51	1.04	3.50	1.05	3.29	1.18	3.42	1.11
Manipulative	2.36	1.14	2.45	1.16	2.22	.96	2.37	1.18	2.39	1.16	2.48	1.17	2.76	1.27	2.24	1.13
Difficulty Trusting Others	3.23	1.12	3.34	1.11	3.35	1.07	3.21	1.15	3.28	1.12	3.33	1.13	3.46	1.10	3.29	1.14
Insensitive to Others	1.77	.86	1.90	.93	1.77	.95	1.80	.88	1.81	.89	1.85	.90	2.12	.97	1.76	.84
Stereotypic Masculine Behavior	1.32	.66	1.37	.72	1.58	1.03	1.34	.71	1.33	.67	1.31	.66	1.46	.77	1.33	.72
Harbors Grudges	2.47	1.05	2.59	1.05	2.46	.98	2.40	1.04	2.51	1.07	2.54	1.06	2.76	1.06	2.56	1.04

	Clinical Scales *(continued)*															
	3 (Hy)		4 (Pd)		5 (Mf)		6 (Pa)		7 (Pt)		8 (Sc)		9 (Ma)		0 (Si)	
	Mean	SD	Mean	SD	Mean	SD	Mean	SD	Mean	SD	Mean	SD	Mean	SD	Mean	SD
Evasive	2.19	1.07	2.30	1.06	2.42	.91	2.19	1.08	2.26	1.09	2.32	1.10	2.71	1.12	2.21	1.04
Disoriented	1.30	.71	1.33	.73	1.30	.67	1.33	.71	1.32	.72	1.34	.73	1.47	.84	1.27	.64
Energetic	2.33	.95	2.44	.97	2.30	.99	2.30	.92	2.29	.94	2.31	.97	2.61	.98	2.19	.88
Lonely	3.02	1.10	2.98	1.06	2.77	1.07	2.95	1.08	3.01	1.05	3.02	1.07	2.81	1.12	2.91	1.04
Family Lacks Love	2.89	1.26	3.03	1.25	3.02	1.28	2.94	1.25	2.95	1.23	3.00	1.24	3.08	1.30	2.91	1.22
Worrier	3.47	1.00	3.40	1.02	3.07	1.03	3.30	1.01	3.48	.97	3.48	.97	3.22	.94	3.48	1.04
Narcissistic	1.99	1.07	2.20	1.15	1.93	.84	2.09	1.12	2.10	1.15	2.16	1.14	2.61	1.23	1.91	.94
Tearful	2.51	1.18	2.40	1.17	2.09	1.17	2.51	1.22	2.48	1.18	2.50	1.20	2.20	1.21	2.51	1.14
Provocative	1.70	.95	1.76	.99	1.81	.93	1.77	1.02	1.72	.98	1.76	.97	1.99	1.12	1.59	.87
Moralistic	2.40	.99	2.28	.95	1.95	.88	2.21	.94	2.32	.97	2.26	.94	2.21	.90	2.34	.98
Socially Awkward	2.44	1.05	2.47	1.03	2.62	.94	2.41	1.01	2.53	1.04	2.55	1.02	2.39	.97	2.73	1.06
Hostile	2.12	1.07	2.22	1.11	2.07	1.07	2.06	1.05	2.11	1.06	2.14	1.07	2.51	1.09	2.12	1.02
Overcontrolled	2.48	1.14	2.46	1.19	2.41	1.09	2.39	1.15	2.50	1.16	2.47	1.17	2.42	1.17	2.50	1.20
Resistant to Interpretations	2.16	.98	2.19	.98	2.17	.83	2.11	.95	2.18	.97	2.22	.99	2.43	1.04	2.15	.96
Antisocial Behavior	1.60	.87	1.75	.97	1.88	.97	1.70	.93	1.65	.89	1.73	.95	2.13	1.10	1.61	.82
Sarcastic	1.86	.97	1.97	1.02	1.93	1.02	1.88	.99	1.88	.97	1.92	.99	2.17	1.15	1.83	.98
Rejects Traditional Gender Role	1.61	.94	1.69	1.00	2.00	1.38	1.63	.94	1.65	.97	1.64	.97	1.90	1.21	1.58	.94
Feels Gets Raw Deal From Life	2.94	1.15	3.00	1.15	2.80	1.16	2.97	1.17	3.02	1.15	3.06	1.18	3.10	1.08	2.95	1.16
Acute Psychological Turmoil	3.08	1.06	3.06	1.07	3.00	1.10	3.04	1.07	3.10	1.08	3.11	1.08	2.95	1.13	2.98	1.06
Does Not Complete Projects	2.16	1.15	2.31	1.13	2.48	1.03	2.17	1.16	2.28	1.11	2.33	1.14	2.49	1.11	2.06	1.01
Uncomfortable with Opposite Sex	2.26	1.17	2.27	1.22	2.22	1.11	2.23	1.19	2.34	1.20	2.29	1.19	2.20	1.19	2.38	1.21
Preoccupied with Health Problems	2.26	1.35	2.02	1.23	2.05	1.17	2.05	1.23	2.14	1.31	2.17	1.30	2.07	1.31	2.07	1.23
Work-Oriented	2.66	1.09	2.71	1.11	2.65	1.29	2.60	1.12	2.63	1.09	2.55	1.10	2.60	1.09	2.61	1.15
Resents Family Members	3.03	1.26	3.14	1.22	3.10	1.22	3.07	1.22	3.05	1.23	3.12	1.22	3.28	1.32	2.97	1.23
Demanding of Attention	2.50	1.08	2.62	1.13	2.22	.99	2.54	1.10	2.57	1.06	2.62	1.07	2.78	1.20	2.40	1.00
Passive	2.68	1.05	2.59	1.07	2.58	1.18	2.58	1.04	2.72	1.04	2.69	1.07	2.43	1.11	2.76	1.12
Self-Punishing	2.75	1.17	2.73	1.15	2.72	1.15	2.70	1.18	2.83	1.15	2.82	1.16	2.63	1.12	2.78	1.20
Needs to Achieve	2.60	1.05	2.66	1.08	2.44	1.10	2.59	1.05	2.64	1.07	2.57	1.06	2.70	1.04	2.37	1.04
Needs to Be with Others	3.11	1.08	3.13	1.04	3.15	.79	3.07	1.09	3.13	1.03	3.14	1.01	3.11	1.04	2.97	1.11
Irritable	2.64	1.07	2.65	1.04	2.60	1.05	2.55	1.06	2.61	1.06	2.68	1.06	2.70	1.06	2.65	1.00
Self-Defeating	3.07	1.09	3.18	1.05	3.17	1.03	3.10	1.11	3.16	1.07	3.23	1.05	3.25	1.10	3.07	1.03
Delusional Thinking	1.30	.78	1.33	.81	1.28	.55	1.34	.83	1.32	.81	1.35	.83	1.50	.98	1.24	.65
Self-Reliant	2.70	.90	2.65	.88	2.63	.69	2.62	.90	2.60	.88	2.55	.87	2.44	.86	2.51	.89
Aggressive	1.98	.95	2.07	.98	2.19	.93	1.98	.94	1.93	.92	2.00	.92	2.40	1.02	1.88	.90
Competitive	2.09	1.00	2.22	1.03	2.10	1.02	2.12	.97	2.10	1.01	2.13	1.02	2.38	1.08	1.92	.92
Suspicious	2.42	1.10	2.47	1.11	2.51	1.16	2.35	1.05	2.44	1.12	2.46	1.12	2.54	1.08	2.38	1.05
Compulsive	2.22	1.11	2.31	1.18	2.07	1.11	2.17	1.09	2.27	1.16	2.26	1.15	2.29	1.12	2.15	1.22

Dependable	3.04	.90	3.00	.90	3.02	.90	2.95	.88	2.99	.91	2.95	.90	2.78	.87	3.02	.87
Multiple Somatic Complaints	2.19	1.30	1.96	1.18	2.00	1.04	1.98	1.20	2.05	1.25	2.08	1.25	2.04	1.25	1.97	1.22
Complains of Lack of Time	2.05	1.15	2.08	1.17	1.83	1.15	2.00	1.09	2.03	1.15	2.03	1.14	2.11	1.12	2.01	1.10
Poor Work Performance	1.77	.99	1.85	.98	1.89	.89	1.82	1.01	1.86	.97	1.87	1.00	2.02	1.03	1.70	.90
Insecure	3.54	.95	3.56	.95	3.47	.93	3.49	.97	3.59	.91	3.61	.92	3.49	.99	3.53	.93
Discusses Problems Openly	3.26	.88	3.27	.84	3.02	.74	3.24	.87	3.20	.84	3.18	.85	3.01	.87	3.09	.82
Sexually Adjusted	2.46	.90	2.53	.88	2.33	.88	2.47	.91	2.51	.89	2.45	.90	2.39	.93	2.41	.84
Exaggerated Need for Affection	2.44	1.16	2.51	1.17	2.10	1.05	2.40	1.17	2.47	1.15	2.47	1.17	2.53	1.20	2.36	1.11
Resentful	2.97	1.09	3.01	1.08	2.85	1.11	2.97	1.08	2.98	1.08	3.03	1.07	3.19	1.06	2.94	1.09
Uses Denial	2.70	1.15	2.81	1.12	2.81	1.02	2.69	1.16	2.76	1.11	2.83	1.11	3.04	1.13	2.72	1.06
Hypochondriacal	1.81	1.09	1.69	1.01	1.64	1.03	1.66	.99	1.73	1.03	1.78	1.06	1.76	1.06	1.71	1.05
Communicates Effectively	3.06	.88	3.09	.88	2.79	.87	3.05	.87	3.02	.88	3.02	.85	2.93	.86	2.91	.87
Has Many Nightmares	2.08	1.17	1.99	1.12	1.84	.90	2.05	1.13	2.08	1.13	2.08	1.10	1.85	1.08	1.99	1.05
Stormy Interpersonal Relationships	3.07	1.22	3.20	1.18	3.10	1.21	3.10	1.21	3.07	1.19	3.14	1.20	3.38	1.06	3.04	1.25
Feigns Remorse When in Trouble	1.65	.92	1.88	1.02	1.97	1.09	1.81	1.03	1.78	1.00	1.89	1.04	2.01	1.09	1.77	1.01
Stereotypic Masculine Interests	1.39	.76	1.49	.82	1.93	1.20	1.43	.79	1.45	.80	1.46	.81	1.55	.86	1.43	.82
Guarded	2.44	1.17	2.49	1.12	2.67	1.02	2.38	1.12	2.52	1.18	2.52	1.17	2.69	1.03	2.49	1.16
Feels Inferior	3.27	1.11	3.27	1.09	2.95	1.15	3.24	1.12	3.34	1.07	3.32	1.09	3.10	1.19	3.42	1.01
Low Frustration Tolerance	2.82	1.07	2.92	1.06	2.95	1.05	2.83	1.08	2.88	1.07	2.93	1.06	3.16	.97	2.79	1.03
Psychotic Symptoms	1.21	.69	1.26	.74	1.14	.42	1.25	.70	1.22	.68	1.25	.71	1.37	.89	1.21	.59
Fired From Past Jobs	1.51	.99	1.61	1.03	1.74	1.05	1.57	.97	1.53	.96	1.66	1.09	1.81	1.17	1.48	.83
Needs Attention	3.03	1.00	3.07	1.01	2.77	.81	2.96	1.04	3.10	1.00	3.10	.99	3.11	1.05	2.95	.97
Acts Out	2.21	1.06	2.39	1.09	2.29	1.01	2.30	1.12	2.29	1.09	2.38	1.11	2.57	1.14	2.23	1.06
Histrionic	2.19	1.11	2.29	1.19	1.87	1.02	2.21	1.19	2.19	1.13	2.32	1.19	2.44	1.36	2.04	1.08
Self-Indulgent	2.10	1.01	2.30	1.10	2.23	.90	2.18	1.05	2.18	1.07	2.28	1.07	2.51	1.09	2.08	.99
Depressed	3.48	.95	3.29	1.01	2.93	1.12	3.33	.99	3.40	.98	3.40	.97	3.10	1.04	3.38	.91
Grandiose	1.59	.90	1.67	.91	1.64	.79	1.59	.90	1.60	.89	1.66	.96	1.96	1.10	1.43	.68
Cynical	2.20	1.06	2.28	1.08	2.29	1.09	2.17	1.04	2.21	1.06	2.27	1.06	2.42	1.18	2.12	1.02
Sociopathic	1.35	.64	1.46	.78	1.34	.76	1.42	.74	1.40	.72	1.45	.76	1.69	.94	1.33	.59
Agitated	2.43	1.05	2.37	1.06	2.40	1.12	2.36	1.07	2.40	1.05	2.42	1.09	2.40	1.09	2.40	1.04
Marital Problems	2.79	1.59	2.69	1.59	2.47	1.37	2.55	1.57	2.66	1.57	2.59	1.55	2.53	1.58	2.70	1.53
Absence of Deep Emotions	1.94	1.10	2.03	1.11	2.12	1.13	1.94	1.04	2.00	1.09	2.06	1.12	2.20	1.16	2.07	1.08
Uncomfortable Dealing with Emotions	2.83	1.17	2.87	1.11	3.00	1.11	2.73	1.13	2.91	1.10	2.90	1.11	3.10	1.09	2.88	1.08
Sad	3.20	.99	3.11	1.03	2.74	1.11	3.13	1.04	3.17	1.00	3.16	1.02	2.86	1.02	3.09	1.00
Self-Degrading	2.60	1.14	2.62	1.13	2.53	1.08	2.63	1.17	2.74	1.14	2.73	1.14	2.53	1.10	2.72	1.10
Unable to Express Negative Feelings	2.29	1.14	2.27	1.11	2.33	1.23	2.17	1.04	2.35	1.14	2.32	1.15	2.31	1.21	2.30	1.10
Concrete in Thinking	2.27	1.07	2.30	1.09	2.56	1.08	2.26	1.10	2.31	1.05	2.35	1.08	2.39	1.09	2.41	1.09
Unable to See Own Limitations	2.09	1.02	2.19	1.03	2.31	.98	2.14	1.00	2.17	1.05	2.22	1.05	2.54	1.06	2.07	.97
Power-Oriented	1.82	.97	1.90	1.01	1.67	.85	1.82	1.01	1.82	.98	1.83	.98	2.04	.97	1.70	.89
Grouchy	2.10	1.01	2.15	.99	2.09	1.06	2.03	.97	2.13	1.01	2.15	1.00	2.23	1.00	2.14	.98
Overbearing in Relationships	2.00	1.01	2.10	1.08	1.88	1.02	2.04	1.07	2.01	1.04	2.10	1.06	2.27	1.08	1.92	1.01
Uncertain About Career	2.85	1.30	2.96	1.32	3.05	1.32	2.93	1.32	2.93	1.31	2.96	1.34	2.95	1.28	2.90	1.38

	Clinical Scales *(continued)*															
	3 (Hy)		4 (Pd)		5 (Mf)		6 (Pa)		7 (Pt)		8 (Sc)		9 (Ma)		0 (Si)	
	Mean	SD	Mean	SD	Mean	SD	Mean	SD	Mean	SD	Mean	SD	Mean	SD	Mean	SD
Likable	3.35	.87	3.35	.87	3.23	.75	3.27	.83	3.30	.85	3.24	.87	3.00	.87	3.21	.82
Procrastinator	2.34	1.03	2.47	1.03	2.46	.98	2.32	.99	2.45	1.01	2.49	1.00	2.46	1.04	2.43	.97
Negative Feelings Toward Opposite Sex	2.57	1.22	2.62	1.23	2.55	1.06	2.59	1.22	2.62	1.22	2.62	1.23	2.71	1.25	2.59	1.19
Defensive	2.69	1.13	2.79	1.09	2.67	1.05	2.62	1.08	2.75	1.09	2.78	1.10	2.95	1.10	2.68	1.00
Empathetic	2.69	.78	2.66	.78	2.62	.76	2.63	.72	2.68	.77	2.64	.76	2.48	.81	2.58	.75
Perfectionistic	2.45	1.12	2.58	1.19	2.37	1.08	2.41	1.14	2.50	1.18	2.46	1.14	2.44	1.06	2.41	1.23
Judgmental	2.47	1.01	2.53	1.03	2.45	.89	2.41	.96	2.50	1.04	2.52	1.01	2.73	.93	2.44	.99
Copes Well with Stress	1.97	.74	2.01	.76	2.00	.72	2.02	.74	1.95	.72	1.94	.74	1.98	.79	1.95	.69
Moody	2.79	1.02	2.79	.99	2.74	.99	2.71	1.02	2.78	.98	2.85	.98	2.88	.97	2.71	.99
Selfish	1.89	.91	2.00	.96	1.84	.79	1.89	.94	1.94	.94	2.00	.96	2.25	1.01	1.88	.91
Gives Up Easily	2.22	1.04	2.24	1.02	2.19	.94	2.23	1.05	2.26	1.03	2.28	1.03	2.40	1.01	2.31	1.01
Physical Symptoms in Response to Stress	2.42	1.28	2.23	1.23	2.26	1.25	2.22	1.21	2.34	1.23	2.34	1.25	2.25	1.22	2.33	1.23
Blames Family For Difficulties	2.68	1.29	2.84	1.29	2.65	1.29	2.77	1.32	2.78	1.30	2.79	1.32	3.11	1.34	2.78	1.31
Bored	2.21	1.12	2.30	1.07	2.40	1.15	2.19	1.07	2.28	1.09	2.28	1.09	2.58	1.13	2.21	1.08
Idealistic	2.47	1.03	2.45	1.05	2.18	.94	2.37	1.01	2.46	1.03	2.41	1.03	2.43	.99	2.28	.98
Difficulty Establishing Therapeutic Rapport	1.84	.94	1.85	.92	2.05	.92	1.75	.85	1.86	.94	1.91	.96	2.07	.91	1.80	.88
Daydreams	1.94	1.04	2.00	1.00	2.27	1.04	1.95	1.00	1.98	1.01	2.04	1.03	1.95	.86	1.89	.95
Concerned About Status	2.10	1.05	2.20	1.11	1.92	.83	2.13	1.10	2.20	1.10	2.18	1.09	2.41	1.16	1.96	1.00
Creates Good First Impression	2.84	.96	2.85	.94	2.63	.87	2.82	.96	2.80	.93	2.76	.95	2.58	1.02	2.63	.91
Complains of Sleep Disturbance	2.92	1.27	2.72	1.27	2.55	1.25	2.73	1.24	2.81	1.21	2.87	1.23	2.50	1.19	2.80	1.16
Has Temper Tantrums	1.98	1.06	2.12	1.09	2.31	1.12	2.04	1.07	2.05	1.06	2.12	1.10	2.35	1.09	2.00	1.02
Overreactive	2.75	1.11	2.85	1.10	2.60	1.03	2.73	1.14	2.81	1.07	2.85	1.09	2.95	.98	2.69	1.08
High Aspirations	2.37	1.12	2.46	1.10	2.26	1.06	2.39	1.13	2.40	1.11	2.37	1.12	2.49	1.20	2.03	1.00
Feels Hopeless	2.83	1.12	2.75	1.18	2.55	1.21	2.76	1.18	2.87	1.17	2.85	1.15	2.52	1.22	2.87	1.09
Keeps Others at a Distance	2.82	1.16	2.89	1.13	3.05	.97	2.79	1.13	2.91	1.12	2.93	1.13	2.94	1.13	2.94	1.11
Argumentative	2.11	1.04	2.22	1.07	2.00	.94	2.13	1.04	2.15	1.04	2.17	1.04	2.34	1.08	2.15	1.02
Paranoid Features	1.73	1.02	1.78	1.03	1.77	1.07	1.70	.98	1.73	1.00	1.79	1.05	1.93	1.03	1.64	.93
Restless	2.56	1.12	2.50	1.11	2.45	.86	2.45	1.07	2.52	1.11	2.55	1.08	2.58	1.13	2.48	1.07
Pessimistic	2.72	1.09	2.69	1.05	2.62	1.06	2.61	1.07	2.74	1.08	2.75	1.04	2.70	1.07	2.80	.98
Feels Like a Failure	3.00	1.11	3.00	1.09	2.74	1.15	2.96	1.13	3.06	1.10	3.04	1.09	2.83	1.08	3.12	1.04
Hallucinations	1.13	.57	1.14	.55	1.05	.22	1.12	.52	1.13	.54	1.14	.55	1.15	.61	1.11	.49
Restricted Affect	2.15	1.10	2.13	1.13	2.28	1.10	2.09	1.10	2.18	1.13	2.21	1.16	2.22	1.24	2.21	1.14
Impatient	2.54	1.05	2.62	1.04	2.60	1.06	2.51	1.06	2.57	1.04	2.61	1.02	2.78	1.06	2.45	.97
Assertive	2.13	.87	2.24	.90	2.00	.73	2.15	.88	2.08	.86	2.13	.87	2.28	.85	1.96	.83
Modest	2.60	.87	2.58	.81	2.70	.91	2.50	.78	2.60	.81	2.58	.83	2.31	.86	2.67	.83
Self-Doubting	3.17	1.02	3.19	1.02	2.93	1.07	3.13	1.00	3.23	1.02	3.22	.99	3.12	1.02	3.22	1.03
Deceptive	1.76	.86	1.91	.95	1.86	.95	1.81	.92	1.79	.88	1.89	.94	2.16	1.01	1.79	.85

Feels That Life is a Strain	3.15	1.05	3.17	1.00	2.95	1.00	3.13	1.07	3.20	1.03	3.24	1.04	3.01	.99	3.13	1.01
Physically Abusive	1.28	.64	1.33	.66	1.41	.89	1.34	.68	1.31	.65	1.34	.67	1.42	.78	1.34	.63
Feels Rejected	3.26	1.09	3.26	1.11	3.12	1.19	3.22	1.16	3.26	1.08	3.29	1.11	3.17	1.17	3.22	1.01
Does Not Get Along with Coworkers	1.60	.86	1.71	.90	1.68	.72	1.64	.87	1.72	.93	1.79	.96	2.04	.95	1.65	.94
Uses Projection	2.28	1.05	2.41	1.09	2.24	1.03	2.35	1.08	2.32	1.06	2.41	1.08	2.59	1.15	2.25	1.02
Complains of Fatigue	2.78	1.32	2.61	1.28	2.24	1.07	2.62	1.25	2.70	1.27	2.73	1.27	2.49	1.25	2.69	1.26
Uses Rationalization	2.64	1.08	2.73	1.08	2.64	1.08	2.57	1.05	2.66	1.03	2.66	1.08	2.79	1.17	2.54	1.02
Critical of Others	2.37	1.05	2.49	1.07	2.33	.97	2.42	1.03	2.44	1.08	2.50	1.07	2.78	.99	2.36	1.05
Egocentric	2.13	1.04	2.28	1.09	2.07	.91	2.18	1.05	2.20	1.10	2.27	1.09	2.61	1.07	2.06	1.03
Overevaluates Own Worth	1.63	.93	1.76	.96	1.57	.77	1.65	.92	1.68	.96	1.74	.98	2.05	1.03	1.53	.78
Optimistic	2.01	.81	2.06	.80	2.10	.79	2.05	.79	2.04	.80	2.04	.79	2.18	.85	1.93	.72
Psychologically Immature	2.69	1.22	2.86	1.16	3.30	1.12	2.77	1.21	2.83	1.17	2.90	1.16	3.18	1.10	2.74	1.17
Poor Judgment	2.70	1.14	2.88	1.16	3.02	1.05	2.81	1.14	2.81	1.14	2.87	1.15	3.14	1.10	2.74	1.14
Low Sex Drive	2.19	1.23	2.18	1.22	2.38	1.20	2.21	1.23	2.25	1.20	2.28	1.20	2.14	1.21	2.37	1.23
Feels Mistreated	3.23	1.15	3.27	1.13	3.05	1.13	3.19	1.12	3.20	1.14	3.24	1.15	3.44	1.05	3.07	1.11
Overly Sensitive to Criticism	3.20	1.15	3.24	1.14	2.90	1.16	3.17	1.14	3.31	1.09	3.33	1.08	3.36	1.04	3.18	1.07
Sentimental	2.65	1.02	2.67	1.05	2.56	1.10	2.64	1.06	2.68	1.05	2.69	1.02	2.66	1.04	2.50	.97
Sexual Preoccupation	1.48	.88	1.60	.96	1.69	1.03	1.59	.99	1.50	.88	1.59	.97	1.87	1.05	1.42	.78
Accelerated Speech	1.70	.98	1.72	1.01	1.70	.91	1.70	1.00	1.66	.93	1.69	.97	1.85	1.01	1.61	.93
Concerns About Homosexuality	1.12	.49	1.19	.66	1.38	1.02	1.18	.66	1.17	.65	1.19	.67	1.23	.67	1.21	.74
Many Specific Fears	2.13	1.07	2.17	1.13	2.02	.96	2.13	1.08	2.16	1.09	2.21	1.08	2.05	1.06	2.24	1.10
Passive in Relationships	2.89	1.15	2.83	1.16	2.90	1.17	2.87	1.14	2.97	1.11	2.93	1.13	2.67	1.25	3.16	1.08
Negative Attitudes Toward Therapy	1.61	.84	1.65	.81	1.88	.92	1.61	.81	1.67	.88	1.70	.87	1.88	.85	1.67	.87
Guilt-Prone	3.13	1.18	3.07	1.18	2.90	1.28	3.05	1.18	3.16	1.15	3.11	1.14	2.95	1.17	3.12	1.13
Nervous	3.05	.98	2.95	.99	2.77	1.00	2.94	.97	3.00	.97	3.00	.99	2.94	.96	3.06	.96
Obsessive	2.46	1.12	2.48	1.15	2.20	1.12	2.39	1.14	2.48	1.17	2.46	1.16	2.45	1.08	2.39	1.19
Shy	2.38	1.15	2.37	1.09	2.44	1.22	2.32	1.11	2.51	1.13	2.45	1.13	2.18	1.10	2.69	1.16
Uses Intellectualization	2.34	1.07	2.36	1.09	2.09	1.00	2.22	1.09	2.33	1.06	2.30	1.08	2.52	1.10	2.13	.99
Has Many Interests	2.19	.91	2.31	.93	2.13	.95	2.25	.94	2.20	.92	2.24	.92	2.17	.89	2.03	.86
Difficulty Making Decisions	2.96	1.13	2.94	1.08	2.88	1.10	2.87	1.09	2.98	1.07	3.00	1.04	2.89	1.10	2.95	1.06
Indirect Expression of Hostility	2.83	1.15	2.88	1.14	2.65	1.12	2.74	1.16	2.83	1.14	2.90	1.11	2.99	1.10	2.75	1.09
Poor Reality Testing	1.46	.86	1.59	.96	1.65	.97	1.53	.96	1.54	.95	1.57	.95	1.81	1.13	1.50	.85
Angry	3.12	1.12	3.10	1.16	2.90	1.27	3.03	1.16	3.07	1.15	3.09	1.17	3.32	1.18	2.94	1.11
Eccentric	1.68	1.00	1.69	.97	1.44	.71	1.67	1.02	1.68	1.00	1.76	1.05	1.93	1.10	1.67	.96
Emotional Lability	2.55	1.10	2.54	1.07	2.29	.97	2.50	1.11	2.53	1.08	2.58	1.08	2.61	1.20	2.35	.99
Dislikes Change	2.65	.97	2.68	.97	2.67	1.01	2.61	.95	2.69	.97	2.75	.94	2.57	.94	2.70	.97
Believes Cannot Be Helped	1.90	.93	1.87	.89	1.90	.93	1.82	.87	1.87	.91	1.93	.90	1.94	.97	1.91	.90
Reliable Informant	3.33	.94	3.30	.91	2.88	.99	3.29	.91	3.29	.92	3.22	.94	3.01	.92	3.23	.89
Ignores Problems	2.36	1.03	2.49	1.05	2.70	.91	2.39	1.05	2.41	1.03	2.46	1.07	2.64	1.11	2.39	1.02
Ruminates	2.94	1.00	2.86	1.03	2.62	1.01	2.80	1.01	2.92	1.01	2.95	.98	2.77	.97	2.79	1.02
Excitable	2.63	1.02	2.70	1.02	2.68	.96	2.57	1.06	2.60	1.00	2.68	1.01	2.69	1.04	2.41	1.02
Conforming	2.56	.96	2.56	.98	2.47	.93	2.53	.92	2.62	.94	2.60	.97	2.35	.92	2.71	1.01

	Clinical Scales *(continued)*															
	3 (Hy)		4 (Pd)		5 (Mf)		6 (Pa)		7 (Pt)		8 (Sc)		9 (Ma)		0 (Si)	
	Mean	SD	Mean	SD	Mean	SD	Mean	SD	Mean	SD	Mean	SD	Mean	SD	Mean	SD
Ineffective at Dealing with Problems	3.03	1.03	3.09	1.01	3.19	1.07	3.01	1.02	3.08	.99	3.15	1.01	3.25	1.01	3.07	1.02
Introverted	2.34	1.09	2.31	1.05	2.35	1.09	2.33	1.03	2.44	1.07	2.42	1.08	2.12	1.04	2.68	1.11
Superficial Relationships	2.61	1.10	2.83	1.08	2.95	.93	2.67	1.11	2.75	1.10	2.82	1.09	3.06	1.05	2.67	1.11
Impulsive	2.60	1.20	2.80	1.21	2.74	1.13	2.69	1.21	2.69	1.18	2.78	1.19	3.11	1.22	2.55	1.16
Stereotypic Feminine Behavior	2.77	1.16	2.82	1.16	2.30	1.15	2.70	1.18	2.80	1.18	2.78	1.17	2.58	1.15	2.70	1.18
Stubborn	2.67	1.06	2.75	1.01	2.65	.95	2.64	1.01	2.70	1.01	2.74	.98	2.96	1.05	2.58	1.02
Hostile Toward Therapist	1.35	.69	1.33	.66	1.42	.76	1.27	.56	1.35	.71	1.35	.68	1.48	.72	1.31	.63
Difficult to Motivate	2.10	1.01	2.14	1.03	2.29	.97	2.06	1.02	2.16	1.08	2.22	1.07	2.51	1.14	2.11	1.01
Suicidal Ideations	1.79	1.00	1.76	.99	1.68	.99	1.84	1.03	1.83	1.01	1.86	1.02	1.73	.94	1.83	.99
Familial Discord	3.41	1.27	3.52	1.20	3.35	1.40	3.46	1.26	3.37	1.22	3.44	1.22	3.63	1.25	3.34	1.23
Dogmatic	2.05	.95	2.08	.98	1.90	.93	2.00	.93	2.01	.97	2.04	.95	2.25	.96	2.02	1.00

Table L-1b. Means and standard deviations for continuous extra-test characteristics (women): High scores on Harris-Lingoes subscales

Extra-test Characteristics	Harris-Lingoes Subscales									
	D_1		D_2		D_3		D_4		D_5	
	Mean	SD	Mean	SD	Mean	SD	Mean	SD	Mean	SD
Intake Information	(n = 417)		(n = 176)		(n = 273)		(n = 388)		(n = 351)	
Axis IV diagnosis	3.04	.99	3.02	1.01	3.07	1.05	3.04	.99	3.02	.99
Axis V - Current Level of Functioning	60.87	9.75	59.66	10.42	60.35	10.08	60.31	9.94	60.46	9.55
Number of Arrests	.37	1.00	.41	1.11	.30	.65	.42	1.14	.40	1.06
Mental Status	(n = 417)		(n = 176)		(n = 273)		(n = 388)		(n = 351)	
Anxiety During Interview	2.44	.70	2.42	.71	2.46	.71	2.45	.71	2.47	.70
Depression During Interview	2.56	.73	2.56	.69	2.62	.73	2.56	.73	2.61	.72
Activity Level During Interview	2.96	.39	2.97	.39	2.97	.42	2.96	.39	2.95	.40
Speech During Interview	2.96	.41	2.96	.42	2.97	.44	2.96	.41	2.95	.42
SCL-90-R Scales	(n = 415)		(n = 175)		(n = 272)		(n = 386)		(n = 349)	
Somatization	1.49	.85	1.46	.88	1.74	.85	1.53	.86	1.53	.86
Obsessive-Compulsive	1.84	.85	1.88	.88	1.97	.90	1.90	.83	1.91	.84
Interpersonal Sensitivity	1.82	.83	1.81	.92	1.88	.88	1.86	.84	1.92	.83
Depression	2.31	.77	2.34	.87	2.39	.81	2.33	.78	2.42	.75
Anxiety	1.70	.90	1.66	.96	1.86	.95	1.73	.91	1.76	.91
Hostility	1.55	.98	1.33	.91	1.64	1.01	1.59	.98	1.63	.99
Phobic Anxiety	1.04	.94	1.06	.99	1.21	.98	1.08	.95	1.10	.97
Paranoid Ideation	1.65	.93	1.52	.96	1.74	.98	1.69	.93	1.74	.92
Psychoticism	1.15	.71	1.12	.72	1.27	.76	1.20	.71	1.24	.72
Initial SCL-90 Analogue	(n = 280)		(n = 117)		(n = 187)		(n = 263)		(n = 236)	
Somatization	2.50	2.73	2.61	2.85	2.83	2.87	2.49	2.65	2.35	2.66
Obsessive-Compulsive	2.64	2.55	2.53	2.53	2.68	2.61	2.72	2.56	2.53	2.48
Interpersonal Sensitivity	5.06	2.59	4.92	2.59	4.97	2.58	5.15	2.56	5.08	2.60
Depression	4.88	2.53	4.84	2.46	4.86	2.56	4.86	2.49	4.85	2.48
Anxiety	4.50	2.70	4.25	2.77	4.64	2.65	4.56	2.68	4.43	2.65
Hostility	2.84	2.61	2.50	2.56	2.72	2.58	2.92	2.55	2.71	2.54
Phobic Anxiety	1.11	1.99	.88	1.70	1.14	2.10	1.12	1.97	.94	1.79
Paranoid Ideation	1.14	1.99	.85	1.49	.96	1.74	1.17	1.98	1.03	1.86
Psychoticism	.64	1.59	.26	.68	.55	1.45	.64	1.53	.55	1.43

Table L-1b. Means and standard deviations for continuous extra-test characteristics (women): High scores on Harris-Lingoes subscales *(continued)*

Extra-test Characteristics	Harris-Lingoes Subscales									
	D_1		D_2		D_3		D_4		D_5	
	Mean	SD	Mean	SD	Mean	SD	Mean	SD	Mean	SD
Patient Description Form Scales	(n = 280)		(n = 118)		(n = 186)		(n = 263)		(n = 236)	
Angry Resentment	2.72	.88	2.64	.87	2.67	.88	2.76	.85	2.67	.85
Critical/Argumentative	2.36	.84	2.33	.88	2.28	.84	2.39	.82	2.32	.85
Narcissistic	2.00	.86	1.90	.79	1.92	.78	2.04	.85	1.95	.84
Defensive	2.50	.81	2.43	.84	2.45	.80	2.55	.81	2.46	.82
Histrionic	2.54	.85	2.37	.81	2.46	.78	2.56	.83	2.51	.84
Aggressive	1.81	.71	1.74	.64	1.79	.70	1.87	.71	1.80	.72
Insecure	3.17	.85	3.12	.87	3.10	.84	3.18	.85	3.16	.87
Anxious	3.00	.80	3.00	.83	3.02	.78	3.01	.79	2.95	.77
Pessimistic	2.31	.87	2.29	.88	2.29	.86	2.34	.88	2.27	.84
Depressed	2.74	.85	2.72	.86	2.76	.85	2.73	.84	2.75	.84
Achievement-Oriented	2.39	.74	2.27	.65	2.28	.70	2.42	.73	2.35	.76
Passive-Submissive	2.67	.89	2.65	.91	2.69	.91	2.68	.91	2.63	.90
Introverted	2.49	.96	2.50	.93	2.47	.95	2.49	.96	2.43	.95
Emotionally Controlled	2.38	.88	2.37	.95	2.29	.85	2.41	.89	2.30	.85
Antisocial	2.07	.78	1.98	.73	1.96	.73	2.12	.79	2.04	.79
Negative Treatment Attitudes	1.91	.71	1.84	.68	1.88	.69	1.96	.72	1.87	.67
Somatic Symptoms	2.25	1.07	2.28	1.10	2.34	1.09	2.25	1.05	2.18	1.05
Psychotic Symptoms	1.28	.55	1.20	.37	1.25	.48	1.31	.57	1.26	.50
Family Problems	3.02	1.09	2.89	1.14	2.99	1.12	3.06	1.09	3.02	1.10
Obsessive-Compulsive	2.61	.86	2.52	.88	2.56	.79	2.65	.83	2.52	.84
Stereotypic Masculine Interests	1.40	.67	1.32	.59	1.37	.70	1.43	.68	1.39	.68
Procrastinates	2.24	.90	2.19	.86	2.12	.88	2.26	.89	2.16	.88
Suspicious	2.46	.92	2.39	.83	2.39	.86	2.52	.92	2.42	.89
Agitated	2.21	.86	2.11	.77	2.19	.82	2.23	.83	2.17	.85
Work Problems	1.66	.84	1.59	.73	1.59	.82	1.67	.79	1.60	.78
Patient Description Form Items	(n = 280)		(n = 118)		(n = 186)		(n = 263)		(n = 236)	
Anxious	3.24	1.02	3.19	1.07	3.27	1.00	3.25	1.02	3.22	1.02
Problems with Authority Figures	2.73	1.23	2.61	1.23	2.67	1.26	2.78	1.21	2.63	1.23
Has Insight Into Own Problems	2.58	.90	2.72	.88	2.56	.91	2.58	.91	2.58	.88
Fears Losing Control	3.19	1.12	3.06	1.13	3.13	1.11	3.19	1.10	3.10	1.14
Extroverted	2.49	1.08	2.32	1.00	2.49	1.04	2.45	1.08	2.46	1.09
Uses Repression	2.79	1.08	2.77	1.05	2.75	1.03	2.86	1.06	2.74	1.09
Submissive	2.81	1.02	2.76	1.00	2.78	1.06	2.81	1.02	2.77	1.01

Difficulty Concentrating	2.77	1.10	2.72	1.07	2.88	1.08	2.80	1.08	2.71	1.07
Rigid	2.45	1.01	2.48	1.03	2.46	.96	2.53	1.01	2.38	.99
Overly Compliant	2.23	1.05	2.27	1.03	2.24	1.06	2.24	1.06	2.21	1.07
Whiny	2.06	1.02	2.01	1.07	1.98	.94	2.09	1.05	2.03	1.02
Feels Overwhelmed	3.53	1.04	3.42	1.09	3.47	1.03	3.51	1.07	3.49	1.05
Manipulative	2.40	1.16	2.23	1.15	2.26	1.08	2.45	1.16	2.36	1.17
Difficulty Trusting Others	3.26	1.14	3.21	1.05	3.23	1.15	3.32	1.12	3.23	1.14
Insensitive to Others	1.83	.89	1.79	.88	1.73	.82	1.86	.91	1.76	.85
Stereotypic Masculine Behavior	1.34	.67	1.25	.57	1.33	.70	1.36	.67	1.33	.67
Harbors Grudges	2.48	1.04	2.47	1.04	2.43	.98	2.54	1.03	2.48	1.05
Evasive	2.26	1.06	2.17	.97	2.15	1.01	2.32	1.06	2.23	1.08
Disoriented	1.31	.71	1.19	.59	1.30	.68	1.35	.75	1.29	.68
Energetic	2.30	.96	2.16	.82	2.21	.94	2.31	.96	2.27	.95
Lonely	2.95	1.05	2.97	1.03	2.95	1.06	2.95	1.06	2.94	1.06
Family Lacks Love	2.92	1.25	2.83	1.24	2.89	1.28	2.94	1.22	2.92	1.26
Worrier	3.46	1.01	3.44	1.06	3.41	1.01	3.46	1.00	3.43	1.02
Narcissistic	2.08	1.12	1.94	1.03	1.96	1.06	2.13	1.15	2.06	1.10
Tearful	2.47	1.16	2.30	1.12	2.47	1.19	2.49	1.17	2.51	1.19
Provocative	1.75	.97	1.68	.94	1.66	.89	1.78	.98	1.70	.97
Moralistic	2.31	.97	2.30	.94	2.34	.92	2.31	.94	2.22	.95
Socially Awkward	2.52	1.04	2.57	1.06	2.54	1.01	2.53	1.03	2.49	1.03
Hostile	2.10	1.05	2.00	1.00	2.03	1.01	2.15	1.05	2.04	1.02
Overcontrolled	2.51	1.17	2.41	1.17	2.39	1.11	2.53	1.18	2.41	1.15
Resistant to Interpretations	2.18	.98	2.12	.99	2.14	.98	2.22	.96	2.12	.94
Antisocial Behavior	1.65	.87	1.54	.77	1.61	.82	1.66	.89	1.64	.88
Sarcastic	1.88	.98	1.85	1.03	1.80	.95	1.91	.99	1.87	.99
Rejects Traditional Gender Role	1.61	.92	1.54	.85	1.57	.94	1.66	.96	1.60	.95
Feels Gets Raw Deal From Life	3.00	1.16	2.95	1.20	2.97	1.09	3.08	1.14	2.97	1.17
Acute Psychological Turmoil	3.08	1.08	3.01	.99	3.04	1.06	3.07	1.06	3.05	1.03
Does Not Complete Projects	2.25	1.12	2.12	.93	2.14	1.05	2.28	1.12	2.21	1.09
Uncomfortable with Opposite Sex	2.29	1.18	2.35	1.21	2.33	1.18	2.34	1.19	2.23	1.17
Preoccupied with Health Problems	2.16	1.33	2.26	1.35	2.32	1.36	2.15	1.28	2.06	1.28
Work-Oriented	2.63	1.12	2.61	1.05	2.49	1.08	2.64	1.09	2.57	1.11
Resents Family Members	3.02	1.22	2.87	1.26	2.99	1.24	3.05	1.23	3.01	1.22
Demanding of Attention	2.57	1.09	2.33	1.08	2.42	1.05	2.62	1.08	2.54	1.09
Passive	2.67	1.06	2.62	.98	2.71	1.06	2.66	1.07	2.62	1.06
Self-Punishing	2.80	1.15	2.75	1.07	2.73	1.14	2.85	1.14	2.78	1.16
Needs to Achieve	2.60	1.07	2.47	1.00	2.46	1.05	2.62	1.05	2.55	1.09
Needs to Be with Others	3.12	1.02	2.91	1.03	3.08	1.03	3.09	1.04	3.08	1.05
Irritable	2.64	1.06	2.60	1.03	2.60	1.02	2.68	1.04	2.60	1.03
Self-Defeating	3.13	1.06	3.10	1.04	3.05	1.03	3.17	1.04	3.11	1.08
Delusional Thinking	1.31	.77	1.18	.43	1.23	.59	1.34	.81	1.26	.70

Table L-1b. Means and standard deviations for continuous extra-test characteristics (women): High scores on Harris-Lingoes subscales *(continued)*

Extra-test Characteristics	Harris-Lingoes Subscales									
	D_1		D_2		D_3		D_4		D_5	
	Mean	SD	Mean	SD	Mean	SD	Mean	SD	Mean	SD
Self-Reliant	2.59	.87	2.66	.82	2.60	.86	2.57	.85	2.58	.88
Aggressive	1.95	.92	1.84	.87	1.90	.88	2.00	.92	1.94	.95
Competitive	2.08	.98	1.92	.89	2.00	.97	2.13	.98	2.05	1.01
Suspicious	2.39	1.10	2.33	1.03	2.32	1.03	2.46	1.11	2.37	1.09
Compulsive	2.25	1.14	2.10	1.15	2.09	1.09	2.29	1.13	2.16	1.11
Dependable	2.99	.90	2.97	.86	2.97	.86	2.93	.87	2.95	.87
Multiple Somatic Complaints	2.07	1.27	2.07	1.31	2.20	1.29	2.07	1.24	2.02	1.24
Complains of Lack of Time	2.06	1.14	1.96	1.12	2.00	1.15	2.10	1.16	1.96	1.07
Poor Work Performance	1.86	.98	1.79	.88	1.79	1.00	1.86	.96	1.84	.97
Insecure	3.57	.93	3.51	.93	3.55	.89	3.56	.94	3.55	.96
Discusses Problems Openly	3.23	.84	3.18	.79	3.23	.85	3.17	.85	3.20	.85
Sexually Adjusted	2.50	.88	2.44	.90	2.38	.85	2.45	.88	2.50	.90
Exaggerated Need for Affection	2.44	1.16	2.28	1.08	2.30	1.06	2.47	1.13	2.42	1.15
Resentful	2.99	1.09	2.95	1.08	2.91	1.08	3.03	1.07	2.97	1.07
Uses Denial	2.75	1.07	2.71	1.09	2.70	1.11	2.80	1.07	2.73	1.09
Hypochondriacal	1.73	1.04	1.79	1.14	1.76	1.04	1.76	1.04	1.69	1.04
Communicates Effectively	3.04	.89	3.03	.80	2.99	.85	3.00	.89	3.04	.87
Has Many Nightmares	2.02	1.10	2.00	1.02	2.08	1.13	2.09	1.08	2.04	1.12
Stormy Interpersonal Relationships	3.11	1.20	2.97	1.17	3.02	1.20	3.10	1.21	3.06	1.21
Feigns Remorse When in Trouble	1.84	1.01	1.75	.97	1.71	.95	1.86	1.01	1.80	1.02
Stereotypic Masculine Interests	1.45	.78	1.38	.78	1.41	.81	1.50	.81	1.44	.79
Guarded	2.49	1.15	2.47	1.17	2.42	1.10	2.54	1.15	2.47	1.14
Feels Inferior	3.30	1.07	3.27	1.08	3.26	1.08	3.30	1.09	3.31	1.07
Low Frustration Tolerance	2.86	1.06	2.77	1.07	2.89	1.04	2.93	1.04	2.85	1.07
Psychotic Symptoms	1.23	.67	1.09	.37	1.16	.47	1.27	.71	1.22	.64
Fired From Past Jobs	1.58	1.03	1.54	.94	1.56	1.00	1.61	1.01	1.51	.90
Needs Attention	3.06	1.02	2.88	1.05	2.99	.96	3.08	.99	3.05	1.01
Acts Out	2.28	1.11	2.20	1.11	2.19	1.05	2.35	1.10	2.29	1.10
Histrionic	2.22	1.17	2.14	1.13	2.10	1.10	2.27	1.17	2.20	1.15
Self-Indulgent	2.18	1.07	2.16	1.03	2.10	.98	2.23	1.05	2.19	1.09
Depressed	3.38	.98	3.39	.94	3.42	.94	3.36	.98	3.38	.96
Grandiose	1.59	.90	1.49	.79	1.54	.84	1.64	.92	1.56	.87
Cynical	2.18	1.03	2.20	1.04	2.14	1.05	2.23	1.02	2.18	1.05
Sociopathic	1.38	.69	1.30	.56	1.31	.55	1.42	.73	1.38	.70
Agitated	2.38	1.07	2.31	.97	2.37	1.03	2.40	1.05	2.36	1.07

Marital Problems	2.69	1.56	2.51	1.55	2.66	1.56	2.71	1.54	2.61	1.54
Absence of Deep Emotions	2.00	1.08	2.05	1.11	1.93	1.05	2.04	1.09	1.94	1.03
Uncomfortable Dealing with Emotions	2.87	1.11	2.86	1.16	2.80	1.12	2.93	1.10	2.82	1.10
Sad	3.13	1.02	3.16	.99	3.12	.98	3.09	1.02	3.14	1.02
Self-Degrading	2.69	1.16	2.69	1.19	2.61	1.11	2.75	1.14	2.74	1.17
Unable to Express Negative Feelings	2.30	1.12	2.28	1.19	2.23	1.07	2.30	1.11	2.23	1.10
Concrete in Thinking	2.33	1.08	2.32	1.11	2.33	1.10	2.35	1.04	2.29	1.07
Unable to See Own Limitations	2.16	1.03	2.04	.96	2.07	.95	2.19	1.03	2.10	1.00
Power-Oriented	1.84	.96	1.63	.85	1.69	.91	1.87	.98	1.81	.99
Grouchy	2.13	.99	2.07	.97	2.06	.98	2.15	.98	2.09	.99
Overbearing in Relationships	2.07	1.07	2.02	1.04	1.96	1.01	2.12	1.05	2.02	1.06
Uncertain About Career	2.92	1.31	2.79	1.33	2.86	1.28	2.91	1.33	2.89	1.34
Likable	3.29	.88	3.26	.84	3.28	.86	3.24	.84	3.24	.83
Procrastinator	2.42	1.01	2.50	1.04	2.30	.96	2.43	.99	2.41	1.02
Negative Feelings Toward Opposite Sex	2.58	1.21	2.54	1.18	2.64	1.21	2.67	1.23	2.52	1.24
Defensive	2.74	1.07	2.63	1.06	2.68	1.03	2.79	1.08	2.70	1.10
Empathetic	2.66	.74	2.60	.72	2.68	.80	2.62	.74	2.63	.73
Perfectionistic	2.50	1.18	2.38	1.11	2.42	1.12	2.53	1.16	2.41	1.17
Judgmental	2.51	1.01	2.49	1.03	2.44	.97	2.57	1.01	2.47	1.01
Copes Well with Stress	1.96	.73	1.93	.70	1.95	.74	1.95	.72	1.95	.72
Moody	2.78	.99	2.83	1.02	2.76	.99	2.84	.95	2.75	.98
Selfish	1.95	.95	1.86	.89	1.88	.87	1.97	.94	1.89	.95
Gives Up Easily	2.26	1.04	2.22	1.01	2.26	1.01	2.25	1.04	2.28	1.05
Physical Symptoms in Response to Stress	2.32	1.24	2.37	1.25	2.45	1.27	2.35	1.24	2.26	1.22
Blames Family For Difficulties	2.75	1.30	2.63	1.26	2.64	1.27	2.85	1.29	2.78	1.31
Bored	2.26	1.09	2.26	1.03	2.25	1.08	2.25	1.11	2.23	1.08
Idealistic	2.39	1.02	2.29	.93	2.34	.99	2.41	.98	2.34	1.02
Difficulty Establishing Therapeutic Rapport	1.87	.96	1.81	.89	1.81	.88	1.92	.98	1.83	.93
Daydreams	1.95	.99	1.95	.96	1.95	.99	2.02	.99	1.93	.97
Concerned About Status	2.18	1.09	2.09	1.01	2.06	1.04	2.25	1.09	2.14	1.10
Creates Good First Impression	2.80	.94	2.78	.86	2.80	.97	2.78	.92	2.74	.93
Complains of Sleep Disturbance	2.80	1.25	2.79	1.27	2.91	1.26	2.80	1.19	2.78	1.20
Has Temper Tantrums	2.05	1.06	1.93	.99	2.01	1.05	2.13	1.05	2.05	1.06
Overreactive	2.78	1.10	2.66	1.09	2.71	1.11	2.83	1.05	2.76	1.10
High Aspirations	2.41	1.12	2.27	1.02	2.19	1.05	2.43	1.13	2.33	1.15
Feels Hopeless	2.84	1.16	2.80	1.13	2.81	1.12	2.83	1.16	2.88	1.13
Keeps Others at a Distance	2.88	1.11	2.93	1.12	2.82	1.08	2.96	1.11	2.88	1.10
Argumentative	2.15	1.04	2.11	1.05	2.04	1.01	2.19	1.02	2.12	1.04
Paranoid Features	1.72	1.02	1.61	.87	1.62	.89	1.76	1.04	1.67	.96
Restless	2.51	1.10	2.45	1.03	2.50	1.06	2.54	1.06	2.47	1.08
Pessimistic	2.73	1.06	2.70	1.03	2.70	1.04	2.75	1.04	2.70	1.01
Feels Like a Failure	3.05	1.10	3.01	1.06	2.96	1.12	3.07	1.09	3.06	1.10

Table L-1b. Means and standard deviations for continuous extra-test characteristics (women): High scores on Harris-Lingoes subscales *(continued)*

Extra-test Characteristics	Harris-Lingoes Subscales									
	D_1		D_2		D_3		D_4		D_5	
	Mean	SD	Mean	SD	Mean	SD	Mean	SD	Mean	SD
Hallucinations	1.11	.49	1.06	.35	1.09	.38	1.11	.49	1.10	.47
Restricted Affect	2.18	1.12	2.18	1.10	2.13	1.08	2.23	1.12	2.08	1.08
Impatient	2.56	1.04	2.57	1.00	2.48	.98	2.61	1.00	2.53	1.04
Assertive	2.12	.88	2.08	.90	2.11	.81	2.12	.88	2.09	.87
Modest	2.61	.84	2.63	.72	2.59	.82	2.58	.86	2.54	.84
Self-Doubting	3.23	1.00	3.14	1.02	3.16	.97	3.24	1.01	3.20	.98
Deceptive	1.83	.91	1.82	.83	1.73	.82	1.84	.90	1.79	.91
Feels That Life is a Strain	3.21	1.05	3.19	1.07	3.18	1.01	3.20	1.04	3.21	1.01
Physically Abusive	1.31	.64	1.29	.59	1.33	.66	1.36	.68	1.30	.65
Feels Rejected	3.23	1.10	3.17	1.07	3.19	1.12	3.24	1.10	3.25	1.10
Does Not Get Along with Coworkers	1.71	.93	1.63	.94	1.67	.89	1.73	.91	1.65	.89
Uses Projection	2.34	1.05	2.31	1.09	2.21	1.02	2.39	1.05	2.24	1.04
Complains of Fatigue	2.76	1.30	2.74	1.27	2.80	1.25	2.75	1.24	2.67	1.25
Uses Rationalization	2.62	1.03	2.60	1.07	2.55	1.04	2.69	1.02	2.56	1.03
Critical of Others	2.44	1.08	2.38	1.09	2.35	1.03	2.52	1.04	2.39	1.06
Egocentric	2.19	1.08	2.14	1.07	2.07	1.02	2.25	1.08	2.14	1.06
Overevaluates Own Worth	1.68	.95	1.57	.92	1.60	.89	1.69	.94	1.61	.91
Optimistic	2.04	.79	1.94	.74	1.99	.77	2.03	.79	2.00	.80
Psychologically Immature	2.82	1.16	2.65	1.10	2.78	1.19	2.90	1.16	2.80	1.18
Poor Judgment	2.77	1.13	2.68	1.14	2.72	1.14	2.79	1.14	2.74	1.15
Low Sex Drive	2.25	1.20	2.38	1.19	2.43	1.25	2.28	1.21	2.24	1.19
Feels Mistreated	3.19	1.15	3.14	1.14	3.19	1.14	3.24	1.11	3.14	1.13
Overly Sensitive to Criticism	3.26	1.08	3.12	1.09	3.22	1.06	3.32	1.05	3.27	1.09
Sentimental	2.68	1.02	2.58	1.00	2.61	1.01	2.62	1.03	2.66	1.04
Sexual Preoccupation	1.51	.90	1.35	.68	1.44	.83	1.55	.94	1.49	.91
Accelerated Speech	1.72	1.00	1.56	.94	1.70	.98	1.75	.98	1.68	.99
Concerns About Homosexuality	1.16	.62	1.13	.55	1.17	.66	1.17	.64	1.16	.63
Many Specific Fears	2.16	1.10	2.24	1.06	2.12	1.06	2.20	1.10	2.13	1.07
Passive in Relationships	2.92	1.11	2.92	1.13	2.98	1.09	2.93	1.13	2.89	1.10
Negative Attitudes Toward Therapy	1.65	.86	1.63	.89	1.63	.83	1.71	.88	1.62	.84
Guilt-Prone	3.12	1.14	3.05	1.10	3.03	1.14	3.14	1.16	3.11	1.15
Nervous	2.97	.99	2.94	1.04	3.01	.94	2.99	.98	2.97	.97
Obsessive	2.47	1.17	2.38	1.21	2.38	1.10	2.49	1.16	2.37	1.14
Shy	2.47	1.13	2.39	1.07	2.43	1.14	2.48	1.13	2.41	1.13
Uses Intellectualization	2.30	1.04	2.17	1.04	2.14	.97	2.34	1.03	2.22	1.05

Has Many Interests	2.24	.93	2.13	.94	2.12	.88	2.24	.93	2.23	.94
Difficulty Making Decisions	2.96	1.07	2.87	.99	2.94	1.05	3.02	1.04	2.92	1.06
Indirect Expression of Hostility	2.79	1.11	2.72	1.13	2.75	1.14	2.88	1.09	2.77	1.09
Poor Reality Testing	1.53	.91	1.46	.89	1.49	.83	1.58	.95	1.48	.86
Angry	3.03	1.17	2.95	1.14	3.02	1.18	3.08	1.15	2.99	1.15
Eccentric	1.65	.95	1.61	.96	1.59	.92	1.73	1.01	1.63	.94
Emotional Lability	2.54	1.08	2.42	.98	2.50	1.06	2.55	1.09	2.52	1.08
Dislikes Change	2.69	.94	2.68	.97	2.71	.95	2.71	.95	2.65	.96
Believes Cannot Be Helped	1.89	.89	1.87	.93	1.88	.91	1.93	.91	1.85	.88
Reliable Informant	3.29	.92	3.27	.87	3.25	.93	3.25	.91	3.27	.91
Ignores Problems	2.40	1.04	2.27	1.05	2.36	1.03	2.44	1.05	2.36	1.03
Ruminates	2.92	1.02	2.88	1.06	2.91	.99	2.95	1.00	2.88	.98
Excitable	2.61	1.02	2.43	.97	2.62	1.00	2.64	1.01	2.58	1.03
Conforming	2.63	.95	2.67	.95	2.64	.90	2.60	.97	2.57	.94
Ineffective at Dealing with Problems	3.08	1.00	2.98	.99	3.08	.98	3.12	1.00	3.02	1.01
Introverted	2.43	1.08	2.52	1.02	2.39	1.06	2.44	1.09	2.38	1.05
Superficial Relationships	2.72	1.07	2.66	1.10	2.67	1.07	2.81	1.07	2.66	1.10
Impulsive	2.68	1.18	2.53	1.12	2.60	1.20	2.74	1.17	2.67	1.20
Stereotypic Feminine Behavior	2.79	1.17	2.75	1.20	2.75	1.15	2.76	1.18	2.76	1.22
Stubborn	2.71	1.00	2.60	1.00	2.67	1.02	2.73	.98	2.66	1.01
Hostile Toward Therapist	1.33	.67	1.30	.67	1.32	.65	1.37	.69	1.29	.62
Difficult to Motivate	2.15	1.05	2.07	.98	2.10	.99	2.20	1.06	2.11	1.05
Suicidal Ideations	1.81	.99	1.88	1.05	1.82	1.03	1.84	.99	1.84	1.02
Familial Discord	3.37	1.23	3.16	1.29	3.33	1.28	3.38	1.22	3.36	1.23
Dogmatic	2.01	.94	2.03	1.03	2.02	.95	2.05	.96	1.95	.93

Harris-Lingoes Subscales *(continued)*

Extra-test Characteristics	Hy_2 Mean	Hy_2 SD	Hy_3 Mean	Hy_3 SD	Hy_4 Mean	Hy_4 SD	Pd_1 Mean	Pd_1 SD	Pd_2 Mean	Pd_2 SD	Pd_4 Mean	Pd_4 SD	Pd_5 Mean	Pd_5 SD	Pa_1 Mean	Pa_1 SD
Intake Information	(n = 20)		(n = 424)		(n = 305)		(n = 286)		(n = 154)		(n = 369)		(n = 372)		(n = 295)	
Axis IV diagnosis	3.15	.93	3.07	.99	3.05	1.01	2.98	.94	3.03	1.00	2.98	.96	3.04	.97	3.02	.99
Axis V - Current Level of Functioning	64.10	8.42	60.57	9.98	60.23	10.04	61.60	9.46	60.89	9.77	61.23	9.69	60.38	9.94	60.69	9.96
Number of Arrests	.37	.76	.40	1.10	.37	.83	.45	1.23	.97	2.40	.47	1.28	.51	1.65	.46	1.27
Mental Status	(n = 20)		(n = 424)		(n = 305)		(n = 286)		(n = 154)		(n = 369)		(n = 372)		(n = 295)	
Anxiety During Interview	2.30	.73	2.43	.70	2.44	.71	2.38	.67	2.40	.75	2.40	.67	2.46	.71	2.41	.70
Depression During Interview	2.20	.70	2.57	.72	2.60	.73	2.45	.71	2.41	.75	2.52	.71	2.58	.73	2.54	.73
Activity Level During Interview	2.85	.37	2.97	.38	2.98	.41	2.95	.37	2.96	.38	2.95	.38	2.97	.38	2.94	.41
Speech During Interview	2.95	.39	2.97	.41	2.97	.42	2.97	.42	2.99	.43	2.96	.40	2.97	.40	2.97	.43
SCL-90-R Scales	(n = 20)		(n = 422)		(n = 304)		(n = 284)		(n = 153)		(n = 367)		(n = 370)		(n = 293)	
Somatization	.41	.55	1.51	.84	1.79	.77	1.41	.86	1.15	.83	1.44	.84	1.49	.84	1.49	.90
Obsessive-Compulsive	.67	.65	1.81	.86	1.96	.86	1.70	.92	1.43	.87	1.80	.88	1.84	.85	1.84	.92
Interpersonal Sensitivity	.56	.55	1.77	.86	1.83	.86	1.76	.92	1.38	.85	1.86	.84	1.87	.83	1.90	.88
Depression	.93	.78	2.28	.79	2.34	.81	2.17	.90	1.80	.97	2.28	.82	2.34	.80	2.28	.87
Anxiety	.49	.64	1.68	.91	1.84	.92	1.57	.96	1.36	.90	1.66	.91	1.70	.90	1.72	.96
Hostility	.28	.36	1.53	.98	1.56	1.00	1.55	1.03	1.20	.95	1.59	1.00	1.60	.96	1.64	1.02
Phobic Anxiety	.11	.32	1.02	.94	1.19	.97	.97	.93	.73	.82	1.02	.93	1.07	.94	1.12	.99
Paranoid Ideation	.33	.38	1.63	.92	1.71	.96	1.68	.95	1.35	.88	1.77	.88	1.72	.91	1.93	.91
Psychoticism	.26	.28	1.14	.72	1.24	.74	1.12	.75	.85	.62	1.18	.72	1.19	.71	1.27	.75
Initial SCL-90 Analogue	(n = 16)		(n = 287)		(n = 204)		(n = 188)		(n = 104)		(n = 248)		(n = 246)		(n = 195)	
Somatization	2.00	2.39	2.50	2.69	2.85	2.78	2.20	2.63	2.12	2.52	2.26	2.51	2.30	2.67	2.21	2.58
Obsessive-Compulsive	3.06	2.26	2.57	2.51	2.59	2.47	2.56	2.52	2.91	2.62	2.51	2.49	2.72	2.61	2.38	2.53
Interpersonal Sensitivity	4.87	2.92	5.01	2.58	4.99	2.58	4.88	2.66	4.85	2.82	4.87	2.68	5.07	2.65	4.85	2.67
Depression	4.44	3.71	4.82	2.51	4.84	2.56	4.49	2.57	4.62	2.58	4.73	2.53	4.86	2.56	4.61	2.57
Anxiety	5.13	2.70	4.47	2.67	4.56	2.70	4.29	2.66	4.57	2.59	4.43	2.68	4.42	2.77	4.33	2.73
Hostility	4.31	2.75	2.87	2.60	2.94	2.58	3.00	2.69	3.55	2.81	3.04	2.60	2.92	2.58	2.90	2.61
Phobic Anxiety	1.25	2.21	1.16	2.11	1.21	2.07	1.13	2.03	1.44	2.32	1.17	2.11	1.19	2.07	1.15	2.15
Paranoid Ideation	1.88	2.31	1.11	1.91	1.15	1.99	1.19	2.02	1.66	2.45	1.19	2.03	1.14	1.87	1.19	2.00
Psychoticism	1.00	1.86	.63	1.61	.61	1.47	.65	1.64	1.02	2.31	.71	1.73	.71	1.73	.67	1.60
Patient Description Form Scales	(n = 16)		(n = 286)		(n = 203)		(n = 189)		(n = 104)		(n = 247)		(n = 246)		(n = 195)	
Angry Resentment	2.98	1.07	2.72	.85	2.71	.90	2.79	.86	2.83	.87	2.74	.85	2.72	.87	2.75	.84
Critical/Argumentative	2.37	.87	2.34	.84	2.31	.85	2.42	.85	2.45	.89	2.39	.86	2.39	.85	2.34	.86

Narcissistic	2.01	.88	1.99	.85	1.92	.78	2.09	.87	2.18	.87	2.03	.85	2.02	.86	2.06	.89
Defensive	2.38	.80	2.50	.80	2.47	.83	2.54	.81	2.68	.81	2.52	.82	2.49	.81	2.54	.84
Histrionic	2.44	.89	2.51	.84	2.51	.79	2.59	.86	2.55	.85	2.50	.85	2.55	.85	2.48	.89
Aggressive	1.57	.62	1.81	.72	1.80	.73	1.90	.74	1.96	.83	1.85	.74	1.85	.72	1.84	.75
Insecure	2.76	1.04	3.13	.84	3.14	.86	3.12	.86	3.19	.93	3.12	.87	3.19	.88	3.05	.86
Anxious	2.83	1.03	2.97	.78	3.05	.79	2.92	.80	2.92	.88	2.91	.76	2.95	.79	2.90	.78
Pessimistic	1.87	.88	2.29	.87	2.33	.90	2.23	.87	2.33	.92	2.27	.87	2.30	.88	2.26	.84
Depressed	2.37	1.05	2.71	.82	2.76	.84	2.59	.87	2.64	.89	2.64	.84	2.72	.89	2.63	.85
Achievement-Oriented	2.99	.93	2.40	.72	2.32	.67	2.42	.77	2.50	.68	2.41	.74	2.42	.74	2.30	.74
Passive-Submissive	2.62	.97	2.68	.88	2.68	.91	2.64	.91	2.53	.93	2.63	.93	2.62	.92	2.64	.92
Introverted	2.22	.98	2.44	.95	2.48	.98	2.44	.94	2.39	.97	2.43	.94	2.42	.97	2.42	.95
Emotionally Controlled	2.22	.97	2.34	.85	2.34	.86	2.35	.87	2.49	.93	2.36	.87	2.33	.90	2.28	.86
Antisocial	1.85	.68	2.06	.78	1.97	.72	2.16	.81	2.38	.88	2.13	.82	2.13	.82	2.12	.87
Negative Treatment Attitudes	1.84	.73	1.91	.71	1.93	.72	1.93	.70	1.94	.63	1.93	.71	1.89	.66	1.94	.73
Somatic Symptoms	1.83	.82	2.22	1.06	2.37	1.10	2.11	1.06	1.98	.90	2.11	.98	2.13	1.04	2.15	1.03
Psychotic Symptoms	1.17	.38	1.25	.50	1.26	.48	1.28	.55	1.42	.81	1.28	.54	1.30	.56	1.28	.52
Family Problems	2.95	1.19	3.04	1.09	3.02	1.10	3.26	1.03	3.28	1.14	3.09	1.07	3.09	1.10	3.07	1.10
Obsessive-Compulsive	2.77	.97	2.56	.81	2.56	.81	2.54	.84	2.68	.96	2.55	.85	2.60	.87	2.47	.84
Stereotypic Masculine Interests	1.28	.58	1.38	.65	1.39	.69	1.37	.63	1.55	.84	1.39	.65	1.42	.71	1.35	.63
Procrastinates	2.36	.94	2.16	.88	2.18	.88	2.17	.91	2.36	1.04	2.20	.86	2.27	.91	2.11	.80
Suspicious	2.46	.86	2.45	.88	2.46	.92	2.49	.90	2.70	.98	2.48	.89	2.48	.89	2.46	.89
Agitated	2.19	.85	2.17	.85	2.19	.82	2.18	.90	2.26	.89	2.15	.84	2.19	.87	2.17	.85
Work Problems	1.24	.30	1.62	.82	1.48	.66	1.66	.90	1.55	.77	1.63	.81	1.69	.82	1.57	.78
Patient Description Form Items	(n = 16)		(n = 286)		(n = 203)		(n = 189)		(n = 104)		(n = 247)		(n = 246)		(n = 195)	
Anxious	2.94	1.12	3.21	1.01	3.28	.98	3.21	.98	3.23	1.03	3.16	.96	3.21	1.00	3.15	.99
Problems with Authority Figures	3.20	1.32	2.71	1.23	2.65	1.25	2.81	1.22	2.96	1.22	2.76	1.24	2.75	1.21	2.74	1.23
Has Insight Into Own Problems	3.00	.97	2.55	.89	2.52	.92	2.59	.89	2.63	.87	2.52	.86	2.61	.89	2.39	.76
Fears Losing Control	2.94	1.34	3.14	1.09	3.16	1.09	3.12	1.10	3.37	1.02	3.10	1.11	3.17	1.07	3.03	1.11
Extroverted	2.69	.95	2.53	1.06	2.47	1.02	2.57	1.10	2.65	1.07	2.53	1.09	2.49	1.09	2.43	1.08
Uses Repression	3.00	1.11	2.83	1.05	2.78	1.07	2.83	1.02	3.03	1.06	2.77	1.07	2.80	1.07	2.74	1.07
Submissive	2.75	1.06	2.84	1.02	2.81	1.04	2.77	1.06	2.66	1.07	2.78	1.04	2.76	1.05	2.82	1.03
Difficulty Concentrating	2.67	1.35	2.76	1.08	2.88	1.10	2.68	1.14	2.74	1.14	2.69	1.07	2.75	1.10	2.76	1.10
Rigid	2.67	.90	2.47	1.00	2.46	1.01	2.42	.98	2.47	1.06	2.43	1.00	2.42	.98	2.41	1.02
Overly Compliant	2.06	.93	2.25	1.04	2.21	1.06	2.20	1.09	2.16	1.04	2.21	1.05	2.21	1.06	2.26	1.06
Whiny	1.93	.96	2.04	1.01	2.07	1.00	2.11	1.08	1.97	1.05	2.01	1.01	2.01	1.05	2.10	1.07
Feels Overwhelmed	3.38	1.41	3.50	.99	3.51	1.03	3.42	1.07	3.34	1.18	3.43	1.02	3.46	1.05	3.38	1.03
Manipulative	2.33	.98	2.39	1.15	2.32	1.10	2.49	1.16	2.57	1.19	2.40	1.19	2.43	1.19	2.43	1.24
Difficulty Trusting Others	3.13	.96	3.25	1.12	3.26	1.13	3.33	1.08	3.45	1.10	3.30	1.10	3.29	1.11	3.21	1.17
Insensitive to Others	2.07	1.03	1.81	.89	1.74	.81	1.86	.89	1.94	.93	1.83	.90	1.80	.90	1.81	.88
Stereotypic Masculine Behavior	1.25	.58	1.32	.64	1.33	.68	1.30	.61	1.45	.82	1.33	.66	1.35	.72	1.31	.66
Harbors Grudges	2.38	.96	2.51	1.02	2.47	1.04	2.63	1.04	2.73	1.07	2.54	1.04	2.50	1.05	2.51	1.02

Extra-test Characteristics	Hy_2 Mean	Hy_2 SD	Hy_3 Mean	Hy_3 SD	Hy_4 Mean	Hy_4 SD	Pd_1 Mean	Pd_1 SD	Pd_2 Mean	Pd_2 SD	Pd_4 Mean	Pd_4 SD	Pd_5 Mean	Pd_5 SD	Pa_1 Mean	Pa_1 SD
	Harris-Lingoes Subscales *(continued)*															
Evasive	2.31	1.14	2.27	1.06	2.23	1.06	2.32	1.09	2.48	1.08	2.28	1.08	2.27	1.06	2.30	1.11
Disoriented	1.19	.54	1.28	.66	1.33	.71	1.34	.74	1.42	.88	1.29	.67	1.33	.73	1.31	.64
Energetic	2.81	1.11	2.34	.96	2.25	.90	2.40	.97	2.59	.90	2.36	.95	2.34	.96	2.26	.91
Lonely	2.87	1.19	2.98	1.03	3.04	1.05	2.87	1.06	2.97	1.08	2.91	1.06	2.93	1.10	2.95	1.05
Family Lacks Love	2.38	1.20	2.89	1.26	2.91	1.28	3.13	1.23	3.13	1.33	2.97	1.26	2.98	1.26	2.92	1.22
Worrier	2.88	.89	3.43	1.00	3.50	.99	3.42	.99	3.22	1.09	3.37	.99	3.41	.99	3.31	1.03
Narcissistic	2.25	1.29	2.10	1.13	1.95	1.00	2.24	1.16	2.31	1.17	2.15	1.13	2.11	1.13	2.17	1.16
Tearful	2.50	1.46	2.44	1.16	2.48	1.18	2.35	1.17	2.38	1.20	2.35	1.16	2.46	1.19	2.43	1.20
Provocative	1.88	1.09	1.72	.93	1.69	.93	1.71	.94	1.91	1.15	1.76	.98	1.76	.99	1.73	.98
Moralistic	3.13	.81	2.33	.95	2.32	.95	2.27	.90	2.27	1.01	2.23	.93	2.17	.90	2.22	.90
Socially Awkward	2.13	1.02	2.46	1.02	2.54	1.05	2.51	1.01	2.47	1.06	2.49	1.03	2.48	1.06	2.46	1.02
Hostile	2.37	1.45	2.10	1.05	2.11	1.05	2.22	1.09	2.34	1.15	2.18	1.09	2.17	1.07	2.11	1.05
Overcontrolled	2.69	1.01	2.47	1.16	2.43	1.14	2.42	1.13	2.48	1.24	2.45	1.17	2.39	1.17	2.33	1.15
Resistant to Interpretations	2.13	.81	2.18	.99	2.19	.96	2.19	.98	2.23	.93	2.17	.98	2.15	.95	2.15	1.02
Antisocial Behavior	1.56	.81	1.67	.90	1.62	.87	1.78	.95	2.04	1.07	1.74	.95	1.75	.97	1.75	.97
Sarcastic	1.69	.79	1.87	.97	1.85	.99	1.91	1.02	2.00	1.07	1.93	1.04	1.96	1.03	1.85	1.03
Rejects Traditional Gender Role	1.56	.63	1.61	.94	1.58	.92	1.67	.99	1.85	1.12	1.64	.98	1.67	.98	1.58	.96
Feels Gets Raw Deal From Life	2.75	1.34	3.00	1.13	2.98	1.15	3.02	1.14	2.99	1.14	3.01	1.12	2.99	1.14	3.04	1.12
Acute Psychological Turmoil	2.50	1.41	3.07	1.03	3.11	1.07	2.97	1.09	3.06	1.16	3.01	1.05	3.10	1.06	3.01	1.07
Does Not Complete Projects	2.00	1.04	2.19	1.08	2.20	1.11	2.23	1.18	2.56	1.23	2.20	1.08	2.34	1.16	2.14	1.06
Uncomfortable with Opposite Sex	1.93	1.07	2.23	1.17	2.30	1.18	2.22	1.15	2.37	1.31	2.26	1.21	2.27	1.19	2.25	1.21
Preoccupied with Health Problems	1.56	1.09	2.15	1.30	2.33	1.35	2.03	1.24	1.83	1.12	1.98	1.16	2.01	1.23	2.05	1.25
Work-Oriented	3.19	1.22	2.68	1.10	2.63	1.07	2.65	1.13	2.69	1.06	2.65	1.09	2.64	1.10	2.47	1.13
Resents Family Members	3.00	1.46	3.05	1.22	3.03	1.25	3.26	1.17	3.31	1.26	3.07	1.21	3.08	1.23	3.07	1.24
Demanding of Attention	2.56	1.09	2.54	1.11	2.46	1.05	2.71	1.13	2.61	1.14	2.57	1.08	2.61	1.10	2.52	1.12
Passive	2.69	1.01	2.66	1.05	2.69	1.05	2.59	1.09	2.46	1.08	2.59	1.06	2.57	1.09	2.62	1.07
Self-Punishing	2.44	1.15	2.76	1.13	2.81	1.16	2.65	1.12	2.80	1.20	2.70	1.14	2.81	1.13	2.60	1.13
Needs to Achieve	3.25	1.24	2.61	1.05	2.52	1.01	2.57	1.06	2.68	1.01	2.56	1.06	2.64	1.06	2.44	1.05
Needs to Be with Others	2.93	1.10	3.10	1.01	3.07	1.03	3.15	1.00	3.24	.99	3.08	1.04	3.10	1.05	3.02	1.07
Irritable	2.69	1.14	2.61	1.04	2.63	1.05	2.68	1.01	2.75	1.08	2.63	1.06	2.66	1.04	2.60	1.04
Self-Defeating	3.00	1.21	3.13	1.05	3.06	1.08	3.12	1.03	3.40	1.11	3.13	1.06	3.18	1.05	3.05	1.06
Delusional Thinking	1.19	.40	1.27	.71	1.28	.70	1.32	.79	1.41	.99	1.32	.79	1.32	.78	1.35	.82
Self-Reliant	3.13	.83	2.63	.88	2.60	.88	2.55	.91	2.62	.95	2.62	.88	2.59	.87	2.54	.92
Aggressive	2.13	1.09	1.96	.92	1.98	.95	2.07	.95	2.25	1.12	2.05	1.00	2.02	.95	2.03	.96
Competitive	2.53	1.06	2.10	1.00	2.03	.95	2.14	.99	2.30	1.00	2.16	.99	2.14	.99	2.06	.99
Suspicious	2.19	1.05	2.40	1.06	2.43	1.12	2.45	1.10	2.68	1.18	2.41	1.08	2.40	1.11	2.41	1.06
Compulsive	2.64	1.34	2.21	1.11	2.18	1.09	2.21	1.13	2.51	1.26	2.20	1.11	2.26	1.12	2.12	1.13

Dependable	3.33	.98	2.99	.90	2.95	.93	2.95	.94	2.87	.87	2.96	.85	2.96	.87	2.93	.87
Multiple Somatic Complaints	1.69	1.01	2.05	1.24	2.23	1.31	1.93	1.18	1.77	1.00	1.95	1.15	1.94	1.19	2.01	1.21
Complains of Lack of Time	2.37	1.36	2.01	1.13	2.03	1.12	2.01	1.12	1.96	1.17	2.07	1.11	2.05	1.11	1.96	1.05
Poor Work Performance	1.50	.94	1.81	.98	1.74	.91	1.87	1.06	1.76	.91	1.82	.97	1.81	.96	1.81	.98
Insecure	3.19	1.11	3.52	.92	3.58	.91	3.53	.91	3.59	.93	3.53	.93	3.57	.98	3.46	.94
Discusses Problems Openly	3.25	.93	3.24	.86	3.17	.87	3.20	.82	3.31	.84	3.20	.83	3.20	.84	3.12	.86
Sexually Adjusted	2.82	.75	2.44	.88	2.46	.89	2.45	.88	2.46	.87	2.46	.89	2.47	.88	2.35	.89
Exaggerated Need for Affection	2.50	1.16	2.46	1.16	2.38	1.12	2.52	1.21	2.51	1.17	2.43	1.16	2.49	1.19	2.33	1.17
Resentful	3.13	1.54	2.99	1.07	2.97	1.09	3.06	1.05	3.17	1.02	2.98	1.08	2.99	1.08	3.02	1.06
Uses Denial	2.63	1.09	2.77	1.10	2.71	1.08	2.80	1.08	3.01	1.15	2.78	1.12	2.73	1.08	2.79	1.15
Hypochondriacal	1.38	.81	1.70	1.02	1.83	1.08	1.68	1.04	1.64	.96	1.66	.93	1.68	1.02	1.66	.93
Communicates Effectively	3.50	.73	3.05	.88	2.95	.85	3.12	.90	3.08	.93	3.00	.83	3.07	.87	2.91	.84
Has Many Nightmares	1.56	.88	2.01	1.08	2.09	1.12	1.87	1.06	2.35	1.17	1.95	1.08	1.99	1.11	2.02	1.12
Stormy Interpersonal Relationships	3.00	1.20	3.11	1.21	3.06	1.24	3.20	1.15	3.26	1.15	3.17	1.15	3.16	1.19	3.08	1.16
Feigns Remorse When in Trouble	1.54	.78	1.81	1.00	1.65	.91	1.87	1.01	1.94	1.09	1.85	1.00	1.83	1.00	1.92	1.06
Stereotypic Masculine Interests	1.31	.60	1.44	.76	1.43	.80	1.43	.78	1.63	.97	1.44	.77	1.48	.83	1.39	.73
Guarded	2.56	1.21	2.47	1.13	2.44	1.12	2.56	1.11	2.62	1.09	2.47	1.11	2.48	1.14	2.47	1.11
Feels Inferior	2.73	1.28	3.26	1.09	3.28	1.10	3.27	1.11	3.24	1.15	3.26	1.10	3.31	1.12	3.17	1.11
Low Frustration Tolerance	2.31	.87	2.86	1.03	2.88	1.06	2.94	1.06	3.12	1.07	2.88	1.04	2.89	1.07	2.86	1.04
Psychotic Symptoms	1.07	.26	1.21	.65	1.22	.63	1.24	.67	1.34	.93	1.25	.71	1.25	.69	1.26	.71
Fired From Past Jobs	1.00	.00	1.61	1.02	1.49	.92	1.74	1.11	1.76	1.11	1.64	1.04	1.63	1.04	1.53	.95
Needs Attention	2.81	1.28	3.04	1.01	3.04	.93	3.14	.96	3.06	1.04	2.96	1.01	3.08	.99	2.92	1.03
Acts Out	1.81	1.05	2.28	1.09	2.20	1.00	2.39	1.13	2.66	1.15	2.35	1.11	2.34	1.13	2.34	1.10
Histrionic	1.88	.89	2.19	1.15	2.17	1.10	2.32	1.22	2.33	1.19	2.19	1.17	2.26	1.21	2.21	1.24
Self-Indulgent	2.38	1.26	2.18	1.07	2.07	.95	2.32	1.06	2.51	1.06	2.25	1.07	2.24	1.06	2.27	1.09
Depressed	2.94	1.48	3.35	.96	3.38	.99	3.18	1.03	3.27	1.13	3.30	1.00	3.35	1.04	3.24	.97
Grandiose	1.50	.73	1.61	.92	1.57	.89	1.68	.93	1.77	.99	1.62	.93	1.61	.92	1.67	.95
Cynical	2.19	1.05	2.18	1.02	2.19	1.04	2.24	1.05	2.41	1.18	2.23	1.09	2.28	1.06	2.15	1.06
Sociopathic	1.25	.45	1.39	.69	1.34	.62	1.45	.72	1.64	.96	1.44	.76	1.42	.75	1.48	.81
Agitated	2.25	1.24	2.33	1.05	2.45	1.05	2.39	1.08	2.47	1.11	2.34	1.04	2.39	1.07	2.34	1.06
Marital Problems	2.87	1.89	2.73	1.56	2.71	1.55	2.60	1.53	2.47	1.63	2.73	1.53	2.60	1.55	2.63	1.55
Absence of Deep Emotions	1.88	1.09	1.99	1.07	1.95	1.09	2.09	1.10	2.25	1.20	2.05	1.10	1.99	1.09	2.00	1.07
Uncomfortable Dealing with Emotions	2.44	1.03	2.85	1.11	2.84	1.11	2.85	1.09	3.00	1.12	2.85	1.12	2.84	1.13	2.76	1.10
Sad	2.94	1.29	3.12	.98	3.14	.99	2.99	1.05	3.10	1.15	3.03	1.00	3.10	1.06	3.03	1.03
Self-Degrading	2.19	.91	2.64	1.15	2.62	1.12	2.56	1.17	2.73	1.21	2.64	1.15	2.74	1.17	2.55	1.08
Unable to Express Negative Feelings	2.06	1.34	2.24	1.10	2.28	1.13	2.25	1.10	2.37	1.25	2.23	1.09	2.25	1.13	2.14	1.07
Concrete in Thinking	1.75	.68	2.30	1.04	2.37	1.12	2.36	1.12	2.45	1.09	2.33	1.10	2.30	1.06	2.36	1.10
Unable to See Own Limitations	2.19	1.11	2.15	1.03	2.12	1.01	2.18	1.02	2.30	1.07	2.19	1.01	2.17	1.04	2.26	1.04
Power-Oriented	2.07	1.03	1.82	.95	1.74	.91	1.81	.95	1.97	.97	1.85	.96	1.87	.97	1.76	.90
Grouchy	2.06	1.06	2.12	.99	2.16	1.01	2.17	.98	2.21	.98	2.09	.99	2.14	.99	2.08	.99
Overbearing in Relationships	1.69	.85	2.07	1.07	2.01	1.04	2.11	1.07	2.06	1.08	2.08	1.06	2.07	1.05	2.06	1.05
Uncertain About Career	2.12	1.41	2.91	1.29	2.91	1.30	2.91	1.31	3.08	1.37	2.98	1.29	3.04	1.32	2.95	1.30

Extra-test Characteristics	Hy_2 Mean	Hy_2 SD	Hy_3 Mean	Hy_3 SD	Hy_4 Mean	Hy_4 SD	Pd_1 Mean	Pd_1 SD	Pd_2 Mean	Pd_2 SD	Pd_4 Mean	Pd_4 SD	Pd_5 Mean	Pd_5 SD	Pa_1 Mean	Pa_1 SD
	Harris-Lingoes Subscales *(continued)*															
Likable	3.56	.81	3.28	.86	3.26	.84	3.29	.88	3.35	.82	3.24	.84	3.31	.86	3.16	.85
Procrastinator	2.60	1.40	2.36	.99	2.36	.97	2.35	.99	2.63	1.17	2.39	1.00	2.50	1.03	2.31	.95
Negative Feelings Toward Opposite Sex	2.54	1.45	2.56	1.22	2.57	1.24	2.58	1.16	2.80	1.29	2.63	1.23	2.60	1.24	2.63	1.26
Defensive	2.81	1.17	2.74	1.08	2.68	1.10	2.81	1.09	2.91	1.16	2.77	1.07	2.73	1.10	2.77	1.06
Empathetic	3.25	.86	2.64	.75	2.67	.76	2.64	.76	2.63	.80	2.61	.73	2.64	.74	2.57	.75
Perfectionistic	2.71	1.27	2.47	1.13	2.38	1.09	2.47	1.17	2.51	1.20	2.48	1.17	2.52	1.16	2.33	1.09
Judgmental	2.69	.87	2.52	1.01	2.46	.98	2.49	1.02	2.64	.97	2.51	1.00	2.53	1.01	2.42	.96
Copes Well with Stress	2.62	.72	2.00	.73	1.94	.72	2.02	.74	1.94	.73	2.03	.75	2.00	.77	1.98	.76
Moody	2.33	.90	2.78	1.00	2.79	1.00	2.85	.97	2.92	1.02	2.75	.98	2.83	1.02	2.72	1.00
Selfish	2.07	.92	1.94	.94	1.88	.89	2.02	.95	2.14	1.02	1.97	.94	1.97	.95	1.98	.99
Gives Up Easily	1.92	.76	2.24	1.03	2.30	1.03	2.24	1.05	2.35	1.11	2.26	1.02	2.28	1.05	2.28	1.02
Physical Symptoms in Response to Stress	2.12	1.36	2.32	1.24	2.50	1.28	2.20	1.24	2.05	1.11	2.20	1.16	2.23	1.23	2.22	1.21
Blames Family For Difficulties	2.56	1.15	2.77	1.27	2.73	1.27	2.98	1.31	3.01	1.31	2.83	1.27	2.83	1.32	2.83	1.32
Bored	2.00	1.21	2.23	1.10	2.28	1.11	2.22	1.14	2.32	1.09	2.29	1.11	2.30	1.11	2.32	1.10
Idealistic	2.69	.95	2.42	1.00	2.35	.96	2.39	1.05	2.43	1.07	2.34	1.03	2.38	1.04	2.34	1.03
Difficulty Establishing Therapeutic Rapport	1.63	.81	1.85	.94	1.88	.95	1.89	.96	1.87	.96	1.88	.94	1.82	.90	1.90	.94
Daydreams	2.09	1.45	1.93	.98	1.96	.99	1.93	.96	2.19	1.09	1.88	.92	1.97	.98	1.93	.96
Concerned About Status	2.85	1.28	2.13	1.06	2.06	1.02	2.15	1.07	2.18	1.13	2.18	1.10	2.25	1.10	2.12	1.08
Creates Good First Impression	3.31	.79	2.82	.93	2.74	.96	2.88	.98	2.85	.91	2.78	.94	2.81	.94	2.66	.97
Complains of Sleep Disturbance	2.47	1.60	2.79	1.24	2.85	1.25	2.57	1.27	2.73	1.27	2.65	1.22	2.73	1.26	2.63	1.21
Has Temper Tantrums	1.71	.83	2.05	1.07	2.06	1.11	2.21	1.08	2.21	1.17	2.11	1.05	2.12	1.08	2.11	1.06
Overreactive	2.44	.89	2.79	1.11	2.79	1.08	2.83	1.10	2.87	1.17	2.74	1.10	2.82	1.10	2.73	1.11
High Aspirations	2.94	1.24	2.40	1.09	2.27	1.04	2.37	1.17	2.51	1.00	2.34	1.10	2.45	1.15	2.21	1.08
Feels Hopeless	2.06	1.12	2.81	1.16	2.85	1.15	2.64	1.21	2.75	1.21	2.74	1.15	2.81	1.20	2.74	1.13
Keeps Others at a Distance	2.50	1.03	2.85	1.11	2.86	1.14	2.86	1.08	3.07	1.18	2.89	1.11	2.89	1.14	2.83	1.13
Argumentative	2.25	1.13	2.14	1.03	2.12	1.04	2.28	1.07	2.23	1.06	2.22	1.05	2.17	1.04	2.20	1.06
Paranoid Features	2.06	1.00	1.68	.96	1.70	1.00	1.67	1.01	1.96	1.17	1.73	1.01	1.73	.99	1.77	1.00
Restless	2.64	1.08	2.47	1.08	2.47	1.02	2.43	1.12	2.59	1.12	2.44	1.08	2.50	1.11	2.41	1.06
Pessimistic	2.19	1.22	2.71	1.06	2.75	1.09	2.65	1.05	2.77	1.07	2.67	1.04	2.74	1.06	2.64	1.03
Feels Like a Failure	2.50	1.10	3.01	1.11	3.03	1.13	2.96	1.06	2.99	1.10	2.98	1.11	3.08	1.14	2.93	1.09
Hallucinations	1.07	.26	1.10	.47	1.10	.42	1.10	.44	1.28	.85	1.10	.48	1.13	.54	1.11	.49
Restricted Affect	2.06	1.24	2.15	1.10	2.17	1.09	2.11	1.14	2.24	1.16	2.19	1.11	2.17	1.13	2.14	1.11
Impatient	2.75	1.06	2.54	1.03	2.55	1.02	2.64	1.01	2.69	1.07	2.58	1.01	2.61	1.03	2.54	1.01
Assertive	2.75	1.13	2.16	.88	2.07	.81	2.18	.84	2.27	.87	2.15	.87	2.12	.89	2.11	.87
Modest	2.60	.74	2.61	.83	2.58	.86	2.61	.84	2.48	.80	2.52	.79	2.57	.84	2.49	.81
Self-Doubting	2.94	1.18	3.19	1.00	3.22	1.02	3.17	.99	3.18	1.16	3.15	1.03	3.26	1.02	3.10	.97
Deceptive	1.67	.82	1.83	.91	1.75	.83	1.93	.99	2.03	1.00	1.88	.94	1.84	.95	1.91	.97

Feels That Life is a Strain	2.63	1.02	3.18	1.02	3.21	1.04	3.12	1.04	3.11	1.07	3.13	1.01	3.17	1.05	3.15	.97
Physically Abusive	1.13	.35	1.31	.65	1.31	.63	1.37	.71	1.45	.81	1.34	.67	1.31	.64	1.33	.69
Feels Rejected	3.00	1.26	3.22	1.07	3.22	1.11	3.24	1.10	3.33	1.13	3.25	1.10	3.27	1.11	3.18	1.09
Does Not Get Along with Coworkers	1.36	.67	1.67	.89	1.61	.88	1.57	.89	1.71	.91	1.71	.91	1.71	.88	1.69	.90
Uses Projection	2.27	.96	2.31	1.05	2.26	1.04	2.36	1.06	2.60	1.04	2.42	1.10	2.36	1.09	2.42	1.10
Complains of Fatigue	2.38	1.09	2.72	1.29	2.83	1.30	2.53	1.29	2.50	1.24	2.62	1.23	2.66	1.27	2.59	1.26
Uses Rationalization	2.63	1.26	2.68	1.04	2.60	1.06	2.72	1.07	2.85	1.11	2.68	1.07	2.68	1.08	2.62	1.08
Critical of Others	2.44	1.15	2.44	1.06	2.35	1.04	2.50	1.04	2.58	1.06	2.49	1.04	2.46	1.05	2.49	1.04
Egocentric	2.13	1.02	2.18	1.06	2.10	1.04	2.31	1.10	2.39	1.12	2.22	1.06	2.21	1.08	2.26	1.11
Overevaluates Own Worth	1.44	.81	1.66	.95	1.60	.88	1.78	.99	1.80	1.03	1.72	.94	1.68	.93	1.76	.97
Optimistic	2.63	1.02	2.04	.81	2.01	.79	2.15	.80	1.99	.77	2.03	.79	2.01	.80	2.08	.81
Psychologically Immature	2.19	1.05	2.81	1.17	2.82	1.22	2.96	1.15	3.07	1.15	2.86	1.16	2.84	1.18	2.90	1.20
Poor Judgment	2.44	.96	2.78	1.13	2.74	1.13	2.95	1.12	3.10	1.15	2.86	1.16	2.87	1.19	2.87	1.16
Low Sex Drive	2.20	1.40	2.22	1.22	2.21	1.29	2.09	1.19	2.28	1.31	2.17	1.17	2.20	1.22	2.28	1.22
Feels Mistreated	3.73	1.22	3.25	1.10	3.21	1.12	3.28	1.11	3.27	1.16	3.22	1.10	3.23	1.11	3.29	1.05
Overly Sensitive to Criticism	3.06	1.34	3.21	1.10	3.17	1.10	3.25	1.12	3.18	1.19	3.19	1.09	3.25	1.10	3.21	1.06
Sentimental	2.80	1.21	2.65	1.02	2.59	.99	2.66	1.04	2.70	1.07	2.56	.99	2.58	1.03	2.63	1.03
Sexual Preoccupation	1.55	.93	1.52	.89	1.51	.91	1.59	.98	1.66	.97	1.58	.97	1.58	.99	1.60	1.01
Accelerated Speech	1.44	.73	1.69	.99	1.66	.94	1.72	1.00	1.72	.96	1.70	.96	1.70	.97	1.75	1.02
Concerns About Homosexuality	1.14	.53	1.14	.60	1.16	.60	1.20	.65	1.17	.67	1.19	.65	1.20	.68	1.17	.66
Many Specific Fears	1.87	1.19	2.12	1.10	2.18	1.08	2.09	1.06	2.23	1.18	2.11	1.05	2.15	1.10	2.13	1.06
Passive in Relationships	2.86	1.17	2.92	1.12	2.93	1.15	2.95	1.15	2.76	1.26	2.90	1.18	2.89	1.16	2.85	1.15
Negative Attitudes Toward Therapy	1.56	.89	1.65	.85	1.67	.88	1.67	.85	1.71	.83	1.66	.85	1.63	.81	1.73	.87
Guilt-Prone	2.88	1.36	3.08	1.14	3.09	1.17	3.01	1.18	3.09	1.22	3.00	1.14	3.10	1.16	2.97	1.16
Nervous	2.73	1.10	2.95	.98	3.02	.98	2.89	1.00	2.95	1.01	2.88	.95	2.90	1.03	2.90	.96
Obsessive	2.54	1.13	2.43	1.13	2.40	1.15	2.40	1.13	2.56	1.21	2.37	1.13	2.45	1.18	2.32	1.11
Shy	2.20	1.15	2.43	1.14	2.46	1.16	2.42	1.13	2.36	1.18	2.40	1.13	2.42	1.14	2.39	1.15
Uses Intellectualization	2.87	1.25	2.25	1.03	2.20	1.00	2.27	1.11	2.62	1.17	2.29	1.08	2.30	1.09	2.16	.98
Has Many Interests	2.80	1.32	2.24	.92	2.10	.84	2.31	.96	2.33	.92	2.20	.91	2.23	.93	2.08	.89
Difficulty Making Decisions	3.07	1.38	2.94	1.10	2.96	1.08	2.94	1.10	3.02	1.14	2.87	1.08	2.96	1.11	2.87	1.06
Indirect Expression of Hostility	3.00	1.24	2.80	1.11	2.78	1.17	2.86	1.11	3.05	1.10	2.84	1.09	2.85	1.12	2.79	1.10
Poor Reality Testing	1.40	.83	1.46	.81	1.51	.88	1.56	.92	1.73	1.12	1.56	.93	1.57	.97	1.55	.90
Angry	3.40	1.30	3.03	1.15	3.04	1.17	3.10	1.13	3.20	1.26	3.06	1.13	3.05	1.15	3.04	1.11
Eccentric	1.57	.76	1.63	.94	1.64	.96	1.70	.98	1.88	1.12	1.68	.99	1.69	1.00	1.69	1.00
Emotional Lability	2.27	1.22	2.53	1.06	2.52	1.06	2.51	1.07	2.55	1.06	2.48	1.08	2.57	1.10	2.47	1.06
Dislikes Change	2.71	1.07	2.64	.97	2.68	.99	2.62	.97	2.68	1.03	2.64	.97	2.68	1.00	2.65	.95
Believes Cannot Be Helped	1.47	.64	1.86	.90	1.91	.91	1.83	.87	1.95	1.00	1.85	.90	1.86	.91	1.87	.88
Reliable Informant	3.93	.88	3.31	.93	3.23	.93	3.24	.89	3.24	.87	3.21	.87	3.27	.90	3.18	.90
Ignores Problems	2.20	1.08	2.40	1.03	2.38	1.04	2.45	1.03	2.48	1.00	2.46	1.05	2.40	1.03	2.49	1.08
Ruminates	2.73	1.16	2.89	1.01	2.89	.99	2.77	1.01	2.85	1.06	2.80	1.02	2.87	1.03	2.75	.97
Excitable	2.47	.99	2.60	1.03	2.62	1.00	2.66	1.05	2.82	1.05	2.56	1.03	2.64	1.06	2.54	1.05
Conforming	2.87	.74	2.62	.95	2.61	.97	2.61	.97	2.40	.98	2.56	.92	2.55	.95	2.56	.94

Extra-test Characteristics	Harris-Lingoes Subscales *(continued)*															
	Hy_2		Hy_3		Hy_4		Pd_1		Pd_2		Pd_4		Pd_5		Pa_1	
	Mean	SD	Mean	SD	Mean	SD	Mean	SD	Mean	SD	Mean	SD	Mean	SD	Mean	SD
Ineffective at Dealing with Problems	2.73	.88	3.07	.99	3.09	.98	3.12	1.01	3.02	1.03	3.07	.98	3.08	1.02	3.12	1.01
Introverted	2.27	1.10	2.40	1.07	2.40	1.09	2.37	1.05	2.34	1.12	2.38	1.08	2.35	1.10	2.39	1.07
Superficial Relationships	2.47	.99	2.73	1.07	2.65	1.08	2.83	1.08	3.05	1.13	2.81	1.08	2.76	1.09	2.78	1.10
Impulsive	2.07	1.00	2.66	1.19	2.64	1.16	2.81	1.21	3.11	1.21	2.74	1.19	2.78	1.22	2.67	1.19
Stereotypic Feminine Behavior	2.93	1.28	2.83	1.17	2.78	1.13	2.87	1.16	2.66	1.15	2.69	1.20	2.71	1.17	2.65	1.21
Stubborn	2.87	1.13	2.72	.99	2.67	1.00	2.77	.99	2.77	.99	2.74	1.00	2.72	1.00	2.66	.99
Hostile Toward Therapist	1.60	.99	1.32	.65	1.34	.67	1.34	.64	1.35	.64	1.34	.67	1.30	.59	1.31	.63
Difficult to Motivate	1.87	.83	2.13	1.03	2.16	1.06	2.09	1.07	2.12	1.04	2.18	1.04	2.12	1.03	2.20	1.07
Suicidal Ideations	1.20	.41	1.77	.97	1.81	1.00	1.70	.96	1.76	.90	1.75	.98	1.86	1.05	1.76	1.01
Familial Discord	3.57	1.45	3.40	1.25	3.38	1.28	3.67	1.12	3.57	1.21	3.48	1.17	3.44	1.21	3.45	1.24
Dogmatic	2.29	.73	2.02	.95	1.99	.94	2.14	.99	2.07	.99	2.02	.96	2.03	.96	2.01	.95

Characteristics	Harris-Lingoes Subscales *(continued)*															
	Pa_2		Pa_3		Sc_1		Sc_2		Sc_3		Sc_4		Sc_5		Sc_6	
	Mean	SD	Mean	SD	Mean	SD	Mean	SD	Mean	SD	Mean	SD	Mean	SD	Mean	SD
Intake Information	(n = 332)		(n = 36)		(n = 339)		(n = 356)		(n = 344)		(n = 393)		(n = 249)		(n = 245)	
Axis IV diagnosis	3.06	.99	2.94	.87	2.98	.96	3.01	.96	3.04	1.00	3.02	.98	2.98	1.00	3.06	1.01
Axis V - Current Level of Functioning	60.54	9.57	62.71	10.40	60.89	9.70	60.50	9.74	60.24	10.00	60.43	9.80	60.29	9.79	60.00	10.38
Number of Arrests	.43	1.20	.40	.67	.49	1.35	.41	1.04	.41	1.16	.44	1.15	.51	1.30	.56	1.79
Mental Status	(n = 332)		(n = 36)		(n = 339)		(n = 356)		(n = 344)		(n = 393)		(n = 249)		(n = 245)	
Anxiety During Interview	2.45	.70	2.26	.71	2.41	.68	2.51	.72	2.48	.72	2.48	.70	2.48	.73	2.47	.73
Depression During Interview	2.56	.73	2.37	.81	2.51	.73	2.60	.73	2.59	.76	2.58	.74	2.56	.73	2.59	.72
Activity Level During Interview	2.96	.38	2.97	.30	2.95	.41	2.97	.37	2.97	.38	2.96	.38	2.97	.40	2.96	.42
Speech During Interview	2.97	.41	3.00	.34	2.96	.42	2.97	.42	2.97	.42	2.96	.42	2.97	.45	2.95	.42
SCL-90-R Scales	(n = 330)		(n = 36)		(n = 337)		(n = 354)		(n = 342)		(n = 391)		(n = 248)		(n = 244)	
Somatization	1.48	.87	.90	.89	1.47	.87	1.53	.85	1.60	.85	1.52	.85	1.59	.83	1.84	.83
Obsessive-Compulsive	1.80	.89	1.15	.90	1.81	.89	1.86	.86	2.01	.81	1.89	.84	1.95	.86	2.08	.84
Interpersonal Sensitivity	1.85	.86	1.22	1.01	1.90	.85	1.88	.85	1.86	.85	1.85	.83	1.91	.88	1.91	.87
Depression	2.32	.83	1.44	1.04	2.29	.85	2.38	.77	2.36	.79	2.32	.78	2.34	.85	2.34	.85
Anxiety	1.70	.93	1.03	.98	1.67	.94	1.74	.92	1.82	.89	1.72	.91	1.91	.91	1.97	.90
Hostility	1.57	.98	.81	.81	1.65	.99	1.59	.98	1.63	.99	1.57	.97	1.75	1.01	1.71	1.03
Phobic Anxiety	1.05	.97	.60	.90	1.07	.95	1.09	.97	1.15	.95	1.08	.94	1.27	.97	1.30	.97
Paranoid Ideation	1.73	.93	.82	.83	1.82	.90	1.70	.96	1.73	.94	1.67	.93	1.88	.92	1.86	.96
Psychoticism	1.20	.73	.58	.57	1.22	.74	1.20	.73	1.25	.70	1.18	.71	1.33	.75	1.35	.75
Initial SCL-90 Analogue	(n = 222)		(n = 27)		(n = 225)		(n = 238)		(n = 237)		(n = 265)		(n = 175)		(n = 165)	
Somatization	2.27	2.55	2.81	3.04	2.25	2.60	2.50	2.74	2.50	2.65	2.50	2.70	2.45	2.69	3.00	2.88
Obsessive-Compulsive	2.69	2.59	2.96	2.68	2.51	2.59	2.70	2.61	2.83	2.61	2.79	2.61	2.91	2.61	2.78	2.48
Interpersonal Sensitivity	5.01	2.62	4.07	2.85	4.97	2.66	5.13	2.60	5.06	2.62	5.17	2.58	5.05	2.56	5.12	2.63
Depression	4.86	2.53	4.81	3.08	4.67	2.62	4.97	2.47	4.74	2.54	4.87	2.53	4.98	2.60	4.79	2.67
Anxiety	4.50	2.68	4.78	2.75	4.32	2.72	4.65	2.68	4.58	2.66	4.56	2.68	4.65	2.65	4.75	2.64
Hostility	3.11	2.63	2.96	2.83	3.10	2.66	3.01	2.60	2.92	2.53	2.95	2.62	2.97	2.63	2.88	2.56
Phobic Anxiety	1.20	2.06	.93	1.88	1.12	2.05	1.16	2.05	1.26	2.14	1.21	2.07	1.22	2.00	1.29	2.07
Paranoid Ideation	1.16	1.96	1.19	1.96	1.23	2.06	1.11	1.95	1.27	2.06	1.21	2.02	1.24	1.87	1.17	1.85
Psychoticism	.69	1.68	1.04	2.34	.67	1.68	.65	1.62	.77	1.75	.69	1.66	.72	1.59	.64	1.43
Patient Description Form Scales	(n = 221)		(n = 27)		(n = 224)		(n = 238)		(n = 237)		(n = 265)		(n = 174)		(n = 164)	
Angry Resentment	2.75	.85	2.60	1.03	2.80	.83	2.75	.86	2.73	.87	2.72	.87	2.73	.86	2.69	.85

Harris-Lingoes Subscales *(continued)*

Characteristics	Pa_2 Mean	Pa_2 SD	Pa_3 Mean	Pa_3 SD	Sc_1 Mean	Sc_1 SD	Sc_2 Mean	Sc_2 SD	Sc_3 Mean	Sc_3 SD	Sc_4 Mean	Sc_4 SD	Sc_5 Mean	Sc_5 SD	Sc_6 Mean	Sc_6 SD
Critical/Argumentative	2.40	.87	2.10	.75	2.43	.86	2.35	.84	2.35	.83	2.35	.84	2.34	.87	2.32	.84
Narcissistic	2.02	.83	1.87	.68	2.06	.87	1.99	.84	2.04	.85	2.03	.87	2.04	.84	2.04	.83
Defensive	2.48	.79	2.30	.81	2.55	.81	2.51	.82	2.55	.84	2.53	.82	2.51	.82	2.51	.81
Histrionic	2.52	.86	2.54	.77	2.52	.87	2.50	.81	2.56	.84	2.56	.84	2.55	.85	2.55	.84
Aggressive	1.86	.73	1.73	.62	1.88	.74	1.81	.71	1.86	.73	1.83	.72	1.87	.76	1.82	.72
Insecure	3.15	.85	3.08	.99	3.11	.89	3.16	.83	3.16	.85	3.19	.85	3.15	.89	3.12	.91
Anxious	2.95	.78	2.96	.90	2.91	.80	2.99	.78	3.02	.81	2.99	.79	3.00	.81	3.05	.82
Pessimistic	2.29	.87	2.08	.93	2.32	.87	2.33	.85	2.31	.88	2.32	.88	2.28	.88	2.34	.93
Depressed	2.72	.86	2.59	1.06	2.66	.89	2.74	.84	2.72	.87	2.73	.86	2.77	.89	2.74	.91
Achievement-Oriented	2.45	.77	2.77	.73	2.36	.74	2.41	.76	2.42	.73	2.42	.72	2.37	.74	2.27	.65
Passive-Submissive	2.60	.89	2.77	.98	2.65	.95	2.66	.91	2.66	.94	2.68	.91	2.67	.96	2.64	.92
Introverted	2.41	.90	2.25	1.10	2.46	.97	2.47	.96	2.47	.98	2.47	.97	2.42	.94	2.42	.95
Emotionally Controlled	2.32	.83	2.37	1.10	2.34	.86	2.35	.87	2.41	.90	2.38	.90	2.36	.93	2.31	.88
Antisocial	2.08	.80	2.06	.62	2.18	.86	2.03	.76	2.11	.80	2.09	.79	2.11	.83	2.09	.77
Negative Treatment Attitudes	1.91	.66	1.70	.63	1.94	.69	1.94	.73	1.95	.71	1.94	.73	1.92	.69	1.93	.72
Somatic Symptoms	2.15	1.02	2.26	1.05	2.13	1.04	2.21	1.07	2.25	1.07	2.23	1.08	2.16	1.02	2.40	1.15
Psychotic Symptoms	1.29	.56	1.48	1.06	1.28	.54	1.27	.51	1.35	.63	1.30	.57	1.35	.61	1.30	.52
Family Problems	3.09	1.10	2.98	1.17	3.18	1.05	3.07	1.06	3.09	1.11	3.03	1.08	3.06	1.17	3.06	1.13
Obsessive-Compulsive	2.59	.85	2.77	.87	2.50	.86	2.57	.84	2.64	.84	2.64	.84	2.59	.85	2.56	.80
Stereotypic Masculine Interests	1.40	.67	1.37	.58	1.38	.64	1.39	.68	1.42	.69	1.42	.68	1.35	.64	1.43	.78
Procrastinates	2.21	.94	2.27	1.05	2.19	.87	2.19	.91	2.25	.91	2.25	.92	2.29	.96	2.26	.86
Suspicious	2.47	.90	2.28	1.03	2.51	.89	2.47	.91	2.51	.93	2.48	.92	2.50	.92	2.47	.92
Agitated	2.23	.86	2.18	.91	2.20	.88	2.17	.84	2.25	.85	2.17	.83	2.24	.88	2.24	.84
Work Problems	1.56	.73	1.62	.77	1.64	.83	1.59	.76	1.65	.78	1.67	.81	1.66	.86	1.69	.89
Patient Description Form Items	(n = 221)		(n = 27)		(n = 224)		(n = 238)		(n = 237)		(n = 265)		(n = 174)		(n = 164)	
Anxious	3.23	.98	3.19	.96	3.19	1.00	3.26	.98	3.27	1.02	3.26	.99	3.29	.99	3.28	1.02
Problems with Authority Figures	2.71	1.21	2.56	1.29	2.78	1.22	2.74	1.23	2.73	1.22	2.73	1.22	2.70	1.21	2.70	1.19
Has Insight Into Own Problems	2.57	.86	2.78	.80	2.46	.81	2.54	.88	2.59	.94	2.59	.89	2.57	.85	2.44	.86
Fears Losing Control	3.13	1.13	3.19	1.33	3.11	1.10	3.17	1.06	3.23	1.14	3.18	1.10	3.20	1.13	3.25	1.07
Extroverted	2.55	1.09	2.44	1.01	2.49	1.08	2.42	1.06	2.49	1.07	2.49	1.08	2.49	1.08	2.49	1.00
Uses Repression	2.78	1.07	2.81	1.17	2.80	1.05	2.83	1.05	2.80	1.09	2.83	1.08	2.77	1.08	2.78	1.04
Submissive	2.74	1.02	2.85	1.06	2.80	1.07	2.78	1.01	2.80	1.06	2.81	1.02	2.78	1.06	2.78	1.03
Difficulty Concentrating	2.75	1.08	2.65	1.35	2.71	1.13	2.77	1.09	2.79	1.12	2.75	1.10	2.85	1.12	2.93	1.09
Rigid	2.43	.97	2.48	.94	2.41	.98	2.44	.99	2.51	1.02	2.48	1.01	2.44	.96	2.45	1.00
Overly Compliant	2.18	1.05	2.12	1.18	2.24	1.06	2.25	1.02	2.23	1.08	2.26	1.06	2.21	1.08	2.23	1.07
Whiny	2.04	1.03	1.77	.71	2.06	1.04	2.02	1.03	2.11	1.06	2.06	1.05	2.08	1.03	2.16	1.07

Feels Overwhelmed	3.43	1.06	3.52	1.09	3.43	1.07	3.48	1.07	3.48	1.05	3.48	1.05	3.38	1.10	3.47	1.08
Manipulative	2.43	1.15	2.24	.97	2.46	1.19	2.41	1.17	2.40	1.17	2.44	1.19	2.45	1.18	2.42	1.12
Difficulty Trusting Others	3.27	1.11	2.85	1.10	3.32	1.10	3.29	1.15	3.29	1.13	3.26	1.13	3.27	1.15	3.25	1.14
Insensitive to Others	1.82	.89	1.73	.78	1.86	.89	1.83	.91	1.81	.86	1.83	.92	1.79	.84	1.84	.91
Stereotypic Masculine Behavior	1.33	.67	1.26	.53	1.32	.66	1.32	.66	1.33	.67	1.34	.67	1.30	.62	1.38	.76
Harbors Grudges	2.48	1.01	2.19	.90	2.61	1.02	2.54	1.03	2.51	1.07	2.50	1.06	2.52	1.02	2.44	1.00
Evasive	2.27	1.04	2.00	1.18	2.33	1.06	2.30	1.05	2.30	1.08	2.29	1.08	2.27	1.05	2.26	1.05
Disoriented	1.35	.72	1.48	1.12	1.32	.67	1.31	.69	1.38	.79	1.32	.72	1.44	.82	1.38	.75
Energetic	2.38	.99	2.48	1.09	2.34	.97	2.30	.95	2.35	.97	2.33	.96	2.38	.95	2.24	.93
Lonely	2.93	1.04	3.04	1.10	2.92	1.08	2.97	1.06	2.95	1.08	2.94	1.04	2.92	1.09	2.98	1.10
Family Lacks Love	2.95	1.27	2.72	1.28	3.01	1.21	2.91	1.22	2.93	1.27	2.90	1.23	3.02	1.29	3.01	1.30
Worrier	3.36	1.00	3.19	1.08	3.36	1.03	3.43	.98	3.50	1.02	3.46	.99	3.43	1.00	3.43	1.03
Narcissistic	2.13	1.13	1.73	.92	2.16	1.12	2.09	1.10	2.10	1.13	2.12	1.13	2.12	1.11	2.10	1.10
Tearful	2.49	1.20	2.38	1.13	2.37	1.17	2.45	1.17	2.48	1.20	2.48	1.18	2.54	1.25	2.49	1.24
Provocative	1.77	.96	1.81	.94	1.70	.95	1.70	.94	1.73	.98	1.76	.98	1.76	.96	1.70	.94
Moralistic	2.30	.95	2.46	.99	2.26	.92	2.30	.94	2.32	.99	2.31	.95	2.24	.93	2.28	.96
Socially Awkward	2.45	.99	2.07	1.24	2.55	1.05	2.49	1.04	2.50	1.04	2.52	1.04	2.52	1.02	2.53	1.04
Hostile	2.18	1.08	2.07	1.30	2.23	1.08	2.14	1.06	2.15	1.05	2.10	1.06	2.15	1.04	2.10	.99
Overcontrolled	2.48	1.10	2.69	1.26	2.41	1.14	2.47	1.17	2.50	1.18	2.52	1.19	2.43	1.18	2.37	1.13
Resistant to Interpretations	2.19	.97	1.96	.71	2.19	.98	2.21	1.01	2.21	.99	2.19	.98	2.18	1.00	2.19	.98
Antisocial Behavior	1.68	.92	1.48	.70	1.78	.99	1.68	.90	1.67	.92	1.67	.90	1.68	.95	1.65	.91
Sarcastic	1.94	1.01	1.63	.84	1.94	1.06	1.87	.95	1.87	.98	1.88	.97	1.88	1.02	1.81	.97
Rejects Traditional Gender Role	1.62	.93	1.48	.64	1.64	.98	1.61	.94	1.68	.99	1.63	.93	1.63	1.01	1.63	1.00
Feels Gets Raw Deal From Life	3.01	1.14	2.62	1.24	3.05	1.13	3.00	1.17	3.03	1.17	3.00	1.16	3.01	1.15	3.02	1.16
Acute Psychological Turmoil	3.06	1.08	3.00	1.26	3.00	1.08	3.06	1.05	3.11	1.05	3.08	1.05	3.09	1.09	3.08	1.09
Does Not Complete Projects	2.25	1.15	2.00	1.23	2.25	1.12	2.24	1.15	2.31	1.15	2.29	1.16	2.38	1.16	2.31	1.11
Uncomfortable with Opposite Sex	2.21	1.17	2.07	1.33	2.30	1.21	2.29	1.14	2.31	1.19	2.28	1.16	2.28	1.20	2.29	1.18
Preoccupied with Health Problems	2.01	1.23	2.00	1.33	2.01	1.23	2.09	1.26	2.18	1.30	2.13	1.29	2.03	1.21	2.36	1.39
Work-Oriented	2.64	1.09	3.04	.90	2.61	1.12	2.63	1.12	2.64	1.11	2.66	1.09	2.54	1.12	2.50	1.08
Resents Family Members	3.07	1.23	2.96	1.34	3.18	1.20	3.10	1.21	3.11	1.23	3.04	1.22	3.04	1.28	3.03	1.27
Demanding of Attention	2.60	1.08	2.58	1.03	2.61	1.11	2.59	1.07	2.58	1.09	2.64	1.08	2.56	1.09	2.56	1.11
Passive	2.57	1.02	2.93	1.04	2.61	1.10	2.68	1.08	2.66	1.09	2.68	1.07	2.70	1.08	2.62	1.08
Self-Punishing	2.72	1.18	2.89	1.28	2.65	1.14	2.74	1.13	2.85	1.18	2.79	1.16	2.77	1.14	2.82	1.15
Needs to Achieve	2.64	1.10	3.07	.87	2.50	1.06	2.59	1.07	2.65	1.04	2.62	1.02	2.53	1.02	2.53	1.01
Needs to Be with Others	3.15	1.04	3.31	1.26	3.08	1.03	3.07	1.06	3.14	1.02	3.15	1.02	3.11	1.06	3.06	.96
Irritable	2.66	1.07	2.37	.93	2.69	1.04	2.64	1.06	2.64	1.05	2.61	1.05	2.62	1.06	2.60	1.06
Self-Defeating	3.13	1.09	3.30	1.17	3.13	1.08	3.13	1.04	3.16	1.08	3.17	1.04	3.10	1.10	3.13	1.11
Delusional Thinking	1.31	.78	1.48	1.19	1.32	.78	1.29	.74	1.38	.87	1.34	.80	1.33	.79	1.33	.79
Self-Reliant	2.64	.89	2.88	.95	2.55	.90	2.62	.90	2.60	.89	2.56	.86	2.59	.88	2.51	.83
Aggressive	2.04	.96	1.92	1.06	2.08	.98	1.94	.91	2.01	.92	1.96	.93	1.98	.92	1.99	.93
Competitive	2.16	1.00	2.36	.95	2.12	1.02	2.12	1.04	2.09	.99	2.12	1.00	2.08	1.02	2.02	.93
Suspicious	2.42	1.09	2.27	1.15	2.45	1.09	2.42	1.10	2.47	1.15	2.42	1.10	2.48	1.12	2.39	1.10

Characteristics	Pa_2 Mean	SD	Pa_3 Mean	SD	Sc_1 Mean	SD	Sc_2 Mean	SD	Sc_3 Mean	SD	Sc_4 Mean	SD	Sc_5 Mean	SD	Sc_6 Mean	SD
	Harris-Lingoes Subscales *(continued)*															
Compulsive	2.26	1.12	2.76	1.13	2.15	1.14	2.20	1.12	2.30	1.17	2.29	1.15	2.25	1.15	2.19	1.07
Dependable	2.97	.91	3.15	.91	2.92	.89	2.98	.90	2.98	.91	2.99	.89	2.94	.84	2.87	.86
Multiple Somatic Complaints	1.96	1.19	2.08	1.38	1.98	1.22	2.03	1.23	2.08	1.24	2.07	1.25	1.98	1.18	2.28	1.34
Complains of Lack of Time	2.03	1.11	2.19	1.21	2.03	1.14	2.00	1.12	2.07	1.16	2.04	1.11	2.09	1.15	2.03	1.12
Poor Work Performance	1.79	.97	1.79	.98	1.80	.99	1.81	.95	1.86	.98	1.84	.96	1.84	.95	1.92	1.05
Insecure	3.55	.92	3.48	.98	3.51	.96	3.55	.93	3.55	.92	3.59	.92	3.57	.97	3.54	.93
Discusses Problems Openly	3.24	.85	3.48	1.09	3.17	.84	3.16	.86	3.19	.86	3.19	.86	3.21	.85	3.20	.82
Sexually Adjusted	2.50	.88	2.67	1.06	2.40	.88	2.40	.87	2.47	.87	2.48	.89	2.47	.88	2.39	.90
Exaggerated Need for Affection	2.43	1.15	2.48	1.08	2.42	1.16	2.41	1.15	2.45	1.18	2.46	1.17	2.44	1.15	2.35	1.14
Resentful	3.03	1.07	3.04	1.15	3.05	1.04	3.04	1.07	3.00	1.08	3.00	1.07	2.98	1.10	2.91	1.04
Uses Denial	2.72	1.09	2.52	1.05	2.78	1.08	2.78	1.10	2.80	1.11	2.79	1.10	2.74	1.12	2.72	1.12
Hypochondriacal	1.67	.98	1.78	1.19	1.68	.98	1.73	1.04	1.74	1.03	1.75	1.06	1.70	1.03	1.87	1.12
Communicates Effectively	3.11	.83	3.27	.96	2.98	.83	3.04	.90	3.04	.86	3.03	.88	3.00	.86	2.95	.80
Has Many Nightmares	2.00	1.09	1.94	1.21	2.04	1.13	1.99	1.10	2.12	1.14	2.01	1.08	2.17	1.18	2.03	1.10
Stormy Interpersonal Relationships	3.13	1.19	3.32	1.35	3.18	1.13	3.09	1.17	3.12	1.22	3.10	1.19	3.11	1.21	3.14	1.22
Feigns Remorse When in Trouble	1.82	.98	1.72	1.10	1.91	1.03	1.77	1.00	1.83	1.01	1.82	1.02	1.79	1.02	1.79	1.01
Stereotypic Masculine Interests	1.46	.79	1.46	.71	1.44	.77	1.47	.81	1.49	.82	1.48	.80	1.40	.77	1.48	.90
Guarded	2.50	1.09	2.30	1.07	2.55	1.10	2.51	1.13	2.51	1.17	2.50	1.16	2.45	1.12	2.42	1.09
Feels Inferior	3.23	1.07	3.22	1.09	3.25	1.12	3.34	1.08	3.27	1.08	3.33	1.09	3.25	1.10	3.22	1.18
Low Frustration Tolerance	2.89	1.07	2.67	1.04	2.92	1.06	2.86	1.05	2.91	1.07	2.89	1.06	2.98	1.06	2.95	1.04
Psychotic Symptoms	1.25	.71	1.31	.97	1.23	.68	1.23	.65	1.29	.75	1.25	.69	1.23	.63	1.23	.62
Fired From Past Jobs	1.50	.92	1.44	1.04	1.63	1.04	1.57	.99	1.57	.98	1.62	1.03	1.59	1.01	1.62	1.07
Needs Attention	3.06	1.03	3.04	1.09	3.03	1.01	3.06	1.00	3.11	1.00	3.11	.99	3.08	1.00	3.04	.97
Acts Out	2.34	1.12	2.11	.93	2.39	1.12	2.31	1.07	2.32	1.10	2.31	1.11	2.37	1.12	2.25	1.01
Histrionic	2.24	1.19	2.19	1.00	2.24	1.20	2.20	1.13	2.22	1.19	2.24	1.19	2.25	1.21	2.22	1.17
Self-Indulgent	2.18	1.04	2.26	.90	2.27	1.09	2.17	1.03	2.19	1.06	2.20	1.06	2.22	1.05	2.15	.98
Depressed	3.38	.99	3.26	1.26	3.26	1.02	3.38	.99	3.33	1.00	3.36	.98	3.36	.98	3.37	1.04
Grandiose	1.62	.92	1.70	.91	1.62	.93	1.58	.88	1.65	.93	1.62	.92	1.66	.96	1.58	.90
Cynical	2.24	1.09	2.11	1.05	2.24	1.09	2.19	1.02	2.20	1.05	2.17	1.02	2.20	1.11	2.20	1.11
Sociopathic	1.41	.71	1.26	.66	1.48	.80	1.39	.67	1.43	.75	1.41	.73	1.42	.74	1.37	.66
Agitated	2.41	1.07	2.41	1.22	2.40	1.08	2.34	1.05	2.43	1.08	2.35	1.06	2.46	1.12	2.44	1.08
Marital Problems	2.63	1.57	2.80	1.85	2.64	1.55	2.65	1.56	2.66	1.55	2.62	1.56	2.53	1.55	2.57	1.53
Absence of Deep Emotions	1.97	1.04	1.93	1.27	2.05	1.08	1.98	1.07	2.06	1.10	2.00	1.10	2.01	1.12	1.98	1.07
Uncomfortable Dealing with Emotions	2.80	1.07	2.56	1.22	2.85	1.06	2.89	1.06	2.91	1.07	2.87	1.09	2.91	1.09	2.87	1.07
Sad	3.11	1.01	3.04	1.37	3.02	1.05	3.14	1.01	3.12	1.04	3.11	1.03	3.13	1.01	3.08	1.05
Self-Degrading	2.65	1.19	2.63	1.31	2.62	1.16	2.64	1.13	2.69	1.15	2.71	1.16	2.72	1.15	2.64	1.16
Unable to Express Negative Feelings	2.19	1.07	2.33	1.30	2.21	1.10	2.28	1.09	2.32	1.14	2.27	1.11	2.27	1.16	2.19	1.12

Concrete in Thinking	2.26	1.08	2.04	1.06	2.41	1.09	2.31	1.06	2.37	1.07	2.34	1.08	2.34	1.05	2.41	1.10
Unable to See Own Limitations	2.14	1.02	1.96	.90	2.22	1.02	2.13	1.02	2.22	1.06	2.18	1.04	2.19	.98	2.19	1.01
Power-Oriented	1.92	1.02	2.04	1.00	1.80	.94	1.81	.96	1.86	.98	1.84	.97	1.85	.96	1.81	.97
Grouchy	2.16	1.01	1.74	.86	2.18	.99	2.16	.99	2.14	.99	2.11	.97	2.10	.95	2.11	.98
Overbearing in Relationships	2.11	1.07	1.91	.95	2.12	1.07	2.02	1.04	2.09	1.04	2.07	1.06	2.05	1.04	2.05	1.02
Uncertain About Career	2.93	1.33	2.52	1.37	2.99	1.33	2.93	1.32	3.00	1.34	2.95	1.34	3.00	1.37	2.97	1.29
Likable	3.30	.85	3.54	.76	3.21	.87	3.28	.87	3.28	.87	3.27	.85	3.27	.84	3.20	.82
Procrastinator	2.36	1.01	2.46	1.22	2.38	.99	2.39	1.01	2.45	.99	2.44	1.02	2.44	1.04	2.44	.97
Negative Feelings Toward Opposite Sex	2.61	1.21	2.52	1.37	2.68	1.24	2.59	1.19	2.67	1.25	2.58	1.22	2.65	1.23	2.60	1.23
Defensive	2.71	1.08	2.48	.94	2.78	1.06	2.73	1.08	2.76	1.10	2.73	1.08	2.71	1.08	2.70	1.08
Empathetic	2.64	.75	2.89	.80	2.58	.75	2.64	.74	2.65	.77	2.63	.74	2.62	.74	2.59	.74
Perfectionistic	2.45	1.15	2.92	1.14	2.39	1.17	2.50	1.14	2.50	1.15	2.55	1.15	2.45	1.15	2.34	1.05
Judgmental	2.51	.99	2.44	.85	2.50	.97	2.49	.98	2.55	1.02	2.52	1.01	2.51	.99	2.52	.96
Copes Well with Stress	2.01	.74	2.22	.75	1.96	.74	1.98	.76	1.95	.72	1.99	.75	1.96	.75	1.92	.73
Moody	2.77	1.00	2.59	.97	2.81	.98	2.79	1.01	2.84	.99	2.80	.98	2.83	1.05	2.81	.98
Selfish	1.94	.91	1.72	.89	2.01	.97	1.91	.93	1.97	.94	1.99	.97	1.94	.93	1.96	.95
Gives Up Easily	2.25	1.04	2.13	1.01	2.32	1.03	2.24	1.04	2.29	1.06	2.26	1.06	2.32	1.06	2.33	1.07
Physical Symptoms in Response to Stress	2.27	1.21	2.30	1.27	2.24	1.22	2.30	1.27	2.35	1.25	2.34	1.27	2.19	1.21	2.46	1.31
Blames Family For Difficulties	2.83	1.31	2.59	1.28	2.93	1.28	2.82	1.28	2.84	1.32	2.79	1.31	2.73	1.35	2.71	1.31
Bored	2.24	1.05	1.88	.88	2.30	1.12	2.27	1.13	2.24	1.10	2.24	1.12	2.31	1.08	2.27	1.11
Idealistic	2.42	1.04	2.70	.95	2.29	1.00	2.40	1.02	2.45	1.04	2.45	1.02	2.45	1.01	2.33	.95
Difficulty Establishing Therapeutic Rapport	1.82	.89	1.48	.70	1.90	.93	1.89	.99	1.89	.96	1.89	.99	1.87	.91	1.86	.93
Daydreams	1.88	.94	2.35	1.50	1.89	.95	1.97	.98	2.03	1.02	2.01	1.01	2.03	1.03	2.03	1.05
Concerned About Status	2.17	1.09	2.40	1.22	2.10	1.06	2.16	1.06	2.21	1.10	2.22	1.08	2.22	1.13	2.10	1.06
Creates Good First Impression	2.83	.96	3.30	.87	2.74	.94	2.79	.96	2.78	.95	2.81	.93	2.73	.91	2.72	.91
Complains of Sleep Disturbance	2.76	1.23	2.59	1.50	2.70	1.28	2.81	1.23	2.79	1.23	2.77	1.24	2.82	1.23	2.81	1.24
Has Temper Tantrums	2.12	1.10	1.88	1.01	2.15	1.05	2.06	1.05	2.10	1.08	2.07	1.05	2.14	1.09	2.08	1.07
Overreactive	2.77	1.09	2.54	1.21	2.81	1.10	2.77	1.05	2.82	1.11	2.81	1.09	2.80	1.08	2.83	1.11
High Aspirations	2.43	1.16	2.96	1.00	2.30	1.10	2.39	1.13	2.40	1.12	2.41	1.12	2.30	1.12	2.23	1.03
Feels Hopeless	2.79	1.20	2.37	1.21	2.79	1.19	2.86	1.14	2.81	1.17	2.82	1.19	2.78	1.19	2.80	1.24
Keeps Others at a Distance	2.89	1.10	2.74	1.13	2.93	1.12	2.95	1.13	2.93	1.13	2.90	1.13	2.91	1.14	2.80	1.11
Argumentative	2.22	1.03	1.77	.95	2.28	1.05	2.17	1.03	2.14	1.01	2.14	1.03	2.08	1.05	2.11	1.01
Paranoid Features	1.70	1.00	1.69	1.19	1.76	1.02	1.72	.99	1.76	1.04	1.75	1.03	1.76	1.00	1.76	1.03
Restless	2.51	1.09	2.46	1.27	2.45	1.12	2.46	1.07	2.57	1.10	2.47	1.08	2.55	1.08	2.58	1.06
Pessimistic	2.73	1.07	2.50	1.27	2.73	1.03	2.76	1.02	2.73	1.05	2.74	1.06	2.68	1.06	2.77	1.15
Feels Like a Failure	3.03	1.09	2.69	1.12	2.99	1.10	3.06	1.09	3.04	1.10	3.09	1.10	2.96	1.12	3.04	1.18
Hallucinations	1.12	.50	1.31	.97	1.11	.50	1.12	.46	1.15	.58	1.13	.51	1.13	.51	1.11	.43
Restricted Affect	2.11	1.08	2.19	1.30	2.16	1.15	2.15	1.12	2.25	1.14	2.19	1.13	2.18	1.15	2.14	1.09
Impatient	2.59	1.04	2.41	1.12	2.57	.99	2.51	1.01	2.61	1.01	2.56	1.03	2.59	1.01	2.65	1.05
Assertive	2.20	.90	2.11	.97	2.13	.85	2.12	.89	2.09	.86	2.11	.86	2.15	.84	2.08	.81
Modest	2.53	.77	2.62	.85	2.53	.82	2.61	.85	2.60	.87	2.62	.84	2.53	.85	2.51	.85
Self-Doubting	3.20	.94	3.19	1.14	3.15	1.02	3.22	.97	3.25	1.01	3.24	1.00	3.20	.99	3.22	1.00

Characteristics	Pa_2 Mean	Pa_2 SD	Pa_3 Mean	Pa_3 SD	Sc_1 Mean	Sc_1 SD	Sc_2 Mean	Sc_2 SD	Sc_3 Mean	Sc_3 SD	Sc_4 Mean	Sc_4 SD	Sc_5 Mean	Sc_5 SD	Sc_6 Mean	Sc_6 SD
	Harris-Lingoes Subscales *(continued)*															
Deceptive	1.87	.89	1.69	.68	1.92	.96	1.82	.91	1.82	.92	1.84	.92	1.86	.94	1.81	.90
Feels That Life is a Strain	3.18	1.05	2.96	1.19	3.17	1.05	3.21	1.05	3.17	1.05	3.17	1.05	3.12	1.03	3.18	1.08
Physically Abusive	1.33	.67	1.32	.75	1.34	.68	1.30	.64	1.35	.68	1.33	.66	1.36	.70	1.29	.65
Feels Rejected	3.28	1.13	3.12	1.34	3.24	1.10	3.24	1.08	3.22	1.09	3.24	1.09	3.27	1.11	3.15	1.13
Does Not Get Along with Coworkers	1.61	.84	1.72	.89	1.73	.91	1.67	.90	1.72	.89	1.73	.92	1.79	.96	1.73	.97
Uses Projection	2.36	1.07	2.27	1.04	2.43	1.07	2.35	1.05	2.38	1.06	2.36	1.06	2.30	1.08	2.31	1.07
Complains of Fatigue	2.67	1.26	2.92	1.09	2.62	1.26	2.70	1.29	2.71	1.29	2.70	1.29	2.67	1.23	2.81	1.31
Uses Rationalization	2.64	1.10	2.70	1.03	2.66	1.06	2.63	1.08	2.63	1.06	2.66	1.04	2.62	1.13	2.66	1.11
Critical of Others	2.50	1.05	2.15	.88	2.52	1.03	2.43	1.04	2.47	1.05	2.48	1.06	2.43	1.01	2.44	1.04
Egocentric	2.23	1.04	1.88	.91	2.29	1.08	2.18	1.06	2.27	1.09	2.25	1.09	2.22	1.04	2.25	1.04
Overevaluates Own Worth	1.68	.90	1.46	.86	1.74	.96	1.61	.88	1.74	.95	1.67	.94	1.71	.91	1.69	.90
Optimistic	2.03	.78	2.44	.97	2.01	.76	1.97	.78	2.06	.80	2.04	.79	2.09	.81	2.03	.79
Psychologically Immature	2.83	1.18	2.54	1.10	2.90	1.19	2.83	1.16	2.91	1.18	2.89	1.17	2.87	1.18	2.92	1.19
Poor Judgment	2.82	1.17	2.74	.94	2.92	1.17	2.78	1.16	2.83	1.17	2.80	1.14	2.86	1.16	2.83	1.10
Low Sex Drive	2.16	1.21	2.21	1.18	2.28	1.22	2.28	1.23	2.30	1.23	2.20	1.21	2.23	1.22	2.18	1.28
Feels Mistreated	3.22	1.13	3.12	1.28	3.28	1.07	3.22	1.07	3.19	1.12	3.19	1.12	3.17	1.13	3.27	1.09
Overly Sensitive to Criticism	3.25	1.07	3.12	1.45	3.23	1.07	3.23	1.10	3.28	1.09	3.31	1.10	3.31	1.06	3.26	1.08
Sentimental	2.68	1.05	2.88	1.30	2.59	1.02	2.61	1.02	2.65	1.05	2.65	1.03	2.64	1.05	2.68	1.01
Sexual Preoccupation	1.55	.94	1.57	.75	1.59	.98	1.51	.87	1.57	.97	1.56	.95	1.62	1.02	1.60	1.04
Accelerated Speech	1.77	1.01	1.59	.93	1.75	1.03	1.70	.98	1.74	.98	1.69	.97	1.72	.98	1.72	.98
Concerns About Homosexuality	1.15	.61	1.09	.42	1.20	.67	1.17	.65	1.18	.63	1.18	.65	1.16	.59	1.17	.65
Many Specific Fears	2.11	1.08	2.00	1.19	2.10	1.05	2.20	1.09	2.22	1.12	2.15	1.08	2.21	1.10	2.19	1.08
Passive in Relationships	2.90	1.13	2.92	1.28	2.93	1.19	2.90	1.15	2.91	1.15	2.93	1.13	2.91	1.18	2.85	1.17
Negative Attitudes Toward Therapy	1.61	.81	1.44	.85	1.71	.83	1.68	.87	1.69	.86	1.69	.88	1.65	.82	1.67	.85
Guilt-Prone	3.06	1.14	3.00	1.30	2.97	1.17	3.13	1.12	3.11	1.19	3.11	1.15	3.05	1.13	3.08	1.17
Nervous	3.00	.96	3.04	1.04	2.90	.99	3.03	.94	3.00	.99	3.00	.97	3.02	.98	3.07	.99
Obsessive	2.44	1.18	2.76	1.27	2.34	1.15	2.41	1.15	2.47	1.17	2.46	1.15	2.46	1.12	2.42	1.13
Shy	2.38	1.08	2.27	1.22	2.41	1.15	2.47	1.11	2.44	1.16	2.47	1.14	2.39	1.11	2.38	1.13
Uses Intellectualization	2.29	1.06	2.65	1.23	2.21	1.07	2.25	1.04	2.30	1.03	2.31	1.04	2.28	1.06	2.19	.99
Has Many Interests	2.27	.94	2.75	1.03	2.20	.91	2.22	.92	2.26	.93	2.27	.94	2.22	.93	2.07	.87
Difficulty Making Decisions	2.92	1.06	3.12	1.17	2.90	1.10	2.93	1.06	3.00	1.07	3.01	1.07	2.99	1.08	2.97	1.05
Indirect Expression of Hostility	2.87	1.14	2.92	1.38	2.88	1.09	2.80	1.11	2.83	1.14	2.81	1.12	2.81	1.15	2.81	1.16
Poor Reality Testing	1.56	.97	1.72	1.31	1.56	.93	1.50	.86	1.65	1.02	1.56	.94	1.69	1.07	1.57	.92
Angry	3.08	1.15	2.92	1.44	3.15	1.13	3.02	1.13	3.05	1.16	3.03	1.16	3.05	1.22	2.99	1.18
Eccentric	1.71	1.03	1.79	1.06	1.71	1.01	1.68	.96	1.77	1.04	1.72	1.01	1.78	1.07	1.72	1.07
Emotional Lability	2.52	1.11	2.31	1.05	2.49	1.07	2.48	1.05	2.55	1.09	2.53	1.10	2.54	1.09	2.51	1.09
Dislikes Change	2.62	.97	2.63	.92	2.64	.96	2.66	.96	2.76	.96	2.70	.96	2.71	.99	2.69	.97

Believes Cannot Be Helped	1.84	.88	1.69	1.09	1.91	.92	1.90	.91	1.89	.91	1.89	.91	1.86	.90	1.91	.91
Reliable Informant	3.30	.88	3.58	.90	3.18	.87	3.26	.92	3.25	.93	3.25	.91	3.26	.87	3.22	.89
Ignores Problems	2.41	1.01	2.16	.85	2.43	1.05	2.44	1.07	2.44	1.06	2.43	1.05	2.41	1.06	2.37	1.03
Ruminates	2.85	.99	2.73	1.00	2.75	1.03	2.90	1.02	2.90	.98	2.92	1.00	2.88	.96	2.85	.97
Excitable	2.60	1.04	2.77	.99	2.59	1.06	2.57	1.01	2.66	1.00	2.61	1.02	2.65	1.02	2.67	1.00
Conforming	2.61	.92	2.65	1.09	2.60	.97	2.63	.96	2.62	.99	2.62	.96	2.58	.95	2.57	.92
Ineffective at Dealing with Problems	3.05	1.01	3.00	.94	3.13	1.00	3.11	1.00	3.09	1.01	3.10	1.01	3.08	1.02	3.09	1.02
Introverted	2.39	1.01	2.36	1.11	2.40	1.09	2.44	1.08	2.43	1.09	2.42	1.09	2.34	1.05	2.32	1.03
Superficial Relationships	2.73	1.09	2.54	.88	2.80	1.08	2.75	1.11	2.76	1.10	2.73	1.10	2.80	1.08	2.73	1.06
Impulsive	2.70	1.21	2.88	1.07	2.75	1.21	2.64	1.17	2.75	1.20	2.70	1.19	2.79	1.24	2.76	1.17
Stereotypic Feminine Behavior	2.80	1.15	2.85	1.22	2.73	1.18	2.76	1.16	2.76	1.20	2.79	1.16	2.68	1.20	2.66	1.14
Stubborn	2.74	1.01	2.32	.99	2.76	.99	2.70	.99	2.73	.97	2.72	.97	2.66	1.02	2.67	1.00
Hostile Toward Therapist	1.33	.63	1.27	.72	1.33	.64	1.34	.67	1.37	.66	1.35	.68	1.34	.63	1.36	.66
Difficult to Motivate	2.16	1.00	1.73	.92	2.22	1.05	2.15	1.04	2.19	1.07	2.16	1.07	2.16	1.06	2.17	1.09
Suicidal Ideations	1.82	1.01	1.81	.98	1.81	1.04	1.84	1.02	1.82	1.03	1.83	1.02	1.91	1.10	1.82	1.01
Familial Discord	3.46	1.22	3.19	1.50	3.55	1.16	3.42	1.21	3.43	1.25	3.36	1.23	3.40	1.27	3.43	1.25
Dogmatic	2.09	.97	1.92	.95	2.04	.97	1.99	.92	2.04	.96	2.05	.96	2.06	.96	2.06	.95

	Harris-Lingoes Subscales *(continued)*							
	Ma_1		Ma_2		Ma_3		Ma_4	
	Mean	SD	Mean	SD	Mean	SD	Mean	SD
Intake Information	(n = 42)		(n = 97)		(n = 31)		(n = 118)	
Axis IV diagnosis	3.05	.90	2.97	.90	2.90	.98	3.00	1.00
Axis V - Current Level of Functioning	60.24	9.05	61.19	9.39	67.07	12.50	61.50	9.41
Number of Arrests	1.21	2.54	.51	1.50	1.26	4.19	.62	1.43
Mental Status	(n = 42)		(n = 97)		(n = 31)		(n = 118)	
Anxiety During Interview	2.29	.74	2.45	.65	1.96	.51	2.41	.67
Depression During Interview	2.33	.69	2.56	.70	1.96	.64	2.45	.66
Activity Level During Interview	2.86	.47	2.98	.39	2.93	.26	2.99	.40
Speech During Interview	2.90	.48	2.98	.46	2.97	.33	3.01	.40
SCL-90-R Scales	(n = 42)		(n = 96)		(n = 30)		(n = 118)	
Somatization	1.16	.79	1.46	.81	.47	.46	1.38	.87
Obsessive-Compulsive	1.55	.83	1.80	.84	.62	.67	1.70	.84
Interpersonal Sensitivity	1.42	.80	1.75	.90	.55	.66	1.88	.78
Depression	1.86	.84	2.06	.85	.76	.80	2.12	.80
Anxiety	1.39	.87	1.77	.90	.41	.51	1.60	.93
Hostility	1.42	.95	1.70	1.08	.43	.56	1.61	1.05
Phobic Anxiety	.86	.90	1.09	.93	.18	.32	1.00	.93
Paranoid Ideation	1.48	.91	1.88	.90	.60	.80	1.92	.87
Psychoticism	.97	.71	1.19	.80	.32	.49	1.24	.75
Initial SCL-90 Analogue	(n = 27)		(n = 65)		(n = 21)		(n = 83)	
Somatization	2.52	3.09	2.29	2.76	1.90	2.72	2.55	2.56
Obsessive-Compulsive	3.52	3.42	2.92	2.46	2.29	2.59	2.89	2.65
Interpersonal Sensitivity	4.93	2.85	4.88	2.88	3.38	2.91	5.01	2.67
Depression	3.74	2.46	4.54	2.72	2.43	2.52	4.72	2.55
Anxiety	4.04	2.59	4.43	2.69	2.86	2.01	4.42	2.74
Hostility	3.52	2.62	3.02	2.67	2.29	2.53	3.43	2.70
Phobic Anxiety	1.41	2.53	1.15	1.97	.67	1.20	1.37	2.29
Paranoid Ideation	1.33	1.75	1.26	1.81	1.76	2.76	1.48	2.21
Psychoticism	1.11	2.42	.64	1.33	.67	1.74	1.04	1.98
Patient Description Form Scales	(n = 27)		(n = 66)		(n = 21)		(n = 83)	
Angry Resentment	2.90	.87	2.84	.77	2.35	.86	2.90	.85
Critical/Argumentative	2.52	.93	2.49	.87	2.32	.83	2.51	.87

Narcissistic	2.28	1.00	2.25	.90	2.24	.73	2.30	.95
Defensive	2.81	.79	2.60	.81	2.60	.91	2.70	.83
Histrionic	2.51	.87	2.71	.92	2.08	.70	2.74	.93
Aggressive	2.10	.87	1.95	.76	2.03	.84	1.98	.78
Insecure	3.02	.91	3.20	.89	2.23	.90	3.20	.83
Anxious	2.87	.77	2.97	.80	2.17	.57	2.95	.80
Pessimistic	2.22	.95	2.30	.93	1.92	.82	2.33	.81
Depressed	2.39	.89	2.62	.83	1.70	.75	2.67	.76
Achievement-Oriented	2.74	.77	2.58	.80	2.67	.89	2.38	.81
Passive-Submissive	2.66	.85	2.54	.93	1.78	.87	2.72	.93
Introverted	2.37	.93	2.38	1.03	1.68	.75	2.49	.93
Emotionally Controlled	2.51	.89	2.42	1.01	2.18	.84	2.42	.93
Antisocial	2.31	.88	2.25	.84	2.30	.87	2.32	.89
Negative Treatment Attitudes	2.07	.67	1.99	.69	2.14	.75	2.08	.74
Somatic Symptoms	2.14	1.15	2.29	1.14	1.84	1.02	2.25	.98
Psychotic Symptoms	1.46	.81	1.31	.58	1.37	.90	1.43	.69
Family Problems	3.32	.90	3.15	1.14	2.62	1.12	3.19	1.08
Obsessive-Compulsive	2.70	.95	2.74	.77	2.16	.73	2.67	.82
Stereotypic Masculine Interests	1.54	.82	1.54	.79	2.00	1.18	1.40	.61
Procrastinates	2.27	.94	2.44	.85	2.24	.96	2.30	.84
Suspicious	2.79	.90	2.62	.95	2.32	1.06	2.60	.98
Agitated	2.21	.82	2.33	.89	1.84	.74	2.30	.93
Work Problems	1.39	.44	1.90	1.03	1.33	.44	1.74	.87
Patient Description Form Items	(n = 27)		(n = 66)		(n = 21)		(n = 83)	
Anxious	3.15	.95	3.27	.95	2.29	.72	3.17	1.11
Problems with Authority Figures	3.22	1.15	3.02	1.15	2.95	1.19	2.89	1.21
Has Insight Into Own Problems	2.59	.84	2.45	.91	2.38	.92	2.36	.85
Fears Losing Control	3.32	1.25	3.31	.92	3.05	.83	3.18	1.12
Extroverted	2.93	1.11	2.71	1.06	3.00	.84	2.55	1.07
Uses Repression	3.00	1.02	2.98	.94	2.60	1.19	2.93	1.13
Submissive	2.85	.97	2.67	1.05	2.10	1.04	2.90	1.07
Difficulty Concentrating	2.64	1.08	2.85	1.21	1.95	.89	2.77	1.10
Rigid	2.74	1.10	2.54	.99	2.95	1.19	2.57	1.07
Overly Compliant	2.42	1.21	2.09	1.08	1.52	.81	2.23	1.08
Whiny	1.81	1.02	2.17	1.16	1.57	.81	2.33	1.12
Feels Overwhelmed	3.38	1.02	3.48	1.00	2.57	1.12	3.41	1.08
Manipulative	2.59	1.31	2.63	1.19	2.50	.89	2.70	1.25
Difficulty Trusting Others	3.50	1.07	3.44	1.14	2.81	1.33	3.32	1.17
Insensitive to Others	2.08	.98	2.02	.96	2.50	1.10	2.01	.97
Stereotypic Masculine Behavior	1.38	.75	1.48	.82	1.90	1.22	1.35	.64
Harbors Grudges	2.65	.98	2.59	.94	2.60	1.05	2.66	1.10

	Harris-Lingoes Subscales *(continued)*							
	Ma_1		Ma_2		Ma_3		Ma_4	
	Mean	SD	Mean	SD	Mean	SD	Mean	SD
Evasive	2.85	1.13	2.45	1.14	2.48	1.25	2.47	1.15
Disoriented	1.52	.94	1.41	.78	1.29	.90	1.49	.85
Energetic	2.85	1.10	2.46	1.00	2.95	.92	2.27	.94
Lonely	2.59	1.05	2.94	1.09	1.90	1.07	2.93	1.02
Family Lacks Love	3.08	1.02	3.06	1.32	2.24	1.26	3.09	1.17
Worrier	3.19	.92	3.38	.94	2.52	1.08	3.43	.97
Narcissistic	2.41	1.25	2.35	1.14	2.52	1.12	2.52	1.25
Tearful	2.26	1.16	2.23	1.15	1.52	.98	2.43	1.12
Provocative	1.89	1.12	1.86	.96	1.86	1.06	1.89	1.05
Moralistic	2.52	1.05	2.19	.81	2.43	1.21	2.26	.96
Socially Awkward	2.33	.88	2.45	1.10	2.00	1.10	2.55	1.04
Hostile	2.59	1.12	2.32	1.07	1.95	.92	2.37	1.12
Overcontrolled	2.30	1.30	2.45	1.21	2.43	1.25	2.54	1.18
Resistant to Interpretations	2.30	.95	2.27	1.03	2.43	1.16	2.36	1.04
Antisocial Behavior	2.12	1.14	1.94	1.00	2.00	1.10	1.91	1.02
Sarcastic	2.07	1.17	2.08	1.12	1.90	.94	1.95	1.08
Rejects Traditional Gender Role	1.89	1.15	1.89	1.22	2.10	1.37	1.73	1.10
Feels Gets Raw Deal From Life	2.76	1.20	3.02	1.08	2.48	1.17	3.11	1.13
Acute Psychological Turmoil	2.81	1.27	3.06	1.12	2.19	.87	3.05	1.10
Does Not Complete Projects	2.47	1.07	2.60	1.12	2.37	1.16	2.40	1.18
Uncomfortable with Opposite Sex	1.96	1.27	2.31	1.22	1.72	1.07	2.29	1.25
Preoccupied with Health Problems	1.96	1.28	2.12	1.27	1.81	1.25	2.10	1.20
Work-Oriented	2.96	.92	2.77	1.10	2.90	1.37	2.52	1.18
Resents Family Members	3.27	1.04	3.09	1.30	2.71	1.10	3.15	1.29
Demanding of Attention	2.42	.99	2.86	1.20	2.48	1.03	2.78	1.15
Passive	2.41	1.01	2.55	1.10	1.71	1.01	2.68	1.08
Self-Punishing	2.73	1.28	2.68	1.13	2.00	.79	2.82	1.12
Needs to Achieve	2.73	.92	2.87	1.01	2.65	1.18	2.57	1.08
Needs to Be with Others	3.31	.93	3.26	.99	2.85	.88	3.21	1.01
Irritable	2.59	1.01	2.65	1.00	2.33	1.02	2.78	1.05
Self-Defeating	3.26	1.13	3.22	1.08	2.76	1.22	3.28	1.02
Delusional Thinking	1.48	.89	1.38	.91	1.48	1.08	1.43	.96
Self-Reliant	2.81	1.00	2.58	.95	2.95	.89	2.44	.96
Aggressive	2.41	1.12	2.08	.96	2.62	1.07	2.21	1.03
Competitive	2.40	1.26	2.32	1.08	2.65	1.18	2.19	1.10
Suspicious	2.81	1.11	2.55	1.14	2.19	1.21	2.60	1.14
Compulsive	2.73	1.25	2.35	1.04	1.94	1.11	2.36	1.15

Dependable	2.88	.82	2.86	.82	3.05	1.03	2.86	.88
Multiple Somatic Complaints	1.78	1.28	2.13	1.23	2.05	1.32	2.14	1.20
Complains of Lack of Time	2.22	1.15	2.11	1.07	2.29	1.35	2.15	1.10
Poor Work Performance	1.63	.68	2.04	1.04	1.75	1.00	1.83	.99
Insecure	3.48	.98	3.67	.93	2.57	1.03	3.62	.86
Discusses Problems Openly	3.11	.80	3.15	.83	2.90	1.04	3.02	.87
Sexually Adjusted	2.72	.67	2.49	.87	2.69	1.01	2.33	.80
Exaggerated Need for Affection	2.13	.99	2.56	1.20	2.16	1.21	2.58	1.21
Resentful	3.27	1.08	3.00	.94	2.62	1.02	3.20	1.05
Uses Denial	2.89	1.12	2.82	1.07	3.10	1.22	2.89	1.05
Hypochondriacal	1.74	.94	1.77	1.10	1.67	1.15	1.73	.89
Communicates Effectively	3.11	.80	3.05	.87	3.19	.98	2.88	.86
Has Many Nightmares	1.68	1.06	1.89	1.13	1.43	.76	2.02	1.15
Stormy Interpersonal Relationships	3.26	1.16	3.26	.92	3.00	1.22	3.23	1.04
Feigns Remorse When in Trouble	1.85	1.08	1.87	1.06	1.89	.90	1.94	1.03
Stereotypic Masculine Interests	1.67	.96	1.58	.83	2.10	1.22	1.44	.71
Guarded	2.85	1.29	2.59	1.10	2.48	1.12	2.59	1.02
Feels Inferior	3.00	1.14	3.15	1.19	2.35	1.23	3.40	1.07
Low Frustration Tolerance	3.08	1.04	3.00	1.02	2.52	1.12	3.11	.93
Psychotic Symptoms	1.33	.88	1.26	.73	1.30	.98	1.41	.93
Fired From Past Jobs	1.29	.61	1.77	1.31	1.42	.79	1.69	1.08
Needs Attention	3.11	.80	3.20	1.01	2.38	.86	3.21	1.00
Acts Out	2.37	.97	2.41	1.09	2.10	.97	2.58	1.08
Histrionic	2.50	1.45	2.45	1.26	1.71	.72	2.49	1.28
Self-Indulgent	2.48	1.16	2.41	1.02	2.33	1.15	2.44	1.07
Depressed	2.89	1.15	3.26	1.04	2.10	1.14	3.22	.94
Grandiose	1.81	1.04	1.74	1.06	1.80	.83	1.90	1.06
Cynical	2.56	1.28	2.34	1.26	2.00	1.05	2.32	1.15
Sociopathic	1.70	1.17	1.56	.91	1.70	.92	1.65	.83
Agitated	2.30	.99	2.38	1.10	1.65	.75	2.39	1.13
Marital Problems	2.77	1.73	2.38	1.52	2.11	1.37	2.65	1.56
Absence of Deep Emotions	2.37	1.28	2.09	1.24	1.80	1.01	2.05	1.13
Uncomfortable Dealing with Emotions	3.19	1.04	2.98	1.13	2.95	1.15	2.89	1.11
Sad	2.70	1.17	3.03	1.04	1.90	.97	3.06	.95
Self-Degrading	2.74	1.35	2.74	1.18	1.65	.67	2.77	1.04
Unable to Express Negative Feelings	2.23	1.07	2.26	1.19	1.75	1.07	2.32	1.18
Concrete in Thinking	2.52	1.22	2.30	1.05	2.05	.83	2.54	1.14
Unable to See Own Limitations	2.56	1.05	2.30	1.10	2.15	1.14	2.50	1.06
Power-Oriented	2.15	1.17	2.02	1.02	2.06	.97	2.06	.97
Grouchy	2.19	1.08	2.14	.97	1.75	.72	2.24	1.00
Overbearing in Relationships	2.12	1.18	2.26	1.15	2.17	1.04	2.22	1.08
Uncertain About Career	2.59	1.22	3.27	1.34	2.65	1.46	3.12	1.34

	Harris-Lingoes Subscales *(continued)*							
	Ma_1		Ma_2		Ma_3		Ma_4	
	Mean	SD	Mean	SD	Mean	SD	Mean	SD
Likable	3.15	.66	3.08	.95	3.10	.64	3.07	.85
Procrastinator	2.48	1.04	2.60	.97	2.40	1.50	2.49	.96
Negative Feelings Toward Opposite Sex	2.25	1.19	2.75	1.18	1.94	1.16	2.74	1.32
Defensive	3.00	1.18	2.80	1.08	2.50	1.10	2.88	1.05
Empathetic	2.58	.58	2.53	.68	2.30	.80	2.63	.76
Perfectionistic	2.68	1.41	2.76	1.16	2.41	1.23	2.51	1.09
Judgmental	2.73	1.04	2.68	.98	2.70	.92	2.63	.95
Copes Well with Stress	2.04	.76	1.97	.78	2.50	.76	1.84	.69
Moody	2.67	1.24	2.92	.98	2.42	1.02	2.84	.91
Selfish	2.24	1.13	2.13	1.02	2.00	.94	2.13	1.03
Gives Up Easily	2.38	1.01	2.43	1.14	1.89	.90	2.49	1.00
Physical Symptoms in Response to Stress	2.20	1.41	2.32	1.28	1.95	1.23	2.29	1.14
Blames Family For Difficulties	2.96	1.16	2.86	1.29	2.60	1.23	2.92	1.33
Bored	2.40	1.04	2.53	1.07	1.75	.97	2.58	1.13
Idealistic	2.62	1.10	2.57	1.00	2.25	1.16	2.43	1.05
Difficulty Establishing Therapeutic Rapport	2.07	1.04	1.97	.89	2.00	.92	1.94	.93
Daydreams	2.14	1.13	1.93	.95	1.67	.98	2.07	.96
Concerned About Status	2.42	1.27	2.47	1.31	2.33	1.28	2.38	1.06
Creates Good First Impression	2.96	.81	2.70	1.02	2.70	1.03	2.60	.97
Complains of Sleep Disturbance	2.48	1.31	2.68	1.26	1.84	1.07	2.67	1.14
Has Temper Tantrums	2.27	1.08	2.26	1.04	2.22	1.11	2.33	1.08
Overreactive	2.92	1.02	2.91	1.11	2.50	.95	2.94	1.09
High Aspirations	2.73	1.04	2.66	1.20	2.74	1.15	2.29	1.16
Feels Hopeless	2.52	1.28	2.75	1.25	1.60	.88	2.78	1.07
Keeps Others at a Distance	3.31	1.35	2.95	1.20	2.58	1.17	2.83	1.06
Argumentative	2.19	1.08	2.20	1.06	2.00	.92	2.35	1.13
Paranoid Features	2.00	1.14	1.85	1.08	1.89	1.15	1.87	1.11
Restless	2.77	1.18	2.75	1.08	2.05	.97	2.59	1.17
Pessimistic	2.62	1.06	2.77	1.14	2.00	.97	2.71	.98
Feels Like a Failure	3.00	1.18	2.97	1.13	2.05	1.03	2.92	1.08
Hallucinations	1.22	.80	1.13	.49	1.15	.67	1.16	.62
Restricted Affect	2.44	1.28	2.31	1.26	1.90	1.07	2.25	1.15
Impatient	2.88	.97	2.87	1.01	2.55	1.00	2.69	1.03
Assertive	2.07	.87	2.32	1.00	2.75	.85	2.06	.87
Modest	2.46	.86	2.51	.90	2.32	.95	2.38	.88
Self-Doubting	3.19	1.08	3.27	1.03	2.26	1.05	3.22	.96
Deceptive	2.27	1.08	1.90	.95	2.00	.91	2.01	.93

Feels That Life is a Strain	2.93	1.04	3.06	.97	2.16	.96	3.14	.95
Physically Abusive	1.42	.90	1.34	.70	1.33	.77	1.38	.73
Feels Rejected	3.00	1.13	3.35	1.11	2.40	1.31	3.29	1.13
Does Not Get Along with Coworkers	1.47	.74	1.98	1.00	1.57	.85	1.86	.97
Uses Projection	2.58	1.17	2.45	1.13	2.45	1.10	2.56	1.05
Complains of Fatigue	2.73	1.22	2.71	1.36	1.75	.85	2.73	1.18
Uses Rationalization	3.12	1.18	2.65	1.16	2.70	1.03	2.72	1.09
Critical of Others	2.62	1.20	2.53	1.01	2.60	.94	2.67	1.00
Egocentric	2.41	1.15	2.48	1.11	2.55	.83	2.46	1.14
Overevaluates Own Worth	1.89	1.05	1.92	1.07	1.89	.81	1.91	1.02
Optimistic	2.30	.78	2.15	.79	2.30	.98	2.11	.80
Psychologically Immature	3.07	.96	3.02	1.14	2.80	1.44	3.14	1.23
Poor Judgment	2.81	.98	2.88	1.09	2.95	1.28	3.05	1.24
Low Sex Drive	2.23	1.24	2.14	1.16	1.69	1.03	2.16	1.13
Feels Mistreated	3.15	1.03	3.28	1.00	2.63	1.30	3.20	1.17
Overly Sensitive to Criticism	3.35	1.06	3.47	1.07	2.47	1.31	3.43	1.03
Sentimental	2.48	.96	2.64	1.01	2.18	1.13	2.77	.97
Sexual Preoccupation	1.70	1.08	1.84	1.20	1.88	1.17	1.79	1.15
Accelerated Speech	1.52	.85	1.80	.96	1.75	.91	1.88	1.04
Concerns About Homosexuality	1.21	.72	1.34	.87	1.11	.46	1.19	.64
Many Specific Fears	1.96	.98	2.02	1.11	1.65	.88	2.17	1.10
Passive in Relationships	2.68	1.22	2.78	1.18	1.68	1.06	2.96	1.17
Negative Attitudes Toward Therapy	1.73	.87	1.68	.83	1.95	.89	1.72	.81
Guilt-Prone	3.11	1.25	3.09	1.11	2.26	1.19	2.96	1.15
Nervous	2.78	.85	3.08	.98	2.05	.76	3.00	.94
Obsessive	2.81	1.41	2.67	1.10	1.94	1.00	2.58	1.13
Shy	2.44	1.15	2.37	1.18	1.45	.51	2.43	1.17
Uses Intellectualization	2.89	1.28	2.56	1.15	2.26	.99	2.45	1.06
Has Many Interests	2.23	1.02	2.28	.94	2.42	1.02	2.12	.95
Difficulty Making Decisions	2.96	1.18	3.13	1.09	2.42	1.12	3.03	1.04
Indirect Expression of Hostility	3.12	1.14	2.85	1.13	2.37	1.07	3.05	1.11
Poor Reality Testing	1.74	1.02	1.70	1.01	1.53	1.12	1.83	1.15
Angry	3.11	1.12	3.14	1.13	2.50	1.05	3.22	1.16
Eccentric	1.96	1.16	1.89	1.20	1.89	.94	1.94	1.15
Emotional Lability	2.41	1.08	2.64	1.04	1.85	.81	2.62	1.16
Dislikes Change	2.79	1.10	2.52	.90	2.39	1.20	2.75	.96
Believes Cannot Be Helped	1.88	1.14	1.81	.92	1.85	1.09	1.92	.81
Reliable Informant	3.08	.93	3.17	.94	3.05	1.05	2.96	.85
Ignores Problems	2.59	.84	2.48	.92	2.85	1.23	2.55	1.11
Ruminates	2.58	1.21	2.91	1.00	2.15	.88	2.88	.91
Excitable	2.69	1.16	2.75	1.08	2.40	.88	2.68	1.05
Conforming	2.69	1.12	2.51	.79	2.15	.88	2.58	1.04

	Harris-Lingoes Subscales *(continued)*							
	Ma_1		Ma_2		Ma_3		Ma_4	
	Mean	SD	Mean	SD	Mean	SD	Mean	SD
Ineffective at Dealing with Problems	3.19	.96	3.09	.94	2.85	1.18	3.29	1.03
Introverted	2.33	1.30	2.27	1.17	1.60	.88	2.41	1.08
Superficial Relationships	2.96	1.17	2.89	1.03	2.79	1.23	2.92	1.10
Impulsive	3.04	1.10	2.95	1.15	3.00	1.20	3.00	1.25
Stereotypic Feminine Behavior	2.63	.97	2.58	1.14	2.25	1.07	2.78	1.21
Stubborn	3.00	.98	2.84	.95	2.89	1.05	2.78	1.01
Hostile Toward Therapist	1.33	.68	1.36	.60	1.30	.47	1.43	.67
Difficult to Motivate	2.35	1.02	2.28	1.16	2.30	1.03	2.50	1.16
Suicidal Ideations	1.48	.58	1.75	.95	1.10	.31	1.73	.89
Familial Discord	3.69	1.05	3.51	1.21	2.95	1.35	3.61	1.12
Dogmatic	2.54	1.17	2.28	.93	2.00	.79	2.11	.93

Table L-1c. Means and standard deviations for continuous extra-test characteristics (women): High scores on Si subscales

Extra-test Characteristics	Si Subscales					
	Si_1		Si_2		Si_3	
	Mean	SD	Mean	SD	Mean	SD
Intake Information	(n = 173)		(n = 211)		(n = 236)	
Axis IV diagnosis	3.00	.99	3.08	1.01	3.00	.89
Axis V - Current Level of Functioning	60.84	8.83	60.40	9.49	60.49	9.97
Number of Arrests	.44	1.21	.37	.78	1.15	2.49
Mental Status	(n = 173)		(n = 211)		(n = 236)	
Anxiety During Interview	2.45	.67	2.44	.67	2.51	.75
Depression During Interview	2.54	.74	2.54	.71	2.42	.73
Activity Level During Interview	2.95	.38	2.94	.40	3.03	.49
Speech During Interview	2.89	.37	2.90	.41	2.91	.43
SCL-90-R Scales	(n = 172)		(n = 210)		(n = 235)	
Somatization	1.52	.83	1.54	.90	1.31	.83
Obsessive-Compulsive	1.96	.85	1.90	.95	1.73	.81
Interpersonal Sensitivity	2.10	.84	1.90	.92	1.70	.84
Depression	2.37	.85	2.28	.91	2.00	.86
Anxiety	1.81	.93	1.75	.97	1.62	.91
Hostility	1.58	.97	1.53	1.02	1.59	1.07
Phobic Anxiety	1.30	.97	1.27	1.01	.82	.71
Paranoid Ideation	1.76	.95	1.67	1.01	1.68	.88
Psychoticism	1.26	.75	1.19	.80	1.21	.72
Initial SCL-90 Analogue	(n = 105)		(n = 138)		(n = 156)	
Somatization	2.27	2.45	2.72	2.84	2.52	2.83
Obsessive-Compulsive	2.60	2.68	2.69	2.64	3.68	2.65
Interpersonal Sensitivity	4.88	2.55	4.99	2.53	4.65	2.51
Depression	4.85	2.44	4.78	2.64	4.55	2.70
Anxiety	4.51	2.76	4.57	2.70	4.72	2.73
Hostility	2.52	2.41	2.73	2.65	3.28	2.81
Phobic Anxiety	1.01	2.00	1.12	1.97	1.49	2.27
Paranoid Ideation	.87	1.52	1.27	2.17	1.22	1.81
Psychoticism	.52	1.36	.92	2.03	.54	1.40

Table L-1c. Means and standard deviations for continuous extra-test characteristics (women): High scores on Si subscales *(continued)*

Extra-test Characteristics	Si Subscales					
	Si_1		Si_2		Si_3	
	Mean	SD	Mean	SD	Mean	SD
Patient Description Form Scales	(n = 106)		(n = 136)		(n = 155)	
Angry Resentment	2.59	.85	2.63	.86	2.77	.94
Critical/Argumentative	2.27	.86	2.27	.83	2.44	.96
Narcissistic	1.85	.76	1.91	.80	2.27	.95
Defensive	2.48	.83	2.50	.83	2.54	.91
Histrionic	2.37	.83	2.38	.86	2.40	.81
Aggressive	1.75	.69	1.76	.67	2.02	.84
Insecure	3.15	.85	3.10	.86	3.04	.80
Anxious	2.97	.84	2.99	.83	2.98	.78
Pessimistic	2.28	.81	2.31	.86	2.34	.87
Depressed	2.75	.84	2.76	.89	2.52	.81
Achievement-Oriented	2.14	.69	2.21	.74	2.59	.72
Passive-Submissive	2.80	.89	2.69	.88	2.36	.81
Introverted	2.77	.95	2.63	.98	2.72	1.02
Emotionally Controlled	2.40	.88	2.37	.90	2.38	1.02
Antisocial	1.99	.71	2.00	.79	2.22	.87
Negative Treatment Attitudes	1.92	.67	1.88	.66	1.91	.79
Somatic Symptoms	2.20	1.02	2.27	1.11	2.17	1.08
Psychotic Symptoms	1.27	.54	1.29	.61	1.22	.38
Family Problems	2.88	1.06	2.93	1.11	2.76	1.15
Obsessive-Compulsive	2.53	.98	2.53	.89	2.87	.81
Stereotypic Masculine Interests	1.35	.61	1.32	.62	2.83	1.13
Procrastinates	2.24	.94	2.11	.88	2.33	1.00
Suspicious	2.35	.83	2.46	.87	2.56	.95
Agitated	2.08	.83	2.20	.86	2.15	.78
Work Problems	1.57	.84	1.58	.78	1.84	.79
Patient Description Form Items	(n = 106)		(n = 136)		(n = 155)	
Anxious	3.28	1.02	3.23	1.03	3.54	.81
Problems with Authority Figures	2.66	1.19	2.56	1.22	3.00	1.17
Has Insight Into Own Problems	2.60	.87	2.54	.85	2.64	.82
Fears Losing Control	3.06	1.18	3.09	1.16	3.30	1.04
Extroverted	2.08	.97	2.23	1.04	2.32	.97
Uses Repression	2.78	.99	2.81	1.05	2.66	1.09
Submissive	2.92	1.05	2.83	1.05	2.38	.91

Difficulty Concentrating	2.70	1.12	2.89	1.11	2.80	1.14
Rigid	2.52	1.03	2.50	1.04	2.70	1.11
Overly Compliant	2.31	1.03	2.18	1.01	2.11	.93
Whiny	1.96	1.01	2.01	1.05	1.91	1.02
Feels Overwhelmed	3.44	1.08	3.42	1.15	3.34	1.16
Manipulative	2.25	1.12	2.23	1.15	2.35	1.16
Difficulty Trusting Others	3.19	1.14	3.31	1.11	3.29	1.21
Insensitive to Others	1.77	.88	1.76	.87	2.21	1.01
Stereotypic Masculine Behavior	1.31	.62	1.28	.62	2.80	1.16
Harbors Grudges	2.43	1.07	2.55	1.05	2.70	1.06
Evasive	2.15	1.03	2.19	1.02	2.23	1.07
Disoriented	1.30	.72	1.36	.80	1.20	.45
Energetic	2.01	.81	2.13	.90	2.43	.84
Lonely	2.85	1.10	2.90	1.05	3.04	1.24
Family Lacks Love	2.77	1.20	2.86	1.27	2.77	1.33
Worrier	3.36	1.08	3.41	1.03	3.35	1.04
Narcissistic	1.88	.91	1.97	1.01	2.44	1.16
Tearful	2.52	1.16	2.50	1.15	1.58	.87
Provocative	1.63	.90	1.60	.89	1.70	.88
Moralistic	2.28	.96	2.45	1.01	2.60	1.04
Socially Awkward	2.67	1.00	2.62	1.06	2.99	1.14
Hostile	2.07	.95	2.04	.93	2.43	1.17
Overcontrolled	2.43	1.17	2.47	1.15	2.61	1.21
Resistant to Interpretations	2.19	.92	2.11	.96	2.08	.97
Antisocial Behavior	1.64	.82	1.61	.88	2.26	1.19
Sarcastic	1.81	1.00	1.79	.98	1.98	1.10
Rejects Traditional Gender Role	1.57	.89	1.58	.94	1.71	1.07
Feels Gets Raw Deal From Life	2.88	1.15	2.98	1.21	2.97	1.20
Acute Psychological Turmoil	2.95	1.13	3.01	1.14	3.10	1.10
Does Not Complete Projects	2.23	1.14	2.11	1.08	2.26	1.14
Uncomfortable with Opposite Sex	2.27	1.19	2.33	1.24	2.27	1.11
Preoccupied with Health Problems	2.11	1.24	2.21	1.31	2.28	1.32
Work-Oriented	2.53	1.12	2.52	1.15	3.03	1.02
Resents Family Members	2.80	1.18	2.92	1.26	2.82	1.35
Demanding of Attention	2.44	.99	2.43	1.09	2.48	1.08
Passive	2.79	1.03	2.71	1.07	2.57	.97
Self-Punishing	2.70	1.14	2.79	1.17	2.47	1.22
Needs to Achieve	2.28	.92	2.42	1.00	2.74	1.00
Needs to Be with Others	2.96	1.08	2.90	1.11	3.00	1.08
Irritable	2.59	1.01	2.69	1.02	2.63	1.07
Self-Defeating	3.06	1.00	3.08	1.08	3.15	1.16
Delusional Thinking	1.26	.69	1.28	.75	1.14	.46

Table L-1c. Means and standard deviations for continuous extra-test characteristics (women): High scores on Si subscales *(continued)*

Extra-test Characteristics	Si Subscales					
	Si_1		Si_2		Si_3	
	Mean	SD	Mean	SD	Mean	SD
Self-Reliant	2.41	.88	2.58	.94	2.61	.84
Aggressive	1.86	.89	1.91	.89	2.35	.94
Competitive	1.87	.92	1.96	.99	2.40	.97
Suspicious	2.25	1.05	2.39	1.09	2.54	1.15
Compulsive	2.11	1.23	2.18	1.18	2.59	1.08
Dependable	2.89	.87	2.95	.93	3.08	.88
Multiple Somatic Complaints	1.99	1.19	2.11	1.28	2.08	1.24
Complains of Lack of Time	2.08	1.10	2.02	1.14	2.02	1.15
Poor Work Performance	1.79	.93	1.73	.92	1.94	1.02
Insecure	3.51	.93	3.47	.94	3.57	.88
Discusses Problems Openly	2.99	.84	3.04	.85	3.08	.78
Sexually Adjusted	2.35	.83	2.31	.83	2.36	.79
Exaggerated Need for Affection	2.35	1.09	2.26	1.16	2.39	1.10
Resentful	2.88	1.08	2.95	1.08	3.00	1.17
Uses Denial	2.79	1.06	2.76	1.11	2.61	1.16
Hypochondriacal	1.72	1.01	1.77	1.09	1.74	.95
Communicates Effectively	2.85	.80	2.96	.91	3.15	.71
Has Many Nightmares	1.94	.99	2.18	1.14	1.85	1.10
Stormy Interpersonal Relationships	2.96	1.20	3.02	1.28	3.00	1.18
Feigns Remorse When in Trouble	1.68	.90	1.70	.99	1.71	.89
Stereotypic Masculine Interests	1.37	.70	1.36	.71	2.83	1.21
Guarded	2.54	1.17	2.59	1.12	2.70	1.31
Feels Inferior	3.41	1.06	3.31	1.09	3.18	1.05
Low Frustration Tolerance	2.79	1.06	2.85	1.06	3.19	1.17
Psychotic Symptoms	1.18	.53	1.28	.76	1.15	.51
Fired From Past Jobs	1.57	.96	1.58	1.00	1.91	.97
Needs Attention	2.92	.95	2.92	1.06	2.92	1.01
Acts Out	2.18	1.03	2.28	1.09	2.40	1.05
Histrionic	2.05	1.08	2.07	1.09	1.90	1.02
Self-Indulgent	2.09	.94	2.13	1.02	2.50	1.11
Depressed	3.39	.93	3.39	.96	3.32	1.05
Grandiose	1.39	.66	1.54	.84	1.86	1.10
Cynical	2.12	.95	2.16	1.00	2.44	1.24
Sociopathic	1.29	.56	1.36	.66	1.62	.81
Agitated	2.34	1.06	2.43	1.06	2.43	1.06

Marital Problems	2.81	1.52	2.69	1.54	2.37	1.59
Absence of Deep Emotions	2.06	1.04	2.02	1.08	1.96	1.13
Uncomfortable Dealing with Emotions	2.87	1.07	2.84	1.12	2.91	1.27
Sad	3.10	1.00	3.14	1.02	2.97	1.02
Self-Degrading	2.68	1.16	2.64	1.11	2.26	1.03
Unable to Express Negative Feelings	2.27	1.05	2.29	1.16	2.21	1.13
Concrete in Thinking	2.34	1.07	2.44	1.10	2.27	1.04
Unable to See Own Limitations	2.13	.94	2.10	1.00	2.28	1.15
Power-Oriented	1.70	.91	1.72	.92	2.07	1.01
Grouchy	2.07	.98	2.19	1.05	2.33	1.04
Overbearing in Relationships	1.88	1.02	2.00	1.04	2.14	1.16
Uncertain About Career	2.85	1.40	2.75	1.38	3.35	1.28
Likable	3.14	.75	3.22	.87	3.25	.73
Procrastinator	2.46	1.01	2.37	.97	2.65	1.16
Negative Feelings Toward Opposite Sex	2.48	1.15	2.57	1.22	2.14	1.11
Defensive	2.65	1.00	2.74	1.04	2.64	1.23
Empathetic	2.50	.74	2.60	.79	2.41	.72
Perfectionistic	2.34	1.23	2.39	1.22	2.49	1.11
Judgmental	2.39	1.00	2.49	.98	2.70	1.15
Copes Well with Stress	1.98	.73	1.91	.74	1.99	.66
Moody	2.68	1.08	2.79	1.01	2.79	1.00
Selfish	1.84	.85	1.93	.94	2.17	1.01
Gives Up Easily	2.34	.97	2.23	1.02	2.33	1.03
Physical Symptoms in Response to Stress	2.32	1.15	2.42	1.31	2.30	1.24
Blames Family For Difficulties	2.66	1.29	2.67	1.35	2.52	1.33
Bored	2.18	1.03	2.16	1.10	2.37	1.11
Idealistic	2.32	1.00	2.33	.99	2.46	1.06
Difficulty Establishing Therapeutic Rapport	1.87	.88	1.84	.91	1.97	1.00
Daydreams	1.92	.96	1.97	1.05	1.98	1.05
Concerned About Status	2.02	1.02	1.88	.92	2.46	1.13
Creates Good First Impression	2.58	.89	2.67	.97	2.69	.79
Complains of Sleep Disturbance	2.77	1.18	2.95	1.29	2.64	1.34
Has Temper Tantrums	1.99	1.02	2.09	1.10	2.27	1.19
Overreactive	2.53	1.10	2.71	1.14	2.72	1.10
High Aspirations	1.96	1.04	2.13	1.11	2.54	1.17
Feels Hopeless	2.80	1.09	2.85	1.17	2.74	1.14
Keeps Others at a Distance	2.93	1.12	2.99	1.14	2.89	1.27
Argumentative	2.07	.98	2.11	1.02	2.27	1.09
Paranoid Features	1.59	.86	1.69	.98	1.84	.92
Restless	2.36	1.07	2.58	1.12	2.65	1.13
Pessimistic	2.73	.96	2.71	1.05	2.89	1.06
Feels Like a Failure	3.03	1.05	3.05	1.12	3.02	1.13

Table L-1c. Means and standard deviations for continuous extra-test characteristics (women): High scores on Si subscales *(continued)*

Extra-test Characteristics	Si Subscales					
	Si_1		Si_2		Si_3	
	Mean	SD	Mean	SD	Mean	SD
Hallucinations	1.08	.38	1.16	.62	1.10	.36
Restricted Affect	2.30	1.14	2.20	1.11	2.22	1.28
Impatient	2.42	.98	2.53	.99	2.66	1.10
Assertive	1.87	.83	2.10	.86	2.33	.85
Modest	2.58	.82	2.63	.84	2.54	.85
Self-Doubting	3.16	1.01	3.12	1.03	3.16	.91
Deceptive	1.80	.78	1.84	.85	1.95	1.05
Feels That Life is a Strain	3.10	1.07	3.19	1.07	3.19	1.07
Physically Abusive	1.36	.66	1.32	.64	1.49	.82
Feels Rejected	3.13	1.02	3.18	1.03	3.24	1.21
Does Not Get Along with Coworkers	1.64	.95	1.60	.82	1.91	.89
Uses Projection	2.21	1.03	2.26	1.04	2.34	1.14
Complains of Fatigue	2.80	1.23	2.83	1.29	2.45	1.35
Uses Rationalization	2.52	1.03	2.58	1.03	2.70	1.09
Critical of Others	2.25	1.06	2.29	1.03	2.52	1.09
Egocentric	2.00	1.07	2.09	1.07	2.53	1.24
Overevaluates Own Worth	1.49	.77	1.60	.89	1.99	1.17
Optimistic	1.89	.72	1.96	.77	2.07	.71
Psychologically Immature	2.71	1.16	2.68	1.19	2.95	1.16
Poor Judgment	2.69	1.02	2.78	1.18	2.92	1.18
Low Sex Drive	2.42	1.17	2.37	1.27	1.74	.94
Feels Mistreated	2.90	1.07	3.00	1.17	2.95	1.05
Overly Sensitive to Criticism	3.17	1.13	3.22	1.08	3.08	1.24
Sentimental	2.39	.91	2.56	.98	2.53	1.03
Sexual Preoccupation	1.42	.78	1.37	.72	1.73	1.14
Accelerated Speech	1.52	.81	1.60	.93	1.43	.82
Concerns About Homosexuality	1.16	.65	1.18	.67	1.51	1.14
Many Specific Fears	2.11	1.05	2.14	1.07	1.84	1.00
Passive in Relationships	3.20	1.04	3.03	1.06	2.40	1.02
Negative Attitudes Toward Therapy	1.70	.87	1.67	.85	1.71	.96
Guilt-Prone	3.08	1.11	3.08	1.18	2.81	1.14
Nervous	3.04	1.02	3.00	.98	3.18	.99
Obsessive	2.30	1.26	2.43	1.22	2.98	1.15
Shy	2.77	1.15	2.61	1.16	2.57	1.20
Uses Intellectualization	2.14	1.06	2.22	1.05	2.52	1.20

Has Many Interests	1.95	.85	2.08	.93	2.41	1.05
Difficulty Making Decisions	2.89	1.09	2.95	1.13	3.07	1.10
Indirect Expression of Hostility	2.73	1.04	2.78	1.08	2.70	1.14
Poor Reality Testing	1.53	.92	1.55	.88	1.60	.75
Angry	2.86	1.09	3.01	1.13	3.07	1.15
Eccentric	1.71	1.00	1.70	.98	1.91	1.28
Emotional Lability	2.30	.98	2.39	1.07	2.26	1.12
Dislikes Change	2.64	1.05	2.64	.95	2.70	1.04
Believes Cannot Be Helped	1.84	.88	1.95	.91	1.80	.88
Reliable Informant	3.21	.89	3.27	.92	3.20	.87
Ignores Problems	2.34	1.03	2.44	1.03	2.27	1.00
Ruminates	2.79	1.08	2.86	1.02	3.30	1.07
Excitable	2.31	1.02	2.48	1.09	2.60	1.06
Conforming	2.69	1.02	2.60	.98	2.55	.81
Ineffective at Dealing with Problems	3.08	1.02	3.11	1.06	2.95	1.10
Introverted	2.83	1.07	2.63	1.08	2.60	1.15
Superficial Relationships	2.59	1.09	2.64	1.10	2.54	1.25
Impulsive	2.49	1.14	2.61	1.19	2.65	1.21
Stereotypic Feminine Behavior	2.65	1.14	2.71	1.24	1.40	.67
Stubborn	2.53	1.01	2.55	1.02	2.69	1.13
Hostile Toward Therapist	1.30	.57	1.30	.56	1.43	.75
Difficult to Motivate	2.25	1.01	2.12	1.00	2.05	.94
Suicidal Ideations	1.88	.98	1.86	1.04	1.79	.98
Familial Discord	3.29	1.19	3.32	1.26	2.96	1.34
Dogmatic	1.92	.94	2.04	.99	2.23	1.16

Table L-1d. Means and standard deviations for continuous extra-test characteristics (women): High scores on content scales

Extra-test Characteristics	Content Scales									
	ANX		FRS		OBS		DEP		HEA	
	Mean	SD	Mean	SD	Mean	SD	Mean	SD	Mean	SD
Intake Information	(n = 396)		(n = 130)		(n = 219)		(n = 376)		(n = 286)	
Axis IV diagnosis	3.04	1.00	3.14	1.03	3.03	.93	3.03	.98	3.09	.99
Axis V - Current Level of Functioning	60.62	9.86	60.63	10.69	60.14	10.13	60.63	9.74	60.12	10.17
Number of Arrests	.38	.99	.46	1.29	.46	1.16	.40	1.03	.35	.77
Mental Status	(n = 396)		(n = 130)		(n = 219)		(n = 376)		(n = 286)	
Anxiety During Interview	2.45	.70	2.46	.72	2.47	.67	2.45	.69	2.46	.72
Depression During Interview	2.57	.73	2.54	.71	2.57	.73	2.59	.73	2.60	.72
Activity Level During Interview	2.97	.39	2.96	.44	2.97	.36	2.95	.37	2.98	.40
Speech During Interview	2.97	.42	2.95	.37	2.96	.38	2.95	.40	2.97	.42
SCL-90-R Scales	(n = 394)		(n = 129)		(n = 218)		(n = 374)		(n = 285)	
Somatization	1.53	.83	1.80	.89	1.64	.81	1.52	.85	1.86	.75
Obsessive-Compulsive	1.89	.83	2.10	.94	2.09	.78	1.87	.86	2.01	.85
Interpersonal Sensitivity	1.85	.84	2.03	.86	2.09	.79	1.90	.83	1.87	.87
Depression	2.34	.77	2.40	.81	2.46	.75	2.41	.74	2.36	.82
Anxiety	1.77	.87	2.00	.97	1.92	.84	1.72	.92	1.89	.91
Hostility	1.60	.98	1.71	1.04	1.75	.98	1.61	.97	1.58	1.00
Phobic Anxiety	1.09	.94	1.61	1.00	1.29	.93	1.06	.95	1.24	.97
Paranoid Ideation	1.73	.91	1.94	.94	1.92	.87	1.74	.93	1.76	.96
Psychoticism	1.19	.71	1.39	.80	1.40	.70	1.21	.71	1.26	.74
Initial SCL-90 Analogue	(n = 263)		(n = 78)		(n = 146)		(n = 255)		(n = 186)	
Somatization	2.44	2.64	2.84	2.98	2.64	2.69	2.41	2.69	3.08	2.86
Obsessive-Compulsive	2.62	2.53	2.47	2.62	2.94	2.61	2.57	2.53	2.69	2.54
Interpersonal Sensitivity	4.94	2.58	5.04	2.57	5.14	2.53	5.04	2.63	4.96	2.61
Depression	4.75	2.55	4.53	2.73	4.82	2.55	4.82	2.49	4.85	2.54
Anxiety	4.41	2.67	4.44	2.73	4.66	2.69	4.39	2.69	4.64	2.68
Hostility	2.79	2.50	2.39	2.55	2.85	2.48	2.82	2.55	2.85	2.55
Phobic Anxiety	1.17	2.02	1.28	2.16	1.28	2.06	1.11	1.96	1.23	2.07
Paranoid Ideation	1.17	1.98	1.08	1.87	1.12	1.72	1.12	1.97	1.03	1.80
Psychoticism	.67	1.56	.66	1.49	.67	1.42	.62	1.52	.57	1.34

Patient Description Form Scales	(n = 263)		(n = 77)		(n = 145)		(n = 255)		(n = 186)	
Angry Resentment	2.69	.85	2.63	.78	2.64	.87	2.73	.85	2.69	.88
Critical/Argumentative	2.30	.84	2.24	.77	2.29	.89	2.38	.84	2.30	.86
Narcissistic	1.97	.85	1.95	.79	1.95	.80	2.01	.85	1.94	.78
Defensive	2.48	.82	2.49	.80	2.46	.81	2.50	.80	2.46	.84
Histrionic	2.51	.85	2.56	.80	2.46	.84	2.51	.83	2.52	.80
Aggressive	1.79	.72	1.71	.67	1.83	.75	1.81	.70	1.77	.72
Insecure	3.13	.86	3.15	.81	3.15	.86	3.19	.84	3.11	.88
Anxious	2.99	.79	3.12	.78	3.01	.82	2.97	.77	3.04	.80
Pessimistic	2.29	.87	2.32	.89	2.26	.90	2.34	.86	2.34	.91
Depressed	2.71	.86	2.79	.94	2.68	.85	2.71	.86	2.75	.84
Achievement-Oriented	2.39	.72	2.19	.71	2.34	.70	2.37	.75	2.30	.68
Passive-Submissive	2.66	.90	2.76	.90	2.77	.95	2.64	.90	2.68	.92
Introverted	2.41	.94	2.54	1.05	2.52	.94	2.49	.95	2.44	.98
Emotionally Controlled	2.35	.88	2.35	.85	2.35	.92	2.35	.84	2.32	.88
Antisocial	2.05	.79	2.02	.76	2.03	.79	2.09	.79	1.96	.72
Negative Treatment Attitudes	1.89	.70	1.91	.67	1.86	.67	1.92	.68	1.93	.73
Somatic Symptoms	2.22	1.07	2.41	1.19	2.18	1.03	2.18	1.05	2.45	1.12
Psychotic Symptoms	1.28	.56	1.30	.47	1.31	.55	1.27	.46	1.26	.48
Family Problems	3.05	1.10	3.13	1.05	3.03	1.15	3.03	1.09	2.97	1.11
Obsessive-Compulsive	2.58	.86	2.71	.80	2.57	.88	2.57	.86	2.59	.82
Stereotypic Masculine Interests	1.39	.66	1.24	.47	1.39	.65	1.40	.68	1.37	.70
Procrastinates	2.17	.89	2.18	.85	2.18	.91	2.23	.89	2.20	.90
Suspicious	2.42	.91	2.50	.88	2.43	.87	2.48	.88	2.44	.91
Agitated	2.17	.85	2.18	.92	2.16	.84	2.19	.84	2.17	.84
Work Problems	1.61	.78	1.51	.69	1.56	.72	1.66	.82	1.58	.78
Patient Description Form Items	(n = 263)		(n = 77)		(n = 145)		(n = 255)		(n = 186)	
Anxious	3.24	1.01	3.35	.97	3.29	.96	3.20	1.00	3.28	1.01
Problems with Authority Figures	2.68	1.23	2.69	1.19	2.73	1.19	2.75	1.22	2.62	1.24
Has Insight Into Own Problems	2.59	.91	2.49	.98	2.58	.88	2.53	.87	2.53	.95
Fears Losing Control	3.15	1.14	3.17	1.14	3.21	1.10	3.15	1.08	3.14	1.12
Extroverted	2.51	1.06	2.40	1.03	2.36	.98	2.45	1.09	2.48	.97
Uses Repression	2.77	1.09	2.81	1.19	2.76	1.06	2.80	1.04	2.81	1.06
Submissive	2.81	1.03	2.97	1.03	2.93	1.09	2.78	1.02	2.83	1.05
Difficulty Concentrating	2.75	1.12	2.88	1.12	2.78	1.10	2.73	1.07	2.86	1.10
Rigid	2.44	1.02	2.41	1.02	2.49	1.00	2.42	.99	2.51	1.02
Overly Compliant	2.21	1.05	2.26	1.03	2.33	1.08	2.21	1.05	2.22	1.07
Whiny	2.05	1.03	2.20	1.05	2.10	1.08	2.03	1.01	2.10	1.00
Feels Overwhelmed	3.50	1.04	3.60	1.00	3.43	1.13	3.47	1.04	3.55	1.04
Manipulative	2.36	1.18	2.29	1.12	2.35	1.17	2.39	1.16	2.33	1.07
Difficulty Trusting Others	3.19	1.16	3.31	1.16	3.27	1.14	3.29	1.12	3.23	1.14

Table L-1d. Means and standard deviations for continuous extra-test characteristics (women): High scores on content scales *(continued)*

Extra-test Characteristics	Content Scales									
	ANX		FRS		OBS		DEP		HEA	
	Mean	SD	Mean	SD	Mean	SD	Mean	SD	Mean	SD
Insensitive to Others	1.76	.87	1.75	.83	1.78	.83	1.82	.89	1.77	.85
Stereotypic Masculine Behavior	1.31	.65	1.20	.49	1.33	.65	1.34	.68	1.34	.70
Harbors Grudges	2.49	1.04	2.51	.92	2.51	1.07	2.54	1.03	2.45	.99
Evasive	2.22	1.06	2.22	1.08	2.21	1.06	2.30	1.04	2.22	1.06
Disoriented	1.32	.72	1.38	.74	1.36	.74	1.28	.63	1.35	.74
Energetic	2.32	.97	2.22	.94	2.27	.85	2.27	.95	2.21	.92
Lonely	2.94	1.05	2.97	1.10	2.92	1.06	3.00	1.06	2.99	1.06
Family Lacks Love	2.90	1.25	2.88	1.27	2.92	1.29	2.90	1.23	2.88	1.29
Worrier	3.45	1.01	3.56	.97	3.43	1.01	3.42	.99	3.47	.96
Narcissistic	2.07	1.11	2.00	1.08	2.04	1.04	2.12	1.12	1.97	1.03
Tearful	2.46	1.18	2.49	1.23	2.51	1.18	2.44	1.17	2.47	1.19
Provocative	1.73	.99	1.57	.88	1.67	.93	1.70	.94	1.67	.91
Moralistic	2.30	.98	2.43	.95	2.30	.96	2.23	.94	2.31	.92
Socially Awkward	2.43	1.02	2.66	1.11	2.55	1.00	2.54	1.04	2.50	1.05
Hostile	2.09	1.04	2.03	.94	2.07	1.03	2.13	1.04	2.07	1.02
Overcontrolled	2.46	1.17	2.51	1.14	2.47	1.21	2.45	1.15	2.38	1.14
Resistant to Interpretations	2.14	.99	2.26	1.00	2.13	.98	2.20	.97	2.18	.98
Antisocial Behavior	1.66	.91	1.52	.87	1.63	.88	1.70	.90	1.62	.85
Sarcastic	1.81	.95	1.77	.93	1.82	1.02	1.88	.98	1.85	1.01
Rejects Traditional Gender Role	1.59	.93	1.41	.74	1.62	.99	1.64	.96	1.59	.95
Feels Gets Raw Deal From Life	2.98	1.15	2.96	1.12	2.93	1.13	3.04	1.14	2.95	1.12
Acute Psychological Turmoil	3.07	1.05	3.17	1.10	2.97	1.06	3.05	1.05	3.07	1.08
Does Not Complete Projects	2.20	1.11	2.33	1.13	2.18	1.13	2.26	1.13	2.22	1.08
Uncomfortable with Opposite Sex	2.24	1.17	2.36	1.26	2.21	1.16	2.27	1.17	2.31	1.17
Preoccupied with Health Problems	2.12	1.30	2.32	1.42	2.12	1.25	2.08	1.27	2.40	1.36
Work-Oriented	2.66	1.12	2.35	1.14	2.72	1.14	2.62	1.12	2.58	1.07
Resents Family Members	3.06	1.23	3.16	1.23	3.02	1.29	3.03	1.21	2.94	1.25
Demanding of Attention	2.55	1.08	2.49	1.07	2.51	1.05	2.54	1.09	2.44	1.04
Passive	2.64	1.06	2.79	1.12	2.74	1.11	2.62	1.06	2.70	1.07
Self-Punishing	2.72	1.17	2.85	1.20	2.81	1.16	2.76	1.12	2.80	1.19
Needs to Achieve	2.57	1.05	2.36	.95	2.59	1.04	2.59	1.09	2.50	.98
Needs to Be with Others	3.13	1.02	3.09	1.06	3.10	1.07	3.08	1.02	3.08	1.05
Irritable	2.58	1.05	2.58	1.05	2.57	1.04	2.64	1.04	2.59	1.04
Self-Defeating	3.07	1.09	3.18	.97	3.11	1.13	3.15	1.04	3.07	1.05
Delusional Thinking	1.32	.80	1.29	.69	1.30	.73	1.29	.68	1.26	.66

Self-Reliant	2.60	.86	2.49	.87	2.52	.90	2.58	.87	2.57	.88
Aggressive	1.95	.95	1.84	.90	1.93	.92	1.97	.93	1.93	.92
Competitive	2.05	.98	1.82	.87	2.01	.95	2.11	1.01	2.02	.95
Suspicious	2.38	1.11	2.43	1.00	2.34	1.08	2.44	1.09	2.40	1.09
Compulsive	2.22	1.17	2.19	1.17	2.24	1.16	2.16	1.11	2.19	1.10
Dependable	3.00	.91	2.95	1.04	2.97	.89	2.93	.85	2.95	.90
Multiple Somatic Complaints	2.08	1.26	2.30	1.39	2.02	1.23	2.00	1.21	2.33	1.35
Complains of Lack of Time	2.05	1.14	2.04	1.08	1.99	1.09	2.02	1.12	2.06	1.14
Poor Work Performance	1.83	.98	1.86	1.00	1.77	.92	1.84	.98	1.81	.95
Insecure	3.52	.93	3.59	.85	3.54	.94	3.58	.93	3.54	.94
Discusses Problems Openly	3.23	.86	3.25	.99	3.14	.84	3.19	.84	3.11	.87
Sexually Adjusted	2.47	.87	2.31	.77	2.50	.87	2.44	.88	2.42	.87
Exaggerated Need for Affection	2.45	1.18	2.42	1.23	2.45	1.15	2.44	1.13	2.41	1.12
Resentful	2.98	1.06	2.99	1.04	2.91	1.09	3.02	1.08	2.93	1.06
Uses Denial	2.74	1.10	2.71	1.08	2.65	1.10	2.75	1.08	2.68	1.11
Hypochondriacal	1.71	1.03	1.93	1.13	1.71	1.05	1.71	1.03	1.88	1.12
Communicates Effectively	3.02	.87	2.89	.91	2.96	.79	3.01	.87	2.96	.84
Has Many Nightmares	2.03	1.11	2.38	1.31	2.00	1.08	2.02	1.09	2.02	1.11
Stormy Interpersonal Relationships	3.09	1.22	3.00	1.12	3.04	1.28	3.12	1.20	3.04	1.20
Feigns Remorse When in Trouble	1.80	1.01	1.80	.94	1.72	.94	1.86	1.03	1.60	.87
Stereotypic Masculine Interests	1.46	.79	1.27	.63	1.44	.80	1.46	.80	1.39	.77
Guarded	2.44	1.12	2.53	1.10	2.43	1.10	2.52	1.12	2.45	1.15
Feels Inferior	3.24	1.09	3.29	.95	3.31	1.12	3.33	1.08	3.26	1.13
Low Frustration Tolerance	2.84	1.09	2.88	1.02	2.85	1.08	2.89	1.04	2.84	1.05
Psychotic Symptoms	1.23	.67	1.24	.67	1.21	.58	1.22	.64	1.21	.57
Fired From Past Jobs	1.56	.98	1.50	.88	1.50	.87	1.60	1.02	1.52	1.00
Needs Attention	3.05	1.01	3.11	.87	2.99	.99	3.06	.99	3.04	.93
Acts Out	2.25	1.10	2.30	1.09	2.22	1.05	2.33	1.10	2.16	.97
Histrionic	2.20	1.17	2.24	1.24	2.14	1.16	2.21	1.16	2.18	1.13
Self-Indulgent	2.15	1.05	2.14	1.04	2.12	1.01	2.22	1.06	2.07	.93
Depressed	3.35	.98	3.33	1.05	3.32	.98	3.35	.99	3.39	.96
Grandiose	1.59	.89	1.51	.78	1.52	.82	1.61	.91	1.59	.88
Cynical	2.12	1.02	2.00	.89	2.22	1.11	2.23	1.05	2.19	1.05
Sociopathic	1.40	.72	1.38	.66	1.37	.66	1.41	.70	1.33	.60
Agitated	2.35	1.07	2.29	1.05	2.38	1.09	2.36	1.05	2.38	1.05
Marital Problems	2.71	1.57	2.53	1.45	2.60	1.59	2.64	1.55	2.66	1.54
Absence of Deep Emotions	2.02	1.08	1.97	1.06	1.97	1.12	1.98	1.05	1.94	1.10
Uncomfortable Dealing with Emotions	2.82	1.10	2.82	1.09	2.83	1.11	2.89	1.08	2.85	1.12
Sad	3.11	1.04	3.14	1.10	3.04	1.01	3.11	1.03	3.13	.99
Self-Degrading	2.62	1.15	2.65	1.12	2.67	1.11	2.71	1.14	2.60	1.13
Unable to Express Negative Feelings	2.26	1.12	2.28	1.11	2.24	1.17	2.26	1.11	2.24	1.13
Concrete in Thinking	2.34	1.08	2.45	1.12	2.32	1.04	2.34	1.07	2.31	1.11

Table L-1d. Means and standard deviations for continuous extra-test characteristics (women): High scores on content scales *(continued)*

Extra-test Characteristics	Content Scales									
	ANX		FRS		OBS		DEP		HEA	
	Mean	SD	Mean	SD	Mean	SD	Mean	SD	Mean	SD
Unable to See Own Limitations	2.18	1.04	2.17	.92	2.17	1.02	2.13	1.02	2.12	1.02
Power-Oriented	1.83	.98	1.68	.92	1.81	.94	1.84	.96	1.79	.93
Grouchy	2.06	.97	2.07	.96	2.09	.97	2.16	.99	2.12	1.00
Overbearing in Relationships	2.03	1.07	2.01	1.10	1.99	1.08	2.08	1.07	1.99	1.04
Uncertain About Career	2.94	1.30	2.89	1.35	2.97	1.35	2.92	1.32	2.94	1.27
Likable	3.28	.85	3.22	.82	3.29	.81	3.26	.85	3.23	.85
Procrastinator	2.36	1.00	2.33	.93	2.41	1.03	2.44	.99	2.38	.99
Negative Feelings Toward Opposite Sex	2.56	1.23	2.63	1.29	2.51	1.25	2.59	1.23	2.57	1.21
Defensive	2.67	1.08	2.72	.96	2.66	1.07	2.74	1.06	2.69	1.09
Empathetic	2.66	.76	2.66	.84	2.67	.78	2.61	.73	2.65	.80
Perfectionistic	2.47	1.17	2.34	1.09	2.43	1.17	2.46	1.17	2.43	1.12
Judgmental	2.49	1.03	2.44	.95	2.45	.98	2.52	1.01	2.48	.98
Copes Well with Stress	1.98	.71	1.84	.67	2.00	.73	1.97	.74	1.92	.71
Moody	2.72	.98	2.79	.95	2.74	1.01	2.79	.97	2.77	1.00
Selfish	1.91	.93	1.97	.91	1.90	.91	1.95	.93	1.86	.87
Gives Up Easily	2.25	1.04	2.46	1.00	2.35	1.06	2.29	1.04	2.31	1.00
Physical Symptoms in Response to Stress	2.33	1.24	2.52	1.31	2.34	1.24	2.27	1.23	2.58	1.31
Blames Family For Difficulties	2.79	1.30	2.95	1.27	2.80	1.30	2.79	1.29	2.66	1.25
Bored	2.22	1.08	2.34	1.10	2.23	1.13	2.28	1.11	2.29	1.11
Idealistic	2.38	1.01	2.38	.93	2.40	.99	2.32	1.03	2.33	.97
Difficulty Establishing Therapeutic Rapport	1.85	.95	1.81	.87	1.77	.88	1.87	.93	1.88	.95
Daydreams	1.96	1.00	2.12	1.12	1.97	1.01	1.94	.97	1.98	1.02
Concerned About Status	2.18	1.13	2.21	1.12	2.15	1.10	2.15	1.08	2.12	1.05
Creates Good First Impression	2.83	.97	2.73	1.06	2.77	.91	2.75	.93	2.72	.95
Complains of Sleep Disturbance	2.78	1.23	2.92	1.23	2.71	1.18	2.74	1.22	2.87	1.24
Has Temper Tantrums	2.02	1.05	2.08	1.14	2.09	1.06	2.08	1.05	2.01	1.07
Overreactive	2.75	1.12	2.89	1.11	2.74	1.08	2.79	1.08	2.78	1.08
High Aspirations	2.35	1.08	2.16	1.03	2.19	1.03	2.37	1.14	2.23	1.03
Feels Hopeless	2.80	1.15	2.89	1.24	2.74	1.17	2.84	1.16	2.82	1.13
Keeps Others at a Distance	2.81	1.12	2.88	1.13	2.79	1.17	2.92	1.11	2.82	1.14
Argumentative	2.15	1.04	2.08	.99	2.09	1.02	2.19	1.03	2.05	1.03
Paranoid Features	1.69	1.00	1.73	1.05	1.67	.95	1.69	.96	1.67	.97
Restless	2.46	1.08	2.47	1.08	2.47	1.10	2.49	1.08	2.49	1.05
Pessimistic	2.70	1.05	2.72	1.03	2.72	1.06	2.78	1.05	2.77	1.11
Feels Like a Failure	3.02	1.10	3.08	1.08	3.01	1.09	3.09	1.09	3.01	1.16

Hallucinations	1.11	.49	1.16	.57	1.11	.46	1.10	.43	1.09	.38
Restricted Affect	2.15	1.11	2.19	1.16	2.21	1.14	2.14	1.09	2.15	1.09
Impatient	2.55	1.04	2.56	1.05	2.49	1.02	2.56	1.01	2.52	1.01
Assertive	2.13	.87	2.05	.79	2.04	.80	2.13	.90	2.06	.81
Modest	2.56	.83	2.57	.85	2.61	.84	2.57	.81	2.55	.85
Self-Doubting	3.19	.99	3.32	.92	3.26	1.03	3.26	.98	3.22	1.03
Deceptive	1.79	.90	1.73	.77	1.78	.87	1.85	.91	1.75	.84
Feels That Life is a Strain	3.19	1.02	3.27	1.01	3.09	1.04	3.22	1.03	3.18	1.03
Physically Abusive	1.31	.64	1.24	.52	1.36	.67	1.32	.64	1.30	.62
Feels Rejected	3.20	1.10	3.20	1.09	3.20	1.08	3.27	1.10	3.19	1.08
Does Not Get Along with Coworkers	1.66	.89	1.50	.80	1.68	.88	1.68	.89	1.73	.95
Uses Projection	2.31	1.05	2.31	1.07	2.25	1.04	2.33	1.04	2.24	1.04
Complains of Fatigue	2.69	1.28	2.74	1.29	2.57	1.25	2.72	1.27	2.92	1.28
Uses Rationalization	2.59	1.05	2.55	.99	2.63	1.09	2.64	1.06	2.60	1.06
Critical of Others	2.39	1.06	2.40	.94	2.35	1.01	2.48	1.05	2.35	1.05
Egocentric	2.19	1.07	2.14	1.00	2.16	1.04	2.21	1.07	2.14	1.04
Overevaluates Own Worth	1.65	.92	1.55	.86	1.58	.81	1.67	.95	1.62	.88
Optimistic	2.03	.78	1.92	.69	2.03	.77	1.97	.80	2.00	.78
Psychologically Immature	2.82	1.19	2.91	1.19	2.82	1.20	2.87	1.18	2.78	1.20
Poor Judgment	2.77	1.16	2.92	1.14	2.78	1.19	2.82	1.16	2.70	1.10
Low Sex Drive	2.24	1.22	2.43	1.33	2.12	1.18	2.26	1.22	2.26	1.28
Feels Mistreated	3.22	1.10	3.25	1.01	3.11	1.09	3.21	1.10	3.23	1.11
Overly Sensitive to Criticism	3.24	1.11	3.37	1.05	3.24	1.08	3.25	1.08	3.21	1.08
Sentimental	2.66	1.02	2.84	.99	2.59	.98	2.59	1.00	2.58	.98
Sexual Preoccupation	1.54	.95	1.45	.91	1.52	.94	1.51	.92	1.48	.88
Accelerated Speech	1.70	.98	1.76	1.07	1.65	.90	1.71	.98	1.64	.91
Concerns About Homosexuality	1.18	.65	1.05	.21	1.17	.62	1.17	.64	1.17	.62
Many Specific Fears	2.17	1.11	2.36	1.23	2.18	1.12	2.18	1.07	2.13	1.07
Passive in Relationships	2.93	1.12	2.96	1.13	3.03	1.18	2.93	1.13	2.91	1.15
Negative Attitudes Toward Therapy	1.63	.84	1.68	.86	1.57	.76	1.66	.84	1.65	.86
Guilt-Prone	3.05	1.16	3.11	1.20	3.08	1.10	3.08	1.12	3.04	1.18
Nervous	2.98	.97	3.15	.93	3.03	.96	2.98	.96	3.04	.98
Obsessive	2.40	1.15	2.43	1.11	2.36	1.11	2.39	1.16	2.43	1.14
Shy	2.41	1.13	2.51	1.21	2.56	1.16	2.49	1.13	2.42	1.16
Uses Intellectualization	2.23	1.04	2.11	.86	2.30	1.10	2.27	1.08	2.22	1.00
Has Many Interests	2.24	.92	2.00	.86	2.14	.86	2.19	.91	2.08	.85
Difficulty Making Decisions	2.92	1.07	3.09	.99	2.93	1.11	2.97	1.05	2.95	1.09
Indirect Expression of Hostility	2.78	1.11	2.75	1.12	2.77	1.16	2.81	1.09	2.82	1.18
Poor Reality Testing	1.55	.92	1.61	.88	1.66	1.04	1.52	.84	1.51	.88
Angry	3.00	1.15	2.91	1.16	2.93	1.16	3.01	1.13	3.02	1.16
Eccentric	1.67	.95	1.65	.92	1.74	1.03	1.67	.97	1.65	.95
Emotional Lability	2.51	1.11	2.53	1.09	2.45	1.09	2.53	1.05	2.50	1.04

Table L-1d. Means and standard deviations for continuous extra-test characteristics (women): High scores on content scales *(continued)*

Extra-test Characteristics	Content Scales									
	ANX		FRS		OBS		DEP		HEA	
	Mean	SD	Mean	SD	Mean	SD	Mean	SD	Mean	SD
Dislikes Change	2.68	.96	2.82	.98	2.68	1.05	2.68	.98	2.68	.99
Believes Cannot Be Helped	1.87	.90	1.94	.92	1.82	.94	1.90	.89	1.90	.93
Reliable Informant	3.31	.91	3.23	.99	3.24	.88	3.25	.89	3.20	.96
Ignores Problems	2.37	1.04	2.40	1.00	2.35	1.05	2.41	1.04	2.35	1.01
Ruminates	2.85	1.00	3.04	1.00	2.78	.95	2.91	1.02	2.85	.98
Excitable	2.59	1.03	2.66	.88	2.48	1.00	2.58	1.01	2.60	1.00
Conforming	2.60	.96	2.73	1.06	2.67	.99	2.59	.96	2.61	.99
Ineffective at Dealing with Problems	3.05	.98	3.09	.96	2.97	1.01	3.09	.98	3.05	1.00
Introverted	2.36	1.05	2.37	1.10	2.44	1.05	2.43	1.07	2.34	1.09
Superficial Relationships	2.68	1.08	2.77	1.06	2.70	1.11	2.77	1.09	2.62	1.07
Impulsive	2.66	1.19	2.70	1.18	2.68	1.22	2.71	1.19	2.61	1.15
Stereotypic Feminine Behavior	2.82	1.19	2.93	1.15	2.65	1.12	2.77	1.19	2.75	1.15
Stubborn	2.67	.99	2.53	.96	2.61	1.05	2.75	1.01	2.65	1.03
Hostile Toward Therapist	1.31	.62	1.21	.47	1.32	.59	1.33	.64	1.35	.68
Difficult to Motivate	2.14	1.05	2.24	1.09	2.13	1.11	2.17	1.02	2.18	1.05
Suicidal Ideations	1.78	1.02	1.92	1.16	1.80	.99	1.82	1.00	1.81	1.01
Familial Discord	3.41	1.24	3.55	1.16	3.38	1.29	3.38	1.23	3.34	1.28
Dogmatic	1.99	.96	2.04	.98	2.00	.97	2.01	.95	1.99	.94

	Content Scales *(continued)*															
	BIZ		ANG		CYN		ASP		TPA		LSE		SOD		FAM	
	Mean	SD	Mean	SD	Mean	SD	Mean	SD	Mean	SD	Mean	SD	Mean	SD	Mean	SD
Intake Information	(n = 161)		(n = 192)		(n = 171)		(n = 158)		(n = 84)		(n = 263)		(n = 202)		(n = 311)	
Axis IV diagnosis	3.01	1.04	3.02	.98	3.06	1.02	3.03	.98	2.91	.96	3.02	.91	2.98	.88	2.93	.91
Axis V - Current Level of Functioning	59.70	10.71	60.26	9.72	60.67	10.68	60.55	10.21	61.94	8.71	60.07	10.56	59.35	11.27	60.75	9.74
Number of Arrests	.52	1.31	.60	1.32	.51	1.27	.77	1.53	.53	1.27	1.48	4.23	1.80	4.72	1.39	3.71
Mental Status	(n = 161)		(n = 192)		(n = 171)		(n = 158)		(n = 84)		(n = 263)		(n = 202)		(n = 311)	
Anxiety During Interview	2.52	.72	2.43	.72	2.39	.68	2.40	.68	2.44	.61	2.56	.76	2.51	.76	2.53	.74
Depression During Interview	2.58	.78	2.52	.69	2.45	.69	2.52	.70	2.51	.70	2.47	.75	2.43	.76	2.39	.69
Activity Level During Interview	2.92	.43	2.97	.39	2.95	.38	2.90	.38	2.94	.33	3.01	.50	3.07	.47	3.01	.46
Speech During Interview	2.94	.45	2.98	.41	2.96	.41	2.96	.44	2.99	.37	2.94	.38	3.00	.35	2.95	.43
SCL-90-R Scales	(n = 160)		(n = 191)		(n = 171)		(n = 157)		(n = 83)		(n = 261)		(n = 201)		(n = 311)	
Somatization	1.67	.90	1.51	.87	1.56	.90	1.34	.80	1.55	.96	1.32	.82	1.15	.74	1.19	.80
Obsessive-Compulsive	2.04	.90	1.80	.88	1.83	.97	1.61	.88	1.94	.94	1.81	.81	1.73	.84	1.60	.83
Interpersonal Sensitivity	1.99	.92	1.92	.89	1.90	.91	1.62	.89	2.02	.85	1.81	.85	1.84	.85	1.62	.87
Depression	2.34	.93	2.29	.83	2.21	.91	2.02	.87	2.23	.89	2.13	.82	2.08	.85	1.94	.87
Anxiety	2.01	.98	1.74	.91	1.76	.98	1.53	.92	1.84	.95	1.68	.91	1.55	.87	1.51	.88
Hostility	1.85	1.02	2.02	.95	1.69	1.06	1.55	1.04	1.87	1.02	1.51	1.03	1.53	1.04	1.62	1.07
Phobic Anxiety	1.35	1.03	1.09	.95	1.21	1.01	.97	.93	1.19	.99	.90	.75	.88	.72	.75	.69
Paranoid Ideation	2.11	.94	1.85	.91	1.98	.94	1.65	.94	2.06	.92	1.66	.87	1.58	.91	1.65	.86
Psychoticism	1.51	.80	1.25	.75	1.34	.81	1.09	.76	1.41	.81	1.26	.72	1.17	.71	1.14	.70
Initial SCL-90 Analogue	(n = 114)		(n = 122)		(n = 114)		(n = 98)		(n = 58)		(n = 174)		(n = 128)		(n = 215)	
Somatization	2.24	2.62	2.35	2.52	2.25	2.52	2.03	2.36	2.48	2.83	2.75	2.92	2.42	2.87	2.21	2.63
Obsessive-Compulsive	2.45	2.59	2.61	2.50	2.41	2.57	2.63	2.82	2.72	2.47	3.37	2.66	3.68	2.78	3.42	2.83
Interpersonal Sensitivity	4.81	2.66	5.10	2.59	4.97	2.65	5.09	2.67	4.59	2.65	5.03	2.25	5.18	2.39	4.88	2.47
Depression	4.70	2.69	4.77	2.63	4.38	2.66	4.35	2.71	4.07	2.46	4.60	2.57	4.68	2.79	4.47	2.62
Anxiety	4.52	2.86	4.52	2.61	4.24	2.67	4.23	2.58	4.19	2.57	4.69	2.75	4.69	2.85	4.58	2.81
Hostility	2.91	2.56	3.12	2.63	2.84	2.73	3.31	3.01	2.81	2.47	3.27	2.74	3.60	2.82	3.40	2.83
Phobic Anxiety	1.37	2.33	1.30	2.04	.98	1.97	1.31	2.21	1.33	2.06	1.56	2.31	1.51	1.90	1.61	2.42
Paranoid Ideation	1.46	2.25	1.30	1.91	1.31	2.12	1.65	2.42	1.03	1.58	1.28	1.85	1.39	1.94	1.45	2.11
Psychoticism	1.00	2.04	.74	1.55	.75	1.76	1.03	2.09	.79	1.60	.52	1.24	.64	1.14	.64	1.59
Patient Description Form Scales	(n = 113)		(n = 123)		(n = 113)		(n = 98)		(n = 58)		(n = 173)		(n = 128)		(n = 214)	
Angry Resentment	2.71	.81	2.81	.85	2.81	.85	3.01	.82	2.73	.89	2.93	.84	3.03	.88	2.88	.91
Critical/Argumentative	2.28	.84	2.46	.86	2.44	.85	2.60	.89	2.38	.90	2.59	.89	2.70	.90	2.54	.92

	Content Scales *(continued)*															
	BIZ		ANG		CYN		ASP		TPA		LSE		SOD		FAM	
	Mean	SD	Mean	SD	Mean	SD	Mean	SD	Mean	SD	Mean	SD	Mean	SD	Mean	SD
Narcissistic	2.13	.92	2.10	.90	2.16	.87	2.35	.92	2.14	.90	2.30	.89	2.37	.84	2.30	.90
Defensive	2.56	.82	2.54	.78	2.62	.80	2.84	.75	2.61	.82	2.65	.89	2.75	.89	2.57	.88
Histrionic	2.53	.91	2.58	.87	2.52	.87	2.64	.81	2.53	.88	2.48	.73	2.49	.69	2.45	.76
Aggressive	1.92	.80	2.00	.80	1.91	.74	2.13	.90	2.02	.83	2.11	.79	2.22	.90	2.24	.92
Insecure	3.04	.92	3.16	.85	3.04	.85	3.18	.82	3.02	.88	3.14	.72	3.20	.73	3.01	.77
Anxious	2.96	.83	2.93	.74	2.88	.82	2.88	.77	2.81	.75	3.08	.77	3.04	.70	2.96	.79
Pessimistic	2.27	.92	2.38	.90	2.31	.90	2.35	.87	2.15	.80	2.56	.94	2.64	1.04	2.38	.94
Depressed	2.68	.91	2.68	.87	2.55	.86	2.57	.85	2.46	.80	2.58	.78	2.68	.78	2.50	.75
Achievement-Oriented	2.24	.69	2.32	.75	2.27	.76	2.39	.73	2.43	.81	2.53	.73	2.54	.69	2.58	.75
Passive-Submissive	2.58	.94	2.56	.93	2.58	.95	2.64	.96	2.44	.97	2.41	.75	2.37	.78	2.20	.84
Introverted	2.41	.99	2.42	.94	2.46	.98	2.44	.94	2.27	.86	2.78	1.04	2.94	.99	2.62	1.04
Emotionally Controlled	2.32	.90	2.33	.80	2.27	.76	2.46	.80	2.46	.91	2.55	1.10	2.72	1.11	2.38	.99
Antisocial	2.21	.90	2.21	.87	2.28	.88	2.52	.91	2.24	.83	2.16	.90	2.30	1.00	2.32	.94
Negative Treatment Attitudes	1.95	.68	1.99	.69	2.06	.70	2.15	.73	2.05	.72	1.98	.81	2.15	.81	1.95	.78
Somatic Symptoms	2.15	.99	2.11	1.00	2.19	1.03	2.07	.82	2.30	1.23	2.27	1.11	2.21	1.09	2.03	1.01
Psychotic Symptoms	1.43	.74	1.29	.51	1.31	.57	1.37	.60	1.35	.57	1.25	.40	1.29	.43	1.27	.47
Family Problems	3.12	1.18	3.13	1.09	3.09	1.10	3.34	1.08	3.11	1.25	2.94	1.04	2.97	1.07	3.01	1.07
Obsessive-Compulsive	2.47	.83	2.58	.79	2.40	.81	2.66	.89	2.55	.85	2.90	.81	2.96	.78	2.85	.79
Stereotypic Masculine Interests	1.42	.68	1.42	.72	1.41	.65	1.56	.83	1.41	.71	2.87	1.03	2.86	1.16	2.76	1.11
Procrastinates	2.13	.83	2.31	.92	2.17	.80	2.38	.92	2.08	.78	2.34	.91	2.46	.83	2.24	.96
Suspicious	2.59	.94	2.58	.87	2.53	.94	2.75	.94	2.45	.83	2.66	.96	2.87	.92	2.63	.93
Agitated	2.25	.92	2.22	.84	2.21	.83	2.34	.86	2.13	.83	2.22	.70	2.27	.80	2.28	.78
Work Problems	1.73	.96	1.70	.81	1.60	.72	1.65	.72	1.60	.55	1.94	.79	2.02	.91	2.06	.90
Patient Description Form Items	(n = 113)		(n = 123)		(n = 113)		(n = 98)		(n = 58)		(n = 173)		(n = 128)		(n = 214)	
Anxious	3.27	1.07	3.21	.93	3.16	1.01	3.16	.96	3.12	.92	3.54	.83	3.58	.75	3.48	.88
Problems with Authority Figures	2.74	1.21	2.83	1.20	2.87	1.21	3.24	1.19	2.93	1.23	3.07	1.17	3.09	1.14	3.04	1.19
Has Insight Into Own Problems	2.43	.89	2.51	.91	2.24	.77	2.36	.86	2.31	.82	2.65	.86	2.66	.86	2.56	.89
Fears Losing Control	3.14	1.13	3.23	.99	3.04	1.10	3.23	1.09	3.20	1.09	3.35	1.06	3.43	.96	3.27	1.04
Extroverted	2.48	1.08	2.57	1.12	2.42	1.03	2.69	1.08	2.58	1.07	2.28	.95	2.17	.95	2.32	.96
Uses Repression	2.80	1.09	2.87	.98	2.82	1.02	3.03	1.03	2.95	1.07	2.69	1.05	2.87	1.05	2.62	1.01
Submissive	2.70	1.07	2.68	1.04	2.74	1.10	2.85	1.05	2.60	1.12	2.39	.89	2.36	.90	2.19	.90
Difficulty Concentrating	2.89	1.13	2.74	1.01	2.76	1.14	2.77	1.09	2.57	1.01	2.86	1.11	2.75	1.09	2.74	1.09
Rigid	2.42	1.08	2.48	.97	2.42	.98	2.59	1.01	2.60	1.08	2.90	1.08	3.00	1.03	2.82	1.08
Overly Compliant	2.19	1.09	2.11	1.05	2.17	1.08	2.23	1.11	2.05	1.07	2.13	.86	2.00	.93	1.98	.93
Whiny	2.13	1.07	2.08	1.08	2.10	1.07	1.99	1.04	2.19	1.05	2.15	1.07	2.11	1.09	1.93	1.03
Feels Overwhelmed	3.33	1.07	3.35	1.00	3.31	1.13	3.31	1.05	3.12	1.10	3.51	1.10	3.42	1.09	3.33	1.10

Manipulative	2.56	1.27	2.48	1.18	2.49	1.21	2.73	1.21	2.46	1.25	2.45	1.12	2.50	1.13	2.40	1.13
Difficulty Trusting Others	3.40	1.15	3.42	1.06	3.32	1.11	3.53	1.11	3.31	1.17	3.42	1.20	3.63	1.13	3.36	1.21
Insensitive to Others	1.83	.89	1.91	.97	1.96	.91	2.05	1.00	1.90	.89	2.22	.97	2.35	1.02	2.22	1.01
Stereotypic Masculine Behavior	1.34	.67	1.39	.72	1.32	.64	1.44	.81	1.38	.77	2.86	1.08	2.87	1.26	2.74	1.15
Harbors Grudges	2.48	1.03	2.63	.95	2.47	.99	2.75	1.04	2.68	1.03	2.87	1.06	3.12	1.09	2.86	1.10
Evasive	2.39	1.17	2.37	1.01	2.42	1.04	2.63	1.06	2.48	1.14	2.35	1.16	2.56	1.16	2.20	1.11
Disoriented	1.47	.81	1.33	.70	1.39	.76	1.44	.80	1.33	.63	1.26	.53	1.32	.62	1.24	.50
Energetic	2.29	.94	2.36	.97	2.33	1.02	2.53	1.06	2.40	.84	2.41	.89	2.35	.81	2.52	.92
Lonely	2.89	1.10	2.84	1.04	2.81	1.08	2.93	1.02	2.86	1.02	3.13	1.23	3.22	1.20	3.02	1.23
Family Lacks Love	3.05	1.30	2.98	1.23	2.95	1.22	3.21	1.28	2.95	1.30	2.99	1.25	3.01	1.23	2.98	1.30
Worrier	3.39	1.06	3.34	.91	3.23	1.03	3.22	1.03	3.38	1.02	3.48	1.01	3.42	1.00	3.32	1.08
Narcissistic	2.18	1.19	2.14	1.17	2.24	1.14	2.40	1.19	2.16	1.21	2.56	1.16	2.57	1.08	2.52	1.14
Tearful	2.45	1.27	2.35	1.21	2.27	1.13	2.35	1.22	2.33	1.11	1.60	.84	1.63	.83	1.55	.82
Provocative	1.80	1.05	1.76	.94	1.72	.92	1.95	1.07	1.81	.95	1.65	.80	1.69	.91	1.73	.91
Moralistic	2.23	.91	2.28	.87	2.12	.88	2.21	.95	2.14	.80	2.62	1.01	2.62	1.03	2.57	1.10
Socially Awkward	2.50	1.07	2.49	1.05	2.50	1.08	2.56	.92	2.38	.95	2.97	1.14	3.11	1.11	2.87	1.20
Hostile	2.02	1.00	2.25	1.07	2.25	1.10	2.36	1.12	2.22	1.08	2.55	1.16	2.72	1.15	2.58	1.18
Overcontrolled	2.33	1.19	2.45	1.11	2.36	1.13	2.36	1.18	2.44	1.10	2.78	1.27	2.89	1.23	2.67	1.23
Resistant to Interpretations	2.19	.96	2.21	.93	2.31	1.00	2.40	.98	2.33	1.03	2.18	1.04	2.37	.97	2.10	1.03
Antisocial Behavior	1.86	1.04	1.91	1.03	1.96	1.04	2.20	1.13	1.86	.94	2.11	1.15	2.24	1.22	2.34	1.27
Sarcastic	1.80	1.03	1.93	1.08	1.87	1.11	2.08	1.18	1.86	.98	2.09	1.10	2.14	1.03	2.02	1.09
Rejects Traditional Gender Role	1.66	1.04	1.71	1.08	1.69	1.08	1.89	1.18	1.76	1.13	1.69	.98	1.79	.98	1.60	1.05
Feels Gets Raw Deal From Life	2.98	1.17	3.00	1.16	3.03	1.13	3.13	1.02	2.96	1.19	3.18	1.11	3.17	1.13	2.98	1.12
Acute Psychological Turmoil	3.07	1.16	3.00	1.08	2.94	1.14	3.01	1.06	2.82	.95	3.22	.95	3.26	.95	3.07	1.03
Does Not Complete Projects	2.39	1.21	2.38	1.17	2.35	1.06	2.52	1.14	2.11	.94	2.27	1.11	2.34	1.02	2.22	1.12
Uncomfortable with Opposite Sex	2.20	1.18	2.31	1.14	2.17	1.20	2.31	1.21	2.16	1.15	2.19	1.10	2.45	1.08	2.12	1.05
Preoccupied with Health Problems	2.04	1.20	1.98	1.21	2.07	1.26	1.94	1.13	2.00	1.27	2.45	1.44	2.44	1.43	2.06	1.24
Work-Oriented	2.40	1.12	2.55	1.12	2.46	1.11	2.52	1.06	2.54	1.13	2.93	1.07	2.99	1.11	3.03	1.08
Resents Family Members	3.13	1.27	3.12	1.19	3.01	1.22	3.32	1.20	3.12	1.36	2.98	1.23	2.97	1.30	3.07	1.26
Demanding of Attention	2.58	1.15	2.63	1.11	2.57	1.09	2.64	1.11	2.60	1.06	2.56	1.07	2.64	1.05	2.49	1.10
Passive	2.55	1.13	2.47	1.10	2.56	1.11	2.49	1.09	2.47	1.05	2.60	.96	2.66	.96	2.38	1.03
Self-Punishing	2.63	1.17	2.71	1.13	2.51	1.06	2.64	1.10	2.69	1.11	2.60	1.23	2.77	1.16	2.44	1.13
Needs to Achieve	2.43	1.04	2.51	1.03	2.49	1.05	2.53	1.00	2.55	1.08	2.71	1.00	2.77	.94	2.75	.97
Needs to Be with Others	3.05	1.07	3.03	1.06	3.12	1.07	3.33	.92	3.04	1.16	2.99	1.06	2.87	.98	2.91	1.05
Irritable	2.62	1.09	2.73	1.05	2.73	1.04	2.78	1.04	2.52	1.06	2.78	1.07	2.83	.98	2.79	1.04
Self-Defeating	3.19	1.05	3.21	1.01	3.11	1.03	3.34	1.08	3.05	1.14	3.16	1.25	3.33	1.06	3.10	1.15
Delusional Thinking	1.48	1.06	1.30	.72	1.27	.74	1.42	.91	1.34	.85	1.25	.59	1.25	.55	1.23	.61

	Content Scales *(continued)*															
	BIZ		ANG		CYN		ASP		TPA		LSE		SOD		FAM	
	Mean	SD	Mean	SD	Mean	SD	Mean	SD	Mean	SD	Mean	SD	Mean	SD	Mean	SD
Self-Reliant	2.43	.87	2.58	.99	2.47	.91	2.45	.91	2.55	.92	2.63	.95	2.60	.93	2.58	.95
Aggressive	2.03	.95	2.09	1.01	2.13	1.02	2.30	1.13	2.09	1.02	2.36	.98	2.46	1.09	2.45	1.07
Competitive	1.91	.91	2.17	1.05	2.02	1.00	2.18	1.10	2.25	1.06	2.41	.98	2.43	.98	2.43	.98
Suspicious	2.50	1.12	2.50	1.05	2.49	1.13	2.71	1.13	2.43	1.06	2.63	1.13	2.92	1.11	2.59	1.14
Compulsive	2.08	1.12	2.19	1.04	2.06	1.07	2.35	1.24	2.22	1.06	2.58	1.13	2.72	1.08	2.53	1.11
Dependable	2.86	.95	2.88	.91	2.75	.86	2.77	.86	2.82	.83	3.08	1.00	2.91	.90	3.01	1.00
Multiple Somatic Complaints	1.98	1.20	1.96	1.18	2.00	1.17	1.84	.98	2.21	1.45	2.20	1.34	2.15	1.38	1.91	1.18
Complains of Lack of Time	1.84	.97	2.01	1.06	1.98	1.06	2.05	1.13	1.98	.97	2.07	1.15	2.07	1.04	2.00	1.17
Poor Work Performance	1.88	1.06	1.84	.99	1.89	.97	1.96	.95	1.89	.87	2.00	1.01	2.02	.98	2.06	1.12
Insecure	3.47	1.02	3.51	.96	3.48	.95	3.64	.86	3.48	1.00	3.63	.85	3.61	.88	3.54	.88
Discusses Problems Openly	3.16	.93	3.13	.86	3.09	.88	3.05	.92	3.02	.81	3.07	.81	3.07	.91	3.01	.87
Sexually Adjusted	2.44	.95	2.36	.89	2.40	.87	2.41	.75	2.25	.84	2.36	.80	2.35	.80	2.36	.93
Exaggerated Need for Affection	2.40	1.23	2.47	1.18	2.43	1.20	2.51	1.11	2.42	1.21	2.40	1.10	2.34	.94	2.28	1.02
Resentful	3.01	1.04	2.99	.99	3.05	1.04	3.28	.98	2.97	1.08	3.15	1.04	3.31	1.06	3.11	1.12
Uses Denial	2.78	1.13	2.79	.98	2.84	1.07	3.15	1.10	2.84	1.05	2.74	1.23	2.94	1.22	2.64	1.22
Hypochondriacal	1.71	.98	1.67	.96	1.70	.94	1.62	.80	1.81	1.12	1.82	1.02	1.82	.92	1.66	.89
Communicates Effectively	2.83	.87	2.93	.88	2.91	.80	2.91	.88	2.95	.89	3.08	.76	3.06	.80	3.02	.80
Has Many Nightmares	2.13	1.21	2.06	1.11	2.01	1.11	2.13	1.07	2.03	1.13	1.84	1.07	1.92	1.17	1.70	.97
Stormy Interpersonal Relationships	3.12	1.25	3.17	1.13	3.12	1.19	3.32	1.08	3.12	1.13	3.17	1.22	3.31	1.19	3.16	1.20
Feigns Remorse When in Trouble	1.91	1.07	1.76	.92	1.92	1.08	2.19	1.09	1.69	.89	1.73	.94	1.95	1.10	1.79	.95
Stereotypic Masculine Interests	1.48	.81	1.43	.80	1.49	.81	1.66	.94	1.45	.75	2.87	1.07	2.85	1.18	2.76	1.16
Guarded	2.45	1.11	2.50	1.06	2.60	1.01	2.90	1.06	2.52	1.13	2.85	1.31	2.96	1.27	2.77	1.28
Feels Inferior	3.10	1.20	3.32	1.05	3.19	1.10	3.32	1.05	3.19	1.09	3.24	.98	3.27	1.03	3.17	1.01
Low Frustration Tolerance	3.11	1.08	3.02	1.02	3.00	1.00	3.19	.98	2.98	1.01	3.12	1.16	3.34	1.04	3.21	1.12
Psychotic Symptoms	1.44	.94	1.27	.67	1.29	.76	1.32	.79	1.22	.68	1.17	.51	1.17	.45	1.19	.59
Fired From Past Jobs	1.76	1.15	1.57	1.06	1.68	1.00	1.76	1.10	1.38	.72	1.93	.97	2.05	1.18	1.99	1.03
Needs Attention	2.91	1.07	3.04	.94	3.07	1.00	3.21	.88	3.07	1.04	2.96	1.02	2.94	.87	2.89	.93
Acts Out	2.39	1.15	2.42	1.14	2.41	1.07	2.64	1.17	2.56	1.05	2.38	1.14	2.47	1.16	2.55	1.18
Histrionic	2.20	1.20	2.22	1.20	2.21	1.18	2.33	1.24	2.35	1.23	1.99	1.02	1.99	.98	1.97	1.06
Self-Indulgent	2.26	1.10	2.24	1.06	2.32	1.06	2.51	1.07	2.28	1.06	2.46	1.11	2.54	1.09	2.47	1.15
Depressed	3.26	1.02	3.27	1.00	3.11	1.04	3.07	1.00	3.09	.90	3.32	1.03	3.47	.90	3.25	1.07
Grandiose	1.75	1.03	1.66	.97	1.63	.89	1.84	1.01	1.72	.97	1.88	1.05	1.99	1.06	1.90	1.03
Cynical	2.11	1.10	2.28	1.12	2.21	1.12	2.48	1.19	2.22	1.16	2.64	1.20	2.75	1.22	2.50	1.18
Sociopathic	1.53	.89	1.50	.81	1.57	.87	1.73	.97	1.45	.71	1.64	.81	1.73	.93	1.68	.87
Agitated	2.42	1.17	2.38	1.09	2.34	1.05	2.48	1.11	2.14	1.05	2.63	1.02	2.66	1.03	2.64	1.09
Marital Problems	2.31	1.51	2.50	1.49	2.53	1.56	2.56	1.50	2.29	1.49	2.68	1.58	2.75	1.62	2.61	1.63
Absence of Deep Emotions	2.06	1.09	1.92	1.04	1.99	1.00	2.27	1.06	2.16	1.15	2.18	1.30	2.37	1.39	1.98	1.17
Uncomfortable Dealing with Emotions	2.82	1.09	2.90	1.05	2.79	.96	3.11	.89	3.00	1.11	3.12	1.30	3.28	1.26	2.95	1.27

Sad	3.06	1.08	3.03	1.00	2.88	1.01	2.86	1.03	2.71	1.01	3.03	.97	3.08	.94	2.97	.99
Self-Degrading	2.57	1.14	2.75	1.15	2.49	1.07	2.69	1.14	2.59	1.08	2.41	.97	2.54	1.03	2.30	1.03
Unable to Express Negative Feelings	2.21	1.13	2.19	1.11	2.04	.99	2.22	1.17	2.41	1.20	2.29	1.16	2.42	1.16	2.09	1.03
Concrete in Thinking	2.43	1.13	2.32	1.03	2.47	1.09	2.54	1.00	2.41	1.09	2.34	1.09	2.36	1.03	2.21	1.01
Unable to See Own Limitations	2.33	1.08	2.21	1.02	2.35	1.08	2.52	.99	2.26	.91	2.37	1.10	2.38	1.06	2.35	1.11
Power-Oriented	1.84	.95	1.91	.98	1.82	.91	1.95	.97	2.04	1.10	2.18	1.06	2.27	1.16	2.28	1.15
Grouchy	2.13	.96	2.25	.99	2.20	1.03	2.30	1.00	2.14	.98	2.45	1.01	2.46	1.09	2.34	1.06
Overbearing in Relationships	2.11	1.10	2.15	1.10	2.13	1.07	2.23	1.13	2.19	1.17	2.28	1.11	2.42	1.08	2.32	1.13
Uncertain About Career	3.12	1.39	2.87	1.29	2.99	1.39	3.07	1.30	3.16	1.13	3.43	1.29	3.60	1.21	3.41	1.23
Likable	3.15	.88	3.18	.90	3.04	.80	3.21	.83	3.00	.79	3.17	.81	3.13	.80	3.15	.84
Procrastinator	2.34	.97	2.46	1.01	2.34	.95	2.61	1.02	2.30	.97	2.58	1.13	2.76	1.06	2.49	1.14
Negative Feelings Toward Opposite Sex	2.63	1.25	2.78	1.24	2.58	1.30	2.84	1.30	2.45	1.19	2.15	1.12	2.45	1.20	2.10	1.13
Defensive	2.68	1.06	2.78	1.06	2.84	1.15	3.13	1.10	2.79	.95	2.74	1.17	2.86	1.14	2.66	1.20
Empathetic	2.56	.76	2.58	.80	2.48	.70	2.52	.76	2.53	.78	2.42	.72	2.26	.72	2.39	.80
Perfectionistic	2.22	1.10	2.47	1.09	2.21	.99	2.48	1.19	2.52	1.27	2.61	1.12	2.75	1.09	2.51	1.13
Judgmental	2.37	.94	2.58	.92	2.43	.94	2.68	.91	2.60	1.01	2.77	1.04	2.84	1.06	2.65	1.12
Copes Well with Stress	1.94	.79	1.94	.74	1.96	.79	1.95	.68	1.98	.76	1.95	.65	1.97	.69	1.95	.65
Moody	2.89	.99	2.82	.93	2.86	.96	2.90	1.02	2.74	.98	2.88	.96	3.03	.93	2.78	.99
Selfish	2.05	1.03	2.07	.98	2.12	1.03	2.30	1.05	1.95	.91	2.18	.95	2.34	.93	2.18	1.00
Gives Up Easily	2.39	1.12	2.31	1.01	2.36	1.02	2.46	1.05	2.27	1.02	2.34	1.04	2.37	.93	2.22	.97
Physical Symptoms in Response to Stress	2.18	1.19	2.19	1.18	2.27	1.19	2.17	1.08	2.42	1.36	2.40	1.27	2.35	1.21	2.21	1.17
Blames Family For Difficulties	2.89	1.43	2.86	1.28	2.88	1.29	3.15	1.27	2.90	1.39	2.57	1.27	2.66	1.32	2.70	1.27
Bored	2.31	1.11	2.33	1.15	2.41	1.11	2.65	1.10	2.44	1.18	2.61	1.15	2.74	1.05	2.40	1.10
Idealistic	2.29	.95	2.30	.96	2.14	.93	2.29	.96	2.35	1.01	2.44	1.10	2.30	1.03	2.38	1.04
Difficulty Establishing Therapeutic Rapport	1.95	.95	1.88	.90	2.01	.94	2.13	1.00	1.93	.90	2.00	.98	2.19	1.10	2.11	1.06
Daydreams	2.06	1.07	2.00	.92	1.92	.94	2.11	.90	1.92	.91	2.00	1.04	2.19	1.12	1.78	1.02
Concerned About Status	2.05	1.08	2.12	1.08	2.15	1.07	2.33	1.13	2.17	1.10	2.42	1.14	2.46	1.09	2.39	1.14
Creates Good First Impression	2.56	.96	2.69	.97	2.62	.93	2.64	.88	2.50	1.05	2.52	.87	2.36	.83	2.45	.93
Complains of Sleep Disturbance	2.72	1.22	2.73	1.14	2.65	1.20	2.69	1.19	2.58	1.18	2.79	1.25	2.76	1.33	2.53	1.25
Has Temper Tantrums	2.19	1.15	2.42	1.15	2.20	1.06	2.49	1.22	2.31	1.06	2.40	1.17	2.42	1.13	2.51	1.23
Overreactive	2.85	1.18	2.87	1.10	2.71	1.09	2.91	1.02	2.84	1.08	2.77	1.01	2.81	1.06	2.79	1.05
High Aspirations	2.21	1.06	2.20	.98	2.13	1.04	2.31	1.04	2.30	1.11	2.48	1.14	2.38	1.07	2.59	1.17
Feels Hopeless	2.74	1.22	2.80	1.20	2.65	1.16	2.69	1.21	2.57	1.08	2.92	1.16	3.06	1.10	2.79	1.09
Keeps Others at a Distance	2.82	1.15	2.96	1.14	2.86	1.09	3.25	1.04	2.93	1.20	3.04	1.25	3.28	1.24	3.07	1.21
Argumentative	2.12	1.04	2.19	1.05	2.21	1.02	2.38	1.09	2.22	1.14	2.41	1.06	2.50	1.05	2.36	1.08
Paranoid Features	1.85	1.13	1.81	1.01	1.74	1.05	1.99	1.07	1.62	.85	1.92	1.00	2.07	1.03	1.91	.99
Restless	2.51	1.13	2.60	1.10	2.47	1.08	2.69	1.08	2.60	1.14	2.67	1.10	2.75	1.14	2.70	1.15
Pessimistic	2.63	1.13	2.77	1.01	2.70	1.06	2.70	.97	2.50	.95	3.12	1.05	3.21	1.09	2.90	1.08
Feels Like a Failure	2.85	1.12	2.96	1.07	2.92	1.10	2.94	1.10	2.68	1.10	3.22	1.07	3.32	1.09	3.05	1.07
Hallucinations	1.24	.78	1.12	.46	1.11	.53	1.15	.59	1.13	.51	1.09	.32	1.08	.28	1.10	.38
Restricted Affect	2.18	1.18	2.15	1.09	2.13	1.09	2.32	1.15	2.33	1.21	2.41	1.37	2.67	1.38	2.20	1.24
Impatient	2.62	1.07	2.63	1.03	2.62	1.01	2.84	1.06	2.60	1.12	2.78	1.12	2.80	1.02	2.80	1.10

	Content Scales (continued)															
	BIZ		ANG		CYN		ASP		TPA		LSE		SOD		FAM	
	Mean	SD	Mean	SD	Mean	SD	Mean	SD	Mean	SD	Mean	SD	Mean	SD	Mean	SD
Assertive	2.20	.84	2.13	.83	2.13	.84	2.19	.85	2.23	.93	2.32	.82	2.32	.82	2.31	.87
Modest	2.46	.83	2.47	.83	2.47	.83	2.42	.85	2.36	.80	2.53	.86	2.56	.81	2.40	.87
Self-Doubting	3.13	.98	3.17	.97	3.15	1.01	3.18	1.03	3.07	1.00	3.27	.88	3.31	.91	3.14	.95
Deceptive	1.99	1.04	1.89	.91	1.99	1.00	2.26	1.00	1.84	.90	1.94	.98	2.07	1.00	1.89	.99
Feels That Life is a Strain	3.06	1.05	3.13	1.06	3.13	.99	3.10	.95	2.91	1.00	3.37	1.05	3.28	1.04	3.17	1.04
Physically Abusive	1.36	.70	1.44	.73	1.36	.69	1.52	.79	1.37	.79	1.51	.75	1.66	.96	1.68	.99
Feels Rejected	3.18	1.20	3.34	1.08	3.14	1.16	3.34	1.12	3.25	1.05	3.30	1.18	3.45	1.04	3.27	1.12
Does Not Get Along with Coworkers	1.83	1.06	1.84	.97	1.73	.89	1.77	.91	1.89	.80	2.09	1.00	2.13	1.06	2.22	1.12
Uses Projection	2.31	1.12	2.33	1.06	2.31	1.09	2.55	1.07	2.35	1.04	2.51	1.13	2.61	1.13	2.46	1.13
Complains of Fatigue	2.53	1.22	2.53	1.26	2.59	1.20	2.55	1.19	2.57	1.24	2.52	1.40	2.55	1.36	2.32	1.31
Uses Rationalization	2.62	1.11	2.73	1.02	2.63	1.12	2.93	1.07	2.54	1.10	2.68	1.03	2.85	1.03	2.69	1.11
Critical of Others	2.42	1.00	2.63	.99	2.52	1.01	2.71	1.07	2.59	1.01	2.65	1.05	2.79	1.15	2.63	1.14
Egocentric	2.31	1.10	2.29	1.13	2.38	1.09	2.52	1.15	2.32	1.14	2.53	1.15	2.60	1.11	2.54	1.18
Overevaluates Own Worth	1.73	.98	1.64	.96	1.75	.93	1.93	1.03	1.80	.94	1.99	1.13	1.94	1.02	1.98	1.11
Optimistic	2.09	.80	1.97	.81	2.05	.75	2.19	.80	2.14	.88	1.99	.78	1.97	.69	2.00	.73
Psychologically Immature	2.97	1.27	2.86	1.27	3.09	1.23	3.30	1.13	2.93	1.18	2.88	1.11	2.86	1.09	2.91	1.17
Poor Judgment	2.98	1.15	2.89	1.15	3.01	1.14	3.17	1.16	3.00	1.24	2.82	1.11	2.94	1.16	2.95	1.21
Low Sex Drive	2.19	1.27	2.30	1.24	2.11	1.17	2.18	1.14	2.15	1.08	1.88	1.11	1.84	.99	1.78	1.10
Feels Mistreated	3.23	1.04	3.27	1.08	3.27	1.07	3.34	1.03	3.12	1.13	3.09	.99	3.20	1.02	3.04	1.04
Overly Sensitive to Criticism	3.25	1.05	3.35	1.07	3.25	1.06	3.35	.95	3.31	1.11	3.34	1.04	3.34	1.00	3.22	1.06
Sentimental	2.77	1.08	2.62	1.01	2.47	1.00	2.68	.99	2.65	1.03	2.60	1.02	2.51	.96	2.42	.98
Sexual Preoccupation	1.73	1.10	1.66	1.03	1.59	.97	1.75	1.02	1.62	1.02	1.93	1.25	1.87	1.15	1.80	1.16
Accelerated Speech	1.84	1.08	1.71	.91	1.77	1.00	1.78	.96	1.70	.91	1.37	.71	1.43	.78	1.50	.79
Concerns About Homosexuality	1.14	.52	1.18	.69	1.17	.66	1.30	.92	1.22	.76	1.54	1.20	1.54	1.13	1.47	1.10
Many Specific Fears	2.22	1.15	2.11	1.09	2.07	1.07	2.08	1.08	2.00	1.03	1.97	1.05	1.95	1.01	1.86	1.06
Passive in Relationships	2.83	1.18	2.84	1.20	2.84	1.18	2.87	1.24	2.66	1.18	2.52	1.02	2.57	1.02	2.25	1.07
Negative Attitudes Toward Therapy	1.63	.80	1.66	.80	1.80	.87	1.89	.92	1.64	.82	1.87	1.04	2.03	1.06	1.73	.98
Guilt-Prone	2.96	1.20	3.01	1.12	2.83	1.09	2.95	1.12	2.77	1.13	2.86	1.12	2.74	1.08	2.56	1.11
Nervous	3.00	1.04	2.95	.92	2.88	.97	2.88	.90	2.96	.89	3.24	.91	3.23	.94	3.09	.93
Obsessive	2.37	1.16	2.43	1.11	2.20	1.11	2.50	1.21	2.47	1.09	2.96	1.12	2.93	1.14	2.92	1.16
Shy	2.35	1.18	2.38	1.12	2.42	1.21	2.44	1.19	2.30	1.02	2.63	1.23	2.76	1.22	2.46	1.21
Uses Intellectualization	2.14	1.00	2.30	.99	2.14	.96	2.39	1.03	2.25	1.07	2.56	1.26	2.68	1.18	2.50	1.24
Has Many Interests	2.15	.93	2.13	.92	2.05	.90	2.17	.89	2.18	1.07	2.29	1.08	2.22	.88	2.26	1.01
Difficulty Making Decisions	2.90	1.12	2.94	1.07	2.88	1.17	2.95	1.09	2.82	.99	3.05	1.05	3.08	1.02	3.00	1.06
Indirect Expression of Hostility	2.87	1.11	2.88	1.11	2.80	1.09	3.08	1.12	2.85	1.08	2.87	1.10	2.99	1.11	2.78	1.15
Poor Reality Testing	1.71	1.09	1.59	.88	1.62	.93	1.76	1.05	1.77	.95	1.62	.72	1.72	.88	1.68	.83
Angry	3.05	1.18	3.15	1.17	3.04	1.13	3.19	1.22	3.07	1.14	3.24	1.04	3.32	1.06	3.24	1.12
Eccentric	1.83	1.15	1.80	1.06	1.73	1.04	1.83	1.03	1.71	.89	1.99	1.27	1.94	1.12	1.96	1.28

Emotional Lability	2.54	1.10	2.62	1.10	2.52	1.05	2.61	1.09	2.25	.97	2.24	.98	2.37	.94	2.36	1.03
Dislikes Change	2.64	.97	2.64	.94	2.58	1.00	2.71	1.04	2.72	1.01	2.79	.97	2.93	.98	2.73	1.06
Believes Cannot Be Helped	1.92	.91	1.97	.96	1.93	.93	2.00	.96	1.78	.85	1.99	1.03	2.07	1.18	1.84	.97
Reliable Informant	3.11	.93	3.13	.89	3.05	.86	3.09	.94	3.07	.78	3.22	.95	3.17	.89	3.12	.92
Ignores Problems	2.53	1.06	2.55	.96	2.50	1.05	2.59	1.00	2.67	1.02	2.22	1.04	2.38	1.07	2.22	1.01
Ruminates	2.75	.98	2.79	.95	2.67	1.06	2.72	1.06	2.79	.91	3.33	1.03	3.31	.98	3.35	.98
Excitable	2.70	1.04	2.72	1.05	2.63	1.02	2.80	1.02	2.58	.98	2.57	.98	2.59	.93	2.72	1.01
Conforming	2.48	.91	2.51	.90	2.54	.95	2.49	.99	2.48	.91	2.51	.85	2.57	.86	2.41	.88
Ineffective at Dealing with Problems	3.08	1.07	3.05	1.02	3.21	1.01	3.20	.94	3.16	1.08	3.09	1.04	3.14	1.05	3.04	1.04
Introverted	2.34	1.07	2.35	1.12	2.44	1.09	2.34	1.14	2.16	.98	2.74	1.14	2.97	1.08	2.53	1.15
Superficial Relationships	2.89	1.06	2.85	1.07	2.88	1.06	3.13	1.05	2.83	1.07	2.72	1.29	2.93	1.18	2.64	1.23
Impulsive	2.85	1.20	2.91	1.26	2.85	1.21	3.09	1.21	2.98	1.15	2.55	1.21	2.72	1.25	2.70	1.21
Stereotypic Feminine Behavior	2.51	1.16	2.65	1.21	2.59	1.22	2.64	1.15	2.51	1.30	1.34	.62	1.37	.74	1.30	.59
Stubborn	2.61	.95	2.75	.99	2.82	.98	3.02	.92	2.74	1.04	2.84	1.00	3.03	1.10	2.74	1.13
Hostile Toward Therapist	1.27	.50	1.38	.65	1.44	.67	1.46	.72	1.42	.63	1.49	.76	1.49	.75	1.41	.66
Difficult to Motivate	2.23	1.16	2.26	1.09	2.39	1.06	2.46	1.14	2.41	1.17	2.21	1.01	2.45	1.04	2.16	1.00
Suicidal Ideations	1.80	1.06	1.82	.98	1.79	1.03	1.74	.95	1.61	.82	1.85	1.05	2.01	1.14	1.78	.96
Familial Discord	3.48	1.24	3.45	1.24	3.51	1.23	3.61	1.24	3.45	1.31	3.07	1.33	3.17	1.30	3.22	1.33
Dogmatic	2.01	.96	1.99	.91	1.98	.88	2.24	.95	2.14	1.03	2.26	1.11	2.36	1.12	2.31	1.15

Content Scales *(continued)*

	WRK		TRT	
	Mean	SD	Mean	SD
Intake Information	(n = 315)		(n = 284)	
Axis IV diagnosis	2.94	.91	2.97	.90
Axis V - Current Level of Functioning	60.46	9.77	60.47	9.71
Number of Arrests	1.40	3.74	1.70	4.11
Mental Status	(n = 315)		(n = 284)	
Anxiety During Interview	2.50	.72	2.51	.73
Depression During Interview	2.46	.71	2.45	.71
Activity Level During Interview	3.00	.47	3.04	.47
Speech During Interview	2.94	.39	2.95	.38
SCL-90-R Scales	(n = 313)		(n = 282)	
Somatization	1.29	.81	1.29	.82
Obsessive-Compulsive	1.74	.82	1.74	.81
Interpersonal Sensitivity	1.70	.83	1.72	.84
Depression	2.06	.78	2.08	.81
Anxiety	1.59	.86	1.62	.87
Hostility	1.54	1.05	1.63	1.05
Phobic Anxiety	.82	.75	.85	.75
Paranoid Ideation	1.66	.86	1.70	.88
Psychoticism	1.20	.70	1.23	.71
Initial SCL-90 Analogue	(n = 209)		(n = 187)	
Somatization	2.54	2.81	2.46	2.75
Obsessive-Compulsive	3.18	2.74	3.45	2.72
Interpersonal Sensitivity	4.74	2.39	4.81	2.47
Depression	4.65	2.66	4.70	2.62
Anxiety	4.44	2.67	4.70	2.75
Hostility	3.23	2.71	3.47	2.84
Phobic Anxiety	1.32	2.13	1.45	2.12
Paranoid Ideation	1.17	1.77	1.28	1.67
Psychoticism	.52	1.31	.42	1.00
Patient Description Form Scales	(n = 208)		(n = 187)	
Angry Resentment	2.83	.93	2.95	.93
Critical/Argumentative	2.55	.95	2.60	.97
Narcissistic	2.31	.96	2.30	.93

Defensive	2.54	.90	2.56	.89
Histrionic	2.40	.79	2.44	.76
Aggressive	2.11	.84	2.15	.88
Insecure	2.97	.78	3.05	.74
Anxious	2.96	.80	3.03	.76
Pessimistic	2.41	.98	2.53	.94
Depressed	2.53	.77	2.63	.78
Achievement-Oriented	2.53	.73	2.55	.74
Passive-Submissive	2.23	.82	2.24	.83
Introverted	2.60	1.04	2.69	1.03
Emotionally Controlled	2.41	1.09	2.47	1.10
Antisocial	2.22	.92	2.30	.93
Negative Treatment Attitudes	1.94	.80	1.97	.79
Somatic Symptoms	2.18	1.07	2.18	1.03
Psychotic Symptoms	1.23	.39	1.26	.40
Family Problems	2.80	1.13	2.86	1.16
Obsessive-Compulsive	2.80	.81	2.87	.80
Stereotypic Masculine Interests	2.76	1.09	2.83	1.14
Procrastinates	2.32	.99	2.35	.93
Suspicious	2.59	.99	2.69	.95
Agitated	2.16	.76	2.23	.77
Work Problems	2.03	.91	1.98	.93
Patient Description Form Items	(n = 208)		(n = 187)	
Anxious	3.50	.84	3.53	.82
Problems with Authority Figures	2.97	1.23	3.11	1.19
Has Insight Into Own Problems	2.63	.86	2.68	.82
Fears Losing Control	3.28	1.03	3.37	1.04
Extroverted	2.29	.94	2.31	.91
Uses Repression	2.59	1.07	2.64	1.06
Submissive	2.21	.91	2.22	.95
Difficulty Concentrating	2.79	1.16	2.85	1.08
Rigid	2.74	1.10	2.81	1.09
Overly Compliant	1.97	.90	1.97	.90
Whiny	1.99	1.09	2.02	1.05
Feels Overwhelmed	3.36	1.12	3.48	1.06
Manipulative	2.41	1.19	2.41	1.18
Difficulty Trusting Others	3.27	1.27	3.45	1.23
Insensitive to Others	2.22	1.03	2.22	.98
Stereotypic Masculine Behavior	2.75	1.13	2.84	1.19
Harbors Grudges	2.78	1.15	2.91	1.10
Evasive	2.24	1.14	2.33	1.11

	Content Scales *(continued)*			
	WRK		TRT	
	Mean	SD	Mean	SD
Disoriented	1.25	.59	1.31	.63
Energetic	2.34	.88	2.34	.86
Lonely	2.98	1.26	3.07	1.27
Family Lacks Love	2.78	1.31	2.87	1.32
Worrier	3.33	1.09	3.38	1.04
Narcissistic	2.47	1.19	2.51	1.18
Tearful	1.53	.83	1.63	.87
Provocative	1.64	.83	1.69	.88
Moralistic	2.45	1.10	2.44	1.03
Socially Awkward	2.79	1.17	2.89	1.14
Hostile	2.47	1.20	2.64	1.22
Overcontrolled	2.61	1.24	2.72	1.24
Resistant to Interpretations	2.10	1.02	2.16	1.00
Antisocial Behavior	2.24	1.24	2.33	1.26
Sarcastic	2.07	1.11	2.08	1.12
Rejects Traditional Gender Role	1.65	1.05	1.71	1.06
Feels Gets Raw Deal From Life	3.05	1.19	3.17	1.17
Acute Psychological Turmoil	3.05	1.07	3.17	1.01
Does Not Complete Projects	2.29	1.19	2.34	1.11
Uncomfortable with Opposite Sex	2.15	1.11	2.17	1.07
Preoccupied with Health Problems	2.35	1.40	2.34	1.38
Work-Oriented	2.85	1.09	2.93	1.09
Resents Family Members	2.83	1.31	2.89	1.35
Demanding of Attention	2.48	1.15	2.48	1.07
Passive	2.47	1.01	2.46	.99
Self-Punishing	2.39	1.19	2.56	1.17
Needs to Achieve	2.71	1.05	2.76	.99
Needs to Be with Others	2.91	1.15	2.90	1.10
Irritable	2.75	1.05	2.82	1.05
Self-Defeating	3.11	1.25	3.26	1.16
Delusional Thinking	1.20	.57	1.25	.63
Self-Reliant	2.67	.92	2.65	.90
Aggressive	2.38	1.02	2.45	1.05
Competitive	2.40	1.01	2.44	.97
Suspicious	2.53	1.16	2.66	1.16
Compulsive	2.49	1.13	2.59	1.11
Dependable	3.02	.96	3.01	.91
Multiple Somatic Complaints	2.15	1.31	2.13	1.29

Complains of Lack of Time	1.99	1.13	2.03	1.13
Poor Work Performance	2.07	1.14	2.05	1.09
Insecure	3.48	.92	3.51	.87
Discusses Problems Openly	3.08	.85	3.07	.81
Sexually Adjusted	2.38	.80	2.40	.81
Exaggerated Need for Affection	2.26	1.13	2.34	1.07
Resentful	3.01	1.13	3.17	1.13
Uses Denial	2.62	1.24	2.68	1.23
Hypochondriacal	1.73	.95	1.72	.91
Communicates Effectively	3.09	.76	3.10	.77
Has Many Nightmares	1.68	1.00	1.83	1.09
Stormy Interpersonal Relationships	3.05	1.25	3.22	1.24
Feigns Remorse When in Trouble	1.68	.93	1.75	.96
Stereotypic Masculine Interests	2.74	1.14	2.81	1.18
Guarded	2.73	1.33	2.80	1.34
Feels Inferior	3.11	1.05	3.17	1.00
Low Frustration Tolerance	3.13	1.17	3.21	1.16
Psychotic Symptoms	1.14	.46	1.13	.41
Fired From Past Jobs	2.04	1.12	2.06	1.20
Needs Attention	2.87	1.04	2.88	1.00
Acts Out	2.43	1.19	2.55	1.18
Histrionic	1.92	1.01	1.97	1.02
Self-Indulgent	2.50	1.13	2.56	1.12
Depressed	3.34	1.02	3.40	.99
Grandiose	1.95	1.12	1.92	1.08
Cynical	2.57	1.31	2.70	1.30
Sociopathic	1.64	.85	1.71	.89
Agitated	2.45	1.05	2.58	1.03
Marital Problems	2.54	1.56	2.66	1.62
Absence of Deep Emotions	2.06	1.29	2.08	1.30
Uncomfortable Dealing with Emotions	2.91	1.30	3.05	1.33
Sad	2.99	1.00	3.06	.98
Self-Degrading	2.24	1.01	2.33	1.00
Unable to Express Negative Feelings	2.20	1.16	2.22	1.16
Concrete in Thinking	2.23	1.03	2.19	1.03
Unable to See Own Limitations	2.28	1.14	2.25	1.09
Power-Oriented	2.16	1.10	2.22	1.13
Grouchy	2.36	1.05	2.43	1.06
Overbearing in Relationships	2.28	1.15	2.27	1.10
Uncertain About Career	3.43	1.27	3.49	1.30
Likable	3.18	.81	3.19	.79
Procrastinator	2.59	1.21	2.63	1.12

	Content Scales *(continued)*			
	WRK		TRT	
	Mean	SD	Mean	SD
Negative Feelings Toward Opposite Sex	2.11	1.16	2.11	1.13
Defensive	2.66	1.20	2.69	1.14
Empathetic	2.33	.76	2.36	.75
Perfectionistic	2.55	1.15	2.53	1.15
Judgmental	2.68	1.14	2.72	1.12
Copes Well with Stress	1.97	.66	1.96	.64
Moody	2.82	1.01	2.83	1.02
Selfish	2.23	1.07	2.20	1.00
Gives Up Easily	2.29	1.05	2.34	1.03
Physical Symptoms in Response to Stress	2.32	1.23	2.31	1.22
Blames Family For Difficulties	2.52	1.29	2.53	1.32
Bored	2.45	1.14	2.54	1.13
Idealistic	2.35	1.07	2.33	1.08
Difficulty Establishing Therapeutic Rapport	2.01	1.06	2.07	1.06
Daydreams	1.86	1.00	1.82	1.03
Concerned About Status	2.42	1.12	2.45	1.16
Creates Good First Impression	2.54	.89	2.53	.88
Complains of Sleep Disturbance	2.64	1.29	2.80	1.29
Has Temper Tantrums	2.33	1.21	2.37	1.15
Overreactive	2.74	1.07	2.81	1.06
High Aspirations	2.46	1.13	2.49	1.13
Feels Hopeless	2.81	1.15	2.94	1.11
Keeps Others at a Distance	2.97	1.30	3.07	1.30
Argumentative	2.34	1.10	2.37	1.08
Paranoid Features	1.93	1.02	1.95	.99
Restless	2.63	1.11	2.70	1.13
Pessimistic	2.92	1.15	3.10	1.08
Feels Like a Failure	3.05	1.13	3.18	1.07
Hallucinations	1.08	.32	1.09	.35
Restricted Affect	2.29	1.32	2.28	1.34
Impatient	2.72	1.10	2.71	1.07
Assertive	2.33	.82	2.32	.83
Modest	2.38	.84	2.48	.83
Self-Doubting	3.11	.93	3.22	.91
Deceptive	1.93	1.02	1.91	.99
Feels That Life is a Strain	3.16	1.14	3.32	1.06
Physically Abusive	1.51	.83	1.58	.90
Feels Rejected	3.15	1.23	3.24	1.20

Does Not Get Along with Coworkers	2.06	1.02	2.01	1.08
Uses Projection	2.46	1.17	2.49	1.15
Complains of Fatigue	2.48	1.35	2.54	1.35
Uses Rationalization	2.68	1.12	2.70	1.07
Critical of Others	2.61	1.14	2.67	1.19
Egocentric	2.52	1.19	2.58	1.20
Overevaluates Own Worth	1.98	1.12	2.01	1.16
Optimistic	1.98	.72	1.93	.65
Psychologically Immature	2.80	1.14	2.80	1.13
Poor Judgment	2.85	1.17	2.98	1.17
Low Sex Drive	1.88	1.17	1.90	1.10
Feels Mistreated	3.01	1.10	3.08	1.09
Overly Sensitive to Criticism	3.10	1.18	3.19	1.16
Sentimental	2.42	1.05	2.49	1.03
Sexual Preoccupation	1.79	1.16	1.86	1.20
Accelerated Speech	1.44	.80	1.44	.80
Concerns About Homosexuality	1.46	1.08	1.51	1.09
Many Specific Fears	1.85	1.03	1.91	1.01
Passive in Relationships	2.29	1.07	2.32	1.06
Negative Attitudes Toward Therapy	1.75	.98	1.81	1.01
Guilt-Prone	2.62	1.14	2.67	1.14
Nervous	3.11	.96	3.16	.95
Obsessive	2.80	1.14	2.91	1.15
Shy	2.47	1.22	2.54	1.24
Uses Intellectualization	2.56	1.30	2.60	1.26
Has Many Interests	2.28	1.03	2.30	1.01
Difficulty Making Decisions	2.98	1.05	3.02	.98
Indirect Expression of Hostility	2.76	1.13	2.77	1.13
Poor Reality Testing	1.60	.78	1.62	.78
Angry	3.11	1.12	3.25	1.12
Eccentric	1.88	1.23	1.94	1.25
Emotional Lability	2.26	1.05	2.37	1.08
Dislikes Change	2.66	1.02	2.75	1.02
Believes Cannot Be Helped	1.88	1.03	1.94	1.00
Reliable Informant	3.20	.92	3.24	.86
Ignores Problems	2.23	1.02	2.24	1.01
Ruminates	3.22	1.02	3.37	.97
Excitable	2.55	1.02	2.61	1.01
Conforming	2.36	.90	2.47	.86
Ineffective at Dealing with Problems	3.03	1.07	3.03	1.04
Introverted	2.56	1.15	2.66	1.13
Superficial Relationships	2.59	1.22	2.63	1.21

	Content Scales *(continued)*			
	WRK		TRT	
	Mean	SD	Mean	SD
Impulsive	2.56	1.20	2.68	1.22
Stereotypic Feminine Behavior	1.32	.62	1.34	.69
Stubborn	2.75	1.13	2.85	1.12
Hostile Toward Therapist	1.41	.68	1.43	.71
Difficult to Motivate	2.14	1.03	2.20	1.00
Suicidal Ideations	1.80	1.00	1.91	1.04
Familial Discord	2.96	1.36	3.10	1.37
Dogmatic	2.20	1.12	2.28	1.11

Table L-1e. Means and standard deviations for continuous extra-test characteristics (women): High scores on Content Component scales

Extra-test Characteristics	Content Component Scales									
	FRS_1		FRS_2		DEP_1		DEP_2		DEP_3	
	Mean	SD	Mean	SD	Mean	SD	Mean	SD	Mean	SD
Intake Information	(n = 178)		(n = 86)		(n = 382)		(n = 422)		(n = 319)	
Axis IV diagnosis	3.07	1.03	3.18	1.08	3.01	.97	3.03	.97	2.98	.96
Axis V - Current Level of Functioning	60.71	9.62	59.07	12.19	60.50	9.55	61.34	9.37	61.06	9.83
Number of Arrests	.55	1.32	.42	1.27	.41	1.04	.39	1.10	.45	1.10
Mental Status	(n = 178)		(n = 86)		(n = 382)		(n = 422)		(n = 319)	
Anxiety During Interview	2.45	.67	2.41	.80	2.44	.70	2.43	.67	2.42	.69
Depression During Interview	2.47	.71	2.48	.75	2.57	.72	2.57	.72	2.55	.74
Activity Level During Interview	2.95	.42	2.98	.47	2.94	.37	2.96	.37	2.96	.36
Speech During Interview	2.94	.38	2.93	.38	2.94	.40	2.96	.39	2.97	.38
SCL-90-R Scales	(n = 177)		(n = 86)		(n = 380)		(n = 419)		(n = 317)	
Somatization	1.63	.88	1.58	.97	1.50	.85	1.43	.86	1.44	.84
Obsessive-Compulsive	1.96	.94	1.85	.97	1.83	.87	1.77	.87	1.83	.87
Interpersonal Sensitivity	1.91	.91	1.78	.87	1.83	.85	1.80	.84	1.91	.84
Depression	2.24	.90	2.21	.91	2.35	.78	2.29	.79	2.35	.79
Anxiety	1.88	1.02	1.73	.96	1.69	.92	1.65	.92	1.68	.92
Hostility	1.64	1.07	1.51	.98	1.59	.98	1.52	.98	1.61	1.00
Phobic Anxiety	1.43	1.02	1.34	1.04	1.04	.94	.98	.94	1.03	.94
Paranoid Ideation	1.79	.98	1.72	.91	1.70	.94	1.64	.91	1.74	.91
Psychoticism	1.26	.82	1.19	.77	1.18	.72	1.12	.72	1.23	.73
Initial SCL-90 Analogue	(n = 118)		(n = 50)		(n = 255)		(n = 285)		(n = 217)	
Somatization	2.77	2.89	2.65	2.66	2.46	2.67	2.29	2.57	2.36	2.69
Obsessive-Compulsive	2.83	2.70	2.76	2.85	2.65	2.53	2.60	2.52	2.70	2.61
Interpersonal Sensitivity	5.11	2.57	4.57	2.49	5.08	2.58	5.00	2.60	5.23	2.66
Depression	4.56	2.70	4.37	2.59	4.78	2.51	4.79	2.51	4.84	2.51
Anxiety	4.67	2.77	3.86	2.79	4.42	2.66	4.35	2.66	4.47	2.71
Hostility	2.77	2.71	2.27	2.27	2.83	2.54	2.94	2.57	2.92	2.57
Phobic Anxiety	1.41	2.41	1.19	2.11	1.04	1.82	1.08	1.98	1.21	2.11
Paranoid Ideation	1.30	2.09	.75	1.41	1.07	1.84	1.11	1.92	1.22	2.07
Psychoticism	.80	1.91	.44	.97	.59	1.39	.59	1.53	.67	1.59

Table L-1e. Means and standard deviations for continuous extra-test characteristics (women): High scores on Content Component scales *(continued)*

Extra-test Characteristics	Content Component Scales									
	FRS_1		FRS_2		DEP_1		DEP_2		DEP_3	
	Mean	SD	Mean	SD	Mean	SD	Mean	SD	Mean	SD
Patient Description Form Scales	(n = 116)		(n = 50)		(n = 256)		(n = 285)		(n = 217)	
Angry Resentment	2.72	.83	2.55	.78	2.73	.85	2.74	.86	2.72	.86
Critical/Argumentative	2.35	.83	2.23	.74	2.37	.83	2.37	.85	2.38	.87
Narcissistic	2.04	.81	1.98	.86	2.01	.85	2.00	.87	2.03	.86
Defensive	2.58	.84	2.48	.72	2.50	.81	2.50	.80	2.52	.80
Histrionic	2.54	.81	2.44	.74	2.49	.82	2.51	.84	2.55	.86
Aggressive	1.81	.70	1.70	.63	1.82	.70	1.82	.71	1.85	.73
Insecure	3.16	.83	2.98	.85	3.13	.86	3.17	.84	3.20	.86
Anxious	3.10	.78	2.94	.76	2.97	.78	2.94	.77	2.96	.76
Pessimistic	2.36	.88	2.23	.89	2.31	.88	2.29	.86	2.34	.87
Depressed	2.76	.89	2.59	.86	2.70	.85	2.70	.85	2.69	.84
Achievement-Oriented	2.28	.67	2.17	.76	2.38	.72	2.44	.77	2.36	.74
Passive-Submissive	2.75	.88	2.62	1.05	2.62	.89	2.62	.89	2.69	.92
Introverted	2.63	.97	2.47	1.10	2.46	.96	2.46	.95	2.48	.94
Emotionally Controlled	2.47	.88	2.29	.81	2.33	.85	2.36	.85	2.36	.87
Antisocial	2.08	.79	2.08	.84	2.07	.79	2.05	.79	2.17	.80
Negative Treatment Attitudes	2.04	.76	1.95	.72	1.93	.70	1.90	.70	1.91	.65
Somatic Symptoms	2.35	1.11	2.34	1.15	2.22	1.05	2.14	1.03	2.12	1.05
Psychotic Symptoms	1.38	.71	1.28	.42	1.27	.46	1.24	.48	1.28	.51
Family Problems	3.16	1.06	2.92	.99	3.05	1.06	3.04	1.06	3.08	1.08
Obsessive-Compulsive	2.73	.83	2.60	.91	2.55	.84	2.57	.84	2.58	.87
Stereotypic Masculine Interests	1.32	.54	1.24	.46	1.40	.69	1.42	.68	1.39	.70
Procrastinates	2.17	.90	2.23	.83	2.18	.88	2.18	.88	2.22	.88
Suspicious	2.57	.94	2.45	.80	2.48	.90	2.45	.88	2.51	.90
Agitated	2.23	.92	1.99	.72	2.17	.83	2.15	.85	2.18	.84
Work Problems	1.55	.81	1.61	.81	1.64	.82	1.60	.77	1.65	.81
Patient Description Form Items	(n = 116)		(n = 50)		(n = 256)		(n = 285)		(n = 217)	
Anxious	3.37	.97	3.06	.91	3.23	1.02	3.18	.99	3.21	.96
Problems with Authority Figures	2.75	1.26	2.58	1.22	2.73	1.22	2.69	1.22	2.79	1.20
Has Insight Into Own Problems	2.47	.90	2.52	.93	2.50	.86	2.62	.92	2.56	.85
Fears Losing Control	3.19	1.15	3.06	1.02	3.13	1.09	3.14	1.09	3.18	1.08
Extroverted	2.34	1.00	2.41	1.00	2.45	1.05	2.50	1.08	2.46	1.07
Uses Repression	2.90	1.12	2.71	1.06	2.82	1.06	2.79	1.06	2.83	1.07

Submissive	2.88	1.03	2.81	1.16	2.76	1.03	2.76	1.01	2.86	1.05
Difficulty Concentrating	2.90	1.13	2.81	1.04	2.74	1.07	2.70	1.08	2.71	1.07
Rigid	2.58	1.03	2.41	.98	2.44	1.00	2.43	1.01	2.42	1.02
Overly Compliant	2.29	1.02	2.15	.99	2.20	1.04	2.17	1.02	2.27	1.06
Whiny	2.15	1.02	2.08	1.07	2.04	1.02	2.04	1.00	2.07	1.07
Feels Overwhelmed	3.50	1.03	3.31	1.04	3.47	1.04	3.44	1.05	3.50	1.02
Manipulative	2.45	1.15	2.29	1.20	2.41	1.16	2.36	1.16	2.48	1.18
Difficulty Trusting Others	3.38	1.08	3.35	1.02	3.29	1.12	3.26	1.12	3.35	1.12
Insensitive to Others	1.84	.90	1.76	.88	1.83	.90	1.82	.91	1.82	.90
Stereotypic Masculine Behavior	1.24	.54	1.27	.60	1.34	.67	1.35	.67	1.33	.71
Harbors Grudges	2.49	1.04	2.56	.85	2.54	1.04	2.54	1.04	2.54	1.04
Evasive	2.28	1.08	2.18	1.04	2.32	1.05	2.27	1.06	2.31	1.07
Disoriented	1.42	.81	1.30	.65	1.30	.65	1.26	.65	1.32	.71
Energetic	2.28	.89	2.06	.91	2.28	.92	2.33	.98	2.33	.94
Lonely	2.92	1.09	2.92	1.10	2.97	1.04	2.95	1.06	2.96	1.05
Family Lacks Love	3.04	1.24	2.48	1.13	2.94	1.20	2.92	1.22	2.97	1.26
Worrier	3.53	1.03	3.48	.97	3.41	1.03	3.41	1.02	3.42	1.00
Narcissistic	2.10	1.11	1.98	1.11	2.13	1.12	2.12	1.13	2.14	1.13
Tearful	2.48	1.20	2.34	1.14	2.43	1.15	2.41	1.18	2.44	1.18
Provocative	1.74	.99	1.56	.88	1.71	.94	1.70	.96	1.76	1.01
Moralistic	2.51	.94	2.40	.92	2.23	.92	2.29	.97	2.23	.93
Socially Awkward	2.69	1.05	2.49	1.18	2.51	1.04	2.49	1.04	2.53	1.03
Hostile	2.19	1.05	2.04	.97	2.13	1.03	2.15	1.07	2.18	1.06
Overcontrolled	2.61	1.16	2.40	1.12	2.45	1.14	2.49	1.18	2.47	1.18
Resistant to Interpretations	2.33	1.04	2.23	.97	2.21	1.00	2.16	.98	2.18	.95
Antisocial Behavior	1.71	.92	1.61	1.06	1.68	.90	1.65	.89	1.77	.94
Sarcastic	1.87	1.04	1.57	.77	1.87	.97	1.89	.98	1.91	1.04
Rejects Traditional Gender Role	1.52	.84	1.27	.49	1.61	.94	1.65	.96	1.63	.96
Feels Gets Raw Deal From Life	2.99	1.15	2.79	1.07	3.02	1.11	2.98	1.14	2.99	1.16
Acute Psychological Turmoil	3.18	1.07	2.88	1.03	3.06	1.04	3.02	1.03	3.02	1.08
Does Not Complete Projects	2.18	1.08	2.46	1.22	2.25	1.11	2.19	1.09	2.28	1.15
Uncomfortable with Opposite Sex	2.25	1.20	2.24	1.13	2.26	1.18	2.28	1.16	2.27	1.19
Preoccupied with Health Problems	2.21	1.35	2.35	1.38	2.14	1.28	2.05	1.25	2.01	1.24
Work-Oriented	2.48	1.15	2.46	1.13	2.62	1.10	2.70	1.13	2.58	1.10
Resents Family Members	3.15	1.23	2.93	1.16	3.06	1.21	3.07	1.18	3.06	1.20
Demanding of Attention	2.49	1.00	2.40	.99	2.52	1.09	2.56	1.11	2.61	1.09
Passive	2.81	1.08	2.78	1.19	2.59	1.05	2.62	1.06	2.63	1.08
Self-Punishing	2.73	1.19	2.63	1.22	2.74	1.10	2.75	1.14	2.83	1.13
Needs to Achieve	2.42	.93	2.27	1.03	2.58	1.06	2.65	1.08	2.57	1.07
Needs to Be with Others	3.10	1.07	2.90	.98	3.02	1.01	3.11	1.02	3.11	1.03
Irritable	2.71	1.05	2.41	.89	2.64	1.04	2.61	1.05	2.65	1.06
Self-Defeating	3.17	1.00	3.08	.99	3.11	1.06	3.10	1.06	3.19	1.03
Delusional Thinking	1.40	.98	1.24	.56	1.28	.67	1.26	.69	1.31	.74

Table L-1e. Means and standard deviations for continuous extra-test characteristics (women): High scores on Content Component scales *(continued)*

Extra-test Characteristics	Content Component Scales									
	FRS_1		FRS_2		DEP_1		DEP_2		DEP_3	
	Mean	SD	Mean	SD	Mean	SD	Mean	SD	Mean	SD
Self-Reliant	2.50	.90	2.51	.92	2.59	.87	2.65	.91	2.59	.90
Aggressive	1.97	.95	1.76	.88	1.99	.93	1.99	.96	2.02	.95
Competitive	1.93	.90	1.80	.91	2.10	1.01	2.14	1.03	2.10	.98
Suspicious	2.49	1.13	2.35	.93	2.44	1.11	2.40	1.08	2.45	1.12
Compulsive	2.30	1.17	2.31	1.29	2.16	1.10	2.22	1.14	2.19	1.13
Dependable	2.95	.97	2.77	.98	2.94	.86	3.03	.89	2.92	.86
Multiple Somatic Complaints	2.22	1.37	2.38	1.41	2.03	1.23	1.97	1.19	1.90	1.16
Complains of Lack of Time	2.10	1.10	1.96	1.02	1.99	1.11	1.97	1.11	1.99	1.09
Poor Work Performance	1.84	1.01	2.06	1.09	1.83	.97	1.83	.96	1.80	.95
Insecure	3.60	.90	3.41	.86	3.54	.95	3.55	.92	3.60	.93
Discusses Problems Openly	3.17	.92	3.10	1.01	3.17	.86	3.25	.85	3.19	.83
Sexually Adjusted	2.38	.80	2.38	.82	2.44	.87	2.49	.87	2.42	.91
Exaggerated Need for Affection	2.39	1.15	2.30	1.10	2.41	1.13	2.47	1.15	2.50	1.15
Resentful	3.01	1.06	2.87	.93	3.01	1.08	3.02	1.07	3.00	1.08
Uses Denial	2.89	1.08	2.73	.91	2.77	1.10	2.74	1.09	2.77	1.08
Hypochondriacal	1.84	1.07	1.77	.97	1.73	1.03	1.66	.97	1.71	1.05
Communicates Effectively	2.86	.88	2.81	.84	3.00	.84	3.09	.90	2.98	.82
Has Many Nightmares	2.33	1.22	1.89	.92	2.04	1.09	1.99	1.08	1.99	1.10
Stormy Interpersonal Relationships	3.05	1.14	2.79	1.07	3.13	1.20	3.11	1.21	3.21	1.20
Feigns Remorse When in Trouble	1.77	.91	1.79	.99	1.81	1.01	1.83	1.00	1.85	1.03
Stereotypic Masculine Interests	1.38	.69	1.21	.46	1.46	.81	1.48	.79	1.44	.81
Guarded	2.63	1.11	2.59	1.06	2.53	1.13	2.53	1.14	2.52	1.11
Feels Inferior	3.34	1.01	3.14	1.04	3.27	1.10	3.30	1.07	3.35	1.09
Low Frustration Tolerance	2.87	.98	2.89	1.05	2.89	1.04	2.88	1.05	2.90	1.09
Psychotic Symptoms	1.32	.82	1.16	.51	1.22	.61	1.19	.61	1.25	.66
Fired From Past Jobs	1.53	.95	1.61	.95	1.61	1.02	1.52	.95	1.66	1.05
Needs Attention	3.05	.94	3.00	.89	3.00	1.00	3.06	1.01	3.10	.97
Acts Out	2.35	1.06	2.23	1.02	2.30	1.07	2.26	1.11	2.39	1.09
Histrionic	2.27	1.23	2.13	1.03	2.21	1.14	2.17	1.15	2.25	1.20
Self-Indulgent	2.19	1.00	2.25	1.14	2.19	1.05	2.21	1.10	2.25	1.07
Depressed	3.35	.99	3.16	1.05	3.34	.99	3.34	.99	3.31	.96
Grandiose	1.53	.79	1.48	.77	1.61	.90	1.60	.90	1.61	.92
Cynical	2.14	.99	2.06	.89	2.23	1.05	2.20	1.05	2.26	1.07
Sociopathic	1.41	.68	1.38	.68	1.41	.70	1.39	.71	1.42	.71
Agitated	2.41	1.12	2.08	.82	2.35	1.05	2.30	1.03	2.38	1.08

Marital Problems	2.54	1.49	2.41	1.52	2.63	1.55	2.66	1.55	2.70	1.55
Absence of Deep Emotions	2.13	1.08	1.96	1.10	1.95	1.04	1.99	1.04	2.02	1.12
Uncomfortable Dealing with Emotions	2.94	1.06	2.71	1.06	2.87	1.09	2.88	1.09	2.87	1.07
Sad	3.09	1.07	2.98	.97	3.09	1.02	3.12	1.01	3.06	1.04
Self-Degrading	2.65	1.16	2.60	1.16	2.64	1.14	2.67	1.16	2.73	1.16
Unable to Express Negative Feelings	2.33	1.13	2.15	1.01	2.21	1.12	2.28	1.08	2.26	1.11
Concrete in Thinking	2.39	1.07	2.38	1.08	2.29	1.05	2.31	1.09	2.36	1.08
Unable to See Own Limitations	2.25	.96	2.14	1.04	2.13	1.00	2.13	1.02	2.17	1.04
Power-Oriented	1.77	.93	1.61	.79	1.84	.98	1.88	1.00	1.84	.96
Grouchy	2.09	.97	2.00	.90	2.15	.99	2.14	.99	2.14	1.04
Overbearing in Relationships	2.06	1.05	1.98	.98	2.08	1.06	2.05	1.06	2.09	1.08
Uncertain About Career	2.81	1.37	2.82	1.32	2.90	1.32	2.90	1.29	3.02	1.30
Likable	3.23	.84	3.12	.85	3.22	.84	3.30	.86	3.28	.84
Procrastinator	2.33	.95	2.33	.93	2.38	1.01	2.40	1.01	2.42	1.00
Negative Feelings Toward Opposite Sex	2.54	1.17	2.39	1.20	2.55	1.23	2.57	1.21	2.63	1.26
Defensive	2.77	1.04	2.73	.93	2.73	1.08	2.74	1.09	2.74	1.08
Empathetic	2.67	.82	2.65	.83	2.60	.72	2.64	.75	2.57	.73
Perfectionistic	2.45	1.10	2.36	1.11	2.45	1.14	2.50	1.19	2.47	1.17
Judgmental	2.49	.94	2.51	.98	2.53	1.01	2.51	1.02	2.52	1.01
Copes Well with Stress	1.91	.68	1.94	.71	1.99	.76	2.02	.72	2.00	.77
Moody	2.81	.95	2.58	.94	2.79	.96	2.78	.97	2.80	1.02
Selfish	1.99	.89	2.00	1.07	1.95	.94	1.97	.96	1.97	.95
Gives Up Easily	2.37	1.02	2.27	1.12	2.27	1.03	2.24	1.03	2.33	1.05
Physical Symptoms in Response to Stress	2.48	1.27	2.38	1.21	2.31	1.23	2.24	1.21	2.22	1.24
Blames Family For Difficulties	2.84	1.31	2.84	1.22	2.81	1.28	2.80	1.27	2.83	1.31
Bored	2.27	1.08	2.39	1.06	2.27	1.09	2.25	1.10	2.27	1.10
Idealistic	2.44	.90	2.28	1.06	2.33	1.02	2.42	1.05	2.32	1.02
Difficulty Establishing Therapeutic Rapport	1.97	.97	1.88	.98	1.91	.95	1.86	.95	1.86	.89
Daydreams	2.11	1.00	2.07	1.01	1.95	.98	1.92	.95	1.92	.93
Concerned About Status	2.19	1.07	2.08	1.08	2.12	1.05	2.18	1.11	2.17	1.10
Creates Good First Impression	2.72	1.03	2.66	1.14	2.73	.91	2.85	.96	2.76	.95
Complains of Sleep Disturbance	2.87	1.24	2.65	1.16	2.78	1.23	2.74	1.24	2.67	1.21
Has Temper Tantrums	2.09	1.08	2.08	1.13	2.06	1.03	2.08	1.07	2.17	1.08
Overreactive	2.82	1.08	2.78	1.13	2.76	1.07	2.75	1.11	2.80	1.09
High Aspirations	2.22	.97	2.23	1.08	2.34	1.12	2.45	1.15	2.33	1.12
Feels Hopeless	2.77	1.22	2.64	1.29	2.83	1.17	2.81	1.15	2.81	1.16
Keeps Others at a Distance	2.87	1.16	2.96	1.00	2.91	1.12	2.89	1.12	2.92	1.12
Argumentative	2.11	1.02	2.12	1.03	2.17	1.00	2.19	1.05	2.21	1.04
Paranoid Features	1.81	1.12	1.64	.94	1.70	.97	1.68	.96	1.74	1.01
Restless	2.51	1.12	2.30	.89	2.48	1.08	2.45	1.10	2.48	1.09
Pessimistic	2.75	1.06	2.66	1.06	2.73	1.08	2.73	1.05	2.79	1.04
Feels Like a Failure	3.00	1.06	3.02	1.13	3.02	1.12	3.04	1.09	3.07	1.11

Table L-1e. Means and standard deviations for continuous extra-test characteristics (women): High scores on Content Component scales *(continued)*

Extra-test Characteristics	Content Component Scales									
	FRS_1		FRS_2		DEP_1		DEP_2		DEP_3	
	Mean	SD	Mean	SD	Mean	SD	Mean	SD	Mean	SD
Hallucinations	1.20	.69	1.08	.44	1.10	.43	1.10	.45	1.11	.46
Restricted Affect	2.29	1.17	2.18	1.12	2.13	1.08	2.15	1.10	2.16	1.13
Impatient	2.61	1.04	2.52	1.05	2.56	1.03	2.55	1.03	2.57	1.03
Assertive	2.07	.77	2.10	.86	2.16	.88	2.17	.89	2.07	.86
Modest	2.60	.85	2.52	.97	2.54	.84	2.61	.82	2.54	.84
Self-Doubting	3.24	.96	3.15	1.07	3.19	1.01	3.21	.97	3.29	.99
Deceptive	1.89	.84	1.72	.90	1.83	.91	1.82	.90	1.88	.96
Feels That Life is a Strain	3.20	.99	3.31	1.01	3.20	1.01	3.15	1.05	3.18	.99
Physically Abusive	1.33	.61	1.15	.42	1.32	.65	1.30	.63	1.29	.60
Feels Rejected	3.17	1.15	2.96	1.06	3.22	1.10	3.28	1.09	3.28	1.08
Does Not Get Along with Coworkers	1.66	.97	1.59	.87	1.69	.92	1.67	.90	1.69	.90
Uses Projection	2.36	1.11	2.23	1.07	2.32	1.06	2.33	1.06	2.37	1.08
Complains of Fatigue	2.83	1.26	2.62	1.34	2.73	1.26	2.65	1.30	2.59	1.26
Uses Rationalization	2.65	1.02	2.61	1.00	2.63	1.06	2.64	1.06	2.67	1.07
Critical of Others	2.46	.99	2.45	1.04	2.49	1.05	2.46	1.07	2.47	1.06
Egocentric	2.31	1.07	2.24	.92	2.22	1.05	2.18	1.08	2.23	1.07
Overevaluates Own Worth	1.67	.82	1.64	.92	1.69	.95	1.65	.94	1.66	.94
Optimistic	2.10	.76	1.90	.75	1.97	.79	2.03	.81	1.98	.77
Psychologically Immature	2.90	1.23	2.84	1.14	2.85	1.19	2.80	1.17	2.92	1.17
Poor Judgment	2.86	1.17	2.86	1.19	2.80	1.15	2.74	1.15	2.91	1.15
Low Sex Drive	2.40	1.29	2.36	1.25	2.26	1.24	2.22	1.21	2.17	1.22
Feels Mistreated	3.19	1.08	3.08	1.13	3.22	1.11	3.22	1.12	3.25	1.11
Overly Sensitive to Criticism	3.36	1.09	3.13	1.15	3.22	1.09	3.27	1.08	3.22	1.09
Sentimental	2.74	1.03	2.64	1.06	2.59	1.02	2.66	1.01	2.49	1.01
Sexual Preoccupation	1.52	.87	1.43	.92	1.51	.92	1.53	.92	1.62	1.01
Accelerated Speech	1.77	1.02	1.59	.96	1.67	.95	1.69	.99	1.69	.94
Concerns About Homosexuality	1.05	.22	1.05	.21	1.16	.62	1.17	.64	1.18	.66
Many Specific Fears	2.34	1.16	2.12	1.25	2.15	1.08	2.10	1.06	2.13	1.08
Passive in Relationships	2.93	1.10	2.70	1.30	2.89	1.14	2.89	1.13	2.95	1.17
Negative Attitudes Toward Therapy	1.82	.95	1.68	.84	1.69	.87	1.65	.85	1.63	.80
Guilt-Prone	3.12	1.18	2.98	1.19	3.06	1.15	3.06	1.13	3.11	1.15
Nervous	3.16	.95	2.88	.97	2.96	.99	2.94	.98	2.93	.96
Obsessive	2.57	1.12	2.40	1.16	2.38	1.13	2.43	1.16	2.41	1.19
Shy	2.63	1.16	2.37	1.20	2.45	1.13	2.44	1.11	2.49	1.11
Uses Intellectualization	2.24	.90	2.15	.85	2.27	1.07	2.27	1.07	2.30	1.09

Has Many Interests	2.11	.89	2.05	.96	2.19	.91	2.29	.94	2.14	.86
Difficulty Making Decisions	3.00	1.06	2.87	1.06	2.94	1.09	2.94	1.08	3.01	1.08
Indirect Expression of Hostility	2.88	1.09	2.79	1.07	2.79	1.10	2.82	1.09	2.83	1.13
Poor Reality Testing	1.66	1.03	1.59	.86	1.52	.84	1.47	.81	1.57	.95
Angry	3.04	1.15	2.78	1.14	3.03	1.13	3.06	1.15	3.03	1.12
Eccentric	1.75	1.00	1.65	1.00	1.69	.98	1.64	.94	1.71	1.01
Emotional Lability	2.51	1.02	2.43	.95	2.53	1.06	2.47	1.08	2.53	1.09
Dislikes Change	2.86	.95	2.57	1.09	2.67	1.00	2.63	.96	2.66	1.00
Believes Cannot Be Helped	1.94	.88	1.83	.90	1.89	.89	1.86	.90	1.88	.92
Reliable Informant	3.17	.90	3.18	.95	3.22	.90	3.33	.91	3.24	.89
Ignores Problems	2.52	1.04	2.43	1.08	2.42	1.04	2.36	1.02	2.48	1.05
Ruminates	3.01	.99	2.84	1.07	2.88	1.02	2.88	1.04	2.84	1.02
Excitable	2.69	.98	2.45	.84	2.57	1.01	2.55	1.03	2.61	1.04
Conforming	2.68	.95	2.64	1.11	2.57	.95	2.60	.95	2.59	.96
Ineffective at Dealing with Problems	3.14	1.01	3.06	1.09	3.08	.99	3.05	.98	3.09	1.02
Introverted	2.54	1.08	2.43	1.17	2.40	1.07	2.42	1.08	2.42	1.06
Superficial Relationships	2.79	1.08	2.79	1.14	2.74	1.09	2.74	1.09	2.83	1.08
Impulsive	2.71	1.18	2.45	1.06	2.70	1.19	2.65	1.23	2.82	1.19
Stereotypic Feminine Behavior	2.88	1.17	2.79	1.22	2.77	1.18	2.82	1.17	2.77	1.19
Stubborn	2.63	.97	2.51	.91	2.72	.98	2.74	1.01	2.69	1.02
Hostile Toward Therapist	1.33	.63	1.24	.52	1.33	.67	1.33	.67	1.31	.61
Difficult to Motivate	2.32	1.10	2.27	1.09	2.14	1.02	2.12	1.03	2.13	1.04
Suicidal Ideations	1.92	1.08	1.73	1.01	1.80	.99	1.77	.99	1.79	.98
Familial Discord	3.51	1.14	3.43	1.14	3.39	1.21	3.40	1.20	3.45	1.21
Dogmatic	2.16	1.02	2.04	1.01	2.02	.95	2.00	.95	2.02	.98

	Content Component Scales (continued)															
	DEP_4		HEA_1		HEA_2		HEA_3		BIZ_1		BIZ_2		ANG_1		ANG_2	
	Mean	SD	Mean	SD	Mean	SD	Mean	SD	Mean	SD	Mean	SD	Mean	SD	Mean	SD
Intake Information	(n = 186)		(n = 301)		(n = 240)		(n = 258)		(n = 134)		(n = 209)		(n = 165)		(n = 270)	
Axis IV diagnosis	3.02	1.02	3.02	.98	3.10	1.00	3.06	1.02	2.91	.94	3.00	1.02	3.08	.97	2.98	1.00
Axis V - Current Level of Functioning	59.27	9.84	61.01	9.85	60.29	9.87	60.28	10.59	60.42	10.49	60.46	10.02	60.79	9.51	61.07	9.48
Number of Arrests	.35	.77	.46	1.59	.43	1.06	.36	.92	.55	1.26	.57	1.54	.64	1.22	.47	1.17
Mental Status	(n = 186)		(n = 301)		(n = 240)		(n = 258)		(n = 134)		(n = 209)		(n = 165)		(n = 270)	
Anxiety During Interview	2.49	.74	2.48	.72	2.45	.71	2.45	.72	2.45	.71	2.47	.71	2.40	.70	2.41	.69
Depression During Interview	2.67	.76	2.55	.73	2.59	.71	2.60	.73	2.50	.78	2.53	.75	2.49	.65	2.51	.74
Activity Level During Interview	2.93	.43	2.97	.41	2.97	.41	2.97	.40	2.93	.41	2.96	.42	2.95	.39	2.97	.37
Speech During Interview	2.93	.44	2.98	.44	2.97	.41	2.98	.42	2.95	.42	2.97	.48	2.97	.41	2.98	.40
SCL-90-R Scales	(n = 185)		(n = 299)		(n = 239)		(n = 257)		(n = 133)		(n = 208)		(n = 164)		(n = 268)	
Somatization	1.67	.84	1.69	.84	1.90	.80	1.82	.81	1.64	.92	1.60	.90	1.52	.88	1.47	.83
Obsessive-Compulsive	2.03	.86	1.85	.88	2.01	.86	1.98	.90	2.01	.90	1.94	.89	1.81	.90	1.82	.86
Interpersonal Sensitivity	2.06	.87	1.77	.86	1.82	.88	1.87	.90	1.97	.90	1.97	.92	1.96	.89	1.88	.87
Depression	2.65	.75	2.22	.88	2.32	.85	2.35	.82	2.31	.91	2.30	.90	2.30	.86	2.30	.82
Anxiety	1.90	.91	1.75	.94	1.91	.92	1.83	.93	1.93	.95	1.89	.95	1.78	.94	1.69	.88
Hostility	1.85	1.01	1.50	1.00	1.62	1.03	1.58	1.01	1.77	1.04	1.81	1.03	2.11	.98	1.83	.96
Phobic Anxiety	1.18	.95	1.10	.98	1.28	.98	1.24	.97	1.30	1.03	1.26	1.00	1.15	.97	1.02	.90
Paranoid Ideation	1.89	.96	1.66	.97	1.77	.97	1.76	.96	2.10	.96	2.01	.92	1.91	.91	1.73	.88
Psychoticism	1.41	.71	1.16	.75	1.26	.76	1.26	.75	1.50	.79	1.39	.77	1.31	.79	1.18	.73
Initial SCL-90 Analogue	(n = 125)		(n = 203)		(n = 159)		(n = 172)		(n = 94)		(n = 142)		(n = 100)		(n = 180)	
Somatization	2.28	2.69	2.79	2.90	3.22	2.88	3.00	2.90	2.16	2.63	2.30	2.69	2.08	2.38	2.25	2.43
Obsessive-Compulsive	2.33	2.57	2.82	2.68	2.80	2.49	2.59	2.46	2.64	2.64	2.73	2.71	2.42	2.49	2.69	2.46
Interpersonal Sensitivity	5.13	2.64	4.97	2.74	5.28	2.55	5.01	2.69	4.78	2.75	4.92	2.73	4.84	2.74	5.07	2.50
Depression	4.96	2.61	4.84	2.64	5.05	2.53	5.01	2.57	4.57	2.53	4.64	2.58	4.53	2.75	4.77	2.53
Anxiety	4.41	2.77	4.66	2.78	4.93	2.60	4.66	2.68	4.56	2.84	4.57	2.76	4.28	2.55	4.61	2.53
Hostility	2.78	2.59	3.01	2.73	3.10	2.63	2.79	2.61	2.88	2.51	2.96	2.56	2.95	2.60	2.89	2.49
Phobic Anxiety	1.22	2.04	1.38	2.27	1.38	2.09	1.20	2.06	1.15	2.23	1.50	2.46	1.19	1.77	1.08	1.87
Paranoid Ideation	1.14	1.87	1.23	2.08	1.24	1.95	1.02	1.84	1.16	1.97	1.44	2.14	1.30	2.03	1.04	1.71
Psychoticism	.54	1.42	.69	1.66	.70	1.49	.60	1.48	.86	1.84	.94	1.93	.78	1.56	.59	1.42
Patient Description Form Scales	(n = 126)		(n = 204)		(n = 157)		(n = 171)		(n = 93)		(n = 141)		(n = 101)		(n = 180)	
Angry Resentment	2.71	.92	2.68	.90	2.77	.83	2.64	.84	2.80	.83	2.76	.84	2.79	.92	2.67	.82
Critical/Argumentative	2.39	.88	2.26	.86	2.38	.83	2.25	.82	2.35	.93	2.35	.87	2.47	.89	2.31	.79

Narcissistic	1.98	.85	1.94	.80	2.00	.77	1.88	.76	2.14	.91	2.12	.91	2.06	.84	2.03	.88
Defensive	2.44	.85	2.45	.85	2.56	.79	2.45	.82	2.61	.86	2.55	.85	2.56	.81	2.47	.78
Histrionic	2.44	.82	2.49	.81	2.58	.80	2.43	.75	2.51	.93	2.52	.89	2.52	.88	2.57	.82
Aggressive	1.77	.74	1.80	.72	1.83	.71	1.72	.67	1.96	.80	1.89	.75	1.98	.84	1.86	.73
Insecure	3.15	.92	3.05	.90	3.20	.85	3.16	.87	2.99	.93	3.07	.92	3.12	.91	3.19	.84
Anxious	2.95	.79	2.97	.84	3.12	.79	3.04	.79	3.01	.86	2.97	.85	2.89	.74	2.96	.75
Pessimistic	2.38	.92	2.25	.91	2.42	.89	2.36	.89	2.31	.90	2.28	.90	2.34	.92	2.27	.84
Depressed	2.85	.88	2.68	.89	2.83	.85	2.81	.84	2.59	.84	2.69	.91	2.64	.92	2.70	.82
Achievement-Oriented	2.23	.73	2.38	.71	2.30	.67	2.23	.67	2.30	.70	2.30	.75	2.26	.72	2.38	.76
Passive-Submissive	2.59	.95	2.58	.93	2.72	.89	2.73	.91	2.67	1.00	2.60	.95	2.57	.97	2.66	.91
Introverted	2.48	.97	2.37	.97	2.52	.99	2.45	.96	2.35	.94	2.47	1.00	2.49	.97	2.43	.93
Emotionally Controlled	2.25	.86	2.29	.89	2.39	.89	2.28	.82	2.30	.96	2.32	.90	2.37	.90	2.32	.84
Antisocial	2.04	.83	1.98	.75	2.04	.74	1.96	.71	2.29	.94	2.19	.88	2.22	.90	2.12	.77
Negative Treatment Attitudes	1.91	.72	1.90	.75	1.95	.67	1.87	.69	1.99	.71	1.94	.67	1.93	.69	1.91	.68
Somatic Symptoms	2.14	1.03	2.30	1.09	2.50	1.11	2.44	1.12	2.09	1.05	2.11	1.01	2.02	1.00	2.13	1.00
Psychotic Symptoms	1.27	.51	1.27	.55	1.31	.53	1.24	.47	1.40	.69	1.40	.69	1.29	.50	1.24	.46
Family Problems	3.01	1.15	3.01	1.13	3.14	1.10	2.97	1.13	3.09	1.19	3.13	1.13	3.13	1.17	3.05	1.09
Obsessive-Compulsive	2.48	.91	2.54	.83	2.64	.80	2.52	.80	2.48	.86	2.52	.89	2.52	.84	2.60	.78
Stereotypic Masculine Interests	1.37	.69	1.41	.70	1.39	.73	1.32	.64	1.37	.67	1.40	.69	1.40	.69	1.42	.74
Procrastinates	2.20	.95	2.14	.94	2.31	.86	2.12	.87	2.13	.88	2.13	.83	2.34	.93	2.21	.87
Suspicious	2.46	.92	2.44	.98	2.55	.91	2.43	.89	2.57	.91	2.61	.98	2.55	.92	2.44	.87
Agitated	2.15	.83	2.16	.86	2.27	.82	2.17	.84	2.25	.88	2.22	.91	2.21	.84	2.20	.82
Work Problems	1.58	.80	1.56	.74	1.58	.81	1.50	.78	1.66	.90	1.65	.89	1.60	.75	1.65	.83
Patient Description Form Items	(n = 126)		(n = 204)		(n = 157)		(n = 171)		(n = 93)		(n = 141)		(n = 101)		(n = 180)	
Anxious	3.13	1.00	3.24	1.02	3.37	1.03	3.26	1.03	3.24	1.05	3.31	1.03	3.13	.87	3.25	.96
Problems with Authority Figures	2.69	1.21	2.66	1.23	2.73	1.23	2.63	1.25	2.82	1.25	2.78	1.26	2.82	1.25	2.70	1.22
Has Insight Into Own Problems	2.44	.85	2.54	.93	2.45	.84	2.51	.90	2.44	.84	2.45	.87	2.49	.90	2.52	.86
Fears Losing Control	3.09	1.15	3.13	1.11	3.24	1.12	3.14	1.12	3.10	1.09	3.21	1.14	3.18	1.00	3.22	1.04
Extroverted	2.33	1.06	2.48	1.02	2.53	1.01	2.42	.97	2.58	1.04	2.45	1.12	2.53	1.10	2.50	1.12
Uses Repression	2.63	1.10	2.77	1.06	2.87	1.02	2.83	1.04	2.75	1.05	2.83	1.13	2.86	1.05	2.83	1.01
Submissive	2.69	1.06	2.70	1.05	2.87	1.02	2.88	1.05	2.80	1.08	2.72	1.08	2.74	1.09	2.81	1.08
Difficulty Concentrating	2.72	1.06	2.82	1.17	2.97	1.08	2.85	1.06	2.90	1.08	2.77	1.12	2.75	.99	2.69	1.04
Rigid	2.36	1.00	2.50	1.00	2.53	1.00	2.49	1.00	2.47	1.10	2.45	1.07	2.44	1.02	2.39	.96
Overly Compliant	2.12	1.07	2.16	1.08	2.26	1.07	2.22	1.04	2.34	1.18	2.20	1.09	2.17	1.13	2.23	1.00
Whiny	2.03	1.07	2.01	1.02	2.15	1.04	2.01	1.01	2.15	1.02	2.10	1.07	2.03	1.11	1.98	1.00
Feels Overwhelmed	3.40	1.10	3.46	1.11	3.59	1.06	3.58	1.03	3.30	1.07	3.40	1.10	3.24	1.04	3.45	1.06
Manipulative	2.36	1.19	2.34	1.10	2.38	1.10	2.29	1.14	2.56	1.31	2.52	1.23	2.42	1.16	2.42	1.16
Difficulty Trusting Others	3.29	1.19	3.17	1.15	3.36	1.12	3.23	1.11	3.33	1.20	3.41	1.17	3.43	1.13	3.28	1.10
Insensitive to Others	1.74	.89	1.80	.91	1.83	.80	1.72	.84	1.97	.85	1.83	.88	1.86	.95	1.85	.93
Stereotypic Masculine Behavior	1.29	.67	1.35	.70	1.36	.72	1.29	.66	1.32	.66	1.33	.69	1.37	.71	1.38	.74
Harbors Grudges	2.51	1.07	2.44	1.02	2.55	.97	2.44	1.01	2.59	.97	2.53	1.08	2.55	1.03	2.49	.98

Content Component Scales *(continued)*

	DEP_4		HEA_1		HEA_2		HEA_3		BIZ_1		BIZ_2		ANG_1		ANG_2	
	Mean	SD	Mean	SD	Mean	SD	Mean	SD	Mean	SD	Mean	SD	Mean	SD	Mean	SD
Evasive	2.25	1.11	2.17	1.04	2.32	1.05	2.20	1.09	2.47	1.11	2.38	1.14	2.33	1.06	2.24	1.02
Disoriented	1.27	.66	1.38	.78	1.40	.77	1.32	.69	1.44	.81	1.44	.79	1.36	.70	1.28	.64
Energetic	2.15	.91	2.29	.91	2.25	.93	2.15	.89	2.42	.92	2.36	.98	2.36	.95	2.34	.98
Lonely	2.98	1.10	2.88	1.07	3.06	1.07	3.00	1.06	2.84	1.09	2.91	1.12	2.80	1.10	2.93	1.06
Family Lacks Love	2.94	1.31	2.88	1.28	3.08	1.27	2.90	1.26	2.95	1.24	3.03	1.29	3.05	1.31	2.89	1.25
Worrier	3.34	.98	3.37	1.01	3.54	.96	3.51	1.00	3.40	1.05	3.40	1.11	3.24	.97	3.42	.96
Narcissistic	2.10	1.15	1.98	1.05	2.06	1.06	1.92	1.05	2.25	1.22	2.22	1.20	2.14	1.13	2.12	1.13
Tearful	2.60	1.23	2.40	1.18	2.48	1.20	2.58	1.20	2.43	1.17	2.40	1.21	2.34	1.19	2.46	1.16
Provocative	1.67	.97	1.72	.95	1.65	.89	1.60	.83	1.97	1.14	1.79	1.02	1.73	.92	1.79	.99
Moralistic	2.26	.98	2.33	.95	2.34	.94	2.34	.95	2.30	.96	2.21	.94	2.19	.89	2.26	.93
Socially Awkward	2.55	1.02	2.46	1.05	2.64	1.05	2.51	1.03	2.48	1.05	2.50	1.08	2.58	1.08	2.44	1.03
Hostile	2.07	1.03	2.15	1.10	2.15	1.00	2.05	.99	2.15	.99	2.09	1.05	2.23	1.10	2.13	1.04
Overcontrolled	2.35	1.13	2.39	1.14	2.46	1.12	2.36	1.13	2.32	1.19	2.41	1.22	2.48	1.15	2.40	1.14
Resistant to Interpretations	2.16	.98	2.17	1.01	2.26	.95	2.14	.98	2.33	1.01	2.22	.97	2.19	.95	2.19	.95
Antisocial Behavior	1.60	.90	1.67	.91	1.63	.88	1.61	.83	1.90	1.02	1.88	1.02	1.87	1.04	1.73	.91
Sarcastic	1.90	1.05	1.81	1.02	1.92	1.04	1.78	.98	1.84	1.08	1.89	1.05	1.94	1.02	1.81	.94
Rejects Traditional Gender Role	1.60	.99	1.63	.98	1.61	.98	1.55	.90	1.59	.98	1.68	1.04	1.68	.98	1.63	1.00
Feels Gets Raw Deal From Life	2.98	1.18	2.90	1.16	3.09	1.08	2.95	1.10	3.02	1.24	2.97	1.18	2.92	1.14	2.94	1.16
Acute Psychological Turmoil	2.97	1.15	3.05	1.10	3.19	1.09	3.11	1.05	3.05	1.13	3.07	1.14	2.92	1.12	3.02	1.04
Does Not Complete Projects	2.26	1.20	2.18	1.14	2.35	1.12	2.15	1.08	2.38	1.16	2.27	1.12	2.37	1.16	2.22	1.07
Uncomfortable with Opposite Sex	2.36	1.25	2.31	1.19	2.39	1.19	2.34	1.21	2.18	1.24	2.23	1.23	2.29	1.15	2.27	1.17
Preoccupied with Health Problems	2.06	1.29	2.21	1.29	2.44	1.38	2.42	1.42	1.98	1.17	2.02	1.20	1.92	1.24	2.02	1.23
Work-Oriented	2.47	1.13	2.65	1.11	2.52	1.06	2.49	1.09	2.50	1.12	2.47	1.12	2.48	1.02	2.65	1.17
Resents Family Members	3.01	1.25	2.99	1.27	3.12	1.24	2.99	1.27	3.08	1.33	3.11	1.23	3.14	1.24	3.07	1.19
Demanding of Attention	2.46	1.05	2.53	1.04	2.51	1.07	2.36	1.02	2.52	1.09	2.57	1.11	2.58	1.10	2.62	1.08
Passive	2.60	1.07	2.62	1.07	2.73	1.09	2.74	1.13	2.56	1.08	2.56	1.11	2.49	1.14	2.62	1.10
Self-Punishing	2.76	1.16	2.66	1.14	2.88	1.17	2.83	1.17	2.62	1.20	2.63	1.23	2.74	1.17	2.75	1.13
Needs to Achieve	2.44	1.09	2.55	.99	2.54	1.02	2.43	1.02	2.45	1.03	2.53	1.04	2.45	1.03	2.61	1.06
Needs to Be with Others	2.90	1.14	3.08	1.07	3.13	.97	3.08	1.03	3.01	1.04	3.04	1.07	3.04	1.12	3.12	1.00
Irritable	2.71	1.06	2.59	1.07	2.68	1.02	2.57	1.03	2.63	1.10	2.62	1.08	2.73	1.08	2.59	1.02
Self-Defeating	3.11	1.08	2.98	1.08	3.14	1.05	3.11	1.06	3.15	1.08	3.14	1.10	3.24	1.03	3.13	1.07
Delusional Thinking	1.27	.70	1.26	.68	1.33	.77	1.24	.66	1.45	.98	1.46	.99	1.28	.73	1.26	.72
Self-Reliant	2.45	.87	2.61	.93	2.55	.88	2.55	.87	2.49	.80	2.49	.90	2.56	.96	2.59	.94
Aggressive	1.88	.92	2.01	.96	2.01	.91	1.89	.88	2.09	.98	2.03	.92	2.12	1.05	2.02	.99
Competitive	1.96	.95	2.12	.99	2.06	.96	1.95	.92	1.98	.93	1.99	.96	2.08	1.00	2.16	1.06
Suspicious	2.37	1.12	2.40	1.16	2.51	1.10	2.37	1.11	2.55	1.09	2.51	1.21	2.43	1.13	2.37	1.07
Compulsive	2.02	1.14	2.23	1.13	2.20	1.05	2.14	1.09	2.06	1.07	2.18	1.17	2.18	1.09	2.24	1.09
Dependable	2.86	.90	3.01	.93	2.88	.86	2.97	.87	2.91	.83	2.93	.95	2.85	.84	2.96	.92

Multiple Somatic Complaints	1.94	1.23	2.17	1.29	2.36	1.33	2.34	1.37	1.91	1.23	1.92	1.17	1.85	1.13	1.92	1.17
Complains of Lack of Time	1.93	1.12	2.03	1.15	2.12	1.12	2.05	1.15	1.90	1.10	1.93	1.04	2.04	1.08	2.06	1.12
Poor Work Performance	1.80	1.04	1.86	1.01	1.81	.98	1.76	.97	1.81	.95	1.83	1.04	1.78	.97	1.83	1.00
Insecure	3.57	.98	3.50	.99	3.60	.93	3.58	.91	3.37	1.01	3.50	.99	3.51	1.01	3.58	.89
Discusses Problems Openly	3.08	.85	3.17	.86	3.18	.78	3.14	.86	3.13	.85	3.20	.89	3.17	.88	3.20	.86
Sexually Adjusted	2.28	.95	2.42	.92	2.41	.86	2.36	.87	2.41	.81	2.40	.96	2.46	.91	2.43	.86
Exaggerated Need for Affection	2.29	1.13	2.39	1.17	2.39	1.12	2.35	1.10	2.34	1.18	2.34	1.21	2.37	1.17	2.54	1.12
Resentful	2.94	1.13	2.90	1.08	2.99	1.01	2.91	1.06	3.16	1.03	3.02	1.08	3.02	1.07	2.89	1.02
Uses Denial	2.60	1.09	2.65	1.11	2.85	1.08	2.69	1.11	2.79	1.18	2.77	1.14	2.86	1.02	2.75	1.04
Hypochondriacal	1.68	1.02	1.77	1.05	1.94	1.14	1.83	1.12	1.68	.98	1.70	.98	1.60	.93	1.69	.97
Communicates Effectively	2.98	.86	3.01	.89	2.95	.81	2.92	.83	2.83	.89	2.94	.87	2.89	.82	3.01	.90
Has Many Nightmares	2.07	1.20	1.98	1.11	2.18	1.13	2.04	1.11	2.11	1.15	2.09	1.22	2.02	1.13	2.08	1.12
Stormy Interpersonal Relationships	2.98	1.27	3.10	1.20	3.14	1.19	3.02	1.17	3.15	1.27	3.16	1.17	3.27	1.20	3.09	1.14
Feigns Remorse When in Trouble	1.85	1.12	1.67	.88	1.70	.93	1.66	.92	2.01	1.06	1.85	1.04	1.85	1.01	1.75	.94
Stereotypic Masculine Interests	1.44	.85	1.46	.80	1.42	.81	1.34	.71	1.43	.79	1.46	.81	1.43	.77	1.45	.83
Guarded	2.44	1.14	2.43	1.17	2.53	1.12	2.41	1.13	2.43	1.10	2.50	1.14	2.56	1.11	2.45	1.11
Feels Inferior	3.31	1.13	3.18	1.15	3.34	1.08	3.37	1.09	3.08	1.21	3.14	1.17	3.27	1.08	3.37	1.06
Low Frustration Tolerance	2.92	1.05	2.84	1.14	2.97	1.00	2.83	1.03	3.11	1.04	2.97	1.10	3.01	1.06	2.89	1.01
Psychotic Symptoms	1.17	.52	1.23	.63	1.24	.66	1.21	.60	1.37	.83	1.35	.83	1.23	.65	1.22	.63
Fired From Past Jobs	1.51	.94	1.54	.95	1.57	1.06	1.50	.98	1.71	1.07	1.63	1.07	1.47	.94	1.53	.98
Needs Attention	2.93	1.02	3.02	.97	3.10	.90	2.98	.92	2.90	1.09	2.99	1.04	2.98	.98	3.08	.95
Acts Out	2.24	1.10	2.15	1.01	2.29	1.03	2.17	1.05	2.43	1.16	2.36	1.11	2.41	1.17	2.35	1.06
Histrionic	2.13	1.16	2.08	1.10	2.25	1.18	2.09	1.09	2.27	1.25	2.23	1.22	2.21	1.22	2.23	1.16
Self-Indulgent	2.17	1.07	2.08	.99	2.10	.93	2.05	.98	2.26	1.09	2.27	1.09	2.21	1.07	2.23	1.01
Depressed	3.48	.97	3.31	1.03	3.45	1.02	3.49	.94	3.17	.96	3.24	1.03	3.19	1.08	3.34	1.01
Grandiose	1.58	.86	1.55	.85	1.61	.93	1.51	.78	1.72	1.00	1.69	.97	1.64	.94	1.58	.90
Cynical	2.25	1.08	2.08	1.05	2.26	1.09	2.15	1.04	2.16	1.11	2.22	1.11	2.30	1.12	2.13	1.00
Sociopathic	1.37	.72	1.38	.66	1.34	.61	1.32	.60	1.53	.82	1.57	.90	1.44	.76	1.42	.74
Agitated	2.39	1.11	2.38	1.09	2.51	1.05	2.37	1.04	2.35	1.08	2.41	1.16	2.43	1.14	2.33	1.06
Marital Problems	2.56	1.55	2.53	1.54	2.67	1.55	2.72	1.56	2.47	1.61	2.43	1.56	2.57	1.46	2.73	1.54
Absence of Deep Emotions	1.91	1.04	1.90	1.08	2.00	1.11	1.87	1.02	2.11	1.14	1.99	1.07	2.08	1.15	1.94	1.03
Uncomfortable Dealing with Emotions	2.77	1.13	2.79	1.15	2.95	1.09	2.83	1.06	2.75	1.16	2.83	1.09	2.89	1.11	2.86	1.09
Sad	3.12	1.06	3.08	1.03	3.21	.99	3.21	1.01	2.94	1.02	3.05	1.10	2.98	1.06	3.10	1.00
Self-Degrading	2.71	1.14	2.50	1.15	2.68	1.12	2.63	1.12	2.48	1.11	2.61	1.16	2.70	1.22	2.72	1.13
Unable to Express Negative Feelings	2.19	1.13	2.17	1.08	2.30	1.13	2.25	1.12	2.16	1.15	2.23	1.15	2.23	1.20	2.22	1.10
Concrete in Thinking	2.25	1.07	2.29	1.14	2.47	1.14	2.33	1.11	2.48	1.11	2.41	1.10	2.34	1.01	2.31	1.01
Unable to See Own Limitations	2.08	.97	2.10	1.04	2.14	1.01	2.07	.95	2.33	1.05	2.25	1.07	2.19	1.01	2.16	1.04
Power-Oriented	1.78	.97	1.81	.91	1.79	.96	1.67	.89	1.86	.95	1.87	1.01	1.83	.93	1.85	.97
Grouchy	2.22	1.04	2.07	.98	2.18	1.02	2.10	1.00	2.19	.97	2.16	1.01	2.24	1.03	2.10	.96
Overbearing in Relationships	1.97	1.00	2.01	1.02	2.03	1.03	1.89	.98	2.12	1.10	2.07	1.08	2.12	1.10	2.06	1.05
Uncertain About Career	2.82	1.33	2.93	1.28	3.06	1.32	2.93	1.25	3.03	1.40	2.98	1.42	2.86	1.34	2.90	1.29
Likable	3.17	.86	3.27	.88	3.26	.84	3.25	.84	3.24	.88	3.23	.89	3.24	.90	3.30	.86

Content Component Scales (*continued*)

	DEP_4		HEA_1		HEA_2		HEA_3		BIZ_1		BIZ_2		ANG_1		ANG_2	
	Mean	SD	Mean	SD	Mean	SD	Mean	SD	Mean	SD	Mean	SD	Mean	SD	Mean	SD
Procrastinator	2.43	1.02	2.31	1.00	2.48	.96	2.33	.96	2.31	.94	2.32	.94	2.49	1.05	2.39	.98
Negative Feelings Toward Opposite Sex	2.51	1.25	2.50	1.27	2.69	1.21	2.64	1.25	2.57	1.26	2.61	1.30	2.71	1.23	2.67	1.22
Defensive	2.75	1.11	2.66	1.12	2.78	1.07	2.67	1.06	2.73	1.08	2.73	1.15	2.78	1.07	2.69	1.05
Empathetic	2.58	.75	2.65	.80	2.67	.75	2.68	.81	2.57	.73	2.58	.76	2.58	.81	2.62	.75
Perfectionistic	2.30	1.16	2.44	1.13	2.42	1.08	2.32	1.09	2.25	1.09	2.36	1.12	2.38	1.08	2.51	1.17
Judgmental	2.46	1.07	2.42	.99	2.58	.95	2.40	.96	2.50	.97	2.46	.98	2.56	.94	2.47	.94
Copes Well with Stress	1.95	.78	2.00	.76	1.90	.73	1.92	.72	1.95	.79	1.94	.79	1.95	.70	1.95	.71
Moody	2.80	1.04	2.75	1.05	2.84	.96	2.72	.98	2.81	1.03	2.83	1.01	2.82	.96	2.72	.90
Selfish	1.91	.94	1.85	.89	1.88	.86	1.83	.87	2.03	1.01	2.02	1.00	2.08	.95	2.00	.96
Gives Up Easily	2.40	1.04	2.20	1.02	2.37	1.00	2.35	1.04	2.26	.96	2.30	1.11	2.36	1.08	2.31	1.05
Physical Symptoms in Response to Stress	2.14	1.18	2.40	1.26	2.57	1.30	2.54	1.29	2.11	1.20	2.14	1.21	2.11	1.22	2.23	1.17
Blames Family For Difficulties	2.70	1.40	2.65	1.31	2.79	1.28	2.66	1.29	2.87	1.34	2.85	1.39	2.83	1.30	2.81	1.29
Bored	2.33	1.10	2.16	1.10	2.36	1.11	2.37	1.11	2.31	1.08	2.21	1.12	2.39	1.11	2.26	1.12
Idealistic	2.24	1.01	2.37	1.03	2.36	.97	2.30	.96	2.29	.91	2.33	1.02	2.33	.94	2.38	1.01
Difficulty Establishing Therapeutic Rapport	1.89	.98	1.88	.98	1.89	.93	1.84	.92	1.89	.85	1.89	.90	1.80	.88	1.79	.90
Daydreams	1.96	1.07	1.95	1.01	2.11	1.07	1.96	1.00	2.03	1.01	2.01	1.06	1.94	.96	1.98	.96
Concerned About Status	2.09	1.04	2.12	1.08	2.09	1.03	2.04	1.01	2.07	1.05	2.07	1.14	2.02	1.04	2.13	1.03
Creates Good First Impression	2.59	.98	2.81	1.01	2.74	.91	2.74	.93	2.66	.94	2.67	1.00	2.70	.90	2.81	.96
Complains of Sleep Disturbance	2.86	1.22	2.78	1.27	3.06	1.21	2.93	1.21	2.62	1.16	2.73	1.25	2.73	1.21	2.76	1.16
Has Temper Tantrums	1.98	1.06	2.02	1.09	2.10	1.06	1.97	1.05	2.16	1.04	2.18	1.09	2.41	1.19	2.21	1.08
Overreactive	2.71	1.05	2.73	1.11	2.87	1.05	2.74	1.07	2.89	1.18	2.84	1.14	2.85	1.14	2.80	1.10
High Aspirations	2.21	1.12	2.35	1.08	2.20	1.05	2.15	1.00	2.21	.99	2.24	1.07	2.16	.98	2.29	1.04
Feels Hopeless	2.98	1.21	2.73	1.20	2.88	1.16	2.89	1.15	2.65	1.09	2.74	1.21	2.73	1.24	2.75	1.16
Keeps Others at a Distance	2.92	1.18	2.76	1.14	2.94	1.09	2.83	1.08	2.77	1.18	2.91	1.19	2.98	1.20	2.82	1.13
Argumentative	2.18	1.04	2.08	1.02	2.13	.99	2.05	1.01	2.28	1.11	2.18	1.04	2.28	1.10	2.11	1.02
Paranoid Features	1.73	.99	1.72	1.03	1.78	1.04	1.66	.98	1.81	1.06	1.89	1.10	1.77	1.02	1.66	.96
Restless	2.48	1.09	2.46	1.06	2.62	1.01	2.52	1.08	2.56	1.11	2.48	1.14	2.55	1.07	2.54	1.06
Pessimistic	2.77	1.10	2.68	1.11	2.86	1.10	2.82	1.09	2.58	1.03	2.69	1.12	2.71	1.02	2.71	1.02
Feels Like a Failure	3.05	1.16	2.91	1.14	3.11	1.14	3.02	1.17	2.82	1.09	2.86	1.15	2.97	1.10	3.01	1.06
Hallucinations	1.11	.46	1.09	.41	1.12	.44	1.11	.45	1.19	.69	1.18	.66	1.13	.47	1.09	.43
Restricted Affect	2.07	1.12	2.15	1.08	2.26	1.12	2.12	1.05	2.18	1.15	2.16	1.19	2.16	1.18	2.12	1.09
Impatient	2.51	1.05	2.49	1.03	2.63	.97	2.46	.99	2.65	1.02	2.63	1.06	2.68	1.08	2.57	1.00
Assertive	2.06	.84	2.09	.83	2.11	.84	2.02	.82	2.16	.83	2.16	.87	2.12	.78	2.06	.85
Modest	2.52	.81	2.54	.86	2.59	.87	2.57	.81	2.46	.82	2.50	.85	2.51	.86	2.57	.87
Self-Doubting	3.18	.96	3.14	1.04	3.33	.99	3.20	1.04	3.09	1.06	3.21	1.01	3.12	1.03	3.23	.99
Deceptive	1.84	1.01	1.73	.85	1.78	.85	1.77	.87	2.03	1.02	1.93	1.01	1.96	.96	1.80	.85
Feels That Life is a Strain	3.17	1.01	3.09	1.09	3.28	1.00	3.21	1.01	3.04	1.00	3.08	1.05	3.11	1.05	3.15	1.04
Physically Abusive	1.33	.64	1.31	.63	1.29	.62	1.29	.64	1.39	.73	1.35	.70	1.41	.71	1.35	.67

Feels Rejected	3.19	1.21	3.12	1.19	3.31	1.07	3.27	1.05	3.12	1.11	3.19	1.18	3.31	1.19	3.27	1.05
Does Not Get Along with Coworkers	1.66	.92	1.65	.91	1.68	.89	1.62	.93	1.78	1.05	1.74	.98	1.76	.91	1.72	.90
Uses Projection	2.24	1.08	2.18	1.04	2.35	1.01	2.23	1.03	2.42	1.14	2.34	1.12	2.45	1.06	2.27	1.00
Complains of Fatigue	2.69	1.25	2.72	1.32	3.01	1.25	2.92	1.28	2.49	1.20	2.55	1.24	2.48	1.24	2.64	1.31
Uses Rationalization	2.57	1.13	2.52	1.05	2.67	1.04	2.63	1.05	2.62	1.14	2.64	1.15	2.84	1.06	2.63	1.02
Critical of Others	2.45	1.10	2.33	1.04	2.49	1.00	2.30	1.03	2.49	1.03	2.48	1.03	2.63	1.01	2.42	1.02
Egocentric	2.24	1.07	2.16	1.07	2.20	.99	2.10	1.00	2.31	1.09	2.36	1.14	2.26	1.06	2.20	1.13
Overevaluates Own Worth	1.63	.89	1.64	.88	1.64	.86	1.56	.86	1.78	.96	1.73	.95	1.63	.88	1.63	.96
Optimistic	1.90	.82	2.02	.78	2.03	.81	1.92	.74	2.14	.81	2.05	.80	2.04	.79	2.05	.82
Psychologically Immature	2.85	1.23	2.74	1.24	2.90	1.18	2.78	1.23	3.03	1.24	2.95	1.26	2.86	1.29	2.83	1.21
Poor Judgment	2.78	1.12	2.71	1.14	2.80	1.08	2.77	1.15	3.03	1.19	2.96	1.14	2.97	1.20	2.84	1.15
Low Sex Drive	2.28	1.25	2.21	1.26	2.35	1.33	2.40	1.30	2.26	1.33	2.26	1.29	2.17	1.19	2.15	1.19
Feels Mistreated	3.24	1.20	3.15	1.11	3.27	1.10	3.23	1.16	3.34	1.07	3.25	1.09	3.22	1.11	3.17	1.12
Overly Sensitive to Criticism	3.29	1.07	3.17	1.15	3.30	1.02	3.19	1.11	3.24	1.06	3.26	1.09	3.28	1.05	3.27	1.08
Sentimental	2.65	1.04	2.53	1.03	2.68	.94	2.66	1.01	2.70	1.09	2.64	1.09	2.67	1.01	2.65	1.02
Sexual Preoccupation	1.60	1.05	1.53	.91	1.47	.89	1.40	.84	1.71	1.06	1.68	1.07	1.62	.94	1.60	1.01
Accelerated Speech	1.62	.92	1.64	.95	1.69	.96	1.62	.91	1.87	1.04	1.77	1.02	1.69	.90	1.72	.98
Concerns About Homosexuality	1.21	.77	1.14	.53	1.19	.67	1.16	.67	1.10	.47	1.18	.65	1.19	.66	1.16	.67
Many Specific Fears	2.23	1.05	2.08	1.10	2.22	1.06	2.17	1.06	2.29	1.15	2.17	1.15	2.13	1.11	2.11	1.05
Passive in Relationships	2.91	1.17	2.79	1.16	2.96	1.10	3.02	1.15	2.87	1.25	2.85	1.15	2.81	1.20	2.92	1.16
Negative Attitudes Toward Therapy	1.64	.85	1.64	.86	1.65	.81	1.66	.86	1.69	.81	1.67	.82	1.63	.78	1.64	.86
Guilt-Prone	3.09	1.18	2.97	1.18	3.17	1.14	3.09	1.15	2.97	1.20	2.95	1.26	3.02	1.18	3.11	1.11
Nervous	2.98	.97	3.01	1.02	3.13	1.00	3.04	.99	3.01	.94	2.97	1.01	2.89	.88	2.99	.93
Obsessive	2.20	1.15	2.38	1.17	2.44	1.11	2.35	1.13	2.45	1.14	2.43	1.17	2.38	1.12	2.43	1.07
Shy	2.42	1.14	2.34	1.15	2.48	1.19	2.45	1.16	2.35	1.17	2.42	1.18	2.45	1.15	2.45	1.12
Uses Intellectualization	2.15	1.07	2.22	1.06	2.25	.98	2.14	.96	2.12	1.01	2.18	1.00	2.29	1.05	2.25	.98
Has Many Interests	2.13	.90	2.20	.93	2.12	.88	2.05	.86	2.18	.89	2.16	.92	2.09	.88	2.22	.94
Difficulty Making Decisions	2.93	1.04	2.92	1.12	3.02	1.06	2.91	1.05	2.87	1.14	2.88	1.11	2.92	1.14	2.98	1.03
Indirect Expression of Hostility	2.83	1.14	2.73	1.19	2.87	1.15	2.76	1.15	2.91	1.07	2.80	1.15	2.84	1.18	2.80	1.11
Poor Reality Testing	1.53	.87	1.50	.94	1.57	.93	1.45	.77	1.71	1.08	1.71	1.08	1.67	1.02	1.45	.77
Angry	2.98	1.13	2.99	1.19	3.12	1.19	3.00	1.14	3.05	1.15	3.08	1.16	3.16	1.25	2.95	1.14
Eccentric	1.69	1.06	1.67	1.00	1.75	1.07	1.60	.90	1.84	1.12	1.85	1.15	1.70	.97	1.67	.98
Emotional Lability	2.58	1.08	2.44	1.09	2.58	1.05	2.49	1.04	2.44	1.10	2.49	1.06	2.62	1.14	2.55	1.04
Dislikes Change	2.69	1.04	2.59	1.02	2.81	.93	2.66	.96	2.62	.99	2.69	1.05	2.67	1.02	2.65	.92
Believes Cannot Be Helped	1.97	.95	1.81	.92	1.97	.91	1.90	.91	2.01	.95	1.87	.86	1.95	.96	1.83	.88
Reliable Informant	3.23	.87	3.24	.91	3.20	.96	3.20	.96	3.07	.91	3.19	.90	3.14	.85	3.23	.89
Ignores Problems	2.38	1.11	2.31	1.02	2.43	1.00	2.32	1.04	2.58	1.14	2.49	1.05	2.47	.97	2.46	.99
Ruminates	2.85	1.05	2.80	1.00	2.92	.98	2.89	.99	2.71	.96	2.80	1.01	2.77	.97	2.84	.97
Excitable	2.54	.99	2.57	1.02	2.65	.99	2.53	.99	2.74	1.02	2.66	1.04	2.72	1.06	2.69	1.01
Conforming	2.47	.96	2.56	.93	2.64	.94	2.61	.98	2.48	.93	2.50	.96	2.49	.94	2.62	.93
Ineffective at Dealing with Problems	3.06	1.04	3.03	1.03	3.14	.99	3.07	.98	3.18	1.10	3.09	1.08	3.05	1.04	3.10	.97
Introverted	2.46	1.10	2.30	1.06	2.40	1.10	2.38	1.07	2.21	.98	2.45	1.10	2.39	1.10	2.42	1.09

	Content Component Scales *(continued)*															
	DEP_4		HEA_1		HEA_2		HEA_3		BIZ_1		BIZ_2		ANG_1		ANG_2	
	Mean	SD	Mean	SD	Mean	SD	Mean	SD	Mean	SD	Mean	SD	Mean	SD	Mean	SD
Superficial Relationships	2.65	1.12	2.60	1.06	2.73	1.01	2.59	1.08	2.86	1.08	2.85	1.10	2.85	1.10	2.73	1.06
Impulsive	2.61	1.21	2.58	1.19	2.76	1.15	2.62	1.17	2.87	1.21	2.79	1.22	2.97	1.27	2.83	1.21
Stereotypic Feminine Behavior	2.60	1.24	2.67	1.18	2.76	1.08	2.79	1.17	2.68	1.19	2.61	1.22	2.65	1.21	2.78	1.17
Stubborn	2.74	1.05	2.62	1.03	2.72	1.00	2.63	1.01	2.66	1.04	2.65	.98	2.76	1.02	2.68	.96
Hostile Toward Therapist	1.35	.68	1.36	.71	1.35	.62	1.31	.66	1.33	.58	1.28	.53	1.32	.57	1.31	.60
Difficult to Motivate	2.19	1.10	2.11	1.04	2.19	1.02	2.13	1.05	2.26	1.10	2.18	1.11	2.21	1.12	2.14	1.04
Suicidal Ideations	2.00	1.10	1.75	1.03	1.90	1.05	1.82	1.03	1.68	.99	1.85	1.05	1.85	1.05	1.77	.95
Familial Discord	3.35	1.27	3.41	1.28	3.51	1.22	3.36	1.28	3.43	1.31	3.51	1.19	3.49	1.28	3.37	1.24
Dogmatic	2.02	.96	2.05	.94	2.10	.95	1.99	.93	2.07	1.01	2.04	.97	2.06	.93	1.91	.90

	Content Component Scales *(continued)*															
	CYN_1 Mean	SD	CYN_2 Mean	SD	ASP_1 Mean	SD	ASP_2 Mean	SD	TPA_1 Mean	SD	TPA_2 Mean	SD	LSE_1 Mean	SD	LSE_2 Mean	SD
Intake Information	(n = 203)		(n = 111)		(n = 88)		(n = 199)		(n = 192)		(n = 111)		(n = 263)		(n = 167)	
Axis IV diagnosis	3.06	1.07	3.05	.96	3.03	1.01	3.06	.97	3.02	1.01	3.01	.98	2.97	.97	2.94	.95
Axis V - Current Level of Functioning	60.72	11.01	61.58	8.39	60.80	10.16	60.29	10.27	60.64	10.34	61.45	10.50	60.12	10.07	60.61	9.80
Number of Arrests	.51	1.23	.58	1.41	.74	1.65	.91	2.19	.44	1.06	.64	1.72	.36	.83	.29	.63
Mental Status	(n = 203)		(n = 111)		(n = 88)		(n = 199)		(n = 192)		(n = 111)		(n = 263)		(n = 167)	
Anxiety During Interview	2.40	.71	2.40	.65	2.36	.70	2.44	.68	2.51	.75	2.42	.61	2.47	.71	2.39	.60
Depression During Interview	2.46	.72	2.45	.70	2.47	.70	2.53	.76	2.57	.79	2.46	.69	2.62	.72	2.55	.71
Activity Level During Interview	2.91	.39	3.03	.29	2.89	.36	2.93	.37	2.98	.42	2.95	.38	2.93	.38	2.96	.37
Speech During Interview	2.95	.43	3.02	.30	2.91	.45	2.95	.44	2.99	.41	3.02	.38	2.95	.40	2.96	.41
SCL-90-R Scales	(n = 202)		(n = 111)		(n = 88)		(n = 198)		(n = 191)		(n = 111)		(n = 261)		(n = 167)	
Somatization	1.47	.87	1.56	.93	1.35	.82	1.28	.79	1.52	.87	1.39	.94	1.55	.82	1.54	.85
Obsessive-Compulsive	1.75	.95	1.86	.92	1.70	.86	1.56	.88	1.90	.90	1.82	.88	1.95	.82	2.00	.86
Interpersonal Sensitivity	1.78	.92	2.00	.83	1.70	.89	1.57	.90	1.94	.87	1.88	.79	2.06	.77	2.12	.81
Depression	2.12	.93	2.27	.84	2.01	.85	1.96	.94	2.26	.86	2.17	.85	2.47	.74	2.40	.82
Anxiety	1.64	.97	1.81	.93	1.60	.96	1.51	.91	1.74	.89	1.65	.91	1.77	.92	1.83	.93
Hostility	1.60	1.03	1.69	1.03	1.63	1.05	1.45	1.02	1.76	.98	1.66	.97	1.72	.99	1.67	.96
Phobic Anxiety	1.07	.95	1.23	.96	1.07	.93	.91	.90	1.18	.97	1.00	.95	1.15	.94	1.24	.98
Paranoid Ideation	1.82	.96	2.03	.90	1.80	.91	1.58	.89	1.76	.92	1.96	.89	1.79	.90	1.88	.93
Psychoticism	1.22	.80	1.40	.76	1.18	.80	1.02	.73	1.22	.73	1.30	.74	1.29	.71	1.39	.77
Initial SCL-90 Analogue	(n = 132)		(n = 74)		(n = 58)		(n = 130)		(n = 130)		(n = 81)		(n = 174)		(n = 108)	
Somatization	2.16	2.36	1.86	2.34	1.86	2.35	2.16	2.60	2.62	2.72	1.99	2.55	2.52	2.73	2.35	2.48
Obsessive-Compulsive	2.56	2.67	2.29	2.40	2.68	2.83	2.74	2.59	2.90	2.57	2.49	2.55	2.88	2.80	2.55	2.48
Interpersonal Sensitivity	5.00	2.55	4.80	2.65	4.95	2.72	5.05	2.71	5.14	2.45	4.75	2.68	5.39	2.61	4.90	2.43
Depression	4.28	2.49	4.27	2.69	4.31	2.79	4.66	2.62	4.88	2.50	4.32	2.66	5.16	2.47	4.85	2.26
Anxiety	4.16	2.63	4.07	2.49	4.34	2.39	4.57	2.51	4.74	2.66	4.10	2.65	4.69	2.79	4.33	2.52
Hostility	2.93	2.64	2.81	2.80	3.02	2.97	3.52	2.68	2.98	2.55	3.11	2.66	2.98	2.68	2.63	2.46
Phobic Anxiety	1.15	2.19	.93	1.75	1.34	2.23	1.34	2.16	1.29	2.22	1.16	1.95	1.34	2.21	1.06	1.83
Paranoid Ideation	1.29	2.15	1.24	2.08	1.47	2.18	1.68	2.37	1.21	2.04	1.27	1.83	1.24	2.06	.90	1.55
Psychoticism	.72	1.70	.72	1.55	.90	1.85	1.05	2.09	.83	1.86	.72	1.56	.74	1.64	.51	1.21
Patient Description Form Scales	(n = 132)		(n = 73)		(n = 58)		(n = 130)		(n = 129)		(n = 80)		(n = 173)		(n = 108)	
Angry Resentment	2.84	.81	2.68	.87	2.87	.77	2.93	.84	2.76	.86	2.80	.88	2.68	.85	2.61	.85

	Content Component Scales *(continued)*															
	CYN_1 Mean	SD	CYN_2 Mean	SD	ASP_1 Mean	SD	ASP_2 Mean	SD	TPA_1 Mean	SD	TPA_2 Mean	SD	LSE_1 Mean	SD	LSE_2 Mean	SD
Critical/Argumentative	2.48	.81	2.39	.90	2.46	.82	2.54	.91	2.45	.84	2.46	.92	2.30	.88	2.27	.89
Narcissistic	2.18	.86	2.11	.93	2.30	.88	2.25	.86	2.07	.84	2.22	.90	1.93	.82	1.89	.82
Defensive	2.65	.75	2.53	.85	2.82	.72	2.71	.79	2.60	.81	2.65	.81	2.47	.83	2.44	.80
Histrionic	2.53	.84	2.47	.87	2.61	.84	2.65	.85	2.65	.87	2.54	.89	2.50	.85	2.45	.86
Aggressive	1.95	.80	1.90	.82	2.02	.84	2.04	.84	1.92	.73	2.03	.84	1.78	.72	1.73	.67
Insecure	3.09	.78	3.00	.87	3.15	.83	3.16	.90	3.25	.83	3.05	.88	3.24	.88	3.13	.84
Anxious	2.89	.74	2.77	.75	2.84	.74	3.00	.84	3.06	.82	2.81	.71	3.00	.80	2.93	.74
Pessimistic	2.36	.86	2.16	.85	2.31	.87	2.33	.92	2.33	.92	2.18	.82	2.33	.87	2.21	.84
Depressed	2.58	.82	2.48	.87	2.55	.92	2.71	.88	2.78	.84	2.51	.84	2.75	.81	2.65	.79
Achievement-Oriented	2.29	.75	2.39	.76	2.31	.74	2.49	.71	2.47	.83	2.49	.82	2.28	.69	2.27	.65
Passive-Submissive	2.58	.96	2.47	.92	2.67	.97	2.60	.95	2.64	.89	2.54	1.00	2.78	.92	2.91	.93
Introverted	2.49	.96	2.28	.95	2.34	1.00	2.48	1.00	2.58	.97	2.28	.84	2.52	.96	2.61	.96
Emotionally Controlled	2.30	.72	2.19	.84	2.37	.79	2.50	.90	2.42	.84	2.40	.84	2.35	.90	2.30	.86
Antisocial	2.28	.87	2.31	.96	2.47	.90	2.43	.90	2.13	.77	2.28	.86	2.05	.78	2.06	.76
Negative Treatment Attitudes	2.09	.69	1.97	.70	2.17	.72	2.03	.70	1.98	.73	2.05	.69	1.88	.66	1.87	.71
Somatic Symptoms	2.15	.97	1.91	.92	2.00	.89	2.05	.98	2.36	1.16	2.03	1.02	2.18	1.01	2.07	.93
Psychotic Symptoms	1.30	.55	1.30	.54	1.38	.64	1.40	.70	1.30	.57	1.31	.52	1.28	.52	1.27	.52
Family Problems	3.07	1.07	3.06	1.20	3.15	1.08	3.36	1.04	3.06	1.10	3.20	1.11	3.07	1.09	2.97	1.10
Obsessive-Compulsive	2.51	.79	2.40	.79	2.50	.82	2.64	.92	2.74	.84	2.55	.81	2.55	.87	2.45	.79
Stereotypic Masculine Interests	1.45	.70	1.36	.61	1.48	.69	1.54	.84	1.46	.78	1.40	.67	1.38	.69	1.35	.64
Procrastinates	2.16	.74	2.16	.79	2.32	.84	2.43	1.01	2.28	.88	2.22	.85	2.13	.86	2.11	.78
Suspicious	2.57	.91	2.42	.88	2.60	.98	2.75	.94	2.56	.89	2.50	.90	2.47	.89	2.36	.82
Agitated	2.18	.79	2.20	.88	2.29	.82	2.33	.90	2.33	.93	2.20	.85	2.19	.83	2.12	.80
Work Problems	1.58	.73	1.50	.55	1.65	.73	1.61	.82	1.68	.81	1.54	.55	1.56	.74	1.60	.86
Patient Description Form Items	(n = 132)		(n = 73)		(n = 58)		(n = 130)		(n = 129)		(n = 80)		(n = 173)		(n = 108)	
Anxious	3.14	.97	3.14	.87	3.12	.88	3.27	.94	3.36	1.04	3.10	.89	3.26	1.02	3.27	.97
Problems with Authority Figures	2.94	1.16	2.90	1.28	3.11	1.19	3.02	1.21	2.68	1.17	3.11	1.20	2.66	1.22	2.75	1.23
Has Insight Into Own Problems	2.24	.74	2.27	.87	2.19	.80	2.57	.85	2.53	.90	2.40	.82	2.56	.82	2.56	.88
Fears Losing Control	3.06	1.09	3.06	1.07	2.93	1.11	3.30	1.07	3.27	1.12	3.12	1.06	3.16	1.07	3.03	1.13
Extroverted	2.46	1.04	2.61	1.03	2.74	1.09	2.63	1.09	2.45	1.11	2.71	1.01	2.31	1.04	2.30	1.02
Uses Repression	2.86	1.03	2.72	1.13	2.89	1.01	3.06	1.00	2.87	1.01	2.91	1.11	2.81	1.09	2.77	1.11
Submissive	2.71	1.08	2.69	1.10	2.84	1.07	2.80	1.09	2.79	1.07	2.72	1.10	2.93	1.06	3.07	1.01
Difficulty Concentrating	2.72	1.05	2.67	1.11	2.69	1.10	2.82	1.15	2.83	1.06	2.64	1.05	2.73	1.05	2.72	1.01
Rigid	2.44	.98	2.32	1.05	2.52	.94	2.47	1.01	2.60	1.02	2.55	1.04	2.48	1.02	2.47	1.04
Overly Compliant	2.23	1.10	2.21	1.07	2.36	1.17	2.13	1.02	2.13	1.01	2.22	1.15	2.31	1.11	2.46	1.19
Whiny	2.10	1.09	2.15	1.10	2.19	1.09	2.07	1.09	2.13	1.08	2.27	1.06	2.08	1.08	2.03	1.01

Feels Overwhelmed	3.35	1.04	3.14	1.08	3.12	1.09	3.44	1.15	3.49	1.09	3.19	1.05	3.51	1.00	3.45	1.01
Manipulative	2.56	1.20	2.45	1.33	2.63	1.25	2.73	1.14	2.37	1.15	2.60	1.25	2.34	1.13	2.33	1.18
Difficulty Trusting Others	3.38	1.06	3.23	1.11	3.25	1.14	3.58	1.13	3.39	1.07	3.37	1.16	3.24	1.14	3.11	1.11
Insensitive to Others	1.98	.92	1.93	.97	2.09	.99	1.98	.94	1.86	.88	1.95	.88	1.73	.83	1.78	.86
Stereotypic Masculine Behavior	1.37	.70	1.29	.62	1.36	.68	1.46	.85	1.42	.79	1.35	.70	1.33	.70	1.31	.70
Harbors Grudges	2.54	1.00	2.51	.99	2.57	1.02	2.80	1.07	2.57	.94	2.64	1.11	2.47	1.05	2.45	1.01
Evasive	2.42	1.03	2.42	1.13	2.64	1.04	2.51	1.09	2.36	1.10	2.47	1.06	2.26	1.10	2.15	1.08
Disoriented	1.36	.72	1.27	.63	1.47	.84	1.45	.83	1.34	.72	1.35	.70	1.30	.68	1.31	.69
Energetic	2.34	.98	2.53	.96	2.55	1.11	2.55	.96	2.34	.99	2.53	1.00	2.25	.94	2.23	.86
Lonely	2.88	1.05	2.77	1.09	2.72	1.07	2.96	1.09	2.88	1.10	2.80	1.05	2.95	1.02	2.93	.98
Family Lacks Love	2.93	1.18	2.80	1.27	2.95	1.19	3.30	1.26	2.88	1.24	3.12	1.19	2.96	1.24	2.85	1.23
Worrier	3.27	.92	3.19	1.09	3.22	.90	3.33	.99	3.64	.93	3.26	1.02	3.45	1.04	3.34	1.01
Narcissistic	2.22	1.12	2.19	1.22	2.44	1.20	2.38	1.13	2.09	1.08	2.43	1.27	1.96	1.04	1.96	1.05
Tearful	2.33	1.14	2.23	1.22	2.40	1.24	2.39	1.25	2.57	1.16	2.30	1.17	2.55	1.16	2.47	1.18
Provocative	1.73	.91	1.68	.98	1.88	.99	1.92	1.11	1.74	.93	1.82	1.02	1.67	.91	1.61	.87
Moralistic	2.22	.86	2.10	.85	2.23	.89	2.18	.94	2.33	.89	2.19	.90	2.22	.92	2.17	.88
Socially Awkward	2.54	1.02	2.37	1.09	2.41	1.03	2.54	1.03	2.65	1.05	2.33	.97	2.58	1.05	2.64	1.04
Hostile	2.25	1.03	2.15	1.15	2.31	1.10	2.33	1.10	2.18	1.07	2.30	1.12	2.08	1.04	2.05	1.11
Overcontrolled	2.36	1.09	2.32	1.13	2.21	1.14	2.51	1.22	2.60	1.16	2.43	1.08	2.47	1.20	2.36	1.13
Resistant to Interpretations	2.36	.95	2.26	1.03	2.34	1.00	2.31	1.00	2.27	.99	2.32	.96	2.11	.95	2.14	.98
Antisocial Behavior	1.95	1.01	1.99	1.09	2.12	1.11	2.12	1.10	1.76	.92	1.89	1.01	1.63	.88	1.71	.89
Sarcastic	1.86	1.05	1.92	1.16	1.96	1.27	2.15	1.13	1.92	1.04	1.92	1.12	1.90	1.05	1.84	1.07
Rejects Traditional Gender Role	1.66	1.03	1.65	1.05	1.81	1.15	1.84	1.15	1.70	1.02	1.78	1.14	1.62	.97	1.53	.94
Feels Gets Raw Deal From Life	3.05	1.07	2.90	1.13	2.98	.97	3.10	1.08	2.98	1.14	2.96	1.03	3.01	1.13	2.97	1.12
Acute Psychological Turmoil	2.97	1.09	2.90	1.04	2.91	1.15	3.12	1.11	3.14	1.07	2.85	1.09	3.03	1.05	2.94	1.01
Does Not Complete Projects	2.33	1.04	2.29	1.02	2.60	.99	2.55	1.26	2.29	1.09	2.28	1.02	2.12	1.10	2.11	1.02
Uncomfortable with Opposite Sex	2.18	1.16	2.13	1.21	2.07	1.17	2.34	1.24	2.28	1.14	2.24	1.23	2.30	1.19	2.21	1.20
Preoccupied with Health Problems	2.09	1.26	1.78	1.08	1.88	1.16	1.90	1.19	2.20	1.33	1.76	1.11	2.09	1.22	1.98	1.18
Work-Oriented	2.43	1.11	2.51	1.06	2.34	1.05	2.67	1.14	2.78	1.20	2.55	1.09	2.60	1.08	2.59	1.03
Resents Family Members	3.02	1.19	3.15	1.30	3.11	1.22	3.39	1.16	3.11	1.25	3.17	1.23	3.05	1.25	2.88	1.26
Demanding of Attention	2.57	1.07	2.54	1.10	2.74	1.03	2.70	1.09	2.61	1.07	2.59	1.09	2.52	1.08	2.50	1.10
Passive	2.52	1.12	2.40	1.02	2.47	1.11	2.61	1.15	2.64	1.06	2.41	.99	2.77	1.08	2.84	1.07
Self-Punishing	2.60	1.08	2.52	1.14	2.58	1.15	2.73	1.20	2.80	1.16	2.68	1.11	2.82	1.19	2.73	1.11
Needs to Achieve	2.49	1.05	2.61	1.02	2.48	.91	2.65	.95	2.64	1.12	2.67	1.13	2.47	1.03	2.50	.96
Needs to Be with Others	3.12	.98	3.06	1.09	3.30	.97	3.29	.96	3.20	1.06	3.10	1.06	3.06	1.07	3.10	1.06
Irritable	2.77	1.00	2.64	1.11	2.57	1.01	2.81	1.07	2.76	1.08	2.59	1.04	2.55	1.04	2.58	1.00
Self-Defeating	3.18	.99	3.08	1.09	3.26	1.09	3.32	1.08	3.19	1.01	3.05	1.14	3.14	1.09	3.06	1.04
Delusional Thinking	1.28	.72	1.27	.77	1.38	.85	1.40	.89	1.30	.78	1.32	.81	1.30	.73	1.26	.72
Self-Reliant	2.47	.92	2.48	.93	2.34	.85	2.64	.90	2.60	.96	2.58	.97	2.53	.87	2.38	.79
Aggressive	2.14	1.04	2.14	1.10	2.19	1.08	2.24	1.12	2.08	.97	2.21	1.04	1.89	.94	1.86	.93
Competitive	2.12	1.05	2.13	1.04	2.04	1.03	2.31	1.04	2.25	1.05	2.27	1.12	1.96	.93	2.01	.91
Suspicious	2.52	1.12	2.38	1.08	2.57	1.14	2.68	1.15	2.51	1.06	2.41	1.14	2.43	1.08	2.35	1.02

	Content Component Scales *(continued)*															
	CYN_1		CYN_2		ASP_1		ASP_2		TPA_1		TPA_2		LSE_1		LSE_2	
	Mean	SD	Mean	SD	Mean	SD	Mean	SD	Mean	SD	Mean	SD	Mean	SD	Mean	SD
Compulsive	2.14	1.13	2.04	1.04	2.30	1.20	2.35	1.22	2.40	1.19	2.23	1.11	2.19	1.16	2.08	1.08
Dependable	2.81	.89	2.71	.93	2.67	.85	2.88	.89	2.98	.90	2.82	.88	3.04	.88	2.98	.91
Multiple Somatic Complaints	2.00	1.16	1.83	1.09	1.79	.98	1.80	1.05	2.17	1.31	1.92	1.24	1.99	1.20	1.86	1.11
Complains of Lack of Time	1.90	1.05	1.89	.90	1.82	.97	2.08	1.18	2.11	1.07	1.96	1.02	2.00	1.07	1.90	.98
Poor Work Performance	1.89	.96	1.70	.89	1.86	.93	1.81	.93	1.97	1.04	1.75	.86	1.80	.90	1.81	.94
Insecure	3.53	.86	3.44	1.03	3.61	.90	3.60	.99	3.69	.93	3.51	.90	3.62	.93	3.54	.95
Discusses Problems Openly	3.05	.85	3.10	.90	3.00	.96	3.20	.86	3.14	.86	3.08	.76	3.16	.83	3.19	.90
Sexually Adjusted	2.42	.87	2.40	.91	2.42	.85	2.49	.88	2.42	.83	2.35	.87	2.35	.92	2.40	.89
Exaggerated Need for Affection	2.44	1.17	2.33	1.16	2.35	1.05	2.58	1.16	2.60	1.21	2.44	1.15	2.45	1.14	2.44	1.15
Resentful	3.07	.99	2.99	1.07	3.13	.94	3.22	1.03	3.06	1.10	3.04	1.07	2.98	1.09	2.86	1.05
Uses Denial	2.90	1.01	2.70	1.17	3.05	.95	3.01	1.08	2.77	1.06	2.84	1.04	2.70	1.08	2.62	1.03
Hypochondriacal	1.65	.94	1.54	.84	1.66	.88	1.68	1.01	1.86	1.11	1.63	.92	1.73	1.03	1.57	.89
Communicates Effectively	2.83	.80	2.95	.88	2.77	.80	3.01	.92	3.03	.95	2.99	.76	2.99	.82	2.93	.79
Has Many Nightmares	1.95	1.08	1.94	1.16	1.97	1.15	2.42	1.20	2.08	1.12	1.83	1.02	1.99	1.15	1.99	1.04
Stormy Interpersonal Relationships	3.18	1.15	3.03	1.20	3.18	1.09	3.46	1.09	3.08	1.14	3.27	1.11	3.06	1.23	3.13	1.26
Feigns Remorse When in Trouble	1.96	1.06	1.82	1.03	2.02	1.03	2.03	1.12	1.71	.85	1.82	.90	1.78	.99	1.78	1.00
Stereotypic Masculine Interests	1.53	.83	1.43	.75	1.57	.78	1.60	.94	1.50	.85	1.43	.73	1.42	.79	1.39	.78
Guarded	2.61	1.00	2.53	1.07	2.74	1.13	2.77	1.12	2.61	1.13	2.54	1.07	2.46	1.14	2.47	1.16
Feels Inferior	3.19	1.03	3.23	1.11	3.23	1.10	3.29	1.10	3.37	1.05	3.17	1.12	3.44	1.11	3.40	1.08
Low Frustration Tolerance	3.02	.96	2.99	.99	3.09	.95	3.10	1.06	2.97	.97	2.99	1.06	2.85	1.09	2.88	1.07
Psychotic Symptoms	1.29	.75	1.26	.69	1.28	.67	1.36	.80	1.30	.80	1.19	.64	1.26	.68	1.25	.67
Fired From Past Jobs	1.62	1.03	1.51	.77	1.56	.88	1.76	1.09	1.52	.94	1.44	.73	1.55	1.00	1.56	.97
Needs Attention	3.07	.94	2.96	1.01	3.18	.91	3.16	.95	3.17	1.00	3.06	1.02	3.02	1.00	2.97	.98
Acts Out	2.47	1.09	2.41	1.18	2.51	1.15	2.69	1.15	2.44	1.10	2.53	1.15	2.24	1.07	2.21	1.07
Histrionic	2.17	1.20	2.18	1.25	2.31	1.32	2.39	1.23	2.36	1.25	2.38	1.24	2.16	1.16	2.13	1.18
Self-Indulgent	2.38	1.07	2.19	1.12	2.58	1.05	2.47	1.03	2.26	1.01	2.34	1.05	2.07	.98	2.07	1.00
Depressed	3.11	1.00	3.04	1.05	3.00	1.02	3.24	1.06	3.37	1.00	3.09	.99	3.40	.92	3.25	.92
Grandiose	1.67	.91	1.64	.92	1.79	.97	1.82	1.01	1.66	.92	1.84	1.02	1.54	.83	1.53	.86
Cynical	2.23	1.09	2.15	1.17	2.29	1.13	2.44	1.16	2.17	1.05	2.34	1.24	2.22	1.10	2.08	1.05
Sociopathic	1.54	.85	1.61	.94	1.71	1.01	1.71	.95	1.45	.73	1.57	.86	1.36	.70	1.36	.60
Agitated	2.33	1.04	2.29	1.05	2.39	1.04	2.53	1.08	2.46	1.10	2.23	1.07	2.39	1.09	2.32	1.04
Marital Problems	2.58	1.52	2.44	1.61	2.35	1.47	2.43	1.54	2.56	1.49	2.53	1.51	2.64	1.55	2.77	1.61
Absence of Deep Emotions	2.00	.99	1.96	1.07	2.18	1.05	2.23	1.16	1.91	1.04	2.13	1.07	1.95	1.05	1.96	1.04
Uncomfortable Dealing with Emotions	2.87	.90	2.64	1.01	2.96	.93	3.09	1.00	3.01	1.12	2.94	1.08	2.88	1.08	2.81	1.02
Sad	2.94	1.00	2.85	1.06	2.79	1.06	3.09	1.10	3.17	1.03	2.84	1.01	3.17	1.00	3.08	1.00
Self-Degrading	2.53	1.06	2.51	1.11	2.74	1.09	2.67	1.15	2.83	1.08	2.62	1.12	2.78	1.21	2.69	1.13
Unable to Express Negative Feelings	2.07	1.05	1.93	1.02	2.16	1.07	2.37	1.22	2.33	1.08	2.33	1.14	2.28	1.15	2.21	1.05
Concrete in Thinking	2.44	1.10	2.40	1.07	2.58	1.05	2.38	.98	2.50	1.10	2.34	1.00	2.37	1.09	2.27	1.08

Unable to See Own Limitations	2.40	1.08	2.25	1.09	2.63	.94	2.40	1.09	2.20	1.07	2.33	1.00	2.09	1.02	2.14	1.03
Power-Oriented	1.87	.90	1.85	1.01	1.93	.93	2.01	1.01	1.97	1.02	2.04	1.08	1.80	.94	1.65	.87
Grouchy	2.25	1.00	2.11	.99	2.12	.97	2.33	1.02	2.29	.99	2.18	1.02	2.09	.98	2.04	.97
Overbearing in Relationships	2.16	1.07	2.09	1.13	2.13	1.09	2.27	1.13	2.21	1.12	2.24	1.07	2.01	1.04	1.89	1.10
Uncertain About Career	3.02	1.34	3.09	1.27	2.89	1.29	3.15	1.30	3.03	1.31	3.18	1.19	2.96	1.35	3.02	1.37
Likable	3.05	.80	3.10	.84	2.98	.83	3.29	.80	3.22	.92	3.11	.81	3.32	.83	3.28	.89
Procrastinator	2.35	.95	2.31	1.04	2.53	1.00	2.67	1.08	2.44	1.01	2.46	1.12	2.39	1.03	2.40	.93
Negative Feelings Toward Opposite Sex	2.60	1.24	2.55	1.42	2.49	1.31	2.75	1.27	2.64	1.21	2.62	1.33	2.64	1.29	2.49	1.22
Defensive	2.91	1.08	2.73	1.15	2.97	1.12	3.02	1.14	2.88	1.05	2.90	1.05	2.67	1.06	2.69	1.04
Empathetic	2.50	.75	2.50	.67	2.44	.68	2.61	.78	2.65	.73	2.60	.76	2.63	.72	2.60	.69
Perfectionistic	2.32	1.08	2.24	.95	2.25	1.00	2.51	1.17	2.64	1.24	2.51	1.18	2.43	1.21	2.35	1.11
Judgmental	2.49	.92	2.49	.95	2.51	.83	2.63	.97	2.62	.98	2.69	1.04	2.42	1.03	2.37	.97
Copes Well with Stress	1.95	.76	2.03	.74	2.03	.75	2.02	.78	1.90	.71	2.06	.72	1.93	.72	2.00	.75
Moody	2.85	.89	2.76	1.02	2.78	1.03	3.00	1.01	2.85	.96	2.87	.97	2.77	1.01	2.75	.98
Selfish	2.12	1.00	2.03	1.07	2.29	.98	2.20	1.00	1.98	.89	2.06	.95	1.84	.93	1.83	.92
Gives Up Easily	2.32	1.03	2.25	1.06	2.51	.99	2.41	1.08	2.39	1.01	2.17	.96	2.35	1.05	2.36	.95
Physical Symptoms in Response to Stress	2.19	1.15	1.99	1.05	2.04	1.15	2.14	1.21	2.50	1.28	2.10	1.18	2.29	1.18	2.23	1.17
Blames Family For Difficulties	2.88	1.27	2.90	1.30	2.93	1.25	3.03	1.30	2.82	1.28	2.89	1.29	2.82	1.32	2.72	1.29
Bored	2.41	1.09	2.23	1.08	2.59	1.07	2.45	1.15	2.34	1.14	2.46	1.10	2.25	1.16	2.21	1.06
Idealistic	2.19	.96	2.19	.88	2.25	1.01	2.45	1.04	2.39	1.02	2.37	1.06	2.33	.99	2.36	1.01
Difficulty Establishing Therapeutic Rapport	2.07	.99	1.95	.93	2.09	.94	2.05	1.00	1.91	.96	2.00	.90	1.81	.89	1.77	.90
Daydreams	1.97	.94	1.77	.85	2.02	.94	2.14	1.01	1.96	.88	1.91	.96	1.98	.99	1.93	.91
Concerned About Status	2.15	1.05	2.16	1.09	2.42	1.15	2.23	1.13	2.26	1.12	2.35	1.20	2.13	1.08	2.07	1.03
Creates Good First Impression	2.59	.97	2.60	.95	2.69	.94	2.72	.82	2.70	1.00	2.71	.98	2.79	.95	2.81	.92
Complains of Sleep Disturbance	2.63	1.14	2.60	1.21	2.59	1.26	2.81	1.30	2.81	1.18	2.57	1.16	2.74	1.17	2.62	1.17
Has Temper Tantrums	2.24	1.09	2.16	1.14	2.32	1.05	2.33	1.18	2.20	1.09	2.24	1.08	2.10	1.08	2.11	1.05
Overreactive	2.79	1.08	2.70	1.05	2.79	1.00	2.92	1.10	2.89	1.13	2.76	1.07	2.77	1.10	2.72	1.11
High Aspirations	2.19	1.06	2.17	1.07	2.21	1.02	2.44	1.05	2.37	1.11	2.35	1.10	2.17	1.05	2.12	.99
Feels Hopeless	2.69	1.18	2.62	1.14	2.60	1.27	2.76	1.17	2.87	1.18	2.58	1.09	2.85	1.14	2.76	1.04
Keeps Others at a Distance	2.97	1.05	2.72	1.20	3.09	1.07	3.16	1.15	2.98	1.14	2.96	1.17	2.82	1.11	2.81	1.10
Argumentative	2.29	1.03	2.25	1.09	2.21	.99	2.33	1.11	2.27	1.10	2.28	1.11	2.13	1.03	2.09	1.08
Paranoid Features	1.78	1.07	1.63	.96	1.91	1.12	2.00	1.08	1.75	1.04	1.73	.90	1.71	.99	1.61	.88
Restless	2.47	1.02	2.44	1.14	2.53	1.04	2.63	1.14	2.68	1.14	2.58	1.12	2.51	1.12	2.41	1.06
Pessimistic	2.76	1.01	2.56	1.03	2.72	1.00	2.74	1.07	2.78	1.00	2.54	1.00	2.78	1.03	2.64	1.02
Feels Like a Failure	2.97	1.06	2.77	1.08	2.95	1.09	2.95	1.13	3.08	1.08	2.78	1.07	3.13	1.06	3.04	1.07
Hallucinations	1.12	.55	1.13	.51	1.14	.52	1.23	.72	1.13	.58	1.09	.43	1.12	.54	1.09	.47
Restricted Affect	2.17	1.09	2.04	1.14	2.26	1.13	2.32	1.19	2.23	1.14	2.14	1.09	2.15	1.14	2.13	1.12
Impatient	2.67	.95	2.57	1.11	2.78	1.04	2.74	1.06	2.75	1.02	2.79	1.06	2.43	1.05	2.50	1.06
Assertive	2.11	.83	2.18	.88	2.05	.79	2.26	.84	2.13	.94	2.23	.89	1.99	.81	1.84	.73
Modest	2.43	.82	2.36	.86	2.42	.86	2.48	.84	2.63	.81	2.36	.83	2.64	.84	2.63	.82
Self-Doubting	3.25	.96	3.06	1.01	3.22	.99	3.15	1.08	3.29	.98	3.16	.99	3.33	1.00	3.20	1.00
Deceptive	2.02	.99	1.94	1.02	2.20	1.05	2.16	1.02	1.80	.88	1.89	.96	1.73	.86	1.78	.87

	Content Component Scales *(continued)*															
	CYN_1		CYN_2		ASP_1		ASP_2		TPA_1		TPA_2		LSE_1		LSE_2	
	Mean	SD	Mean	SD	Mean	SD	Mean	SD	Mean	SD	Mean	SD	Mean	SD	Mean	SD
Feels That Life is a Strain	3.16	.92	2.99	1.03	2.93	1.02	3.13	1.01	3.19	1.05	2.92	1.00	3.23	1.00	3.01	1.00
Physically Abusive	1.43	.77	1.34	.75	1.49	.79	1.38	.70	1.38	.72	1.41	.80	1.32	.66	1.26	.56
Feels Rejected	3.18	1.08	3.15	1.19	3.19	1.16	3.35	1.11	3.36	1.03	3.16	1.18	3.31	1.13	3.22	1.05
Does Not Get Along with Coworkers	1.73	.89	1.66	.81	1.70	.81	1.77	.95	1.78	.96	1.82	.82	1.66	.88	1.67	.93
Uses Projection	2.44	1.06	2.30	1.13	2.44	1.09	2.65	1.08	2.42	1.12	2.40	1.04	2.26	1.05	2.20	1.05
Complains of Fatigue	2.61	1.17	2.27	1.15	2.33	1.12	2.61	1.31	2.77	1.34	2.46	1.16	2.68	1.26	2.59	1.15
Uses Rationalization	2.71	1.09	2.57	1.16	2.79	1.16	2.88	1.08	2.68	1.02	2.75	1.11	2.59	1.10	2.52	1.03
Critical of Others	2.58	1.04	2.59	1.03	2.50	1.04	2.64	1.07	2.57	1.03	2.69	1.07	2.34	1.08	2.27	1.03
Egocentric	2.44	1.07	2.31	1.10	2.46	1.13	2.46	1.14	2.25	1.10	2.44	1.08	2.18	1.09	2.01	1.06
Overevaluates Own Worth	1.81	.96	1.71	.91	1.84	.97	1.84	.99	1.66	.89	1.90	.96	1.55	.85	1.52	.87
Optimistic	2.02	.74	2.08	.80	2.16	.81	2.07	.78	2.07	.81	2.19	.77	1.95	.77	2.03	.76
Psychologically Immature	3.11	1.16	2.99	1.25	3.29	1.15	3.04	1.22	2.89	1.16	3.16	1.16	2.83	1.23	2.79	1.18
Poor Judgment	2.99	1.14	3.10	1.22	3.11	1.03	3.15	1.12	2.82	1.22	3.03	1.17	2.74	1.16	2.75	1.10
Low Sex Drive	2.16	1.19	1.85	1.00	2.04	1.00	2.16	1.26	2.36	1.22	2.14	1.11	2.31	1.29	2.16	1.06
Feels Mistreated	3.26	1.04	3.27	1.12	3.32	1.03	3.32	1.08	3.14	1.18	3.32	1.06	3.24	1.10	3.12	1.08
Overly Sensitive to Criticism	3.26	.98	3.24	1.15	3.39	.95	3.24	1.11	3.42	1.06	3.33	1.05	3.25	1.13	3.20	1.07
Sentimental	2.56	.97	2.49	1.05	2.75	1.02	2.68	1.03	2.72	1.05	2.70	1.04	2.60	1.03	2.59	.97
Sexual Preoccupation	1.56	.94	1.61	.97	1.69	1.00	1.77	1.09	1.61	.92	1.71	1.11	1.53	.97	1.46	.87
Accelerated Speech	1.71	.96	1.85	1.07	1.90	.99	1.79	.97	1.83	1.09	1.85	.98	1.69	.97	1.63	.94
Concerns About Homosexuality	1.15	.61	1.17	.63	1.28	.84	1.23	.78	1.18	.71	1.21	.75	1.18	.71	1.17	.64
Many Specific Fears	2.09	1.09	1.89	.97	2.02	.99	2.27	1.18	2.27	1.18	1.95	.97	2.18	1.13	2.03	1.00
Passive in Relationships	2.80	1.21	2.69	1.15	2.82	1.12	2.86	1.22	2.96	1.12	2.75	1.24	3.09	1.11	3.20	1.13
Negative Attitudes Toward Therapy	1.81	.88	1.69	.88	1.93	.92	1.80	.85	1.68	.90	1.73	.80	1.63	.82	1.61	.81
Guilt-Prone	2.90	1.09	2.79	1.11	2.90	1.18	2.98	1.17	3.20	1.05	2.78	1.11	3.15	1.15	3.00	1.07
Nervous	2.87	.91	2.86	.86	2.83	.86	2.98	1.04	3.14	1.04	2.84	.88	3.05	.98	2.89	.91
Obsessive	2.31	1.11	2.20	1.15	2.37	1.19	2.53	1.18	2.63	1.17	2.40	1.12	2.37	1.18	2.27	1.13
Shy	2.47	1.18	2.22	1.06	2.29	1.17	2.49	1.22	2.57	1.12	2.24	1.00	2.50	1.15	2.60	1.19
Uses Intellectualization	2.18	.93	2.21	1.03	2.29	.96	2.48	1.11	2.37	1.07	2.32	1.06	2.17	1.06	2.14	1.01
Has Many Interests	2.11	.87	2.19	.97	2.16	.99	2.28	.86	2.22	.99	2.21	.99	2.10	.87	2.15	.92
Difficulty Making Decisions	2.92	1.11	2.83	1.09	2.95	1.08	2.93	1.14	3.13	1.03	2.89	1.03	2.99	1.05	2.96	1.07
Indirect Expression of Hostility	2.86	1.06	2.63	1.16	2.91	1.10	2.97	1.11	2.86	1.08	2.95	1.03	2.83	1.15	2.78	1.11
Poor Reality Testing	1.59	.89	1.68	.99	1.81	1.00	1.77	1.13	1.59	.95	1.73	1.01	1.58	.96	1.55	1.01
Angry	3.06	1.11	2.90	1.22	2.97	1.15	3.23	1.20	3.05	1.17	3.13	1.19	3.00	1.16	2.91	1.10
Eccentric	1.72	1.06	1.75	1.04	1.84	1.10	1.86	1.11	1.71	1.02	1.80	1.07	1.70	1.05	1.53	.86
Emotional Lability	2.52	1.04	2.49	1.07	2.51	1.09	2.65	1.10	2.60	1.10	2.39	1.09	2.47	1.07	2.42	1.05
Dislikes Change	2.68	.97	2.61	1.01	2.56	1.00	2.68	.99	2.75	.92	2.69	1.01	2.67	1.01	2.63	.93
Believes Cannot Be Helped	1.97	.92	1.77	.85	1.88	.93	1.94	.96	1.89	1.00	1.79	.83	1.90	.93	1.79	.84
Reliable Informant	2.99	.88	3.01	.85	2.86	.85	3.25	.88	3.28	.90	3.15	.81	3.32	.90	3.19	.95

Ignores Problems	2.51	1.04	2.40	1.02	2.59	.96	2.53	.99	2.48	.99	2.48	1.00	2.39	1.07	2.37	1.04
Ruminates	2.77	1.00	2.81	1.02	2.68	1.09	2.83	1.08	2.98	.98	2.74	.95	2.78	1.00	2.70	.96
Excitable	2.66	.98	2.66	1.01	2.64	1.00	2.78	1.08	2.72	1.01	2.63	1.05	2.53	1.02	2.39	1.05
Conforming	2.51	.98	2.48	.96	2.50	1.02	2.39	.99	2.70	.92	2.49	.90	2.68	.97	2.74	1.02
Ineffective at Dealing with Problems	3.20	.98	3.07	1.07	3.22	.88	3.13	.98	3.13	1.05	3.08	.97	3.07	1.00	3.10	.96
Introverted	2.44	1.10	2.26	1.06	2.33	1.21	2.41	1.17	2.50	1.10	2.25	.99	2.48	1.08	2.57	1.03
Superficial Relationships	2.90	1.04	2.81	1.06	3.13	1.01	2.99	1.07	2.78	1.01	2.97	1.09	2.72	1.11	2.60	1.10
Impulsive	2.84	1.19	2.96	1.26	3.11	1.14	2.99	1.20	2.87	1.19	3.01	1.18	2.66	1.23	2.64	1.14
Stereotypic Feminine Behavior	2.67	1.19	2.56	1.22	2.63	1.20	2.68	1.13	2.78	1.20	2.70	1.24	2.76	1.20	2.84	1.21
Stubborn	2.93	.89	2.76	.97	2.95	.89	2.84	1.02	2.80	1.01	2.85	.97	2.62	1.02	2.63	1.06
Hostile Toward Therapist	1.43	.68	1.35	.59	1.41	.68	1.42	.71	1.36	.70	1.51	.71	1.28	.57	1.30	.59
Difficult to Motivate	2.43	1.07	2.21	1.11	2.52	1.19	2.25	1.13	2.22	1.09	2.33	1.14	2.22	1.10	2.11	1.09
Suicidal Ideations	1.76	.95	1.70	.95	1.84	.99	1.82	.98	1.80	1.00	1.73	.96	1.83	.98	1.75	.90
Familial Discord	3.46	1.18	3.44	1.37	3.45	1.19	3.75	1.11	3.44	1.25	3.55	1.16	3.42	1.25	3.42	1.22
Dogmatic	2.04	.84	1.92	.91	2.21	.94	2.15	.93	2.12	1.00	2.19	1.03	1.98	.99	1.90	.94

	Content Component Scales *(continued)*											
	SOD_1		SOD^2		FAM_1		FAM_2		TRT_1		TRT_2	
	Mean	SD	Mean	SD	Mean	SD	Mean	SD	Mean	SD	Mean	SD
Intake Information	(n = 224)		(n = 176)		(n = 239)		(n = 275)		(n = 299)		(n = 162)	
Axis IV diagnosis	3.07	.99	2.99	.98	2.96	.92	3.01	1.00	3.02	1.00	3.04	1.02
Axis V - Current Level of Functioning	59.97	9.84	60.68	9.30	61.82	9.12	61.73	9.31	60.27	9.46	59.94	10.06
Number of Arrests	.41	.99	.47	1.24	.57	1.49	.57	1.87	.36	.88	.61	1.48
Mental Status	(n = 224)		(n = 176)		(n = 239)		(n = 275)		(n = 299)		(n = 162)	
Anxiety During Interview	2.45	.66	2.47	.70	2.38	.67	2.40	.68	2.42	.69	2.40	.68
Depression During Interview	2.57	.73	2.52	.75	2.43	.71	2.46	.72	2.59	.75	2.54	.73
Activity Level During Interview	2.93	.42	2.94	.40	2.98	.40	2.94	.38	2.92	.41	2.96	.41
Speech During Interview	2.90	.39	2.90	.39	2.97	.41	2.95	.40	2.94	.42	2.92	.47
SCL-90-R Scales	(n = 223)		(n = 175)		(n = 239)		(n = 274)		(n = 297)		(n = 161)	
Somatization	1.56	.91	1.50	.84	1.43	.85	1.39	.85	1.54	.86	1.52	.78
Obsessive-Compulsive	1.95	.93	1.92	.90	1.76	.87	1.68	.92	1.93	.86	1.89	.89
Interpersonal Sensitivity	1.97	.91	2.01	.87	1.87	.87	1.72	.92	1.95	.80	1.99	.84
Depression	2.36	.90	2.32	.89	2.24	.85	2.13	.91	2.43	.78	2.38	.83
Anxiety	1.80	.97	1.78	.96	1.66	.95	1.55	.96	1.78	.91	1.83	.97
Hostility	1.61	1.02	1.56	1.00	1.72	.98	1.45	1.02	1.63	.96	1.71	1.02
Phobic Anxiety	1.28	1.02	1.28	.98	1.07	.96	.94	.92	1.13	.94	1.24	1.00
Paranoid Ideation	1.73	1.00	1.68	.95	1.81	.91	1.64	.95	1.77	.92	1.84	.89
Psychoticism	1.25	.79	1.19	.73	1.22	.77	1.11	.75	1.28	.71	1.35	.74
Initial SCL-90 Analogue	(n = 148)		(n = 112)		(n = 165)		(n = 190)		(n = 197)		(n = 107)	
Somatization	2.73	2.81	2.37	2.52	2.17	2.56	2.29	2.60	2.52	2.63	2.22	2.43
Obsessive-Compulsive	2.67	2.64	2.69	2.69	2.53	2.56	2.74	2.72	2.63	2.55	2.69	2.53
Interpersonal Sensitivity	5.05	2.48	4.88	2.54	4.91	2.73	5.17	2.64	5.03	2.61	5.07	2.30
Depression	4.88	2.58	4.66	2.44	4.64	2.62	4.50	2.46	4.78	2.55	5.04	2.44
Anxiety	4.47	2.76	4.45	2.62	4.33	2.74	4.30	2.53	4.47	2.72	4.74	2.50
Hostility	2.80	2.65	2.56	2.40	2.98	2.68	3.00	2.56	2.75	2.49	2.99	2.65
Phobic Anxiety	1.16	2.04	1.04	1.95	1.17	2.08	1.06	1.97	1.18	2.03	1.18	2.03
Paranoid Ideation	1.21	1.97	.91	1.60	1.14	1.97	1.28	2.11	1.08	1.90	1.12	1.87
Psychoticism	.76	1.81	.53	1.39	.63	1.49	.55	1.48	.54	1.30	.66	1.45
Patient Description Form Scales	(n = 147)		(n = 113)		(n = 164)		(n = 190)		(n = 197)		(n = 106)	
Angry Resentment	2.66	.84	2.59	.83	2.79	.84	2.81	.81	2.67	.87	2.75	.86

Critical/Argumentative	2.30	.83	2.26	.87	2.46	.86	2.47	.80	2.29	.87	2.32	.87
Narcissistic	1.88	.78	1.86	.79	2.08	.88	2.12	.90	1.99	.87	1.94	.77
Defensive	2.49	.81	2.48	.84	2.52	.79	2.61	.79	2.47	.81	2.49	.75
Histrionic	2.38	.82	2.35	.83	2.56	.87	2.61	.85	2.51	.88	2.44	.84
Aggressive	1.82	.69	1.75	.67	1.95	.75	1.92	.72	1.75	.71	1.84	.74
Insecure	3.14	.83	3.10	.81	3.12	.86	3.13	.81	3.17	.86	3.16	.81
Anxious	3.00	.82	2.95	.83	2.92	.77	2.95	.74	3.01	.80	3.01	.75
Pessimistic	2.32	.85	2.23	.81	2.27	.88	2.28	.83	2.36	.88	2.34	.87
Depressed	2.78	.88	2.71	.83	2.65	.89	2.64	.78	2.72	.88	2.73	.85
Achievement-Oriented	2.21	.74	2.17	.73	2.43	.80	2.49	.79	2.25	.71	2.29	.78
Passive-Submissive	2.66	.88	2.76	.88	2.60	.92	2.66	.88	2.73	.94	2.79	.97
Introverted	2.63	.97	2.72	.91	2.42	.91	2.48	.94	2.50	.98	2.63	.92
Emotionally Controlled	2.39	.88	2.41	.90	2.32	.85	2.41	.85	2.31	.87	2.38	.86
Antisocial	2.03	.77	2.00	.75	2.15	.83	2.18	.84	2.08	.83	2.06	.80
Negative Treatment Attitudes	1.86	.64	1.91	.75	1.91	.66	2.00	.76	1.89	.70	1.95	.62
Somatic Symptoms	2.26	1.09	2.17	1.04	2.02	1.04	2.16	1.03	2.19	1.05	2.06	.98
Psychotic Symptoms	1.27	.58	1.28	.56	1.25	.46	1.25	.47	1.27	.48	1.32	.51
Family Problems	2.96	1.10	2.91	1.03	3.18	1.08	3.25	.99	3.04	1.09	3.15	1.12
Obsessive-Compulsive	2.53	.88	2.55	.95	2.54	.85	2.63	.81	2.55	.86	2.51	.88
Stereotypic Masculine Interests	1.38	.68	1.35	.64	1.40	.65	1.43	.75	1.36	.69	1.31	.62
Procrastinates	2.11	.85	2.22	.95	2.17	.91	2.22	.85	2.20	.89	2.19	.86
Suspicious	2.46	.84	2.37	.87	2.46	.86	2.57	.90	2.43	.88	2.58	.80
Agitated	2.20	.82	2.07	.83	2.18	.88	2.23	.84	2.18	.85	2.20	.84
Work Problems	1.53	.75	1.62	.87	1.67	.86	1.54	.80	1.58	.83	1.55	.68
Patient Description Form Items	(n = 147)		(n = 113)		(n = 164)		(n = 190)		(n = 197)		(n = 106)	
Anxious	3.18	1.05	3.27	1.03	3.18	.99	3.21	.96	3.24	1.04	3.30	.95
Problems with Authority Figures	2.59	1.17	2.63	1.23	2.80	1.21	2.82	1.19	2.69	1.20	2.69	1.24
Has Insight Into Own Problems	2.57	.84	2.62	.93	2.60	.90	2.57	.90	2.49	.87	2.62	.88
Fears Losing Control	3.16	1.15	3.08	1.16	3.15	1.07	3.19	1.10	3.15	1.09	3.12	1.13
Extroverted	2.26	1.03	2.15	.96	2.58	1.12	2.59	1.11	2.40	1.05	2.40	1.02
Uses Repression	2.78	1.03	2.83	1.06	2.77	.99	2.91	1.07	2.77	1.08	2.88	1.07
Submissive	2.82	1.05	2.88	1.05	2.70	1.03	2.78	1.04	2.87	1.08	2.94	1.15
Difficulty Concentrating	2.89	1.12	2.66	1.13	2.72	1.12	2.76	1.09	2.78	1.09	2.82	.96
Rigid	2.51	1.04	2.50	1.08	2.40	.98	2.51	1.00	2.45	1.02	2.52	.91
Overly Compliant	2.19	.98	2.25	1.06	2.26	1.06	2.26	1.06	2.27	1.10	2.35	1.11
Whiny	2.01	1.05	1.96	1.01	2.09	1.08	2.13	1.07	2.07	1.06	2.06	1.07
Feels Overwhelmed	3.47	1.12	3.42	1.06	3.39	1.04	3.42	1.02	3.52	1.07	3.38	1.01
Manipulative	2.23	1.14	2.24	1.18	2.45	1.16	2.55	1.17	2.36	1.18	2.27	1.11
Difficulty Trusting Others	3.32	1.12	3.18	1.17	3.36	1.09	3.46	1.08	3.22	1.15	3.44	1.07
Insensitive to Others	1.77	.85	1.76	.92	1.84	.91	1.86	.95	1.75	.84	1.79	.83
Stereotypic Masculine Behavior	1.33	.68	1.31	.64	1.36	.65	1.37	.75	1.30	.68	1.26	.61

	Content Component Scales (continued)											
	SOD_1		SOD_2		FAM_1		FAM_2		TRT_1		TRT_2	
	Mean	SD	Mean	SD	Mean	SD	Mean	SD	Mean	SD	Mean	SD
Harbors Grudges	2.57	1.01	2.45	1.08	2.63	1.04	2.66	1.04	2.45	1.02	2.59	.95
Evasive	2.16	1.01	2.14	1.05	2.29	1.05	2.39	1.08	2.27	1.04	2.27	.99
Disoriented	1.31	.73	1.31	.72	1.29	.66	1.30	.66	1.28	.66	1.36	.72
Energetic	2.10	.86	2.12	.86	2.42	1.02	2.47	.99	2.20	.92	2.32	.97
Lonely	2.97	1.08	2.79	1.00	2.80	1.05	3.02	1.06	3.01	1.07	2.98	1.05
Family Lacks Love	2.90	1.23	2.78	1.21	3.02	1.25	3.17	1.18	2.92	1.22	3.03	1.27
Worrier	3.39	1.05	3.38	1.07	3.40	.98	3.38	.95	3.48	1.01	3.41	1.01
Narcissistic	1.96	1.01	1.92	.99	2.23	1.14	2.29	1.18	2.09	1.12	2.03	1.01
Tearful	2.51	1.15	2.50	1.18	2.45	1.17	2.43	1.13	2.53	1.21	2.58	1.21
Provocative	1.57	.87	1.59	.90	1.80	.99	1.80	1.03	1.69	.98	1.60	.87
Moralistic	2.41	.99	2.21	.94	2.29	.90	2.32	.94	2.26	1.00	2.26	.87
Socially Awkward	2.66	1.07	2.66	1.00	2.49	1.00	2.56	1.01	2.55	1.05	2.63	.94
Hostile	2.06	.92	2.02	1.00	2.23	1.05	2.23	1.05	2.08	1.01	2.20	1.06
Overcontrolled	2.50	1.17	2.41	1.18	2.42	1.13	2.49	1.11	2.44	1.16	2.49	1.18
Resistant to Interpretations	2.10	.94	2.17	.99	2.12	.94	2.29	1.00	2.18	.96	2.22	.94
Antisocial Behavior	1.60	.86	1.66	.85	1.77	.96	1.77	.98	1.69	.94	1.72	.93
Sarcastic	1.81	.99	1.75	.97	1.99	1.07	1.96	1.01	1.80	.98	1.87	1.05
Rejects Traditional Gender Role	1.57	.93	1.61	.97	1.74	1.05	1.75	1.07	1.54	.94	1.57	.90
Feels Gets Raw Deal From Life	2.97	1.14	2.86	1.13	2.98	1.14	3.13	1.09	2.98	1.13	3.11	1.15
Acute Psychological Turmoil	3.03	1.07	2.94	1.07	3.00	1.07	3.02	1.01	3.00	1.08	3.18	1.04
Does Not Complete Projects	2.10	1.06	2.20	1.14	2.28	1.20	2.27	1.13	2.25	1.16	2.29	1.10
Uncomfortable with Opposite Sex	2.37	1.22	2.27	1.18	2.25	1.19	2.36	1.19	2.25	1.20	2.30	1.15
Preoccupied with Health Problems	2.20	1.33	2.07	1.20	1.96	1.20	2.10	1.26	2.14	1.30	1.96	1.15
Work-Oriented	2.50	1.17	2.59	1.17	2.71	1.13	2.72	1.15	2.56	1.12	2.55	1.19
Resents Family Members	2.92	1.24	2.86	1.15	3.20	1.22	3.23	1.14	3.05	1.24	3.13	1.21
Demanding of Attention	2.44	1.05	2.39	1.01	2.69	1.08	2.74	1.11	2.53	1.13	2.43	1.03
Passive	2.66	1.09	2.74	1.03	2.53	1.07	2.58	1.09	2.71	1.11	2.71	1.14
Self-Punishing	2.76	1.18	2.68	1.12	2.68	1.16	2.75	1.12	2.77	1.14	2.80	1.12
Needs to Achieve	2.42	1.05	2.30	.97	2.59	1.04	2.65	1.12	2.46	1.08	2.53	1.05
Needs to Be with Others	2.90	1.08	2.95	1.05	3.10	1.01	3.19	1.01	3.09	1.06	3.02	1.04
Irritable	2.68	.98	2.58	1.02	2.66	1.03	2.72	.97	2.57	1.07	2.67	1.03
Self-Defeating	3.12	1.08	3.08	1.04	3.14	1.05	3.17	1.07	3.13	1.08	3.11	1.07
Delusional Thinking	1.22	.64	1.23	.63	1.29	.68	1.26	.70	1.30	.72	1.26	.69
Self-Reliant	2.64	.95	2.47	.94	2.56	.93	2.67	.97	2.47	.88	2.60	.93
Aggressive	1.97	.90	1.89	.91	2.09	.95	2.12	.97	1.90	.94	2.05	.94
Competitive	1.97	1.00	1.91	.97	2.21	1.06	2.23	1.04	1.97	.99	2.07	1.01
Suspicious	2.38	1.04	2.31	1.08	2.37	1.05	2.52	1.09	2.39	1.08	2.56	.98
Compulsive	2.18	1.19	2.18	1.28	2.19	1.13	2.32	1.16	2.11	1.13	2.25	1.22

Dependable	2.96	.90	2.93	.90	3.01	.95	2.91	.94	2.91	.88	2.87	.92
Multiple Somatic Complaints	2.13	1.31	1.99	1.21	1.88	1.17	2.01	1.23	2.02	1.22	1.94	1.14
Complains of Lack of Time	1.94	1.09	2.03	1.10	1.99	1.07	2.01	1.10	1.95	1.09	1.94	1.09
Poor Work Performance	1.71	.92	1.78	.93	1.81	1.03	1.80	1.03	1.81	.99	1.77	.90
Insecure	3.51	.90	3.52	.89	3.52	.92	3.59	.87	3.60	.92	3.52	.91
Discusses Problems Openly	3.12	.84	3.01	.86	3.18	.83	3.17	.84	3.18	.88	3.14	.88
Sexually Adjusted	2.38	.84	2.42	.84	2.41	.92	2.45	.87	2.41	.86	2.39	.88
Exaggerated Need for Affection	2.25	1.12	2.30	1.13	2.39	1.20	2.61	1.22	2.48	1.18	2.40	1.12
Resentful	2.97	1.06	2.86	1.07	3.02	1.03	3.06	.98	2.92	1.10	3.01	1.08
Uses Denial	2.73	1.07	2.74	1.06	2.72	1.07	2.87	1.06	2.65	1.08	2.76	1.01
Hypochondriacal	1.80	1.10	1.72	1.02	1.61	.93	1.72	1.03	1.71	1.04	1.69	1.00
Communicates Effectively	2.94	.89	2.93	.89	3.10	.91	3.13	.89	2.94	.84	2.96	.80
Has Many Nightmares	2.17	1.16	2.00	1.05	1.90	1.05	2.06	1.09	1.95	1.08	2.08	1.10
Stormy Interpersonal Relationships	3.06	1.25	3.03	1.21	3.20	1.15	3.24	1.15	3.04	1.21	3.19	1.24
Feigns Remorse When in Trouble	1.74	.99	1.64	.92	1.84	.98	1.87	1.03	1.85	1.02	1.66	.86
Stereotypic Masculine Interests	1.42	.79	1.39	.74	1.45	.77	1.49	.86	1.41	.81	1.35	.71
Guarded	2.56	1.13	2.59	1.22	2.49	1.07	2.63	1.14	2.44	1.12	2.50	1.03
Feels Inferior	3.36	1.04	3.34	1.06	3.28	1.13	3.29	1.08	3.30	1.09	3.39	1.02
Low Frustration Tolerance	2.87	1.03	2.75	1.07	2.91	1.03	2.97	.99	2.84	1.07	2.89	1.02
Psychotic Symptoms	1.22	.63	1.21	.59	1.20	.58	1.23	.67	1.22	.62	1.26	.67
Fired From Past Jobs	1.51	.92	1.58	.95	1.64	1.08	1.67	1.05	1.58	1.03	1.54	.87
Needs Attention	2.92	1.04	2.90	.92	3.09	.97	3.15	.97	3.04	1.02	3.03	.90
Acts Out	2.29	1.09	2.19	1.05	2.33	1.06	2.44	1.10	2.26	1.11	2.36	1.05
Histrionic	2.09	1.06	2.05	1.13	2.24	1.17	2.33	1.22	2.25	1.22	2.15	1.16
Self-Indulgent	2.11	1.04	2.11	1.00	2.27	1.06	2.33	1.11	2.16	1.08	2.16	.99
Depressed	3.43	.97	3.34	.94	3.24	1.05	3.26	.96	3.32	1.02	3.30	.94
Grandiose	1.49	.77	1.41	.73	1.62	.92	1.71	.96	1.59	.94	1.51	.79
Cynical	2.16	1.02	2.14	.99	2.24	1.06	2.31	1.05	2.13	1.05	2.12	1.05
Sociopathic	1.36	.60	1.36	.60	1.46	.78	1.48	.75	1.38	.68	1.36	.64
Agitated	2.44	1.04	2.29	1.08	2.37	1.06	2.39	1.00	2.37	1.08	2.49	1.09
Marital Problems	2.58	1.55	2.86	1.50	2.60	1.55	2.66	1.55	2.76	1.60	2.65	1.60
Absence of Deep Emotions	2.01	1.07	2.08	1.09	2.04	1.05	2.08	1.10	1.96	1.07	1.99	1.05
Uncomfortable Dealing with Emotions	2.88	1.09	2.91	1.09	2.82	1.09	2.97	1.07	2.86	1.09	2.85	.98
Sad	3.14	1.02	3.05	.98	3.02	1.01	3.05	.98	3.10	1.05	3.11	.97
Self-Degrading	2.71	1.11	2.64	1.13	2.65	1.16	2.60	1.10	2.68	1.14	2.67	1.12
Unable to Express Negative Feelings	2.30	1.12	2.26	1.07	2.13	1.04	2.30	1.12	2.20	1.11	2.30	1.09
Concrete in Thinking	2.47	1.08	2.32	1.08	2.38	1.09	2.35	1.07	2.37	1.10	2.30	1.03
Unable to See Own Limitations	2.12	1.00	2.17	1.02	2.18	1.00	2.22	1.05	2.08	1.01	2.20	.99
Power-Oriented	1.73	.94	1.70	.92	1.89	1.00	1.88	1.00	1.78	.98	1.75	.95
Grouchy	2.19	1.00	2.04	.97	2.22	1.01	2.19	.95	2.10	.99	2.21	1.00
Overbearing in Relationships	2.05	1.04	1.88	1.02	2.21	1.10	2.19	1.06	2.04	1.11	2.01	1.11
Uncertain About Career	2.79	1.38	2.83	1.43	2.95	1.32	2.99	1.33	2.92	1.33	2.85	1.36

	Content Component Scales *(continued)*											
	SOD_1		SOD_2		FAM_1		FAM_2		TRT_1		TRT_2	
	Mean	SD	Mean	SD	Mean	SD	Mean	SD	Mean	SD	Mean	SD
Likable	3.21	.84	3.15	.80	3.24	.89	3.27	.85	3.21	.82	3.24	.84
Procrastinator	2.42	1.01	2.46	1.07	2.31	1.02	2.48	1.04	2.42	1.03	2.41	.97
Negative Feelings Toward Opposite Sex	2.61	1.22	2.51	1.17	2.61	1.21	2.69	1.17	2.55	1.25	2.68	1.23
Defensive	2.74	.99	2.70	1.06	2.77	1.05	2.87	1.12	2.67	1.07	2.72	1.02
Empathetic	2.61	.75	2.50	.72	2.61	.76	2.64	.78	2.58	.75	2.59	.78
Perfectionistic	2.40	1.23	2.36	1.24	2.53	1.22	2.59	1.18	2.41	1.20	2.39	1.21
Judgmental	2.50	.98	2.42	1.01	2.55	.98	2.58	.98	2.45	1.03	2.48	.97
Copes Well with Stress	1.92	.72	2.01	.76	2.04	.74	2.01	.73	1.95	.77	1.97	.71
Moody	2.80	.98	2.67	1.05	2.87	1.03	2.87	.90	2.71	.99	2.74	1.00
Selfish	1.89	.90	1.87	.88	2.09	.97	2.09	1.01	1.92	.98	1.90	.86
Gives Up Easily	2.25	1.03	2.33	.97	2.21	1.05	2.27	1.06	2.36	1.07	2.39	.98
Physical Symptoms in Response to Stress	2.37	1.24	2.33	1.20	2.12	1.20	2.27	1.20	2.31	1.23	2.20	1.18
Blames Family For Difficulties	2.72	1.31	2.65	1.27	2.91	1.27	3.03	1.27	2.78	1.30	2.88	1.31
Bored	2.20	1.08	2.12	1.03	2.26	1.13	2.26	1.13	2.32	1.10	2.15	.96
Idealistic	2.29	.94	2.32	.99	2.37	1.03	2.48	1.05	2.26	1.04	2.22	.97
Difficulty Establishing Therapeutic Rapport	1.80	.88	1.88	.99	1.85	.83	1.98	1.04	1.84	.94	1.85	.85
Daydreams	1.89	1.02	1.87	.91	1.87	.92	2.01	.96	1.91	.98	1.89	.96
Concerned About Status	1.91	.97	1.93	1.00	2.17	1.11	2.17	1.12	2.09	1.07	2.05	1.06
Creates Good First Impression	2.66	.94	2.61	.94	2.83	.99	2.83	.97	2.71	.93	2.74	1.04
Complains of Sleep Disturbance	2.92	1.26	2.77	1.17	2.68	1.25	2.68	1.20	2.73	1.23	2.85	1.19
Has Temper Tantrums	2.06	1.07	2.02	1.01	2.20	1.05	2.14	1.08	1.98	1.05	2.11	1.04
Overreactive	2.69	1.12	2.56	1.12	2.84	1.07	2.79	1.08	2.71	1.14	2.68	1.11
High Aspirations	2.13	1.10	1.99	1.05	2.35	1.16	2.43	1.16	2.16	1.10	2.08	1.03
Feels Hopeless	2.86	1.14	2.79	1.09	2.72	1.20	2.69	1.12	2.86	1.18	2.82	1.12
Keeps Others at a Distance	3.03	1.12	2.93	1.14	2.89	1.11	3.00	1.10	2.83	1.13	2.96	1.08
Argumentative	2.14	.98	2.04	.98	2.30	1.07	2.25	1.01	2.14	1.03	2.17	1.00
Paranoid Features	1.69	.92	1.63	.92	1.63	.93	1.73	1.01	1.69	.97	1.75	.98
Restless	2.55	1.10	2.38	1.06	2.47	1.15	2.53	1.11	2.49	1.09	2.50	1.05
Pessimistic	2.74	1.02	2.71	.98	2.65	1.03	2.68	1.03	2.79	1.06	2.78	1.03
Feels Like a Failure	3.03	1.09	2.96	1.05	2.98	1.07	3.02	1.06	3.11	1.11	3.03	1.08
Hallucinations	1.12	.54	1.11	.47	1.06	.28	1.10	.47	1.07	.39	1.12	.49
Restricted Affect	2.24	1.09	2.30	1.14	2.15	1.14	2.14	1.10	2.11	1.10	2.21	1.15
Impatient	2.51	.97	2.42	1.02	2.65	1.03	2.71	1.03	2.49	1.03	2.50	.98
Assertive	2.08	.86	1.94	.83	2.20	.89	2.22	.89	2.04	.87	2.10	.80
Modest	2.63	.78	2.56	.78	2.52	.87	2.60	.86	2.57	.87	2.53	.87
Self-Doubting	3.17	.99	3.10	1.02	3.20	.99	3.17	.98	3.25	.98	3.21	.96
Deceptive	1.80	.82	1.76	.82	1.87	.94	1.94	.96	1.76	.89	1.85	.85
Feels That Life is a Strain	3.14	1.06	3.03	1.09	3.09	1.06	3.12	1.00	3.17	1.05	3.24	1.03

Physically Abusive	1.34	.66	1.33	.64	1.34	.68	1.31	.64	1.27	.61	1.32	.65
Feels Rejected	3.23	1.03	3.14	1.03	3.24	1.10	3.26	1.04	3.25	1.11	3.37	1.08
Does Not Get Along with Coworkers	1.63	.88	1.73	1.04	1.70	.91	1.65	.90	1.63	.91	1.68	.89
Uses Projection	2.31	1.00	2.20	1.07	2.41	1.04	2.48	1.07	2.29	1.06	2.28	1.04
Complains of Fatigue	2.78	1.25	2.67	1.25	2.45	1.27	2.62	1.21	2.68	1.28	2.53	1.23
Uses Rationalization	2.59	1.00	2.56	1.05	2.73	1.08	2.77	1.02	2.60	1.09	2.50	1.06
Critical of Others	2.37	1.04	2.29	1.09	2.65	1.04	2.60	1.05	2.38	1.09	2.36	1.00
Egocentric	2.11	1.05	2.03	1.09	2.33	1.08	2.35	1.12	2.16	1.06	2.13	1.05
Overevaluates Own Worth	1.56	.87	1.51	.83	1.73	.94	1.80	1.00	1.62	.95	1.57	.80
Optimistic	1.92	.77	1.91	.78	2.04	.77	2.07	.79	1.95	.80	1.95	.76
Psychologically Immature	2.69	1.16	2.73	1.17	2.88	1.17	3.04	1.17	2.85	1.23	2.71	1.21
Poor Judgment	2.79	1.14	2.71	1.10	2.88	1.18	2.93	1.16	2.82	1.18	2.83	1.17
Low Sex Drive	2.33	1.22	2.39	1.19	2.23	1.29	2.07	1.14	2.22	1.22	2.26	1.25
Feels Mistreated	3.04	1.14	2.95	1.10	3.25	1.08	3.28	1.12	3.24	1.12	3.19	1.09
Overly Sensitive to Criticism	3.24	1.03	3.15	1.17	3.25	1.12	3.31	1.08	3.28	1.07	3.23	1.07
Sentimental	2.56	.96	2.40	.91	2.62	1.03	2.70	1.06	2.67	1.02	2.44	.98
Sexual Preoccupation	1.39	.72	1.40	.77	1.68	1.06	1.68	1.08	1.57	1.02	1.50	.91
Accelerated Speech	1.63	.96	1.50	.80	1.73	1.02	1.75	1.00	1.70	.99	1.63	.90
Concerns About Homosexuality	1.15	.62	1.16	.61	1.23	.74	1.19	.68	1.16	.65	1.13	.48
Many Specific Fears	2.18	1.06	2.13	1.07	2.09	1.07	2.13	1.09	2.24	1.12	2.23	1.18
Passive in Relationships	2.98	1.07	3.14	1.04	2.89	1.17	2.98	1.12	3.05	1.16	3.11	1.13
Negative Attitudes Toward Therapy	1.64	.82	1.70	.94	1.64	.80	1.74	.93	1.61	.83	1.69	.79
Guilt-Prone	3.10	1.14	3.03	1.09	2.99	1.15	3.04	1.14	3.12	1.10	3.04	1.09
Nervous	2.99	1.00	3.02	1.01	2.94	.95	2.90	.95	3.03	.97	3.10	.88
Obsessive	2.41	1.21	2.29	1.21	2.34	1.13	2.46	1.12	2.34	1.14	2.34	1.20
Shy	2.59	1.15	2.70	1.13	2.38	1.09	2.42	1.10	2.50	1.16	2.66	1.16
Uses Intellectualization	2.20	1.02	2.22	1.07	2.25	1.10	2.35	1.08	2.20	1.05	2.12	1.02
Has Many Interests	2.08	.89	2.05	.90	2.31	.98	2.33	.94	2.10	.88	2.16	.93
Difficulty Making Decisions	2.91	1.08	2.91	1.14	2.91	1.11	3.00	1.10	3.00	1.05	2.81	1.08
Indirect Expression of Hostility	2.78	1.06	2.72	1.07	2.82	1.07	2.96	1.07	2.81	1.13	2.81	1.08
Poor Reality Testing	1.51	.85	1.54	.94	1.52	.85	1.52	.88	1.55	.89	1.68	1.02
Angry	2.99	1.15	2.91	1.07	3.13	1.07	3.11	1.07	2.95	1.16	3.03	1.21
Eccentric	1.73	1.01	1.69	.99	1.73	1.01	1.71	1.02	1.66	.98	1.69	.97
Emotional Lability	2.44	1.04	2.28	1.03	2.51	1.10	2.56	1.06	2.47	1.12	2.37	1.07
Dislikes Change	2.65	.92	2.68	1.02	2.59	.98	2.72	.95	2.69	.99	2.67	.98
Believes Cannot Be Helped	1.92	.92	1.78	.85	1.88	.90	1.90	.86	1.93	.92	1.90	.91
Reliable Informant	3.28	.91	3.18	.94	3.25	.91	3.20	.92	3.25	.92	3.16	1.01
Ignores Problems	2.35	1.02	2.38	1.04	2.40	1.02	2.49	1.05	2.35	1.07	2.39	1.00
Ruminates	2.88	1.00	2.81	1.03	2.83	.98	2.85	.97	2.86	1.04	2.68	1.00
Excitable	2.47	1.05	2.36	1.05	2.67	1.06	2.67	1.04	2.53	1.03	2.53	1.01
Conforming	2.61	.94	2.63	1.04	2.54	.95	2.60	.99	2.62	.99	2.66	.96
Ineffective at Dealing with Problems	3.08	1.03	3.07	1.04	3.09	1.02	3.14	.99	3.12	1.03	3.11	.98

	Content Component Scales *(continued)*											
	SOD_1		SOD_2		FAM_1		FAM_2		TRT_1		TRT_2	
	Mean	SD	Mean	SD	Mean	SD	Mean	SD	Mean	SD	Mean	SD
Introverted	2.63	1.09	2.76	1.04	2.38	1.06	2.43	1.10	2.44	1.11	2.56	1.06
Superficial Relationships	2.65	1.08	2.64	1.14	2.75	1.08	2.86	1.11	2.72	1.09	2.78	1.06
Impulsive	2.63	1.16	2.50	1.15	2.83	1.19	2.85	1.23	2.70	1.24	2.69	1.25
Stereotypic Feminine Behavior	2.66	1.21	2.61	1.21	2.76	1.19	2.81	1.18	2.82	1.20	2.68	1.20
Stubborn	2.59	1.00	2.53	1.02	2.78	.98	2.85	.93	2.66	1.03	2.66	1.03
Hostile Toward Therapist	1.31	.61	1.34	.71	1.32	.56	1.41	.75	1.30	.63	1.33	.58
Difficult to Motivate	2.15	1.01	2.23	1.08	2.15	1.05	2.21	1.09	2.18	1.09	2.26	1.05
Suicidal Ideations	1.87	1.06	1.77	.96	1.78	1.02	1.72	.89	1.82	1.00	1.83	.99
Familial Discord	3.30	1.23	3.33	1.16	3.56	1.21	3.57	1.10	3.38	1.25	3.52	1.28
Dogmatic	2.03	.98	1.89	.97	2.10	.98	2.15	.98	1.95	.98	1.99	.97

Table L-1f. Means and standard deviations for continuous extra-test characteristics (women): High scores on supplementary scales

Extra-test Characteristics	Supplementary Scales									
	A		R		Es		MAC-R		AAS	
	Mean	SD	Mean	SD	Mean	SD	Mean	SD	Mean	SD
Intake Information	(n = 300)		(n = 129)		(n = 382)		(n = 121)		(n = 192)	
Axis IV diagnosis	3.02	.99	2.96	1.01	2.87	.89	3.10	1.04	2.97	.96
Axis V - Current Level of Functioning	60.09	10.08	61.35	9.64	65.43	9.01	59.79	11.35	60.31	10.33
Number of Arrests	.40	1.08	.57	2.21	.60	1.90	1.03	1.95	.69	1.40
Mental Status	(n = 300)		(n = 129)		(n = 382)		(n = 121)		(n = 192)	
Anxiety During Interview	2.47	.68	2.45	.70	2.24	.57	2.46	.71	2.39	.71
Depression During Interview	2.60	.74	2.54	.80	2.17	.73	2.54	.75	2.51	.77
Activity Level During Interview	2.96	.39	2.98	.39	2.98	.28	2.93	.41	2.95	.37
Speech During Interview	2.95	.40	2.96	.41	3.01	.32	3.00	.45	2.98	.41
SCL-90-R Scales	(n = 298)		(n = 128)		(n = 380)		(n = 120)		(n = 191)	
Somatization	1.57	.82	1.33	.91	.58	.49	1.41	.87	1.39	.81
Obsessive-Compulsive	2.01	.82	1.69	1.02	.80	.63	1.62	.96	1.71	.90
Interpersonal Sensitivity	2.05	.78	1.59	1.01	.93	.72	1.51	.90	1.66	.88
Depression	2.48	.74	2.06	1.05	1.18	.82	2.01	.98	2.12	.92
Anxiety	1.85	.87	1.52	1.07	.67	.65	1.59	.99	1.60	.90
Hostility	1.71	.97	1.28	.99	.73	.71	1.46	1.00	1.52	1.00
Phobic Anxiety	1.19	.94	1.07	1.06	.24	.39	.94	.93	.92	.88
Paranoid Ideation	1.86	.88	1.36	1.03	.87	.74	1.63	.95	1.59	.93
Psychoticism	1.31	.70	.95	.75	.44	.41	1.15	.82	1.12	.75
Initial SCL-90 Analogue	(n = 195)		(n = 92)		(n = 256)		(n = 75)		(n = 124)	
Somatization	2.35	2.56	2.90	2.93	1.71	2.13	2.12	2.43	2.13	2.67
Obsessive-Compulsive	2.69	2.56	2.77	2.62	2.68	2.61	2.99	2.62	2.94	2.63
Interpersonal Sensitivity	5.04	2.62	5.24	2.43	4.10	2.74	4.64	2.51	4.85	2.66
Depression	4.82	2.58	4.88	2.50	3.96	2.55	4.51	2.55	4.62	2.57
Anxiety	4.49	2.68	4.82	2.67	3.98	2.50	4.49	2.53	4.46	2.50
Hostility	2.79	2.48	2.80	2.60	2.98	2.56	3.39	2.75	2.96	2.51
Phobic Anxiety	1.20	2.02	1.13	1.89	1.02	1.86	1.51	2.36	1.11	1.99
Paranoid Ideation	1.11	1.79	1.02	1.87	1.08	1.79	1.52	2.00	1.21	1.97
Psychoticism	.61	1.51	.63	1.70	.74	1.58	1.03	1.90	.85	1.95

Table L-1f. Means and standard deviations for continuous extra-test characteristics (women): High scores on supplementary scales *(continued)*

Extra-test Characteristics	A Mean	A SD	R Mean	R SD	Es Mean	Es SD	MAC-R Mean	MAC-R SD	AAS Mean	AAS SD
Patient Description Form Scales	(n = 195)		(n = 93)		(n = 256)		(n = 74)		(n = 125)	
Angry Resentment	2.67	.86	2.69	.84	2.61	.89	2.95	.85	2.82	.89
Critical/Argumentative	2.32	.89	2.31	.78	2.30	.84	2.53	.89	2.51	.91
Narcissistic	2.00	.88	2.05	.80	2.07	.85	2.27	.87	2.24	.88
Defensive	2.47	.83	2.57	.78	2.45	.82	2.69	.75	2.58	.81
Histrionic	2.48	.88	2.52	.79	2.39	.86	2.67	.86	2.67	.85
Aggressive	1.74	.72	1.86	.67	1.89	.75	2.16	.86	1.95	.78
Insecure	3.18	.88	3.21	.73	2.84	.90	3.17	.94	3.19	.88
Anxious	2.98	.78	3.12	.81	2.69	.78	3.08	.86	3.00	.78
Pessimistic	2.30	.89	2.36	.88	2.02	.87	2.32	.89	2.33	.92
Depressed	2.72	.87	2.79	.85	2.25	.81	2.66	.89	2.73	.88
Achievement-Oriented	2.36	.73	2.27	.69	2.78	.75	2.51	.74	2.59	.79
Passive-Submissive	2.73	.92	2.74	.90	2.40	.90	2.66	.90	2.59	.91
Introverted	2.51	.97	2.76	.85	2.18	.92	2.39	.91	2.44	.94
Emotionally Controlled	2.38	.89	2.42	.87	2.34	.89	2.42	.85	2.50	.96
Antisocial	2.05	.79	2.14	.81	2.16	.82	2.48	.92	2.33	.87
Negative Treatment Attitudes	1.91	.71	1.90	.69	1.92	.75	2.01	.61	1.97	.69
Somatic Symptoms	2.15	1.02	2.39	1.13	1.84	.85	2.09	.93	2.05	1.02
Psychotic Symptoms	1.26	.51	1.27	.62	1.28	.65	1.48	.71	1.38	.66
Family Problems	3.04	1.11	2.90	1.12	2.95	1.04	3.43	1.04	3.29	1.04
Obsessive-Compulsive	2.58	.89	2.62	.81	2.56	.86	2.74	.88	2.70	.89
Stereotypic Masculine Interests	1.36	.63	1.42	.75	1.55	.76	1.56	.82	1.50	.76
Procrastinates	2.19	.91	2.16	.79	2.20	.93	2.43	.95	2.46	.98
Suspicious	2.43	.88	2.44	.85	2.33	.88	2.74	.90	2.60	.89
Agitated	2.16	.85	2.26	.84	2.04	.83	2.37	.89	2.28	.88
Work Problems	1.63	.81	1.52	.78	1.54	.67	1.68	.76	1.68	.83
Patient Description Form Items	(n = 195)		(n = 93)		(n = 256)		(n = 74)		(n = 125)	
Anxious	3.26	.98	3.30	1.06	2.95	.92	3.36	.99	3.27	.93
Problems with Authority Figures	2.70	1.22	2.83	1.21	2.72	1.19	3.17	1.16	2.93	1.16
Has Insight Into Own Problems	2.56	.91	2.44	.81	2.73	.91	2.54	.85	2.76	.90
Fears Losing Control	3.13	1.11	3.20	1.13	3.03	1.11	3.45	1.04	3.31	1.08
Extroverted	2.37	1.07	2.31	1.01	2.78	1.06	2.88	1.05	2.72	1.06
Uses Repression	2.74	1.08	2.93	1.02	2.86	1.07	2.97	1.04	2.94	1.06

Submissive	2.85	1.05	2.93	1.09	2.57	1.02	2.85	1.03	2.75	1.12
Difficulty Concentrating	2.74	1.09	2.90	1.18	2.37	1.08	2.92	1.18	2.75	1.15
Rigid	2.43	1.01	2.56	1.04	2.42	1.06	2.59	1.03	2.39	1.01
Overly Compliant	2.25	1.08	2.33	1.05	2.01	.95	2.27	1.06	2.19	1.10
Whiny	2.06	1.06	2.20	1.13	1.85	.96	2.04	1.06	2.05	1.09
Feels Overwhelmed	3.48	1.06	3.67	1.06	3.15	1.14	3.29	1.11	3.43	1.09
Manipulative	2.37	1.21	2.38	1.10	2.43	1.06	2.69	1.18	2.70	1.19
Difficulty Trusting Others	3.24	1.13	3.26	1.10	3.07	1.12	3.49	1.17	3.48	1.08
Insensitive to Others	1.77	.87	1.87	.94	1.98	.98	2.03	.95	1.96	.90
Stereotypic Masculine Behavior	1.29	.62	1.38	.77	1.48	.78	1.49	.82	1.41	.73
Harbors Grudges	2.51	1.09	2.59	.99	2.47	1.02	2.75	.98	2.62	1.05
Evasive	2.25	1.07	2.28	1.08	2.30	1.13	2.46	1.06	2.43	1.11
Disoriented	1.29	.67	1.29	.73	1.25	.69	1.49	.80	1.39	.77
Energetic	2.27	.92	2.15	.85	2.74	.97	2.64	.96	2.51	.92
Lonely	2.94	1.08	3.05	1.06	2.63	1.10	2.91	1.12	2.96	1.11
Family Lacks Love	2.94	1.27	2.73	1.23	2.75	1.20	3.34	1.27	3.26	1.23
Worrier	3.45	1.00	3.52	.97	3.04	1.04	3.35	1.08	3.41	.94
Narcissistic	2.11	1.13	2.05	1.01	2.16	1.12	2.36	1.09	2.39	1.16
Tearful	2.50	1.20	2.61	1.27	2.04	1.12	2.36	1.28	2.43	1.19
Provocative	1.68	.95	1.76	.96	1.94	1.08	1.92	1.06	1.93	1.12
Moralistic	2.24	.96	2.56	.91	2.29	1.02	2.27	.91	2.17	.88
Socially Awkward	2.51	1.04	2.81	1.04	2.18	1.01	2.53	.92	2.45	1.01
Hostile	2.08	1.04	2.05	.96	2.23	1.14	2.36	1.17	2.24	1.09
Overcontrolled	2.50	1.19	2.37	1.11	2.57	1.13	2.32	1.20	2.46	1.18
Resistant to Interpretations	2.15	1.00	2.13	.93	2.18	1.03	2.39	.94	2.20	.99
Antisocial Behavior	1.66	.92	1.64	.95	1.79	.98	2.21	1.12	1.96	.99
Sarcastic	1.85	1.00	1.79	.91	1.89	.99	2.04	1.14	2.12	1.09
Rejects Traditional Gender Role	1.60	.95	1.53	.81	1.77	1.00	1.82	1.16	1.91	1.11
Feels Gets Raw Deal From Life	2.97	1.17	3.00	1.20	2.60	1.14	3.08	1.08	3.02	1.15
Acute Psychological Turmoil	3.02	1.09	3.05	1.06	2.67	1.03	3.18	1.08	3.14	1.08
Does Not Complete Projects	2.22	1.14	2.06	.99	2.17	1.18	2.48	1.16	2.51	1.22
Uncomfortable with Opposite Sex	2.23	1.14	2.39	1.19	1.99	1.10	2.17	1.19	2.17	1.16
Preoccupied with Health Problems	2.04	1.22	2.39	1.44	1.66	1.00	1.97	1.16	1.90	1.16
Work-Oriented	2.68	1.12	2.53	1.11	3.06	1.07	2.75	1.11	2.80	1.19
Resents Family Members	3.03	1.24	3.00	1.25	2.94	1.19	3.42	1.18	3.31	1.12
Demanding of Attention	2.55	1.12	2.52	1.09	2.54	1.07	2.60	1.09	2.73	1.07
Passive	2.70	1.06	2.74	1.06	2.43	1.11	2.47	1.09	2.55	1.03
Self-Punishing	2.77	1.16	2.75	1.05	2.43	1.08	2.76	1.22	2.87	1.19
Needs to Achieve	2.58	1.07	2.48	1.01	2.88	1.04	2.60	1.04	2.81	1.07
Needs to Be with Others	3.10	1.06	3.02	1.01	3.06	1.00	3.38	.92	3.31	.97
Irritable	2.59	1.06	2.70	1.00	2.49	1.02	2.76	1.03	2.77	1.08
Self-Defeating	3.09	1.09	3.24	.95	2.98	1.08	3.44	1.12	3.36	1.08

Table L-1f. Means and standard deviations for continuous extra-test characteristics (women): High scores on supplementary scales *(continued)*

Extra-test Characteristics	Supplementary Scales									
	A		R		Es		MAC-R		AAS	
	Mean	SD	Mean	SD	Mean	SD	Mean	SD	Mean	SD
Delusional Thinking	1.30	.76	1.33	.84	1.33	.85	1.49	.97	1.42	.88
Self-Reliant	2.52	.88	2.48	.86	2.90	.96	2.65	.93	2.72	.97
Aggressive	1.86	.93	1.98	.98	2.23	1.04	2.33	1.09	2.18	1.00
Competitive	2.03	1.01	2.04	.92	2.46	1.02	2.26	1.04	2.30	1.09
Suspicious	2.37	1.08	2.34	1.04	2.30	1.09	2.65	1.08	2.55	1.13
Compulsive	2.21	1.14	2.26	1.20	2.51	1.19	2.36	1.08	2.44	1.12
Dependable	2.92	.90	2.94	.89	3.18	.87	2.91	.80	3.02	.91
Multiple Somatic Complaints	1.96	1.18	2.21	1.35	1.65	.97	1.92	1.08	1.84	1.13
Complains of Lack of Time	1.98	1.11	2.07	1.09	2.05	1.13	2.16	1.17	2.20	1.19
Poor Work Performance	1.82	.98	1.73	.91	1.66	.85	1.90	.94	1.88	.98
Insecure	3.57	.92	3.65	.83	3.23	1.02	3.55	.98	3.69	.92
Discusses Problems Openly	3.17	.85	3.12	.85	3.24	.88	3.35	.78	3.28	.84
Sexually Adjusted	2.45	.88	2.33	.80	2.72	.84	2.52	.80	2.63	.91
Exaggerated Need for Affection	2.46	1.19	2.40	1.17	2.28	1.14	2.40	1.11	2.62	1.17
Resentful	2.94	1.11	3.02	1.04	2.93	1.08	3.18	1.02	3.10	1.12
Uses Denial	2.68	1.13	2.83	1.07	2.78	1.11	3.03	1.11	2.83	1.11
Hypochondriacal	1.69	1.02	1.89	1.19	1.51	.89	1.68	.93	1.69	1.04
Communicates Effectively	3.03	.85	2.88	.85	3.24	.94	2.91	.74	3.19	.86
Has Many Nightmares	2.01	1.09	2.25	1.13	1.73	.93	2.29	1.20	2.23	1.22
Stormy Interpersonal Relationships	3.06	1.23	3.04	1.16	3.09	1.13	3.48	1.11	3.40	1.08
Feigns Remorse When in Trouble	1.80	.98	1.94	1.10	1.84	.97	2.02	1.04	1.95	1.01
Stereotypic Masculine Interests	1.43	.78	1.44	.85	1.61	.84	1.62	.92	1.59	.89
Guarded	2.48	1.14	2.53	1.10	2.50	1.09	2.59	1.05	2.67	1.17
Feels Inferior	3.33	1.11	3.43	.93	2.91	1.15	3.29	1.21	3.28	1.13
Low Frustration Tolerance	2.82	1.11	2.90	1.00	2.66	1.04	3.30	.95	3.01	1.07
Psychotic Symptoms	1.20	.61	1.22	.71	1.23	.73	1.47	.89	1.28	.70
Fired From Past Jobs	1.54	.93	1.49	1.03	1.46	.92	1.72	1.02	1.67	1.08
Needs Attention	3.05	1.02	3.02	.94	2.82	1.06	3.09	.89	3.22	.98
Acts Out	2.25	1.08	2.41	1.15	2.24	1.10	2.66	1.16	2.52	1.13
Histrionic	2.20	1.18	2.22	1.17	2.13	1.16	2.42	1.27	2.48	1.30
Self-Indulgent	2.17	1.06	2.32	1.10	2.33	1.10	2.45	1.05	2.52	1.07
Depressed	3.36	.99	3.37	.98	2.83	1.10	3.11	1.08	3.30	1.04
Grandiose	1.57	.92	1.59	.84	1.74	.95	1.82	.96	1.75	.96
Cynical	2.18	1.09	2.10	.96	2.09	1.00	2.36	1.18	2.43	1.14
Sociopathic	1.41	.71	1.39	.76	1.44	.80	1.71	.94	1.58	.82

Agitated	2.35	1.09	2.49	1.05	2.10	1.02	2.56	1.11	2.45	1.06
Marital Problems	2.61	1.56	2.70	1.58	2.59	1.61	2.56	1.60	2.50	1.60
Absence of Deep Emotions	2.03	1.09	2.09	1.05	1.97	1.10	2.25	1.17	2.24	1.22
Uncomfortable Dealing with Emotions	2.88	1.07	2.91	1.10	2.81	1.16	3.03	1.04	3.11	1.11
Sad	3.11	1.04	3.18	.98	2.69	1.07	2.97	1.05	3.15	1.06
Self-Degrading	2.73	1.16	2.67	.98	2.26	1.09	2.64	1.19	2.75	1.14
Unable to Express Negative Feelings	2.27	1.14	2.42	1.08	2.26	1.08	2.29	1.14	2.39	1.24
Concrete in Thinking	2.31	1.06	2.57	1.05	2.11	1.06	2.38	1.05	2.29	1.02
Unable to See Own Limitations	2.14	1.02	2.15	.99	2.12	1.06	2.41	1.01	2.38	1.10
Power-Oriented	1.81	.95	1.73	.99	2.03	.99	1.96	.92	2.08	1.05
Grouchy	2.09	.98	2.14	1.00	1.93	.91	2.31	.90	2.24	1.05
Overbearing in Relationships	1.96	1.05	2.08	1.04	2.08	1.09	2.31	1.13	2.23	1.13
Uncertain About Career	2.97	1.39	2.81	1.33	2.70	1.33	3.24	1.24	3.05	1.38
Likable	3.26	.86	3.25	.81	3.49	.77	3.27	.82	3.40	.85
Procrastinator	2.42	1.00	2.49	1.01	2.39	1.14	2.60	.98	2.69	1.10
Negative Feelings Toward Opposite Sex	2.56	1.20	2.59	1.25	2.32	1.12	2.76	1.26	2.64	1.21
Defensive	2.68	1.08	2.78	1.01	2.57	1.04	2.93	1.08	2.88	1.19
Empathetic	2.58	.75	2.60	.76	2.66	.76	2.74	.75	2.71	.67
Perfectionistic	2.48	1.22	2.35	1.18	2.65	1.19	2.56	1.19	2.66	1.21
Judgmental	2.47	1.04	2.52	.99	2.58	.97	2.70	.91	2.62	1.00
Copes Well with Stress	1.95	.73	1.92	.79	2.37	.73	1.96	.77	2.08	.75
Moody	2.73	1.01	2.80	.95	2.61	.98	2.92	.98	2.98	1.03
Selfish	1.95	.97	2.01	.91	2.00	.95	2.15	1.00	2.21	.99
Gives Up Easily	2.33	1.05	2.25	1.01	1.95	.93	2.52	1.06	2.47	1.07
Physical Symptoms in Response to Stress	2.28	1.20	2.47	1.27	1.99	1.09	2.13	1.13	2.13	1.23
Blames Family For Difficulties	2.79	1.34	2.68	1.30	2.73	1.21	3.01	1.23	2.90	1.31
Bored	2.24	1.11	2.19	1.06	2.16	1.09	2.57	1.11	2.41	1.15
Idealistic	2.37	1.05	2.43	.92	2.54	1.04	2.44	.94	2.52	1.06
Difficulty Establishing Therapeutic Rapport	1.84	.93	1.88	.91	1.81	.91	1.97	.90	1.96	.93
Daydreams	1.89	.97	2.05	1.09	1.86	.91	2.27	.90	2.13	.97
Concerned About Status	2.14	1.11	2.08	1.07	2.38	1.15	2.25	1.19	2.36	1.17
Creates Good First Impression	2.74	.93	2.76	.98	3.15	.94	2.73	.84	2.93	.90
Complains of Sleep Disturbance	2.72	1.22	2.92	1.27	2.23	1.20	2.80	1.28	2.74	1.31
Has Temper Tantrums	1.98	1.03	2.13	1.11	2.05	1.08	2.38	1.20	2.15	1.09
Overreactive	2.70	1.10	2.75	1.10	2.56	1.08	3.00	1.03	2.89	1.08
High Aspirations	2.27	1.12	2.20	.98	2.81	1.11	2.36	.99	2.60	1.23
Feels Hopeless	2.85	1.19	2.83	1.21	2.27	1.12	2.67	1.14	2.71	1.19
Keeps Others at a Distance	2.85	1.14	3.00	1.07	2.77	1.15	3.09	1.14	3.07	1.21
Argumentative	2.12	1.05	2.16	.95	2.12	1.04	2.29	1.05	2.29	1.10
Paranoid Features	1.69	.97	1.70	.96	1.63	.93	2.03	1.07	1.79	.98
Restless	2.47	1.09	2.58	1.05	2.30	1.10	2.66	1.12	2.65	1.17
Pessimistic	2.75	1.08	2.76	1.01	2.35	1.08	2.71	1.01	2.76	1.09

Table L-1f. Means and standard deviations for continuous extra-test characteristics (women): High scores on supplementary scales *(continued)*

Extra-test Characteristics	Supplementary Scales									
	A		R		*Es*		MAC-R		AAS	
	Mean	SD	Mean	SD	Mean	SD	Mean	SD	Mean	SD
Feels Like a Failure	3.07	1.14	3.12	.99	2.64	1.06	2.99	1.16	3.02	1.12
Hallucinations	1.11	.47	1.13	.62	1.09	.48	1.24	.77	1.16	.58
Restricted Affect	2.18	1.13	2.24	1.14	2.06	1.11	2.26	1.21	2.31	1.22
Impatient	2.51	1.02	2.62	.98	2.63	1.09	2.79	1.09	2.69	1.02
Assertive	2.07	.87	2.10	.88	2.37	.91	2.25	.88	2.26	.92
Modest	2.58	.83	2.68	.70	2.55	.80	2.48	.83	2.55	.79
Self-Doubting	3.24	1.03	3.21	.93	2.89	1.05	3.18	1.07	3.23	1.07
Deceptive	1.81	.91	1.90	.82	1.89	.89	2.15	.98	2.02	.99
Feels That Life is a Strain	3.14	1.07	3.32	1.04	2.73	1.06	3.20	.97	3.16	1.01
Physically Abusive	1.34	.66	1.29	.59	1.27	.65	1.48	.83	1.37	.65
Feels Rejected	3.25	1.11	3.15	1.01	2.93	1.13	3.28	1.19	3.34	1.13
Does Not Get Along with Coworkers	1.73	.94	1.59	.95	1.62	.87	1.76	.99	1.69	.85
Uses Projection	2.25	1.06	2.39	1.04	2.43	1.08	2.71	1.04	2.51	1.09
Complains of Fatigue	2.65	1.30	2.82	1.22	2.24	1.17	2.60	1.22	2.60	1.35
Uses Rationalization	2.58	1.08	2.67	.95	2.71	1.05	2.96	1.15	2.85	1.15
Critical of Others	2.40	1.09	2.45	1.07	2.48	1.02	2.76	1.01	2.54	1.11
Egocentric	2.20	1.11	2.27	1.07	2.23	1.07	2.48	1.06	2.39	1.10
Overevaluates Own Worth	1.66	.96	1.62	.83	1.72	.96	1.93	1.00	1.87	1.05
Optimistic	1.99	.81	2.07	.74	2.33	.82	2.16	.76	2.16	.85
Psychologically Immature	2.84	1.20	2.93	1.22	2.68	1.21	3.12	1.14	2.85	1.15
Poor Judgment	2.80	1.18	2.83	1.13	2.76	1.09	3.27	1.11	3.02	1.18
Low Sex Drive	2.18	1.17	2.51	1.20	1.89	1.08	2.03	1.29	2.16	1.26
Feels Mistreated	3.15	1.12	3.16	1.10	2.94	1.20	3.38	1.06	3.24	1.13
Overly Sensitive to Criticism	3.26	1.08	3.21	1.14	2.87	1.22	3.24	1.06	3.24	1.14
Sentimental	2.60	1.00	2.72	.90	2.55	1.07	2.70	1.01	2.56	1.04
Sexual Preoccupation	1.57	1.01	1.43	.80	1.62	.93	1.88	1.21	1.91	1.06
Accelerated Speech	1.66	.94	1.68	1.03	1.69	.96	1.90	1.01	1.73	.95
Concerns About Homosexuality	1.18	.64	1.14	.65	1.13	.52	1.17	.70	1.19	.60
Many Specific Fears	2.17	1.07	2.36	1.08	1.82	1.00	2.44	1.18	2.27	1.06
Passive in Relationships	3.05	1.12	2.96	1.03	2.55	1.22	2.91	1.26	2.88	1.16
Negative Attitudes Toward Therapy	1.66	.85	1.76	.93	1.68	.88	1.68	.79	1.66	.86
Guilt-Prone	3.07	1.14	3.22	1.07	2.88	1.21	2.99	1.13	3.15	1.13
Nervous	3.02	.97	3.05	1.03	2.65	.95	3.07	.95	2.99	.98
Obsessive	2.39	1.15	2.48	1.08	2.39	1.11	2.69	1.20	2.53	1.12
Shy	2.52	1.14	2.68	.99	2.21	1.04	2.40	1.20	2.48	1.13

Uses Intellectualization	2.23	1.09	2.16	.95	2.57	1.11	2.36	1.10	2.61	1.26
Has Many Interests	2.19	.94	2.16	.79	2.67	.93	2.28	.93	2.40	.94
Difficulty Making Decisions	2.96	1.08	3.06	1.02	2.79	1.17	3.04	1.15	3.08	1.18
Indirect Expression of Hostility	2.78	1.11	2.91	1.12	2.82	1.16	3.04	1.09	2.85	1.20
Poor Reality Testing	1.55	.93	1.53	.94	1.53	.99	1.89	1.19	1.74	1.12
Angry	2.97	1.12	2.96	1.15	2.95	1.14	3.24	1.17	3.16	1.14
Eccentric	1.71	1.04	1.71	.99	1.66	.94	1.93	1.19	1.81	1.09
Emotional Lability	2.48	1.10	2.52	.97	2.27	1.08	2.67	1.08	2.64	1.09
Dislikes Change	2.67	1.03	2.73	.88	2.46	1.01	2.67	.99	2.73	1.01
Believes Cannot Be Helped	1.85	.91	1.99	.94	1.72	.93	1.93	.96	1.91	.96
Reliable Informant	3.26	.92	3.30	.88	3.34	.95	3.25	.81	3.33	.89
Ignores Problems	2.36	1.07	2.38	1.02	2.53	1.03	2.59	1.00	2.56	.98
Ruminates	2.85	1.00	3.02	.92	2.62	1.05	2.82	1.06	2.87	1.04
Excitable	2.46	1.03	2.59	.99	2.54	1.07	2.97	1.03	2.71	1.04
Conforming	2.66	.98	2.69	1.01	2.51	.91	2.51	.91	2.53	1.00
Ineffective at Dealing with Problems	3.04	1.01	3.21	.98	2.93	1.06	3.23	.99	3.14	1.09
Introverted	2.48	1.08	2.71	.96	2.16	1.08	2.25	1.08	2.36	1.06
Superficial Relationships	2.71	1.11	2.78	1.05	2.66	1.11	3.10	1.05	3.04	1.11
Impulsive	2.65	1.22	2.69	1.10	2.78	1.21	3.25	1.25	3.05	1.18
Stereotypic Feminine Behavior	2.77	1.19	2.91	1.15	2.81	1.12	2.78	1.00	2.74	1.16
Stubborn	2.64	1.04	2.70	.97	2.69	1.03	2.92	1.01	2.83	1.07
Hostile Toward Therapist	1.34	.66	1.25	.63	1.34	.70	1.42	.69	1.37	.70
Difficult to Motivate	2.18	1.09	2.19	1.06	1.97	1.03	2.24	1.03	2.21	1.13
Suicidal Ideations	1.80	.98	1.84	1.04	1.40	.76	1.86	.98	1.84	.95
Familial Discord	3.36	1.22	3.28	1.25	3.32	1.26	3.86	1.11	3.63	1.16
Dogmatic	1.97	.97	2.17	.91	2.05	.97	2.26	.94	2.14	.98

Extra-test Characteristics	Supplementary Scales (continued)											
	APS		O-H		Do		Re		MDS		PK	
	Mean	SD	Mean	SD	Mean	SD	Mean	SD	Mean	SD	Mean	SD
Intake Information	(n = 87)		(n = 64)		(n = 396)		(n = 274)		(n = 426)		(n = 379)	
Axis IV diagnosis	2.94	.92	3.10	1.00	2.88	.95	2.97	.95	2.95	.95	3.05	.99
Axis V - Current Level of Functioning	61.96	9.76	64.76	10.02	64.82	9.12	63.15	9.70	61.39	9.86	60.43	9.51
Number of Arrests	.43	.75	.58	1.00	.50	1.79	.27	.71	.41	1.19	.44	1.16
Mental Status	(n = 87)		(n = 64)		(n = 396)		(n = 274)		(n = 426)		(n = 379)	
Anxiety During Interview	2.52	.78	2.21	.64	2.29	.62	2.35	.66	2.40	.68	2.44	.70
Depression During Interview	2.49	.67	2.15	.62	2.27	.70	2.37	.73	2.50	.73	2.58	.72
Activity Level During Interview	2.94	.42	3.00	.26	2.99	.32	2.99	.34	2.97	.36	2.96	.39
Speech During Interview	2.98	.34	3.05	.28	3.01	.29	2.99	.36	2.97	.41	2.96	.43
SCL-90-R Scales	(n = 87)		(n = 63)		(n = 394)		(n = 273)		(n = 424)		(n = 377)	
Somatization	1.38	.90	.78	.85	.78	.70	1.11	.88	1.40	.84	1.54	.83
Obsessive-Compulsive	1.70	.81	.85	.85	.96	.78	1.36	.94	1.73	.89	1.86	.84
Interpersonal Sensitivity	1.63	.81	.80	.81	1.02	.78	1.32	.89	1.77	.86	1.86	.83
Depression	2.10	.89	1.11	.98	1.36	.94	1.74	1.01	2.22	.84	2.36	.77
Anxiety	1.60	.91	.83	1.07	.82	.79	1.17	.95	1.59	.93	1.74	.88
Hostility	1.52	.99	.67	.86	.82	.81	1.00	.90	1.52	.98	1.65	.97
Phobic Anxiety	.86	.86	.50	.91	.32	.51	.64	.86	.95	.91	1.09	.94
Paranoid Ideation	1.59	.87	.83	.90	.95	.79	1.12	.90	1.66	.92	1.74	.91
Psychoticism	1.01	.71	.44	.60	.54	.52	.74	.66	1.12	.72	1.21	.71
Initial SCL-90 Analogue	(n = 63)		(n = 49)		(n = 262)		(n = 177)		(n = 288)		(n = 249)	
Somatization	2.79	2.69	2.35	2.75	1.80	2.33	2.30	2.58	2.27	2.60	2.37	2.66
Obsessive-Compulsive	3.31	2.24	2.87	2.57	2.71	2.65	2.67	2.56	2.56	2.54	2.66	2.58
Interpersonal Sensitivity	5.38	2.50	4.04	2.94	4.28	2.75	4.60	2.70	4.83	2.64	5.08	2.64
Depression	4.89	2.49	3.96	2.49	4.06	2.62	4.45	2.45	4.66	2.53	4.77	2.57
Anxiety	5.02	2.67	4.24	2.70	3.98	2.61	4.19	2.57	4.36	2.71	4.42	2.71
Hostility	3.13	2.32	2.40	2.46	2.85	2.66	2.69	2.53	3.12	2.65	2.93	2.64
Phobic Anxiety	1.43	2.22	.60	1.45	.91	1.83	.91	1.79	1.18	2.12	1.14	2.00
Paranoid Ideation	1.10	1.37	.90	1.90	1.01	1.80	.88	1.59	1.24	2.07	1.17	2.01
Psychoticism	.61	1.41	.69	1.63	.68	1.69	.55	1.36	.70	1.68	.66	1.62
Patient Description Form Scales	(n = 63)		(n = 49)		(n = 262)		(n = 178)		(n = 287)		(n = 248)	
Angry Resentment	2.87	.83	2.49	.76	2.58	.90	2.51	.90	2.75	.86	2.73	.86

Critical/Argumentative	2.48	.88	2.09	.73	2.25	.83	2.18	.81	2.37	.86	2.37	.85
Narcissistic	2.30	.89	1.95	.73	1.92	.77	1.85	.76	2.02	.86	1.99	.85
Defensive	2.56	.77	2.42	.83	2.34	.83	2.36	.83	2.49	.82	2.50	.81
Histrionic	2.78	.81	2.33	.82	2.31	.85	2.33	.80	2.51	.87	2.53	.86
Aggressive	2.03	.72	1.91	.71	1.82	.71	1.71	.66	1.85	.74	1.85	.76
Insecure	3.35	.90	2.77	.86	2.88	.96	2.96	.88	3.10	.88	3.16	.85
Anxious	3.15	.78	2.83	.82	2.69	.81	2.81	.77	2.93	.78	2.96	.77
Pessimistic	2.40	.98	1.95	.80	2.00	.89	2.11	.87	2.26	.87	2.29	.86
Depressed	2.82	.91	2.27	.82	2.34	.84	2.48	.83	2.63	.84	2.72	.86
Achievement-Oriented	2.77	.84	2.53	.67	2.78	.76	2.55	.76	2.44	.75	2.37	.73
Passive-Submissive	2.68	.88	2.59	.94	2.38	.88	2.57	.91	2.61	.91	2.64	.91
Introverted	2.26	.95	2.21	.74	2.12	.88	2.32	.95	2.41	.96	2.44	.94
Emotionally Controlled	2.57	.97	2.24	.86	2.24	.89	2.30	.89	2.32	.87	2.34	.85
Antisocial	2.33	.78	2.05	.74	1.95	.72	1.89	.69	2.09	.81	2.09	.81
Negative Treatment Attitudes	1.97	.67	1.89	.68	1.80	.69	1.85	.72	1.91	.72	1.91	.68
Somatic Symptoms	2.20	1.03	2.07	1.09	1.85	.87	2.07	1.01	2.12	1.02	2.17	1.04
Psychotic Symptoms	1.35	.54	1.31	.70	1.23	.60	1.21	.51	1.27	.52	1.27	.50
Family Problems	3.26	1.08	2.83	1.02	2.88	1.07	2.82	1.08	3.10	1.05	3.09	1.09
Obsessive-Compulsive	2.87	.85	2.42	.77	2.56	.90	2.52	.81	2.54	.85	2.56	.82
Stereotypic Masculine Interests	1.48	.70	1.38	.62	1.49	.80	1.40	.71	1.39	.68	1.41	.69
Procrastinates	2.43	.98	2.18	.98	2.16	.95	2.09	.87	2.16	.88	2.21	.87
Suspicious	2.53	.90	2.29	.81	2.28	.88	2.24	.83	2.47	.90	2.47	.89
Agitated	2.40	.93	2.09	.86	1.99	.84	2.02	.79	2.15	.86	2.21	.85
Work Problems	1.79	.95	1.41	.50	1.43	.60	1.46	.66	1.58	.79	1.61	.77
Patient Description Form Items	(n = 63)		(n = 49)		(n = 262)		(n = 178)		(n = 287)		(n = 248)	
Anxious	3.51	.90	3.12	.95	3.00	.97	3.05	.95	3.19	1.00	3.21	.99
Problems with Authority Figures	2.89	1.29	2.64	1.21	2.51	1.15	2.47	1.18	2.70	1.23	2.71	1.21
Has Insight Into Own Problems	2.78	.94	2.73	.86	2.81	.90	2.69	.93	2.56	.91	2.55	.88
Fears Losing Control	3.51	1.11	3.10	1.22	3.06	1.17	3.02	1.14	3.09	1.11	3.12	1.11
Extroverted	2.98	1.00	2.73	.84	2.73	.99	2.55	1.02	2.55	1.09	2.52	1.10
Uses Repression	2.90	1.03	2.71	1.15	2.73	1.12	2.75	1.06	2.77	1.09	2.79	1.05
Submissive	2.84	.96	2.80	1.12	2.57	.99	2.69	1.04	2.74	1.05	2.78	1.05
Difficulty Concentrating	2.92	1.16	2.44	1.11	2.40	1.09	2.51	1.10	2.67	1.09	2.75	1.09
Rigid	2.49	1.00	2.49	1.17	2.37	1.12	2.41	1.04	2.42	1.02	2.42	.97
Overly Compliant	2.26	1.04	2.20	1.12	1.99	.92	2.15	1.04	2.21	1.05	2.23	1.05
Whiny	2.16	1.10	2.10	1.12	1.77	.87	1.88	.96	2.04	1.02	2.04	1.05
Feels Overwhelmed	3.62	1.11	3.31	.87	3.12	1.15	3.32	1.08	3.43	1.04	3.47	1.06
Manipulative	2.73	1.06	2.29	1.09	2.26	1.05	2.17	1.02	2.42	1.18	2.39	1.18
Difficulty Trusting Others	3.40	1.21	3.04	1.10	3.00	1.12	2.96	1.06	3.27	1.11	3.29	1.11
Insensitive to Others	2.05	.94	1.96	.91	1.79	.90	1.74	.85	1.80	.88	1.78	.87
Stereotypic Masculine Behavior	1.41	.69	1.39	.73	1.43	.80	1.36	.71	1.33	.68	1.34	.68

Extra-test Characteristics	Supplementary Scales *(continued)*											
	APS		O-H		Do		Re		MDS		PK	
	Mean	SD	Mean	SD	Mean	SD	Mean	SD	Mean	SD	Mean	SD
Harbors Grudges	2.53	1.05	2.48	.99	2.38	1.02	2.36	1.01	2.55	1.04	2.51	1.04
Evasive	2.43	1.16	2.10	1.10	2.14	1.04	2.15	1.07	2.29	1.08	2.28	1.05
Disoriented	1.49	.84	1.31	.80	1.25	.69	1.19	.56	1.28	.64	1.32	.71
Energetic	2.62	1.01	2.69	.80	2.73	.99	2.48	.95	2.38	.97	2.32	.97
Lonely	3.02	1.10	2.44	1.03	2.65	1.11	2.79	1.10	2.93	1.06	2.94	1.08
Family Lacks Love	3.21	1.34	2.54	1.21	2.66	1.24	2.66	1.21	2.93	1.23	2.98	1.24
Worrier	3.67	.92	3.18	1.15	3.07	1.12	3.27	1.06	3.40	1.01	3.42	1.00
Narcissistic	2.40	1.15	1.92	.98	1.99	1.08	1.96	1.03	2.12	1.12	2.11	1.12
Tearful	2.52	1.28	2.08	1.13	2.17	1.18	2.23	1.12	2.37	1.18	2.45	1.17
Provocative	2.06	1.01	1.71	1.00	1.77	1.00	1.65	.88	1.71	.97	1.73	.98
Moralistic	2.37	.96	2.61	.95	2.39	1.10	2.44	.99	2.29	.97	2.22	.94
Socially Awkward	2.25	1.05	2.19	.84	2.11	.99	2.30	1.05	2.47	1.05	2.51	1.01
Hostile	2.17	1.09	1.96	.91	2.13	1.14	2.02	1.06	2.19	1.09	2.11	1.04
Overcontrolled	2.76	1.27	2.39	1.11	2.56	1.19	2.49	1.13	2.45	1.16	2.44	1.15
Resistant to Interpretations	2.27	1.00	2.10	.98	2.09	.99	2.10	1.00	2.16	.99	2.17	.98
Antisocial Behavior	1.92	1.07	1.69	.92	1.61	.90	1.51	.77	1.71	.93	1.69	.93
Sarcastic	2.00	1.02	1.63	.83	1.80	.95	1.72	.89	1.90	1.02	1.88	.99
Rejects Traditional Gender Role	1.79	1.11	1.49	.71	1.70	.97	1.54	.84	1.63	.97	1.62	.96
Feels Gets Raw Deal From Life	2.97	1.14	2.60	1.10	2.56	1.15	2.64	1.17	2.95	1.15	3.02	1.15
Acute Psychological Turmoil	3.16	1.10	2.78	1.03	2.73	1.07	2.82	1.02	2.99	1.07	3.07	1.06
Does Not Complete Projects	2.33	1.17	2.09	1.14	2.09	1.13	2.04	1.05	2.18	1.11	2.24	1.11
Uncomfortable with Opposite Sex	2.08	1.11	1.96	1.02	2.00	1.12	2.09	1.08	2.26	1.18	2.30	1.19
Preoccupied with Health Problems	2.00	1.12	2.00	1.32	1.69	1.06	2.01	1.23	2.04	1.25	2.05	1.25
Work-Oriented	2.98	1.17	2.77	1.12	3.07	1.10	2.81	1.11	2.70	1.12	2.61	1.12
Resents Family Members	3.26	1.16	2.85	1.15	2.91	1.25	2.79	1.23	3.12	1.19	3.08	1.22
Demanding of Attention	2.87	.98	2.28	1.06	2.35	1.06	2.40	1.06	2.56	1.10	2.57	1.10
Passive	2.63	1.10	2.61	1.10	2.40	1.06	2.60	1.07	2.57	1.07	2.60	1.07
Self-Punishing	2.98	1.24	2.43	1.14	2.44	1.15	2.55	1.12	2.67	1.16	2.77	1.12
Needs to Achieve	2.94	1.02	2.65	1.00	2.94	1.10	2.74	1.10	2.62	1.07	2.57	1.05
Needs to Be with Others	3.40	.89	3.09	.90	3.01	1.02	2.95	1.01	3.10	1.01	3.10	1.02
Irritable	2.62	1.07	2.25	.91	2.43	1.02	2.41	1.00	2.62	1.06	2.66	1.04
Self-Defeating	3.48	1.11	2.98	1.18	2.89	1.14	2.89	1.07	3.07	1.09	3.13	1.06
Delusional Thinking	1.30	.66	1.31	.74	1.24	.74	1.24	.69	1.30	.76	1.28	.71
Self-Reliant	2.81	1.06	2.77	.83	2.98	.97	2.81	.93	2.65	.92	2.59	.87
Aggressive	2.16	.88	2.12	.95	2.10	1.00	1.93	.91	2.04	.97	2.00	.96
Competitive	2.52	1.10	2.15	.92	2.39	1.06	2.21	.99	2.16	1.02	2.09	1.01
Suspicious	2.46	1.09	2.24	.97	2.24	1.11	2.21	1.04	2.41	1.11	2.41	1.11
Compulsive	2.62	1.15	2.43	1.25	2.49	1.24	2.30	1.15	2.19	1.13	2.18	1.11

Dependable	2.98	.87	3.04	.91	3.27	.89	3.17	.90	2.99	.92	2.97	.87
Multiple Somatic Complaints	1.95	1.12	2.00	1.35	1.70	1.05	1.95	1.19	1.95	1.19	2.00	1.22
Complains of Lack of Time	2.34	1.19	2.12	1.20	2.05	1.16	2.00	1.10	2.01	1.10	2.08	1.14
Poor Work Performance	2.06	1.10	1.66	.73	1.56	.83	1.66	.90	1.75	.96	1.81	.97
Insecure	3.63	1.04	3.24	.97	3.24	1.05	3.30	.98	3.51	.94	3.57	.95
Discusses Problems Openly	3.41	.89	3.29	.91	3.29	.84	3.23	.83	3.19	.86	3.21	.85
Sexually Adjusted	2.76	.92	2.61	.70	2.74	.78	2.63	.84	2.45	.87	2.44	.89
Exaggerated Need for Affection	2.72	1.05	1.98	1.07	2.27	1.14	2.22	1.10	2.42	1.17	2.46	1.18
Resentful	3.14	1.06	2.90	1.01	2.87	1.10	2.81	1.13	3.03	1.06	3.00	1.07
Uses Denial	2.98	1.05	2.90	1.12	2.67	1.14	2.66	1.12	2.73	1.11	2.77	1.08
Hypochondriacal	1.77	.98	1.61	1.04	1.47	.82	1.62	.97	1.66	.99	1.67	1.00
Communicates Effectively	3.17	.93	3.22	.94	3.39	.91	3.19	.87	3.06	.87	3.02	.85
Has Many Nightmares	1.89	.98	2.22	1.15	1.80	1.01	1.77	.97	1.95	1.09	2.09	1.12
Stormy Interpersonal Relationships	3.47	1.05	3.02	1.09	3.06	1.21	2.89	1.21	3.15	1.19	3.14	1.19
Feigns Remorse When in Trouble	1.92	.96	1.67	.82	1.64	.82	1.60	.87	1.80	.99	1.83	.99
Stereotypic Masculine Interests	1.54	.82	1.35	.64	1.54	.87	1.44	.79	1.44	.78	1.47	.82
Guarded	2.62	1.13	2.43	1.02	2.40	1.09	2.39	1.12	2.49	1.13	2.47	1.13
Feels Inferior	3.35	1.12	2.92	1.13	2.90	1.13	3.07	1.12	3.23	1.11	3.28	1.07
Low Frustration Tolerance	3.05	1.02	2.63	1.00	2.57	1.02	2.60	1.04	2.85	1.06	2.88	1.07
Psychotic Symptoms	1.14	.50	1.20	.64	1.14	.60	1.15	.56	1.23	.68	1.22	.64
Fired From Past Jobs	1.58	1.03	1.45	.78	1.34	.75	1.41	.80	1.55	.99	1.56	.99
Needs Attention	3.30	.91	2.67	.94	2.77	1.08	2.86	1.02	3.00	1.00	3.06	1.00
Acts Out	2.52	.98	2.20	1.12	2.08	1.01	2.05	1.00	2.32	1.12	2.33	1.13
Histrionic	2.53	1.08	2.14	1.24	2.00	1.03	2.00	1.07	2.21	1.19	2.24	1.19
Self-Indulgent	2.50	1.10	2.31	1.14	2.19	1.03	2.07	1.02	2.21	1.07	2.20	1.07
Depressed	3.35	.99	2.84	1.05	3.01	1.12	3.13	1.05	3.26	1.01	3.34	.99
Grandiose	1.87	1.03	1.67	.69	1.62	.83	1.57	.83	1.63	.92	1.58	.91
Cynical	2.44	1.18	2.02	.90	2.12	1.05	2.03	.99	2.20	1.07	2.22	1.07
Sociopathic	1.58	.84	1.35	.66	1.33	.66	1.27	.54	1.41	.74	1.41	.73
Agitated	2.57	1.10	2.20	1.06	2.01	1.02	2.18	1.00	2.33	1.07	2.41	1.07
Marital Problems	2.68	1.69	2.84	1.65	2.64	1.59	2.67	1.58	2.69	1.58	2.66	1.55
Absence of Deep Emotions	2.21	1.27	1.84	1.01	1.84	1.03	1.91	1.06	1.97	1.07	2.00	1.07
Uncomfortable Dealing with Emotions	3.11	1.25	2.73	1.13	2.67	1.20	2.75	1.16	2.82	1.12	2.86	1.08
Sad	3.21	1.03	2.67	1.07	2.79	1.05	2.94	1.04	3.05	1.02	3.10	1.02
Self-Degrading	2.89	1.26	2.12	1.11	2.36	1.15	2.42	1.15	2.58	1.16	2.68	1.15
Unable to Express Negative Feelings	2.48	1.15	2.22	1.09	2.14	1.08	2.26	1.08	2.20	1.10	2.24	1.11
Concrete in Thinking	2.25	1.08	2.27	1.09	2.00	1.02	2.20	1.13	2.35	1.13	2.31	1.06
Unable to See Own Limitations	2.24	1.06	2.20	1.06	1.99	1.00	2.00	1.00	2.13	1.03	2.17	1.04
Power-Oriented	2.40	1.12	1.83	.96	2.04	1.08	1.84	.99	1.87	1.01	1.84	.96
Grouchy	2.06	1.07	1.68	.78	1.91	.93	1.89	.90	2.13	.98	2.14	.99
Overbearing in Relationships	2.43	1.18	1.98	1.02	2.05	1.08	1.91	1.01	2.08	1.06	2.08	1.07
Uncertain About Career	3.11	1.37	2.58	1.16	2.71	1.35	2.67	1.31	2.96	1.29	2.96	1.29

Extra-test Characteristics	Supplementary Scales (continued)											
	APS		O-H		Do		Re		MDS		PK	
	Mean	SD	Mean	SD	Mean	SD	Mean	SD	Mean	SD	Mean	SD
Likable	3.33	.92	3.56	.74	3.53	.75	3.42	.79	3.28	.85	3.28	.86
Procrastinator	2.53	1.01	2.30	1.20	2.38	1.17	2.33	1.07	2.36	1.02	2.39	.97
Negative Feelings Toward Opposite Sex	2.65	1.27	2.36	1.15	2.29	1.20	2.30	1.16	2.59	1.22	2.64	1.23
Defensive	2.73	1.07	2.46	.90	2.54	1.02	2.51	1.06	2.71	1.10	2.74	1.09
Empathetic	2.66	.75	2.75	.79	2.77	.80	2.71	.76	2.67	.75	2.62	.74
Perfectionistic	2.92	1.22	2.20	1.10	2.65	1.24	2.53	1.19	2.48	1.18	2.47	1.14
Judgmental	2.78	.96	2.35	.98	2.53	1.03	2.42	1.02	2.50	1.02	2.48	1.00
Copes Well with Stress	2.21	.81	2.37	.70	2.34	.74	2.22	.76	2.03	.73	1.95	.72
Moody	2.76	1.07	2.39	1.06	2.57	1.01	2.53	1.01	2.76	.99	2.79	.98
Selfish	2.17	1.01	1.79	.78	1.87	.87	1.81	.85	1.97	.95	1.94	.95
Gives Up Easily	2.53	1.16	1.86	.90	1.90	.90	2.00	.94	2.22	1.04	2.25	1.05
Physical Symptoms in Response to Stress	2.32	1.23	2.17	1.26	2.04	1.10	2.19	1.18	2.22	1.21	2.26	1.23
Blames Family For Difficulties	2.78	1.24	2.54	1.11	2.56	1.21	2.53	1.25	2.83	1.27	2.79	1.32
Bored	2.35	1.12	2.00	1.05	2.08	1.04	2.07	1.07	2.26	1.10	2.23	1.09
Idealistic	2.66	1.12	2.69	.95	2.60	1.10	2.55	1.06	2.36	1.03	2.34	1.00
Difficulty Establishing Therapeutic Rapport	1.90	.91	1.81	.79	1.65	.82	1.76	.91	1.86	.95	1.85	.93
Daydreams	2.16	1.10	1.94	.93	1.78	.95	1.82	.94	1.87	.94	1.96	.99
Concerned About Status	2.77	1.28	2.04	1.11	2.32	1.13	2.17	1.09	2.15	1.09	2.12	1.06
Creates Good First Impression	3.06	1.05	3.29	.77	3.14	.95	3.05	.97	2.83	.96	2.78	.94
Complains of Sleep Disturbance	2.82	1.28	2.49	1.38	2.32	1.26	2.50	1.30	2.65	1.24	2.80	1.24
Has Temper Tantrums	2.18	1.02	2.19	1.14	1.92	1.02	1.84	.96	2.11	1.09	2.12	1.11
Overreactive	3.02	1.05	2.71	1.13	2.52	1.08	2.51	1.07	2.75	1.13	2.78	1.12
High Aspirations	2.81	1.27	2.55	.95	2.82	1.09	2.53	1.13	2.39	1.11	2.34	1.10
Feels Hopeless	2.93	1.24	2.17	1.00	2.36	1.16	2.50	1.16	2.69	1.16	2.82	1.18
Keeps Others at a Distance	3.03	1.25	2.54	1.01	2.70	1.18	2.73	1.12	2.85	1.14	2.90	1.10
Argumentative	2.16	1.05	1.90	1.04	2.00	.96	1.97	.95	2.22	1.05	2.17	1.04
Paranoid Features	1.73	.90	1.62	.87	1.58	.86	1.53	.85	1.71	.99	1.70	.98
Restless	2.78	1.17	2.22	1.07	2.33	1.07	2.29	1.03	2.43	1.11	2.51	1.08
Pessimistic	2.89	1.14	2.10	.95	2.34	1.13	2.45	1.09	2.66	1.06	2.70	1.04
Feels Like a Failure	3.30	.99	2.53	1.02	2.59	1.15	2.82	1.11	2.96	1.11	3.02	1.10
Hallucinations	1.10	.30	1.08	.58	1.09	.45	1.07	.39	1.10	.48	1.11	.47
Restricted Affect	2.29	1.21	2.02	1.09	1.97	1.09	2.09	1.06	2.12	1.12	2.14	1.11
Impatient	2.78	1.13	2.45	1.06	2.61	1.08	2.45	1.02	2.59	1.03	2.58	1.01
Assertive	2.27	.94	2.45	.77	2.40	.86	2.16	.87	2.18	.88	2.14	.88
Modest	2.47	.90	2.59	.79	2.58	.84	2.65	.79	2.55	.84	2.54	.84
Self-Doubting	3.37	1.05	2.71	1.02	2.91	1.06	3.05	1.03	3.16	1.01	3.21	.99
Deceptive	2.00	.96	1.87	.82	1.73	.81	1.69	.82	1.85	.94	1.82	.93
Feels That Life is a Strain	3.32	.95	2.73	1.09	2.75	1.10	2.93	1.10	3.11	1.05	3.19	1.05

Physically Abusive	1.30	.64	1.30	.62	1.22	.61	1.25	.64	1.31	.65	1.35	.68
Feels Rejected	3.35	1.08	2.75	1.12	2.96	1.20	3.01	1.14	3.23	1.13	3.24	1.10
Does Not Get Along with Coworkers	1.76	.92	1.39	.62	1.54	.79	1.53	.80	1.66	.89	1.67	.86
Uses Projection	2.54	1.09	2.46	.98	2.34	1.09	2.26	1.03	2.39	1.08	2.33	1.05
Complains of Fatigue	2.70	1.41	2.37	1.30	2.25	1.22	2.48	1.27	2.60	1.26	2.70	1.28
Uses Rationalization	2.95	1.08	2.73	1.08	2.69	1.07	2.58	1.05	2.65	1.07	2.65	1.06
Critical of Others	2.63	1.07	2.31	.96	2.40	1.00	2.25	1.02	2.48	1.05	2.45	1.05
Egocentric	2.48	1.02	2.06	.92	2.06	.96	2.03	.97	2.23	1.07	2.20	1.07
Overevaluates Own Worth	1.92	1.05	1.63	.76	1.59	.86	1.54	.81	1.70	.95	1.65	.92
Optimistic	2.13	.83	2.57	.74	2.26	.79	2.15	.80	2.05	.79	1.99	.79
Psychologically Immature	2.75	1.02	2.69	1.21	2.49	1.15	2.54	1.19	2.83	1.20	2.83	1.18
Poor Judgment	3.03	1.11	2.76	1.09	2.57	1.14	2.54	1.11	2.79	1.17	2.81	1.18
Low Sex Drive	2.17	1.42	2.08	1.12	1.91	1.17	2.08	1.14	2.20	1.22	2.28	1.23
Feels Mistreated	3.40	1.11	3.02	1.19	2.98	1.24	2.95	1.22	3.23	1.13	3.22	1.11
Overly Sensitive to Criticism	3.54	1.01	2.67	1.18	2.89	1.23	2.95	1.18	3.19	1.11	3.25	1.08
Sentimental	2.73	1.04	2.66	.96	2.68	1.08	2.57	1.04	2.61	1.02	2.63	1.01
Sexual Preoccupation	1.96	1.13	1.32	.84	1.52	.89	1.35	.70	1.56	.97	1.54	.96
Accelerated Speech	1.87	1.03	1.82	.99	1.61	.92	1.59	.91	1.69	.97	1.72	1.01
Concerns About Homosexuality	1.11	.42	1.03	.16	1.12	.51	1.12	.52	1.18	.65	1.19	.67
Many Specific Fears	2.17	1.11	2.04	1.11	1.83	1.02	1.91	.99	2.12	1.08	2.15	1.07
Passive in Relationships	2.98	1.19	2.73	1.20	2.52	1.21	2.80	1.15	2.88	1.16	2.92	1.14
Negative Attitudes Toward Therapy	1.52	.72	1.83	.91	1.53	.77	1.60	.85	1.66	.87	1.64	.83
Guilt-Prone	3.39	1.11	3.00	1.04	2.98	1.26	3.03	1.17	3.03	1.16	3.09	1.15
Nervous	3.31	.97	2.71	.97	2.71	1.01	2.81	.96	2.91	.99	2.94	.96
Obsessive	2.87	1.08	2.36	1.07	2.47	1.17	2.35	1.11	2.36	1.14	2.38	1.13
Shy	2.35	1.15	2.15	.82	2.10	1.00	2.31	1.06	2.38	1.13	2.42	1.13
Uses Intellectualization	2.77	1.27	2.38	.98	2.51	1.13	2.32	1.07	2.26	1.08	2.25	1.02
Has Many Interests	2.47	1.06	2.49	.80	2.67	.97	2.44	.93	2.28	.93	2.21	.94
Difficulty Making Decisions	3.25	1.12	2.56	1.10	2.74	1.19	2.84	1.11	2.88	1.10	2.95	1.06
Indirect Expression of Hostility	2.98	1.07	2.59	1.09	2.74	1.17	2.69	1.16	2.84	1.13	2.82	1.09
Poor Reality Testing	1.73	1.06	1.63	1.08	1.43	.90	1.41	.81	1.53	.91	1.52	.91
Angry	3.24	1.11	2.79	.97	2.91	1.18	2.89	1.16	3.07	1.14	3.07	1.17
Eccentric	1.95	1.11	1.57	.90	1.63	.96	1.58	.90	1.68	1.00	1.67	.99
Emotional Lability	2.59	1.13	2.29	1.09	2.30	1.10	2.32	1.04	2.51	1.09	2.55	1.09
Dislikes Change	2.63	1.11	2.67	.92	2.48	1.02	2.55	.97	2.64	.97	2.68	.98
Believes Cannot Be Helped	1.90	1.07	1.85	1.00	1.65	.95	1.76	.91	1.85	.91	1.87	.88
Reliable Informant	3.44	.95	3.33	.91	3.49	.92	3.35	.97	3.26	.92	3.25	.87
Ignores Problems	2.63	.93	2.52	1.09	2.34	1.05	2.37	1.06	2.40	1.08	2.40	1.04
Ruminates	3.07	.87	2.67	1.00	2.65	1.07	2.78	1.03	2.81	1.04	2.88	.99
Excitable	2.84	1.09	2.58	1.03	2.51	1.08	2.38	.97	2.60	1.04	2.62	1.05
Conforming	2.61	.94	2.58	.85	2.52	.87	2.69	.89	2.58	.96	2.57	.95
Ineffective at Dealing with Problems	3.08	1.00	2.94	.95	2.76	1.02	2.93	1.04	3.07	.99	3.08	.98

Extra-test Characteristics	Supplementary Scales *(continued)*											
	APS		O-H		Do		Re		MDS		PK	
	Mean	SD	Mean	SD	Mean	SD	Mean	SD	Mean	SD	Mean	SD
Introverted	2.15	1.04	2.26	.97	2.13	.99	2.33	1.07	2.38	1.08	2.37	1.07
Superficial Relationships	2.86	1.06	2.58	1.05	2.47	1.07	2.43	1.07	2.73	1.09	2.73	1.08
Impulsive	3.13	1.16	2.73	1.09	2.59	1.21	2.47	1.16	2.71	1.20	2.70	1.22
Stereotypic Feminine Behavior	2.90	1.16	3.19	.96	2.76	1.14	2.86	1.16	2.78	1.17	2.72	1.18
Stubborn	2.85	.99	2.53	1.00	2.63	1.05	2.60	1.04	2.74	1.01	2.70	.99
Hostile Toward Therapist	1.35	.63	1.27	.49	1.27	.61	1.29	.64	1.33	.66	1.32	.62
Difficult to Motivate	2.08	1.03	2.04	1.13	1.88	.96	1.95	.97	2.14	1.05	2.16	1.05
Suicidal Ideations	1.81	.97	1.33	.63	1.37	.71	1.52	.86	1.74	.96	1.82	1.03
Familial Discord	3.65	1.22	3.35	1.31	3.28	1.28	3.22	1.29	3.49	1.21	3.47	1.21
Dogmatic	2.25	1.04	2.04	.83	2.05	.98	2.03	.95	2.04	.97	2.00	.95

Table L-2a. Means and standard deviations for continuous extra-test characteristics (men): High scores on clinical scales

Extra-test Characteristics	Total Sample Mean	Total Sample SD	Valid MMPI-2 Mean	Valid MMPI-2 SD	WNL Mean	WNL SD	Clinical Scales 1 (Hs) Mean	1 (Hs) SD	Clinical Scales 2 (D) Mean	2 (D) SD
Intake Information	(n = 1,035)		(n = 410)		(n = 48)		(n = 169)		(n = 227)	
Axis IV diagnosis	2.89	.92	2.88	.91	2.85	.94	3.03	.95	2.94	.91
Axis V - Current Level of Functioning	60.59	11.79	62.96	10.09	68.34	9.52	60.43	10.07	60.17	10.03
Number of Arrests	1.91	5.09	1.40	3.29	1.51	2.14	1.36	2.47	1.10	2.16
Mental Status	(n = 1,035)		(n = 410)		(n = 48)		(n = 169)		(n = 227)	
Anxiety During Interview	2.38	.72	2.41	.70	2.24	.68	2.43	.67	2.48	.72
Depression During Interview	2.30	.75	2.26	.71	1.86	.56	2.46	.73	2.44	.71
Activity Level During Interview	2.99	.47	3.01	.43	3.02	.41	2.97	.46	3.00	.46
Speech During Interview	2.94	.47	2.96	.40	2.91	.53	2.95	.37	2.94	.37
SCL-90-R Scales	(n = 520)		(n = 403)		(n = 48)		(n = 166)		(n = 222)	
Somatization	1.05	.89	.91	.78	.26	.28	1.52	.78	1.26	.80
Obsessive-Compulsive	1.42	.99	1.23	.87	.53	.42	1.72	.88	1.71	.82
Interpersonal Sensitivity	1.34	1.00	1.17	.90	.48	.42	1.61	.94	1.60	.89
Depression	1.60	1.01	1.46	.96	.53	.40	2.02	.88	2.02	.81
Anxiety	1.25	.99	1.08	.90	.28	.29	1.63	.92	1.54	.87
Hostility	1.26	1.10	1.10	1.03	.40	.48	1.41	1.03	1.38	1.02
Phobic Anxiety	.73	.85	.54	.66	.08	.18	.86	.79	.78	.74
Paranoid Ideation	1.38	1.03	1.19	.92	.53	.53	1.54	.94	1.51	.94
Psychoticism	.99	.88	.80	.72	.21	.25	1.21	.79	1.15	.74
Initial SCL-90 Analogue	(n = 468)		(n = 272)		(n = 38)		(n = 104)		(n = 145)	
Somatization	1.99	2.60	1.96	2.65	.68	1.25	3.60	3.07	2.79	3.01
Obsessive-Compulsive	3.03	2.67	3.15	2.72	2.24	2.38	3.40	2.64	3.51	2.88
Interpersonal Sensitivity	4.48	2.53	4.39	2.57	3.21	2.53	4.50	2.37	4.92	2.49
Depression	4.00	2.59	3.85	2.67	2.08	1.84	4.86	2.68	4.95	2.65
Anxiety	4.20	2.62	4.05	2.70	2.16	1.95	4.83	2.65	4.99	2.69
Hostility	3.24	2.80	3.09	2.82	2.29	2.56	3.27	2.75	3.33	2.83
Phobic Anxiety	1.25	2.06	1.25	2.11	.58	1.00	1.57	2.48	1.52	2.29
Paranoid Ideation	1.48	2.10	1.29	1.97	.66	1.21	1.40	1.96	1.37	2.05
Psychoticism	.72	1.41	.63	1.38	.42	1.00	.63	1.47	.74	1.53
Patient Description Form Scales	(n = 469)		(n = 274)		(n = 38)		(n = 107)		(n = 147)	
Angry Resentment	2.73	.99	2.70	.97	2.16	.85	2.89	.92	2.83	.96

Table L-2a. Means and standard deviations for continuous extra-test characteristics (men): High scores on clinical scales *(continued)*

Extra-test Characteristics	Total Sample		Valid MMPI-2		WNL		Clinical Scales 1 (Hs)		Clinical Scales 2 (D)	
	Mean	SD	Mean	SD	Mean	SD	Mean	SD	Mean	SD
Critical/Argumentative	2.45	.93	2.45	.92	1.96	.71	2.59	.87	2.54	.95
Narcissistic	2.36	.91	2.38	.89	2.33	.63	2.29	.93	2.31	.93
Defensive	2.64	.89	2.59	.86	2.39	.71	2.62	.85	2.61	.92
Histrionic	2.32	.78	2.29	.79	1.86	.73	2.41	.75	2.38	.79
Aggressive	2.19	.95	2.16	.90	1.94	.79	2.14	.84	2.05	.83
Insecure	2.80	.85	2.77	.82	2.22	.81	2.93	.77	3.04	.78
Anxious	2.78	.81	2.71	.82	1.98	.68	3.04	.78	3.03	.77
Pessimistic	2.27	.93	2.23	.93	1.56	.65	2.59	.90	2.54	.94
Depressed	2.25	.81	2.20	.81	1.42	.43	2.60	.76	2.59	.75
Achievement-Oriented	2.56	.72	2.70	.70	3.00	.59	2.50	.74	2.54	.74
Passive-Submissive	2.13	.80	2.16	.81	2.03	.79	2.30	.80	2.28	.84
Introverted	2.58	1.01	2.50	.98	2.22	.91	2.56	.96	2.70	1.03
Emotionally Controlled	2.35	.96	2.39	.98	2.19	.87	2.42	1.01	2.48	1.05
Antisocial	2.39	.96	2.31	.92	2.25	.65	2.20	.93	2.23	.96
Negative Treatment Attitudes	2.05	.82	2.03	.81	1.95	.77	2.06	.82	2.06	.85
Somatic Symptoms	1.91	1.02	1.91	1.03	1.29	.45	2.57	1.13	2.25	1.12
Psychotic Symptoms	1.35	.54	1.27	.45	1.14	.30	1.31	.46	1.31	.49
Family Problems	2.65	1.17	2.61	1.17	2.04	1.08	2.73	1.24	2.73	1.14
Obsessive-Compulsive	2.62	.82	2.68	.83	2.19	.77	2.85	.81	2.86	.80
Stereotypic Masculine Interests	2.90	1.10	2.93	1.12	3.11	1.06	2.91	1.10	2.72	1.13
Procrastinates	2.17	.90	2.20	.92	1.91	.83	2.40	1.00	2.32	.95
Suspicious	2.56	1.03	2.51	1.01	2.01	.79	2.63	.97	2.59	1.04
Agitated	2.15	.81	2.10	.81	1.60	.61	2.29	.81	2.25	.83
Work Problems	1.94	1.00	1.92	.91	1.32	.44	1.97	.95	2.05	1.01
Patient Description Form Items	(n = 469)		(n = 274)		(n = 38)		(n = 107)		(n = 147)	
Anxious	3.22	.95	3.18	.99	2.32	.77	3.53	.88	3.58	.87
Problems with Authority Figures	3.06	1.24	2.99	1.21	2.62	.92	2.99	1.20	2.96	1.25
Has Insight Into Own Problems	2.44	.89	2.54	.87	2.58	.83	2.57	.86	2.60	.84
Fears Losing Control	3.09	1.11	3.12	1.13	2.62	1.13	3.39	1.09	3.31	1.03
Extroverted	2.35	1.00	2.49	.98	2.74	.95	2.42	.91	2.27	.92
Uses Repression	2.61	1.05	2.62	1.01	2.77	.88	2.72	1.06	2.62	1.03
Submissive	2.13	.89	2.18	.90	2.21	.84	2.29	.86	2.23	.92
Difficulty Concentrating	2.67	1.13	2.53	1.12	1.79	.93	2.94	1.02	2.84	1.13
Rigid	2.74	1.12	2.72	1.12	2.27	1.07	2.90	.98	2.85	1.07
Overly Compliant	1.84	.87	1.90	.89	1.89	.84	2.04	.93	1.97	.90

Whiny	1.85	1.00	1.79	.98	1.45	.76	2.10	1.06	2.01	1.09
Feels Overwhelmed	3.12	1.15	3.04	1.16	2.16	1.04	3.42	1.10	3.41	1.13
Manipulative	2.53	1.19	2.52	1.13	2.58	1.05	2.44	1.13	2.45	1.16
Difficulty Trusting Others	3.21	1.25	3.17	1.25	2.68	1.18	3.32	1.25	3.27	1.26
Insensitive to Others	2.34	1.10	2.31	1.08	2.35	.89	2.20	1.12	2.23	1.10
Stereotypic Masculine Behavior	2.91	1.14	2.91	1.14	3.11	1.06	2.84	1.13	2.71	1.16
Harbors Grudges	2.73	1.20	2.70	1.15	2.39	1.14	2.81	1.07	2.75	1.15
Evasive	2.42	1.18	2.38	1.15	2.49	1.15	2.31	1.04	2.32	1.18
Disoriented	1.31	.65	1.23	.54	1.13	.41	1.32	.58	1.30	.61
Energetic	2.50	.94	2.60	.94	3.03	.85	2.26	.96	2.33	.89
Lonely	2.74	1.24	2.73	1.24	2.16	1.14	2.86	1.22	3.03	1.26
Family Lacks Love	2.58	1.33	2.53	1.32	1.76	1.02	2.75	1.38	2.74	1.30
Worrier	3.06	1.11	3.04	1.10	2.14	.89	3.37	1.03	3.37	1.07
Narcissistic	2.55	1.18	2.59	1.15	2.49	1.04	2.47	1.18	2.51	1.19
Tearful	1.47	.80	1.42	.73	1.11	.31	1.57	.86	1.57	.84
Provocative	1.63	.90	1.67	.90	1.49	.77	1.70	.88	1.70	.94
Moralistic	2.41	1.07	2.49	1.07	2.20	.83	2.58	1.03	2.55	1.10
Socially Awkward	2.83	1.16	2.71	1.14	2.37	1.17	2.73	1.07	2.88	1.16
Hostile	2.44	1.22	2.38	1.20	1.87	1.02	2.51	1.15	2.50	1.18
Overcontrolled	2.50	1.17	2.61	1.17	2.47	1.08	2.71	1.27	2.72	1.21
Resistant to Interpretations	2.24	1.07	2.22	1.01	2.17	1.03	2.31	1.06	2.24	1.05
Antisocial Behavior	2.45	1.27	2.35	1.21	2.45	1.06	2.25	1.23	2.16	1.22
Sarcastic	1.97	1.07	2.00	1.04	1.61	.82	2.09	1.07	2.08	1.09
Rejects Traditional Gender Role	1.55	.99	1.57	1.01	1.30	.57	1.60	1.03	1.70	1.09
Feels Gets Raw Deal From Life	2.86	1.23	2.79	1.20	1.97	.91	3.13	1.10	3.07	1.22
Acute Psychological Turmoil	2.86	1.09	2.84	1.09	2.00	.91	3.04	1.06	3.16	1.06
Does Not Complete Projects	2.28	1.17	2.19	1.14	1.76	1.00	2.43	1.19	2.33	1.16
Uncomfortable with Opposite Sex	2.05	1.08	2.00	1.03	1.58	.71	1.97	.99	2.19	1.10
Preoccupied with Health Problems	2.04	1.32	1.95	1.29	1.22	.42	2.78	1.43	2.40	1.44
Work-Oriented	2.88	1.10	3.11	1.04	3.59	.83	2.93	1.13	2.88	1.06
Resents Family Members	2.61	1.31	2.61	1.31	1.92	1.11	2.72	1.35	2.74	1.31
Demanding of Attention	2.43	1.16	2.41	1.14	1.97	1.04	2.50	1.12	2.46	1.11
Passive	2.29	1.04	2.27	.98	2.03	.93	2.45	.96	2.46	.98
Self-Punishing	2.27	1.13	2.24	1.10	1.64	.76	2.50	1.19	2.44	1.17
Needs to Achieve	2.74	1.04	2.85	1.01	3.03	.92	2.68	1.01	2.78	1.06
Needs to Be with Others	2.85	.99	2.91	.95	2.92	.76	2.93	1.02	2.88	1.08
Irritable	2.63	1.11	2.57	1.08	1.89	.83	2.83	1.04	2.73	1.04
Self-Defeating	3.09	1.18	3.07	1.16	2.76	1.14	3.18	1.17	3.17	1.18
Delusional Thinking	1.37	.75	1.29	.66	1.18	.46	1.31	.74	1.35	.75
Self-Reliant	2.65	.90	2.79	.90	3.00	.77	2.74	.96	2.64	.90
Aggressive	2.53	1.11	2.51	1.08	2.43	1.04	2.41	1.04	2.35	1.01
Competitive	2.43	.99	2.56	.98	2.86	.83	2.42	1.03	2.38	.99

Table L-2a. Means and standard deviations for continuous extra-test characteristics (men): High scores on clinical scales *(continued)*

Extra-test Characteristics	Total Sample Mean	Total Sample SD	Valid MMPI-2 Mean	Valid MMPI-2 SD	WNL Mean	WNL SD	Clinical Scales 1 (Hs) Mean	1 (Hs) SD	2 (D) Mean	2 (D) SD
Suspicious	2.56	1.19	2.49	1.21	1.97	1.00	2.64	1.19	2.56	1.21
Compulsive	2.45	1.14	2.50	1.13	2.25	1.05	2.61	1.14	2.60	1.13
Dependable	2.91	.92	3.07	.91	3.11	.73	3.06	.97	3.01	.93
Multiple Somatic Complaints	1.82	1.24	1.80	1.22	1.17	.38	2.54	1.37	2.19	1.37
Complains of Lack of Time	1.79	1.03	1.92	1.08	1.89	.99	2.05	1.17	1.98	1.09
Poor Work Performance	2.04	1.16	2.00	1.12	1.40	.67	2.09	1.21	2.10	1.19
Insecure	3.31	1.05	3.27	1.03	2.83	1.18	3.30	1.02	3.49	.96
Discusses Problems Openly	2.96	.92	2.99	.88	2.89	.89	2.98	.84	2.98	.89
Sexually Adjusted	2.48	.87	2.52	.85	2.80	.55	2.47	.85	2.33	.82
Exaggerated Need for Affection	2.15	1.02	2.18	1.02	1.86	.85	2.25	1.07	2.29	1.11
Resentful	2.96	1.21	2.94	1.17	2.49	1.20	3.14	1.13	3.05	1.14
Uses Denial	2.81	1.15	2.77	1.15	2.63	.97	2.79	1.20	2.77	1.22
Hypochondriacal	1.56	.91	1.60	.93	1.22	.48	2.03	1.09	1.81	.99
Communicates Effectively	2.93	.87	3.03	.81	2.89	.69	3.08	.72	3.05	.75
Has Many Nightmares	1.65	1.05	1.53	.90	1.32	.75	1.71	.99	1.70	1.00
Stormy Interpersonal Relationships	2.97	1.24	2.95	1.27	2.56	1.37	3.05	1.23	3.03	1.22
Feigns Remorse When in Trouble	1.89	1.00	1.86	.96	1.89	.81	1.76	.94	1.73	.93
Stereotypic Masculine Interests	2.88	1.17	2.94	1.19	3.11	1.16	2.96	1.17	2.73	1.18
Guarded	2.79	1.23	2.77	1.23	2.50	.98	2.92	1.29	2.78	1.33
Feels Inferior	3.03	1.08	2.91	1.02	2.25	1.05	3.09	.99	3.13	1.05
Low Frustration Tolerance	3.08	1.16	2.98	1.14	2.50	.75	3.05	1.14	3.14	1.15
Psychotic Symptoms	1.29	.67	1.20	.56	1.08	.27	1.24	.58	1.24	.61
Fired From Past Jobs	2.07	1.22	1.96	1.13	1.59	.89	2.05	1.15	2.07	1.20
Needs Attention	2.84	1.01	2.79	1.00	2.43	.96	2.86	1.05	2.88	1.02
Acts Out	2.55	1.22	2.43	1.18	2.18	.98	2.40	1.19	2.44	1.19
Histrionic	1.81	.99	1.81	1.00	1.34	.71	2.01	.97	1.94	.98
Self-Indulgent	2.59	1.14	2.58	1.11	2.73	.93	2.47	1.11	2.46	1.13
Depressed	2.95	1.07	2.92	1.10	1.95	.73	3.41	1.01	3.42	.99
Grandiose	1.93	1.08	1.96	1.08	1.74	.89	1.94	1.07	1.96	1.07
Cynical	2.36	1.22	2.37	1.20	1.59	.83	2.66	1.22	2.59	1.27
Sociopathic	1.78	.98	1.71	.93	1.53	.77	1.67	.92	1.67	.92
Agitated	2.45	1.12	2.31	1.08	1.66	.97	2.63	1.11	2.52	1.06
Marital Problems	2.36	1.53	2.45	1.58	1.89	1.30	2.67	1.60	2.60	1.62
Absence of Deep Emotions	2.10	1.18	2.09	1.17	1.89	.90	2.01	1.21	2.07	1.23
Uncomfortable Dealing with Emotions	2.91	1.21	2.91	1.22	2.63	.97	2.95	1.30	3.01	1.31
Sad	2.70	1.05	2.67	1.03	1.82	.80	3.05	1.01	3.03	1.00

Self-Degrading	2.04	1.06	2.01	1.00	1.42	.68	2.21	1.04	2.31	1.07
Unable to Express Negative Feelings	2.14	1.11	2.17	1.11	2.14	1.08	2.18	1.14	2.25	1.18
Concrete in Thinking	2.38	1.13	2.21	1.02	2.08	.95	2.28	.99	2.22	1.04
Unable to See Own Limitations	2.38	1.14	2.32	1.11	2.06	.79	2.36	1.14	2.37	1.19
Power-Oriented	2.21	1.07	2.31	1.07	2.55	.95	2.19	1.07	2.14	1.08
Grouchy	2.19	1.07	2.20	1.05	1.65	.72	2.48	1.04	2.38	1.07
Overbearing in Relationships	2.27	1.16	2.30	1.14	2.00	1.14	2.34	1.07	2.26	1.10
Uncertain About Career	3.17	1.30	3.21	1.28	2.84	1.22	3.50	1.30	3.50	1.25
Likable	3.09	.79	3.16	.77	3.21	.58	3.19	.80	3.16	.81
Procrastinator	2.46	1.13	2.46	1.11	2.14	.94	2.57	1.18	2.56	1.19
Negative Feelings Toward Opposite Sex	2.01	1.11	2.03	1.10	1.74	.86	2.06	1.14	2.15	1.18
Defensive	2.64	1.18	2.66	1.18	2.26	.89	2.72	1.16	2.76	1.26
Empathetic	2.21	.79	2.27	.76	2.03	.55	2.35	.77	2.35	.81
Perfectionistic	2.33	1.12	2.47	1.12	2.24	1.02	2.50	1.14	2.56	1.18
Judgmental	2.59	1.15	2.65	1.09	2.19	.86	2.70	1.07	2.72	1.13
Copes Well with Stress	2.03	.71	2.12	.67	2.50	.61	2.03	.67	1.96	.68
Moody	2.65	1.04	2.61	1.02	2.20	.83	2.81	1.02	2.80	1.02
Selfish	2.28	1.04	2.31	1.00	2.43	.88	2.20	.99	2.26	1.04
Gives Up Easily	2.24	1.08	2.11	1.00	1.65	.95	2.29	1.04	2.28	1.01
Physical Symptoms in Response to Stress	2.03	1.18	2.01	1.18	1.34	.73	2.69	1.27	2.33	1.26
Blames Family For Difficulties	2.37	1.32	2.34	1.33	1.84	1.21	2.46	1.39	2.49	1.32
Bored	2.33	1.12	2.32	1.14	1.87	.93	2.64	1.15	2.53	1.14
Idealistic	2.22	1.06	2.30	1.05	2.03	.93	2.28	1.05	2.35	1.06
Difficulty Establishing Therapeutic Rapport	2.16	1.11	2.12	1.07	2.03	1.00	2.09	1.01	2.07	1.09
Daydreams	1.85	.98	1.84	.96	1.62	.73	1.88	.95	1.91	.96
Concerned About Status	2.41	1.08	2.48	1.08	2.57	.90	2.37	1.18	2.43	1.14
Creates Good First Impression	2.51	.95	2.65	.94	2.89	.76	2.60	.98	2.51	.92
Complains of Sleep Disturbance	2.29	1.29	2.20	1.24	1.32	.75	2.80	1.22	2.67	1.26
Has Temper Tantrums	2.37	1.28	2.24	1.20	1.83	1.13	2.27	1.09	2.21	1.12
Overreactive	2.70	1.15	2.60	1.16	2.06	1.24	2.70	1.07	2.66	1.11
High Aspirations	2.46	1.13	2.60	1.12	2.76	.93	2.43	1.11	2.46	1.15
Feels Hopeless	2.47	1.14	2.40	1.15	1.39	.64	2.85	1.10	2.88	1.10
Keeps Others at a Distance	2.92	1.20	2.93	1.19	2.64	1.05	3.04	1.23	3.04	1.27
Argumentative	2.28	1.13	2.25	1.11	1.82	.93	2.33	.96	2.33	1.07
Paranoid Features	1.90	1.11	1.83	1.06	1.37	.71	1.92	1.03	1.94	1.10
Restless	2.50	1.13	2.51	1.14	1.89	.89	2.77	1.15	2.72	1.18
Pessimistic	2.70	1.12	2.66	1.12	1.65	.82	3.13	1.04	3.09	1.07
Feels Like a Failure	2.83	1.14	2.74	1.11	1.94	.92	3.06	1.12	3.12	1.11
Hallucinations	1.15	.50	1.09	.37	1.03	.16	1.10	.35	1.12	.42
Restricted Affect	2.18	1.23	2.20	1.23	1.87	1.12	2.28	1.20	2.35	1.28
Impatient	2.70	1.12	2.65	1.10	2.26	.92	2.72	1.13	2.69	1.12
Assertive	2.27	.83	2.40	.83	2.43	.60	2.41	.88	2.34	.83

Table L-2a. Means and standard deviations for continuous extra-test characteristics (men): High scores on clinical scales *(continued)*

Extra-test Characteristics	Total Sample Mean	Total Sample SD	Valid MMPI-2 Mean	Valid MMPI-2 SD	WNL Mean	WNL SD	Clinical Scales 1 (Hs) Mean	1 (Hs) SD	2 (D) Mean	2 (D) SD
Modest	2.35	.84	2.38	.83	2.22	.75	2.54	.76	2.44	.82
Self-Doubting	2.90	1.02	2.88	.99	2.32	.97	3.04	.95	3.14	.91
Deceptive	2.06	1.06	2.05	1.05	2.22	1.08	1.97	.98	1.96	1.03
Feels That Life is a Strain	2.91	1.11	2.86	1.13	1.94	.89	3.27	1.09	3.30	1.07
Physically Abusive	1.65	1.08	1.57	.98	1.29	.67	1.56	.92	1.52	.91
Feels Rejected	2.93	1.23	2.91	1.29	2.19	1.27	3.08	1.26	3.25	1.26
Does Not Get Along with Coworkers	1.84	1.09	1.86	1.04	1.33	.66	2.02	1.11	2.01	1.08
Uses Projection	2.46	1.17	2.43	1.14	2.09	.95	2.51	1.15	2.45	1.21
Complains of Fatigue	2.16	1.24	2.21	1.29	1.45	.72	2.82	1.43	2.64	1.40
Uses Rationalization	2.78	1.10	2.85	1.05	2.84	1.05	2.72	1.05	2.78	1.11
Critical of Others	2.54	1.15	2.56	1.12	2.25	1.00	2.63	1.09	2.60	1.12
Egocentric	2.61	1.15	2.62	1.13	2.47	.89	2.50	1.13	2.55	1.19
Overevaluates Own Worth	1.96	1.06	1.99	1.06	1.68	.66	1.98	1.10	1.99	1.09
Optimistic	2.05	.79	2.14	.79	2.32	.90	1.93	.70	1.92	.70
Psychologically Immature	2.90	1.21	2.85	1.14	2.74	.95	2.72	1.08	2.83	1.15
Poor Judgment	3.04	1.20	2.96	1.16	2.97	1.00	2.81	1.18	2.87	1.19
Low Sex Drive	1.70	1.09	1.70	1.07	1.17	.48	2.18	1.31	1.94	1.18
Feels Mistreated	2.89	1.19	2.86	1.17	2.28	1.03	3.08	1.13	3.08	1.18
Overly Sensitive to Criticism	2.98	1.16	2.95	1.13	2.31	1.14	3.09	1.08	3.16	1.14
Sentimental	2.27	1.02	2.30	.99	2.11	.93	2.47	1.01	2.43	1.02
Sexual Preoccupation	1.82	1.19	1.83	1.20	1.90	1.35	1.77	1.09	1.83	1.14
Accelerated Speech	1.49	.88	1.47	.83	1.24	.49	1.51	.81	1.52	.87
Concerns About Homosexuality	1.35	.94	1.33	.93	1.14	.58	1.29	.85	1.44	1.05
Many Specific Fears	1.73	.98	1.69	.95	1.36	.76	1.94	1.08	1.90	1.00
Passive in Relationships	2.25	1.06	2.28	1.09	1.94	.98	2.39	1.07	2.44	1.11
Negative Attitudes Toward Therapy	1.86	1.04	1.84	.98	1.68	.88	1.92	1.02	1.92	1.04
Guilt-Prone	2.38	1.15	2.45	1.11	2.14	.99	2.63	1.11	2.67	1.12
Nervous	2.87	1.00	2.85	1.03	2.08	.78	3.14	.97	3.22	.97
Obsessive	2.54	1.17	2.64	1.16	2.00	1.00	2.89	1.08	2.87	1.15
Shy	2.43	1.19	2.37	1.12	2.18	1.01	2.45	1.18	2.53	1.22
Uses Intellectualization	2.40	1.23	2.56	1.22	2.37	1.13	2.58	1.24	2.66	1.25
Has Many Interests	2.27	.97	2.44	.99	2.81	1.05	2.24	.94	2.28	.99
Difficulty Making Decisions	2.73	1.06	2.76	1.07	2.22	.98	2.96	1.05	3.05	1.05
Indirect Expression of Hostility	2.66	1.18	2.69	1.19	2.51	1.46	2.82	1.10	2.80	1.19
Poor Reality Testing	1.69	.90	1.59	.80	1.28	.51	1.64	.78	1.67	.86
Angry	2.98	1.23	2.91	1.22	2.24	1.12	3.13	1.11	3.05	1.14

Eccentric	1.88	1.13	1.86	1.17	1.42	.68	1.80	1.10	1.99	1.29
Emotional Lability	2.22	1.08	2.14	1.05	1.58	.76	2.27	1.06	2.30	1.09
Dislikes Change	2.60	1.01	2.60	1.01	2.19	.86	2.76	.91	2.71	1.03
Believes Cannot Be Helped	1.83	.99	1.78	.97	1.43	.87	2.02	1.00	1.98	1.05
Reliable Informant	3.10	.96	3.19	.93	3.03	.68	3.21	.94	3.18	.93
Ignores Problems	2.34	1.03	2.36	1.02	2.42	1.11	2.31	1.06	2.33	1.07
Ruminates	3.03	1.13	3.00	1.12	2.17	1.10	3.23	1.08	3.24	1.01
Excitable	2.57	1.05	2.48	1.02	1.97	.84	2.48	1.01	2.46	1.00
Conforming	2.36	.88	2.41	.89	2.49	.80	2.46	.89	2.40	.92
Ineffective at Dealing with Problems	3.00	1.07	2.93	1.04	2.42	.95	3.06	1.04	3.09	1.07
Introverted	2.46	1.13	2.43	1.12	2.11	.86	2.51	1.08	2.69	1.15
Superficial Relationships	2.65	1.16	2.63	1.18	2.27	1.13	2.57	1.20	2.69	1.21
Impulsive	2.78	1.20	2.72	1.18	2.63	.97	2.52	1.18	2.57	1.22
Stereotypic Feminine Behavior	1.29	.66	1.33	.67	1.24	.43	1.32	.64	1.37	.69
Stubborn	2.81	1.13	2.78	1.13	2.43	1.12	2.90	.99	2.83	1.13
Hostile Toward Therapist	1.42	.75	1.44	.76	1.24	.59	1.54	.78	1.53	.81
Difficult to Motivate	2.29	1.16	2.23	1.07	2.11	1.11	2.26	1.07	2.27	1.08
Suicidal Ideations	1.57	.90	1.55	.90	1.08	.28	1.81	1.00	1.82	1.00
Familial Discord	2.94	1.36	2.87	1.38	2.39	1.40	2.91	1.42	2.91	1.39
Dogmatic	2.19	1.08	2.24	1.09	1.92	.94	2.26	1.13	2.27	1.09

Extra-test Characteristics	Clinical Scales *(continued)* 3 (Hy) Mean	SD	4 (Pd) Mean	SD	5 (Mf) Mean	SD	6 (Pa) Mean	SD	7 (Pt) Mean	SD	8 (Sc) Mean	SD	9 (Ma) Mean	SD	0 (Si) Mean	SD
Intake Information	(n = 181)		(n = 243)		(n = 56)		(n = 194)		(n = 213)		(n = 218)		(n = 101)		(n = 145)	
Axis IV diagnosis	2.98	.92	2.88	.88	2.86	.88	3.01	.90	2.95	.88	2.94	.88	2.81	.86	2.99	.91
Axis V - Current Level of Functioning	60.61	9.98	61.73	9.60	61.37	9.29	60.69	9.74	60.72	9.79	60.45	9.83	61.46	8.79	59.86	10.65
Number of Arrests	1.35	2.58	1.57	3.62	.63	1.50	1.50	3.72	1.17	2.36	1.22	3.35	1.31	2.31	1.53	4.33
Mental Status	(n = 181)		(n = 243)		(n = 56)		(n = 194)		(n = 213)		(n = 218)		(n = 101)		(n = 145)	
Anxiety During Interview	2.44	.67	2.45	.72	2.48	.66	2.46	.67	2.50	.71	2.48	.71	2.44	.68	2.54	.73
Depression During Interview	2.46	.71	2.37	.68	2.46	.74	2.45	.74	2.46	.70	2.43	.73	2.32	.72	2.50	.76
Activity Level During Interview	2.98	.46	3.01	.40	3.05	.40	3.00	.45	3.01	.46	3.02	.48	3.07	.41	3.02	.48
Speech During Interview	2.96	.35	2.98	.36	3.02	.40	2.95	.43	2.95	.39	2.95	.39	2.97	.36	2.96	.39
SCL-90-R Scales	(n = 179)		(n = 239)		(n = 54)		(n = 189)		(n = 209)		(n = 213)		(n = 60)		(n = 141)	
Somatization	1.41	.82	1.13	.79	1.15	.77	1.22	.81	1.24	.82	1.27	.82	1.12	.82	1.31	.82
Obsessive-Compulsive	1.67	.89	1.54	.83	1.62	.76	1.63	.83	1.71	.83	1.72	.83	1.39	.86	1.79	.84
Interpersonal Sensitivity	1.50	.92	1.49	.88	1.71	.89	1.65	.87	1.62	.88	1.61	.87	1.28	.84	1.84	.85
Depression	1.99	.87	1.85	.87	2.00	.85	1.95	.86	2.03	.81	2.00	.85	1.61	.96	2.09	.83
Anxiety	1.55	.92	1.38	.89	1.47	.86	1.50	.91	1.55	.88	1.53	.88	1.25	.89	1.67	.88
Hostility	1.31	.99	1.42	1.04	1.26	.83	1.52	1.04	1.40	1.06	1.46	1.05	1.55	1.14	1.59	1.07
Phobic Anxiety	.79	.78	.71	.73	.64	.63	.78	.78	.80	.74	.81	.74	.60	.66	.93	.76
Paranoid Ideation	1.43	.93	1.50	.89	1.56	.97	1.71	.88	1.52	.92	1.61	.90	1.57	.90	1.67	.92
Psychoticism	1.14	.79	1.08	.74	1.24	.68	1.20	.76	1.17	.74	1.20	.72	1.01	.74	1.20	.72
Initial SCL-90 Analogue	(n = 119)		(n = 153)		(n = 42)		(n = 117)		(n = 128)		(n = 136)		(n = 60)		(n = 87)	
Somatization	3.21	3.06	2.17	2.71	1.86	2.47	2.36	2.66	2.64	2.96	2.44	2.82	2.08	2.63	2.72	2.96
Obsessive-Compulsive	3.53	2.91	3.35	2.82	3.33	2.89	3.41	2.77	3.59	2.80	3.60	2.84	3.32	2.71	3.78	2.68
Interpersonal Sensitivity	4.75	2.46	5.01	2.39	4.69	2.73	4.97	2.42	5.07	2.46	4.85	2.48	4.64	2.60	5.02	2.41
Depression	4.85	2.60	4.47	2.68	4.24	2.53	4.64	2.48	4.96	2.63	4.72	2.65	4.17	2.99	4.72	2.66
Anxiety	4.77	2.62	4.58	2.70	4.45	2.62	4.80	2.63	4.92	2.62	4.75	2.69	4.19	2.73	4.79	2.72
Hostility	3.47	2.87	3.52	2.91	3.05	2.77	3.72	2.92	3.33	2.87	3.32	2.87	3.90	3.05	3.37	2.84
Phobic Anxiety	1.65	2.46	1.45	2.27	1.39	1.79	1.50	2.15	1.49	2.31	1.49	2.37	1.53	2.43	1.49	2.27
Paranoid Ideation	1.47	2.05	1.44	2.17	1.12	1.31	1.50	2.12	1.33	2.04	1.34	1.98	1.80	2.30	1.07	1.62
Psychoticism	.66	1.49	.74	1.56	.45	.89	.68	1.40	.68	1.52	.72	1.59	1.09	2.11	.44	1.10
Patient Description Form Scales	(n = 123)		(n = 156)		(n = 41)		(n = 118)		(n = 128)		(n = 136)		(n = 59)		(n = 88)	
Angry Resentment	2.91	.97	2.85	.95	2.75	.92	2.94	.93	2.79	.95	2.83	.96	2.94	.95	2.98	.92
Critical/Argumentative	2.63	.91	2.53	.94	2.45	.93	2.59	.94	2.48	.93	2.53	.97	2.70	.96	2.61	.92

Narcissistic	2.43	.97	2.33	.90	2.41	.97	2.39	.95	2.24	.94	2.34	.97	2.59	.97	2.31	.88
Defensive	2.66	.85	2.54	.89	2.52	.91	2.60	.84	2.54	.91	2.56	.88	2.68	.81	2.66	.89
Histrionic	2.43	.77	2.40	.75	2.50	.84	2.44	.77	2.37	.76	2.40	.75	2.51	.75	2.46	.71
Aggressive	2.19	.86	2.24	.96	1.98	.74	2.24	.93	2.04	.86	2.14	.94	2.53	.90	2.17	.89
Insecure	2.85	.75	2.96	.81	3.03	.76	3.04	.75	3.04	.78	2.99	.75	2.82	.70	3.11	.70
Anxious	2.96	.82	2.90	.82	2.89	.77	2.96	.79	3.07	.78	3.04	.75	2.81	.75	3.12	.70
Pessimistic	2.48	.89	2.39	.94	2.24	.96	2.46	.91	2.43	.91	2.47	.95	2.31	.91	2.51	.90
Depressed	2.53	.75	2.42	.81	2.38	.76	2.53	.79	2.61	.75	2.58	.76	2.41	.86	2.65	.77
Achievement-Oriented	2.59	.76	2.59	.70	2.67	.71	2.52	.76	2.51	.71	2.55	.71	2.65	.71	2.57	.73
Passive-Submissive	2.20	.81	2.17	.84	2.27	.77	2.22	.87	2.23	.84	2.19	.80	2.09	.84	2.37	.79
Introverted	2.49	.94	2.60	1.00	2.57	.84	2.61	1.01	2.61	1.00	2.63	.97	2.42	.92	2.88	1.02
Emotionally Controlled	2.44	.98	2.38	1.03	2.39	1.01	2.34	1.06	2.38	1.02	2.38	1.04	2.32	.99	2.63	1.12
Antisocial	2.31	.94	2.35	1.00	2.21	.86	2.37	1.02	2.21	.97	2.31	1.01	2.64	.87	2.17	.96
Negative Treatment Attitudes	2.07	.81	1.94	.81	1.89	.74	1.99	.80	1.95	.82	1.96	.81	2.06	.75	2.08	.82
Somatic Symptoms	2.42	1.15	2.01	1.04	2.05	.96	2.09	1.03	2.21	1.10	2.19	1.05	1.88	1.05	2.30	1.11
Psychotic Symptoms	1.28	.44	1.34	.51	1.27	.41	1.31	.51	1.29	.47	1.32	.50	1.44	.57	1.22	.37
Family Problems	2.69	1.18	2.82	1.17	2.97	1.25	2.91	1.17	2.74	1.16	2.87	1.19	2.95	1.05	2.92	1.12
Obsessive-Compulsive	2.82	.77	2.78	.80	2.80	.75	2.85	.79	2.85	.78	2.87	.77	2.77	.77	2.97	.77
Stereotypic Masculine Interests	2.85	1.13	2.74	1.14	2.06	.96	2.77	1.11	2.70	1.14	2.73	1.16	3.00	1.09	2.80	1.14
Procrastinates	2.34	.99	2.23	.90	2.46	1.05	2.25	.94	2.29	.98	2.30	.94	2.33	.97	2.42	.85
Suspicious	2.65	1.01	2.59	1.03	2.62	1.01	2.64	1.01	2.61	1.06	2.65	1.01	2.74	.94	2.69	.92
Agitated	2.26	.81	2.21	.83	2.12	.73	2.23	.79	2.20	.79	2.23	.80	2.37	.72	2.23	.76
Work Problems	2.04	1.01	2.16	.98	1.90	.72	2.11	.94	1.96	.93	2.05	.96	2.30	1.01	1.91	.88
Patient Description Form Items	(n = 123)		(n = 156)		(n = 41)		(n = 118)		(n = 128)		(n = 136)		(n = 59)		(n = 88)	
Anxious	3.46	.91	3.38	.96	3.39	.80	3.50	.85	3.64	.84	3.57	.80	3.32	.97	3.69	.78
Problems with Authority Figures	3.07	1.26	3.05	1.26	2.90	1.41	3.13	1.27	2.90	1.27	3.00	1.27	3.41	1.17	3.02	1.16
Has Insight Into Own Problems	2.58	.88	2.67	.94	2.73	.81	2.57	.85	2.66	.86	2.61	.87	2.55	.92	2.71	.85
Fears Losing Control	3.36	1.11	3.30	1.07	3.39	.92	3.20	1.03	3.35	1.05	3.36	1.03	3.19	.95	3.39	1.02
Extroverted	2.46	.92	2.31	.92	2.54	.84	2.35	.96	2.30	.92	2.32	.91	2.63	1.08	2.23	.93
Uses Repression	2.64	1.03	2.52	1.04	2.70	.94	2.54	1.07	2.59	1.07	2.56	1.03	2.42	.98	2.76	1.12
Submissive	2.16	.87	2.15	.93	2.24	.83	2.15	.93	2.22	.93	2.18	.90	2.09	.94	2.35	.94
Difficulty Concentrating	2.77	1.12	2.68	1.13	2.68	1.11	2.74	1.07	2.90	1.11	2.87	1.08	2.80	.96	2.89	1.07
Rigid	2.90	1.02	2.78	1.08	2.66	1.02	2.85	1.09	2.77	1.06	2.81	1.05	2.66	1.12	2.94	1.07
Overly Compliant	1.95	.91	1.93	.92	1.95	.97	1.96	.91	1.93	.90	1.91	.89	1.93	.91	2.08	.90
Whiny	2.02	1.02	1.91	1.06	1.98	1.04	1.97	1.07	1.93	1.02	1.93	1.01	1.86	1.07	2.07	1.08
Feels Overwhelmed	3.38	1.11	3.24	1.13	3.24	1.16	3.31	1.11	3.42	1.11	3.43	1.09	3.19	1.06	3.52	1.04
Manipulative	2.58	1.13	2.51	1.14	2.34	1.15	2.53	1.21	2.35	1.14	2.45	1.20	2.67	1.14	2.37	1.19
Difficulty Trusting Others	3.34	1.25	3.28	1.26	3.39	1.26	3.30	1.24	3.28	1.27	3.35	1.24	3.39	1.10	3.42	1.17
Insensitive to Others	2.33	1.12	2.30	1.11	2.22	1.08	2.34	1.15	2.22	1.12	2.30	1.15	2.41	1.11	2.25	1.04
Stereotypic Masculine Behavior	2.80	1.18	2.73	1.17	2.05	.97	2.74	1.14	2.69	1.18	2.73	1.21	2.98	1.11	2.82	1.21
Harbors Grudges	2.83	1.16	2.85	1.18	2.64	1.01	2.95	1.16	2.65	1.15	2.76	1.20	2.80	1.13	2.90	1.09

Extra-test Characteristics	Clinical Scales (*continued*)															
	3 (Hy)		4 (Pd)		5 (Mf)		6 (Pa)		7 (Pt)		8 (Sc)		9 (Ma)		0 (Si)	
	Mean	SD	Mean	SD	Mean	SD	Mean	SD	Mean	SD	Mean	SD	Mean	SD	Mean	SD
Evasive	2.38	1.11	2.26	1.10	2.17	1.05	2.25	1.10	2.26	1.14	2.27	1.14	2.48	1.11	2.39	1.17
Disoriented	1.30	.61	1.31	.61	1.24	.54	1.25	.51	1.30	.63	1.32	.63	1.22	.49	1.24	.55
Energetic	2.36	.94	2.51	.91	2.44	.84	2.42	.99	2.29	.91	2.34	.91	2.51	.90	2.36	.80
Lonely	2.80	1.15	2.91	1.26	3.07	1.17	2.98	1.24	3.05	1.27	2.99	1.25	2.91	1.23	3.15	1.21
Family Lacks Love	2.65	1.29	2.83	1.34	2.90	1.41	2.91	1.38	2.78	1.30	2.87	1.37	2.85	1.35	2.92	1.23
Worrier	3.28	1.07	3.25	1.07	3.39	1.00	3.32	1.09	3.42	1.05	3.38	1.04	3.19	.99	3.55	.96
Narcissistic	2.71	1.23	2.61	1.17	2.73	1.20	2.67	1.24	2.48	1.22	2.56	1.22	2.93	1.22	2.48	1.16
Tearful	1.57	.84	1.51	.81	1.61	.77	1.63	.90	1.63	.88	1.58	.86	1.53	.88	1.64	.91
Provocative	1.76	.95	1.71	.93	1.76	.94	1.70	.93	1.72	.96	1.75	.97	1.90	.98	1.64	.82
Moralistic	2.52	1.08	2.51	1.13	2.61	1.14	2.54	1.08	2.46	1.12	2.47	1.09	2.52	1.20	2.67	1.06
Socially Awkward	2.65	1.03	2.85	1.15	2.68	1.04	2.85	1.14	2.85	1.14	2.85	1.10	2.78	1.08	3.07	1.13
Hostile	2.59	1.19	2.56	1.22	2.44	1.14	2.61	1.25	2.48	1.17	2.52	1.21	2.73	1.23	2.62	1.18
Overcontrolled	2.74	1.24	2.60	1.22	2.68	1.23	2.61	1.28	2.67	1.22	2.61	1.22	2.46	1.13	2.84	1.22
Resistant to Interpretations	2.33	1.05	2.10	1.03	2.10	.97	2.20	1.01	2.17	1.04	2.15	1.02	2.31	1.00	2.30	1.03
Antisocial Behavior	2.31	1.26	2.39	1.34	2.05	1.06	2.47	1.37	2.17	1.26	2.32	1.33	2.80	1.28	2.16	1.22
Sarcastic	2.21	1.09	2.05	1.06	2.22	1.08	2.07	1.08	2.03	1.09	2.08	1.12	2.31	1.19	2.03	1.10
Rejects Traditional Gender Role	1.64	1.12	1.61	1.08	2.32	1.29	1.68	1.12	1.70	1.14	1.70	1.15	1.67	1.19	1.75	.97
Feels Gets Raw Deal From Life	3.15	1.20	2.95	1.16	2.88	1.14	3.09	1.15	3.02	1.20	3.01	1.21	2.98	1.16	3.10	1.25
Acute Psychological Turmoil	3.03	1.09	3.06	1.10	3.07	1.08	3.06	1.10	3.15	1.09	3.15	1.09	3.00	1.08	3.22	.98
Does Not Complete Projects	2.34	1.16	2.28	1.11	2.53	1.22	2.26	1.12	2.32	1.22	2.30	1.14	2.49	1.14	2.33	1.08
Uncomfortable with Opposite Sex	1.97	.99	2.05	1.05	2.08	1.02	2.08	1.05	2.14	1.09	2.16	1.06	2.02	1.10	2.40	1.08
Preoccupied with Health Problems	2.55	1.45	2.05	1.34	2.02	1.19	2.13	1.32	2.36	1.43	2.36	1.43	2.00	1.34	2.49	1.42
Work-Oriented	2.99	1.11	2.97	1.02	2.90	1.04	2.90	1.03	2.90	1.07	2.96	1.04	2.92	1.04	3.03	1.10
Resents Family Members	2.75	1.32	2.86	1.32	3.15	1.37	2.94	1.33	2.78	1.32	2.92	1.36	2.90	1.18	2.92	1.34
Demanding of Attention	2.59	1.10	2.55	1.13	2.65	1.29	2.56	1.15	2.45	1.12	2.52	1.13	2.71	1.09	2.53	1.07
Passive	2.37	.97	2.29	.97	2.51	.87	2.41	1.01	2.41	.96	2.40	.96	2.22	1.08	2.61	.96
Self-Punishing	2.44	1.15	2.42	1.16	2.51	1.19	2.49	1.21	2.46	1.15	2.43	1.16	2.23	1.04	2.67	1.19
Needs to Achieve	2.80	1.05	2.79	.96	2.90	1.07	2.70	1.02	2.74	1.01	2.76	1.01	2.81	1.04	2.77	.92
Needs to Be with Others	2.87	1.02	2.88	1.01	2.90	1.04	2.81	1.02	2.90	1.07	2.88	1.08	3.10	.90	2.94	.99
Irritable	2.81	1.05	2.74	1.06	2.51	.93	2.76	1.04	2.72	1.01	2.75	1.02	2.76	1.06	2.74	1.03
Self-Defeating	3.20	1.18	3.21	1.17	3.17	1.16	3.15	1.18	3.23	1.19	3.21	1.17	3.15	1.11	3.20	1.14
Delusional Thinking	1.32	.73	1.34	.75	1.38	.75	1.32	.77	1.29	.71	1.31	.75	1.46	.83	1.14	.38
Self-Reliant	2.75	.91	2.65	.89	2.59	1.00	2.57	.94	2.63	.87	2.62	.86	2.71	1.05	2.63	.94
Aggressive	2.54	1.06	2.56	1.07	2.20	.87	2.50	1.08	2.32	1.00	2.41	1.06	2.73	1.06	2.38	1.08
Competitive	2.52	1.03	2.45	.95	2.37	.97	2.44	.99	2.32	.99	2.41	1.01	2.53	.94	2.42	1.01
Suspicious	2.67	1.21	2.56	1.24	2.59	1.30	2.61	1.22	2.61	1.28	2.63	1.25	2.79	1.20	2.68	1.12
Compulsive	2.61	1.11	2.60	1.15	2.55	1.11	2.50	1.15	2.59	1.10	2.63	1.10	2.40	1.01	2.74	1.16
Dependable	3.09	.94	2.99	.94	3.07	1.03	2.97	.95	3.08	.91	3.01	.93	2.81	.96	3.00	.90

Multiple Somatic Complaints	2.37	1.38	1.90	1.23	1.88	1.19	1.99	1.26	2.11	1.33	2.12	1.33	1.90	1.31	2.22	1.33
Complains of Lack of Time	2.07	1.18	1.90	1.09	2.20	1.14	1.97	1.11	1.92	1.13	1.96	1.14	2.05	1.13	2.06	1.08
Poor Work Performance	2.10	1.21	2.18	1.20	2.15	1.18	2.19	1.17	2.02	1.11	2.08	1.15	2.41	1.37	2.02	.99
Insecure	3.30	.95	3.39	.98	3.51	.93	3.55	.88	3.53	.95	3.46	.89	3.37	1.00	3.61	.85
Discusses Problems Openly	2.94	.84	3.09	.92	3.00	.71	3.00	.84	3.09	.90	3.04	.85	2.90	.76	3.06	.88
Sexually Adjusted	2.47	.81	2.43	.90	2.30	.88	2.32	.79	2.37	.82	2.30	.84	2.57	.96	2.33	.79
Exaggerated Need for Affection	2.25	1.09	2.27	1.06	2.70	1.11	2.35	1.08	2.32	1.12	2.24	1.08	2.33	1.04	2.38	1.02
Resentful	3.15	1.15	3.10	1.13	3.00	1.20	3.18	1.14	3.02	1.17	3.09	1.17	3.07	1.08	3.20	1.19
Uses Denial	2.80	1.16	2.65	1.21	2.73	1.20	2.72	1.23	2.65	1.23	2.62	1.22	2.69	1.12	2.70	1.21
Hypochondriacal	1.95	1.09	1.65	.92	1.80	.93	1.64	.86	1.76	.99	1.72	.89	1.45	.73	1.81	.96
Communicates Effectively	3.12	.74	3.03	.82	3.27	.90	3.05	.80	3.06	.75	3.03	.78	2.95	.90	3.01	.78
Has Many Nightmares	1.61	.93	1.62	.95	1.56	.89	1.77	1.07	1.75	1.05	1.76	1.05	1.57	.84	1.87	1.16
Stormy Interpersonal Relationships	2.98	1.22	3.22	1.22	2.85	1.24	3.19	1.22	3.01	1.20	3.07	1.20	3.50	1.04	3.13	1.24
Feigns Remorse When in Trouble	1.86	.96	1.88	.99	1.70	.85	1.85	1.02	1.66	.95	1.78	1.01	1.94	.92	1.76	1.00
Stereotypic Masculine Interests	2.88	1.18	2.75	1.19	2.07	1.03	2.78	1.17	2.70	1.19	2.72	1.21	2.96	1.16	2.77	1.18
Guarded	2.99	1.27	2.76	1.27	2.66	1.24	2.79	1.28	2.73	1.33	2.79	1.33	2.93	1.24	2.84	1.41
Feels Inferior	2.99	1.01	3.14	.98	3.12	1.02	3.22	.95	3.14	1.06	3.12	1.01	3.00	.88	3.19	.99
Low Frustration Tolerance	3.02	1.17	3.12	1.16	2.76	1.11	3.18	1.16	3.12	1.16	3.14	1.13	3.25	1.09	3.28	1.10
Psychotic Symptoms	1.18	.52	1.26	.65	1.13	.41	1.22	.61	1.20	.54	1.23	.63	1.39	.82	1.12	.39
Fired From Past Jobs	2.06	1.17	2.15	1.21	1.84	1.11	2.11	1.12	1.99	1.13	2.12	1.17	2.14	1.01	1.90	1.10
Needs Attention	2.90	1.02	2.88	1.00	2.97	1.10	2.90	.95	2.88	1.02	2.90	.99	2.95	.90	2.86	.91
Acts Out	2.45	1.16	2.53	1.25	2.54	1.14	2.55	1.24	2.44	1.22	2.49	1.24	2.84	1.18	2.43	1.16
Histrionic	2.03	1.01	1.89	.97	2.17	1.14	1.88	.98	1.91	.98	1.95	1.02	1.93	1.10	1.94	1.00
Self-Indulgent	2.57	1.16	2.47	1.14	2.59	1.16	2.52	1.22	2.40	1.10	2.53	1.16	2.77	1.17	2.47	1.09
Depressed	3.37	.98	3.18	1.08	3.20	.95	3.26	1.04	3.46	.98	3.41	1.00	3.10	1.21	3.41	.93
Grandiose	2.04	1.09	1.89	1.02	2.15	1.09	1.89	1.06	1.86	1.01	1.97	1.11	2.34	1.24	1.90	1.05
Cynical	2.72	1.23	2.53	1.25	2.46	1.21	2.61	1.24	2.54	1.24	2.60	1.31	2.66	1.29	2.63	1.28
Sociopathic	1.79	.97	1.77	1.00	1.56	.87	1.78	.99	1.66	.92	1.72	.95	1.79	.89	1.63	.88
Agitated	2.58	1.05	2.59	1.07	2.29	.96	2.59	1.07	2.52	1.08	2.54	1.08	2.55	1.11	2.59	1.01
Marital Problems	2.69	1.57	2.77	1.64	2.17	1.48	2.61	1.65	2.61	1.59	2.51	1.61	2.61	1.73	2.65	1.62
Absence of Deep Emotions	2.07	1.15	2.10	1.23	1.93	1.08	1.97	1.22	1.99	1.21	2.06	1.26	2.12	1.18	2.22	1.35
Uncomfortable Dealing with Emotions	2.98	1.26	2.89	1.31	2.85	1.24	2.91	1.31	2.88	1.28	2.93	1.28	2.90	1.26	3.19	1.32
Sad	2.98	.98	2.91	1.02	2.85	.94	2.98	.98	3.05	1.01	3.04	.99	2.83	1.00	3.13	.95
Self-Degrading	2.16	1.00	2.31	1.07	2.44	.92	2.25	1.05	2.32	1.09	2.26	1.04	1.97	.87	2.36	1.00
Unable to Express Negative Feelings	2.18	1.12	2.15	1.14	2.39	1.22	2.05	1.08	2.14	1.11	2.10	1.10	2.05	1.11	2.38	1.19
Concrete in Thinking	2.21	.98	2.14	.97	2.27	.98	2.18	1.04	2.20	1.05	2.26	1.04	2.29	1.12	2.31	1.08
Unable to See Own Limitations	2.39	1.13	2.29	1.11	2.20	1.08	2.29	1.09	2.30	1.16	2.29	1.13	2.62	1.15	2.40	1.15
Power-Oriented	2.29	1.10	2.24	1.08	2.03	1.03	2.27	1.13	2.10	1.03	2.21	1.11	2.59	1.16	2.18	1.13
Grouchy	2.48	1.05	2.31	1.08	2.20	1.04	2.41	1.08	2.33	1.11	2.35	1.09	2.41	1.10	2.46	1.10
Overbearing in Relationships	2.36	1.04	2.31	1.13	2.11	.99	2.36	1.15	2.25	1.12	2.31	1.15	2.70	1.17	2.32	1.05
Uncertain About Career	3.34	1.34	3.28	1.29	3.26	1.23	3.32	1.30	3.46	1.24	3.43	1.28	3.38	1.19	3.63	1.18
Likable	3.16	.78	3.10	.80	3.28	.78	3.11	.84	3.20	.80	3.16	.82	3.08	.79	3.19	.80

Extra-test Characteristics	Clinical Scales (continued)															
	3 (Hy)		4 (Pd)		5 (Mf)		6 (Pa)		7 (Pt)		8 (Sc)		9 (Ma)		0 (Si)	
	Mean	SD	Mean	SD	Mean	SD	Mean	SD	Mean	SD	Mean	SD	Mean	SD	Mean	SD
Procrastinator	2.49	1.18	2.47	1.13	2.85	1.27	2.46	1.13	2.57	1.19	2.56	1.12	2.46	1.07	2.64	1.06
Negative Feelings Toward Opposite Sex	2.07	1.13	2.17	1.19	2.13	1.08	2.18	1.19	2.12	1.20	2.13	1.15	2.02	1.21	2.24	1.17
Defensive	2.80	1.17	2.64	1.19	2.70	1.20	2.77	1.14	2.71	1.20	2.66	1.18	2.85	1.20	2.77	1.19
Empathetic	2.34	.82	2.29	.82	2.43	.87	2.35	.89	2.40	.82	2.33	.80	2.17	.77	2.33	.72
Perfectionistic	2.54	1.12	2.47	1.12	2.53	1.18	2.50	1.11	2.56	1.13	2.56	1.15	2.48	1.13	2.69	1.15
Judgmental	2.76	1.07	2.69	1.14	2.62	1.08	2.75	1.17	2.68	1.13	2.69	1.16	2.81	1.21	2.80	1.01
Copes Well with Stress	2.04	.66	2.00	.66	2.03	.62	1.94	.59	1.95	.65	1.94	.63	2.00	.62	1.93	.66
Moody	2.77	1.03	2.76	.99	2.65	1.00	2.77	1.00	2.80	1.00	2.79	1.00	2.71	1.04	3.02	.98
Selfish	2.35	1.05	2.23	.99	2.33	1.05	2.23	1.03	2.16	1.03	2.21	1.01	2.39	1.05	2.23	.95
Gives Up Easily	2.20	1.01	2.24	.99	2.35	.92	2.30	1.01	2.31	1.01	2.27	.98	2.22	.92	2.38	.98
Physical Symptoms in Response to Stress	2.54	1.30	2.16	1.21	2.16	1.20	2.27	1.22	2.33	1.27	2.30	1.21	1.93	1.14	2.43	1.23
Blames Family For Difficulties	2.44	1.35	2.56	1.33	2.70	1.42	2.62	1.33	2.45	1.30	2.54	1.32	2.63	1.24	2.59	1.35
Bored	2.56	1.16	2.34	1.11	2.45	1.18	2.40	1.15	2.48	1.18	2.51	1.16	2.36	1.09	2.65	1.13
Idealistic	2.36	1.08	2.31	1.07	2.59	1.14	2.34	1.08	2.32	1.09	2.36	1.07	2.48	.96	2.42	1.02
Difficulty Establishing Therapeutic Rapport	2.14	.99	2.05	1.08	1.98	1.03	2.11	1.08	1.95	1.01	2.00	1.07	2.15	1.06	2.15	1.05
Daydreams	1.78	.92	1.87	1.00	1.93	.96	1.80	.97	1.92	1.01	1.88	.99	1.82	1.01	2.04	1.05
Concerned About Status	2.45	1.17	2.42	1.11	2.55	1.01	2.37	1.17	2.41	1.10	2.43	1.14	2.53	1.11	2.42	1.09
Creates Good First Impression	2.67	1.00	2.56	.93	2.78	.86	2.47	.98	2.53	.90	2.50	.93	2.37	.89	2.48	.82
Complains of Sleep Disturbance	2.64	1.22	2.38	1.25	2.31	1.24	2.57	1.30	2.66	1.27	2.64	1.27	2.48	1.25	2.84	1.31
Has Temper Tantrums	2.30	1.15	2.41	1.22	2.41	1.12	2.45	1.22	2.20	1.13	2.28	1.19	2.71	1.33	2.33	1.17
Overreactive	2.76	1.14	2.74	1.09	2.65	1.05	2.75	1.07	2.67	1.10	2.69	1.08	2.85	.98	2.78	1.04
High Aspirations	2.57	1.18	2.51	1.08	2.79	1.23	2.47	1.16	2.44	1.12	2.54	1.13	2.72	1.20	2.45	1.04
Feels Hopeless	2.75	1.10	2.69	1.09	2.68	1.14	2.82	1.12	2.85	1.11	2.85	1.12	2.59	1.13	2.88	1.06
Keeps Others at a Distance	3.07	1.22	3.00	1.22	2.80	1.16	2.92	1.26	2.97	1.25	2.98	1.25	3.03	1.20	3.19	1.30
Argumentative	2.37	1.06	2.34	1.11	2.20	.94	2.38	1.10	2.26	1.02	2.24	1.06	2.49	1.15	2.43	1.04
Paranoid Features	1.94	1.06	1.94	1.12	1.82	.96	1.99	1.07	1.94	1.10	1.96	1.09	2.03	1.14	1.91	.97
Restless	2.72	1.18	2.60	1.15	2.60	1.10	2.72	1.16	2.68	1.12	2.68	1.16	2.93	1.06	2.72	1.13
Pessimistic	3.01	1.09	2.90	1.09	2.68	1.08	3.02	1.03	3.00	1.10	3.02	1.12	2.79	1.07	3.10	1.04
Feels Like a Failure	2.93	1.11	3.03	1.10	2.95	1.02	3.10	1.06	3.07	1.13	3.10	1.12	3.03	1.10	3.18	1.06
Hallucinations	1.07	.31	1.13	.44	1.10	.37	1.14	.48	1.10	.35	1.12	.44	1.18	.54	1.08	.31
Restricted Affect	2.27	1.19	2.22	1.24	2.10	1.18	2.17	1.28	2.23	1.26	2.20	1.25	2.08	1.21	2.51	1.37
Impatient	2.75	1.16	2.69	1.08	2.66	1.06	2.77	1.17	2.71	1.13	2.66	1.10	2.97	1.07	2.74	1.03
Assertive	2.48	.88	2.30	.82	2.46	.78	2.25	.85	2.32	.81	2.33	.85	2.53	.86	2.26	.82
Modest	2.42	.81	2.44	.88	2.39	.83	2.34	.84	2.40	.82	2.43	.81	2.24	.86	2.55	.90
Self-Doubting	2.96	.89	3.07	.99	3.07	.96	3.13	.89	3.14	.91	3.14	.92	2.85	.89	3.26	.84
Deceptive	2.04	.96	1.97	1.04	1.98	.92	1.97	1.06	1.87	.99	1.94	1.04	2.09	1.00	1.95	1.03
Feels That Life is a Strain	3.19	1.12	3.08	1.12	3.00	1.02	3.25	1.08	3.21	1.11	3.21	1.10	2.90	1.12	3.33	1.08
Physically Abusive	1.58	.96	1.74	1.10	1.35	.81	1.69	1.06	1.52	.92	1.62	1.01	1.92	1.09	1.57	.87

Feels Rejected	3.01	1.24	3.20	1.24	3.32	1.17	3.32	1.24	3.25	1.28	3.24	1.23	3.10	1.32	3.33	1.12
Does Not Get Along with Coworkers	2.04	1.11	2.11	1.14	2.00	.98	2.16	1.17	1.95	1.03	2.03	1.12	2.33	1.24	2.03	1.02
Uses Projection	2.57	1.18	2.51	1.19	2.65	1.12	2.53	1.19	2.41	1.17	2.45	1.17	2.61	1.03	2.48	1.17
Complains of Fatigue	2.66	1.40	2.35	1.31	2.49	1.23	2.43	1.40	2.59	1.40	2.56	1.38	2.29	1.36	2.64	1.38
Uses Rationalization	2.84	1.10	2.76	1.10	2.78	1.15	2.81	1.13	2.71	1.12	2.71	1.14	2.90	1.08	2.81	1.09
Critical of Others	2.70	1.16	2.59	1.15	2.49	1.16	2.68	1.19	2.52	1.10	2.63	1.18	2.95	1.19	2.67	1.13
Egocentric	2.68	1.20	2.60	1.12	2.83	1.26	2.69	1.21	2.52	1.19	2.60	1.21	2.79	1.20	2.51	1.13
Overevaluates Own Worth	2.13	1.14	2.01	1.09	2.12	1.12	2.11	1.15	1.92	1.03	2.02	1.09	2.37	1.20	1.99	1.10
Optimistic	2.01	.74	1.99	.75	2.05	.63	1.94	.73	1.87	.67	1.93	.68	2.17	.83	1.97	.69
Psychologically Immature	2.79	1.12	2.80	1.16	2.80	1.14	2.93	1.16	2.78	1.15	2.85	1.18	3.03	1.08	2.90	1.07
Poor Judgment	2.91	1.14	2.96	1.20	2.76	1.14	2.97	1.22	2.81	1.20	2.90	1.22	3.36	1.11	2.77	1.20
Low Sex Drive	2.04	1.27	1.76	1.07	1.71	1.08	1.80	1.10	1.78	1.13	1.85	1.17	1.40	.74	1.96	1.10
Feels Mistreated	3.07	1.17	3.06	1.12	2.88	1.12	3.18	1.09	3.06	1.14	3.01	1.13	3.03	1.16	3.09	1.09
Overly Sensitive to Criticism	3.08	1.15	3.15	1.08	3.29	1.19	3.29	1.05	3.12	1.13	3.08	1.11	2.98	1.15	3.26	1.02
Sentimental	2.41	1.02	2.29	.98	2.54	1.07	2.46	1.03	2.47	1.06	2.43	.97	2.28	.99	2.51	.98
Sexual Preoccupation	1.84	1.12	1.89	1.23	2.17	1.28	1.80	1.17	1.74	1.11	1.80	1.15	1.80	1.13	1.75	1.11
Accelerated Speech	1.53	.84	1.47	.85	1.44	.71	1.41	.72	1.44	.79	1.49	.82	1.66	.90	1.40	.78
Concerns About Homosexuality	1.35	.88	1.39	1.01	1.86	1.31	1.36	.96	1.44	1.04	1.44	1.03	1.47	1.06	1.37	.93
Many Specific Fears	1.87	1.06	1.81	1.01	1.72	.86	1.90	1.07	1.88	1.03	1.87	1.04	1.67	.98	2.00	1.06
Passive in Relationships	2.28	1.06	2.29	1.11	2.44	1.07	2.34	1.14	2.38	1.10	2.29	1.03	2.07	.98	2.49	.98
Negative Attitudes Toward Therapy	1.90	1.00	1.74	.97	1.68	.91	1.78	.97	1.77	.96	1.80	.97	1.78	.99	1.94	1.03
Guilt-Prone	2.56	1.09	2.55	1.13	2.83	1.22	2.59	1.16	2.70	1.12	2.59	1.12	2.57	1.06	2.76	1.11
Nervous	3.07	1.01	3.02	1.01	2.98	.82	3.10	.97	3.24	.96	3.15	.94	2.93	.95	3.26	.93
Obsessive	2.86	1.09	2.78	1.13	2.88	1.21	2.97	1.12	2.92	1.12	2.91	1.11	2.84	1.12	3.05	1.08
Shy	2.36	1.16	2.41	1.14	2.54	1.05	2.45	1.19	2.40	1.19	2.46	1.19	2.19	1.13	2.69	1.22
Uses Intellectualization	2.66	1.26	2.60	1.24	2.85	1.22	2.59	1.26	2.54	1.23	2.55	1.26	2.79	1.27	2.68	1.22
Has Many Interests	2.34	1.04	2.35	1.01	2.72	1.05	2.28	1.05	2.29	.97	2.26	.99	2.38	1.00	2.31	.95
Difficulty Making Decisions	2.89	1.06	2.88	1.08	3.07	.93	2.97	1.06	3.01	1.02	3.00	1.03	3.02	1.12	3.07	1.00
Indirect Expression of Hostility	2.87	1.08	2.77	1.14	2.68	1.01	2.80	1.15	2.69	1.14	2.71	1.16	2.84	1.03	2.85	1.16
Poor Reality Testing	1.64	.83	1.71	.88	1.66	.79	1.68	.86	1.68	.88	1.70	.88	1.98	.91	1.60	.81
Angry	3.11	1.14	3.16	1.17	3.02	1.11	3.17	1.18	3.03	1.13	3.08	1.17	3.19	1.22	3.26	1.15
Eccentric	1.89	1.17	1.95	1.22	1.95	1.26	1.91	1.21	1.92	1.28	1.99	1.27	2.26	1.38	1.93	1.20
Emotional Lability	2.25	1.10	2.32	1.06	2.41	1.05	2.33	1.13	2.31	1.10	2.30	1.08	2.50	1.16	2.34	1.01
Dislikes Change	2.68	.93	2.68	.99	2.55	1.01	2.70	1.00	2.69	1.00	2.73	.99	2.61	1.00	2.84	1.02
Believes Cannot Be Helped	1.93	.90	1.86	.99	1.80	1.03	1.88	1.00	1.84	.94	1.90	.98	1.75	.97	1.91	.97
Reliable Informant	3.25	.95	3.19	.93	3.24	.99	3.20	1.01	3.23	.92	3.18	.91	3.03	.92	3.19	.93
Ignores Problems	2.27	1.05	2.21	1.00	2.10	.80	2.22	1.00	2.20	1.04	2.21	1.02	2.48	.98	2.26	1.06
Ruminates	3.21	1.00	3.18	1.06	3.18	1.00	3.27	1.00	3.26	1.05	3.27	1.05	3.23	1.05	3.35	.97
Excitable	2.54	1.03	2.62	.97	2.55	.93	2.60	1.01	2.45	.96	2.53	.96	2.86	.99	2.59	.98
Conforming	2.37	.90	2.35	.85	2.33	.89	2.37	.89	2.40	.86	2.36	.89	2.28	.82	2.57	.92
Ineffective at Dealing with Problems	3.04	1.02	3.01	1.06	2.83	1.08	3.10	1.02	3.04	1.05	3.04	1.01	3.14	.94	3.12	1.05
Introverted	2.48	1.06	2.55	1.15	2.53	.99	2.54	1.21	2.59	1.14	2.61	1.09	2.30	1.18	2.89	1.13

Extra-test Characteristics	Clinical Scales *(continued)*															
	3 (Hy)		4 (Pd)		5 (Mf)		6 (Pa)		7 (Pt)		8 (Sc)		9 (Ma)		0 (Si)	
	Mean	SD	Mean	SD	Mean	SD	Mean	SD	Mean	SD	Mean	SD	Mean	SD	Mean	SD
Superficial Relationships	2.65	1.19	2.68	1.25	2.54	1.17	2.60	1.23	2.55	1.21	2.61	1.19	2.82	1.15	2.80	1.20
Impulsive	2.62	1.16	2.71	1.25	2.59	1.07	2.62	1.28	2.54	1.23	2.64	1.25	3.03	1.08	2.59	1.24
Stereotypic Feminine Behavior	1.34	.68	1.31	.69	1.59	.74	1.34	.72	1.38	.74	1.37	.73	1.36	.69	1.40	.74
Stubborn	2.93	1.04	2.83	1.10	2.80	1.10	2.88	1.10	2.75	1.12	2.77	1.12	2.91	1.14	2.84	1.07
Hostile Toward Therapist	1.59	.80	1.42	.74	1.44	.63	1.41	.73	1.47	.75	1.44	.74	1.47	.71	1.48	.77
Difficult to Motivate	2.27	1.03	2.16	.99	2.24	1.14	2.25	1.03	2.19	1.07	2.18	1.02	2.17	.96	2.24	.99
Suicidal Ideations	1.76	.98	1.72	.99	1.63	.90	1.79	.98	1.83	.99	1.86	1.02	1.84	1.03	1.90	1.06
Familial Discord	2.89	1.38	3.08	1.40	3.08	1.42	3.04	1.42	2.95	1.37	3.09	1.37	3.32	1.18	3.05	1.33
Dogmatic	2.33	1.10	2.32	1.12	2.17	1.09	2.33	1.17	2.25	1.13	2.30	1.11	2.59	1.11	2.34	1.09

Table L-2b. Means and standard deviations for continuous extra-test characteristics (men): High scores on Harris-Lingoes subscales

Extra-test Characteristics	Harris-Lingoes Subscales									
	D_1		D_2		D_3		D_4		D_5	
	Mean	SD	Mean	SD	Mean	SD	Mean	SD	Mean	SD
Intake Information	(n = 246)		(n = 149)		(n = 187)		(n = 221)		(n = 208)	
Axis IV diagnosis	2.91	.91	2.99	.99	3.00	.91	2.96	.90	2.94	.91
Axis V - Current Level of Functioning	60.56	9.76	59.63	11.36	59.90	10.32	60.23	9.85	60.26	9.77
Number of Arrests	1.31	3.42	1.05	2.13	1.28	2.54	1.31	3.49	1.40	3.66
Mental Status	(n = 246)		(n = 149)		(n = 187)		(n = 221)		(n = 208)	
Anxiety During Interview	2.47	.72	2.49	.75	2.50	.72	2.46	.71	2.49	.72
Depression During Interview	2.43	.70	2.44	.77	2.40	.72	2.45	.71	2.48	.72
Activity Level During Interview	3.02	.44	3.01	.51	3.00	.48	3.00	.46	3.02	.45
Speech During Interview	2.95	.38	2.99	.39	2.96	.39	2.94	.40	2.96	.37
SCL-90-R Scales	(n = 241)		(n = 145)		(n = 184)		(n = 217)		(n = 203)	
Somatization	1.22	.80	1.13	.79	1.38	.82	1.28	.81	1.23	.80
Obsessive-Compulsive	1.67	.80	1.60	.83	1.68	.89	1.73	.80	1.70	.81
Interpersonal Sensitivity	1.59	.87	1.49	.91	1.60	.91	1.59	.89	1.68	.84
Depression	2.00	.78	1.89	.88	2.00	.86	2.02	.80	2.09	.77
Anxiety	1.49	.85	1.42	.87	1.58	.90	1.55	.88	1.55	.87
Hostility	1.49	1.06	1.11	.92	1.48	1.06	1.52	1.04	1.56	1.04
Phobic Anxiety	.77	.73	.78	.71	.82	.74	.79	.75	.77	.71
Paranoid Ideation	1.54	.90	1.35	.89	1.56	.93	1.55	.91	1.61	.89
Psychoticism	1.13	.71	1.05	.73	1.17	.78	1.16	.71	1.20	.70
Initial SCL-90 Analogue	(n = 155)		(n = 93)		(n = 120)		(n = 132)		(n = 132)	
Somatization	2.66	2.94	2.75	3.07	2.96	3.08	2.76	2.93	2.50	2.83
Obsessive-Compulsive	3.50	2.83	3.61	2.65	3.41	2.76	3.44	2.80	3.52	2.77
Interpersonal Sensitivity	4.94	2.45	4.97	2.50	4.79	2.55	4.83	2.46	5.08	2.43
Depression	4.93	2.66	4.83	2.67	4.63	2.68	4.87	2.70	4.97	2.65
Anxiety	4.86	2.68	5.00	2.68	4.69	2.61	4.73	2.70	4.82	2.71
Hostility	3.46	2.83	3.30	2.74	3.62	2.86	3.38	2.77	3.55	2.90
Phobic Anxiety	1.46	2.21	1.80	2.47	1.48	2.25	1.40	2.14	1.48	2.20
Paranoid Ideation	1.43	2.10	1.70	2.28	1.39	1.93	1.24	1.89	1.34	1.96
Psychoticism	.69	1.47	.89	1.62	.62	1.48	.62	1.42	.57	1.35

Table L-2b. Means and standard deviations for continuous extra-test characteristics (men): High scores on Harris-Lingoes subscales *(continued)*

Extra-test Characteristics	Harris-Lingoes Subscales									
	D_1		D_2		D_3		D_4		D_5	
	Mean	SD	Mean	SD	Mean	SD	Mean	SD	Mean	SD
Patient Description Form Scales	(n = 157)		(n = 95)		(n = 123)		(n = 135)		(n = 133)	
Angry Resentment	2.88	.95	2.79	.96	2.97	.92	2.86	.94	2.93	.93
Critical/Argumentative	2.60	.95	2.55	.97	2.64	.91	2.56	.95	2.62	.95
Narcissistic	2.34	.93	2.27	.87	2.36	.88	2.36	.96	2.34	.96
Defensive	2.61	.89	2.58	.92	2.65	.85	2.61	.92	2.61	.90
Histrionic	2.43	.76	2.31	.76	2.47	.76	2.42	.76	2.46	.79
Aggressive	2.18	.91	2.00	.86	2.28	.90	2.15	.88	2.18	.90
Insecure	3.02	.77	3.00	.78	2.97	.77	3.02	.76	3.06	.79
Anxious	3.01	.77	2.94	.77	2.99	.79	3.02	.78	3.03	.79
Pessimistic	2.52	.97	2.46	.99	2.52	.90	2.50	.98	2.53	.98
Depressed	2.60	.75	2.52	.77	2.56	.79	2.61	.75	2.63	.77
Achievement-Oriented	2.54	.72	2.52	.65	2.59	.74	2.54	.70	2.53	.74
Passive-Submissive	2.22	.83	2.29	.74	2.23	.84	2.26	.82	2.22	.83
Introverted	2.66	1.01	2.73	.99	2.55	1.02	2.67	1.01	2.63	1.03
Emotionally Controlled	2.45	1.05	2.54	1.07	2.39	1.02	2.53	1.09	2.40	1.08
Antisocial	2.28	.98	2.15	.94	2.26	.91	2.31	.96	2.30	1.00
Negative Treatment Attitudes	2.03	.81	2.03	.85	2.00	.77	2.05	.83	2.01	.82
Somatic Symptoms	2.22	1.10	2.32	1.16	2.33	1.15	2.27	1.07	2.13	1.05
Psychotic Symptoms	1.31	.48	1.35	.52	1.29	.44	1.29	.44	1.27	.44
Family Problems	2.82	1.13	2.71	1.18	2.80	1.18	2.79	1.15	2.83	1.16
Obsessive-Compulsive	2.86	.79	2.87	.81	2.79	.81	2.86	.79	2.86	.81
Stereotypic Masculine Interests	2.74	1.14	2.74	1.12	2.88	1.14	2.77	1.14	2.78	1.13
Procrastinates	2.34	.93	2.40	.89	2.33	.94	2.38	.97	2.31	.94
Suspicious	2.65	1.01	2.64	1.04	2.63	.99	2.62	1.01	2.66	1.03
Agitated	2.23	.79	2.17	.85	2.23	.77	2.20	.76	2.23	.80
Work Problems	2.07	.96	2.03	1.04	2.01	.89	2.03	.96	2.06	.99
Patient Description Form Items	(n = 157)		(n = 95)		(n = 123)		(n = 135)		(n = 133)	
Anxious	3.55	.85	3.45	.87	3.45	.93	3.54	.84	3.56	.86
Problems with Authority Figures	3.01	1.26	2.88	1.24	3.10	1.17	3.05	1.23	3.01	1.30
Has Insight Into Own Problems	2.59	.83	2.67	.87	2.56	.88	2.63	.84	2.59	.83
Fears Losing Control	3.31	1.01	3.28	1.11	3.32	1.06	3.36	1.05	3.32	1.08
Extroverted	2.26	.91	2.31	.92	2.46	.99	2.27	.93	2.33	.94
Uses Repression	2.62	1.06	2.68	.99	2.63	1.03	2.71	1.06	2.59	1.09

Submissive	2.17	.89	2.21	.86	2.23	.92	2.24	.91	2.19	.93
Difficulty Concentrating	2.82	1.11	2.76	1.13	2.87	1.10	2.87	1.11	2.82	1.14
Rigid	2.82	1.07	2.86	1.07	2.89	1.01	2.83	1.07	2.86	1.09
Overly Compliant	1.95	.91	1.90	.89	1.98	.90	1.98	.90	1.96	.90
Whiny	1.99	1.07	1.85	.99	2.05	1.07	1.98	1.01	2.05	1.10
Feels Overwhelmed	3.42	1.09	3.22	1.19	3.42	1.12	3.44	1.11	3.43	1.11
Manipulative	2.48	1.21	2.33	1.09	2.47	1.11	2.52	1.21	2.49	1.21
Difficulty Trusting Others	3.35	1.24	3.31	1.22	3.37	1.23	3.36	1.27	3.30	1.26
Insensitive to Others	2.26	1.04	2.23	1.08	2.21	1.05	2.24	1.06	2.30	1.10
Stereotypic Masculine Behavior	2.73	1.18	2.76	1.17	2.84	1.17	2.77	1.19	2.77	1.16
Harbors Grudges	2.80	1.16	2.71	1.11	2.90	1.09	2.83	1.16	2.85	1.16
Evasive	2.32	1.14	2.34	1.21	2.37	1.09	2.36	1.20	2.32	1.18
Disoriented	1.31	.63	1.35	.65	1.29	.57	1.30	.63	1.30	.64
Energetic	2.32	.86	2.31	.84	2.44	.96	2.32	.85	2.32	.88
Lonely	3.02	1.26	3.02	1.12	2.98	1.21	3.07	1.24	3.04	1.26
Family Lacks Love	2.80	1.30	2.76	1.33	2.74	1.30	2.83	1.31	2.79	1.35
Worrier	3.38	1.04	3.21	1.01	3.34	1.08	3.41	1.05	3.42	1.06
Narcissistic	2.54	1.20	2.46	1.14	2.56	1.20	2.53	1.21	2.52	1.23
Tearful	1.56	.82	1.47	.77	1.57	.89	1.56	.82	1.61	.85
Provocative	1.69	.90	1.68	1.02	1.70	.92	1.72	.89	1.71	.97
Moralistic	2.52	1.09	2.47	1.10	2.59	1.06	2.43	1.07	2.47	1.09
Socially Awkward	2.88	1.16	2.85	1.12	2.77	1.15	2.85	1.14	2.86	1.18
Hostile	2.56	1.19	2.45	1.14	2.61	1.20	2.54	1.16	2.63	1.22
Overcontrolled	2.69	1.22	2.87	1.23	2.62	1.27	2.76	1.24	2.62	1.21
Resistant to Interpretations	2.21	1.02	2.24	1.03	2.27	.97	2.22	1.03	2.18	1.02
Antisocial Behavior	2.26	1.28	2.09	1.08	2.24	1.21	2.31	1.28	2.27	1.30
Sarcastic	2.08	1.08	2.10	1.07	2.14	1.10	2.06	1.10	2.09	1.10
Rejects Traditional Gender Role	1.69	1.08	1.63	1.02	1.67	1.14	1.73	1.12	1.71	1.11
Feels Gets Raw Deal From Life	3.07	1.18	3.06	1.20	3.15	1.17	3.05	1.20	3.15	1.18
Acute Psychological Turmoil	3.15	1.09	3.11	1.09	3.06	1.06	3.13	1.13	3.16	1.11
Does Not Complete Projects	2.37	1.14	2.30	1.11	2.37	1.14	2.42	1.13	2.32	1.16
Uncomfortable with Opposite Sex	2.20	1.10	2.10	.98	2.10	1.08	2.18	1.10	2.21	1.10
Preoccupied with Health Problems	2.33	1.41	2.47	1.50	2.55	1.48	2.43	1.41	2.27	1.40
Work-Oriented	2.90	1.10	2.90	1.02	2.93	1.07	2.91	1.06	2.83	1.07
Resents Family Members	2.80	1.30	2.79	1.33	2.77	1.32	2.80	1.32	2.84	1.33
Demanding of Attention	2.51	1.12	2.45	1.06	2.61	1.10	2.50	1.09	2.55	1.18
Passive	2.40	.99	2.47	.89	2.38	1.01	2.49	.99	2.43	.99
Self-Punishing	2.51	1.17	2.52	1.03	2.45	1.21	2.53	1.18	2.53	1.22
Needs to Achieve	2.76	1.02	2.77	.93	2.83	1.04	2.75	1.03	2.76	1.03
Needs to Be with Others	2.89	1.05	2.74	.99	3.00	.99	2.95	1.07	2.92	1.11
Irritable	2.79	1.05	2.74	1.06	2.83	1.04	2.77	1.03	2.83	1.03
Self-Defeating	3.23	1.19	3.18	1.13	3.13	1.19	3.30	1.20	3.28	1.19

Table L-2b. Means and standard deviations for continuous extra-test characteristics (men): High scores on Harris-Lingoes subscales *(continued)*

Extra-test Characteristics	Harris-Lingoes Subscales									
	D_1		D_2		D_3		D_4		D_5	
	Mean	SD	Mean	SD	Mean	SD	Mean	SD	Mean	SD
Delusional Thinking	1.32	.74	1.40	.77	1.29	.71	1.28	.67	1.27	.67
Self-Reliant	2.62	.88	2.59	.84	2.72	.95	2.61	.86	2.59	.90
Aggressive	2.42	1.03	2.34	1.06	2.55	1.04	2.39	1.01	2.43	1.05
Competitive	2.41	.98	2.41	1.05	2.46	1.00	2.42	1.02	2.38	1.00
Suspicious	2.60	1.18	2.64	1.21	2.64	1.21	2.57	1.20	2.66	1.22
Compulsive	2.62	1.12	2.73	1.10	2.53	1.11	2.61	1.11	2.57	1.13
Dependable	2.96	.93	3.05	.95	3.03	.94	2.98	.94	3.01	.95
Multiple Somatic Complaints	2.15	1.33	2.29	1.41	2.33	1.41	2.22	1.33	2.05	1.30
Complains of Lack of Time	1.97	1.10	2.00	1.05	1.98	1.13	2.01	1.13	1.97	1.09
Poor Work Performance	2.14	1.15	1.97	1.12	2.12	1.14	2.10	1.17	2.13	1.16
Insecure	3.49	.94	3.46	.93	3.37	.98	3.49	.91	3.54	.91
Discusses Problems Openly	3.00	.85	3.02	.99	2.97	.84	3.04	.85	3.08	.88
Sexually Adjusted	2.38	.83	2.37	.76	2.38	.81	2.36	.81	2.36	.82
Exaggerated Need for Affection	2.31	1.09	2.26	1.01	2.32	1.07	2.34	1.10	2.37	1.11
Resentful	3.08	1.15	3.07	1.18	3.18	1.14	3.09	1.16	3.11	1.15
Uses Denial	2.74	1.22	2.88	1.18	2.79	1.17	2.73	1.23	2.72	1.25
Hypochondriacal	1.78	.96	1.84	1.02	1.84	1.03	1.80	.95	1.71	.90
Communicates Effectively	3.06	.75	3.07	.75	3.08	.81	3.09	.75	3.09	.79
Has Many Nightmares	1.74	1.01	1.61	1.01	1.75	1.06	1.81	1.08	1.79	1.06
Stormy Interpersonal Relationships	3.05	1.24	2.97	1.20	3.18	1.22	3.11	1.24	3.12	1.24
Feigns Remorse When in Trouble	1.77	.98	1.70	.91	1.77	.90	1.80	.99	1.76	.99
Stereotypic Masculine Interests	2.74	1.18	2.73	1.17	2.90	1.21	2.77	1.19	2.78	1.17
Guarded	2.78	1.31	2.71	1.37	2.88	1.31	2.81	1.36	2.74	1.33
Feels Inferior	3.14	1.02	3.03	.98	3.13	1.01	3.12	1.02	3.15	1.03
Low Frustration Tolerance	3.18	1.17	3.01	1.16	3.25	1.18	3.22	1.11	3.27	1.12
Psychotic Symptoms	1.21	.56	1.31	.69	1.19	.53	1.18	.51	1.16	.44
Fired From Past Jobs	2.09	1.16	2.07	1.22	2.05	1.10	2.10	1.17	2.10	1.21
Needs Attention	2.89	.99	2.78	.96	2.98	1.01	2.91	1.00	2.92	1.00
Acts Out	2.51	1.24	2.20	1.04	2.49	1.20	2.52	1.20	2.56	1.24
Histrionic	1.95	1.00	1.89	.92	1.97	1.02	2.00	1.00	1.95	1.02
Self-Indulgent	2.50	1.12	2.43	1.09	2.57	1.07	2.60	1.13	2.50	1.19
Depressed	3.40	1.00	3.34	1.02	3.34	1.07	3.43	.99	3.46	.99
Grandiose	1.98	1.08	2.00	1.09	1.98	1.09	1.99	1.10	1.92	1.11
Cynical	2.63	1.26	2.56	1.26	2.64	1.25	2.60	1.31	2.67	1.28
Sociopathic	1.70	.93	1.67	.90	1.67	.92	1.71	.93	1.69	.96

Agitated	2.53	1.09	2.39	1.10	2.57	1.09	2.51	1.04	2.53	1.08
Marital Problems	2.65	1.59	2.53	1.55	2.69	1.63	2.63	1.59	2.60	1.59
Absence of Deep Emotions	2.08	1.24	2.12	1.28	2.00	1.20	2.17	1.29	2.05	1.29
Uncomfortable Dealing with Emotions	3.01	1.30	3.03	1.31	3.01	1.30	3.04	1.33	2.95	1.34
Sad	3.05	.98	2.97	.96	3.08	1.00	3.06	.99	3.06	1.01
Self-Degrading	2.32	1.05	2.27	1.04	2.24	1.03	2.32	1.01	2.34	1.08
Unable to Express Negative Feelings	2.19	1.14	2.19	1.17	2.18	1.15	2.27	1.19	2.14	1.16
Concrete in Thinking	2.21	1.02	2.16	.98	2.26	1.03	2.32	1.02	2.20	1.05
Unable to See Own Limitations	2.35	1.14	2.25	1.11	2.40	1.14	2.32	1.14	2.37	1.16
Power-Oriented	2.22	1.13	2.11	1.09	2.26	1.08	2.20	1.09	2.23	1.13
Grouchy	2.42	1.10	2.35	1.10	2.51	1.09	2.40	1.08	2.45	1.10
Overbearing in Relationships	2.32	1.09	2.29	1.12	2.50	1.08	2.33	1.11	2.36	1.12
Uncertain About Career	3.52	1.18	3.53	1.21	3.45	1.29	3.57	1.21	3.54	1.23
Likable	3.11	.82	3.20	.77	3.20	.81	3.16	.79	3.17	.84
Procrastinator	2.59	1.15	2.76	1.12	2.53	1.16	2.63	1.16	2.56	1.17
Negative Feelings Toward Opposite Sex	2.15	1.19	2.11	1.15	2.11	1.13	2.17	1.17	2.20	1.20
Defensive	2.75	1.21	2.67	1.23	2.73	1.20	2.70	1.23	2.75	1.21
Empathetic	2.32	.77	2.29	.73	2.33	.74	2.33	.76	2.31	.80
Perfectionistic	2.58	1.16	2.55	1.19	2.52	1.15	2.59	1.15	2.54	1.18
Judgmental	2.78	1.13	2.74	1.10	2.82	1.08	2.75	1.14	2.82	1.15
Copes Well with Stress	1.96	.66	1.98	.70	2.01	.68	1.97	.66	1.92	.63
Moody	2.83	1.00	2.74	1.00	2.81	1.01	2.83	1.00	2.87	1.01
Selfish	2.26	1.02	2.21	.94	2.26	.96	2.25	1.04	2.26	1.05
Gives Up Easily	2.30	.99	2.31	1.06	2.26	.97	2.37	1.02	2.35	.99
Physical Symptoms in Response to Stress	2.32	1.25	2.37	1.21	2.45	1.27	2.37	1.22	2.24	1.22
Blames Family For Difficulties	2.54	1.31	2.37	1.33	2.54	1.37	2.47	1.29	2.55	1.32
Bored	2.51	1.15	2.61	1.17	2.54	1.12	2.56	1.16	2.47	1.19
Idealistic	2.36	1.05	2.35	1.05	2.45	1.08	2.34	1.05	2.35	1.07
Difficulty Establishing Therapeutic Rapport	2.04	1.06	2.01	1.07	2.00	1.00	2.08	1.08	2.06	1.08
Daydreams	1.91	1.01	2.05	.98	1.87	.99	1.94	1.03	1.91	1.02
Concerned About Status	2.47	1.12	2.44	1.07	2.46	1.18	2.42	1.14	2.46	1.16
Creates Good First Impression	2.49	.93	2.52	.86	2.55	.88	2.53	.90	2.50	.94
Complains of Sleep Disturbance	2.72	1.25	2.62	1.31	2.74	1.24	2.73	1.28	2.72	1.30
Has Temper Tantrums	2.37	1.19	2.10	1.12	2.37	1.22	2.35	1.16	2.37	1.18
Overreactive	2.76	1.10	2.61	1.12	2.77	1.12	2.74	1.06	2.79	1.11
High Aspirations	2.53	1.15	2.48	1.14	2.55	1.14	2.51	1.11	2.49	1.15
Feels Hopeless	2.88	1.11	2.85	1.18	2.84	1.15	2.90	1.13	2.91	1.15
Keeps Others at a Distance	3.06	1.25	3.04	1.23	3.02	1.26	3.07	1.29	3.01	1.30
Argumentative	2.38	1.09	2.29	1.10	2.40	1.05	2.34	1.06	2.42	1.10
Paranoid Features	1.99	1.09	1.99	1.22	1.87	1.02	1.93	1.06	1.98	1.10
Restless	2.71	1.12	2.67	1.13	2.72	1.15	2.67	1.14	2.70	1.14
Pessimistic	3.04	1.11	3.02	1.15	3.05	1.03	3.01	1.12	3.07	1.12

Table L-2b. Means and standard deviations for continuous extra-test characteristics (men): High scores on Harris-Lingoes subscales *(continued)*

Extra-test	Harris-Lingoes Subscales									
	D_1		D_2		D_3		D_4		D_5	
Characteristics	Mean	SD	Mean	SD	Mean	SD	Mean	SD	Mean	SD
Feels Like a Failure	3.13	1.11	3.02	1.15	3.09	1.07	3.10	1.13	3.17	1.13
Hallucinations	1.11	.41	1.13	.45	1.08	.32	1.10	.35	1.08	.30
Restricted Affect	2.33	1.27	2.48	1.32	2.16	1.20	2.43	1.33	2.25	1.31
Impatient	2.72	1.10	2.63	1.08	2.78	1.12	2.73	1.10	2.77	1.10
Assertive	2.34	.82	2.36	.80	2.46	.91	2.32	.81	2.29	.82
Modest	2.44	.82	2.45	.80	2.44	.83	2.44	.82	2.39	.84
Self-Doubting	3.13	.91	3.09	.88	3.06	.94	3.13	.92	3.16	.94
Deceptive	1.96	1.03	1.89	.95	1.96	.93	1.99	1.03	1.94	1.05
Feels That Life is a Strain	3.27	1.10	3.19	1.15	3.25	1.11	3.23	1.12	3.24	1.13
Physically Abusive	1.66	1.03	1.51	.92	1.65	1.03	1.63	.96	1.58	.97
Feels Rejected	3.20	1.25	3.19	1.24	3.22	1.24	3.22	1.21	3.27	1.27
Does Not Get Along with Coworkers	2.09	1.11	1.93	1.09	2.05	1.13	2.02	1.06	2.02	1.13
Uses Projection	2.47	1.16	2.44	1.19	2.51	1.12	2.48	1.19	2.52	1.19
Complains of Fatigue	2.60	1.37	2.72	1.41	2.64	1.42	2.64	1.38	2.55	1.38
Uses Rationalization	2.76	1.11	2.77	1.04	2.80	1.01	2.73	1.09	2.74	1.13
Critical of Others	2.67	1.15	2.62	1.14	2.76	1.12	2.63	1.13	2.70	1.18
Egocentric	2.58	1.19	2.53	1.10	2.62	1.13	2.56	1.20	2.61	1.23
Overevaluates Own Worth	2.03	1.11	1.85	1.00	2.09	1.11	2.06	1.12	2.01	1.14
Optimistic	1.92	.68	1.95	.71	2.02	.75	1.93	.68	1.88	.69
Psychologically Immature	2.86	1.16	2.74	1.10	2.87	1.15	2.86	1.16	2.86	1.18
Poor Judgment	2.91	1.18	2.77	1.19	2.93	1.17	2.92	1.17	2.92	1.22
Low Sex Drive	1.90	1.16	2.00	1.16	1.84	1.14	1.84	1.16	1.84	1.14
Feels Mistreated	3.06	1.15	2.92	1.15	3.16	1.09	3.05	1.14	3.12	1.13
Overly Sensitive to Criticism	3.15	1.12	3.16	1.13	3.23	1.08	3.11	1.14	3.20	1.12
Sentimental	2.37	1.01	2.42	.92	2.47	.98	2.41	1.03	2.44	.99
Sexual Preoccupation	1.81	1.13	1.70	1.02	1.78	1.23	1.90	1.20	1.84	1.17
Accelerated Speech	1.48	.81	1.46	.88	1.43	.76	1.44	.78	1.47	.81
Concerns About Homosexuality	1.48	1.08	1.45	1.08	1.34	.89	1.51	1.14	1.45	1.06
Many Specific Fears	1.90	1.02	1.86	1.02	1.88	1.06	1.90	.99	1.93	1.05
Passive in Relationships	2.35	1.09	2.51	1.01	2.36	1.08	2.36	1.06	2.33	1.07
Negative Attitudes Toward Therapy	1.88	1.01	1.86	1.03	1.84	1.00	1.88	1.03	1.83	1.01
Guilt-Prone	2.64	1.10	2.76	1.08	2.65	1.17	2.70	1.11	2.66	1.17
Nervous	3.13	.99	3.17	.96	3.09	.98	3.13	.96	3.15	.96
Obsessive	2.85	1.13	2.82	1.14	2.83	1.14	2.89	1.12	2.92	1.16
Shy	2.48	1.20	2.60	1.18	2.41	1.24	2.51	1.23	2.44	1.21

Uses Intellectualization	2.58	1.22	2.71	1.21	2.62	1.28	2.61	1.26	2.55	1.25
Has Many Interests	2.27	.97	2.26	.88	2.24	.93	2.27	.95	2.30	1.02
Difficulty Making Decisions	3.01	1.03	3.01	1.05	2.95	1.12	3.05	.99	3.01	1.04
Indirect Expression of Hostility	2.79	1.13	2.86	1.22	2.80	1.10	2.82	1.16	2.74	1.13
Poor Reality Testing	1.68	.86	1.67	.91	1.67	.82	1.67	.84	1.64	.86
Angry	3.14	1.16	3.07	1.11	3.29	1.12	3.13	1.14	3.17	1.16
Eccentric	1.95	1.23	1.96	1.23	1.91	1.25	1.92	1.23	1.92	1.23
Emotional Lability	2.32	1.08	2.18	1.03	2.33	1.09	2.28	1.09	2.39	1.11
Dislikes Change	2.72	.98	2.78	1.00	2.70	.92	2.72	1.03	2.72	1.03
Believes Cannot Be Helped	1.97	1.05	1.86	1.05	1.96	1.01	1.97	1.05	1.96	1.05
Reliable Informant	3.17	.91	3.16	.92	3.20	.95	3.19	.90	3.23	.90
Ignores Problems	2.30	1.03	2.32	1.07	2.31	1.01	2.39	1.09	2.26	1.05
Ruminates	3.24	1.02	3.20	1.02	3.15	1.07	3.24	1.04	3.30	1.00
Excitable	2.55	1.01	2.41	1.00	2.65	1.04	2.51	.99	2.56	1.03
Conforming	2.37	.90	2.50	.85	2.40	.90	2.39	.87	2.37	.90
Ineffective at Dealing with Problems	3.10	1.06	2.99	1.08	3.10	1.08	3.10	1.05	3.08	1.06
Introverted	2.64	1.13	2.74	1.12	2.48	1.13	2.66	1.13	2.61	1.16
Superficial Relationships	2.64	1.16	2.65	1.23	2.68	1.21	2.65	1.18	2.61	1.19
Impulsive	2.66	1.22	2.52	1.22	2.70	1.21	2.70	1.20	2.67	1.27
Stereotypic Feminine Behavior	1.34	.68	1.38	.76	1.35	.70	1.35	.69	1.35	.69
Stubborn	2.83	1.10	2.86	1.13	2.94	1.06	2.80	1.13	2.85	1.14
Hostile Toward Therapist	1.49	.73	1.54	.86	1.47	.75	1.48	.75	1.47	.74
Difficult to Motivate	2.26	1.03	2.23	1.07	2.20	1.00	2.27	1.07	2.27	1.05
Suicidal Ideations	1.86	1.03	1.75	1.00	1.81	1.01	1.88	1.02	1.93	1.04
Familial Discord	3.06	1.39	2.92	1.39	3.07	1.40	3.01	1.40	3.07	1.40
Dogmatic	2.30	1.10	2.31	1.12	2.36	1.14	2.26	1.10	2.34	1.14

	Harris-Lingoes Subscales *(continued)*															
	Hy_2 Mean	Hy_2 SD	Hy_3 Mean	Hy_3 SD	Hy_4 Mean	Hy_4 SD	Pd_1 Mean	Pd_1 SD	Pd_2 Mean	Pd_2 SD	Pd_4 Mean	Pd_4 SD	Pd_5 Mean	Pd_5 SD	Pa_1 Mean	Pa_1 SD
Intake Information	(n = 19)		(n = 261)		(n = 171)		(n = 219)		(n = 100)		(n = 222)		(n = 227)		(n = 189)	
Axis IV diagnosis	2.63	.83	2.95	.92	3.02	.98	2.89	.90	2.82	.84	2.89	.90	2.96	.86	2.96	.92
Axis V - Current Level of Functioning	68.32	9.05	60.51	9.61	60.20	10.32	61.73	9.50	63.30	8.60	61.95	9.12	60.71	9.35	60.59	9.50
Number of Arrests	1.32	1.97	1.45	3.55	1.13	2.09	1.50	3.68	2.55	3.87	1.29	3.31	1.41	3.55	1.54	3.73
Mental Status	(n = 19)		(n = 261)		(n = 171)		(n = 219)		(n = 100)		(n = 222)		(n = 227)		(n = 189)	
Anxiety During Interview	2.26	.73	2.45	.70	2.45	.69	2.42	.70	2.33	.71	2.47	.73	2.47	.73	2.47	.71
Depression During Interview	2.11	.74	2.43	.69	2.45	.71	2.32	.68	2.16	.62	2.38	.71	2.44	.69	2.40	.72
Activity Level During Interview	3.00	.00	3.00	.45	2.96	.47	3.02	.41	2.96	.45	3.01	.44	3.01	.44	2.96	.47
Speech During Interview	3.05	.23	2.96	.36	2.94	.37	2.97	.39	2.97	.39	2.94	.41	2.96	.36	2.91	.45
SCL-90-R Scales	(n = 19)		(n = 256)		(n = 167)		(n = 216)		(n = 99)		(n = 217)		(n = 222)		(n = 184)	
Somatization	.39	.36	1.22	.79	1.55	.74	1.07	.77	.83	.75	1.15	.78	1.18	.79	1.25	.83
Obsessive-Compulsive	.59	.50	1.62	.81	1.80	.85	1.47	.86	1.09	.76	1.61	.83	1.63	.81	1.66	.86
Interpersonal Sensitivity	.43	.41	1.55	.88	1.67	.89	1.46	.88	1.01	.76	1.62	.85	1.56	.85	1.67	.89
Depression	.79	.70	1.95	.80	2.04	.85	1.77	.89	1.29	.89	1.94	.86	1.99	.80	1.93	.90
Anxiety	.46	.37	1.47	.86	1.69	.89	1.34	.91	.94	.77	1.42	.89	1.48	.87	1.50	.96
Hostility	.22	.28	1.46	1.05	1.49	1.02	1.45	1.05	1.22	1.08	1.48	1.04	1.48	1.04	1.60	1.05
Phobic Anxiety	.17	.31	.75	.72	.88	.76	.65	.68	.43	.57	.70	.68	.74	.72	.82	.78
Paranoid Ideation	.38	.55	1.51	.92	1.60	.88	1.49	.91	1.20	.82	1.66	.85	1.53	.88	1.82	.83
Psychoticism	.21	.39	1.12	.71	1.23	.74	1.02	.71	.70	.63	1.12	.72	1.15	.71	1.20	.77
Initial SCL-90 Analogue	(n = 16)		(n = 160)		(n = 107)		(n = 140)		(n = 66)		(n = 142)		(n = 138)		(n = 115)	
Somatization	1.00	1.21	2.80	2.99	3.26	3.09	2.07	2.46	1.20	1.84	2.22	2.68	2.55	2.89	2.26	2.65
Obsessive-Compulsive	3.50	3.01	3.62	2.82	3.64	2.76	3.31	2.68	2.85	2.58	3.21	2.77	3.56	2.77	3.19	2.53
Interpersonal Sensitivity	4.63	2.22	4.83	2.52	4.78	2.50	4.72	2.45	4.59	2.45	4.82	2.41	4.84	2.37	4.79	2.37
Depression	3.81	2.59	4.80	2.68	4.91	2.55	4.24	2.60	3.45	2.52	4.52	2.60	4.73	2.73	4.47	2.54
Anxiety	4.38	2.92	4.70	2.71	4.99	2.57	4.38	2.73	3.54	2.62	4.44	2.74	4.64	2.73	4.50	2.67
Hostility	2.38	2.90	3.41	2.80	3.35	2.78	3.24	2.75	3.85	2.91	3.39	2.85	3.53	2.86	3.59	3.01
Phobic Anxiety	.69	1.08	1.56	2.33	1.66	2.43	1.29	2.06	1.09	1.56	1.29	2.07	1.59	2.38	1.37	2.20
Paranoid Ideation	.94	2.29	1.39	2.02	1.38	1.79	1.23	1.80	1.37	1.63	1.36	2.05	1.43	2.16	1.40	2.13
Psychoticism	.69	1.40	.66	1.46	.55	1.34	.57	1.30	.71	1.20	.54	1.21	.69	1.55	.61	1.41
Patient Description Form Scales	(n = 16)		(n = 163)		(n = 109)		(n = 143)		(n = 68)		(n = 143)		(n = 140)		(n = 116)	
Angry Resentment	2.41	.88	2.89	.96	2.91	.92	2.83	.90	2.95	.84	2.86	.93	2.87	.99	2.88	.91
Critical/Argumentative	2.30	.79	2.60	.95	2.58	.92	2.53	.89	2.59	.79	2.56	.94	2.58	.96	2.52	.92
Narcissistic	2.42	.90	2.37	.96	2.33	.92	2.39	.92	2.63	.82	2.31	.89	2.31	.90	2.31	.90

Defensive	2.28	.73	2.64	.90	2.60	.85	2.59	.85	2.70	.77	2.60	.87	2.60	.89	2.60	.87
Histrionic	2.27	.75	2.47	.77	2.41	.77	2.45	.77	2.47	.74	2.40	.78	2.44	.76	2.41	.76
Aggressive	2.00	.76	2.20	.88	2.16	.80	2.25	.89	2.60	.97	2.16	.90	2.18	.90	2.23	.95
Insecure	2.74	1.02	3.00	.79	2.93	.71	2.96	.78	2.78	.79	2.98	.76	3.03	.81	2.99	.71
Anxious	2.69	.77	3.00	.78	3.08	.75	2.90	.79	2.62	.79	2.84	.79	3.00	.79	2.91	.78
Pessimistic	1.94	.81	2.49	.95	2.48	.89	2.35	.91	2.24	.87	2.37	.95	2.51	1.01	2.38	.88
Depressed	2.03	.80	2.56	.75	2.58	.71	2.39	.76	2.14	.84	2.46	.77	2.57	.82	2.46	.75
Achievement-Oriented	3.18	.63	2.56	.73	2.53	.79	2.63	.72	2.73	.68	2.56	.72	2.56	.71	2.53	.72
Passive-Submissive	2.13	.84	2.23	.80	2.28	.75	2.20	.80	1.93	.84	2.17	.85	2.23	.82	2.17	.84
Introverted	2.23	1.09	2.62	1.01	2.60	.97	2.57	1.02	2.50	.94	2.65	1.00	2.65	.99	2.61	.97
Emotionally Controlled	2.31	.92	2.48	1.04	2.41	1.00	2.41	.98	2.45	.99	2.34	1.00	2.44	1.06	2.29	1.01
Antisocial	2.04	.71	2.26	.95	2.21	.91	2.34	.90	2.84	.84	2.29	.96	2.32	.96	2.38	.97
Negative Treatment Attitudes	1.82	.73	2.03	.82	2.02	.80	1.95	.74	2.04	.72	1.97	.79	1.97	.82	1.93	.79
Somatic Symptoms	1.34	.29	2.25	1.11	2.45	1.16	1.98	.97	1.68	.69	2.04	1.05	2.17	1.08	2.01	1.02
Psychotic Symptoms	1.16	.34	1.30	.47	1.27	.41	1.30	.50	1.34	.45	1.27	.46	1.32	.49	1.31	.50
Family Problems	2.41	1.20	2.80	1.13	2.76	1.17	2.91	1.13	2.92	1.14	2.88	1.13	2.83	1.17	2.89	1.14
Obsessive-Compulsive	2.85	.72	2.88	.77	2.85	.78	2.84	.76	2.62	.74	2.81	.82	2.86	.81	2.80	.79
Stereotypic Masculine Interests	2.81	1.17	2.81	1.13	2.87	1.11	2.73	1.08	3.11	1.18	2.75	1.13	2.89	1.12	2.87	1.08
Procrastinates	2.19	.94	2.34	.92	2.37	.98	2.26	.90	2.21	.83	2.23	.94	2.31	.93	2.21	.92
Suspicious	2.00	.95	2.64	1.02	2.62	.94	2.57	.89	2.73	.89	2.64	.99	2.69	1.01	2.62	.98
Agitated	1.96	.96	2.25	.78	2.30	.75	2.22	.75	2.26	.75	2.17	.82	2.26	.81	2.22	.76
Work Problems	1.73	1.30	2.05	.95	2.00	.86	2.13	.96	2.15	.95	2.12	.95	2.03	.93	2.13	.94
Patient Description Form Items	(n = 16)		(n = 163)		(n = 109)		(n = 143)		(n = 68)		(n = 143)		(n = 140)		(n = 116)	
Anxious	3.06	1.18	3.50	.88	3.58	.84	3.38	.91	3.01	.89	3.34	.89	3.46	.88	3.41	.81
Problems with Authority Figures	2.71	1.14	3.04	1.24	3.00	1.17	3.11	1.18	3.34	1.09	3.03	1.22	3.05	1.27	3.09	1.22
Has Insight Into Own Problems	2.81	.98	2.59	.88	2.58	.80	2.58	.92	2.63	.93	2.55	.85	2.63	.90	2.53	.81
Fears Losing Control	3.40	1.06	3.33	1.05	3.42	1.06	3.27	1.06	3.10	1.12	3.18	1.03	3.30	1.05	3.18	1.04
Extroverted	2.81	.75	2.36	.96	2.35	.93	2.45	.96	2.63	1.04	2.25	.94	2.33	.94	2.31	.97
Uses Repression	2.20	.86	2.65	1.05	2.70	1.00	2.64	1.00	2.61	.94	2.64	1.04	2.65	1.06	2.61	1.02
Submissive	2.19	.91	2.18	.88	2.25	.83	2.18	.87	1.94	.92	2.13	.92	2.25	.94	2.15	.95
Difficulty Concentrating	2.47	1.13	2.77	1.14	2.90	1.04	2.61	1.06	2.59	1.02	2.63	1.11	2.83	1.12	2.75	1.08
Rigid	2.63	1.15	2.86	1.07	2.83	1.05	2.74	1.05	2.72	1.02	2.82	1.06	2.77	1.07	2.83	1.07
Overly Compliant	1.94	.77	1.98	.90	2.03	.89	1.97	.89	1.66	.86	1.89	.90	1.96	.89	1.93	.90
Whiny	1.69	.87	2.03	1.07	2.06	1.04	1.99	1.06	1.69	.95	1.92	1.03	1.96	1.05	1.86	.99
Feels Overwhelmed	2.94	1.00	3.40	1.10	3.51	1.07	3.26	1.13	2.99	1.19	3.22	1.14	3.39	1.14	3.26	1.15
Manipulative	2.80	1.01	2.52	1.22	2.42	1.10	2.53	1.17	2.70	1.09	2.45	1.15	2.47	1.16	2.43	1.12
Difficulty Trusting Others	2.75	1.13	3.36	1.26	3.32	1.21	3.38	1.18	3.56	1.16	3.33	1.22	3.38	1.24	3.30	1.26
Insensitive to Others	2.12	1.09	2.29	1.09	2.29	1.10	2.30	1.05	2.54	.99	2.31	1.04	2.29	1.06	2.28	1.07
Stereotypic Masculine Behavior	2.75	1.13	2.80	1.17	2.83	1.15	2.71	1.10	3.15	1.23	2.75	1.14	2.88	1.15	2.86	1.12
Harbors Grudges	2.29	1.14	2.87	1.16	2.82	1.08	2.78	1.11	2.92	1.06	2.85	1.15	2.83	1.16	2.90	1.18
Evasive	2.00	.97	2.39	1.16	2.27	1.08	2.27	1.05	2.35	.88	2.31	1.09	2.31	1.13	2.25	1.11

Harris-Lingoes Subscales *(continued)*

	Hy_2		Hy_3		Hy_4		Pd_1		Pd_2		Pd_4		Pd_5		Pa_1	
	Mean	SD	Mean	SD	Mean	SD	Mean	SD	Mean	SD	Mean	SD	Mean	SD	Mean	SD
Disoriented	1.25	.58	1.30	.62	1.29	.57	1.26	.55	1.32	.63	1.29	.61	1.31	.62	1.23	.48
Energetic	2.81	.98	2.37	.88	2.26	.91	2.58	.93	2.72	.87	2.40	.89	2.39	.84	2.45	.94
Lonely	2.63	1.36	3.03	1.23	2.87	1.17	3.01	1.22	2.81	1.31	3.00	1.19	3.03	1.28	2.94	1.22
Family Lacks Love	2.29	1.14	2.78	1.29	2.68	1.30	2.90	1.34	2.90	1.33	2.84	1.33	2.79	1.35	2.83	1.40
Worrier	3.19	1.17	3.37	1.03	3.42	1.04	3.27	1.06	2.76	1.14	3.22	1.06	3.35	.99	3.26	1.06
Narcissistic	2.63	1.20	2.61	1.22	2.56	1.19	2.61	1.15	2.92	1.18	2.49	1.11	2.52	1.20	2.54	1.15
Tearful	1.63	.81	1.56	.83	1.61	.87	1.51	.77	1.47	.75	1.52	.80	1.54	.83	1.51	.79
Provocative	1.50	.63	1.76	.95	1.67	.86	1.78	.91	1.85	.80	1.70	.97	1.74	.97	1.74	.98
Moralistic	2.67	1.35	2.55	1.10	2.53	1.02	2.50	1.10	2.23	.96	2.54	1.14	2.53	1.07	2.55	1.04
Socially Awkward	2.44	1.26	2.83	1.14	2.76	1.08	2.83	1.17	2.74	1.06	2.87	1.15	2.86	1.13	2.86	1.10
Hostile	2.00	.97	2.57	1.18	2.57	1.21	2.53	1.16	2.79	1.20	2.49	1.22	2.55	1.26	2.53	1.22
Overcontrolled	2.87	1.25	2.72	1.20	2.75	1.24	2.62	1.20	2.60	1.16	2.55	1.18	2.63	1.22	2.50	1.19
Resistant to Interpretations	2.06	.93	2.24	1.01	2.25	1.02	2.14	.96	2.24	1.01	2.13	.99	2.17	1.04	2.07	1.03
Antisocial Behavior	2.00	1.00	2.25	1.27	2.24	1.20	2.38	1.23	2.96	1.27	2.34	1.27	2.37	1.33	2.47	1.31
Sarcastic	2.06	1.18	2.12	1.09	2.04	1.07	2.03	1.05	2.06	.95	2.07	1.05	2.09	1.09	1.96	1.05
Rejects Traditional Gender Role	1.69	1.25	1.66	1.07	1.67	1.05	1.68	1.11	1.50	.95	1.65	1.04	1.68	1.06	1.63	1.06
Feels Gets Raw Deal From Life	2.31	1.08	3.09	1.17	3.08	1.19	2.96	1.13	2.81	1.18	3.06	1.13	3.04	1.21	3.02	1.13
Acute Psychological Turmoil	2.75	.77	3.12	1.09	3.09	1.03	2.96	1.04	2.82	1.02	2.96	1.07	3.14	1.09	3.00	1.06
Does Not Complete Projects	2.00	1.35	2.36	1.13	2.24	1.10	2.27	1.08	2.28	1.06	2.24	1.13	2.36	1.15	2.22	1.14
Uncomfortable with Opposite Sex	1.75	.93	2.13	1.08	2.06	1.02	2.17	1.07	1.83	.87	2.11	1.07	2.11	1.01	2.11	1.04
Preoccupied with Health Problems	1.19	.40	2.37	1.41	2.64	1.45	2.00	1.22	1.61	.95	2.08	1.33	2.29	1.43	2.08	1.29
Work-Oriented	3.44	1.15	2.91	1.08	3.01	1.12	3.02	1.01	3.04	1.02	2.98	1.08	2.99	1.10	2.97	1.00
Resents Family Members	2.19	1.22	2.82	1.29	2.79	1.29	2.91	1.33	2.83	1.26	2.92	1.31	2.82	1.30	2.96	1.32
Demanding of Attention	2.63	1.26	2.59	1.16	2.48	1.08	2.54	1.13	2.58	1.10	2.51	1.15	2.54	1.12	2.51	1.13
Passive	1.94	.93	2.40	.96	2.47	.90	2.35	.99	2.07	1.00	2.37	1.01	2.39	.97	2.35	1.02
Self-Punishing	2.27	1.16	2.51	1.14	2.51	1.21	2.40	1.11	2.33	1.11	2.37	1.13	2.55	1.18	2.35	1.17
Needs to Achieve	3.50	.97	2.78	1.04	2.68	1.08	2.77	.98	2.87	.89	2.75	1.03	2.77	1.02	2.75	.99
Needs to Be with Others	3.25	.77	2.94	1.06	2.86	1.02	2.94	1.05	3.01	.91	2.77	1.07	2.95	1.03	2.90	1.00
Irritable	2.25	.86	2.80	1.05	2.85	1.03	2.74	1.05	2.76	.96	2.73	1.06	2.77	1.07	2.76	1.05
Self-Defeating	3.06	1.06	3.23	1.21	3.08	1.14	3.17	1.18	3.26	1.10	3.13	1.17	3.24	1.22	3.08	1.17
Delusional Thinking	1.13	.34	1.32	.73	1.26	.68	1.31	.71	1.38	.76	1.25	.67	1.28	.69	1.30	.73
Self-Reliant	3.44	1.03	2.62	.88	2.72	.94	2.64	.91	2.78	.94	2.65	.89	2.61	.90	2.63	.91
Aggressive	2.67	1.05	2.44	1.04	2.48	1.03	2.51	1.02	3.03	1.06	2.44	1.01	2.51	1.05	2.46	1.06
Competitive	3.06	1.00	2.44	1.02	2.42	1.00	2.45	.94	2.69	.94	2.43	.96	2.47	.97	2.41	.99
Suspicious	1.88	1.31	2.62	1.22	2.61	1.15	2.52	1.12	2.66	1.12	2.59	1.19	2.68	1.23	2.60	1.22
Compulsive	2.67	1.11	2.65	1.11	2.62	1.13	2.60	1.11	2.49	1.16	2.52	1.13	2.62	1.13	2.42	1.10
Dependable	3.31	.87	2.99	.96	3.08	.97	3.00	.93	2.84	.78	3.00	.99	2.96	.93	3.01	.98
Multiple Somatic Complaints	1.13	.34	2.21	1.35	2.39	1.38	1.82	1.13	1.50	.87	1.94	1.25	2.11	1.33	1.90	1.18

Complains of Lack of Time	2.06	.85	1.99	1.12	2.15	1.20	1.96	1.10	2.04	1.09	1.93	1.08	1.95	1.09	1.92	1.07
Poor Work Performance	1.80	1.14	2.12	1.17	2.09	1.16	2.17	1.15	2.27	1.15	2.16	1.15	2.12	1.16	2.11	1.17
Insecure	3.56	1.09	3.44	.95	3.38	.93	3.47	.90	3.25	1.01	3.46	.91	3.44	.97	3.52	.85
Discusses Problems Openly	3.38	1.09	3.04	.88	2.97	.82	3.09	.84	2.97	.86	3.05	.87	3.11	.90	3.01	.84
Sexually Adjusted	2.85	1.07	2.38	.82	2.36	.78	2.45	.89	2.71	.78	2.39	.82	2.38	.85	2.36	.83
Exaggerated Need for Affection	2.19	1.22	2.37	1.08	2.24	1.06	2.34	1.05	2.33	1.02	2.28	1.03	2.32	1.07	2.28	1.01
Resentful	2.69	1.01	3.13	1.16	3.12	1.11	3.11	1.14	3.21	1.07	3.11	1.12	3.08	1.17	3.15	1.13
Uses Denial	2.56	.81	2.77	1.22	2.71	1.20	2.73	1.19	2.99	1.11	2.72	1.23	2.71	1.24	2.69	1.22
Hypochondriacal	1.31	.60	1.83	1.02	1.99	1.11	1.68	.94	1.48	.71	1.65	.91	1.75	.93	1.61	.86
Communicates Effectively	3.38	1.09	3.08	.77	3.16	.75	3.07	.78	2.96	.92	2.99	.81	3.02	.77	2.97	.83
Has Many Nightmares	1.33	.52	1.73	1.01	1.72	1.07	1.69	.94	1.54	.95	1.57	.89	1.79	1.05	1.63	.92
Stormy Interpersonal Relationships	2.64	1.39	3.11	1.22	3.03	1.16	3.26	1.18	3.42	1.22	3.05	1.24	3.10	1.28	3.16	1.21
Feigns Remorse When in Trouble	1.46	.66	1.80	.97	1.72	.93	1.85	.94	2.13	.88	1.81	.99	1.80	.99	1.80	.98
Stereotypic Masculine Interests	2.88	1.26	2.82	1.18	2.90	1.17	2.74	1.14	3.07	1.20	2.75	1.19	2.88	1.19	2.88	1.14
Guarded	2.56	1.21	2.84	1.31	2.87	1.30	2.78	1.19	2.91	1.14	2.76	1.25	2.81	1.32	2.75	1.29
Feels Inferior	2.87	1.13	3.10	1.04	3.06	1.01	3.09	1.03	2.96	.97	3.16	.99	3.14	1.03	3.21	.93
Low Frustration Tolerance	2.75	.86	3.19	1.14	3.06	1.10	3.17	1.11	3.24	1.09	3.11	1.12	3.17	1.15	3.16	1.12
Psychotic Symptoms	1.19	.54	1.21	.55	1.19	.54	1.22	.63	1.19	.53	1.17	.51	1.22	.58	1.21	.60
Fired From Past Jobs	1.50	.90	2.06	1.15	2.06	1.13	2.09	1.15	2.27	1.30	2.12	1.19	2.06	1.15	2.17	1.13
Needs Attention	3.06	1.00	2.94	1.01	2.83	1.00	2.90	.99	2.99	1.02	2.86	.98	2.91	.99	2.89	.96
Acts Out	2.40	.91	2.49	1.19	2.41	1.14	2.66	1.18	2.99	1.20	2.52	1.21	2.54	1.21	2.61	1.22
Histrionic	1.94	1.06	2.01	1.03	1.97	1.01	1.99	1.05	1.86	.88	1.91	1.01	1.96	.99	1.88	1.03
Self-Indulgent	2.69	1.08	2.56	1.14	2.54	1.17	2.57	1.13	3.00	1.03	2.48	1.13	2.53	1.13	2.54	1.16
Depressed	2.63	.96	3.38	.98	3.43	.91	3.15	1.05	2.73	1.12	3.27	1.02	3.39	1.02	3.26	1.01
Grandiose	2.00	.97	2.01	1.11	1.94	1.05	1.95	1.09	2.09	1.09	1.92	1.03	1.94	1.04	1.85	1.03
Cynical	2.50	.97	2.62	1.25	2.65	1.25	2.49	1.18	2.46	1.15	2.52	1.26	2.62	1.28	2.46	1.22
Sociopathic	1.67	.98	1.69	.92	1.65	.92	1.68	.88	2.03	1.04	1.72	.93	1.71	.94	1.74	.93
Agitated	2.13	1.26	2.58	1.07	2.64	1.05	2.53	1.07	2.54	1.08	2.45	1.05	2.59	1.10	2.53	1.07
Marital Problems	2.69	1.82	2.62	1.61	2.58	1.56	2.68	1.62	2.80	1.60	2.70	1.62	2.72	1.60	2.70	1.64
Absence of Deep Emotions	1.93	1.03	2.11	1.24	1.98	1.19	2.11	1.18	2.28	1.23	1.97	1.17	2.09	1.26	1.96	1.19
Uncomfortable Dealing with Emotions	2.69	1.01	3.02	1.31	2.92	1.29	2.91	1.20	3.01	1.20	2.89	1.27	3.03	1.31	2.88	1.31
Sad	2.56	1.09	3.02	.98	3.00	.95	2.87	1.01	2.61	1.03	2.99	.96	2.97	1.01	2.96	.95
Self-Degrading	2.00	1.21	2.29	1.05	2.16	.99	2.31	1.05	2.10	1.02	2.25	1.04	2.34	1.04	2.19	1.00
Unable to Express Negative Feelings	2.12	1.36	2.25	1.17	2.19	1.06	2.19	1.08	2.16	1.09	2.12	1.08	2.21	1.15	2.03	1.05
Concrete in Thinking	1.56	.81	2.22	1.01	2.27	1.01	2.16	.96	2.28	.98	2.18	.99	2.24	.99	2.24	1.03
Unable to See Own Limitations	2.19	1.22	2.40	1.16	2.38	1.13	2.38	1.09	2.46	1.03	2.34	1.11	2.36	1.13	2.37	1.09
Power-Oriented	2.50	.97	2.29	1.12	2.20	1.13	2.32	1.09	2.70	1.04	2.16	1.09	2.24	1.09	2.22	1.11
Grouchy	1.94	1.00	2.43	1.09	2.51	1.06	2.27	1.04	2.23	.99	2.32	1.06	2.41	1.09	2.32	1.03
Overbearing in Relationships	2.31	1.20	2.40	1.11	2.32	1.04	2.38	1.13	2.60	1.20	2.26	1.11	2.29	1.14	2.30	1.15
Uncertain About Career	3.54	1.33	3.45	1.28	3.39	1.31	3.34	1.23	3.30	1.25	3.30	1.30	3.39	1.27	3.36	1.31
Likable	3.69	.70	3.15	.82	3.21	.75	3.15	.82	3.21	.71	3.14	.81	3.13	.82	3.16	.79
Procrastinator	2.50	1.26	2.59	1.14	2.55	1.15	2.51	1.13	2.37	.98	2.51	1.17	2.60	1.13	2.47	1.12

Harris-Lingoes Subscales *(continued)*

	Hy_2		Hy_3		Hy_4		Pd_1		Pd_2		Pd_4		Pd_5		Pa_1	
	Mean	SD	Mean	SD	Mean	SD	Mean	SD	Mean	SD	Mean	SD	Mean	SD	Mean	SD
Negative Feelings Toward Opposite Sex	1.81	1.11	2.17	1.18	2.09	1.10	2.17	1.12	2.14	1.12	2.16	1.18	2.16	1.16	2.13	1.13
Defensive	2.33	.98	2.78	1.20	2.75	1.16	2.67	1.13	2.77	1.09	2.76	1.18	2.72	1.22	2.68	1.22
Empathetic	2.80	1.08	2.35	.77	2.38	.82	2.34	.81	2.15	.79	2.31	.78	2.34	.79	2.32	.77
Perfectionistic	3.00	1.26	2.60	1.14	2.48	1.19	2.59	1.08	2.29	1.02	2.47	1.12	2.57	1.12	2.41	1.11
Judgmental	2.56	.96	2.82	1.14	2.68	1.06	2.70	1.08	2.63	1.04	2.72	1.17	2.74	1.14	2.63	1.19
Copes Well with Stress	2.38	.50	1.98	.68	2.00	.67	2.01	.65	2.18	.60	1.97	.65	1.99	.66	1.97	.60
Moody	2.53	.92	2.84	1.00	2.80	1.02	2.76	.95	2.63	.88	2.79	1.01	2.88	1.00	2.78	.95
Selfish	2.47	1.25	2.27	1.04	2.25	.99	2.30	1.04	2.57	.93	2.21	.98	2.21	1.00	2.16	.99
Gives Up Easily	1.62	.77	2.29	.98	2.25	1.02	2.24	.96	2.16	.95	2.27	1.02	2.33	1.04	2.28	1.01
Physical Symptoms in Response to Stress	1.15	.38	2.36	1.25	2.55	1.33	2.12	1.15	1.84	.95	2.17	1.22	2.31	1.23	2.14	1.20
Blames Family For Difficulties	2.13	1.36	2.51	1.29	2.50	1.37	2.57	1.30	2.61	1.33	2.57	1.30	2.54	1.32	2.58	1.33
Bored	1.88	.96	2.56	1.15	2.59	1.18	2.37	1.06	2.36	1.15	2.39	1.13	2.51	1.15	2.36	1.15
Idealistic	2.47	1.30	2.41	1.07	2.33	1.04	2.35	1.02	2.17	1.00	2.40	1.06	2.38	1.05	2.35	1.03
Difficulty Establishing Therapeutic Rapport	1.81	.83	2.07	1.06	2.10	1.06	2.08	.99	2.18	.98	2.04	1.07	2.05	1.07	2.02	1.09
Daydreams	1.80	.79	1.89	1.01	1.81	.94	1.85	.98	1.79	.85	1.84	1.02	1.96	1.04	1.77	.97
Concerned About Status	3.00	1.00	2.45	1.16	2.36	1.18	2.47	1.11	2.39	1.12	2.42	1.08	2.44	1.12	2.35	1.11
Creates Good First Impression	3.50	.82	2.56	.96	2.59	.92	2.55	.97	2.43	.91	2.50	.92	2.56	.89	2.46	.94
Complains of Sleep Disturbance	1.56	.73	2.68	1.23	2.76	1.23	2.38	1.21	2.10	1.26	2.43	1.26	2.66	1.27	2.50	1.27
Has Temper Tantrums	1.93	1.16	2.38	1.18	2.30	1.10	2.45	1.22	2.71	1.21	2.36	1.21	2.29	1.16	2.47	1.24
Overreactive	2.50	1.10	2.79	1.08	2.72	1.11	2.70	1.04	2.79	1.15	2.76	1.09	2.79	1.10	2.75	1.06
High Aspirations	3.07	1.16	2.52	1.16	2.44	1.18	2.58	1.12	2.50	1.04	2.51	1.12	2.49	1.08	2.43	1.09
Feels Hopeless	2.20	1.08	2.82	1.13	2.77	1.09	2.62	1.14	2.34	1.05	2.69	1.14	2.86	1.19	2.71	1.11
Keeps Others at a Distance	2.63	.96	3.06	1.25	3.01	1.26	3.04	1.18	3.14	1.18	3.03	1.23	3.01	1.25	2.91	1.26
Argumentative	2.00	1.10	2.39	1.07	2.33	1.02	2.36	1.09	2.45	1.05	2.38	1.13	2.35	1.12	2.37	1.13
Paranoid Features	1.38	.81	1.94	1.07	1.90	.99	1.82	.95	1.96	1.02	1.97	1.09	1.99	1.12	1.93	1.05
Restless	2.13	1.15	2.72	1.15	2.84	1.15	2.62	1.08	2.78	1.07	2.61	1.12	2.73	1.12	2.71	1.08
Pessimistic	2.50	1.10	3.01	1.08	3.03	1.05	2.82	1.08	2.56	1.03	2.85	1.10	3.01	1.15	2.90	1.01
Feels Like a Failure	2.47	1.25	3.08	1.11	3.03	1.08	2.90	1.07	2.82	1.01	3.04	1.08	3.14	1.15	3.09	1.06
Hallucinations	1.06	.25	1.10	.39	1.07	.32	1.13	.47	1.12	.45	1.10	.40	1.12	.38	1.13	.47
Restricted Affect	1.94	1.12	2.34	1.25	2.23	1.16	2.20	1.20	2.16	1.15	2.20	1.27	2.27	1.30	2.10	1.27
Impatient	2.88	1.02	2.80	1.12	2.73	1.16	2.78	1.06	2.82	.94	2.70	1.07	2.70	1.08	2.69	1.10
Assertive	2.73	.88	2.38	.84	2.39	.90	2.34	.84	2.43	.74	2.27	.79	2.33	.81	2.22	.78
Modest	2.25	.86	2.45	.83	2.47	.77	2.43	.89	2.29	.86	2.40	.85	2.45	.83	2.36	.86
Self-Doubting	2.81	1.22	3.09	.93	3.06	.86	3.06	.93	2.87	1.03	3.09	.89	3.19	.93	3.12	.86
Deceptive	2.00	1.07	1.99	1.00	1.94	.97	2.04	1.02	2.15	.97	1.96	1.02	1.99	1.07	1.93	1.04
Feels That Life is a Strain	2.63	1.15	3.23	1.11	3.28	1.05	3.00	1.08	2.71	.99	3.14	1.09	3.21	1.14	3.25	1.06
Physically Abusive	1.07	.26	1.62	.95	1.52	.91	1.62	.98	2.07	1.30	1.60	.98	1.64	.93	1.72	1.06
Feels Rejected	2.81	1.38	3.24	1.21	3.06	1.25	3.22	1.17	2.89	1.29	3.21	1.19	3.26	1.25	3.22	1.22

Does Not Get Along with Coworkers	1.44	1.01	2.05	1.08	2.04	1.03	2.16	1.12	2.05	1.15	2.14	1.13	1.98	1.07	2.17	1.14
Uses Projection	2.69	1.20	2.49	1.15	2.50	1.14	2.49	1.12	2.78	1.06	2.49	1.15	2.50	1.14	2.49	1.19
Complains of Fatigue	1.75	.86	2.59	1.37	2.71	1.41	2.26	1.25	2.17	1.17	2.37	1.33	2.52	1.32	2.33	1.32
Uses Rationalization	3.00	.63	2.79	1.09	2.72	1.08	2.78	1.08	3.10	1.04	2.76	1.10	2.75	1.09	2.72	1.08
Critical of Others	2.31	.95	2.70	1.17	2.67	1.16	2.61	1.13	2.73	1.10	2.61	1.12	2.65	1.15	2.59	1.14
Egocentric	2.69	1.20	2.64	1.21	2.54	1.17	2.62	1.19	2.84	1.08	2.58	1.15	2.54	1.10	2.56	1.19
Overevaluates Own Worth	1.80	.94	2.09	1.14	1.97	1.10	2.05	1.14	2.09	1.03	2.02	1.14	1.99	1.06	2.03	1.15
Optimistic	2.19	.75	1.98	.72	1.95	.67	2.10	.79	2.22	.77	1.96	.73	1.95	.74	1.97	.72
Psychologically Immature	2.53	1.13	2.87	1.15	2.81	1.08	2.90	1.11	3.03	1.10	2.83	1.15	2.88	1.11	2.91	1.14
Poor Judgment	2.69	.95	2.88	1.18	2.83	1.18	2.94	1.16	3.41	1.05	2.88	1.20	2.93	1.18	3.02	1.19
Low Sex Drive	1.50	.80	1.85	1.15	2.11	1.31	1.84	1.12	1.41	.85	1.90	1.14	1.80	1.05	1.72	1.01
Feels Mistreated	3.00	1.41	3.08	1.14	3.07	1.09	3.05	1.06	2.91	1.03	3.06	1.08	3.06	1.11	3.10	1.04
Overly Sensitive to Criticism	2.93	1.10	3.15	1.13	3.16	1.09	3.12	1.07	2.91	.98	3.18	1.13	3.11	1.13	3.21	1.11
Sentimental	2.38	1.19	2.40	1.00	2.43	1.00	2.43	.99	2.11	.91	2.37	1.01	2.41	1.00	2.37	1.00
Sexual Preoccupation	1.92	1.00	1.87	1.16	1.74	1.13	1.96	1.30	2.09	1.36	1.79	1.15	1.88	1.21	1.94	1.27
Accelerated Speech	1.62	.96	1.49	.82	1.44	.76	1.51	.78	1.46	.78	1.45	.82	1.48	.81	1.43	.74
Concerns About Homosexuality	1.31	1.11	1.42	1.02	1.31	.87	1.40	1.00	1.12	.59	1.43	1.04	1.48	1.08	1.38	1.03
Many Specific Fears	1.44	.81	1.91	1.03	1.94	1.07	1.83	1.02	1.67	.91	1.81	1.01	1.95	1.04	1.87	1.05
Passive in Relationships	2.36	1.39	2.35	1.05	2.39	1.05	2.31	1.09	2.08	1.10	2.29	1.09	2.36	1.07	2.23	1.04
Negative Attitudes Toward Therapy	1.50	.63	1.88	1.01	1.83	.99	1.73	.95	1.72	.91	1.75	.95	1.83	.99	1.72	.96
Guilt-Prone	2.53	1.51	2.65	1.08	2.64	1.09	2.57	1.10	2.44	1.15	2.52	1.11	2.69	1.09	2.52	1.13
Nervous	2.81	1.22	3.11	.98	3.19	.91	3.02	.93	2.62	.90	2.99	.97	3.12	.99	3.03	.97
Obsessive	3.00	1.18	2.92	1.11	2.91	1.06	2.88	1.13	2.46	1.12	2.80	1.20	2.83	1.13	2.83	1.15
Shy	2.19	1.17	2.44	1.20	2.47	1.16	2.41	1.19	2.40	1.16	2.50	1.17	2.49	1.19	2.48	1.16
Uses Intellectualization	3.38	1.15	2.66	1.22	2.56	1.21	2.68	1.22	2.67	1.31	2.47	1.19	2.59	1.23	2.43	1.19
Has Many Interests	2.69	.95	2.32	.98	2.28	1.00	2.40	1.10	2.43	1.00	2.30	1.05	2.35	1.00	2.30	1.02
Difficulty Making Decisions	2.60	.99	2.99	1.04	3.04	1.02	2.89	1.04	2.69	.99	2.94	1.07	3.04	1.04	2.93	1.04
Indirect Expression of Hostility	2.40	1.35	2.82	1.13	2.78	1.12	2.79	1.09	2.92	1.01	2.69	1.14	2.77	1.16	2.69	1.13
Poor Reality Testing	1.19	.40	1.67	.85	1.59	.74	1.63	.80	1.73	.78	1.65	.84	1.70	.86	1.70	.84
Angry	2.56	1.41	3.15	1.12	3.15	1.15	3.18	1.10	3.32	1.15	3.09	1.12	3.16	1.19	3.13	1.14
Eccentric	1.87	1.09	1.98	1.25	1.88	1.21	1.93	1.22	1.88	1.10	1.90	1.19	1.99	1.23	1.89	1.25
Emotional Lability	2.00	.89	2.31	1.08	2.25	1.08	2.31	1.03	2.53	1.00	2.30	1.09	2.34	1.08	2.29	1.09
Dislikes Change	2.47	.52	2.72	.99	2.69	.98	2.68	.97	2.71	.91	2.72	1.02	2.71	1.00	2.73	1.00
Believes Cannot Be Helped	1.38	.72	1.94	1.03	1.90	.97	1.84	.95	1.89	1.00	1.86	1.01	1.99	1.06	1.84	.95
Reliable Informant	3.81	1.11	3.20	.92	3.19	.95	3.17	.91	3.12	.81	3.22	.92	3.19	.88	3.18	.91
Ignores Problems	2.19	1.05	2.30	1.05	2.22	1.04	2.24	.99	2.39	.97	2.30	1.01	2.28	1.01	2.23	.99
Ruminates	2.88	1.15	3.30	1.01	3.28	1.00	3.25	1.00	2.95	.96	3.24	1.07	3.31	1.06	3.33	1.03
Excitable	2.19	.91	2.58	1.01	2.53	1.01	2.64	.98	2.79	.91	2.57	1.00	2.63	.97	2.61	.99
Conforming	2.47	1.06	2.39	.85	2.44	.90	2.36	.88	2.25	.81	2.34	.89	2.40	.86	2.37	.86
Ineffective at Dealing with Problems	2.69	1.01	3.09	1.06	3.03	1.08	3.00	1.02	3.00	1.03	2.98	1.02	3.03	1.07	3.00	1.01
Introverted	2.06	1.29	2.60	1.13	2.56	1.13	2.47	1.11	2.34	1.09	2.58	1.14	2.62	1.12	2.51	1.13
Superficial Relationships	2.44	1.09	2.71	1.21	2.59	1.23	2.74	1.21	3.02	1.05	2.63	1.23	2.62	1.22	2.63	1.21

	Harris-Lingoes Subscales *(continued)*															
	Hy_2		Hy_3		Hy_4		Pd_1		Pd_2		Pd_4		Pd_5		Pa_1	
	Mean	SD	Mean	SD	Mean	SD	Mean	SD	Mean	SD	Mean	SD	Mean	SD	Mean	SD
Impulsive	2.40	1.06	2.64	1.21	2.53	1.18	2.69	1.17	3.16	.98	2.65	1.23	2.72	1.21	2.72	1.25
Stereotypic Feminine Behavior	1.69	.95	1.33	.67	1.31	.60	1.33	.65	1.24	.58	1.32	.68	1.33	.67	1.29	.66
Stubborn	2.69	1.08	2.87	1.11	2.84	1.04	2.81	1.08	2.95	.98	2.84	1.12	2.85	1.09	2.80	1.12
Hostile Toward Therapist	1.38	.81	1.50	.76	1.50	.73	1.39	.63	1.36	.60	1.43	.72	1.44	.72	1.39	.71
Difficult to Motivate	2.00	1.10	2.25	1.04	2.16	.99	2.14	.96	2.34	.99	2.22	.99	2.17	1.03	2.20	1.00
Suicidal Ideations	1.38	.89	1.82	1.01	1.79	.98	1.68	.93	1.48	.88	1.73	.96	1.93	1.05	1.73	.95
Familial Discord	2.86	1.46	3.05	1.37	2.93	1.40	3.13	1.33	3.29	1.32	3.10	1.37	3.15	1.38	3.09	1.37
Dogmatic	2.31	1.01	2.34	1.10	2.25	1.12	2.31	1.08	2.33	1.05	2.28	1.16	2.34	1.10	2.25	1.17

	Harris-Lingoes Subscales *(continued)*															
	Pa_2		Pa_3		Sc_1		Sc_2		Sc_3		Sc_4		Sc_5		Sc_6	
	Mean	SD	Mean	SD	Mean	SD	Mean	SD	Mean	SD	Mean	SD	Mean	SD	Mean	SD
Intake Information	(n = 179)		(n = 23)		(n = 196)		(n = 218)		(n = 205)		(n = 225)		(n = 129)		(n = 176)	
Axis IV diagnosis	2.96	.92	2.74	.96	2.96	.90	2.97	.93	2.94	.90	2.92	.89	2.96	.88	2.96	.91
Axis V - Current Level of Functioning	60.48	9.65	67.17	9.23	60.46	10.07	60.00	9.61	60.43	9.94	60.85	9.99	60.22	9.70	60.43	9.99
Number of Arrests	1.25	3.63	.73	1.03	1.45	3.71	1.48	3.63	1.43	3.83	1.18	3.31	1.20	2.13	1.39	3.73
Mental Status	(n = 179)		(n = 23)		(n = 196)		(n = 218)		(n = 205)		(n = 225)		(n = 129)		(n = 176)	
Anxiety During Interview	2.51	.71	2.17	.65	2.50	.71	2.50	.72	2.47	.74	2.46	.71	2.53	.72	2.44	.68
Depression During Interview	2.45	.73	2.13	.81	2.42	.73	2.46	.72	2.44	.73	2.47	.72	2.42	.76	2.41	.73
Activity Level During Interview	3.02	.47	3.04	.56	2.98	.49	3.00	.45	3.03	.46	3.00	.45	3.04	.46	3.01	.43
Speech During Interview	2.94	.39	2.96	.37	2.93	.44	2.94	.40	2.97	.38	2.95	.37	2.95	.44	2.95	.39
SCL-90-R Scales	(n = 174)		(n = 23)		(n = 192)		(n = 213)		(n = 200)		(n = 220)		(n = 126)		(n = 171)	
Somatization	1.28	.79	.38	.32	1.25	.82	1.23	.80	1.28	.80	1.25	.80	1.40	.80	1.48	.78
Obsessive-Compulsive	1.68	.82	.67	.60	1.67	.84	1.64	.83	1.77	.80	1.74	.80	1.79	.84	1.76	.85
Interpersonal Sensitivity	1.69	.85	.47	.63	1.71	.86	1.58	.89	1.58	.88	1.64	.85	1.68	.87	1.62	.87
Depression	2.07	.84	.93	.72	1.97	.85	2.01	.82	1.98	.84	2.05	.79	1.99	.85	1.97	.88
Anxiety	1.61	.86	.57	.59	1.55	.91	1.54	.90	1.53	.89	1.54	.86	1.68	.95	1.62	.91
Hostility	1.60	1.07	.28	.42	1.59	1.09	1.50	1.05	1.57	1.07	1.53	1.03	1.73	1.11	1.55	1.05
Phobic Anxiety	.79	.71	.12	.33	.83	.76	.79	.76	.81	.71	.77	.75	.90	.81	.83	.76
Paranoid Ideation	1.67	.86	.37	.44	1.73	.87	1.55	.91	1.62	.90	1.58	.90	1.73	.89	1.68	.87
Psychoticism	1.21	.68	.24	.30	1.19	.72	1.16	.74	1.19	.69	1.18	.72	1.29	.78	1.23	.75
Initial SCL-90 Analogue	(n = 106)		(n = 16)		(n = 124)		(n = 134)		(n = 129)		(n = 140)		(n = 80)		(n = 109)	
Somatization	2.35	2.61	1.94	2.52	2.39	2.78	2.60	2.97	2.41	2.79	2.56	2.81	2.64	2.69	2.79	2.96
Obsessive-Compulsive	3.50	2.70	3.81	2.71	3.60	2.78	3.69	2.71	3.56	2.75	3.57	2.82	3.62	2.72	3.44	2.66
Interpersonal Sensitivity	4.98	2.50	4.75	2.93	4.85	2.52	4.90	2.60	4.79	2.47	4.94	2.48	4.53	2.42	4.70	2.47
Depression	4.53	2.67	3.06	1.95	4.59	2.64	4.83	2.76	4.63	2.74	4.81	2.71	4.62	2.68	4.69	2.68
Anxiety	4.57	2.71	3.81	2.76	4.80	2.77	4.68	2.79	4.45	2.69	4.75	2.71	4.51	2.55	4.64	2.66
Hostility	3.48	2.90	2.69	2.89	3.43	3.00	3.35	2.83	3.36	2.79	3.45	2.84	3.54	3.01	3.46	2.83
Phobic Anxiety	1.42	2.10	1.50	1.67	1.62	2.41	1.68	2.48	1.31	2.04	1.58	2.32	1.32	2.28	1.63	2.41
Paranoid Ideation	1.40	1.84	.81	.98	1.50	2.11	1.42	2.11	1.26	1.87	1.30	1.94	1.44	2.09	1.40	1.96
Psychoticism	.57	1.24	1.00	1.41	.64	1.47	.62	1.47	.67	1.55	.65	1.46	.72	1.70	.65	1.56
Patient Description Form Scales	(n = 107)		(n = 15)		(n = 125)		(n = 136)		(n = 130)		(n = 140)		(n = 81)		(n = 110)	
Angry Resentment	2.95	.95	2.37	.91	2.86	.95	2.88	.95	2.83	.98	2.86	.96	2.89	.97	2.95	.95
Critical/Argumentative	2.67	.96	2.24	.82	2.53	.96	2.57	.93	2.55	1.00	2.57	.96	2.60	1.00	2.64	.95

	Harris-Lingoes Subscales *(continued)*															
	Pa_2		Pa_3		Sc_1		Sc_2		Sc_3		Sc_4		Sc_5		Sc_6	
	Mean	SD	Mean	SD	Mean	SD	Mean	SD	Mean	SD	Mean	SD	Mean	SD	Mean	SD
Narcissistic	2.39	.91	2.33	.76	2.29	.87	2.36	.93	2.37	.95	2.36	.95	2.38	1.01	2.38	.93
Defensive	2.64	.87	2.27	.54	2.58	.87	2.63	.89	2.60	.90	2.58	.89	2.60	.89	2.63	.84
Histrionic	2.48	.78	2.13	.83	2.42	.78	2.45	.78	2.42	.77	2.43	.78	2.42	.75	2.45	.71
Aggressive	2.26	.92	1.92	.62	2.20	.94	2.18	.90	2.15	.92	2.17	.92	2.34	.96	2.24	.88
Insecure	3.05	.71	2.50	.94	3.01	.74	3.01	.81	2.98	.76	3.03	.81	2.94	.77	2.90	.75
Anxious	3.01	.77	2.45	.69	3.02	.72	2.98	.81	2.98	.78	3.00	.79	3.02	.76	2.99	.77
Pessimistic	2.47	.97	1.87	.79	2.47	.99	2.44	.96	2.43	.95	2.46	.97	2.45	.92	2.49	.93
Depressed	2.63	.75	1.76	.60	2.53	.76	2.58	.79	2.56	.79	2.61	.77	2.60	.82	2.56	.77
Achievement-Oriented	2.57	.74	2.94	.57	2.51	.72	2.56	.74	2.55	.70	2.56	.73	2.53	.74	2.55	.73
Passive-Submissive	2.25	.85	2.35	.96	2.25	.82	2.22	.80	2.24	.82	2.22	.80	2.17	.78	2.23	.84
Introverted	2.63	1.00	2.58	.97	2.74	1.01	2.64	.99	2.64	.96	2.63	.98	2.52	1.01	2.62	.99
Emotionally Controlled	2.46	1.04	2.39	.82	2.37	1.05	2.44	1.03	2.46	1.07	2.45	1.05	2.35	1.05	2.44	1.07
Antisocial	2.26	.93	2.08	.72	2.31	.98	2.28	.94	2.32	.94	2.28	.96	2.38	.99	2.30	.93
Negative Treatment Attitudes	2.05	.81	1.94	.55	1.97	.80	2.01	.81	1.99	.80	1.98	.81	2.02	.81	2.04	.79
Somatic Symptoms	2.16	1.04	1.78	.97	2.08	1.04	2.20	1.09	2.16	1.05	2.20	1.06	2.22	1.11	2.35	1.09
Psychotic Symptoms	1.27	.42	1.21	.36	1.30	.48	1.31	.48	1.31	.48	1.29	.47	1.31	.48	1.31	.50
Family Problems	2.90	1.18	2.59	1.12	2.95	1.16	2.75	1.14	2.87	1.21	2.81	1.14	2.81	1.16	2.90	1.18
Obsessive-Compulsive	2.89	.78	2.50	.63	2.87	.78	2.84	.81	2.87	.79	2.85	.81	2.84	.75	2.86	.78
Stereotypic Masculine Interests	2.77	1.22	2.80	.98	2.69	1.12	2.86	1.09	2.81	1.15	2.79	1.10	2.79	1.13	2.85	1.10
Procrastinates	2.28	.97	2.38	.73	2.29	.95	2.31	.91	2.36	.96	2.33	.94	2.30	1.00	2.37	.96
Suspicious	2.68	1.01	1.96	.64	2.69	.97	2.66	1.00	2.65	.99	2.60	1.00	2.65	1.01	2.66	.92
Agitated	2.28	.77	1.96	.80	2.25	.78	2.29	.78	2.19	.78	2.22	.78	2.32	.83	2.28	.77
Work Problems	2.06	.90	1.95	1.31	2.11	.92	2.05	.95	2.02	.93	2.05	.97	2.09	1.03	2.06	.93
Patient Description Form Items	(n = 107)		(n = 15)		(n = 125)		(n = 136)		(n = 130)		(n = 140)		(n = 81)		(n = 110)	
Anxious	3.47	.87	2.93	1.03	3.55	.80	3.51	.87	3.45	.83	3.51	.86	3.58	.83	3.45	.86
Problems with Authority Figures	3.15	1.21	3.00	1.20	3.06	1.22	3.07	1.27	3.06	1.25	3.07	1.26	3.19	1.22	3.19	1.17
Has Insight Into Own Problems	2.58	.89	2.93	.88	2.56	.89	2.53	.86	2.64	.84	2.62	.84	2.65	.85	2.59	.89
Fears Losing Control	3.31	1.02	3.29	.83	3.31	1.07	3.32	1.05	3.31	1.01	3.32	1.06	3.21	1.09	3.28	1.01
Extroverted	2.36	.94	2.67	.62	2.22	.91	2.29	.95	2.32	.94	2.36	.96	2.43	.96	2.36	.96
Uses Repression	2.63	1.05	2.27	1.03	2.61	1.03	2.69	1.06	2.64	1.05	2.59	1.08	2.61	.97	2.63	1.02
Submissive	2.15	.92	2.27	.96	2.25	.91	2.20	.91	2.24	.91	2.19	.89	2.11	.84	2.21	.89
Difficulty Concentrating	2.83	1.06	1.93	.73	2.81	1.05	2.79	1.10	2.84	1.11	2.78	1.15	2.91	1.06	2.91	1.02
Rigid	2.92	1.15	2.60	1.18	2.83	1.09	2.84	1.08	2.79	1.11	2.77	1.09	2.80	1.10	2.83	1.08
Overly Compliant	1.95	.90	1.87	.99	1.95	.93	1.95	.88	2.01	.92	1.99	.89	1.94	.88	1.97	.91
Whiny	2.02	1.08	1.67	.98	1.95	1.05	1.95	1.05	1.98	1.03	1.97	1.05	1.90	.94	2.03	.98
Feels Overwhelmed	3.41	1.10	2.93	.96	3.35	1.09	3.36	1.14	3.38	1.15	3.39	1.11	3.44	1.08	3.44	1.09

Manipulative	2.48	1.18	2.60	.99	2.40	1.13	2.46	1.17	2.49	1.20	2.47	1.19	2.55	1.20	2.47	1.14
Difficulty Trusting Others	3.38	1.26	2.67	.98	3.35	1.23	3.31	1.29	3.37	1.24	3.27	1.26	3.35	1.25	3.36	1.18
Insensitive to Others	2.26	1.07	2.40	1.18	2.25	1.04	2.30	1.08	2.28	1.10	2.24	1.06	2.35	1.07	2.31	1.06
Stereotypic Masculine Behavior	2.73	1.25	2.73	.96	2.67	1.15	2.85	1.16	2.79	1.19	2.76	1.14	2.78	1.19	2.83	1.14
Harbors Grudges	2.91	1.14	2.23	1.01	2.76	1.14	2.85	1.16	2.83	1.18	2.80	1.16	2.86	1.14	2.87	1.09
Evasive	2.36	1.08	2.20	.94	2.26	1.08	2.35	1.14	2.34	1.16	2.30	1.15	2.40	1.15	2.36	1.08
Disoriented	1.27	.58	1.33	.62	1.27	.53	1.30	.64	1.30	.62	1.27	.61	1.23	.48	1.26	.55
Energetic	2.34	.94	3.07	.70	2.40	.93	2.35	.91	2.32	.87	2.36	.90	2.38	.87	2.29	.89
Lonely	3.02	1.23	2.73	1.16	2.97	1.20	2.93	1.26	3.09	1.26	3.06	1.23	2.91	1.22	2.92	1.23
Family Lacks Love	2.92	1.34	2.21	1.19	2.97	1.35	2.71	1.36	2.92	1.33	2.81	1.33	2.78	1.37	2.83	1.36
Worrier	3.36	1.02	2.60	1.06	3.38	1.00	3.35	1.04	3.34	1.08	3.38	1.04	3.27	1.00	3.25	1.04
Narcissistic	2.55	1.16	2.53	1.13	2.50	1.14	2.56	1.20	2.58	1.20	2.57	1.23	2.61	1.29	2.58	1.22
Tearful	1.71	.90	1.27	.46	1.58	.84	1.55	.83	1.55	.83	1.57	.85	1.64	.91	1.51	.82
Provocative	1.72	.91	1.33	.49	1.73	.95	1.76	.96	1.71	.93	1.71	.94	1.78	.89	1.70	.89
Moralistic	2.52	1.10	2.40	1.18	2.60	1.08	2.48	1.02	2.55	1.12	2.46	1.05	2.54	1.02	2.52	1.04
Socially Awkward	2.82	1.13	2.87	1.25	2.94	1.15	2.88	1.14	2.85	1.10	2.85	1.14	2.72	1.13	2.79	1.08
Hostile	2.61	1.28	2.20	1.01	2.52	1.22	2.54	1.21	2.49	1.21	2.57	1.21	2.64	1.30	2.59	1.23
Overcontrolled	2.75	1.20	2.80	1.08	2.61	1.23	2.64	1.22	2.67	1.23	2.64	1.21	2.62	1.26	2.71	1.24
Resistant to Interpretations	2.29	1.00	2.07	.70	2.13	1.01	2.18	1.02	2.17	1.02	2.17	1.00	2.25	1.07	2.25	1.02
Antisocial Behavior	2.21	1.19	2.13	1.06	2.35	1.28	2.28	1.28	2.34	1.27	2.25	1.30	2.43	1.36	2.35	1.25
Sarcastic	2.15	1.11	2.00	1.13	2.00	1.08	2.01	1.06	2.10	1.13	2.08	1.11	2.10	1.12	2.14	1.08
Rejects Traditional Gender Role	1.73	1.12	1.40	.63	1.66	1.06	1.62	1.01	1.71	1.12	1.70	1.12	1.72	1.09	1.66	1.06
Feels Gets Raw Deal From Life	3.17	1.17	2.00	1.00	3.02	1.19	3.06	1.17	2.99	1.22	3.04	1.21	2.99	1.20	3.01	1.20
Acute Psychological Turmoil	3.10	1.06	2.67	.82	3.14	1.07	3.14	1.08	3.07	1.13	3.14	1.11	3.10	1.12	3.03	1.08
Does Not Complete Projects	2.26	1.11	2.15	1.07	2.26	1.12	2.29	1.09	2.36	1.10	2.35	1.16	2.32	1.13	2.32	1.10
Uncomfortable with Opposite Sex	2.12	1.06	1.93	1.03	2.13	1.10	2.10	1.02	2.18	1.11	2.18	1.10	2.06	1.04	2.08	1.05
Preoccupied with Health Problems	2.28	1.35	1.80	1.37	2.21	1.35	2.32	1.38	2.31	1.41	2.32	1.39	2.33	1.39	2.53	1.44
Work-Oriented	2.98	1.12	3.33	1.05	2.96	1.03	3.04	1.10	2.95	1.05	2.93	1.04	2.89	1.07	2.94	1.09
Resents Family Members	2.93	1.33	2.73	1.39	2.98	1.35	2.74	1.30	2.90	1.36	2.85	1.32	2.84	1.32	2.90	1.32
Demanding of Attention	2.59	1.14	2.27	1.16	2.53	1.15	2.50	1.07	2.54	1.14	2.55	1.15	2.49	1.06	2.53	1.03
Passive	2.49	1.04	2.33	1.05	2.47	.99	2.40	.98	2.46	.98	2.42	.97	2.43	.94	2.47	1.01
Self-Punishing	2.62	1.13	2.07	.88	2.48	1.17	2.50	1.17	2.47	1.20	2.50	1.15	2.46	1.13	2.45	1.17
Needs to Achieve	2.77	1.01	3.53	.83	2.71	.97	2.82	1.04	2.77	1.04	2.81	1.04	2.67	1.07	2.67	1.05
Needs to Be with Others	2.80	1.08	2.80	.68	2.82	1.00	2.92	1.07	2.95	1.08	2.96	1.09	2.86	1.05	2.85	1.01
Irritable	2.86	1.04	2.13	.83	2.74	1.06	2.81	1.08	2.74	1.05	2.73	1.05	2.84	1.08	2.83	1.05
Self-Defeating	3.21	1.13	3.07	.96	3.16	1.17	3.23	1.23	3.20	1.15	3.24	1.22	3.11	1.18	3.13	1.13
Delusional Thinking	1.27	.69	1.33	.49	1.29	.74	1.28	.69	1.30	.68	1.29	.72	1.36	.82	1.29	.73
Self-Reliant	2.64	.96	3.07	1.22	2.54	.92	2.56	.82	2.63	.86	2.60	.87	2.74	.93	2.64	.91
Aggressive	2.45	1.08	2.47	.92	2.43	1.08	2.46	1.05	2.41	1.02	2.44	1.06	2.51	1.13	2.52	1.06
Competitive	2.42	.93	2.80	.94	2.39	.97	2.45	.98	2.42	.99	2.41	1.00	2.35	1.01	2.49	.98
Suspicious	2.65	1.21	1.87	.99	2.67	1.17	2.62	1.19	2.63	1.21	2.58	1.20	2.63	1.17	2.64	1.11
Compulsive	2.59	1.12	2.71	.99	2.61	1.14	2.61	1.06	2.63	1.12	2.61	1.12	2.55	1.09	2.58	1.08

Harris-Lingoes Subscales *(continued)*

	Pa_2		Pa_3		Sc_1		Sc_2		Sc_3		Sc_4		Sc_5		Sc_6	
	Mean	SD	Mean	SD	Mean	SD	Mean	SD	Mean	SD	Mean	SD	Mean	SD	Mean	SD
Dependable	2.99	.93	3.07	.88	2.98	.97	3.00	.97	2.96	.90	2.98	.92	2.96	1.01	2.95	.98
Multiple Somatic Complaints	2.07	1.25	1.80	1.42	2.02	1.29	2.10	1.28	2.10	1.30	2.11	1.29	2.17	1.32	2.33	1.37
Complains of Lack of Time	2.05	1.14	2.27	.88	1.96	1.15	1.97	1.12	2.01	1.12	1.98	1.13	2.08	1.18	2.08	1.14
Poor Work Performance	2.17	1.10	2.21	1.48	2.16	1.17	2.05	1.13	2.09	1.12	2.07	1.16	2.22	1.19	2.21	1.18
Insecure	3.46	.88	3.00	1.13	3.49	.90	3.47	.97	3.45	.91	3.48	.94	3.40	.88	3.34	.95
Discusses Problems Openly	3.03	.83	3.27	.96	2.99	.84	3.03	.91	3.08	.84	3.09	.88	2.99	.81	2.95	.82
Sexually Adjusted	2.36	.83	2.71	.73	2.29	.90	2.38	.81	2.38	.82	2.43	.81	2.32	.85	2.37	.83
Exaggerated Need for Affection	2.36	1.08	2.20	1.15	2.28	1.06	2.32	1.04	2.32	1.12	2.32	1.09	2.25	1.07	2.27	1.05
Resentful	3.17	1.13	2.80	1.21	3.07	1.16	3.10	1.17	3.10	1.18	3.07	1.16	3.06	1.24	3.17	1.13
Uses Denial	2.76	1.22	2.47	.64	2.66	1.24	2.70	1.19	2.66	1.18	2.68	1.23	2.65	1.20	2.72	1.20
Hypochondriacal	1.75	.92	1.33	.62	1.68	.90	1.76	.97	1.70	.88	1.72	.90	1.70	.88	1.81	.95
Communicates Effectively	3.05	.82	3.00	.85	3.00	.80	3.04	.72	3.03	.79	3.11	.77	3.19	.82	3.01	.81
Has Many Nightmares	1.83	1.08	1.00	.00	1.75	1.05	1.75	1.03	1.80	1.05	1.79	1.05	1.93	1.14	1.70	1.01
Stormy Interpersonal Relationships	3.12	1.25	3.07	1.33	3.03	1.21	3.05	1.30	3.16	1.19	3.11	1.25	3.14	1.19	3.12	1.15
Feigns Remorse When in Trouble	1.78	.99	1.77	.93	1.82	1.00	1.78	.97	1.80	.98	1.75	.96	1.87	.93	1.77	.94
Stereotypic Masculine Interests	2.79	1.26	2.87	1.06	2.70	1.17	2.86	1.13	2.80	1.20	2.80	1.17	2.79	1.14	2.85	1.15
Guarded	2.82	1.32	2.33	.72	2.74	1.30	2.79	1.31	2.80	1.34	2.72	1.31	2.93	1.39	2.91	1.30
Feels Inferior	3.14	.94	2.60	1.06	3.16	.99	3.10	1.05	3.08	1.02	3.11	1.04	3.06	.99	3.03	1.00
Low Frustration Tolerance	3.29	1.12	2.53	1.06	3.12	1.15	3.18	1.16	3.20	1.13	3.22	1.16	3.12	1.11	3.11	1.12
Psychotic Symptoms	1.17	.51	1.14	.53	1.22	.60	1.20	.57	1.22	.62	1.19	.57	1.22	.58	1.24	.66
Fired From Past Jobs	2.07	1.14	1.73	1.19	2.06	1.09	2.08	1.15	2.01	1.15	2.09	1.15	2.17	1.13	2.10	1.13
Needs Attention	2.87	.98	2.80	1.01	2.87	1.00	2.89	1.00	2.94	.99	2.91	1.01	2.88	.95	2.90	.93
Acts Out	2.50	1.21	2.27	.96	2.51	1.22	2.51	1.18	2.52	1.20	2.48	1.20	2.54	1.20	2.49	1.18
Histrionic	2.02	1.05	1.73	.96	1.90	1.04	1.97	1.03	1.98	1.03	1.96	1.00	1.91	.99	1.98	1.00
Self-Indulgent	2.50	1.09	2.73	1.03	2.47	1.13	2.54	1.12	2.62	1.12	2.52	1.14	2.56	1.19	2.54	1.14
Depressed	3.40	.99	2.40	.74	3.32	1.03	3.39	1.02	3.35	1.05	3.42	1.01	3.42	1.06	3.36	1.01
Grandiose	1.99	1.05	1.87	.74	1.81	.96	1.93	1.08	1.98	1.10	1.97	1.10	2.04	1.23	2.07	1.12
Cynical	2.74	1.26	2.07	1.03	2.54	1.26	2.54	1.23	2.60	1.33	2.60	1.29	2.70	1.31	2.73	1.29
Sociopathic	1.67	.89	1.40	.63	1.70	.92	1.71	.89	1.72	.91	1.68	.92	1.81	.97	1.71	.91
Agitated	2.64	1.07	2.20	1.15	2.56	1.08	2.62	1.06	2.49	1.08	2.56	1.08	2.68	1.16	2.61	1.08
Marital Problems	2.77	1.59	2.69	1.97	2.56	1.62	2.66	1.59	2.57	1.65	2.57	1.58	2.65	1.63	2.62	1.63
Absence of Deep Emotions	2.05	1.21	1.93	1.10	2.00	1.22	2.10	1.24	2.15	1.30	2.09	1.24	2.06	1.23	2.13	1.28
Uncomfortable Dealing with Emotions	2.95	1.28	3.00	1.13	2.89	1.31	3.02	1.31	3.02	1.31	2.99	1.30	2.89	1.34	3.00	1.32
Sad	2.93	.98	2.20	.77	3.00	.96	2.99	1.02	2.96	1.01	3.03	1.03	3.09	1.01	3.00	.97
Self-Degrading	2.39	1.03	1.87	.92	2.30	1.02	2.31	1.08	2.25	1.04	2.32	1.08	2.23	.95	2.18	.95
Unable to Express Negative Feelings	2.23	1.10	2.13	1.30	2.11	1.09	2.18	1.10	2.23	1.14	2.22	1.17	2.06	1.06	2.15	1.11
Concrete in Thinking	2.22	1.04	1.60	.74	2.26	1.02	2.25	.99	2.29	1.02	2.21	1.02	2.28	1.06	2.30	1.03
Unable to See Own Limitations	2.35	1.06	2.13	.99	2.28	1.10	2.40	1.12	2.32	1.13	2.35	1.15	2.34	1.11	2.39	1.12

Power-Oriented	2.26	1.13	2.20	.86	2.12	1.09	2.28	1.10	2.25	1.13	2.25	1.11	2.26	1.14	2.25	1.13
Grouchy	2.42	1.10	1.87	.83	2.32	1.09	2.44	1.08	2.39	1.10	2.39	1.10	2.42	1.11	2.53	1.06
Overbearing in Relationships	2.45	1.14	2.13	.99	2.26	1.10	2.28	1.12	2.38	1.17	2.34	1.15	2.53	1.19	2.45	1.10
Uncertain About Career	3.44	1.24	3.08	1.31	3.41	1.23	3.48	1.20	3.36	1.30	3.55	1.22	3.44	1.31	3.37	1.25
Likable	3.12	.86	3.47	.52	3.07	.81	3.14	.80	3.13	.76	3.16	.82	3.16	.77	3.11	.77
Procrastinator	2.47	1.11	2.60	.99	2.51	1.13	2.59	1.11	2.63	1.13	2.59	1.16	2.49	1.14	2.61	1.13
Negative Feelings Toward Opposite Sex	2.20	1.17	1.73	.80	2.13	1.17	2.13	1.18	2.16	1.17	2.17	1.20	2.11	1.17	2.07	1.09
Defensive	2.87	1.12	2.27	.88	2.66	1.19	2.73	1.18	2.65	1.25	2.71	1.21	2.77	1.21	2.77	1.18
Empathetic	2.40	.82	2.47	.92	2.31	.78	2.36	.78	2.34	.78	2.35	.79	2.27	.75	2.32	.78
Perfectionistic	2.70	1.09	2.47	1.13	2.51	1.13	2.56	1.11	2.57	1.12	2.58	1.18	2.55	1.15	2.52	1.12
Judgmental	2.87	1.13	2.53	.92	2.70	1.14	2.72	1.11	2.75	1.19	2.75	1.14	2.65	1.17	2.71	1.11
Copes Well with Stress	1.94	.63	2.47	.64	1.93	.66	1.98	.62	1.98	.66	1.96	.66	1.96	.58	1.97	.62
Moody	2.79	1.04	2.60	.91	2.79	1.00	2.88	.99	2.82	.98	2.84	1.01	2.77	1.07	2.87	.97
Selfish	2.24	.94	2.33	.98	2.18	.99	2.24	.99	2.27	1.05	2.25	1.02	2.26	1.01	2.26	1.00
Gives Up Easily	2.32	1.00	1.93	.92	2.30	.97	2.30	.99	2.30	.95	2.34	1.01	2.23	.99	2.27	.98
Physical Symptoms in Response to Stress	2.33	1.21	1.62	.87	2.22	1.19	2.27	1.23	2.22	1.16	2.30	1.22	2.46	1.29	2.44	1.23
Blames Family For Difficulties	2.57	1.33	2.27	1.28	2.61	1.34	2.39	1.27	2.58	1.33	2.49	1.31	2.51	1.28	2.61	1.32
Bored	2.50	1.14	2.40	1.06	2.46	1.13	2.52	1.14	2.48	1.13	2.49	1.13	2.41	1.20	2.50	1.16
Idealistic	2.42	1.09	2.27	.88	2.37	1.05	2.35	1.07	2.41	1.05	2.35	1.08	2.32	1.08	2.39	1.03
Difficulty Establishing Therapeutic Rapport	2.10	1.12	2.00	.65	2.06	1.08	2.08	1.06	2.01	1.10	2.02	1.05	2.14	1.07	2.11	1.05
Daydreams	1.78	.91	2.00	.82	1.85	1.03	1.86	1.03	1.98	1.04	1.90	1.02	1.83	.99	1.83	.93
Concerned About Status	2.44	1.13	2.36	.84	2.28	1.06	2.47	1.10	2.42	1.08	2.49	1.16	2.41	1.17	2.39	1.09
Creates Good First Impression	2.51	.94	3.07	.46	2.45	.90	2.51	.91	2.48	.86	2.53	.91	2.57	.97	2.44	.92
Complains of Sleep Disturbance	2.77	1.22	1.67	1.29	2.55	1.27	2.68	1.27	2.67	1.28	2.69	1.27	2.74	1.36	2.76	1.25
Has Temper Tantrums	2.44	1.16	2.00	1.13	2.45	1.25	2.39	1.20	2.29	1.19	2.35	1.20	2.53	1.18	2.41	1.15
Overreactive	2.81	1.05	2.40	1.12	2.73	1.07	2.83	1.10	2.72	1.05	2.75	1.09	2.72	1.04	2.76	1.00
High Aspirations	2.54	1.13	2.64	.84	2.45	1.11	2.57	1.13	2.52	1.11	2.54	1.13	2.47	1.23	2.51	1.16
Feels Hopeless	2.86	1.04	1.87	1.06	2.82	1.14	2.85	1.17	2.83	1.13	2.90	1.14	2.85	1.13	2.85	1.14
Keeps Others at a Distance	3.04	1.28	2.93	1.03	3.01	1.23	3.05	1.26	2.98	1.30	3.00	1.27	3.06	1.30	3.08	1.27
Argumentative	2.46	1.08	2.07	1.10	2.29	1.05	2.40	1.06	2.27	1.09	2.36	1.09	2.47	1.15	2.41	1.06
Paranoid Features	1.99	1.06	1.33	.49	1.99	1.09	2.00	1.04	1.92	1.04	1.92	1.04	1.98	1.11	1.96	1.07
Restless	2.73	1.13	2.27	1.03	2.73	1.14	2.77	1.13	2.65	1.14	2.68	1.14	2.80	1.23	2.76	1.14
Pessimistic	2.99	1.13	2.40	1.06	2.95	1.12	2.96	1.15	2.97	1.12	2.99	1.14	3.02	1.04	3.05	1.07
Feels Like a Failure	3.10	1.03	2.47	.83	3.09	1.12	3.07	1.14	3.03	1.11	3.10	1.17	3.15	1.13	3.04	1.09
Hallucinations	1.11	.42	1.07	.26	1.11	.43	1.11	.41	1.13	.45	1.09	.40	1.08	.31	1.14	.48
Restricted Affect	2.30	1.28	2.07	1.03	2.22	1.27	2.29	1.27	2.27	1.30	2.30	1.28	2.10	1.23	2.23	1.25
Impatient	2.87	1.15	2.53	1.06	2.61	1.07	2.79	1.11	2.70	1.12	2.72	1.09	2.85	1.25	2.76	1.15
Assertive	2.36	.89	2.27	.70	2.29	.84	2.34	.82	2.32	.84	2.35	.82	2.37	.84	2.38	.86
Modest	2.38	.81	2.47	.83	2.44	.83	2.50	.82	2.47	.81	2.43	.84	2.37	.82	2.45	.78
Self-Doubting	3.09	.86	2.53	1.13	3.13	.90	3.16	.92	3.09	.92	3.11	.94	3.04	.86	3.06	.87
Deceptive	1.88	.95	1.93	.80	1.92	1.03	1.95	.98	1.95	1.03	1.92	.99	1.99	.99	1.94	.98
Feels That Life is a Strain	3.25	1.09	2.53	.99	3.22	1.04	3.25	1.12	3.14	1.13	3.20	1.17	3.24	1.12	3.18	1.13

Harris-Lingoes Subscales *(continued)*

	Pa_2		Pa_3		Sc_1		Sc_2		Sc_3		Sc_4		Sc_5		Sc_6	
	Mean	SD	Mean	SD	Mean	SD	Mean	SD	Mean	SD	Mean	SD	Mean	SD	Mean	SD
Physically Abusive	1.62	1.03	1.07	.26	1.69	1.07	1.61	.97	1.62	.96	1.62	.95	1.79	1.10	1.62	.94
Feels Rejected	3.33	1.20	2.80	1.37	3.24	1.18	3.22	1.24	3.24	1.23	3.28	1.25	3.19	1.27	3.05	1.28
Does Not Get Along with Coworkers	2.15	1.10	1.70	1.06	2.16	1.13	2.09	1.09	2.00	1.08	2.04	1.04	2.09	1.12	2.03	1.09
Uses Projection	2.59	1.17	2.13	1.06	2.45	1.19	2.42	1.12	2.45	1.17	2.47	1.15	2.49	1.19	2.48	1.13
Complains of Fatigue	2.48	1.40	2.00	1.31	2.40	1.34	2.52	1.37	2.57	1.37	2.55	1.36	2.53	1.45	2.69	1.39
Uses Rationalization	2.77	1.07	2.93	.70	2.70	1.13	2.72	1.09	2.71	1.07	2.75	1.10	2.79	1.13	2.76	1.07
Critical of Others	2.73	1.16	2.53	.92	2.63	1.19	2.59	1.15	2.63	1.18	2.63	1.15	2.65	1.21	2.73	1.18
Egocentric	2.68	1.17	2.40	.99	2.51	1.18	2.59	1.17	2.57	1.20	2.61	1.20	2.54	1.20	2.60	1.11
Overevaluates Own Worth	2.14	1.14	1.73	.80	1.98	1.10	2.01	1.12	2.05	1.09	2.06	1.12	2.09	1.15	2.10	1.12
Optimistic	1.94	.75	2.33	.72	1.93	.74	1.95	.76	2.02	.70	1.96	.72	1.94	.70	1.95	.68
Psychologically Immature	2.90	1.13	2.53	.92	2.86	1.16	2.89	1.14	2.89	1.17	2.88	1.15	2.78	1.14	2.84	1.06
Poor Judgment	2.85	1.11	2.87	.83	2.93	1.22	2.94	1.17	2.94	1.17	2.89	1.18	2.99	1.22	2.91	1.18
Low Sex Drive	2.00	1.24	1.45	.82	1.81	1.05	1.87	1.13	1.76	1.07	1.80	1.08	1.90	1.11	2.03	1.25
Feels Mistreated	3.15	1.13	2.73	1.33	3.01	1.09	3.01	1.12	2.98	1.14	3.02	1.16	3.05	1.11	3.08	1.07
Overly Sensitive to Criticism	3.26	1.03	2.67	1.05	3.19	1.14	3.15	1.11	3.08	1.15	3.10	1.17	3.06	1.15	3.08	1.11
Sentimental	2.50	1.00	2.08	1.04	2.41	.98	2.38	1.00	2.41	1.00	2.36	.98	2.34	1.03	2.39	1.01
Sexual Preoccupation	1.71	1.05	1.90	1.10	1.75	1.16	1.77	1.09	1.86	1.16	1.85	1.18	1.67	1.05	1.67	1.05
Accelerated Speech	1.50	.78	1.40	.83	1.46	.76	1.48	.82	1.46	.80	1.44	.79	1.54	.87	1.51	.82
Concerns About Homosexuality	1.46	1.04	1.07	.27	1.45	1.09	1.43	1.03	1.48	1.08	1.49	1.09	1.29	.76	1.36	.92
Many Specific Fears	1.94	1.00	1.60	1.06	1.88	1.04	1.90	1.04	1.84	1.00	1.89	1.03	1.86	1.05	1.89	1.08
Passive in Relationships	2.38	1.12	2.69	1.38	2.34	1.05	2.31	1.03	2.27	1.02	2.29	1.01	2.26	1.04	2.27	1.05
Negative Attitudes Toward Therapy	1.85	1.00	1.67	.82	1.81	1.03	1.85	1.01	1.81	.98	1.81	.99	1.84	.99	1.87	1.01
Guilt-Prone	2.62	1.11	2.27	1.22	2.61	1.13	2.61	1.10	2.69	1.08	2.65	1.12	2.62	1.15	2.62	1.13
Nervous	3.09	.94	2.53	1.13	3.20	.89	3.07	.97	3.05	.97	3.13	.98	3.12	.95	3.11	.94
Obsessive	2.92	1.11	2.57	1.02	2.94	1.13	2.89	1.11	2.91	1.15	2.88	1.13	2.96	1.06	2.90	1.07
Shy	2.46	1.19	2.40	.99	2.58	1.20	2.44	1.16	2.45	1.18	2.46	1.18	2.43	1.16	2.51	1.19
Uses Intellectualization	2.61	1.20	3.40	1.24	2.48	1.23	2.50	1.21	2.60	1.25	2.62	1.25	2.58	1.31	2.62	1.25
Has Many Interests	2.28	1.07	3.00	.76	2.24	.99	2.24	.97	2.30	1.02	2.31	.99	2.26	.97	2.31	1.03
Difficulty Making Decisions	2.98	1.00	2.60	1.06	3.01	1.03	2.96	1.09	3.04	1.03	2.99	1.07	3.00	1.13	3.04	1.08
Indirect Expression of Hostility	2.76	1.11	2.60	1.40	2.71	1.12	2.76	1.15	2.70	1.17	2.80	1.15	2.69	1.17	2.79	1.10
Poor Reality Testing	1.64	.78	1.47	.64	1.68	.82	1.66	.86	1.69	.84	1.66	.87	1.73	.84	1.67	.80
Angry	3.17	1.13	2.53	1.13	3.18	1.17	3.13	1.16	3.07	1.21	3.13	1.14	3.26	1.14	3.20	1.16
Eccentric	1.90	1.20	1.87	1.06	1.96	1.28	1.91	1.21	1.98	1.27	1.91	1.23	1.92	1.27	1.92	1.18
Emotional Lability	2.37	1.11	2.00	1.07	2.29	1.02	2.37	1.10	2.25	1.08	2.31	1.12	2.44	1.10	2.34	1.06
Dislikes Change	2.72	1.04	2.47	.74	2.74	1.02	2.75	1.04	2.71	.99	2.69	1.03	2.64	.99	2.73	1.00
Believes Cannot Be Helped	1.94	1.00	1.33	.62	1.95	1.05	1.91	.97	1.86	.97	1.91	1.01	1.88	.98	1.93	.99
Reliable Informant	3.16	.92	3.20	.77	3.16	.91	3.12	.88	3.18	.90	3.17	.91	3.27	1.05	3.16	.94
Ignores Problems	2.30	1.00	2.60	1.12	2.24	1.02	2.30	1.03	2.26	1.01	2.26	1.04	2.36	1.03	2.30	1.02

Ruminates	3.29	.99	2.13	.74	3.33	1.02	3.25	1.03	3.23	1.08	3.20	1.06	3.29	1.03	3.23	1.04
Excitable	2.63	1.04	2.00	.93	2.62	.98	2.59	1.01	2.56	.99	2.54	1.02	2.69	1.03	2.62	1.02
Conforming	2.38	.94	2.60	.91	2.38	.88	2.41	.87	2.37	.87	2.39	.89	2.40	.85	2.45	.89
Ineffective at Dealing with Problems	3.08	.99	2.73	1.10	3.06	1.03	3.08	1.04	3.01	1.01	3.08	1.06	3.03	1.03	3.05	1.01
Introverted	2.61	1.17	2.47	1.25	2.70	1.13	2.59	1.13	2.63	1.11	2.58	1.10	2.44	1.13	2.59	1.16
Superficial Relationships	2.64	1.19	2.43	.85	2.66	1.23	2.63	1.21	2.65	1.19	2.66	1.20	2.59	1.21	2.68	1.17
Impulsive	2.62	1.22	2.60	1.18	2.62	1.24	2.69	1.18	2.71	1.23	2.68	1.21	2.68	1.18	2.64	1.17
Stereotypic Feminine Behavior	1.36	.72	1.33	.62	1.33	.67	1.33	.67	1.37	.71	1.34	.68	1.40	.74	1.36	.71
Stubborn	2.91	1.11	2.67	1.18	2.71	1.11	2.81	1.10	2.79	1.16	2.80	1.14	2.80	1.13	2.90	1.05
Hostile Toward Therapist	1.50	.73	1.33	.82	1.41	.71	1.49	.78	1.45	.74	1.46	.74	1.46	.73	1.50	.74
Difficult to Motivate	2.27	1.02	2.00	1.00	2.17	.99	2.19	1.00	2.22	1.04	2.20	1.02	2.09	.92	2.22	1.01
Suicidal Ideations	1.88	1.04	1.13	.52	1.82	.99	1.90	1.03	1.84	1.03	1.88	1.03	1.87	.99	1.83	.98
Familial Discord	3.02	1.39	2.93	1.38	3.10	1.38	3.03	1.36	3.06	1.40	3.00	1.37	3.05	1.40	3.13	1.35
Dogmatic	2.36	1.17	2.13	.92	2.27	1.16	2.26	1.09	2.31	1.14	2.29	1.12	2.27	1.11	2.37	1.13

	Harris-Lingoes Subscales *(continued)*							
	Ma_1		Ma_2		Ma_3		Ma_4	
	Mean	SD	Mean	SD	Mean	SD	Mean	SD
Intake Information	(n = 80)		(n = 41)		(n = 39)		(n = 74)	
Axis IV diagnosis	3.04	.90	2.85	.88	2.79	.86	2.84	.98
Axis V - Current Level of Functioning	60.62	8.15	60.68	9.23	65.79	10.20	61.51	8.07
Number of Arrests	2.18	5.06	1.40	2.17	1.34	1.97	1.22	2.13
Mental Status	(n = 80)		(n = 41)		(n = 39)		(n = 74)	
Anxiety During Interview	2.61	.81	2.66	.79	2.37	.79	2.41	.66
Depression During Interview	2.41	.74	2.39	.77	1.71	.69	2.34	.69
Activity Level During Interview	3.09	.46	3.20	.56	3.03	.54	3.01	.42
Speech During Interview	2.94	.41	3.02	.52	3.00	.46	2.92	.46
SCL-90-R Scales	(n = 80)		(n = 40)		(n = 38)		(n = 72)	
Somatization	1.07	.80	1.11	.70	.52	.63	1.13	.84
Obsessive-Compulsive	1.35	.83	1.45	.77	.65	.62	1.55	.82
Interpersonal Sensitivity	1.24	.80	1.40	.76	.42	.52	1.48	.88
Depression	1.58	.91	1.62	.75	.60	.58	1.72	.90
Anxiety	1.22	.89	1.34	.78	.47	.57	1.38	.92
Hostility	1.59	1.10	1.85	1.14	.46	.67	1.60	1.22
Phobic Anxiety	.61	.66	.54	.46	.22	.32	.61	.58
Paranoid Ideation	1.46	.80	1.63	.79	.69	.75	1.76	.95
Psychoticism	1.00	.70	.98	.55	.36	.43	1.07	.77
Initial SCL-90 Analogue	(n = 46)		(n = 23)		(n = 30)		(n = 45)	
Somatization	2.27	2.28	2.57	2.97	1.50	2.70	2.57	2.98
Obsessive-Compulsive	3.98	2.66	3.43	2.73	2.93	2.82	3.45	2.40
Interpersonal Sensitivity	4.91	2.40	4.91	2.52	3.77	3.06	4.35	2.54
Depression	4.02	2.75	4.65	2.81	2.63	2.51	4.48	2.74
Anxiety	3.74	2.78	4.57	2.86	3.40	2.66	4.86	2.82
Hostility	3.46	2.92	4.83	2.50	2.63	2.94	3.48	2.77
Phobic Anxiety	1.53	2.03	1.87	2.42	.87	2.26	1.30	2.11
Paranoid Ideation	1.29	1.65	1.78	2.49	1.40	2.24	1.73	2.13
Psychoticism	.82	1.59	1.13	2.28	.90	1.90	.67	1.61
Patient Description Form Scales	(n = 46)		(n = 24)		(n = 30)		(n = 44)	
Angry Resentment	2.82	.95	3.00	.75	2.61	1.06	2.87	.92
Critical/Argumentative	2.65	.93	2.74	.92	2.52	1.05	2.57	.88
Narcissistic	2.66	.93	2.63	1.00	2.48	.99	2.53	.93

Defensive	2.68	.70	2.68	.76	2.81	1.08	2.66	.84
Histrionic	2.47	.68	2.40	.64	2.22	.84	2.57	.89
Aggressive	2.51	.92	2.46	.68	2.44	1.00	2.23	.82
Insecure	2.89	.73	2.78	.68	2.36	.80	2.94	.72
Anxious	2.72	.76	2.71	.61	2.28	.74	2.95	.75
Pessimistic	2.31	.96	2.23	.92	2.10	.88	2.21	.80
Depressed	2.39	.77	2.33	.82	1.73	.61	2.48	.85
Achievement-Oriented	2.67	.75	2.79	.73	2.89	.55	2.75	.73
Passive-Submissive	2.24	.87	2.17	.97	2.04	.83	2.25	.92
Introverted	2.56	.84	2.36	.76	2.39	1.04	2.48	1.04
Emotionally Controlled	2.60	.96	2.50	.94	2.31	.95	2.32	.93
Antisocial	2.60	.81	2.51	.68	2.77	.96	2.35	.82
Negative Treatment Attitudes	2.12	.72	2.12	.70	2.24	.94	1.95	.75
Somatic Symptoms	1.95	.85	1.98	.89	1.60	1.03	2.15	1.08
Psychotic Symptoms	1.27	.38	1.34	.45	1.39	.53	1.27	.50
Family Problems	3.05	1.12	3.10	.88	2.49	1.30	2.76	1.20
Obsessive-Compulsive	2.85	.67	2.67	.69	2.49	.82	2.87	.84
Stereotypic Masculine Interests	3.01	.94	3.00	1.06	3.35	.83	2.80	1.18
Procrastinates	2.38	.90	2.48	1.16	2.10	.97	2.49	1.04
Suspicious	2.70	.84	2.67	.90	2.53	1.18	2.60	.86
Agitated	2.25	.64	2.29	.67	2.02	.90	2.34	.74
Work Problems	2.05	.99	2.08	.73	2.06	.92	2.07	.69
Patient Description Form Items	(n = 46)		(n = 24)		(n = 30)		(n = 44)	
Anxious	3.28	.89	3.25	.85	2.70	1.02	3.34	.96
Problems with Authority Figures	3.33	1.14	3.42	.97	3.18	1.36	3.19	1.09
Has Insight Into Own Problems	2.52	.78	2.75	.94	2.20	.76	2.70	.83
Fears Losing Control	3.20	.97	3.17	.87	2.97	1.15	3.16	.99
Extroverted	2.46	1.03	2.67	1.01	2.60	.89	2.80	.95
Uses Repression	2.77	1.07	2.58	1.06	2.52	.83	2.67	.98
Submissive	2.18	.94	2.17	1.01	2.03	.96	2.36	1.03
Difficulty Concentrating	2.63	.95	2.88	.85	2.32	1.16	2.89	.84
Rigid	2.74	1.16	2.71	1.08	2.70	1.21	2.86	1.07
Overly Compliant	1.96	.88	2.00	1.14	1.80	.96	2.17	.91
Whiny	1.85	1.09	1.79	.98	1.57	.94	2.00	1.08
Feels Overwhelmed	3.17	1.00	3.25	.90	2.60	1.04	3.36	1.12
Manipulative	2.68	1.27	2.65	1.23	2.60	1.35	2.61	1.07
Difficulty Trusting Others	3.52	1.13	3.46	1.02	3.17	1.28	3.25	1.06
Insensitive to Others	2.58	1.06	2.65	1.07	2.66	1.34	2.33	1.08
Stereotypic Masculine Behavior	3.02	1.00	3.00	1.22	3.27	.83	2.70	1.23
Harbors Grudges	2.77	1.14	3.05	1.13	2.64	1.19	2.74	1.04
Evasive	2.43	1.11	2.71	1.23	2.50	1.38	2.33	1.08

	Harris-Lingoes Subscales *(continued)*							
	Ma_1		Ma_2		Ma_3		Ma_4	
	Mean	SD	Mean	SD	Mean	SD	Mean	SD
Disoriented	1.22	.51	1.25	.53	1.10	.31	1.16	.37
Energetic	2.50	.86	2.42	1.02	2.83	.83	2.55	.95
Lonely	2.98	1.23	2.91	.95	2.19	1.14	2.95	1.23
Family Lacks Love	3.07	1.40	3.10	1.09	2.25	1.32	2.76	1.28
Worrier	2.96	1.13	3.00	.88	2.53	1.07	3.43	.97
Narcissistic	2.93	1.00	2.83	1.20	2.59	1.27	2.72	1.18
Tearful	1.49	.79	1.50	.93	1.17	.47	1.68	1.01
Provocative	1.83	.95	2.00	.93	1.69	.97	1.95	.94
Moralistic	2.42	1.05	2.22	1.17	2.53	1.22	2.60	1.07
Socially Awkward	2.89	.99	2.58	.78	2.57	1.25	2.70	1.15
Hostile	2.54	1.22	2.71	.95	2.40	1.35	2.50	1.28
Overcontrolled	2.65	1.12	2.88	1.08	2.43	1.10	2.61	1.20
Resistant to Interpretations	2.39	.98	2.46	.93	2.37	1.03	2.07	.94
Antisocial Behavior	2.70	1.28	2.75	1.22	2.87	1.04	2.41	1.19
Sarcastic	2.11	1.14	2.25	1.11	2.13	1.17	2.11	1.04
Rejects Traditional Gender Role	1.56	1.08	1.55	1.14	1.50	.94	1.83	1.24
Feels Gets Raw Deal From Life	2.84	1.22	2.87	1.06	2.63	1.16	3.05	1.15
Acute Psychological Turmoil	2.98	1.09	3.04	1.12	2.60	1.00	2.91	1.05
Does Not Complete Projects	2.51	1.15	2.45	1.14	1.96	1.07	2.56	1.17
Uncomfortable with Opposite Sex	2.18	1.01	2.00	.97	1.85	1.16	2.10	1.14
Preoccupied with Health Problems	1.89	1.10	2.04	1.26	1.60	1.16	2.19	1.31
Work-Oriented	2.85	.99	3.04	1.04	3.30	1.02	3.07	1.04
Resents Family Members	2.98	1.31	3.00	.98	2.43	1.37	2.79	1.34
Demanding of Attention	2.69	1.12	2.52	1.08	2.38	1.08	2.55	1.11
Passive	2.41	1.13	2.38	1.13	2.00	1.02	2.35	1.15
Self-Punishing	2.35	1.10	2.33	1.05	1.77	.77	2.31	1.16
Needs to Achieve	2.80	1.08	2.92	1.10	3.00	.80	2.84	1.01
Needs to Be with Others	2.93	1.06	2.88	.90	3.03	.78	3.07	1.02
Irritable	2.82	1.11	2.78	.90	2.57	1.28	2.77	1.09
Self-Defeating	3.38	1.07	3.04	1.16	3.00	.98	3.23	1.20
Delusional Thinking	1.25	.58	1.22	.67	1.57	.86	1.23	.62
Self-Reliant	2.70	.87	2.63	.71	2.93	.94	2.61	.87
Aggressive	2.74	.98	2.79	.78	2.76	1.21	2.60	1.03
Competitive	2.59	.97	2.74	1.05	2.86	.74	2.65	.95
Suspicious	2.69	1.12	2.75	1.29	2.43	1.33	2.58	.98
Compulsive	2.67	1.09	2.57	.84	2.31	1.04	2.59	1.02
Dependable	2.95	.91	2.88	.99	2.77	.97	3.18	.81
Multiple Somatic Complaints	1.89	1.04	2.17	1.27	1.43	1.07	2.02	1.27

Complains of Lack of Time	2.05	1.08	2.23	1.27	2.03	1.15	2.21	1.26
Poor Work Performance	2.16	1.11	2.25	1.37	2.17	1.23	2.00	1.05
Insecure	3.46	.84	3.29	.86	3.03	1.27	3.39	.92
Discusses Problems Openly	2.98	.86	2.92	.83	2.77	.90	2.98	.73
Sexually Adjusted	2.56	.70	2.50	.71	2.71	1.00	2.41	.91
Exaggerated Need for Affection	2.27	.99	2.30	.97	1.85	.86	2.45	1.09
Resentful	3.07	1.08	3.13	1.08	2.83	1.17	3.02	1.07
Uses Denial	2.78	1.01	2.67	1.01	3.03	1.15	2.77	1.05
Hypochondriacal	1.53	.63	1.48	.73	1.48	.99	1.67	1.04
Communicates Effectively	3.11	.90	3.13	.99	2.83	.83	3.11	.78
Has Many Nightmares	1.87	1.06	1.64	.93	1.33	.69	1.86	1.06
Stormy Interpersonal Relationships	3.35	1.17	3.38	.88	2.93	1.36	3.16	1.13
Feigns Remorse When in Trouble	1.82	1.00	1.82	1.01	2.33	1.24	1.75	.81
Stereotypic Masculine Interests	2.93	1.04	2.91	1.04	3.43	.94	2.86	1.21
Guarded	2.89	1.14	2.92	1.21	3.03	1.27	2.91	1.20
Feels Inferior	2.96	.88	3.00	.95	2.67	1.06	3.09	.96
Low Frustration Tolerance	3.33	1.11	3.25	.68	3.04	1.32	3.27	1.15
Psychotic Symptoms	1.16	.53	1.26	.75	1.37	.85	1.24	.66
Fired From Past Jobs	1.94	.96	2.15	.88	2.05	1.17	2.03	.89
Needs Attention	2.93	.80	3.04	.75	2.93	1.05	2.98	.95
Acts Out	2.96	1.13	2.83	.94	2.62	1.37	2.49	1.05
Histrionic	2.09	1.01	2.00	1.10	1.55	.87	2.16	1.22
Self-Indulgent	3.00	1.08	2.83	1.20	2.76	1.15	2.72	1.01
Depressed	3.04	1.07	3.17	1.09	2.30	1.12	3.16	1.19
Grandiose	2.20	1.32	2.50	1.35	2.00	1.17	2.14	1.25
Cynical	2.64	1.30	2.87	1.29	2.28	1.22	2.51	1.16
Sociopathic	1.80	.84	1.70	.70	2.03	1.12	1.63	.79
Agitated	2.40	1.05	2.43	1.08	2.07	1.08	2.44	1.01
Marital Problems	2.82	1.67	2.95	1.56	2.04	1.54	2.51	1.60
Absence of Deep Emotions	2.44	1.25	2.21	1.14	2.17	1.17	1.93	1.00
Uncomfortable Dealing with Emotions	3.22	1.09	2.96	1.12	2.97	1.21	2.84	1.26
Sad	2.83	.88	2.83	.87	2.17	.79	2.98	1.00
Self-Degrading	2.15	.99	1.92	.72	1.73	.74	2.00	.86
Unable to Express Negative Feelings	2.30	1.03	2.29	1.16	1.90	1.09	2.11	1.04
Concrete in Thinking	2.31	.95	2.30	1.06	2.37	1.16	2.28	.98
Unable to See Own Limitations	2.48	.98	2.52	1.12	2.60	1.38	2.49	1.08
Power-Oriented	2.56	1.16	2.61	1.16	2.27	1.08	2.51	1.14
Grouchy	2.37	.95	2.46	.93	2.24	1.15	2.41	1.06
Overbearing in Relationships	2.59	1.19	2.55	1.05	2.41	1.05	2.42	1.03
Uncertain About Career	3.37	1.23	3.30	1.33	2.71	1.15	3.52	1.21
Likable	3.11	.82	3.12	.74	3.10	.84	3.20	.79
Procrastinator	2.56	.99	2.71	1.23	2.46	1.21	2.60	1.19

	Harris-Lingoes Subscales *(continued)*							
	Ma_1		Ma_2		Ma_3		Ma_4	
	Mean	SD	Mean	SD	Mean	SD	Mean	SD
Negative Feelings Toward Opposite Sex	2.24	1.26	2.24	1.22	1.88	1.11	1.93	1.07
Defensive	2.72	1.13	2.88	1.03	2.93	1.39	2.68	1.23
Empathetic	2.31	.79	2.21	.72	2.07	.65	2.43	.76
Perfectionistic	2.63	1.09	2.58	1.18	2.26	.81	2.63	1.16
Judgmental	2.83	1.23	2.87	1.26	2.67	1.09	2.84	1.14
Copes Well with Stress	2.11	.53	2.08	.58	2.17	.79	2.05	.61
Moody	2.87	.89	2.83	.94	2.45	.99	2.72	.96
Selfish	2.51	.98	2.52	.99	2.38	.94	2.33	1.05
Gives Up Easily	2.40	1.05	2.38	1.06	1.88	.93	2.26	1.09
Physical Symptoms in Response to Stress	2.14	1.07	2.09	1.11	1.64	1.06	2.32	1.25
Blames Family For Difficulties	2.53	1.33	2.88	1.12	2.41	1.62	2.57	1.37
Bored	2.62	1.09	2.50	1.10	2.10	1.16	2.51	1.14
Idealistic	2.37	.95	2.17	.89	2.30	.88	2.63	.99
Difficulty Establishing Therapeutic Rapport	2.26	1.00	2.33	1.13	2.30	1.26	2.02	1.00
Daydreams	1.92	1.02	1.81	.91	1.90	1.02	1.75	1.00
Concerned About Status	2.64	1.06	2.65	1.27	2.57	.90	2.67	1.19
Creates Good First Impression	2.48	.94	2.71	.91	2.73	1.11	2.61	.87
Complains of Sleep Disturbance	2.73	1.21	2.36	1.22	1.75	1.14	2.71	1.27
Has Temper Tantrums	2.64	1.28	2.76	1.22	2.34	1.32	2.42	1.26
Overreactive	2.85	.97	2.79	.88	2.63	1.35	2.86	1.13
High Aspirations	2.77	1.24	2.83	1.30	2.83	.99	2.81	1.05
Feels Hopeless	2.35	1.10	2.58	1.21	1.87	.86	2.64	1.16
Keeps Others at a Distance	3.16	1.12	3.04	1.02	2.97	1.18	2.95	1.15
Argumentative	2.41	1.09	2.38	1.10	2.40	1.28	2.41	1.02
Paranoid Features	1.89	.82	1.79	1.02	2.03	1.22	1.93	1.04
Restless	2.78	.94	3.00	1.06	2.37	1.16	2.91	1.05
Pessimistic	2.71	1.12	2.71	1.08	2.37	.96	2.77	1.02
Feels Like a Failure	2.80	1.07	3.04	1.12	2.41	.87	2.93	1.07
Hallucinations	1.07	.34	1.09	.42	1.17	.59	1.17	.54
Restricted Affect	2.41	1.33	2.17	1.13	2.17	1.32	2.09	1.22
Impatient	3.02	.93	2.92	.88	2.57	1.25	2.91	.98
Assertive	2.39	.77	2.62	.65	2.40	.67	2.61	.87
Modest	2.39	.83	2.37	.92	2.50	.64	2.40	.93
Self-Doubting	2.91	.89	2.88	.90	2.45	1.09	3.14	.85
Deceptive	2.14	.98	2.13	.81	2.48	1.30	1.95	.96
Feels That Life is a Strain	2.80	.94	2.87	1.06	2.55	1.06	3.14	1.13
Physically Abusive	1.83	1.07	1.90	.91	1.97	1.40	1.49	.87
Feels Rejected	3.16	1.22	3.13	1.22	2.31	1.23	3.19	1.10

Does Not Get Along with Coworkers	2.08	1.09	2.06	1.06	2.00	1.11	2.48	1.09
Uses Projection	2.66	1.03	2.74	.92	2.54	1.10	2.57	1.11
Complains of Fatigue	2.33	1.31	2.50	1.10	1.97	1.33	2.66	1.45
Uses Rationalization	3.04	.94	2.96	1.04	3.13	1.04	3.02	.95
Critical of Others	2.84	1.13	3.09	1.16	2.73	1.20	2.72	1.03
Egocentric	2.93	1.03	2.88	1.12	2.72	1.22	2.75	1.24
Overevaluates Own Worth	2.13	1.19	2.25	1.15	2.07	1.23	2.26	1.20
Optimistic	2.24	.77	2.13	.68	2.57	.86	2.36	.87
Psychologically Immature	3.17	.95	3.04	1.04	3.17	1.28	3.14	1.19
Poor Judgment	3.30	.84	3.08	.88	3.43	1.04	3.05	1.24
Low Sex Drive	1.65	.88	1.33	.65	1.33	.59	1.96	1.19
Feels Mistreated	2.98	1.11	3.08	.97	2.59	1.38	3.11	1.04
Overly Sensitive to Criticism	2.93	1.08	2.96	1.23	2.79	1.26	3.19	1.18
Sentimental	2.47	.96	2.17	.98	2.14	.93	2.63	.94
Sexual Preoccupation	1.93	1.20	1.75	1.00	1.96	1.33	1.91	1.33
Accelerated Speech	1.63	.93	1.54	.98	1.63	1.03	1.73	1.02
Concerns About Homosexuality	1.36	.83	1.58	1.22	1.36	1.18	1.68	1.28
Many Specific Fears	1.67	.90	1.52	.68	1.50	.79	1.88	.99
Passive in Relationships	2.23	1.08	2.12	1.03	2.21	1.10	2.15	1.10
Negative Attitudes Toward Therapy	1.93	.95	1.83	.98	2.10	1.18	1.70	.89
Guilt-Prone	2.54	1.05	2.61	1.12	2.24	1.09	2.73	1.17
Nervous	2.87	1.00	2.83	.96	2.34	1.14	3.14	.95
Obsessive	2.87	.98	2.79	.93	2.23	1.17	2.98	1.12
Shy	2.26	1.08	2.25	.99	2.27	1.08	2.34	1.26
Uses Intellectualization	2.63	1.20	2.79	1.35	2.43	1.10	2.77	1.32
Has Many Interests	2.35	1.07	2.48	.99	2.52	.87	2.58	1.12
Difficulty Making Decisions	2.87	1.08	2.78	1.24	2.56	1.09	3.18	1.19
Indirect Expression of Hostility	2.73	.89	2.79	1.02	2.52	1.35	2.70	1.06
Poor Reality Testing	1.74	.77	1.92	.83	1.73	.83	1.66	.81
Angry	3.17	1.14	3.50	.93	2.62	1.42	3.20	1.07
Eccentric	1.87	1.06	1.78	1.20	2.00	1.49	2.09	1.39
Emotional Lability	2.44	1.12	2.42	1.10	2.10	1.08	2.53	1.22
Dislikes Change	2.78	.89	2.24	1.00	2.74	1.10	2.57	1.02
Believes Cannot Be Helped	1.84	.95	1.75	1.07	1.79	.94	1.64	.78
Reliable Informant	3.20	.91	3.12	.90	3.00	1.08	3.02	.82
Ignores Problems	2.50	.98	2.46	.88	2.80	.81	2.43	.93
Ruminates	3.13	1.02	3.04	1.11	2.62	1.08	3.29	1.09
Excitable	2.80	.98	2.74	.96	2.59	1.27	2.98	1.05
Conforming	2.28	.86	2.54	.72	2.57	.90	2.51	.91
Ineffective at Dealing with Problems	3.04	.82	3.13	1.01	3.13	1.11	3.00	1.05
Introverted	2.52	1.05	2.35	1.11	2.33	1.18	2.39	1.10
Superficial Relationships	2.83	.96	2.73	1.12	2.64	1.31	2.63	1.24

	Harris-Lingoes Subscales *(continued)*							
	Ma_1		Ma_2		Ma_3		Ma_4	
	Mean	SD	Mean	SD	Mean	SD	Mean	SD
Impulsive	3.20	1.02	3.00	.83	3.10	1.09	2.89	1.08
Stereotypic Feminine Behavior	1.33	.63	1.33	.70	1.23	.43	1.59	.84
Stubborn	2.82	1.11	3.00	1.10	2.69	1.17	2.89	1.08
Hostile Toward Therapist	1.41	.58	1.46	.59	1.60	1.04	1.55	.79
Difficult to Motivate	2.27	.99	2.25	.90	2.27	1.26	2.09	.94
Suicidal Ideations	1.76	.93	1.74	.92	1.13	.43	1.68	.83
Familial Discord	3.40	1.20	3.54	1.02	2.67	1.54	2.98	1.35
Dogmatic	2.30	1.11	2.50	1.18	2.37	1.16	2.57	1.13

Table L-2c. Means and standard deviations for continuous extra-test characteristics (men): High scores on Si subscales

Extra-test Characteristics	Si Subscales					
	Si_1		Si_2		Si_3	
	Mean	SD	Mean	SD	Mean	SD
Intake Information	(n = 116)		(n = 112)		(n = 162)	
Axis IV diagnosis	2.96	.87	3.04	.92	3.00	.89
Axis V - Current Level of Functioning	60.25	11.23	58.65	10.43	60.49	9.97
Number of Arrests	1.31	2.99	1.74	4.72	1.15	2.49
Mental Status	(n = 116)		(n = 112)		(n = 162)	
Anxiety During Interview	2.48	.72	2.55	.77	2.51	.75
Depression During Interview	2.42	.74	2.48	.70	2.42	.73
Activity Level During Interview	3.04	.51	3.05	.47	3.03	.49
Speech During Interview	2.97	.39	3.01	.35	2.91	.43
SCL-90-R Scales	(n = 112)		(n = 110)		(n = 159)	
Somatization	1.13	.77	1.13	.79	1.31	.83
Obsessive-Compulsive	1.67	.86	1.57	.88	1.73	.81
Interpersonal Sensitivity	1.77	.90	1.60	.94	1.70	.84
Depression	1.98	.87	1.88	.94	2.00	.86
Anxiety	1.55	.90	1.43	.96	1.62	.91
Hostility	1.49	1.09	1.41	1.04	1.59	1.07
Phobic Anxiety	.86	.73	.84	.77	.82	.71
Paranoid Ideation	1.46	.93	1.47	.94	1.68	.88
Psychoticism	1.09	.74	1.03	.74	1.21	.72
Initial SCL-90 Analogue	(n = 69)		(n = 72)		(n = 96)	
Somatization	2.33	2.64	2.54	3.03	2.52	2.83
Obsessive-Compulsive	3.71	2.67	3.58	2.85	3.68	2.65
Interpersonal Sensitivity	4.88	2.25	4.79	2.61	4.65	2.51
Depression	4.28	2.63	4.47	2.69	4.55	2.70
Anxiety	4.77	2.78	4.37	2.74	4.72	2.73
Hostility	3.04	2.63	3.47	2.77	3.28	2.81
Phobic Anxiety	1.54	2.15	1.50	2.07	1.49	2.27
Paranoid Ideation	1.14	1.60	1.49	2.02	1.22	1.81
Psychoticism	.51	.98	.83	1.38	.54	1.40

Table L-2c. Means and standard deviations for continuous extra-test characteristics (men): High scores on Si subscales *(continued)*

Extra-test Characteristics	Si Subscales					
	Si_1		Si_2		Si_3	
	Mean	SD	Mean	SD	Mean	SD
Patient Description Form Scales	(n = 69)		(n = 73)		(n = 96)	
Angry Resentment	2.83	.88	2.84	.91	2.77	.94
Critical/Argumentative	2.48	.79	2.56	.93	2.44	.96
Narcissistic	2.20	.76	2.38	.90	2.27	.95
Defensive	2.55	.85	2.73	.95	2.54	.91
Histrionic	2.32	.70	2.35	.78	2.40	.81
Aggressive	2.06	.83	2.24	.87	2.02	.84
Insecure	3.07	.73	2.96	.80	3.04	.80
Anxious	3.06	.67	2.90	.86	2.98	.78
Pessimistic	2.32	.95	2.53	1.04	2.34	.87
Depressed	2.54	.78	2.50	.80	2.52	.81
Achievement-Oriented	2.60	.66	2.48	.66	2.59	.72
Passive-Submissive	2.41	.80	2.28	.85	2.36	.81
Introverted	2.93	1.03	2.77	1.09	2.72	1.02
Emotionally Controlled	2.64	1.09	2.63	1.11	2.38	1.02
Antisocial	2.03	.87	2.39	.99	2.22	.87
Negative Treatment Attitudes	1.96	.74	2.19	.92	1.91	.79
Somatic Symptoms	2.16	1.04	2.19	1.17	2.17	1.08
Psychotic Symptoms	1.20	.33	1.35	.46	1.22	.38
Family Problems	2.83	1.06	2.79	1.04	2.76	1.15
Obsessive-Compulsive	2.91	.76	2.88	.78	2.87	.81
Stereotypic Masculine Interests	2.76	1.15	2.81	1.20	2.83	1.13
Procrastinates	2.28	.80	2.36	.90	2.33	1.00
Suspicious	2.61	.88	2.76	1.02	2.56	.95
Agitated	2.15	.75	2.19	.85	2.15	.78
Work Problems	1.87	.83	2.08	.96	1.84	.79
Patient Description Form Items	(n = 69)		(n = 73)		(n = 96)	
Anxious	3.62	.77	3.37	.96	3.54	.81
Problems with Authority Figures	2.84	1.12	3.04	1.07	3.00	1.17
Has Insight Into Own Problems	2.76	.87	2.55	.88	2.64	.82
Fears Losing Control	3.48	1.04	3.40	1.06	3.30	1.04
Extroverted	2.14	.93	2.14	.90	2.32	.97
Uses Repression	2.78	1.06	2.83	1.06	2.66	1.09

Submissive	2.42	.92	2.20	.96	2.38	.91
Difficulty Concentrating	2.67	1.08	2.74	1.13	2.80	1.14
Rigid	2.83	1.04	2.96	1.16	2.70	1.11
Overly Compliant	2.12	.99	1.92	.96	2.11	.93
Whiny	1.99	1.05	1.96	1.06	1.91	1.02
Feels Overwhelmed	3.36	1.00	3.31	1.24	3.34	1.16
Manipulative	2.24	1.06	2.58	1.24	2.35	1.16
Difficulty Trusting Others	3.38	1.16	3.46	1.21	3.29	1.21
Insensitive to Others	2.16	.96	2.47	1.16	2.21	1.01
Stereotypic Masculine Behavior	2.78	1.22	2.85	1.25	2.80	1.16
Harbors Grudges	2.77	1.08	2.97	1.19	2.70	1.06
Evasive	2.36	1.08	2.56	1.31	2.23	1.07
Disoriented	1.25	.50	1.32	.60	1.20	.45
Energetic	2.39	.81	2.28	.86	2.43	.84
Lonely	3.09	1.20	2.94	1.22	3.04	1.24
Family Lacks Love	2.77	1.23	2.70	1.18	2.77	1.33
Worrier	3.51	.88	3.19	1.19	3.35	1.04
Narcissistic	2.40	1.00	2.59	1.15	2.44	1.16
Tearful	1.59	.85	1.59	.81	1.58	.87
Provocative	1.51	.72	1.60	.91	1.70	.88
Moralistic	2.48	1.04	2.50	1.02	2.60	1.04
Socially Awkward	3.10	1.21	2.90	1.25	2.99	1.14
Hostile	2.47	1.11	2.50	1.16	2.43	1.17
Overcontrolled	2.86	1.22	2.71	1.26	2.61	1.21
Resistant to Interpretations	2.22	1.03	2.37	1.07	2.08	.97
Antisocial Behavior	2.03	1.16	2.29	1.20	2.26	1.19
Sarcastic	1.99	.98	2.00	1.02	1.98	1.10
Rejects Traditional Gender Role	1.73	.98	1.68	1.00	1.71	1.07
Feels Gets Raw Deal From Life	2.91	1.18	3.06	1.23	2.97	1.20
Acute Psychological Turmoil	3.10	.94	3.16	1.05	3.10	1.10
Does Not Complete Projects	2.09	1.01	2.32	1.05	2.26	1.14
Uncomfortable with Opposite Sex	2.38	1.07	2.16	1.03	2.27	1.11
Preoccupied with Health Problems	2.25	1.31	2.40	1.51	2.28	1.32
Work-Oriented	3.06	1.08	3.00	1.11	3.03	1.02
Resents Family Members	2.87	1.24	2.79	1.31	2.82	1.35
Demanding of Attention	2.32	.99	2.47	1.16	2.48	1.08
Passive	2.63	.98	2.43	1.02	2.57	.97
Self-Punishing	2.66	1.16	2.46	1.16	2.47	1.22
Needs to Achieve	2.76	.88	2.74	.98	2.74	1.00
Needs to Be with Others	2.86	.93	2.70	.91	3.00	1.08
Irritable	2.62	.94	2.77	1.07	2.63	1.07
Self-Defeating	3.19	1.06	3.19	1.09	3.15	1.16
Delusional Thinking	1.13	.38	1.35	.72	1.14	.46

Table L-2c. Means and standard deviations for continuous extra-test characteristics (men): High scores on Si subscales *(continued)*

Extra-test Characteristics	Si Subscales					
	Si_1		Si_2		Si_3	
	Mean	SD	Mean	SD	Mean	SD
Self-Reliant	2.64	.86	2.63	.94	2.61	.84
Aggressive	2.31	.97	2.50	1.06	2.35	.94
Competitive	2.47	.96	2.46	1.01	2.40	.97
Suspicious	2.55	1.09	2.75	1.21	2.54	1.15
Compulsive	2.85	1.17	2.63	1.15	2.59	1.08
Dependable	3.12	.91	2.99	.92	3.08	.88
Multiple Somatic Complaints	2.03	1.24	2.19	1.46	2.08	1.24
Complains of Lack of Time	1.91	.95	1.97	1.10	2.02	1.15
Poor Work Performance	1.98	1.00	2.02	1.00	1.94	1.02
Insecure	3.59	.83	3.38	.97	3.57	.88
Discusses Problems Openly	3.17	.80	2.92	.98	3.08	.78
Sexually Adjusted	2.42	.80	2.21	.82	2.36	.79
Exaggerated Need for Affection	2.21	.91	2.13	.95	2.39	1.10
Resentful	3.09	1.15	3.14	1.07	3.00	1.17
Uses Denial	2.67	1.21	2.90	1.24	2.61	1.16
Hypochondriacal	1.78	.94	1.76	.99	1.74	.95
Communicates Effectively	3.17	.79	2.97	.82	3.15	.71
Has Many Nightmares	1.98	1.21	1.69	1.05	1.85	1.10
Stormy Interpersonal Relationships	2.97	1.29	3.20	1.20	3.00	1.18
Feigns Remorse When in Trouble	1.69	.90	1.98	1.14	1.71	.89
Stereotypic Masculine Interests	2.75	1.19	2.78	1.25	2.83	1.21
Guarded	2.70	1.25	2.96	1.25	2.70	1.31
Feels Inferior	3.17	1.04	3.06	1.02	3.18	1.05
Low Frustration Tolerance	3.09	1.14	3.30	1.05	3.19	1.17
Psychotic Symptoms	1.13	.38	1.25	.55	1.15	.51
Fired From Past Jobs	1.95	1.08	2.24	1.21	1.91	.97
Needs Attention	2.72	.82	2.74	.94	2.92	1.01
Acts Out	2.30	1.06	2.47	1.13	2.40	1.05
Histrionic	1.78	.84	1.96	1.08	1.90	1.02
Self-Indulgent	2.36	1.11	2.56	1.08	2.50	1.11
Depressed	3.32	.87	3.27	.93	3.32	1.05
Grandiose	1.85	.93	1.97	1.06	1.86	1.10
Cynical	2.46	1.13	2.56	1.22	2.44	1.24
Sociopathic	1.52	.80	1.85	1.03	1.62	.81
Agitated	2.46	1.04	2.50	1.03	2.43	1.06

Marital Problems	2.48	1.56	2.78	1.59	2.37	1.59
Absence of Deep Emotions	2.24	1.36	2.25	1.30	1.96	1.13
Uncomfortable Dealing with Emotions	3.12	1.19	3.18	1.33	2.91	1.27
Sad	3.06	.90	2.94	.99	2.97	1.02
Self-Degrading	2.41	1.03	2.29	.98	2.26	1.03
Unable to Express Negative Feelings	2.46	1.12	2.44	1.14	2.21	1.13
Concrete in Thinking	2.17	1.01	2.30	1.04	2.27	1.04
Unable to See Own Limitations	2.18	1.04	2.35	1.10	2.28	1.15
Power-Oriented	2.17	1.13	2.14	1.13	2.07	1.01
Grouchy	2.26	1.07	2.34	1.10	2.33	1.04
Overbearing in Relationships	2.19	1.03	2.40	1.06	2.14	1.16
Uncertain About Career	3.47	1.22	3.44	1.27	3.35	1.28
Likable	3.24	.78	3.14	.79	3.25	.73
Procrastinator	2.66	1.01	2.62	1.08	2.65	1.16
Negative Feelings Toward Opposite Sex	2.29	1.09	2.35	1.19	2.14	1.11
Defensive	2.63	1.10	2.84	1.19	2.64	1.23
Empathetic	2.24	.72	2.15	.75	2.41	.72
Perfectionistic	2.76	1.12	2.54	1.14	2.49	1.11
Judgmental	2.71	.99	2.72	1.11	2.70	1.15
Copes Well with Stress	2.06	.72	1.92	.66	1.99	.66
Moody	2.97	1.00	2.85	1.04	2.79	1.00
Selfish	2.18	.89	2.32	1.01	2.17	1.01
Gives Up Easily	2.32	1.03	2.25	.94	2.33	1.03
Physical Symptoms in Response to Stress	2.39	1.25	2.27	1.24	2.30	1.24
Blames Family For Difficulties	2.49	1.27	2.51	1.24	2.52	1.33
Bored	2.56	1.07	2.63	1.12	2.37	1.11
Idealistic	2.30	1.04	2.29	1.02	2.46	1.06
Difficulty Establishing Therapeutic Rapport	1.99	.95	2.26	1.13	1.97	1.00
Daydreams	2.14	1.00	1.98	1.11	1.98	1.05
Concerned About Status	2.45	1.11	2.30	1.11	2.46	1.13
Creates Good First Impression	2.55	.84	2.47	.83	2.69	.79
Complains of Sleep Disturbance	2.70	1.36	2.58	1.34	2.64	1.34
Has Temper Tantrums	2.27	1.16	2.34	1.10	2.27	1.19
Overreactive	2.63	1.06	2.78	1.17	2.72	1.10
High Aspirations	2.47	1.08	2.29	1.05	2.54	1.17
Feels Hopeless	2.76	1.09	2.75	1.10	2.74	1.14
Keeps Others at a Distance	3.12	1.23	3.21	1.30	2.89	1.27
Argumentative	2.33	.98	2.32	1.08	2.27	1.09
Paranoid Features	1.84	.93	2.08	1.09	1.84	.92
Restless	2.61	1.09	2.63	1.21	2.65	1.13
Pessimistic	2.88	1.08	3.01	1.14	2.89	1.06
Feels Like a Failure	3.09	1.09	3.10	1.12	3.02	1.13

Table L-2c. Means and standard deviations for continuous extra-test characteristics (men): High scores on Si subscales *(continued)*

Extra-test Characteristics	Si Subscales					
	Si_1		Si_2		Si_3	
	Mean	SD	Mean	SD	Mean	SD
Hallucinations	1.09	.28	1.11	.36	1.10	.36
Restricted Affect	2.57	1.37	2.64	1.33	2.22	1.28
Impatient	2.65	1.06	2.72	1.12	2.66	1.10
Assertive	2.28	.84	2.25	.86	2.33	.85
Modest	2.63	.90	2.39	.83	2.54	.85
Self-Doubting	3.25	.86	3.14	.98	3.16	.91
Deceptive	1.94	.98	2.14	1.11	1.95	1.05
Feels That Life is a Strain	3.09	1.05	3.26	1.10	3.19	1.07
Physically Abusive	1.48	.73	1.74	1.05	1.49	.82
Feels Rejected	3.25	1.11	3.18	1.10	3.24	1.21
Does Not Get Along with Coworkers	1.98	.96	2.05	1.09	1.91	.89
Uses Projection	2.46	1.09	2.54	1.24	2.34	1.14
Complains of Fatigue	2.46	1.23	2.57	1.42	2.45	1.35
Uses Rationalization	2.78	1.03	2.89	1.12	2.70	1.09
Critical of Others	2.46	.95	2.65	1.21	2.52	1.09
Egocentric	2.42	.96	2.58	1.15	2.53	1.24
Overevaluates Own Worth	1.77	.89	1.89	.95	1.99	1.17
Optimistic	2.06	.64	1.95	.66	2.07	.71
Psychologically Immature	2.70	1.03	2.95	1.22	2.95	1.16
Poor Judgment	2.65	1.20	3.10	1.13	2.92	1.18
Low Sex Drive	1.89	1.01	1.95	1.10	1.74	.94
Feels Mistreated	2.97	1.05	3.05	1.08	2.95	1.05
Overly Sensitive to Criticism	3.15	1.00	3.25	1.06	3.08	1.24
Sentimental	2.48	1.00	2.33	.94	2.53	1.03
Sexual Preoccupation	1.73	1.09	1.86	1.23	1.73	1.14
Accelerated Speech	1.36	.66	1.45	.88	1.43	.82
Concerns About Homosexuality	1.37	.98	1.44	1.07	1.51	1.14
Many Specific Fears	1.98	.99	1.85	1.02	1.84	1.00
Passive in Relationships	2.55	1.00	2.56	1.07	2.40	1.02
Negative Attitudes Toward Therapy	1.76	.92	2.04	1.09	1.71	.96
Guilt-Prone	2.71	1.06	2.52	1.11	2.81	1.14
Nervous	3.28	.93	3.08	1.06	3.18	.99
Obsessive	2.91	1.02	2.90	1.11	2.98	1.15
Shy	2.80	1.21	2.56	1.20	2.57	1.20
Uses Intellectualization	2.64	1.15	2.53	1.18	2.52	1.20

Has Many Interests	2.27	.83	2.05	.80	2.41	1.05
Difficulty Making Decisions	2.90	.97	3.04	1.00	3.07	1.10
Indirect Expression of Hostility	2.76	1.19	3.03	1.12	2.70	1.14
Poor Reality Testing	1.49	.68	1.76	.91	1.60	.75
Angry	3.12	1.16	3.11	1.16	3.07	1.15
Eccentric	1.83	1.07	2.03	1.27	1.91	1.28
Emotional Lability	2.27	.95	2.24	.99	2.26	1.12
Dislikes Change	2.75	1.05	2.88	1.02	2.70	1.04
Believes Cannot Be Helped	1.75	1.01	2.04	1.13	1.80	.88
Reliable Informant	3.29	.89	3.10	.94	3.20	.87
Ignores Problems	2.24	1.05	2.44	1.14	2.27	1.00
Ruminates	3.24	1.00	3.20	.95	3.30	1.07
Excitable	2.52	.98	2.53	1.03	2.60	1.06
Conforming	2.57	.95	2.44	.82	2.55	.81
Ineffective at Dealing with Problems	2.90	.97	3.21	1.11	2.95	1.10
Introverted	2.90	1.10	2.86	1.17	2.60	1.15
Superficial Relationships	2.72	1.18	2.88	1.18	2.54	1.25
Impulsive	2.55	1.19	2.73	1.24	2.65	1.21
Stereotypic Feminine Behavior	1.41	.75	1.32	.70	1.40	.67
Stubborn	2.73	1.06	2.96	1.11	2.69	1.13
Hostile Toward Therapist	1.33	.59	1.52	.91	1.43	.75
Difficult to Motivate	2.09	.88	2.44	1.16	2.05	.94
Suicidal Ideations	1.75	1.03	1.87	1.09	1.79	.98
Familial Discord	3.00	1.26	3.04	1.36	2.96	1.34
Dogmatic	2.09	1.05	2.22	1.07	2.23	1.16

Table L-2d. Means and standard deviations for continuous extra-test characteristics (men): High scores on Content Scales

	Content Scales									
	ANX		FRS		OBS		DEP		HEA	
	Mean	SD	Mean	SD	Mean	SD	Mean	SD	Mean	SD
Intake Information	(n = 236)		(n = 64)		(n = 143)		(n = 252)		(n = 171)	
Axis IV diagnosis	2.95	.91	2.97	.99	2.98	.91	2.92	.91	3.03	.97
Axis V - Current Level of Functioning	60.66	9.63	60.56	10.74	60.26	10.23	60.51	9.67	60.02	10.64
Number of Arrests	1.39	3.51	1.51	2.76	1.35	2.63	1.47	3.58	1.43	3.79
Mental Status	(n = 236)		(n = 64)		(n = 143)		(n = 252)		(n = 171)	
Anxiety During Interview	2.50	.73	2.56	.76	2.54	.71	2.46	.71	2.44	.67
Depression During Interview	2.43	.69	2.29	.73	2.50	.72	2.43	.70	2.45	.73
Activity Level During Interview	3.02	.45	3.02	.49	3.02	.50	3.02	.45	2.98	.43
Speech During Interview	2.96	.38	3.02	.28	2.94	.41	2.96	.37	2.96	.37
SCL-90-R Scales	(n = 232)		(n = 62)		(n = 140)		(n = 247)		(n = 167)	
Somatization	1.25	.80	1.25	.90	1.31	.82	1.20	.80	1.57	.71
Obsessive-Compulsive	1.67	.81	1.59	.96	1.88	.76	1.64	.81	1.79	.86
Interpersonal Sensitivity	1.60	.86	1.51	.87	1.78	.83	1.59	.85	1.65	.88
Depression	1.99	.81	1.73	.94	2.06	.80	1.99	.79	2.02	.85
Anxiety	1.54	.85	1.42	.98	1.70	.87	1.48	.87	1.70	.88
Hostility	1.55	1.06	1.10	.95	1.61	1.09	1.50	1.05	1.52	1.03
Phobic Anxiety	.77	.73	.94	.76	.87	.70	.76	.73	.91	.75
Paranoid Ideation	1.61	.88	1.40	.91	1.72	.88	1.56	.90	1.62	.90
Psychoticism	1.15	.71	1.13	.81	1.21	.69	1.13	.71	1.21	.74
Initial SCL-90 Analogue	(n = 146)		(n = 40)		(n = 85)		(n = 158)		(n = 106)	
Somatization	2.62	2.91	2.54	2.97	2.24	2.71	2.59	2.92	3.50	3.15
Obsessive-Compulsive	3.50	2.80	3.41	2.49	3.31	2.83	3.42	2.79	3.72	2.66
Interpersonal Sensitivity	4.83	2.46	4.33	2.65	4.55	2.51	4.92	2.44	4.86	2.44
Depression	4.68	2.74	4.56	2.41	4.30	2.71	4.82	2.69	4.97	2.60
Anxiety	4.64	2.63	4.55	2.39	4.74	2.72	4.64	2.72	5.05	2.54
Hostility	3.47	2.83	2.85	2.72	3.49	2.94	3.43	2.83	3.42	2.78
Phobic Anxiety	1.34	2.16	1.05	1.72	1.37	2.26	1.41	2.22	1.80	2.48
Paranoid Ideation	1.28	1.91	1.71	2.18	1.16	1.93	1.38	2.10	1.38	1.80
Psychoticism	.59	1.43	.54	1.26	.47	1.43	.63	1.44	.60	1.35

Patient Description Form Scales	(n = 148)		(n = 40)		(n = 84)		(n = 159)		(n = 107)	
Angry Resentment	2.88	.96	2.77	.94	2.81	1.01	2.88	.95	2.97	.93
Critical/Argumentative	2.59	.95	2.42	.92	2.47	.99	2.57	.95	2.67	.91
Narcissistic	2.35	.93	2.25	.87	2.25	.98	2.31	.94	2.38	.91
Defensive	2.59	.89	2.59	.94	2.48	.93	2.59	.90	2.68	.87
Histrionic	2.43	.78	2.22	.78	2.36	.82	2.41	.77	2.50	.75
Aggressive	2.25	.91	1.89	.67	2.07	.88	2.18	.89	2.27	.83
Insecure	2.96	.75	2.82	.82	2.99	.82	3.02	.79	2.97	.72
Anxious	2.96	.78	3.02	.81	2.97	.81	2.97	.80	3.11	.74
Pessimistic	2.41	.93	2.51	.87	2.38	.95	2.49	.97	2.60	.94
Depressed	2.55	.77	2.38	.78	2.51	.85	2.57	.77	2.61	.73
Achievement-Oriented	2.59	.73	2.46	.69	2.57	.75	2.55	.73	2.52	.77
Passive-Submissive	2.20	.81	2.36	.86	2.18	.83	2.21	.84	2.30	.81
Introverted	2.57	1.00	2.60	1.11	2.62	1.07	2.60	1.03	2.64	1.00
Emotionally Controlled	2.39	1.03	2.26	1.00	2.35	1.14	2.40	1.07	2.48	1.05
Antisocial	2.31	.94	2.17	.87	2.16	.95	2.26	.98	2.30	.94
Negative Treatment Attitudes	1.98	.80	2.00	.78	1.90	.80	2.00	.82	2.09	.83
Somatic Symptoms	2.20	1.10	2.26	1.12	2.12	1.08	2.17	1.09	2.52	1.13
Psychotic Symptoms	1.27	.42	1.31	.49	1.22	.42	1.29	.45	1.30	.41
Family Problems	2.82	1.14	2.44	1.06	2.84	1.20	2.80	1.15	2.85	1.19
Obsessive-Compulsive	2.82	.80	2.79	.78	2.76	.89	2.83	.81	2.90	.77
Stereotypic Masculine Interests	2.84	1.12	2.65	1.12	2.86	1.14	2.81	1.13	2.88	1.15
Procrastinates	2.31	.92	2.23	.93	2.29	1.05	2.29	.96	2.42	.97
Suspicious	2.59	.98	2.70	.99	2.51	.99	2.65	1.03	2.70	.92
Agitated	2.24	.78	2.17	.74	2.17	.84	2.22	.77	2.35	.76
Work Problems	2.06	.97	1.92	.86	1.79	.83	2.06	.96	2.01	.88
Patient Description Form Items	(n = 148)		(n = 40)		(n = 84)		(n = 159)		(n = 107)	
Anxious	3.49	.85	3.48	.82	3.52	.86	3.48	.88	3.64	.82
Problems with Authority Figures	2.98	1.24	2.95	1.10	2.90	1.22	3.01	1.28	3.10	1.18
Has Insight Into Own Problems	2.54	.82	2.30	.69	2.73	.86	2.63	.89	2.55	.82
Fears Losing Control	3.26	1.01	3.05	1.21	3.14	1.16	3.25	1.08	3.44	1.03
Extroverted	2.36	.94	2.30	.91	2.35	1.02	2.32	.93	2.36	.90
Uses Repression	2.62	1.06	2.77	.99	2.44	1.07	2.60	1.07	2.75	1.04
Submissive	2.19	.87	2.42	.96	2.17	.89	2.17	.92	2.29	.86
Difficulty Concentrating	2.78	1.11	2.97	1.19	2.71	1.18	2.75	1.12	3.00	.98
Rigid	2.78	1.11	2.80	1.02	2.70	1.12	2.78	1.07	2.94	1.04
Overly Compliant	1.98	.89	2.02	1.00	1.98	.90	1.96	.89	2.06	.91
Whiny	1.97	1.04	1.92	.97	1.92	1.03	1.98	1.04	2.15	1.08
Feels Overwhelmed	3.40	1.12	3.35	1.17	3.35	1.16	3.39	1.12	3.51	1.09
Manipulative	2.43	1.15	2.35	1.08	2.32	1.10	2.48	1.19	2.54	1.12
Difficulty Trusting Others	3.29	1.25	3.30	1.32	3.18	1.27	3.34	1.26	3.41	1.21

Table L-2d. Means and standard deviations for continuous extra-test characteristics (men): High scores on Content Scales *(continued)*

	Content Scales									
	ANX		FRS		OBS		DEP		HEA	
	Mean	SD	Mean	SD	Mean	SD	Mean	SD	Mean	SD
Insensitive to Others	2.27	1.06	2.23	1.10	2.20	1.10	2.26	1.09	2.27	1.12
Stereotypic Masculine Behavior	2.83	1.15	2.63	1.13	2.84	1.20	2.78	1.17	2.83	1.19
Harbors Grudges	2.80	1.14	2.62	.98	2.75	1.14	2.85	1.17	2.87	1.09
Evasive	2.28	1.13	2.38	1.11	2.18	1.14	2.32	1.15	2.36	1.11
Disoriented	1.27	.61	1.25	.49	1.20	.53	1.30	.62	1.31	.57
Energetic	2.42	.91	2.42	.81	2.49	.94	2.36	.87	2.32	.95
Lonely	2.94	1.25	2.88	1.24	2.96	1.28	2.99	1.26	2.92	1.22
Family Lacks Love	2.75	1.32	2.36	1.20	2.83	1.26	2.78	1.34	2.84	1.35
Worrier	3.36	1.04	3.35	1.03	3.32	1.12	3.35	1.07	3.48	1.00
Narcissistic	2.52	1.19	2.35	1.10	2.48	1.24	2.53	1.21	2.59	1.18
Tearful	1.57	.84	1.40	.71	1.58	.89	1.57	.84	1.60	.87
Provocative	1.66	.86	1.62	.74	1.63	.88	1.70	.93	1.71	.87
Moralistic	2.49	1.08	2.62	1.02	2.44	1.01	2.52	1.11	2.53	1.05
Socially Awkward	2.81	1.16	2.85	1.31	2.75	1.16	2.82	1.18	2.79	1.08
Hostile	2.52	1.21	2.33	1.16	2.51	1.28	2.58	1.22	2.64	1.22
Overcontrolled	2.61	1.18	2.52	1.26	2.64	1.33	2.64	1.25	2.76	1.26
Resistant to Interpretations	2.19	1.01	2.08	.94	2.05	.96	2.17	1.02	2.31	1.03
Antisocial Behavior	2.28	1.28	1.98	1.07	2.17	1.27	2.27	1.31	2.30	1.26
Sarcastic	2.08	1.10	1.98	.95	2.02	1.11	2.06	1.08	2.12	1.09
Rejects Traditional Gender Role	1.63	1.03	1.79	1.10	1.65	1.06	1.66	1.07	1.63	.99
Feels Gets Raw Deal From Life	3.10	1.18	3.05	1.28	3.02	1.28	3.10	1.17	3.15	1.14
Acute Psychological Turmoil	3.08	1.09	2.93	1.10	3.04	1.15	3.11	1.10	3.15	1.04
Does Not Complete Projects	2.29	1.12	2.21	1.02	2.23	1.16	2.33	1.16	2.33	1.10
Uncomfortable with Opposite Sex	2.12	1.07	2.21	1.07	2.13	1.14	2.13	1.09	2.11	1.05
Preoccupied with Health Problems	2.28	1.39	2.40	1.39	2.29	1.38	2.28	1.41	2.74	1.44
Work-Oriented	2.98	1.08	2.80	1.02	2.96	1.05	2.93	1.09	3.00	1.14
Resents Family Members	2.84	1.32	2.59	1.32	2.85	1.36	2.79	1.31	2.83	1.32
Demanding of Attention	2.50	1.13	2.20	1.07	2.45	1.07	2.50	1.13	2.56	1.10
Passive	2.38	.98	2.60	.93	2.39	1.02	2.40	.99	2.47	.97
Self-Punishing	2.43	1.19	2.38	1.14	2.47	1.28	2.47	1.18	2.57	1.19
Needs to Achieve	2.78	1.03	2.51	1.07	2.69	1.06	2.79	1.05	2.67	1.07
Needs to Be with Others	2.91	1.07	2.48	.93	2.89	1.12	2.91	1.06	2.91	1.03
Irritable	2.79	1.06	2.75	1.13	2.70	1.03	2.76	1.05	2.95	1.03
Self-Defeating	3.18	1.16	3.13	1.18	2.89	1.22	3.18	1.25	3.18	1.14
Delusional Thinking	1.24	.61	1.38	.77	1.16	.54	1.29	.70	1.30	.70

Self-Reliant	2.68	.90	2.80	.85	2.63	.82	2.62	.89	2.68	.93
Aggressive	2.49	1.05	2.23	.86	2.36	1.12	2.43	1.06	2.56	1.05
Competitive	2.44	.99	2.29	1.01	2.38	1.09	2.40	1.00	2.44	1.03
Suspicious	2.55	1.19	2.68	1.12	2.48	1.14	2.61	1.22	2.71	1.15
Compulsive	2.55	1.11	2.29	.90	2.50	1.17	2.56	1.13	2.69	1.08
Dependable	3.00	.96	3.10	.81	3.10	.89	3.03	.97	3.03	.96
Multiple Somatic Complaints	2.13	1.31	2.17	1.28	2.08	1.29	2.12	1.32	2.50	1.38
Complains of Lack of Time	2.01	1.12	1.95	1.07	2.00	1.17	1.94	1.11	2.17	1.21
Poor Work Performance	2.12	1.15	2.00	1.11	1.95	1.10	2.10	1.17	2.13	1.15
Insecure	3.43	.90	3.33	.97	3.51	.95	3.49	.95	3.36	.94
Discusses Problems Openly	3.05	.83	3.00	.75	3.05	.85	3.08	.88	2.95	.81
Sexually Adjusted	2.43	.83	2.19	.91	2.35	.80	2.38	.84	2.38	.81
Exaggerated Need for Affection	2.27	1.05	2.03	1.00	2.32	1.13	2.29	1.07	2.30	1.04
Resentful	3.09	1.16	3.03	1.18	3.04	1.22	3.08	1.16	3.15	1.12
Uses Denial	2.68	1.17	2.75	1.24	2.58	1.20	2.70	1.24	2.77	1.23
Hypochondriacal	1.76	.95	1.93	1.00	1.67	.90	1.75	.95	2.02	1.09
Communicates Effectively	3.05	.76	3.05	.68	3.10	.82	3.08	.79	3.07	.73
Has Many Nightmares	1.68	1.01	1.79	.98	1.74	1.12	1.76	1.05	1.75	1.08
Stormy Interpersonal Relationships	3.10	1.24	2.86	1.26	3.07	1.21	3.07	1.27	3.12	1.22
Feigns Remorse When in Trouble	1.79	.97	1.80	.90	1.66	.93	1.76	.97	1.82	1.00
Stereotypic Masculine Interests	2.84	1.18	2.67	1.19	2.85	1.20	2.82	1.18	2.91	1.21
Guarded	2.73	1.32	2.90	1.35	2.65	1.43	2.79	1.31	2.93	1.31
Feels Inferior	3.08	1.01	3.08	1.12	3.16	1.05	3.15	1.03	3.09	1.02
Low Frustration Tolerance	3.18	1.17	2.88	1.24	3.18	1.17	3.13	1.16	3.10	1.12
Psychotic Symptoms	1.15	.48	1.26	.64	1.16	.54	1.19	.51	1.18	.52
Fired From Past Jobs	2.12	1.16	2.12	1.08	1.84	1.04	2.09	1.17	2.07	1.14
Needs Attention	2.88	.98	2.53	.96	2.89	1.03	2.89	.99	2.90	.99
Acts Out	2.54	1.23	2.30	1.02	2.33	1.17	2.50	1.22	2.53	1.19
Histrionic	1.99	1.05	1.75	1.01	1.82	1.00	1.92	.99	2.08	1.03
Self-Indulgent	2.54	1.13	2.53	1.04	2.43	1.16	2.48	1.16	2.52	1.13
Depressed	3.33	1.04	3.28	1.04	3.23	1.07	3.39	1.01	3.44	.95
Grandiose	1.97	1.09	1.67	.97	1.86	1.10	1.92	1.08	1.96	1.06
Cynical	2.61	1.27	2.43	1.13	2.47	1.30	2.59	1.27	2.74	1.24
Sociopathic	1.65	.87	1.65	.95	1.57	.83	1.72	.95	1.69	.92
Agitated	2.53	1.10	2.42	1.11	2.49	1.08	2.57	1.08	2.70	1.03
Marital Problems	2.67	1.62	2.14	1.53	2.36	1.59	2.68	1.61	2.66	1.59
Absence of Deep Emotions	2.08	1.26	1.87	1.07	1.94	1.30	2.04	1.25	2.09	1.26
Uncomfortable Dealing with Emotions	2.93	1.30	2.78	1.21	2.87	1.40	2.94	1.33	3.02	1.32
Sad	2.99	.99	2.98	.97	2.96	1.03	3.04	.99	3.06	.96
Self-Degrading	2.25	1.00	2.10	1.01	2.18	1.01	2.30	1.06	2.22	1.01
Unable to Express Negative Feelings	2.14	1.09	1.93	.94	2.14	1.16	2.16	1.12	2.25	1.11
Concrete in Thinking	2.24	1.02	2.25	.98	2.17	1.09	2.21	1.03	2.38	1.02

Table L-2d. Means and standard deviations for continuous extra-test characteristics (men): High scores on Content Scales *(continued)*

	Content Scales									
	ANX		FRS		OBS		DEP		HEA	
	Mean	SD	Mean	SD	Mean	SD	Mean	SD	Mean	SD
Unable to See Own Limitations	2.40	1.14	2.28	1.01	2.31	1.19	2.34	1.15	2.46	1.13
Power-Oriented	2.26	1.13	1.93	1.00	2.16	1.14	2.24	1.09	2.20	1.11
Grouchy	2.45	1.09	2.33	1.12	2.30	1.08	2.38	1.10	2.59	1.07
Overbearing in Relationships	2.40	1.12	1.97	1.03	2.22	1.12	2.33	1.12	2.41	1.05
Uncertain About Career	3.42	1.24	3.49	1.19	3.31	1.32	3.44	1.25	3.45	1.26
Likable	3.18	.79	3.12	.79	3.20	.79	3.15	.84	3.16	.82
Procrastinator	2.54	1.13	2.51	1.12	2.56	1.25	2.53	1.17	2.62	1.13
Negative Feelings Toward Opposite Sex	2.10	1.15	2.03	1.13	2.08	1.15	2.11	1.20	2.12	1.13
Defensive	2.73	1.22	2.55	1.22	2.58	1.26	2.75	1.20	2.79	1.15
Empathetic	2.34	.75	2.17	.68	2.38	.82	2.35	.80	2.36	.80
Perfectionistic	2.58	1.13	2.29	1.01	2.48	1.18	2.55	1.15	2.54	1.16
Judgmental	2.76	1.14	2.55	1.04	2.60	1.19	2.74	1.14	2.70	1.08
Copes Well with Stress	1.97	.65	1.92	.66	1.96	.70	1.97	.65	1.95	.62
Moody	2.84	1.01	2.63	.98	2.78	1.08	2.81	1.02	2.86	1.01
Selfish	2.27	1.03	2.28	1.00	2.18	1.10	2.21	1.01	2.28	.96
Gives Up Easily	2.28	.99	2.14	1.08	2.29	1.04	2.30	1.02	2.29	.99
Physical Symptoms in Response to Stress	2.30	1.24	2.33	1.26	2.28	1.24	2.31	1.24	2.64	1.29
Blames Family For Difficulties	2.51	1.32	2.21	1.14	2.63	1.44	2.52	1.30	2.55	1.33
Bored	2.43	1.16	2.40	1.13	2.40	1.23	2.51	1.16	2.65	1.15
Idealistic	2.41	1.02	2.21	1.04	2.30	1.11	2.36	1.09	2.34	1.03
Difficulty Establishing Therapeutic Rapport	2.01	1.05	2.07	.97	1.95	.99	2.06	1.08	2.17	1.07
Daydreams	1.81	.99	1.83	.95	1.87	.98	1.84	1.02	1.77	.92
Concerned About Status	2.45	1.11	2.35	1.12	2.36	1.16	2.44	1.15	2.37	1.13
Creates Good First Impression	2.56	.89	2.68	.86	2.52	.90	2.53	.95	2.55	.93
Complains of Sleep Disturbance	2.69	1.27	2.53	1.36	2.65	1.41	2.64	1.29	2.83	1.20
Has Temper Tantrums	2.41	1.22	2.10	1.02	2.23	1.20	2.35	1.17	2.41	1.12
Overreactive	2.79	1.09	2.42	1.03	2.68	1.08	2.73	1.09	2.83	1.06
High Aspirations	2.54	1.14	2.23	1.11	2.41	1.20	2.52	1.16	2.44	1.12
Feels Hopeless	2.79	1.13	2.55	1.13	2.79	1.09	2.84	1.14	2.85	1.11
Keeps Others at a Distance	3.01	1.24	2.95	1.36	2.84	1.35	2.99	1.27	3.07	1.26
Argumentative	2.37	1.12	2.28	1.11	2.35	1.15	2.39	1.10	2.42	.99
Paranoid Features	1.89	1.00	2.13	1.04	1.87	1.02	1.97	1.11	1.95	.98
Restless	2.71	1.15	2.58	1.11	2.64	1.22	2.68	1.13	2.91	1.13
Pessimistic	2.95	1.10	3.00	1.01	2.95	1.15	3.01	1.12	3.10	1.07
Feels Like a Failure	3.04	1.09	2.77	1.17	3.02	1.15	3.11	1.11	3.10	1.08

Hallucinations	1.08	.32	1.10	.38	1.11	.39	1.08	.32	1.07	.32
Restricted Affect	2.22	1.23	2.20	1.38	2.15	1.34	2.26	1.30	2.32	1.21
Impatient	2.78	1.12	2.75	1.19	2.71	1.14	2.72	1.13	2.80	1.12
Assertive	2.39	.83	2.23	.89	2.30	.90	2.33	.83	2.44	.91
Modest	2.39	.82	2.42	.90	2.40	.91	2.44	.84	2.51	.76
Self-Doubting	3.07	.90	3.20	.79	3.10	.98	3.14	.92	3.07	.88
Deceptive	1.96	1.03	2.03	1.09	1.84	1.02	1.94	1.02	1.99	1.00
Feels That Life is a Strain	3.18	1.13	3.20	.97	3.15	1.11	3.22	1.12	3.30	1.08
Physically Abusive	1.65	.99	1.32	.53	1.54	.89	1.60	.95	1.59	.96
Feels Rejected	3.18	1.24	2.82	1.17	3.25	1.20	3.21	1.27	3.15	1.24
Does Not Get Along with Coworkers	2.03	1.09	2.08	1.09	1.89	.95	2.07	1.12	2.01	1.07
Uses Projection	2.48	1.14	2.40	1.10	2.41	1.20	2.47	1.16	2.53	1.13
Complains of Fatigue	2.54	1.36	2.50	1.32	2.45	1.43	2.51	1.37	2.77	1.40
Uses Rationalization	2.75	1.11	2.70	1.09	2.73	1.15	2.74	1.11	2.73	1.04
Critical of Others	2.69	1.19	2.45	1.18	2.55	1.19	2.63	1.17	2.74	1.18
Egocentric	2.58	1.17	2.47	1.09	2.54	1.27	2.56	1.17	2.61	1.17
Overevaluates Own Worth	2.05	1.11	1.95	1.06	1.95	1.14	2.00	1.11	2.06	1.14
Optimistic	1.96	.68	1.85	.62	2.00	.76	1.92	.73	1.94	.68
Psychologically Immature	2.86	1.15	2.80	1.11	2.80	1.21	2.79	1.16	2.85	1.11
Poor Judgment	2.95	1.17	3.05	1.20	2.75	1.24	2.88	1.21	2.92	1.17
Low Sex Drive	1.87	1.16	2.25	1.14	1.73	1.01	1.88	1.17	2.11	1.31
Feels Mistreated	3.01	1.14	2.95	1.15	3.01	1.12	3.08	1.13	3.15	1.08
Overly Sensitive to Criticism	3.11	1.15	3.08	1.09	3.16	1.22	3.16	1.11	3.18	1.07
Sentimental	2.42	.99	2.46	1.10	2.34	1.05	2.40	1.04	2.49	1.01
Sexual Preoccupation	1.71	1.08	2.00	1.26	1.65	1.12	1.85	1.20	1.83	1.21
Accelerated Speech	1.49	.80	1.50	.72	1.45	.83	1.45	.78	1.48	.78
Concerns About Homosexuality	1.47	1.09	1.47	1.13	1.46	1.12	1.45	1.06	1.27	.78
Many Specific Fears	1.85	1.02	1.87	1.00	1.91	1.05	1.89	1.04	1.96	1.07
Passive in Relationships	2.26	1.06	2.43	1.09	2.26	1.05	2.33	1.10	2.35	1.09
Negative Attitudes Toward Therapy	1.82	.99	1.85	.98	1.75	.97	1.85	1.01	1.96	1.05
Guilt-Prone	2.58	1.08	2.37	1.10	2.70	1.19	2.63	1.13	2.69	1.10
Nervous	3.05	.97	3.15	.95	3.23	.97	3.09	.96	3.22	.90
Obsessive	2.86	1.14	2.87	1.14	2.80	1.18	2.85	1.14	2.98	1.06
Shy	2.41	1.19	2.38	1.19	2.46	1.26	2.43	1.21	2.53	1.18
Uses Intellectualization	2.52	1.22	2.38	1.15	2.63	1.30	2.58	1.25	2.58	1.23
Has Many Interests	2.32	1.00	2.05	.94	2.40	1.05	2.28	.99	2.26	.96
Difficulty Making Decisions	2.96	1.06	3.05	1.06	2.96	1.17	2.97	1.06	3.06	1.01
Indirect Expression of Hostility	2.74	1.12	2.69	1.20	2.74	1.21	2.77	1.16	2.84	1.10
Poor Reality Testing	1.65	.83	1.60	.74	1.57	.80	1.66	.86	1.69	.77
Angry	3.14	1.20	2.93	.97	3.11	1.27	3.14	1.15	3.21	1.14
Eccentric	1.88	1.20	1.95	1.24	1.83	1.29	1.94	1.22	1.92	1.22
Emotional Lability	2.34	1.08	2.28	.96	2.24	1.09	2.34	1.08	2.36	1.05

Table L-2d. Means and standard deviations for continuous extra-test characteristics (men): High scores on Content Scales *(continued)*

	Content Scales									
	ANX		FRS		OBS		DEP		HEA	
	Mean	SD	Mean	SD	Mean	SD	Mean	SD	Mean	SD
Dislikes Change	2.65	.98	2.72	.92	2.58	1.06	2.70	1.02	2.79	.99
Believes Cannot Be Helped	1.86	.97	2.03	.92	1.80	.95	1.96	1.04	2.06	1.03
Reliable Informant	3.18	.92	3.10	.87	3.24	.89	3.21	.93	3.17	.92
Ignores Problems	2.29	1.00	2.26	1.09	2.19	1.05	2.25	1.04	2.24	1.06
Ruminates	3.21	1.04	3.36	1.09	3.14	1.09	3.27	1.02	3.26	1.03
Excitable	2.63	1.06	2.58	1.06	2.52	1.10	2.53	1.01	2.59	1.01
Conforming	2.37	.88	2.43	.90	2.51	.83	2.40	.88	2.46	.88
Ineffective at Dealing with Problems	3.05	1.05	2.97	1.07	2.99	1.12	3.05	1.07	3.15	1.08
Introverted	2.51	1.12	2.58	1.06	2.63	1.18	2.57	1.15	2.62	1.12
Superficial Relationships	2.59	1.17	2.49	1.07	2.49	1.27	2.59	1.22	2.71	1.23
Impulsive	2.68	1.20	2.43	1.15	2.55	1.26	2.65	1.24	2.62	1.19
Stereotypic Feminine Behavior	1.29	.59	1.38	.59	1.36	.67	1.31	.66	1.31	.59
Stubborn	2.82	1.13	2.63	.95	2.73	1.15	2.81	1.14	2.91	1.04
Hostile Toward Therapist	1.45	.70	1.48	.78	1.42	.66	1.47	.73	1.54	.79
Difficult to Motivate	2.16	1.00	2.25	1.03	2.10	.99	2.22	1.01	2.27	1.02
Suicidal Ideations	1.83	1.01	1.55	.85	1.81	.99	1.86	1.03	1.88	1.02
Familial Discord	3.10	1.38	2.51	1.30	3.05	1.38	3.05	1.41	3.04	1.38
Dogmatic	2.31	1.13	2.15	1.05	2.17	1.19	2.27	1.10	2.30	1.12

	Content Scales *(continued)*															
	BIZ		ANG		CYN		ASP		TPA		LSE		SOD		FAM	
	Mean	SD	Mean	SD	Mean	SD	Mean	SD	Mean	SD	Mean	SD	Mean	SD	Mean	SD
Intake Information	(n = 96)		(n = 136)		(n = 133)		(n = 113)		(n = 57)		(n = 147)		(n = 118)		(n = 181)	
Axis IV diagnosis	2.98	.94	2.93	.86	3.05	.94	2.88	.90	3.00	.91	3.02	.91	2.98	.88	2.93	.91
Axis V - Current Level of Functioning	59.65	9.66	61.43	8.46	59.69	9.69	60.92	9.07	62.58	6.50	60.07	10.56	59.35	11.27	60.75	9.74
Number of Arrests	1.80	4.77	1.96	4.53	1.70	4.50	2.25	4.81	1.58	3.28	1.48	4.23	1.80	4.72	1.39	3.71
Mental Status	(n = 96)		(n = 136)		(n = 133)		(n = 113)		(n = 57)		(n = 147)		(n = 118)		(n = 181)	
Anxiety During Interview	2.52	.71	2.44	.68	2.48	.70	2.45	.71	2.44	.66	2.56	.76	2.51	.76	2.53	.74
Depression During Interview	2.43	.74	2.38	.69	2.42	.76	2.40	.70	2.28	.70	2.47	.75	2.43	.76	2.39	.69
Activity Level During Interview	3.01	.47	3.05	.41	3.00	.49	2.97	.44	3.04	.38	3.01	.50	3.07	.47	3.01	.46
Speech During Interview	2.95	.42	2.99	.37	2.89	.44	2.91	.38	2.89	.41	2.94	.38	3.00	.35	2.95	.43
SCL-90-R Scales	(n = 94)		(n = 134)		(n = 131)		(n = 113)		(n = 56)		(n = 143)		(n = 114)		(n = 178)	
Somatization	1.55	.82	1.25	.81	1.25	.85	1.12	.81	1.49	.84	1.32	.82	1.15	.74	1.19	.80
Obsessive-Compulsive	1.90	.89	1.64	.85	1.61	.88	1.42	.83	1.90	.83	1.81	.81	1.73	.84	1.60	.83
Interpersonal Sensitivity	1.79	.94	1.55	.88	1.59	.91	1.36	.83	1.82	.77	1.81	.85	1.84	.85	1.62	.87
Depression	2.03	.89	1.89	.83	1.81	.94	1.67	.89	1.97	.95	2.13	.82	2.08	.85	1.94	.87
Anxiety	1.84	.91	1.53	.86	1.51	.95	1.31	.94	1.80	.97	1.68	.91	1.55	.87	1.51	.88
Hostility	1.69	.97	2.03	1.03	1.66	1.14	1.65	1.11	2.26	1.15	1.51	1.03	1.53	1.04	1.62	1.07
Phobic Anxiety	1.01	.85	.67	.68	.82	.79	.63	.68	.85	.85	.90	.75	.88	.72	.75	.69
Paranoid Ideation	1.99	.87	1.71	.90	1.77	.93	1.60	.83	2.06	.78	1.66	.87	1.58	.91	1.65	.86
Psychoticism	1.48	.81	1.12	.69	1.11	.74	.99	.66	1.27	.74	1.26	.72	1.17	.71	1.14	.70
Initial SCL-90 Analogue	(n = 60)		(n = 80)		(n = 82)		(n = 63)		(n = 33)		(n = 92)		(n = 72)		(n = 116)	
Somatization	2.45	2.87	2.25	2.65	2.52	2.88	2.11	2.40	2.67	2.51	2.75	2.92	2.42	2.87	2.21	2.63
Obsessive-Compulsive	3.40	2.69	3.32	2.42	3.40	2.51	3.62	2.64	3.06	2.28	3.37	2.66	3.68	2.78	3.42	2.83
Interpersonal Sensitivity	4.58	2.57	4.63	2.37	4.43	2.43	4.94	2.28	4.19	2.09	5.03	2.25	5.18	2.39	4.88	2.47
Depression	4.33	2.61	4.16	2.66	4.33	2.75	4.21	2.63	3.61	2.62	4.60	2.57	4.68	2.79	4.47	2.62
Anxiety	4.64	2.75	4.30	2.63	4.27	2.84	4.18	2.62	4.18	2.65	4.69	2.75	4.69	2.85	4.58	2.81
Hostility	3.17	2.77	3.84	2.88	3.12	2.90	3.92	2.72	3.30	3.04	3.27	2.74	3.60	2.82	3.40	2.83
Phobic Anxiety	1.52	2.64	1.20	1.98	1.36	2.16	1.62	2.11	.88	1.83	1.56	2.31	1.51	1.90	1.61	2.42
Paranoid Ideation	1.46	2.42	1.19	1.62	1.22	1.59	1.58	1.82	.88	1.19	1.28	1.85	1.39	1.94	1.45	2.11
Psychoticism	.91	2.02	.46	1.15	.44	.99	.70	1.42	.42	1.00	.52	1.24	.64	1.14	.64	1.59
Patient Description Form Scales	(n = 61)		(n = 80)		(n = 82)		(n = 64)		(n = 34)		(n = 92)		(n = 72)		(n = 118)	
Angry Resentment	2.83	.96	3.06	.94	2.78	.96	2.98	.92	2.91	.95	2.93	.84	3.03	.88	2.88	.91
Critical/Argumentative	2.50	.99	2.64	.89	2.49	1.00	2.61	.94	2.61	.93	2.59	.89	2.70	.90	2.54	.92

	Content Scales *(continued)*															
	BIZ		ANG		CYN		ASP		TPA		LSE		SOD		FAM	
	Mean	SD	Mean	SD	Mean	SD	Mean	SD	Mean	SD	Mean	SD	Mean	SD	Mean	SD
Narcissistic	2.38	1.07	2.36	.90	2.39	.89	2.49	.87	2.45	.91	2.30	.89	2.37	.84	2.30	.90
Defensive	2.61	.92	2.57	.82	2.62	.84	2.72	.77	2.56	.84	2.65	.89	2.75	.89	2.57	.88
Histrionic	2.44	.82	2.46	.69	2.39	.78	2.50	.72	2.43	.66	2.48	.73	2.49	.69	2.45	.76
Aggressive	2.26	.97	2.55	.96	2.20	.92	2.50	1.02	2.38	.88	2.11	.79	2.22	.90	2.24	.92
Insecure	2.95	.73	2.95	.70	2.92	.65	3.04	.71	2.82	.76	3.14	.72	3.20	.73	3.01	.77
Anxious	2.98	.76	2.87	.69	2.92	.78	2.88	.75	3.03	.84	3.08	.77	3.04	.70	2.96	.79
Pessimistic	2.33	.85	2.39	.92	2.38	.93	2.41	.94	2.36	.99	2.56	.94	2.64	1.04	2.38	.94
Depressed	2.45	.72	2.52	.81	2.44	.80	2.43	.78	2.39	.87	2.58	.78	2.68	.78	2.50	.75
Achievement-Oriented	2.44	.79	2.64	.69	2.57	.72	2.48	.73	2.89	.73	2.53	.73	2.54	.69	2.58	.75
Passive-Submissive	2.16	.80	2.03	.77	2.22	.75	2.22	.80	2.10	.71	2.41	.75	2.37	.78	2.20	.84
Introverted	2.58	.89	2.50	.90	2.66	.86	2.65	.93	2.53	.98	2.78	1.04	2.94	.99	2.62	1.04
Emotionally Controlled	2.26	1.09	2.45	1.04	2.41	1.04	2.55	1.00	2.46	1.06	2.55	1.10	2.72	1.11	2.38	.99
Antisocial	2.48	1.00	2.46	.94	2.40	.88	2.63	.83	2.38	.86	2.16	.90	2.30	1.00	2.32	.94
Negative Treatment Attitudes	2.02	.84	1.95	.79	2.00	.80	2.03	.81	1.95	.78	1.98	.81	2.15	.81	1.95	.78
Somatic Symptoms	2.17	1.11	2.10	.97	2.17	1.13	1.94	.96	2.30	1.07	2.27	1.11	2.21	1.09	2.03	1.01
Psychotic Symptoms	1.42	.62	1.26	.42	1.26	.44	1.32	.48	1.25	.44	1.25	.40	1.29	.43	1.27	.47
Family Problems	2.94	1.21	3.07	1.08	2.79	1.14	3.20	1.03	3.05	1.08	2.94	1.04	2.97	1.07	3.01	1.07
Obsessive-Compulsive	2.83	.78	2.78	.71	2.80	.75	2.82	.72	2.86	.75	2.90	.81	2.96	.78	2.85	.79
Stereotypic Masculine Interests	2.71	1.06	3.06	1.11	2.97	1.04	3.10	1.04	2.93	1.07	2.87	1.03	2.86	1.16	2.76	1.11
Procrastinates	2.41	1.13	2.38	.97	2.37	1.00	2.36	.90	2.41	1.16	2.34	.91	2.46	.83	2.24	.96
Suspicious	2.67	.96	2.63	.94	2.58	.90	2.75	.86	2.47	.96	2.66	.96	2.87	.92	2.63	.93
Agitated	2.31	.87	2.29	.73	2.22	.78	2.32	.72	2.38	.66	2.22	.70	2.27	.80	2.28	.78
Work Problems	1.99	1.00	2.09	.91	2.06	.87	2.20	.95	2.15	.98	1.94	.79	2.02	.91	2.06	.90
Patient Description Form Items	(n = 61)		(n = 80)		(n = 82)		(n = 64)		(n = 34)		(n = 92)		(n = 72)		(n = 118)	
Anxious	3.52	.83	3.28	.83	3.38	.88	3.33	.84	3.44	.93	3.54	.83	3.58	.75	3.48	.88
Problems with Authority Figures	3.05	1.21	3.21	1.20	3.20	1.09	3.34	1.04	3.42	.97	3.07	1.17	3.09	1.14	3.04	1.19
Has Insight Into Own Problems	2.46	.87	2.64	.80	2.56	.82	2.45	.66	2.79	.95	2.65	.86	2.66	.86	2.56	.89
Fears Losing Control	3.12	1.04	3.33	.97	3.25	1.07	3.28	.97	3.26	1.02	3.35	1.06	3.43	.96	3.27	1.04
Extroverted	2.46	.96	2.54	1.01	2.41	.98	2.31	1.01	2.76	1.05	2.28	.95	2.17	.95	2.32	.96
Uses Repression	2.72	1.10	2.70	1.05	2.82	.97	2.83	1.01	2.70	1.05	2.69	1.05	2.87	1.05	2.62	1.01
Submissive	2.12	.92	2.05	.83	2.26	.83	2.30	.89	2.21	.84	2.39	.89	2.36	.90	2.19	.90
Difficulty Concentrating	2.84	.99	2.75	1.02	2.82	1.01	2.73	1.01	2.82	1.09	2.86	1.11	2.75	1.09	2.74	1.09
Rigid	2.69	1.12	2.80	1.07	2.80	1.08	2.85	1.07	2.74	1.08	2.90	1.08	3.00	1.03	2.82	1.08
Overly Compliant	1.90	.87	1.87	.90	1.97	.85	1.95	.80	2.03	.85	2.13	.86	2.00	.93	1.98	.93
Whiny	1.98	.97	1.89	.94	1.93	1.01	1.86	1.08	2.00	1.02	2.15	1.07	2.11	1.09	1.93	1.03
Feels Overwhelmed	3.36	1.08	3.38	1.08	3.28	1.18	3.27	1.03	3.38	1.18	3.51	1.10	3.42	1.09	3.33	1.10

Manipulative	2.47	1.26	2.53	1.20	2.54	1.18	2.54	1.26	2.61	1.12	2.45	1.12	2.50	1.13	2.40	1.13
Difficulty Trusting Others	3.30	1.19	3.50	1.22	3.33	1.19	3.52	1.20	3.24	1.23	3.42	1.20	3.63	1.13	3.36	1.21
Insensitive to Others	2.25	1.15	2.22	.96	2.23	.93	2.39	.91	2.06	.89	2.22	.97	2.35	1.02	2.22	1.01
Stereotypic Masculine Behavior	2.72	1.14	3.06	1.15	2.96	1.09	3.11	1.11	2.85	1.13	2.86	1.08	2.87	1.26	2.74	1.15
Harbors Grudges	2.77	1.11	3.04	1.08	2.78	1.10	3.00	1.16	2.85	1.05	2.87	1.06	3.12	1.09	2.86	1.10
Evasive	2.33	1.19	2.22	.97	2.35	1.12	2.40	1.07	2.24	.99	2.35	1.16	2.56	1.16	2.20	1.11
Disoriented	1.28	.55	1.28	.59	1.23	.48	1.31	.59	1.24	.50	1.26	.53	1.32	.62	1.24	.50
Energetic	2.34	1.01	2.52	.93	2.41	.86	2.44	.73	2.85	.96	2.41	.89	2.35	.81	2.52	.92
Lonely	2.93	1.23	3.05	1.23	2.88	1.19	3.23	1.21	2.82	1.29	3.13	1.23	3.22	1.20	3.02	1.23
Family Lacks Love	2.98	1.49	3.05	1.25	2.77	1.42	3.11	1.33	2.97	1.30	2.99	1.25	3.01	1.23	2.98	1.30
Worrier	3.28	1.10	3.29	.97	3.29	1.07	3.21	1.02	3.50	.96	3.48	1.01	3.42	1.00	3.32	1.08
Narcissistic	2.66	1.37	2.50	1.17	2.54	1.12	2.71	1.07	2.71	1.19	2.56	1.16	2.57	1.08	2.52	1.14
Tearful	1.50	.87	1.53	.84	1.46	.72	1.45	.71	1.47	.71	1.60	.84	1.63	.83	1.55	.82
Provocative	1.73	.92	1.74	.84	1.74	.90	1.71	.81	1.76	.82	1.65	.80	1.69	.91	1.73	.91
Moralistic	2.56	1.09	2.56	1.00	2.71	1.02	2.47	.90	2.59	1.02	2.62	1.01	2.62	1.03	2.57	1.10
Socially Awkward	2.85	1.06	2.80	1.06	2.96	.97	3.00	1.10	2.71	1.06	2.97	1.14	3.11	1.11	2.87	1.20
Hostile	2.47	1.27	2.74	1.35	2.45	1.29	2.64	1.30	2.50	1.33	2.55	1.16	2.72	1.15	2.58	1.18
Overcontrolled	2.43	1.24	2.72	1.23	2.66	1.24	2.77	1.16	2.82	1.22	2.78	1.27	2.89	1.23	2.67	1.23
Resistant to Interpretations	2.21	1.11	2.15	1.01	2.17	1.02	2.23	1.08	2.09	1.03	2.18	1.04	2.37	.97	2.10	1.03
Antisocial Behavior	2.61	1.35	2.56	1.40	2.46	1.27	2.86	1.32	2.41	1.31	2.11	1.15	2.24	1.22	2.34	1.27
Sarcastic	1.90	1.09	2.04	1.05	1.93	1.13	1.91	1.08	1.94	1.07	2.09	1.10	2.14	1.03	2.02	1.09
Rejects Traditional Gender Role	1.77	1.23	1.51	.97	1.73	1.10	1.47	.91	1.56	1.11	1.69	.98	1.79	.98	1.60	1.05
Feels Gets Raw Deal From Life	2.92	1.14	3.13	1.10	2.96	1.17	2.97	1.09	2.91	1.19	3.18	1.11	3.17	1.13	2.98	1.12
Acute Psychological Turmoil	3.02	1.13	3.04	1.02	3.09	1.00	3.10	1.04	2.85	1.05	3.22	.95	3.26	.95	3.07	1.03
Does Not Complete Projects	2.48	1.28	2.54	1.15	2.38	1.21	2.41	1.07	2.37	1.33	2.27	1.11	2.34	1.02	2.22	1.12
Uncomfortable with Opposite Sex	2.08	1.09	2.08	1.04	2.16	1.07	2.12	.94	2.07	1.03	2.19	1.10	2.45	1.08	2.12	1.05
Preoccupied with Health Problems	2.33	1.40	2.11	1.27	2.33	1.39	1.97	1.22	2.27	1.33	2.45	1.44	2.44	1.43	2.06	1.24
Work-Oriented	2.82	1.10	3.02	1.11	3.00	1.03	2.86	.98	3.32	1.12	2.93	1.07	2.99	1.11	3.03	1.08
Resents Family Members	2.97	1.37	3.13	1.30	2.79	1.38	3.10	1.27	3.00	1.35	2.98	1.23	2.97	1.30	3.07	1.26
Demanding of Attention	2.51	1.24	2.55	1.12	2.44	1.12	2.57	1.16	2.39	1.12	2.56	1.07	2.64	1.05	2.49	1.10
Passive	2.48	.96	2.17	.91	2.46	.92	2.41	.98	2.21	.91	2.60	.96	2.66	.96	2.38	1.03
Self-Punishing	2.32	1.18	2.44	1.23	2.26	1.13	2.54	1.19	2.32	1.25	2.60	1.23	2.77	1.16	2.44	1.13
Needs to Achieve	2.51	.99	2.70	.95	2.66	.95	2.57	.95	2.94	.92	2.71	1.00	2.77	.94	2.75	.97
Needs to Be with Others	2.80	1.12	3.01	.97	2.96	.95	3.03	1.05	3.03	.80	2.99	1.06	2.87	.98	2.91	1.05
Irritable	2.77	1.08	2.85	1.09	2.61	1.14	2.75	1.14	2.79	1.09	2.78	1.07	2.83	.98	2.79	1.04
Self-Defeating	3.11	1.24	3.25	1.24	3.15	1.18	3.37	1.21	3.09	1.19	3.16	1.25	3.33	1.06	3.10	1.15
Delusional Thinking	1.51	.93	1.23	.60	1.27	.65	1.24	.64	1.15	.50	1.25	.59	1.25	.55	1.23	.61
Self-Reliant	2.54	.96	2.72	.95	2.63	.90	2.63	.88	2.94	.95	2.63	.95	2.60	.93	2.58	.95
Aggressive	2.47	1.10	2.76	1.09	2.53	1.07	2.75	1.05	2.71	1.06	2.36	.98	2.46	1.09	2.45	1.07
Competitive	2.28	.99	2.56	.92	2.41	.92	2.39	.93	2.56	.96	2.41	.98	2.43	.98	2.43	.98
Suspicious	2.67	1.16	2.50	1.20	2.52	1.09	2.68	1.10	2.36	1.08	2.63	1.13	2.92	1.11	2.59	1.14
Compulsive	2.38	1.06	2.51	1.16	2.49	1.09	2.60	1.11	2.61	1.17	2.58	1.13	2.72	1.08	2.53	1.11

	Content Scales *(continued)*															
	BIZ		ANG		CYN		ASP		TPA		LSE		SOD		FAM	
	Mean	SD	Mean	SD	Mean	SD	Mean	SD	Mean	SD	Mean	SD	Mean	SD	Mean	SD
Dependable	2.83	1.03	2.85	.90	3.00	.89	2.84	.84	3.12	.95	3.08	1.00	2.91	.90	3.01	1.00
Multiple Somatic Complaints	2.11	1.32	1.98	1.20	2.15	1.31	1.92	1.15	2.21	1.25	2.20	1.34	2.15	1.38	1.91	1.18
Complains of Lack of Time	2.05	1.20	2.05	1.18	2.00	1.13	1.93	1.09	2.38	1.34	2.07	1.15	2.07	1.04	2.00	1.17
Poor Work Performance	2.29	1.29	2.25	1.17	2.10	1.15	2.28	1.18	2.32	1.38	2.00	1.01	2.02	.98	2.06	1.12
Insecure	3.48	.91	3.36	.85	3.49	.81	3.63	.83	3.29	.87	3.63	.85	3.61	.88	3.54	.88
Discusses Problems Openly	2.93	.83	3.14	.79	3.02	.82	3.08	.80	3.09	.75	3.07	.81	3.07	.91	3.01	.87
Sexually Adjusted	2.29	.89	2.68	.75	2.42	.86	2.56	.81	2.74	.81	2.36	.80	2.35	.80	2.36	.93
Exaggerated Need for Affection	2.11	1.04	2.29	.97	2.24	.98	2.38	1.04	2.26	.96	2.40	1.10	2.34	.94	2.28	1.02
Resentful	3.22	1.14	3.35	1.15	3.04	1.18	3.23	1.07	3.03	1.14	3.15	1.04	3.31	1.06	3.11	1.12
Uses Denial	2.68	1.31	2.69	1.18	2.70	1.16	2.84	1.17	2.59	1.26	2.74	1.23	2.94	1.22	2.64	1.22
Hypochondriacal	1.74	1.02	1.59	.82	1.73	.99	1.58	.76	1.71	.87	1.82	1.02	1.82	.92	1.66	.89
Communicates Effectively	2.92	.88	3.03	.75	3.07	.75	2.94	.77	3.24	.89	3.08	.76	3.06	.80	3.02	.80
Has Many Nightmares	1.63	.94	1.89	1.15	1.93	1.10	1.96	1.13	1.78	1.06	1.84	1.07	1.92	1.17	1.70	.97
Stormy Interpersonal Relationships	3.22	1.23	3.39	1.19	3.09	1.27	3.49	1.23	3.16	1.37	3.17	1.22	3.31	1.19	3.16	1.20
Feigns Remorse When in Trouble	1.89	1.09	1.83	.97	1.81	.91	1.91	1.01	1.88	.91	1.73	.94	1.95	1.10	1.79	.95
Stereotypic Masculine Interests	2.68	1.07	3.03	1.16	2.98	1.08	3.06	1.08	3.00	1.10	2.87	1.07	2.85	1.18	2.76	1.16
Guarded	2.85	1.34	2.74	1.28	2.83	1.28	2.88	1.20	2.79	1.37	2.85	1.31	2.96	1.27	2.77	1.28
Feels Inferior	3.12	.94	3.06	.96	3.05	.90	3.08	.86	3.00	.95	3.24	.98	3.27	1.03	3.17	1.01
Low Frustration Tolerance	3.17	1.17	3.41	1.09	3.15	1.11	3.43	.97	3.24	.92	3.12	1.16	3.34	1.04	3.21	1.12
Psychotic Symptoms	1.40	.84	1.13	.44	1.18	.53	1.20	.57	1.18	.63	1.17	.51	1.17	.45	1.19	.59
Fired From Past Jobs	2.13	1.13	2.18	1.10	2.12	1.03	2.13	1.08	2.32	1.04	1.93	.97	2.05	1.18	1.99	1.03
Needs Attention	2.84	.99	2.90	.91	2.78	.88	2.94	.86	2.85	.86	2.96	1.02	2.94	.87	2.89	.93
Acts Out	2.64	1.21	2.76	1.22	2.62	1.15	2.92	1.11	2.47	1.08	2.38	1.14	2.47	1.16	2.55	1.18
Histrionic	1.98	1.10	1.91	.97	1.93	1.08	1.94	.98	1.91	1.03	1.99	1.02	1.99	.98	1.97	1.06
Self-Indulgent	2.70	1.20	2.71	1.13	2.66	1.08	2.92	1.11	2.67	1.14	2.46	1.11	2.54	1.09	2.47	1.15
Depressed	3.15	1.06	3.18	1.06	3.16	1.07	3.14	1.03	3.15	1.08	3.32	1.03	3.47	.90	3.25	1.07
Grandiose	2.05	1.23	1.92	.96	1.98	1.17	1.98	1.08	2.00	1.04	1.88	1.05	1.99	1.06	1.90	1.03
Cynical	2.49	1.32	2.65	1.24	2.44	1.33	2.49	1.27	2.79	1.39	2.64	1.20	2.75	1.22	2.50	1.18
Sociopathic	1.83	.97	1.69	.89	1.73	.89	1.79	.82	1.68	.81	1.64	.81	1.73	.93	1.68	.87
Agitated	2.62	1.22	2.72	1.09	2.45	1.10	2.63	1.18	2.71	1.12	2.63	1.02	2.66	1.03	2.64	1.09
Marital Problems	2.53	1.72	2.80	1.61	2.47	1.61	2.94	1.65	2.57	1.76	2.68	1.58	2.75	1.62	2.61	1.63
Absence of Deep Emotions	1.98	1.30	2.17	1.31	2.04	1.18	2.25	1.30	2.18	1.34	2.18	1.30	2.37	1.39	1.98	1.17
Uncomfortable Dealing with Emotions	2.83	1.38	2.96	1.26	2.95	1.20	3.16	1.20	2.82	1.22	3.12	1.30	3.28	1.26	2.95	1.27
Sad	2.92	1.01	2.97	.99	2.80	1.02	2.88	.93	2.85	1.10	3.03	.97	3.08	.94	2.97	.99
Self-Degrading	2.05	.94	2.24	1.02	2.01	.92	2.14	1.02	1.94	.95	2.41	.97	2.54	1.03	2.30	1.03
Unable to Express Negative Feelings	2.03	1.12	2.22	1.08	2.20	1.07	2.27	1.02	2.26	1.05	2.29	1.16	2.42	1.16	2.09	1.03
Concrete in Thinking	2.42	1.11	2.29	1.04	2.41	1.04	2.42	1.02	2.29	1.06	2.34	1.09	2.36	1.03	2.21	1.01
Unable to See Own Limitations	2.43	1.20	2.38	1.11	2.35	1.06	2.42	1.03	2.47	1.21	2.37	1.10	2.38	1.06	2.35	1.11

Power-Oriented	2.12	1.15	2.41	1.16	2.23	1.10	2.41	1.16	2.41	1.13	2.18	1.06	2.27	1.16	2.28	1.15
Grouchy	2.33	1.08	2.46	1.11	2.26	1.05	2.44	1.06	2.50	1.05	2.45	1.01	2.46	1.09	2.34	1.06
Overbearing in Relationships	2.37	1.26	2.56	1.15	2.29	1.23	2.41	1.33	2.48	1.34	2.28	1.11	2.42	1.08	2.32	1.13
Uncertain About Career	3.36	1.36	3.57	1.24	3.43	1.23	3.37	1.29	3.41	1.34	3.43	1.29	3.60	1.21	3.41	1.23
Likable	3.07	.81	3.19	.75	3.13	.75	3.09	.75	3.24	.74	3.17	.81	3.13	.80	3.15	.84
Procrastinator	2.61	1.27	2.52	1.12	2.63	1.19	2.62	1.09	2.52	1.25	2.58	1.13	2.76	1.06	2.49	1.14
Negative Feelings Toward Opposite Sex	2.02	1.12	2.11	1.11	2.00	1.08	2.11	1.18	1.93	1.09	2.15	1.12	2.45	1.20	2.10	1.13
Defensive	2.68	1.21	2.63	1.14	2.50	1.11	2.64	1.15	2.53	1.08	2.74	1.17	2.86	1.14	2.66	1.20
Empathetic	2.27	.83	2.39	.75	2.33	.71	2.31	.76	2.50	.75	2.42	.72	2.26	.72	2.39	.80
Perfectionistic	2.31	1.09	2.47	1.05	2.45	1.18	2.33	1.02	2.79	1.17	2.61	1.12	2.75	1.09	2.51	1.13
Judgmental	2.60	1.21	2.84	1.02	2.68	1.15	2.79	1.19	2.74	1.14	2.77	1.04	2.84	1.06	2.65	1.12
Copes Well with Stress	1.87	.62	1.99	.59	2.06	.62	2.03	.54	1.94	.60	1.95	.65	1.97	.69	1.95	.65
Moody	2.64	.89	2.86	1.01	2.76	.98	2.84	.86	2.71	1.09	2.88	.96	3.03	.93	2.78	.99
Selfish	2.12	1.08	2.29	1.02	2.22	.93	2.40	.97	2.36	1.08	2.18	.95	2.34	.93	2.18	1.00
Gives Up Easily	2.39	1.07	2.38	.98	2.22	1.04	2.49	1.04	2.36	1.03	2.34	1.04	2.37	.93	2.22	.97
Physical Symptoms in Response to Stress	2.32	1.21	2.32	1.17	2.29	1.26	2.22	1.15	2.67	1.27	2.40	1.27	2.35	1.21	2.21	1.17
Blames Family For Difficulties	2.55	1.32	2.77	1.29	2.45	1.22	2.70	1.27	2.76	1.32	2.57	1.27	2.66	1.32	2.70	1.27
Bored	2.38	1.08	2.39	1.09	2.42	1.06	2.54	1.00	2.32	1.12	2.61	1.15	2.74	1.05	2.40	1.10
Idealistic	2.36	1.13	2.33	.95	2.37	1.01	2.27	.96	2.55	.97	2.44	1.10	2.30	1.03	2.38	1.04
Difficulty Establishing Therapeutic Rapport	2.10	1.14	2.04	1.06	2.12	1.12	2.19	1.08	2.09	1.06	2.00	.98	2.19	1.10	2.11	1.06
Daydreams	1.93	1.10	1.82	1.02	1.92	1.11	1.97	1.10	1.73	1.03	2.00	1.04	2.19	1.12	1.78	1.02
Concerned About Status	2.35	1.15	2.38	1.12	2.44	1.10	2.34	1.10	2.59	1.16	2.42	1.14	2.46	1.09	2.39	1.14
Creates Good First Impression	2.31	1.01	2.61	.90	2.51	.80	2.44	.89	2.85	.89	2.52	.87	2.36	.83	2.45	.93
Complains of Sleep Disturbance	2.51	1.24	2.70	1.38	2.65	1.32	2.44	1.31	2.65	1.43	2.79	1.25	2.76	1.33	2.53	1.25
Has Temper Tantrums	2.49	1.27	2.78	1.26	2.39	1.25	2.72	1.28	2.64	1.29	2.40	1.17	2.42	1.13	2.51	1.23
Overreactive	2.79	1.10	2.95	1.06	2.70	1.12	2.90	1.07	2.68	.91	2.77	1.01	2.81	1.06	2.79	1.05
High Aspirations	2.40	1.21	2.51	1.00	2.53	1.11	2.33	1.11	2.64	1.08	2.48	1.14	2.38	1.07	2.59	1.17
Feels Hopeless	2.75	1.11	2.82	1.17	2.72	1.19	2.66	1.12	2.53	1.02	2.92	1.16	3.06	1.10	2.79	1.09
Keeps Others at a Distance	2.88	1.32	3.13	1.27	2.97	1.26	3.13	1.23	3.03	1.36	3.04	1.25	3.28	1.24	3.07	1.21
Argumentative	2.44	1.19	2.46	1.11	2.27	1.08	2.38	1.15	2.35	1.07	2.41	1.06	2.50	1.05	2.36	1.08
Paranoid Features	2.05	1.19	1.86	.93	1.88	.95	2.03	.91	1.79	1.04	1.92	1.00	2.07	1.03	1.91	.99
Restless	2.77	1.16	2.80	1.10	2.74	1.05	2.89	.96	2.94	.98	2.67	1.10	2.75	1.14	2.70	1.15
Pessimistic	2.85	1.00	2.92	1.08	2.84	1.08	2.84	1.06	2.88	1.20	3.12	1.05	3.21	1.09	2.90	1.08
Feels Like a Failure	3.08	1.11	3.03	1.06	3.02	1.13	3.10	1.13	2.97	1.24	3.22	1.07	3.32	1.09	3.05	1.07
Hallucinations	1.22	.62	1.11	.39	1.11	.39	1.13	.43	1.12	.41	1.09	.32	1.08	.28	1.10	.38
Restricted Affect	2.02	1.22	2.19	1.28	2.23	1.34	2.33	1.27	2.21	1.34	2.41	1.37	2.67	1.38	2.20	1.24
Impatient	2.72	1.19	2.84	1.05	2.65	1.07	2.97	1.01	2.88	.91	2.78	1.12	2.80	1.02	2.80	1.10
Assertive	2.18	.83	2.43	.83	2.41	.82	2.22	.68	2.65	.88	2.32	.82	2.32	.82	2.31	.87
Modest	2.32	.89	2.46	.83	2.52	.73	2.51	.74	2.41	.82	2.53	.86	2.56	.81	2.40	.87
Self-Doubting	3.03	.82	3.08	.94	3.09	.86	3.11	.92	3.03	.97	3.27	.88	3.31	.91	3.14	.95
Deceptive	1.97	1.08	2.07	1.05	2.02	1.02	2.15	1.08	2.18	1.16	1.94	.98	2.07	1.00	1.89	.99
Feels That Life is a Strain	3.28	.95	3.18	1.11	3.17	1.13	3.15	.95	3.18	1.22	3.37	1.05	3.28	1.04	3.17	1.04

	Content Scales *(continued)*															
	BIZ		ANG		CYN		ASP		TPA		LSE		SOD		FAM	
	Mean	SD	Mean	SD	Mean	SD	Mean	SD	Mean	SD	Mean	SD	Mean	SD	Mean	SD
Physically Abusive	1.74	1.03	1.96	1.09	1.64	.93	2.04	1.10	1.72	.92	1.51	.75	1.66	.96	1.68	.99
Feels Rejected	3.15	1.28	3.27	1.08	3.02	1.14	3.34	1.17	3.12	1.23	3.30	1.18	3.45	1.04	3.27	1.12
Does Not Get Along with Coworkers	2.13	1.18	2.15	1.09	2.11	1.06	2.23	1.09	2.17	1.11	2.09	1.00	2.13	1.06	2.22	1.12
Uses Projection	2.49	1.15	2.53	1.07	2.44	1.12	2.64	1.11	2.62	1.18	2.51	1.13	2.61	1.13	2.46	1.13
Complains of Fatigue	2.45	1.42	2.47	1.31	2.41	1.37	2.10	1.19	2.48	1.42	2.52	1.40	2.55	1.36	2.32	1.31
Uses Rationalization	2.69	1.19	2.81	1.02	2.77	1.02	2.91	1.02	2.97	1.06	2.68	1.03	2.85	1.03	2.69	1.11
Critical of Others	2.58	1.21	2.80	1.10	2.70	1.19	2.77	1.15	2.88	1.12	2.65	1.05	2.79	1.15	2.63	1.14
Egocentric	2.58	1.29	2.56	1.11	2.60	1.15	2.63	1.07	2.59	1.05	2.53	1.15	2.60	1.11	2.54	1.18
Overevaluates Own Worth	2.25	1.27	2.08	1.08	2.07	1.20	1.97	1.07	2.18	1.10	1.99	1.13	1.94	1.02	1.98	1.11
Optimistic	2.02	.81	2.07	.73	2.11	.75	2.08	.62	2.26	.79	1.99	.78	1.97	.69	2.00	.73
Psychologically Immature	2.88	1.17	2.87	1.14	2.91	1.07	3.17	.94	2.82	1.03	2.88	1.11	2.86	1.09	2.91	1.17
Poor Judgment	3.08	1.14	3.15	1.11	3.17	1.15	3.36	1.04	3.06	1.28	2.82	1.11	2.94	1.16	2.95	1.21
Low Sex Drive	1.69	.95	1.84	1.01	1.80	1.07	1.59	.95	1.95	1.18	1.88	1.11	1.84	.99	1.78	1.10
Feels Mistreated	3.02	1.10	3.11	1.08	2.93	1.08	3.06	.96	3.18	1.11	3.09	.99	3.20	1.02	3.04	1.04
Overly Sensitive to Criticism	3.14	1.13	3.10	1.09	3.03	1.20	3.02	1.07	2.97	1.17	3.34	1.04	3.34	1.00	3.22	1.06
Sentimental	2.41	1.11	2.44	.94	2.47	1.02	2.47	.97	2.35	.91	2.60	1.02	2.51	.96	2.42	.98
Sexual Preoccupation	1.97	1.27	1.62	1.03	1.85	1.22	1.72	1.16	1.43	.93	1.93	1.25	1.87	1.15	1.80	1.16
Accelerated Speech	1.59	.92	1.39	.74	1.48	.88	1.47	.80	1.50	.71	1.37	.71	1.43	.78	1.50	.79
Concerns About Homosexuality	1.42	.99	1.29	.82	1.41	.95	1.27	.72	1.26	.71	1.54	1.20	1.54	1.13	1.47	1.10
Many Specific Fears	2.02	1.14	1.77	.95	1.89	1.05	1.88	1.08	1.87	1.06	1.97	1.05	1.95	1.01	1.86	1.06
Passive in Relationships	2.21	1.04	2.08	1.02	2.28	1.01	2.27	1.06	2.13	1.01	2.52	1.02	2.57	1.02	2.25	1.07
Negative Attitudes Toward Therapy	1.85	1.01	1.71	.99	1.80	1.02	1.79	1.05	1.71	.94	1.87	1.04	2.03	1.06	1.73	.98
Guilt-Prone	2.66	1.20	2.46	1.05	2.53	1.09	2.65	.96	2.38	.95	2.86	1.12	2.74	1.08	2.56	1.11
Nervous	3.12	1.00	2.94	1.00	3.04	1.00	2.98	.95	3.15	1.08	3.24	.91	3.23	.94	3.09	.93
Obsessive	3.03	1.21	2.84	1.09	2.87	1.13	2.78	1.10	2.88	1.01	2.96	1.12	2.93	1.14	2.92	1.16
Shy	2.39	1.14	2.33	1.08	2.55	1.09	2.50	1.08	2.53	1.13	2.63	1.23	2.76	1.22	2.46	1.21
Uses Intellectualization	2.59	1.36	2.57	1.21	2.51	1.28	2.48	1.22	2.88	1.19	2.56	1.26	2.68	1.18	2.50	1.24
Has Many Interests	2.26	1.09	2.40	.96	2.36	1.03	2.25	.98	2.75	1.08	2.29	1.08	2.22	.88	2.26	1.01
Difficulty Making Decisions	3.11	1.05	2.91	.94	2.96	.96	3.03	.98	2.88	1.07	3.05	1.05	3.08	1.02	3.00	1.06
Indirect Expression of Hostility	2.63	1.12	2.67	1.05	2.65	1.16	2.81	1.04	2.76	1.13	2.87	1.10	2.99	1.11	2.78	1.15
Poor Reality Testing	1.80	.91	1.59	.71	1.59	.72	1.71	.76	1.56	.70	1.62	.72	1.72	.88	1.68	.83
Angry	3.05	1.19	3.46	1.17	3.13	1.19	3.30	1.14	3.35	1.25	3.24	1.04	3.32	1.06	3.24	1.12
Eccentric	2.07	1.42	1.66	.95	1.99	1.30	1.79	1.06	1.88	1.15	1.99	1.27	1.94	1.12	1.96	1.28
Emotional Lability	2.35	1.19	2.34	1.08	2.26	1.08	2.40	1.13	2.24	1.02	2.24	.98	2.37	.94	2.36	1.03
Dislikes Change	2.66	1.07	2.67	.98	2.68	1.01	2.79	.93	2.58	1.09	2.79	.97	2.93	.98	2.73	1.06
Believes Cannot Be Helped	1.80	.93	1.84	.96	1.86	.99	1.89	1.06	1.79	1.02	1.99	1.03	2.07	1.18	1.84	.97
Reliable Informant	3.11	1.03	3.22	.84	3.17	.86	3.11	.76	3.24	.85	3.22	.95	3.17	.89	3.12	.92
Ignores Problems	2.34	1.00	2.44	1.03	2.37	1.02	2.45	1.01	2.50	1.13	2.22	1.04	2.38	1.07	2.22	1.01

Ruminates	3.34	1.03	3.13	1.02	3.32	1.02	3.24	.95	3.21	1.11	3.33	1.03	3.31	.98	3.35	.98
Excitable	2.79	1.08	2.83	1.04	2.71	1.01	2.76	.98	3.09	.79	2.57	.98	2.59	.93	2.72	1.01
Conforming	2.45	.85	2.32	.88	2.54	.91	2.52	.82	2.53	.83	2.51	.85	2.57	.86	2.41	.88
Ineffective at Dealing with Problems	3.10	1.03	3.01	1.05	2.95	1.05	3.06	.99	3.00	1.03	3.09	1.04	3.14	1.05	3.04	1.04
Introverted	2.49	1.10	2.36	1.08	2.48	1.01	2.45	1.08	2.35	1.20	2.74	1.14	2.97	1.08	2.53	1.15
Superficial Relationships	2.63	1.28	2.64	1.19	2.65	1.20	2.89	1.12	2.65	1.25	2.72	1.29	2.93	1.18	2.64	1.23
Impulsive	2.74	1.21	2.85	1.19	2.81	1.16	3.03	1.14	2.71	.97	2.55	1.21	2.72	1.25	2.70	1.21
Stereotypic Feminine Behavior	1.43	.81	1.25	.56	1.41	.74	1.22	.49	1.29	.63	1.34	.62	1.37	.74	1.30	.59
Stubborn	2.75	1.08	2.95	1.01	2.77	1.19	2.95	1.11	2.91	1.06	2.84	1.00	3.03	1.10	2.74	1.13
Hostile Toward Therapist	1.38	.69	1.34	.65	1.39	.68	1.31	.59	1.35	.65	1.49	.76	1.49	.75	1.41	.66
Difficult to Motivate	2.21	1.05	2.07	1.02	2.16	.98	2.19	1.05	1.97	.90	2.21	1.01	2.45	1.04	2.16	1.00
Suicidal Ideations	1.72	.88	1.80	1.02	1.78	1.02	1.87	.98	1.76	.99	1.85	1.05	2.01	1.14	1.78	.96
Familial Discord	3.14	1.42	3.26	1.35	2.96	1.32	3.52	1.15	3.24	1.26	3.07	1.33	3.17	1.30	3.22	1.33
Dogmatic	2.44	1.22	2.39	1.12	2.37	1.14	2.46	1.10	2.38	1.10	2.26	1.11	2.36	1.12	2.31	1.15

	Content Scales *(continued)*			
	WRK		TRT	
	Mean	SD	Mean	SD
Intake Information	(n = 208)		(n = 196)	
Axis IV diagnosis	2.94	.91	2.97	.90
Axis V - Current Level of Functioning	60.46	9.77	60.47	9.71
Number of Arrests	1.40	3.74	1.70	4.11
Mental Status	(n = 208)		(n = 196)	
Anxiety During Interview	2.50	.72	2.51	.73
Depression During Interview	2.46	.71	2.45	.71
Activity Level During Interview	3.00	.47	3.04	.47
Speech During Interview	2.94	.39	2.95	.38
SCL-90-R Scales	(n = 205)		(n = 191)	
Somatization	1.29	.81	1.29	.82
Obsessive-Compulsive	1.74	.82	1.74	.81
Interpersonal Sensitivity	1.70	.83	1.72	.84
Depression	2.06	.78	2.08	.81
Anxiety	1.59	.86	1.62	.87
Hostility	1.54	1.05	1.63	1.05
Phobic Anxiety	.82	.75	.85	.75
Paranoid Ideation	1.66	.86	1.70	.88
Psychoticism	1.20	.70	1.23	.71
Initial SCL-90 Analogue	(n = 131)		(n = 119)	
Somatization	2.54	2.81	2.46	2.75
Obsessive-Compulsive	3.18	2.74	3.45	2.72
Interpersonal Sensitivity	4.74	2.39	4.81	2.47
Depression	4.65	2.66	4.70	2.62
Anxiety	4.44	2.67	4.70	2.75
Hostility	3.23	2.71	3.47	2.84
Phobic Anxiety	1.32	2.13	1.45	2.12
Paranoid Ideation	1.17	1.77	1.28	1.67
Psychoticism	.52	1.31	.42	1.00
Patient Description Form Scales	(n = 131)		(n = 120)	
Angry Resentment	2.83	.93	2.95	.93
Critical/Argumentative	2.55	.95	2.60	.97
Narcissistic	2.31	.96	2.30	.93

Defensive	2.54	.90	2.56	.89
Histrionic	2.40	.79	2.44	.76
Aggressive	2.11	.84	2.15	.88
Insecure	2.97	.78	3.05	.74
Anxious	2.96	.80	3.03	.76
Pessimistic	2.41	.98	2.53	.94
Depressed	2.53	.77	2.63	.78
Achievement-Oriented	2.53	.73	2.55	.74
Passive-Submissive	2.23	.82	2.24	.83
Introverted	2.60	1.04	2.69	1.03
Emotionally Controlled	2.41	1.09	2.47	1.10
Antisocial	2.22	.92	2.30	.93
Negative Treatment Attitudes	1.94	.80	1.97	.79
Somatic Symptoms	2.18	1.07	2.18	1.03
Psychotic Symptoms	1.23	.39	1.26	.40
Family Problems	2.80	1.13	2.86	1.16
Obsessive-Compulsive	2.80	.81	2.87	.80
Stereotypic Masculine Interests	2.76	1.09	2.83	1.14
Procrastinates	2.32	.99	2.35	.93
Suspicious	2.59	.99	2.69	.95
Agitated	2.16	.76	2.23	.77
Work Problems	2.03	.91	1.98	.93
Patient Description Form Items	(n = 131)		(n = 120)	
Anxious	3.50	.84	3.53	.82
Problems with Authority Figures	2.97	1.23	3.11	1.19
Has Insight Into Own Problems	2.63	.86	2.68	.82
Fears Losing Control	3.28	1.03	3.37	1.04
Extroverted	2.29	.94	2.31	.91
Uses Repression	2.59	1.07	2.64	1.06
Submissive	2.21	.91	2.22	.95
Difficulty Concentrating	2.79	1.16	2.85	1.08
Rigid	2.74	1.10	2.81	1.09
Overly Compliant	1.97	.90	1.97	.90
Whiny	1.99	1.09	2.02	1.05
Feels Overwhelmed	3.36	1.12	3.48	1.06
Manipulative	2.41	1.19	2.41	1.18
Difficulty Trusting Others	3.27	1.27	3.45	1.23
Insensitive to Others	2.22	1.03	2.22	.98
Stereotypic Masculine Behavior	2.75	1.13	2.84	1.19
Harbors Grudges	2.78	1.15	2.91	1.10
Evasive	2.24	1.14	2.33	1.11

Content Scales (*continued*)

	WRK		TRT	
	Mean	SD	Mean	SD
Disoriented	1.25	.59	1.31	.63
Energetic	2.34	.88	2.34	.86
Lonely	2.98	1.26	3.07	1.27
Family Lacks Love	2.78	1.31	2.87	1.32
Worrier	3.33	1.09	3.38	1.04
Narcissistic	2.47	1.19	2.51	1.18
Tearful	1.53	.83	1.63	.87
Provocative	1.64	.83	1.69	.88
Moralistic	2.45	1.10	2.44	1.03
Socially Awkward	2.79	1.17	2.89	1.14
Hostile	2.47	1.20	2.64	1.22
Overcontrolled	2.61	1.24	2.72	1.24
Resistant to Interpretations	2.10	1.02	2.16	1.00
Antisocial Behavior	2.24	1.24	2.33	1.26
Sarcastic	2.07	1.11	2.08	1.12
Rejects Traditional Gender Role	1.65	1.05	1.71	1.06
Feels Gets Raw Deal From Life	3.05	1.19	3.17	1.17
Acute Psychological Turmoil	3.05	1.07	3.17	1.01
Does Not Complete Projects	2.29	1.19	2.34	1.11
Uncomfortable with Opposite Sex	2.15	1.11	2.17	1.07
Preoccupied with Health Problems	2.35	1.40	2.34	1.38
Work-Oriented	2.85	1.09	2.93	1.09
Resents Family Members	2.83	1.31	2.89	1.35
Demanding of Attention	2.48	1.15	2.48	1.07
Passive	2.47	1.01	2.46	.99
Self-Punishing	2.39	1.19	2.56	1.17
Needs to Achieve	2.71	1.05	2.76	.99
Needs to Be with Others	2.91	1.15	2.90	1.10
Irritable	2.75	1.05	2.82	1.05
Self-Defeating	3.11	1.25	3.26	1.16
Delusional Thinking	1.20	.57	1.25	.63
Self-Reliant	2.67	.92	2.65	.90
Aggressive	2.38	1.02	2.45	1.05
Competitive	2.40	1.01	2.44	.97
Suspicious	2.53	1.16	2.66	1.16
Compulsive	2.49	1.13	2.59	1.11
Dependable	3.02	.96	3.01	.91
Multiple Somatic Complaints	2.15	1.31	2.13	1.29

Complains of Lack of Time	1.99	1.13	2.03	1.13
Poor Work Performance	2.07	1.14	2.05	1.09
Insecure	3.48	.92	3.51	.87
Discusses Problems Openly	3.08	.85	3.07	.81
Sexually Adjusted	2.38	.80	2.40	.81
Exaggerated Need for Affection	2.26	1.13	2.34	1.07
Resentful	3.01	1.13	3.17	1.13
Uses Denial	2.62	1.24	2.68	1.23
Hypochondriacal	1.73	.95	1.72	.91
Communicates Effectively	3.09	.76	3.10	.77
Has Many Nightmares	1.68	1.00	1.83	1.09
Stormy Interpersonal Relationships	3.05	1.25	3.22	1.24
Feigns Remorse When in Trouble	1.68	.93	1.75	.96
Stereotypic Masculine Interests	2.74	1.14	2.81	1.18
Guarded	2.73	1.33	2.80	1.34
Feels Inferior	3.11	1.05	3.17	1.00
Low Frustration Tolerance	3.13	1.17	3.21	1.16
Psychotic Symptoms	1.14	.46	1.13	.41
Fired From Past Jobs	2.04	1.12	2.06	1.20
Needs Attention	2.87	1.04	2.88	1.00
Acts Out	2.43	1.19	2.55	1.18
Histrionic	1.92	1.01	1.97	1.02
Self-Indulgent	2.50	1.13	2.56	1.12
Depressed	3.34	1.02	3.40	.99
Grandiose	1.95	1.12	1.92	1.08
Cynical	2.57	1.31	2.70	1.30
Sociopathic	1.64	.85	1.71	.89
Agitated	2.45	1.05	2.58	1.03
Marital Problems	2.54	1.56	2.66	1.62
Absence of Deep Emotions	2.06	1.29	2.08	1.30
Uncomfortable Dealing with Emotions	2.91	1.30	3.05	1.33
Sad	2.99	1.00	3.06	.98
Self-Degrading	2.24	1.01	2.33	1.00
Unable to Express Negative Feelings	2.20	1.16	2.22	1.16
Concrete in Thinking	2.23	1.03	2.19	1.03
Unable to See Own Limitations	2.28	1.14	2.25	1.09
Power-Oriented	2.16	1.10	2.22	1.13
Grouchy	2.36	1.05	2.43	1.06
Overbearing in Relationships	2.28	1.15	2.27	1.10
Uncertain About Career	3.43	1.27	3.49	1.30
Likable	3.18	.81	3.19	.79
Procrastinator	2.59	1.21	2.63	1.12

	Content Scales *(continued)*			
	WRK		TRT	
	Mean	SD	Mean	SD
Negative Feelings Toward Opposite Sex	2.11	1.16	2.11	1.13
Defensive	2.66	1.20	2.69	1.14
Empathetic	2.33	.76	2.36	.75
Perfectionistic	2.55	1.15	2.53	1.15
Judgmental	2.68	1.14	2.72	1.12
Copes Well with Stress	1.97	.66	1.96	.64
Moody	2.82	1.01	2.83	1.02
Selfish	2.23	1.07	2.20	1.00
Gives Up Easily	2.29	1.05	2.34	1.03
Physical Symptoms in Response to Stress	2.32	1.23	2.31	1.22
Blames Family For Difficulties	2.52	1.29	2.53	1.32
Bored	2.45	1.14	2.54	1.13
Idealistic	2.35	1.07	2.33	1.08
Difficulty Establishing Therapeutic Rapport	2.01	1.06	2.07	1.06
Daydreams	1.86	1.00	1.82	1.03
Concerned About Status	2.42	1.12	2.45	1.16
Creates Good First Impression	2.54	.89	2.53	.88
Complains of Sleep Disturbance	2.64	1.29	2.80	1.29
Has Temper Tantrums	2.33	1.21	2.37	1.15
Overreactive	2.74	1.07	2.81	1.06
High Aspirations	2.46	1.13	2.49	1.13
Feels Hopeless	2.81	1.15	2.94	1.11
Keeps Others at a Distance	2.97	1.30	3.07	1.30
Argumentative	2.34	1.10	2.37	1.08
Paranoid Features	1.93	1.02	1.95	.99
Restless	2.63	1.11	2.70	1.13
Pessimistic	2.92	1.15	3.10	1.08
Feels Like a Failure	3.05	1.13	3.18	1.07
Hallucinations	1.08	.32	1.09	.35
Restricted Affect	2.29	1.32	2.28	1.34
Impatient	2.72	1.10	2.71	1.07
Assertive	2.33	.82	2.32	.83
Modest	2.38	.84	2.48	.83
Self-Doubting	3.11	.93	3.22	.91
Deceptive	1.93	1.02	1.91	.99
Feels That Life is a Strain	3.16	1.14	3.32	1.06
Physically Abusive	1.51	.83	1.58	.90
Feels Rejected	3.15	1.23	3.24	1.20

Does Not Get Along with Coworkers	2.06	1.02	2.01	1.08
Uses Projection	2.46	1.17	2.49	1.15
Complains of Fatigue	2.48	1.35	2.54	1.35
Uses Rationalization	2.68	1.12	2.70	1.07
Critical of Others	2.61	1.14	2.67	1.19
Egocentric	2.52	1.19	2.58	1.20
Overevaluates Own Worth	1.98	1.12	2.01	1.16
Optimistic	1.98	.72	1.93	.65
Psychologically Immature	2.80	1.14	2.80	1.13
Poor Judgment	2.85	1.17	2.98	1.17
Low Sex Drive	1.88	1.17	1.90	1.10
Feels Mistreated	3.01	1.10	3.08	1.09
Overly Sensitive to Criticism	3.10	1.18	3.19	1.16
Sentimental	2.42	1.05	2.49	1.03
Sexual Preoccupation	1.79	1.16	1.86	1.20
Accelerated Speech	1.44	.80	1.44	.80
Concerns About Homosexuality	1.46	1.08	1.51	1.09
Many Specific Fears	1.85	1.03	1.91	1.01
Passive in Relationships	2.29	1.07	2.32	1.06
Negative Attitudes Toward Therapy	1.75	.98	1.81	1.01
Guilt-Prone	2.62	1.14	2.67	1.14
Nervous	3.11	.96	3.16	.95
Obsessive	2.80	1.14	2.91	1.15
Shy	2.47	1.22	2.54	1.24
Uses Intellectualization	2.56	1.30	2.60	1.26
Has Many Interests	2.28	1.03	2.30	1.01
Difficulty Making Decisions	2.98	1.05	3.02	.98
Indirect Expression of Hostility	2.76	1.13	2.77	1.13
Poor Reality Testing	1.60	.78	1.62	.78
Angry	3.11	1.12	3.25	1.12
Eccentric	1.88	1.23	1.94	1.25
Emotional Lability	2.26	1.05	2.37	1.08
Dislikes Change	2.66	1.02	2.75	1.02
Believes Cannot Be Helped	1.88	1.03	1.94	1.00
Reliable Informant	3.20	.92	3.24	.86
Ignores Problems	2.23	1.02	2.24	1.01
Ruminates	3.22	1.02	3.37	.97
Excitable	2.55	1.02	2.61	1.01
Conforming	2.36	.90	2.47	.86
Ineffective at Dealing with Problems	3.03	1.07	3.03	1.04
Introverted	2.56	1.15	2.66	1.13
Superficial Relationships	2.59	1.22	2.63	1.21

Content Scales *(continued)*

	WRK		TRT	
	Mean	SD	Mean	SD
Impulsive	2.56	1.20	2.68	1.22
Stereotypic Feminine Behavior	1.32	.62	1.34	.69
Stubborn	2.75	1.13	2.85	1.12
Hostile Toward Therapist	1.41	.68	1.43	.71
Difficult to Motivate	2.14	1.03	2.20	1.00
Suicidal Ideations	1.80	1.00	1.91	1.04
Familial Discord	2.96	1.36	3.10	1.37
Dogmatic	2.20	1.12	2.28	1.11

Table L-2e. Means and standard deviations for continuous extra-test characteristics (men): High scores on Content Component scales

Extra-test Characteristics	Content Component Scales									
	FRS_1		FRS_2		DEP_1		DEP_2		DEP_3	
	Mean	SD	Mean	SD	Mean	SD	Mean	SD	Mean	SD
Intake Information	(n = 79)		(n = 65)		(n = 228)		(n = 241)		(n = 119)	
Axis IV diagnosis	3.00	.95	2.92	.88	2.95	.90	2.91	.92	2.95	.90
Axis V - Current Level of Functioning	59.63	9.91	61.69	10.51	60.37	9.95	60.77	9.64	60.47	10.00
Number of Arrests	1.53	3.01	1.21	2.40	1.39	3.54	1.30	3.43	1.48	3.73
Mental Status	(n = 79)		(n = 65)		(n = 228)		(n = 241)		(n = 119)	
Anxiety During Interview	2.59	.71	2.41	.71	2.47	.73	2.48	.71	2.47	.74
Depression During Interview	2.42	.69	2.22	.66	2.45	.71	2.44	.70	2.46	.72
Activity Level During Interview	3.03	.43	3.03	.44	3.02	.46	3.03	.43	3.00	.44
Speech During Interview	2.94	.37	2.98	.34	2.96	.37	2.95	.39	2.95	.41
SCL-90-R Scales	(n = 77)		(n = 64)		(n = 223)		(n = 236)		(n = 117)	
Somatization	1.39	.90	1.05	.77	1.26	.80	1.16	.82	1.16	.80
Obsessive-Compulsive	1.80	.98	1.46	.84	1.69	.82	1.61	.84	1.60	.81
Interpersonal Sensitivity	1.71	.95	1.41	.80	1.61	.85	1.57	.88	1.57	.86
Depression	1.89	.99	1.64	.92	2.02	.81	1.98	.83	1.96	.83
Anxiety	1.76	1.03	1.15	.80	1.53	.87	1.47	.89	1.44	.89
Hostility	1.53	1.12	1.07	1.00	1.56	1.06	1.45	1.05	1.44	1.01
Phobic Anxiety	1.21	.88	.74	.66	.78	.74	.73	.74	.73	.71
Paranoid Ideation	1.71	1.00	1.31	.93	1.57	.91	1.54	.94	1.54	.90
Psychoticism	1.33	.91	.97	.76	1.17	.73	1.12	.73	1.13	.72
Initial SCL-90 Analogue	(n = 50)		(n = 35)		(n = 143)		(n = 153)		(n = 77)	
Somatization	2.86	3.02	2.67	3.17	2.79	2.95	2.59	2.92	2.56	2.89
Obsessive-Compulsive	3.45	2.61	3.09	2.65	3.43	2.69	3.61	2.83	3.42	2.61
Interpersonal Sensitivity	4.56	2.48	4.38	2.73	4.87	2.45	5.01	2.49	4.86	2.41
Depression	4.34	2.42	4.65	2.70	4.83	2.73	4.87	2.69	4.76	2.70
Anxiety	4.74	2.58	4.55	2.68	4.70	2.72	4.74	2.70	4.66	2.70
Hostility	2.98	2.68	2.62	2.71	3.30	2.78	3.38	2.89	3.40	2.79
Phobic Anxiety	1.59	2.77	.97	1.42	1.53	2.28	1.45	2.20	1.40	2.22
Paranoid Ideation	1.43	2.09	1.56	2.09	1.40	2.06	1.33	2.04	1.30	1.94
Psychoticism	.69	1.61	.48	1.09	.70	1.59	.62	1.46	.61	1.27

Table L-2e. Means and standard deviations for continuous extra-test characteristics (men): High scores on Content Component scales *(continued)*

Extra-test Characteristics	FRS_1 Mean	FRS_1 SD	FRS_2 Mean	FRS_2 SD	DEP_1 Mean	DEP_1 SD	DEP_2 Mean	DEP_2 SD	DEP_3 Mean	DEP_3 SD
Patient Description Form Scales	(n = 52)		(n = 35)		(n = 144)		(n = 154)		(n = 78)	
Angry Resentment	2.83	1.01	2.57	.89	2.86	.98	2.86	.97	2.89	.95
Critical/Argumentative	2.49	.96	2.21	.85	2.56	.97	2.57	.97	2.56	.95
Narcissistic	2.24	.98	2.17	.84	2.35	.94	2.33	.96	2.33	.88
Defensive	2.58	.92	2.48	.88	2.60	.91	2.60	.91	2.62	.89
Histrionic	2.35	.82	2.14	.80	2.45	.78	2.42	.79	2.45	.76
Aggressive	2.16	.87	1.74	.60	2.17	.90	2.12	.90	2.18	.88
Insecure	2.87	.77	2.71	.81	3.01	.78	3.00	.80	3.08	.78
Anxious	3.06	.88	2.94	.80	2.99	.80	2.96	.79	3.00	.80
Pessimistic	2.36	.92	2.34	.84	2.49	.97	2.46	.97	2.51	.97
Depressed	2.38	.73	2.29	.76	2.60	.77	2.57	.78	2.57	.80
Achievement-Oriented	2.46	.73	2.49	.69	2.54	.71	2.61	.74	2.53	.69
Passive-Submissive	2.23	.71	2.32	.99	2.24	.81	2.24	.84	2.28	.84
Introverted	2.62	1.03	2.59	1.11	2.62	1.00	2.62	.99	2.68	1.03
Emotionally Controlled	2.28	1.10	2.11	.87	2.46	1.06	2.41	1.02	2.46	1.09
Antisocial	2.20	.89	2.10	.82	2.29	.94	2.25	.98	2.31	.98
Negative Treatment Attitudes	1.97	.78	1.90	.72	2.01	.81	2.01	.83	2.03	.81
Somatic Symptoms	2.39	1.18	2.16	1.10	2.28	1.11	2.15	1.09	2.15	1.08
Psychotic Symptoms	1.31	.56	1.24	.38	1.30	.48	1.28	.46	1.30	.45
Family Problems	2.72	1.20	2.22	1.04	2.82	1.15	2.75	1.14	2.78	1.13
Obsessive-Compulsive	2.75	.86	2.60	.81	2.85	.83	2.87	.79	2.87	.79
Stereotypic Masculine Interests	2.63	1.03	2.41	1.17	2.82	1.11	2.76	1.12	2.86	1.14
Procrastinates	2.35	1.06	2.23	.91	2.40	.95	2.29	.93	2.32	.90
Suspicious	2.59	.99	2.57	.97	2.64	1.00	2.61	1.05	2.65	1.00
Agitated	2.27	.89	2.03	.72	2.23	.80	2.23	.80	2.23	.80
Work Problems	1.89	1.05	1.92	.86	2.07	.97	1.98	.93	2.06	.96
Patient Description Form Items	(n = 52)		(n = 35)		(n = 144)		(n = 154)		(n = 78)	
Anxious	3.62	.93	3.46	.85	3.50	.88	3.51	.86	3.49	.90
Problems with Authority Figures	2.96	1.22	2.97	1.02	3.04	1.29	3.03	1.28	3.05	1.25
Has Insight Into Own Problems	2.42	.70	2.29	.79	2.64	.86	2.59	.87	2.61	.88
Fears Losing Control	3.26	1.24	2.97	1.22	3.31	1.07	3.26	1.06	3.35	1.06
Extroverted	2.38	.91	2.14	.94	2.35	.96	2.33	.95	2.27	.90
Uses Repression	2.49	1.02	2.76	1.07	2.67	1.07	2.61	1.06	2.66	1.05
Submissive	2.27	.83	2.49	.98	2.22	.90	2.19	.91	2.26	.94

Content Component Scales

Difficulty Concentrating	2.98	1.06	2.77	1.17	2.83	1.10	2.76	1.15	2.84	1.10
Rigid	2.85	1.07	2.71	1.02	2.76	1.10	2.79	1.09	2.81	1.05
Overly Compliant	1.90	.81	1.94	1.10	1.96	.91	1.99	.91	2.04	.91
Whiny	1.98	1.00	1.80	.90	2.02	1.04	1.99	1.05	2.05	1.07
Feels Overwhelmed	3.42	1.09	3.26	1.20	3.42	1.11	3.33	1.17	3.39	1.08
Manipulative	2.27	1.22	2.29	.91	2.50	1.16	2.48	1.19	2.49	1.17
Difficulty Trusting Others	3.17	1.29	3.23	1.19	3.35	1.24	3.27	1.27	3.34	1.24
Insensitive to Others	2.10	1.07	2.14	1.03	2.24	1.06	2.27	1.10	2.28	1.03
Stereotypic Masculine Behavior	2.65	1.12	2.31	1.13	2.81	1.15	2.73	1.15	2.84	1.16
Harbors Grudges	2.63	1.11	2.30	.92	2.80	1.15	2.72	1.17	2.89	1.09
Evasive	2.18	1.09	2.29	1.05	2.33	1.16	2.32	1.16	2.35	1.14
Disoriented	1.27	.56	1.23	.49	1.33	.65	1.28	.61	1.32	.64
Energetic	2.40	.77	2.43	.98	2.38	.87	2.41	.90	2.30	.85
Lonely	2.90	1.17	2.60	1.26	3.01	1.23	3.01	1.27	3.10	1.27
Family Lacks Love	2.57	1.30	2.13	1.04	2.81	1.33	2.73	1.34	2.80	1.34
Worrier	3.38	1.17	3.37	1.11	3.40	1.06	3.36	1.00	3.37	1.04
Narcissistic	2.45	1.25	2.31	1.08	2.55	1.19	2.54	1.22	2.49	1.17
Tearful	1.42	.70	1.37	.65	1.58	.83	1.58	.85	1.59	.86
Provocative	1.73	.91	1.54	.74	1.73	.95	1.73	.95	1.74	.97
Moralistic	2.54	.98	2.50	1.05	2.46	1.08	2.56	1.07	2.57	1.09
Socially Awkward	2.88	1.13	2.83	1.34	2.82	1.15	2.85	1.14	2.91	1.16
Hostile	2.33	1.18	2.06	1.03	2.55	1.21	2.55	1.23	2.57	1.22
Overcontrolled	2.56	1.32	2.29	1.15	2.67	1.25	2.66	1.20	2.63	1.23
Resistant to Interpretations	2.08	1.04	2.09	.92	2.20	1.01	2.18	1.04	2.21	1.05
Antisocial Behavior	2.15	1.14	1.83	1.04	2.31	1.28	2.26	1.31	2.36	1.29
Sarcastic	1.92	1.03	1.74	.89	2.09	1.08	2.09	1.11	2.04	1.08
Rejects Traditional Gender Role	1.62	.90	1.74	1.14	1.68	1.08	1.68	1.11	1.68	1.04
Feels Gets Raw Deal From Life	2.94	1.39	2.91	1.17	3.05	1.20	3.11	1.16	3.08	1.18
Acute Psychological Turmoil	2.96	1.03	2.91	1.20	3.08	1.14	3.12	1.10	3.15	1.04
Does Not Complete Projects	2.28	1.24	2.07	1.09	2.42	1.15	2.33	1.17	2.35	1.13
Uncomfortable with Opposite Sex	2.11	.97	2.03	1.09	2.14	1.05	2.17	1.09	2.15	1.06
Preoccupied with Health Problems	2.61	1.40	2.23	1.35	2.41	1.44	2.24	1.39	2.22	1.37
Work-Oriented	2.83	1.02	3.00	1.00	2.93	1.04	3.01	1.05	2.90	1.09
Resents Family Members	2.76	1.44	2.19	1.17	2.80	1.32	2.75	1.31	2.73	1.29
Demanding of Attention	2.35	1.14	2.09	1.06	2.49	1.11	2.53	1.15	2.53	1.14
Passive	2.45	.83	2.51	1.07	2.45	.97	2.40	.99	2.42	.99
Self-Punishing	2.42	1.23	2.26	1.15	2.49	1.19	2.47	1.17	2.53	1.17
Needs to Achieve	2.50	.96	2.56	1.05	2.76	1.02	2.88	1.05	2.75	.98
Needs to Be with Others	2.65	.97	2.57	.95	2.96	1.05	2.98	1.02	2.91	1.05
Irritable	2.75	1.14	2.51	1.07	2.76	1.07	2.73	1.08	2.73	1.09
Self-Defeating	3.13	1.24	3.14	1.19	3.26	1.21	3.19	1.22	3.23	1.19
Delusional Thinking	1.37	.80	1.31	.76	1.29	.69	1.28	.69	1.28	.66

Table L-2e. Means and standard deviations for continuous extra-test characteristics (men): High scores on Content Component scales *(continued)*

Extra-test Characteristics	Content Component Scales									
	FRS_1		FRS_2		DEP_1		DEP_2		DEP_3	
	Mean	SD	Mean	SD	Mean	SD	Mean	SD	Mean	SD
Self-Reliant	2.65	.93	2.77	.81	2.62	.86	2.65	.88	2.60	.87
Aggressive	2.29	.99	2.11	.83	2.43	1.03	2.40	1.09	2.46	1.02
Competitive	2.24	1.01	2.30	.88	2.40	.96	2.42	.99	2.45	.91
Suspicious	2.50	1.09	2.50	1.13	2.59	1.22	2.58	1.25	2.64	1.20
Compulsive	2.37	1.13	2.27	1.04	2.58	1.10	2.60	1.10	2.58	1.16
Dependable	2.94	.99	3.09	.82	2.99	.96	3.03	.95	3.01	.93
Multiple Somatic Complaints	2.37	1.39	2.11	1.25	2.22	1.37	2.05	1.30	2.07	1.31
Complains of Lack of Time	2.06	1.21	1.94	.98	2.01	1.12	1.97	1.13	1.94	1.05
Poor Work Performance	2.21	1.24	1.87	1.12	2.10	1.15	2.03	1.15	2.14	1.12
Insecure	3.47	.97	3.14	1.03	3.46	.95	3.49	.94	3.50	.95
Discusses Problems Openly	2.98	.75	2.91	.66	3.06	.86	3.05	.90	3.11	.90
Sexually Adjusted	2.38	.79	2.35	.94	2.39	.82	2.42	.83	2.38	.82
Exaggerated Need for Affection	2.08	1.10	2.06	1.04	2.30	1.07	2.33	1.07	2.33	1.05
Resentful	3.19	1.21	2.79	1.07	3.03	1.18	3.07	1.19	3.09	1.14
Uses Denial	2.65	1.31	2.63	1.19	2.70	1.24	2.69	1.23	2.74	1.25
Hypochondriacal	1.94	1.11	1.89	1.08	1.82	1.00	1.74	.96	1.72	.95
Communicates Effectively	2.98	.64	3.06	.68	3.07	.75	3.09	.80	3.05	.80
Has Many Nightmares	1.74	1.10	1.50	.74	1.78	1.05	1.69	1.01	1.78	1.04
Stormy Interpersonal Relationships	2.94	1.33	2.57	1.28	3.13	1.21	3.01	1.26	3.14	1.25
Feigns Remorse When in Trouble	1.68	.91	1.71	.82	1.77	.95	1.76	.97	1.83	.97
Stereotypic Masculine Interests	2.62	1.03	2.51	1.29	2.82	1.17	2.77	1.19	2.86	1.20
Guarded	2.79	1.45	2.71	1.18	2.78	1.32	2.79	1.32	2.80	1.29
Feels Inferior	2.92	1.04	2.94	1.11	3.11	1.01	3.13	1.06	3.20	1.01
Low Frustration Tolerance	2.94	1.26	2.57	1.12	3.19	1.17	3.12	1.16	3.16	1.16
Psychotic Symptoms	1.27	.73	1.21	.41	1.20	.57	1.18	.51	1.17	.47
Fired From Past Jobs	1.94	1.08	2.09	1.00	2.11	1.14	1.99	1.13	2.03	1.18
Needs Attention	2.56	1.06	2.49	.92	2.90	.97	2.91	1.02	2.91	.98
Acts Out	2.35	1.06	2.31	1.13	2.52	1.17	2.47	1.21	2.51	1.24
Histrionic	1.90	1.07	1.80	1.05	2.01	1.01	1.94	1.02	1.96	.98
Self-Indulgent	2.47	1.14	2.29	1.05	2.56	1.15	2.47	1.15	2.54	1.11
Depressed	3.12	1.06	3.26	1.07	3.43	.98	3.42	1.01	3.36	1.03
Grandiose	1.83	1.08	1.57	.88	2.00	1.13	1.96	1.10	1.88	1.00
Cynical	2.46	1.26	2.23	1.06	2.61	1.28	2.62	1.28	2.61	1.23
Sociopathic	1.54	.80	1.69	.93	1.70	.89	1.70	.95	1.72	.95
Agitated	2.56	1.23	2.26	1.04	2.54	1.08	2.51	1.08	2.55	1.07

Marital Problems	2.18	1.56	1.91	1.48	2.61	1.59	2.61	1.60	2.76	1.59
Absence of Deep Emotions	1.92	1.21	1.69	.90	2.10	1.26	2.05	1.22	2.10	1.29
Uncomfortable Dealing with Emotions	2.81	1.30	2.69	1.21	2.99	1.31	2.95	1.28	3.01	1.33
Sad	2.88	.96	2.89	.99	3.08	.98	3.00	1.04	3.02	1.03
Self-Degrading	2.02	.96	2.00	.97	2.32	1.06	2.32	1.08	2.35	1.04
Unable to Express Negative Feelings	1.94	1.00	1.94	1.00	2.22	1.14	2.16	1.13	2.26	1.17
Concrete in Thinking	2.21	1.11	2.23	1.03	2.26	1.00	2.20	1.04	2.21	1.00
Unable to See Own Limitations	2.52	1.13	2.17	.98	2.33	1.12	2.37	1.13	2.34	1.14
Power-Oriented	2.16	1.14	1.80	.90	2.24	1.09	2.25	1.12	2.16	1.01
Grouchy	2.45	1.12	2.20	1.13	2.38	1.12	2.37	1.11	2.42	1.10
Overbearing in Relationships	2.24	1.14	1.77	.94	2.39	1.13	2.28	1.14	2.33	1.11
Uncertain About Career	3.48	1.18	3.45	1.20	3.49	1.24	3.45	1.25	3.38	1.33
Likable	3.10	.70	3.06	.73	3.16	.83	3.15	.82	3.16	.83
Procrastinator	2.48	1.22	2.55	1.12	2.66	1.13	2.52	1.18	2.61	1.11
Negative Feelings Toward Opposite Sex	1.90	1.05	1.82	1.01	2.14	1.16	2.13	1.18	2.19	1.16
Defensive	2.53	1.24	2.46	1.12	2.72	1.21	2.77	1.18	2.78	1.21
Empathetic	2.32	.71	2.09	.74	2.33	.77	2.35	.81	2.36	.77
Perfectionistic	2.32	1.07	2.18	.98	2.57	1.17	2.65	1.14	2.49	1.11
Judgmental	2.59	1.10	2.43	1.07	2.73	1.14	2.78	1.15	2.78	1.13
Copes Well with Stress	1.92	.66	1.97	.62	1.95	.65	1.98	.61	1.99	.63
Moody	2.72	1.01	2.43	.95	2.80	1.03	2.80	1.03	2.83	.99
Selfish	2.12	1.03	2.18	.95	2.23	1.02	2.24	1.04	2.22	.99
Gives Up Easily	2.20	1.02	2.12	1.05	2.37	1.00	2.27	.99	2.34	1.04
Physical Symptoms in Response to Stress	2.49	1.32	2.26	1.26	2.39	1.25	2.27	1.27	2.27	1.25
Blames Family For Difficulties	2.42	1.28	2.09	1.16	2.50	1.29	2.46	1.30	2.51	1.29
Bored	2.44	1.26	2.14	1.00	2.54	1.14	2.44	1.18	2.50	1.19
Idealistic	2.37	1.03	2.21	1.17	2.32	1.06	2.40	1.11	2.39	1.05
Difficulty Establishing Therapeutic Rapport	2.06	.97	2.00	.94	2.08	1.06	2.03	1.06	2.10	1.07
Daydreams	1.81	1.08	1.54	.81	1.93	1.05	1.87	1.00	1.96	1.08
Concerned About Status	2.29	1.10	2.23	1.03	2.43	1.14	2.51	1.14	2.46	1.13
Creates Good First Impression	2.53	.81	2.74	.89	2.54	.93	2.59	.94	2.54	.94
Complains of Sleep Disturbance	2.67	1.33	2.20	1.11	2.71	1.26	2.63	1.28	2.67	1.23
Has Temper Tantrums	2.40	1.21	2.06	.98	2.33	1.20	2.27	1.16	2.30	1.14
Overreactive	2.69	1.09	2.23	1.06	2.78	1.10	2.74	1.13	2.81	1.08
High Aspirations	2.46	1.16	2.24	1.13	2.52	1.12	2.62	1.19	2.42	1.03
Feels Hopeless	2.61	1.08	2.49	1.09	2.87	1.15	2.88	1.13	2.84	1.18
Keeps Others at a Distance	2.82	1.39	2.85	1.26	3.03	1.26	3.02	1.26	3.02	1.25
Argumentative	2.35	1.07	2.09	1.04	2.37	1.13	2.38	1.07	2.40	1.12
Paranoid Features	2.06	1.12	1.94	1.03	1.96	1.08	1.94	1.09	1.94	1.06
Restless	2.75	1.25	2.31	1.05	2.69	1.13	2.70	1.15	2.67	1.13
Pessimistic	2.87	1.07	2.83	1.04	3.01	1.10	2.98	1.13	3.00	1.11
Feels Like a Failure	2.92	1.19	2.86	1.19	3.08	1.12	3.07	1.12	3.16	1.14

Table L-2e. Means and standard deviations for continuous extra-test characteristics (men): High scores on Content Component scales *(continued)*

Extra-test Characteristics	Content Component Scales									
	FRS_1		FRS_2		DEP_1		DEP_2		DEP_3	
	Mean	SD	Mean	SD	Mean	SD	Mean	SD	Mean	SD
Hallucinations	1.10	.41	1.06	.24	1.10	.36	1.09	.33	1.09	.33
Restricted Affect	2.13	1.33	1.97	1.12	2.31	1.29	2.23	1.29	2.32	1.30
Impatient	2.75	1.15	2.46	1.12	2.72	1.13	2.75	1.12	2.68	1.08
Assertive	2.40	.89	2.11	.90	2.34	.86	2.38	.83	2.28	.79
Modest	2.39	.85	2.57	.85	2.47	.81	2.44	.82	2.49	.88
Self-Doubting	3.10	.87	3.03	.92	3.13	.92	3.12	.93	3.19	.93
Deceptive	1.90	1.02	1.94	1.01	1.96	1.02	1.97	1.01	2.00	1.07
Feels That Life is a Strain	3.19	1.05	2.97	.98	3.21	1.15	3.20	1.14	3.24	1.10
Physically Abusive	1.53	.89	1.28	.59	1.58	.93	1.56	.95	1.62	.94
Feels Rejected	2.94	1.29	2.62	1.16	3.19	1.22	3.21	1.24	3.22	1.27
Does Not Get Along with Coworkers	2.12	1.32	2.09	1.12	2.05	1.11	1.96	1.04	2.07	1.07
Uses Projection	2.40	1.18	2.23	1.19	2.49	1.13	2.41	1.17	2.46	1.14
Complains of Fatigue	2.46	1.42	2.37	1.24	2.64	1.37	2.50	1.35	2.57	1.34
Uses Rationalization	2.65	1.17	2.63	1.11	2.78	1.09	2.76	1.11	2.73	1.09
Critical of Others	2.62	1.21	2.26	1.09	2.60	1.18	2.65	1.18	2.59	1.15
Egocentric	2.46	1.18	2.37	1.14	2.57	1.16	2.58	1.23	2.56	1.11
Overevaluates Own Worth	1.98	1.13	1.89	1.08	2.05	1.12	2.05	1.13	1.99	1.10
Optimistic	1.94	.73	1.77	.69	1.97	.71	1.93	.74	1.96	.73
Psychologically Immature	2.90	1.14	2.66	1.11	2.83	1.14	2.83	1.16	2.86	1.12
Poor Judgment	2.94	1.21	2.91	1.17	2.95	1.19	2.86	1.22	2.92	1.21
Low Sex Drive	2.12	1.24	2.05	1.24	1.91	1.20	1.84	1.11	1.93	1.17
Feels Mistreated	2.88	1.13	2.89	1.16	3.05	1.14	3.08	1.16	3.05	1.12
Overly Sensitive to Criticism	3.10	1.11	2.97	1.14	3.14	1.14	3.13	1.14	3.21	1.09
Sentimental	2.49	1.02	2.26	1.12	2.40	1.01	2.40	1.02	2.48	1.02
Sexual Preoccupation	1.59	1.02	1.88	1.27	1.78	1.13	1.75	1.08	1.93	1.23
Accelerated Speech	1.48	.75	1.51	.74	1.49	.84	1.48	.83	1.48	.82
Concerns About Homosexuality	1.21	.61	1.53	1.20	1.49	1.09	1.43	1.02	1.40	.98
Many Specific Fears	1.90	1.13	1.76	.89	1.89	1.04	1.84	1.00	1.94	1.05
Passive in Relationships	2.34	.98	2.42	1.15	2.34	1.05	2.36	1.10	2.40	1.11
Negative Attitudes Toward Therapy	1.83	.90	1.80	.93	1.83	1.00	1.84	1.01	1.85	.99
Guilt-Prone	2.46	1.15	2.29	1.15	2.64	1.14	2.65	1.12	2.71	1.11
Nervous	3.08	1.03	3.09	.89	3.10	1.00	3.10	1.00	3.14	1.00
Obsessive	2.78	1.18	2.70	1.13	2.87	1.15	2.88	1.15	2.89	1.14
Shy	2.40	1.22	2.43	1.17	2.46	1.20	2.48	1.19	2.49	1.22
Uses Intellectualization	2.44	1.29	2.18	1.00	2.59	1.24	2.58	1.23	2.54	1.22

Has Many Interests	2.31	1.02	2.09	.98	2.25	1.01	2.39	1.00	2.29	.95
Difficulty Making Decisions	3.04	1.01	2.89	1.11	3.02	1.08	2.96	1.05	3.01	1.05
Indirect Expression of Hostility	2.70	1.25	2.38	1.10	2.75	1.15	2.73	1.17	2.80	1.15
Poor Reality Testing	1.65	.88	1.46	.66	1.70	.88	1.62	.85	1.67	.84
Angry	3.10	1.12	2.66	.97	3.14	1.17	3.08	1.16	3.16	1.17
Eccentric	1.88	1.22	1.91	1.22	1.97	1.24	1.97	1.25	1.96	1.24
Emotional Lability	2.27	1.00	2.09	.98	2.38	1.10	2.30	1.10	2.34	1.06
Dislikes Change	2.69	1.06	2.50	.99	2.72	1.01	2.67	1.03	2.77	.99
Believes Cannot Be Helped	1.82	.97	1.86	.88	1.95	1.04	1.92	1.01	2.01	1.05
Reliable Informant	3.10	.96	3.17	.89	3.21	.90	3.23	.92	3.21	.90
Ignores Problems	2.16	1.07	2.00	.85	2.29	1.06	2.31	1.04	2.29	1.06
Ruminates	3.20	1.06	3.03	1.06	3.25	1.05	3.30	1.02	3.36	1.00
Excitable	2.62	1.05	2.49	1.07	2.57	1.01	2.56	1.02	2.61	.99
Conforming	2.47	.97	2.46	.98	2.41	.87	2.38	.90	2.41	.90
Ineffective at Dealing with Problems	3.00	.99	2.89	.99	3.06	1.05	3.04	1.04	3.04	1.09
Introverted	2.56	1.09	2.51	1.07	2.58	1.13	2.57	1.12	2.64	1.17
Superficial Relationships	2.58	1.16	2.33	1.08	2.67	1.20	2.55	1.22	2.67	1.21
Impulsive	2.52	1.08	2.46	1.17	2.70	1.23	2.63	1.24	2.71	1.25
Stereotypic Feminine Behavior	1.29	.50	1.34	.59	1.35	.70	1.37	.71	1.35	.67
Stubborn	2.73	1.01	2.43	.92	2.76	1.15	2.81	1.14	2.85	1.10
Hostile Toward Therapist	1.48	.75	1.37	.69	1.47	.76	1.49	.78	1.46	.73
Difficult to Motivate	2.13	.95	2.11	1.05	2.22	1.00	2.23	1.05	2.25	1.04
Suicidal Ideations	1.65	.81	1.54	.89	1.89	1.03	1.87	1.03	1.87	1.04
Familial Discord	2.78	1.42	2.35	1.30	3.07	1.39	2.99	1.38	3.04	1.36
Dogmatic	2.31	1.04	1.94	1.03	2.30	1.12	2.33	1.12	2.31	1.08

	Content Component Scales *(continued)*															
	DEP_4		HEA_1		HEA_2		HEA_3		BIZ_1		BIZ_2		ANG_1		ANG_2	
	Mean	SD	Mean	SD	Mean	SD	Mean	SD	Mean	SD	Mean	SD	Mean	SD	Mean	SD
Intake Information	(n = 119)		(n = 145)		(n = 164)		(n = 214)		(n = 89)		(n = 121)		(n = 156)		(n = 132)	
Axis IV diagnosis	3.09	.95	2.99	.92	2.99	.95	2.92	.99	3.10	.89	3.00	.93	2.96	.88	3.04	.86
Axis V - Current Level of Functioning	59.27	10.28	61.55	9.28	59.94	10.59	61.24	10.17	60.53	10.25	59.08	9.99	61.20	8.43	60.97	9.26
Number of Arrests	1.38	4.07	1.17	2.10	1.29	2.89	1.40	3.66	1.34	2.17	1.67	4.46	2.02	4.41	1.57	4.29
Mental Status	(n = 119)		(n = 145)		(n = 164)		(n = 214)		(n = 89)		(n = 121)		(n = 156)		(n = 132)	
Anxiety During Interview	2.55	.72	2.47	.66	2.45	.69	2.42	.70	2.46	.69	2.51	.77	2.43	.68	2.47	.67
Depression During Interview	2.56	.76	2.37	.71	2.45	.73	2.39	.73	2.39	.73	2.40	.81	2.37	.68	2.44	.70
Activity Level During Interview	3.00	.45	2.99	.41	2.96	.46	3.00	.45	2.98	.45	2.99	.49	3.01	.45	3.00	.45
Speech During Interview	2.97	.37	2.96	.35	2.96	.38	2.97	.39	2.94	.38	2.95	.46	2.95	.42	2.94	.35
SCL-90-R Scales	(n = 117)		(n = 142)		(n = 159)		(n = 210)		(n = 88)		(n = 119)		(n = 153)		(n = 130)	
Somatization	1.41	.85	1.43	.84	1.53	.77	1.33	.79	1.45	.87	1.37	.85	1.19	.83	1.42	.81
Obsessive-Compulsive	1.85	.85	1.61	.93	1.77	.88	1.63	.87	1.76	.96	1.76	.89	1.56	.90	1.76	.81
Interpersonal Sensitivity	1.80	.89	1.55	.97	1.61	.91	1.53	.89	1.71	.94	1.71	.93	1.49	.92	1.70	.81
Depression	2.34	.77	1.92	.93	1.98	.89	1.86	.88	1.92	1.00	1.94	.93	1.78	.90	2.05	.79
Anxiety	1.74	.94	1.57	.96	1.64	.91	1.47	.89	1.70	1.02	1.67	.95	1.42	.90	1.68	.85
Hostility	1.63	.99	1.43	1.14	1.48	1.04	1.36	1.02	1.53	.98	1.59	1.08	1.93	1.05	2.00	1.01
Phobic Anxiety	.88	.81	.78	.75	.89	.77	.76	.72	.97	.86	.91	.81	.67	.72	.79	.74
Paranoid Ideation	1.75	.88	1.55	.99	1.57	.92	1.48	.90	1.93	.89	1.85	.90	1.59	.93	1.79	.86
Psychoticism	1.40	.78	1.14	.82	1.19	.76	1.09	.76	1.40	.89	1.31	.79	1.07	.74	1.21	.70
Initial SCL-90 Analogue	(n = 77)		(n = 94)		(n = 97)		(n = 137)		(n = 53)		(n = 74)		(n = 87)		(n = 84)	
Somatization	2.37	2.76	2.92	2.99	3.44	3.19	3.02	3.08	2.31	2.76	2.57	2.86	2.34	2.57	2.54	2.72
Obsessive-Compulsive	3.39	2.57	3.28	2.63	3.37	2.62	3.47	2.84	3.04	2.61	3.61	2.71	3.48	2.50	3.30	2.53
Interpersonal Sensitivity	4.88	2.48	4.45	2.47	4.63	2.56	4.76	2.42	4.33	2.52	4.73	2.63	4.84	2.27	4.78	2.29
Depression	4.91	2.72	4.67	2.65	4.89	2.64	4.57	2.61	4.26	2.50	4.39	2.60	4.16	2.54	4.55	2.59
Anxiety	4.86	2.80	4.65	2.58	4.82	2.56	4.63	2.63	4.60	2.78	4.51	2.65	4.33	2.49	4.61	2.55
Hostility	3.68	3.09	3.47	2.89	3.20	2.67	3.24	2.70	3.13	2.99	3.53	2.92	4.00	2.76	3.61	2.83
Phobic Anxiety	1.29	2.29	1.25	2.19	1.55	2.40	1.57	2.34	1.12	2.24	1.46	2.44	1.26	1.99	1.32	1.97
Paranoid Ideation	1.40	2.14	1.22	1.76	1.33	1.81	1.35	1.97	1.27	1.98	1.62	2.26	1.30	1.66	1.16	1.56
Psychoticism	.55	1.27	.57	1.49	.65	1.51	.72	1.56	.71	1.50	.90	1.89	.56	1.18	.46	1.13
Patient Description Form Scales	(n = 78)		(n = 95)		(n = 99)		(n = 140)		(n = 53)		(n = 76)		(n = 88)		(n = 84)	
Angry Resentment	3.06	.86	2.92	.97	2.90	.93	2.89	.92	2.72	.94	2.83	.98	3.11	.83	3.02	.94
Critical/Argumentative	2.69	.87	2.61	.91	2.61	.95	2.59	.89	2.42	.93	2.56	1.02	2.67	.84	2.67	.93
Narcissistic	2.43	.92	2.43	.94	2.38	.94	2.35	.88	2.30	1.00	2.45	1.01	2.41	.89	2.38	.89

Defensive	2.70	.87	2.66	.87	2.66	.86	2.59	.84	2.49	.80	2.67	.90	2.62	.80	2.61	.83
Histrionic	2.58	.73	2.42	.83	2.47	.72	2.41	.78	2.33	.79	2.46	.82	2.50	.67	2.51	.70
Aggressive	2.35	.98	2.29	.88	2.16	.78	2.15	.83	2.21	1.02	2.25	.97	2.61	.92	2.40	.91
Insecure	3.17	.76	2.87	.80	2.91	.74	2.92	.75	2.77	.73	2.96	.76	2.98	.68	2.99	.71
Anxious	3.18	.71	2.89	.80	3.06	.78	2.99	.77	2.87	.82	2.97	.75	2.89	.72	2.98	.70
Pessimistic	2.79	.95	2.44	.97	2.54	.92	2.44	.89	2.24	.88	2.36	.89	2.40	.92	2.42	.94
Depressed	2.81	.76	2.52	.82	2.61	.73	2.49	.78	2.36	.77	2.44	.77	2.53	.80	2.60	.80
Achievement-Oriented	2.50	.71	2.64	.77	2.52	.78	2.60	.71	2.49	.81	2.51	.77	2.60	.70	2.66	.70
Passive-Submissive	2.23	.83	2.15	.78	2.30	.81	2.19	.79	2.02	.74	2.19	.79	2.12	.83	2.20	.80
Introverted	2.72	1.06	2.47	1.01	2.58	1.01	2.55	.98	2.49	.89	2.54	.90	2.56	.96	2.61	.92
Emotionally Controlled	2.38	1.08	2.40	.98	2.41	1.05	2.42	.99	2.03	.95	2.31	1.06	2.52	1.03	2.51	1.05
Antisocial	2.43	1.05	2.34	.93	2.21	.87	2.25	.93	2.40	.99	2.53	.97	2.53	.93	2.33	.94
Negative Treatment Attitudes	2.05	.81	2.06	.81	2.06	.80	2.03	.78	1.89	.74	2.02	.81	2.00	.77	1.98	.81
Somatic Symptoms	2.21	1.05	2.26	1.16	2.52	1.14	2.36	1.15	2.08	1.08	2.13	1.08	2.07	.96	2.23	1.00
Psychotic Symptoms	1.35	.52	1.24	.39	1.28	.44	1.28	.47	1.42	.64	1.39	.57	1.32	.43	1.23	.36
Family Problems	2.85	1.21	2.69	1.18	2.76	1.18	2.83	1.16	2.74	1.28	2.94	1.24	3.08	1.03	3.04	1.07
Obsessive-Compulsive	2.92	.80	2.76	.84	2.86	.77	2.84	.81	2.72	.76	2.83	.75	2.84	.75	2.89	.66
Stereotypic Masculine Interests	2.96	1.12	3.07	1.12	2.89	1.10	2.86	1.12	2.77	1.05	2.82	1.06	3.10	1.10	2.93	1.08
Procrastinates	2.28	.85	2.30	1.02	2.40	.93	2.37	.97	2.22	1.02	2.42	1.06	2.32	.97	2.41	.93
Suspicious	2.71	1.01	2.61	1.00	2.62	.92	2.57	.94	2.62	.91	2.70	.94	2.68	.90	2.65	.92
Agitated	2.40	.75	2.24	.82	2.33	.77	2.20	.78	2.20	.82	2.30	.83	2.32	.70	2.31	.72
Work Problems	2.19	.97	1.97	.91	2.03	.89	1.95	.85	1.99	1.02	1.93	.88	2.04	.90	2.04	.88
Patient Description Form Items	(n = 78)		(n = 95)		(n = 99)		(n = 140)		(n = 53)		(n = 76)		(n = 88)		(n = 84)	
Anxious	3.68	.76	3.49	.94	3.57	.86	3.48	.89	3.45	.82	3.50	.84	3.35	.84	3.42	.85
Problems with Authority Figures	3.19	1.25	3.11	1.24	3.06	1.14	3.00	1.20	2.98	1.28	3.08	1.27	3.21	1.09	3.16	1.18
Has Insight Into Own Problems	2.55	.90	2.45	.88	2.55	.82	2.67	.87	2.38	.86	2.45	.82	2.66	.81	2.73	.78
Fears Losing Control	3.47	1.06	3.17	1.09	3.41	1.02	3.31	1.04	2.98	1.09	3.26	1.01	3.37	.97	3.33	.98
Extroverted	2.34	.90	2.45	1.04	2.42	.96	2.48	.97	2.47	1.01	2.43	.93	2.53	.98	2.44	.97
Uses Repression	2.70	1.10	2.69	1.04	2.67	1.00	2.62	1.05	2.48	.93	2.70	1.07	2.75	.99	2.74	1.00
Submissive	2.17	.97	2.11	.89	2.29	.88	2.19	.87	2.06	.84	2.20	.92	2.14	.90	2.18	.89
Difficulty Concentrating	2.99	.99	2.76	1.09	2.97	1.01	2.81	1.06	2.74	1.11	2.87	.98	2.84	1.06	2.86	.99
Rigid	2.92	1.00	2.87	1.05	2.89	1.05	2.80	1.04	2.64	1.02	2.83	1.10	2.82	1.05	2.87	1.04
Overly Compliant	1.99	.92	1.90	.85	2.09	.92	1.92	.88	1.75	.85	1.92	.84	1.93	.89	2.00	.92
Whiny	2.19	1.11	2.08	1.15	2.17	.99	1.96	1.00	1.91	.99	1.93	.96	1.78	.88	1.98	1.01
Feels Overwhelmed	3.60	1.05	3.25	1.13	3.53	1.13	3.40	1.09	3.11	1.20	3.42	1.06	3.40	1.05	3.39	1.06
Manipulative	2.71	1.24	2.54	1.16	2.54	1.12	2.44	1.12	2.38	1.18	2.51	1.21	2.50	1.17	2.55	1.21
Difficulty Trusting Others	3.36	1.24	3.31	1.20	3.34	1.20	3.28	1.20	3.11	1.14	3.32	1.19	3.50	1.18	3.51	1.18
Insensitive to Others	2.35	1.13	2.31	1.14	2.24	1.07	2.22	1.02	2.17	1.12	2.42	1.12	2.31	.96	2.18	.94
Stereotypic Masculine Behavior	2.97	1.16	3.01	1.15	2.85	1.14	2.81	1.15	2.79	1.10	2.84	1.10	3.09	1.16	2.93	1.12
Harbors Grudges	3.01	1.12	2.85	1.07	2.85	1.06	2.81	1.07	2.62	1.05	2.83	1.06	3.13	1.04	2.98	1.06
Evasive	2.47	1.18	2.36	1.12	2.43	1.10	2.32	1.09	2.12	.98	2.37	1.22	2.27	.94	2.24	1.08

	Content Component Scales *(continued)*															
	DEP_4		HEA_1		HEA_2		HEA_3		BIZ_1		BIZ_2		ANG_1		ANG_2	
	Mean	SD	Mean	SD	Mean	SD	Mean	SD	Mean	SD	Mean	SD	Mean	SD	Mean	SD
Disoriented	1.32	.63	1.23	.55	1.28	.55	1.28	.56	1.25	.52	1.29	.56	1.33	.60	1.21	.49
Energetic	2.29	.93	2.45	.97	2.22	.92	2.43	.95	2.51	1.14	2.32	.96	2.49	.84	2.57	.88
Lonely	3.19	1.27	2.89	1.32	2.93	1.24	2.91	1.19	2.77	1.19	2.92	1.26	3.09	1.24	3.08	1.21
Family Lacks Love	2.90	1.40	2.70	1.31	2.71	1.33	2.79	1.33	2.74	1.54	2.99	1.43	3.02	1.26	3.04	1.33
Worrier	3.53	.96	3.24	1.13	3.38	1.05	3.29	1.10	3.00	1.18	3.28	1.08	3.22	.96	3.43	.99
Narcissistic	2.68	1.24	2.66	1.23	2.58	1.20	2.58	1.18	2.60	1.35	2.72	1.29	2.60	1.16	2.51	1.15
Tearful	1.65	.94	1.57	.83	1.58	.86	1.51	.82	1.33	.62	1.56	.84	1.55	.82	1.67	.88
Provocative	1.83	1.02	1.73	.90	1.66	.85	1.68	.88	1.71	.96	1.79	.98	1.77	.85	1.74	.84
Moralistic	2.57	.97	2.57	1.06	2.53	1.00	2.59	1.10	2.42	1.10	2.58	1.12	2.49	1.01	2.69	.98
Socially Awkward	3.05	1.13	2.65	1.14	2.82	1.07	2.71	1.07	2.74	1.06	2.78	1.09	2.90	1.09	2.83	1.04
Hostile	2.78	1.22	2.62	1.22	2.55	1.14	2.53	1.18	2.34	1.29	2.49	1.25	2.80	1.26	2.67	1.27
Overcontrolled	2.62	1.27	2.54	1.18	2.68	1.27	2.72	1.25	2.13	1.16	2.49	1.25	2.82	1.19	2.80	1.19
Resistant to Interpretations	2.25	1.09	2.24	1.04	2.27	1.03	2.24	.97	2.06	1.03	2.18	1.08	2.22	1.01	2.15	.99
Antisocial Behavior	2.45	1.45	2.43	1.25	2.23	1.19	2.21	1.19	2.56	1.33	2.61	1.28	2.60	1.37	2.38	1.33
Sarcastic	2.12	1.09	2.14	1.07	2.07	1.07	2.08	1.04	1.83	1.05	2.01	1.11	2.02	1.04	2.08	1.10
Rejects Traditional Gender Role	1.66	1.10	1.62	1.07	1.61	1.00	1.60	1.02	1.63	1.19	1.82	1.23	1.47	.91	1.63	1.05
Feels Gets Raw Deal From Life	3.27	1.09	3.11	1.24	3.06	1.21	3.05	1.18	2.96	1.13	2.96	1.16	3.10	1.10	3.02	1.15
Acute Psychological Turmoil	3.24	1.01	2.92	1.01	3.07	1.04	3.01	1.08	2.75	1.05	3.14	1.08	3.11	1.01	3.12	1.05
Does Not Complete Projects	2.34	1.14	2.28	1.22	2.27	1.05	2.38	1.17	2.33	1.31	2.44	1.19	2.46	1.16	2.44	1.14
Uncomfortable with Opposite Sex	2.18	1.00	1.90	1.00	2.04	.97	2.07	1.03	1.89	.96	2.00	1.05	2.06	1.06	2.15	.97
Preoccupied with Health Problems	2.32	1.39	2.35	1.46	2.72	1.46	2.50	1.47	2.25	1.39	2.29	1.40	2.14	1.24	2.23	1.28
Work-Oriented	2.91	1.08	3.01	1.15	2.91	1.11	3.01	1.09	2.91	1.08	2.84	1.13	3.05	1.10	3.05	1.06
Resents Family Members	2.81	1.40	2.66	1.33	2.77	1.31	2.83	1.29	2.85	1.45	2.96	1.40	3.10	1.21	3.05	1.32
Demanding of Attention	2.63	1.14	2.48	1.14	2.52	1.07	2.48	1.14	2.42	1.13	2.56	1.26	2.59	1.12	2.53	1.12
Passive	2.45	.96	2.34	.99	2.45	.96	2.38	.98	2.26	.88	2.46	.94	2.26	.99	2.37	.98
Self-Punishing	2.71	1.22	2.43	1.19	2.53	1.21	2.46	1.13	2.24	1.15	2.36	1.15	2.52	1.20	2.55	1.22
Needs to Achieve	2.76	1.01	2.76	1.11	2.69	1.12	2.79	1.03	2.57	1.07	2.66	1.05	2.68	.90	2.80	.95
Needs to Be with Others	3.06	1.13	2.92	1.06	2.96	1.06	2.90	1.00	2.60	.97	2.86	1.12	3.02	.95	3.06	.92
Irritable	3.01	1.05	2.80	1.14	2.83	1.07	2.81	1.03	2.68	1.12	2.76	1.10	2.93	1.01	2.82	1.04
Self-Defeating	3.44	1.20	3.15	1.14	3.16	1.09	3.16	1.14	2.98	1.23	3.11	1.15	3.33	1.16	3.18	1.19
Delusional Thinking	1.38	.84	1.27	.65	1.26	.62	1.29	.72	1.56	.98	1.39	.84	1.30	.68	1.14	.38
Self-Reliant	2.60	.94	2.91	.93	2.68	.93	2.72	.91	2.81	1.08	2.57	.96	2.72	.91	2.69	.94
Aggressive	2.55	1.11	2.59	1.05	2.48	.94	2.46	1.03	2.50	1.15	2.49	1.07	2.80	1.07	2.61	1.05
Competitive	2.43	.89	2.49	1.03	2.50	.98	2.44	.99	2.33	1.09	2.44	1.01	2.55	.99	2.54	.90
Suspicious	2.67	1.23	2.64	1.23	2.60	1.11	2.53	1.15	2.73	1.14	2.73	1.16	2.59	1.13	2.52	1.19
Compulsive	2.66	1.13	2.47	1.07	2.55	1.06	2.59	1.13	2.35	1.04	2.47	1.04	2.52	1.21	2.57	1.12
Dependable	2.96	.97	3.09	.97	3.06	.99	3.05	.93	3.12	1.02	2.89	1.00	2.89	.91	2.89	.90
Multiple Somatic Complaints	2.06	1.28	2.19	1.39	2.48	1.40	2.33	1.40	2.02	1.29	2.11	1.34	1.92	1.14	2.13	1.22

Complains of Lack of Time	1.91	1.10	1.99	1.19	2.13	1.19	2.06	1.17	1.87	1.14	2.07	1.17	2.05	1.18	2.10	1.20
Poor Work Performance	2.17	1.13	2.22	1.20	2.11	1.16	2.03	1.11	2.11	1.29	2.27	1.24	2.21	1.19	2.12	1.11
Insecure	3.53	.95	3.28	1.10	3.34	.91	3.28	.97	3.26	.92	3.50	.93	3.42	.85	3.44	.78
Discusses Problems Openly	3.05	.91	2.97	.84	2.99	.83	2.93	.85	2.98	.87	3.00	.86	3.09	.77	3.07	.77
Sexually Adjusted	2.32	.87	2.53	.84	2.31	.85	2.47	.80	2.41	.94	2.39	.84	2.60	.74	2.63	.79
Exaggerated Need for Affection	2.46	1.10	2.25	1.12	2.22	1.05	2.30	1.03	1.98	.95	2.18	1.05	2.30	.98	2.34	.93
Resentful	3.33	1.09	3.03	1.16	3.12	1.10	3.14	1.16	3.10	1.14	3.15	1.12	3.34	1.05	3.31	1.18
Uses Denial	2.85	1.31	2.77	1.22	2.71	1.21	2.77	1.18	2.52	1.21	2.72	1.25	2.74	1.20	2.65	1.18
Hypochondriacal	1.68	.89	1.79	1.12	2.03	1.10	1.89	1.06	1.63	.93	1.67	.94	1.61	.81	1.76	.88
Communicates Effectively	3.04	.73	3.11	.83	3.11	.84	3.06	.74	3.04	.83	2.95	.91	2.98	.73	3.11	.76
Has Many Nightmares	1.82	1.17	1.60	.93	1.64	1.02	1.66	1.00	1.61	.92	1.60	.90	1.96	1.20	1.96	1.15
Stormy Interpersonal Relationships	3.23	1.22	3.03	1.22	3.11	1.15	3.02	1.18	2.98	1.31	3.18	1.21	3.40	1.16	3.30	1.17
Feigns Remorse When in Trouble	1.89	1.01	1.83	.94	1.75	.91	1.78	.92	1.84	.98	1.87	1.05	1.88	.95	1.79	.97
Stereotypic Masculine Interests	2.96	1.14	3.11	1.17	2.91	1.16	2.89	1.18	2.75	1.09	2.77	1.12	3.09	1.14	2.91	1.16
Guarded	2.92	1.31	2.89	1.32	2.97	1.31	2.84	1.27	2.70	1.15	2.82	1.33	2.75	1.24	2.76	1.35
Feels Inferior	3.36	1.02	3.11	.98	3.03	1.00	3.07	.96	2.96	.93	3.11	.96	3.10	.92	3.09	.93
Low Frustration Tolerance	3.29	1.20	3.06	1.19	3.07	1.10	3.01	1.15	2.91	1.20	3.15	1.18	3.40	1.02	3.38	1.07
Psychotic Symptoms	1.24	.57	1.14	.49	1.20	.59	1.22	.62	1.37	.79	1.33	.76	1.19	.47	1.10	.37
Fired From Past Jobs	2.38	1.23	2.01	1.14	2.03	1.11	2.00	1.08	2.11	1.17	1.86	.99	2.21	1.12	2.10	1.06
Needs Attention	2.99	1.03	2.85	1.03	2.89	1.00	2.88	1.00	2.66	.96	2.89	1.01	2.94	.93	2.93	.87
Acts Out	2.64	1.32	2.54	1.20	2.39	1.11	2.46	1.16	2.50	1.20	2.66	1.27	2.80	1.19	2.65	1.16
Histrionic	2.01	1.01	1.97	1.00	2.03	1.04	1.97	1.00	1.83	1.02	2.01	1.08	1.90	.91	2.05	1.03
Self-Indulgent	2.63	1.21	2.57	1.17	2.60	1.11	2.53	1.11	2.56	1.26	2.71	1.16	2.72	1.14	2.55	1.11
Depressed	3.52	.98	3.28	1.09	3.42	.96	3.25	1.06	3.11	1.10	3.17	1.12	3.24	1.02	3.30	1.00
Grandiose	1.90	1.05	1.97	1.08	2.05	1.15	1.99	1.06	1.85	1.10	2.04	1.15	1.89	.95	2.02	1.06
Cynical	2.78	1.22	2.66	1.28	2.73	1.26	2.60	1.22	2.46	1.29	2.55	1.27	2.68	1.19	2.71	1.30
Sociopathic	1.79	1.02	1.70	.91	1.60	.85	1.68	.90	1.73	.91	1.82	.97	1.74	.91	1.65	.88
Agitated	2.82	1.04	2.46	1.14	2.65	1.05	2.48	1.08	2.42	1.18	2.59	1.22	2.78	1.03	2.66	1.03
Marital Problems	2.55	1.62	2.53	1.59	2.58	1.64	2.59	1.57	2.32	1.62	2.45	1.67	2.87	1.58	2.81	1.59
Absence of Deep Emotions	2.08	1.31	2.00	1.14	2.06	1.28	2.01	1.14	1.81	1.17	1.97	1.22	2.23	1.31	2.14	1.26
Uncomfortable Dealing with Emotions	2.97	1.34	3.01	1.28	2.97	1.36	2.96	1.28	2.56	1.27	2.97	1.35	3.00	1.23	2.99	1.27
Sad	3.29	.95	3.04	.96	3.05	.99	2.97	1.01	2.87	1.02	2.89	1.01	2.95	.93	3.05	.99
Self-Degrading	2.49	1.13	2.16	1.02	2.13	.98	2.18	1.03	1.94	.97	2.12	.91	2.26	1.00	2.33	1.01
Unable to Express Negative Feelings	2.06	1.10	2.23	1.12	2.16	1.09	2.21	1.10	1.81	.96	2.04	1.14	2.24	1.07	2.33	1.12
Concrete in Thinking	2.22	1.04	2.31	1.05	2.35	1.02	2.17	.97	2.32	.98	2.37	1.06	2.35	1.09	2.39	1.06
Unable to See Own Limitations	2.46	1.12	2.49	1.18	2.41	1.16	2.30	1.09	2.28	1.06	2.51	1.12	2.48	1.12	2.34	1.08
Power-Oriented	2.39	1.07	2.24	1.06	2.23	1.12	2.24	1.08	1.98	1.05	2.16	1.12	2.47	1.12	2.35	1.15
Grouchy	2.58	1.07	2.47	1.08	2.52	1.10	2.48	1.06	2.21	1.00	2.35	1.10	2.49	1.05	2.46	1.11
Overbearing in Relationships	2.43	1.13	2.42	1.08	2.36	1.12	2.37	1.06	2.22	1.22	2.38	1.22	2.58	1.18	2.51	1.11
Uncertain About Career	3.64	1.19	3.37	1.36	3.40	1.30	3.43	1.23	3.25	1.29	3.29	1.36	3.49	1.31	3.46	1.32
Likable	3.12	.87	3.26	.73	3.17	.76	3.19	.83	3.13	.81	3.09	.75	3.14	.77	3.23	.79
Procrastinator	2.57	1.12	2.57	1.21	2.61	1.10	2.60	1.15	2.45	1.19	2.72	1.20	2.45	1.06	2.64	1.07

Content Component Scales (*continued*)

	DEP_4 Mean	DEP_4 SD	HEA_1 Mean	HEA_1 SD	HEA_2 Mean	HEA_2 SD	HEA_3 Mean	HEA_3 SD	BIZ_1 Mean	BIZ_1 SD	BIZ_2 Mean	BIZ_2 SD	ANG_1 Mean	ANG_1 SD	ANG_2 Mean	ANG_2 SD
Negative Feelings Toward Opposite Sex	2.16	1.21	2.06	1.11	1.98	1.03	2.06	1.10	1.82	.98	2.13	1.14	2.16	1.16	2.14	1.06
Defensive	2.79	1.15	2.81	1.21	2.79	1.17	2.71	1.18	2.52	1.13	2.72	1.29	2.69	1.10	2.63	1.17
Empathetic	2.29	.78	2.31	.77	2.46	.78	2.42	.78	2.33	.84	2.26	.79	2.36	.74	2.47	.73
Perfectionistic	2.53	1.13	2.44	1.15	2.49	1.13	2.53	1.18	2.27	1.11	2.34	1.06	2.48	1.10	2.64	1.04
Judgmental	2.82	1.10	2.72	1.13	2.70	1.10	2.74	1.06	2.43	1.15	2.71	1.24	2.80	1.03	2.90	1.04
Copes Well with Stress	1.86	.56	2.05	.65	2.01	.62	2.01	.64	1.94	.53	1.93	.62	2.01	.60	2.00	.63
Moody	2.90	.94	2.79	1.07	2.81	1.02	2.76	.95	2.58	.96	2.70	.91	2.83	.92	2.93	.95
Selfish	2.26	.98	2.34	1.03	2.26	1.03	2.27	.97	2.10	1.11	2.24	1.06	2.33	.95	2.33	1.02
Gives Up Easily	2.31	.95	2.17	.97	2.28	1.01	2.22	.97	2.14	1.00	2.38	.98	2.42	1.05	2.38	.97
Physical Symptoms in Response to Stress	2.33	1.26	2.39	1.34	2.65	1.32	2.49	1.26	2.15	1.19	2.29	1.20	2.32	1.17	2.44	1.18
Blames Family For Difficulties	2.38	1.32	2.43	1.32	2.47	1.34	2.55	1.32	2.38	1.39	2.55	1.36	2.74	1.29	2.69	1.25
Bored	2.58	1.12	2.54	1.13	2.60	1.19	2.54	1.15	2.30	1.07	2.42	1.12	2.44	1.07	2.51	1.15
Idealistic	2.47	1.13	2.35	1.06	2.38	1.05	2.38	1.10	2.27	1.05	2.43	1.07	2.31	.92	2.45	1.01
Difficulty Establishing Therapeutic Rapport	2.14	1.14	2.10	1.05	2.14	1.05	2.13	1.05	2.00	1.00	2.12	1.13	2.09	1.02	2.09	1.09
Daydreams	1.87	1.03	1.75	.88	1.83	.96	1.83	.95	1.74	1.00	2.02	1.09	1.82	.93	1.92	1.00
Concerned About Status	2.49	1.16	2.52	1.13	2.41	1.22	2.39	1.09	2.23	1.12	2.41	1.09	2.32	1.13	2.42	1.19
Creates Good First Impression	2.39	.96	2.66	.99	2.53	.94	2.60	.94	2.51	1.01	2.41	.94	2.59	.90	2.62	.86
Complains of Sleep Disturbance	2.95	1.25	2.67	1.29	2.84	1.16	2.57	1.25	2.52	1.32	2.47	1.21	2.63	1.38	2.84	1.36
Has Temper Tantrums	2.57	1.22	2.44	1.22	2.27	1.05	2.28	1.14	2.39	1.27	2.45	1.26	2.87	1.20	2.64	1.21
Overreactive	2.99	1.12	2.81	1.16	2.78	1.02	2.70	1.12	2.66	1.07	2.82	1.07	2.95	1.00	2.95	1.00
High Aspirations	2.57	1.13	2.57	1.15	2.50	1.20	2.55	1.10	2.35	1.15	2.51	1.20	2.44	1.01	2.62	1.08
Feels Hopeless	3.16	1.09	2.67	1.05	2.87	1.14	2.75	1.14	2.51	1.17	2.74	1.16	2.80	1.12	2.84	1.13
Keeps Others at a Distance	3.10	1.25	3.00	1.26	3.02	1.28	3.03	1.21	2.69	1.23	2.92	1.27	3.13	1.26	3.10	1.27
Argumentative	2.52	1.02	2.39	1.02	2.39	1.05	2.36	1.00	2.32	1.17	2.41	1.17	2.52	1.05	2.46	1.07
Paranoid Features	2.08	1.13	1.87	1.03	1.93	.97	1.85	1.05	2.04	1.13	2.05	1.12	1.90	.95	1.85	.90
Restless	2.82	1.10	2.77	1.14	2.81	1.16	2.72	1.13	2.66	1.14	2.80	1.12	2.80	1.05	2.85	1.10
Pessimistic	3.40	.99	2.97	1.08	3.10	1.06	2.99	1.06	2.72	1.06	2.83	1.03	2.91	1.09	2.94	1.04
Feels Like a Failure	3.38	1.05	2.97	1.09	3.06	1.14	3.00	1.09	2.87	1.16	3.07	1.13	3.07	1.01	3.07	1.12
Hallucinations	1.13	.41	1.07	.29	1.09	.38	1.10	.43	1.23	.65	1.19	.57	1.10	.34	1.10	.34
Restricted Affect	2.21	1.33	2.26	1.20	2.23	1.18	2.20	1.16	1.81	1.06	2.08	1.21	2.31	1.32	2.29	1.31
Impatient	2.86	1.14	2.81	1.20	2.78	1.17	2.73	1.12	2.51	1.22	2.73	1.19	2.91	1.05	2.83	1.02
Assertive	2.29	.81	2.51	.89	2.38	.92	2.44	.86	2.28	.89	2.25	.80	2.37	.79	2.42	.87
Modest	2.43	.79	2.48	.82	2.49	.78	2.48	.78	2.19	.82	2.37	.87	2.48	.80	2.48	.82
Self-Doubting	3.28	.95	2.99	.93	3.06	.92	3.04	.84	2.88	.78	3.05	.87	3.06	.89	3.10	.91
Deceptive	2.03	1.11	2.01	.99	1.94	.98	1.96	.94	1.86	1.06	2.04	1.11	2.04	.95	2.06	1.06
Feels That Life is a Strain	3.46	1.10	3.23	1.05	3.23	1.12	3.17	1.10	3.08	1.06	3.27	.96	3.15	1.04	3.22	1.15
Physically Abusive	1.81	1.15	1.64	1.02	1.50	.82	1.52	.92	1.76	1.10	1.73	1.06	2.04	1.08	1.75	1.00
Feels Rejected	3.44	1.22	3.00	1.28	3.05	1.26	3.10	1.23	2.96	1.30	3.15	1.31	3.31	1.15	3.28	1.11

Does Not Get Along with Coworkers	2.07	1.10	1.95	.97	2.03	1.07	1.97	1.09	1.97	1.04	2.08	1.15	2.09	1.10	2.08	1.04
Uses Projection	2.47	1.15	2.53	1.10	2.48	1.14	2.48	1.10	2.37	1.11	2.51	1.16	2.63	1.04	2.54	1.11
Complains of Fatigue	2.57	1.39	2.61	1.41	2.79	1.36	2.66	1.40	2.27	1.37	2.51	1.38	2.37	1.33	2.58	1.32
Uses Rationalization	2.81	1.08	2.84	1.03	2.69	1.06	2.79	1.03	2.66	1.18	2.71	1.16	2.81	1.02	2.82	1.03
Critical of Others	2.68	1.13	2.68	1.13	2.69	1.24	2.67	1.10	2.53	1.10	2.64	1.27	2.83	1.10	2.82	1.15
Egocentric	2.76	1.20	2.73	1.20	2.59	1.15	2.58	1.14	2.58	1.24	2.62	1.26	2.59	1.11	2.61	1.12
Overevaluates Own Worth	2.14	1.16	2.04	1.16	2.08	1.17	1.99	1.06	2.08	1.19	2.18	1.21	2.09	1.06	2.08	1.14
Optimistic	1.78	.68	2.04	.76	1.94	.70	2.04	.70	1.94	.84	2.03	.77	2.02	.64	2.11	.71
Psychologically Immature	2.86	1.19	2.86	1.17	2.82	1.12	2.77	1.11	2.77	1.17	3.00	1.14	2.94	1.10	2.95	1.07
Poor Judgment	3.15	1.21	2.96	1.25	2.88	1.18	2.81	1.16	3.00	1.24	3.08	1.15	3.15	1.09	3.04	1.18
Low Sex Drive	1.89	1.18	1.97	1.23	2.22	1.33	1.90	1.18	1.86	.94	1.64	.92	1.83	1.10	1.88	1.02
Feels Mistreated	3.18	1.09	3.14	1.18	3.03	1.09	3.07	1.08	2.92	1.12	2.99	1.10	3.15	1.03	3.11	1.10
Overly Sensitive to Criticism	3.21	1.01	3.07	1.15	3.15	1.07	3.18	1.01	2.94	1.19	3.24	1.14	3.13	1.03	3.17	1.06
Sentimental	2.61	.96	2.46	1.04	2.45	.99	2.45	1.00	2.32	1.08	2.49	1.05	2.49	.95	2.53	.97
Sexual Preoccupation	1.96	1.24	1.65	1.02	1.79	1.13	1.90	1.27	1.86	1.25	1.94	1.25	1.79	1.23	1.66	1.04
Accelerated Speech	1.55	.85	1.53	.82	1.56	.85	1.43	.79	1.53	.77	1.55	.87	1.39	.72	1.42	.76
Concerns About Homosexuality	1.33	.95	1.23	.73	1.32	.90	1.27	.80	1.22	.64	1.33	.90	1.19	.63	1.37	.94
Many Specific Fears	2.12	1.10	1.74	.93	1.89	1.06	1.90	1.06	1.92	1.10	1.91	1.10	1.78	.94	1.88	1.00
Passive in Relationships	2.28	1.12	2.24	1.10	2.36	1.07	2.25	1.03	2.06	.99	2.24	1.07	2.19	1.06	2.26	1.05
Negative Attitudes Toward Therapy	1.91	1.05	1.86	1.04	1.94	1.01	1.86	1.02	1.70	.91	1.83	1.01	1.78	.97	1.76	.98
Guilt-Prone	2.69	1.14	2.51	1.13	2.62	1.14	2.64	1.15	2.38	1.13	2.68	1.14	2.51	1.02	2.57	1.11
Nervous	3.18	.98	3.02	1.04	3.15	.98	3.11	.96	2.98	.98	3.04	.99	2.94	1.01	3.08	.97
Obsessive	3.00	1.14	2.73	1.12	2.87	1.06	2.88	1.13	2.81	1.19	2.96	1.20	2.85	1.10	2.95	1.05
Shy	2.53	1.31	2.31	1.16	2.41	1.24	2.45	1.19	2.34	1.13	2.36	1.14	2.42	1.14	2.49	1.11
Uses Intellectualization	2.62	1.22	2.46	1.26	2.58	1.22	2.67	1.28	2.28	1.26	2.56	1.35	2.59	1.23	2.64	1.23
Has Many Interests	2.29	1.01	2.31	.95	2.25	.99	2.32	.96	2.32	1.17	2.26	1.01	2.31	.90	2.46	.98
Difficulty Making Decisions	2.95	1.04	2.88	1.11	3.06	1.04	2.96	1.08	2.89	1.09	3.12	1.03	2.91	.97	2.96	.98
Indirect Expression of Hostility	2.87	1.10	2.78	1.16	2.74	1.14	2.83	1.13	2.54	1.09	2.72	1.13	2.78	1.09	2.80	1.09
Poor Reality Testing	1.66	.87	1.58	.71	1.61	.74	1.63	.82	1.72	.89	1.82	.86	1.72	.76	1.62	.73
Angry	3.33	1.10	3.19	1.12	3.12	1.17	3.09	1.10	2.94	1.26	3.11	1.21	3.44	1.10	3.39	1.16
Eccentric	2.00	1.28	1.89	1.28	1.99	1.28	1.87	1.23	1.96	1.33	2.11	1.42	1.71	.98	1.81	1.11
Emotional Lability	2.53	1.07	2.30	1.10	2.33	1.04	2.32	1.08	2.21	1.13	2.39	1.15	2.48	1.06	2.40	1.06
Dislikes Change	2.87	.98	2.77	1.01	2.79	.97	2.67	.93	2.61	.96	2.74	1.01	2.81	.96	2.72	.93
Believes Cannot Be Helped	2.15	1.12	1.89	1.05	1.97	1.00	1.88	.97	1.75	.86	1.87	.98	1.88	.94	1.89	1.03
Reliable Informant	3.17	.96	3.26	.96	3.20	.96	3.22	.95	3.19	1.00	3.17	.97	3.23	.81	3.26	.88
Ignores Problems	2.24	1.03	2.38	1.07	2.21	1.05	2.28	.99	2.23	.97	2.33	.97	2.42	1.00	2.36	1.07
Ruminates	3.42	1.00	3.16	1.15	3.29	1.01	3.18	1.03	3.17	1.10	3.27	1.03	3.25	.96	3.23	1.02
Excitable	2.63	.94	2.59	1.08	2.66	1.00	2.53	1.03	2.70	1.15	2.77	.99	2.82	.97	2.82	.94
Conforming	2.31	.91	2.35	.95	2.47	.88	2.39	.86	2.28	.86	2.45	.86	2.40	.87	2.40	.89
Ineffective at Dealing with Problems	3.19	1.05	3.04	1.10	3.08	1.01	3.08	1.07	2.81	.92	3.11	1.01	3.03	.99	2.94	1.00
Introverted	2.58	1.23	2.46	1.16	2.52	1.13	2.50	1.14	2.40	1.06	2.52	1.08	2.37	1.11	2.53	1.07
Superficial Relationships	2.66	1.21	2.70	1.19	2.65	1.24	2.69	1.21	2.45	1.06	2.67	1.25	2.71	1.16	2.69	1.23

	Content Component Scales (*continued*)															
	DEP_4		HEA_1		HEA_2		HEA_3		BIZ_1		BIZ_2		ANG_1		ANG_2	
	Mean	SD	Mean	SD	Mean	SD	Mean	SD	Mean	SD	Mean	SD	Mean	SD	Mean	SD
Impulsive	2.76	1.27	2.72	1.16	2.58	1.17	2.64	1.21	2.60	1.17	2.87	1.22	2.91	1.17	2.75	1.20
Stereotypic Feminine Behavior	1.37	.74	1.39	.72	1.35	.70	1.31	.64	1.32	.73	1.45	.77	1.20	.48	1.31	.62
Stubborn	2.91	1.02	2.94	1.05	2.87	1.08	2.85	1.05	2.68	1.00	2.84	1.11	2.93	.97	2.87	1.06
Hostile Toward Therapist	1.47	.77	1.51	.76	1.53	.76	1.47	.74	1.26	.59	1.39	.69	1.35	.66	1.37	.67
Difficult to Motivate	2.27	.97	2.25	1.03	2.25	.99	2.25	1.02	2.11	.99	2.24	1.00	2.15	1.01	2.16	1.02
Suicidal Ideations	2.17	1.10	1.82	1.05	1.85	.98	1.70	.96	1.67	.94	1.76	.92	1.79	1.01	1.89	1.02
Familial Discord	3.05	1.41	2.90	1.38	3.03	1.38	3.01	1.37	2.90	1.51	3.15	1.37	3.31	1.23	3.24	1.38
Dogmatic	2.42	1.10	2.41	1.17	2.33	1.12	2.35	1.12	2.23	1.15	2.45	1.22	2.42	1.07	2.32	1.11

	Content Component Scales *(continued)*															
	CYN_1		CYN_2		ASP_1		ASP_2		TPA_1		TPA_2		LSE_1		LSE_2	
	Mean	SD	Mean	SD	Mean	SD	Mean	SD	Mean	SD	Mean	SD	Mean	SD	Mean	SD
Intake Information	(n = 101)		(n = 89)		(n = 76)		(n = 152)		(n = 54)		(n = 53)		(n = 202)		(n = 86)	
Axis IV diagnosis	3.00	.94	3.09	.94	3.04	.96	2.80	.88	2.91	.95	3.04	.90	2.95	.91	3.06	.87
Axis V - Current Level of Functioning	60.05	9.69	58.73	10.50	59.91	9.48	61.95	9.24	61.52	8.20	60.58	8.21	60.51	10.30	60.49	10.87
Number of Arrests	1.75	4.84	1.73	5.01	2.44	5.46	2.48	4.82	1.14	2.35	1.57	3.27	1.47	3.88	1.32	3.00
Mental Status	(n = 101)		(n = 89)		(n = 76)		(n = 152)		(n = 54)		(n = 53)		(n = 202)		(n = 86)	
Anxiety During Interview	2.56	.72	2.48	.76	2.55	.74	2.35	.68	2.52	.75	2.45	.67	2.48	.76	2.55	.81
Depression During Interview	2.36	.72	2.43	.81	2.38	.70	2.28	.67	2.42	.75	2.25	.73	2.44	.76	2.40	.76
Activity Level During Interview	3.03	.50	3.04	.47	3.03	.50	2.99	.42	3.08	.47	3.08	.47	3.01	.47	2.96	.53
Speech During Interview	2.89	.45	2.92	.48	2.89	.43	2.95	.35	2.96	.39	2.87	.52	2.94	.39	2.93	.43
SCL-90-R Scales	(n = 99)		(n = 87)		(n = 76)		(n = 149)		(n = 54)		(n = 52)		(n = 197)		(n = 85)	
Somatization	1.13	.84	1.26	.79	1.19	.82	.99	.77	1.44	.86	1.17	.86	1.23	.83	1.24	.85
Obsessive-Compulsive	1.48	.91	1.73	.94	1.50	.87	1.28	.82	1.84	.85	1.71	.89	1.66	.85	1.77	.83
Interpersonal Sensitivity	1.49	.92	1.71	.92	1.41	.84	1.22	.87	1.85	.86	1.64	.91	1.65	.87	1.78	.87
Depression	1.68	.99	1.91	.99	1.69	.89	1.53	.90	2.14	.85	1.80	.96	2.02	.84	1.97	.91
Anxiety	1.39	.99	1.64	.97	1.39	1.01	1.16	.84	1.86	.93	1.49	1.00	1.52	.92	1.58	.97
Hostility	1.63	1.17	1.61	1.06	1.79	1.14	1.40	1.07	2.24	1.14	1.80	1.25	1.47	1.05	1.39	1.10
Phobic Anxiety	.77	.75	.87	.79	.75	.77	.54	.64	.85	.73	.75	.76	.78	.76	.89	.78
Paranoid Ideation	1.66	.96	1.86	.92	1.65	.82	1.35	.87	2.00	.90	1.82	.96	1.55	.91	1.63	.85
Psychoticism	1.05	.75	1.22	.83	1.06	.66	.86	.66	1.24	.77	1.14	.77	1.17	.74	1.18	.77
Initial SCL-90 Analogue	(n = 63)		(n = 55)		(n = 44)		(n = 94)		(n = 29)		(n = 33)		(n = 129)		(n = 48)	
Somatization	2.69	2.84	1.91	2.53	2.52	2.49	1.92	2.58	3.28	2.95	2.36	2.64	2.36	2.70	2.63	2.89
Obsessive-Compulsive	3.60	2.45	3.17	2.47	3.75	2.53	3.18	2.62	3.10	2.18	3.03	2.48	3.52	2.70	3.30	2.67
Interpersonal Sensitivity	4.44	2.30	4.74	2.41	4.56	2.50	4.52	2.39	4.96	2.03	4.16	1.95	4.85	2.36	4.79	2.26
Depression	4.32	2.73	4.09	2.65	3.80	2.78	3.90	2.65	4.10	2.73	3.88	2.62	4.60	2.67	4.48	2.63
Anxiety	4.03	2.82	4.24	2.76	3.98	2.87	4.04	2.66	4.14	2.40	4.36	2.74	4.52	2.70	4.64	2.87
Hostility	2.92	2.80	3.42	2.81	3.55	2.92	4.09	2.78	2.97	2.77	3.00	2.88	3.37	2.81	3.00	2.73
Phobic Anxiety	1.18	2.09	1.35	2.16	1.61	2.15	1.20	1.81	.90	1.74	.88	1.75	1.31	2.14	1.37	2.34
Paranoid Ideation	1.24	1.65	1.22	1.71	1.43	1.65	1.47	2.03	.69	1.14	.91	1.16	1.23	1.87	.96	1.67
Psychoticism	.53	1.14	.50	1.09	.63	1.13	.65	1.27	.41	.91	.42	1.00	.56	1.24	.24	.74
Patient Description Form Scales	(n = 64)		(n = 56)		(n = 45)		(n = 95)		(n = 29)		(n = 34)		(n = 130)		(n = 48)	
Angry Resentment	2.73	.91	2.87	.96	2.91	.98	2.99	.88	2.93	.88	2.74	.94	2.92	.91	2.79	.84
Critical/Argumentative	2.40	.91	2.56	1.05	2.70	1.03	2.60	.89	2.66	1.00	2.51	.91	2.63	.92	2.39	.79

	Content Component Scales *(continued)*															
	CYN_1		CYN_2		ASP_1		ASP_2		TPA_1		TPA_2		LSE_1		LSE_2	
	Mean	SD	Mean	SD	Mean	SD	Mean	SD	Mean	SD	Mean	SD	Mean	SD	Mean	SD
Narcissistic	2.33	.83	2.39	.97	2.60	.90	2.57	.81	2.38	.92	2.41	1.00	2.36	.92	2.25	.87
Defensive	2.63	.86	2.56	.86	2.74	.76	2.70	.77	2.63	.91	2.50	.72	2.62	.89	2.61	.83
Histrionic	2.39	.77	2.39	.81	2.41	.75	2.49	.72	2.48	.76	2.42	.74	2.49	.74	2.40	.75
Aggressive	2.27	.99	2.16	.90	2.54	1.15	2.53	.95	2.24	.85	2.17	.77	2.18	.89	2.11	.72
Insecure	2.98	.66	2.92	.71	2.92	.70	2.90	.76	2.93	.80	2.90	.60	3.07	.77	2.99	.76
Anxious	2.96	.80	2.87	.79	2.94	.76	2.72	.78	3.04	.89	2.99	.69	3.04	.76	3.06	.87
Pessimistic	2.40	.93	2.33	.94	2.54	1.01	2.38	.95	2.45	1.10	2.26	.88	2.50	.96	2.33	.91
Depressed	2.49	.77	2.29	.79	2.39	.75	2.29	.84	2.46	.79	2.35	.83	2.56	.78	2.47	.86
Achievement-Oriented	2.50	.66	2.72	.75	2.53	.64	2.60	.67	2.74	.70	2.88	.72	2.57	.72	2.43	.67
Passive-Submissive	2.25	.74	2.16	.74	2.11	.61	2.00	.78	1.97	.59	2.23	.73	2.23	.79	2.49	.75
Introverted	2.74	.86	2.61	.89	2.61	.82	2.45	.89	2.43	1.13	2.64	.85	2.69	1.00	2.58	1.07
Emotionally Controlled	2.44	1.03	2.28	1.04	2.66	1.02	2.50	1.00	2.59	1.14	2.24	.89	2.48	1.07	2.43	1.05
Antisocial	2.41	.91	2.33	.88	2.69	.83	2.75	.86	2.12	.83	2.33	.84	2.29	.97	2.16	.84
Negative Treatment Attitudes	1.98	.84	1.92	.78	2.13	.76	2.03	.79	1.98	.87	1.84	.63	2.00	.81	1.90	.79
Somatic Symptoms	2.19	1.13	2.06	1.10	2.12	1.01	1.88	.93	2.36	1.06	2.28	1.11	2.13	1.05	2.20	1.15
Psychotic Symptoms	1.30	.49	1.25	.46	1.31	.50	1.38	.53	1.20	.37	1.28	.50	1.29	.48	1.20	.35
Family Problems	2.70	1.11	2.86	1.16	3.16	.99	2.92	1.16	2.98	1.03	2.79	1.22	2.81	1.08	2.85	1.10
Obsessive-Compulsive	2.89	.71	2.75	.79	2.87	.66	2.66	.79	2.91	.78	2.83	.71	2.92	.79	2.80	.78
Stereotypic Masculine Interests	3.05	1.08	2.89	1.08	3.13	1.07	3.15	1.16	2.66	1.06	2.71	.99	2.87	1.14	2.82	.98
Procrastinates	2.44	.98	2.33	1.14	2.40	.77	2.29	.87	2.36	1.04	2.51	1.11	2.34	.89	2.22	.91
Suspicious	2.59	.86	2.52	.90	2.68	.78	2.79	.95	2.54	.91	2.52	.85	2.68	.99	2.46	.84
Agitated	2.20	.79	2.25	.80	2.24	.74	2.29	.75	2.29	.65	2.26	.73	2.31	.78	2.10	.68
Work Problems	2.23	.97	1.91	.76	2.40	.94	2.20	.97	2.05	.93	2.09	.88	2.02	.93	2.11	.77
Patient Description Form Items	(n = 64)		(n = 56)		(n = 45)		(n = 95)		(n = 29)		(n = 34)		(n = 130)		(n = 48)	
Anxious	3.39	.92	3.34	.86	3.33	.80	3.12	.91	3.52	.91	3.41	.78	3.53	.85	3.52	.90
Problems with Authority Figures	3.25	1.05	3.09	1.13	3.39	.97	3.33	1.10	3.25	1.04	3.21	.96	3.10	1.27	2.89	1.12
Has Insight Into Own Problems	2.52	.85	2.61	.85	2.40	.58	2.56	.84	2.79	1.05	2.74	.83	2.64	.88	2.45	.85
Fears Losing Control	3.23	1.12	3.13	1.06	3.39	1.02	3.12	1.06	3.38	1.15	3.12	.98	3.35	1.07	3.33	1.16
Extroverted	2.36	1.06	2.46	.87	2.42	.94	2.57	1.00	2.52	.95	2.62	.99	2.31	.94	2.40	.96
Uses Repression	2.98	.95	2.58	1.05	2.81	1.02	2.81	.99	2.57	1.03	2.55	.87	2.66	1.07	2.77	1.04
Submissive	2.28	.86	2.24	.88	2.18	.72	2.03	.88	2.00	.80	2.41	.86	2.21	.90	2.47	.97
Difficulty Concentrating	2.83	1.05	2.68	1.05	2.71	1.04	2.73	1.00	2.72	1.13	2.76	.89	2.81	1.12	2.88	1.20
Rigid	2.77	1.05	2.78	1.08	2.77	1.08	2.81	1.00	2.83	1.04	2.56	.89	2.82	1.03	2.71	1.01
Overly Compliant	1.97	.87	1.94	.76	1.79	.71	1.71	.80	1.93	.72	2.00	.83	1.96	.88	2.26	.88
Whiny	1.97	1.03	1.87	1.02	1.84	1.10	1.80	1.07	2.21	1.05	1.82	.94	2.02	1.05	2.08	1.11
Feels Overwhelmed	3.27	1.17	3.25	1.18	3.39	.92	3.13	1.14	3.34	1.34	3.35	1.04	3.44	1.10	3.38	1.16

Manipulative	2.61	1.19	2.38	1.16	2.67	1.36	2.74	1.16	2.75	1.29	2.39	1.12	2.46	1.17	2.41	1.18
Difficulty Trusting Others	3.37	1.18	3.16	1.19	3.47	1.18	3.65	1.11	3.45	1.21	3.15	.96	3.39	1.22	3.23	1.17
Insensitive to Others	2.16	.90	2.25	1.01	2.51	.89	2.48	1.04	2.10	.90	2.21	1.04	2.29	.99	2.23	.93
Stereotypic Masculine Behavior	3.05	1.12	2.91	1.18	3.16	1.13	3.17	1.17	2.62	1.08	2.71	1.09	2.88	1.16	2.77	.99
Harbors Grudges	2.75	1.15	2.80	1.10	2.95	1.21	3.15	1.10	2.93	1.07	2.56	1.05	2.85	1.09	2.77	.95
Evasive	2.39	1.18	2.36	1.18	2.52	1.07	2.43	1.03	2.41	1.21	2.15	.99	2.32	1.13	2.31	1.17
Disoriented	1.33	.56	1.18	.43	1.29	.55	1.42	.71	1.21	.49	1.18	.39	1.32	.66	1.21	.50
Energetic	2.42	.87	2.54	.83	2.47	.73	2.67	.85	2.69	1.04	2.74	.83	2.39	.88	2.35	.91
Lonely	2.98	1.18	2.93	1.22	3.02	1.08	3.00	1.27	2.93	1.33	2.94	1.25	3.06	1.28	2.75	1.18
Family Lacks Love	2.77	1.43	2.73	1.43	3.08	1.36	2.94	1.36	2.96	1.37	2.48	1.29	2.83	1.29	2.74	1.39
Worrier	3.34	1.04	3.30	1.08	3.25	.92	2.94	1.05	3.55	1.02	3.53	.99	3.42	.95	3.37	1.10
Narcissistic	2.52	1.05	2.61	1.14	2.76	1.03	2.84	1.13	2.45	1.15	2.53	1.26	2.53	1.17	2.36	1.05
Tearful	1.52	.78	1.38	.65	1.31	.51	1.44	.71	1.59	.82	1.41	.70	1.50	.74	1.67	.97
Provocative	1.73	.84	1.71	.93	1.75	.87	1.91	.94	1.66	.77	1.79	.95	1.77	.94	1.60	.82
Moralistic	2.69	.98	2.70	1.01	2.47	.93	2.30	.93	2.59	1.09	2.56	.93	2.56	1.03	2.60	.92
Socially Awkward	3.11	.99	2.89	.98	3.02	1.03	2.72	1.09	2.62	1.15	2.79	.91	2.94	1.13	2.88	1.18
Hostile	2.38	1.27	2.48	1.33	2.58	1.37	2.77	1.24	2.52	1.06	2.24	1.30	2.60	1.20	2.33	1.06
Overcontrolled	2.64	1.23	2.66	1.24	2.84	1.13	2.60	1.20	2.93	1.25	2.56	1.16	2.65	1.22	2.54	1.34
Resistant to Interpretations	2.14	1.11	2.02	1.00	2.39	1.02	2.20	1.01	2.14	1.09	1.85	.82	2.12	1.01	2.17	1.05
Antisocial Behavior	2.48	1.31	2.36	1.27	2.80	1.34	2.91	1.24	2.21	1.15	2.41	1.35	2.26	1.26	2.06	1.08
Sarcastic	1.73	1.01	2.02	1.17	2.04	1.22	2.06	1.02	1.97	1.09	1.88	1.15	2.08	1.07	1.96	1.03
Rejects Traditional Gender Role	1.63	1.05	1.74	1.10	1.44	.88	1.48	.94	1.71	1.12	1.75	1.24	1.65	1.02	1.81	1.01
Feels Gets Raw Deal From Life	2.94	1.05	2.95	1.18	2.98	1.10	2.92	1.17	2.93	1.16	2.82	1.19	3.09	1.18	2.98	1.17
Acute Psychological Turmoil	3.06	.98	3.02	1.05	2.93	.99	2.95	1.05	2.86	.99	2.76	1.07	3.18	.98	3.06	1.02
Does Not Complete Projects	2.50	1.20	2.19	1.30	2.50	1.05	2.49	1.04	2.35	1.30	2.37	1.30	2.37	1.15	2.26	1.16
Uncomfortable with Opposite Sex	2.13	1.06	2.17	1.12	2.39	.93	1.98	.94	2.04	.96	2.36	1.10	2.17	1.08	2.07	1.04
Preoccupied with Health Problems	2.27	1.39	2.25	1.32	2.30	1.37	1.89	1.17	2.48	1.43	2.39	1.39	2.20	1.35	2.42	1.43
Work-Oriented	2.97	1.02	3.18	.97	2.82	.97	2.90	1.04	3.10	1.11	3.26	.96	2.93	1.06	2.85	1.17
Resents Family Members	2.73	1.39	2.91	1.36	3.02	1.30	2.86	1.32	3.21	1.34	2.70	1.42	2.82	1.27	3.00	1.35
Demanding of Attention	2.38	1.14	2.53	1.15	2.47	1.14	2.63	1.16	2.64	1.22	2.39	1.09	2.57	1.09	2.53	.97
Passive	2.45	.83	2.30	.87	2.32	.83	2.17	.95	2.07	.84	2.35	.88	2.42	.97	2.72	.93
Self-Punishing	2.19	1.11	2.38	1.18	2.36	1.12	2.42	1.18	2.48	1.30	2.12	1.30	2.58	1.17	2.45	1.27
Needs to Achieve	2.58	.92	2.91	1.01	2.60	.85	2.71	.90	2.90	.94	2.97	.94	2.78	1.00	2.51	1.00
Needs to Be with Others	2.97	.91	2.95	1.00	2.91	.98	3.03	.96	3.10	1.01	3.12	.77	2.93	1.04	3.08	1.05
Irritable	2.55	1.15	2.70	1.11	2.80	1.20	2.81	1.00	2.90	1.01	2.65	1.10	2.81	1.07	2.65	1.06
Self-Defeating	3.22	1.23	2.91	1.15	3.34	1.08	3.33	1.18	3.07	1.13	3.03	1.17	3.22	1.20	3.23	1.24
Delusional Thinking	1.30	.71	1.19	.62	1.25	.65	1.38	.75	1.10	.31	1.24	.71	1.28	.69	1.19	.50
Self-Reliant	2.61	.85	2.63	.89	2.64	.77	2.77	.90	2.72	.96	2.85	.86	2.63	.90	2.46	.87
Aggressive	2.57	1.12	2.52	1.11	2.73	1.07	2.86	1.04	2.48	.91	2.44	1.08	2.45	1.06	2.34	.94
Competitive	2.35	.90	2.45	1.01	2.36	.85	2.57	1.00	2.38	.86	2.56	1.02	2.40	.98	2.31	.90
Suspicious	2.49	1.03	2.51	1.15	2.65	1.02	2.69	1.22	2.43	1.17	2.42	1.06	2.62	1.16	2.43	1.04
Compulsive	2.52	1.12	2.45	1.03	2.68	1.03	2.58	1.17	2.68	1.31	2.52	1.06	2.67	1.18	2.41	1.15

	Content Component Scales (*continued*)															
	CYN_1		CYN_2		ASP_1		ASP_2		TPA_1		TPA_2		LSE_1		LSE_2	
	Mean	SD	Mean	SD	Mean	SD	Mean	SD	Mean	SD	Mean	SD	Mean	SD	Mean	SD
Dependable	3.03	.89	3.07	.91	2.77	.61	2.86	.79	2.93	1.10	3.18	.90	2.98	.96	3.16	1.02
Multiple Somatic Complaints	2.13	1.26	2.07	1.32	2.20	1.23	1.74	1.08	2.31	1.31	2.21	1.34	2.01	1.26	2.08	1.30
Complains of Lack of Time	1.97	1.15	2.15	1.22	1.93	.91	1.94	1.01	2.25	1.24	2.28	1.25	2.02	1.06	1.74	1.01
Poor Work Performance	2.30	1.21	1.85	1.05	2.35	1.17	2.32	1.21	2.09	1.35	2.35	1.30	2.14	1.10	2.15	1.06
Insecure	3.54	.80	3.54	.85	3.48	.76	3.41	.96	3.34	.86	3.50	.75	3.52	.93	3.56	.82
Discusses Problems Openly	3.13	.83	3.04	.81	2.96	.74	3.02	.84	3.07	.92	3.21	.64	3.10	.87	3.12	.94
Sexually Adjusted	2.50	.86	2.37	.86	2.69	.84	2.61	.79	2.65	.75	2.65	.71	2.45	.84	2.35	.79
Exaggerated Need for Affection	2.23	1.01	2.21	.97	2.23	.91	2.44	1.02	2.31	1.00	2.26	.99	2.39	1.04	2.37	1.20
Resentful	3.00	1.15	3.27	1.12	3.23	1.14	3.24	1.11	3.21	1.15	2.94	1.18	3.13	1.10	3.08	1.13
Uses Denial	2.80	1.22	2.52	1.19	2.91	1.10	2.91	1.15	2.90	1.47	2.47	1.02	2.73	1.25	2.71	1.24
Hypochondriacal	1.75	1.05	1.64	.96	1.70	.79	1.59	.88	1.79	.94	1.65	.95	1.68	.91	1.85	1.07
Communicates Effectively	3.06	.77	3.09	.79	2.96	.74	2.93	.82	3.14	.95	3.24	.78	3.06	.78	3.08	.71
Has Many Nightmares	2.00	1.13	1.73	1.00	2.20	1.11	1.74	1.03	2.00	1.21	1.73	.96	1.73	1.01	1.93	1.00
Stormy Interpersonal Relationships	3.18	1.38	3.04	1.27	3.46	1.27	3.51	1.15	3.32	1.12	2.81	1.35	3.17	1.26	3.13	1.10
Feigns Remorse When in Trouble	1.82	.94	1.79	1.01	2.03	1.08	2.12	1.00	1.70	.87	1.74	.86	1.80	.98	1.64	.84
Stereotypic Masculine Interests	3.06	1.14	2.88	1.06	3.11	1.09	3.14	1.22	2.69	1.14	2.71	.97	2.86	1.20	2.85	1.08
Guarded	2.83	1.28	2.79	1.30	3.04	1.19	2.85	1.23	2.97	1.40	2.59	1.23	2.77	1.33	2.79	1.25
Feels Inferior	3.08	.90	3.18	.88	3.00	.80	3.09	.92	3.11	.99	3.15	.86	3.16	1.03	3.06	1.01
Low Frustration Tolerance	3.19	1.15	3.09	1.03	3.51	.96	3.41	.92	3.24	.99	3.09	.97	3.17	1.15	3.06	1.19
Psychotic Symptoms	1.23	.58	1.19	.59	1.21	.64	1.26	.64	1.10	.41	1.24	.66	1.18	.52	1.16	.42
Fired From Past Jobs	2.33	1.10	2.00	1.02	2.31	.97	2.29	1.27	2.19	1.05	2.25	1.07	2.01	1.19	2.10	.90
Needs Attention	2.79	.86	2.82	.88	2.87	.73	3.01	.98	2.83	1.07	3.03	.72	2.91	1.01	2.98	1.08
Acts Out	2.67	1.18	2.45	1.11	2.93	1.10	2.95	1.12	2.34	1.08	2.44	1.08	2.55	1.23	2.52	1.18
Histrionic	1.87	1.04	1.95	1.10	1.98	1.05	1.92	.90	2.07	1.07	1.91	1.16	1.96	.97	1.90	.99
Self-Indulgent	2.68	1.05	2.55	1.14	2.95	1.03	3.00	1.02	2.48	1.15	2.64	1.14	2.52	1.13	2.65	1.08
Depressed	3.19	1.05	3.07	1.05	3.07	1.01	3.00	1.10	3.28	.92	3.15	1.10	3.33	1.05	3.13	.98
Grandiose	1.83	1.07	2.11	1.25	2.16	1.24	1.99	.98	1.93	1.03	2.06	1.32	1.96	1.09	1.74	.99
Cynical	2.36	1.25	2.50	1.39	2.67	1.35	2.53	1.17	2.93	1.33	2.53	1.40	2.65	1.20	2.33	1.10
Sociopathic	1.76	.91	1.61	.82	1.73	.76	2.01	1.01	1.41	.68	1.62	.82	1.71	.92	1.58	.85
Agitated	2.48	1.15	2.48	1.13	2.51	1.22	2.64	1.03	2.86	1.03	2.29	1.09	2.64	1.02	2.43	1.06
Marital Problems	2.64	1.62	2.50	1.67	2.76	1.60	2.72	1.57	2.46	1.53	2.37	1.65	2.71	1.57	2.70	1.63
Absence of Deep Emotions	2.05	1.23	1.96	1.17	2.44	1.33	2.31	1.27	2.28	1.41	1.94	1.13	2.13	1.29	2.09	1.16
Uncomfortable Dealing with Emotions	2.95	1.13	2.75	1.27	3.22	1.13	3.11	1.16	2.93	1.31	2.74	1.08	3.06	1.29	2.96	1.27
Sad	2.84	1.03	2.77	1.04	2.71	.87	2.82	1.00	2.90	1.11	2.88	1.01	2.99	1.03	2.92	1.03
Self-Degrading	2.06	.99	2.04	.95	2.13	1.06	2.20	1.07	2.34	1.04	1.85	.86	2.39	1.06	2.17	.95
Unable to Express Negative Feelings	2.23	1.05	2.05	1.07	2.32	1.05	2.22	1.08	2.48	1.24	2.03	.90	2.24	1.13	2.29	1.13
Concrete in Thinking	2.45	1.05	2.27	1.02	2.25	.92	2.33	.99	2.00	.89	2.26	1.08	2.19	1.04	2.42	1.18
Unable to See Own Limitations	2.31	1.06	2.41	1.02	2.40	1.00	2.41	1.07	2.41	1.09	2.41	1.18	2.40	1.14	2.36	1.11

Power-Oriented	2.17	1.03	2.30	1.16	2.44	1.24	2.57	1.02	2.41	1.05	2.36	1.19	2.23	1.07	2.08	.94
Grouchy	2.14	1.04	2.37	1.09	2.43	1.09	2.39	1.03	2.45	1.09	2.27	1.01	2.50	1.07	2.34	.96
Overbearing in Relationships	2.34	1.27	2.25	1.19	2.59	1.35	2.60	1.25	2.52	1.12	2.15	1.08	2.34	1.13	2.14	1.05
Uncertain About Career	3.45	1.27	3.30	1.33	3.56	1.12	3.33	1.31	3.18	1.61	3.37	1.29	3.44	1.29	3.34	1.20
Likable	3.17	.77	3.09	.77	3.00	.77	3.11	.80	3.17	.76	3.27	.67	3.16	.79	3.08	.74
Procrastinator	2.71	1.17	2.59	1.24	2.65	.98	2.49	1.09	2.64	1.19	2.72	1.30	2.59	1.10	2.57	1.19
Negative Feelings Toward Opposite Sex	2.04	1.06	1.94	1.06	2.20	1.13	2.26	1.21	2.04	1.00	1.73	.92	2.19	1.17	2.13	1.04
Defensive	2.44	1.07	2.50	1.16	2.58	1.03	2.71	1.10	2.76	1.06	2.33	1.14	2.81	1.20	2.56	1.17
Empathetic	2.33	.72	2.30	.76	2.23	.71	2.22	.73	2.41	.73	2.39	.79	2.37	.74	2.43	.74
Perfectionistic	2.37	1.15	2.48	1.13	2.48	1.09	2.29	1.04	2.90	1.14	2.73	1.13	2.57	1.15	2.39	1.06
Judgmental	2.59	1.09	2.71	1.25	2.86	1.19	2.66	1.07	2.90	1.18	2.70	1.24	2.81	1.10	2.69	.93
Copes Well with Stress	2.03	.62	2.07	.66	2.05	.57	2.03	.59	1.83	.54	2.00	.61	1.95	.61	2.02	.73
Moody	2.76	.94	2.68	.94	2.77	.89	2.74	.91	2.83	1.00	2.85	1.00	2.88	.98	2.87	.88
Selfish	2.16	.87	2.15	.99	2.47	.98	2.50	.91	2.43	1.10	2.41	1.16	2.25	1.00	2.09	.95
Gives Up Easily	2.40	1.09	2.17	1.04	2.55	.99	2.30	.97	2.25	1.04	2.28	.89	2.30	.98	2.22	1.00
Physical Symptoms in Response to Stress	2.36	1.27	2.19	1.23	2.34	1.17	2.07	1.11	2.86	1.30	2.47	1.22	2.23	1.21	2.32	1.34
Blames Family For Difficulties	2.23	1.11	2.61	1.25	2.57	1.17	2.55	1.30	2.69	1.26	2.53	1.39	2.46	1.27	2.48	1.28
Bored	2.43	1.00	2.36	1.07	2.52	.98	2.42	1.09	2.34	1.20	2.42	1.12	2.50	1.19	2.35	1.18
Idealistic	2.38	1.05	2.47	.96	2.24	.89	2.15	.94	2.43	1.10	2.56	.91	2.40	1.06	2.32	1.07
Difficulty Establishing Therapeutic Rapport	2.09	1.14	2.04	1.14	2.38	1.13	2.15	1.11	2.07	1.19	1.85	.83	2.04	1.03	1.96	.99
Daydreams	1.95	1.15	1.86	1.03	2.12	1.19	1.94	.96	1.82	1.07	1.79	.92	1.91	1.06	1.96	1.20
Concerned About Status	2.37	1.04	2.68	1.10	2.55	1.09	2.30	1.11	2.45	1.12	2.76	1.12	2.46	1.11	2.21	1.02
Creates Good First Impression	2.53	.82	2.57	.81	2.47	.87	2.46	.91	2.76	.95	2.82	.73	2.53	.90	2.58	.92
Complains of Sleep Disturbance	2.67	1.34	2.30	1.19	2.68	1.29	2.24	1.26	2.86	1.41	2.50	1.38	2.66	1.23	2.77	1.39
Has Temper Tantrums	2.44	1.27	2.33	1.23	2.74	1.36	2.71	1.21	2.52	1.19	2.47	1.27	2.38	1.18	2.42	1.20
Overreactive	2.71	1.16	2.66	1.13	2.77	1.12	2.86	1.06	2.76	1.02	2.67	1.02	2.84	1.04	2.67	1.04
High Aspirations	2.40	1.00	2.65	1.21	2.51	1.12	2.42	.99	2.54	1.00	2.78	1.10	2.50	1.09	2.30	1.04
Feels Hopeless	2.73	1.15	2.59	1.17	2.61	1.19	2.52	1.11	2.66	1.11	2.48	1.15	2.87	1.13	2.46	1.20
Keeps Others at a Distance	3.00	1.25	2.87	1.29	3.29	1.13	3.13	1.18	3.07	1.36	2.97	1.14	3.09	1.26	2.85	1.30
Argumentative	2.23	1.09	2.36	1.20	2.36	1.23	2.45	1.13	2.59	1.12	2.18	1.04	2.48	1.11	2.29	1.01
Paranoid Features	1.89	.96	1.88	.92	1.91	.82	1.98	1.11	1.69	.81	1.88	1.02	1.97	1.06	1.71	.80
Restless	2.67	1.01	2.79	1.02	2.71	.89	2.78	1.10	2.72	1.00	2.88	.99	2.77	1.12	2.50	1.07
Pessimistic	2.84	1.10	2.78	1.10	2.89	1.13	2.83	1.02	2.90	1.21	2.79	1.07	3.02	1.10	2.92	1.09
Feels Like a Failure	3.11	1.14	2.96	1.14	2.98	1.25	2.96	1.03	3.07	1.31	3.06	1.10	3.19	1.10	2.94	1.08
Hallucinations	1.13	.42	1.11	.42	1.16	.48	1.16	.50	1.07	.26	1.15	.51	1.10	.41	1.10	.31
Restricted Affect	2.34	1.37	1.98	1.26	2.44	1.32	2.27	1.27	2.31	1.42	1.94	1.18	2.31	1.32	2.31	1.37
Impatient	2.66	1.14	2.73	1.05	2.93	.96	2.85	1.06	2.86	1.06	2.50	.93	2.79	1.08	2.71	1.13
Assertive	2.31	.83	2.37	.82	2.34	.75	2.45	.78	2.52	.91	2.50	.83	2.33	.80	2.23	.88
Modest	2.54	.76	2.46	.79	2.44	.69	2.38	.78	2.52	.91	2.53	.75	2.46	.89	2.37	.88
Self-Doubting	3.14	.87	3.05	.86	3.05	.89	3.00	.96	3.14	.95	3.24	.78	3.20	.90	3.13	.95
Deceptive	2.06	1.07	1.95	.97	2.26	1.06	2.24	1.01	2.32	1.09	2.12	1.11	1.98	1.04	1.93	1.08
Feels That Life is a Strain	3.24	1.10	3.16	1.06	3.18	.97	2.99	1.13	3.24	1.33	3.00	1.13	3.26	1.07	3.10	1.12

	Content Component Scales (continued)															
	CYN_1		CYN_2		ASP_1		ASP_2		TPA_1		TPA_2		LSE_1		LSE_2	
	Mean	SD	Mean	SD	Mean	SD	Mean	SD	Mean	SD	Mean	SD	Mean	SD	Mean	SD
Physically Abusive	1.70	1.02	1.60	.91	1.97	1.23	1.99	1.16	1.60	.76	1.61	.88	1.60	.92	1.49	.74
Feels Rejected	3.06	1.15	3.13	1.16	3.16	1.11	3.17	1.28	3.17	1.07	2.94	1.23	3.20	1.27	3.19	1.18
Does Not Get Along with Coworkers	2.18	1.05	2.13	1.07	2.30	1.15	2.00	1.04	2.10	.91	2.09	1.11	2.11	1.08	2.10	.96
Uses Projection	2.45	1.13	2.46	1.16	2.59	1.09	2.67	1.08	2.55	1.24	2.62	1.18	2.48	1.15	2.30	1.12
Complains of Fatigue	2.35	1.25	2.21	1.37	2.16	1.18	2.19	1.24	2.62	1.37	2.47	1.40	2.53	1.32	2.40	1.32
Uses Rationalization	2.77	.99	2.73	1.05	3.00	.93	2.99	.98	2.93	1.07	2.88	1.07	2.77	1.12	2.60	.98
Critical of Others	2.54	1.06	2.77	1.25	2.95	1.16	2.78	1.06	2.72	1.25	2.82	1.11	2.68	1.11	2.37	.98
Egocentric	2.50	1.04	2.64	1.18	2.78	1.17	2.82	1.04	2.45	1.12	2.56	1.16	2.60	1.17	2.37	1.16
Overevaluates Own Worth	1.92	1.10	2.15	1.21	2.11	1.17	2.04	1.02	2.07	1.09	1.91	1.08	2.05	1.12	1.87	1.08
Optimistic	2.12	.75	2.11	.80	2.18	.61	2.09	.74	2.21	.82	2.29	.76	1.95	.74	2.06	.78
Psychologically Immature	2.91	1.06	2.82	1.10	3.18	.91	3.07	1.03	2.72	1.10	3.00	1.10	2.81	1.11	2.98	1.06
Poor Judgment	3.17	1.19	2.96	1.14	3.36	.98	3.39	1.03	2.76	1.18	3.12	1.27	2.88	1.20	2.83	1.06
Low Sex Drive	1.78	1.06	1.76	1.06	1.44	.78	1.67	.97	1.88	1.17	1.72	1.18	1.89	1.12	2.11	1.29
Feels Mistreated	2.92	1.02	3.07	.95	3.02	.95	3.07	1.03	3.14	1.03	3.00	1.10	3.06	1.06	2.96	1.01
Overly Sensitive to Criticism	3.03	1.14	3.13	1.19	2.98	1.03	3.02	1.03	3.21	.90	2.88	1.15	3.19	1.08	3.16	1.07
Sentimental	2.56	1.02	2.48	.97	2.40	.87	2.28	.97	2.35	1.02	2.52	.89	2.43	1.00	2.67	1.12
Sexual Preoccupation	2.00	1.34	1.79	1.26	1.63	1.10	1.82	1.22	1.71	1.16	1.62	1.24	1.89	1.21	1.97	1.24
Accelerated Speech	1.44	.83	1.48	.89	1.51	.92	1.44	.78	1.28	.53	1.56	.86	1.50	.83	1.42	.74
Concerns About Homosexuality	1.34	.94	1.41	.96	1.41	.95	1.21	.72	1.38	1.07	1.31	.85	1.39	.99	1.55	1.22
Many Specific Fears	1.91	1.08	1.87	1.07	2.08	1.13	1.72	.93	1.88	1.03	1.84	1.05	1.92	1.02	2.00	1.10
Passive in Relationships	2.31	1.03	2.24	1.03	2.19	.92	2.09	1.04	2.12	.95	2.28	.96	2.33	1.03	2.55	1.04
Negative Attitudes Toward Therapy	1.79	1.07	1.69	.96	1.88	1.07	1.79	.99	1.83	1.04	1.56	.70	1.83	1.00	1.81	.99
Guilt-Prone	2.52	1.09	2.62	1.06	2.47	.91	2.40	1.02	2.43	1.03	2.59	1.10	2.73	1.09	2.67	1.06
Nervous	3.06	1.07	3.02	.94	2.98	1.06	2.80	1.00	3.41	.98	3.06	.95	3.18	.93	3.29	1.01
Obsessive	2.97	1.14	2.79	1.09	2.89	1.03	2.62	1.16	3.03	1.12	2.71	1.00	2.93	1.13	2.91	1.19
Shy	2.63	1.09	2.52	1.10	2.44	.99	2.32	1.07	2.41	1.27	2.59	1.10	2.52	1.19	2.38	1.31
Uses Intellectualization	2.48	1.24	2.55	1.30	2.70	1.23	2.55	1.21	3.04	1.29	2.73	1.33	2.64	1.24	2.40	1.28
Has Many Interests	2.29	.97	2.53	1.05	2.31	1.00	2.26	.95	2.85	1.20	2.79	1.08	2.35	1.02	2.36	1.11
Difficulty Making Decisions	2.94	.81	3.00	1.06	2.84	.86	2.80	.99	2.72	1.03	3.06	1.10	3.02	1.01	3.00	1.02
Indirect Expression of Hostility	2.70	1.15	2.64	1.21	2.77	1.01	2.83	1.12	2.93	1.19	2.50	1.05	2.82	1.14	2.78	1.07
Poor Reality Testing	1.60	.75	1.64	.75	1.64	.75	1.73	.88	1.52	.74	1.59	.70	1.65	.86	1.42	.58
Angry	3.08	1.16	3.13	1.19	3.16	1.20	3.36	1.13	3.38	1.12	2.88	1.30	3.17	1.13	3.10	1.06
Eccentric	1.89	1.25	1.98	1.34	1.84	1.12	1.82	.99	1.76	1.12	2.12	1.34	2.00	1.24	1.77	1.21
Emotional Lability	2.24	1.10	2.29	1.14	2.34	1.12	2.48	.97	2.28	1.00	2.35	1.10	2.38	1.05	2.15	1.03
Dislikes Change	2.83	.97	2.58	.97	2.85	.93	2.70	.97	2.74	1.10	2.52	.85	2.73	1.01	2.70	1.03
Believes Cannot Be Helped	1.89	.96	1.80	1.02	2.07	1.12	1.93	1.12	2.00	1.22	1.67	.92	1.96	1.01	1.75	.91
Reliable Informant	3.20	.89	3.07	.85	3.07	.69	3.15	.79	3.21	.98	3.35	.85	3.22	.89	3.13	1.00
Ignores Problems	2.39	1.08	2.23	.91	2.53	.87	2.41	.98	2.34	1.14	2.38	.92	2.29	1.05	2.21	1.08

Ruminates	3.48	.97	3.19	1.10	3.26	.94	3.00	1.00	3.19	1.08	3.12	.99	3.32	.97	3.36	1.07
Excitable	2.68	1.01	2.78	.98	2.73	1.04	2.69	.91	2.82	.86	2.76	.96	2.61	1.01	2.46	.97
Conforming	2.53	.85	2.56	.83	2.39	.65	2.22	.82	2.41	.95	2.56	.93	2.41	.91	2.58	.87
Ineffective at Dealing with Problems	2.98	1.07	2.80	1.03	3.07	.95	3.04	.97	2.75	.97	2.91	.80	3.05	1.05	3.15	1.13
Introverted	2.50	1.01	2.44	1.01	2.41	1.00	2.33	1.03	2.32	1.25	2.53	1.05	2.62	1.15	2.48	1.13
Superficial Relationships	2.72	1.23	2.48	1.21	2.97	1.08	2.94	1.08	2.69	1.35	2.55	1.12	2.71	1.19	2.43	1.19
Impulsive	2.79	1.18	2.71	1.13	3.20	1.11	3.16	1.10	2.48	1.09	2.76	1.02	2.67	1.23	2.64	1.28
Stereotypic Feminine Behavior	1.33	.71	1.36	.64	1.22	.52	1.24	.56	1.34	.61	1.44	.79	1.30	.65	1.42	.65
Stubborn	2.70	1.17	2.91	1.17	2.88	1.17	2.92	1.05	2.86	1.13	2.76	1.10	2.90	1.10	2.61	.91
Hostile Toward Therapist	1.36	.76	1.41	.65	1.29	.51	1.40	.69	1.38	.68	1.29	.46	1.46	.75	1.35	.60
Difficult to Motivate	2.10	.93	2.18	.99	2.32	1.03	2.28	1.10	2.10	.98	2.03	.97	2.25	1.03	1.96	.95
Suicidal Ideations	1.81	1.01	1.80	.93	1.90	1.03	1.71	1.04	1.71	.98	1.76	.96	1.88	1.06	1.77	1.07
Familial Discord	2.89	1.32	3.07	1.34	3.43	1.17	3.22	1.33	3.10	1.23	3.06	1.27	3.05	1.30	3.04	1.38
Dogmatic	2.32	1.11	2.40	1.21	2.42	1.14	2.40	1.09	2.24	1.15	2.32	1.04	2.35	1.08	2.02	1.00

	Content Component Scales *(continued)*											
	SOD_1		SOD_2		FAM_1		FAM_2		TRT_1		TRT_2	
	Mean	SD	Mean	SD	Mean	SD	Mean	SD	Mean	SD	Mean	SD
Intake Information	(n = 126)		(n = 81)		(n = 171)		(n = 180)		(n = 206)		(n = 99)	
Axis IV diagnosis	3.00	.92	3.06	.87	2.91	.89	2.92	.92	2.94	.92	2.95	.92
Axis V - Current Level of Functioning	59.14	11.07	58.90	11.63	61.45	9.57	61.78	10.31	60.37	9.90	60.21	10.64
Number of Arrests	1.81	4.62	1.48	3.31	1.45	3.80	1.62	3.92	1.30	2.57	1.75	2.98
Mental Status	(n = 126)		(n = 81)		(n = 171)		(n = 180)		(n = 206)		(n = 99)	
Anxiety During Interview	2.53	.77	2.49	.77	2.48	.69	2.45	.76	2.52	.73	2.41	.77
Depression During Interview	2.42	.72	2.36	.76	2.32	.68	2.34	.73	2.45	.71	2.41	.74
Activity Level During Interview	3.07	.44	3.06	.49	2.99	.45	3.02	.45	3.03	.49	3.05	.46
Speech During Interview	3.01	.33	2.92	.42	2.95	.43	2.96	.39	2.96	.44	2.94	.40
SCL-90-R Scales	(n = 122)		(n = 78)		(n = 169)		(n = 177)		(n = 201)		(n = 98)	
Somatization	1.11	.75	1.20	.74	1.17	.78	1.03	.77	1.27	.82	1.28	.82
Obsessive-Compulsive	1.62	.83	1.74	.86	1.54	.81	1.40	.84	1.70	.80	1.58	.80
Interpersonal Sensitivity	1.68	.88	1.80	.86	1.58	.87	1.46	.88	1.64	.86	1.57	.85
Depression	1.97	.90	2.02	.83	1.87	.88	1.77	.91	2.05	.81	1.88	.90
Anxiety	1.44	.87	1.61	.85	1.46	.90	1.28	.92	1.57	.88	1.47	.92
Hostility	1.48	1.07	1.56	1.09	1.66	1.03	1.34	1.04	1.51	1.07	1.54	1.14
Phobic Anxiety	.80	.71	.94	.74	.72	.69	.64	.66	.80	.75	.66	.65
Paranoid Ideation	1.49	.93	1.50	.92	1.65	.89	1.48	.91	1.59	.91	1.53	.86
Psychoticism	1.08	.70	1.13	.70	1.09	.71	1.01	.74	1.19	.72	1.08	.66
Initial SCL-90 Analogue	(n = 82)		(n = 45)		(n = 108)		(n = 118)		(n = 129)		(n = 59)	
Somatization	2.55	3.03	2.84	2.98	2.07	2.55	2.03	2.49	2.53	2.88	2.55	2.75
Obsessive-Compulsive	3.74	2.90	3.60	2.62	3.38	2.69	3.13	2.63	3.42	2.75	3.40	2.73
Interpersonal Sensitivity	4.98	2.49	5.04	2.24	4.91	2.52	4.64	2.38	4.88	2.57	4.89	2.39
Depression	4.63	2.79	4.42	2.82	4.23	2.61	4.09	2.66	4.70	2.74	4.53	2.60
Anxiety	4.76	2.78	4.73	2.94	4.49	2.78	4.22	2.82	4.60	2.84	4.62	2.75
Hostility	3.60	2.80	3.07	2.75	3.32	2.82	3.15	2.75	3.25	2.78	3.41	2.83
Phobic Anxiety	1.60	2.11	1.76	2.27	1.55	2.27	1.29	2.17	1.50	2.24	1.09	1.55
Paranoid Ideation	1.46	1.97	1.29	1.70	1.35	1.94	1.21	1.84	1.34	2.01	1.43	1.81
Psychoticism	.70	1.24	.53	.99	.49	1.26	.55	1.31	.60	1.45	.47	1.03
Patient Description Form Scales	(n = 83)		(n = 46)		(n = 109)		(n = 120)		(n = 129)		(n = 59)	
Angry Resentment	2.97	.90	2.82	.89	2.92	.90	2.76	.95	2.85	.93	2.97	.97
Critical/Argumentative	2.68	.92	2.50	.78	2.55	.88	2.44	.94	2.55	.96	2.59	.96
Narcissistic	2.40	.92	2.20	.81	2.37	.89	2.28	.89	2.32	.94	2.38	.92

Defensive	2.73	.91	2.51	.81	2.60	.86	2.51	.87	2.56	.92	2.69	.88
Histrionic	2.45	.76	2.37	.69	2.48	.75	2.36	.76	2.43	.80	2.44	.83
Aggressive	2.26	.91	2.14	.84	2.31	.93	2.18	.92	2.10	.84	2.17	.96
Insecure	3.11	.71	3.00	.68	2.97	.75	2.93	.79	3.05	.81	2.96	.82
Anxious	2.99	.74	3.04	.67	2.90	.79	2.82	.80	2.99	.79	2.97	.71
Pessimistic	2.58	1.02	2.36	.86	2.37	.95	2.28	.95	2.48	.97	2.54	.97
Depressed	2.60	.80	2.48	.81	2.44	.74	2.37	.80	2.57	.76	2.58	.80
Achievement-Oriented	2.63	.72	2.57	.60	2.58	.71	2.62	.75	2.56	.75	2.55	.72
Passive-Submissive	2.30	.77	2.51	.81	2.20	.86	2.14	.80	2.22	.79	2.29	.70
Introverted	2.83	.99	2.86	.95	2.63	1.05	2.56	1.01	2.64	1.03	2.67	.96
Emotionally Controlled	2.65	1.07	2.60	1.08	2.46	1.01	2.39	.99	2.47	1.07	2.62	1.07
Antisocial	2.37	1.04	2.11	.92	2.31	.94	2.26	.90	2.27	.92	2.33	.88
Negative Treatment Attitudes	2.14	.85	1.97	.76	1.98	.78	1.93	.78	1.97	.80	2.13	.79
Somatic Symptoms	2.23	1.18	2.32	1.16	2.04	.99	1.91	.96	2.19	1.06	2.26	1.08
Psychotic Symptoms	1.32	.46	1.20	.29	1.29	.48	1.27	.46	1.26	.45	1.29	.45
Family Problems	2.87	1.10	2.70	.99	3.06	1.08	2.95	1.09	2.79	1.15	2.94	1.20
Obsessive-Compulsive	2.96	.78	2.78	.74	2.84	.77	2.76	.83	2.86	.83	2.90	.79
Stereotypic Masculine Interests	2.92	1.19	2.74	1.14	2.74	1.07	2.76	1.15	2.80	1.13	2.70	1.09
Procrastinates	2.43	.86	2.27	.78	2.27	.93	2.20	.88	2.36	.99	2.44	1.02
Suspicious	2.80	.97	2.63	.88	2.63	.92	2.57	.94	2.63	1.01	2.78	.89
Agitated	2.31	.88	2.11	.73	2.23	.77	2.17	.82	2.23	.81	2.25	.78
Work Problems	2.04	.93	1.85	.94	2.05	.90	1.94	.90	1.98	.93	1.93	.91
Patient Description Form Items	(n = 83)		(n = 46)		(n = 109)		(n = 120)		(n = 129)		(n = 59)	
Anxious	3.53	.82	3.57	.75	3.37	.92	3.37	.88	3.51	.86	3.49	.75
Problems with Authority Figures	3.09	1.14	2.93	1.05	3.08	1.16	3.03	1.29	2.98	1.25	3.24	1.28
Has Insight Into Own Problems	2.63	.87	2.82	.91	2.56	.90	2.64	.92	2.66	.85	2.61	.83
Fears Losing Control	3.49	.97	3.52	1.07	3.24	1.04	3.26	1.05	3.38	1.04	3.36	1.07
Extroverted	2.27	.99	2.22	.94	2.35	.97	2.40	1.00	2.36	.94	2.32	.84
Uses Repression	2.81	1.06	2.82	1.05	2.65	1.01	2.60	1.00	2.64	1.04	2.74	.99
Submissive	2.25	.88	2.52	.88	2.19	.93	2.14	.86	2.23	.92	2.31	.80
Difficulty Concentrating	2.73	1.07	2.70	1.01	2.69	1.09	2.58	1.08	2.78	1.14	2.81	1.01
Rigid	3.01	1.06	2.80	1.02	2.80	1.08	2.74	1.10	2.76	1.11	2.88	1.05
Overly Compliant	2.00	.93	2.27	.99	2.02	.94	1.92	.89	1.94	.88	1.88	.80
Whiny	2.04	1.09	1.96	1.03	1.99	1.06	1.89	.99	2.02	1.07	1.95	1.01
Feels Overwhelmed	3.40	1.12	3.39	1.00	3.28	1.15	3.19	1.16	3.43	1.07	3.41	1.05
Manipulative	2.57	1.21	2.32	1.07	2.48	1.16	2.41	1.14	2.45	1.17	2.51	1.15
Difficulty Trusting Others	3.52	1.17	3.37	1.10	3.38	1.18	3.41	1.25	3.33	1.27	3.54	1.25
Insensitive to Others	2.36	1.07	2.24	.95	2.27	1.04	2.25	.98	2.24	1.03	2.37	.89
Stereotypic Masculine Behavior	2.93	1.25	2.73	1.19	2.75	1.11	2.75	1.20	2.80	1.18	2.68	1.17
Harbors Grudges	3.06	1.14	2.81	1.07	2.95	1.08	2.80	1.14	2.83	1.15	2.89	1.13
Evasive	2.59	1.22	2.24	.95	2.25	1.06	2.28	1.09	2.32	1.17	2.49	1.12

	Content Component Scales *(continued)*											
	SOD_1		SOD_2		FAM_1		FAM_2		TRT_1		TRT_2	
	Mean	SD	Mean	SD	Mean	SD	Mean	SD	Mean	SD	Mean	SD
Disoriented	1.33	.61	1.26	.44	1.24	.47	1.26	.54	1.29	.62	1.32	.63
Energetic	2.38	.87	2.33	.79	2.52	.94	2.54	.94	2.32	.86	2.27	.85
Lonely	3.12	1.21	2.98	1.09	2.98	1.25	3.02	1.24	3.03	1.29	2.97	1.30
Family Lacks Love	2.87	1.26	2.73	1.19	2.98	1.34	2.98	1.32	2.83	1.33	2.83	1.41
Worrier	3.37	1.05	3.39	.86	3.28	1.02	3.23	1.11	3.37	1.03	3.29	1.08
Narcissistic	2.59	1.18	2.34	1.01	2.57	1.10	2.47	1.12	2.51	1.20	2.53	1.19
Tearful	1.60	.81	1.54	.86	1.52	.81	1.53	.80	1.58	.84	1.61	.72
Provocative	1.65	.92	1.46	.66	1.72	.88	1.76	.96	1.73	.93	1.75	.92
Moralistic	2.67	1.06	2.43	.93	2.58	1.02	2.53	1.15	2.45	1.07	2.46	.93
Socially Awkward	3.04	1.15	3.07	1.10	2.87	1.20	2.78	1.15	2.84	1.18	2.93	1.17
Hostile	2.66	1.17	2.44	1.14	2.54	1.17	2.48	1.19	2.52	1.18	2.64	1.21
Overcontrolled	2.87	1.24	2.85	1.17	2.71	1.19	2.55	1.24	2.71	1.24	2.86	1.27
Resistant to Interpretations	2.35	.99	2.15	1.01	2.16	1.03	2.08	1.02	2.15	1.02	2.40	.99
Antisocial Behavior	2.31	1.27	2.13	1.17	2.32	1.25	2.33	1.26	2.30	1.23	2.32	1.32
Sarcastic	2.11	1.08	2.00	.94	2.02	1.00	1.98	1.07	2.09	1.08	2.14	1.09
Rejects Traditional Gender Role	1.70	1.00	1.71	.92	1.62	1.04	1.52	.97	1.69	1.05	1.90	1.13
Feels Gets Raw Deal From Life	3.13	1.11	2.91	1.22	2.99	1.11	2.90	1.18	3.06	1.17	3.10	1.23
Acute Psychological Turmoil	3.23	.94	3.11	.95	2.99	1.04	2.98	1.05	3.12	1.05	3.15	1.08
Does Not Complete Projects	2.36	1.05	2.06	.94	2.37	1.15	2.20	1.09	2.34	1.17	2.39	1.10
Uncomfortable with Opposite Sex	2.32	1.05	2.39	.89	2.15	1.10	2.01	1.01	2.12	1.04	2.15	.91
Preoccupied with Health Problems	2.44	1.48	2.41	1.42	2.04	1.23	1.90	1.17	2.34	1.39	2.24	1.33
Work-Oriented	3.05	1.13	3.00	1.12	3.06	1.02	3.08	1.07	2.92	1.08	2.93	1.01
Resents Family Members	2.84	1.33	2.67	1.19	3.18	1.24	2.96	1.30	2.82	1.32	3.00	1.40
Demanding of Attention	2.57	1.10	2.33	.90	2.59	1.18	2.43	1.11	2.49	1.11	2.52	1.08
Passive	2.49	1.00	2.76	1.00	2.35	1.04	2.31	1.01	2.41	.96	2.53	.84
Self-Punishing	2.69	1.12	2.66	1.16	2.37	1.15	2.39	1.13	2.53	1.19	2.43	1.17
Needs to Achieve	2.90	.96	2.64	.83	2.76	.96	2.76	.97	2.79	1.02	2.74	.98
Needs to Be with Others	2.87	.96	2.91	.91	2.91	.98	2.87	1.04	2.90	1.13	2.95	1.04
Irritable	2.84	1.01	2.67	.97	2.76	1.02	2.67	1.06	2.76	1.05	2.73	1.05
Self-Defeating	3.29	1.07	3.24	1.08	3.16	1.13	3.06	1.18	3.20	1.19	3.29	1.10
Delusional Thinking	1.30	.62	1.13	.34	1.24	.66	1.26	.66	1.24	.62	1.29	.73
Self-Reliant	2.67	.94	2.59	.86	2.58	.95	2.72	.95	2.64	.88	2.69	.81
Aggressive	2.55	1.11	2.38	.96	2.51	1.07	2.46	1.03	2.37	1.00	2.38	1.01
Competitive	2.56	1.01	2.43	.87	2.49	.96	2.50	1.00	2.44	.99	2.35	.90
Suspicious	2.81	1.14	2.61	1.11	2.60	1.14	2.54	1.18	2.60	1.21	2.79	1.10
Compulsive	2.71	1.12	2.80	1.05	2.56	1.13	2.50	1.13	2.56	1.11	2.68	1.10
Dependable	3.00	.94	3.18	.90	3.00	1.00	3.01	1.00	3.02	.95	2.98	.90
Multiple Somatic Complaints	2.22	1.44	2.28	1.38	1.89	1.17	1.78	1.11	2.13	1.31	2.08	1.30

Complains of Lack of Time	2.05	1.06	2.02	.90	1.95	1.14	1.92	1.08	2.03	1.13	2.21	1.20
Poor Work Performance	2.03	1.03	2.00	1.04	2.09	1.12	1.92	1.04	2.00	1.14	2.07	1.15
Insecure	3.49	.92	3.48	.84	3.49	.85	3.37	.94	3.50	.94	3.44	.95
Discusses Problems Openly	3.01	.92	3.07	.80	2.97	.84	3.09	.89	3.10	.89	2.92	.79
Sexually Adjusted	2.34	.83	2.47	.80	2.41	.91	2.52	.89	2.36	.82	2.50	.74
Exaggerated Need for Affection	2.26	.95	2.27	.92	2.30	1.04	2.19	.94	2.33	1.10	2.42	1.03
Resentful	3.24	1.07	3.09	1.15	3.23	1.13	3.07	1.17	3.05	1.12	3.19	1.22
Uses Denial	2.92	1.22	2.63	1.14	2.71	1.21	2.61	1.18	2.71	1.24	2.83	1.21
Hypochondriacal	1.78	.99	1.93	1.03	1.65	.89	1.63	.89	1.76	.97	1.83	.93
Communicates Effectively	3.04	.83	3.11	.71	2.99	.79	3.08	.76	3.07	.78	3.15	.85
Has Many Nightmares	1.83	1.12	1.90	1.14	1.69	1.01	1.54	.85	1.74	1.02	1.97	1.21
Stormy Interpersonal Relationships	3.26	1.20	3.02	1.20	3.24	1.19	3.11	1.25	3.11	1.27	3.11	1.29
Feigns Remorse When in Trouble	2.00	1.10	1.82	.98	1.84	.97	1.75	.91	1.76	.93	1.85	.93
Stereotypic Masculine Interests	2.91	1.22	2.76	1.19	2.73	1.12	2.76	1.20	2.78	1.17	2.73	1.11
Guarded	2.95	1.29	2.67	1.25	2.80	1.22	2.72	1.24	2.78	1.34	3.00	1.25
Feels Inferior	3.17	.93	3.00	1.03	3.13	1.00	3.03	1.02	3.15	1.04	3.07	.96
Low Frustration Tolerance	3.29	1.07	3.13	1.06	3.28	1.09	3.08	1.14	3.13	1.18	3.14	1.14
Psychotic Symptoms	1.23	.53	1.13	.34	1.18	.55	1.17	.53	1.18	.56	1.18	.47
Fired From Past Jobs	2.08	1.19	2.03	1.05	2.04	1.05	1.90	1.06	2.05	1.15	2.05	1.13
Needs Attention	2.87	.89	2.80	.83	2.93	.93	2.81	.96	2.90	1.02	2.78	1.00
Acts Out	2.53	1.20	2.35	1.08	2.61	1.19	2.46	1.16	2.49	1.16	2.49	1.17
Histrionic	1.99	1.00	1.87	.86	1.97	1.07	1.92	1.04	1.96	1.02	1.95	1.04
Self-Indulgent	2.56	1.12	2.41	1.07	2.54	1.14	2.50	1.12	2.57	1.13	2.56	1.16
Depressed	3.39	.94	3.30	.87	3.19	.99	3.07	1.12	3.40	.97	3.46	.99
Grandiose	2.04	1.15	1.82	.89	1.94	1.05	1.88	1.03	1.98	1.14	1.86	.97
Cynical	2.72	1.22	2.50	1.11	2.50	1.18	2.44	1.18	2.63	1.25	2.78	1.22
Sociopathic	1.83	.99	1.63	.80	1.68	.91	1.65	.84	1.70	.86	1.59	.79
Agitated	2.65	1.07	2.44	.94	2.58	1.07	2.48	1.08	2.55	1.10	2.61	1.08
Marital Problems	2.74	1.61	2.40	1.50	2.73	1.62	2.73	1.60	2.55	1.57	2.60	1.60
Absence of Deep Emotions	2.23	1.31	2.31	1.35	2.15	1.21	2.04	1.20	2.08	1.26	2.34	1.28
Uncomfortable Dealing with Emotions	3.23	1.28	3.04	1.21	2.96	1.22	2.94	1.22	3.01	1.30	3.19	1.29
Sad	3.05	.91	2.96	.90	2.94	.96	2.83	1.02	3.01	.97	3.00	1.00
Self-Degrading	2.40	.96	2.41	1.00	2.32	1.03	2.25	1.04	2.36	1.04	2.22	.95
Unable to Express Negative Feelings	2.41	1.14	2.35	1.16	2.20	1.08	2.17	1.07	2.23	1.16	2.25	1.11
Concrete in Thinking	2.28	1.02	2.22	.99	2.28	1.02	2.15	.97	2.20	1.00	2.31	1.00
Unable to See Own Limitations	2.41	1.11	2.18	.98	2.35	1.07	2.23	1.07	2.30	1.11	2.37	1.00
Power-Oriented	2.34	1.20	2.18	1.08	2.36	1.18	2.24	1.13	2.22	1.10	2.19	1.03
Grouchy	2.48	1.09	2.32	1.07	2.38	1.05	2.16	1.05	2.39	1.07	2.46	1.09
Overbearing in Relationships	2.42	1.06	2.27	1.00	2.42	1.13	2.28	1.15	2.31	1.14	2.28	1.11
Uncertain About Career	3.63	1.21	3.50	1.15	3.31	1.23	3.36	1.26	3.46	1.29	3.64	1.25
Likable	3.19	.77	3.31	.76	3.09	.82	3.19	.80	3.22	.80	3.17	.67
Procrastinator	2.71	1.08	2.49	.95	2.51	1.11	2.49	1.08	2.64	1.19	2.64	1.15

	Content Component Scales *(continued)*											
	SOD_1		SOD_2		FAM_1		FAM_2		TRT_1		TRT_2	
	Mean	SD	Mean	SD	Mean	SD	Mean	SD	Mean	SD	Mean	SD
Negative Feelings Toward Opposite Sex	2.33	1.15	2.26	.99	2.11	1.14	2.14	1.13	2.16	1.17	2.17	1.04
Defensive	2.82	1.19	2.53	1.06	2.67	1.15	2.59	1.17	2.69	1.18	2.76	1.19
Empathetic	2.27	.72	2.32	.74	2.34	.79	2.36	.76	2.37	.76	2.29	.70
Perfectionistic	2.72	1.13	2.55	1.02	2.53	1.09	2.50	1.14	2.57	1.14	2.56	1.08
Judgmental	2.91	1.07	2.70	.93	2.72	1.06	2.61	1.15	2.71	1.15	2.76	1.06
Copes Well with Stress	1.96	.67	2.09	.70	1.96	.63	2.05	.70	1.98	.66	1.97	.59
Moody	2.93	.98	3.02	.96	2.78	.98	2.69	.98	2.82	1.02	2.81	1.12
Selfish	2.31	.96	2.25	.92	2.30	1.02	2.16	.98	2.22	1.02	2.42	1.02
Gives Up Easily	2.31	.97	2.34	.91	2.27	.98	2.17	.96	2.32	1.07	2.47	1.10
Physical Symptoms in Response to Stress	2.32	1.27	2.51	1.32	2.25	1.17	2.01	1.10	2.33	1.24	2.47	1.29
Blames Family For Difficulties	2.57	1.31	2.31	1.20	2.73	1.31	2.58	1.27	2.46	1.29	2.66	1.37
Bored	2.73	1.09	2.69	1.14	2.43	1.09	2.38	1.14	2.53	1.14	2.64	1.22
Idealistic	2.38	1.05	2.32	.99	2.34	1.05	2.30	1.02	2.33	1.11	2.25	1.05
Difficulty Establishing Therapeutic Rapport	2.20	1.12	2.00	.93	2.13	1.05	2.08	1.08	2.05	1.06	2.32	.99
Daydreams	2.06	1.14	2.11	.99	1.81	.99	1.72	.94	1.92	1.04	2.13	1.06
Concerned About Status	2.51	1.15	2.43	1.00	2.40	1.09	2.36	1.11	2.48	1.18	2.46	1.10
Creates Good First Impression	2.45	.84	2.60	.96	2.45	.93	2.52	.93	2.57	.93	2.68	.90
Complains of Sleep Disturbance	2.69	1.35	2.63	1.40	2.48	1.30	2.39	1.21	2.67	1.27	2.70	1.39
Has Temper Tantrums	2.38	1.13	2.33	1.16	2.53	1.23	2.36	1.23	2.26	1.13	2.42	1.16
Overreactive	2.83	1.12	2.67	1.07	2.79	1.05	2.67	1.06	2.78	1.10	2.66	1.21
High Aspirations	2.54	1.14	2.50	.95	2.55	1.15	2.55	1.13	2.50	1.17	2.47	1.20
Feels Hopeless	2.95	1.10	2.67	1.11	2.72	1.16	2.59	1.14	2.90	1.15	2.78	1.15
Keeps Others at a Distance	3.22	1.27	3.16	1.20	3.10	1.22	3.01	1.19	3.04	1.28	3.21	1.26
Argumentative	2.41	1.06	2.29	.92	2.44	1.10	2.25	1.07	2.36	1.10	2.39	1.07
Paranoid Features	2.08	1.08	1.87	.92	1.88	.99	1.77	.94	1.95	1.07	1.97	.87
Restless	2.77	1.21	2.49	1.06	2.64	1.14	2.61	1.17	2.69	1.14	2.75	1.18
Pessimistic	3.10	1.10	2.96	1.03	2.89	1.08	2.76	1.14	3.01	1.12	3.03	1.11
Feels Like a Failure	3.29	1.10	3.07	1.06	2.94	1.03	2.92	1.11	3.12	1.16	3.10	1.14
Hallucinations	1.12	.37	1.11	.31	1.11	.39	1.10	.42	1.09	.37	1.10	.36
Restricted Affect	2.54	1.33	2.46	1.29	2.28	1.30	2.24	1.22	2.31	1.30	2.46	1.33
Impatient	2.82	1.04	2.78	1.00	2.80	1.10	2.69	1.11	2.77	1.12	2.71	1.19
Assertive	2.40	.87	2.28	.89	2.31	.86	2.37	.88	2.33	.81	2.34	.78
Modest	2.54	.77	2.69	.73	2.39	.85	2.45	.88	2.46	.85	2.53	.80
Self-Doubting	3.27	.88	3.13	.88	3.06	.92	3.05	.98	3.19	.95	3.14	1.01
Deceptive	2.10	1.06	2.00	1.07	1.99	1.00	1.86	.92	1.94	.96	2.22	1.04
Feels That Life is a Strain	3.27	1.04	2.93	1.07	3.11	1.09	3.06	1.10	3.24	1.06	3.25	1.06
Physically Abusive	1.70	1.03	1.51	.80	1.74	1.04	1.65	1.03	1.52	.84	1.64	.99
Feels Rejected	3.31	1.09	3.16	1.02	3.24	1.16	3.19	1.11	3.22	1.22	3.10	1.31

Does Not Get Along with Coworkers	2.14	1.15	1.76	.96	2.21	1.10	2.11	1.15	2.02	1.09	2.05	1.00
Uses Projection	2.58	1.16	2.43	1.15	2.49	1.14	2.44	1.13	2.51	1.15	2.55	1.17
Complains of Fatigue	2.60	1.44	2.59	1.38	2.32	1.30	2.29	1.28	2.55	1.34	2.69	1.38
Uses Rationalization	2.88	1.04	2.67	1.01	2.78	1.06	2.67	1.08	2.74	1.08	2.80	1.10
Critical of Others	2.82	1.18	2.54	.86	2.66	1.10	2.52	1.16	2.59	1.17	2.66	1.18
Egocentric	2.66	1.16	2.33	.92	2.54	1.16	2.53	1.16	2.57	1.19	2.47	1.15
Overevaluates Own Worth	2.00	1.13	1.74	.91	2.06	1.09	1.97	1.12	2.03	1.15	2.00	1.08
Optimistic	2.05	.76	2.04	.63	2.06	.76	2.07	.77	1.96	.73	1.90	.61
Psychologically Immature	2.84	1.21	2.76	1.04	2.95	1.14	2.74	1.13	2.81	1.17	2.90	1.17
Poor Judgment	3.00	1.21	2.63	1.16	2.97	1.16	2.87	1.17	2.92	1.16	3.02	1.06
Low Sex Drive	1.89	.97	1.96	1.25	1.87	1.14	1.65	.95	1.82	1.08	1.90	1.06
Feels Mistreated	3.13	1.04	3.02	1.02	3.05	1.06	2.95	1.08	3.02	1.07	3.10	1.14
Overly Sensitive to Criticism	3.30	1.01	2.96	.98	3.23	1.04	3.10	1.09	3.19	1.17	3.14	1.17
Sentimental	2.49	.93	2.57	.93	2.43	1.00	2.30	.97	2.47	1.03	2.47	1.01
Sexual Preoccupation	1.85	1.19	1.71	1.14	1.88	1.21	1.90	1.23	1.97	1.23	1.76	1.13
Accelerated Speech	1.53	.94	1.41	.69	1.46	.75	1.46	.79	1.49	.86	1.41	.70
Concerns About Homosexuality	1.48	1.07	1.31	.90	1.44	1.04	1.37	1.00	1.54	1.16	1.57	1.19
Many Specific Fears	1.90	1.03	1.98	1.03	1.83	1.03	1.75	.99	1.88	.98	1.82	.96
Passive in Relationships	2.49	1.04	2.53	1.06	2.28	1.11	2.18	1.05	2.31	1.03	2.49	1.05
Negative Attitudes Toward Therapy	2.00	1.07	1.78	.93	1.79	.97	1.73	.95	1.80	1.01	1.95	1.00
Guilt-Prone	2.71	1.10	2.74	1.00	2.50	1.06	2.55	1.10	2.71	1.17	2.61	1.16
Nervous	3.21	.95	3.22	.88	3.05	.95	2.90	.97	3.16	.97	3.03	.91
Obsessive	3.03	1.15	2.84	.97	2.91	1.17	2.78	1.15	2.87	1.17	2.84	1.01
Shy	2.64	1.15	2.72	1.17	2.48	1.23	2.41	1.13	2.46	1.21	2.47	1.13
Uses Intellectualization	2.73	1.23	2.57	1.07	2.58	1.22	2.47	1.24	2.63	1.29	2.60	1.21
Has Many Interests	2.27	.91	2.28	.85	2.28	1.01	2.27	1.08	2.29	1.02	2.25	1.00
Difficulty Making Decisions	3.06	1.00	2.74	.98	2.92	1.06	2.87	1.09	3.00	1.04	2.97	1.11
Indirect Expression of Hostility	2.98	1.11	2.68	1.18	2.80	1.10	2.68	1.14	2.80	1.17	2.75	1.14
Poor Reality Testing	1.72	.88	1.48	.66	1.69	.87	1.61	.79	1.63	.84	1.59	.67
Angry	3.22	1.14	3.07	1.10	3.22	1.13	3.13	1.19	3.13	1.10	3.25	1.24
Eccentric	2.01	1.23	1.67	.79	1.85	1.15	1.88	1.16	1.95	1.27	1.83	1.16
Emotional Lability	2.38	1.06	2.27	.95	2.27	1.01	2.27	1.03	2.36	1.08	2.41	1.03
Dislikes Change	2.86	.98	2.80	1.00	2.71	1.03	2.69	1.03	2.76	1.07	2.84	1.01
Believes Cannot Be Helped	2.05	1.15	1.76	.85	1.85	1.03	1.76	.95	1.95	1.03	2.05	1.02
Reliable Informant	3.16	.91	3.22	.81	3.13	.91	3.18	.91	3.23	.91	3.17	.89
Ignores Problems	2.43	1.08	2.29	1.12	2.23	.98	2.20	1.01	2.22	1.02	2.45	1.10
Ruminates	3.34	.95	3.02	1.00	3.28	1.00	3.18	1.07	3.30	1.00	3.25	1.02
Excitable	2.60	1.00	2.57	.96	2.67	1.00	2.58	1.02	2.55	1.02	2.54	1.02
Conforming	2.54	.88	2.61	.83	2.37	.90	2.31	.85	2.44	.86	2.46	.88
Ineffective at Dealing with Problems	3.15	1.07	2.87	.98	2.99	1.05	2.92	1.03	3.01	1.06	2.98	.92
Introverted	2.84	1.12	2.78	1.07	2.53	1.17	2.48	1.17	2.62	1.14	2.59	1.04
Superficial Relationships	2.91	1.20	2.71	1.14	2.74	1.20	2.70	1.25	2.68	1.27	2.75	1.19

	Content Component Scales *(continued)*											
	SOD_1		SOD_2		FAM_1		FAM_2		TRT_1		TRT_2	
	Mean	SD	Mean	SD	Mean	SD	Mean	SD	Mean	SD	Mean	SD
Impulsive	2.77	1.29	2.63	1.16	2.66	1.22	2.64	1.20	2.66	1.21	2.80	1.17
Stereotypic Feminine Behavior	1.34	.70	1.37	.61	1.25	.55	1.28	.61	1.33	.69	1.37	.58
Stubborn	3.01	1.12	2.67	.97	2.78	1.09	2.68	1.14	2.80	1.17	2.83	1.10
Hostile Toward Therapist	1.48	.79	1.37	.64	1.39	.64	1.39	.68	1.44	.74	1.39	.62
Difficult to Motivate	2.39	1.07	2.11	.91	2.21	1.06	2.14	.99	2.19	1.02	2.29	1.00
Suicidal Ideations	1.95	1.12	1.65	1.02	1.70	.91	1.68	.98	1.84	1.00	1.88	.98
Familial Discord	3.14	1.35	2.98	1.12	3.24	1.31	3.24	1.32	3.02	1.35	3.07	1.45
Dogmatic	2.46	1.15	2.02	.95	2.28	1.09	2.22	1.08	2.30	1.15	2.25	1.11

Table L-2f. Means and standard deviations for continuous extra-test characteristics (men): High scores on supplementary scales

Extra-test Characteristics	Supplementary Scales									
	A		R		Es		MAC-R		AAS	
	Mean	SD	Mean	SD	Mean	SD	Mean	SD	Mean	SD
Intake Information	(n = 190)		(n = 48)		(n = 239)		(n = 79)		(n = 127)	
Axis IV diagnosis	2.98	.91	2.85	1.00	2.82	.87	2.87	.95	2.95	.92
Axis V - Current Level of Functioning	60.22	9.85	59.94	11.67	66.35	9.41	59.95	9.63	60.95	9.40
Number of Arrests	1.18	2.50	1.44	4.18	1.30	2.80	2.42	3.51	2.09	4.52
Mental Status	(n = 190)		(n = 48)		(n = 239)		(n = 79)		(n = 127)	
Anxiety During Interview	2.49	.73	2.56	.77	2.33	.66	2.41	.63	2.50	.75
Depression During Interview	2.47	.71	2.38	.77	2.05	.66	2.32	.74	2.44	.73
Activity Level During Interview	3.02	.47	2.96	.62	3.02	.39	3.01	.47	3.02	.43
Speech During Interview	2.94	.38	2.91	.35	2.99	.43	2.92	.31	2.93	.36
SCL-90-R Scales	(n = 185)		(n = 48)		(n = 234)		(n = 78)		(n = 125)	
Somatization	1.30	.81	1.06	.87	.41	.38	1.24	.80	1.14	.83
Obsessive-Compulsive	1.78	.80	1.32	1.01	.63	.48	1.41	.81	1.48	.85
Interpersonal Sensitivity	1.74	.80	1.45	1.04	.56	.49	1.23	.81	1.39	.89
Depression	2.10	.80	1.68	1.08	.81	.67	1.72	.96	1.75	.88
Anxiety	1.66	.84	1.11	.99	.46	.50	1.39	.97	1.37	.90
Hostility	1.57	1.07	.87	.96	.60	.71	1.54	1.13	1.62	1.12
Phobic Anxiety	.84	.72	.81	.92	.16	.26	.63	.75	.69	.77
Paranoid Ideation	1.68	.87	1.10	.90	.66	.62	1.41	.87	1.53	.88
Psychoticism	1.24	.69	.97	.93	.31	.35	1.03	.75	1.07	.73
Initial SCL-90 Analogue	(n = 120)		(n = 29)		(n = 150)		(n = 46)		(n = 62)	
Somatization	2.40	2.72	3.14	3.06	1.04	1.78	2.04	2.47	2.25	2.51
Obsessive-Compulsive	3.36	2.71	3.90	3.24	2.86	2.55	2.80	2.04	4.00	2.48
Interpersonal Sensitivity	4.71	2.41	5.21	2.53	4.04	2.67	4.18	2.48	5.16	2.05
Depression	4.55	2.62	5.24	2.59	2.90	2.47	3.63	2.69	4.32	2.66
Anxiety	4.53	2.66	4.90	2.43	3.19	2.52	4.00	2.65	4.45	2.58
Hostility	3.18	2.79	2.90	2.81	2.70	2.81	3.91	2.76	3.74	2.62
Phobic Anxiety	1.36	2.19	1.83	2.33	.93	1.69	1.20	2.02	1.48	2.08
Paranoid Ideation	1.23	1.80	1.48	2.11	1.10	1.81	1.43	1.82	1.38	1.67
Psychoticism	.47	1.26	.97	1.45	.58	1.16	.61	1.26	.82	1.44

Table L-2f. Means and standard deviations for continuous extra-test characteristics (men): High scores on supplementary scales *(continued)*

Extra-test Characteristics	A		R		Es		MAC-R		AAS	
	Mean	SD	Mean	SD	Mean	SD	Mean	SD	Mean	SD
Patient Description Form Scales	(n = 119)		(n = 30)		(n = 151)		(n = 47)		(n = 64)	
Angry Resentment	2.82	.92	2.70	.93	2.46	.97	3.01	.92	2.97	.91
Critical/Argumentative	2.51	.97	2.55	.90	2.30	.86	2.66	.91	2.58	.82
Narcissistic	2.30	.95	2.17	.84	2.42	.81	2.54	.96	2.50	.77
Defensive	2.55	.89	2.89	.93	2.58	.84	2.66	.79	2.66	.73
Histrionic	2.39	.77	2.27	.66	2.16	.81	2.46	.71	2.53	.74
Aggressive	2.11	.86	1.94	.81	2.13	.91	2.54	.98	2.46	.91
Insecure	2.98	.77	2.97	.74	2.56	.86	2.78	.69	3.07	.66
Anxious	2.97	.76	3.15	.80	2.41	.76	2.86	.79	2.93	.67
Pessimistic	2.38	.94	2.70	.95	1.96	.86	2.36	.91	2.43	.90
Depressed	2.57	.77	2.52	.77	1.81	.69	2.30	.82	2.47	.77
Achievement-Oriented	2.57	.76	2.42	.57	2.85	.62	2.55	.68	2.61	.68
Passive-Submissive	2.25	.83	2.48	.82	2.06	.77	1.92	.76	2.29	.83
Introverted	2.60	1.02	2.96	1.05	2.37	.95	2.45	.96	2.74	.93
Emotionally Controlled	2.38	1.06	2.85	1.04	2.37	.90	2.43	.97	2.67	.95
Antisocial	2.21	.90	2.19	.99	2.30	.82	2.72	.80	2.60	.83
Negative Treatment Attitudes	1.91	.79	2.30	.97	2.03	.78	1.98	.71	2.07	.70
Somatic Symptoms	2.13	1.04	2.53	1.31	1.48	.70	1.96	.90	2.01	.93
Psychotic Symptoms	1.24	.39	1.41	.54	1.21	.36	1.39	.53	1.32	.40
Family Problems	2.78	1.16	2.30	1.03	2.29	1.15	2.85	1.20	2.87	1.06
Obsessive-Compulsive	2.85	.79	3.13	.80	2.50	.85	2.61	.81	2.87	.65
Stereotypic Masculine Interests	2.81	1.12	2.79	1.28	3.11	1.10	3.34	1.16	2.96	1.03
Procrastinates	2.31	.96	2.43	.96	2.06	.85	2.25	.79	2.36	.86
Suspicious	2.60	.96	2.92	1.16	2.30	1.01	2.79	.87	2.73	.85
Agitated	2.19	.77	2.25	.95	1.95	.76	2.40	.71	2.44	.66
Work Problems	1.98	.95	2.08	1.11	1.76	.78	2.18	.91	2.20	.95
Patient Description Form Items	(n = 119)		(n = 30)		(n = 151)		(n = 47)		(n = 64)	
Anxious	3.52	.80	3.70	.92	2.78	.97	3.17	.89	3.39	.83
Problems with Authority Figures	2.97	1.18	2.97	1.19	2.90	1.22	3.51	1.20	3.31	1.10
Has Insight Into Own Problems	2.65	.85	2.47	.90	2.51	.89	2.45	.72	2.75	.80
Fears Losing Control	3.30	1.03	3.46	.96	2.95	1.20	3.28	1.07	3.44	.85
Extroverted	2.36	1.01	2.00	.79	2.71	.99	2.68	1.07	2.48	.99
Uses Repression	2.56	1.04	2.89	1.07	2.64	1.02	2.68	1.02	2.90	.89

Supplementary Scales: A, R, Es, MAC-R, AAS.

Submissive	2.19	.92	2.46	1.04	2.16	.89	2.09	.90	2.30	.97
Difficulty Concentrating	2.79	1.14	3.10	1.06	2.22	1.03	2.81	1.04	2.88	.88
Rigid	2.73	1.08	3.27	.83	2.62	1.18	2.81	1.10	2.73	1.10
Overly Compliant	2.03	.93	2.00	.95	1.79	.83	1.72	.83	2.03	.92
Whiny	1.97	1.02	1.87	1.01	1.63	.92	1.85	1.04	1.80	.99
Feels Overwhelmed	3.38	1.12	3.40	1.13	2.64	1.11	3.26	1.09	3.23	1.00
Manipulative	2.33	1.18	2.45	1.15	2.58	1.05	2.69	1.18	2.61	1.04
Difficulty Trusting Others	3.28	1.24	3.66	1.20	2.96	1.26	3.64	1.11	3.61	1.06
Insensitive to Others	2.19	1.04	2.33	1.03	2.40	1.11	2.40	1.06	2.41	.89
Stereotypic Masculine Behavior	2.79	1.15	2.76	1.27	3.10	1.12	3.34	1.17	2.95	1.12
Harbors Grudges	2.78	1.13	2.75	1.27	2.52	1.15	3.18	1.07	2.95	1.14
Evasive	2.23	1.12	2.73	1.31	2.43	1.16	2.41	1.00	2.44	1.08
Disoriented	1.26	.60	1.47	.68	1.15	.44	1.38	.71	1.34	.60
Energetic	2.36	.90	2.23	.90	2.86	.96	2.53	.86	2.59	.83
Lonely	3.03	1.28	2.87	1.22	2.47	1.22	2.94	1.41	3.11	1.18
Family Lacks Love	2.75	1.33	2.37	1.24	2.20	1.24	2.83	1.45	3.05	1.33
Worrier	3.39	1.03	3.30	1.06	2.70	1.05	3.11	.98	3.20	.96
Narcissistic	2.46	1.21	2.31	1.07	2.64	1.08	2.68	1.25	2.78	1.06
Tearful	1.58	.84	1.47	.86	1.29	.60	1.36	.53	1.57	.80
Provocative	1.62	.83	1.77	1.04	1.72	.93	1.89	.84	1.94	.89
Moralistic	2.44	1.06	2.79	1.18	2.48	1.05	2.43	1.03	2.38	1.02
Socially Awkward	2.82	1.15	3.10	1.18	2.55	1.13	2.81	1.17	3.00	1.10
Hostile	2.43	1.15	2.38	1.08	2.19	1.17	2.89	1.32	2.69	1.23
Overcontrolled	2.59	1.21	3.07	1.25	2.53	1.08	2.53	1.20	2.81	1.13
Resistant to Interpretations	2.08	1.03	2.57	1.14	2.22	.96	2.24	.97	2.25	.98
Antisocial Behavior	2.20	1.24	2.07	1.05	2.35	1.09	3.04	1.25	2.77	1.28
Sarcastic	2.03	1.12	1.93	.94	1.87	.97	2.13	1.06	2.03	1.05
Rejects Traditional Gender Role	1.69	1.05	1.62	1.18	1.41	.88	1.29	.66	1.59	1.05
Feels Gets Raw Deal From Life	3.03	1.20	2.93	1.20	2.45	1.13	2.96	1.12	2.92	1.13
Acute Psychological Turmoil	3.06	1.05	3.20	1.03	2.54	1.03	2.89	1.01	3.20	1.03
Does Not Complete Projects	2.19	1.11	2.46	1.25	2.01	1.08	2.51	.98	2.44	1.06
Uncomfortable with Opposite Sex	2.15	1.10	2.39	1.10	1.81	.94	1.73	.78	2.21	.95
Preoccupied with Health Problems	2.30	1.37	2.83	1.62	1.39	.82	1.96	1.14	1.95	1.14
Work-Oriented	2.98	1.07	2.93	1.14	3.36	.91	2.83	1.11	3.00	1.02
Resents Family Members	2.82	1.35	2.22	1.09	2.26	1.24	2.82	1.32	2.90	1.21
Demanding of Attention	2.45	1.10	2.27	1.05	2.31	1.15	2.54	1.11	2.64	1.11
Passive	2.44	.98	2.60	1.00	2.07	.96	2.09	.95	2.47	1.04
Self-Punishing	2.42	1.22	2.55	1.02	2.00	.97	2.39	1.19	2.73	1.13
Needs to Achieve	2.77	1.07	2.70	.75	3.03	.90	2.65	.85	2.79	.97
Needs to Be with Others	2.95	1.10	2.47	.63	2.97	.81	3.13	1.01	3.00	1.01
Irritable	2.63	1.04	2.77	1.10	2.37	1.05	2.85	1.08	2.92	.97
Self-Defeating	3.10	1.17	3.13	1.14	2.97	1.10	3.40	1.19	3.52	1.10
Delusional Thinking	1.21	.57	1.45	.74	1.21	.52	1.36	.76	1.32	.67

Table L-2f. Means and standard deviations for continuous extra-test characteristics (men): High scores on supplementary scales *(continued)*

Extra-test Characteristics	Supplementary Scales									
	A		R		Es		MAC-R		AAS	
	Mean	SD	Mean	SD	Mean	SD	Mean	SD	Mean	SD
Self-Reliant	2.66	.92	2.80	.81	2.97	.89	2.83	1.03	2.67	.94
Aggressive	2.35	.99	2.20	.92	2.59	1.12	2.79	1.08	2.78	1.03
Competitive	2.39	1.01	2.32	.82	2.71	.91	2.60	.92	2.52	.84
Suspicious	2.61	1.18	2.90	1.30	2.29	1.21	2.78	1.08	2.66	1.10
Compulsive	2.51	1.13	2.76	1.21	2.45	1.17	2.46	1.07	2.85	1.13
Dependable	3.02	.95	3.07	.80	3.12	.84	2.72	.83	2.87	.87
Multiple Somatic Complaints	2.03	1.23	2.53	1.57	1.32	.79	1.72	1.04	1.94	1.13
Complains of Lack of Time	2.03	1.16	1.97	1.05	1.87	1.03	1.80	.88	2.13	1.06
Poor Work Performance	2.04	1.12	2.10	.94	1.85	1.00	2.39	1.26	2.22	1.13
Insecure	3.46	.84	3.47	.90	3.08	1.12	3.23	.98	3.50	.80
Discusses Problems Openly	3.12	.86	2.70	.99	2.99	.91	3.19	.68	3.13	.79
Sexually Adjusted	2.36	.81	2.00	.91	2.75	.82	2.71	.91	2.67	.72
Exaggerated Need for Affection	2.24	1.08	2.00	.94	2.10	.99	2.30	1.05	2.37	.92
Resentful	3.04	1.15	2.80	.96	2.72	1.18	3.17	1.20	3.19	1.08
Uses Denial	2.56	1.22	3.07	1.23	2.88	1.05	2.83	1.13	2.91	1.05
Hypochondriacal	1.69	.88	1.97	1.12	1.35	.78	1.62	.90	1.70	.94
Communicates Effectively	3.14	.76	2.83	.79	3.00	.87	3.02	.77	3.09	.75
Has Many Nightmares	1.73	1.06	1.47	.80	1.29	.63	1.75	.94	1.84	1.00
Stormy Interpersonal Relationships	3.05	1.26	2.86	1.27	2.83	1.33	3.65	1.15	3.37	1.15
Feigns Remorse When in Trouble	1.69	.91	1.76	.97	1.90	.93	2.02	.96	1.93	.93
Stereotypic Masculine Interests	2.81	1.18	2.83	1.34	3.12	1.18	3.34	1.22	2.92	1.06
Guarded	2.69	1.35	3.30	1.21	2.73	1.14	3.00	1.20	2.89	1.21
Feels Inferior	3.09	1.05	3.20	1.06	2.73	1.04	2.98	.87	3.21	.94
Low Frustration Tolerance	3.15	1.18	3.14	1.27	2.82	1.10	3.32	.98	3.33	.94
Psychotic Symptoms	1.13	.47	1.34	.67	1.15	.44	1.28	.66	1.18	.47
Fired From Past Jobs	2.07	1.17	2.00	1.30	1.74	.98	2.41	1.21	2.30	1.18
Needs Attention	2.86	.97	2.60	.86	2.72	1.04	2.89	1.01	2.97	.86
Acts Out	2.42	1.15	2.17	1.02	2.32	1.13	2.96	1.14	2.92	1.10
Histrionic	1.88	1.01	1.87	.97	1.70	.97	1.83	.89	2.16	1.00
Self-Indulgent	2.47	1.12	2.23	.94	2.63	1.08	2.96	1.18	2.89	1.10
Depressed	3.34	1.01	3.53	.82	2.42	1.00	3.06	1.15	3.24	1.01
Grandiose	1.95	1.12	1.86	.99	1.93	1.06	2.09	1.14	1.87	.92
Cynical	2.60	1.32	2.67	1.12	2.09	1.03	2.64	1.22	2.60	1.10
Sociopathic	1.57	.82	1.90	1.09	1.67	.89	1.94	.89	1.78	.83
Agitated	2.46	1.04	2.38	.86	2.09	1.04	2.77	1.13	2.76	1.06

Marital Problems	2.54	1.59	2.42	1.50	2.36	1.55	2.64	1.66	2.75	1.57
Absence of Deep Emotions	2.03	1.25	2.30	1.21	2.15	1.09	2.36	1.31	2.42	1.28
Uncomfortable Dealing with Emotions	2.93	1.31	3.37	1.10	2.80	1.10	3.02	1.31	3.22	1.15
Sad	2.98	1.02	2.83	.89	2.25	.90	2.72	.95	2.83	.97
Self-Degrading	2.24	1.04	2.30	.99	1.80	.97	2.00	1.00	2.36	.97
Unable to Express Negative Feelings	2.18	1.13	2.70	1.15	2.19	1.11	2.06	.96	2.50	.99
Concrete in Thinking	2.24	1.09	2.50	1.20	2.21	.99	2.23	.96	2.37	.91
Unable to See Own Limitations	2.38	1.17	2.23	1.17	2.29	1.06	2.43	1.10	2.32	.93
Power-Oriented	2.18	1.12	1.79	.86	2.43	1.01	2.57	1.14	2.40	1.05
Grouchy	2.29	1.08	2.40	1.07	1.99	.98	2.55	1.02	2.52	1.00
Overbearing in Relationships	2.28	1.16	2.00	1.00	2.26	1.19	2.72	1.32	2.51	1.15
Uncertain About Career	3.46	1.27	3.44	1.26	2.89	1.28	3.31	1.29	3.48	1.25
Likable	3.25	.76	3.03	.76	3.20	.69	3.17	.76	3.19	.69
Procrastinator	2.61	1.15	2.57	1.20	2.37	1.05	2.41	1.02	2.58	1.08
Negative Feelings Toward Opposite Sex	2.06	1.14	2.31	1.23	1.94	1.06	2.02	1.17	2.18	1.12
Defensive	2.67	1.20	3.03	1.19	2.59	1.16	2.70	1.10	2.69	1.05
Empathetic	2.39	.77	2.34	.86	2.21	.71	2.23	.76	2.35	.72
Perfectionistic	2.57	1.18	2.93	1.04	2.44	1.11	2.38	1.07	2.52	.96
Judgmental	2.67	1.15	2.93	1.00	2.59	1.05	2.85	1.14	2.67	.95
Copes Well with Stress	1.97	.66	1.90	.71	2.32	.63	2.15	.55	2.05	.58
Moody	2.81	1.04	2.76	1.09	2.39	.98	2.68	1.00	2.90	.80
Selfish	2.19	1.04	2.07	1.00	2.42	1.00	2.41	1.09	2.44	.86
Gives Up Easily	2.32	1.06	2.21	1.18	1.89	.97	2.36	1.00	2.44	1.01
Physical Symptoms in Response to Stress	2.25	1.21	2.46	1.40	1.53	.87	2.26	1.10	2.17	1.09
Blames Family For Difficulties	2.50	1.32	1.96	1.14	2.03	1.30	2.50	1.24	2.41	1.19
Bored	2.45	1.14	2.60	1.16	2.07	1.05	2.34	1.15	2.54	.96
Idealistic	2.39	1.05	2.31	.97	2.21	1.05	2.13	.99	2.33	.96
Difficulty Establishing Therapeutic Rapport	1.97	1.05	2.43	1.10	2.15	1.04	2.09	.97	2.30	1.09
Daydreams	1.83	.99	2.32	1.11	1.76	.87	1.61	.83	1.84	.92
Concerned About Status	2.46	1.15	2.20	1.03	2.55	.98	2.40	1.15	2.37	1.09
Creates Good First Impression	2.59	.85	2.57	.90	2.82	.92	2.49	1.02	2.51	.91
Complains of Sleep Disturbance	2.75	1.30	2.76	1.24	1.65	.93	2.36	1.31	2.51	1.18
Has Temper Tantrums	2.27	1.15	1.97	1.02	2.18	1.27	2.67	1.19	2.73	1.18
Overreactive	2.73	1.08	2.57	1.22	2.40	1.22	2.85	.98	2.90	1.06
High Aspirations	2.51	1.16	2.27	.98	2.66	1.04	2.26	.95	2.47	1.04
Feels Hopeless	2.84	1.13	2.83	1.12	1.93	1.01	2.62	1.19	2.67	1.14
Keeps Others at a Distance	2.95	1.30	3.23	1.17	2.82	1.12	3.27	1.25	3.19	1.13
Argumentative	2.27	1.08	2.27	1.14	2.14	1.12	2.60	1.21	2.38	1.04
Paranoid Features	1.85	.95	2.23	1.30	1.65	.99	1.94	1.07	1.87	.98
Restless	2.69	1.16	2.73	1.20	2.31	1.04	2.89	1.01	3.03	.90
Pessimistic	2.92	1.13	3.30	.95	2.28	1.04	2.91	1.02	2.95	1.06
Feels Like a Failure	3.06	1.10	3.10	1.12	2.43	1.04	2.96	1.14	3.16	1.01

Table L-2f. Means and standard deviations for continuous extra-test characteristics (men): High scores on supplementary scales *(continued)*

Extra-test Characteristics	Supplementary Scales									
	A		R		Es		MAC-R		AAS	
	Mean	SD	Mean	SD	Mean	SD	Mean	SD	Mean	SD
Hallucinations	1.07	.31	1.13	.35	1.03	.18	1.21	.55	1.11	.37
Restricted Affect	2.18	1.28	2.87	1.38	2.15	1.21	2.19	1.23	2.39	1.22
Impatient	2.68	1.10	2.62	1.15	2.62	1.11	2.98	1.21	2.84	.95
Assertive	2.34	.85	2.17	.83	2.45	.79	2.38	.85	2.28	.74
Modest	2.42	.86	2.60	.77	2.36	.85	2.36	.79	2.48	.84
Self-Doubting	3.13	.93	3.33	.92	2.67	1.04	2.85	.91	3.17	.88
Deceptive	1.87	1.00	2.07	1.03	2.13	1.06	2.15	1.03	2.03	.86
Feels That Life is a Strain	3.19	1.15	3.34	.97	2.45	1.02	3.00	1.06	3.08	.96
Physically Abusive	1.54	.85	1.54	.99	1.49	.96	2.07	1.13	1.93	1.02
Feels Rejected	3.19	1.24	2.79	1.21	2.67	1.33	3.04	1.30	3.24	1.24
Does Not Get Along with Coworkers	1.96	1.00	2.00	1.25	1.72	.94	2.15	1.10	2.24	1.02
Uses Projection	2.37	1.18	2.43	1.32	2.39	1.10	2.71	1.04	2.73	1.04
Complains of Fatigue	2.47	1.36	2.97	1.56	1.81	1.02	2.17	1.18	2.32	1.08
Uses Rationalization	2.66	1.10	2.80	1.06	2.98	.96	2.91	1.06	2.78	.83
Critical of Others	2.58	1.16	2.53	1.01	2.44	1.08	2.79	1.12	2.67	1.08
Egocentric	2.53	1.22	2.40	1.07	2.67	1.05	2.61	1.14	2.70	1.06
Overevaluates Own Worth	2.03	1.14	1.83	.91	1.89	.92	2.13	1.15	2.03	1.00
Optimistic	1.98	.71	2.03	.67	2.36	.88	2.11	.76	2.14	.73
Psychologically Immature	2.88	1.16	2.97	1.25	2.82	1.12	2.87	1.12	3.02	.86
Poor Judgment	2.87	1.19	2.97	1.22	3.01	1.09	3.43	1.02	3.38	.98
Low Sex Drive	1.88	1.11	2.60	1.59	1.38	.81	1.62	.97	1.65	.88
Feels Mistreated	2.96	1.12	3.23	1.19	2.62	1.19	2.89	1.07	3.00	1.10
Overly Sensitive to Criticism	3.12	1.16	3.27	1.11	2.76	1.13	2.74	1.04	3.03	1.02
Sentimental	2.49	1.04	2.62	.98	2.19	.93	2.11	.98	2.45	.95
Sexual Preoccupation	1.81	1.17	1.69	.95	1.82	1.23	1.69	1.12	1.95	1.20
Accelerated Speech	1.42	.79	1.70	1.24	1.46	.80	1.53	.80	1.53	.78
Concerns About Homosexuality	1.53	1.12	1.38	1.02	1.19	.75	1.12	.33	1.27	.76
Many Specific Fears	1.80	1.00	2.04	1.09	1.47	.75	1.86	.98	1.93	.94
Passive in Relationships	2.33	1.04	2.87	1.04	2.20	1.10	1.91	1.00	2.38	1.06
Negative Attitudes Toward Therapy	1.73	.96	2.14	1.06	1.79	.93	1.72	.99	1.79	.94
Guilt-Prone	2.66	1.15	2.60	.97	2.27	1.06	2.36	.97	2.73	.96
Nervous	3.12	.97	3.48	1.12	2.52	.99	2.91	1.00	3.06	.91
Obsessive	2.91	1.13	3.14	1.11	2.37	1.13	2.61	1.04	2.97	.97
Shy	2.46	1.22	2.77	1.17	2.29	1.02	2.32	1.14	2.64	1.10
Uses Intellectualization	2.53	1.27	2.90	1.32	2.57	1.21	2.72	1.26	2.75	1.16

Has Many Interests	2.32	1.05	1.96	.71	2.59	.99	2.26	.98	2.39	.88
Difficulty Making Decisions	3.03	1.02	3.17	1.05	2.49	1.04	2.70	.95	2.95	.97
Indirect Expression of Hostility	2.66	1.16	2.90	1.35	2.55	1.23	2.70	.99	2.87	.98
Poor Reality Testing	1.61	.79	1.80	1.03	1.48	.71	1.72	.77	1.78	.72
Angry	3.07	1.16	2.83	1.23	2.63	1.26	3.36	1.19	3.33	1.08
Eccentric	1.91	1.25	2.37	1.33	1.77	1.08	1.96	1.07	1.89	1.09
Emotional Lability	2.23	1.07	2.27	.94	1.94	.99	2.47	1.06	2.48	1.11
Dislikes Change	2.69	1.05	2.97	.93	2.44	1.01	2.59	1.09	2.73	.94
Believes Cannot Be Helped	1.81	.97	2.10	1.12	1.61	.94	1.81	1.01	1.91	.95
Reliable Informant	3.23	.91	3.24	1.02	3.24	.95	3.15	.81	3.16	.78
Ignores Problems	2.19	1.00	2.45	1.09	2.43	.97	2.53	1.02	2.42	.87
Ruminates	3.28	1.00	3.48	.99	2.68	1.18	3.00	1.06	3.25	.98
Excitable	2.56	1.03	2.57	1.01	2.36	1.02	2.79	1.06	2.83	.95
Conforming	2.44	.90	2.67	.96	2.45	.91	2.23	.89	2.38	.90
Ineffective at Dealing with Problems	3.00	1.04	3.27	1.11	2.78	1.00	2.87	.86	3.11	.98
Introverted	2.54	1.14	3.00	1.26	2.25	1.11	2.21	1.10	2.59	1.11
Superficial Relationships	2.57	1.23	2.93	1.28	2.63	1.19	2.74	1.16	2.93	1.09
Impulsive	2.59	1.21	2.47	1.25	2.77	1.11	3.00	1.14	3.02	1.03
Stereotypic Feminine Behavior	1.34	.68	1.50	.94	1.30	.64	1.13	.34	1.27	.60
Stubborn	2.74	1.15	3.00	1.15	2.76	1.16	2.98	1.11	2.79	.99
Hostile Toward Therapist	1.39	.67	1.63	1.00	1.37	.76	1.34	.70	1.38	.58
Difficult to Motivate	2.11	.99	2.48	1.24	2.22	1.13	2.09	1.06	2.27	.94
Suicidal Ideations	1.81	.98	1.67	1.12	1.30	.73	1.74	.99	1.79	1.02
Familial Discord	2.93	1.39	2.54	1.26	2.59	1.33	3.22	1.35	3.13	1.25
Dogmatic	2.25	1.15	2.43	.94	2.22	1.05	2.49	1.14	2.28	.92

	Supplementary Scales *(continued)*											
	APS		O-H		Do		Re		MDS		PK	
	Mean	SD	Mean	SD	Mean	SD	Mean	SD	Mean	SD	Mean	SD
Intake Information	(n = 80)		(n = 51)		(n = 227)		(n = 195)		(n = 249)		(n = 235)	
Axis IV diagnosis	2.85	.83	2.94	.99	2.76	.87	2.85	.90	2.90	.91	2.93	.89
Axis V - Current Level of Functioning	62.70	9.33	64.72	11.90	66.04	9.78	64.18	10.82	61.22	9.36	60.72	9.36
Number of Arrests	1.77	3.26	1.60	2.22	1.29	2.73	.87	2.16	1.27	3.26	1.46	3.56
Mental Status	(n = 80)		(n = 51)		(n = 227)		(n = 195)		(n = 249)		(n = 235)	
Anxiety During Interview	2.42	.67	2.31	.65	2.35	.63	2.40	.69	2.45	.71	2.50	.71
Depression During Interview	2.37	.67	1.88	.74	2.09	.65	2.18	.72	2.39	.69	2.43	.69
Activity Level During Interview	3.04	.38	3.00	.49	3.03	.41	3.03	.44	3.00	.42	3.02	.45
Speech During Interview	3.00	.36	2.94	.37	3.00	.41	3.00	.41	2.95	.40	2.95	.38
SCL-90-R Scales	(n = 79)		(n = 50)		(n = 223)		(n = 192)		(n = 245)		(n = 230)	
Somatization	.96	.68	.69	.80	.62	.61	.78	.75	1.18	.81	1.25	.81
Obsessive-Compulsive	1.48	.80	.85	.98	.83	.66	1.07	.87	1.60	.84	1.68	.80
Interpersonal Sensitivity	1.38	.78	.83	.95	.80	.73	.94	.86	1.56	.88	1.62	.86
Depression	1.72	.78	.96	1.00	1.01	.80	1.27	.98	1.92	.84	2.01	.80
Anxiety	1.33	.81	.71	.90	.68	.67	.88	.85	1.43	.90	1.52	.87
Hostility	1.30	.95	.60	.89	.75	.91	.73	.80	1.50	1.05	1.56	1.06
Phobic Anxiety	.59	.64	.45	.78	.29	.52	.44	.61	.71	.71	.78	.73
Paranoid Ideation	1.34	.84	.91	.99	.85	.79	.84	.79	1.55	.89	1.62	.89
Psychoticism	.94	.68	.60	.85	.49	.53	.64	.68	1.12	.72	1.18	.71
Initial SCL-90 Analogue	(n = 47)		(n = 28)		(n = 148)		(n = 120)		(n = 156)		(n = 146)	
Somatization	2.26	2.82	1.54	2.22	1.42	2.19	1.97	2.70	2.27	2.67	2.49	2.83
Obsessive-Compulsive	3.17	2.85	2.86	2.65	2.75	2.65	3.01	2.78	3.42	2.76	3.55	2.84
Interpersonal Sensitivity	4.70	2.40	3.64	2.82	4.02	2.61	4.00	2.61	4.87	2.45	5.00	2.51
Depression	4.26	2.77	2.93	1.84	3.23	2.42	3.46	2.49	4.39	2.70	4.74	2.60
Anxiety	4.13	2.71	3.50	2.13	3.56	2.58	3.75	2.53	4.39	2.72	4.74	2.65
Hostility	3.68	2.87	2.82	2.97	2.66	2.58	2.36	2.40	3.54	2.86	3.61	2.97
Phobic Anxiety	1.23	1.83	1.11	1.93	1.04	1.73	1.19	2.11	1.35	2.11	1.58	2.33
Paranoid Ideation	1.49	2.02	1.57	1.99	1.20	1.83	1.11	1.71	1.31	2.00	1.47	2.10
Psychoticism	.87	1.68	.93	1.33	.60	1.13	.62	1.28	.54	1.35	.66	1.57
Patient Description Form Scales	(n = 47)		(n = 30)		(n = 149)		(n = 121)		(n = 158)		(n = 147)	
Angry Resentment	2.88	.87	2.55	.93	2.53	.94	2.49	.94	2.87	.93	2.91	.96
Critical/Argumentative	2.59	.91	2.31	.89	2.36	.88	2.33	.87	2.58	.93	2.60	.97
Narcissistic	2.52	.95	2.29	.90	2.41	.92	2.33	.92	2.39	.91	2.36	.96

Defensive	2.65	.80	2.67	.93	2.54	.87	2.54	.91	2.61	.87	2.62	.90
Histrionic	2.50	.66	2.04	.66	2.15	.79	2.20	.83	2.45	.76	2.45	.78
Aggressive	2.37	.83	2.09	1.06	2.05	.85	1.94	.78	2.22	.93	2.24	.95
Insecure	2.86	.79	2.45	.88	2.54	.81	2.68	.86	2.96	.80	3.02	.74
Anxious	2.77	.71	2.51	.69	2.46	.77	2.65	.85	2.88	.81	3.00	.77
Pessimistic	2.26	.87	2.12	.84	2.04	.82	2.10	.88	2.42	.98	2.49	.97
Depressed	2.38	.72	1.88	.55	1.91	.69	2.08	.77	2.46	.78	2.60	.76
Achievement-Oriented	2.72	.73	2.50	.75	2.81	.70	2.78	.68	2.57	.73	2.54	.73
Passive-Submissive	2.15	.85	2.11	.88	2.11	.82	2.29	.82	2.14	.80	2.22	.83
Introverted	2.43	.98	2.50	1.08	2.36	.98	2.48	1.01	2.57	1.03	2.63	1.03
Emotionally Controlled	2.45	.95	2.25	.89	2.33	.91	2.38	.92	2.41	1.03	2.43	1.05
Antisocial	2.45	.93	2.45	1.03	2.24	.87	2.09	.82	2.32	.96	2.34	1.02
Negative Treatment Attitudes	1.98	.74	2.20	.91	2.07	.80	2.03	.80	1.99	.78	2.01	.82
Somatic Symptoms	1.88	.96	1.69	.93	1.63	.82	1.91	1.11	2.05	1.03	2.15	1.06
Psychotic Symptoms	1.34	.38	1.40	.58	1.26	.41	1.21	.37	1.29	.47	1.31	.48
Family Problems	2.91	1.13	2.27	1.24	2.33	1.10	2.34	1.13	2.85	1.14	2.90	1.16
Obsessive-Compulsive	2.71	.71	2.57	.78	2.53	.81	2.63	.87	2.80	.82	2.87	.78
Stereotypic Masculine Interests	2.89	1.26	2.77	1.18	2.86	1.09	2.78	1.07	2.79	1.17	2.79	1.11
Procrastinates	2.25	.96	1.90	.79	2.10	.90	2.12	.89	2.23	.92	2.29	.94
Suspicious	2.67	1.02	2.59	1.12	2.39	1.05	2.32	.97	2.63	.96	2.69	1.01
Agitated	2.31	.76	2.01	.79	1.98	.80	1.96	.81	2.23	.80	2.24	.80
Work Problems	2.04	.92	1.90	.88	1.71	.80	1.70	.83	2.12	.96	2.11	.97
Patient Description Form Items	(n = 47)		(n = 30)		(n = 149)		(n = 121)		(n = 158)		(n = 147)	
Anxious	3.23	.98	3.13	.94	2.86	1.01	3.13	1.02	3.37	.91	3.54	.81
Problems with Authority Figures	3.11	1.14	2.97	1.21	2.79	1.20	2.77	1.19	3.03	1.24	3.03	1.27
Has Insight Into Own Problems	2.72	.95	2.27	.78	2.54	.87	2.50	.87	2.60	.90	2.54	.88
Fears Losing Control	3.20	.98	3.03	1.22	2.85	1.17	3.06	1.19	3.25	1.05	3.31	1.03
Extroverted	2.72	1.12	2.37	.85	2.64	.97	2.56	.97	2.34	.97	2.24	.93
Uses Repression	2.40	.95	2.60	1.00	2.54	.97	2.59	1.04	2.60	1.03	2.59	1.05
Submissive	2.13	.85	2.13	.97	2.07	.86	2.29	.89	2.14	.87	2.19	.91
Difficulty Concentrating	2.66	1.09	2.25	1.04	2.26	1.07	2.41	1.14	2.64	1.12	2.80	1.13
Rigid	2.68	1.09	2.69	1.11	2.63	1.15	2.66	1.15	2.83	1.08	2.82	1.09
Overly Compliant	2.06	.92	1.66	.86	1.83	.88	2.03	.94	1.90	.88	1.94	.91
Whiny	1.89	.89	1.41	.68	1.62	.85	1.75	.94	2.00	1.06	1.98	1.07
Feels Overwhelmed	3.15	1.12	2.66	.90	2.82	1.12	2.93	1.19	3.25	1.15	3.39	1.09
Manipulative	2.65	1.16	2.27	1.14	2.52	1.14	2.46	1.11	2.54	1.17	2.44	1.20
Difficulty Trusting Others	3.34	1.24	3.03	1.30	3.01	1.28	2.87	1.21	3.35	1.22	3.36	1.24
Insensitive to Others	2.51	1.21	2.38	1.32	2.33	1.12	2.21	1.09	2.34	1.06	2.30	1.12
Stereotypic Masculine Behavior	2.94	1.28	2.77	1.19	2.85	1.12	2.73	1.08	2.79	1.18	2.80	1.15
Harbors Grudges	2.83	1.14	2.56	1.25	2.54	1.16	2.42	1.12	2.91	1.15	2.89	1.17
Evasive	2.36	1.07	2.37	1.13	2.38	1.15	2.38	1.23	2.33	1.09	2.32	1.16

	Supplementary Scales (*continued*)											
	APS		O-H		Do		Re		MDS		PK	
	Mean	SD	Mean	SD	Mean	SD	Mean	SD	Mean	SD	Mean	SD
Disoriented	1.17	.38	1.20	.41	1.18	.46	1.15	.41	1.31	.62	1.32	.63
Energetic	2.55	.83	2.52	.91	2.73	.91	2.69	.96	2.48	.92	2.36	.88
Lonely	3.04	1.28	2.38	1.18	2.48	1.13	2.58	1.17	2.98	1.25	3.02	1.24
Family Lacks Love	3.00	1.33	2.17	1.17	2.21	1.17	2.21	1.19	2.86	1.31	2.83	1.34
Worrier	2.98	.94	2.62	.86	2.76	1.11	2.99	1.12	3.27	1.04	3.39	1.03
Narcissistic	2.62	1.28	2.45	1.12	2.60	1.20	2.49	1.15	2.62	1.17	2.55	1.22
Tearful	1.61	.83	1.28	.65	1.31	.60	1.36	.69	1.51	.77	1.59	.85
Provocative	1.83	.79	1.66	.86	1.59	.79	1.54	.82	1.74	.95	1.71	.96
Moralistic	2.48	1.17	2.34	1.29	2.48	1.10	2.50	1.07	2.47	1.13	2.50	1.09
Socially Awkward	2.72	1.16	2.41	1.12	2.47	1.11	2.63	1.16	2.78	1.17	2.88	1.18
Hostile	2.53	1.12	2.28	1.28	2.21	1.13	2.11	1.06	2.58	1.20	2.58	1.24
Overcontrolled	2.62	1.11	2.64	.99	2.57	1.13	2.64	1.14	2.60	1.23	2.66	1.21
Resistant to Interpretations	2.17	.94	2.31	1.14	2.24	.98	2.22	.99	2.16	1.01	2.20	1.03
Antisocial Behavior	2.40	1.30	2.55	1.15	2.20	1.09	2.05	1.02	2.31	1.26	2.33	1.33
Sarcastic	2.21	1.14	1.79	.92	1.93	.96	1.91	1.02	2.09	1.06	2.06	1.09
Rejects Traditional Gender Role	1.50	.96	1.62	1.18	1.48	.96	1.61	1.02	1.66	1.09	1.68	1.09
Feels Gets Raw Deal From Life	2.79	1.06	2.55	1.12	2.57	1.16	2.62	1.20	3.06	1.15	3.10	1.21
Acute Psychological Turmoil	2.98	1.07	2.69	.85	2.54	1.05	2.65	1.08	3.02	1.06	3.10	1.11
Does Not Complete Projects	2.38	1.09	1.84	1.03	2.08	1.10	1.97	1.08	2.29	1.09	2.33	1.13
Uncomfortable with Opposite Sex	2.02	1.10	1.85	1.16	1.88	1.02	2.01	1.04	2.08	1.08	2.20	1.12
Preoccupied with Health Problems	1.89	1.20	1.86	1.21	1.63	1.02	1.94	1.33	2.16	1.34	2.30	1.40
Work-Oriented	2.98	1.01	2.82	.82	3.25	1.06	3.22	.99	2.99	1.08	2.91	1.06
Resents Family Members	2.87	1.22	2.37	1.33	2.29	1.19	2.34	1.25	2.87	1.32	2.90	1.33
Demanding of Attention	2.79	1.10	2.07	1.05	2.26	1.12	2.26	1.08	2.55	1.14	2.51	1.15
Passive	2.36	1.03	2.14	.95	2.17	.99	2.33	1.01	2.30	.98	2.45	.99
Self-Punishing	2.41	1.05	1.97	.87	2.05	.96	2.18	1.02	2.43	1.18	2.49	1.20
Needs to Achieve	2.91	1.13	2.71	.90	3.01	.99	2.94	1.04	2.76	1.02	2.74	1.03
Needs to Be with Others	3.19	1.08	2.61	.79	2.84	.92	2.91	.94	2.87	1.07	2.86	1.07
Irritable	2.68	.81	2.38	1.08	2.45	1.03	2.42	1.05	2.78	1.05	2.78	1.07
Self-Defeating	3.30	1.08	2.66	1.01	2.88	1.13	2.91	1.15	3.15	1.17	3.20	1.20
Delusional Thinking	1.38	.77	1.59	.95	1.32	.68	1.27	.63	1.26	.66	1.30	.71
Self-Reliant	2.85	.93	2.76	.95	2.94	.87	2.84	.88	2.65	.92	2.61	.89
Aggressive	2.68	1.09	2.61	1.40	2.36	1.11	2.28	1.03	2.51	1.08	2.46	1.09
Competitive	2.72	1.10	2.39	1.10	2.59	1.00	2.54	.96	2.44	1.00	2.40	1.01
Suspicious	2.68	1.25	2.62	1.24	2.36	1.24	2.33	1.14	2.63	1.15	2.68	1.23
Compulsive	2.46	1.11	2.50	1.23	2.39	1.11	2.51	1.10	2.59	1.13	2.58	1.11
Dependable	2.96	.92	2.83	.76	3.11	.88	3.21	.88	3.01	.96	2.98	.96
Multiple Somatic Complaints	1.77	1.13	1.52	1.06	1.53	1.00	1.83	1.28	1.96	1.24	2.10	1.32

Complains of Lack of Time	2.07	1.10	1.52	.70	1.93	1.05	1.90	1.08	1.93	1.12	1.94	1.13
Poor Work Performance	2.33	1.26	1.95	1.00	1.84	1.02	1.75	.99	2.14	1.20	2.16	1.18
Insecure	3.38	.95	3.00	1.22	3.03	1.04	3.13	1.06	3.43	.93	3.52	.89
Discusses Problems Openly	3.15	.83	2.70	.95	2.94	.89	2.97	.88	3.06	.90	3.05	.87
Sexually Adjusted	2.61	.82	2.40	1.05	2.70	.83	2.51	.86	2.41	.86	2.29	.82
Exaggerated Need for Affection	2.55	1.13	1.70	.87	2.03	.96	2.08	1.01	2.31	1.07	2.32	1.09
Resentful	3.22	1.17	2.86	1.09	2.80	1.17	2.75	1.18	3.10	1.13	3.08	1.16
Uses Denial	2.81	1.10	3.00	1.22	2.81	1.10	2.72	1.16	2.74	1.19	2.72	1.23
Hypochondriacal	1.68	.91	1.41	.78	1.48	.85	1.67	1.03	1.69	.93	1.71	.91
Communicates Effectively	3.11	.84	2.97	.81	3.10	.87	3.10	.78	3.04	.82	3.04	.78
Has Many Nightmares	1.58	.81	1.24	.75	1.33	.67	1.35	.72	1.59	.92	1.76	1.05
Stormy Interpersonal Relationships	3.39	1.16	2.72	1.22	2.74	1.24	2.58	1.22	3.18	1.25	3.13	1.22
Feigns Remorse When in Trouble	2.00	.96	1.81	1.17	1.91	.94	1.76	.90	1.82	.97	1.81	1.01
Stereotypic Masculine Interests	2.83	1.32	2.77	1.22	2.89	1.15	2.82	1.15	2.78	1.24	2.77	1.15
Guarded	2.85	1.23	2.97	1.16	2.77	1.19	2.69	1.23	2.79	1.26	2.78	1.32
Feels Inferior	2.93	1.06	2.73	1.20	2.71	1.01	2.77	1.05	3.08	1.00	3.15	1.00
Low Frustration Tolerance	3.13	.95	2.73	1.23	2.74	1.07	2.78	1.14	3.17	1.10	3.23	1.14
Psychotic Symptoms	1.24	.57	1.30	.75	1.20	.51	1.17	.52	1.19	.56	1.20	.56
Fired From Past Jobs	2.09	1.11	2.04	1.30	1.85	1.10	1.82	1.06	2.08	1.16	2.17	1.18
Needs Attention	3.09	.97	2.63	1.10	2.67	1.02	2.71	1.01	2.94	.99	2.93	.97
Acts Out	2.62	1.21	2.14	1.06	2.24	1.14	2.17	1.07	2.57	1.21	2.57	1.26
Histrionic	1.77	.76	1.48	.75	1.76	1.03	1.81	1.04	1.94	1.04	1.93	1.03
Self-Indulgent	2.77	1.07	2.50	1.04	2.56	1.12	2.43	1.11	2.54	1.12	2.55	1.18
Depressed	3.30	1.00	2.70	.99	2.60	1.02	2.79	1.06	3.22	1.05	3.40	.99
Grandiose	2.21	1.30	1.93	1.14	2.03	1.16	1.98	1.14	1.97	1.09	1.96	1.09
Cynical	2.57	1.28	2.21	1.18	2.24	1.12	2.21	1.10	2.62	1.23	2.65	1.30
Sociopathic	1.77	1.05	2.00	1.13	1.68	.94	1.58	.82	1.73	.92	1.72	.95
Agitated	2.64	.97	2.13	.86	2.13	1.06	2.05	.95	2.60	1.09	2.57	1.09
Marital Problems	2.88	1.62	2.00	1.44	2.33	1.57	2.28	1.53	2.70	1.63	2.65	1.62
Absence of Deep Emotions	2.30	1.21	1.79	1.15	2.07	1.11	2.02	1.10	2.09	1.24	2.09	1.27
Uncomfortable Dealing with Emotions	2.89	1.20	2.62	1.12	2.79	1.14	2.86	1.20	2.96	1.28	2.99	1.31
Sad	2.87	.92	2.43	.82	2.41	.95	2.54	1.01	2.94	1.00	3.04	.97
Self-Degrading	2.15	.93	1.87	1.07	1.84	.95	1.92	.96	2.30	1.08	2.31	1.03
Unable to Express Negative Feelings	2.19	1.10	1.93	.91	2.10	1.09	2.16	1.09	2.17	1.11	2.14	1.11
Concrete in Thinking	2.26	1.01	2.27	1.08	2.06	1.03	2.20	1.06	2.20	1.03	2.25	1.05
Unable to See Own Limitations	2.49	1.12	2.37	1.19	2.24	1.12	2.23	1.13	2.36	1.12	2.34	1.14
Power-Oriented	2.57	1.16	2.20	1.16	2.37	1.07	2.23	1.03	2.28	1.11	2.25	1.14
Grouchy	2.36	1.03	1.86	.95	2.02	.97	2.07	1.01	2.36	1.06	2.41	1.09
Overbearing in Relationships	2.70	1.26	2.11	.99	2.28	1.10	2.14	1.05	2.37	1.15	2.39	1.11
Uncertain About Career	3.24	1.42	2.85	1.08	2.95	1.29	3.17	1.28	3.30	1.28	3.43	1.25
Likable	3.23	.79	2.83	.83	3.19	.76	3.25	.75	3.11	.81	3.12	.80
Procrastinator	2.41	1.11	2.21	1.13	2.35	1.10	2.42	1.08	2.48	1.15	2.54	1.15

	Supplementary Scales *(continued)*											
	APS		O-H		Do		Re		MDS		PK	
	Mean	SD	Mean	SD	Mean	SD	Mean	SD	Mean	SD	Mean	SD
Negative Feelings Toward Opposite Sex	2.27	1.27	1.96	1.18	1.88	1.01	1.91	1.00	2.16	1.17	2.20	1.20
Defensive	2.91	1.10	2.69	1.17	2.61	1.12	2.61	1.22	2.72	1.16	2.73	1.21
Empathetic	2.15	.78	2.00	.80	2.24	.72	2.32	.74	2.30	.80	2.29	.80
Perfectionistic	2.63	1.16	2.45	.99	2.47	1.11	2.54	1.11	2.50	1.12	2.55	1.14
Judgmental	2.81	1.23	2.73	.98	2.60	1.08	2.58	1.04	2.73	1.14	2.76	1.17
Copes Well with Stress	2.04	.59	2.30	.79	2.26	.64	2.19	.71	1.97	.64	1.94	.64
Moody	2.81	.95	2.31	.89	2.40	.99	2.48	1.04	2.82	1.01	2.84	1.02
Selfish	2.53	.97	2.10	1.05	2.41	1.04	2.28	1.06	2.30	1.02	2.25	1.03
Gives Up Easily	2.22	.89	1.93	1.12	1.89	.89	1.96	.96	2.24	.98	2.30	.99
Physical Symptoms in Response to Stress	2.13	1.18	1.78	1.05	1.73	.97	1.96	1.24	2.18	1.19	2.27	1.22
Blames Family For Difficulties	2.62	1.33	2.21	1.45	2.10	1.29	2.11	1.29	2.55	1.33	2.62	1.32
Bored	2.40	1.21	2.20	1.16	2.17	1.10	2.31	1.18	2.42	1.12	2.48	1.15
Idealistic	2.34	1.03	2.10	.82	2.23	1.06	2.35	1.08	2.35	1.08	2.38	1.07
Difficulty Establishing Therapeutic Rapport	2.13	1.06	2.27	1.11	2.15	1.06	2.10	1.01	2.08	1.03	2.06	1.08
Daydreams	1.71	.78	1.79	.83	1.72	.81	1.86	.93	1.82	.97	1.89	1.01
Concerned About Status	2.57	1.21	2.21	.98	2.50	1.05	2.57	1.07	2.41	1.12	2.43	1.13
Creates Good First Impression	2.66	.96	2.43	.97	2.78	1.00	2.83	.91	2.49	.94	2.47	.91
Complains of Sleep Disturbance	2.27	1.25	1.64	.99	1.81	1.05	2.07	1.19	2.46	1.26	2.67	1.29
Has Temper Tantrums	2.42	.99	1.96	1.26	2.12	1.16	1.99	1.09	2.40	1.20	2.42	1.23
Overreactive	2.64	.94	2.33	1.06	2.36	1.15	2.44	1.20	2.76	1.05	2.81	1.09
High Aspirations	2.46	1.17	2.33	1.06	2.70	1.19	2.72	1.14	2.52	1.13	2.51	1.17
Feels Hopeless	2.55	1.12	2.00	.83	2.11	1.05	2.21	1.10	2.73	1.13	2.88	1.13
Keeps Others at a Distance	3.15	1.17	2.73	1.11	2.88	1.14	2.84	1.17	3.05	1.23	3.04	1.26
Argumentative	2.43	1.14	2.03	1.10	2.18	1.07	2.08	1.04	2.38	1.12	2.34	1.10
Paranoid Features	2.00	1.22	2.07	1.20	1.74	1.07	1.74	.97	1.91	1.06	2.00	1.09
Restless	2.70	1.21	2.37	1.10	2.30	1.12	2.32	1.14	2.64	1.14	2.70	1.16
Pessimistic	2.79	1.08	2.50	1.01	2.44	1.03	2.48	1.14	2.93	1.13	3.03	1.11
Feels Like a Failure	3.02	1.05	2.34	.77	2.50	1.01	2.53	1.06	2.99	1.14	3.10	1.09
Hallucinations	1.09	.28	1.21	.62	1.08	.35	1.06	.33	1.09	.35	1.10	.37
Restricted Affect	2.23	1.13	2.20	1.27	2.12	1.17	2.21	1.16	2.26	1.26	2.26	1.29
Impatient	2.81	1.15	2.37	1.07	2.59	1.12	2.58	1.10	2.80	1.12	2.76	1.15
Assertive	2.43	.83	2.33	.84	2.49	.82	2.39	.87	2.36	.85	2.33	.85
Modest	2.43	.77	2.14	.88	2.35	.80	2.41	.82	2.37	.84	2.41	.82
Self-Doubting	2.83	.87	2.55	.99	2.65	.99	2.81	1.03	3.06	.92	3.13	.89
Deceptive	2.11	.91	2.14	1.13	2.08	1.03	2.01	1.03	1.94	.96	1.95	1.02
Feels That Life is a Strain	2.79	1.06	2.69	.97	2.59	1.07	2.68	1.14	3.12	1.09	3.21	1.08
Physically Abusive	1.74	.96	1.72	1.28	1.46	.90	1.31	.74	1.65	1.01	1.71	1.05
Feels Rejected	3.31	1.40	2.64	1.34	2.57	1.29	2.78	1.29	3.21	1.21	3.23	1.24

Does Not Get Along with Coworkers	1.88	.93	1.79	.98	1.67	.99	1.60	.87	2.11	1.10	2.07	1.13
Uses Projection	2.69	1.12	2.41	1.30	2.42	1.09	2.29	1.13	2.53	1.18	2.51	1.18
Complains of Fatigue	2.15	1.11	1.90	1.23	1.94	1.12	2.12	1.28	2.34	1.31	2.50	1.35
Uses Rationalization	2.72	1.12	2.97	1.10	2.91	1.02	2.80	1.05	2.77	1.10	2.76	1.13
Critical of Others	2.68	1.14	2.40	1.10	2.51	1.14	2.42	1.07	2.65	1.16	2.71	1.20
Egocentric	2.63	1.08	2.59	1.12	2.69	1.17	2.59	1.16	2.62	1.17	2.60	1.22
Overevaluates Own Worth	2.02	.99	1.97	1.00	2.00	1.07	1.92	1.03	2.06	1.11	2.05	1.12
Optimistic	2.17	.92	2.20	.89	2.28	.80	2.25	.82	2.00	.79	1.93	.69
Psychologically Immature	2.83	1.19	2.79	1.18	2.72	1.18	2.76	1.19	2.85	1.14	2.94	1.20
Poor Judgment	3.15	1.02	3.03	1.27	2.90	1.10	2.76	1.14	2.92	1.20	2.98	1.24
Low Sex Drive	1.55	.72	1.52	1.08	1.65	1.09	1.77	1.19	1.79	1.11	1.84	1.13
Feels Mistreated	2.98	1.09	2.71	1.27	2.70	1.21	2.72	1.20	3.07	1.09	3.07	1.12
Overly Sensitive to Criticism	2.85	1.11	2.55	1.12	2.72	1.07	2.83	1.10	3.20	1.08	3.22	1.12
Sentimental	2.30	1.05	2.03	.94	2.15	.97	2.33	.97	2.32	1.00	2.40	1.01
Sexual Preoccupation	1.97	1.07	1.55	1.10	1.82	1.20	1.80	1.13	1.86	1.20	1.81	1.18
Accelerated Speech	1.60	.88	1.53	.97	1.49	.82	1.54	.90	1.47	.81	1.46	.80
Concerns About Homosexuality	1.26	.72	1.14	.47	1.23	.76	1.28	.87	1.47	1.09	1.47	1.09
Many Specific Fears	1.59	.90	1.64	.91	1.55	.82	1.63	.92	1.83	1.02	1.86	1.03
Passive in Relationships	2.11	1.08	2.52	1.27	2.30	1.15	2.44	1.12	2.26	1.07	2.32	1.06
Negative Attitudes Toward Therapy	1.77	.94	2.00	1.02	1.87	.94	1.86	.94	1.81	1.00	1.83	1.02
Guilt-Prone	2.53	.97	2.17	.93	2.24	1.09	2.48	1.16	2.55	1.11	2.63	1.12
Nervous	3.02	.82	2.61	1.10	2.59	.98	2.79	1.02	3.03	.95	3.15	.94
Obsessive	2.76	1.08	2.48	1.09	2.42	1.11	2.53	1.11	2.82	1.18	2.89	1.15
Shy	2.34	1.18	2.52	1.12	2.33	1.10	2.39	1.13	2.40	1.21	2.44	1.21
Uses Intellectualization	2.70	1.27	2.48	1.24	2.65	1.18	2.56	1.22	2.57	1.25	2.55	1.24
Has Many Interests	2.43	1.00	2.21	.83	2.55	.98	2.50	.96	2.26	1.01	2.26	1.01
Difficulty Making Decisions	2.89	1.02	2.61	1.07	2.52	1.05	2.69	1.11	2.93	1.09	3.01	1.05
Indirect Expression of Hostility	2.78	1.07	2.64	1.19	2.62	1.18	2.61	1.22	2.81	1.14	2.77	1.14
Poor Reality Testing	1.87	.77	1.66	.81	1.52	.73	1.48	.68	1.66	.86	1.71	.88
Angry	3.15	1.10	2.86	1.30	2.67	1.19	2.58	1.14	3.18	1.14	3.18	1.19
Eccentric	1.93	1.16	1.79	1.20	1.85	1.11	1.90	1.22	1.93	1.21	1.97	1.27
Emotional Lability	2.45	1.04	2.14	1.01	2.04	1.02	2.03	1.08	2.32	1.04	2.34	1.09
Dislikes Change	2.49	.99	2.48	1.05	2.50	.98	2.51	1.03	2.67	1.03	2.75	1.01
Believes Cannot Be Helped	1.72	.99	1.62	.85	1.62	.87	1.67	.83	1.89	1.02	1.93	1.03
Reliable Informant	3.30	.93	2.93	.96	3.23	.98	3.24	.96	3.19	.91	3.18	.94
Ignores Problems	2.32	.98	2.45	.87	2.40	.97	2.32	1.05	2.25	1.00	2.27	1.01
Ruminates	3.07	1.00	2.79	1.01	2.77	1.08	2.86	1.15	3.21	1.06	3.32	1.01
Excitable	2.61	.91	2.45	.95	2.36	1.03	2.33	1.05	2.60	1.02	2.60	1.03
Conforming	2.28	.95	2.39	.88	2.49	.87	2.54	.93	2.31	.87	2.37	.89
Ineffective at Dealing with Problems	2.93	.99	2.90	.98	2.82	.95	2.87	1.03	3.03	1.05	3.08	1.08
Introverted	2.28	1.07	2.48	1.21	2.30	1.12	2.40	1.12	2.53	1.17	2.60	1.15
Superficial Relationships	2.84	1.16	2.61	1.29	2.60	1.17	2.53	1.19	2.72	1.25	2.63	1.20

	Supplementary Scales *(continued)*											
	APS		O-H		Do		Re		MDS		PK	
	Mean	SD	Mean	SD	Mean	SD	Mean	SD	Mean	SD	Mean	SD
Impulsive	2.64	1.19	2.79	1.17	2.63	1.13	2.50	1.14	2.68	1.24	2.69	1.28
Stereotypic Feminine Behavior	1.23	.48	1.41	.91	1.35	.69	1.39	.71	1.31	.70	1.32	.67
Stubborn	2.96	1.14	2.79	1.10	2.71	1.15	2.65	1.10	2.88	1.12	2.83	1.14
Hostile Toward Therapist	1.38	.71	1.55	1.02	1.42	.77	1.48	.82	1.46	.72	1.46	.73
Difficult to Motivate	2.09	1.02	2.41	1.18	2.34	1.14	2.18	1.07	2.24	.98	2.23	1.03
Suicidal Ideations	1.57	.86	1.18	.48	1.30	.68	1.40	.76	1.78	1.02	1.90	1.03
Familial Discord	3.17	1.31	2.41	1.34	2.65	1.39	2.58	1.37	3.08	1.36	3.13	1.40
Dogmatic	2.30	1.14	2.11	.96	2.18	1.02	2.14	1.02	2.34	1.14	2.34	1.15

Table L-3. Means and standard deviations for continuous extra-test characteristics (men and women combined): Two- and three-point code types

Extra-test Characteristics	Total Sample		Valid MMPI-2		WNL		Code Types			
							12/21		13/31	
	Mean	SD	Mean	SD	Mean	SD	Mean	SD	Mean	SD
Intake Information	(n = 2,482)		(n = 1,020)		(n = 90)		(n = 15)		(n = 20)	
Axis IV diagnosis	2.94	.94	2.93	.95	2.80	.93	2.87	1.19	2.95	.97
Axis V - Current Level of Functioning	60.87	11.08	62.58	9.97	68.23	9.30	59.40	9.29	64.85	8.17
Number of Arrests	1.09	3.60	.86	2.41	.98	1.73	.18	.40	.25	.44
Mental Status	(n = 2,482)		(n = 1,020)		(n = 90)		(n = 15)		(n = 20)	
Anxiety During Interview	2.40	.69	2.39	.68	2.25	.64	2.57	.85	2.25	.64
Depression During Interview	2.37	.75	2.35	.73	1.94	.65	2.79	.70	2.15	.49
Activity Level During Interview	2.99	.44	2.98	.39	2.99	.33	3.00	.55	2.90	.55
Speech During Interview	2.97	.44	2.97	.39	2.94	.39	2.79	.43	3.05	.39
SCL-90-R Scales	(n = 1,266)		(n = 1,008)		(n = 90)		(n = 15)		(n = 20)	
Somatization	1.18	.91	1.09	.85	.31	.28	1.88	.69	1.59	.83
Obsessive-Compulsive	1.51	.99	1.39	.92	.52	.42	1.67	.59	1.15	.88
Interpersonal Sensitivity	1.47	.98	1.36	.92	.56	.49	1.42	.67	.68	.46
Depression	1.79	1.02	1.71	.99	.64	.48	1.92	.71	1.12	.62
Anxiety	1.35	1.01	1.23	.95	.31	.30	1.39	.57	.91	.70
Hostility	1.30	1.06	1.19	1.00	.42	.43	.82	.84	.55	.63
Phobic Anxiety	.82	.94	.68	.82	.10	.20	.89	.67	.43	.53
Paranoid Ideation	1.43	1.02	1.30	.94	.59	.54	1.33	.88	.52	.44
Psychoticism	1.00	.85	.87	.72	.26	.31	.84	.47	.44	.38
Initial SCL-90 Analogue	(n = 1,184)		(n = 697)		(n = 73)		(n = 10)		(n = 17)	
Somatization	2.14	2.59	2.12	2.60	.84	1.26	3.10	2.18	4.47	3.24
Obsessive-Compulsive	2.75	2.63	2.85	2.66	2.05	2.23	2.50	2.51	2.82	2.32
Interpersonal Sensitivity	4.64	2.64	4.58	2.67	3.41	2.62	4.20	2.66	4.76	2.93
Depression	4.21	2.59	4.20	2.62	2.56	1.99	5.30	2.71	4.41	2.32
Anxiety	4.25	2.60	4.19	2.66	2.75	2.15	4.40	2.72	4.71	2.57
Hostility	3.01	2.67	2.95	2.67	2.23	2.42	2.90	2.85	2.71	2.39
Phobic Anxiety	1.20	2.07	1.16	2.06	.55	1.04	.00	.00	1.94	2.90
Paranoid Ideation	1.32	2.03	1.19	1.94	.59	1.15	.80	1.48	1.29	2.31
Psychoticism	.72	1.53	.67	1.55	.37	.89	.10	.32	1.06	2.11

Table L-3. Means and standard deviations for continuous extra-test characteristics (men and women combined): Two- and three-point code types *(continued)*

Extra-test Characteristics	Total Sample		Valid MMPI-2		WNL		Code Types 12/21		Code Types 13/31	
	Mean	SD	Mean	SD	Mean	SD	Mean	SD	Mean	SD
Patient Description Form Scales	(n = 1,183)		(n = 699)		(n = 73)		(n = 10)		(n = 17)	
Angry Resentment	2.70	.93	2.67	.91	2.20	.82	2.35	1.11	2.67	.78
Critical/Argumentative	2.36	.88	2.36	.87	1.94	.71	2.12	.93	2.33	.68
Narcissistic	2.11	.87	2.15	.88	2.05	.71	1.79	.61	2.10	.89
Defensive	2.54	.86	2.52	.84	2.25	.77	2.43	.67	2.57	.87
Histrionic	2.40	.82	2.38	.83	1.92	.72	2.03	.72	2.54	.77
Aggressive	1.97	.85	1.95	.81	1.81	.70	1.72	.68	1.86	.72
Insecure	2.94	.88	2.93	.87	2.37	.85	2.48	.84	2.83	.90
Anxious	2.88	.81	2.81	.82	2.21	.72	2.73	.88	3.11	.92
Pessimistic	2.23	.90	2.20	.90	1.65	.75	2.05	.90	2.03	.76
Depressed	2.43	.84	2.41	.86	1.66	.61	2.35	.84	2.42	.71
Achievement-Oriented	2.47	.74	2.57	.74	2.97	.60	2.31	.79	2.59	.74
Passive-Submissive	2.40	.92	2.42	.90	2.14	.82	2.53	1.01	2.58	.97
Introverted	2.44	.99	2.42	.96	2.14	.87	2.33	1.05	2.14	.81
Emotionally Controlled	2.32	.92	2.36	.92	2.23	.88	2.06	.88	2.56	.82
Antisocial	2.19	.89	2.17	.86	2.08	.70	1.63	.56	1.87	.57
Negative Treatment Attitudes	1.97	.77	1.96	.75	1.83	.75	1.75	.64	1.93	.76
Somatic Symptoms	2.03	1.03	2.02	1.03	1.39	.57	2.52	.77	2.86	1.27
Psychotic Symptoms	1.33	.59	1.27	.54	1.10	.25	1.10	.14	1.38	.80
Family Problems	2.87	1.14	2.85	1.14	2.39	1.14	2.48	1.18	2.98	1.01
Obsessive-Compulsive	2.60	.83	2.60	.84	2.25	.76	2.37	.65	2.70	.73
Stereotypic Masculine Interests	2.00	1.15	2.02	1.16	2.31	1.24	2.00	1.27	2.21	1.20
Procrastinates	2.18	.91	2.19	.91	1.96	.89	2.19	.73	2.22	1.13
Suspicious	2.48	.96	2.44	.94	2.00	.75	2.23	.83	2.45	.99
Agitated	2.14	.81	2.11	.83	1.68	.70	1.83	.65	2.31	.82
Work Problems	1.74	.90	1.70	.84	1.33	.50	1.33	.41	1.42	.57
Patient Description Form Items	(n = 1,183)		(n = 699)		(n = 73)		(n = 10)		(n = 17)	
Anxious	3.20	.96	3.15	.99	2.58	.85	3.00	1.05	3.24	1.03
Problems with Authority Figures	2.83	1.23	2.81	1.22	2.47	.98	2.70	1.06	2.59	1.33
Has Insight Into Own Problems	2.51	.90	2.58	.89	2.79	.85	2.60	.84	2.47	.94
Fears Losing Control	3.09	1.11	3.11	1.12	2.84	1.12	2.80	.92	3.47	1.23
Extroverted	2.42	1.01	2.54	1.01	2.71	.96	2.70	.82	2.94	.97
Uses Repression	2.71	1.09	2.74	1.05	2.82	.90	2.60	.70	3.18	1.01

Submissive	2.50	1.04	2.52	1.02	2.29	.94	2.60	1.07	2.59	1.18
Difficulty Concentrating	2.69	1.12	2.59	1.12	1.81	.91	2.60	1.17	2.71	1.45
Rigid	2.54	1.08	2.54	1.08	2.18	1.07	2.60	.84	3.06	.83
Overly Compliant	2.03	1.00	2.07	.99	1.86	.83	2.30	1.25	2.25	1.06
Whiny	1.95	1.02	1.90	1.00	1.50	.86	1.70	.67	2.12	1.05
Feels Overwhelmed	3.28	1.13	3.22	1.14	2.49	1.14	3.40	1.26	3.47	1.18
Manipulative	2.40	1.15	2.42	1.13	2.32	1.05	2.30	1.06	2.41	1.00
Difficulty Trusting Others	3.18	1.17	3.17	1.17	2.72	1.10	2.70	1.16	3.24	1.03
Insensitive to Others	2.02	1.01	2.02	1.00	2.01	.87	1.80	.79	1.82	.73
Stereotypic Masculine Behavior	1.97	1.18	1.97	1.18	2.31	1.26	1.90	1.20	2.12	1.27
Harbors Grudges	2.60	1.11	2.56	1.08	2.33	.98	2.50	.85	2.50	.82
Evasive	2.33	1.12	2.31	1.11	2.18	1.14	2.00	.67	2.18	1.13
Disoriented	1.32	.68	1.27	.64	1.11	.36	1.10	.32	1.35	.86
Energetic	2.45	.98	2.51	.96	3.00	.86	2.10	.74	2.59	1.33
Lonely	2.78	1.17	2.78	1.15	2.18	1.10	2.80	1.03	2.35	1.06
Family Lacks Love	2.74	1.30	2.72	1.28	2.12	1.17	2.10	1.10	2.81	1.22
Worrier	3.23	1.07	3.20	1.08	2.51	.98	3.10	1.20	3.65	1.00
Narcissistic	2.24	1.14	2.27	1.15	2.12	1.06	1.80	.63	2.18	1.07
Tearful	1.96	1.11	1.95	1.11	1.47	.83	1.90	.99	2.24	1.25
Provocative	1.68	.94	1.72	.96	1.55	.82	1.60	.84	1.53	.80
Moralistic	2.34	1.01	2.38	1.02	2.24	.92	2.70	.95	3.12	.99
Socially Awkward	2.55	1.13	2.51	1.09	2.17	1.07	2.10	.99	2.29	1.05
Hostile	2.25	1.15	2.22	1.13	1.89	1.02	2.00	1.15	2.06	1.20
Overcontrolled	2.43	1.17	2.53	1.16	2.48	1.07	2.10	.99	2.94	.97
Resistant to Interpretations	2.19	1.04	2.19	1.00	2.06	1.01	2.00	.94	2.44	1.09
Antisocial Behavior	2.00	1.15	1.96	1.10	2.04	1.04	1.50	.97	1.59	.80
Sarcastic	1.87	1.00	1.89	1.01	1.57	.92	1.70	1.06	1.76	.90
Rejects Traditional Gender Role	1.58	.96	1.61	.97	1.42	.79	1.30	.48	1.71	.85
Feels Gets Raw Deal From Life	2.85	1.20	2.81	1.18	2.09	1.02	2.60	1.35	2.71	1.21
Acute Psychological Turmoil	2.91	1.07	2.89	1.08	2.11	.87	2.80	1.14	2.94	1.09
Does Not Complete Projects	2.24	1.14	2.19	1.13	1.74	1.00	2.00	.67	2.07	1.22
Uncomfortable with Opposite Sex	2.10	1.12	2.11	1.11	1.75	.95	1.90	.88	2.07	1.07
Preoccupied with Health Problems	2.01	1.27	1.97	1.25	1.32	.65	2.70	.95	2.88	1.58
Work-Oriented	2.74	1.11	2.88	1.10	3.44	.96	2.80	1.48	2.71	1.26
Resents Family Members	2.85	1.28	2.85	1.27	2.31	1.21	2.50	1.51	3.00	1.21
Demanding of Attention	2.46	1.12	2.46	1.10	2.06	.99	2.10	.88	2.53	.87
Passive	2.46	1.10	2.46	1.06	2.10	1.00	2.40	.97	2.71	1.26
Self-Punishing	2.46	1.14	2.47	1.14	1.82	.86	2.20	1.03	2.35	1.22
Needs to Achieve	2.64	1.03	2.73	1.04	2.95	.87	2.40	1.17	2.59	1.06

Table L-3. Means and standard deviations for continuous extra-test characteristics (men and women combined): Two- and three-point code types *(continued)*

Extra-test Characteristics	Total Sample		Valid MMPI-2		WNL		Code Types 12/21		13/31	
	Mean	SD	Mean	SD	Mean	SD	Mean	SD	Mean	SD
Needs to Be with Others	2.97	1.00	3.01	.98	2.93	.77	2.60	.84	3.00	1.00
Irritable	2.60	1.05	2.55	1.05	1.95	.88	2.20	.92	2.47	.72
Self-Defeating	3.05	1.13	3.05	1.12	2.66	1.08	2.40	.97	2.81	1.22
Delusional Thinking	1.35	.78	1.30	.74	1.11	.36	1.10	.32	1.59	1.06
Self-Reliant	2.61	.93	2.73	.91	3.19	.83	2.70	1.25	3.00	1.00
Aggressive	2.20	1.06	2.21	1.04	2.19	1.04	2.20	1.23	2.29	1.10
Competitive	2.22	.99	2.34	1.01	2.71	.84	2.10	1.29	2.29	.92
Suspicious	2.47	1.16	2.41	1.14	2.04	1.04	2.30	1.06	2.24	1.20
Compulsive	2.34	1.15	2.38	1.16	2.33	1.16	2.20	.79	2.50	1.15
Dependable	2.95	.93	3.05	.90	3.23	.74	3.30	.67	3.13	1.09
Multiple Somatic Complaints	1.89	1.23	1.88	1.20	1.27	.56	2.70	.95	3.24	1.48
Complains of Lack of Time	1.91	1.09	1.99	1.11	1.94	1.04	1.90	.88	2.35	1.50
Poor Work Performance	1.89	1.07	1.84	1.02	1.39	.70	1.50	.55	1.77	1.17
Insecure	3.40	1.00	3.36	1.00	2.83	1.06	2.60	.97	3.06	1.20
Discusses Problems Openly	3.07	.90	3.13	.87	3.15	.88	3.40	.70	3.24	.75
Sexually Adjusted	2.49	.86	2.53	.85	2.79	.64	2.80	.63	2.54	.78
Exaggerated Need for Affection	2.27	1.10	2.28	1.10	1.88	.92	1.90	.88	2.41	1.00
Resentful	2.94	1.12	2.94	1.12	2.55	1.08	2.80	1.23	2.88	.99
Uses Denial	2.77	1.14	2.77	1.13	2.57	.99	2.60	.84	2.82	1.07
Hypochondriacal	1.63	.97	1.62	.96	1.25	.55	1.80	.79	2.35	1.41
Communicates Effectively	3.00	.89	3.07	.86	3.15	.78	3.00	.67	3.00	.94
Has Many Nightmares	1.85	1.08	1.79	1.02	1.45	.80	1.71	.76	2.00	.94
Stormy Interpersonal Relationships	3.06	1.19	3.04	1.22	2.72	1.23	2.60	.84	2.50	1.26
Feigns Remorse When in Trouble	1.82	.98	1.82	.97	1.73	.85	1.44	.53	1.73	.80
Stereotypic Masculine Interests	2.03	1.19	2.06	1.21	2.31	1.29	2.10	1.37	2.29	1.21
Guarded	2.62	1.18	2.59	1.17	2.37	1.03	2.30	1.25	2.47	1.18
Feels Inferior	3.09	1.10	3.05	1.09	2.36	1.00	2.50	.97	2.76	1.30
Low Frustration Tolerance	2.91	1.11	2.85	1.10	2.30	.85	2.70	.82	2.41	.87
Psychotic Symptoms	1.28	.72	1.21	.64	1.04	.20	1.10	.32	1.31	.79
Fired From Past Jobs	1.77	1.11	1.70	1.05	1.48	.78	1.17	.41	1.50	.76
Needs Attention	2.91	1.02	2.88	1.01	2.49	.92	2.80	.92	2.65	1.06
Acts Out	2.36	1.16	2.31	1.13	2.08	.97	1.70	.82	2.12	1.11
Histrionic	2.01	1.11	2.01	1.10	1.48	.82	1.60	.97	2.47	.94
Self-Indulgent	2.34	1.11	2.36	1.10	2.43	1.00	2.00	.82	2.06	.97

Depressed	3.07	1.06	3.05	1.08	2.17	.80	3.10	.99	3.24	.90
Grandiose	1.73	.97	1.76	.98	1.62	.85	1.40	.70	1.71	1.10
Cynical	2.22	1.13	2.22	1.11	1.63	.82	2.20	1.23	1.94	.97
Sociopathic	1.53	.85	1.52	.83	1.38	.67	1.20	.63	1.47	.72
Agitated	2.38	1.06	2.28	1.07	1.75	.93	2.10	.99	2.29	1.21
Marital Problems	2.51	1.56	2.57	1.58	2.44	1.48	2.20	1.62	2.31	1.54
Absence of Deep Emotions	2.01	1.13	2.03	1.12	1.84	.96	1.60	.84	2.24	1.09
Uncomfortable Dealing with Emotions	2.83	1.17	2.86	1.16	2.72	1.08	2.40	1.17	2.88	1.17
Sad	2.85	1.07	2.84	1.05	2.03	.89	2.80	1.14	2.88	.93
Self-Degrading	2.31	1.13	2.31	1.12	1.65	.89	2.00	.94	2.12	.78
Unable to Express Negative Feelings	2.16	1.11	2.22	1.11	2.16	1.00	2.10	.99	2.47	1.01
Concrete in Thinking	2.33	1.11	2.24	1.06	1.92	.95	2.80	.92	2.35	1.00
Unable to See Own Limitations	2.25	1.08	2.22	1.07	1.86	.86	2.10	1.10	2.12	1.22
Power-Oriented	1.95	1.00	2.04	1.03	2.23	1.01	1.90	.99	2.06	1.03
Grouchy	2.11	1.01	2.09	1.00	1.57	.68	1.89	1.05	2.18	.81
Overbearing in Relationships	2.10	1.09	2.13	1.10	1.94	1.11	2.00	.87	2.35	1.06
Uncertain About Career	3.00	1.32	2.99	1.31	2.81	1.29	2.33	1.00	2.65	1.17
Likable	3.21	.83	3.27	.81	3.38	.62	3.10	.57	3.35	.70
Procrastinator	2.43	1.12	2.42	1.08	2.17	1.04	2.56	1.24	2.31	1.20
Negative Feelings Toward Opposite Sex	2.28	1.19	2.31	1.19	1.89	1.00	1.60	.70	2.15	1.41
Defensive	2.64	1.14	2.67	1.12	2.28	.91	2.50	.97	2.76	1.25
Empathetic	2.47	.81	2.51	.78	2.37	.76	2.40	.52	2.88	.70
Perfectionistic	2.38	1.13	2.48	1.14	2.32	1.01	1.89	.60	2.71	1.16
Judgmental	2.51	1.07	2.55	1.04	2.22	.84	2.30	1.06	2.82	.95
Copes Well with Stress	2.02	.74	2.11	.72	2.53	.61	2.60	.84	2.24	.75
Moody	2.68	1.02	2.66	1.00	2.23	.84	2.67	.87	2.65	.70
Selfish	2.06	.99	2.08	.98	2.06	.89	1.80	.79	2.00	.97
Gives Up Easily	2.21	1.06	2.13	1.01	1.66	.92	1.90	.99	1.76	.75
Physical Symptoms in Response to Stress	2.15	1.20	2.13	1.20	1.51	.82	2.50	.85	2.94	1.43
Blames Family For Difficulties	2.61	1.30	2.58	1.31	2.08	1.23	2.70	1.34	2.59	1.28
Bored	2.24	1.10	2.25	1.11	1.80	.99	2.10	1.10	2.47	1.18
Idealistic	2.31	1.05	2.38	1.04	2.19	.98	2.10	.88	2.71	1.10
Difficulty Establishing Therapeutic Rapport	1.98	1.03	1.95	.99	1.89	1.01	1.70	.82	2.00	1.22
Daydreams	1.89	.98	1.89	.97	1.61	.72	1.88	.83	2.14	1.29
Concerned About Status	2.26	1.09	2.31	1.10	2.47	.99	2.00	1.05	2.65	1.32
Creates Good First Impression	2.72	.97	2.81	.96	3.19	.87	2.80	.92	3.06	1.09
Complains of Sleep Disturbance	2.49	1.27	2.43	1.26	1.50	.86	2.50	1.27	2.88	1.02
Has Temper Tantrums	2.19	1.17	2.11	1.12	1.83	1.02	1.67	.71	1.63	.81
Overreactive	2.69	1.13	2.64	1.13	2.07	1.09	1.80	.92	2.88	1.05
High Aspirations	2.41	1.10	2.52	1.11	2.80	1.00	2.20	1.03	2.47	1.18
Feels Hopeless	2.56	1.14	2.51	1.17	1.61	.91	2.20	.92	2.24	1.03
Keeps Others at a Distance	2.86	1.17	2.86	1.15	2.57	1.06	2.60	1.17	2.88	.93

Table L-3. Means and standard deviations for continuous extra-test characteristics (men and women combined): Two- and three-point code types *(continued)*

Extra-test Characteristics	Total Sample Mean	Total Sample SD	Valid MMPI-2 Mean	Valid MMPI-2 SD	WNL Mean	WNL SD	Code Types 12/21 Mean	Code Types 12/21 SD	Code Types 13/31 Mean	Code Types 13/31 SD
Argumentative	2.17	1.07	2.16	1.05	1.78	.86	1.70	.82	2.35	1.00
Paranoid Features	1.78	1.04	1.74	1.01	1.27	.65	1.70	.82	1.88	1.17
Restless	2.43	1.08	2.45	1.11	1.86	.87	2.20	.92	2.71	1.10
Pessimistic	2.65	1.10	2.60	1.10	1.81	.86	2.60	1.35	2.35	.86
Feels Like a Failure	2.84	1.13	2.81	1.12	2.04	1.00	2.30	1.06	2.71	.85
Hallucinations	1.16	.57	1.10	.46	1.01	.12	1.00	.00	1.18	.53
Restricted Affect	2.14	1.16	2.16	1.16	1.92	1.07	2.10	1.10	2.29	.99
Impatient	2.61	1.07	2.59	1.06	2.36	.98	2.10	.57	2.71	1.05
Assertive	2.18	.84	2.27	.86	2.35	.66	2.60	.97	2.29	.92
Modest	2.50	.85	2.50	.83	2.42	.76	2.90	.74	2.62	.89
Self-Doubting	3.03	1.03	3.00	1.02	2.48	.97	2.90	.99	2.75	1.13
Deceptive	1.92	.99	1.92	.97	1.94	1.08	1.60	.70	1.88	.93
Feels That Life is a Strain	2.98	1.10	2.94	1.10	2.13	1.03	3.20	1.23	3.12	1.05
Physically Abusive	1.46	.90	1.40	.80	1.24	.55	1.10	.32	1.18	.39
Feels Rejected	3.03	1.18	3.02	1.20	2.44	1.23	2.56	1.13	2.88	1.02
Does Not Get Along with Coworkers	1.70	.97	1.72	.95	1.39	.71	1.14	.38	1.38	.65
Uses Projection	2.39	1.10	2.38	1.09	2.07	.97	2.20	.92	2.41	.94
Complains of Fatigue	2.40	1.26	2.39	1.29	1.54	.86	2.90	1.20	2.88	1.41
Uses Rationalization	2.67	1.08	2.74	1.07	2.74	1.02	2.30	.82	2.76	1.15
Critical of Others	2.45	1.10	2.47	1.07	2.21	.92	2.50	1.35	2.41	.80
Egocentric	2.34	1.12	2.35	1.11	2.14	.95	1.90	.88	2.41	1.18
Overevaluates Own Worth	1.75	.97	1.79	.98	1.54	.67	1.30	.67	2.00	1.00
Optimistic	2.05	.80	2.13	.80	2.35	.81	2.20	.92	2.47	1.01
Psychologically Immature	2.83	1.20	2.80	1.18	2.56	1.06	2.50	1.18	2.76	1.39
Poor Judgment	2.90	1.19	2.85	1.16	2.68	1.05	1.80	.63	2.59	1.00
Low Sex Drive	1.97	1.18	1.95	1.16	1.52	.98	2.17	1.17	3.00	1.53
Feels Mistreated	3.03	1.17	3.01	1.16	2.46	1.12	2.80	1.14	3.29	1.05
Overly Sensitive to Criticism	3.06	1.15	3.03	1.14	2.37	1.08	3.00	1.12	3.24	1.20
Sentimental	2.48	1.02	2.48	1.03	2.15	.97	2.40	.84	2.75	1.06
Sexual Preoccupation	1.63	1.03	1.65	1.05	1.61	1.13	1.20	.63	1.54	.66
Accelerated Speech	1.61	.93	1.60	.91	1.40	.76	1.20	.42	1.94	.90
Concerns About Homosexuality	1.22	.74	1.21	.73	1.07	.41	1.00	.00	1.00	.00
Many Specific Fears	1.94	1.05	1.90	1.04	1.48	.83	1.60	1.07	2.25	1.29
Passive in Relationships	2.58	1.17	2.60	1.17	2.22	1.14	2.67	1.00	2.59	1.18

Negative Attitudes Toward Therapy	1.73	.95	1.73	.91	1.58	.84	1.70	.95	1.76	.97
Guilt-Prone	2.74	1.21	2.79	1.18	2.41	1.18	2.30	.82	3.06	1.39
Nervous	2.91	.98	2.86	1.00	2.28	.86	2.70	.82	3.12	.99
Obsessive	2.45	1.15	2.49	1.15	1.97	.95	2.20	.79	2.71	1.05
Shy	2.37	1.15	2.36	1.11	2.07	.94	2.56	1.42	2.06	.90
Uses Intellectualization	2.31	1.14	2.42	1.13	2.36	1.05	2.00	.67	2.71	1.21
Has Many Interests	2.28	.94	2.39	.96	2.88	.95	2.20	.79	2.41	.71
Difficulty Making Decisions	2.85	1.07	2.83	1.09	2.38	1.02	2.50	1.08	2.50	1.37
Indirect Expression of Hostility	2.69	1.15	2.75	1.15	2.54	1.32	2.40	.97	3.06	1.09
Poor Reality Testing	1.62	.92	1.56	.89	1.27	.61	1.20	.42	1.53	1.01
Angry	2.97	1.18	2.94	1.18	2.39	1.10	2.40	1.35	3.00	.87
Eccentric	1.73	1.04	1.74	1.06	1.36	.68	1.60	.84	1.76	1.09
Emotional Lability	2.34	1.08	2.30	1.07	1.71	.80	2.10	.88	2.35	1.11
Dislikes Change	2.63	1.00	2.60	1.00	2.25	.92	2.56	.73	2.76	1.03
Believes Cannot Be Helped	1.81	.95	1.80	.94	1.47	.90	1.50	.71	1.71	.77
Reliable Informant	3.18	.97	3.25	.93	3.31	.80	3.00	1.15	3.35	1.06
Ignores Problems	2.35	1.03	2.40	1.03	2.32	1.05	2.10	.99	2.18	.88
Ruminates	2.89	1.08	2.86	1.07	2.18	1.01	2.80	1.23	2.88	.99
Excitable	2.57	1.03	2.52	1.03	2.03	.87	2.20	.92	2.88	1.05
Conforming	2.49	.93	2.52	.92	2.54	.81	2.50	.53	2.82	.95
Ineffective at Dealing with Problems	3.02	1.06	2.98	1.03	2.48	.92	2.40	1.07	3.18	1.19
Introverted	2.38	1.12	2.38	1.09	2.17	.93	2.20	1.03	2.06	.90
Superficial Relationships	2.62	1.12	2.66	1.12	2.26	1.08	1.90	.88	2.71	.99
Impulsive	2.69	1.21	2.69	1.19	2.58	1.12	2.10	.74	2.31	.95
Stereotypic Feminine Behavior	2.18	1.23	2.21	1.22	1.86	1.05	2.30	1.34	2.41	1.18
Stubborn	2.72	1.06	2.71	1.06	2.35	1.07	2.40	.97	3.06	.97
Hostile Toward Therapist	1.36	.69	1.37	.70	1.24	.62	1.20	.42	1.47	.62
Difficult to Motivate	2.21	1.12	2.14	1.06	1.83	.99	1.80	.79	2.12	1.05
Suicidal Ideations	1.60	.91	1.60	.91	1.10	.34	1.60	1.07	1.35	.61
Familial Discord	3.19	1.32	3.18	1.33	2.83	1.48	2.60	1.43	3.41	1.37
Dogmatic	2.06	.99	2.11	1.01	1.87	.91	2.10	.74	2.35	1.06

Code Types (*continued*)

	23/32		24/42		26/62		27/72		34/43		46/64		48/84		49/94	
	Mean	SD	Mean	SD	Mean	SD	Mean	SD	Mean	SD	Mean	SD	Mean	SD	Mean	SD
Intake Information	(n = 20)		(n = 30)		(n = 15)		(n = 35)		(n = 15)		(n = 35)		(n = 16)		(n = 12)	
Axis IV diagnosis	3.47	1.17	2.59	.91	3.21	.97	2.75	.98	2.79	.89	2.82	.83	3.07	.88	2.83	.83
Axis V - Current Level of Functioning	54.84	15.50	65.13	5.46	59.64	11.34	60.94	11.74	65.53	4.85	62.03	6.74	58.80	9.14	62.70	8.97
Number of Arrests	.13	.52	.90	2.21	.27	.46	.28	.63	1.53	2.20	.67	1.11	1.71	2.64	1.40	3.06
Mental Status	(n = 20)		(n = 30)		(n = 15)		(n = 35)		(n = 15)		(n = 35)		(n = 16)		(n = 12)	
Anxiety During Interview	2.74	.99	2.23	.57	2.27	.80	2.44	.66	2.13	.35	2.59	.74	2.25	.68	2.50	.90
Depression During Interview	2.94	.87	2.13	.51	2.67	.82	2.64	.70	2.27	.46	2.41	.66	2.31	.60	2.50	.90
Activity Level During Interview	3.00	.49	3.03	.41	2.87	.52	2.97	.39	3.07	.26	2.97	.30	2.81	.40	3.08	.29
Speech During Interview	3.11	.47	3.10	.48	2.73	.46	2.91	.38	3.07	.26	3.09	.45	2.69	.48	3.00	.43
SCL-90-R Scales	(n = 20)		(n = 30)		(n = 15)		(n = 35)		(n = 15)		(n = 35)		(n = 16)		(n = 11)	
Somatization	1.70	.73	.77	.56	1.23	.80	.98	.61	1.01	.57	.74	.51	1.16	.52	.35	.32
Obsessive-Compulsive	2.02	.83	1.21	.51	1.71	.76	1.70	.85	1.19	.77	1.21	.56	1.70	.79	.81	.53
Interpersonal Sensitivity	1.40	.91	1.41	.52	2.10	.85	1.50	.71	1.23	.80	1.60	.83	1.34	.78	.97	.72
Depression	2.25	.63	1.99	.69	2.54	.82	2.14	.81	1.69	.83	1.82	.87	2.02	1.03	1.08	.61
Anxiety	1.77	.91	1.07	.57	1.49	.77	1.43	.72	1.17	.71	1.07	.79	1.32	.75	.70	.54
Hostility	1.48	.80	1.18	.64	1.80	1.06	1.28	.94	1.09	.77	1.19	.94	1.25	.99	.97	.85
Phobic Anxiety	.74	.86	.43	.50	1.01	.91	.88	.87	.32	.53	.40	.53	.65	.68	.26	.34
Paranoid Ideation	1.42	.90	1.47	.71	2.03	.95	.94	.67	1.16	.96	1.83	.98	1.58	.77	1.24	.83
Psychoticism	.95	.61	.82	.51	1.15	.54	.79	.50	.68	.48	.90	.61	1.20	.70	.47	.45
Initial SCL-90 Analogue	(n = 13)		(n = 15)		(n = 10)		(n = 24)		(n = 12)		(n = 25)		(n = 10)		(n = 9)	
Somatization	3.54	3.10	1.50	1.87	2.20	2.44	2.22	2.95	2.27	2.00	1.08	2.48	2.00	2.16	1.56	2.01
Obsessive-Compulsive	2.08	2.10	3.71	3.07	2.50	2.80	3.09	3.12	2.67	2.53	2.08	2.60	3.90	2.56	1.67	2.06
Interpersonal Sensitivity	4.31	2.43	5.79	2.78	4.40	3.20	4.38	2.50	5.00	2.52	4.08	2.69	5.80	2.25	5.67	3.04
Depression	4.85	2.54	5.64	2.62	4.40	2.17	5.04	2.56	3.92	2.61	3.80	2.22	5.67	2.35	4.22	3.23
Anxiety	3.92	2.40	5.07	2.53	4.30	3.37	4.13	2.94	3.67	2.02	3.48	2.99	5.70	2.36	3.33	1.94
Hostility	2.08	2.29	2.64	2.41	1.80	2.53	2.22	2.50	3.36	2.46	3.64	2.96	4.70	2.75	4.56	3.13
Phobic Anxiety	.15	.55	1.57	2.44	1.00	1.70	1.17	2.15	1.27	1.56	.60	2.12	1.70	1.77	.44	.73
Paranoid Ideation	.15	.38	.93	1.49	.60	.84	.96	1.72	1.64	2.38	.72	1.90	3.20	3.22	3.44	3.13
Psychoticism	.08	.28	.07	.27	.20	.63	.57	1.56	1.00	1.34	.20	.65	2.50	3.27	1.87	3.00
Patient Description Form Scales	(n = 13)		(n = 15)		(n = 10)		(n = 24)		(n = 12)		(n = 25)		(n = 10)		(n = 9)	
Angry Resentment	2.52	.81	3.04	.80	2.61	.97	2.28	1.00	3.00	.79	2.76	.91	2.62	.68	2.86	.99
Critical/Argumentative	2.21	.60	2.69	.80	2.37	1.09	2.14	.96	2.56	.68	2.42	.96	2.15	.64	2.81	1.09
Narcissistic	1.64	.50	2.29	.73	2.13	.89	1.76	.97	2.27	.86	2.08	.87	2.69	1.16	2.74	1.03

Defensive	2.35	.76	2.77	.94	2.50	1.04	2.36	.94	2.33	.87	2.34	.82	2.76	.94	2.94	.61
Histrionic	2.48	.71	2.80	.79	2.28	.84	2.24	.89	2.72	.80	2.22	.79	2.69	1.06	2.72	.87
Aggressive	1.77	.51	2.19	.72	1.70	.57	1.79	.90	1.98	.56	2.01	.93	2.46	.70	2.43	1.30
Insecure	3.30	.93	3.42	.78	2.77	.95	2.95	.74	2.99	.61	2.63	.88	3.33	.52	3.02	1.07
Anxious	2.90	.86	3.18	.69	2.56	.72	2.86	.79	2.83	.71	2.43	.81	2.94	.55	2.42	.85
Pessimistic	2.42	1.00	2.54	.80	2.10	.74	2.11	1.00	2.14	.55	2.02	.92	2.38	.83	2.28	.83
Depressed	2.85	.97	2.60	.74	2.52	.67	2.71	.74	2.31	.60	2.22	.79	2.95	1.00	2.19	.84
Achievement-Oriented	2.53	.61	2.54	.79	2.29	.85	2.26	.70	2.99	.56	2.73	.82	2.36	.76	2.38	.99
Passive-Submissive	2.71	.95	2.66	.94	2.68	1.11	2.54	.73	2.25	.75	1.81	.70	2.72	.65	2.44	1.34
Introverted	2.11	.86	2.74	1.34	2.60	1.18	2.68	.90	2.27	.66	1.78	.80	2.37	.79	2.26	.66
Emotionally Controlled	2.17	.78	2.53	.80	2.02	1.04	2.47	1.05	2.42	.85	1.92	.86	2.42	.86	2.47	1.10
Antisocial	1.77	.42	2.45	.78	2.02	.97	1.90	.92	2.43	.63	2.17	1.11	2.65	1.05	2.83	.89
Negative Treatment Attitudes	1.78	.60	1.96	.61	2.03	.79	1.94	.82	1.86	.62	1.69	.71	1.80	.53	2.31	.90
Somatic Symptoms	2.65	1.33	1.71	.76	2.20	.84	2.19	1.10	2.02	1.12	1.57	.79	2.04	.71	1.44	.51
Psychotic Symptoms	1.11	.23	1.26	.41	1.24	.40	1.37	.83	1.34	.41	1.19	.52	1.71	.71	1.69	1.25
Family Problems	2.79	1.07	3.23	1.02	2.28	.93	2.31	1.11	2.95	1.05	3.26	1.16	3.22	.93	3.50	1.18
Obsessive-Compulsive	2.50	.62	2.82	.83	2.44	.89	2.39	.86	2.63	.68	2.27	.85	2.43	.70	2.43	.94
Stereotypic Masculine Interests	1.65	1.13	1.86	1.05	1.55	.76	1.64	.74	1.54	.84	2.20	1.21	2.00	1.08	1.89	1.54
Procrastinates	2.07	.92	2.22	.83	2.19	.71	2.11	.88	2.13	.87	1.88	.69	1.83	.46	2.33	.82
Suspicious	1.94	.58	2.69	.81	2.50	1.15	2.33	.93	2.67	1.04	2.39	.97	3.10	1.10	2.81	1.14
Agitated	2.05	1.01	2.31	.74	2.10	.74	2.21	.92	2.25	.89	1.83	.76	2.63	.94	2.15	.97
Work Problems	1.11	.17	1.61	.90	1.89	.69	1.83	1.19	1.87	1.15	1.67	.56	1.83	.24	1.89	1.02
Patient Description Form Items	(n = 13)		(n = 15)		(n = 10)		(n = 24)		(n = 12)		(n = 25)		(n = 10)		(n = 9)	
Anxious	3.31	1.11	3.80	.86	3.20	1.03	3.21	1.06	2.92	.67	2.80	1.08	3.50	.85	2.33	.71
Problems with Authority Figures	2.17	1.11	3.40	1.40	2.70	1.42	2.43	1.16	2.83	1.27	2.72	1.14	2.90	.99	3.67	.87
Has Insight Into Own Problems	2.62	1.19	2.73	.96	2.50	.53	2.63	.97	3.33	1.23	2.60	1.12	2.50	.85	2.22	.97
Fears Losing Control	3.23	1.17	3.60	1.12	2.50	.71	2.91	1.08	3.17	.83	2.56	1.12	3.44	.73	2.88	.99
Extroverted	2.92	1.04	2.73	1.33	2.60	.84	1.96	1.00	3.08	.79	2.83	1.20	2.60	1.26	2.89	1.36
Uses Repression	2.50	.90	2.93	1.14	2.89	1.05	2.75	1.11	2.67	.78	2.08	1.14	3.67	1.00	3.11	1.27
Submissive	2.46	.88	2.67	1.23	2.80	1.14	2.74	1.05	2.33	.89	2.00	.96	2.89	.93	2.67	1.50
Difficulty Concentrating	2.33	.98	2.79	.97	2.40	1.07	2.57	1.12	2.58	1.16	2.24	1.13	2.80	.63	2.56	.88
Rigid	2.38	.96	2.47	.83	2.50	1.43	2.52	.85	2.25	.75	2.28	1.06	2.60	1.07	3.00	1.32
Overly Compliant	2.54	.88	2.33	1.05	2.60	1.26	2.05	.86	2.00	1.21	1.68	.75	2.40	1.07	1.89	1.17
Whiny	1.54	.78	1.93	.88	2.10	1.10	2.00	1.18	2.00	.95	1.60	.82	1.90	.99	2.56	1.42
Feels Overwhelmed	3.54	1.13	3.73	1.10	3.00	1.33	3.33	1.09	3.33	.89	2.72	1.02	3.50	.97	3.00	1.41
Manipulative	1.83	.72	2.40	.91	2.10	.88	2.05	1.09	2.42	1.00	2.64	1.29	3.10	1.45	3.33	1.22
Difficulty Trusting Others	2.77	.93	3.87	1.19	2.90	1.37	3.04	1.16	3.17	1.11	3.20	1.29	3.60	.97	3.44	1.01
Insensitive to Others	1.54	.66	1.93	.70	2.30	.95	1.82	1.14	2.00	.95	2.12	1.27	2.30	1.25	2.22	1.09
Stereotypic Masculine Behavior	1.62	.96	1.87	.99	1.50	.71	1.52	.85	1.50	.80	2.08	1.25	1.90	1.10	1.89	1.54
Harbors Grudges	2.17	.72	2.80	1.01	2.60	.97	2.17	1.15	2.83	1.11	2.92	1.35	2.67	1.12	2.67	1.41
Evasive	2.00	.71	2.60	1.12	2.10	.88	2.13	1.19	2.08	1.00	2.16	1.21	2.60	1.58	2.78	.97

	Code Types (continued)															
	23/32		24/42		26/62		27/72		34/43		46/64		48/84		49/94	
	Mean	SD	Mean	SD	Mean	SD	Mean	SD	Mean	SD	Mean	SD	Mean	SD	Mean	SD
Disoriented	1.15	.38	1.27	.80	1.10	.32	1.46	1.02	1.42	.90	1.12	.33	1.70	.82	1.67	1.32
Energetic	2.15	.80	2.87	1.25	2.00	.94	1.96	.88	3.08	.90	2.88	1.24	2.60	1.26	2.56	.88
Lonely	3.08	1.04	3.00	1.41	2.90	1.45	2.46	1.14	3.00	1.04	2.60	1.08	3.30	1.06	2.78	.83
Family Lacks Love	2.46	1.20	3.33	1.11	2.10	1.10	2.39	1.27	3.00	1.28	3.21	1.32	3.50	1.08	3.33	1.22
Worrier	3.54	1.13	3.80	.94	3.20	1.14	3.25	1.07	3.50	.80	2.72	1.17	3.50	.97	2.78	1.09
Narcissistic	1.69	.85	2.33	.90	2.20	1.23	1.67	.92	2.42	1.31	2.36	1.15	2.90	1.45	3.44	1.24
Tearful	2.46	1.39	2.00	1.07	1.70	.82	2.33	1.24	1.82	.75	2.04	1.17	2.30	1.34	1.89	1.54
Provocative	1.31	.63	2.00	1.00	1.50	.71	1.63	1.06	1.50	.67	1.75	1.15	1.80	.92	2.22	1.64
Moralistic	2.75	.97	2.40	1.12	2.60	1.35	2.13	.69	2.10	.99	2.28	1.24	1.90	.88	2.33	1.22
Socially Awkward	2.08	.79	2.93	1.49	2.70	1.34	2.54	1.02	2.42	.79	2.08	1.00	2.90	.88	2.33	1.12
Hostile	1.69	.63	2.40	1.24	2.00	1.15	1.92	.93	2.33	1.15	2.24	1.20	2.40	1.35	2.56	1.42
Overcontrolled	2.58	1.16	2.93	1.16	2.20	1.03	2.61	1.16	2.42	1.08	2.08	1.19	2.30	1.25	2.11	1.27
Resistant to Interpretations	2.08	.86	2.13	.99	2.40	1.07	2.22	1.09	2.17	1.03	1.96	.93	1.90	.99	2.67	1.22
Antisocial Behavior	1.25	.45	1.93	.88	2.00	1.15	1.48	.90	2.08	.90	2.24	1.42	2.60	1.58	2.44	1.01
Sarcastic	1.62	.77	2.13	1.06	2.00	1.15	1.83	1.07	1.92	1.08	2.12	1.13	1.70	.82	2.22	1.39
Rejects Traditional Gender Role	1.46	.52	2.20	1.15	1.60	.97	1.39	.58	1.92	1.44	1.44	.71	1.90	1.29	2.11	1.69
Feels Gets Raw Deal From Life	2.92	1.32	3.20	.94	3.00	1.33	2.43	1.20	2.75	1.22	2.92	1.19	3.20	1.23	3.11	1.05
Acute Psychological Turmoil	3.23	1.01	3.20	1.21	2.70	1.16	2.96	1.12	2.92	1.16	2.64	.91	3.70	.82	2.56	.88
Does Not Complete Projects	2.00	.94	2.10	.88	2.22	.97	2.00	.97	2.13	1.13	2.10	.97	2.29	.76	2.88	1.13
Uncomfortable with Opposite Sex	1.92	1.00	2.86	1.29	2.30	1.42	2.10	1.09	2.00	.89	1.57	.73	2.00	.94	3.00	1.58
Preoccupied with Health Problems	2.77	1.64	1.53	.74	2.60	1.26	1.86	1.35	2.17	1.27	1.20	.50	1.90	.74	1.33	.71
Work-Oriented	2.77	.93	3.13	1.13	2.60	.97	2.48	.79	3.33	.65	3.16	1.31	2.50	.97	2.38	1.51
Resents Family Members	2.69	1.18	3.20	1.15	2.30	1.06	2.32	1.21	2.82	1.33	3.42	1.32	3.10	1.29	3.33	1.50
Demanding of Attention	2.54	1.27	2.80	1.01	2.60	1.17	2.29	1.19	2.92	1.00	2.44	1.16	3.00	1.25	3.11	1.54
Passive	2.69	.95	2.53	1.13	2.60	1.35	2.65	1.11	2.42	1.00	1.64	.64	2.50	1.08	2.67	1.66
Self-Punishing	2.92	1.00	2.87	1.30	2.50	.85	2.35	1.15	2.55	.82	2.09	1.16	2.60	.97	2.44	1.42
Needs to Achieve	2.75	1.06	2.79	1.12	2.30	.95	2.18	1.01	3.27	.79	2.96	1.24	2.60	1.07	2.75	1.16
Needs to Be with Others	3.46	.97	2.93	1.03	2.10	.99	2.83	1.05	3.42	.67	2.67	.96	3.10	.57	3.00	1.12
Irritable	2.23	.83	2.93	.59	2.80	.92	2.58	.93	2.67	.98	2.44	1.12	2.50	1.18	2.56	1.24
Self-Defeating	3.00	1.08	3.40	.99	3.00	1.41	2.83	1.05	3.00	.95	2.80	1.22	3.60	1.35	3.56	1.13
Delusional Thinking	1.08	.28	1.20	.41	1.30	.67	1.25	.85	1.42	.67	1.21	.83	2.20	1.40	1.67	1.41
Self-Reliant	2.77	.60	2.53	.99	2.40	.84	2.54	.78	3.42	.90	2.79	1.02	2.60	.52	2.33	1.41
Aggressive	1.83	.72	2.40	.91	2.00	.82	1.87	.99	2.58	.79	2.52	1.36	2.30	.82	2.33	1.32
Competitive	2.09	1.04	2.38	.87	2.30	.95	1.92	.93	2.73	.79	2.68	1.14	2.22	.97	2.33	1.50
Suspicious	1.83	1.03	2.53	.83	2.90	1.29	2.33	1.13	3.00	1.28	2.40	1.19	3.00	1.41	2.44	1.42
Compulsive	2.17	.83	2.54	1.20	1.89	.93	2.20	1.28	2.73	1.19	2.18	1.33	2.80	.92	2.11	1.27
Dependable	3.08	1.04	3.13	.83	2.60	.84	2.87	.95	3.25	1.14	3.29	1.04	3.50	.71	2.25	1.28
Multiple Somatic Complaints	2.69	1.55	1.47	.74	2.30	1.25	1.82	1.33	1.92	.90	1.36	.91	1.90	.88	1.22	.44

Complains of Lack of Time	1.77	.93	2.14	1.23	2.00	.82	1.87	1.06	2.08	1.08	1.75	.99	1.50	.71	1.44	.73
Poor Work Performance	1.50	.76	1.70	1.06	1.75	.89	2.00	1.08	1.90	.74	1.70	1.02	1.50	.84	1.80	1.10
Insecure	3.38	1.04	3.93	.70	3.50	1.18	3.46	.93	3.17	.83	3.16	1.21	3.60	.97	3.33	1.00
Discusses Problems Openly	3.38	.87	3.33	.49	3.30	.67	2.96	.95	3.58	.90	3.08	1.00	3.60	.70	3.00	.87
Sexually Adjusted	2.75	1.14	2.50	.80	2.33	.71	2.39	.85	2.33	1.00	2.17	.72	2.56	.88	2.29	1.25
Exaggerated Need for Affection	2.17	.83	2.57	1.09	2.00	.87	2.26	1.10	2.42	1.16	2.23	1.19	2.70	1.25	2.67	1.00
Resentful	2.85	.99	3.33	.98	3.00	1.05	2.27	1.12	2.92	.90	3.00	1.22	3.00	.94	3.00	1.12
Uses Denial	2.92	1.04	2.93	1.10	2.60	1.26	2.83	1.13	2.42	1.08	2.60	1.38	3.10	1.29	3.67	.71
Hypochondriacal	1.85	.99	1.47	.74	1.80	1.03	1.64	1.09	1.75	1.14	1.24	.72	2.10	1.29	1.22	.44
Communicates Effectively	3.23	.83	3.20	.94	2.90	.57	2.88	.85	3.42	1.16	3.20	.96	3.30	.67	3.56	.73
Has Many Nightmares	1.67	.82	1.50	.76	1.71	.76	2.00	1.00	1.29	.49	1.38	.89	2.13	1.13	1.60	.89
Stormy Interpersonal Relationships	2.85	1.34	3.40	1.24	2.90	1.20	2.61	1.50	3.42	1.31	3.08	1.18	3.70	.95	3.67	1.41
Feigns Remorse When in Trouble	1.17	.39	2.08	1.04	1.60	.84	1.80	1.01	2.10	.99	1.91	1.19	2.40	1.26	2.00	1.12
Stereotypic Masculine Interests	1.69	1.32	1.93	1.21	1.60	.84	1.73	.83	1.58	.90	2.33	1.37	2.10	1.10	1.89	1.54
Guarded	2.00	1.00	2.67	1.18	2.50	1.27	2.46	1.35	2.58	1.16	2.60	1.29	2.60	1.17	2.89	.93
Feels Inferior	3.42	1.08	3.86	.95	3.00	1.49	3.00	1.06	2.92	.90	2.92	1.19	3.50	.85	3.25	1.28
Low Frustration Tolerance	2.69	.85	3.00	1.07	2.90	1.37	2.82	1.14	2.83	1.19	2.84	1.07	3.11	1.17	3.22	1.09
Psychotic Symptoms	1.08	.28	1.07	.26	1.20	.42	1.21	.66	1.50	1.00	1.21	.72	2.20	1.23	1.56	1.33
Fired From Past Jobs	1.00	.00	1.43	.79	1.50	.76	1.77	1.36	2.00	1.53	1.89	1.08	2.25	.96	1.60	.89
Needs Attention	3.08	.86	3.20	1.01	2.60	1.07	2.75	1.03	3.25	.87	2.63	1.10	3.20	.92	3.00	1.12
Acts Out	1.58	.67	2.93	1.33	2.20	1.23	2.09	1.34	2.58	.79	2.48	1.26	2.90	1.37	2.78	1.48
Histrionic	1.85	.80	2.87	1.06	2.20	.92	1.86	1.13	2.08	1.00	1.84	1.07	2.70	1.57	2.33	1.66
Self-Indulgent	1.92	.86	2.80	1.26	2.30	.95	1.78	1.04	2.50	.80	2.33	1.24	2.78	1.39	2.67	1.32
Depressed	3.31	1.18	3.40	.91	3.40	.97	3.50	.83	2.73	.79	2.92	.95	3.33	1.22	2.78	1.56
Grandiose	1.38	.65	2.00	.93	1.80	1.23	1.52	1.04	1.92	1.16	1.50	.78	2.40	.97	2.44	1.13
Cynical	2.00	.82	2.40	1.12	2.20	1.14	2.09	1.08	2.58	1.08	2.32	1.14	1.90	.57	2.78	1.39
Sociopathic	1.17	.39	1.60	.63	1.40	.70	1.27	.70	1.58	1.00	1.68	1.11	2.00	1.25	1.89	1.36
Agitated	2.15	1.14	2.60	.63	2.50	1.08	2.35	1.03	2.67	.98	2.12	.83	2.80	1.03	2.00	.87
Marital Problems	3.62	1.61	3.33	1.61	2.44	1.74	2.40	1.19	2.64	1.43	2.14	1.52	2.13	1.25	3.71	1.89
Absence of Deep Emotions	1.75	.97	2.13	.83	1.80	1.03	2.13	1.25	2.17	1.40	1.71	1.04	2.30	.82	2.22	1.48
Uncomfortable Dealing with Emotions	2.38	1.04	2.93	1.16	2.50	1.35	2.96	1.20	2.83	1.03	2.40	1.41	3.00	1.15	3.56	1.13
Sad	3.23	1.24	3.07	.96	2.60	.97	3.00	.88	2.92	.79	2.72	1.14	3.10	1.20	2.89	1.05
Self-Degrading	2.54	1.39	2.87	1.06	2.20	.92	2.70	1.11	2.33	.98	2.20	1.00	2.40	.70	2.22	1.39
Unable to Express Negative Feelings	2.08	.86	2.60	.99	1.70	1.16	2.23	1.07	2.42	1.00	1.88	.93	2.30	1.34	2.44	1.51
Concrete in Thinking	2.38	1.33	2.80	1.15	2.20	1.40	2.13	1.06	2.27	1.27	1.88	1.05	2.60	.97	2.33	1.32
Unable to See Own Limitations	2.23	1.01	2.53	.99	2.30	1.25	2.23	1.41	1.83	1.19	2.16	1.03	2.70	.95	2.00	.87
Power-Oriented	1.46	.78	1.93	1.00	1.70	1.25	1.77	.97	2.42	.90	2.28	1.17	2.50	1.18	2.71	1.25
Grouchy	2.00	.91	2.33	.72	2.20	1.23	1.96	.95	2.25	.87	2.00	.96	2.20	.92	2.33	1.00
Overbearing in Relationships	2.00	.71	2.50	.94	1.90	1.10	1.81	1.12	2.33	1.07	2.43	1.16	2.70	1.16	2.33	1.41
Uncertain About Career	2.92	1.38	2.62	1.12	2.70	1.25	2.96	1.43	2.83	1.27	2.68	1.18	3.50	1.18	2.78	1.56
Likable	3.62	.77	3.33	.98	3.00	.47	3.21	.78	3.67	1.07	3.24	1.09	3.30	.67	3.44	.53
Procrastinator	2.36	1.03	2.67	.98	2.22	.97	2.43	1.12	2.36	.81	1.82	.85	2.38	.74	3.00	1.41

	Code Types *(continued)*															
	23/32		24/42		26/62		27/72		34/43		46/64		48/84		49/94	
	Mean	SD	Mean	SD	Mean	SD	Mean	SD	Mean	SD	Mean	SD	Mean	SD	Mean	SD
Negative Feelings Toward Opposite Sex	2.31	1.25	2.87	1.25	2.60	1.07	2.14	1.28	2.33	1.15	2.04	.98	2.44	1.42	3.11	1.69
Defensive	2.33	1.07	3.20	1.15	2.80	1.23	2.67	1.20	2.73	1.10	2.64	1.15	2.80	1.23	3.33	1.12
Empathetic	3.33	.65	2.73	.70	2.30	.48	2.39	.84	2.58	.90	2.44	.87	2.50	.85	2.33	1.00
Perfectionistic	2.18	.98	2.93	1.33	2.33	1.12	2.32	1.17	2.90	.99	2.42	1.14	2.10	.74	2.50	1.41
Judgmental	2.23	1.09	2.93	1.10	2.50	1.27	2.17	1.03	2.42	.90	2.28	1.14	2.30	1.06	2.67	1.41
Copes Well with Stress	2.00	.71	1.80	.77	1.80	.79	1.87	.74	2.42	.67	2.28	.54	1.90	.88	2.11	.78
Moody	2.42	.90	2.93	.96	2.40	1.07	2.67	1.24	2.83	1.03	2.40	1.00	3.00	.94	3.00	.87
Selfish	1.75	.75	2.36	1.01	1.80	.79	1.81	1.03	2.50	.90	1.96	1.00	2.50	1.18	2.89	1.36
Gives Up Easily	2.08	1.00	2.31	1.18	1.70	.82	2.35	.93	1.92	.90	1.67	.73	2.67	1.32	2.63	1.30
Physical Symptoms in Response to Stress	2.92	1.55	1.73	.80	2.10	1.10	2.52	1.25	2.00	1.25	1.92	1.18	1.89	1.05	1.67	.71
Blames Family For Difficulties	2.54	1.33	3.00	1.07	2.30	1.34	2.32	1.39	2.42	1.16	3.08	1.47	3.00	1.33	3.22	1.56
Bored	2.08	1.38	2.00	1.00	2.20	.63	2.33	1.13	2.45	1.13	1.67	.96	3.00	.94	2.67	1.32
Idealistic	2.83	.72	2.27	.96	1.90	.99	2.30	.92	2.33	1.30	1.88	.93	2.70	1.16	2.56	1.24
Difficulty Establishing Therapeutic Rapport	1.62	.65	2.00	.85	1.70	.82	2.12	1.08	2.17	1.11	1.72	1.02	1.70	1.06	2.22	1.09
Daydreams	1.67	.82	2.00	.87	1.56	.88	1.95	.91	1.67	.82	1.28	.57	2.63	1.06	2.00	1.00
Concerned About Status	2.00	.85	2.07	.83	2.30	1.16	2.35	1.03	2.18	1.25	2.29	1.33	2.50	1.08	2.75	1.49
Creates Good First Impression	3.77	.73	3.07	.96	2.20	.79	2.63	.92	3.33	.89	2.72	1.17	2.90	.99	2.33	.71
Complains of Sleep Disturbance	3.08	1.55	2.33	1.05	3.10	1.10	2.96	1.12	2.10	1.66	2.00	1.09	3.11	1.05	2.00	.82
Has Temper Tantrums	1.92	1.00	2.47	1.19	1.80	.92	2.27	1.32	2.17	1.03	1.92	1.10	2.63	1.19	2.44	1.42
Overreactive	2.92	1.19	3.27	1.03	2.50	1.18	2.52	.99	2.92	1.16	2.48	1.08	3.30	1.34	2.89	1.05
High Aspirations	2.67	.89	2.43	.94	2.30	1.34	2.32	.99	3.09	.94	2.88	1.13	2.40	1.07	2.25	1.04
Feels Hopeless	2.67	1.23	2.80	1.01	2.90	1.29	2.75	.99	2.33	.65	2.24	.97	3.30	1.49	2.78	1.39
Keeps Others at a Distance	2.69	.95	3.33	1.23	2.90	1.29	2.83	1.17	2.75	.97	2.57	1.16	3.10	.88	3.00	1.41
Argumentative	2.38	.96	2.87	1.19	2.20	1.23	1.88	.99	2.42	1.24	2.32	1.22	2.20	1.14	2.56	1.33
Paranoid Features	1.15	.38	1.67	.82	1.70	1.06	1.62	.92	1.83	1.11	1.56	1.00	2.70	1.49	2.56	1.33
Restless	2.23	1.17	2.67	1.18	2.30	.82	2.52	1.04	2.33	.98	2.00	1.18	3.00	.94	2.78	1.39
Pessimistic	2.62	.96	2.80	.86	2.30	.82	2.54	1.18	2.58	.79	2.40	1.15	2.89	1.05	2.78	1.09
Feels Like a Failure	3.58	1.16	3.14	.66	2.70	1.16	2.83	1.13	2.92	1.08	2.48	1.00	3.50	.85	3.13	1.13
Hallucinations	1.00	.00	1.00	.00	1.00	.00	1.13	.61	1.09	.30	1.08	.41	1.70	1.06	1.33	1.00
Restricted Affect	2.08	.95	2.07	1.16	1.90	1.37	2.43	1.27	2.25	1.06	1.72	1.02	2.20	1.14	2.00	1.32
Impatient	2.38	.96	2.93	1.03	2.30	.95	2.18	.96	2.83	.94	2.42	1.10	3.10	1.20	2.78	1.20
Assertive	2.25	.75	2.43	.85	2.20	.63	1.79	.78	2.83	.72	2.68	.99	2.40	.70	2.44	1.13
Modest	2.75	.75	2.64	.74	2.22	.83	2.57	.73	2.67	.78	2.04	.95	2.90	.57	2.22	.97
Self-Doubting	3.31	.85	3.21	1.05	2.70	.95	3.04	.81	3.33	.65	2.60	.91	3.40	.70	3.25	1.28
Deceptive	1.42	.51	2.07	1.00	1.50	.53	1.77	.92	1.92	.79	1.88	1.13	2.80	1.40	2.25	1.16
Feels That Life is a Strain	3.46	1.51	3.36	.93	3.00	1.15	2.79	.93	3.00	.60	2.72	1.02	3.40	1.07	2.87	.83
Physically Abusive	1.33	.65	1.46	.78	1.10	.32	1.43	.81	1.10	.32	1.35	.83	1.89	1.17	1.71	1.50
Feels Rejected	3.31	1.03	3.43	1.09	2.70	1.25	2.92	1.10	3.25	1.14	2.88	1.13	3.80	.92	3.22	1.20

Does Not Get Along with Coworkers	1.22	.44	1.57	.79	2.22	1.30	1.89	1.08	1.43	.79	1.53	.61	1.50	.58	2.25	1.50
Uses Projection	2.31	.95	2.54	.97	2.40	.97	2.14	1.21	2.91	1.14	2.63	1.35	2.50	1.18	2.33	1.41
Complains of Fatigue	3.00	1.47	2.50	1.09	2.20	1.14	2.87	1.25	2.33	1.23	2.00	1.14	2.50	1.27	1.78	.83
Uses Rationalization	2.92	.95	2.93	.83	2.60	1.17	2.54	1.14	2.75	1.06	2.64	1.25	3.20	1.32	3.22	1.39
Critical of Others	1.85	.69	2.86	1.03	2.60	1.43	2.18	1.10	2.33	.98	2.60	1.04	2.60	.97	3.00	1.12
Egocentric	1.92	.64	2.57	.85	2.50	1.43	2.00	1.20	2.42	1.08	2.52	1.08	3.10	1.45	2.78	1.39
Overevaluates Own Worth	1.17	.39	2.21	1.05	2.00	1.63	1.39	.72	2.00	1.13	1.75	.90	2.30	1.16	2.11	1.36
Optimistic	2.00	.41	2.07	.73	2.00	.82	1.92	.83	2.33	.49	2.08	.95	2.30	.82	2.00	1.00
Psychologically Immature	2.75	1.14	3.00	1.30	3.00	1.33	2.63	1.28	2.58	1.24	2.36	1.08	3.10	1.37	3.56	1.42
Poor Judgment	2.62	.77	3.14	1.03	2.50	1.18	2.42	1.25	2.92	1.08	2.72	1.34	3.60	1.35	3.89	1.27
Low Sex Drive	3.00	1.53	2.56	1.13	2.40	.89	2.27	.96	1.57	1.13	1.69	1.03	1.67	1.21	1.67	.82
Feels Mistreated	3.38	1.45	3.50	1.09	2.90	1.52	2.71	1.20	3.42	1.00	3.16	1.07	2.90	.88	3.22	1.48
Overly Sensitive to Criticism	3.25	1.42	3.36	1.08	3.00	1.41	3.00	1.13	2.92	1.16	3.08	1.18	2.89	1.27	3.67	1.22
Sentimental	3.00	1.25	2.75	.97	2.11	.93	2.18	1.01	2.27	1.01	2.32	1.18	2.78	1.30	3.00	1.29
Sexual Preoccupation	1.18	.60	2.18	1.17	1.38	1.06	1.33	.58	2.17	1.17	1.54	.97	2.33	1.75	2.63	1.41
Accelerated Speech	1.77	1.09	1.77	1.09	1.50	.97	1.62	1.13	1.75	1.06	1.40	.76	2.10	1.29	1.67	1.12
Concerns About Homosexuality	1.00	.00	1.18	.60	1.22	.67	1.14	.47	1.22	.67	1.00	.00	1.17	.41	1.33	1.00
Many Specific Fears	1.91	1.14	1.93	1.00	1.78	.67	2.00	1.17	1.70	1.06	1.68	1.11	2.22	1.30	1.63	1.19
Passive in Relationships	3.00	1.35	3.07	1.14	2.70	1.16	2.95	.74	2.25	.97	1.88	1.08	2.70	.95	2.56	1.74
Negative Attitudes Toward Therapy	1.46	.78	1.79	.70	1.80	1.14	1.87	.97	1.33	.49	1.48	.82	1.70	.95	1.89	.78
Guilt-Prone	3.25	1.42	3.21	1.37	2.60	1.26	3.00	1.02	3.00	1.26	2.20	1.32	3.10	.88	2.50	1.20
Nervous	2.85	1.14	2.93	.92	2.60	.97	3.04	1.16	2.55	.69	2.40	1.04	2.78	.44	2.33	.71
Obsessive	2.33	1.44	2.86	1.10	2.44	1.33	2.22	1.28	2.36	1.03	2.37	1.21	2.89	1.17	1.78	1.09
Shy	2.08	1.12	2.86	1.41	2.60	1.26	2.63	1.01	2.36	.81	1.58	.88	2.22	1.09	2.00	.87
Uses Intellectualization	2.31	1.03	2.29	.99	2.30	1.06	2.17	1.19	3.27	1.42	2.20	1.08	2.00	1.12	3.63	.52
Has Many Interests	2.58	.67	2.50	.94	2.10	.99	2.00	1.00	2.40	.84	2.42	1.06	2.38	1.19	2.13	.99
Difficulty Making Decisions	3.08	.51	2.92	1.08	2.80	1.03	2.75	1.15	3.00	1.26	2.26	1.01	2.63	.74	2.78	1.20
Indirect Expression of Hostility	2.67	1.07	2.86	.86	2.70	1.06	2.52	1.12	3.27	1.19	2.61	1.23	3.22	1.30	2.89	1.36
Poor Reality Testing	1.23	.44	1.71	.99	1.60	.84	1.78	1.38	1.82	.75	1.33	.76	1.78	.83	2.22	1.64
Angry	2.85	1.07	3.36	1.15	2.70	.95	2.83	1.43	3.27	1.10	3.04	1.17	3.00	1.22	3.33	1.66
Eccentric	1.31	.63	1.86	1.03	1.90	1.20	1.57	.90	1.90	1.10	1.40	.65	2.11	1.45	2.67	1.32
Emotional Lability	2.69	1.03	2.93	1.14	1.80	.63	2.35	1.23	2.91	.94	2.16	1.11	2.78	1.20	2.78	1.09
Dislikes Change	2.92	.90	2.85	1.07	2.40	1.07	2.32	.84	2.33	.71	2.30	.93	2.50	.93	2.88	.99
Believes Cannot Be Helped	2.23	1.17	2.29	.91	1.90	.88	1.74	1.01	1.64	.81	1.64	.91	1.89	.78	1.78	.83
Reliable Informant	3.69	.85	3.21	.70	3.10	.99	3.13	1.19	4.00	.67	3.21	.93	3.13	.83	3.00	1.00
Ignores Problems	2.46	1.20	2.50	.85	2.40	1.07	2.12	1.03	2.09	.83	2.04	1.30	2.89	1.05	2.78	1.56
Ruminates	3.15	.99	3.43	1.02	3.00	1.05	2.71	.81	3.00	1.00	2.64	1.11	2.44	1.13	2.67	.87
Excitable	3.00	1.00	3.00	1.18	2.60	1.26	2.22	1.13	3.00	1.10	2.60	1.08	2.67	1.22	2.44	1.33
Conforming	3.00	1.04	2.64	1.08	2.90	.99	2.63	.92	2.36	1.03	1.87	.74	2.88	.64	2.11	1.36
Ineffective at Dealing with Problems	3.23	1.01	3.00	.96	3.10	1.20	2.88	.99	2.82	.87	2.72	1.17	3.22	.83	3.50	1.20
Introverted	2.15	.99	2.50	1.51	2.50	1.18	2.88	.95	1.91	.83	1.75	.94	2.00	.71	2.44	1.42
Superficial Relationships	2.54	1.13	3.21	1.05	2.40	1.43	2.39	1.20	3.30	1.06	2.35	1.11	2.78	1.09	3.75	1.49

	Code Types *(continued)*															
	23/32		24/42		26/62		27/72		34/43		46/64		48/84		49/94	
	Mean	SD	Mean	SD	Mean	SD	Mean	SD	Mean	SD	Mean	SD	Mean	SD	Mean	SD
Impulsive	2.64	1.12	2.93	1.27	2.33	1.12	2.21	1.14	3.27	.79	2.42	1.35	3.22	1.09	4.00	1.22
Stereotypic Feminine Behavior	3.08	1.32	2.64	1.50	2.10	1.29	2.27	1.20	2.45	1.44	1.88	1.17	2.33	1.32	2.67	1.80
Stubborn	3.15	.90	3.07	1.07	2.40	1.26	2.32	1.09	2.91	1.04	2.72	1.14	2.78	.97	3.13	1.46
Hostile Toward Therapist	1.15	.55	1.50	.76	1.30	.67	1.38	.77	1.27	.47	1.24	.52	1.22	.44	1.78	.83
Difficult to Motivate	1.92	1.04	1.79	.70	2.60	1.17	2.37	1.13	1.91	.70	1.83	.92	1.89	1.05	2.56	1.59
Suicidal Ideations	1.69	.85	1.86	.95	1.40	.70	1.87	1.06	1.27	.65	1.40	.76	2.33	1.32	1.44	.73
Familial Discord	3.46	1.39	3.50	1.22	2.40	1.07	2.71	1.30	3.45	1.37	3.25	1.45	3.89	.93	4.11	.93
Dogmatic	2.08	1.00	2.29	.73	2.10	1.45	1.87	1.01	2.00	1.26	1.92	1.15	2.44	.88	2.33	1.32

	Code Types (continued)													
	68/86		78/87		123		247		278		468		478	
	Mean	SD	Mean	SD	Mean	SD	Mean	SD	Mean	SD	Mean	SD	Mean	SD
Intake Information	(n = 28)		(n = 20)		(n = 27)		(n = 17)		(n = 29)		(n = 20)		(n = 12)	
Axis IV diagnosis	3.07	.96	2.70	.66	3.12	1.28	2.69	1.08	3.15	.82	2.84	.83	3.25	1.14
Axis V - Current Level of Functioning	57.74	9.62	64.25	9.22	58.65	10.41	65.94	6.64	56.50	12.34	60.79	7.50	55.00	12.61
Number of Arrests	2.65	8.27	.26	.45	.17	.38	.40	.83	.31	.84	3.93	10.54	.64	.92
Mental Status	(n = 28)		(n = 20)		(n = 27)		(n = 17)		(n = 29)		(n = 20)		(n = 12)	
Anxiety During Interview	2.48	.70	2.40	.60	2.67	.83	2.00	.00	2.48	.57	2.35	.59	2.67	1.07
Depression During Interview	2.44	.80	2.20	.52	2.48	.58	2.25	.45	2.59	.63	2.40	.75	2.50	.90
Activity Level During Interview	2.89	.42	3.00	.32	2.93	.47	3.00	.00	2.90	.41	2.95	.22	2.92	.51
Speech During Interview	3.00	.27	2.90	.45	3.00	.55	3.00	.00	2.86	.44	2.90	.31	3.00	.60
SCL-90-R Scales	(n = 25)		(n = 20)		(n = 27)		(n = 17)		(n = 28)		(n = 20)		(n = 12)	
Somatization	1.53	.97	1.33	.72	2.02	.91	1.01	.53	1.46	.69	1.21	.61	1.04	.74
Obsessive-Compulsive	2.00	1.09	2.13	.86	1.77	.89	1.83	.69	2.37	.66	1.47	.65	1.82	.75
Interpersonal Sensitivity	1.79	.98	2.09	1.00	1.26	.79	1.88	.71	2.32	.75	1.73	.77	1.86	1.00
Depression	2.06	1.06	2.09	.93	2.01	.70	2.38	.60	2.64	.72	2.17	.81	2.20	1.02
Anxiety	1.83	1.11	2.00	1.05	1.67	.96	1.28	.76	1.98	.82	1.56	.62	1.80	1.15
Hostility	1.83	.98	1.48	1.15	1.00	.88	1.48	1.03	1.50	.86	2.00	1.02	1.51	1.29
Phobic Anxiety	1.33	1.08	1.14	.99	1.09	1.05	.87	.64	1.44	.74	1.05	.85	.87	.69
Paranoid Ideation	1.99	1.01	1.65	1.00	1.06	.92	1.54	.70	1.64	.84	2.07	.75	1.61	.92
Psychoticism	1.50	.95	1.29	.85	.87	.64	.95	.56	1.57	.66	1.53	.74	1.32	.94
Initial SCL-90 Analogue	(n = 17)		(n = 13)		(n = 19)		(n = 8)		(n = 17)		(n = 16)		(n = 10)	
Somatization	1.53	2.35	2.15	2.64	5.53	3.41	2.00	2.20	2.82	2.38	2.33	2.82	1.11	1.45
Obsessive-Compulsive	3.00	2.65	4.23	3.09	2.21	2.51	3.13	3.14	3.06	2.49	3.13	2.70	3.22	3.93
Interpersonal Sensitivity	3.76	2.17	5.46	2.63	4.37	3.27	5.38	3.25	5.47	2.32	4.44	2.13	4.78	2.22
Depression	3.94	2.14	4.23	3.17	4.84	2.41	4.75	2.76	5.47	2.27	4.63	2.45	3.44	1.74
Anxiety	3.06	2.22	4.92	2.56	4.47	2.82	4.50	2.39	4.65	2.74	3.87	2.77	4.00	2.18
Hostility	2.47	2.37	2.77	2.95	1.58	2.12	3.75	2.92	3.06	2.19	2.50	2.53	2.67	1.80
Phobic Anxiety	.71	1.36	1.46	2.47	1.05	2.04	1.29	1.89	1.71	2.31	1.40	2.87	2.11	3.72
Paranoid Ideation	1.12	1.32	1.23	2.24	.47	.84	.43	.79	1.29	1.76	1.75	2.82	1.56	2.60
Psychoticism	.82	1.29	1.31	2.18	.42	.69	.14	.38	.41	.71	.87	1.92	1.56	3.32
Patient Description Form Scales	(n = 17)		(n = 13)		(n = 19)		(n = 8)		(n = 17)		(n = 16)		(n = 10)	
Angry Resentment	2.84	.89	2.44	1.05	2.29	1.04	3.02	1.15	2.53	.97	3.22	.71	3.01	.70
Critical/Argumentative	2.41	1.01	2.24	1.02	2.11	.93	2.73	1.19	2.41	.73	2.90	.84	2.67	.76

	Code Types (continued)													
	68/86		78/87		123		247		278		468		478	
	Mean	SD	Mean	SD	Mean	SD	Mean	SD	Mean	SD	Mean	SD	Mean	SD
Narcissistic	2.55	.96	1.81	.77	1.80	.58	1.98	1.04	1.91	.74	2.61	1.10	2.28	.71
Defensive	2.73	.96	2.42	.90	2.49	.88	2.69	1.41	2.27	.57	2.97	.67	3.03	.71
Histrionic	2.55	.74	2.22	.75	2.30	.76	2.22	.86	2.27	.68	3.10	.91	2.89	.81
Aggressive	2.25	1.22	1.60	.58	1.42	.60	1.72	.97	1.79	.72	2.63	.94	2.06	.99
Insecure	2.88	.82	3.13	1.00	2.79	1.00	3.02	1.08	3.32	.84	3.46	.64	3.59	.65
Anxious	2.73	.61	3.19	.97	2.89	.83	3.04	.98	3.05	.77	3.22	.61	3.54	.68
Pessimistic	2.56	.95	2.35	.88	2.58	1.14	2.56	.86	2.26	.73	2.72	.89	2.45	.76
Depressed	2.46	.62	2.47	1.09	2.65	.73	2.46	.91	2.86	.60	2.87	.50	2.60	.89
Achievement-Oriented	2.12	.74	2.40	.53	1.96	.61	2.44	.67	2.38	.70	2.47	.70	2.38	.60
Passive-Submissive	2.30	.82	2.54	1.02	2.56	.63	2.53	1.25	2.22	.86	2.48	1.05	2.83	.66
Introverted	2.78	.77	2.87	1.23	2.44	.93	3.00	1.31	2.63	.99	2.48	.64	3.27	.83
Emotionally Controlled	2.50	1.38	2.38	1.25	2.27	.79	2.60	1.18	2.38	.95	2.60	1.16	3.20	.98
Antisocial	2.51	1.19	2.05	.88	1.76	.65	1.88	1.23	1.81	.57	3.14	1.07	2.58	.78
Negative Treatment Attitudes	2.12	.79	1.71	.81	2.02	.75	2.06	1.01	1.66	.42	2.21	.82	2.05	.62
Somatic Symptoms	1.89	.95	2.14	1.07	3.49	1.04	1.98	.87	2.39	.95	1.97	1.24	1.71	.61
Psychotic Symptoms	1.32	.51	1.45	.99	1.20	.29	1.35	.55	1.16	.25	1.53	.71	1.84	1.02
Family Problems	3.16	1.26	2.79	1.22	2.19	1.04	2.97	1.61	2.78	1.18	3.65	.81	3.63	.82
Obsessive-Compulsive	2.81	.82	2.89	.74	2.36	.71	2.73	1.11	2.65	.78	3.18	.75	3.38	.85
Stereotypic Masculine Interests	2.22	1.39	2.31	.90	1.89	1.28	2.13	.88	1.71	1.15	2.25	1.26	1.85	.85
Procrastinates	2.30	.78	2.19	1.36	2.19	.92	2.13	.87	2.31	.72	2.59	.88	2.78	.81
Suspicious	2.67	.86	2.62	1.33	2.16	1.09	2.54	1.22	2.37	.78	3.00	.58	2.93	.75
Agitated	1.94	.67	2.21	.81	2.09	.83	2.17	1.15	2.12	.64	2.56	.81	2.63	.81
Work Problems	2.11	1.50	1.67	.85	1.75	.82	1.95	1.19	1.25	.30	2.52	1.51	1.78	1.07
Patient Description Form Items	(n = 17)		(n = 13)		(n = 19)		(n = 8)		(n = 17)		(n = 16)		(n = 10)	
Anxious	2.88	.86	3.62	1.12	3.16	1.26	3.63	1.06	3.29	.85	3.38	.96	3.80	.63
Problems with Authority Figures	3.24	1.25	2.85	1.14	2.28	1.27	3.25	1.67	2.56	1.03	3.60	1.12	3.22	.97
Has Insight Into Own Problems	2.41	1.06	3.00	.71	2.11	.94	2.63	.92	2.88	.93	2.44	1.03	2.60	.70
Fears Losing Control	3.06	1.18	3.83	1.03	3.32	1.25	3.00	.93	3.25	1.29	3.47	.99	3.33	.87
Extroverted	2.18	1.01	2.08	.64	2.00	.69	1.88	.64	2.18	1.07	2.75	1.06	2.30	.82
Uses Repression	3.00	1.10	2.38	1.19	2.68	1.11	2.75	1.67	2.53	1.01	3.33	.90	3.00	1.12
Submissive	2.25	1.13	2.69	1.03	2.44	.86	2.75	1.58	2.44	1.03	2.50	1.21	3.10	.74
Difficulty Concentrating	2.47	1.07	2.92	1.26	2.74	1.28	2.75	1.39	2.94	1.20	2.94	.77	3.60	.97
Rigid	2.88	1.45	2.46	1.05	2.53	1.22	2.88	1.13	2.65	1.00	2.81	.98	3.10	1.29
Overly Compliant	1.88	.93	2.38	1.12	2.11	.99	2.50	1.07	1.94	.85	2.25	1.13	2.30	.67
Whiny	2.00	1.06	1.77	.93	2.21	1.13	2.25	1.16	1.94	1.09	2.38	1.20	2.30	.82
Feels Overwhelmed	3.31	1.01	3.31	1.32	3.16	1.21	3.38	1.30	3.41	1.06	3.25	1.00	3.60	.84

Manipulative	3.13	1.46	2.23	1.09	2.05	1.08	2.13	1.46	1.94	.85	3.19	1.52	2.60	.84
Difficulty Trusting Others	3.65	1.06	3.23	1.30	2.72	1.27	3.38	1.41	3.06	1.14	3.94	.93	3.90	.88
Insensitive to Others	2.41	1.12	1.77	.83	1.58	.77	1.88	.99	1.88	1.11	2.00	1.07	2.10	.74
Stereotypic Masculine Behavior	2.12	1.41	2.08	1.12	1.89	1.29	2.13	.99	1.76	1.20	2.19	1.22	1.70	.95
Harbors Grudges	3.13	1.02	2.31	1.03	1.82	1.07	3.00	1.41	2.69	1.20	3.00	.96	2.90	.88
Evasive	2.82	1.38	2.38	1.50	2.21	1.08	2.63	1.60	2.00	.94	2.87	.96	2.50	.71
Disoriented	1.35	.49	1.31	.85	1.32	.58	1.50	1.07	1.12	.33	1.38	.62	1.80	.92
Energetic	2.12	.78	2.62	.65	1.68	.67	2.63	.92	2.24	.90	2.25	.93	2.20	.63
Lonely	3.06	1.25	2.54	1.27	3.21	1.08	2.88	1.25	3.06	1.14	3.37	.96	3.40	1.07
Family Lacks Love	3.44	1.26	2.69	1.55	2.12	1.05	2.88	1.36	2.71	1.21	3.53	1.55	3.70	1.16
Worrier	3.24	.83	3.77	1.09	3.32	1.16	3.38	1.06	3.65	1.06	3.63	.81	3.80	.92
Narcissistic	2.88	1.31	1.85	.99	1.58	.77	1.88	.99	1.94	1.03	2.80	1.26	2.40	.97
Tearful	1.47	.80	1.69	.85	1.79	1.08	1.88	1.13	2.18	1.07	2.20	1.01	1.60	.70
Provocative	1.71	.77	1.46	.88	1.37	.83	1.87	.99	1.29	.59	2.27	1.28	2.00	1.05
Moralistic	2.13	.96	2.69	.85	2.28	1.07	2.63	1.19	2.41	.87	2.33	1.11	2.60	.70
Socially Awkward	2.76	.83	3.08	1.44	2.47	1.02	3.00	1.41	2.71	1.21	2.81	.91	3.50	.85
Hostile	2.12	1.41	2.15	1.14	1.58	1.02	2.75	1.28	2.00	1.00	2.50	1.10	2.50	1.18
Overcontrolled	2.37	1.31	2.46	1.39	2.28	1.02	2.75	1.04	2.06	1.20	2.60	1.12	3.10	1.29
Resistant to Interpretations	2.41	1.12	1.92	1.04	2.32	.95	2.25	1.28	1.88	.70	2.81	1.28	2.40	.70
Antisocial Behavior	2.41	1.50	1.69	.75	1.53	.70	1.63	1.41	1.47	.87	2.73	1.58	2.30	1.42
Sarcastic	1.76	.97	2.08	1.19	1.58	.90	2.25	1.16	2.00	.87	2.38	1.09	2.10	.74
Rejects Traditional Gender Role	1.63	1.15	1.62	1.12	1.32	.48	1.50	.76	1.29	.69	1.63	.81	2.20	1.55
Feels Gets Raw Deal From Life	3.13	1.20	2.46	1.56	2.72	1.27	3.50	1.41	2.76	1.25	3.75	.93	3.40	.97
Acute Psychological Turmoil	2.94	1.00	3.31	1.32	2.95	1.22	3.00	1.20	3.00	.87	3.37	.96	3.40	1.07
Does Not Complete Projects	2.36	1.03	2.38	1.61	2.31	1.14	2.38	1.19	1.85	.90	2.90	1.45	3.00	.89
Uncomfortable with Opposite Sex	2.00	1.21	2.62	1.33	2.20	.94	3.12	1.46	2.44	1.21	2.00	1.04	1.90	1.10
Preoccupied with Health Problems	1.94	1.48	2.31	1.32	3.74	1.37	2.00	1.20	2.41	1.33	1.69	1.14	1.80	1.03
Work-Oriented	2.12	1.11	2.77	.93	2.26	1.28	2.63	.92	3.00	1.00	2.69	1.20	2.70	.95
Resents Family Members	3.18	1.51	2.85	1.34	1.94	.83	2.88	1.64	2.94	1.39	3.73	.96	3.50	1.08
Demanding of Attention	2.71	1.16	2.15	.99	2.22	1.00	2.25	1.28	2.44	.81	3.73	1.10	2.90	.74
Passive	2.82	.73	2.69	1.38	2.79	.79	2.50	1.41	2.13	1.09	2.50	1.03	2.60	.84
Self-Punishing	2.27	.96	2.69	1.25	2.29	1.16	2.50	.93	2.88	1.41	2.75	.93	3.40	1.26
Needs to Achieve	2.00	.87	2.77	1.09	2.28	.89	2.75	1.04	2.88	1.09	2.47	.92	2.90	1.10
Needs to Be with Others	2.81	1.05	3.00	1.00	2.67	1.03	2.50	.76	2.71	1.05	3.25	1.06	3.70	1.06
Irritable	2.65	1.00	2.54	1.20	2.21	1.18	2.88	1.13	2.59	.80	2.87	1.02	3.00	1.05
Self-Defeating	3.31	1.14	3.38	.96	2.79	.98	3.13	1.46	3.13	1.31	3.44	1.09	4.00	.82
Delusional Thinking	1.50	1.10	1.54	1.20	1.16	.50	1.25	.46	1.12	.33	1.63	1.15	1.80	1.32
Self-Reliant	2.24	.90	2.46	.66	2.79	.98	2.50	.53	2.88	.86	2.56	1.09	2.30	.48
Aggressive	2.18	1.29	1.77	.73	1.74	.87	1.88	.99	1.94	.97	2.67	1.18	2.30	.82
Competitive	1.88	.96	2.00	.82	1.71	.85	2.00	.76	2.24	1.03	2.64	1.01	2.00	.93
Suspicious	2.47	.94	2.54	1.45	2.22	1.31	2.50	1.31	2.24	.90	3.00	.97	2.80	.92
Compulsive	2.47	1.18	2.58	1.24	1.94	.85	2.25	1.16	2.53	1.46	2.60	1.12	3.22	1.30

	Code Types *(continued)*													
	68/86		78/87		123		247		278		468		478	
	Mean	SD	Mean	SD	Mean	SD	Mean	SD	Mean	SD	Mean	SD	Mean	SD
Dependable	2.76	1.09	3.31	.63	3.06	.80	3.00	.76	3.06	.97	2.47	.99	3.20	.79
Multiple Somatic Complaints	1.94	1.34	2.15	1.14	3.74	1.24	1.63	.74	2.12	1.17	1.88	1.36	1.40	.70
Complains of Lack of Time	1.94	.97	1.83	1.11	2.00	1.05	1.38	.52	2.07	1.03	2.13	1.19	1.90	1.10
Poor Work Performance	2.33	1.50	1.90	.88	2.00	1.03	2.00	1.15	1.42	.90	2.70	1.49	2.00	1.00
Insecure	3.29	.85	3.69	.85	3.11	1.20	3.75	.89	3.41	.87	3.75	.93	4.00	.67
Discusses Problems Openly	2.88	1.05	3.15	.69	2.63	.76	2.75	1.04	3.24	.90	2.94	.85	3.40	.84
Sexually Adjusted	2.33	.78	2.50	.97	2.46	.78	2.13	.83	2.33	.98	2.30	1.06	2.17	.75
Exaggerated Need for Affection	2.25	1.13	1.91	.83	1.76	.56	2.38	1.19	2.06	1.06	3.00	1.52	2.88	1.13
Resentful	3.18	1.01	2.69	1.11	2.28	.89	3.25	1.39	3.00	1.22	3.47	.92	3.30	1.06
Uses Denial	2.94	1.44	2.38	1.19	2.74	1.15	2.63	1.60	2.59	.71	3.27	1.39	2.70	1.06
Hypochondriacal	1.44	.73	1.85	.90	2.63	1.30	1.75	.89	1.76	.90	1.53	.92	1.40	.52
Communicates Effectively	2.76	1.09	3.08	.90	2.74	.73	2.50	.76	3.24	.66	2.88	.96	3.00	.94
Has Many Nightmares	1.29	.49	2.00	1.41	1.69	.75	1.50	.84	2.00	1.41	2.43	.98	2.60	1.52
Stormy Interpersonal Relationships	3.18	1.38	2.83	1.03	2.29	1.16	3.25	1.39	2.76	1.39	3.73	1.33	3.30	1.34
Feigns Remorse When in Trouble	2.23	1.36	1.92	1.38	1.35	.70	1.63	1.06	1.29	.59	2.50	1.45	2.38	.74
Stereotypic Masculine Interests	2.31	1.45	2.54	1.13	1.89	1.29	2.13	.83	1.65	1.17	2.31	1.35	2.00	1.05
Guarded	3.06	1.30	2.54	1.51	2.47	1.31	2.88	1.81	2.24	1.35	3.06	1.12	3.50	1.18
Feels Inferior	3.12	1.05	3.31	1.38	2.84	1.07	3.25	1.49	3.47	1.07	3.44	1.09	3.60	.84
Low Frustration Tolerance	3.37	.89	3.08	1.26	2.50	1.20	3.38	1.30	2.81	1.17	3.53	.92	3.40	.70
Psychotic Symptoms	1.29	.77	1.33	.89	1.11	.32	1.00	.00	1.18	.39	1.44	.89	1.60	1.35
Fired From Past Jobs	1.82	1.25	1.75	1.39	1.44	.73	1.86	1.46	1.11	.33	2.30	1.25	1.50	1.00
Needs Attention	2.88	.86	2.69	1.03	2.68	1.06	2.63	.92	2.71	.85	3.38	1.02	3.50	1.08
Acts Out	2.50	1.32	2.31	1.11	1.89	.94	2.00	1.31	2.13	.96	3.47	1.19	2.50	1.27
Histrionic	2.13	.96	2.08	1.19	1.95	1.03	2.00	1.20	1.63	.96	2.80	1.52	2.40	1.17
Self-Indulgent	2.82	.95	2.15	.90	1.74	.81	2.00	.93	2.06	1.09	2.67	1.40	2.56	1.01
Depressed	2.94	.75	2.92	1.44	3.37	.90	3.38	1.06	3.65	.93	3.44	.81	3.30	.95
Grandiose	1.71	1.05	1.62	1.19	1.53	.61	1.75	1.16	1.47	1.01	2.31	1.30	2.00	.82
Cynical	2.41	1.42	2.15	1.41	2.05	1.08	2.63	1.60	2.29	1.05	2.73	1.16	2.80	1.14
Sociopathic	1.82	.95	1.62	1.04	1.21	.42	1.50	1.07	1.29	.47	2.00	1.07	1.60	.84
Agitated	2.35	1.00	2.46	1.13	2.21	1.08	2.38	1.06	2.41	.80	2.63	1.02	2.90	1.10
Marital Problems	2.50	1.86	1.78	1.20	2.33	1.46	2.83	2.04	3.06	1.39	2.93	1.82	2.00	1.60
Absence of Deep Emotions	2.65	1.62	2.17	1.47	1.74	.93	2.25	1.39	1.81	1.33	2.50	1.51	3.40	1.26
Uncomfortable Dealing with Emotions	3.00	1.50	2.92	1.26	3.05	1.18	2.88	1.36	3.24	.83	3.40	1.18	4.10	1.10
Sad	2.87	1.09	2.92	1.55	2.89	.94	3.00	.93	3.18	.81	3.31	.95	3.20	1.23
Self-Degrading	2.18	.95	2.62	1.26	2.53	1.26	2.63	1.41	2.82	1.29	2.88	1.26	3.40	.97
Unable to Express Negative Feelings	2.29	1.31	2.23	1.24	2.22	1.06	2.50	1.20	2.47	1.12	2.00	1.15	2.40	1.17
Concrete in Thinking	2.47	1.12	2.23	1.01	2.32	1.06	2.25	1.28	2.18	1.07	2.56	.96	2.80	.92
Unable to See Own Limitations	2.29	1.16	1.85	.69	2.16	1.07	2.25	1.58	2.00	1.06	2.69	1.20	2.60	1.35

Power-Oriented	1.94	1.12	1.69	.75	1.32	.58	2.25	1.04	1.76	1.15	2.37	1.02	2.10	.88
Grouchy	2.24	.97	2.23	1.09	1.89	.99	2.25	1.39	2.18	1.13	2.53	.99	2.60	.97
Overbearing in Relationships	2.47	1.41	1.77	1.09	1.61	.61	1.88	.99	2.19	1.22	3.07	1.44	2.25	1.39
Uncertain About Career	3.07	1.54	3.38	1.26	3.17	1.42	3.43	1.51	3.13	1.31	3.53	1.60	3.80	1.55
Likable	2.82	.95	3.38	.87	2.95	.52	2.75	.71	3.29	.85	2.94	1.12	3.30	.67
Procrastinator	2.75	.77	2.31	1.44	2.36	1.22	2.63	1.41	2.73	1.03	2.93	.83	3.22	.83
Negative Feelings Toward Opposite Sex	2.36	1.08	2.23	1.24	2.13	1.02	2.75	1.91	2.38	1.26	2.93	1.16	2.60	1.07
Defensive	2.59	.94	2.77	1.36	2.74	1.15	3.00	1.77	2.41	.94	3.33	.82	3.30	.95
Empathetic	2.35	.61	2.54	.66	2.37	.60	2.50	.53	2.35	.79	2.47	.74	2.60	.52
Perfectionistic	2.06	1.09	2.83	1.34	1.94	.90	2.63	.92	2.50	1.29	2.86	1.10	2.89	1.17
Judgmental	2.69	1.20	2.46	1.05	2.22	.88	2.75	1.04	2.65	.79	2.88	1.02	2.90	1.29
Copes Well with Stress	2.00	.61	1.85	.55	1.84	.83	2.00	.76	2.00	.71	1.81	.75	1.80	.63
Moody	2.94	.68	2.38	.87	2.74	1.10	3.00	1.07	3.06	1.06	3.07	.96	3.30	.95
Selfish	2.06	.85	1.62	.77	1.81	.83	2.13	.99	1.94	.97	2.36	1.22	2.38	1.06
Gives Up Easily	3.07	.92	2.00	.91	2.18	1.13	2.50	1.07	2.24	.97	2.77	1.17	2.60	1.07
Physical Symptoms in Response to Stress	2.00	1.15	2.00	1.08	3.61	1.04	2.25	1.28	2.47	1.07	2.20	1.42	1.56	.73
Blames Family For Difficulties	2.56	1.36	2.77	1.30	2.21	1.27	3.12	1.89	2.35	1.17	3.25	1.13	3.00	1.41
Bored	2.63	1.09	2.00	1.15	2.78	1.11	2.57	.98	2.38	1.15	2.31	.95	2.70	1.42
Idealistic	2.31	.79	2.31	1.18	2.06	.94	2.25	1.04	2.12	.99	2.63	.96	2.80	1.03
Difficulty Establishing Therapeutic Rapport	2.41	1.23	1.69	.85	2.16	.83	2.00	1.07	1.53	.62	2.19	1.28	1.90	.74
Daydreams	2.33	.98	2.11	1.17	2.07	.92	2.38	1.06	1.70	1.06	2.44	1.01	2.17	.98
Concerned About Status	2.07	1.03	2.00	1.00	1.94	1.00	2.75	1.16	1.94	1.18	2.44	1.15	2.30	1.16
Creates Good First Impression	2.18	.95	2.85	.80	2.42	.77	2.50	.93	2.47	.80	2.13	.96	2.70	.67
Complains of Sleep Disturbance	2.60	1.12	2.77	1.42	3.26	1.33	2.13	1.36	3.24	1.15	2.69	1.01	2.70	1.42
Has Temper Tantrums	2.63	1.31	1.77	.73	1.56	.73	1.75	1.04	2.00	1.25	2.93	1.03	2.10	1.10
Overreactive	2.81	1.05	2.54	1.13	2.67	1.14	2.00	.93	2.81	1.05	3.25	1.00	3.50	.85
High Aspirations	1.94	.93	2.31	1.11	1.67	.91	2.25	1.04	2.24	.97	2.69	1.25	2.30	.95
Feels Hopeless	2.73	.80	2.54	1.27	2.84	1.17	2.75	1.16	3.00	1.22	3.13	1.02	2.70	1.25
Keeps Others at a Distance	3.06	1.43	2.92	1.55	3.00	1.15	3.13	1.64	3.29	1.05	3.27	1.16	3.80	.63
Argumentative	2.06	1.09	2.08	1.04	1.89	1.10	2.75	1.28	2.18	1.07	2.69	1.20	2.50	.97
Paranoid Features	1.88	1.05	2.08	1.55	1.58	.90	1.75	1.16	1.82	.88	2.06	1.06	2.10	1.10
Restless	2.29	.99	2.54	1.05	2.58	1.02	2.38	1.41	2.65	1.00	3.13	1.02	2.90	1.20
Pessimistic	3.13	1.15	3.00	1.00	2.95	1.35	3.25	1.16	2.94	.90	3.13	.96	2.90	.99
Feels Like a Failure	3.06	1.18	3.00	1.00	3.21	1.47	3.00	1.31	3.24	1.15	3.73	.59	3.30	.95
Hallucinations	1.06	.25	1.50	1.00	1.00	.00	1.00	.00	1.06	.24	1.31	.87	1.50	1.27
Restricted Affect	2.53	1.70	2.00	1.35	2.32	1.06	2.63	1.60	2.18	1.01	2.31	1.45	3.00	1.63
Impatient	2.69	1.08	2.69	1.03	2.24	1.20	2.88	1.13	2.12	.70	3.07	1.03	2.90	.88
Assertive	1.76	.56	2.08	.86	1.68	.82	1.75	.71	2.12	.93	2.19	.91	2.00	.82
Modest	2.41	.94	2.31	.75	2.50	.79	2.88	.99	2.53	.87	2.43	.94	2.75	.89
Self-Doubting	2.94	.83	3.38	1.04	3.11	1.08	3.13	1.25	3.29	.92	3.33	1.11	3.80	1.03
Deceptive	2.00	1.06	1.54	.97	1.72	.83	1.63	1.06	1.53	.51	2.57	1.22	2.20	1.03
Feels That Life is a Strain	3.40	1.06	3.15	1.34	3.53	1.12	3.50	1.41	3.06	1.20	3.50	1.09	3.50	.53

	Code Types (continued)													
	68/86		78/87		123		247		278		468		478	
	Mean	SD	Mean	SD	Mean	SD	Mean	SD	Mean	SD	Mean	SD	Mean	SD
Physically Abusive	1.87	1.30	1.08	.29	1.24	.75	1.38	1.06	1.14	.36	1.86	1.10	1.70	1.06
Feels Rejected	3.06	1.24	2.62	1.56	2.65	1.17	3.75	1.28	3.53	.80	3.87	.74	3.50	1.27
Does Not Get Along with Coworkers	2.00	1.18	1.70	1.25	1.75	.77	2.00	1.15	1.64	1.03	2.30	1.42	1.75	.96
Uses Projection	2.50	1.15	2.08	1.19	2.11	1.08	2.25	1.28	2.24	1.09	2.67	1.11	3.00	.94
Complains of Fatigue	2.75	1.34	2.38	1.56	3.37	1.34	2.25	1.04	3.18	1.29	2.33	1.23	2.50	1.35
Uses Rationalization	2.53	1.07	2.46	1.27	2.50	.86	2.75	1.49	2.53	1.07	2.87	1.26	2.90	.88
Critical of Others	2.76	1.25	2.15	.90	2.12	.86	2.75	1.28	2.24	.90	3.06	1.06	2.50	1.08
Egocentric	2.71	1.16	1.77	1.01	2.00	.84	2.38	1.30	2.24	1.09	2.53	.92	2.80	.92
Overevaluates Own Worth	2.06	1.09	1.46	.78	1.56	.86	1.75	1.16	1.41	.71	2.44	1.36	2.20	.79
Optimistic	1.94	.66	2.00	.60	1.84	.76	1.88	.35	1.65	.79	1.87	.81	2.20	.63
Psychologically Immature	2.94	.90	2.77	1.17	2.79	1.08	3.00	1.41	2.12	.93	2.93	.88	3.70	.95
Poor Judgment	3.12	1.17	2.46	1.05	2.72	1.23	2.50	1.60	2.35	1.06	3.50	1.41	3.50	1.18
Low Sex Drive	1.50	.76	1.75	.89	2.25	.89	2.13	.99	2.22	1.48	1.70	.82	2.00	.82
Feels Mistreated	3.12	1.05	2.62	1.19	2.83	1.42	3.57	1.13	2.59	1.00	3.53	.99	3.30	.95
Overly Sensitive to Criticism	3.18	1.07	3.38	1.12	2.94	1.30	3.50	1.51	3.06	.77	3.47	.99	3.80	.79
Sentimental	2.56	.81	2.54	1.20	2.35	1.11	2.38	1.06	2.65	.86	2.54	1.05	2.89	.60
Sexual Preoccupation	1.91	1.04	1.55	.93	1.30	.95	1.50	.76	1.62	1.19	2.50	.97	2.14	1.35
Accelerated Speech	1.18	.39	1.62	1.12	1.47	1.12	1.75	1.39	1.29	.69	1.94	.85	2.10	.88
Concerns About Homosexuality	1.21	.43	1.08	.28	1.00	.00	1.43	.79	1.00	.00	1.08	.29	1.67	1.41
Many Specific Fears	1.93	1.10	2.15	1.28	1.89	1.10	1.88	.99	2.12	1.17	2.64	1.22	2.89	1.27
Passive in Relationships	2.35	1.00	2.38	1.04	2.83	.79	2.38	1.19	2.38	1.02	2.47	1.19	3.11	.93
Negative Attitudes Toward Therapy	1.62	.89	1.46	.78	1.79	.98	2.00	1.07	1.35	.61	1.94	1.00	1.60	.70
Guilt-Prone	2.56	1.09	3.31	1.18	2.63	1.26	2.71	.95	3.47	1.23	2.88	.81	3.50	1.08
Nervous	2.75	.93	3.38	1.12	3.05	.91	3.25	1.28	2.88	.86	3.13	.92	3.50	.85
Obsessive	2.94	1.18	3.17	.83	2.18	.95	2.75	1.58	2.38	1.09	3.06	1.29	3.00	1.33
Shy	2.82	.95	2.62	1.39	2.37	1.01	2.88	1.64	2.59	1.23	2.50	.82	3.10	1.29
Uses Intellectualization	2.24	1.20	2.62	1.61	2.11	.88	2.63	1.41	2.53	1.07	2.56	1.21	2.80	1.32
Has Many Interests	1.93	.88	2.31	1.03	1.76	.97	2.00	.76	1.81	.83	2.14	1.17	2.13	.64
Difficulty Making Decisions	3.00	.76	3.15	1.14	2.94	1.14	3.00	1.41	3.06	.83	3.31	.75	3.78	.83
Indirect Expression of Hostility	2.81	1.11	2.83	1.40	2.24	1.25	3.00	1.69	2.93	1.22	3.13	.92	3.20	.79
Poor Reality Testing	1.82	1.01	1.77	1.24	1.42	.61	2.00	1.41	1.35	.49	1.88	1.09	2.50	1.43
Angry	2.94	1.00	2.62	1.33	2.58	1.22	3.00	.93	2.71	1.10	3.40	.99	3.10	1.10
Eccentric	2.06	1.29	2.08	1.61	1.56	.86	1.75	1.04	1.82	1.38	2.27	1.10	3.00	1.49
Emotional Lability	2.59	.87	2.08	1.12	2.33	1.08	2.13	1.25	2.59	.94	2.80	1.08	2.70	.95
Dislikes Change	3.06	1.06	2.46	.88	2.95	1.03	2.50	1.20	2.47	.87	3.00	1.07	3.56	1.01
Believes Cannot Be Helped	2.00	1.03	1.69	.85	2.17	1.10	1.88	.99	1.59	.80	2.31	1.01	2.00	.82
Reliable Informant	3.06	1.00	3.46	.78	2.84	.96	3.00	.76	3.18	1.13	3.06	1.00	3.20	.63
Ignores Problems	2.59	1.00	1.92	1.16	2.32	1.00	2.25	1.16	2.25	.77	2.63	.81	2.80	1.14

Ruminates	3.19	.75	2.92	1.19	3.00	.91	3.25	1.28	2.82	.95	3.38	.96	3.30	1.25
Excitable	2.88	.78	2.62	.96	2.44	1.10	2.13	.99	2.19	.75	3.00	.82	3.20	.79
Conforming	2.31	.70	2.38	.77	2.67	.97	2.75	1.16	2.53	1.07	2.19	.91	2.80	1.03
Ineffective at Dealing with Problems	3.35	.93	3.00	.91	3.26	1.10	3.25	1.39	2.76	.90	3.44	.89	3.60	.84
Introverted	2.76	1.09	2.92	1.12	2.47	.96	3.13	1.25	2.59	1.12	2.13	.81	3.20	.79
Superficial Relationships	2.75	1.13	2.46	1.20	2.75	1.00	2.87	1.46	2.47	1.07	3.33	1.11	3.60	1.07
Impulsive	2.94	1.14	2.31	1.11	2.13	.92	2.00	1.41	2.18	1.07	3.27	1.28	3.40	1.17
Stereotypic Feminine Behavior	2.12	1.32	1.92	1.04	2.05	1.22	1.75	1.16	2.12	1.36	2.13	1.41	2.60	1.07
Stubborn	2.81	1.11	2.46	1.27	2.61	1.29	3.13	1.36	2.67	.98	3.00	.85	3.10	.88
Hostile Toward Therapist	1.29	.59	1.46	.66	1.37	.76	1.75	.89	1.18	.39	1.38	.72	1.20	.42
Difficult to Motivate	2.59	.94	1.85	1.07	2.06	.94	2.13	1.13	1.82	.95	2.31	1.01	2.40	1.26
Suicidal Ideations	1.62	.96	2.00	1.15	1.74	1.15	1.63	.74	1.94	.83	2.06	1.18	2.10	1.10
Familial Discord	3.18	1.51	2.85	1.34	2.39	1.46	3.00	1.69	3.12	1.32	3.93	.96	4.30	.67
Dogmatic	2.38	1.15	2.00	1.22	1.83	.86	2.50	.93	1.82	.95	2.38	1.09	2.50	1.18

Index

John R. Graham currently teaches in and is chair of the Department of Psychology at Kent State University. He was previously on the faculty and directed the counseling center at Lake Forest College. Dr. Graham completed his graduate work at the University of North Carolina at Chapel Hill. He was involved in the development of the MMPI-2 and MMPI-A and has published numerous journal articles and books on the MMPI instruments.

Yossef S. Ben-Porath teaches in the Department of Psychology at Kent State University. He obtained his doctoral training in clinical psychology at the University of Minnesota. He was involved in the development of several new scales for the MMPI-2 and continues to focus his research efforts on clinical applications of the MMPI-2. He has published journal articles and books in the area of applied psychological assessment. He maintains an active clinical practice in forensic consulting and assessment and is a frequent presenter at continuing education workshops. He is presently associate editor of *Psychological Assessment.*

John L. McNulty is a postdoctoral fellow in the Department of Psychology at Kent State University. He obtained his doctoral training in clinical psychology at the University of Tulsa. His research interests include objective assessment of adult and adolescent personality and psychopathology as well as exploration of the utility of dimensional models of personality in clinical populations.

James N. Butcher is professor of psychology at the University of Minnesota and a consultant to the test division of the University of Minnesota Press. He is the author of many articles and books on the MMPI and the MMPI-2, and served on the MMPI Restandardization Project and Adolescent Project Committees.